THE LEGAL ORDE
THE OCEANS

This compendium of documents brings together, for the first time in an affordable format, the essential documents needed to gain a thorough knowledge of the laws of the sea. There has been a long felt need for such a collection to provide students, scholars and practitioners with a working library of the key materials. This collection integrates documents of the International Maritime Organisation (which are not available anywhere on the web in consolidated form), of regional fisheries organizations, security related documents, treaties concerning resource exploitation, environmental protection measures and much more, into the framework created by the Law of the Sea Convention. The book is aimed at teachers and practitioners in the area and can be used as a class room companion for law of the sea courses.

DOCUMENTS IN INTERNATIONAL LAW

GENERAL EDITOR: PROFESSOR STEFAN TALMON
Professor of Public International Law in the University of
Oxford and Fellow of St. Anne's College

OTHER TITLES IN THE SERIES

THE OCCUPATION OF IRAQ:
THE OFFICIAL DOCUMENTS OF THE COALITION PROVISIONAL
AUTHORITY
Stefan Talmon (Forthcoming December 2009)

THE IRAN NUCLEAR ISSUE
Yael Ronen (Forthcoming 2010)

TERRORISM
Ben Saul (Forthcoming 2010)

THE LEGAL ORDER OF
THE OCEANS

BASIC DOCUMENTS ON LAW OF THE SEA

Edited by

Vaughan Lowe and Stefan Talmon

HART
PUBLISHING

OXFORD AND PORTLAND, OREGON
2009

Published in North America (US and Canada) by
Hart Publishing
c/o International Specialized Book Services
920 NE 58th Avenue, Suite 300
Portland, OR 97213-3786
USA
Tel: +1 503 287 3093 or toll-free: (1) 800 944 6190
Fax: +1 503 280 8832
E-mail: orders@isbs.com
Website: http://www.isbs.com

Hart Publishing Ltd, 16C Worcester Place, Oxford, OX1 2JW
Telephone: +44 (0)1865 517530 Fax: +44 (0)1865 510710
E-mail: mail@hartpub.co.uk
Website: http://www.hartpub.co.uk

British Library Cataloguing in Publication Data
Data Available

ISBN: 978-184113-823-7

Typeset by Tatiana Galarza
Printed and bound in Great Britain by
Antony Rowe, Chippenham, Wilts

CONTENTS

II. List of Documents Arranged According to Subject Matter
[Document numbers can be found in the top outside corner of each page]

Contents

EDITORS' PREFACE

One of the most striking characteristics of the Law of the Sea is the richness of its documentary sources. Its framework treaty, the monumental 1982 UN Convention on the Law of the Sea, is truly a framework (and one with many significant gaps) which holds together an extensive network of treaties, standards and other measures adopted by international and regional organizations, rooted in a fertile mulch of State practice and case-law. By no means all of this material is readily available, and our simple aim in this volume is to put the most commonly used materials between two covers and to supplement them with a comprehensive subject index for ease of reference.

The documents are organized in chronological order. Subsequent protocols as well as supplementary and implementation agreements are listed immediately following the main treaty. Each document is allocated a unique document number in the table of contents and thereafter navigation within the book is by document number, not page number. References to documents in the list of documents, footnotes and the subject index also use this document number, which can be found at the top outside corner of each page.

We must thank Lydia-Maria Bolani, Bilyana Tsvetkova and Pierre Zickert for their assistance in preparing the volume, and the Law Faculty, All Souls College and St Anne's College for supporting the project.

Vaughan Lowe
Stefan Talmon
Oxford, June 2009

ABBREVIATIONS

A/[UN Doc No]	General Assembly
ACP	African, Caribbean and Pacific [group of States]
AMSA	Australian Maritime Safety Authority
ATS	Australian Treaty Series
AUD	Australian Dollar
ASEAN	Association of South East Asian Nations
B	breadth
BBC, SWB	British Broadcasting Corporation, Summary of World Broadcasts
BCN	biological, chemical and nuclear [weapons]
BOD	Biochemical Oxygen Demand
BYBIL	British Year Book of International Law
CAMP	Comprehensive Atmospheric Monitoring Programme
CFCs	chlorofluorocarbons
Chinese JIL	Chinese Journal of International Law
Circ.	Circular
CLC 92	International Convention on Civil Liability for Oil Pollution Damage, 1992
CLCS	Commission on the Limits of the Continental Shelf
CNIS	Channel Navigation Information Service
COD	Chemical Oxygen Demand
COFI	Committee on Fisheries
COLREG 72	Convention on the International Regulations for Preventing Collisions at Sea, 1972
COSS	Committee on Safe Seas and the Prevention of Pollution from Ships
CSCE	Conference on Security and Co-operation in Europe
DO	Dissolved Oxygen
DPR	Democratic People's Republic
DR	Democratic Republic
DSB	Department of State Bulletin
DSI	Departement des Systèmes d'Information
DW	Deadweight
EC	European Community
ECDIS	Electronic Chart Display and Information Systems
EEC	European Economic Community
EEZ	Exclusive Economic Zone
ETA	Estimated Time of Arrival
FAO	Food and Agriculture Organization
FCO	Foreign and Commonwealth Office, United Kingdom
FM	Frequency Modulation
FPSOs	Floating Production, Storage and Offloading Facilities
FR	Federal Register
FSUs	Floating Storage Units
FYR	Former Yugoslav Republic
GESAMP	Group of Experts on the Scientific Aspects of Marine Environmental Protection
GIS	Geographical Information System
GMDSS	Global Maritime Distress and Safety System

HCFCs	hydrochlorofluorocarbons
IA 1994	Agreement Relating to the Implementation of Part XI of the United Nations Convention on the Law of the Sea
IA 1995	Agreement for the Implementation of the Provisions of the United Nations Convention on the Law of the Sea Relating to the Conservation and Management of Straddling Fish Stocks and Highly Migratory Fish Stocks
IAEA	International Atomic Energy Agency
IALA	International Association of Lighthouse Authorities
IAMSAR	International Aeronautical and Maritime Search and Rescue
IBC Code	International Code for the Construction and Equipment of Ships Carrying Dangerous Chemicals in Bulk
ICE	International Electronics Commission
ICES	International Council for the Exploration of the Sea
ICNAF	International Convention for the Northwest Atlantic Fisheries
ICPO	International Criminal Police Organization
ICZM	Integrated Coastal Zone Management
IGC Code	International Code for the Construction and Equipment of Ships Carrying Liquified Gases in Bulk
IHO	International Hydrographic Organization
ILO	International Labour Organization
IOC	Intergovernmental Oceanographic Commission
IMDG	International Maritime Dangerous Goods
IMO	International Maritime Organization
INTERCO	International Code of Signals
IPOA	International Plan of Action
ISBA	International Sea Bed Authority
ISM	International Safety Management
ISPS	International Ship and Port Facility Security
ITC 69	International Convention on Tonnage Measurement of Ships, 1969
IUA	International Unitisation Agreement
IUU	Illegal, Unreported and Unregulated
JHA	Justice and Home Affairs
JPDA	Joint Petroleum Development Area
L	Length
LBS	Land-Based Sources
LC	London Convention
LIBOR	London Interbank Offered Rate
LL 66	International Convention on Load Lines, 1966
LL PROT 88	Protocol of 1988 relating to the International Convention on Load Lines
LNTS	League of Nations Treaty Series
LOSB	Law of the Sea Bulletin
MARPOL	International Convention for the Prevention of Pollution from Ships
MCS	Monitoring, Control and Surveillance
MEPC	Marine Environment Protection Committee
MMSI	Maritime Mobile Service Identification
MODU	Mobile Offshore Drilling Unit
MOU	Memorandum of Understanding
MSC	Maritime Safety Committee

NAFO	Northwest Atlantic Fisheries Organization
NGO	Non-Governmental Organization
NLS	Noxious Liquid Substances
No	Number
OECD	Organization for Economic Co-operation and Development
OJ	Official Journal, European Union
OSPAR	Convention Convention for the Protection of the Marine Environment of the North-East Atlantic
PAHs	polycyclic aromatic hydrocarbons
PDR	People's Democratic Republic
PEEs	Pre-Enactment Explorers
ppm	parts per million
PROT	Protocol
PSSA	Particularly Sensitive Sea Area
PSC	Port State Control
PSI	Proliferation Security Initiative
RCC	Rescue Co-ordination Centre
REMPEC	Regional Marine Pollution Emergency Response Centre for the Mediterranean Sea
RES	Resolution
S/[UN Doc No]	Security Council
SAN	National Air Service, Panama
SAR	Search and Rescue
SIReNaC	Système d'Information Relatif aux Navires Contrôlés
SMN	National Maritime Service, Panama
SOLAS 74	International Convention for the Safety of Life at Sea, 1974
SPA	Specially Protected Area
SPAMI	Specially Protected Areas of Mediterranean Importance
SPLOS	States Parties to the United Nations Convention on the Law of the Sea
STCW 78	International Convention on Standards of Training, Certification and Watchkeeping for Seafarers, 1978
SUA Convention	Convention for the Suppression of Unlawful Acts Against the Safety of Maritime Navigation
TEMA	Training, Education and Mutual Assistance
TFG	Transitional Federal Government [Somalia]
UKMIL	United Kingdom Materials on International Law
UNCED	United Nations Conference on Environment and Development
UNCITRAL	United Nations Commission on International Trade Law
UNCLOS	United Nations Convention on the Law of the Sea
UNEP	United Nations Environment Programme
UNESCO	United Nations Educational, Scientific and Cultural Organization
UNODC	United Nations Office on Drugs and Crime
UNTS	United Nations Treaty Series
USD	US Dollar
VHF	Very High Frequency
VMS	Vessel Monitoring System
VTS	Vessel Traffic Services
WETREP	West European Tanker Reporting System
WFP	World Food Programme
WGS	World Geodetic System

WHO	World Health Organization
WIG	Wing-in-Ground
WMD	Weapons of Mass Destruction
WMO	World Meteorological Organization
WTO	World Trade Organization

Convention and Statute on the International Regime of Maritime Ports

Done at Geneva, 9 December 1923; entry into force, 26 July 1926
58 LNTS 285 [Registration Number 1379]

Germany, Belgium, Brazil, the British Empire (with New Zealand and India), Bulgaria, Chile, Denmark, Spain, Esthonia, Greece, Hungary, Italy, Japan, Lithuania, Norway, the Netherlands, Salvador, Kingdom of the Serbs, Croats and Slovenes, Siam, Sweden, Switzerland, Czechoslovakia and Uruguay,

Desirous of ensuring in the fullest measure possible the freedom of communications mentioned in Article 23(e) of the Covenant by guaranteeing in the maritime ports situated under their sovereignty or authority and for purposes of international trade equality of treatment between the ships of all the Contracting States, their cargoes and passengers;

Considering that the best method of achieving their present purpose is by means of a general convention to which the greatest possible number of States can later accede;

And whereas the Conference which met at Genoa on 10 April 1922 requested, in a resolution which was transmitted to the competent organisations of the League of Nations with the approval of the Council and the Assembly of the League, that the International Conventions relating to the Regime of Communications provided for in the Treaties of Peace should be concluded and put into operation as soon as possible, and whereas, Article 379 of the Treaty of Versailles and the corresponding Articles of the other Treaties provide for the preparation of a General Convention on the International Regime of Ports;

Having accepted the invitation of the League of Nations to take part in a Conference which met at Geneva on 15 November 1923;

Desirous of bringing into force the provisions of the Statute relating to the International Regime of Ports adopted thereat, and of concluding a General Convention for this purpose, the High Contracting Parties have appointed as their plenipotentiaries [...]:[1]

Who, after communicating their full powers, found in good and due form, have agreed as follows:

Article 1

The Contracting States declare that they accept the Statute on the International Regime of Maritime Ports, annexed hereto, adopted by the Second General Conference on Communications and Transit which met at Geneva on 15 November 1923.

This Statute shall be deemed to constitute an integral part of the present Convention.

Consequently, they hereby declare that they accept the obligations and undertakings of the said Statute in conformity with the terms and in accordance with the conditions set out therein.

[...][2]

In faith whereof the above-named plenipotentiaries have signed the present Convention.

Done at Geneva the ninth day of December, one thousand nine hundred and twenty-three, in a single copy which shall remain deposited in the archives of the Secretariat of the League of Nations.

---

[1] Names of plenipotentiaries omitted.
[2] Articles 2 to 10 of the Convention omitted.

STATUTE

Article 1

All ports which are normally frequented by sea-going vessels and used for foreign trade shall be deemed to be maritime ports within the meaning of the present Statute.

Article 2

Subject to the principle of reciprocity and to the reservation set out in the first paragraph of Article 8, every Contracting State undertakes to grant the vessels of every other Contracting State equality of treatment with its own vessels, or those of any other State whatsoever, in the maritime ports situated under its sovereignty or authority, as regards freedom of access to the port, the use of the port, and the full enjoyment of the benefits as regards navigation and commercial operations which it affords to vessels, their cargoes and passengers.

The equality of treatment thus established shall cover facilities of all kinds, such as allocation of berths, loading and unloading facilities, as well as dues and charges of all kinds levied in the name or for the account of the Government, public authorities, concessionaries or undertakings of any kind.

Article 3

The provisions of the preceding Article in no way restrict the liberty of the competent port authorities to take such measures as they may deem expedient for the proper conduct of the business of the port provided that these measures comply with the principle of equality of treatment as defined in the said Article.

Article 4

All dues and charges levied for the use of maritime ports shall be duly published before coming into force.

The same shall apply to the by-laws and regulations of the port.

In each maritime port, the port authority shall keep open for inspection by all persons concerned a table of the dues and charges in force, as well as a copy of the by-laws and regulations.

Article 5

In assessing and applying Customs and other analogous duties, local octroi or consumption duties, or incidental charges, levied on the importation or exportation of goods through the maritime ports situated under the sovereignty or authority of the Contracting States, the flag of the vessel must not be taken into account, and accordingly no distinction may be made to the detriment of the flag of any Contracting State whatsoever as between that flag and the flag of the State under whose sovereignty or authority the port is situated, or the flag of any other State whatsoever.

Article 6

In order that the principle of equal treatment in maritime ports laid down in Article 2 may not be rendered ineffective in practice by the adoption of other methods of discrimination against the vessels of a Contracting State using such ports, each Contracting State undertakes to apply the provisions of Articles 4, 20, 21 and 22 of the Statute annexed to the Convention on the International Regime of Railways, signed at Geneva on 9 December 1923, so far as they are applicable to traffic to or from a maritime port, whether or not such Contracting State is a party to the said Convention on the International Regime of Railways. The aforesaid Articles are to be interpreted in conformity with the provisions of the Protocol of Signature of the said Convention. (See Annex.).[3]

Article 7

Unless there are special reasons justifying an exception, such as those based upon special geographical, economic, or technical conditions, the Customs duties levied in any maritime port situated under the sovereignty or authority of a Contracting State may not exceed the duties levied on the other Customs frontiers of the said State on goods of the same kind, source or destination.

If, for special reasons as set out above, a Contracting State grants special Customs facilities on other routes for the importation or exportation of goods, it shall not use these facilities as a means of discrimination unfairly against importation or exportation through the maritime ports situated under its sovereignty or authority.

Article 8

Each of the Contracting States reserves the power, after giving notice through diplomatic channels, of suspending the benefit of equality of treatment from any vessel of a State which does not effectively apply, in any maritime port situated under its sovereignty or authority, the provisions of this Statute to the vessels of the said Contracting State, their cargoes and passengers.

In the event of action being taken as provided in the preceding paragraph, the State which has taken action and the State against which action is taken, shall both alike have the right of applying to the Permanent Court of International Justice by an application addressed to the Registrar; and the Court shall settle the matter in accordance with the rules of summary procedure.

Every Contracting State shall, however, have the right at the time of signing or ratifying this Convention, of declaring that it renounces the right of taking action as provided in the first paragraph of this Article against any other State which may make a similar declaration.

Article 9

This Statute does not in any way apply to the maritime coasting trade.

Article 10

Each Contracting State reserves the right to make such arrangements for towage in its maritime ports as it thinks fit, provided that the provisions of Articles 2 and 4 are not thereby infringed.

Article 11

Each Contracting State reserves the right to organise and administer pilotage services as it thinks fit. Where pilotage is compulsory, the dues and facilities offered shall be subject to the provisions of Articles 2 and 4, but each Contracting State may exempt from the obligation of compulsory pilotage such as its nationals as possess the necessary technical qualifications.

Article 12

Each Contracting State shall have the power, at the time of signing or ratifying this Convention, of declaring that it reserves the right of limiting the transport of emigrants, in accordance with the provisions of its own legislation to vessels which have been granted

---

[3] Annex omitted.

special authorisation as fulfilling the requirements of the said legislation. In exercising this right, however, the Contracting State shall be guided, as far as possible, by the principles of this Statute.

The vessels so authorised to transport emigrants shall enjoy all the benefits of this Statute in all maritime ports.

Article 13

This Statute applies to all vessels, whether publicly or privately owned or controlled.

It does not, however, apply in any way to warships or vessels performing police or administrative functions, or, in general, exercising any kind of public authority, or any other vessels which for the time being are exclusively employed for the purposes of the naval, military or air forces of a State.

Article 14

This Statute does not in any way apply to fishing vessels or to their catches.

Article 15

Where in virtue of a treaty, convention or agreement, a Contracting State has granted special rights to another State within a defined area in any of its maritime ports for the purpose of facilitating the transit of goods or passengers to or from the territory of the said State, no other Contracting State can invoke the stipulations of this Statute in support of any claim for similar special rights.

Every Contracting State which enjoys the aforesaid special rights in a maritime port of another State, whether Contracting or not, shall conform to the provisions of this Statute in its treatment of the vessels trading with it, and their cargoes and passengers.

Every Contracting State which grants the aforesaid special rights to a non-Contracting State is bound to impose, as one of the conditions of the grant, an obligation on the State which is to enjoy the aforesaid rights to conform to the provisions of this Statute in its treatment of the vessels trading with it, and their cargoes and passengers.

Article 16

Measures of a general or particular character which a Contracting State is obliged to take in case of an emergency affecting the safety of the State or the vital interests of the country may, in exceptional cases, and for as short a period as possible, involve a deviation from the provisions of Articles 2 to 7 inclusive; it being understood that the principles of the present Statute must be observed to the utmost possible extent.

Article 17

No Contracting State shall be bound by this Statute to permit the transit of passengers whose admission to its territories is forbidden, or of goods of a kind of which the importation is prohibited, either on grounds of public health or security, or as a precaution against diseases of animals or plants. As regards traffic other than traffic in transit, no Contracting State shall be bound by this Statute to permit the transport of passengers whose admission to its territories is forbidden, or of goods of which the import or export is prohibited, by its national laws.

Each Contracting State shall be entitled to take the necessary precautionary measures in respect of the transport of dangerous goods or goods of a similar character, as well as general police measures, including the control of emigrants entering or leaving its territory, it being understood that such measures must not result in any discrimination contrary to the principles of the present Statute.

Nothing in this Statute shall affect the measures which one of the Contracting States is or may feel called upon to take in pursuance of general international conventions to which it is a party, or which may be concluded hereafter, particularly conventions concluded under the auspices of the League of Nations, relating to the traffic in women and children, the transit, export or import of particular kinds of articles such as opium or other dangerous drugs, arms, or the produce of fisheries, or in pursuance of general conventions intended to prevent any infringement of industrial, literary or artistic property, or relating to false marks, false indications of origin or other methods of unfair competition.

Article 18

This Statute does not prescribe the rights and duties of belligerents and neutrals in time of war. The Statute shall, however, continue in force in time of war so far as such rights and duties permit.

Article 19

The Contracting States undertake to introduce into those Conventions in force on 9 December 1923, which contravene the provisions of this Statute, so soon as circumstances permit and in any case on the expiry of such conventions, the modifications required to bring them into harmony with such provisions, so far as the geographical, economic or technical circumstance of the countries or areas concerned allow.

The same shall apply to concessions granted before 9 December 1923 for the total or partial exploitation of maritime ports.

Article 20

This Statute does not entail in any way the withdrawal of facilities which are greater than those provided for in the Statute and which have been granted in respect of the use of maritime ports under conditions consistent with its principles. This Statute also entails no prohibition of such grant of greater facilities in the future.

Article 21

Without prejudice to the provisions of the second paragraph of Article 8, disputes which may arise between Contracting States as to the interpretation or the application of the present Statute shall be settled in the following manner:

Should it prove impossible to settle such dispute either directly between the Parties or by any other method of amicable settlement, the Parties to the dispute may, before resorting to any procedure of arbitration or to a judicial settlement, submit the dispute for an advisory opinion to the body established by the League of Nations as the advisory and technical organisation of Members of the League for matters of communications and transit. In urgent cases a preliminary opinion may be given recommending temporary measures, including measures to restore the facilities for international traffic which existed before the act or occurrence which gave rise to the dispute.

Should it prove impossible to settle the dispute by any of the methods of procedure enumerated in the preceding paragraph, the Contracting States shall submit their dispute to arbitration, unless they have decided or shall decide, under an agreement between them, to bring it before the Permanent Court of International Justice.

Article 22

If the case is submitted to the Permanent Court of International Justice, it shall be heard and determined under the conditions laid down in Article 27 of the Statute of the Court.

If the arbitration is resorted to, and unless the Parties decide otherwise, each Party shall appoint an arbitrator, and a third member of the arbitral tribunal shall be elected by the arbitrators, or, in case the latter are unable to agree, shall be selected by the Council of the League of Nations from the list of assessors for Communications and Transit cases mentioned in Article 27 of the Statute of the Permanent Court of International Justice; in such latter case, the third arbitrator shall be selected in accordance with the provisions of the penultimate paragraph of Article 4 and the first paragraph of Article 5 of the Covenant of the League.

The arbitral tribunal shall judge the case on the basis of the terms of reference mutually agreed upon between the Parties. If the parties have failed to reach an agreement, the arbitral tribunal, acting unanimously, shall itself draw up terms of reference after considering the claims formulated by the Parties; if unanimity cannot be obtained, the Council of the League of Nations shall decide the terms of reference under the conditions laid down in the preceding paragraph. If the procedure is not determined by the terms of reference, it shall be settled by the arbitral tribunal.

During the course of the arbitration the Parties, in the absence of any contrary provision in the terms of reference, are bound to submit to the Permanent Court of International Justice any question of international law or question as to the legal meaning of this Statute the solution of which the arbitral tribunal, at the request of one of the Parties, pronounces to be a necessary preliminary to the settlement of the dispute.

Article 23

It is understood that this Statute must not be interpreted as regulating in any way rights and obligations inter se of territories forming part of or placed under the protection of the same sovereign State, whether or not these territories are individually Contracting States.

Article 24

Nothing in the preceding Articles is to be construed as affecting in any way the rights or duties of a Contracting State as Member of the League of Nations.[4]

---

[4] The Protocol of Signature attached to the Convention provides: 'At the moment of signing the Convention of today's date relating to the International Regime of Maritime Ports, the undersigned, duly authorised, have agreed as follows:

1. It is understood that the provisions of the present Statute shall apply to ports of refuge specially constructed for that purpose.

2. It is understood that the British Government's reservation as to the provisions of Section 24 of the 'Pilotage Act' of 1913 is accepted.

3. It is understood that the obligations laid down in French Law in regard to ship-brokers shall not be regarded as contrary to the principle and spirit of the Statute on the International Regime of Maritime Ports.

4. It is understood that the condition of reciprocity laid down in Article 2 of the Statute on the International Regime of Maritime Ports shall not exclude from the benefit of the said Statute Contracting States which have no maritime ports and do not enjoy in any zone of a maritime port of another State the rights mentioned in Article 15 of the said Statute.

5. In the event of the flag or nationality of a Contracting State being identical with the flag or nationality of a State or territory which is outside the Convention, no claim can be advanced on behalf of the latter State or territory to the benefits assured by this Statute to the flags or nationals of Contracting States.

The present Protocol will have the same force, effect and duration as the Statute of today's date, of which it is to be considered as an integral part.

In faith whereof the above-named plenipotentiaries have signed the present Protocol.

Done at Geneva, the ninth day of December, One thousand nine hundred and twenty-three in a single copy which will remain deposited in the archives of the Secretariat of the League of Nations; certified copies will be transmitted to all the States represented at the Conference.'

Convention between the United States of America and the United Kingdom Respecting the Regulation of the Liquor Traffic

Done at Washington, 23 January 1924; entry into force, 22 May 1924
27 LNTS 182 [Registration Number 681]

His Majesty the King of the United Kingdom of Great Britain and Ireland and of the British Dominions beyond the Seas, Emperor of India and the President of the United States of America; being desirous of avoiding any difficulties which might arise between them in connection with the laws in force in the United States on the subject of alcoholic beverages; have decided to conclude a Convention for that purpose and have appointed as their Plenipotentiaries [...]:[1]

Who, having communicated their full powers, found in good and due form, have agreed as follows:

Article 1

The High Contracting Parties declare that it is their firm intention to uphold the principle that three marine miles extending from the coastline outwards and measures from low-water mark constitute the proper limits of territorial waters.

Article 2

1. His Britannic Majesty agrees that he will raise no objection to the boarding of private vessels under the British flag outside the limits of territorial waters by the authorities of the United States, its territories or possessions, in order that enquiries may be addressed to those on board and an examination be made of the ship's papers for the purpose of ascertaining whether the vessel or those on board are endeavouring to import or have imported alcoholic beverages into the United States, its territories or possessions in violation of the laws there in force. When such enquiries and examination show a reasonable ground for suspicion, a search of the vessel may be instituted.

2. If there is reasonable cause for belief that the vessel has committed or is committing or attempting to commit an offence against the laws of the United States, its territories or possessions prohibiting the importation of alcoholic beverages, the vessel may be seized and taken into a port of the United States, its territories or possessions for adjudication in accordance with such laws.

3. The rights conferred by this article shall not be exercised at a greater distance from the coast of the United States, its territories or possessions that can be traversed in one hour by the vessel suspected or endeavouring to commit the offence. In cases, however, in which the liquor is intended to be conveyed to the United States, its territories or possessions, by a vessel other than the one boarded and searched, it shall be the speed of such other vessel and not the speed of the vessel boarded which shall determine the distance from the coast at which the right under this article can be exercised.

Article 3

No penalty or forfeiture under the laws of the United States shall be applicable or attach to alcoholic liquors or to vessels or persons by reason of the carriage of such liquors, when such liquors are listed as sea stores or cargo destined for a port foreign to the United States, its territories or possessions, on board British vessels voyaging to or from ports of

---

[1] Names of plenipotentiaries omitted.

the United States, or its territories or possessions, or passing through the territorial waters thereof, and such carriage shall be as now provided by law with respect to the transit of such liquors through the Panama Canal, provided that such liquors shall be kept under seal continuously while the vessel on which they are carried remains within said territorial waters and that no part of such liquors shall at any time or place be unladen within the United States, its territories or possessions.

Article 4

Any claim by a British vessel for compensation on the grounds that it has suffered loss or injury through the improper or unreasonable exercise of the rights conferred by Article 2 of this Treaty or on the ground that it has not been given the benefit of Article 3 shall be referred for the joint consideration of two persons, one of whom shall be nominated by each of the High Contracting Parties.

Effect shall be given to the recommendations contained in any such joint report. If no joint report can be agreed upon, the claim shall be referred to the Claims Commission established under the provisions of the Agreement for the Settlement of Outstanding Pecuniary Claims signed at Washington, the 18th August 1910, but the claim shall not, before submission to the tribunal, require to be included in a schedule of claims confirmed in the manner therein provided.

Article 5

This treaty shall be subject to ratification and shall remain in force for a period of one year from the date of the exchange of ratifications.

Three months before the expiration of the said period of one year, either of the High Contracting Parties may give notice of its desire to propose modifications in the terms of the Treaty.

If such modifications have not been agreed upon before the expiration of the term of one year mentioned above, the Treaty shall lapse.

If no notice is given on either side of the desire to propose modifications, the Treaty shall remain in force for another year, and so on automatically, but subject always in respect of each such period of a year to the right on either side to propose as provided above three months before its expiration modifications in the Treaty and to the provision that, if such modifications are not agreed upon before the close of the period of one year, the Treaty shall lapse.

Article 6

In the event that either of the High Contracting Parties shall be prevented either by judicial decision or legislative action from giving full effect to the provisions of the present Treaty the said Treaty shall automatically lapse, and on such lapse or whenever the Treaty shall cease to be in force, each High Contracting Party shall enjoy all the rights which it would have possessed had this Treaty not been concluded.

The present Convention shall be duly ratified by His Britannic Majesty and the President of the United States of America, by and with the advice and consent of the Senate thereof; and the ratifications shall be exchanged at Washington as soon as possible.

In witness whereof the respective Plenipotentiaries have signed the present Convention in duplicate and have thereunto affixed their seals.

Done at the city of Washington, this twenty-third day of January, in the year of our Lord one thousand nine hundred and twenty-four.

Convention Regarding the Regime of the Straits

Done at Montreux, 20 July 1936; entry into force, 9 November 1936
173 LNTS 213 [Registration Number 4015][1]

His Majesty the King of the Bulgarians, the President of the French Republic, His Majesty the King of Great Britain, Ireland and the British Dominions beyond the Seas, Emperor of India, His Majesty the King of the Hellenes, His Majesty the Emperor of Japan, His Majesty the King of Romania, the President of the Turkish Republic, the Central Executive Committee of the Union of Soviet Socialist Republics, and His Majesty the King of Yugoslavia;

Desiring to regulate transit and navigation in the Straits of the Dardanelles, the Sea of Marmora and the Bosphorus comprised under the general term 'Straits' in such manner as to safeguard, within the framework of Turkish security and of the security, in the Black Sea, of the riparian States, the principle enshrined in Article 23 of the Treaty of Peace signed at Lausanne on 24 July 1923;

Have resolved to replace by the present Convention the Convention signed at Lausanne on 24 July 1923, and have appointed as their Plenipotentiaries [...]:[2]

Who, after having exhibited their full powers, found in good and due form, have agreed on the following provisions:

Article 1

The High Contracting Parties recognise and affirm the principle of freedom of transit and navigation by sea in the Straits.

The exercise of this freedom shall henceforth be regulated by the provisions of the present Convention.

SECTION I MERCHANT VESSELS

Article 2

In time of peace, merchant vessels shall enjoy complete freedom of transit and navigation in the Straits, by day and by night, under any flag and with any kind of cargo, without any formalities, except as provided in Article 3 below. No taxes or charges other than those authorised by Annex I to the present Convention shall be levied by the Turkish authorities on these vessels when passing in transit without calling at a port in the Straits.

In order to facilitate the collection of these taxes or charges merchant vessels passing through the Straits shall communicate to the officials at the stations referred to in Article 3 their name, nationality, tonnage, destination and last port of call (provenance).

Pilotage and towage remain optional.

Article 3

All ships entering the Straits by the Aegean Sea or by the Black Sea shall stop at a sanitary station near the entrance to the Straits for the purposes of the sanitary control prescribed by Turkish law within the framework of international sanitary regulations. This control, in the case of ships possessing a clean bill of health or presenting a declaration of health testifying that they do not fall within the scope of the provisions of the second paragraph of the present Article, shall be carried out by day and by night with all possible

---

[1] Annexes I-III omitted.
[2] Names of plenipotentiaries omitted.

speed, and the vessels in question shall not be required to make any other stop during their passage through the Straits.

Vessels which have on board cases of plague, cholera, yellow fever, exanthematic typhus or smallpox, or which have had such cases on board during the previous seven days, and vessels which have left an infected port within less than five times twenty-four hours shall stop at the sanitary stations indicated in the preceding paragraph in order to embark such sanitary guards as the Turkish authorities may direct. No tax or charge shall be levied in respect of these sanitary guards and they shall be disembarked at a sanitary station on departure from the Straits.

Article 4

In time of war, Turkey not being belligerent, merchant vessels, under any flag or with any kind of cargo, shall enjoy freedom of transit and navigation in the Straits subject to the provisions of Articles 2 and 3.

Pilotage and towage remain optional.

Article 5

In time of war, Turkey being belligerent, merchant vessels not belonging to a country at war with Turkey shall enjoy freedom of transit and navigation in the Straits on condition that they do not in any way assist the enemy.

Such vessels shall enter the Straits by day and their transit shall be effected by the route which shall in each case be indicated by the Turkish authorities.

Article 6

Should Turkey consider herself to be threatened with imminent danger of war, the provisions of Article 2 shall nevertheless continue to be applied except that vessels must enter the Straits by day and that their transit must be effected by the route which shall, in each case, be indicated by the Turkish authorities.

Pilotage may, in this case, be made obligatory, but no charge shall be levied.

Article 7

The term 'merchant vessels' applies to all vessels which are not covered by Section II of the present Convention.

SECTION II VESSELS OF WAR

Article 8

For the purposes of the present Convention, the definitions of vessels of war and of their specification together with those relating to the calculation of tonnage shall be as set forth in Annex II to the present Convention.

Article 9

Naval auxiliary vessels specifically designed for the carriage of fuel, liquid or non-liquid, shall not be subject to the provisions of Article 13 regarding notification, nor shall they be counted for the purpose of calculating the tonnage which is subject to limitation under Articles 14 and 18, on condition that they shall pass through the Straits singly. They shall, however, continue to be on the same footing as vessels of war for the purpose of the remaining provisions governing transit.

The auxiliary vessels specified in the preceding paragraph shall only be entitled to benefit by the exceptional status therein contemplated if their armament does not include: for use against floating targets, more than two guns of a maximum calibre of 105 millimetres; for use against aerial targets, more than two guns of a maximum calibre of 75 millimetres.

Article 10

In time of peace, light surface vessels, minor war vessels and auxiliary vessels, whether belonging to Black Sea or non-Black Sea Powers, and whatever their flag, shall enjoy freedom of transit through the Straits without any taxes or charges whatever, provided that such transit is begun during daylight and subject to the conditions laid down in Article 13 and the Articles following thereafter.

Vessels of war other than those which fall within the categories specified in the preceding paragraph shall only enjoy a right of transit under the special conditions provided by Articles 11 and 12.

Article 11

Black Sea Powers may send through the Straits capital ships of a tonnage greater than that laid down in the first paragraph of Article 14, on condition that these vessels pass through the Straits singly, escorted by not more than two destroyers.

Article 12

Black Sea Powers shall have the right to send through the Straits, for the purpose of rejoining their base, submarines constructed or purchased outside the Black Sea, provided that adequate notice of the laying down or purchase of such submarines shall have been given to Turkey.

Submarines belonging to the said Powers shall also be entitled to pass through the Straits to be repaired in dockyards outside the Black Sea on condition that detailed information on the matter is given to Turkey.

In either case, the said submarines must travel by day and on the surface, and must pass through the Straits singly.

Article 13

The transit of vessels of war through the Straits shall be preceded by a notification given to the Turkish Government through the diplomatic channel. The normal period of notice shall be eight days; but it is desirable that in the case of non-Black Sea Powers this period should be increased to fifteen days. The notification shall specify the destination, name, type and number of the vessels, as also the date of entry for the outward passage and, if necessary, for the return journey. Any change of date shall be subject to three days' notice.

Entry into the Straits for the outward passage shall take place within a period of five days from the date given in the original notification. After the expiry of this period, a new notification shall be given under the same conditions as for the original notification.

When effecting transit, the commander of the naval force shall, without being under any obligation to stop, communicate a signal station at the entrance to the Dardanelles or the Bosphorus the exact composition of the force under his orders.

Article 14

The maximum aggregate tonnage of all foreign naval forces which may be in course of transit through the Straits shall not exceed 15,000 tons, except in the cases provided for in Article 11 and in Annex III to the present Convention.

The forces specified in the preceding paragraph shall not, however, comprise more than nine vessels.

Vessels, whether belonging to Black Sea or non-Black Sea Powers, paying visits to a port in the Straits, in accordance with the provisions of Article 17, shall not be included in this tonnage.

Neither shall vessels of war which have suffered damage during their passage through the Straits be included in this tonnage; such vessels, while undergoing repair, shall be subject to any special provisions relating to security laid down by Turkey.

Article 15

Vessels of war in transit through the Straits shall in no circumstances make use of any aircraft which they may be carrying.

Article 16

Vessels of war in transit through the Straits shall not, except in the event of damage or peril of the sea, remain therein longer than is necessary for them to effect the passage.

Article 17

Nothing in the provisions of the preceding Articles shall prevent a naval force of any tonnage or composition from paying a courtesy visit of limited duration to a port in the Straits, at the invitation of the Turkish Government. Any such force must leave the Straits by the same route as that by which it entered, unless it fulfils the conditions required for passage in transit through the Straits as laid down by Articles 10, 14 and 18.

Article 18

1. The aggregate tonnage which non-Black Sea Powers may have in that sea in time of peace shall be limited as follows:

    (a) Except as provided in paragraph (b) below, the aggregate tonnage of the said Powers shall not exceed 30,000 tons;

    (b) If at any time the tonnage of the strongest fleet in the Black Sea shall exceed by at least 10,000 tons the tonnage of the strongest fleet in that sea at the date of the signature of the present Convention, the aggregate tonnage of 30,000 tons mentioned in paragraph (a) shall be increased by the same amount, up to a maximum of 45,000 tons. For this purpose, each Black Sea Power shall, in conformity with Annex IV[3] to the present Convention, inform the Turkish Government, on 1 January and 1 July of each year, of the total tonnage of its fleet in the Black Sea; and the Turkish Government shall transmit this information to the other High Contracting Parties and to the Secretary-General of the League of Nations;

    (c) The tonnage which any one non-Black Sea Power may have in the Black Sea shall be limited to two-thirds of the aggregate tonnage provided for in paragraphs (a) and (b) above;

    (d) In the event, however, of one or more non-Black Sea Powers desiring to send naval forces into the Black Sea, for a humanitarian purpose, the said forces, which shall in no case exceed 8,000 tons altogether, shall be allowed to enter the Black Sea without having to give the notification provided for in Article 13 of the present Convention, provided an authorisation is obtained from the Turkish Government in the following circumstances: if the figure of the aggregate tonnage specified in paragraphs (a) and (b) above has not been

---

[3] Annex IV omitted.

reached and will not be exceeded by the despatch of the forces which it is desired to send, the Turkish Government shall grant the said authorisation within the shortest possible time after receiving the request which has been addressed to it; if the said figure has already been reached or if the despatch of the forces which it is desired to send will cause it to be exceeded, the Turkish Government will immediately inform the other Black Sea Powers of the request for authorisation, and if the said Powers make no objection within twenty-four hours of having received this information, the Turkish Government shall, within forty-eight hours at the latest, inform the interested Powers of the reply which it has decided to make to their request.

Any further entry into the Black Sea of naval forces of non-Black Sea Powers shall only be effected within the available limits of the aggregate tonnage provided for in paragraphs (a) and (b) above.

2. Vessels of war belonging to non-Black Sea Powers shall not remain in the Black Sea more than twenty-one days, whatever be the object of their presence there.

Article 19

In time of war, Turkey not being belligerent, warships shall enjoy complete freedom of transit and navigation through the Straits under the same conditions as those laid down in Articles 10 to 18.

Vessels of war belonging to belligerent Powers shall not, however, pass through the Straits except in cases arising out of the application of Article 25 of the present Convention, and in cases of assistance rendered to a State victim of aggression in virtue of a treaty of mutual assistance binding Turkey, concluded within the framework of the Covenant of the League of Nations, and registered and published in accordance with the provisions of Article 18 of the Covenant.

In the exceptional cases provided for in the preceding paragraph, the limitations laid down in Articles 10 to 18 of the present Convention shall not be applicable.

Notwithstanding the prohibition of passage laid down in paragraph 2 above, vessels of war belonging to belligerent Powers, whether they are Black Sea Powers or not, which have become separated from their bases, may return thereto.

Vessels of war belonging to belligerent Powers shall not make any capture, exercise the right of visit and search, or carry out any hostile act in the Straits.

Article 20

In time of war, Turkey being belligerent, the provisions of Articles 10 to 18 shall not be applicable; the passage of warships shall be left entirely to the discretion of the Turkish Government.

Article 21

Should Turkey consider herself to be threatened with imminent danger of war she shall have the right to apply the provisions of Article 20 of the present Convention.

Vessels which have passed through the Straits before Turkey has made use of the powers conferred upon her by the preceding paragraph, and which thus find themselves separated from their bases, may return thereto. It is, however, understood that Turkey may deny this right to vessels of war belonging to the State whose attitude has given rise to the application of the present Article.

Should the Turkish Government make use of the powers conferred by the first paragraph of the present Article, a notification to that effect shall be addressed to the High Contracting Parties and to the Secretary-General of the League of Nations.

If the Council of the League of Nations decide by a majority of two-thirds that the measures thus taken by Turkey are not justified, and if such should also be the opinion of the majority of the High Contracting Parties signatories to the present Convention, the Turkish Government undertakes to discontinue the measures in question as also any measures which may have been taken under Article 6 of the present Convention.

Article 22

Vessels of war which have on board cases of plague, cholera, yellow fever, exanthematic typhus or smallpox or which have had such cases on board within the last seven days and vessels of war which have left an infected port within less than five times twenty-four hours must pass through the Straits in quarantine and apply by the means on board such prophylactic measures as are necessary in order to prevent any possibility of the Straits being infected.

SECTION III AIRCRAFT

Article 23

In order to assure the passage of civil aircraft between the Mediterranean and the Black Sea, the Turkish Government will indicate the air routes available for this purpose, outside the forbidden zones which may be established in the Straits. Civil aircraft may use these routes provided that they give the Turkish Government, as regards occasional flights, a notification of three days, and as regards flights on regular services, a general notification of the dates of passage.

The Turkish Government moreover undertake, notwithstanding any re-militarisation of the Straits, to furnish the necessary facilities for the safe passage of civil aircraft authorised under the air regulations in force in Turkey to fly across Turkish territory between Europe and Asia. The route which is to be followed in the Straits zone by aircraft which have obtained an authorisation shall be indicated from time to time.

SECTION IV GENERAL PROVISIONS

Article 24

The functions of the International Commission set up under the Convention relating to the regime of the Straits of 24 July 1923 are hereby transferred to the Turkish Government.

The Turkish Government undertake to collect statistics and to furnish information concerning the application of Articles 11, 12, 14 and 18 of the present Convention.

They will supervise the execution of all the provisions of the present Convention relating to the passage of vessels of war through the Straits.

As soon as they have been notified of the intended passage through the Straits of a foreign naval force the Turkish Government shall inform the representatives at Angora of the High Contracting Parties of the composition of that force, its tonnage, the date fixed for its entry into the Straits, and, if necessary, the probable date of its return.

The Turkish Government shall address to the Secretary-General of the League of Nations and to the High Contracting Parties an annual report giving details regarding the movements of foreign vessels of war through the Straits and furnishing all information which may be of service to commerce and navigation, both by sea and by air, for which provision is made in the present Convention.

Article 25

Nothing in the present Convention shall prejudice the rights and obligations of Turkey, or of any of the other High Contracting Parties members of the League of Nations, arising out of the Covenant of the League of Nations.

SECTION V FINAL PROVISIONS

Article 26

The present Convention shall be ratified as soon as possible.

The ratifications shall be deposited in the archives of the Government of the French Republic in Paris.

The Japanese Government shall be entitled to inform the Government of the French Republic through their diplomatic representative in Paris that the ratification has been given, and in that case they shall transmit the instrument of ratification as soon as possible.

A *procès-verbal* of the deposit of ratifications shall be drawn up as soon as six instruments of ratification, including that of Turkey, shall have been deposited. For this purpose the notification provided for in the preceding paragraph shall be taken as the equivalent of the deposit of an instrument of ratification.

The present Convention shall come into force on the date of the said *procès-verbal*.

The French Government will transmit to all the High Contracting Parties an authentic copy of the *procès-verbal* provided for in the preceding paragraph and of the *procès-verbaux* of the deposit of any subsequent ratifications.

Article 27

The present Convention shall, as from the date of its entry into force, be open to accession by any Power signatory to the Treaty of Peace at Lausanne signed on 24 July 1923.

Each accession shall be notified, through the diplomatic channel, to the Government of the French Republic, and by the latter to all the High Contracting Parties.

Accessions shall come into force as from the date of notification to the French Government.

Article 28

The present Convention shall remain in force for twenty years from the date of its entry into force.

The principle of freedom of transit and navigation affirmed in Article 1 of the present Convention shall however continue without limit of time.

If, two years prior to the expiry of the said period of twenty years, no High Contracting Party shall have given notice of denunciation to the French Government the present Convention shall continue in force until two years after such notice shall have been given. Any such notice shall be communicated by the French Government to the High Contracting Parties.

In the event of the present Convention being denounced in accordance with the provisions of the present Article, the High Contracting Parties agree to be represented at a conference for the purpose of concluding a new Convention.

Article 29

At the expiry of each period of five years from the date of the entry into force of the present Convention each of the High Contracting Parties shall be entitled to initiate a proposal for amending one or more of the provisions of the present Convention.

To be valid, any request for revision formulated by one of the High Contracting Parties must be supported, in the case of modifications to Articles 14 or 18, by one other High Contracting Party, and, in the case of modifications to any other Article, by two other High Contracting Parties.

Any request for revision thus supported must be notified to all the High Contracting Parties three months prior to the expiry of the current period of five years. This notification shall contain details of the proposed amendments and the reasons which have given rise to them.

Should it be found impossible to reach an agreement on these proposals through the diplomatic channel, the High Contracting Parties agree to be represented at a conference to be summoned for this purpose.

Such a conference may only take decisions by a unanimous vote, except as regards cases of revision involving Articles 14 and 18, for which a majority of three-quarters of the High Contracting Parties shall be sufficient.

The said majority shall include three-quarters of the High Contracting Parties which are Black Sea Powers, including Turkey.

In witness whereof, the abovementioned Plenipotentiaries have signed the present Convention.

Done at Montreux the 20th July, 1936, in eleven copies, of which the first copy, to which the seals of the Plenipotentiaries have been affixed, will be deposited in the archives of the Government of the French Republic and of which the remaining copies have been transmitted to the signatory Powers.

Treaty between the Great Britain and Northern Ireland and Venezuela Relating to the Submarine Areas of the Gulf of Paria

Signed at Caracas, 26 February 1942; entry into force, 22 September 1942
Terminated, 23 July 1991[1]
205 LNTS 122 [Registration Number 4829]

HIS MAJESTY THE KING OF GREAT BRITAIN, IRELAND AND THE BRITISH DOMINIONS BEYOND THE SEAS, EMPEROR OF INDIA, and THE PRESIDENT OF THE UNITED STATES OF VENEZUELA,

Desiring in a spirit of goodwill to make provision for and to define as between themselves their respective interests in the submarine areas of the Gulf of Paria,

Have decided to conclude a Treaty for that purpose and, to that end, have named as their Plenipotentiaries [...]:[2]

Who, having communicated to each other their full powers, found in good and due form, have agreed as follows:

Article 1

In this treaty the term 'submarine areas in the Gulf Paria' denotes the sea-bed and sub-soil outside of the territorial waters of the High Contracting Parties to one or the other side of the lines A-B, B-Y and Y-X.

---

[1] Article 12 of the Treaty between the Republic of Venezuela and the Republic of Trinidad and Tobago on the delimitation of marine and submarine areas, signed at Caracas on 18 April 1990, which came into force on 23 July 1991, provides for the termination of the Treaty (1654 UNTS 614).
[2] Names of plenipotentiaries omitted.

Article 2

1. His Majesty The King declares that he for his part will not assert any claim to sovereignty or control over those parts of the submarine areas of the Gulf of Paria which lie westerly of the line A-B, or southerly of the lines B-Y and Y-X respectively described in Article 3 of the present Treaty, and that he will recognise any rights of sovereignty or control which have been or may hereafter be lawfully acquired by the United States of Venezuela over the said parts of the submarine areas of the Gulf of Paria.

2. The President of the United States of Venezuela declares that he for his part will not assert any claim to sovereignty or control over those parts of the submarine areas of the Gulf of Paria which lie easterly of the line A-B or northerly of the lines B-Y and Y-X respectively, described in Article 3 of the present Treaty, and that he will recognise any rights of sovereignty or control which have been or may hereafter be lawfully acquired by His Majesty The King over the said parts of the submarine areas of the Gulf of Paria.

Article 3

The lines A-B, B-Y and Y-X mentioned in the preceding Article are drawn on the annexed map[3] and are defined as follows:

Line A-B runs from point A, which is the intersection of the central meridian of the island of Patos with the southern limit of the territorial waters of the said Island, the approximate co-ordinates of which are: Latitude 10° 35′ 04″ N., Longitude 61° 51′ 53″ W. From there the line runs straight to Point B which is situated at the limit of the territorial waters of Venezuela at the point of their intersection with the meridian of 62° 05′ 08″ W., the approximate latitude of which is 10° 02′ 24″ N.

Line B-Y runs from Point B, already established, and follows the limits of the territorial waters of Venezuela to Point Y, where the said limits intersect the parallel of 9° 57′ 30″ N., the approximate longitude of which is 61° 56′ 40″ W.

Line Y-X runs from the point Y, already established, and follows the parallel of 9° 57′ 30″ N. to Point X, situated on the meridian of 61° 30′ 00″ W.

The longitude of the central meridian of the Island of Patos to which this Article refers shall be determined by taking the mathematical half of the most eastern and the most western longitudes of the said Island.

Should the straight lines A-B or Y-X described in this Article intersect in their course the outside limit of the territorial waters of either of the two High Contracting Parties, the dividing line shall follow along the said limit until it reaches again the intersecting straight line in conformity with the stipulations in Articles 1 and 5 of this Treaty, which exclude the bed of the sea and the sub-soil of territorial waters.

The co-ordinates of points A, B and Y which are here given approximately shall be determined with exactness by the Commission provided for in Article 4 of this Treaty.

Article 4

1. The High Contracting Parties shall, as soon as practicable after the coming into force of this Treaty, appoint a mixed Commission to take all necessary steps to demarcate the lines A-B, B-Y and Y-X by means of buoys or other visible methods on the surface of the sea or on the land as the case may be. Any buoys or other means employed shall, however, conform in all respects to the provisions of Article 6 of this Treaty.

2. The manner in which this mixed Commission shall be constituted and the instructions to which it shall be subject for the fulfillment of its duties shall be laid down in a special protocol or by an exchange of notes.

---

[3] Map not reproduced.

Article 5

This Treaty refers solely to the submarine areas of the Gulf of Paria, and nothing herein shall be held to affect in any way the status of the islands, islets or rocks above the surface of the sea together with the territorial waters thereof.

Article 6

Nothing in this Treaty shall be held to affect in any way the status of the waters of the Gulf of Paria or any rights of passage or navigation on the surface of the seas outside the territorial waters of the Contracting Parties. In particular, passage or navigation shall not be closed or be impeded by any works or installations which may be erected, which shall be of such a nature and shall be constructed, placed, marked, buoyed and lighted, as not to constitute a danger or obstruction to shipping.

Article 7

Each of the High Contracting Parties shall take all practical measures to prevent the exploitation of any submarine areas claimed or occupied by him in the Gulf from causing the pollution of the territorial waters of the other by oil, mud or any other fluid or substance liable to contaminate the navigable waters or the foreshore and shall concert with the other to make the said measures as effective as possible.

Article 8

Each of the High Contracting Parties shall cause to be inserted in any concession which may be granted for the exploitation of submarine areas in the Gulf of Paria stipulations for securing the effective observance of the two preceding Articles, including a requirement for the use by the concessionaire of modern equipment, and shall cause the operation of any such concession to be supervised in order to ensure that the provisions of the present Treaty are complied with.

Article 9

All differences between the High Contracting Parties relating to the interpretation or execution of this Treaty shall be settled by such peaceful means as are recognised in International Law.

Article 10

The present Treaty shall be ratified in conformity with the respective laws of the High Contracting Parties and shall come into force upon the exchange of ratifications which shall take place in London.

In witness whereof the above-named Plenipotentiaries have signed the present Treaty and have affixed thereto their seals.

Done in duplicate in the English and Spanish languages at Caracas, the 26th day of February, 1942.

US Presidential Proclamation No 2667
Policy of the United States with Respect to the Natural Resources of the Subsoil and Sea Bed of the Continental Shelf

Done at Washington, 28 September 1945
10 FR 12303, (1945) 13 DSB 485

Whereas the Government of the United States of America, aware of the long range world-wide need for new sources of petroleum and other minerals, holds the view that efforts to discover and make available new supplies of these resources should be encouraged; and

Whereas its competent experts are of the opinion that such resources underlie many parts of the continental shelf off the coasts of the United States of America, and that with modern technological progress their utilization is already practicable or will become so at an early date; and

Whereas recognized jurisdiction over these resources is required in the interest of their conservation and prudent utilization when and as development is undertaken; and

Whereas it is the view of the Government of the United States that the exercise of jurisdiction over the natural resources of the subsoil and sea bed of the continental shelf by the contiguous nation is reasonable and just, since the effectiveness of measures to utilize or conserve these resources would be contingent upon cooperation and protection from the shore, since the continental shelf may be regarded as an extension of the land-mass of the coastal nation and thus naturally appurtenant to it, since these resources frequently form a seaward extension of a pool or deposit lying within the territory, and since self-protection compels the coastal nation to keep close watch over activities off its shores which are of the nature necessary for utilization of these resources;

Now, therefore, I Harry S. Truman, President of the United States of America, de hereby proclaim the following policy of the United States of America with respect to the natural resources of the subsoil and sea bed of the continental shelf.

Having concern for the urgency of conserving and prudently utilizing its natural resources, the Government of the United States regards the natural resources of the subsoil and sea bed of the continental shelf beneath the high seas but contiguous to the coasts of the United States as appertaining to the United States, subject to its jurisdiction and control. In cases where the continental shelf extends to the shores of another State, or is shared with an adjacent State, the boundary shall be determined by the United States and the State concerned in accordance with equitable principles. The character as high seas of the waters above the continental shelf and the right to their free and unimpeded navigation are in no way thus affected.

In witness whereof, I have hereunto set my hand and caused the seal of the United States of America to be affixed.

Done at the city of Washington this 28th day of September, in the year of our Lord nineteen hundred and forty-five, and of the Independence of the United States of America the one hundred and seventieth.

Harry S. Truman

US Presidential Proclamation No 2668
Policy of the United States with Respect to Coastal Fisheries in Certain Areas of the High Seas

Done at Washington, 28 September 1945
10 FR 12304, (1945) 13 DSB 486

Whereas for some years the Government of the United States of America has viewed with concern the inadequacy of present arrangements for the protection and perpetuation of the fishery resources contiguous to its coasts, and in view of the potentially disturbing effect of the situation, has carefully studied the possibility of improving the jurisdictional basis for conservation measures and international cooperation in this field; and

Whereas such fishery resources have a special importance to coastal communities as a source of livelihood and to the nation as a food and industrial resource; and

Whereas the progressive development of new methods and techniques contributes to intensified fishing over wide sea areas and in certain cases seriously threatens fisheries with depletion; and

Whereas there is an urgent need to protect coastal fishery resources from destructive exploitation, having due regards to conditions peculiar to each region and situation and to the special rights and equities of the coastal State and of any other State which may have established a legitimate interest therein;

Now, therefore, I, Harry S. Truman, President of the United States of America, do hereby proclaim the following policy of the United States of America with respect to coastal fisheries in certain areas of the high seas:

In view of the pressing need for conservation and protection of fishery resources, the Government of the United States regards it as proper to establish conservation zones in those areas of the high seas contiguous to the coasts of the United States wherein fishing activities have been or in the future may be developed and maintained on a substantial scale. Where such activities have been or shall hereafter be developed and maintained by its nationals alone, the United States regards it as proper to establish explicitly bounded conservation zones in which fishing activities shall be subject to the regulation and control of the United States. Where such activities have been or shall hereafter be legitimately developed and maintained jointly by nationals of the United States and nationals of other States, explicitly bounded conservation zones may be established under agreements between the United States and such other States; and all fishing activities in such zones shall be subject to regulation and control as provided in such agreements. The right of any State to establish conservation zones off its shores in accordance with the above principles is conceded, provided that corresponding recognition is given to any fishing interests of nationals of the United States which may exist in such areas. The character as high seas of the areas in which such conservation zones are established and the right to their free and unimpeded navigation are in no way thus affected.

In witness whereof, I have hereunto set my hand and caused the seal of the United States of America to be affixed.

Done at the City of Washington this 28th day of September, in the year of our Lord nineteen hundred of forty-five, and of the Independence of the United States of America the one hundred and seventieth.

Harry S. Truman

International Convention for the Regulation of Whaling

Signed at Washington, 2 December 1946; entry into force, 10 November 1948
161 UNTS 74 [Registration Number 2124][1]

The Governments whose duly authorised representatives have subscribed hereto,

Recognizing the interest of the nations of the world in safeguarding for future generations the great natural resources represented by the whale stocks;

Considering that the history of whaling has seen over-fishing of one area after another and of one species of whale after another to such a degree that it is essential to protect all species of whales from further overfishing;

Recognizing that the whale stocks are susceptible of natural increases if whaling is properly regulated, and that increases in the size of whale stocks will permit increases in the number of whales which may be captured without endangering these natural resources;

Recognizing that it is in the common interest to achieve the optimum level of whale stocks as rapidly as possible without causing wide-spread economic and nutritional distress;

Recognizing that in the course of achieving these objectives, whaling operations should be confined to those species best able to sustain exploitation in order to give an interval for recovery to certain species of whales now depleted in numbers;

Desiring to establish a system of international regulation for the whale fisheries to ensure proper and effective conservation and development of whale stocks on the basis of the principles embodied in the provisions of the International Agreement for the Regulation of Whaling, signed in London on June 8, 1937, and the protocols to that Agreement signed in London on June 24, 1938, and November 26, 1945; and

Having decided to conclude a convention to provide for the proper conservation of whale stocks and thus make possible the orderly development of the whaling industry;

Have agreed as follows:

Article I

1. This Convention includes the Schedule attached thereto which forms an integral part thereof. All references to 'Convention' shall be understood as including the said Schedule either in its present terms or as amended in accordance with the provisions of Article V.

2. This Convention applies to factory ships, land stations, and whale catchers under the jurisdiction of the Contracting Governments and to all waters in which whaling is prosecuted by such factory ships, land stations, and whale catchers.

Article II

As used in this Convention:

1. 'factory ship' means a ship in which or on which whales are treated either wholly or in part;

2. 'land station' means a factory on the land at which whales are treated whether wholly or in part;

---

[1] The text of the Whaling Convention was amended by the Protocol to the International Convention for the Regulation of Whaling, signed at Washington on 19 November 1956. The Protocol extended the application of that Convention to helicopters and other aircraft. It entered into force on 4 May 1959 (338 UNTS 366). The text of the Whaling Convention reproduced is a consolidated version incorporating the amendments made by the Protocol.

3. 'whale catcher' means a helicopter, or other aircraft, or a ship, used for the purpose of hunting, taking, killing, towing, holding on to, or scouting for whales;

4. 'Contracting Government' means any Government which has deposited an instrument of ratification or has given notice of adherence to this Convention.

Article III

1. The Contracting Governments agree to establish an International Whaling Commission, hereinafter referred to as the Commission, to be composed of one member from each Contracting Government. Each member shall have one vote and may be accompanied by one or more experts and advisers.

2. The Commission shall elect from its own members a Chairman and Vice-Chairman and shall determine its own Rules of Procedure. Decisions of the Commission shall be taken by a simple majority of those members voting except that a three-fourths majority of those members voting shall be required for action in pursuance of Article V. The Rules of Procedure may provide for decisions otherwise than at meetings of the Commission.

3. The Commission may appoint its own Secretary and staff.

4. The Commission may set up, from among its own members and experts or advisers, such committees as it considers desirable to perform such functions as it may authorize.

5. The expenses of each member of the Commission and of his experts and advisers shall be determined and paid by his own Government.

6. Recognizing that specialized agencies related to the United Nations will be concerned with the conservation and development of whale fisheries and the products arising therefrom and desiring to avoid duplication of functions, the Contracting Governments will consult among themselves within two years after the coming into force of this Convention to decide whether the Commission shall be brought within the framework of a specialized agency related to the United Nations.

7. In the meantime the Government of the United Kingdom of Great Britain and Northern Ireland shall arrange, in consultation with the other Contracting Governments, to convene the first meeting of the Commission, and shall initiate the consultation referred to in paragraph 6 above.

8. Subsequent meetings of the Commission shall be convened as the Commission may determine.

Article IV

1. The Commission may either in collaboration with or through independent agencies of the Contracting Governments or other public or private agencies, establishments, or organizations, or independently

    (a) encourage, recommend, or if necessary, organize studies and investigations relating to whales and whaling;

    (b) collect and analyze statistical information concerning the current condition and trend of the whale stocks and the effects of whaling activities thereon;

    (c) study, appraise, and disseminate information concerning methods of maintaining and increasing the populations of whale stocks.

2. The Commission shall arrange for the publication of reports of its activities, and it may publish independently or in collaboration with the International Bureau for Whaling Statistics at Sandefjord in Norway and other organizations and agencies such reports as it deems appropriate, as well as statistical, scientific, and other pertinent information relating to whales and whaling.

Article V

1. The Commission may amend from time to time the provisions of the Schedule by adopting regulations with respect to the conservation and utilization of whale resources, fixing (a) protected and unprotected species; (b) open and closed seasons; (c) open and closed waters, including the designation of sanctuary areas; (d) size limits for each species; (e) time, methods, and intensity of whaling (including the maximum catch of whales to be taken in any one season); (f) types and specifications of gear and apparatus and appliances which may be used; (g) methods of measurement; (h) catch returns and other statistical and biological records; and (i) methods of inspection.

2. These amendments of the Schedule (a) shall be such as are necessary to carry out the objectives and purposes of this Convention and to provide for the conservation, development, and optimum utilization of the whale resources; (b) shall be based on scientific findings; (c) shall not involve restrictions on the number or nationality of factory ships or land stations, nor allocate specific quotas to any factory ship or land station or to any group of factory ships or land stations; and (d) shall take into consideration the interests of the consumers of whale products and the whaling industry.

3. Each of such amendments shall become effective with respect to the Contracting Governments ninety days following notification of the amendment by the Commission to each of the Contracting Governments, except that (a) if any Government presents to the Commission objection to any amendment prior to the expiration of this ninety-day period, the amendment shall not become effective with respect to any of the Governments for an additional ninety days; (b) thereupon, any other Contracting Government may present objection to the amendment at any time prior to the expiration of the additional ninety-day period, or before the expiration of thirty days from the date of receipt of the last objection received during such additional ninety-day period, whichever date shall be the later; and (c) thereafter, the amendment shall become effective with respect to all Contracting Governments which have not presented objection but shall not become effective with respect to any Government which has so objected until such date as the objection is withdrawn. The Commission shall notify each Contracting Government immediately upon receipt of each objection and withdrawal and each Contracting Government shall acknowledge receipt of all notifications of amendments, objections, and withdrawals.

4. No amendments shall become effective before July 1, 1949.

Article VI

The Commission may from time to time make recommendations to any or all Contracting Governments on any matters which relate to whales or whaling and to the objectives and purposes of this Convention.

Article VII

The Contracting Governments shall ensure prompt transmission to the International Bureau for Whaling Statistics at Sandefjord in Norway, or to such other body as the Commission may designate, of notifications and statistical and other information required by this Convention in such form and manner as may be prescribed by the Commission.

Article VIII

1. Notwithstanding anything contained in this Convention, any Contracting Government may grant to any of its nationals a special permit authorizing that national to kill, take, and treat whales for purposes of scientific research subject to such restrictions

as to number and subject to such other conditions as the Contracting Government thinks fit, and the killing, taking, and treating of whales in accordance with the provisions of this Article shall be exempt from the operation of this Convention. Each Contracting Government shall report at once to the Commission all such authorizations which it has granted. Each Contracting Government may at any time revoke any such special permit which it has granted.

2. Any whales taken under these special permits shall so far as practicable be processed and the proceeds shall be dealt with in accordance with directions issued by the Government by which the permit was granted.

3. Each Contracting Government shall transmit to such body as may be designated by the Commission, in so far as practicable, and at intervals of not more than one year, scientific information available to that Government with respect to whales and whaling, including the results of research conducted pursuant to paragraph 1 of this Article and to Article IV.

4. Recognizing that continuous collection and analysis of biological data in connection with the operations of factory ships and land stations are indispensable to sound and constructive management of the whale fisheries, the Contracting Governments will take all practicable measures to obtain such data.

Article IX

1. Each Contracting Government shall take appropriate measures to ensure the application of the provisions of this Convention and the punishment of infractions against the said provisions in operations carried out by persons or by vessels under its jurisdiction.

2. No bonus or other remuneration calculated with relation to the results of their work shall be paid to the gunners and crews of whale catchers in respect of any whales the taking of which is forbidden by this Convention.

3. Prosecution for infractions against or contraventions of this Convention shall be instituted by the Government having jurisdiction over the offence.

4. Each Contracting Government shall transmit to the Commission full details of each infraction of the provisions of this Convention by persons or vessels under the jurisdiction of that Government as reported by its inspectors. This information shall include a statement of measures taken for dealing with the infraction and of penalties imposed.

Article X

1. This Convention shall be ratified and the instruments of ratifications shall be deposited with the Government of the United States of America.

2. Any Government which has not signed this Convention may adhere thereto after it enters into force by a notification in writing to the Government of the United States of America.

3. The Government of the United States of America shall inform all other signatory Governments and all adhering Governments of all ratifications deposited and adherences received.

4. This Convention shall, when instruments of ratification have been deposited by at least six signatory Governments, which shall include the Governments of the Netherlands, Norway, the Union of Soviet Socialist Republics, the United Kingdom of Great Britain and Northern Ireland, and the United States of America, enter into force with respect to those Governments and shall enter into force with respect to each Government which subsequently ratifies or adheres on the date of the deposit of its instrument of ratification or the receipt of its notification of adherence.

5. The provisions of the Schedule shall not apply prior to July 1, 1948. Amendments to the Schedule adopted pursuant to Article V shall not apply prior to July 1, 1949.

Article XI

Any Contracting Government may withdraw from this Convention on June thirtieth of any year by giving notice on or before January first of the same year to the depository Government, which upon receipt of such a notice shall at once communicate it to the other Contracting Governments. Any other Contracting Government may, in like manner, within one month of the receipt of a copy of such a notice from the depository Government, give notice of withdrawal, so that the Convention shall cease to be in force on June thirtieth of the same year with respect to the Government giving such notice of withdrawal.

This Convention shall bear the date on which it is opened for signature and shall remain open for signature for a period of fourteen days thereafter.

IN WITNESS WHEREOF the undersigned, being duly authorized, have signed this Convention.

DONE in Washington this second day of December, 1946, in the English language, the original of which shall be deposited in the archives of the Government of the United States of America. The Government of the United States of America shall transmit certified copies thereof to all the other signatory and adhering Governments.

Convention on the International Maritime Organization

Done at Geneva, 6 March 1948; entry into force, 17 March 1958
289 UNTS 48 [Registration Number 4214][1]

The States Parties to the present Convention hereby establish the International Maritime Organization (hereinafter referred to as the 'Organization').

PART I
PURPOSES OF THE ORGANIZATION

Article 1

The purposes of the Organization are:

(a) To provide machinery for co-operation among Governments in the field of governmental regulation and practices relating to technical matters of all kinds affecting shipping engaged in international trade; to encourage and facilitate the general adoption of the highest practicable standards in matters concerning the maritime safety, efficiency of navigation and prevention and control of marine pollution from ships; and to deal with administrative and legal matters related to the purposes set out in this Article;

(b) To encourage the removal of discriminatory action and unnecessary restrictions by Governments affecting shipping engaged in international trade so as to promote the availability of shipping services to the commerce of the world

---

[1] The present text is a consolidated version of the original Convention on the Intergovernmental Maritime Consultative Organization, done in Geneva on 6 March 1948, as modified by amendments adopted by the Assembly on 15 September 1964 (A.69(ES.II)), 28 September 1965 (A.70(IV)), 17 October 1974 (A.315 (ES.V)), 14 November 1975 (A.358 (IX)), 17 November 1977 (A.400 (X)), 15 November 1979 (A.450 (XI)), 7 November 1991 (A.724(17)), 4 November 1993 (A.735 (18)). In 1982, the name of the Organization was changed to International Maritime Organization (IMO). Appendix I and II omitted.

without discrimination; assistance and encouragement given by a Government for the development of its national shipping and for purposes of security does not in itself constitute discrimination, provided that such assistance and encouragement is not based on measures designed to restrict the freedom of shipping of all flags to take part in international trade;

(c) To provide for the consideration by the Organization of matters concerning unfair restrictive practices by shipping concerns in accordance with part II;

(d) To provide for the consideration by the Organization of any matters concerning shipping and the effect of shipping on the marine environment that may be referred to it by an organ or specialized agency of the United Nations;

(e) To provide for the exchange of information among Governments on matters under consideration of the Organization.

PART II
FUNCTIONS

Article 2

In order to achieve the purposes set out in part I, the Organization shall:

(a) Subject to the provisions of Article 3, consider and make recommendations upon matters arising under Article 1(a), (b) and (c) that may be remitted to it by Members, by any organ or specialized agency of the United Nations or by any other intergovernmental organization or upon matters referred to it under Article 1(d);

(b) Provide for the drafting of conventions, agreements, or other suitable instruments, and recommend these to Governments and to intergovernmental organizations, and convene such conferences as may be necessary;

(c) Provide machinery for consultation among Members and the exchange of information among Governments;

(d) Perform functions arising in connection with paragraphs (a), (b) and (c) of this Article, in particular those assigned to it by or under international instruments relating to maritime matters and the effect of shipping on the marine environment;

(e) Facilitate as necessary, and in accordance with part X, technical co-operation within the scope of the Organization.

Article 3

In those matters which appear to the Organization capable of settlement through the normal processes of international shipping business the Organization shall so recommend. When, in the opinion of the Organization, any matter concerning unfair restrictive practices by shipping concerns is incapable of settlement through the normal processes of international shipping business, or has in fact so proved, and provided it shall first have been the subject of direct negotiations between the Members concerned, the Organization shall, at the request of one of those Members, consider the matter.

PART III
MEMBERSHIP

Article 4

Membership in the Organization shall be open to all States, subject to the provisions of part III.

Article 5

Members of the United Nations may become Members of the Organization by becoming Parties to the Convention in accordance with the provisions of Article 76.

Article 6

States not Members of the United Nations which have been invited to send representatives to the United Nations Maritime Conference convened in Geneva on 19 February 1948, may become Members by becoming Parties to the Convention in accordance with the provisions of Article 76.

Article 7

Any State not entitled to become a Member under Article 5 or 6 may apply through the Secretary-General of the Organization to become a Member and shall be admitted as a Member upon its becoming a Party to the Convention in accordance with the provisions of Article 76, provided that, upon the recommendation of the Council, its application has been approved by two thirds of the Members other then Associate Members.

Article 8

Any Territory or group of Territories to which the Convention has been made applicable under Article 77, by the Member having responsibility for its international relations or by the United Nations, may become an Associate Member of the Organization by notification in writing given by such Member or by the United Nations, as the case may be, to the Secretary-General of the United Nations.

Article 9

An Associate Member shall have the rights and obligations of a Member under the Convention except that it shall not have the right to vote or be eligible for membership on the Council and subject to this the word 'Member' in the Convention shall be deemed to include Associate Member unless the context otherwise requires.

Article 10

No State or Territory may become or remain a Member of the Organization contrary to a resolution of the General Assembly of the United Nations.

PART IV
ORGANS

Article 11

The Organization shall consist of an Assembly, a Council, a Maritime Safety Committee, a Legal Committee, a Marine Environment Protection Committee, a Technical Co-operation Committee, a Facilitation Committee and such subsidiary organs as the Organization may at any time consider necessary; and a Secretariat.

PART V
THE ASSEMBLY

Article 12

The Assembly shall consist of all the Members.

Article 13

Regular sessions of the Assembly shall take place once every two years. Extraordinary sessions shall be convened after a notice of sixty days whenever one third of the Members give notice to the Secretary-General that they desire a session to be arranged, or at any time if deemed necessary by the Council, after notice of sixty days.

Article 14

A majority of the Members other than the Associate Members shall continue a quorum for the meetings of the Assembly.

Article 15

The functions of the Assembly shall be:

(a) To elect at each regular session from among its Members, other than Associate Members, its President and two Vice-Presidents who shall hold office until the next regular session;

(b) To determine its own Rules of Procedure except as otherwise provided in the Convention;

(c) To establish any temporary or, upon recommendation of the Council, permanent subsidiary bodies it may consider to be necessary;

(d) To elect the members to be represented on the Council as provided in Article 17;

(e) To receive and consider the reports of the Council, and to decide upon any question referred to it by the Council;

(f) To approve the work programme of the Organization;

(g) To vote the budget and determine the financial arrangements of the Organization, in accordance with part XIII;

(h) To review the expenditures and approve the accounts of the Organization;

(i) To perform the functions of the Organization, provided that in matters relating to Article 2(a) and (b), the Assembly shall refer such matters to the Council for formulation by it of any recommendations or instruments thereon; provided further that any recommendations or instruments submitted to the Assembly by the Council and not accepted by the Assembly shall be referred back to the Council for further consideration with such observations as the Assembly may make;

(j) To recommend to Members for adoption, regulations and guidelines concerning maritime safety, the prevention and control of marine pollution from ships and other matters concerning the effect of shipping on the marine environment assigned to the Organization by or under international instruments, or amendments to such regulations and guidelines which have been referred to it;

(k) To take such action as it may deem appropriate to promote technical co-operation in accordance with Article 2(e), taking into account the special needs of developing countries;

(l) To take decisions in regard to convening any international conference or following any other appropriate procedure for the adoption of international conventions or of amendments to any international conventions which have been developed by the Maritime Safety Committee, the Legal Committee, the Marine Environment Protection Committee, the Technical Co-operation Committee, the Facilitation Committee, or other organs of the Organization;

(m) To refer to the Council for consideration or decision any matters within the scope of the Organization, except that the function of making recommendations under paragraph (j) of this Article shall not be delegated.

PART VI
THE COUNCIL

Article 16

The Council shall be composed of forty Members elected by the Assembly.

Article 17

In electing the Members of the Council, the Assembly shall observe the following criteria:

    (a)   Ten shall be States with the largest interest in providing international shipping services;

    (b)   Ten shall be other States with the largest interest in international seaborne trade;

    (c)   Twenty shall be States not elected under (a) or (b) above which have special interests in maritime transport or navigation, and whose election to the Council will ensure the representation of all major geographic areas of the world.

Article 18

Members represented on the Council in accordance with Article 16 shall hold office until the end of the next regular session of the Assembly. Members shall be eligible for re-election.

Article 19

    (a)   The Council shall elect its Chairman and adopt its own Rules of Procedure except as otherwise provided in the Convention.

    (b)   Twenty-six Members of the Council shall constitute a quorum.

    (c)   The Council shall meet upon one month's notice as often as may be necessary for the efficient discharge of its duties upon the summons of its Chairman or upon request by not less than four of its Members. It shall meet at such places as may be convenient.

Article 20

The Council shall invite any Member to participate, without vote, in its deliberations on any matter of particular concern to that Member.

Article 21

    (a)   The Council shall consider the draft work programme and budget estimates prepared by the Secretary-General in the light of the proposals of the Maritime Safety Committee, the Legal Committee, the Marine Environment Protection Committee, the Technical Co-operation Committee, the Facilitation Committee and other organs of the Organization and, taking these into account, shall establish and submit to the Assembly the work programme and budget of the Organization, having regard to the general interest and priorities of the Organization.

    (b)   The Council shall receive the reports, proposals and recommendations of the Maritime Safety Committee, the Legal Committee, the Marine Environment Protection Committee, the Technical Co-operation Committee, the Facilitation Committee and other organs of the Organization and shall transmit them to the Assembly and, when the Assembly is not in session, to the Members for information, together with the comments and recommendations of the Council.

    (c)   Matters within the scope of Articles 28, 33, 38, 43 and 48 shall be considered by the Council only after obtaining the views of the Maritime Safety Committee, the Legal

Committee, the Marine Environment Protection Committee, the Technical Co-operation Committee or the Facilitation Committee, as may be appropriate.

Article 22

The Council, with the approval of the Assembly, shall appoint the Secretary-General. The Council shall also make provision for the appointment of such other personnel as may be necessary, and determine the terms and conditions of service of the Secretary-General and other personnel, which terms and conditions shall conform as far as possible with those of the United Nations and its specialized agencies.

Article 23

The Council shall make a report to the Assembly at each regular session on the work performed by the Organization since the previous regular session of the Assembly.

Article 24

The Council shall submit to the Assembly financial statements of the Organization, together with the Council's comments and recommendations.

Article 25

(a)   The Council may enter into agreements or arrangements covering the relationship of the Organization with other organizations, as provided for in part XVI. Such agreements or arrangements shall be subject to approval by the Assembly.

(b)   Having regard to the provisions of part XVI and to the relations maintained with other bodies by the respective Committees under Articles 28, 33, 38, 43 and 48, the Council shall between sessions of the Assembly, be responsible for relations with other organizations.

Article 26

Between sessions of the Assembly, the Council shall perform all the functions of the Organization, except the function of making recommendations under Article 15(j). In particular, the Council shall co-ordinate the activities of the organs of the Organization and may make such adjustments in the work programme as are strictly necessary to ensure the efficient functioning of the Organization.

PART VII

MARITIME SAFETY COMMITTEE

Article 27

The Maritime Safety Committee shall consist of all the Members.

Article 28

(a)   The Maritime Safety Committee shall consider any matter within the scope of the Organization concerned with aids to navigation, construction and equipment of vessels, manning from a safety standpoint, rules for the prevention of collisions, handling of dangerous cargoes, maritime safety procedures and requirements, hydrographic information, log-books and navigational records, maritime casualty investigation, salvage and rescue, and any other matters directly affecting maritime safety.

(b)   The Maritime Safety Committee shall provide machinery for performing any duties assigned to it by this Convention, the Assembly or the Council, or any duty within the scope of this Article which may be assigned to it by or under any other international instrument and accepted by the Organization.

(c)   Having regard to the provisions of Article 25, the Maritime Safety Committee, upon request by the Assembly or the Council or, if it deems such action useful in the interests of its own work, shall maintain such close relationship with other bodies as may further the purposes of the Organization.

Article 29
The Maritime Safety Committee shall submit to the Council:
(a)   Proposals for safety regulations or for amendments to safety regulations which the Committee has developed;
(b)   Recommendations and guidelines which the Committee has developed;
(c)   A report on the work of the Committee since the previous session of the Council.

Article 30
The Maritime Safety Committee shall meet at least once a year. It shall elect its officers once a year and shall adopt its own Rules of Procedure.

Article 31
Notwithstanding anything to the contrary in this Convention but subject to the provisions of Article 27, the Maritime Safety when exercising the functions conferred upon it by or under any international convention or other instrument, shall conform to the relevant provisions of the convention or instrument in question, particularly as regards the rules governing the procedure to be followed.

PART VIII
LEGAL COMMITTEE

Article 32
The Legal Committee shall consist of all the Members.

Article 33
(a)   The Legal Committee shall consider any legal matters within the scope of the Organization.
(b)   The Legal Committee shall take all necessary steps to perform any duties assigned to it by this Convention or by the Assembly or the Council, or any duty within the scope of this Article which may be assigned to it by or under any other international instrument and accepted by the Organization
(c)   Having regard to the provisions of Article 25, the Legal Committee, upon request by the Assembly or the Council or, if it deems such action useful in the interests of its own work, shall maintain such close relationship with other bodies as may further the purposes of the Organization.

Article 34
The Legal Committee shall submit to the Council:
(a)   Drafts of international conventions and of amendments to international conventions which the Committee has developed;
(b)   A report on the work of the Committee since the previous session of the Council.

Article 35

The Legal Committee shall meet at least once a year. It shall elect its officers once a year and shall adopt its own Rules of Procedure.

Article 36

Notwithstanding anything to the contrary in this Convention, but subject to the provisions of Article 32, the Legal Committee, when exercising the functions conferred upon it by or under any international convention or other instrument, shall conform to the relevant provisions of the convention or instrument in question, particularly as regards the rules governing the procedures to be followed.

PART IX
MARINE ENVIRONMENT PROTECTION COMMITTEE

Article 37

The Marine Environment Protection Committee shall consist of all the Members.

Article 38

The Marine Environment Protection Committee shall consider any matter within the scope of the Organization concerned with the prevention and control of marine pollution from ships and in particular shall:

  (a) Perform such functions as are or may be conferred upon the Organization by or under international conventions for the prevention and control of marine pollution from ships, particularly with respect to the adoption and amendment of regulations or other provisions, as provided for in such conventions;

  (b) Consider appropriate measures to facilitate the enforcement of the conventions referred to in paragraph (a) above;

  (c) Provide for the acquisition of scientific, technical and any other practical information on the prevention and control of marine pollution from ships for dissemination to States, in particular to developing countries and, where appropriate, make recommendations and develop guidelines;

  (d) Promote co-operation with regional organizations concerned with the prevention and control of marine pollution from ships, having regard to the provisions of Article 25;

  (e) Consider and take appropriate action with respect to any other matters falling within the scope of the Organization which would contribute to the prevention and control of marine pollution from ships including co-operation on environmental matters with other international organizations, having regard to the provisions of Article 25.

Article 39

The Marine Environment Protection Committee shall submit to the Council:

  (a) Proposals for regulations for the prevention and control of marine pollution from ships and for amendments to such regulations which the Committee has developed;

  (b) Recommendations and guidelines which the Committee has developed;

  (c) A report on the work of the Committee since the previous session of the Council.

Article 40

The Marine Environment Protection Committee shall meet at least once a year. It shall elect its officers once a year and shall adopt its own Rules of Procedure.

Article 41

Notwithstanding anything to the contrary in this Convention, but subject to the provisions of Article 37, the Marine Environment Protection Committee, when exercising the functions conferred upon it by or under any international convention or other instrument, shall conform to the relevant provisions of the convention or instrument in question, particularly as regards the rules governing the procedures to be followed.

PART X

TECHNICAL CO-OPERATION COMMITTEE

Article 42

The Technical Co-operation Committee shall consist of all the Members.

Article 43

(a) The Technical Co-operation Committee shall consider, as appropriate, any matter within the scope of the Organization concerned with the implementation of technical co-operation projects funded by the relevant United Nations programme for which the Organization acts as the executing or co-operating agency or by funds-in-trust voluntarily provided to the Organization, and any other matters related to the Organization's activities in the technical co-operation field.

(b) The Technical Co-operation Committee shall keep under review the work of the Secretariat concerning technical co-operation.

(c) The Technical Co-operation Committee shall perform those functions assigned to it by this Convention or by the Assembly or the Council, or any duty within the scope of this Article which may be assigned to it by or under any other international instrument and accepted by the Organization.

(d) Having regard to the provisions of Article 25, the Technical Co-operation Committee, upon request by the Assembly or the Council or, if it deems such action useful in the interests of its own work, shall maintain such close relationships with other bodies as may further the purposes of the Organization.

Article 44

The Technical Co-operation Committee shall submit to the Council:
(a) Recommendations which the Committee has developed;
(b) A report on the work of the Committee since the previous sessions of the Council.

Article 45

The Technical Co-operation Committee shall meet at least once a year. It shall elect its officers once a year and shall adopt its own Rules of Procedure.

Article 46

Notwithstanding anything contrary in this Convention, but subject to the provisions of Article 42, the Technical Co-operation Committee, when exercising the functions conferred upon it by or under any international convention or other instrument, shall conform to the relevant provisions of the convention or instrument in question, particularly as regards the rules governing the procedures to be followed.

PART XI
THE FACILITATION COMMITTEE

Article 47

The Facilitation Committee shall consist of all the Members.

Article 48

The Facilitation Committee shall consider any matter within the scope of the Organization concerned with the facilitation of international maritime traffic and in particular shall:

(a) Perform such functions as are or may be conferred upon the Organization by or under international conventions for the facilitation of international maritime traffic, particularly with respect to the adoption and amendment of measures or other provisions, as provided for in such conventions.

(b) Having regard to the provisions of Article 25, the Facilitation Committee, upon request by the Assembly or the Council or if it deems such action useful in the interests of its own work, shall maintain such close relationship with other bodies as may further the purposes of the Organization.

Article 49

The Facilitation Committee shall submit to the Council:

(a) Recommendations and guidelines which the Committee has developed.

(b) A report on the work of the Committee since the previous session of the Council.

Article 50

The Facilitation Committee shall meet at least once a year. It shall elect its officers once a year and shall adopt its own Rules of Procedure.

Article 51

Notwithstanding anything to the contrary in this Convention, but subject to the provisions of Article 47, the Facilitation Committee, when exercising the functions conferred upon it by or under any international convention or other instrument, shall conform to the relevant provisions of the convention or instrument in question, particularly as regards the rules governing the procedure to be followed.

PART XII
THE SECRETARIAT

Article 52

The Secretariat shall comprise the Secretary-General and such other personnel as the Organization may require. The Secretary-General shall be the chief administrative officer of the Organization and shall, subject to the provisions of Article 22, appoint the above-mentioned personnel.

Article 53

The Secretariat shall maintain all such records as may be necessary for the efficient discharge of the functions of the Organization and shall prepare, collect and circulate the papers, documents, agenda, minutes and information that may be required for the work of the Organization.

Article 54

The Secretary-General shall prepare and submit to the Council the financial statements for each year and the budget estimates on a biennial basis, with the estimates for each year shown separately.

Article 55

The Secretary-General shall keep Members informed with respect to the activities of the Organization. Each Member may appoint one or more representatives for the purpose of communication with the Secretary-General.

Article 56

In the performance of their duties the Secretary-General and the staff shall not seek or receive instructions from any Government or from any authority external to the Organization. They shall refrain from any action which might reflect on their position as international officials. Each Member on its part undertakes to respect the exclusively international character of the responsibilities of the Secretary-General and the staff and not to seek to influence them in the discharge of their responsibilities.

Article 57

The Secretary-General shall assume any other functions which may be assigned to him by the Convention, the Assembly or the Council.

PART XIII
FINANCES

Article 58

Each Member shall bear the salary, travel and other expenses of its own delegation to the meetings held by the Organization.

Article 59

The Council shall consider the financial statements and budget estimates prepared by the Secretary-General and submit them to the Assembly with its comments and recommendations.

Article 60

(a) Subject to any agreement between the Organization and the United Nations, the Assembly shall review and approve the budget estimates.

(b) The Assembly shall apportion the expenses among the Members in accordance with a scale to be fixed by it after consideration of the proposals of the Council thereon.

Article 61

Any Member which fails to discharge its financial obligation to the Organization within one year from the date on which it is due, shall have no vote in the Assembly, the Council, the Maritime Safety Committee, the Legal Committee, the Marine Environment

Protection Committee, the Technical Co-operation Committee or the Facilitation Committee unless the Assembly, at its discretion, waives this provision.

PART XIV
VOTING

Article 62

Except as otherwise provided in the Convention or in any international agreement which confers functions on the Assembly, the Council, the Maritime Safety Committee, the Legal Committee, the Marine Environment Protection Committee, or the Technical Co-operation Committee, or the Facilitation Committee, the following provisions shall apply to voting in these organs:

(a)   Each member shall have one vote.

(b)   Decisions shall be by a majority vote of the Members present and voting and, for decisions where a two-thirds majority vote is required, by a two-thirds majority vote of those present.

(c)   For the purpose of the Convention, the phrase 'Members present and voting' means 'Members present and casting an affirmative or negative vote'. Members, which abstain from voting, shall be considered as 'not voting'.

PART XV
HEADQUARTERS OF THE ORGANIZATION

Article 63

(a)   The Headquarters of the Organization shall be established in London.

(b)   The Assembly may by a two-thirds majority vote change the site of the Headquarters if necessary.

(c)   The Assembly may hold sessions in any place other than the Headquarters if the Council deems it necessary.

PART XVI
RELATIONSHIP WITH THE UNITED NATIONS AND OTHER ORGANIZATIONS

Article 64

The Organization shall be brought into relationship with the United Nations in accordance with Article 57 of the Charter of the United Nations as the specialized agency in the field of shipping and the effect of shipping on the marine environment. This relationship shall be effected through an agreement with the United Nations under Article 63 of the Charter of the United Nations, which agreement shall be concluded as provided in Article 25.

Article 65

The Organization shall co-operate with any specialized agency of the United Nations in matters which may be the common concern of the Organization and of such specialized agency, and shall consider such matters and act with respect to them in accord with such specialized agency.

Article 66

The Organization may, on matters within its scope, co-operate with other intergovernmental organizations which are not specialized agencies of the United Nations, but whose interests and activities are related to the purposes of the Organization.

Article 67

The Organization may, on matters within its scope, make suitable arrangements for consultation and co-operation with non-governmental international organizations.

Article 68

Subject to approval by a two-thirds majority vote of the Assembly, the Organization may take over from any other international organizations, governmental or non-governmental, such functions, resources and obligations within the scope of the Organization as may be transferred to the Organization by international agreements or by mutually acceptable arrangements entered into between competent authorities of the respective organizations. Similarly, the Organization may take over any administrative functions which are within its scope and which have been entrusted to a Government under the terms of any international instrument.

PART XVII
LEGAL CAPACITY, PRIVILEGES AND IMMUNITIES

Article 69

The legal capacity, privileges and immunities to be accorded to, or in connection with, the Organization, shall be derived from and governed by the General Convention on the Privileges and Immunities of the Specialized Agencies approved by the General Assembly of the United Nations on 21 November 1947, subject to such modifications as may be set forth in the final (or revised) text of the Annex approved by the Organization in accordance with Sections 36 and 38 of the said General Convention.

Article 70

Pending its accession to the said General Convention in respect of the Organization, each Member undertakes to apply the provisions of appendix II[2] to the present Convention.

PART XVIII
AMENDMENTS

Article 71

Texts of proposed amendments to the Convention shall be communicated by the Secretary-General to Members at least six months in advance of their consideration by the Assembly. Amendments shall be adopted by a two-thirds majority vote of the Assembly. Twelve months after its acceptance by two thirds of the Members of the Organization, other than Associate Members, each amendment shall come into force for all Members. If within the first 60 days of this period of twelve months a Member gives notification of withdrawal from the Organization on account of an amendment the withdrawal shall, notwithstanding the provisions of Article 78 of the Convention, take effect on the date on which such amendment comes into force.

Article 72

Any amendment adopted under Article 71 shall be deposited with the Secretary-General of the United Nations, who will immediately forward a copy of the amendment to all Members.

---

[2] Appendix omitted.

Article 73

A declaration or acceptance under Article 71 shall be made by the communication of an instrument to the Secretary-General for deposit with the Secretary-General of the United Nations. The Secretary-General will notify Members of the receipt of any such instrument and of the date when the amendment enters into force.

PART XIX

INTERPRETATION

Article 74

Any question or dispute concerning the interpretation or application of the Convention shall be referred to the Assembly for settlement, or shall be settled in such other manner as the parties to the dispute may agree. Nothing in this Article shall preclude any organ of the Organization from settling any such question or dispute that may arise during the exercise of its functions.

Article 75

Any legal question which cannot be settled as provided in Article 74 shall be referred by the Organization to the International Court of Justice for an advisory opinion in accordance with Article 96 of the Charter of the United Nations.

PART XX

MISCELLANEOUS PROVISIONS

Article 76 Signature and acceptance

Subject to the provisions of part III the present Convention shall remain open for signature or acceptance and States may become Parties to the Convention by:

(a)   Signature without reservation as to acceptance;

(b)   Signature subject to acceptance followed by acceptance; or

(c)   Acceptance.

Acceptance shall be effected by the deposit of an instrument with the Secretary-General of the United Nations.

Article 77 Territories

(a)   Members may make a declaration at any time that their participation in the Convention includes all or a group or single one of the Territories for whose international relations they are responsible.

(b)   The Convention does not apply to Territories for whose international relations Members are responsible unless a declaration to that effect has been made on their behalf under the provisions of paragraph (a) of this Article.

(c)   A declaration made under paragraph (a) of this Article shall be communicated to the Secretary-General of the United Nations and a copy of it will be forwarded by him to all States invited to the United Nations Maritime Conference and to such other States as may have become Members.

(d)   In cases where under a Trusteeship Agreement the United Nations is the administering authority, the United Nations may accept the Convention on behalf of one, several, or all of the Trust Territories in accordance with the procedure set forth in Article 76.

Article 78 Withdrawal

(a)　Any Member may withdraw from the Organization by written notification given to the Secretary-General of the United Nations, who will immediately inform the other Members and the Secretary-General of the Organization of such notification. Notification of withdrawal may be given at any time after the expiration of twelve months from the date on which the Convention has come into force. The withdrawal shall take effect upon the expiration of twelve months from the date on which such written notification is received by the Secretary-General of the United Nations.

(b)　The application of the Convention to a Territory or group of Territories under Article 77 may at any time be terminated by written notification given to the Secretary-General of the United Nations by the Member responsible for its international relations or, in the case of a Trust Territory of which the United Nations is the administering authority, by the United Nations. The Secretary-General of the United Nations will immediately inform all Members and the Secretary-General of the Organization of such notification. The notification shall take effect upon the expiration of twelve months from the date on which it is received by the Secretary-General of the United Nations.

PART XXI
ENTRY INTO FORCE

Article 79

The present Convention shall enter into force on the date when 21 States, of which seven shall each have a total tonnage of not less than 1,000,000 gross tons of shipping, have become Parties to the Convention in accordance with Article 76.

Article 80

The Secretary-General of the United Nations will inform all States invited to the United Nations Maritime Conference and such other States as may have become Members, of the date when each State becomes Party to the Convention, and also of the date on which the Convention enters into force.

Article 81

The present Convention, of which the English, French and Spanish texts are equally authentic, shall be deposited with the Secretary-General of the United Nations, who will transmit certified copies thereof to each of the States invited to the United Nations Maritime Conference and to such other States as may have become Members.

Article 82

The United Nations is authorized to effect registration of the Convention as soon as it comes into force.

IN WITNESS WHEREOF the undersigned being duly authorized by their respective Governments for that purpose have signed the present Convention.

DONE in Geneva on 6 March 1948.

Convention on the Territorial Sea and the Contiguous Zone

Done at Geneva, 29 April 1958; entry into force, 10 September 1964
516 UNTS 206 [Registration Number 7477]

The States Parties to this Convention,
Have agreed as follows:

PART I
TERRITORIAL SEA

Section I. General

Article 1

1. The sovereignty of a State extends, beyond its land territory and its internal waters, to a belt of sea adjacent to its coast, described as the territorial sea.

2. This sovereignty is exercised subject to the provisions of these articles and to other rules of international law.

Article 2

The sovereignty of a coastal State extends to the air space over the territorial sea as well as to its bed and subsoil.

Section II. Limits of the Territorial Sea

Article 3

Except where otherwise provided in these articles, the normal baseline for measuring the breadth of the territorial sea is the low-water line along the coast as marked on large-scale charts officially recognized by the coastal State.

Article 4

1. In localities where the coast line is deeply indented and cut into, or if there is a fringe of islands along the coast in its immediate vicinity, the method of straight baselines joining appropriate points may be employed in drawing the baseline from which the breadth of the territorial sea is measured.

2. The drawing of such baselines must not depart to any appreciable extent from the general direction of the coast, and the sea areas lying within the lines must be sufficiently closely linked to the land domain to be subject to the regime of internal waters.

3. Baselines shall not be drawn to and from low-tide elevations, unless lighthouses or similar installations which are permanently above sea level have been built on them.

4. Where the method of straight baselines is applicable under the provisions of paragraph 1, account may be taken, in determining particular baselines, of economic interests peculiar to the region concerned, the reality and the importance of which are clearly evidenced by a long usage.

5. The system of straight baselines may not be applied by a State in such a manner as to cut off from the high seas the territorial sea of another State.

6. The coastal State must clearly indicate straight baselines on charts, to which due publicity must be given.

Article 5

    1. Waters on the landward side of the baseline of the territorial sea form part of the internal waters of the State.

    2. Where the establishment of a straight baseline in accordance with article 4 has the effect of enclosing as internal waters areas which previously had been considered as part of the territorial sea or of the high seas, a right of innocent passage, as provided in articles 14 to 23, shall exist in those waters.

Article 6

    The outer limit of the territorial sea is the line every point of which is at a distance from the nearest point of the baseline equal to the breadth of the territorial sea.

Article 7

    1. This article relates only to bays the coasts of which belong to a single State.

    2. For the purposes of these articles, a bay is a well-marked indentation whose penetration is in such proportion to the width of its mouth as to contain landlocked waters and constitute more than a mere curvature of the coast. An indentation shall not, however, be regarded as a bay unless its area is as large as, or larger than, that of the semi-circle whose diameter is a line drawn across the mouth of that indentation.

    3. For the purpose of measurement, the area of an indentation is that lying between the low-water mark around the shore of the indentation and a line joining the low-water marks of its natural entrance points. Where, because of the presence of islands, an indentation has more than one mouth, the semi-circle shall be drawn on a line as long as the sum total of the lengths of the lines across the different mouths. Islands within an indentation shall be included as if they were part of the water areas of the indentation.

    4. If the distance between the low-water marks of the natural entrance points of a bay does not exceed twenty-four miles, a closing line may be drawn between these two low-water marks, and the waters enclosed thereby shall be considered as internal waters.

    5. Where the distance between the low-water marks of the natural entrance points of a bay exceeds twenty-four miles, a straight baseline of twenty-four miles shall be drawn within the bay in such a manner as to enclose the maximum area of water that is possible with a line of that length.

    6. The foregoing provisions shall not apply to so-called 'historic' bays, or in any case where the straight baseline system provided for in article 4 is applied.

Article 8

    For the purpose of delimiting the territorial sea, the outermost permanent harbour works which form an integral part of the harbour system shall be regarded as forming part of the coast.

Article 9

    Roadsteads which are normally used for the loading, unloading and anchoring of ships, and which would otherwise be situated wholly or partly outside the outer limit of the territorial sea, are included in the territorial sea. The coastal State must clearly demarcate such roadsteads and indicate them on charts together with their boundaries, to which due publicity must be given.

Article 10

1. An island is a naturally-formed area of land, surrounded by water, which is above water at high-tide.

2. The territorial sea of an island is measured in accordance with the provisions of these articles.

Article 11

1. A low-tide elevation is a naturally-formed area of land which is surrounded by and above water at low-tide but submerged at high-tide. Where a low-tide elevation is situated wholly or partly at a distance not exceeding the breadth of the territorial sea from the mainland or an island, the low-water line on that elevation may be used as the baseline for measuring the breadth of the territorial sea.

2. Where a low-tide elevation is wholly situated at a distance exceeding the breadth of the territorial sea from the mainland or an island, it has no territorial sea of its own.

Article 12

1. Where the coasts of two States are opposite or adjacent to each other, neither of the two States is entitled, failing agreement between them to the contrary, to extend its territorial sea beyond the median line every point of which is equidistant from the nearest points on the baselines from which the breadth of the territorial seas of each of the two States is measured. The provisions of this paragraph shall not apply, however, where it is necessary by reason of historic title or other special circumstances to delimit the territorial seas of the two States in a way which is at variance with this provision.

2. The line of delimitation between the territorial seas of two States lying opposite to each other or adjacent to each other shall be marked on large-scale charts officially recognized by the coastal States.

Article 13

If a river flows directly into the sea, the baseline shall be a straight line across the mouth of the river between points on the low-tide line of its banks.

SECTION III. RIGHT OF INNOCENT PASSAGE

Sub-Section A. Rules Applicable to all Ships

Article 14

1. Subject to the provisions of these articles, ships of all States, whether coastal or not, shall enjoy the right of innocent passage through the territorial sea.

2. Passage means navigation through the territorial sea for the purpose either of traversing that sea without entering internal waters, or of proceeding to internal waters, or of making for the high seas from internal waters.

3. Passage includes stopping and anchoring, but only in so far as the same are incidental to ordinary navigation or are rendered necessary by force majeure or by distress.

4. Passage is innocent so long as it is not prejudicial to the peace, good order or security of the coastal State. Such passage shall take place in conformity with these articles and with other rules of international law.

5. Passage of foreign fishing vessels shall not be considered innocent if they do not observe such laws and regulations as the coastal State may make and publish in order to prevent these vessels from fishing in the territorial sea.

6. Submarines are required to navigate on the surface and to show their flag.

Article 15

1. The coastal State must not hamper innocent passage through the territorial sea.

2. The coastal State is required to give appropriate publicity to any dangers to navigation, of which it has knowledge, within its territorial sea.

Article 16

1. The coastal State may take the necessary steps in its territorial sea to prevent passage which is not innocent.

2. In the case of ships proceeding to internal waters, the coastal State shall also have the right to take the necessary steps to prevent any breach of the conditions to which admission of those ships to those waters is subject.

3. Subject to the provisions of paragraph 4, the coastal State may, without discrimination amongst foreign ships, suspend temporarily in specified areas of its territorial sea the innocent passage of foreign ships if such suspension is essential for the protection of its security. Such suspension shall take effect only after having been duly published.

4. There shall be no suspension of the innocent passage of foreign ships through straits which are used for international navigation between one part of the high seas and another part of the high seas or the territorial sea of a foreign State.

Article 17

Foreign ships exercising the right of innocent passage shall comply with the laws and regulations enacted by the coastal State in conformity with these articles and other rules of international law and, in particular, with such laws and regulations relating to transport and navigation.

Sub-Section B. Rules Applicable to Merchant Ships

Article 18

1. No charge may be levied upon foreign ships by reason only of their passage through the territorial sea.

2. Charges may be levied upon a foreign ship passing through the territorial sea as payment only for specific services rendered to the ship. These charges shall be levied without discrimination.

Article 19

1. The criminal jurisdiction of the coastal State should not be exercised on board a foreign ship passing through the territorial sea to arrest any person or to conduct any investigation in connexion with any crime committed on board the ship during its passage, save only in the following cases:

 (a)   If the consequences of the crime extend to the coastal State; or

 (b)   If the crime is of a kind to disturb the peace of the country or the good order of the territorial sea; or

 (c)   If the assistance of the local authorities has been requested by the captain of the ship or by the consul of the country whose flag the ship flies; or

 (d)   If it is necessary for the suppression of illicit traffic in narcotic drugs.

2. The above provisions do not affect the right of the coastal State to take any steps authorized by its laws for the purpose of an arrest or investigation on board a foreign ship passing through the territorial sea after leaving internal waters.

3. In the cases provided for in paragraphs 1 and 2 of this article, the coastal State shall, if the captain so requests, advise the consular authority of the flag State before taking any steps, and shall facilitate contact between such authority and the ship's crew. In cases of emergency this notification may be communicated while the measures are being taken.

4. In considering whether or how an arrest should be made, the local authorities shall pay due regard to the interests of navigation.

5. The coastal State may not take any steps on board a foreign ship passing through the territorial sea to arrest any person or to conduct any investigation in connexion with any crime committed before the ship entered the territorial sea, if the ship, proceeding from a foreign port, is only passing through the territorial sea without entering internal waters.

Article 20

1. The coastal State should not stop or divert a foreign ship passing through the territorial sea for the purpose of exercising civil jurisdiction in relation to a person on board the ship.

2. The coastal State may not levy execution against or arrest the ship for the purpose of any civil proceedings, save only in respect of obligations or liabilities assumed or incurred by the ship itself in the course or for the purpose of its voyage through the waters of the coastal State.

3. The provisions of the previous paragraph are without prejudice to the right of the coastal State, in accordance with its laws, to levy execution against or to arrest, for the purpose of any civil proceedings, a foreign ship lying in the territorial sea, or passing through the territorial sea after leaving internal waters.

Sub-Section C. Rules Applicable to Government Ships Other than Warships

Article 21

The rules contained in sub-sections A and B shall also apply to government ships operated for commercial purposes.

Article 22

1. The rules contained in sub-section A and in article 18 shall apply to government ships operated for non-commercial purposes.

2. With such exceptions as are contained in the provisions referred to in the preceding paragraph, nothing in these articles affects the immunities which such ships enjoy under these articles or other rules of international law.

Sub-Section D. Rules Applicable to Warships

Article 23

If any warship does not comply with the regulations of the coastal State concerning passage through the territorial sea and disregards any request for compliance which is made to it, the coastal State may require the warship to leave the territorial sea.

PART II
CONTIGUOUS ZONE

Article 24

1. In a zone of the high seas contiguous to its territorial sea, the coastal State may exercise the control necessary to:

    (a) Prevent infringement of its customs, fiscal, immigration or sanitary regulations within its territory or territorial sea;

    (b) Punish infringement of the above regulations committed within its territory or territorial sea.

2. The contiguous zone may not extend beyond twelve miles from the baseline from which the breadth of the territorial sea is measured.

3. Where the coasts of two States are opposite or adjacent to each other, neither of the two States is entitled, failing agreement between them to the contrary, to extend its contiguous zone beyond the median line every point of which is equidistant from the nearest points on the baselines from which the breadth of the territorial seas of the two States is measured.

PART III
FINAL ARTICLES

Article 25

The provisions of this Convention shall not affect conventions or other international agreements already in force, as between States Parties to them.

Article 26

This Convention shall, until 31 October 1958, be open for signature by all States Members of the United Nations or of any of the specialized agencies, and by any other State invited by the General Assembly of the United Nations to become a Party to the Convention.

Article 27

This Convention is subject to ratification. The instruments of ratification shall be deposited with the Secretary-General of the United Nations.

Article 28

This Convention shall be open for accession by any States belonging to any of the categories mentioned in article 26. The instruments of accession shall be deposited with the Secretary-General of the United Nations.

Article 29

1. This Convention shall come into force on the thirtieth day following the date of deposit of the twenty-second instrument of ratification or accession with the Secretary-General of the United Nations.

2. For each State ratifying or acceding to the Convention after the deposit of the twenty-second instrument of ratification or accession, the Convention shall enter into force on the thirtieth day after deposit by such State of its instrument of ratification or accession.

Article 30

1. After the expiration of a period of five years from the date on which this Convention shall enter into force, a request for the revision of this Convention may be made at any time by any Contracting Party by means of a notification in writing addressed to the Secretary-General of the United Nations.

2. The General Assembly of the United Nations shall decide upon the steps, if any, to be taken in respect of such request.

Article 31

The Secretary-General of the United Nations shall inform all States Members of the United Nations and the other States referred to in article 26:

(a) Of signatures to this Convention and of the deposit of instruments of ratification or accession, in accordance with articles 26, 27 and 28;

(b) Of the date on which this Convention will come into force, in accordance with article 29;

(c) Of requests for revision in accordance with article 30.

Article 32

The original of this Convention, of which the Chinese, English, French, Russian and Spanish texts are equally authentic, shall be deposited with the Secretary-General of the United Nations, who shall send certified copies thereof to all States referred to in article 26.

IN WITNESS WHEREOF the undersigned Plenipotentiaries, being duly authorized thereto by their respective Governments, have signed this Convention.

DONE at Geneva, this twenty-ninth day of April one thousand nine hundred and fifty-eight.

Convention on the High Seas

Done at Geneva, 29 April 1958; entry into force, 30 September 1962
450 UNTS 82 [Registration Number 6465]

The States Parties to this Convention,

Desiring to codify the rules of international law relating to the high seas,

Recognizing that the United Nations Conference on the Law of the Sea, held at Geneva from 24 February to 27 April 1958, adopted the following provisions as generally declaratory of established principles of international law,

Have agreed as follows:

Article 1

The term 'high seas' means all parts of the sea that are not included in the territorial sea or in the internal waters of a State.

Article 2

The high seas being open to all nations, no State may validly purport to subject any part of them to its sovereignty. Freedom of the high seas is exercised under the conditions laid down by these articles and by the other rules of international law. It comprises, *inter alia*, both for coastal and non-coastal States:

(1) Freedom of navigation;

(2) Freedom of fishing;

(3) Freedom to lay submarine cables and pipelines;

(4) Freedom to fly over the high seas.

These freedoms, and others which are recognized by the general principles of international law, shall be exercised by all States with reasonable regard to the interests of other States in their exercise of the freedom of the high seas.

Article 3

1. In order to enjoy the freedom of the seas on equal terms with coastal States, States having no sea-coast should have free access to the sea. To this end States situated between the sea and a State having no sea-coast shall by common agreement with the latter, and in conformity with existing international conventions, accord:

(a) To the State having no sea-coast, on a basis of reciprocity, free transit through their territory; and

(b) To ships flying the flag of that State treatment equal to that accorded to their own ships, or to the ships of any other States, as regards access to seaports and the use of such ports.

2. States situated between the sea and a State having no sea-coast shall settle, by mutual agreement with the latter, and taking into account the rights of the coastal State or State of transit and the special conditions of the State having no sea-coast, all matters relating to freedom of transit and equal treatment in ports, in case such States are not already parties to existing international conventions.

Article 4

Every State, whether coastal or not, has the right to sail ships under its flag on the high seas.

Article 5

1. Each State shall fix the conditions for the grant of its nationality to ships, for the registration of ships in its territory, and for the right to fly its flag. Ships have the nationality of the State whose flag they are entitled to fly. There must exist a genuine link between the State and the ship; in particular, the State must effectively exercise its jurisdiction and control in administrative, technical and social matters over ships flying its flag.

2. Each State shall issue to ships to which it has granted the right to fly its flag documents to that effect.

Article 6

1. Ships shall sail under the flag of one State only and, save in exceptional cases expressly provided for in international treaties or in these articles, shall be subject to its exclusive jurisdiction on the high seas. A ship may not change its flag during a voyage or while in a port of call, save in the case of a real transfer of ownership or change of registry.

2. A ship which sails under the flags of two or more States, using them according to convenience, may not claim any of the nationalities in question with respect to any other State, and may be assimilated to a ship without nationality.

Article 7

The provisions of the preceding articles do not prejudice the question of ships employed on the official service of an inter-governmental organization flying the flag of the organization.

Article 8

1. Warships on the high seas have complete immunity from the jurisdiction of any State other than the flag State.

2. For the purposes of these articles, the term 'warship' means a ship belonging to the naval forces of a State and bearing the external marks distinguishing warships of its nationality, under the command of an officer duly commissioned by the government and whose name appears in the Navy List, and manned by a crew who are under regular naval discipline.

Article 9

Ships owned or operated by a State and used only on government non-commercial service shall, on the high seas, have complete immunity from the jurisdiction of any State other than the flag State.

Article 10

1. Every State shall take such measures for ships under its flag as are necessary to ensure safety at sea with regard *inter alia* to:
    (a) The use of signals, the maintenance of communications and the prevention of collisions;
    (b) The manning of ships and labour conditions for crews taking into account the applicable international labour instruments;
    (c) The construction, equipment and seaworthiness of ships.

2. In taking such measures each State is required to conform to generally accepted international standards and to take any steps which may be necessary to ensure their observance.

Article 11

1. In the event of a collision or of any other incident of navigation concerning a ship on the high seas, involving the penal or disciplinary responsibility of the master or of any other person in the service of the ship, no penal or disciplinary proceedings may be instituted against such persons except before the judicial or administrative authorities either of the flag State or of the State of which such person is a national.

2. In disciplinary matters, the State which has issued a master's certificate or a certificate of competence or licence shall alone be competent, after due legal process, to pronounce the withdrawal of such certificates, even if the holder is not a national of the State which issued them.

3. No arrest or detention of the ship, even as a measure of investigation, shall be ordered by any authorities other than those of the flag State.

Article 12

1. Every State shall require the master of a ship sailing under its flag, in so far as he can do so without serious danger to the ship, the crew or the passengers,
    (a) To render assistance to any person found at sea in danger of being lost;
    (b) To proceed with all possible speed to the rescue of persons in distress if informed of their need of assistance, in so far as such action may reasonably be expected of him;
    (c) After a collision, to render assistance to the other ship, her crew and her passengers and, where possible, to inform the other ship of the name of his own ship, her port of registry and the nearest port at which she will call.

2. Every coastal State shall promote the establishment and maintenance of an adequate and effective search and rescue service regarding safety on and over the sea and where circumstances so require by way of mutual regional arrangements co-operate with neighbouring States for this purpose.

Article 13

Every State shall adopt effective measures to prevent and punish the transport of slaves in ships authorized to fly its flag, and to prevent the unlawful use of its flag for that purpose. Any slave taking refuge on board any ship, whatever its flag, shall *ipso facto* be free.

Article 14

All States shall co-operate to the fullest possible extent in the repression of piracy on the high seas or in any other place outside the jurisdiction of any State.

Article 15

Piracy consists of any of the following acts:

1. Any illegal acts of violence, detention or any act of depredation, committed for private ends by the crew or the passengers of a private ship or a private aircraft, and directed:

   (a) On the high seas, against another ship or aircraft, or against persons or property on board such ship or aircraft;

   (b) Against a ship, aircraft, persons or property in a place outside the jurisdiction of any State;

2. Any act of voluntary participation in the operation of a ship or of an aircraft with knowledge of facts making it a pirate ship or aircraft;

3. Any act of inciting or of intentionally facilitating an act described in sub-paragraph 1 or sub-paragraph 2 of this article.

Article 16

The acts of piracy, as defined in article 15, committed by a warship, government ship or government aircraft whose crew has mutinied and taken control of the ship or aircraft are assimilated to acts committed by a private ship.

Article 17

A ship or aircraft is considered a pirate ship or aircraft if it is intended by the persons in dominant control to be used for the purpose of committing one of the acts referred to in article 15. The same applies if the ship or aircraft has been used to commit any such act, so long as it remains under the control of the persons guilty of that act.

Article 18

A ship or aircraft may retain its nationality although it has become a pirate ship or aircraft. The retention or loss of nationality is determined by the law of the State from which such nationality was derived.

Article 19

On the high seas, or in any other place outside the jurisdiction of any State, every State may seize a pirate ship or aircraft, or a ship taken by piracy and under the control of pirates, and arrest the persons and seize the property on board. The courts of the State which carried out the seizure may decide upon the penalties to be imposed, and may also determine the action to be taken with regard to the ships, aircraft or property, subject to the rights of third parties acting in good faith.

Article 20

Where the seizure of a ship or aircraft on suspicion of piracy has been effected without adequate grounds, the State making the seizure shall be liable to the State the nationality of which is possessed by the ship or aircraft, for any loss or damage caused by the seizure.

Article 21

A seizure on account of piracy may only be carried out by warships or military aircraft, or other ships or aircraft on government service authorized to that effect.

Article 22

1. Except where acts of interference derive from powers conferred by treaty, a warship which encounters a foreign merchant ship on the high seas is not justified in boarding her unless there is reasonable ground for suspecting:
    (a) That the ship is engaged in piracy; or
    (b) That the ship is engaged in the slave trade; or
    (c) That though flying a foreign flag or refusing to show its flag, the ship is, in reality, of the same nationality as the warship.

2. In the cases provided for in sub-paragraphs (a), (b) and (c) above, the warship may proceed to verify the ship's right to fly its flag. To this end, it may send a boat under the command of an officer to the suspected ship. If suspicion remains after the documents have been checked, it may proceed to a further examination on board the ship, which must be carried out with all possible consideration.

3. If the suspicions prove to be unfounded, and provided that the ship boarded has not committed any act justifying them, it shall be compensated for any loss or damage that may have been sustained.

Article 23

1. The hot pursuit of a foreign ship may be undertaken when the competent authorities of the coastal State have good reason to believe that the ship has violated the laws and regulations of that State. Such pursuit must be commenced when the foreign ship or one of its boats is within the internal waters or the territorial sea or the contiguous zone of the pursuing State, and may only be continued outside the territorial sea or the contiguous zone if the pursuit has not been interrupted. It is not necessary that, at the time when the foreign ship within the territorial sea or the contiguous zone receives the order to stop, the ship giving the order should likewise be within the territorial sea or the contiguous zone. If the foreign ship is within a contiguous zone, as defined in article 24 of the Convention on the Territorial Sea and the Contiguous Zone, the pursuit may only be undertaken if there has been a violation of the rights for the protection of which the zone was established.

2. The right of hot pursuit ceases as soon as the ship pursued enters the territorial sea of its own country or of a third State.

3. Hot pursuit is not deemed to have begun unless the pursuing ship has satisfied itself by such practicable means as may be available that the ship pursued or one of its boats or other craft working as a team and using the ship pursued as a mother ship are within the limits of the territorial sea, or as the case may be within the contiguous zone. The pursuit may only be commenced after a visual or auditory signal to stop has been given at a distance which enables it to be seen or heard by the foreign ship.

4. The right of hot pursuit may be exercised only by warships or military aircraft, or other ships or aircraft on government service specially authorized to that effect.

5. Where hot pursuit is effected by an aircraft:

(a) The provisions of paragraph 1 to 3 of this article shall apply *mutatis mutandis*;

(b) The aircraft giving the order to stop must itself actively pursue the ship until a ship or aircraft of the coastal State, summoned by the aircraft, arrives to take over the pursuit, unless the aircraft is itself able to arrest the ship. It does not suffice to justify an arrest on the high seas that the ship was merely sighted by the aircraft as an offender or suspected offender, if it was not both ordered to stop and pursued by the aircraft itself or other aircraft or ships which continue the pursuit without interruption.

6. The release of a ship arrested within the jurisdiction of a State and escorted to a port of that State for the purposes of an enquiry before the competent authorities may not be claimed solely on the ground that the ship, in the course of its voyage, was escorted across a portion of the high seas, if the circumstances rendered this necessary.

7. Where a ship has been stopped or arrested on the high seas in circumstances which do not justify the exercise of the right of hot pursuit, it shall be compensated for any loss or damage that may have been thereby sustained.

Article 24

Every State shall draw up regulations to prevent pollution of the seas by the discharge of oil from ships or pipelines or resulting from the exploitation and exploration of the seabed and its subsoil, taking account of existing treaty provisions on the subject.

Article 25

1. Every State shall take measures to prevent pollution of the seas from the dumping of radioactive waste, taking into account any standards and regulations which may be formulated by the competent international organizations.

2. All States shall co-operate with the competent international organizations in taking measures for the prevention of pollution of the seas or air space above, resulting from any activities with radioactive materials or other harmful agents.

Article 26

1. All States shall be entitled to lay submarine cables and pipelines on the bed of the high seas.

2. Subject to its right to take reasonable measures for the exploration of the continental shelf and the exploitation of its natural resources, the coastal State may not impede the laying or maintenance of such cables or pipelines.

3. When laying such cables or pipelines the State in question shall pay due regard to cables or pipelines already in position on the seabed. In particular, possibilities of repairing existing cables or pipelines shall not be prejudiced.

Article 27

Every State shall take the necessary legislative measures to provide that the breaking or injury by a ship flying its flag or by a person subject to its jurisdiction of a submarine cable beneath the high seas done wilfully or through culpable negligence, in such a manner as to be liable to interrupt or obstruct telegraphic or telephonic communications, and similarly the breaking or injury of a submarine pipeline or high-voltage power cable shall be a punishable offence. This provision shall not apply to any break or injury caused by persons who acted merely with the legitimate object of saving their lives or their ships, after having taken all necessary precautions to avoid such break or injury.

Article 28

Every State shall take the necessary legislative measures to provide that, if persons subject to its jurisdiction who are the owners of a cable or pipeline beneath the high seas, in laying or repairing that cable or pipeline, cause a break in or injury to another cable or pipeline, they shall bear the cost of the repairs.

Article 29

Every State shall take the necessary legislative measures to ensure that the owners of ships who can prove that they have sacrificed an anchor, a net or any other fishing gear, in order to avoid injuring a submarine cable or pipeline, shall be indemnified by the owner of the cable or pipeline, provided that the owner of the ship has taken all reasonable precautionary measures beforehand.

Article 30

The provisions of this Convention shall not affect conventions or other international agreements already in force, as between States Parties to them.

Article 31

This Convention shall, until 31 October 1958, be open for signature by all States Members of the United Nations or of any of the specialized agencies, and by any other State invited by the General Assembly of the United Nations to become a Party to the Convention.

Article 32

This Convention is subject to ratification. The instruments of ratification shall be deposited with the Secretary-General of the United Nations.

Article 33

This Convention shall be open for accession by any States belonging to any of the categories mentioned in article 31. The instruments of accession shall be deposited with the Secretary-General of the United Nations.

Article 34

1. This Convention shall come into force on the thirtieth day following the date of deposit of the twenty-second instrument of ratification or accession with the Secretary-General of the United Nations.

2. For each State ratifying or acceding to the Convention after the deposit of the twenty-second instrument of ratification or accession, the Convention shall enter into force on the thirtieth day after deposit by such State of its instrument of ratification or accession.

Article 35

1. After the expiration of a period of five years from the date on which this Convention shall enter into force, a request for the revision of this Convention may be made at any time by any Contracting Party by means of a notification in writing addressed to the Secretary-General of the United Nations.

2. The General Assembly of the United Nations shall decide upon the steps, if any, to be taken in respect of such request.

Article 36

The Secretary-General of the United Nations shall inform all States Members of the United Nations and the other States referred to in article 31:

    (a) Of signatures to this Convention and of the deposit of instruments of ratification or accession, in accordance with articles 31, 32 and 33;

    (b) Of the date on which this Convention will come into force, in accordance with article 34;

    (c) Of requests for revision in accordance with article 35.

Article 37

The original of this Convention, of which the Chinese, English, French, Russian and Spanish texts are equally authentic, shall be deposited with the Secretary-General of the United Nations, who shall send certified copies thereof to all States referred to in article 31.

IN WITNESS WHEREOF the undersigned Plenipotentiaries, being duly authorized thereto by their respective Governments, have signed this Convention.

DONE at Geneva, this twenty-ninth day of April one thousand nine hundred and fifty-eight.

Convention on Fishing and Conservation of the Living Resources of the High Seas

Done at Geneva, 29 April 1958; entry into force, 20 March 1966
559 UNTS 286 [Registration Number 8164]

The States Parties to this Convention,

Considering that the development of modern techniques for the exploitation of the living resources of the sea, increasing man's ability to meet the need of the world's expanding population for food, has exposed some of these resources to the danger of being over-exploited,

Considering also that the nature of the problems involved in the conservation of the living resources of the high seas is such that there is a clear necessity that they be solved, whenever possible, on the basis of international co-operation through the concerted action of all the States concerned,

Have agreed as follows:

Article 1

1. All States have the right for their nationals to engage in fishing on the high seas, subject (a) to their treaty obligations, (b) to the interests and rights of coastal States as provided for in this Convention, and (c) to the provisions contained in the following articles concerning conservation of the living resources of the high seas.

2. All States have the duty to adopt, or to co-operate with other States in adopting, such measures for their respective nationals as may be necessary for the conservation of the living resources of the high seas.

Article 2

As employed in this Convention, the expression 'conservation of the living resources of the high seas' means the aggregate of the measures rendering possible the optimum sustainable yield from those resources so as to secure a maximum supply of food and other marine products. Conservation programmes should be formulated with a view to securing in the first place a supply of food for human consumption.

Article 3

A State whose nationals are engaged in fishing any stock or stocks of fish or other living marine resources in any area of the high seas where the nationals of other States are not thus engaged shall adopt, for its own nationals, measures in that area when necessary for the purpose of the conservation of the living resources affected.

Article 4

1. If the nationals of two or more States are engaged in fishing the same stock or stocks of fish or other living marine resources in any area or areas of the high seas, these States shall, at the request of any of them, enter into negotiations with a view to prescribing by agreement for their nationals the necessary measures for the conservation of the living resources affected.

2. If the States concerned do not reach agreement within twelve months, any of the parties may initiate the procedure contemplated by article 9.

Article 5

1. If, subsequent to the adoption of the measures referred to in articles 3 and 4, nationals of other States engage in fishing the same stock or stocks of fish or other living marine resources in any area or areas of the high seas, the other States shall apply the measures, which shall not be discriminatory in form or in fact, to their own nationals not later than seven months after the date on which the measures shall have been notified to the Director-General of the Food and Agriculture Organization of the United Nations. The Director-General shall notify such measures to any State which so requests and, in any case, to any State specified by the State initiating the measure.

2. If these other States do not accept the measures so adopted and if no agreement can be reached within twelve months, any of the interested parties may initiate the procedure contemplated by article 9. Subject to paragraph 2 of article 10, the measures adopted shall remain obligatory pending the decision of the special commission.

Article 6

1. A coastal State has a special interest in the maintenance of the productivity of the living resources in any area of the high seas adjacent to its territorial sea.

2. A coastal State is entitled to take part on an equal footing in any system of research and regulation for purposes of conservation of the living resources of the high seas in that area, even though its nationals do not carry on fishing there.

3. A State whose nationals are engaged in fishing in any area of the high seas adjacent to the territorial sea of a State shall, at the request of that coastal State, enter into negotiations with a view to prescribing by agreement the measures necessary for the conservation of the living resources of the high seas in that area.

4. A State whose nationals are engaged in fishing in any area of the high seas adjacent to the territorial sea of a coastal State shall not enforce conservation measures in that area which are opposed to those which have been adopted by the coastal State, but may enter into negotiations with the coastal State with a view to prescribing by agreement the measures necessary for the conservation of the living resources of the high seas in that area.

5. If the States concerned do not reach agreement with respect to conservation measures within twelve months, any of the parties may initiate the procedure contemplated by article 9.

Article 7

1. Having regard to the provisions of paragraph 1 of article 6, any coastal State may, with a view to the maintenance of the productivity of the living resources of the sea, adopt unilateral measures of conservation appropriate to any stock of fish or other marine resources in any area of the high seas adjacent to its territorial sea, provided that negotiations to that effect with the other States concerned have not led to an agreement within six months.

2. The measures which the coastal State adopts under the previous paragraph shall be valid as to other States only if the following requirements are fulfilled:

(a)　That there is a need for urgent application of conservation measures in the light of the existing knowledge of the fishery;

(b)　That the measures adopted are based on appropriate scientific findings;

(c)　That such measures do not discriminate in form or in fact against foreign fishermen.

3. These measures shall remain in force pending the settlement, in accordance with the relevant provisions of this Convention, of any disagreement as to their validity.

4. If the measures are not accepted by the other States concerned, any of the parties may initiate the procedure contemplated by article 9. Subject to paragraph 2 of article 10, the measures adopted shall remain obligatory pending the decision of the special commission.

5. The principles of geographical demarcation as defined in article 12 of the Convention on the Territorial Sea and the Contiguous Zone shall be adopted when coasts of different States are involved.

Article 8

1. Any State which, even if its nationals are not engaged in fishing in an area of the high seas not adjacent to its coast, has a special interest in the conservation of the living resources of the high seas in that area, may request the State or States whose nationals are engaged in fishing there to take the necessary measures of conservation under articles 3 and 4 respectively, at the same time mentioning the scientific reasons which in its opinion make such measures necessary, and indicating its special interest.

2. If no agreement is reached within twelve months, such State may initiate the procedure contemplated by article 9.

Article 9

1. Any dispute which may arise between States under articles 4, 5, 6, 7 and 8 shall, at the request of any of the parties, be submitted for settlement to a special commission of five members, unless the parties agree to seek a solution by another method of peaceful settlement, as provided for in Article 33 of the Charter of the United Nations.

2. The members of the commission, one of whom shall be designated as chairman, shall be named by agreement between the States in dispute within three months of the request for settlement in accordance with the provisions of this article. Failing agreement they shall, upon the request of any State party, be named by the Secretary-General of the United Nations, within a further three-month period, in consultation with the States in dispute and with the President of the International Court of Justice and the Director-General of the Food and Agriculture Organization of the United Nations, from amongst

well-qualified persons being nationals of States not involved in the dispute and specializing in legal, administrative or scientific questions relating to fisheries, depending upon the nature of the dispute to be settled. Any vacancy arising after the original appointment shall be filled in the same manner as provided for the initial selection.

3. Any State party to proceedings under these articles shall have the right to name one of its nationals to the special commission, with the right to participate fully in the proceedings on the same footing as a member of the commission, but without the right to vote or to take part in the writing of the commission's decision.

4. The commission shall determine is own procedure, assuring each party to the proceedings a full opportunity to be heard and to present its case. It shall also determine how the costs and expenses shall be divided between the parties to the dispute, failing agreement by the parties on this matter.

5. The special commission shall render its decision within a period of five months from the time it is appointed unless it decides, in case of necessity, to extend the time limit for a period not exceeding three months.

6. The special commission shall, in reaching its decisions, adhere to these articles and to any special agreements between the disputing parties regarding settlement of the dispute.

7. Decisions of the commission shall be by majority vote.

Article 10

1. The special commission shall, in disputes arising under article 7, apply the criteria listed in paragraph 2 of that article. In disputes under articles 4, 5, 6 and 8, the commission shall apply the following criteria, according to the issues involved in the dispute:

    (a)   Common to the determination of disputes arising under articles 4, 5 and 6 are the requirements:
        (i)   That scientific findings demonstrate the necessity of conservation measures;
        (ii) That the specific measures are based on scientific findings and are practicable; and
        (iii) That the measures do not discriminate, in form or in fact, against fishermen of other States;

    (b)   Applicable to the determination of disputes arising under article 8 is the requirement that scientific findings demonstrate the necessity for conservation measures, or that the conservation programme is adequate, as the case may be.

2. The special commission may decide that pending its award the measures in dispute shall not be applied, provided that, in the case of disputes under article 7, the measures shall only be suspended when it is apparent to the commission on the basis of prima facie evidence that the need for the urgent application of such measures does not exist.

Article 11

The decisions of the special commission shall be binding on the States concerned and the provisions of paragraph 2 of Article 94 of the Charter of the United Nations shall be applicable to those decisions. If the decisions are accompanied by any recommendations, they shall receive the greatest possible consideration.

Article 12

1. If the factual basis of the award of the special commission is altered by substantial changes in the conditions of the stock or stocks of fish or other living marine resources or in methods of fishing, any of the States concerned may request the other States to enter

into negotiations with a view to prescribing by agreement the necessary modifications in the measures of conservation.

2. If no agreement is reached within a reasonable period of time, any of the States concerned may again resort to the procedure contemplated by article 9 provided that at least two years have elapsed from the original award.

Article 13

1. The regulation of fisheries conducted by means of equipment embedded in the floor of the sea in areas of the high seas adjacent to the territorial sea of a State may be undertaken by that State where such fisheries have long been maintained and conducted by its nationals, provided that non-nationals are permitted to participate in such activities on an equal footing with nationals except in areas where such fisheries have by long usage been exclusively enjoyed by such nationals. Such regulations will not, however, affect the general status of the areas as high seas.

2. In this article, the expression 'fisheries conducted by means of equipment embedded in the floor of the sea' means those fisheries using gear with supporting members embedded in the sea floor, constructed on a site and left there to operate permanently or, if removed, restored each season on the same site.

Article 14

In articles 1, 3, 4, 5, 6 and 8, the terms 'nationals' means fishing boats or craft of any size having the nationality of the State concerned, according to the law of that State, irrespective of the nationality of the members of their crews.

Article 15

This Convention shall, until 31 October 1958, be open for signature by all States Members of the United Nations or of any of the specialized agencies, and by any other State invited by the General Assembly of the United Nations to become a Party to the Convention.

Article 16

This Convention is subject to ratification. The instruments of ratification shall be deposited with the Secretary-General of the United Nations.

Article 17

This Convention shall be open for accession by any States belonging to any of the categories mentioned in article 15. The instruments of accession shall be deposited with the Secretary-General of the United Nations.

Article 18

1. This Convention shall come into force on the thirtieth day following the date of deposit of the twenty-second instrument of ratification or accession with the Secretary-General of the United Nations.

2. For each State ratifying or acceding to the Convention after the deposit of the twenty-second instrument of ratification or accession, the Convention shall enter into force on the thirtieth day after deposit by such State of its instrument of ratification or accession.

Article 19

1. At the time of signature, ratification or accession, any State may make reservations to articles of the Convention other than to articles 6, 7, 9, 10, 11 and 12.

2. Any contracting State making a reservation in accordance with the preceding paragraph may at any time withdraw the reservation by a communication to that effect addressed to the Secretary-General of the United Nations.

Article 20

1. After the expiration of a period of five years from the date on which this Convention shall enter into force, a request for the revision of this Convention may be made at any time by any contracting party by means of a notification in writing addressed to the Secretary-General of the United Nations.

2. The General Assembly of the United Nations shall decide upon the steps, if any, to be taken in respect of such request.

Article 21

The Secretary-General of the United Nations shall inform all States Members of the United Nations and the other States referred to in article 15:

    (a)   Of signatures to this Convention and of the deposit of instruments of ratification or accession, in accordance with articles 15, 16 and 17;

    (b)   Of the date on which this Convention will come into force, in accordance with article 18;

    (c)   Of requests for revision in accordance with article 20;

    (d)   Of reservations to this Convention, in accordance with article 19.

Article 22

The original of this Convention, of which the Chinese, English, French, Russian, and Spanish texts are equally authentic, shall be deposited with the Secretary-General of the United Nations, who shall send certified copies thereof to all States referred to in article 15.

IN WITNESS WHEREOF the undersigned plenipotentiaries, being duly authorized thereto by their respective governments, have signed this Convention.

DONE at Geneva, this twenty-ninth day of April one thousand nine hundred and fifty-eight.

Convention on the Continental Shelf

Done at Geneva, 29 April 1958; entry into force, 10 June 1964
499 UNTS 312 [Registration Number 7302]

The States Parties to this Convention,
Have agreed as follows:

Article 1

For the purpose of these articles, the term 'continental shelf' is used as referring (a) to the seabed and subsoil of the submarine areas adjacent to the coast but outside the area of the territorial sea, to a depth of 200 metres or, beyond that limit, to where the depth of the superjacent waters admits of the exploitation of the natural resources of the said areas; (b) to the seabed and subsoil of similar submarine areas adjacent to the coasts of islands.

Article 2

1. The coastal State exercises over the continental shelf sovereign rights for the purpose of exploring it and exploiting its natural resources.

2. The rights referred to in paragraph 1 of this article are exclusive in the sense that if the coastal State does not explore the continental shelf or exploit its natural resources, no one may undertake these activities, or make a claim to the continental shelf, without the express consent of the coastal State.

3. The rights of the coastal State over the continental shelf do not depend on occupation, effective or notional, or on any express proclamation.

4. The natural resources referred to in these articles consist of the mineral and other non-living resources of the seabed and subsoil together with living organisms belonging to sedentary species, that is to say, organisms which, at the harvestable stage, either are immobile on or under the seabed or are unable to move except in constant physical contact with the seabed or the subsoil.

Article 3

The rights of the coastal State over the continental shelf do not affect the legal status of the superjacent waters as high seas, or that of the airspace above those waters.

Article 4

Subject to its right to take reasonable measures for the exploration of the continental shelf and the exploitation of its natural resources, the coastal State may not impede the laying or maintenance of submarine cables or pipe lines on the continental shelf.

Article 5

1. The exploration of the continental shelf and the exploitation of its natural resources must not result in any unjustifiable interference with navigation, fishing or the conservation of the living resources of the sea, nor result in any interference with fundamental oceanographic or other scientific research carried out with the intention of open publication.

2. Subject to the provisions of paragraphs 1 and 6 of this article, the coastal State is entitled to construct and maintain or operate on the continental shelf installations and other devices necessary for its exploration and the exploitation of its natural resources, and to establish safety zones around such installations and devices and to take in those zones measures necessary for their protection.

3. The safety zones referred to in paragraph 2 of this article may extend to a distance of 500 metres around the installations and other devices which have been erected, measured from each point of their outer edge. Ships of all nationalities must respect these safety zones.

4. Such installations and devices, though under the jurisdiction of the coastal State, do not possess the status of islands. They have no territorial sea of their own, and their presence does not affect the delimitation of the territorial sea of the coastal State.

5. Due notice must be given of the construction of any such installations, and permanent means for giving warning of their presence must be maintained. Any installations which are abandoned or disused must be entirely removed.

6. Neither the installations or devices, nor the safety zones around them, may be established where interference may be caused to the use of recognized sea lanes essential to international navigation.

7. The coastal State is obliged to undertake, in the safety zones, all appropriate measures for the protection of the living resources of the sea from harmful agents.

8. The consent of the coastal State shall be obtained in respect of any research concerning the continental shelf and undertaken there. Nevertheless the coastal State shall not normally withhold its consent if the request is submitted by a qualified institution with a view to purely scientific research into the physical or biological characteristics of the continental shelf, subject to the proviso that the coastal State shall have the right, if it so desires, to participate or to be represented in the research, and that in any event the results shall be published.

Article 6

1. Where the same continental shelf is adjacent to the territories of two or more States whose coasts are opposite each other, the boundary of the continental shelf appertaining to such States shall be determined by agreement between them. In the absence of agreement, and unless another boundary line is justified by special circumstances, the boundary is the median line, every point of which is equidistant from the nearest points of the baselines from which the breadth of the territorial sea of each State is measured.

2. Where the same continental shelf is adjacent to the territories of two adjacent States, the boundary of the continental shelf shall be determined by agreement between them. In the absence of agreement, and unless another boundary line is justified by special circumstances, the boundary shall be determined by application of the principle of equidistance from the nearest points of the baselines from which the breadth of the territorial sea of each State is measured.

3. In delimiting the boundaries of the continental shelf, any lines which are drawn in accordance with the principles set out in paragraphs 1 and 2 of this article should be defined with reference to charts and geographical features as they exist at a particular date, and reference should be made to fixed permanent identifiable points on the land.

Article 7

The provisions of these articles shall not prejudice the right of the coastal State to exploit the subsoil by means of tunnelling irrespective of the depth of water above the subsoil.

Article 8

This Convention shall, until 31 October 1958, be open for signature by all States Members of the United Nations or of any of the specialized agencies, and by any other State invited by the General Assembly of the United Nations to become a Party to the Convention.

Article 9

This Convention is subject to ratification. The instruments of ratification shall be deposited with the Secretary-General of the United Nations.

Article 10

This Convention shall be open for accession by any States belonging to any of the categories mentioned in article 8. The instruments of accession shall be deposited with the Secretary-General of the United Nations.

Article 11

1. This Convention shall come into force on the thirtieth day following the date of deposit of the twenty-second instrument of ratification or accession with the Secretary-General of the United Nations.

2. For each State ratifying or acceding to the Convention after the deposit of the twenty-second instrument of ratification or accession, the Convention shall enter into force on the thirtieth day after deposit by such State of its instrument of ratification or accession.

Article 12

1. At the time of signature, ratification or accession, any State may make reservations to articles of the Convention other than to articles 1 to 3 inclusive.

2. Any Contracting State making a reservation in accordance with the preceding paragraph may at any time withdraw the reservation by a communication to that effect addressed to the Secretary-General of the United Nations.

Article 13

1. After the expiration of a period of five years from the date on which this Convention shall enter into force, a request for the revision of this Convention may be made at any time by any Contracting Party by means of a notification in writing addressed to the Secretary-General of the United Nations.

2. The General Assembly of the United Nations shall decide upon the steps, if any, to be taken in respect of such request.

Article 14

The Secretary-General of the United Nations shall inform all States Members of the United Nations and the other States referred to in article 8:

(a) Of signatures to this Convention and of the deposit of instruments of ratification or accession, in accordance with articles 8, 9 and 10;

(b) Of the date on which this Convention will come into force, in accordance with article 11;

(c) Of requests for revision in accordance with article 13;

(d) Of reservations to this Convention, in accordance with article 12.

Article 15

The original of this Convention, of which the Chinese, English, French, Russian and Spanish texts are equally authentic, shall be deposited with the Secretary-General of the United Nations, who shall send certified copies thereof to all States referred to in article 8.

IN WITNESS WHEREOF the undersigned Plenipotentiaries, being duly authorized thereto by their respective Governments, have signed this Convention.

DONE at Geneva, this twenty-ninth day of April one thousand nine hundred and fifty-eight.

Optional Protocol of Signature Concerning the Compulsory Settlement of Disputes Arising from the Law of the Sea Conventions

Opened for signature, 29 April 1958; entry into force, 30 September 1962
450 UNTS 170 [Registration Number 6466]

The States Parties to this Protocol and to any one or more of the Conventions on the Law of the Sea adopted by the United Nations Conference on the Law of the Sea held at Geneva from 24 February to 27 April 1958,

Expressing their wish to resort, in all matters concerning them in respect of any dispute arising out of the interpretation or application of any article of any Convention on the Law of the Sea of 29 April 1958, to the compulsory jurisdiction of the International Court of Justice, unless some other form of settlement is provided in the Convention or has been agreed upon by the Parties within a reasonable period,

Have agreed as follows:

Article I

Disputes arising out of the interpretation or application of any Convention on the Law of the Sea shall lie within the compulsory jurisdiction of the International Court of Justice, and may accordingly be brought before the Court by an application made by any party to the dispute being a Party to this Protocol.

Article II

This undertaking relates to all the provisions of any Convention on the Law of the Sea except, in the Convention on Fishing and Conservation of the Living Resources of the High Seas, articles 4, 5, 6, 7 and 8, to which articles 9, 10, 11 and 12 of that Convention remain applicable.

Article III

The Parties may agree, within a period of two months after one party has notified its opinion to the other that a dispute exists, to resort not to the International Court of Justice but to an arbitral tribunal. After the expiry of the said period, either Party to this Protocol may bring the dispute before the Court by an application.

Article IV

1. Within the same period of two months, the Parties to this Protocol may agree to adopt a conciliation procedure before resorting to the International Court of Justice.

2. The conciliation commission shall make its recommendations within five months after its appointment. If its recommendations are not accepted by the parties to the dispute within two months after they have been delivered, either party may bring the dispute before the Court by an application.

Article V

This Protocol shall remain open for signature by all States who become Parties to any Convention on the Law of the Sea adopted by the United Nations Conference on the Law of the Sea and is subject to ratification, where necessary, according to the constitutional requirements of the signatory States.

Article VI

The Secretary-General of the United Nations shall inform all States who become Parties to any Convention on the Law of the Sea of signatures to this Protocol and of the deposit of instruments of ratification in accordance with article V.

Article VII

The original of this Protocol, of which the Chinese, English, French, Russian and Spanish texts are equally authentic, shall be deposited with the Secretary-General of the United Nations, who shall send certified copies thereof to all States referred to in article V.

IN WITNESS WHEREOF the undersigned Plenipotentiaries, being duly authorized thereto by their respective Governments, have signed this Protocol.

DONE at Geneva, this twenty-ninth day of April one thousand nine hundred and fifty-eight.

International Convention Relating to Intervention on the High Seas in Cases of Oil Pollution Casualties

Done at Brussels, 29 November 1969; entry into force, 6 May 1975
970 UNTS 212 [Registration Number 14049]

The States Parties to the present Convention,

Conscious of the need to protect the interests of their peoples against the grave consequences of a maritime casualty resulting in danger of oil pollution of sea and coastlines,

Convinced that under these circumstances measures of an exceptional character to protect such interests might be necessary on the high seas and that these measures do not affect the principle of freedom of the high seas,

Have agreed as follows:

Article I

1. Parties to the present Convention may take such measures on the high seas as may be necessary to prevent, mitigate or eliminate grave and imminent danger to their coastline or related interests from pollution or threat of pollution of the sea by oil, following upon a maritime casualty or acts related to such a casualty, which may reasonably be expected to result in major harmful consequences.

2. However, no measures shall be taken under the present Convention against any warship or other ship owned or operated by a State and used, for the time being, only on government non-commercial service.

Article II

For the purposes of the present Convention:

1. 'Maritime casualty' means a collision of ships, stranding or other incident of navigation, or other occurrence on board a ship or external to it resulting in material damage or imminent threat of material damage to a ship or cargo.

2. 'Ship' means:

(a) any sea-going vessel of any type whatsoever, and

(b) any floating craft, with the exception of an installation or device engaged in the exploration and exploitation of the resources of the sea-bed and the ocean floor and the subsoil thereof.

3. 'Oil' means crude oil, fuel oil, diesel oil and lubricating oil.

4. 'Related interests' means the interests of a coastal State directly affected or threatened by the maritime casualty, such as:

(a) maritime coastal, port or estuarine activities, including fisheries activities, constituting an essential means of livelihood of the persons concerned;

(b) tourist attractions of the area concerned;

(c) the health of the coastal population and the well-being of the area concerned, including conservation of living marine resources and of wildlife.

5. 'Organization' means the Inter-Governmental Maritime Consultative Organization.

Article III

When a coastal State is exercising the right to take measures in accordance with Article I, the following provisions shall apply:

(a)   before taking any measures, a coastal State shall proceed to consultations with other States affected by the maritime casualty, particularly with the flag State or States;

(b)   the coastal State shall notify without delay the proposed measures to any persons physical or corporate known to the coastal State, or made known to it during the consultations, to have interests which can reasonably be expected to be affected by those measures. The coastal State shall take into account any views they may submit;

(c)   before any measure is taken, the coastal State may proceed to a consultation with independent experts, whose names shall be chosen from a list maintained by the Organization;

(d)   in cases of extreme urgency requiring measures to be taken immediately, the coastal State may take measures rendered necessary by the urgency of the situation, without prior notification or consultation or without continuing consultations already begun;

(e)   a coastal State shall, before taking such measures and during their course, use its best endeavours to avoid any risk to human life, and to afford persons in distress any assistance of which they may stand in need, and in appropriate cases to facilitate repatriation of ships' crews, and to raise no obstacle thereto;

(f)   measures which have been taken in application of Article I shall be notified without delay to the States and to the known physical or corporate persons concerned, as well as to the Secretary-General of the Organization.

Article IV

1.   Under the supervision of the Organization, there shall be set up and maintained the list of experts contemplated by Article III of the present Convention, and the Organization shall make necessary and appropriate regulations in connexion therewith, including the determination of the required qualifications.

2.   Nominations to the list may be made by Member States of the Organization and by Parties to this Convention. The experts shall be paid on the basis of services rendered by the States utilizing those services.

Article V

1.   Measures taken by the coastal State in accordance with Article I shall be proportionate to the damage actual or threatened to it.

2.   Such measures shall not go beyond what is reasonably necessary to achieve the end mentioned in Article I and shall cease as soon as that end has been achieved; they shall not unnecessarily interfere with the rights and interests of the flag State, third States and of any persons, physical or corporate, concerned.

3.   In considering whether the measures are proportionate to the damage, account shall be taken of:

(a)   the extent and probability of imminent damage if those measures are not taken; and

(b)   the likelihood of those measures being effective; and

(c)   the extent of the damage which may be caused by such measures.

Article VI

Any party which has taken measures in contravention of the provisions of the present Convention causing damage to others, shall be obliged to pay compensation to the extent of the damage caused by measures which exceed those reasonably necessary to achieve the end mentioned in Article I.

Article VII

Except as specifically provided, nothing in the present Convention shall prejudice any otherwise applicable right, duty, privilege or immunity or deprive any of the Parties or any interested physical or corporate person of any remedy otherwise applicable.

Article VIII

1. Any controversy between the Parties as to whether measures taken under Article I were in contravention of the provisions of the present Convention, to whether compensation is obliged to be paid under Article VI, and to the amount of such compensation shall, if settlement by negotiation between the Parties involved or between the Party which took the measures and the physical or corporate claimants has not been possible, and if the Parties do not otherwise agree, be submitted upon request of any of the Parties concerned to conciliation or, if conciliation does not succeed, to arbitration, as set out in the Annex to the present Convention.

2. The Party which took the measures shall not be entitled to refuse a request for conciliation or arbitration under provisions of the preceding paragraph solely on the grounds that any remedies under municipal law in its own courts have not been exhausted.

Article IX

1. The present Convention shall remain open for signature until 31 December 1970 and shall thereafter remain open for accession.

2. States Members of the United Nations or any of the Specialized Agencies or of the International Atomic Energy Agency or Parties to the Statute of the International Court of Justice may become Parties to this Convention by:

    (a)   signature without reservation as to ratification, acceptance or approval;

    (b)   signature subject to ratification, acceptance or approval followed by ratification, acceptance or approval; or

    (c)   accession.

Article X

1. Ratification, acceptance, approval or accession shall be effected by the deposit of a formal instrument to that effect with the Secretary-General of the Organization.

2. Any instrument of ratification, acceptance, approval or accession deposited after the entry into force of an amendment to the present Convention with respect to all existing Parties or after the completion of all measures required for the entry into force of the amendment with respect to those Parties shall be deemed to apply to the Convention as modified by the amendment.

Article XI

1. The present Convention shall enter into force on the ninetieth day following the date on which Governments of fifteen States have either signed it without reservation as to ratification, acceptance or approval or have deposited instruments of ratification, acceptance, approval or accession with the Secretary-General of the Organization.

2. For each State which subsequently ratifies, accepts, approves or accedes to it the present Convention shall come into force on the ninetieth day after deposit by such State of the appropriate instrument.

Article XII

1. The present Convention may be denounced by any Party at any time after the date on which the Convention comes into force for that State.

2. Denunciation shall be effected by the deposit of an instrument with the Secretary-General of the Organization.

3. A denunciation shall take effect one year, or such longer period as may be specified in the instrument of denunciation, after its deposit with the Secretary-General of the Organization.

Article XIII

1. The United Nations where it is the administering authority for a territory, or any State Party to the present Convention responsible for the international relations of a territory, shall as soon as possible consult with the appropriate authorities of such territories or take such other measures as may be appropriate, in order to extend the present Convention to that territory and may at any time by notification in writing to the Secretary-General of the Organization declare that the present Convention shall extend to such territory.

2. The present Convention shall, from the date of receipt of the notification or from such other date as may be specified in the notification, extend to the territory named therein.

3. The United Nations, or any Party which has made a declaration under paragraph 1 of this Article may at any time after the date on which the Convention has been so extended to any territory declare by notification in writing to the Secretary-General of the Organization that the present Convention shall cease to extend to any such territory named in the notification.

4. The present Convention shall cease to extend to any territory mentioned in such notification one year, or such longer period as may be specified therein, after the date of receipt of the notification by the Secretary-General of the Organization.

Article XIV

1. A Conference for the purpose of revising or amending the present Convention may be convened by the Organization.

2. The Organization shall convene a Conference of the States Parties to the present Convention for revising or amending the present Convention at the request of not less than one-third of the Parties.

Article XV

1. The present Convention shall be deposited with the Secretary-General of the Organization.

2. The Secretary-General of the Organization shall:

(a)   inform all States which have signed or acceded to the Convention of:
    (i)   each new signature or deposit of instrument together with the date thereof;
    (ii)   the deposit of any instrument of denunciation of this Convention together with the date of the deposit;
    (iii) the extension of the present Convention to any territory under paragraph 1 of Article XIII and of the termination of any such extension under the provisions of paragraph 4 of that Article stating in each case the date on which the present Convention has been or will cease to be so extended;

(b)   transmit certified true copies of the present Convention to all Signatory States and to all States which accede to the present Convention.

Article XVI

As soon as the present Convention comes into force, the text shall be transmitted by the Secretary-General of the Organization to the Secretariat of the United Nations for registration and publication in accordance with Article 102 of the Charter of the United Nations.

Article XVII

The present Convention is established in a single copy in the English and French languages, both texts being equally authentic. Official translations in the Russian and Spanish languages shall be prepared and deposited with the signed original.

IN WITNESS WHEREOF the undersigned being duly authorized by their respective Governments for that purpose have signed the present Convention.

DONE at Brussels this twenty-ninth day of November 1969.

ANNEX

CHAPTER I. CONCILIATION

Article 1

Provided the Parties concerned do not decide otherwise, the procedure for conciliation shall be in accordance with the rules set out in this Chapter.

Article 2

1. A Conciliation Commission shall be established upon the request of one Party addressed to another in application of Article VIII of the Convention.

2. The request for conciliation submitted by a Party shall consist of a statement of the case together with any supporting documents.

3. If a procedure has been initiated between two Parties, any other Party the nationals or property of which have been affected by the same measures, or which is a coastal State having taken similar measures, may join in the conciliation procedure by giving written notice to the Parties which have originally initiated the procedure unless either of the latter Parties object to such joinder.

Article 3

1. The Conciliation Commission shall be composed of three members: one nominated by the coastal State which took the measures, one nominated by the State the nationals or property of which have been affected by those measures and a third, who shall preside over the Commission and shall be nominated by agreement between the two original members.

2. The Conciliators shall be selected from a list previously drawn up in accordance with the procedure set out in Article 4 below.

3. If within a period of 60 days from the date of receipt of the request for conciliation, the Party to which such request is made has not given notice to the other Party to the controversy of the nomination of the Conciliator for whose selection it is responsible, or if, within a period of 30 days from the date of nomination of the second of the members of the Commission to be designated by the Parties, the first two Conciliators have not been able to designate by common agreement the Chairmen of the Commission, the Secretary-General of the Organization shall upon request of either Party and within a period of 30 days, proceed to the required nomination. The members of the Commission thus nominated shall be selected from the list prescribed in the preceding paragraph.

4. In no case shall the Chairman of the Commission be or have been a national of one of the original Parties to the procedure, whatever the method of his nomination.

Article 4

1. The list prescribed in Article 3 above shall consist of qualified persons designated by the Parties and shall be kept up to date by the Organization. Each Party may designate for inclusion on the list four persons, who shall not necessarily be its nationals. The nominations shall be for periods of six years each and shall be renewable.

2. In the case of the decease or resignation of a person whose name appears on the list, the Party which nominated such persons shall be permitted to nominate a replacement for the remainder of the term of office.

Article 5

1. Provided the Parties do not agree otherwise, the Conciliation Commission shall establish its own procedures, which shall in all cases permit a fair hearing. As regards examination, the Commission, unless it unanimously decides otherwise, shall conform with the provisions of Chapter III of The Hague Convention for the Peaceful Settlement of International Disputes of 18 October 1907.

2. The Parties shall be represented before the Conciliation Commission by agents whose duty shall be to act as intermediaries between the Parties and the Commission. Each of the Parties may seek also the assistance of advisers and experts nominated by it for this purpose and may request the hearing of all persons whose evidence the Party considers useful.

3. The Commission shall have the right to request explanations from agents, advisers and experts of the Parties as well as from any persons whom, with the consent of their Governments, it may deem useful to call.

Article 6

Provided the Parties do not agree otherwise, decisions of the Conciliation Commission shall be taken by a majority vote and the Commission shall not pronounce on the substance of the controversy unless all its members are present.

Article 7

The Parties shall facilitate the work of the Conciliation Commission and in particular, in accordance with their legislation, and using all means at their disposal:
    (a)   provide the Commission with the necessary documents and information;
    (b)   enable the Commission to enter their territory, to hear witnesses or experts, and to visit the scene.

Article 8

The task of the Conciliation Commission will be to clarify the matters under dispute, to assemble for this purpose all relevant information by means of examination or other means, and to endeavour to reconcile the Parties. After examining the case, the Commission shall communicate to the Parties a recommendation which appears to the Commission to be appropriate to the matter and shall fix a period of not more than 90 days within which the Parties are called upon to state whether or not they accept the recommendation.

Article 9

The recommendation shall be accompanied by a statement of reasons. If the recommendation does not represent in whole or in part the unanimous opinion of the Commission, any Conciliator shall be entitled to deliver a separate opinion.

Article 10

A conciliation shall be deemed unsuccessful if, 90 days after the Parties have been notified of the recommendation, either Party shall not have notified the other Party of its acceptance of the recommendation. Conciliation shall likewise be deemed unsuccessful if the Commission shall not have been established within the period prescribed in the third paragraph of Article 3 above, or provided the Parties have not agreed otherwise, if the Commission shall not have issued its recommendation within one year from the date on which the Chairman of the Commission was nominated.

Article 11

1. Each member of the Commission shall receive the remuneration for his work, such remuneration to be fixed by agreement between the Parties which shall each contribute an equal proportion.

2. Contributions for miscellaneous expenditure incurred by the work of the Commission shall be apportioned in the same manner.

Article 12

The parties to the controversy may at any time during the conciliation procedure decide in agreement to have recourse to a different procedure for settlement of disputes.

CHAPTER II. ARBITRATION

Article 13

1. Arbitration procedure, unless the Parties decide otherwise, shall be in accordance with the rules set out in this Chapter.

2. Where conciliation is unsuccessful, a request for arbitration may only be made within a period of 180 days following the failure of conciliation.

Article 14

The Arbitration Tribunal shall consist of three members: one Arbitrator nominated by the coastal State which took the measures, one Arbitrator nominated by the State the nationals or property of which have been affected by those measures, and another Arbitrator who shall be nominated by agreement between the two first-named, and shall act as its Chairman.

Article 15

1. If, at the end of a period of 60 days from the nomination of the second Arbitrator, the Chairman of the Tribunal shall not have been nominated, the Secretary-General of the Organization upon request of either Party shall within a further period of 60 days proceed to such nomination, selecting from a list of qualified persons previously drawn up on accordance with the provisions of Article 4 above. This list shall be separate from the list of experts prescribed in Article IV of the Convention and from the list of Conciliators prescribed in Article 4 of the present Annex; the name of the same person may, however, appear both on the list of Conciliators and on the list of Arbitrators. A person who has acted as Conciliator in a dispute may not, however, be chosen to act as Arbitrator in the same matter.

2. If, within a period of 60 days from the date of the receipt of the request, one of the Parties shall not have nominated the member of the Tribunal for whose designation it is responsible, the other Party may directly inform the Secretary-General of the Organization who shall nominate the Chairman of the Tribunal within a period of 60 days, selecting him from the list prescribed in paragraph 1 of the present Article.

3. The Chairman of the Tribunal shall, upon nomination, request the Party which has not provided an Arbitrator, to do so in the same manner and under the same conditions. If the Party does not make the required nomination, the Chairman of the Tribunal shall request the Secretary-General of the Organization to make the nomination in the form and conditions prescribed in the preceding paragraph.

4. The Chairman of the Tribunal, if nominated under the provisions of the present Article, shall not be or have been a national of one of the Parties concerned, except with the consent of the other Party or Parties.

5. In the case of the decease or default of an Arbitrator for whose nomination one of the Parties is responsible, the said Party shall nominate a replacement within a period of 60 days from the date of decease or default. Should the said party not make the nomination, the arbitration shall proceed under the remaining Arbitrators. In the case of decease or default of the Chairman of the Tribunal, a replacement shall be nominated in accordance with the provisions of Article 14 above, or in the absence of agreement between the members of the Tribunal within a period of 60 days of the decease or default according to the provisions of the present Article.

Article 16

If a procedure has been initiated between two Parties, any other Party, the nationals or property of which have been affected by the same measures or which is a coastal State having taken similar measures, may join in the arbitration procedure by giving written notice to the Parties which have originally initiated the procedure unless either of the latter Parties object to such joinder.

Article 17

Any Arbitration Tribunal established under the provisions of the present Annex shall decide its own rules of procedure.

Article 18

1. Decisions of the Tribunal both as to its procedure and its place of meeting and as to any controversy laid before it, shall be taken by majority vote of its members; the absence or abstention of one of the members of the Tribunal for whose nomination the Parties were responsible shall not constitute an impediment to the Tribunal reaching a decision. In cases of equal voting, the Chairman shall cast the deciding vote.

2. The Parties shall facilitate the work of the Tribunal and in particular, in accordance with their legislation, and using all means at their disposal:

    (a) provide the Tribunal with the necessary documents and information;
    (b) enable the Tribunal to enter their territory, to hear witnesses or experts, and to visit the scene.

3. Absence or default of one Party shall not constitute an impediment to the procedure.

Article 19

1. The award of the Tribunal shall be accompanied by a statement of reasons. It shall be final and without appeal. The Parties shall immediately comply with the award.

2. Any controversy which may arise between the Parties as regards interpretation and execution of the award may be submitted by either Party for judgment to the Tribunal which made the award, or, if it is not available, to another Tribunal constituted for this purpose in the same manner as the original Tribunal.

Protocol Relating to Intervention on the High Seas in Cases of Pollution by Substances Other than Oil

Done at London, 2 November 1973; entry into force, 30 March 1983
1313 UNTS 4 [Registration Number 21886]

The Parties to the present Protocol,

Being parties to the International Convention relating to Intervention on the High Seas in Cases of Oil Pollution Casualties, done in Brussels on 29 November 1969,

Taking into account the Resolution on International Co-operation concerning Pollutants other than Oil adopted by the International Legal Conference on Marine Pollution Damage, 1969,

Further taking into account that, pursuant to the Resolution, the Inter-Governmental Maritime Consultative Organization has intensified its work, in collaboration with all interested international organizations, on all aspects of pollution by substances other than oil,

Have agreed as follows:

Article I

1. Parties to the present Protocol may take such measures on the high seas as may be necessary to prevent, mitigate or eliminate grave and imminent danger to their coastline or related interests from pollution or threat of pollution by substances other than oil following upon a maritime casualty or acts related to such a casualty, which may reasonably be expected to result in major harmful consequences.

2. 'Substances other than oil' as referred to in paragraph 1 shall be:
(a) Those substances enumerated in a list which shall be established by an appropriate body designated by the Organization and which shall be annexed to the present Protocol,[1] and
(b) Those other substances which are liable to create hazards to human health, to harm living resources and marine life, to damage amenities or to interfere with other legitimate uses of the sea.

3. Whenever an intervening Party takes action with regard to a substance referred to in paragraph 2(b) above that Party shall have the burden of establishing that the substance, under the circumstances present at the time of the intervention, could reasonably pose a grave and imminent danger analogous to that posed by any of the substances enumerated in the list referred to in paragraph 2(a) above.

Article II

1. The provisions of paragraph 2 of article I and of articles II to VIII of the Convention Relating to Intervention on the High Seas in Cases of Oil Pollution Casualties, 1969, and

---

[1] Annex relating to the list of substances established by the Marine Environment Protection Committee of the Organization in accordance with Paragraph 2(a) of Article 1 omitted. The list of substances was revised and amended in 1991, 1996 and 2002.

the annex thereto as they relate to oil, shall be applicable with regard to the substances referred to in article I of the present Protocol.

2. For the purpose of the present Protocol the list of experts referred to in articles III(c) and IV of the Convention shall be extended to include experts qualified to give advice in relation to substances other than oil. Nominations to the list may be made by Member States of the Organization and by Parties to the present Protocol.

Article III

1. The list referred to in paragraph 2(a) of article I shall be maintained by the appropriate body designated by the Organization.

2. Any amendment to the list proposed by a Party to the present Protocol shall be submitted to the Organization and circulated by it to all Members of the Organization and all Parties to the present Protocol at least three months prior to its consideration by the appropriate body.

3. Parties to the present Protocol whether or not Members of the Organization shall be entitled to participate in the proceedings of the appropriate body.

4. Amendments shall be adopted by a two-thirds majority of only the Parties to the present Protocol present and voting.

5. If adopted in accordance with paragraph 4 above, the amendment shall be communicated by the Organization to all Parties to the present Protocol for acceptance.

6. The amendment shall be deemed to have been accepted at the end of a period of six months after it has been communicated, unless within that period an objection to the amendment has been communicated to the Organization by not less than one-third of the Parties to the present Protocol.

7. An amendment deemed to have been accepted in accordance with paragraph 6 above shall enter into force three months after its acceptance for all Parties to the present Protocol, with the exception of those which before that date have made a declaration of non-acceptance of the said amendment.

Article IV

1. The present Protocol shall be open for signature by the States which have signed the Convention referred to in article II or acceded thereto, and by any State invited to be represented at the International Conference on Marine Pollution 1973. The Protocol shall remain open for signature from 15 January 1974 until 31 December 1974 at the Headquarters of the Organization.

2. Subject to paragraph 4 of this article, the present Protocol shall be subject to ratification, acceptance or approval by the States which have signed it.

3. Subject to paragraph 4, this Protocol shall be open for accession by States which did not sign it.

4. The present Protocol may be ratified, accepted, approved or acceded to only by States which have ratified, accepted, approved or acceded to the Convention referred to in article II.

Article V

1. Ratification, acceptance, approval or accession shall be effected by the deposit of a formal instrument to that effect with the Secretary-General of the Organization.

2. Any instrument of ratification, acceptance, approval or accession deposited after the entry into force of an amendment to the present Protocol with respect to all existing Parties or after the completion of all measures required for the entry into force of the amendment with respect to all existing Parties shall be deemed to apply to the Protocol as modified by the amendment.

Article VI

1. The present Protocol shall enter into force on the ninetieth day following the date on which fifteen States have deposited instruments of ratification, acceptance, approval or accession with the Secretary-General of the Organization, provided however that the present Protocol shall not enter into force before the Convention referred to in article II has entered into force.

2. For each State which subsequently ratifies, accepts, approves or accedes to it, the present Protocol shall enter into force on the ninetieth day after the deposit by such State of the appropriate instrument.

Article VII

1. The present Protocol may be denounced by any Party at any time after the date on which the Protocol enters into force for that Party.

2. Denunciation shall be effected by the deposit of an instrument to that effect with the Secretary-General of the Organization.

3. Denunciation shall take effect one year, or such longer period as may be specified in the instrument of denunciation, after its deposit with the Secretary-General of the Organization.

4. Denunciation of the Convention referred to in article II by a Party shall be deemed to be a denunciation of the present Protocol by that Party. Such denunciation shall take effect on the same day as the denunciation of the Convention takes effect in accordance with paragraph 3 of article XII of that Convention.

Article VIII

1. A conference for the purpose of revising or amending the present Protocol may be convened by the Organization.

2. The Organization shall convene a conference of Parties to the present Protocol for the purpose of revising or amending it at the request of not less than one-third of the Parties.

Article IX

1. The present Protocol shall be deposited with the Secretary-General of the Organization.

2. The Secretary-General of the Organization shall:

(a) Inform all States which have signed the present Protocol or acceded thereto of:

    (i) Each new signature or deposit of an instrument together with the date thereof;

    (ii) The date of entry into force of the present Protocol;

    (iii) The deposit of any instrument of denunciation of the present Protocol together with the date on which the denunciation takes effect;

    (iv) Any amendments to the present Protocol or its annex and any objection or declaration of non-acceptance of the said amendment;

(b) Transmit certified true copies of the present Protocol to all States which have signed the present Protocol or acceded thereto.

Article X

As soon as the present Protocol enters into force, a certified true copy thereof shall be transmitted by the Secretary-General of the Organization to the Secretariat of the United Nations for registration and publication in accordance with Article 102 of the Charter of the United Nations.

Article XI

The present Protocol is established in a single original in the English, French, Russian and Spanish languages, all four texts being equally authentic.

In witness whereof the undersigned being duly authorized for that purpose have signed the present Protocol.

Done at London this second day of November one thousand nine hundred and seventy-three.

UN General Assembly Resolution 2574 D (XXIV)
(Moratorium Resolution)
Question of the Reservation Exclusively for Peaceful Purposes of the Sea-Bed and the Ocean Floor, and the Subsoil Thereof, Underlying the High Seas Beyond the Limits of Present National Jurisdiction, and the Use of Their Resources in the Interests of Mankind

Adopted at the 1833rd plenary meeting, 15 December 1969,
62 in favour, 28 against, with 28 abstentions
UN Doc. A/RES/2574 (XXIV), 15 January 1970

The General Assembly,

Recalling its resolution 2467 A (XXIII) of 21 December 1968 to the effect that the exploitation of the resources of the sea-bed and the ocean floor, and the subsoil thereof, beyond the limits of national jurisdiction should be carried out for the benefit of mankind as a whole, irrespective of the geographical location of States, taking into account the special interests and needs of the developing countries,

Convinced that it is essential, for the achievement of this purpose, that such activities be carried out under an international régime including appropriate international machinery,

Noting that this matter is under consideration by the Committee on the Peaceful Uses of the Sea-Bed and the Ocean Floor beyond the Limits of National Jurisdiction,

Recalling its resolution 2340 (XXII) of 18 December 1967 on the importance of preserving the sea-bed and the ocean floor, and the subsoil thereof, beyond the limits of national jurisdiction from actions and uses which might be detrimental to the common interests of mankind,

Declares that, pending the establishment of the aforementioned international régime:

(a)   States and persons, physical or juridical, are bound to refrain from all activities of exploitation of the resources of the area of the sea-bed and ocean floor, and the subsoil thereof, beyond the limits of national jurisdiction;

(b)   No claim to any part of that area or its resources shall be recognized.

UN General Assembly Resolution 2749 (XXV) (Declaration of Principles)
Declaration of Principles Governing the Sea-Bed and the Ocean Floor, and the Subsoil Thereof, Beyond the Limits of National Jurisdiction

Adopted at the 1933rd plenary meeting, 17 December 1970,
108 in favour, none against, with 14 abstentions
UN Doc. A/RES/2749 (XXV)

The General Assembly,

Recalling its resolutions 2340 (XXII) of 18 December 1967, 2467 (XXIII) of 21 December 1968 and 2574 (XXIV) of 15 December 1969, concerning the area to which the title of the item refers,

Affirming that there is an area of the sea-bed and the ocean floor, and the subsoil thereof, beyond the limits of national jurisdiction, the precise limits of which are yet to be determined,

Recognizing that the existing legal régime of the high seas does not provide substantive rules for regulating the exploration of the aforesaid area and the exploitation of its resources,

Convinced that the area shall be reserved exclusively for peaceful purposes and that the exploration of the area and the exploitation of its resources shall be carried out for the benefit of mankind as a whole,

Believing it essential that an international régime applying to the area and its resources and including appropriate international machinery should be established as soon as possible,

Bearing in mind that the development and use of the area and its resources shall be undertaken in such a manner as to foster the healthy development of the world economy and balanced growth of international trade, and to minimize any adverse economic effects caused by the fluctuation of prices of raw materials resulting from such activities,

Solemnly declares that:

1. The sea-bed and ocean floor, and the subsoil thereof, beyond the limits of national jurisdiction (hereinafter referred to as the area), as well as the resources of the area, are the common heritage of mankind.

2. The area shall not be subject to appropriation by any means by States or persons, natural or juridical, and no State shall claim or exercise sovereignty or sovereign rights over any part thereof.

3. No State or person, natural or juridical, shall claim, exercise or acquire rights with respect to the area or its resources incompatible with the international régime to be established and the principles of this Declaration.

4. All activities regarding the exploration and exploitation of the resources of the area and other related activities shall be governed by the international régime to be established.

5. The area shall be open to use exclusively for peaceful purposes by all States, whether coastal or land-locked, without discrimination, in accordance with the international régime to be established.

6. States shall act in the area in accordance with the applicable principles and rules of international law, including the Charter of the United Nations and the Declaration on

Principles of International Law concerning Friendly Relations and Co-operation among States in accordance with the Charter of the United Nations, adopted by the General Assembly on 24 October 1970, in the interests of maintaining international peace and security and promoting international co-operation and mutual understanding.

7. The exploration of the area and the exploitation of its resources shall be carried out for the benefit of mankind as a whole, irrespective of the geographical location of States, whether land-locked or coastal, and taking into particular consideration the interests and needs of the developing countries.

8. The area shall be reserved exclusively for peaceful purposes, without prejudice to any measures which have been or may be agreed upon in the context of international negotiations undertaken in the field of disarmament and which may be applicable to a broader area. One or more international agreements shall be concluded as soon as possible in order to implement effectively this principle and to constitute a step towards the exclusion of the sea-bed, the ocean floor and the subsoil thereof from the arms race.

9. On the basis of the principles of this Declaration, an international régime applying to the area its resources and including appropriate international machinery to give effect to its provisions shall be established by an international treaty of a universal character, generally agreed upon. The régime shall, *inter alia*, provide for the orderly and safe development and rational management of the area and its resources and for expanding opportunities in the use thereof, and ensure the equitable sharing by States in the benefits derived therefrom, taking into particular consideration the interests and needs of the developing countries, whether land-locked or coastal.

10. States shall promote international co-operation in scientific research exclusively for peaceful purposes:

    (a) By participation in international programmes and by encouraging co-operation in scientific research by personnel of different countries;

    (b) Through effective publication of research programmes and dissemination of the results of research through international channels;

    (c) By co-operation in measure to strengthen research capabilities of developing countries, including the participation of their nationals in research programmes.

No such activity shall form the legal basis for any claims with respect to any part of the area or its resources.

11. With respect to activities in the area and acting in conformity with the international régime to be established, State shall take appropriate measures for and shall co-operate in the adoption and implementation of international rules, standards and procedures for, *inter alia*:

    (a) The prevention of pollution and contamination, and other hazards to the marine environment, including the coastline, and of interference with the ecological balance of the marine environment;

    (b) The protection and conservation of the natural resources of the area and the prevention of damage to the flora and fauna of the marine environment.

12. In their activities in the area, including those relating to its resources, States shall pay due regard to the rights and legitimate interests of coastal States in the region of such activities, as well as of all other States, which may be affected by such activities. Consultations shall be maintained with the coastal States concerned with respect to activities relating to the exploration of the area and the exploitation of its resources with a view to avoiding infringement of such rights and interests.

13.   Nothing herein shall affect:

(a)   The legal status of the waters superjacent to the area or that or the air space above those waters;

(b)   The rights of coastal States with respect to measures to prevent, mitigate or eliminate grave and imminent danger to their coastline or related interests from pollution or threat thereof or from other hazardous occurrences resulting from or caused by any activities in the area, subject to the international régime to be established.

14.   Every State shall have the responsibility to ensure that activities in the area, including those relating to its resources, whether undertaken by governmental agencies, or non-governmental entities or persons under its jurisdiction, or acting on its behalf, shall be carried out in conformity with the international régime to be established. The same responsibility applies to international organizations and their members for activities undertaken by such organizations or on their behalf. Damage caused by such activities shall entail liability.

15.   The parties to any dispute relating to activities in the area and its resources shall resolve such dispute by the measures mentioned in Article 33 of the Charter of the United Nations and such procedures for settling disputes as may be agreed upon in the international régime to be established.

Convention on the Prevention of Marine Pollution by Dumping of Wastes and Other Matter

Done at London, 29 December 1972; entry into force 30 August 1975
1046 UNTS 138 [Registration Number 15749][1]

The Contracting Parties to this Convention,

Recognizing that the marine environment and the living organisms which it supports are of vital importance to humanity, and all people have an interest in assuring that it is so managed that its quality and resources are not impaired;

Recognizing that the capacity of the sea to assimilate wastes and render them harmless, and its ability to regenerate natural resources, is not unlimited;

Recognizing that States have, in accordance with the Charter of the United Nations and the principles of international law, the sovereign right to exploit their own resources pursuant to their own environmental policies, and the responsibility to ensure that activities within their jurisdiction or control do not cause damage to the environment of other States or of areas beyond the limits of national jurisdiction;

Recalling Resolution 2749 (XXV) of the General Assembly of the United Nations on the principles governing the sea-bed and the ocean floor and the subsoil thereof, beyond the limits of national jurisdiction;

Noting that marine pollution originates in many sources, such as dumping and discharges through the atmosphere, rivers, estuaries, outfalls and pipelines, and that it is important that States use the best practicable means to prevent such pollution and develop products and processes which will reduce the amount of harmful wastes to be disposed of;

---

[1] The text of the Convention was amended on 12 October 1978, 24 September 1980, 3 November 1989, and 12 November 1993. The text of the Convention reproduced is a consolidated version incorporating the various amendments. Annexes omitted.

Being convinced that international action to control the pollution of the sea by dumping can and must be taken without delay but that this action should not preclude discussion of measures to control other sources of marine pollution as soon as possible; and

Wishing to improve protection of the marine environment by encouraging States with a common interest in particular geographical areas to enter into appropriate agreements supplementary to this Convention;

Have agreed as follows:

Article I

Contracting Parties shall individually and collectively promote the effective control of all sources of pollution of the marine environment, and pledge themselves especially to take all practicable steps to prevent the pollution of the sea by the dumping of waste and other matter that is liable to create hazards to human health, to harm living resources and marine life, to damage amenities or to interfere with other legitimate uses of the sea.

Article II

Contracting Parties shall, as provided for in the following Articles, take effective measures individually, according to their scientific, technical and economic capabilities, and collectively, to prevent marine pollution caused by dumping and shall harmonize their policies in this regard.

Article III

For the purposes of this Convention:

1. (a) 'Dumping' means:
    (i)   any deliberate disposal at sea of wastes or other matter from vessels, aircraft, platforms or other man-made structures at sea;
    (ii) any deliberate disposal at sea of vessels, aircraft, platforms or other man-made structures at sea.
    (b) 'Dumping' does not include:
    (i)   the disposal at sea of wastes or other matter incidental to, or derived from the normal operations of vessels, aircraft, platforms or other man-made structures at sea and their equipment, other than wastes or other matter transported by or to vessels, aircraft, platforms or other man-made structures at sea, operating for the purpose of disposal of such matter or derived from the treatment of such wastes or other matter on such vessels, aircraft, platforms or structures;
    (ii) placement of matter for a purpose other than the mere disposal thereof, provided that such placement is not contrary to the aims of this Convention.
    (c) The disposal of wastes or other matter directly arising from, or related to the exploration, exploitation and associated off-shore processing of sea-bed mineral resources will not be covered by the provisions of this Convention.

2. 'Vessels and aircraft' means waterborne or airborne craft of any type whatsoever. This expression includes air-cushioned craft and floating craft, whether self-propelled or not.

3. 'Sea' means all marine waters other than the internal waters of States.

4. 'Wastes or other matter' means material and substance of any kind, form or description.

5. 'Special permit' means permission granted specifically on application in advance and in accordance with Annex II and Annex III.

6. 'General permit' means permission granted in advance and in accordance with Annex III.

7. 'The Organisation' means the Organisation designated by the Contracting Parties in accordance with Article XIV (2).

Article IV

1. In accordance with the provisions of this Convention, Contracting Parties shall prohibit the dumping of any wastes or other matter in whatever form or condition except as otherwise specified below:

(a) the dumping of wastes or other matter listed in Annex I is prohibited;

(b) the dumping of wastes or other matter listed in Annex II requires a prior special permit;

(c) the dumping of all other wastes or matter requires a prior general permit.

2. Any permit shall be issued only after careful consideration of all the factors set forth in Annex III, including prior studies of the characteristics of the dumping site, as set forth in Sections B and C of that Annex.

3. No provision of this Convention is to be interpreted as preventing a Contracting Party from prohibiting, insofar as that Party is concerned, the dumping of wastes or other matter not mentioned in Annex I. That Party shall notify such measures to the Organisation.

Article V

1. The provisions of Article IV shall not apply when it is necessary to secure the safety of human life or of vessels, aircraft, platforms or other man-made structures at sea in cases of *force majeure* caused by stress of weather, or in any case which constitutes a danger to human life or a real threat to vessels, aircraft, platforms or other man-made structures at sea, if dumping appears to be the only way of averting the threat and if there is every probability that the damage consequent upon such dumping will be less than would otherwise occur. Such dumping shall be so conducted as to minimize the likelihood of damage to human or marine life and shall be reported forthwith to the Organisation.

2. A Contracting Party may issue a special permit as an exception to Article IV (1) (a), in emergencies, posing unacceptable risk relating to human health and admitting no other feasible solution. Before doing so the Party shall consult any other country or countries that are likely to be affected and the Organisation which, after consulting other Parties, and international organisations as appropriate, shall, in accordance with Article XIV promptly recommend to the Party the most appropriate procedures to adopt. The Party shall follow these recommendations to the maximum extent feasible consistent with the time within which action must be taken and with the general obligation to avoid damage to the marine environment and shall inform the Organisation of the action it takes. The Parties pledge themselves to assist one another in such situations.

3. Any Contracting Party may waive its rights under paragraph (2) at the time of, or subsequent to ratification of, or accession to this Convention.

Article VI

1. Each Contracting Party shall designate an appropriate authority or authorities to:

(a) issue special permits which shall be required prior to, and for, the dumping of matter listed in Annex II and in the circumstances provided for in Article V (2);

(b)   issue general permits which shall be required prior to, and for, the dumping of all other matter;

(c)   keep records of the nature and quantities of all matter permitted to be dumped and the location, time and method of dumping;

(d)   monitor individually, or in collaboration with other Parties and competent international organisations, the condition of the seas for the purposes of this Convention.

2.   The appropriate authority or authorities of a contracting Party shall issue prior special or general permits in accordance with paragraph (1) in respect of matter intended for dumping:

(a)   loaded in its territory;

(b)   loaded by a vessel or aircraft registered in its territory or flying its flag, when the loading occurs in the territory of a State not party to this Convention.

3.   In issuing permits under sub-paragraphs (1) (a) and (b) above, the appropriate authority or authorities shall comply with Annex III, together with such additional criteria, measures and requirements as they may consider relevant.

4.   Each Contracting Party, directly or through a Secretariat established under a regional agreement, shall report to the Organisation, and where appropriate to other Parties, the information specified in sub-paragraphs (c) and (d) of paragraph (1) above, and the criteria, measures and requirements it adopts in accordance with paragraph (3) above. The procedure to be followed and the nature of such reports shall be agreed by the Parties in consultation.

Article VII

1.   Each Contracting Party shall apply the measures required to implement the present Convention to all:

(a)   vessels and aircraft registered in its territory or flying its flag;

(b)   vessels and aircraft loading in its territory or territorial seas matter which is to be dumped;

(c)   vessels and aircraft and fixed or floating platforms under its jurisdiction believed to be engaged in dumping.

2.   Each Party shall take in its territory appropriate measures to prevent and punish conduct in contravention of the provisions of this Convention.

3.   The Parties agree to co-operate in the development of procedures for the effective application of this Convention particularly on the high seas, including procedures for the reporting of vessels and aircraft observed dumping in contravention of the Convention.

4.   This Convention shall not apply to those vessels and aircraft entitled to sovereign immunity under international law. However, each Party shall ensure by the adoption of appropriate measures that such vessels and aircraft owned or operated by it act in a manner consistent with the object and purpose of this Convention, and shall inform the Organisation accordingly.

5.   Nothing in this Convention shall affect the right of each Party to adopt other measures, in accordance with the principles of international law, to prevent dumping at sea.

Article VIII

In order to further the objectives of this Convention, the Contracting Parties with common interests to protect in the marine environment in a given geographical area shall endeavour, taking into account characteristic regional features, to enter into regional agreements consistent with this Convention for the prevention of pollution, especially by dumping. The Contracting Parties to the present Convention shall endeavour to act consistently with the objectives and provisions of such regional agreements, which shall be notified to them by the Organisation. Contracting Parties shall seek to co-operate with the Parties to regional agreements in order to develop harmonized procedures to be followed by Contracting Parties to the different conventions concerned. Special attention shall be given to co-operation in the field of monitoring and scientific research.

Article IX

The Contracting Parties shall promote, through collaboration within the Organisation and other international bodies, support for those Parties which request it for:
(a) the training of scientific and technical personnel;
(b) the supply of necessary equipment and facilities for research and monitoring;
(c) the disposal and treatment of waste and other measures to prevent or mitigate pollution caused by dumping;
preferably within the countries concerned, so furthering the aims and purposes of this Convention.

Article X

In accordance with the principles of international law regarding State responsibility for damage to the environment of other States or to any other area of the environment, caused by dumping of wastes and other matter of all kinds, the Contracting Parties undertake to develop procedures for the assessment of liability and the settlement of disputes regarding dumping.

Article XI

The Contracting Parties shall at their first consultative meeting consider procedures for the settlement of disputes concerning the interpretation and application of this Convention.

Article XII

The Contracting Parties pledge themselves to promote, within the competent specialised agencies and other international bodies, measures to protect the marine environment against pollution caused by:
(a) hydrocarbons, including oil and their wastes;
(b) other noxious or hazardous matter transported by vessels for purposes other than dumping;
(c) wastes generated in the course of operation of vessels, aircraft, platforms and other man-made structures at sea;
(d) radio-active pollutants from all sources, including vessels;
(e) agents of chemical and biological warfare;
(f) wastes or other matter directly arising from, or related to the exploration, exploitation and associated offshore processing of sea-bed mineral resources.
The Parties will also promote, within the appropriate international organisation, the codification of signals to be used by vessels engaged in dumping.

Article XIII

Nothing in this Convention shall prejudice the codification and development of the law of the sea by the United Nations Conference on the Law of the Sea convened pursuant to Resolution 2750 C (XXV) of the General Assembly of the United Nations nor the present or future claims and legal views of any State concerning the law of the sea and the nature and extent of coastal and flag State jurisdiction. The Contracting Parties agree to consult at a meeting to be convened by the Organisation after the Law of the Sea Conference, and in any case not later than 1976, with a view to defining the nature and extent of the right and the responsibility of a coastal State to apply the Convention in a zone adjacent to its coast.

Article XIV

1. The Government of the United Kingdom of Great Britain and Northern Ireland as a depositary shall call a meeting of the Contracting Parties not later than three months after the entry into force of this Convention to decide on organisational matters.

2. The Contracting Parties shall designate a competent Organisation existing at the time of that meeting to be responsible for Secretariat duties in relation to this Convention. Any Party to this Convention not being a member of this Organisation shall make an appropriate contribution to the expenses incurred by the Organisation in performing these duties.

3. The Secretariat duties of the Organisation shall include:

(a)   the convening of consultative meetings of the Contracting Parties not less frequently than once every two years and of special meetings of the Parties at any time on the request of two thirds of the Parties;

(b)   preparing and assisting, in consultation with the Contracting Parties and appropriate International Organisations, in the development and implementation of procedures referred to in sub-paragraph (4) (e) of this Article;

(c)   considering enquiries by, and information from the Contracting Parties, consulting with them and with the appropriate International Organisations, and providing recommendations to the Parties on questions related to, but not specifically covered by the Convention;

(d)   conveying to the Parties concerned all notifications received by the Organisation in accordance with Articles IV (3), V (1) and (2), VI (4), XV, XX and XXI.

Prior to the designation of the Organisation these functions shall, as necessary, be performed by the depositary, who for this purpose shall be the Government of the United Kingdom of Great Britain and Northern Ireland.

4. Consultative or special meetings of the Contracting Parties shall keep under continuing review the implementation of this Convention and may, *inter alia*:

(a)   review and adopt amendments to this Convention and its Annexes in accordance with Article XV;

(b)   invite the appropriate scientific body or bodies to collaborate with and to advise the Parties or the Organisation on any scientific or technical aspect relevant to this Convention, including particularly the content of the Annexes;

(c)   receive and consider reports made pursuant to Article VI (4);

(d)   promote co-operation with and between regional organisations concerned with the prevention of marine pollution;

(e)   develop or adopt, in consultation with appropriate International Organisations, procedures referred to in Article V (2), including basic criteria for determining exceptional and emergency situations, and procedures for consultative advice and the safe disposal of matter in such circumstances, including the designation of appropriate dumping areas, and recommend accordingly;

(f)   consider any additional action that may be required.

5. The Contracting Parties at their first consultative meeting shall establish rules of procedure as necessary.

Article XV

    1. (a) At meetings of the Contracting Parties called in accordance with Article XIV amendments to this Convention may be adopted by a two-thirds majority of those present. An amendment shall enter into force for the Parties which have accepted it on the sixtieth day after two thirds of the Parties shall have deposited an instrument of acceptance of the amendment with the Organisation. Thereafter the amendment shall enter into force for any other Party 30 days after that Party deposits its instrument of acceptance of the amendment.

        (b) The Organisation shall inform all Contracting Parties of any request made for a special meeting under Article XIV and of any amendments adopted at meetings of the Parties and of the date on which each such amendment enters into force for each Party.

    2. Amendments to the Annexes will be based on scientific or technical considerations. Amendments to the Annexes approved by a two-thirds majority of those present at a meeting called in accordance with Article XIV shall enter into force for each Contracting Party immediately on notification of its acceptance to the Organisation and 100 days after approval by the meeting for all other Parties except for those which before the end of the 100 days make a declaration that they are not able to accept the amendment at that time. Parties should endeavour to signify their acceptance of an amendment to the Organisation as soon as possible after approval at a meeting. A Party may at any time substitute an acceptance for a previous declaration of objection and the amendment previously objected to shall thereupon enter into force for that Party.

    3. An acceptance or declaration of objection under this Article shall be made by the deposit of an instrument with the Organisation. The Organisation shall notify all Contracting Parties of the receipt of such instruments.

    4. Prior to the designation of the Organisation, the Secretarial functions herein attributed to it shall be performed temporarily by the Government of the United Kingdom of Great Britain and Northern Ireland, as one of the depositaries of this Convention.

Article XVI

    This Convention shall be open for signature by any State at London, Mexico City, Moscow and Washington from 29 December 1972 until 31 December 1973.

Article XVII

    This Convention shall be subject to ratification. The instruments of ratification shall be deposited with the Governments of Mexico, the Russian Federation, the United Kingdom of Great Britain and Northern Ireland, and the United States of America.

Article XVIII

    After 31 December 1973, this Convention shall be open for accession by any State. The instruments of accession shall be deposited with the Governments of Mexico, the Russian Federation, the United Kingdom of Great Britain and Northern Ireland, and the United States of America.

Article XIX

    1. This Convention shall enter into force on the thirtieth day following the date of deposit of the fifteenth instrument of ratification or accession.

    2. For each Contracting Party ratifying or acceding to the Convention after the deposit of the fifteenth instrument of ratification or accession, the Convention shall enter

into force on the thirtieth day after deposit by such Party of its instrument of ratification or accession.

Article XX

The depositaries shall inform Contracting Parties:

(a)   of signatures to this Convention and of the deposit of instruments of ratification, accession or withdrawal, in accordance with Articles XVI, XVII, XVIII and XXI, and

(b)   of the date on which this Convention will enter into force, in accordance with Article XIX.

Article XXI

Any Contracting Party may withdraw from this Convention by giving six months' notice in writing to a depositary, which shall promptly inform all Parties of such notice.

Article XXII

The original of this Convention of which the English, French, Russian and Spanish texts are equally authentic, shall be deposited with the Governments of Mexico, the Russian Federation, the United Kingdom of Great Britain and Northern Ireland and the United States of America who shall send certified copies thereof to all States.

IN WITNESS WHEREOF the undersigned Plenipotentiaries, being duly authorised thereto by their respective Governments, have signed the present Convention.

DONE in quadruplicate at London, Mexico City, Moscow and Washington, this twenty-ninth day of December, 1972.

Protocol to the Convention on the Prevention of Marine Pollution by Dumping of Wastes and Other Matter

Done at London, 7 November 1996; entry into force, 24 March 2006
IMO Doc. LC/SM 1/6, 14 November 1996[1]

The Contracting Parties to this Protocol,

Stressing the need to protect the marine environment and to promote the sustainable use and conservation of marine resources,

Noting in this regard the achievements within the framework of the Convention on the Prevention of Marine Pollution by Dumping of Wastes and Other Matter, 1972 and especially the evolution towards approaches based on precaution and prevention,

Noting further the contribution in this regard by complementary regional and national instruments which aim to protect the marine environment and which take account of specific circumstances and needs of those regions and States,

Reaffirming the value of a global approach to these matters and in particular the importance of continuing co-operation and collaboration between Contracting Parties in implementing the Convention and the Protocol,

---

[1] The text of the Protocol was amended on 2 November 2006 by the first meeting of the Contracting Parties through resolution LP.1(1). The amendment entered into force on 10 February 2007. The text of the Protocol reproduced is a consolidated version incorporating that amendment. Annex 2 (Assessment of wastes or other matter that may be considered for dumping) and Annex 3 (Arbitral procedure) omitted.

Recognizing that it may be desirable to adopt, on a national or regional level, more stringent measures with respect to prevention and elimination of pollution of the marine environment from dumping at sea than are provided for in international conventions or other types of agreements with a global scope,

Taking into account relevant international agreements and actions, especially the United Nations Convention on the Law of the Sea, 1982, the Rio Declaration on Environment and Development and Agenda 21,

Recognizing also the interests and capacities of developing States and in particular small island developing States,

Being convinced that further international action to prevent, reduce and where practicable eliminate pollution of the sea caused by dumping can and must be taken without delay to protect and preserve the marine environment and to manage human activities in such a manner that the marine ecosystem will continue to sustain the legitimate uses of the sea and will continue to meet the needs of present and future generations,

Have agreed as follows:

Article 1 Definitions

For the purposes of this Protocol:

1. 'Convention' means the Convention on the Prevention of Marine Pollution by Dumping of Wastes and Other Matter, 1972, as amended.

2. 'Organization' means the International Maritime Organization.

3. 'Secretary-General' means the Secretary-General of the Organization.

4. (a) 'Dumping' means:
   (i) any deliberate disposal into the sea of wastes or other matter from vessels, aircraft, platforms or other man-made structures at sea;
   (ii) any deliberate disposal into the sea of vessels, aircraft, platforms or other man-made structures at sea;
   (iii) any storage of wastes or other matter in the sea-bed and the subsoil thereof from vessels, aircraft, platforms or other man-made structures at sea; and
   (iv) any abandonment or toppling at site of platforms or other man-made structures at sea, for the sole purpose of deliberate disposal.

   (b) Dumping does not include:
   (i) the disposal into the sea of wastes or other matter incidental to, or derived from the normal operations of vessels, aircraft, platforms or other man-made structures at sea and their equipment, other than wastes or other matter transported by or to vessels, aircraft, platforms or other man-made structures at sea, operating for the purpose of disposal of such matter or derived from the treatment of such wastes or other matter on such vessels, aircraft, platforms or other man-made structures;
   (ii) placement of matter for a purpose other than the mere disposal thereof, provided that such placement is not contrary to the aims of this Protocol; and
   (iii) notwithstanding paragraph 4 (a) (iv), abandonment in the sea of matter (e.g., cables, pipelines and marine research devices) placed for a purpose other than the mere disposal thereof.

   (c) The disposal or storage of wastes or other matter directly arising from, or related to the exploration, exploitation and associated off-shore processing of sea-bed mineral resources is not covered by the provisions of this Protocol.

5. (a) 'Incineration' at sea means the combustion on board a vessel, platform or other man-made structure at sea of wastes or other matter for the purpose of their deliberate disposal by thermal destruction.

(b) Incineration at sea does not include the incineration of wastes or other matter on board a vessel, platform, or other man-made structure at sea if such wastes or other matter were generated during the normal operation of that vessel, platform or other man-made structure at sea.

6. 'Vessels and aircraft' means waterborne or airborne craft of any type whatsoever. This expression includes air-cushioned craft and floating craft, whether self-propelled or not.

7. 'Sea' means all marine waters other than the internal waters of States, as well as the sea-bed and the subsoil thereof; it does not include sub-sea-bed repositories accessed only from land.

8. 'Wastes or other matter' means material and substance of any kind, form or description.

9. 'Permit' means permission granted in advance and in accordance with relevant measures adopted pursuant to Article 4 (a) (ii) or 8 (2).

10. 'Pollution' means the introduction, directly or indirectly, by human activity, of wastes or other matter into the sea which results or is likely to result in such deleterious effects as harm to living resources and marine ecosystems, hazards to human health, hindrance to marine activities, including fishing and other legitimate uses of the sea, impairment of quality for use of sea water and reduction of amenities.

Article 2 Objectives

Contracting Parties shall individually and collectively protect and preserve the marine environment from all sources of pollution and take effective measures, according to their scientific, technical and economic capabilities, to prevent, reduce and where practicable eliminate pollution caused by dumping or incineration at sea of wastes or other matter. Where appropriate, they shall harmonize their policies in this regard.

Article 3 General obligations

1. In implementing this Protocol, Contracting Parties shall apply a precautionary approach to environmental protection from dumping of wastes or other matter whereby appropriate preventative measures are taken when there is reason to believe that wastes or other matter introduced into the marine environment are likely to cause harm even when there is no conclusive evidence to prove a causal relation between inputs and their effects.

2. Taking into account the approach that the polluter should, in principle, bear the cost of pollution, each Contracting Party shall endeavour to promote practices whereby those it has authorized to engage in dumping or incineration at sea bear the cost of meeting the pollution prevention and control requirements for the authorized activities, having due regard to the public interest.

3 In implementing the provisions of this Protocol, Contracting Parties shall act so as not to transfer, directly or indirectly, damage or likelihood of damage from one part of the environment to another or transform one type of pollution into another.

4. No provision of this Protocol shall be interpreted as preventing Contracting Parties from taking, individually or jointly, more stringent measures in accordance with international law with respect to the prevention, reduction and where practicable elimination of pollution.

Article 4 Dumping of wastes or other matter

    1. (a)   Contracting Parties shall prohibit the dumping of any wastes or other matter with the exception of those listed in Annex 1.

       (b)   The dumping of wastes or other matter listed in Annex 1 shall require a permit. Contracting Parties shall adopt administrative or legislative measures to ensure that issuance of permits and permit conditions comply with provisions of Annex 2. Particular attention shall be paid to opportunities to avoid dumping in favour of environmentally preferable alternatives.

    2. No provision of this Protocol shall be interpreted as preventing a Contracting Party from prohibiting, insofar as that Contracting Party is concerned, the dumping of wastes or other matter mentioned in Annex 1. That Contracting Party shall notify the Organization of such measures.

Article 5 Incineration at sea

    Contracting Parties shall prohibit incineration at sea of wastes or other matter.

Article 6 Export of waste or other matter

    Contracting Parties shall not allow the export of wastes or other matter to other countries for dumping or incineration at sea.

Article 7 Internal waters

    1. Notwithstanding any other provision of this Protocol, this Protocol shall relate to internal waters only to the extent provided for in paragraphs (2) and (3).

    2. Each Contracting Party shall at its discretion either apply the provisions of this Protocol or adopt other effective permitting and regulatory measures to control the deliberate disposal of wastes or other matter in marine internal waters where such disposal would be 'dumping' or 'incineration at sea' within the meaning of Article 1, if conducted at sea.

    3. Each Contracting Party should provide the Organization with information on legislation and institutional mechanisms regarding implementation, compliance and enforcement in marine internal waters. Contracting Parties should also use their best efforts to provide on a voluntary basis summary reports on the type and nature of the materials dumped in marine internal waters.

Article 8 Exceptions

    1. The provisions of Articles 4 (a) and 5 shall not apply when it is necessary to secure the safety of human life or of vessels, aircraft, platforms or other man-made structures at sea in cases of *force majeure* caused by stress of weather, or in any case which constitutes a danger to human life or a real threat to vessels, aircraft, platforms or other man-made structures at sea, if dumping or incineration at sea appears to be the only way of averting the threat and if there is every probability that the damage consequent upon such dumping or incineration at sea will be less than would otherwise occur. Such dumping or incineration at sea shall be conducted so as to minimize the likelihood of damage to human or marine life and shall be reported forthwith to the Organization.

    2. A Contracting Party may issue a permit as an exception to Articles 4 (a) and 5, in emergencies posing an unacceptable threat to human health, safety, or the marine environment and admitting of no other feasible solution. Before doing so the Contracting Party shall consult any other country or countries that are likely to be affected and the Organization which, after consulting other Contracting Parties, and competent international organizations as appropriate, shall, in accordance with Article 18 (1) (f)

promptly recommend to the Contracting Party the most appropriate procedures to adopt. The Contracting Party shall follow these recommendations to the maximum extent feasible consistent with the time within which action must be taken and with the general obligation to avoid damage to the marine environment and shall inform the Organization of the action it takes. The Contracting Parties pledge themselves to assist one another in such situations.

3. Any Contracting Party may waive its rights under paragraph (2) at the time of, or subsequent to ratification of, or accession to this Protocol.

Article 9 Issuance of permits and reporting

1. Each Contracting Party shall designate an appropriate authority or authorities to:
   (a)   issue permits in accordance with this Protocol;
   (b)   keep records of the nature and quantities of all wastes or other matter for which dumping permits have been issued and where practicable the quantities actually dumped and the location, time and method of dumping; and
   (c)   monitor individually, or in collaboration with other Contracting Parties and competent international organizations, the condition of the sea for the purposes of this Protocol.

2. The appropriate authority or authorities of a Contracting Party shall issue permits in accordance with this Protocol in respect of wastes or other matter intended for dumping or, as provided for in Article 8 (2), incineration at sea:
   (a)   loaded in its territory; and
   (b)   loaded onto a vessel or aircraft registered in its territory or flying its flag, when the loading occurs in the territory of a State not a Contracting Party to this Protocol.

3. In issuing permits, the appropriate authority or authorities shall comply with the requirements of Article 4, together with such additional criteria, measures and requirements as they may consider relevant.

4. Each Contracting Party, directly or through a secretariat established under a regional agreement, shall report to the Organization and where appropriate to other Contracting Parties:
   (a)   the information specified in paragraphs (1) (b) and (1) (c);
   (b)   the administrative and legislative measures taken to implement the provisions of this Protocol, including a summary of enforcement measures; and
   (c)   the effectiveness of the measures referred to in paragraph (4) (b) and any problems encountered in their application.

The information referred to in paragraphs (1) (b) and (1) (c) shall be submitted on an annual basis. The information referred to in paragraphs (4) (b) and (4) (c) shall be submitted on a regular basis.

5. Reports submitted under paragraphs (4) (b) and (4) (c) shall be evaluated by an appropriate subsidiary body as determined by the Meeting of Contracting Parties. This body will report its conclusions to an appropriate Meeting or Special Meeting of Contracting Parties.

Article 10 Application and enforcement

1. Each Contracting Party shall apply the measures required to implement this Protocol to all:
   (a)   vessels and aircraft registered in its territory or flying its flag;
   (b)   vessels and aircraft loading in its territory the wastes or other matter which are to be dumped or incinerated at sea; and

(c) vessels, aircraft and platforms or other man-made structures believed to be engaged in dumping or incineration at sea in areas within which it is entitled to exercise jurisdiction in accordance with international law.

2. Each Contracting Party shall take appropriate measures in accordance with international law to prevent and if necessary punish acts contrary to the provisions of this Protocol.

3. Contracting Parties agree to co-operate in the development of procedures for the effective application of this Protocol in areas beyond the jurisdiction of any State, including procedures for the reporting of vessels and aircraft observed dumping or incinerating at sea in contravention of this Protocol.

4. This Protocol shall not apply to those vessels and aircraft entitled to sovereign immunity under international law. However, each Contracting Party shall ensure by the adoption of appropriate measures that such vessels and aircraft owned or operated by it act in a manner consistent with the object and purpose of this Protocol and shall inform the Organization accordingly.

5. A State may, at the time it expresses its consent to be bound by this Protocol, or at any time thereafter, declare that it shall apply the provisions of this Protocol to its vessels and aircraft referred to in paragraph (4), recognizing that only that State may enforce those provisions against such vessels and aircraft.

Article 11 Compliance procedures

1. No later than two years after the entry into force of this Protocol, the Meeting of Contracting Parties shall establish those procedures and mechanisms necessary to assess and promote compliance with this Protocol. Such procedures and mechanisms shall be developed with a view to allowing for the full and open exchange of information, in a constructive manner.

2. After full consideration of any information submitted pursuant to this Protocol and any recommendations made through procedures or mechanisms established under paragraph (1), the Meeting of Contracting Parties may offer advice, assistance or co-operation to Contracting Parties and non-Contracting Parties.

Article 12 Regional co-operation

In order to further the objectives of this Protocol, Contracting Parties with common interests to protect the marine environment in a given geographical area shall endeavour, taking into account characteristic regional features, to enhance regional co-operation including the conclusion of regional agreements consistent with this Protocol for the prevention, reduction and where practicable elimination of pollution caused by dumping or incineration at sea of wastes or other matter. Contracting Parties shall seek to co-operate with the parties to regional agreements in order to develop harmonized procedures to be followed by Contracting Parties to the different conventions concerned.

Article 13 Technical co-operation and assistance

1. Contracting Parties shall, through collaboration within the Organization and in co-ordination with other competent international organizations, promote bilateral and multilateral support for the prevention, reduction and where practicable elimination of pollution caused by dumping as provided for in this Protocol to those Contracting Parties that request it for:

(a) training of scientific and technical personnel for research, monitoring and enforcement, including as appropriate the supply of necessary equipment and facilities, with a view to strengthening national capabilities;

(b)   advice on implementation of this Protocol;

(c)   information and technical co-operation relating to waste minimization and clean production processes;

(d)   information and technical co-operation relating to the disposal and treatment of waste and other measures to prevent, reduce and where practicable eliminate pollution caused by dumping; and

(e)   access to and transfer of environmentally sound technologies and corresponding know-how, in particular to developing countries and countries in transition to market economies, on favourable terms, including on concessional and preferential terms, as mutually agreed, taking into account the need to protect intellectual property rights as well as the special needs of developing countries and countries in transition to market economies.

2.   The Organization shall perform the following functions:

(a)   forward requests from Contracting Parties for technical co-operation to other Contracting Parties, taking into account such factors as technical capabilities;

(b)   co-ordinate requests for assistance with other competent international organizations, as appropriate; and

(c)   subject to the availability of adequate resources, assist developing countries and those in transition to market economies, which have declared their intention to become Contracting Parties to this Protocol, to examine the means necessary to achieve full implementation.

Article 14 Scientific and technical research

1.   Contracting Parties shall take appropriate measures to promote and facilitate scientific and technical research on the prevention, reduction and where practicable elimination of pollution by dumping and other sources of marine pollution relevant to this Protocol. In particular, such research should include observation, measurement, evaluation and analysis of pollution by scientific methods.

2.   Contracting Parties shall, to achieve the objectives of this Protocol, promote the availability of relevant information to other Contracting Parties who request it on:

(a)   scientific and technical activities and measures undertaken in accordance with this Protocol;

(b)   marine scientific and technological programmes and their objectives; and

(c)   the impacts observed from the monitoring and assessment conducted pursuant to Article 9 (1) (c).

Article 15 Responsibility and liability

In accordance with the principles of international law regarding State responsibility for damage to the environment of other States or to any other area of the environment, the Contracting Parties undertake to develop procedures regarding liability arising from the dumping or incineration at sea of wastes or other matter.

Article 16 Settlement of disputes

1.   Any disputes regarding the interpretation or application of this Protocol shall be resolved in the first instance through negotiation, mediation or conciliation, or other peaceful means chosen by parties to the dispute.

2.   If no resolution is possible within twelve months after one Contracting Party has notified another that a dispute exists between them, the dispute shall be settled, at the request of a party to the dispute, by means of the Arbitral procedure set forth in Annex 3, unless the parties to the dispute agree to use one of the procedures listed in paragraph (1)

of Article 287 of the 1982 United Nations Convention on the Law of the Sea. The parties to the dispute may so agree, whether or not they are also States Parties to the 1982 United Nations Convention on the Law of the Sea.

3. In the event an agreement to use one of the procedures listed in paragraph (1) of Article 287 of the 1982 United Nations Convention on the Law of the Sea is reached, the provisions set forth in Part XV of that Convention that are related to the chosen procedure would also apply, *mutatis mutandis.*

4. The twelve month period referred to in paragraph (2) may be extended for another twelve months by mutual consent of the parties concerned.

5. Notwithstanding paragraph (2), any State may, at the time it expresses its consent to be bound by this Protocol, notify the Secretary-General that, when it is a party to a dispute about the interpretation or application of Article 3 (1) or 3 (2), its consent will be required before the dispute may be settled by means of the Arbitral procedure set forth in Annex 3.

Article 17 International co-operation

Contracting Parties shall promote the objectives of this Protocol within the competent international organizations.

Article 18 Meetings of Contracting Parties

1. Meetings of Contracting Parties or Special Meetings of Contracting Parties shall keep under continuing review the implementation of this Protocol and evaluate its effectiveness with a view to identifying means of strengthening action, where necessary, to prevent, reduce and where practicable eliminate pollution caused by dumping and incineration at sea of wastes or other matter. To these ends, Meetings of Contracting Parties or Special Meetings of Contracting Parties may:

    (a)   review and adopt amendments to this Protocol in accordance with Articles 21 and 22;

    (b)   establish subsidiary bodies, as required, to consider any matter with a view to facilitating the effective implementation of this Protocol;

    (c)   invite appropriate expert bodies to advise the Contracting Parties or the Organization on matters relevant to this Protocol;

    (d)   promote co-operation with competent international organizations concerned with the prevention and control of pollution;

    (e)   consider the information made available pursuant to Article 9 (4);

    (f)   develop or adopt, in consultation with competent international organizations, procedures referred to in Article 8 (2), including basic criteria for determining exceptional and emergency situations, and procedures for consultative advice and the safe disposal of matter at sea in such circumstances;

    (g)   consider and adopt resolutions; and

    (h)   consider any additional action that may be required.

2. The Contracting Parties at their first Meeting shall establish rules of procedure as necessary.

Article 19 Duties of the Organization

1. The Organization shall be responsible for Secretariat duties in relation to this Protocol. Any Contracting Party to this Protocol not being a member of this Organization shall make an appropriate contribution to the expenses incurred by the Organization in performing these duties.

2. Secretariat duties necessary for the administration of this Protocol include:

(a)   convening Meetings of Contracting Parties once per year, unless otherwise decided by Contracting Parties, and Special Meetings of Contracting Parties at any time on the request of two thirds of the Contracting Parties;

(b)   providing advice on request on the implementation of this Protocol and on guidance and procedures developed thereunder;

(c)   considering enquiries by, and information from Contracting Parties, consulting with them and with the competent international organizations, and providing recommendations to Contracting Parties on questions related to, but not specifically covered by, this Protocol;

(d)   preparing and assisting, in consultation with Contracting Parties and the competent international organizations, in the development and implementation of procedures referred to in Article 18 (6);

(e)   conveying to the Contracting Parties concerned all notifications received by the Organization in accordance with this Protocol; and

(f)   preparing, every two years, a budget and a financial account for the administration of this Protocol which shall be distributed to all Contracting Parties.

3. The Organization shall, subject to the availability of adequate resources, in addition to the requirements set out in Article 13 (2) (c):

(a)   collaborate in assessments of the state of the marine environment; and

(b)   co-operate with competent international organizations concerned with the prevention and control of pollution.

Article 20 Annexes

Annexes to this Protocol form an integral part of this Protocol.

Article 21 Amendment of the protocol

1. Any Contracting Party may propose amendments to the Articles of this Protocol. The text of a proposed amendment shall be communicated to Contracting Parties by the Organization at least six months prior to its consideration at a Meeting of Contracting Parties or a Special Meeting of Contracting Parties.

2. Amendments to the Articles of this Protocol shall be adopted by a two-thirds majority vote of the Contracting Parties which are present and voting at the Meeting of Contracting Parties or Special Meeting of Contracting Parties designated for this purpose.

3. An amendment shall enter into force for the Contracting Parties which have accepted it on the sixtieth day after two thirds of the Contracting Parties shall have deposited an instrument of acceptance of the amendment with the Organization. Thereafter the amendment shall enter into force for any other Contracting Party on the sixtieth day after the date on which that Contracting Party has deposited its instrument of acceptance of the amendment.

4. The Secretary-General shall inform Contracting Parties of any amendments adopted at Meetings of Contracting Parties and of the date on which such amendments enter into force generally and for each Contracting Party.

5. After entry into force of an amendment to this Protocol, any State that becomes a Contracting Party to this Protocol shall become a Contracting Party to this Protocol as amended, unless two thirds of the Contracting Parties present and voting at the Meeting or Special Meeting of Contracting Parties adopting the amendment agree otherwise.

Article 22 Amendment of the Annexes

1. Any Contracting Party may propose amendments to the Annexes to this Protocol. The text of a proposed amendment shall be communicated to Contracting Parties by the

Organization at least six months prior to its consideration by a Meeting of Contracting Parties or Special Meeting of Contracting Parties.

2. Amendments to the Annexes other than Annex 3 will be based on scientific or technical considerations and may take into account legal, social and economic factors as appropriate. Such amendments shall be adopted by a two-thirds majority vote of the Contracting Parties present and voting at a Meeting of Contracting Parties or Special Meeting of Contracting Parties designated for this purpose.

3. The Organization shall without delay communicate to Contracting Parties amendments to the Annexes that have been adopted at a Meeting of Contracting Parties or Special Meeting of Contracting Parties.

4. Except as provided in paragraph (7), amendments to the Annexes shall enter into force for each Contracting Party immediately on notification of its acceptance to the Organization or 100 days after the date of their adoption at a Meeting of Contracting Parties, if that is later, except for those Contracting Parties which before the end of the 100 days make a declaration that they are not able to accept the amendment at that time. A Contracting Party may at any time substitute an acceptance for a previous declaration of objection and the amendment previously objected to shall thereupon enter into force for that Contracting Party.

5. The Secretary-General shall without delay notify Contracting Parties of instruments of acceptance or objection deposited with the Organization.

6. A new Annex or an amendment to an Annex which is related to an amendment to the Articles of this Protocol shall not enter into force until such time as the amendment to the Articles of this Protocol enters into force.

7. With regard to amendments to Annex 3 concerning the Arbitral procedure and with regard to the adoption and entry into force of new Annexes the procedures on amendments to the Articles of this Protocol shall apply.

Article 23 Relationship between the Protocol and the Convention

This Protocol will supersede the Convention as between Contracting Parties to this Protocol which are also Parties to the Convention.[2]

Article 24 Signature, ratification, acceptance, approval and accession

1. This Protocol shall be open for signature by any State at the Headquarters of the Organization from 1 April 1997 to 31 March 1998 and shall thereafter remain open for accession by any State.

2. States may become Contracting Parties to this Protocol by:
    (a) signature not subject to ratification, acceptance or approval; or
    (b) signature subject to ratification, acceptance or approval, followed by ratification, acceptance or approval; or
    (c) accession.

3. Ratification, acceptance, approval or accession shall be effected by the deposit of an instrument to that effect with the Secretary-General.

Article 25 Entry into force

1. This Protocol shall enter into force on the thirtieth day following the date on which:
    (a) at least 26 States have expressed their consent to be bound by this Protocol in accordance with Article 24; and
    (b) at least 15 Contracting Parties to the Convention are included in the number of States referred to in paragraph 1 (a).

---

[2] As at 1 June 2009, of the 85 parties to the Convention 37 were also parties to the Protocol.

2. For each State that has expressed its consent to be bound by this Protocol in accordance with Article 24 following the date referred to in paragraph (1), this Protocol shall enter into force on the thirtieth day after the date on which such State expressed its consent.

Article 26   Transitional period

1. Any State that was not a Contracting Party to the Convention before 31 December 1996 and that expresses its consent to be bound by this Protocol prior to its entry into force or within five years after its entry into force may, at the time it expresses its consent, notify the Secretary-General that, for reasons described in the notification, it will not be able to comply with specific provisions of this Protocol other than those provided in paragraph (2), for a transitional period that shall not exceed that described in paragraph (4).

2. No notification made under paragraph (1) shall affect the obligations of a Contracting Party to this Protocol with respect to incineration at sea or the dumping of radioactive wastes or other radioactive matter.

3. Any Contracting Party to this Protocol that has notified the Secretary-General under paragraph (1) that, for the specified transitional period, it will not be able to comply, in part or in whole, with Article 4 (1) or article 9 shall nonetheless during that period prohibit the dumping of wastes or other matter for which it has not issued a permit, use its best efforts to adopt administrative or legislative measures to ensure that issuance of permits and permit conditions comply with the provisions of Annex 2, and notify the Secretary-General of any permits issued.

4. Any transitional period specified in a notification made under paragraph (1) shall not extend beyond five years after such notification is submitted.

5. Contracting Parties that have made a notification under paragraph (1) shall submit to the first Meeting of Contracting Parties occurring after deposit of their instrument of ratification, acceptance, approval or accession a programme and timetable to achieve full compliance with this Protocol, together with any requests for relevant technical co-operation and assistance in accordance with Article 13 of this Protocol.

6. Contracting Parties that have made a notification under paragraph (1) shall establish procedures and mechanisms for the transitional period to implement and monitor submitted programmes designed to achieve full compliance with this Protocol. A report on progress toward compliance shall be submitted by such Contracting Parties to each Meeting of Contracting Parties held during their transitional period for appropriate action.

Article 27   Withdrawal

1. Any Contracting Party may withdraw from this Protocol at any time after the expiry of two years from the date on which this Protocol enters into force for that Contracting Party.

2. Withdrawal shall be effected by the deposit of an instrument of withdrawal with the Secretary-General.

3. A withdrawal shall take effect one year after receipt by the Secretary-General of the instrument of withdrawal or such longer period as may be specified in that instrument.

Article 28   Depositary

1. This Protocol shall be deposited with the Secretary-General.

2. In addition to the functions specified in Articles 10 (5), 16 (5), 21 (4), 22 (5) and 26 (5), the Secretary-General shall:

(a)   inform all States which have signed this Protocol or acceded thereto of:
    (i)   each new signature or deposit of an instrument of ratification, acceptance, approval or accession, together with the date thereof;

(ii) the date of entry into force of this Protocol; and

(iii) the deposit of any instrument of withdrawal from this Protocol together with the date on which it was received and the date on which the withdrawal takes effect.

(b) transmit certified copies of this Protocol to all States which have signed this Protocol or acceded thereto.

3. As soon as this Protocol enters into force, a certified true copy thereof shall be transmitted by the Secretary-General to the Secretariat of the United Nations for registration and publication in accordance with Article 102 of the Charter of the United Nations.

Article 29 Authentic texts

This Protocol is established in a single original in the Arabic, Chinese, English, French, Russian and Spanish languages, each text being equally authentic.

IN WITNESS WHEREOF the undersigned being duly authorized by their respective Governments for that purpose have signed this Protocol.

DONE at London, this seventh day of November, one thousand nine hundred and ninety-six.

ANNEX 1
WASTES OR OTHER MATTER THAT MAY BE CONSIDERED FOR DUMPING

1 The following wastes or other matter are those that may be considered for dumping being mindful of the objectives and general obligations of this Protocol set out in articles 2 and 3:

.1 dredged material;

.2 sewage sludge;

.3 fish waste, or material resulting from industrial fish processing operations;

.4 vessels and platforms or other man-made structures at sea;

.5 inert, organic geological material;

.6 organic material of natural origin;

.7 bulky items primarily comprising iron, steel, concrete and similarly unharmful materials for which the concern is physical impact, and limited to those circumstances where such wastes are generated at locations, such as small islands with isolated communities, having no practicable access to disposal options other than dumping; and

.8 Carbon dioxide streams from carbon dioxide capture processes for sequestration.

2 The wastes or other matter listed in paragraphs 1.4 and 1.7 may be considered for dumping, provided that material capable of creating floating debris or otherwise contributing to pollution of the marine environment has been removed to the maximum extent and provided that the material dumped poses no serious obstacle to fishing or navigation.

3 Notwithstanding the above, materials listed in paragraphs 1.1 to 1.8 containing levels of radioactivity greater than *de minimis* (exempt) concentrations as defined by the IAEA and adopted by Contracting Parties, shall not be considered eligible for dumping; provided further that within 25 years of 20 February 1994, and at each 25-year interval thereafter, Contracting Parties shall complete a scientific study relating to all radioactive wastes and other radioactive matter other than high-level wastes or matter, taking into account such other factors as Contracting Parties consider appropriate and shall review the prohibition on dumping of such substances in accordance with the procedures set forth in article 22.

4   Carbon dioxide streams referred to in paragraph 1.8 may only be considered for dumping, if:

.1   disposal is into a sub-seabed geological formation; and

.2   they consist overwhelmingly of carbon dioxide. They may contain incidental associated substances derived from the source material and the capture and sequestration processes used; and

.3   no wastes or other matter are added for the purpose of disposing of those wastes or other matter.

Convention on the International Regulations for Preventing Collisions at Sea (COLREG)

Done at London, 20 October 1972; entry into force, 15 July 1977
1050 UNTS 18 [Registration Number 15824][1]

The Parties to the present Convention,

Desiring to maintain a high level of safety at sea,

Mindful of the need to revise and bring up to date the International Regulations for Preventing Collisions at Sea annexed to the Final Act of the International Conference on Safety of Life at Sea, 1960,

Having considered those Regulations in the light of developments since they were approved,

Have agreed as follows:

Article I General Obligations

The Parties to the present Convention undertake to give effect to the Rules and other Annexes constituting the International Regulations for Preventing Collisions at Sea, 1972, (hereinafter referred to as 'the Regulations') attached hereto.

Article VI Amendments to the Regulations

1.   Any amendment to the Regulations proposed by a Contracting Party shall be considered in the Organization at the request of that Party.

2.   If adopted by a two-thirds majority of those present and voting in the Maritime Safety Committee of the Organization, such amendment shall be communicated to all Contracting Parties and Members of the Organization at least six months prior to its consideration by the Assembly of the Organization. Any Contracting Party which is not a Member of the Organization shall be entitled to participate when the amendment is considered by the Assembly.

3.   If adopted by a two-thirds majority of those present and voting in the Assembly, the amendment shall be communicated by the Secretary-General to all Contracting Parties for their acceptance.

---

[1] The Convention was amended on 19 November 1981 (A.464 (XII)), 19 November 1987 (A.626(15)), 19 October 1989 (A.678(16)), 4 November 1993 (A.737(18)), and 29 November 2001 (A.910(22)). The text of the Convention reproduced is a consolidated version incorporating the various amendments. Articles II to V and Annexes omitted. The four annexes deal with Positioning and technical details of lights and shapes (Annex I), Additional signals for fishing vessels fishing in close proximity (Annex II), Technical details of sounds signal appliances (Annex III), and Distress signals, which lists the signals indicating distress and need of assistance (Annex IV).

4. Such an amendment shall enter into force on a date to be determined by the Assembly at the time of the its adoption unless, by a prior date determined by the Assembly at the same time, more than one third of the Contracting Parties notify the Organization of their objection to the amendment. Determination by the Assembly of the dates referred to in this paragraph shall be by a two-thirds majority of those present and voting.

5. On entry into force any amendment shall, for all Contracting Parties which have not objected to the amendment, replace and supersede any previous provision to which the amendment refers.

6. The Secretary-General shall inform all Contracting Parties and Members of the Organization of any request and communication under this Article and the date on which any amendment enters intro force.

Article VII Denunciation

1. The present Convention may be denounced by a Contracting Party at any time after the expiry of five years from the date on which the Convention entered into force for that Party.

2. Denunciation shall be effected by the deposit of an instrument with the Organization. The Secretary-General shall inform all other Contracting Parties of the receipt of the instrument of denunciation and of the date of its deposit.

3. A denunciation shall take effect, one year, or such longer period as may be specified in the instrument, after its deposit.

Article VIII Deposit and Registration

1. The present Convention and the Regulations shall be deposited with the Organization, and the Secretary-General shall transmit certified true copies thereof to all Governments of States that have signed this Convention or acceded to it.

2. When the present Convention enters into force, the text shall be transmitted by the Secretary-General to the Secretariat of the United Nations for registration and publication in accordance with Article 102 of the Charter of the United Nations.

Article IX Languages

The present Convention is established, together with the Regulations, in a single copy in the English and French languages, both texts being equally authentic. Official translations in the Russian and Spanish languages shall be prepared and deposited with the signed original.

IN WITNESS WHEREOF the undersigned, being duly authorized by their respective Governments for that purpose, have signed the present Convention.

DONE at London this twentieth day of October one thousand nine hundred and seventy-two.

INTERNATIONAL REGULATIONS FOR PREVENTING COLLISIONS AT SEA, 1972[2]

PART A. GENERAL

Rule 1 Application

(a) These Rules shall apply to all vessels upon the high seas and in all waters connected therewith navigable by seagoing vessels.

---

[2] Parts C (Lights and Shapes – Rules 20-31), D (Sound and Light Signals – Rules 32-37) and E Exemptions – Rule 38) omitted.

(b)   Nothing in these Rules shall interfere with the operation of special rules made by an appropriate authority for roadsteads, harbours, rivers, lakes or inland waterways connected with the high seas and navigable by seagoing vessels. Such special rules shall conform as closely as possible to the Rules.

(c)   Nothing in these Rules shall interfere with the operation of any special rules made by the Government of any State with respect to additional station or signal lights, shapes or whistle signals for ships of war and vessels proceeding under convoy, or with respect to additional station or signal lights or shapes for fishing vessels engaged in fishing as a fleet. These additional station or signal lights, shapes or whistle signals shall, so far as possible, be such that they cannot be mistaken for any light, shape or signal authorized elsewhere under these Rules.

(d)   Traffic separation schemes may be adopted by the Organization for the purpose of these Rules.

(e)   Whenever the Government concerned shall have determined that a vessel of special construction or purpose cannot comply fully with the provisions of any of these Rules with respect to the number, position, range or arc of visibility of lights or shapes, as well as to the disposition and characteristics of sound-signalling appliances, such vessel shall comply with such other provisions in regard to the number, position, range or arc of visibility of lights or shapes, as well as to the disposition and characteristics of sound-signalling appliances, as her Government shall have determined to be the closest possible compliance with these Rules in respect of that vessel.

Rule 2 Responsibility

(a)   Nothing in these Rules shall exonerate any vessel, or the owner, master or crew thereof, from the consequences of any neglect to comply with these Rules or of the neglect of any precaution which may be required by the ordinary practice of seamen, or by the special circumstances of the case.

(b)   In construing and complying with these Rules due regard shall be had to all dangers of navigation and collision and to any special circumstances, including the limitations of the vessels involved, which may make a departure form these Rules necessary to avoid immediate danger.

Rule 3 General definitions

For the purpose of these Rules, except where the context otherwise requires:

(a)   The word 'vessel' includes every description of water craft, including non-displacement craft, WIG craft and seaplanes, used or capable of being used as a means of transportation on water.

(b)   The term 'power-driven vessel' means any vessel propelled by machinery.

(c)   The term 'sailing vessel' means any vessel under sail provided that propelling machinery, if fitted, is not being used.

(d)   The term 'vessel engaged in fishing' means any vessel fishing with nets, lines, trawls or other fishing apparatus which restrict manoeuvrability, but does not include a vessel fishing with trolling lines or other fishing apparatus which do not restrict manoeuvrability.

(e)   The word 'seaplane' includes any aircraft designed to manoeuvre on the water.

(f)   The term 'vessel not under command' means a vessel which through some exceptional circumstance is unable to manoeuvre as required by these Rules and is therefore unable to keep out of the way of another vessel.

(g)   The term 'vessel restricted in her ability to manoeuvre' means a vessel which from the nature of her work is restricted in her ability to manoeuvre as required be these

Rules and is therefore unable to keep out of the way of another vessel. The term 'vessels restricted in their ability to manoeuvre' shall include but not limited to:

    (i)   a vessel engaged in laying, servicing or picking up a navigation mark, submarine cable or pipeline;

    (ii)   a vessel engaged in dredging, surveying or underwater operations;

    (iii)   a vessel engaged in replenishment or transferring persons, provisions or cargo while underway;

    (iv)   a vessel engaged in the launching or recovery of aircraft;

    (v)   a vessel engaged in mine clearance operations;

    (vi)   a vessel engaged in a towing operation such as severely restricts the towing vessel and her tow in their ability to deviate from their course.

    (h)   The term 'vessel constrained by her draught' means a power-driven vessel, which because of her draught in relation to the available depth and width of navigable water, is severely restricted in her ability to deviate from the course she is following.

    (i)   The word 'underway' means that a vessel is not at anchor, or made fast to the shore, or aground.

    (j)   The words 'length' and 'breadth' of a vessel mean her length overall and greatest breadth.

    (k)   Vessels shall be deemed to be in sight of one another only when one can be observed visually from the other.

    (l)   The term 'restricted visibility' means any condition in which visibility is restricted by fog, mist, falling snow, heavy rainstorms, sandstorms or any other similar causes.

    (m)   The term 'Wing-in-Ground (WIG)' craft means a multimodal craft which, in its main operational mode, flies in close proximity to the surface by utilizing surface-effect action.

PART B. STEERING AND SAILING RULES

Section I. Conduct of Vessels in Any Condition of Visibility

Rule 4 Application

    Rules in this Section apply in any condition of visibility.

Rule 5 Look-out

    Every vessel shall at all times maintain a proper look-out by sight and hearing as well as by all available means appropriate in the prevailing circumstances and conditions so as to make a full appraisal of the situation and of the risk of collision.

Rule 6 Safe speed

    Every vessel shall at all times proceed at a safe speed so that she can take proper and effective action to avoid collision and be stopped within a distance appropriate to the prevailing circumstances and conditions.

    In determining a safe speed the following factors shall be among those taken into account:

    (a)   by all vessels:

        (i)   the sate of visibility;

        (ii)   the traffic density including concentrations of dishing vessels or any other vessels;

        (iii)   the manoeuvrability of the vessel with special reference to stopping distance and turning ability in the prevailing conditions;

> > (iv)   at night the presence of background light such as from shore lights or from backscatter of her own lights;
> > (v)   the state of wind, sea and current, and the proximity of navigational hazards;
> > (vi)   the draught in relation to the available depth of water;
>
> (b)   additionally, by vessels with operational radar:
> > (i)   the characteristics, efficiency and limitations of the radar equipment;
> > (ii)   any constraints imposed by the radar range scale in use;
> > (iii)   the effect on radar detection of the sea state, weather and other sources of interference;
> > (iv)   the possibility that small vessels, ice and other floating objects may not be detected by radar at an adequate range;
> > (v)   the number, location and movement of vessels detected by radar;
> > (vi)   the more exact assessment of the visibility that may be possible when radar is used to determine the range of vessels or other objects in the vicinity.

Rule 7   Risk of collision

(a)   Every vessel shall use all available means appropriate to the prevailing circumstances and conditions to determine if risk of collision exists. If there is any doubt such risk shall be deemed to exist.

(b)   Proper use shall be made of radar equipment if fitted and operational, including long-range scanning to obtain early warning of risk of collision and radar plotting or equivalent systematic observation of detected objects.

(c)   Assumptions shall not be made on the basis of scant information, especially scanty radar information.

(d)   In determining if risk of collision exists the following considerations shall be among those taken into account:
> (i)   such risk shall be deemed to exist if the compass bearing of an approaching vessel does not appreciably change;
> (ii)   such risk may sometimes exist even when an appreciable bearing change is evident, particularly when approaching a very large vessel or a tow or when approaching a vessel at close range.

Rule 8   Action to avoid collision

(a) Any action to avoid collision shall be taken in accordance with the Rules of this Part and shall, if the circumstances of the case admit, be positive, made in ample time and with due regard to the observance of good seamanship.

(b) Any alteration of course and/or speed to avoid collision shall, if the circumstances of the case admit, be large enough to be readily apparent to another vessel observing visually or by radar; a succession of small alterations of course and/or speed should be avoided.

(c) If there is sufficient sea-room, alteration of course alone may be the most effective action to avoid a close-quarters situation provided that it is made in good time, is substantial and does not result in another close-quarters situation.

(d) Action taken to avoid collision with another vessel shall be such as to result in passing at a safe distance. The effectiveness of the action shall be carefully checked until the other vessel is finally past and clear.

(e) If necessary to avoid collision or allow more time to assess the situation, a vessel shall slacken her speed or take all way off by stopping or reversing her means of propulsion.

> (f)   (i)   A vessel which by any of these Rules, is required not to impede the passage or safe passage of another vessel shall, when required by the

circumstances of the case, take early action to allow sufficient sea-room for the safe passage of the other vessel.

(ii) A vessel required not to impede the passage or safe passage of another vessel is not relieved of this obligation if approaching the other vessel so as to involve risk of collision and shall, when taking action, have full regard to the action which may be required by the Rules of this Part.

(iii) A vessel the passage of which is not to be impeded remains fully obliged to comply with the Rules of this Part when two vessels are approaching one another so as to involve risk of collision.

Rule 9 Narrow channels

(a) A vessel proceeding along the course of a narrow channel or fairway shall keep as near to the outer limit of the channel or fairway which lies on her starboard as is safe and practicable.

(b) A vessel of less than 20m in length or a sailing vessel shall not impede the passage of a vessel which can safely navigate only within a narrow channel or fairway.

(c) A vessel engaged in fishing shall not impede the passage of any other vessel navigating within a narrow channel or fairway.

(d) A vessel shall not cross a narrow channel or fairway if such crossing impedes the passage of a vessel which can safely navigate only within such channel or fairway. The latter vessel may use the sound signal prescribed in Rule 34(d) if in doubt as to the intention of the crossing vessel.

(e) (i) In a narrow channel or fairway when overtaking can take place only if the vessel to be overtaken has to take action to permit safe passing, the vessel intending to overtake shall indicate her intention by sounding the appropriate sound signal prescribed in Rule 34(c)(i). The vessel to be overtaken shall, if in agreement, sound the appropriate signal prescribed in Rule 34(c)(ii) and take steps to permit safe passing. If in doubt she may sound the signals prescribed in Rule 34(d).

(ii) This Rule does not relieve the overtaking vessel of her obligation under Rule 13.

(f) A vessel nearing a bend or an area of a narrow channel or fairway where other vessels may be obscured by an intervening obstruction shall navigate with particular alertness and shall sound the appropriate signal prescribed in Rule 34(e).

(g) Any vessel shall, if the circumstances of the case admit, avoid anchoring in a narrow channel.

Rule 10 Traffic separation schemes

(a) This Rule applies to traffic separation schemes adopted by the Organization and does not relieve any vessel of her obligation under any other rule.

(b) A vessel using a traffic separation scheme shall:

(i) proceed in the appropriate traffic lane in the general direction of traffic flow for that lane;

(ii) so far as practicable keep clear of a traffic separation line or separation zone;

(iii) normally join or leave a traffic lane at the termination of the lane, but when joining or leaving from either side shall do so at as small an angle to the general direction of traffic flow as practicable.

(c) A vessel shall, so far as practicable, avoid crossing traffic lanes but if obliged to do so shall cross on a heading as nearly as practicable at right angles to the general direction or traffic flow.

(d) (i)   A vessel shall not use an inshore traffic zone when she can safely use the appropriate traffic lane within the adjacent traffic separation scheme. However, vessels of less than 20m in length, sailing vessels and vessels engaged in fishing may use the inshore traffic zone.

(ii)   Notwithstanding subparagraph (d)(i), a vessel may use an inshore traffic zone when *en route* to or from a port, offshore installation or structure, pilot station or any other place situated within the inshore traffic zone, or to avoid immediate danger.

(e)   A vessel other than a crossing vessel or a vessel joining or leaving a lane shall not normally enter a separation zone or cross a separation line except:

(i)   in cases of emergency to avoid immediate danger;

(ii)   to engage in fishing within a separation zone.

(f)   A vessel navigating in areas near the terminations of traffic separation schemes shall do so with particular caution.

(g)   A vessel shall so far as practicable avoid anchoring in a traffic separation scheme or in areas near its terminations.

(h)   A vessel not using a traffic separation scheme shall avoid it by as wide a margin as is practicable.

(i)   A vessel engaged in fishing shall not impede the passage of any vessel following a traffic lane.

(j)   A vessel of less than 20m in length or a sailing vessel shall not impede the safe passage of a power-driven vessel following a traffic lane.

(k)   A vessel restricted in her ability to manoeuvre when engaged in an operation for the maintenance of safety of navigation in a traffic separation scheme is exempted from complying with this Rule to the extent necessary to carry out the operation.

(l)   A vessel restricted in her ability to manoeuvre when engaged in an operation for the laying, servicing or picking up of a submarine cable, within a traffic separation scheme, is exempted from complying with this Rule to the extent necessary to carry out the operation.

SECTION II. CONDUCT OF VESSELS IN SIGHT OF ONE ANOTHER

Rule 11 Application
Rules in this Section apply to vessels in sight of one another.

Rule 12 Sailing vessels
(a)   When two sailing vessels are approaching one another, so as to involve risk of collision, one of them shall keep out of the way of the other as follows:

(i)   when each has the wind on a different side, the vessel which has the wind on the port side shall out of the way of the other;

(ii)   when both have the wind on the same side, the vessel which is to windward shall keep out of the way of the vessel which is to leeward;

(iii)   if a vessel with the wind on the port side sees a vessel to windward and cannot determine with certainty whether the other vessel has the wind on the port or on the starboard side, she shall keep out of the way of the other.

(b)   For the purpose of this Rule the windward side shall be deemed to be the side opposite to that on which the mainsail is carried or, in the case of a square-rigged vessel, the side opposite to that on which the largest for-and-aft sail is carried.

Rule 13 Overtaking
(a)   Notwithstanding anything contained in the Rules of Part B, Sections I and II, any vessel overtaking any other shall keep out of the way of the vessel being overtaken.

(b)   A vessel shall be deemed to be overtaking when coming up with another vessel from a direction more than 22.5° abaft her beam, that is, in such a position with reference to the vessel she is overtaking, that at night she would be able to see only the sternlight of that vessel but neither of her sidelights.

(c)   When a vessel is in any doubt as to whether she is overtaking another, she shall assume that this is the case and act accordingly.

(d)   Any subsequent alteration of the bearing between the two vessels shall not make the overtaking vessel a crossing vessel within the meaning of these Rules or relieve her of the duty of keeping clear of the overtaken vessel until she is finally past and clear.

Rule 14 Head-on situation

(a)   When two power-driven vessels are meeting on reciprocal or nearly reciprocal courses so as to involve risk of collision each shall alter her course to starboard so that each shall pass on the port side of the other.

(b)   Such a situation shall be deemed to exist when a vessel sees the other ahead or nearly ahead and by night she could see the masthead lights of the other in a line or nearly in a line and/or both sidelights and by day she observes the corresponding aspect of the other vessel.

(c)   When a vessel is in any doubt as to whether such a situation exists she shall assume that it does exist and act accordingly.

Rule 15 Crossing situation

When two power-driven vessels are crossing so as to involve risk of collision, the vessel which has the other on her own starboard side shall keep out of the way and shall, if the circumstances of the case admit, avoid crossing ahead of the other vessel.

Rule 16 Action by give-way vessel

Every vessel which is directed to keep out of the way of another vessel shall, so far as possible, take early and substantial action to keep well clear.

Rule 17 Action by stand-on vessel

(a)   (i)   When one of two vessels is to keep out of the way the other shall keep her course and speed.

(ii)   The latter vessel may, however, take action to avoid collision by her manoeuvre alone, as soon as it becomes apparent to her that the vessel required to keep out of the way is not taking appropriate action in compliance with these Rules.

(b)   When, from any cause, the vessel required to keep her course and speed finds herself so close that collision cannot be avoided by the action of the give-way vessel alone, she shall take such action as will best aid to avoid collision.

(c)   A power-driven vessel which takes action in a crossing situation in accordance with subparagraph (a)(ii) of this Rule to avoid collision with another power-driven vessel shall, if the circumstances of the case admit, not alter course to port for a vessel on her own port side.

(d)   This Rule does not relieve the give-way vessel of her obligation to keep out of the way.

Rule 18 Responsibilities between vessels

Except where Rules 9, 10 and 13 otherwise require:

(a)   A power-driven vessel underway shall keep out of the way of:

       (i)   a vessel not under command;
       (ii)   a vessel restricted in her ability to manoeuvre;
       (iii) a vessel engaged in fishing;
       (iv) a sailing vessel.

  (b)   A sailing vessel underway shall keep out of the way of:
       (i)   a vessel not under command;
       (ii)   a vessel restricted in her ability to manoeuvre;
       (iii) a vessel engaged in fishing.

  (c)   A vessel engaged in fishing when underway shall, so far as possible, keep out of the way of:
       (i)   a vessel not under command;
       (ii)   a vessel restricted in her ability to manoeuvre.

  (d) (i)   Any vessel other than a vessel not under command or a vessel restricted in her ability to manoeuvre shall, if the circumstances of the case admit, avoid impending the safe passage of a vessel constrained by her draught, exhibiting the signals in Rule 28.

      (ii)   A vessel constrained by her draught shall navigate with particular caution having full regard to her special condition.

  (e)   A seaplane on the water shall, in general, keep well clear of all vessels and avoid impeding their navigation. In circumstances, however, where risk of collision exists, she shall comply with the Rules of this Part.

  (f) (i)   A WIG craft, when taking off, landing and in flight near the surface, shall keep well clear of all other vessels and avoid impeding their navigation;

      (ii)   A WIG craft operating on the water surface shall comply with the Rules of this Part as a power-driven vessel.

SECTION II. CONDUCT OF VESSELS IN RESTRICTED VISIBILITY

Rule 19 Conduct of vessels in restricted visibility

    (a)   This Rule applies to vessels not in sight of one another when navigating on or near an area of restricted visibility.

    (b)   Every vessel shall proceed at a safe speed adapted to the prevailing circumstances and conditions of restricted visibility. A power-driven vessel shall have her engines ready for immediate manoeuvre.

    (c)   Every vessel shall have due regard to the prevailing circumstances and conditions of restricted visibility when complying with the Rules of Section I of this Part.

    (d)   A vessel which detects by radar alone the presence of another vessel shall determine if a close-quarters situation is developing and/or risk of collision exists. If so, she shall take avoiding action in ample time, provided that when such action consists of an alteration of course, so far as possible the following shall be avoided:
       (i)   an alteration of course to port for a vessel forward of the beam, other than for a vessel being overtaken;
       (ii)   an alteration of course towards a vessel abeam of abaft the beam.

    (e)   Except where it has been determined that a risk of collision does not exist, every vessel which hears apparently forward of her beam the fog signal of another vessel, or which cannot avoid a close-quarters situation with another vessel forward of her beam, shall reduce her speed to the minimum at which she can be kept on her course. She shall if necessary take all her way off and in any event navigate with extreme caution until danger of collision is over.

International Convention for the Prevention of Pollution from Ships, as Modified by the Protocol of 1978 Relating Thereto (MARPOL 73/78)

Done at London, 2 November 1973 and 17 February 1978; entry into force,
2 October 1983
1340 UNTS 62 [Registration Number 22484][1]

The Parties to the Convention,

Being conscious of the need to preserve the human environment in general and the marine environment in particular,

Recognizing that deliberate, negligent or accidental release of oil and other harmful substances from ships constitutes a serious source of pollution,

Recognizing also the importance of the International Convention for the Prevention of Pollution of the Sea by Oil, 1954, as being the first multilateral instrument to be concluded with the prime objective protecting the environment, and appreciating the significant contribution which that Convention has made in preserving the seas and coastal environment from pollution,

Desiring to achieve the complete elimination of international pollution of the marine environment by oil and other harmful substances and the minimization of accidental discharge of such substances,

Considering that this object may best be achieved by establishing rules not limited to oil pollution having a universal purport,

Have agreed as follows:

Article 1 General obligations under the Convention

1. The Parties to the Convention undertake to give effect to the provisions of the present Convention and those Annexes thereto by which they are bound, in order to prevent the pollution of the marine environment by the discharge of harmful substances or effluents containing such substances in contravention of the Convention.

2. Unless expressly provided otherwise, a reference to the present Convention constitutes at the same time a reference to its Protocols and to the Annexes.

Article 2 Definitions

For the purposes of the present Convention, unless expressly provided otherwise:

1. 'Regulation' means the regulations contained in the Annexes to the present Convention.

2. 'Harmful substance' means any substance which, if introduced into the sea, is liable to create hazards to human health, to harm living resources and marine life, to damage amenities or to interfere with other legitimate uses of the sea, and includes any substance subject to control by the present Convention.

3. (a) 'Discharge', in relation to harmful substances or effluents containing such substances, means any release howsoever caused from a ship and includes any escape, disposal, spilling, leaking, pumping, emitting or emptying;

---

[1] The Convention was amended several times between 1984 and 2008. The text of the Convention reproduced is a consolidated version incorporating the various amendments in force as at 1 June 2009. The Convention includes six technical Annexes – Annex I: Regulations for the Prevention of Pollution by Oil, Annex II: Regulations for the Control of Pollution by Noxious Liquid Substances in Bulk, Annex III: Prevention of Pollution by Harmful Substances Carried by Sea in Packaged Form, Annex IV: Prevention of Pollution by Sewage from Ships, Annex V: Prevention of Pollution by Garbage from Ships, and Annex VI: Prevention of Air Pollution from Ships – of which only parts of Annex I (without Appendixes I-III) and V are reproduced here.

(b)   'Discharge' does not include:

    (i)   dumping within the meaning of the Convention on the Prevention of Marine Pollution by Dumping of Wastes and Other Matter, done at London on 13 November 1972; or

    (ii)   release of harmful substances directly arising from the exploration, exploitation and associated offshore processing of sea-bed mineral resources; or

    (iii)   release of harmful substances for purposes of legitimate scientific research into pollution abatement or control.

4.   'Ship' means a vessel of any type whatsoever operating in the marine environment and includes hydrofoil boats, air-cushion vehicles, submersibles, floating craft and fixed or floating platforms.

5.   'Administration' means the Government of the State under whose authority the ship is operating. With respect to a ship entitled to fly a flag of any State, the Administration is the Government of that State. With respect to fixed a floating platforms engaged in exploration and exploitation of the sea-bed and subsoil thereof adjacent to the coast over which the coastal State exercises sovereign rights for the purposes of exploration and exploitation of their natural resources, the Administration is the Government of the coastal State concerned.

6.   'Incident' means an event involving the actual or probable discharge into the sea of a harmful substance, or effluents containing such a substance.

7.   'Organization' means the Inter-Governmental Maritime Consultative Organization.

Article 3 Application

1.   The present Convention shall apply to:

(a)   Ships entitled to fly the flag of a Party to the Convention; and

(b)   Ships not entitled to fly the flag of a Party but which operate under the authority of a Party.

2.   Nothing in the present Article shall be construed as derogating from or extending the sovereign rights of the Parties under international law over the sea-bed and subsoil thereof adjacent to their coasts for the purposes of exploration and exploitation of their natural resources.

3.   The present Convention shall not apply to any warship, naval auxiliary or other ship owned or operated by a State and used, for the time being, only on government non-commercial service. However, each Party shall ensure by the adoption of appropriate measures not impairing the operations or operational capabilities of such ships owned or operated by it, that such ships act in a manner consistent, so far as is reasonable and practicable, with the present Convention.

Article 4 Violation

1.   Any violation of the requirements of the present Convention shall be prohibited and sanctions shall be established therefore under the law of the Administration of the ship concerned wherever the violation occurs. If the Administration is informed of such a violation and is satisfied that sufficient evidence is available to enable proceedings to be brought in respect of the alleged violation, it shall cause such proceedings to be taken as soon as possible, in accordance with its law.

2.   Any violation of the requirements of the present Convention within the jurisdiction of any Party to the Convention shall be prohibited and sanctions shall be established therefor under the law of that Party. Whenever such a violation occurs, that Party shall either:

(a)   Cause proceedings to be taken in accordance with its law; or

(b)   Furnish to the Administration of the ship such information and evidence as may be in its possession that a violation has occurred.

3.   Where information or evidence with respect to any violation of the present Convention by a ship is furnished to the Administration of that ship, the Administration shall promptly inform the Party which has furnished the information or evidence, and the Organization, of the action taken.

4.   The penalties specified under the law of a Party pursuant to the present Article shall be adequate in severity to discourage violations of the present Convention and shall be equally severe irrespective of where the violations occur.

Article 5 Certificates and special rules on inspection of ships

1.   Subject to the provisions of paragraph (2) of the present Article a certificate issued under the authority of a Party to the Convention in accordance with the provisions of the Regulations shall be accepted by the other Parties and regarded for all purposes covered by the present Convention as having the same validity as a certificate issued by them.

2.   A ship required to hold a certificate in accordance with the provisions of the Regulations is subject, while in the ports or offshore terminals under the jurisdiction of a Party, to inspection by officers duly authorized by that Party. Any such inspection shall be limited to verifying that there is on board a valid certificate, unless there are clear grounds for believing that the condition of the ship or its equipment does not correspond substantially with the particulars of that certificate. In that case, or if the ship does not carry a valid certificate, the Party carrying out the inspection shall take such steps as will ensure that the ship shall not sail until it can proceed to sea without presenting an unreasonable threat of harm to the marine environment. That Party may, however, grant such a ship permission to leave the port or offshore terminal for the purpose of proceeding to the nearest appropriate repair yard available.

3.   If a Party denies a foreign ship entry to the ports or offshore terminals under its jurisdiction or takes any action against such a ship for the reason that the ship does not comply with the provisions of the present Convention, the Party shall immediately inform the consul or diplomatic representative of the Party whose flag the ship is entitled to fly, or if this is not possible, the Administration of the ship concerned. Before denying entry or taking such action the Party may request consultation with the Administration of the ship concerned. Information shall also be given to the Administration when a ship does not carry a valid certificate in accordance with the provisions of the Regulations.

4.   With respect to the ship of non-Parties to the Convention, Parties shall apply the requirements of the present Convention as may be necessary to ensure that no more favourable treatment is given to such ships.

Article 6 Detection of violations and enforcement of the Convention

1.   Parties to the Convention shall co-operate in the detection of violations and the enforcement of the provisions of the present Convention, using all appropriate and practicable measures of detection and environmental monitoring, adequate procedures for reporting and accumulation of evidence.

2.   A ship to which the present Convention applies may, in any port or offshore terminal of a Party, be subject to inspection by officers appointed or authorized by that Party for the purpose of verifying whether the ship has discharged any harmful substances in violation of the provisions of the Regulations. If an inspection indicates a violation of the Convention, a report shall be forwarded to the Administration for any appropriate action.

3. Any Party shall furnish to the Administration evidence, if any, that the ship has discharged harmful substances or effluents containing such substances in violation of the provisions of the Regulations. If it is practicable to do so, the competent authority of the former Party shall notify the master of the ship of the alleged violation.

4. Upon receiving such evidence, the Administration so informed shall investigate the matter, and may request the other Party to furnish further or better evidence of the alleged contravention. If the Administration is satisfied that sufficient evidence is available to enable proceedings to be brought in respect of the alleged violation, it shall cause such proceedings to be taken in accordance with its law as soon as possible. The Administration shall promptly inform the Party which has reported the alleged violation, as well as the Organization, of the action taken.

5. A Party may also inspect a ship to which the present Convention applies when it enters the ports of offshore terminals under its jurisdiction, if a request for an investigation is received from any Party together with sufficient evidence that the ship has discharged harmful substances or effluents containing such substances in any place. The report of such investigation shall be sent to the Party requesting it and to the Administration so that the appropriate action may be taken under the present Convention.

Article 7 Undue delay to ships

1. All possible efforts shall be made to avoid a ship being unduly detained or delayed under Articles 4, 5 or 6 of the present Convention.

2. When a ship is unduly detained or delayed under Articles 4, 5 or 6 of the present Convention, it shall be entitled to compensation for any loss or damage suffered.

Article 8 Reports on incidents involving harmful substances

1. A report of an incident shall be made without delay to the fullest extent possible in accordance with the provisions of Protocol I to the present Convention.

2. Each Party to the Convention shall:
(a) Make all arrangements necessary for an appropriate officer or agency to receive and process all reports on incidents; and
(b) Notify the Organization with complete details of such arrangements for circulation to other Parties and Member States of the Organization.

3. Whenever a Party receives a report under the provisions of the present Article, that Party shall relay the report without delay to:
(a) The Administration of the ship involved; and
(b) Any other State which may be affected.

4. Each Party to the Convention undertakes to issue instructions to its maritime inspection vessels and aircraft and to other appropriate services, to report to its authorities any incident referred to in Protocol I to the present Convention. That Party shall, if it considers it appropriate, report accordingly to the Organization and to any other Party concerned.

Article 9 Other treaties and interpretation

1. Upon its entry into force, the present Convention supersedes the International Convention for the Prevention of Pollution of the Sea by Oil, 1954, as amended, as between Parties to that Convention.

2. Nothing in the present Convention shall prejudice the codification and development of the law of the sea by the United Nations Conference on the Law of the Sea convened pursuant to Resolution 2750 C(XXV) of the General Assembly of the United Nations nor the present or future claims and legal views of any State concerning the law of the sea and the nature and extent of coastal and flag State jurisdiction.

3. The term 'jurisdiction' in the present Convention shall be construed in the light of international law in force at the time of application or interpretation of the present Convention.

Article 10 Settlement of disputes

Any dispute between two or more Parties to the Convention concerning the interpretation or application of the present Convention shall, if settlement by negotiation between the Parties involved has not been possible, and if these Parties do not otherwise agree, be submitted upon request of any of them to arbitration as set out in Protocol II to the present Convention.

Article 11 Communication of information

1. The Parties to the Convention undertake to communicate to the Organization:
   (a) The text of laws, orders, decrees and regulations and other instruments which have been promulgated on the various matters within the scope of the present Convention;
   (b) A list of nominated surveyors or recognized organizations which are authorized to act on their behalf in the administration of matters relating to the design, construction, equipment and operation of ships carrying harmful substances in accordance with the provisions of the Regulations for circulation to the Parties for information of their officers. The Administration shall therefore notify the Organization of the specific responsibilities and conditions of the authority delegated to nominated surveyors or recognized organizations;
   (c) A sufficient number of specimens of their certificates issued under the provisions of the Regulations;
   (d) A list of reception facilities including their location, capacity and available facilities and other characteristics;
   (e) Official reports or summaries of official reports in so far as they show the results of the application of the present Convention; and
   (f) An annual statistical report, in a form standardized by the Organization, of penalties actually imposed for infringement of the present Convention.

2. The Organization shall notify Parties of the receipt of any communications under the present Article and circulate to all Parties any information communicated to it under sub-paragraphs 1(b) to (f) of the present Article.

Article 12 Casualties to ships

1. Each Administration undertakes to conduct an investigation of any casualty occurring to any of its ships subject to the provisions of the Regulations if such casualty has produced a major deleterious effect upon the marine environment.

2. Each Party to the Convention undertakes to supply the Organization with information concerning the findings of such investigation, when it judges that such information may assist in determining what changes in the present Convention might be desirable.

Article 13 Signature, ratification, acceptance, approval and accession

1. The present Convention shall remain open for signature at the Headquarters of the Organization from 15 January 1974 until 31 December 1974 and shall thereafter remain open for accession. States may become Parties to the present Convention by:
   (a) signature without reservation as to ratification, acceptance or approval;
   (b) signature subject to ratification, acceptance or approval, followed by ratification, acceptance or approval; or
   (c) accession.

2. Ratification, acceptance, approval or accession shall be effected by the deposit of an instrument to that effect with the Secretary-General of the Organization.

3. The Secretary-General of the Organization shall inform all States which have signed the present Convention or acceded to it of any signature or of the deposit of any new instrument of ratification, acceptance, approval or accession and the date of its deposit.

Article 14 Optional Annexes

1. A State may at the time of signing, ratifying, accepting, approving or acceding to the present Convention declare that it does not accept any one or all of Annexes III, IV and V (hereinafter referred to as 'Optional Annexes') of the present Convention, Subject to the above, Parties to the Convention shall be bound by any Annex in its entirety.

2. A State which has declared that it is not bound by an Optional Annex may at any time accept such Annex by depositing with the Organization an instrument of the kind referred to in Article 13(2).

3. A State which makes a declaration under paragraph 1 of the present Article in respect of an Optional Annex and which has not subsequently accepted that Annex in accordance with paragraph 2 of the present Article shall not be under any obligation nor entitled to claim any privileges under the present Convention in respect of matters related to such Annex and all references to Parties in the present Convention shall not include that State in so far as matters related to such Annex are concerned.

4. The Organization shall inform the States which have signed or acceded to the present Convention of any declaration under the present Article as well as the receipt of any instrument deposited in accordance with the provisions of paragraph (2) of the present Article.

Article 15 Entry in force

1. The present Convention shall enter into force 12 months after the date on which not less than 15 States, the combined merchant fleets of which constitute not less than 50 per cent of the gross tonnage of the world's merchant shipping, have become Parties to it in accordance with Article 13.

2. An Optional Annex shall enter into force 12 months after the date on which the conditions stipulated in paragraph 1 of the present Article have been satisfied in relation to that Annex.

3. The Organization shall inform the States which have signed the present Convention or acceded to it of the date on which it enters into force and of the date on which an Optional Annex enters into force in accordance with paragraph (2) of the present Article.

4. For States which have deposited an instrument of ratification, acceptance, approval or accession in respect of the present Convention or any Optional Annex after the requirements for entry into force thereof have been met prior to the date of entry into force, the ratification, acceptance, approval or accession shall take effect on the date of entry into force of the Convention or such Annex or three months after the date of deposit of the instrument whichever is the later date.

5. For States which have deposited an instrument of ratification, acceptance, approval or accession after the date on which the Convention or an Optional Annex entered into force, the Convention or the Optional Annex shall become effective three months after the date of deposit of the instrument.

6. After the date on which all the conditions required under Article 16 to bring an amendment to the present Convention or an Optional Annex into force have been fulfilled, any instrument of ratification, acceptance, approval or accession deposited shall apply to the Convention or Annex as amended.

Article 16 Amendments

1. The present Convention may be amended by any of the procedures specified in the following paragraphs.

2. Amendments after consideration by the Organization:

(a) Any amendment proposed by a Party to the Convention shall be submitted to the Organization and circulated by its Secretary-General to all Members of the Organization and all Parties at least six months prior to its consideration;

(b) Any amendment proposed and circulated as above shall be submitted to an appropriate body by the Organization for consideration;

(c) Parties to the Convention, whether or not Members of the Organization, shall be entitled to participate in the proceedings of the appropriate body;

(d) Amendments shall be adopted by a two-thirds majority of only the Parties to the Convention present and voting;

(e) If adopted in accordance with sub-paragraph (d) above, amendments shall be communicated by the Secretary-General of the Organization to all the Parties to the Convention for acceptance;

(f) An amendment shall be deemed to have been accepted in the following circumstances:

(i) An amendment to an Article of the Convention shall be deemed to have been accepted on the date on which it is accepted by two thirds of the Parties, the combined merchant fleets of which constitute not less than 50 per cent of the gross tonnage of the world's merchant fleet;

(ii) An amendment to an Annex to the Convention shall be deemed to have been accepted in accordance with the procedure specified in sub-paragraph (f)(iii) unless the appropriate body, at the time of its adoption, determines that the amendment shall be deemed to have been accepted on the date on which it is accepted by two thirds of the Parties, the combined merchant fleets of which constitute not less than 50 per cent of the of the gross tonnage of the world's merchant fleet. Nevertheless, at any time before the entry into force of an amendment to an Annex to the Convention, a Party may notify the Secretary-General of the Organization that its express approval will be necessary before the amendment enters into force for it. The latter shall bring such notification and the date of its receipt to the notice of Parties;

(iii) An amendment to an Appendix to an Annex to the Convention shall be deemed to have been accepted at the end of a period to be determined by the appropriate body at the time of its adoption, which period shall be not less than ten months, unless within that period an objection is communicated to the Organization by not less than one third of the Parties or by the Parties the combined merchant fleets of which constitute not less than 50 per cent of the gross tonnage of the world's merchant fleet whichever condition is fulfilled;

(iv) An amendment to Protocol I to the Convention shall be subject to the same procedures as for the amendments to the Annexes to the Convention, as provided for in sub-paragraphs (f)(i) or (f)(iii) above;

(v) An amendment to Protocol II to the Convention shall be subject to the same procedures as for the amendments to an Article of the Convention, as provided for in sub-paragraph (f)(i) above;

(g) The amendment shall enter into force under the following conditions:

    (i)   In the case of an amendment to an Article of the Convention, to Protocol II, or to Protocol I or to an Annex to the Convention not under the procedure specified in sub-paragraph (f)(iii), the amendment accepted in conformity with the foregoing provisions shall enter into force six months after the date of its acceptance with respect to the Parties which have declared that they have accepted it;

    (ii) In the case of an amendment to Protocol I, to an Appendix to an Annex or to an Annex to the Convention under the procedure specified in sub-paragraph (f)(iii), the amendment deemed to have been accepted in accordance with the foregoing conditions shall enter into force six months after its acceptance for all the Parties with the exception of those which, before that date, have made a declaration that they do not accept it or a declaration under sub-paragraph (f)(ii), that their express approval is necessary.

3. Amendment by a Conference:

(a) Upon the request of a Party, concurred in by at least one third of the Parties, the Organization shall convene a Conference of Parties to the Convention to consider amendments to the present Convention;

(b) Every amendment adopted by such a Conference by a two-thirds majority of those present and voting of the Parties shall be communicated by the Secretary-General of the Organization to all contracting Parties for their acceptance;

(c) Unless the Conference decides otherwise, the amendment shall be deemed to have been accepted and to have entered into force in accordance with the procedures specified for that purpose in paragraph (2)(f) and (g) above.

4. (a) In the case of an amendment to an Optional Annex, a reference in the present Article to a 'Party to the Convention' shall be deemed to mean a reference to a Party bound by that Annex;

    (b) Any Party which has declined to accept an amendment to an Annex shall be treated as a non-Party only for the purpose of application of that amendment.

5. The adoption and entry into force of a new Annex shall be subject to the same procedures as for the adoption and entry into force of an amendment to an Article of the Convention.

6. Unless expressly provided otherwise, any amendment to the present Convention made under this Article, which relates to the structure of a ship, shall apply only to ships for which the building contract is placed, or in the absence of a building contract, the keel of which is laid, on or after the date on which the amendment comes into force.

7. Any amendment to a Protocol or to an Annex shall relate to the substance of that Protocol or Annex and shall be consistent with the Articles of the present Convention.

8. The Secretary-General of the Organization shall inform all Parties of any amendments which enter into force under the present Article, together with the date on which each such amendment enters into force.

9. Any declaration of acceptance or of objection to an amendment under the present Article shall be notified in writing to the Secretary-General of the Organization. The latter shall bring such notification and the date of its receipt to the notice of the Parties to the Convention.

Article 17 Promotion of technical co-operation

The Parties to the Convention shall promote, in consultation with the Organization and other international bodies, with assistance and co-ordination by the Executive Director of the United Nations Environment Programme, support for those Parties which request technical assistance for:

(a) The training of scientific and technical personnel;

(b) The supply of necessary equipment and facilities for reception and monitoring;

(c) The facilitation of other measures and arrangements to prevent or mitigate pollution of the marine environment by ships; and

(d) The encouragement of research;

preferably within the countries concerned, so furthering the aims and purposes of the present Convention.

Article 18 Denunciation

1. The present Convention or any Optional Annex may be denounced by any Parties to the Convention at any time after the expiry of five years from the date on which the Convention or such Annex enters into force for that Party.

2. Denunciation shall be affected by notification in writing to the Secretary-General of the Organization who shall inform all the other Parties of any such notification received and of the date of its receipt as well as the date on which such denunciation takes effect.

3. A denunciation shall take effect 12 months after receipt of the notification of denunciation by the Secretary-General of the Organization or after the expiry of any other longer period which may be indicated in the notification.

Article 19 Deposit and registration

1. The present Convention shall be deposited with the Secretary-General of the Organization who shall transmit certified true copies thereof to all States which have signed the present Convention or acceded to it.

2. As soon as the present Convention enters into force, the text shall be transmitted by the Secretary-General of the Organization to the Secretary-General of the United Nations for registration and publication in accordance with Article 102 of the Charter of the United Nations.

Article 20 Languages

The present Convention is established in a single copy in the English, French, Russian and Spanish languages, each text being equally authentic. Official translations in the Arabic, German, Italian and Japanese languages shall be prepared and deposited with the signed original.

IN WITNESS WHEREOF the undersigned being duly authorized by their respective Governments for that purpose have signed the present Convention.

DONE at London this second day of November, one thousand nine hundred and seventy-three.

PROTOCOL I

PROVISIONS CONCERNING REPORTS ON
INCIDENTS INVOLVING HARMFUL SUBSTANCES
(in accordance with Article 8 of the Convention)

Article I Duty to report

1. The master or other person having charge of any ship involved in an incident referred to in Article II of this Protocol shall report the particulars of such incident without delay and to the fullest extent possible in accordance with the provisions of this Protocol.

2. In the event of the ship referred to in paragraph (1) of this Article being abandoned, or in the event of a report from such a ship being incomplete or unobtainable, the owner, charterer, manager or operator of the ship, or their agent shall, to the fullest extent possible, assume the obligations placed upon the master under the provisions of this Protocol.

Article II When to make reports

1. The report shall be made when an incident involves:
    (a) A discharge above the permitted level or probable discharge of oil or of noxious liquid substances for whatever reason including those for the purpose of securing the safety of the ship or for saving life at sea; or
    (b) A discharge or probable discharge of harmful substances in packaged form, including those in freight containers, portable tanks, road and rail vehicles and shipborne barges; or
    (c) Damage, failure or breakdown of a ship of 15 metres in length or above which:
        (i) Affects the safety of the ship; including but not limited to collision, grounding, fire, explosion, structural failure, flooding and cargo shifting; or
        (ii) Results in impairment of the safety of navigation; including but not limited to, failure or breakdown of steering gear, propulsion plant, electrical generating system, and essential shipborne navigational aids; or
    (d) A discharge during the operation of the ship of oil or noxious liquid substances in excess of the quantity or instantaneous rate permitted under the present Convention.
2. For the purposes of this Protocol:
    (a) 'Oil' referred to in sub-paragraph (1)(a) of this Article means oil as defined in Regulation 1(1) of Annex I of the Convention.
    (b) 'Noxious liquid substances' referred to in sub-paragraph (1)(a) of this Article means noxious liquid substances as defined in Regulation 1 (6) of Annex II of the Convention.
    (c) 'Harmful substances' in packaged form referred to in sub-paragraph (1)(b) of this Article means substances which are identified as marine pollutants in the International Maritime Dangerous Goods Code (IMDG Code).

Article III Contents of report

Reports shall in any case include:
(a) Identity of ships involved;
(b) Time, type and location of incident;
(c) Quantity and type of harmful substance involved;
(d) Assistance and salvage measures.

Article IV Supplementary report

Any person who is obliged under the provisions of this Protocol to send a report, shall when possible:
(a) Supplement the initial report, as necessary, and provide information concerning further developments; and
(b) Comply as fully as possible with requests from affected States for additional information.

Article V Reporting procedures

1. Reports shall be made by the fastest telecommunications channels available with the highest possible priority to the nearest coastal State.

2. In order to implement the provisions of this Protocol, Parties to the present Convention shall issue, or cause to be issued, regulations or instructions on the procedures to be followed in reporting incidents involving harmful substances, based on guidelines developed by the Organization.

PROTOCOL II

ARBITRATION

(in accordance with Article 10 of the Convention)

Article I

Arbitration procedure, unless the Parties to the dispute decide otherwise, shall be in accordance with the rules set out in this Protocol.

Article II

1. An Arbitration Tribunal shall be established upon the request of one Party to the Convention addressed to another in application of Article 10 of the present Convention. The request for arbitration shall consist of a statement of the case together with any supporting documents.

2. The requesting Party shall inform the Secretary-general of the Organization of the fact that it has applied for the establishment of a Tribunal, of the names of the Parties to the dispute, and of the Articles of the Convention or Regulations over which there is in its opinion disagreement concerning their interpretation or application. The Secretary-General shall transmit this information to all Parties.

Article III

The Tribunal shall consist of three members: one Arbitrator nominated by each Party to the dispute and a third Arbitrator who shall be nominated by agreement between the two first named, and shall act as its Chairman.

Article IV

1. If, at the end of a period of 60 days from the nomination of the second arbitrator, the Chairman of the Tribunal shall not have been nominated, the Secretary-General of the Organization upon request of either Party shall within a further period of 60 days proceed to such nomination, selecting him from a list of qualified persons previously drawn up by the Council of the Organization.

2. If, within a period of 60 days from the date of the receipt of the request, one of the Parties shall not have nominated the member of the Tribunal for whose designation it is responsible, the other Party may directly inform the Secretary-General of the Organization who shall nominate the Chairman if the Tribunal within a period of 60 days, selecting him from the list prescribed in paragraph (1) of the present Article.

3. The Chairman of the Tribunal shall, upon nomination, request the Party which has not provided an Arbitrator, to do so in the same manner and under the same conditions. If the Party does not make the required nomination, the Chairman of the Tribunal shall request the Secretary-General of the Organization to make the nomination in the form and conditions prescribed in the preceding paragraph.

4. The Chairman of the Tribunal, if nominated under the provisions of the present Article, shall not be or have been a national of one of the Parties concerned, except with the consent of the other Party.

5.   In the case of the decease or default of an Arbitrator for whose nomination one of the Parties is responsible, the said Party shall nominate a replacement within a period of 60 days from the date of decease or default. Should the said Party not make the nomination, the arbitration shall proceed under the remaining Arbitrators. In case of the decease or default of the Chairman of the Tribunal, replacement shall be nominated in accordance with the provisions of Article III above, or in the absence of an agreement between the members of the Tribunal within a period of 60 days of the decease or default, according to the provisions of the present Article.

Article V

The Tribunal may hear and determine counter-claims arising directly out of the subject matter of the dispute.

Article VI

Each Party shall be responsible for the remuneration of its Arbitrator and connected costs and for the costs entailed by the preparation of its own case. The remuneration of the Chairman of the Tribunal and of all general expenses incurred by the Arbitration shall be borne equally by the Parties. The Tribunal shall keep a record of all its expenses and shall furnish a final statement thereof.

Article VII

Any Party to the Convention which has an interest of a legal nature and which may be affected by the decision in the case may, after giving written notice to the Parties which have originally initiated the procedure, join in the arbitration procedure with the consent of the tribunal.

Article VIII

Any Arbitration Tribunal established under the provisions of the present Protocol shall decide its own rules of procedure.

Article IX

1.   Decisions of the Tribunal both as to its procedure and its place of meeting and as to any question laid before it, shall be taken by majority votes of its members; the absence or abstention of one of the members of the Tribunal for whose nomination the Parties were responsible, shall not constitute an impediment to the Tribunal reaching a decision. In cases of equal voting, the vote of the Chairman shall be decisive.

2.   The Parties shall facilitate the work of the Tribunal and in particular, in accordance with their legislation, and using all means at their disposal:

(a)   Provide the tribunal with the necessary documents and information;

(b)   Enable the Tribunal to enter their territory, to hear witnesses or experts, and to visit the scene.

3.   Absence or default of one Party shall not constitute an impediment to the procedure.

Article X

1.   The Tribunal shall render its award within a period of five months from the time it is established unless it decides, in the case of necessity, to extend the time limit for a further period not exceeding three months. The award of the Tribunal shall be accompanied by a statement of reasons. It shall be final and without appeal and shall be communicated to the Secretary-General of the Organization. The Parties shall immediately comply with the award.

2. Any controversy which may arise between the Parties as regards interpretation or execution of the award may be submitted by either Party for judgment to the Tribunal which made the award, or, if it is not available to another Tribunal constituted for this purpose, in the same manner as the original Tribunal.

ANNEX I
REGULATIONS FOR THE PREVENTION OF POLLUTION BY OIL[2]

CHAPTER 1. GENERAL

Regulation 1 Definitions

For the purposes of this Annex:

1. 'Oil' means petroleum in any form including crude oil, fuel oil, sludge, oil refuse and refined products (other than those petrochemicals which are subject to the provisions of Annex II of the present Convention) and, without limiting the generality of the foregoing, includes the substances listed in Appendix I to this Annex.

2. 'Crude oil' means any liquid hydrocarbon mixture occurring naturally in the earth whether or not treated to render it suitable for transportation and includes:

(a) Crude oil from which certain distillate fractions may have been removed; and

(b) Crude oil to which certain distillate fractions may have been added.

3. 'Oily mixture' means a mixture with any oil content.

4. 'Oil fuel' means any oil used as fuel in connection with the propulsion and auxiliary machinery of the ship in which such oil is carried.

5. 'Oil tanker' means a ship constructed or adapted primarily to carry oil in bulk in its cargo spaces and includes combination carriers, any 'NLS tanker' as defined in Annex II of the present Convention and any gas carrier as defined in Regulation 3 (20) of Chapter II-1 of SOLAS 74 (as amended), when carrying a cargo or part cargo of oil in bulk.

6. 'Crude oil tanker' means an oil tanker engaged in the trade of carrying crude oil.

7. 'Product carrier' means an oil tanker engaged in the trade of carrying oil other than crude oil.

8. 'Combination carrier' means a ship designed to carry either oil or solid cargoes in bulk.

9. 'Major conversion':

(a) Means a conversion of a ship:

    (i) Which substantially alters the dimensions or carrying capacity of the ship; or

    (ii) Which changes the type of the ship; or

    (iii) The intent of which in the opinion of the Administration is substantially to prolong its life; or

    (iv) Which otherwise so alters the ship that, if it were a new ship, it would become subject to relevant provisions of the present Convention not applicable to it as an existing ship.

(b) Notwithstanding the provisions of this definition:

    (i) Conversion of an oil tanker of 20,000 tones deadweight and above delivered on or before 1 June 1982, as defined in Regulation 1 (28)(c) to meet the requirements of Regulation 18 of this Annex shall not be deemed to constitute a major conversion for the purpose of this Annex; and

    (ii) Conversion of an oil tanker delivered before 6 July 1996, as defined in Regulation 1 (28)(e), to meet the requirements of Regulation 19 or 20 of

---

[2] Regulations 2, 3, 5-10, 12-14, 16-19, 22-33, 35-37 omitted.

this Annex shall not be deemed to constitute a major conversion for the purpose of the Annex.

10. 'Nearest land'. The term 'from the nearest land' means from the baseline from which the territorial sea of the territory in question is established in accordance with international law, except that, for the purposes of the present Convention 'from the nearest land' off the north-eastern coast of Australia shall mean a line drawn from a point on the coast of Australia [...].[3]

11. 'Special area' means a sea area where for recognized technical reasons in relation to its oceanographical and ecological condition and to the particular character of its traffic the adoption of special mandatory methods for the prevention of sea pollution by oil is required.

For the purposes of this Annex, the special areas are defined as follows:

(a) 'The Mediterranean Sea area' means the Mediterranean Sea proper including the gulfs and seas therein with the boundary between the Mediterranean and the Black Sea constituted by the 41° N parallel and bounded to the west by the Straits of Gibraltar at the meridian of 005°36′ W;

(b) 'The Baltic Sea area' means the Baltic Sea proper with the Gulf of Bothnia, the Gulf of Finland and the entrance to the Baltic Sea bounded by the parallel of the Skaw in the Skagerrak at 57°44′.8 N;

(c) 'The Black Sea area' means the Black Sea proper with the boundary between the Mediterranean Sea and the Black Sea constituted by the parallel 41° N;

(d) 'The Red Sea area' means the Red Sea proper including the Gulfs of Suez and Aqaba bounded at the south by the rhumb line between Ras si Ane (12°28.5′ N, 043°19′.6 E) and Husn Murad (12°40′.4 N, 043°30′.2 E);

(e) 'The Gulfs area 'means the sea area located north-west of the rhumb line between Ras al Hadd (22°30′ N, 059°48′ E) and Ras al Fasteh (25°04′ N, 061°25′ E);

(f) 'The Gulf of Aden area' means that part of the Gulf of Aden between the Red Sea and the Arabian Sea bounded to the west by the rhumb line between Ras si Ane (12°28.5′ N, 043°19′.6 E) and Husn Murad (12°40′.4 N, 043°30′.2 E) and to the east by the rhumb line between Ras Asir (11°50′ N, 051°16′.9 E) and the Ras Fartak (15°35′ N, 052°13′.8 E);

(g) 'The Antarctic area' means the sea area south of latitude 60° S; and

(h) 'The North West European waters' include the North Sea and its approaches, the Irish Sea and its approaches, the Celtic Sea, the English Channel and its approaches and part of the North East Atlantic immediately to the west of Ireland [...].[4]

(i) 'The Oman area of the Arabian Sea' means the sea enclosed by the following co-ordinates [...].[5]

12. 'Instantaneous rate of discharge of oil content' means the rate of discharge of oil in litres per hour at any instant divided by the speed of the ship in knots at the same instant.

13. 'Tank' means an enclosed space which is formed by the permanent structure of a ship and which is designed for the carriage of liquid in bulk.

14. 'Wing tank' means any tank adjacent to the side shell plating.

15. 'Centre tank' means any tank inboard of a longitudinal bulkhead.

16. 'Slop tank' means a tank specifically designated for the collection of tank draining, tank washings and other oily mixtures.

---

[3] Co-ordinates omitted.
[4] Co-ordinates omitted.
[5] Co-ordinates omitted.

17.   'Clean ballast' means the ballast in a tank which, since oil was last carried therein, has been so cleaned that effluent therefrom if it were discharged from a ship which is stationary into clean calm water on a clear day would not produce visible traces of oil on the surface of the water or on adjoining shorelines or cause a sludge or emulsion to be deposited beneath the surface of the water or upon adjoining shorelines. If the ballast is discharged through an oil discharge monitoring and control system approved by the Administration, evidence based on such a system to the effect that the oil content of the effluent did not exceed 15 parts per million shall be determinative that the ballast was clean, notwithstanding the presence of visible traces.

18.   'Segregated ballast' means the ballast water introduced into a tank which is completely separated from the cargo oil and oil fuel system and which is permanently allocated to the carriage of ballast or cargoes other than oil or noxious liquid substances as variously defined in the Annexes of the present Convention.

19.   'Length (L)' means 96 per cent of the total length on waterline at 85 per cent of the least moulded depth measured from the top of the keel, or the length from the foreside of the stem to the axis of rudder stock on that waterline, if that be greater. In ships designed with a rake of keel the waterline on which this length is measured shall be parallel to the designed waterline. The length (L) shall be measured in metres.

20.   'Forward and after perpendiculars' shall be taken at the forward and after ends of the length (L). The forward perpendicular shall coincide with the foreside of the stem on the waterline on which the length is measured.

21.   'Amidships' is at the middles of the length (L).

22.   'Breadth (B)' means the maximum breadth of the ship, measured amidships to the moulded line of the frame in a ship with a metal shell and to the outer surface of the hull in a ship with a shell of any other material. The breadth (B) shall be measured in metres.

23.   'Deadweight (DW)' means the difference in tones between the displacement of a ship in water of a relative density of 1.025 at the load waterline corresponding to the assigned summer freeboard and the lightweight of the ship.

24.   'Lightweight' means the displacement of a ship in tones without cargo, fuel, lubricating oil, ballast water, fresh water and feed water in tanks, consumable stores, and passengers and crew and their effects.

25.   'Permeability' of a space means the ratio of the volume within that space which is assumed to be occupied by water to the total volume of that space.

26.   'Volumes and areas' in a ship shall be calculated in all cases to moulded lines.

27.   'Anniversary date' means the day and the month of each year, which will correspond to the date of expiry of the International Oil Pollution Prevention Certificate.

28.   [...].[6]

29.   'Parts per million (ppm)' means parts of oil per million parts of water by volume.

30.   'Constructed' means a ship the keel of which is laid or which is at a similar stage of construction.

Regulation 4 Exceptions

Regulations 15 and 34 of this Annex shall not apply to:

(a)   The discharge into the sea of oil or oily mixture necessary for the purpose of securing the safety of a ship or saving life at sea; or

(b)   The discharge into the sea of oil or oily mixture resulting from damage to a ship or its equipment:

---

[6] Paragraph 28 omitted.

        (i)   Provided that all reasonable precautions have been taken after the occurrence of the damage or discovery of the discharge for the purpose of preventing or minimizing the discharge; and

        (ii)   Except if the owner or the master acted either with intent to cause damage, or recklessly and with knowledge that damage would probably result; or

(c)   The discharge into the sea of substances containing oil, approved by the Administration, when being used for the purpose of combating specific pollution incidents in order to minimize the damage from pollution. Any such discharge shall be subject to the approval of any Government in whose jurisdiction it is contemplated the discharge will occur.

CHAPTER 2. SURVEYS AND CERTIFICATION

Regulation 11 Port State control on operational requirements

1.   A ship when in port or an offshore terminal of another Party is subject to inspection by officers duly authorized by such Party concerning operational requirements under this Annex, where there are clear grounds for believing that the master or crew are not familiar with essential shipboard procedures relating to the prevention of pollution by oil.

2.   In the circumstances given in paragraph (1) of this Regulation, the Party shall take such steps as will ensure that the ship shall not sail until the situation has been brought to order in accordance with the requirements of this Annex.

3.   Procedures relating to the port State control prescribed in Article 5 of the present Convention shall apply to this Regulation.

4.   Nothing in this Regulation shall be construed to limit the rights and obligations of a Party carrying out control over operational requirements specifically provided for in the present Convention.

CHAPTER 3. REQUIREMENTS FOR MACHINERY SPACES OF ALL SHIPS

PART C. CONTROL OF OPERATIONAL DISCHARGE OF OIL

Regulation 15 Control of discharge of oil

1.   Subject to the provisions of Regulation 4 of this Annex and paragraphs (2), (3) and (6) of this Regulation, any discharge into the sea of oil or oily mixtures from ships shall be prohibited.

A Discharges outside special areas

2.   Any discharge into the sea of oil or oily mixtures from ships of 400 gross tonnage and above shall be prohibited except when all the following conditions are satisfied:

(a)   The ship is proceeding *en route*;

(b)   The oily mixture is processed through an oil filtering equipment meeting the requirements of Regulation 14 of this Annex;

(c)   The oil content of the effluent without dilution does not exceed 15 parts per million;

(d)   The oily mixture does not originate from cargo pump-room bilges on oil tankers; and

(e)   The oily mixture, in case of oil tankers, is not mixed with oil cargo residues.

B Discharges in special areas

3. Any discharge into the sea of oil or oily mixtures from ships of 400 gross tonnage and above shall be prohibited except when all of the following conditions are satisfied:

(a) The ship is proceeding *en route*;

(b) The oily mixture is processed through an oil filtering equipment meeting the requirements of Regulation 14 (7) of this Annex;

(c) The oil content of the effluent without dilution does not exceed 15 parts per million;

(d) The oily mixture does not originate from cargo pump-room bilges on oil tankers; and

(e) The oily mixture, in case of oil tankers, is not mixed with oil cargo residues.

4. In respect of the Antarctic area, any discharge into the sea of oil or oily mixtures from any ship shall be prohibited.

5. Nothing in this Regulation shall prohibit a ship on a voyage only part of which is in a special area from discharging outside a special area in accordance with paragraph (2) of this Regulation.

C Requirements for ships of less than 400 gross tonnage in all areas except the Antarctic area

6. In the case of a ship of less than 400 gross tonnage, oil and all oily mixtures shall either be retained on board for subsequent discharge to reception facilities or discharged into the sea in accordance with the following provisions:

(a) The ship is proceeding *en route*;

(b) The ship has in operation equipment of a design approved by the Administration that ensures that the oil content of the effluent without dilution does not exceed 15 parts per million;

(c) The oily mixture does not originate from cargo pump-room bilges on oil tankers; and

(d) The oily mixture, in case of oil tankers, is not mixed with oil cargo residues.

D General requirements

7. Whenever visible traces of oil are observed on or below the surface of the water in the immediate vicinity of a ship or its wake, Governments of Parties to the present Convention should, to the extent they are reasonably able to so do, promptly investigate the facts bearing on the issue of whether there has been a violation of the provisions of this Regulation. The investigation should include, in particular, the wind and sea conditions, the track and speed of the ship, other possible sources of the visible traces in the vicinity, and any relevant oil discharge records.

8. No discharge into the sea shall contain chemicals or other substances in quantities or concentrations which are hazardous to the marine environment or chemicals or other substances introduced for the purpose of circumventing the conditions of discharge specified in this Regulation.

9. The oil residues which cannot be discharged into the sea in compliance with this Regulation shall be retained on board for subsequent discharge to reception facilities.

CHAPTER 4. REQUIREMENTS FOR THE CARGO AREA OF OIL TANKERS

PART A. CONSTRUCTION

Regulation 20 Double hull and double bottom requirements for oil tankers delivered before 6 July 1996

1. Unless expressly provided otherwise this Regulation shall:
   (a) Apply to oil tankers of 5,000 tonnes deadweight and above, which are delivered before 6 July 1996, as defined in Regulation 1 (28)(e) of this Annex; and
   (b) Not apply to oil tankers complying with Regulation 19 and Regulation 28 in respect of paragraph (6), which are delivered before 6 July 1996, as defined in Regulation 1 (28)(5) of this Annex; and
   (c) Not apply to oil tankers covered by sub-paragraph (a) above which comply with Regulation 19 (3)(a) and 19 (3)(b) or 19 (4) or 19 (5) of this Annex, except that the requirement for minimum distances between the cargo tank boundaries and the ship side and bottom plating need not be met in all respects. In that event, the side protection distances shall not be less than those specified in the International Bulk Chemical Code for type 2 cargo tank location and the bottom protection distances at centerline shall comply with Regulation 18 (15)(b) of this Annex.

2. For the purpose of this Regulation:
   (a) 'Heavy diesel oil' means diesel oil other than those distillates of which more than 50 per cent by volume distils at a temperature not exceeding 340°C when tested by the method acceptable to the Organization.
   (b) 'Fuel oil' means heavy distillates or residues from crude oil or blends of such materials intended for use as a fuel for the production of heat or power of a quality equivalent to the specification acceptable to the Organization.

3. For the purpose of this Regulation, oil tankers are divided into the following categories:
   (a) 'Category 1 oil tanker' means an oil tanker of 20,000 tonnes deadweight and above carrying crude oil, fuel oil, heavy diesel oil or lubricating oil as cargo, and of 30,000 tonnes deadweight and above carrying oil other than the above, which does not comply with the requirements for oil tankers delivered after 1 June 1982, as defined in Regulation 1 (28)(d) of this Annex;
   (b) 'Category 2 oil tanker' means an oil tanker of 20,000 tonnes deadweight and above carrying crude oil, fuel oil, heavy diesel oil or lubricating oil as cargo, and of 30,000 tonnes deadweight and above carrying oil other than the above, which complies with the requirements for oil tankers delivered after 1 June 1982, as defined in Regulation 1 (28)(d) of this Annex; and
   (c) 'Category 3 oil tanker' means an oil tanker of 5,000 tonnes deadweight and above but less than that specified in sub-paragraph (a) or (b) of this paragraph.

4. An oil tanker to which this Regulation applies shall comply with the requirements of paragraphs (2) to (5), (7) and (8) of Regulation 19 and Regulation 28 in respect of paragraph (6) of this Annex not later than 5 April 2005 or the anniversary of the date of delivery of the ship on the date or in the year specified in the following table:

Category of oil tanker	Date or year
Category 1	– 5 April 2005 for ships delivered on 5 April 1982 or earlier – 2005 for ships delivered after 5 April 1982
Category 2 and Category 3	– 5 April 2005 for ships delivered on 5 April 1977 or earlier 2005 for ships delivered after 5 April 1977 but before 1 January 1978 – 2006 for ships delivered in 1978 and 1979 – 2007 for ships delivered in 1980 and 1981 – 2008 for ships delivered in 1982 – 2009 for ships delivered in 1983 – 2010 for ships delivered in 1984 or later

5. Notwithstanding the provisions of paragraph (4) of this Regulation, in the case of Category 2 or 3 oil tanker fitted with only double bottoms or double sides not used for the carriage of oil and extending to the entire cargo tank length or double hull spaces which are not used for the carriage of oil and extend to the entire cargo tank length, but which does not fulfil conditions for being exempted from the provisions of paragraph (1)(c) of this Regulation, the Administration may allow continued operation of such a ship beyond the date specified in paragraph (4) of this Regulation provided that:

(a) The ship was in service on 1 July 2001;

(b) The Administration is satisfied by verification of the official records that the ship complied with the conditions specified above;

(c) The conditions of the ship specified above remain unchanged; and

(d) Such continued operation does not go beyond the date on which the ship reaches 25 years after the date of its delivery.

6. A Category 2 or 3 oil tanker of 15 years and over after the date of its delivery shall comply with the Condition Assessment Scheme adopted by the Marine Environment Protection Committee by Resolution MEPC.94(46), as amended, provided that such amendments shall be adopted, brought into force and take effect in accordance with the provisions of Article 16 of the present Convention relating to amendment procedures applicable to an Appendix to an Annex.

7. The Administration may allow continued operation of a Category 2 or 3 oil tanker beyond the date specified in paragraph (4) of this Regulation, if satisfactory results of the Condition Assessment Scheme warrant that, in the opinion of the Administration, the ship is fit to continue such operation, provided that the operation shall not go beyond the anniversary of the date of delivery of the ship in 2015 or the date on which the ship reaches 25 years after the date of its delivery, whichever is the earlier date.

8.1 The Administration of a Party to the present Convention which allows the application of paragraph (5) of this Regulation, or allows, suspends, withdraws or declines the application of paragraph (7) of this Regulation, to a ship entitled to fly its flag shall forthwith communicate to the Organization for circulation to the Parties to the present Convention particulars thereof, for their information and appropriate action, if any.

8.2 A Party to the present Convention shall be entitled to deny entry into the ports or offshore terminals under its jurisdiction of oil tankers operating in accordance with the provisions of:

(a) Paragraph (5) of this Regulation beyond the anniversary of the date of delivery of the ship in 2015; or

(b) Paragraph (7) of this Regulation.

In such cases, that Party shall communicate to the Organization for circulation to the Parties to the present Convention particulars thereof for their information.

Regulation 21 Prevention of oil pollution from oil tankers carrying heavy grade oil as cargo

1. This Regulation shall:
(a)   Apply to oil tankers of 600 tonnes deadweight and above carrying heavy grade oil as cargo regardless of the date of delivery; and
(b)   Not apply to oil tankers covered by sub-paragraph (a) above which comply with Regulations 19 (3)(a) and 19 (3)(b) or 19 (4) or 19 (5) of this Annex, except that the requirement for minimum distances between the cargo tank boundaries and the ship side and bottom plating need not be met in all respects. In that event, the side protection distances shall not be less than those specified in the International Bulk Chemical Code for type 2 cargo tank location and the bottom protection distances as centreline shall comply with the Regulation 18 (15)(b) of this Annex.

2. For the purpose of this Regulation 'heavy grade oil' means any of the following:
(a)   Crude oils having a density at 15°C higher than 900 kg/m³;
(b)   Oils, other than crude oils, having either a density at 15°C higher than 900 kg/m³ or kinematic viscosity at 50°C higher than 180 mm²/s; or
(c)   Bitumen, tar and their emulsions.

3. An oil taker to which this Regulation applies shall comply with the provisions of paragraphs (4) to (8) of this Regulation in addition to complying with the applicable provisions of Regulation 20.

4. Subject to the provisions of paragraphs (5), (6) and (7) of this Regulation, an oil tanker to which this Regulation applies shall:
(a)   If 5,000 tonnes deadweight and above, comply with the requirements of Regulation 19 of this Annex not later than 5 April 2005; or
(b)   If 600 tonnes deadweight and above but less than 5,000 tonnes deadweight, be fitted with both double bottom tanks or spaces complying with the provisions of Regulation 19 (6)(a) of this Annex, and wing tanks or spaces arranged in accordance with Regulation 19 (3)(a) and complying with the requirement for distance *w* as referred to in Regulation 19 (6)(b), not later than the anniversary of the date of delivery of the ship in the year 2008.

5. In the case of an oil tanker of 5,000 tonnes deadweight and above, carrying heavy grade oil as cargo fitted with only double bottoms or double sides not used for the carriage of oil and extending to the entire cargo tank length or double hull spaces which are not used for the carriage of oil and extend to the entire cargo tank length, but which does not fulfil conditions for being exempted from the provisions of paragraph (1)(b) of this Regulation, the Administration may allow continued operation of such a ship beyond the date specified in paragraph (4) of this Regulation, provided that:
(a)   The ship was in service on 4 December 2003;
(b)   The Administration is satisfied by verification of the official records that the ship complied with the conditions specified above;
(c)   The conditions of the ship specified above remain unchanged; and
(d)   Such continued operation does not go beyond the date on which the ship reaches 25 years after the date of its delivery.
6. (a)   The Administration may allow continued operation of an oil tanker of 5,000 tonnes deadweight and above, carrying such crude oil having a density at 15°C higher than 900kg/m³ but lower than 945 kg/m³, beyond the date

specified in paragraph (4)(a) of this Regulation, if satisfactory results of the Condition Assessment Scheme referred to in Regulation 20 (6) warrant that, in the opinion of the Administration, the ship is fit to continue such operation, having regard to the size, age, operational area and structural conditions of the ship and provided that the operation shall not go beyond the date on which the ship reaches 25 years after the date of its delivery.

(b)   The Administration may allow continued operation of an oil tanker of 600 tonnes deadweight and above but less than 5,000 tones deadweight, carrying heavy grade oil as cargo, beyond the date specified in paragraph (4)(b) of this Regulation, if, in the opinion of the Administration, the ship is fit to continue such operation, having regard to the size, age, operational area and structural conditions of the ship, provided that the operation shall not go beyond the date on which the ship reached 25 years after the date of its delivery.

7.   The Administration of a Party to the present Convention may exempt an oil tanker of 600 tonnes deadweight and above carrying heavy grade oil as cargo from the provisions of this Regulation if the oil tanker:

(a)   Either is engaged in voyages exclusively within an area under its jurisdiction, or operates as a floating storage unit of heavy grade oil located within an area under its jurisdiction; or

(b)   Either is engaged in voyages exclusively within an area under the jurisdiction of another Party, or operates as a floating storage unit of heavy grade oil located within an area under the jurisdiction of another Party, provided that the Party within whose jurisdiction the oil tanker will be operating agrees to the operation of the oil tanker within an area under its jurisdiction.

8.   (a)   The Administration of a Party to the present Convention which allows, suspends, withdraws or declines the application of paragraph (5), (6) or (7) of this Regulation to a ship entitled to fly its flag shall forthwith communicate to the Organization for circulation to the Parties to the present Convention particulars thereof, for their information and appropriate action, if any.

(b)   Subject to the provisions of international law, a Party to the present Convention shall be entitled to deny entry of oil tankers operating in accordance with the provisions of paragraph (5) or (6) of this Regulation into the ports or offshore terminals under its jurisdiction, or deny ship-to-ship transfer of heavy grade oil in areas under its jurisdiction except when this is necessary for the purpose of securing the safety of a ship or saving life at sea. In such cases, that Party shall communicate to the Organization for circulation to the Parties to the present Convention particulars thereof for their information.

PART C. CONTROL OF OPERATIONAL DISCHARGES OF OIL

Regulation 34
A Discharges outside special areas

1.   Subject to the provisions of Regulation 4 of this Annex and paragraph (2) of this Regulation, any discharge into the sea of oil or oily mixtures from the cargo area of an oil tanker shall be prohibited except when all the following conditions are satisfied:

(a)   The tanker is not within a special area;

(b)   The tanker is more than 50 nautical miles from the nearest land;

(c)   The tanker is proceeding *en route*;

(d)   The instantaneous rate of discharge of oil content does not exceed 30 litres per nautical mile;

(e)   The total quantity of oil discharged into the sea does not exceed for tankers delivered on or before 31 December 1979, as defined in Regulation 1 (28) (a), 1/15,000 of the total quantity of the particular cargo of which the residue formed a part, and for tankers delivered after 31 December 1979, as defined in Regulation 1 (28)(b), 1/30,000 of the total quantity of the particular cargo of which the residue formed a part; and

(f)   The tanker has in operation an oil discharge monitoring and control system and a slop tank arrangement as required by Regulations 29 and 31 of this Annex.

2.   The provisions of paragraph (1) of this Regulation shall not apply to the discharge of clean or segregated ballast.

B Discharges in special areas

3.   Subject to the provisions of paragraph (4) of this Regulation, any discharge into the sea of oil or oily mixture from the cargo area of an oil tanker shall be prohibited while in a special area.

4.   The provisions of paragraph (3) of this Regulation shall not apply to the discharge of clean or segregated ballast.

5.   Nothing in this Regulation shall prohibit a ship on a voyage only part of which is in a special area from discharging outside the special area in accordance with paragraph (1) of this Regulation.

C Requirements for oil tankers of less than 150 gross tonnage

6.   The requirements of Regulations 29, 31 and 32 of this Annex shall not apply to oil tankers of less than 150 gross tonnage, for which the control of discharge of oil under this Regulation shall be effected by the retention of oil on board with subsequent discharge of all contaminated washings to reception facilities. The total quantity of oil and water used for washing and returned to a storage tank shall be discharged to reception facilities unless adequate arrangements are made to ensure that any effluent which is allowed to be discharged into the sea is effectively monitored to ensure that the provisions of this Regulation are complied with.

D General requirements

7.   Whenever visible traces of oil are observed on or below the surface of the water in the immediate vicinity of a ship or its wake, the Governments of Parties to the present Convention should, to the extent they are reasonably able to do so, promptly investigate the facts bearing on the issue of whether there has been a violation of the provisions of this Regulation. The investigation should include, in particular, the wind and sea conditions, the track and speed of the ship, other possible sources of the visible traces in the vicinity, and any relevant oil discharge records.

8.   No discharge into the sea shall contain chemicals or other substances in quantities or concentrations which are hazardous to the marine environment or chemicals or other substances introduced for the purpose of circumventing the conditions of discharge specified in this Regulation.

9.   The oil residues which cannot be discharged into the sea in compliance with paragraphs (1) and (3) of this Regulation shall be retained on board for subsequent discharge to reception facilities.

CHAPTER 6. RECEPTION FACILITIES

Regulation 38 Reception facilities

A Reception facilities outside special areas

1.   The Government of each Party to the present Convention undertakes to ensure the provision at oil loading terminals, repair ports, and in other ports in which ships have oily residues to discharge, of facilities for the reception of such residues and oily mixtures as remain from oil tankers and other ships adequate to meet the needs of the ships using them without causing undue delay to ships.

2.   Reception facilities in accordance with paragraph (1) of this Regulation shall be provided in:

(a)   All ports and terminals in which crude oil is loaded into oil tankers where such tankers have immediately prior to arrival completed a ballast voyage of not more than 72 hours or not more than 1200 nautical miles;

(b)   All ports and terminals in which oil other than crude oil in bulk is loaded at an average quantity of more than 1000 tonnes per day;

(c)   All ports having ship repair yards or tank cleaning facilities;

(d)   All ports and terminals which handle ships provided with the sludge tank(s) required by Regulation 12 of this Annex;

(e)   All ports in respect of oily bilge waters and other residues which cannot be discharged in accordance with Regulations 15 and 34 of this Annex; and

(f)   All loading ports of bulk cargoes in respect of oil residues from combination carriers which cannot be discharged in accordance with Regulation 34 of this Annex;

3.   The capacity for the reception facilities shall be as follows:

(a)   Crude oil loading terminals shall have sufficient reception facilities to receive oil and oily mixtures which cannot be discharged in accordance with the provisions of Regulation 34 (1) of this Annex from all oil tankers on voyages as described in paragraph (2)(a) of this Regulation.

(b)   Loading ports and terminals referred to in paragraph (2)(b) of this Regulation shall have sufficient reception facilities to receive oil and oily mixtures which cannot be discharged in accordance with the provisions of Regulation 34 (1) of this Annex from oil tankers which load oil other than crude oil in bulk.

(c)   All ports having ship repair yards or tank cleaning facilities shall have sufficient reception facilities to receive all residues and oily mixtures which remain on board for disposal from ships prior to entering such yards or facilities.

(d)   All facilities provided in ports and terminals under paragraph (2)(d) of this Regulation shall be sufficient to receive all residues retained according to Regulation 12 of this Annex from all ships that may reasonably be expected to call at such ports and terminals.

(e)   All facilities provided in ports and terminals under this Regulation shall be sufficient to receive oily bilge waters and other residues which cannot be discharged in accordance with Regulation 15 of this Annex.

(f)   The facilities provided in loading ports for bulk cargoes shall take into account the special problems of combination carriers as appropriate.

B Reception facilities within special areas

4.   The Government of each Party to the present Convention the coastline of which borders on any given special area shall ensure that all oil loading terminals and repair ports within the special area are provided with facilities adequate for the reception and

treatment of all the dirty ballast and tank washing water from oil tankers. In addition, all ports within the special area shall be provided with adequate reception facilities for other residues and oily mixtures from all ships. Such facilities shall have adequate capacity to meet the needs of the ships using them without causing undue delay.

5. The Government of each Party to the present Convention having under its jurisdiction entrances to seawater courses with low depth contour which might require a reduction of draught by the discharge of ballast shall ensure the provision of the facilities referred to in paragraph (4) of this Regulation but with the proviso that ships required to discharge slops or dirty ballast could be subject to some delay.

6. With regard to the Red Sea area, Gulfs area, Gulf of Aden area and Oman area of the Arabian Sea:

(a) Each Party shall notify the Organization of the measures taken pursuant to provisions of paragraphs (4) and (5) of this Regulation. Upon receipt of sufficient notifications, the Organization shall establish a date from which the discharge requirements of Regulation 15 and 34 of this Annex in respect of the area in question shall take effect. The Organization shall notify all the Parties of the date so established no less than twelve months in advance of that date.

(b) During the period between the entry into force of the present Convention and the date so established, ships while navigating in the special area shall comply with the requirements of Regulations 15 and 34 of this Annex as regards discharges outside special areas.

(c) After such date, oil tankers loading in ports in these special areas where such facilities are not yet available shall also fully comply with the requirements of Regulations 15 and 34 of this Annex as regards discharges within special areas. However, oil tankers entering those special areas for the purpose of loading shall make every effort to enter the area with only clean ballast on board.

(d) After the date on which the requirements for the special area in question take effect, each Party shall notify the Organization for transmission to the Parties concerned of all cases where the facilities are alleged to be inadequate.

(e) At least the reception facilities as prescribed in paragraphs (1), (2) and (3) of this Regulation shall be provided one year after the date of entry into force of the present Convention.

7. Notwithstanding paragraphs (4), (5) and (6) of this Regulation the following rules apply to the Antarctic area:

(a) The Government of each Party to the present Convention at whose ports ships depart *en route* to or arrive from the Antarctic area undertakes to ensure that as soon as practicable adequate facilities are provided for the reception of all sludge, dirty ballast, tank washing water, and other oily residues and mixtures from all ships, without causing undue delay, and according to the needs of the ships using them.

(b) The Government of each Party to the present Convention shall ensure that all ships entitled to fly its flag, before entering the Antarctic area, are fitted with a tank or tanks of sufficient capacity on board for the retention of all sludge, dirty ballast, tank washing water and other oily residues and mixtures while operating in the area and have concluded arrangements to discharge such oily residues at a reception facility after leaving the area.

C General requirements

8. Each Party shall notify the Organization for transmission to the Parties concerned of all cases where the facilities provided under this Regulation are alleged to be inadequate.

CHAPTER 7. SPECIAL REQUIREMENTS FOR FIXED OR FLOATING PLATFORMS

Regulation 39 Special Requirements for fixed or floating platforms

1. This Regulation applies to fixed or floating platforms including drilling rigs, floating production, storage and offloading facilities (FPSOs) used for the offshore production and storage of oil, and floating storage units (FSUs) used for the offshore storage of produced oil.

2. Fixed or floating platforms when engaged in the exploration, exploitation and associated offshore processing of sea-bed mineral resources and other platforms shall comply with the requirements of this Annex applicable to ships of 400 gross tonnage and above other than oil tankers, except that:

   (a) They shall be equipped as far as practicable with the installations required in Regulations 12 and 14 of this Annex;

   (b) They shall keep a record of all operations involving oil or oily mixture discharges, in a form approved by the Administration; and

   (c) Subject to the provisions of Regulation 4 of this Annex, the discharge into the sea of oil or oily mixture shall be prohibited except when the oil content of the discharge without dilution does not exceed 15 parts per million.

3. In verifying compliance with this Annex in relation to platforms configured as FPSOs or FSUs, in addition to the requirements of paragraph (2), Administrations should take account of the Guidelines developed by the Organization.

ANNEX V
REGULATIONS FOR THE PREVENTION OF POLLUTION
BY GARBAGE FROM SHIP[7]

Regulation 1 Definitions

For the purposes of this Annex:

1. 'Garbage' means all kinds of victual, domestic and operational waste excluding fresh fish and parts thereof, generated during the normal operation of the ship and liable to be disposed of continuously or periodically except those substances which are defined or listed in other Annexes to the present Convention.

2. 'Nearest land'. The term 'from the nearest land' means from the baseline from which the territorial sea of the territory in question is established in accordance with international law, except that, for the purposes of the present Convention, 'from the nearest land' off the north-eastern coast of Australia shall mean from a line drawn from a point on the coast of Australia [...].[8]

3. 'Special area' means a sea area where for recognized technical reasons in relation to its oceanographical and ecological condition and to the particular character of its traffic the adoption of special mandatory methods for the prevention of sea pollution by garbage is required. Special areas shall include those listed in Regulation 5 of this Annex.

---

[7] Regulation 9 omitted.
[8] Co-ordinates omitted.

Regulation 2 Application

Unless expressly provided otherwise, the provisions of this Annex shall apply to all ships.

Regulation 3 Disposal of garbage outside special areas

1. Subject to the provisions of Regulations 4, 5 and 6 of this Annex:

(a) The disposal into the sea of all plastics, including but not limited to synthetic ropes, synthetic fishing nets, plastic garbage bags and incinerator ashes from plastic products which may contain toxic or heavy metal residues, is prohibited;

(b) The disposal into the sea of the following garbage shall be made as far as practicable from the nearest land but in any case is prohibited if the distance from the nearest land is less than:

    (i) 25 nautical miles for dunnage, lining and packing materials which will float;

    (ii) 12 nautical miles for food wastes and all other garbage including paper products, rags, glass, metal, bottles, crockery and similar refuse;

(c) Disposal into the sea of garbage specified in sub-paragraph (b)(ii) of this Regulation may be permitted when it has passed through a comminuter or grinder and made as far as practicable from the nearest land but in any case is prohibited if the distance from the nearest land is less than 3 nautical miles. Such comminuted or ground garbage shall be capable of passing through a screen with openings no greater than 25 mm.

2. When the garbage is mixed with other discharges having different disposal or discharge requirements the more stringent requirements shall apply.

Regulation 4 Special requirements for disposal of garbage

1. Subject to the provisions of paragraph (2) of this Regulation, the disposal of any materials regulated by this Annex is prohibited from fixed or floating platforms engaged in the exploration, exploitation and associated offshore processing of sea-bed mineral resources, and from all other ships when alongside or within 500 m of such platforms.

2. The disposal into the sea of food wastes may be permitted when they have been passed through a comminuter or grinder from such fixed or floating platforms located more than 12 nautical miles from land and all other ships when alongside or within 500 m of such platforms. Such comminuted or ground food wastes shall be capable of passing through a screen with openings no greater than 25 mm.

Regulation 5 Disposal of garbage within special areas

1. For the purposes of this Annex the special areas are the Mediterranean Sea area, the Baltic Sea area, the Black Sea area, the Red Sea area, the 'Gulfs area', the North Sea area, the Antarctic area and the Wider Caribbean Region, including the Gulf of Mexico and the Caribbean Sea, which are defined as follows:

(a) The 'Mediterranean Sea area' means the Mediterranean Sea proper including the gulfs and seas therein with the boundary between the Mediterranean and the Black Sea constituted by the 41° N parallel and bounded to the west by the Straits of Gibraltar at the meridian of 5°36′ W;

(b) The 'Baltic Sea area' means the Baltic Sea proper with the Gulf of Bothnia, the Gulf of Finland and the entrance to the Baltic Sea bounded by the parallel of the Skaw in the Skagerrak at 57°44′.8 N;

(c)   The 'Black Sea area' means the Black Sea proper with the boundary between the Mediterranean and the Black Sea constituted by the parallel 41° N;

(d)   The 'Red Sea area' means the Red Sea proper including the Gulfs of Suez and Aqaba bounded at the south by the rhumb line between Ras si Ane (12°28.5′ N, 43°19′.6 E) and Husn Murad (12°40′.4 N, 43°30′.2 E);

(e)   The 'Gulfs area' means the sea area located north-west of the rhumb line between Ras al Hadd (22°30′ N, 59°48′ E) and Ras al Fasteh (25°04′ N, 61°25′ E);

(f)   The 'North Sea area' means the North Sea proper including seas therein with the boundary between:

    (i)   The North Sea southwards of latitude 62° N and eastwards of longitude 4° W;

    (ii)   The Skagerrak, the southern limit of which is determined east of the Skaw by latitude 57°44.8′ N; and

    (iii)   The English Channel and its approaches eastwards of longitude 5° W and northwards of latitude 48°30′ N.

(g)   The 'Antarctic area' means the sea area south of latitude 60° S;

(h)   The 'Wider Caribbean Region', as defined in Article 2, paragraph (1) of the Convention for the Protection and Development of the Marine Environment of the Wider Caribbean Region (Cartagena de Indias, 1983), means the Gulf of Mexico and Caribbean Sea proper including the bays and sea therein and that portion of the Atlantic Ocean within the boundary constituted by the 30° N parallel from Florida eastward to 77°30′ W meridian, thence a rhumb line to the intersection of 20° N parallel and 59° W meridian, thence a rhumb line to the intersection of 7°20′ N parallel and 50° W meridian, thence a rhumb line drawn south-westerly to the eastern boundary of French Guiana.

2.   Subject to the provisions of Regulation 6 of this Annex:

(a)   Disposal into the sea of the following is prohibited:

    (i)   All plastics, including but not limited to synthetic ropes, synthetic fishing nets, plastic garbage bags and incinerator ashes from plastic products which may contain toxic or heavy metal residues; and

    (ii)   All other garbage, including paper products, rags, glass, metal, bottles, crockery, dunnage, lining and packing materials;

(b)   Except as provided in sub-paragraph (c) of this paragraph, disposal into the sea of food wastes shall be made as far as practicable from land, but in any case not less than 12 nautical miles from the nearest land;

(c)   Disposal into the Wider Caribbean Region of food wastes which have been passed through a comminuter or grinder shall be made as far as practicable from land, but in any case not less than 3 nautical miles from the nearest land. Such comminuted or ground food wastes shall be capable of passing through a screen with openings no greater than 25 mm.

3.   When the garbage is mixed with other discharges having different disposal or discharge requirements the more stringent requirements shall apply.

4.   Reception facilities within special areas:

(a)   The Government of each Party to the Convention, the coastline of which borders a special area, undertakes to ensure that as soon as possible in all ports within a special area adequate reception facilities are provided in accordance with Regulation 7 of this Annex, taking into account the special needs of ships operating in these areas.

(b) The Government of each Party concerned shall notify the Organization of such measures taken pursuant to sub-paragraph (a) of this Regulation. Upon receipt of sufficient notifications the Organization shall establish a date from which the requirements of this Regulation in respect of the area in question shall take effect. The Organization shall notify all Parties of the date so established no less than twelve months in advance of that date.

(c) After the date so established, ships calling at ports in these special areas where such facilities are not yet available, shall fully comply with the requirements of this Regulation.

5. Notwithstanding paragraph (4) of this Regulation, the following rules apply to the Antarctic area:

(a) The Government of each Party to the Convention at whose ports ships depart *en route* to or arrive from the Antarctic area undertakes to ensure that as soon as practicable adequate facilities are provided for the reception of all garbage from all ships, without causing undue delay, and according to the needs of the ships using them.

(b) The Government of each Party to the Convention shall ensure that all ships entitled to fly its flag, before entering the Antarctic area, have sufficient capacity on board for the retention of all garbage while operating in the area and have concluded arrangements to discharge such garbage at a reception facility after leaving the area.

Regulation 6 Exceptions

Regulations 3, 4 and 5 of this Annex shall not apply to:

(a) The disposal of garbage from a ship necessary for the purpose of securing the safety of a ship and those on board or saving life at sea; or

(b) The escape of garbage resulting from damage to a ship or its equipment provided all reasonable precautions have been taken before and after the occurrence of the damage, for the purpose of preventing or minimizing the escape; or

(c) The accidental loss of synthetic fishing nets, provided that all reasonable precautions have been taken to prevent such loss.

Regulation 7 Reception facilities

1. The Government of each Party to the Convention undertakes to ensure the provision of facilities at ports and terminals for the reception of garbage, without causing undue delay to ships, and according to the needs of the ships using them.

2. The Government of each Party shall notify the Organization for transmission to the Parties concerned of all cases where the facilities provided under this Regulation are alleged to be inadequate.

Regulation 8 Port State control on operational requirements

1. A ship when in a port of another Party is subject to inspection by officers duly authorized by such Party concerning operational requirements under this Annex, where there are clear grounds for believing that the master or crew are not familiar with essential shipboard procedures relating to the prevention of pollution by garbage.

2. In the circumstances given in paragraph (1) of this Regulation, the Party shall take such steps as will ensure that the ship shall not sail until the situation has been brought to order in accordance with the requirements of this Annex.

3. Procedures relating to the port State control prescribed in Article 5 of the present Convention shall apply to this Regulation.

4. Nothing in this Regulation shall be construed to limit the rights and obligation of a Party carrying out control over operational requirements specifically provided for in the present Convention.

International Convention for the Safety of Life at Sea (SOLAS)

Done at London, 1 November 1974; entry into force, 25 May 1980
1184 UNTS 278 [Registration Number 18961][1]

The Contracting Governments,

Being desirous of promoting safety of life at sea by establishing in common agreement uniform principles and rules directed thereto,

Considering that this end may best be achieved by the conclusion of a Convention to replace the International Convention for the Safety of Life at Sea, 1960, taking account of developments since that Convention was concluded,

Have agreed as follows:

Article I General obligations under the Convention[2]

(a) The Contracting Governments undertake to give effect to the provisions of the present Convention and the Annex thereto, which shall constitute an integral part of the present Convention. Every reference to the present Convention constitutes at the same time a reference to the Annex.

(b) The Contracting Governments undertake to promulgate all laws, decrees, orders and regulations and to take all other steps which may be necessary to give the present Convention full and complete effect, so as to ensure that, from the point of view of safety of life, a ship is fit for the service for which it is intended.

Article II Application

The present Convention shall apply to ships entitled to fly the flag of States the Governments of which are Contracting Governments.

Article III Laws, regulations

The Contracting Governments undertake to communicate to and deposit with the Secretary-General of the Inter-Governmental Maritime Consultative Organization (hereinafter referred to as 'the Organization'):

(a) A list of non-governmental agencies which are authorized to act in their behalf in the administration of measures for safety of life at sea for circulation to the Contracting Governments for the information of their officers;

(b) The text of laws, decrees, orders and regulations which shall have been promulgated on the various matters within the scope of the present Convention;

(c) A sufficient number of specimens of their Certificates issued under the provisions of the present Convention for circulation to the Contracting Governments for the information of their officers.

---

[1] The SOLAS Convention has been updated and amended on numerous occasions between 1981 and 2008. The text of the Convention reproduced is a consolidated version incorporating the various amendments in force as at 1 June 2009.

[2] Article I (3) of the 1988 Protocol Relating to the SOLAS Convention provides: 'With respect to ships entitled to fly the flag of a State which is not a Party to the Convention and the present Protocol, the Parties to the present Protocol shall apply the requirements of the Convention and the present Protocol as may be necessary to ensure that no more favourable treatment is given to such ships.'

Article IV Cases of *force majeure*

(a)   A ship, which is not subject to the provisions of the present Convention at the time of its departure on any voyage, shall not become subject to the provisions of the present Convention on account of any deviation from its intended voyage due to stress of weather or any other case of *force majeure.*

(b)   Persons who are on board a ship by reason of *force majeure* or in consequence of the obligation laid upon the master to carry shipwrecked or other persons shall not be taken into account for the purpose of ascertaining the application to a ship of any provisions of the present Convention.

Article V Carriage of persons in emergencies

(a)   For the purpose of evacuating persons in order to avoid a threat to the security of their lives a Contracting Government may permit the carriage of a larger number of persons in its ships than is otherwise permissible under the present Convention.

(b)   Such permission shall not deprive other Contracting Governments of any right of control under the present Convention over such ships which come within their ports.

(c)   Notice of any such permission, together with a statement of the circumstances, shall be sent to the Secretary-General of the Organization by the Contracting Government granting such permission.

Article VI Prior treaties and conventions

(a)   As between the Contracting Governments, the present Convention replaces and abrogates the International Convention for the Safety of Life at Sea which was signed in London on 17 June 1960.

(b)   All other treaties, conventions and arrangements relating to safety of life at sea, or matters appertaining thereto, at present in force between Governments Parties to the present Convention shall continue to have full and complete effect during the terms thereof as regards:

(i)   Ships to which the present Convention does not apply;

(ii)   Ships to which the present Convention applies, in respect of matters for which it has not expressly provided.

(c)   To the extent, however, that such treaties, conventions or arrangements conflict with the provisions of the present Convention, the provisions of the present Convention shall prevail.

(d)   All matters which are not expressly provided for in the present Convention remain subject to the legislation of the Contracting Governments.

Article VII Special rules drawn up by agreement

When in accordance with the present Convention special rules are drawn up by agreement between all or some of the Contracting Governments, such rules shall be communicated to the Secretary-General of the Organization for circulation to all Contracting Governments.

Article VIII Amendments

(a)   The present Convention may be amended by either of the procedures specified in the following paragraphs.

(b)   Amendments after consideration within the Organization:

(i)   Any amendment proposed by a Contracting Government shall be submitted to the Secretary-General of the Organization, who shall then circulate it to all Members of the Organization and all Contracting Governments at least six months prior to its consideration.

(ii) Any amendment proposed and circulated as above shall be referred to the Maritime Safety Committee of the Organization for consideration.

(iii) Contracting Governments of States, whether or not Members of the Organization, shall be entitled to participate in the proceedings of the Maritime Safety Committee for the consideration and adoption of amendments.

(iv) Amendments shall be adopted by a two-thirds majority of the Contracting Governments present and voting in the Maritime Safety Committee expanded as provided for in sub-paragraph (iii) of this paragraph (hereinafter referred to as 'the expanded Maritime Safety Committee') on condition that at least one-third of the Contracting Governments shall be present at the time of voting.

(v) Amendments adopted in accordance with sub-paragraph (iv) of this paragraph shall be communicated by the Secretary-General of the Organization to all Contracting Governments for acceptance.

(vi) (1) An amendment to an Article of the Convention or to Chapter I of the Annex shall be deemed to have been accepted on the date on which it is accepted by two-thirds of the Contracting Governments.

    (2) An amendment to the Annex other than Chapter I shall be deemed to have been accepted:

        (aa) At the end of two years from the date on which it is communicated to Contracting Governments for acceptance; or

        (bb) At the end of a different period, which shall not be less than one year, if so determined at the time of its adoption by a two-thirds majority of the Contracting Governments present and voting in the expanded Maritime Safety Committee.

However, if within the specified period either more than one-third of Contracting Governments, or Contracting Governments the combined merchant fleets of which constitute not less than fifty per cent of the gross tonnage of the world's merchant fleet, notify the Secretary-General of the Organization that they object to the amendment, it shall be deemed not to have been accepted.

(vii) (1) An amendment to an Article of the Convention or to Chapter I of the Annex shall enter into force with respect to those Contracting Governments which have accepted it, six months after the date on which it is deemed to have been accepted, and with respect to each Contracting Government which accepts it after that date, six months after the date of that Contracting Government's acceptance.

    (2) An amendment to the Annex other than Chapter I shall enter into force with respect to all Contracting Governments, except those which have objected to the amendment under sub-paragraph (vi)(2) of this paragraph and which have not withdrawn such objections, six months after the date on which it is deemed to have been accepted. However, before the date set for entry into force, any Contracting Government may give notice to the Secretary-General of the Organization that it exempts itself from giving effect to that amendment for a period not longer than one year from the date of its entry into force, or for such longer period as may be determined by a two-thirds majority of the Contracting Governments present and voting in the expanded Maritime Safety Committee at the time of the adoption of the amendment.

(c) Amendment by a Conference:

(i) Upon the request of a Contracting Government concurred in by at least one-third of the Contracting Governments, the Organization shall convene a

Conference of Contracting Governments to consider amendments to the present Convention.

(ii)   Every amendment adopted by such a Conference by a two-thirds majority of the Contracting Governments present and voting shall be communicated by the Secretary-General of the Organization to all Contracting Governments for acceptance.

(iii) Unless the Conference decides otherwise, the amendment shall be deemed to have been accepted and shall enter into force in accordance with the procedures specified in sub-paragraphs (b)(vi) and (b)(vii) respectively of this Article, provided that references in these paragraphs to the expanded Maritime Safety Committee shall be taken to mean references to the Conference.

(d) (i)   A Contracting Government which has accepted an amendment to the Annex which has entered into force shall not be obliged to extend the benefit of the present Convention in respect of the certificates issued to a ship entitled to fly the flag of a State the Government of which, pursuant to the provisions of sub-paragraph (b)(vi)(2) of this Article, has objected to the amendment and has not withdrawn such an objection, but only to the extent that such certificates relate to matters covered by the amendment in question.

(ii) A Contracting Government which has accepted an amendment to the Annex which has entered into force shall extend the benefit of the present Convention in respect of the certificates issued to a ship entitled to fly the flag of a State the Government of which, pursuant to the provisions of sub-paragraph (b)(vii)(2) of this Article, has notified the Secretary-General of the Organization that it exempts itself from giving effect to the amendment.

(e)   Unless expressly provided otherwise, any amendment to the present Convention made under this Article, which relates to the structure of a ship, shall apply only to ships the keels of which are laid or which are at a similar stage of construction, on or after the date on which the amendment enters into force.

(f)   Any declaration of acceptance of, or objection to, an amendment or any notice given under sub-paragraph (b)(vii)(2) of this Article shall be submitted in writing to the Secretary-General of the Organization, who shall inform all Contracting Governments of any such submission and the date of its receipt.

(g)   The Secretary-General of the Organization shall inform all Contracting Governments of any amendments which enter into force under this Article, together with the date on which each such amendment enters into force.

Article IX Signature, ratification, acceptance, approval and accession

(a)   The present Convention shall remain open for signature at the Headquarters of the Organization from 1 November 1974 until 1 July 1975 and shall thereafter remain open for accession. States may become Parties to the present Convention by:

(i)   Signature without reservation as to ratification, acceptance or approval; or

(ii)   Signature subject to ratification, acceptance or approval, followed by ratification, acceptance or approval; or

(iii) Accession.

(b)   Ratification, acceptance, approval or accession shall be effected by the deposit of an instrument to that effect with the Secretary-General of the Organization.

(c)   The Secretary-General of the Organization shall inform the Governments of all States which have signed the present Convention or acceded to it of any signature or of the deposit of any instrument of ratification, acceptance, approval or accession and the date of its deposit.

Article X   Entry into force

(a)   The present Convention shall enter into force twelve months after the date on which not less than twenty-five States, the combined merchant fleets of which constitute not less than fifty per cent of the gross tonnage of the world's merchant shipping, have become Parties to it in accordance with Article IX.

(b)   Any instrument of ratification, acceptance, approval or accession deposited after the date on which the present Convention enters into force shall take effect three months after the date of deposit.

(c)   After the date on which an amendment to the present Convention is deemed to have been accepted under Article VIII, any instrument of ratification, acceptance, approval or accession deposited shall apply to the Convention as amended.

Article XI   Denunciation

(a)   The present Convention may be denounced by any Contracting Government at any time after the expiry of five years from the date on which the Convention enters into force for that Government.

(b)   Denunciation shall be effected by the deposit of an instrument of denunciation with the Secretary-General of the Organization who shall notify all the other Contracting Governments of any instrument of denunciation received and of the date of its receipt as well as the date on which such denunciation takes effect.

(c)   A denunciation shall take effect one year, or such longer period as may be specified in the instrument of denunciation, after its receipt by the Secretary-General of the Organization.

Article XII   Deposit and registration

(a)   The present Convention shall be deposited with the Secretary-General of the Organization who shall transmit certified true copies thereof to the Governments of all States which have signed the present Convention or acceded to it.

(b)   As soon as the present Convention enters into force, the text shall be transmitted by the Secretary-General of the Organization to the Secretary-General of the United Nations for registration and publication, in accordance with Article 102 of the Charter of the United Nations.

Article XIII   Languages

The present Convention is established in a single copy in the Chinese, English, French, Russian and Spanish languages, each text being equally authentic. Official translations in the Arabic, German and Italian languages shall be prepared and deposited with the signed original.

IN WITNESS WHEREOF the undersigned, being duly authorized by their respective Governments for that purpose, have signed the present Convention.

DONE at London this first day of November one thousand nine hundred and seventy-four.

ANNEX[3]

CHAPTER I. GENERAL PROVISIONS[4]

PART A. APPLICATION, DEFINITIONS ETC

Regulation 1 Application

(a) Unless expressly provided otherwise, the present Regulations apply only to ships engaged on international voyages.

(b) The classes of ships to which each Chapter applies are more precisely defined, and the extent of the application is shown, in each Chapter.

Regulation 2 Definitions

For the purpose of the present Regulations, unless expressly provided otherwise:

(a) 'Regulations' means the Regulations contained in the Annex to the present Convention.

(b) 'Administration' means the Government of the State whose flag the ship is entitled to fly.

(c) 'Approved' means approved by the Administration.

(d) 'International voyage' means a voyage from a country to which the present Convention applies to a port outside such country, or conversely.

(e) A passenger is every person other than:

   (i) The master and the members of the crew or other persons employed or engaged in any capacity on board a ship on the business of that ship; and

   (ii) A child under one year of age.

(f) A passenger ship is a ship which carries more than twelve passengers.

(g) A cargo ship is any ship which is not a passenger ship.

(h) A tanker is a cargo ship constructed or adapted for the carriage in bulk of liquid cargoes of an inflammable nature.

(i) A fishing vessel is a vessel used for catching fish, whales, seals, walrus or other living resources of the sea.

(j) A nuclear ship is a ship provided with a nuclear power plant.

(k) 'New ship' means a ship the keel of which is laid or which is at a similar stage of construction on or after 25 May 1980.

(l) 'Existing ship' means a ship which is not a new ship.

(m) A mile is 1,852 m or 6,080 ft.

(n) Anniversary date means the day and the month of each year which will correspond to the date of expiry of the relevant certificate.

Regulation 3 Exceptions

(a) The present Regulations, unless expressly provided otherwise, do not apply to:

   (i) Ships of war and troopships.

   (ii) Cargo ships of less than 500 gross tonnage.

---

[3] The Annex includes 12 Chapters: I: General Provisions; II-1: Construction – Subdivision and Stability, Machinery and Electrical Installations; II-2: Fire Protection, Fire Detection and Fire Extinction; III: Life-Saving Appliances and Arrangements; IV: Radiocommunications; V: Safety of Navigation; VI: Carriage of Cargoes; VII: Carriage of Dangerous Goods; VIII: Nuclear Ships; IX: Management for the Safe Operation of Ships; X: Safety Measures for High-Speed Craft; XI-1: Special Measures to Enhance Maritime Safety; XI-2: Special Measures to Enhance Maritime Security; XII: Additional safety measures for bulk carriers. Only parts of Chapters I, V, VIII and XI-2 are reproduced here.

[4] Chapter I, Regulations 4, 5, 7-18 and 21 omitted.

(iii) Ships not propelled by mechanical means.

(iv) Wooden ships of primitive build.

(v) Pleasure yachts not engaged in trade.

(vi) Fishing vessels.

(b) Except as expressly provided in Chapter V, nothing herein shall apply to ships solely navigating the Great Lakes of North America and the River St Lawrence as far east as a straight line drawn from Cap des Rosiers to West Point, Anticosti Island and, on the north side of Anticosti Island, the 63rd meridian.

PART B. SURVEYS AND CERTIFICATES

Regulation 6 Inspection and survey

(a) The inspection and survey of ships, so far as regards the enforcement of the provisions of the present Regulations and the granting of exemptions therefrom, shall be carried out by officers of the Administration. The Administration may, however, entrust the inspections and surveys either to surveyors nominated for the purpose or to organizations recognized by it.

(b) An Administration nominating surveyors or recognizing organizations to conduct inspections and surveys as set forth in paragraph (a) shall as a minimum empower any nominated surveyor or recognized organization to:

(i) Require repairs to a ship;

(ii) Carry out inspections and surveys if requested by the appropriate authorities of a port State.

The Administration shall notify the Organization of the specific responsibilities and conditions of the authority delegated to nominated surveyors or recognized organizations.

(c) When a nominated surveyor or recognized organization determines that the condition of the ship or its equipment does not correspond substantially with the particulars of the certificate or is such that the ship is not fit to proceed to sea without danger to the ship, or persons on board, such surveyor or organization shall immediately ensure that corrective action is taken and shall in due course notify the Administration. If such corrective action is not taken the relevant certificate should be withdrawn and the Administration shall be notified immediately; and, if the ship is in the port of another Party, the appropriate authorities of the port State shall also be notified immediately. When an officer of the Administration, a nominated surveyor or a recognized organization has notified the appropriate authorities of the port State, the Government of the port State concerned shall give such officer, surveyor or organization any necessary assistance to carry out their obligations under this Regulation. When applicable, the Government of the port State concerned shall ensure that the ship shall not sail until it can proceed to sea, or leave port for the purpose of proceeding to the appropriate repair yard, without danger to the ship or persons on board.

(d) In every case, the Administration shall fully guarantee the completeness and efficiency of the inspection and survey, and shall undertake to ensure the necessary arrangements to satisfy this obligation.

Regulation 19 Control

(a) Every ship when in a port of another Contracting Government is subject to control by officers duly authorized by such Government in so far as this control is directed towards verifying that the certificates issued under Regulation 12 or Regulation 13 are valid.

(b)   Such certificates, if valid, shall be accepted unless there are clear grounds for believing that the condition of the ship or of its equipment does not correspond substantially with the particulars of any of the certificates or that the ship and its equipment are not in compliance with the provisions of Regulation 11(a) and (b).

(c)   In the circumstances given in paragraph (b) or where a certificate has expired or ceased to be valid, the officer carrying out the control shall take steps to ensure that the ship shall not sail until it can proceed to sea or leave the port for the purpose of proceeding to the appropriate repair yard without danger to the ship or persons on board.

(d)   In the event of this control giving rise to an intervention of any kind, the officer carrying out the control shall forthwith inform, in writing, the Consul or, in his absence, the nearest diplomatic representative of the State whose flag the ship is entitled to fly of all the circumstances in which intervention was deemed necessary. In addition, nominated surveyors or recognized organizations responsible for the issue of the certificates shall also be notified. The facts concerning the intervention shall be reported to the Organization.

(e)   The port State authority concerned shall notify all relevant information about the ship to the authorities of the next port of call, in addition to parties mentioned in paragraph (d), if it is unable to take action as specified in paragraphs (c) and (d) or if the ship has been allowed to proceed to the next port of call.

(f)   When exercising control under this Regulation all possible efforts shall be made to avoid a ship being unduly detained or delayed. If a ship is thereby unduly detained or delayed it shall be entitled to compensation for any loss or damage suffered.

Regulation 20 Privileges

The privileges of the present Convention may not be claimed in favour of any ship unless it holds appropriate valid certificates.

CHAPTER V. SAFETY OF NAVIGATION[5]

Regulation 1 Application

(a)   Unless expressly provided otherwise, this Chapter shall apply to all ships on all voyages, except:

    (i)   Warships, naval auxiliaries and other ships owned or operated by a Contracting Government and used only on Government non-commercial service; and

    (ii)   Ships solely navigating the Great Lakes of North America and their connecting and tributary waters as far east as the lower exit of the St. Lambert Lock at Montreal in the Province of Quebec, Canada.

However, warships, naval auxiliaries or other ships owned or operated by a Contracting Government and used only on Government non-commercial service are encouraged to act in a manner consistent, so far as reasonable and practicable, with this Chapter.

(b)   The Administration may decide to what extent this Chapter shall apply to ships operating solely in waters landward of the baselines which are established in accordance with international law.

(c)   A rigidly connected composite unit of a pushing vessel and associated pushed vessel, when designed as a dedicated and integrated tug and barge combination, shall be regarded as a single ship for the purpose of this chapter.

(d)   The Administration shall determine to what extent the provisions of Regulations 15, 16, 17, 18, 19, 20, 21, 22, 23, 24, 25, 26, 27 and 28 do not apply to the following categories of ships:

    (i)   Ships below 150 gross tonnage engaged on any voyage;

---

[5] Chapter V, Regulations 14 to 32 and 34 to 35 omitted.

(ii)   Ships below 500 gross tonnage not engaged on international voyages; and

(iii) Fishing vessels.

Regulation 2 Definitions

For the purpose of this Chapter:

(a)   'Constructed' in respect of a ship means a stage of construction where:

(i)   The keel is laid; or

(ii)   Construction identifiable with a specific ship begins; or

(iii) Assembly of the ship has commenced comprising at least 50 tonnes or 1% of the estimated mass of all structural material, whichever is less.

(b)   'Nautical chart or nautical publication' is a special-purpose map or book, or a specially compiled database from which such a map or book is derived, that is issued officially by or on the authority of a Government, authorized Hydrographic Office or other relevant government institution and is designed to meet the requirements of marine navigation.

(c)   'All ships' means any ship, vessel or craft irrespective of type and purpose.

(d)   'Length' of a ship means its length overall.

(e)   'Search and rescue service'. The performance of distress monitoring, communication, co-ordination and search and rescue functions, including provision of medical advice, initial medical assistance, or medical evacuation, through the use of public and private resources including co-operating aircraft, ships, vessels and other craft and installations.

(f)   'High-speed craft' means a craft as defined in Regulation X/1(c).

(g)   'Mobile offshore drilling unit' means a mobile offshore drilling unit as defined in Regulation XI-2/1(a)(v).

Regulation 3 Exemptions and equivalents

(a)   The Administration may grant general exemptions from the requirements of Regulations 15, 17, 18, 19 (except 19(2)(a)(vii)), 20, 22, 24, 25, 26, 27 and 28 to ships without mechanical means of propulsion.

(b)   The Administration may grant to individual ships exemptions or equivalents of a partial or conditional nature, when any such ship is engaged on a voyage where the maximum distance of the ship from the shore, the length and nature of the voyage, the absence of general navigational hazards, and other conditions affecting safety are such as to render the full application of this Chapter unreasonable or unnecessary, provided that the Administration has taken into account the effect such exemptions and equivalents may have upon the safety of all other ships.

(c)   Each Administration shall submit to the Organization, as soon as possible after 1 January in each year, a report summarizing all new exemptions and equivalents granted under paragraph (b) of this Regulation during the previous calendar year and giving the reasons for granting such exemptions and equivalents. The Organization shall circulate such particulars to other Contracting Governments for information.

Regulation 4 Navigational warnings

Each Contracting Government shall take all steps necessary to ensure that, when intelligence of any dangers is received from whatever reliable source, it shall be promptly brought to the knowledge of those concerned and communicated to other interested Governments.

Regulation 5 Meteorological services and warnings

(a)   Contracting Governments undertake to encourage the collection of meteorological data by ships at sea and to arrange for their examination, dissemination and exchange in the manner most suitable for the purpose of aiding navigation. Administrations shall encourage the use of meteorological instruments of a high degree of accuracy and shall facilitate the checking of such instruments upon request. Arrangements may be made by appropriate national meteorological services for this checking to be undertaken, free of charge to the ship.

(b)   In particular, Contracting Governments undertake to carry out, in co-operation, the following meteorological arrangements:

(i)   To warn ships of gales, storms and tropical cyclones by the issue of information in text and, as far as practicable, graphic form, using the appropriate shore-based facilities for terrestrial and space radiocommunication services;

(ii)   To issue, at least twice daily, by terrestrial and space radiocommunication services, as appropriate, weather information suitable for shipping containing data, analyses, warnings and forecasts of weather, waves and ice. Such information shall be transmitted in text and, as far as practicable, graphic form, including meteorological analysis and prognosis charts transmitted by facsimile or in digital form for reconstitution on board the ship's data processing system;

(iii) To prepare and issue such publications as may be necessary for the efficient conduct of meteorological work at sea and to arrange, if practicable, for the publication and making available of daily weather charts for the information of departing ships;

(iv)   To arrange for a selection of ships to be equipped with tested marine meteorological instruments (such as a barometer, a barograph, a psychrometer and suitable apparatus for measuring sea temperature) for use in this service, and to take, record and transmit meteorological observations at the main standard times for surface synoptic observations (i.e. at least four times daily, whenever circumstances permit) and to encourage other ships to take, record and transmit observations in a modified form, particularly when in areas where shipping is sparse;

(v)   To encourage companies to involve as many of their ships as practicable in the making and recording of weather observations; these observations to be transmitted using the ship's terrestrial or space radiocommunication facilities for the benefit of the various national meteorological services;

(vi)   The transmission of these weather observations is free of charge to the ships concerned;

(vii) When in the vicinity of a tropical cyclone, or of a suspected tropical cyclone, ships should be encouraged to take and transmit their observations at more frequent intervals whenever practicable, bearing in mind navigational preoccupations of ships' officers during storm conditions;

(viii) To arrange for the reception and transmission of weather messages from and to ships, using the appropriate shore-based facilities for terrestrial and space radiocommunication services;

(ix)   To encourage masters to inform ships in the vicinity and also shore stations whenever they experience a wind speed of 50 knots or more (force 10 on the Beaufort scale);

(x)   To endeavour to obtain a uniform procedure in regard to the international meteorological services already specified, and as far as practicable, to conform to the technical regulations and recommendations made by the World Meteorological Organization, to which Contracting Governments may refer, for study and advice, any meteorological question which may arise in carrying out the present Convention.

(c)   The information provided for in this Regulation shall be furnished in a form for transmission and be transmitted in the order of priority prescribed by the Radio Regulations. During transmission 'to all stations' of meteorological information, forecasts and warnings, all ship stations must conform to the provisions of the Radio Regulations.

(d)   Forecasts, warnings, synoptic and other meteorological data intended for ships shall be issued and disseminated by the national meteorological service in the best position to serve various coastal and high seas areas, in accordance with mutual arrangements made by Contracting Governments, in particular as defined by the World Meteorological Organization's system for the preparation and dissemination of meteorological forecasts and warnings for the high seas under the global maritime distress and safety system (GMDSS).

Regulation 6 Ice Patrol Service

(a)   The Ice Patrol contributes to safety of life at sea, safety and efficiency of navigation and protection of the marine environment in the North Atlantic. Ships transiting the region of icebergs guarded by the Ice Patrol during the ice season are required to make use of the services provided by the Ice Patrol.

(b)   The Contracting Governments undertake to continue an ice patrol and a service for study and observation of ice conditions in the North Atlantic. During the whole of the ice season, i.e., for the period from 15 February through 1 July of each year, the south-eastern, southern and south-western limits of the region of icebergs in the vicinity of the Grand Banks of Newfoundland shall be guarded for the purpose of informing passing ships of the extent of this dangerous region; for the study of ice conditions in general; and for the purpose of affording assistance to ships and crews requiring aid within the limits of operation of the patrol ships and aircraft. During the rest of the year the study and observation of ice conditions shall be maintained as advisable.

(c)   Ships and aircraft used for the Ice Patrol Service and the study and observation of ice conditions may be assigned other duties provided that such other duties do not interfere with the primary purpose or increase the cost of this service.

(d)   The Government of the United States of America agrees to continue the overall management of the Ice Patrol Service and the study and observation of ice conditions, including the dissemination of information therefrom.

(e)   The terms and conditions governing the management, operation and financing of the Ice Patrol are set forth in the Rules for the management, operation and financing of the North Atlantic Ice Patrol appended[6] to this Chapter, which shall form an integral part of this Chapter.

(f)   If, at any time, the United States and/or Canadian Governments should desire to discontinue providing these services, it may do so and the Contracting Governments shall settle the question of continuing these services in accordance with their mutual interests. The United States and/or Canadian Governments shall provide 18 months' written notice to all Contracting Governments whose ships entitled to fly their flag and whose ships are registered in territories to which those Contracting Governments have extended this regulation benefit from these services before discontinuing providing these services.

Regulation 7 Search and rescue services

(a)   Each Contracting Government undertakes to ensure that necessary arrangements are made for distress communication and co-ordination in their area of responsibility and for the rescue of persons in distress at sea around its coasts. These arrangements shall include the establishment, operation and maintenance of such search and rescue facilities

---

[6] Appendix omitted.

as are deemed practicable and necessary, having regard to the density of the seagoing traffic and the navigational dangers, and shall, so far as possible, provide adequate means of locating and rescuing such persons.

(b)   Each Contracting Government undertakes to make available information to the Organization concerning its existing search and rescue facilities and the plans for changes therein, if any.

(c)   Passenger ships to which Chapter I applies shall have on board a plan for co-operation with appropriate search and rescue services in the event of an emergency. The plan shall be developed in co-operation between the ship, the company, as defined in Regulation IX/1, and the search and rescue services. The plan shall include provisions for periodic exercises to be undertaken to test its effectiveness. The plan shall be developed based on the guidelines developed by the Organization.

Regulation 8 Life-saving signals

Contracting Governments undertake to arrange that life-saving signals are used by search and rescue facilities engaged in search and rescue operations when communicating with ships or persons in distress.

Regulation 9 Hydrographic services

(a)   Contracting Governments undertake to arrange for the collection and compilation of hydrographic data and the publication, dissemination and keeping up to date of all nautical information necessary for safe navigation.

(b)   In particular, Contracting Governments undertake to co-operate in carrying out, as far as possible, the following nautical and hydrographic services, in the manner most suitable for the purpose of aiding navigation:

(i)   To ensure that hydrographic surveying is carried out, as far as possible, adequate to the requirements of safe navigation;

(ii)   To prepare and issue nautical charts, sailing directions, lists of lights, tide tables and other nautical publications, where applicable, satisfying the needs of safe navigation;

(iii)   To promulgate notices to mariners in order that nautical charts and publications are kept, as far as possible, up to date; and

(iv)   To provide data management arrangements to support these services.

(c)   Contracting Governments undertake to ensure the greatest possible uniformity in charts and nautical publications and to take into account, whenever possible, relevant international resolutions and recommendations.

(d)   Contracting Governments undertake to co-ordinate their activities to the greatest possible degree in order to ensure that hydrographic and nautical information is made available on a world-wide scale as timely, reliably, and unambiguously as possible.

Regulation 10 Ships' routeing

(a)   Ships' routeing systems contribute to safety of life at sea, safety and efficiency of navigation and/or protection of the marine environment. Ships' routeing systems are recommended for use by, and may be made mandatory for, all ships, certain categories of ships or ships carrying certain cargoes, when adopted and implemented in accordance with the guidelines and criteria developed by the Organization.

(b)   The Organization is recognized as the only international body for developing guidelines, criteria and regulations on an international level for ships' routeing systems. Contracting Governments shall refer proposals for the adoption of ships' routeing systems to the Organization. The Organization will collate and disseminate to Contracting Governments all relevant information with regard to any adopted ships' routeing systems.

(c)   The initiation of action for establishing a ships' routeing system is the responsibility of the Government or Governments concerned. In developing such systems for adoption by the Organization, the guidelines and criteria developed by the Organization shall be taken into account.

(d)   Ships' routeing systems should be submitted to the Organization for adoption. However, a Government or Governments implementing ships' routeing systems not intended to be submitted to the Organization for adoption or which have not been adopted by the Organization are encouraged to take into account, wherever possible, the guidelines and criteria developed by the Organization.

(e)   Where two or more Governments have a common interest in a particular area, they should formulate joint proposals for the delineation and use of a routeing system therein on the basis of an agreement between them. Upon receipt of such proposal and before proceeding with consideration of it for adoption, the Organization shall ensure that details of the proposal are disseminated to the Governments which have a common interest in the area, including countries in the vicinity of the proposed ships' routeing system.

(f)   Contracting Governments shall adhere to the measures adopted by the Organization concerning ships' routeing. They shall promulgate all information necessary for the safe and effective use of adopted ships' routeing systems. A Government or Governments concerned may monitor traffic in those systems. Contracting Governments shall do everything in their power to secure the appropriate use of ships' routeing systems adopted by the Organization.

(g)   A ship shall use a mandatory ships' routeing system adopted by the Organization as required for its category or cargo carried and in accordance with the relevant provisions in force unless there are compelling reasons not to use a particular ships' routeing system. Any such reason shall be recorded in the ships' log.

(h)   Mandatory ships' routeing systems shall be reviewed by the Contracting Government or Governments concerned in accordance with the guidelines and criteria developed by the Organization.

(i)   All adopted ships' routeing systems and actions taken to enforce compliance with those systems shall be consistent with international law, including the relevant provisions of the 1982 United Nations Convention on the Law of the Sea.

(j)   Nothing in this Regulation nor its associated guidelines and criteria shall prejudice the rights and duties of Governments under international law or the legal regimes of straits used for international navigation and archipelagic sea lanes.

Regulation 11 Ship reporting systems

(a)   Ship reporting systems contribute to safety of life at sea, safety and efficiency of navigation and/or protection of the marine environment. A ship reporting system, when adopted and implemented in accordance with the guidelines and criteria developed by the Organization pursuant to this regulation, shall be used by all ships or certain categories of ships or ships carrying certain cargoes in accordance with the provisions of each system so adopted.

(b)   The Organization is recognized as the only international body for developing guidelines, criteria and regulations on an international level for ship reporting systems. Contracting Government shall refer proposals for the adoption of ship reporting systems to the Organization. The Organization will collate and disseminate to Contracting Governments all relevant information with regard to any adopted ship reporting system.

(c)   The initiation of action for establishing a ship reporting system is the responsibility of the Government or Governments concerned. In developing such systems, provision of the guidelines and criteria developed by the Organization shall be taken into account.

(d)   Ship reporting systems not submitted to the Organization for adoption do not necessarily need to comply with this Regulation. However, Governments implementing such systems are encouraged to follow, wherever possible, the guidelines and criteria developed by the Organization. Contracting Governments may submit such systems to the Organization for recognition.

(e)   Where two or more Governments have a common interest in a particular area, they should formulate proposals for a co-ordinated ship reporting system on the basis of agreement between them. Before proceeding with a proposal for adoption of a ship reporting system, the Organization shall disseminate details of the proposal to those Governments which have a common interest in the area covered by the proposed system. Where a co-ordinated ship reporting system is adopted and established, it shall have uniform procedures and operations.

(f)   After adoption of a ship reporting system in accordance with this Regulation, the Government or Governments concerned shall take all measures necessary for the promulgation of any information needed for the efficient and effective use of the system. Any adopted ship reporting system shall have the capability of interaction and the ability to assist ships with information when necessary. Such systems shall be operated in accordance with the guidelines and criteria developed by the Organization pursuant to this Regulation.

(g)   The master of a ship shall comply with the requirements of adopted ship reporting systems and report to the appropriate authority all information required in accordance with the provisions of each such system.

(h)   All adopted ship reporting systems and actions taken to enforce compliance with those systems shall be consistent with international law, including the relevant provisions of the United Nations Convention on the Law of the Sea.

(i)   Nothing in this Regulation or its associated guidelines and criteria shall prejudice the rights and duties of Governments under international law or the legal regimes of straits used for international navigation and archipelagic sea lanes.

(j)   The participation of ships in accordance with the provisions of adopted ship reporting systems shall be free of charge to the ships concerned.

(k)   The Organization shall ensure that adopted ship reporting systems are reviewed under the guidelines and criteria developed by the Organization.

Regulation 12 Vessel traffic services

(a)   Vessel traffic services (VTS) contribute to safety of life at sea, safety and efficiency of navigation and protection of the marine environment, adjacent shore areas, work sites and offshore installations from possible adverse effects of maritime traffic.

(b)   Contracting Governments undertake to arrange for the establishment of VTS where, in their opinion, the volume of traffic or the degree of risk justifies such services.

(c)   Contracting Governments planning and implementing VTS shall, wherever possible, follow the guidelines developed by the Organization. The use of VTS may only be made mandatory in sea areas within the territorial seas of a coastal State.

(d)   Contracting Governments shall endeavour to secure the participation in, and compliance with, the provisions of vessel traffic services by ships entitled to fly their flag.

(e)   Nothing in this Regulation or the guidelines adopted by the Organization shall prejudice the rights and duties of Governments under international law or the legal regimes of straits used for international navigation and archipelagic sea lanes.

Regulation 13 Establishment and operation of aids to navigation

(a)   Each Contracting Government undertakes to provide, as it deems practical and necessary, either individually or in co-operation with other Contracting Governments, such aids to navigation as the volume of traffic justifies and the degree of risk requires.

(b)   In order to obtain the greatest possible uniformity in aids to navigation, Contracting Governments undertake to take into account the international recommendations and guidelines when establishing such aids.

(c)   Contracting Governments undertake to arrange for information relating to aids to navigation to be made available to all concerned. Changes in the transmissions of position-fixing systems which could adversely affect the performance of receivers fitted in ships shall be avoided as far as possible and only be effected after timely and adequate notice has been promulgated.

Regulation 33 Distress situations: obligations and procedures

(a)   The master of a ship at sea which is in a position to be able to provide assistance, on receiving information from any source that persons are in distress at sea, is bound to proceed with all speed to their assistance, if possible informing them or the search and rescue service that the ship is doing so. This obligation to provide assistance applies regardless of the nationality or status of such persons or the circumstances in which they are found. If the ship receiving the distress alert is unable or, in the special circumstances of the case, considers it unreasonable or unnecessary to proceed to their assistance, the master must enter in the log-book the reason for failing to proceed to the assistance of the persons in distress, taking into account the recommendation of the Organization to inform the appropriate search and rescue service accordingly.

Contracting Governments shall co-ordinate and co-operate to ensure that masters of ships providing assistance by embarking persons in distress at sea are released from their obligations with minimum further deviation from the ships' intended voyage, provided that releasing the master of the ship from the obligations under the current regulation does not further endanger the safety of life at sea. The Contracting Government responsible for the search and rescue region in which such assistance is rendered shall exercise primary responsibility for ensuring such co-ordination and co-operation occurs, so that survivors assisted are disembarked from the assisting ship and delivered to a place of safety, taking into account the particular circumstances of the case and guidelines developed by the Organization. In these cases the relevant Contracting Governments shall arrange for such disembarkation to be effected as soon as reasonably practicable.

(b)   The master of a ship in distress or the search and rescue service concerned, after consultation, so far as may be possible, with the masters of ships which answer the distress alert, has the right to requisition one or more of those ships as the master of the ship in distress or the search and rescue service considers best able to render assistance, and it shall be the duty of the master or masters of the ship or ships requisitioned to comply with the requisition by continuing to proceed with all speed to the assistance of persons in distress.

(c)   Masters of ships shall be released from the obligation imposed by paragraph (a) on learning that their ships have not been requisitioned and that one or more other ships have been requisitioned and are complying with the requisition. This decision shall, if possible, be communicated to the other requisitioned ships and to the search and rescue service.

(d)   The master of a ship shall be released from the obligation imposed by paragraph (a) and, if his ship has been requisitioned, from the obligation imposed by paragraph (b) on being informed by the persons in distress or by the search and rescue service or by the master of another ship which has reached such persons that assistance is no longer necessary.

(e)   The provisions of this Regulation do not prejudice the Convention for the Unification of Certain Rules of Law relating to Assistance and Salvage at Sea, signed at Brussels on 23 September 1910, particularly the obligation to render assistance imposed by Article 11 of that Convention.

(f)   Masters of ships who have embarked persons in distress at sea shall treat them with humanity, within the capabilities and limitations of the ship.

CHAPTER VIII. NUCLEAR SHIPS[7]

Regulation 1 Application
This chapter applies to all nuclear ships except ships of war.

Regulation 2 Application of other Chapters
The Regulations contained in the other Chapters of the present Convention apply to nuclear ships except as modified by this Chapter.

Regulation 3 Exemptions
A nuclear ship shall not, in any circumstances, be exempted from compliance with any Regulations of this Convention.

Regulation 11 Special control
In addition to the control established by Regulation 19 of Chapter I, nuclear ships shall be subject to special control before entering the ports and in the ports of Contracting Governments, directed towards verifying that there is on board a valid Nuclear Ship Safety Certificate and that there are no unreasonable radiation or other hazards at sea or in port, to the crew, passengers or public, or to the waterways or food or water resources.

Regulation 12 Casualties
In the event of any accident likely to lead to an environmental hazard the master of a nuclear ship shall immediately inform the Administration. The master shall also immediately inform the competent governmental authority of the country in whose waters the ship may be, or whose waters the ship approaches in a damaged condition.

CHAPTER XI-2. SPECIAL MEASURES TO ENHANCE MARITIME SECURITY

Regulation 1 Definitions
(a)   For the purpose of this Chapter, unless expressly provided otherwise:
(i)   'Bulk carrier' means a bulk carrier as defined in Regulation IX/1(f).
(ii)   'Chemical tanker' means a chemical tanker as defined in Regulation VII/8(b).
(iii) 'Gas carrier' means a gas carrier as defined in Regulation VII/11(b).
(iv)   'High-speed craft' means a craft as defined in Regulation X/1(b).
(v)   'Mobile offshore drilling unit' means a mechanically propelled mobile offshore drilling unit, as defined in Regulation IX/1, not on location.
(vi)   'Oil tanker' means an oil tanker as defined in Regulation II-1/2(v).
(vii) 'Company' means a Company as defined in Regulation IX/1.
(viii) 'Ship/port interface' means the interactions that occur when a ship is directly and immediately affected by actions involving the movement of persons, goods or the provisions of port services to or from the ship.

---

[7] Chapter VIII, Regulations 4 to 10 omitted.

(ix) 'Port facility' is a location, as determined by the Contracting Government or by the Designated Authority, where the ship/port interface takes place. This includes areas such as anchorages, waiting berths and approaches from seaward, as appropriate.

(x) 'Ship to ship activity' means any activity not related to a port facility that involves the transfer of goods or persons from one ship to another.

(xi) 'Designated Authority' means the organization(s) or the administration(s) identified, within the Contracting Government, as responsible for ensuring the implementation of the provisions of this Chapter pertaining to port facility security and ship/port interface, from the point of view of the port facility.

(xii) 'International Ship and Port Facility Security (ISPS) Code' means the International Code for the Security of Ships and of Port Facilities consisting of Part A (the provisions of which shall be treated as mandatory) and part B (the provisions of which shall be treated as recommendatory), as adopted, on 12 December 2002, by Resolution 2 of the Conference of Contracting Governments to the International Convention for the Safety of Life at Sea, 1974 as may be amended by the Organization, provided that:

    (1) Amendments to part A of the Code are adopted, brought into force and take effect in accordance with Article VIII of the present Convention concerning the amendment procedures applicable to the Annex other than Chapter I; and

    (2) Amendments to part B of the Code are adopted by the Maritime Safety Committee in accordance with its Rules of Procedure.

(xiii) 'Security incident' means any suspicious act or circumstance threatening the security of a ship, including a mobile offshore drilling unit and a high speed craft, or of a port facility or of any ship/port interface or any ship to ship activity.

(xiv) 'Security level' means the qualification of the degree of risk that a security incident will be attempted or will occur.

(xv) 'Declaration of security' means an agreement reached between a ship and either a port facility or another ship with which it interfaces specifying the security measures each will implement.

(xvi) 'Recognized security organization' means an organization with appropriate expertise in security matters and with appropriate knowledge of ship and port operations authorized to carry out an assessment, or a verification, or an approval or a certification activity, required by this Chapter or by part A of the ISPS Code.

(b) The term 'ship', when used in Regulations 3 to 13, includes mobile offshore drilling units and high-speed craft.

(c) The term 'all ships', when used in this Chapter, means any ship to which this Chapter applies.

(d) The term 'Contracting Government', when used in Regulations 3, 4, 7, and 10 to 13 includes a reference to the 'Designated Authority'.

Regulation 2 Application

(a) This Chapter applies to:

    (i) The following types of ships engaged on international voyages:

        (1) Passenger ships, including high-speed passenger craft;

        (2) Cargo ships, including high-speed craft, of 500 gross tonnage and upwards; and

(3)   Mobile offshore drilling units; and

(ii)   Port facilities serving such ships engaged on international voyages.

(b)   Notwithstanding the provisions of paragraph (a)(ii), Contracting Governments shall decide the extent of application of this Chapter and of the relevant sections of part A of the ISPS Code to those port facilities within their territory which, although used primarily by ships not engaged on international voyages, are required, occasionally, to serve ships arriving or departing on an international voyage.

    (i)   Contracting Governments shall base their decisions, under paragraph (b), on a port facility security assessment carried out in accordance with the provisions of part A of the ISPS Code.

    (ii)   Any decision which a Contracting Government makes, under paragraph (b), shall not compromise the level of security intended to be achieved by this Chapter or by part A of the ISPS Code.

(c)   This Chapter does not apply to warships, naval auxiliaries or other ships owned or operated by a Contracting Government and used only on Government non-commercial service.

(d)   Nothing in this Chapter shall prejudice the rights or obligations of States under international law.

Regulation 3   Obligations of Contracting Governments with respect to security

(a)   Administrations shall set security levels and ensure the provision of security level information to ships entitled to fly their flag. When changes in security level occur, security level information shall be updated as the circumstance dictates.

(b)   Contracting Governments shall set security levels and ensure the provision of security level information to port facilities within their territory, and to ships prior to entering a port or whilst in a port within their territory. When changes in security level occur, security level information shall be updated as the circumstance dictates.

Regulation 4   Requirements for Companies and ships

(a)   Companies shall comply with the relevant requirements of this Chapter and of part A of the ISPS Code, taking into account the guidance given in part B of the ISPS Code.

(b)   Ships shall comply with the relevant requirements of this Chapter and of part A of the ISPS Code, taking into account the guidance given in part B of the ISPS Code, and such compliance shall be verified and certified as provided for in part A of the ISPS Code.

(c)   Prior to entering a port or whilst in a port within the territory of a Contracting Government, a ship shall comply with the requirements for the security level set by that Contracting Government, if such security level is higher than the security level set by the Administration for that ship.

(d)   Ships shall respond without undue delay to any change to a higher security level.

(e)   Where a ship is not in compliance with the requirements of this Chapter or of part A of the ISPS Code, or cannot comply with the requirements of the security level set by the Administration or by another Contracting Government and applicable to that ship, then the ship shall notify the appropriate competent authority prior to conducting any ship/port interface or prior to entry into port, whichever occurs earlier.

Regulation 5   Specific responsibility of Companies

The Company shall ensure that the master has available on board, at all times, information through which officers duly authorized by a Contracting Government can establish:

(i)   Who is responsible for appointing the members of the crew or other persons currently employed or engaged on board the ship in any capacity on the business of that ship;

(ii) Who is responsible for deciding the employment of the ship; and

(iii) In cases where the ship is employed under the terms of charter party(ies), who are the parties to such charter party(ies).

Regulation 6 Ship security alert system

(a)   All ships shall be provided with a ship security alert system, as follows:

(i)   Ships constructed on or after 1 July 2004;

(ii) Passenger ships, including high-speed passenger craft, constructed before 1 July 2004, not later than the first survey of the radio installation after 1 July 2004;

(iii) Oil tankers, chemical tankers, gas carriers, bulk carriers and cargo high speed craft, of 500 gross tonnage and upwards constructed before 1 July 2004, not later than the first survey of the radio installation after 1 July 2004; and

(iv) Other cargo ships of 500 gross tonnage and upward and mobile offshore drilling units constructed before 1 July 2004, not later than the first survey of the radio installation after 1 July 2006.

(b)   The ship security alert system, when activated, shall:

(i)   Initiate and transmit a ship-to-shore security alert to a competent authority designated by the Administration, which in these circumstances may include the Company, identifying the ship, its location and indicating that the security of the ship is under threat or it has been compromised;

(ii) Not send the ship security alert to any other ships;

(iii) Not raise any alarm on-board the ship; and

(iv) Continue the ship security alert until deactivated and/or reset.

(c)   The ship security alert system shall:

(i)   Be capable of being activated from the navigation bridge and in at least one other location; and

(ii) Conform to performance standards not inferior to those adopted by the Organization.

(d)   The ship security alert system activation points shall be designed so as to prevent the inadvertent initiation of the ship security alert.

(e)   The requirement for a ship security alert system may be complied with by using the radio installation fitted for compliance with the requirements of Chapter IV, provided all requirements of this regulation are complied with.

(f)   When an Administration receives notification of a ship security alert, that Administration shall immediately notify the State(s) in the vicinity of which the ship is presently operating.

(g)   When a Contracting Government receives notification of a ship security alert from a ship which is not entitled to fly its flag, that Contracting Government shall immediately notify the relevant Administration and, if appropriate, the State(s) in the vicinity of which the ship is presently operating.

Regulation 7 Threats to ships

(a)   Contracting Governments shall set security levels and ensure the provision of security level information to ships operating in their territorial sea or having communicated an intention to enter their territorial sea.

(b)   Contracting Governments shall provide a point of contact through which such ships can request advice or assistance and to which such ships can report any security concerns about other ships, movements or communications.

(c)   Where a risk of attack has been identified, the Contracting Government concerned shall advise the ships concerned and their Administrations of:

(i)   The current security level;

(ii)   Any security measures that should be put in place by the ships concerned to protect themselves from attack, in accordance with the provisions of part A of the ISPS Code; and

(iii)   Security measures that the coastal State has decided to put in place, as appropriate.

Regulation 8   Master's discretion for ship safety and security

(a)   The master shall not be constrained by the Company, the charterer or any other person from taking or executing any decision which, in the professional judgement of the master, is necessary to maintain the safety and security of the ship. This includes denial of access to persons (except those identified as duly authorized by a Contracting Government) or their effects and refusal to load cargo, including containers or other closed cargo transport units.

(b)   If, in the professional judgement of the master, a conflict between any safety and security requirements applicable to the ship arises during its operations, the master shall give effect to those requirements necessary to maintain the safety of the ship. In such cases, the master may implement temporary security measures and shall forthwith inform the Administration and, if appropriate, the Contracting Government in whose port the ship is operating or intends to enter. Any such temporary security measures under this Regulation shall, to the highest possible degree, be commensurate with the prevailing security level. When such cases are identified, the Administration shall ensure that such conflicts are resolved and that the possibility of recurrence is minimized.

Regulation 9   Control and compliance measures

(a)   Control of ships in port

(i)   For the purpose of this Chapter, every ship to which this Chapter applies is subject to control when in a port of another Contracting Government by officers duly authorized by that Government, who may be the same as those carrying out the functions of Regulation I/19. Such control shall be limited to verifying that there is onboard a valid International Ship Security Certificate or a valid Interim International Ships Security Certificate issued under the provisions of part A of the ISPS Code (Certificate), which if valid shall be accepted, unless there are clear grounds for believing that the ship is not in compliance with the requirements of this Chapter or part A of the ISPS Code.

(ii)   When there are such clear grounds, or where no valid Certificate is produced when required, the officers duly authorized by the Contracting Government shall impose any one or more control measures in relation to that ship as provided in paragraph (a)(iii). Any such measures imposed must be proportionate, taking into account the guidance given in part B of the ISPS Code.

(iii)   Such control measures are as follows: inspection of the ship, delaying the ship, detention of the ship, restriction of operations including movement within the port, or expulsion of the ship from port. Such control measures may additionally or alternatively include other lesser administrative or corrective measures.

(b)   Ships intending to enter a port of another Contracting Government

(i)   For the purpose of this Chapter, a Contracting Government may require that ships intending to enter its ports provide the following information to officers duly authorized by that Government to ensure compliance with this Chapter prior to entry into port with the aim of avoiding the need to impose control measures or steps:

    (1)   That the ship possesses a valid Certificate and the name of its issuing authority;

    (2)   The security level at which the ship is currently operating;

    (3)   The security level at which the ship operated in any previous port where it has conducted a ship/port interface within the time frame specified in paragraph (b)(iii);

    (4)   Any special or additional security measures that were taken by the ship in any previous port where it has conducted a ship/port interface within the time frame specified in paragraph (b)(iii);

    (5)   That the appropriate ship security procedures were maintained during any ship to ship activity within the time frame specified in paragraph (b)(iii); or

    (6)   Other practical security related information (but not details of the ship security plan), taking into account the guidance given in part B of the ISPS Code. If requested by the Contracting Government, the ship or the Company shall provide confirmation, acceptable to that Contracting Government, of the information required above.

(ii)   Every ship to which this Chapter applies intending to enter the port of another Contracting Government shall provide the information described in paragraph (b)(i) on the request of the officers duly authorized by that Government. The master may decline to provide such information on the understanding that failure to do so may result in denial of entry into port.

(iii)   The ship shall keep records of the information referred to in paragraph (b)(i) for the last 10 calls at port facilities.

(iv)   If, after receipt of the information described in paragraph (b)(i), officers duly authorized by the Contracting Government of the port in which the ship intends to enter have clear grounds for believing that the ship is in non-compliance with the requirements of this Chapter or part A of the ISPS Code, such officers shall attempt to establish communication with and between the ship and the Administration in order to rectify the non-compliance. If such communication does not result in rectification, or if such officers have clear grounds otherwise for believing that the ship is in non-compliance with the requirements of this Chapter or part A of the ISPS Code, such officers may take steps in relation to that ship as provided in paragraph (b)(v). Any such steps taken must be proportionate, taking into account the guidance given in part B of the ISPS Code.

(v)   Such steps are as follows:

    (1)   A requirement for the rectification of the non-compliance;

    (2)   A requirement that the ship proceed to a location specified in the territorial sea or internal waters of that Contracting Government;

    (3)   Inspection of the ship, if the ship is in the territorial sea of the Contracting Government the port of which the ship intends to enter; or

    (4)   Denial of entry into port. Prior to initiating any such steps, the ship shall be informed by the Contracting Government of its intentions. Upon this information the master may withdraw the intention to enter that port. In such cases, this Regulation shall not apply.

(c)   Additional provisions

(i)   In the event:

    (1)   Of the imposition of a control measure, other than a lesser administrative or corrective measure, referred to in paragraph (a)(iii); or

    (2)   Any of the steps referred to in paragraph (b)(v) are taken, an officer duly authorized by the Contracting Government shall forthwith inform in writing the Administration specifying which control measures have been imposed or steps taken and the reasons thereof. The Contracting Government imposing the control measures or steps shall also notify the recognized security organization, which issued the Certificate relating to the ship concerned and the Organization when any such control measures have been imposed or steps taken.

(ii)   When entry into port is denied or the ship is expelled from port, the authorities of the port State should communicate the appropriate facts to the authorities of the State of the next appropriate ports of call, when known, and any other appropriate coastal States, taking into account guidelines to be developed by the Organization. Confidentiality and security of such notification shall be ensured.

(iii)   Denial of entry into port, pursuant to paragraphs (b)(iv) and (b)(v), or expulsion from port, pursuant to paragraphs (a)(i) to (a)(iii), shall only be imposed where the officers duly authorized by the Contracting Government have clear grounds to believe that the ship poses an immediate threat to the security or safety of persons, or of ships or other property and there are no other appropriate means for removing that threat.

(iv)   The control measures referred to in paragraph (a)(iii) and the steps referred to in paragraph (b)(v) shall only be imposed, pursuant to this Regulation, until the non-compliance giving rise to the control measures or steps has been corrected to the satisfaction of the Contracting Government, taking into account actions proposed by the ship or the Administration, if any.

(v)   When Contracting Governments exercise control under paragraph (a) or take steps under paragraph (b):

    (1)   All possible efforts shall be made to avoid a ship being unduly detained or delayed. If a ship is thereby unduly detained, or delayed, it shall be entitled to compensation for any loss or damage suffered; and

    (2)   Necessary access to the ship shall not be prevented for emergency or humanitarian reasons and for security purposes.

Regulation 10   Requirements for port facilities

(a)   Port facilities shall comply with the relevant requirements of this Chapter and part A of the ISPS Code, taking into account the guidance given in part B of the ISPS Code.

(b)   Contracting Governments with a port facility or port facilities within their territory, to which this Regulation applies, shall ensure that:

(i)   Port facility security assessments are carried out, reviewed and approved in accordance with the provisions of part A of the ISPS Code; and Appendix 1

(ii)   Port facility security plans are developed, reviewed, approved and implemented in accordance with the provisions of part A of the ISPS Code 3 Contracting Governments shall designate and communicate the measures required to be addressed in a port facility security plan for the various security levels, including when the submission of a Declaration of Security will be required.

Regulation 11 Alternative security agreements

(a)   Contracting Governments may, when implementing this Chapter and part A of the ISPS Code, conclude in writing bilateral or multilateral agreements with other Contracting Governments on alternative security arrangements covering short international voyages on fixed routes between port facilities located within their territories.

(b)   Any such agreement shall not compromise the level of security of other ships or of port facilities not covered by the agreement.

(c)   No ship covered by such an agreement shall conduct any ship-to-ship activities with any ship not covered by the agreement.

(d)   Such agreements shall be reviewed periodically, taking into account the experience gained as well as any changes in the particular circumstances or the assessed threats to the security of the ships, the port facilities or the routes covered by the agreement.

Regulation 12 Equivalent security arrangements

(a)   An Administration may allow a particular ship or a group of ships entitled to fly its flag to implement other security measures equivalent to those prescribed in this Chapter or in part A of the ISPS Code, provided such security measures are at least as effective as those prescribed in this Chapter or part A of the ISPS Code. The Administration, which allows such security measures, shall communicate to the Organization particulars thereof.

(b)   When implementing this Chapter and part A of the ISPS Code, a Contracting Government may allow a particular port facility or a group of port facilities located within its territory, other than those covered by an agreement concluded under Regulation 11, to implement security measures equivalent to those prescribed in this Chapter or in Part A of the ISPS Code, provided such security measures are at least as effective as those prescribed in this Chapter or part A of the ISPS Code. The Contracting Government, which allows such security measures, shall communicate to the Organization particulars thereof.

Regulation 13 Communication of information

(a)   Contracting Governments shall, not later than 1 July 2004, communicate to the Organization and shall make available for the information of Companies and ships:

(i)   The names and contact details of their national authority or authorities responsible for ship and port facility security;

(ii)   The locations within their territory covered by the approved port facility security plans;

(iii) The names and contact details of those who have been designated to be available at all times to receive and act upon the ship-to-shore security alerts, referred to in Regulation 6(b)(i);

(iv)   The names and contact details of those who have been designated to be available at all times to receive and act upon any communications from Contracting Governments exercising control and compliance measures, referred to in Regulation 9(c)(i); and

(v)   The names and contact details of those who have been designated to be available at all times to provide advice or assistance to ships and to whom ships can report any security concerns, referred to in Regulation 7(b); and thereafter update such information as and when changes relating thereto occur. The Organization shall circulate such particulars to other Contracting Governments for the information of their officers.

(b)   Contracting Governments shall, not later than 1 July 2004, communicate to the Organization the names and contact details of any recognized security organizations authorized to act on their behalf together with details of the specific responsibility and conditions of authority delegated to such organizations. Such information shall be updated as and when changes relating thereto occur. The Organization shall circulate such particulars to other Contracting Governments for the information of their officers.

(c)   Contracting Governments shall, not later than 1 July 2004 communicate to the Organization a list showing the approved port facility security plans for the port facilities located within their territory together with the location or locations covered by each approved port facility security plan and the corresponding date of approval and thereafter shall further communicate when any of the following changes take place:

(i)   Changes in the location or locations covered by an approved port facility security plan are to be introduced or have been introduced. In such cases the information to be communicated shall indicate the changes in the location or locations covered by the plan and the date as of which such changes are to be introduced or were implemented;

(ii)   An approved port facility security plan, previously included in the list submitted to the Organization, is to be withdrawn or has been withdrawn. In such cases, the information to be communicated shall indicate the date on which the withdrawal will take effect or was implemented. In these cases, the communication shall be made to the Organization as soon as is practically possible; and

(iii)   Additions are to be made to the list of approved port facility security plans. In such cases, the information to be communicated shall indicate the location or locations covered by the plan and the date of approval.

(d)   Contracting Governments shall, at five year intervals after 1 July 2004, communicate to the Organization a revised and updated list showing all the approved port facility security plans for the port facilities located within their territory together with the location or locations covered by each approved port facility security plan and the corresponding date of approval (and the date of approval of any amendments thereto) which will supersede and replace all information communicated to the Organization, pursuant to paragraph (c), during the preceding five years.

(e)   Contracting Governments shall communicate to the Organization information that an agreement under Regulation 11 has been concluded. The information communicated shall include:

(i)   The names of the Contracting Governments which have concluded the agreement;

(ii)   The port facilities and the fixed routes covered by the agreement;

(iii)   The periodicity of review of the agreement;

(iv)   The date of entry into force of the agreement; and

(v)   Information on any consultations which have taken place with other Contracting Governments; and thereafter shall communicate, as soon as practically possible, to the Organization information when the agreement has been amended or has ended.

(f)   Any Contracting Government which allows, under the provisions of Regulation 12, any equivalent security arrangements with respect to a ship entitled to fly its flag or with respect to a port facility located within its territory, shall communicate to the Organization particulars thereof.

(g)   The Organization shall make available the information communicated under paragraph (c) to other Contracting Governments upon request.

Convention for the Protection of the Marine Environment and the Coastal Region of the Mediterranean (Barcelona Convention)

Done at Barcelona, 16 February 1976, and amended at Barcelona, 10 June 1995;
entry into force on 12 February 1978 and 9 July 2004, respectively
1102 UNTS 45 [Registration Number 16908] and (1996) 31 LOSB 65[1]

The Contracting Parties,

Conscious of the economic, social, health and cultural value of the marine environment of the Mediterranean Sea Area,

Fully aware of their responsibility to preserve and sustainably develop this common heritage for the benefit and enjoyment of present and future generations,

Recognizing the threat posed by pollution to the marine environment, its ecological equilibrium, resources and legitimate uses,

Mindful of the special hydrographic and ecological characteristics of the Mediterranean Sea Area and its particular vulnerability to pollution,

Noting that existing international conventions on the subject do not cover, in spite of the progress achieved, all aspects and sources of marine pollution and do not entirely meet the special requirements of the Mediterranean Sea Area,

Realizing fully the need for close cooperation among the States and international organizations concerned in a coordinated and comprehensive regional approach for the protection and enhancement of the marine environment in the Mediterranean Sea Area,

Fully aware that the Mediterranean Action Plan, since its adoption in 1975 and through its evolution, has contributed to the process of sustainable development in the Mediterranean region and has represented a substantive and dynamic tool for the implementation of the activities related to the Convention and its Protocols by the Contracting Parties,

Taking into account the results of the United Nations Conference on Environment and Development, held in Rio de Janeiro from 4 to 14 June 1992,

Also taking into account the Declaration of Genoa of 1985, the Charter of Nicosia of 1990, the Declaration of Cairo of 1992 on Euro-Mediterranean Cooperation on the Environment within the Mediterranean Basin, the recommendations of the Conference of Casablanca of 1993, and the Declaration of Tunis of 1994 on the Sustainable Development of the Mediterranean,

Bearing in mind the relevant provisions of the United Nations Convention on the Law of the Sea, done at Montego Bay on 10 December 1982 and signed by many Contracting Parties,

Have agreed as follows:

Article 1 Geographical coverage

1. For the purposes of this Convention, the Mediterranean Sea Area shall mean the maritime waters of the Mediterranean Sea proper, including its gulfs and seas, bounded to the west by the meridian passing through Cape Spartel lighthouse, at the entrance of the Straits of Gibraltar, and to the east by the southern limits of the Straits of the Dardanelles between Mehmetcik and Kumkale lighthouses.

---

[1] The Convention for the Protection of the Mediterranean Sea against Pollution was adopted in Barcelona on 16 February 1976 and entered into force on 12 February 1978. It was modified by amendments adopted in Barcelona on 10 June 1995. The amended Convention, renamed the Convention for the Protection of the Marine Environment and the Coastal Region of the Mediterranean, entered into force on 9 July 2004. The text of the Protocol reproduced is a consolidated version incorporating the 1995 amendment. Annex A omitted.

2. The application of the Convention may be extended to coastal areas as defined by each Contracting Party within its own territory.

3. Any Protocol to this Convention may extend the geographical coverage to which that particular Protocol applies.

Article 2 Definitions

For the purposes of this Convention:
(a) 'Pollution' means the introduction by man, directly or indirectly, of substances or energy into the marine environment, including estuaries, which results, or is likely to result, in such deleterious effects as harm to living resources and marine life, hazards to human health, hindrance to marine activities, including fishing and other legitimate uses of the sea, impairment of quality for use of seawater and reduction of amenities;
(b) 'Organization' means the body designated as responsible for carrying out secretariat functions pursuant to Article 17 of this Convention.

Article 3 General provisions

1. The Contracting Parties, when applying this Convention and its related Protocols, shall act in conformity with international law.

2. The Contracting Parties may enter into bilateral or multilateral agreements, including regional or sub-regional agreements for the promotion of sustainable development, the protection of the environment, the conservation and preservation of natural resources in the Mediterranean Sea Area, provided that such agreements are consistent with this Convention and the Protocols and conform to international law. Copies of such agreements shall be communicated to the Organization. As appropriate, Contracting Parties should make use of existing organizations, agreements or arrangements in the Mediterranean Sea Area.

3. Nothing in this Convention and its Protocols shall prejudice the rights and positions of any State concerning the United Nations Convention on the Law of the Sea of 1982.

4. The Contracting Parties shall take individual or joint initiatives compatible with international law through the relevant international organizations to encourage the implementation of the provisions of this Convention and its Protocols by all the non-party States.

5. Nothing in this Convention and its Protocols shall affect the sovereign immunity of warships or other ships owned or operated by a State while engaged in government non-commercial service. However, each Contracting Party shall ensure that its vessels and aircraft, entitled to sovereign immunity under international law, act in a manner consistent with this Protocol.

Article 4 General obligations

1. The Contracting Parties shall individually or jointly take all appropriate measures in accordance with the provisions of this Convention and those Protocols in force to which they are party to prevent, abate, combat and to the fullest possible extent eliminate pollution of the Mediterranean Sea Area and to protect and enhance the marine environment in that Area so as to contribute towards its sustainable development.

2. The Contracting Parties pledge themselves to take appropriate measures to implement the Mediterranean Action Plan and, further, to pursue the protection of the marine environment and the natural resources of the Mediterranean Sea Area as an integral part of the development process, meeting the needs of present and future generations

in an equitable manner. For the purpose of implementing the objectives of sustainable development the Contracting Parties shall take fully into account the recommendations of the Mediterranean Commission on Sustainable Development established within the framework of the Mediterranean Action Plan.

3. In order to protect the environment and contribute to the sustainable development of the Mediterranean Sea Area, the Contracting Parties shall:

(a) apply, in accordance with their capabilities, the precautionary principle, by virtue of which where there are threats of serious or irreversible damage, lack of full scientific certainty shall not be used as a reason for postponing cost-effective measures to prevent environmental degradation;

(b) apply the polluter pays principle, by virtue of which the costs of pollution prevention, control and reduction measures are to be borne by the polluter, with due regard to the public interest;

(c) undertake environmental impact assessment for proposed activities that are likely to cause a significant adverse impact on the marine environment and are subject to an authorization by competent national authorities;

(d) promote cooperation between and among States in environmental impact assessment procedures related to activities under their jurisdiction or control which are likely to have a significant adverse effect on the marine environment of other States or areas beyond the limits of national jurisdiction, on the basis of notification, exchange of information and consultation;

(e) commit themselves to promote the integrated management of the coastal zones, taking into account the protection of areas of ecological and landscape interest and the rational use of natural resources.

4. In implementing the Convention and the related Protocols, the Contracting Parties shall:

(a) adopt programmes and measures which contain, where appropriate, time limits for their completion;

(b) utilize the best available techniques and the best environmental practices and promote the application of, access to and transfer of environmentally sound technology, including clean production technologies, taking into account the social, economic and technological conditions.

5. The Contracting Parties shall cooperate in the formulation and adoption of Protocols, prescribing agreed measures, procedures and standards for the implementation of this Convention.

6. The Contracting Parties further pledge themselves to promote, within the international bodies considered to be competent by the Contracting Parties, measures concerning the implementation of programmes of sustainable development, the protection, conservation and rehabilitation of the environment and of the natural resources in the Mediterranean Sea Area.

Article 5 Pollution caused by dumping from ships and aircraft or incineration at sea

The Contracting Parties shall take all appropriate measures to prevent, abate and to the fullest possible extent eliminate pollution of the Mediterranean Sea Area caused by dumping from ships and aircraft or incineration at sea.

Article 6 Pollution from ships

The Contracting Parties shall take all measures in conformity with international law to prevent, abate, combat and to the fullest possible extent eliminate pollution of the Mediterranean Sea Area caused by discharges from ships and to ensure the effective implementation in that Area of the rules which are generally recognized at the international level relating to the control of this type of pollution.

Article 7 Pollution resulting from exploration and exploitation of the continental shelf and the seabed and its subsoil

The Contracting Parties shall take all appropriate measures to prevent, abate, combat and to the fullest possible extent eliminate pollution of the Mediterranean Sea Area resulting from exploration and exploitation of the continental shelf and the seabed and its subsoil.

Article 8 Pollution from land-based sources

The Contracting Parties shall take all appropriate measures to prevent, abate, combat and to the fullest possible extent eliminate pollution of the Mediterranean Sea Area and to draw up and implement plans for the reduction and phasing out of substances that are toxic, persistent and liable to bioaccumulate arising from land-based sources. These measures shall apply:

(a)   to pollution from land-based sources originating within the territories of the Parties, and reaching the sea:

–   directly from outfalls discharging into the sea or through coastal disposal;

–   indirectly through rivers, canals or other watercourses, including underground watercourses, or through run-off;

(b)   to pollution from land-based sources transported by the atmosphere.

Article 9 Cooperation in dealing with pollution emergencies

1. The Contracting Parties shall cooperate in taking the necessary measures for dealing with pollution emergencies in the Mediterranean Sea Area, whatever the causes of such emergencies, and reducing or eliminating damage resulting therefrom.

2. Any Contracting Party which becomes aware of any pollution emergency in the Mediterranean Sea Area shall without delay notify the Organization and, either through the Organization or directly, any Contracting Party likely to be affected by such emergency.

Article 10 Conservation of biological diversity

The Contracting Parties shall, individually or jointly, take all appropriate measures to protect and preserve biological diversity, rare or fragile ecosystems, as well as species of wild fauna and flora which are rare, depleted, threatened or endangered and their habitats, in the area to which this Convention applies.

Article 11 Pollution resulting from the transboundary movements of hazardous wastes and their disposal

The Contracting Parties shall take all appropriate measures to prevent, abate and to the fullest possible extent eliminate pollution of the environment which can be caused by transboundary movements and disposal of hazardous wastes, and to reduce to a minimum, and if possible eliminate, such transboundary movements.

Article 12 Monitoring

1. The Contracting Parties shall endeavour to establish, in close cooperation with the international bodies which they consider competent, complementary or joint programmes, including, as appropriate, programmes at the bilateral or multilateral levels, for pollution

monitoring in the Mediterranean Sea Area and shall endeavour to establish a pollution monitoring system for that Area.

2. For this purpose, the Contracting Parties shall designate the competent authorities responsible for pollution monitoring within areas under their national jurisdiction and shall participate as far as practicable in international arrangements for pollution monitoring in areas beyond national jurisdiction.

3. The Contracting Parties undertake to cooperate in the formulation, adoption and implementation of such Annexes to this Convention as may be required to prescribe common procedures and standards for pollution monitoring.

Article 13 Scientific and technological cooperation

1. The Contracting Parties undertake as far as possible to cooperate directly, or when appropriate through competent regional or other international organizations, in the fields of science and technology and to exchange data as well as other scientific information for the purpose of this Convention.

2. The Contracting Parties undertake to promote the research on, access to and transfer of environmentally sound technology, including clean production technologies, and to cooperate in the formulation, establishment and implementation of clean production processes.

3. The Contracting Parties undertake to cooperate in the provision of technical and other possible assistance in fields relating to marine pollution, with priority to be given to the special needs of developing countries in the Mediterranean region.

Article 14 Environmental legislation

1. The Contracting Parties shall adopt legislation implementing the Convention and the Protocols.

2. The Secretariat may, upon request from a Contracting Party, assist that Party in the drafting of environmental legislation in compliance with the Convention and the Protocols.

Article 15 Public information and participation

1. The Contracting Parties shall ensure that their competent authorities shall give to the public appropriate access to information on the environmental state in the field of application of the Convention and the Protocols, on activities or measures adversely affecting or likely to affect it and on activities carried out or measures taken in accordance with the Convention and the Protocols.

2. The Contracting Parties shall ensure that the opportunity is given to the public to participate in decision-making processes relevant to the field of application of the Convention and the Protocols, as appropriate.

3. The provision of paragraph 1 of this Article shall not prejudice the right of Contracting Parties to refuse, in accordance with their legal systems and applicable international regulations, to provide access to such information on the ground of confidentiality, public security or investigation proceedings, stating the reasons for such a refusal.

Article 16 Liability and compensation

The Contracting Parties undertake to cooperate in the formulation and adoption of appropriate rules and procedures for the determination of liability and compensation for damage resulting from pollution of the marine environment in the Mediterranean Sea Area.

Article 17 Institutional arrangements

The Contracting Parties designate the United Nations Environment Programme as responsible for carrying out the following secretariat functions:

(a) to convene and prepare the meetings of Contracting Parties and conferences provided for in Articles 18, 21 and 22;

(b) to transmit to the Contracting Parties notifications, reports and other information received in accordance with Articles 3, 9 and 26;

(c) to receive, consider and reply to enquiries and information from the Contracting Parties;

(d) to receive, consider and reply to enquiries and information from non-governmental organizations and the public when they relate to subjects of common interest or to activities carried out at the regional level; in this case, the Contracting Parties concerned shall be informed;

(e) to perform the functions assigned to it by the Protocols to this Convention;

(f) to regularly report to the Contracting Parties on the implementation of the Convention and of the Protocols;

(g) to perform such other functions as may be assigned to it by the Contracting Parties;

(h) to ensure the necessary coordination with other international bodies which the Contracting Parties consider competent, and in particular, to enter into such administrative arrangements as may be required for the effective discharge of the secretariat functions.

Article 18 Meetings of the Contracting Parties

1. The Contracting Parties shall hold ordinary meetings once every two years and extraordinary meetings at any other time deemed necessary, upon the request of the Organization or at the request of any Contracting Party, provided that such requests are supported by at least two Contracting Parties.

2. It shall be the function of the meetings of the Contracting Parties to keep under review the implementation of this Convention and the Protocols and, in particular:

(a) to review generally the inventories carried out by Contracting Parties and competent international organizations on the state of marine pollution and its effects in the Mediterranean Sea Area;

(b) to consider reports submitted by the Contracting Parties under Article 26;

(c) to adopt, review and amend as required the Annexes to this Convention and to the Protocols, in accordance with the procedure established in Article 23;

(d) to make recommendations regarding the adoption of any additional protocols or any amendments to this Convention or the Protocols in accordance with the provisions of Articles 21 and 22;

(e) to establish working groups as required to consider any matters related to this Convention and the Protocols and Annexes;

(f) to consider and undertake any additional action that may be required for the achievement of the purposes of this Convention and the Protocols.

(g) to approve the Programme Budget.

Article 19 Bureau

1. The Bureau of the Contracting Parties shall be composed of representatives of the Contracting Parties elected by the Meetings of the Contracting Parties. In electing the members of the Bureau, the Meetings of the Contracting Parties shall observe the principle of equitable geographical distribution.

2. The functions of the Bureau and the terms and conditions upon which it shall operate shall be set in the Rules of Procedure adopted by the Meetings of the Contracting Parties.

Article 20 Observers

1. The Contracting Parties may decide to admit as observers at their meetings and conferences:

(a)   any State which is not a Contracting Party to the Convention;

(b)   any international governmental organization or any non-governmental organization the activities of which are related to the Convention.

2. Such observers may participate in meetings without the right to vote and may present any information or report relevant to the objectives of the Convention.

3. The conditions for the admission and participation of observers shall be established in the Rules of Procedure adopted by the Contracting Parties.

Article 21 Adoption of additional protocols

1. The Contracting Parties, at a diplomatic conference, may adopt additional protocols to this Convention pursuant to paragraph 5 of Article 4.

2. A diplomatic conference for the purpose of adopting additional protocols shall be convened by the Organization at the request of two thirds of the Contracting Parties.

Article 22 Amendment of the Convention or Protocols

1. Any Contracting Party to this Convention may propose amendments to the Convention. Amendments shall be adopted by a diplomatic conference which shall be convened by the Organization at the request of two thirds of the Contracting Parties.

2. Any Contracting Party to this Convention may propose amendments to any Protocol. Such amendments shall be adopted by a diplomatic conference which shall be convened by the Organization at the request of two thirds of the Contracting Parties to the Protocol concerned.

3. Amendments to this Convention shall be adopted by a three-fourths majority vote of the Contracting Parties to the Convention which are represented at the diplomatic conference and shall be submitted by the Depositary for acceptance by all Contracting Parties to the Convention. Amendments to any Protocol shall be adopted by a three-fourths majority vote of the Contracting Parties to such Protocol which are represented at the diplomatic conference and shall be submitted by the Depositary for acceptance by all Contracting Parties to such Protocol.

4. Acceptance of amendments shall be notified to the Depositary in writing. Amendments adopted in accordance with paragraph 3 of this Article shall enter into force between Contracting Parties having accepted such amendments on the thirtieth day following the receipt by the Depositary of notification of their acceptance by at least three fourths of the Contracting Parties to this Convention or to the protocol concerned, as the case may be.

5. After the entry into force of an amendment to this Convention or to a Protocol, any new Contracting Party to this Convention or such Protocol shall become a Contracting Party to the instrument as amended.

Article 23 Annexes and amendments to Annexes

1. Annexes to this Convention or to any Protocol shall form an integral part of the Convention or such Protocol, as the case may be.

2. Except as may be otherwise provided in any Protocol, the following procedure shall apply to the adoption and entry into force of any amendments to Annexes to this Convention or to any Protocol, with the exception of amendments to the Annex on Arbitration:

(a)   any Contracting Party may propose amendments to the Annexes to this Convention or to any Protocol at the meetings referred to in Article 18;

(b)   such amendments shall be adopted by a three-fourths majority vote of the Contracting Parties to the instrument in question;

(c)   the Depositary shall without delay communicate the amendments so adopted to all Contracting Parties;

(d)   any Contracting Party that is unable to approve an amendment to the Annexes to this Convention or to any protocol shall so notify in writing the Depositary within a period determined by the Contracting Parties concerned when adopting the amendment;

(e)   the Depositary shall without delay notify all Contracting Parties of any notification received pursuant to the preceding subparagraph;

(f)   on expiry of the period referred to in subparagraph (d) above, the amendment to the Annex shall become effective for all Contracting Parties to this Convention or to the Protocol concerned which have not submitted a notification in accordance with the provisions of that subparagraph.

3. The adoption and entry into force of a new Annex to this Convention or to any Protocol shall be subject to the same procedure as for the adoption and entry into force of an amendment to an Annex in accordance with the provisions of paragraph 2 of this Article, provided that, if any amendment to the Convention or the Protocol concerned is involved, the new Annex shall not enter into force until such time as the amendment to the Convention or the Protocol concerned enters into force.

4. Amendments to the Annex on Arbitration shall be considered to be amendments to this Convention and shall be proposed and adopted in accordance with the procedures set out in Article 22 above.

Article 24 Rules of Procedure and Financial Rules

1. The Contracting Parties shall adopt Rules of Procedure for their meetings and conferences envisaged in Articles 18, 21 and 22 above.

2. The Contracting Parties shall adopt Financial Rules, prepared in consultation with the Organization, to determine, in particular, their financial participation in the Trust Fund.

Article 25 Special exercise of voting right

Within the areas of their competence, the European Economic Community and any regional economic grouping referred to in Article 30 of this Convention shall exercise their right to vote with a number of votes equal to the number of their member States which are Contracting Parties to this Convention and to one or more Protocols; the European Economic Community and any grouping as referred to above shall not exercise their right to vote in cases where the member States concerned exercise theirs, and conversely.

Article 26 Reports

1. The Contracting Parties shall transmit to the Organization reports on:

(a)   the legal, administrative or other measures taken by them for the implementation of this Convention, the Protocols and of the recommendations adopted by their meetings;

(b)   the effectiveness of the measures referred to in subparagraph (a) and problems encountered in the implementation of the instruments as mentioned above.

2. The reports shall be submitted in such form and at such intervals as the Meetings of Contracting Parties may determine.

Article 27 Compliance control
The meetings of the Contracting Parties shall, on the basis of periodical reports referred to in Article 26 and any other report submitted by the Contracting Parties, assess the compliance with the Convention and the Protocols as well as the measures and recommendations. They shall recommend, when appropriate, the necessary steps to bring about full compliance with the Convention and the Protocols and promote the implementation of the decisions and recommendations.

Article 28 Settlement of disputes
1. In case of a dispute between Contracting Parties as to the interpretation or application of this Convention or the Protocols, they shall seek a settlement of the dispute through negotiation or any other peaceful means of their own choice.
2. If the Parties concerned cannot settle their dispute through the means mentioned in the preceding paragraph, the dispute shall upon common agreement be submitted to arbitration under the conditions laid down in Annex A to this Convention.
3. Nevertheless, the Contracting Parties may at any time declare that they recognize as compulsory *ipso facto* and without special agreement, in relation to any other Party accepting the same obligation, the application of the arbitration procedure in conformity with the provisions of Annex A. Such declaration shall be notified in writing to the Depositary, who shall communicate it to the other Parties.

Article 29 Relationship between the Convention and Protocols
1. No one may become a Contracting Party to this Convention unless it becomes at the same time a Contracting Party to at least one of the Protocols. No one may become a Contracting Party to a Protocol unless it is, or becomes at the same time, a Contracting Party to this Convention.
2. Any Protocol to this Convention shall be binding only on the Contracting Parties to the Protocol in question.
3. Decisions concerning any Protocol pursuant to Articles 18, 22 and 23 of this Convention shall be taken only by the Parties to the Protocol concerned.

Article 30 Signature
This Convention, the Protocol for the Prevention of Pollution of the Mediterranean Sea by Dumping from Ships and Aircraft and the Protocol concerning Cooperation in Combating Pollution of the Mediterranean Sea by Oil and Other Harmful Substances in Cases of Emergency shall be open for signature in Barcelona on 16 February 1976 and in Madrid from 17 February 1976 to 16 February 1977 by any State invited as a participant in the Conference of Plenipotentiaries of the Coastal States of the Mediterranean Region on the Protection of the Mediterranean Sea, held in Barcelona from 2 to 16 February 1976, and by any State entitled to sign any Protocol in accordance with the provisions of such Protocol. They shall also be open until the same date for signature by the European Economic Community and by any similar regional economic grouping at least one member of which is a coastal State of the Mediterranean Sea Area and which exercise competence in fields covered by this Convention, as well as by any Protocol affecting them.

Article 31 Ratification, acceptance or approval
This Convention and any Protocol thereto shall be subject to ratification, acceptance, or approval. Instruments of ratification, acceptance or approval shall be deposited with the Government of Spain, which will assume the functions of Depositary.

Article 32 Accession

1. As from 17 February 1977, the present Convention, the Protocol for the Prevention of Pollution of the Mediterranean Sea by Dumping from Ships and Aircraft, and the Protocol concerning Cooperation in Combating Pollution of the Mediterranean Sea by Oil and other Harmful Substances in Cases of Emergency shall be open for accession by the States, by the European Economic Community and by any grouping as referred to in Article 30.

2. After the entry into force of the Convention and of any Protocol, any State not referred to in Article 30 may accede to this Convention and to any Protocol, subject to prior approval by three fourths of the Contracting Parties to the Protocol concerned.

3. Instruments of accession shall be deposited with the Depositary.

Article 33 Entry into force

1. This Convention shall enter into force on the same date as the Protocol first entering into force.

2. The Convention shall also enter into force with regard to the States, the European Economic Community and any regional economic grouping referred to in Article 30 if they have complied with the formal requirements for becoming Contracting Parties to any other Protocol not yet entered into force.

3. Any Protocol to this Convention, except as otherwise provided in such Protocol, shall enter into force on the thirtieth day following the date of deposit of at least six instruments of ratification, acceptance, or approval of, or accession to such Protocol by the Parties referred to in Article 30.

4. Thereafter, this Convention and any Protocol shall enter into force with respect to any State, the European Economic Community and any regional economic grouping referred to in Article 30 on the thirtieth day following the date of deposit of the instruments of ratification, acceptance, approval or accession.

Article 34 Withdrawal

1. At any time after three years from the date of entry into force of this Convention, any Contracting Party may withdraw from this Convention by giving written notification of withdrawal.

2. Except as may be otherwise provided in any Protocol to this Convention, any Contracting Party may, at any time after three years from the date of entry into force of such Protocol, withdraw from such Protocol by giving written notification of withdrawal.

3. Withdrawal shall take effect 90 days after the date on which notification of withdrawal is received by the Depositary.

4. Any Contracting Party which withdraws from this Convention shall be considered as also having withdrawn from any Protocol to which it was a Party.

5. Any Contracting Party which, upon its withdrawal from a Protocol, is no longer a Party to any Protocol to this Convention, shall be considered as also having withdrawn from this Convention.

Article 35 Responsibilities of the Depositary

1. The Depositary shall inform the Contracting Parties, any other Party referred to in Article 30, and the Organization:

(a) of the signature of this Convention and of any Protocol thereto, and of the deposit of instruments of ratification, acceptance, approval or accession in accordance with Articles 30, 31 and 32;

(b)   of the date on which the Convention and any Protocol will come into force in accordance with the provisions of Article 33;

(c)   of notifications of withdrawal made in accordance with Article 34;

(d)   of the amendments adopted with respect to the Convention and to any Protocol, their acceptance by the Contracting Parties and the date of entry into force of those amendments in accordance with the provisions of Article 22;

(e)   of the adoption of new Annexes and of the amendment of any Annex in accordance with Article 23;

(f)   of declarations recognizing as compulsory the application of the arbitration procedure mentioned in paragraph 3 of Article 28.

2.   The original of this Convention and of any Protocol thereto shall be deposited with the Depositary, the Government of Spain, which shall send certified copies thereof to the Contracting Parties, to the Organization, and to the Secretary-General of the United Nations for registration and publication in accordance with Article 102 of the United Nations Charter.

IN WITNESS THEREOF the undersigned, being duly authorized by their respective Governments, have signed this Convention.

DONE at Barcelona on 16 February 1976 in a single copy in the Arabic, English, French and Spanish languages, the four texts being equally authoritative.

Protocol for the Prevention and Elimination of Pollution of the Mediterranean Sea by Dumping from Ships and Aircraft or Incineration at Sea (Dumping Protocol)

Done at Barcelona, 16 February 1976, and amended at Barcelona, 10 June 1995;
entry into force, 12 February 1978; amendments not yet in force
UNEP, Mediterranean Action Plan, *Convention for the Protection of the Marine Environment and the Coastal Region of the Mediterranean and its Protocols*, 2005, 23[1]

The Contracting Parties to the present Protocol,

Being Parties to the Convention for the Protection of the Mediterranean Sea against Pollution,

Recognizing the danger posed to the marine environment by the dumping or incineration of wastes or other matter,

Considering that the coastal States of the Mediterranean Sea have a common interest in protecting the marine environment from this danger,

Bearing in mind that Chapter 17 of Agenda 21 of UNCED calls on the Contracting Parties to the Convention on the Prevention of Marine Pollution by Dumping of Wastes and other Matter (London, 1972) to take the necessary measures to end dumping in the ocean and the incineration of hazardous substances,

Taking into account Resolutions LC 49(16) and LC 50(16), approved by the 16th Consultative Meeting of the 1972 London Convention, which prohibit the dumping and incineration of industrial wastes at sea,

Have agreed as follows:

---

[1] The Protocol for the Prevention of Pollution of the Mediterranean Sea by Dumping from Ships and Aircraft was adopted in Barcelona on 16 February 1976 and entered into force on 12 February 1978 (1102 UNTS 92 [Registration Number 16908]). The original Dumping Protocol was amended in Barcelona on 10 June 1995 and was renamed Protocol for the Prevention and Elimination of Pollution of the Mediterranean Sea by Dumping from Ships and Aircraft or Incineration at Sea. The text of the Protocol reproduced is a consolidated version incorporating the 1995 amendment.

Article 1

The Contracting Parties to this Protocol (hereinafter referred to as 'the Parties) shall take all appropriate measures to prevent, abate and eliminate to the fullest extent possible pollution of the Mediterranean Sea caused by dumping from ships and aircraft or incineration at sea.

Article 2

The area to which this Protocol applies shall be the Mediterranean Sea Area as defined in Article 1 of the Convention for the Protection of the Marine Environment and the Coastal Region of the Mediterranean (hereinafter referred to as 'the Convention').

Article 3

For the purposes of this Protocol:

1. 'Ships and aircraft' means waterborne or airborne craft of any type whatsoever. This expression includes air-cushioned craft and floating craft, whether self-propelled or not, and platforms and other man-made structures at sea and their equipment.

2. 'Wastes or other matter' means material and substances of any kind, form or description.

3. 'Dumping' means:

(a) any deliberate disposal at sea of wastes or other matter from ships or aircraft;

(b) any deliberate disposal at sea of ships or aircraft;

(c) any deliberate disposal or storage and burial of wastes or other matter on the seabed or in the marine subsoil from ships or aircraft.

4. 'Dumping' does not include:

(a) the disposal at sea of wastes or other matter incidental to, or derived from, the normal operations of vessels or aircraft and their equipment, other than wastes or other matter transported by or to vessels or aircraft, operating for the purpose of disposal of such matter, or derived from the treatment of such wastes or other matter on such vessels or aircraft;

(b) placement of matter for a purpose other than the mere disposal thereof, provided that such placement is not contrary to the aims of this Protocol.

5. 'Incineration at sea' means the deliberate combustion of wastes or other matter in the maritime waters of the Mediterranean Sea, with the aim of thermal destruction and does not include activities incidental to the normal operations of ships or aircraft.

6. 'Organization' means the body referred to in Article 17 of the Convention.

Article 4

1. The dumping of wastes or other matter, with the exception of those listed in paragraph 2 of this Article, is prohibited.

2. The following is the list referred to in the preceding paragraph:

(a) dredged material;

(b) fish waste or organic materials resulting from the processing of fish and other marine organisms;

(c) vessels, until 31 December 2000;

(d) platforms and other man-made structures at sea, provided that material capable of creating floating debris or otherwise contributing to pollution of the marine environment has been removed to the maximum extent, without prejudice to the provisions of the Protocol concerning Pollution Resulting from Exploration and Exploitation of the Continental Shelf, the Seabed and its Subsoil;

(e) inert uncontaminated geological materials the chemical constituents of which are unlikely to be released into the marine environment.

Article 5

The dumping of the wastes or other matter listed in Article 4 paragraph 2 requires a prior special permit from the competent national authorities.

Article 6

1. The permit referred to in Article 5 shall be issued only after careful consideration of the factors set forth in the Annex[2] to this Protocol or the criteria, guidelines and relevant procedures adopted by the meeting of the Contracting Parties pursuant to paragraph 2 below:

2. The Contracting Parties shall draw up and adopt criteria, guidelines and procedures for the dumping of wastes or other matter listed in Article 4 paragraph 2 so as to prevent, abate and eliminate pollution.

Article 7

Incineration at sea is prohibited.

Article 8

The provisions of Articles 4, 5 and 6 shall not apply in case of *force majeure* due to stress of weather or any other cause when human life or the safety of a ship or aircraft is threatened. Such dumpings shall immediately be reported to the Organization and, either through the Organization or directly, to any Party or Parties likely to be affected, together with full details of the circumstances and of the nature and quantities of the wastes or other matter dumped.

Article 9

If a Party in a critical situation of an exceptional nature considers that wastes or other matter not listed in Article 4 paragraph 2 of this Protocol cannot be disposed of on land without unacceptable danger or damage, above all for the safety of human life, the Party concerned shall forthwith consult the Organization. The Organization, after consulting the Parties to this Protocol, shall recommend methods of storage or the most satisfactory means of destruction or disposal under the prevailing circumstances. The Party shall inform the Organization of the steps adopted in pursuance of these recommendations. The Parties pledge themselves to assist one another in such situations.

Article 10

1. Each Party shall designate one or more competent authorities to:
(a) issue the permits provided for in Article 5;
(b) keep records of the nature and quantities of the wastes or other matter permitted to be dumped and of the location, date and method of dumping.

2. The competent authorities of each Party shall issue the permits provided for in Article 5 in respect of the wastes or other matter intended for dumping:
(a) loaded in its territory;
(b) loaded by a ship or aircraft registered in its territory or flying its flag, when the loading occurs in the territory of a State not Party to this Protocol.

---

[2] Annex omitted.

Article 11

Each Party shall apply the measures required to implement this Protocol to all:

(a)   ships and aircraft registered in its territory or flying its flag;

(b)   ships and aircraft loading in its territory wastes or other matter which are to be dumped;

(c)   ships and aircraft believed to be engaged in dumping in areas under its jurisdiction in this matter.

Article 12

Each Party undertakes to issue instructions to its maritime inspection ships and aircraft and to other appropriate services to report to its authorities any incidents or conditions in the Mediterranean Sea Area which give rise to suspicions that dumping in contravention of the provisions of this Protocol has occurred or is about to occur. That Party shall, if it considers it appropriate, report accordingly to any other Party concerned.

Article 13

Nothing in this Protocol shall affect the right of each Party to adopt other measures, in accordance with international law, to prevent pollution due to dumping.

Article 14

1.   Ordinary meetings of the Parties to this Protocol shall be held in conjunction with ordinary meetings of the Contracting Parties to the Convention held pursuant to Article 18 of the Convention. The Parties to this Protocol may also hold extraordinary meetings in conformity with Article 18 of the Convention.

2.   It shall be the function of the meetings of the Parties to this Protocol:

(a)   to keep under review the implementation of this Protocol, and to consider the efficacy of the measures adopted and the need for any other measures, in particular in the form of Annexes;

(b)   to study and consider the records of the permits issued in accordance with Articles 5, 6 and 7 and of the dumping which has taken place;

(c)   to review and amend as required any Annex to this Protocol;

(d)   to discharge such other functions as may be appropriate for the implementation of this Protocol.

3.   The adoption of amendments to the Annex to this Protocol pursuant to Article 23 of the Convention shall require a three-fourths majority vote of the Parties.

Article 15

1.   The provisions of the Convention relating to any Protocol shall apply with respect to the present Protocol.

2.   The rules or procedure and the financial rules adopted pursuant to Article 24 of the Convention shall apply with respect to this Protocol, unless the Parties to this Protocol agree otherwise.

IN WITNESS WHEREOF the undersigned, being duly authorized by their respective Governments, have signed this Protocol.

DONE at Barcelona on 16 February 1976 in a single copy in the Arabic, English, French and Spanish languages, the four texts being equally authoritative.

Protocol for the Protection of the Mediterranean Sea against Pollution from Land-Based Sources and Activities (LBS Protocol)

Done at Athens, 17 May 1980, and amended at Syracuse, 7 March 1996;
entry into force on 17 June 1983 and 11 May 2008, respectively
UNEP, Mediterranean Action Plan, *Convention for the Protection of the Marine Environment and the Coastal Region of the Mediterranean and its Protocols*, 2005, 49[1]

The Contracting Parties to the present Protocol,

Being Parties to the Convention for the Protection of the Mediterranean Sea against Pollution, adopted at Barcelona on 16 February 1976 and amended on 10 June 1995,

Desirous of implementing Article 4, paragraph 5, and Articles 8 and 21 of the said Convention,

Noting the increasing environmental pressures resulting from human activities in the Mediterranean Sea Area, particularly in the fields of industrialization and urbanization, as well as the seasonal increase in the coastal population due to tourism,

Recognizing the danger posed to the marine environment, living resources and human health by pollution from land-based sources and activities and the serious problems resulting therefrom in many coastal waters and river estuaries of the Mediterranean Sea, primarily due to the release of untreated, insufficiently treated or inadequately disposed of domestic or industrial discharges containing substances that are toxic, persistent and liable to bioaccumulate,

Applying the precautionary principle and the polluter pays principle, undertaking environmental impact assessment and utilizing the best available techniques and the best environmental practice, including clean production technologies, as provided for in Article 4 of the Convention,

Recognizing the difference in levels of development between the coastal States, and taking account of the economic and social imperatives of the developing countries,

Determined to take, in close cooperation, the necessary measures to protect the Mediterranean Sea against pollution from land-based sources and activities,

Taking into consideration the Global Programme of Action for the Protection of the Marine Environment from Land-Based Activities, adopted in Washington, D.C., on 3 November 1995,

Have agreed as follows:

Article 1 General provision

The Contracting Parties to this Protocol (hereinafter referred to as 'the Parties') shall take all appropriate measures to prevent, abate, combat and eliminate to the fullest possible extent pollution of the Mediterranean Sea Area caused by discharges from rivers, coastal establishments or outfalls, or emanating from any other land-based sources and activities within their territories, giving priority to the phasing out of inputs of substances that are toxic, persistent and liable to bioaccumulate.

---

[1] The Protocol for the Protection of the Mediterranean Sea against Pollution from Land-Based Sources was adopted in Athens on 17 May 1980 and entered into force on 17 June 1983 (1328 UNTS 120 [Registration Number 22281]). The original LBS Protocol was amended in Syracuse on 7 March 1996 and was renamed Protocol for the Protection of the Mediterranean Sea against Pollution from Land-Based Sources and Activities. The amendment entered into for on 11 May 2008. The text of the Protocol reproduced is a consolidated version incorporating the 1996 amendment. Annex I-IV omitted.

Article 2 Definitions

For the purposes of this Protocol:

(a) 'The Convention' means the Convention for the Protection of the Mediterranean Sea against Pollution, adopted at Barcelona on 16 February 1976 and amended on 10 June 1995;

(b) 'Organization' means the body referred to in Article 17 of the Convention;

(c) 'Freshwater limit' means the place in watercourses where, at low tides and in a period of low freshwater flow, there is an appreciable increase in salinity due to the presence of sea-water;

(d) The 'Hydrologic Basin' means the entire watershed area within the territories of the Contracting Parties, draining into the Mediterranean Sea Area as defined in Article 1 of the Convention.

Article 3 Protocol Area

The area to which this Protocol applies (hereinafter referred to as the 'Protocol Area') shall be:

(a) the Mediterranean Sea Area as defined in Article 1 of the Convention;

(b) the hydrologic basin of the Mediterranean Sea Area;

(c) waters on the landward side of the baselines from which the breadth of the territorial sea is measured and extending, in the case of watercourses, up to the freshwater limit;

(d) brackish waters, coastal salt waters including marshes and coastal lagoons, and ground waters communicating with the Mediterranean Sea.

Article 4 Protocol application

1. This Protocol shall apply:

(a) to discharges originating from land-based point and diffuse sources and activities within the territories of the Contracting Parties that may affect directly or indirectly the Mediterranean Sea Area. These discharges shall include those which reach the Mediterranean Area, as defined in Article 3 (a), (c) and (d) of this Protocol, through coastal disposals, rivers, outfalls, canals, or other watercourses, including ground water flow, or through run-off and disposal under the seabed with access from land;

(b) to inputs of polluting substances transported by the atmosphere to the Mediterranean Sea Area from land-based sources or activities within the territories of the Contracting Parties under the conditions defined in Annex III to this Protocol.

2. This Protocol shall also apply to polluting discharges from fixed man-made offshore structures which are under the jurisdiction of a Party and which serve purposes other than exploration and exploitation of mineral resources of the continental shelf and the sea-bed and its subsoil.

3. The Parties shall invite States that are not Parties to the Protocol and have in their territories parts of the hydrologic basin of the Mediterranean Area to cooperate in the implementation of the Protocol.

Article 5 General obligations

1. The Parties undertake to eliminate pollution deriving from land-based sources and activities, in particular to phase out inputs of the substances that are toxic, persistent and liable to bioaccumulate listed in Annex I.

2. To this end, they shall elaborate and implement, individually or jointly, as appropriate, national and regional action plans and programmes, containing measures and timetables for their implementation.

3. The priorities and timetables for implementing the action plans, programmes and measures shall be adopted by the Parties taking into account the elements set out in Annex I and shall be periodically reviewed.

4. When adopting action plans, programmes and measures, the Parties shall take into account, either individually or jointly, the best available techniques and the best environmental practice including, where appropriate, clean production technologies, taking into account the criteria set forth in Annex IV.

5. The Parties shall take preventive measures to reduce to the minimum the risk of pollution caused by accidents.

Article 6 Authorization or regulation system

1. Point source discharges into the Protocol Area, and releases into water or air that reach and may affect the Mediterranean Area, as defined in Article 3 (a), (c) and (d) of this Protocol, shall be strictly subject to authorization or regulation by the competent authorities of the Parties, taking due account of the provisions of this Protocol and Annex II thereto, as well as the relevant decisions or recommendations of the meetings of the Contracting Parties.

2. To this end, the Parties shall provide for systems of inspection by their competent authorities to assess compliance with authorizations and regulations.

3. The Parties may be assisted by the Organization, upon request, in establishing new, or strengthening existing, competent structures for inspection of compliance with authorizations and regulations. Such assistance shall include special training of personnel.

4. The Parties establish appropriate sanctions in case of non-compliance with the authorizations and regulations and ensure their application.

Article 7 Common guidelines, standards and criteria

1. The Parties shall progressively formulate and adopt, in cooperation with the competent international organizations, common guidelines and, as appropriate, standards or criteria dealing in particular with:

(a)   the length, depth and position of pipelines for coastal outfalls, taking into account, in particular, the methods used for pretreatment of effluents;

(b)   special requirements for effluents necessitating separate treatment;

(c)   the quality of sea-water used for specific purposes that is necessary for the protection of human health, living resources and ecosystems;

(d)   the control and progressive replacement of products, installations and industrial and other processes causing significant pollution of the marine environment;

(e)   specific requirements concerning the quantities of the substances discharged (listed in Annex I), their concentration in effluents and methods of discharging them.

2. Without prejudice to the provisions of Article 5 of this Protocol, such common guidelines, standards or criteria shall take into account local ecological, geographical and physical characteristics, the economic capacity of the Parties and their need for development, the level of existing pollution and the real absorptive capacity of the marine environment.

3. The action plans, programmes and measures referred to in Articles 5 and 15 of this Protocol shall be adopted by taking into account, for their progressive implementation, the

capacity to adapt and reconvert existing installations, the economic capacity of the Parties and their need for development.

Article 8 Monitoring

Within the framework of the provisions of, and the monitoring programmes provided for in Article 12 of the Convention, and if necessary in cooperation with the competent international organizations, the Parties shall carry out at the earliest possible date monitoring activities and make access to the public of the findings in order:

    (a)   systematically to assess, as far as possible, the levels of pollution along their coasts, in particular with regard to the sectors of activity and categories of substances listed in Annex I, and periodically to provide information in this respect;

    (b)   to evaluate the effectiveness of action plans, programmes and measures implemented under this Protocol to eliminate to the fullest possible extent pollution of the marine environment.

Article 9 Scientific and technical cooperation

In conformity with Article 13 of the Convention, the Parties shall cooperate in scientific and technological fields related to pollution from land-based sources and activities, particularly research on inputs, pathways and effects of pollutants and on the development of new methods for their treatment, reduction or elimination, as well as the development of clean production processes to this effect. To this end, the Parties shall, in particular, endeavour to:

    (a)   exchange scientific and technical information;

    (b)   coordinate their research programmes;

    (c)   promote access to, and transfer of, environmentally sound technology including clean production technology.

Article 10 Technical assistance

1. The Parties shall, directly or with the assistance of competent regional or other international organizations, bilaterally or multilaterally, cooperate with a view to formulating and, as far as possible, implementing programmes of assistance to developing countries, particularly in the fields of science, education and technology, with a view to preventing, reducing or, as appropriate, phasing out inputs of pollutants from land-based sources and activities and their harmful effects in the marine environment.

2. Technical assistance would include, in particular, the training of scientific and technical personnel, as well as the acquisition, utilization and production by those countries of appropriate equipment and, as appropriate, clean production technologies, on advantageous terms to be agreed upon among the Parties concerned.

Article 11 Transboundary pollution

1. If discharges from a watercourse which flows through the territories of two or more Parties or forms a boundary between them are likely to cause pollution of the marine environment of the Protocol Area, the Parties in question, respecting the provisions of this Protocol in so far as each of them is concerned, are called upon to cooperate with a view to ensuring its full application.

2. A Party shall not be responsible for any pollution originating on the territory of a non-contracting State. However, the said Party shall endeavour to cooperate with the said State so as to make possible full application of the Protocol.

Article 12 Settlement of disputes
1. Taking into account Article 28, paragraph 1, of the Convention, when land-based pollution originating from the territory of one Party is likely to prejudice directly the interests of one or more of the other Parties, the Parties concerned shall, at the request of one or more of them, undertake to enter into consultation with a view to seeking a satisfactory solution.
2. At the request of any Party concerned, the matter shall be placed on the agenda of the next meeting of the Parties held in accordance with Article 14 of this Protocol; the meeting may make recommendations with a view to reaching a satisfactory solution.

Article 13 Reports
1. The Parties shall submit reports every two years, unless decided otherwise by the Meeting of the Contracting Parties, to the meetings of the Contracting Parties, through the Organization, of measures taken, results achieved and, if the case arises, of difficulties encountered in the application of this Protocol. Procedures for the submission of such reports shall be determined at the meetings of the Parties.
2. Such reports shall include, *inter alia*:
   (a) statistical data on the authorizations granted in accordance with Article 6 of this Protocol;
   (b) data resulting from monitoring as provided for in Article 8 of this Protocol;
   (c) quantities of pollutants discharged from their territories;
   (d) action plans, programmes and measures implemented in accordance with Articles 5, 7 and 15 of this Protocol.

Article 14 Meetings
1. Ordinary meetings of the Parties shall take place in conjunction with ordinary meetings of the Contracting Parties to the Convention held pursuant to Article 18 of the Convention. The Parties may also hold extraordinary meetings in accordance with Article 18 of the Convention.
2. The functions of the meetings of the Parties to this Protocol shall be, *inter alia*:
   (a) to keep under review the implementation of this Protocol and to consider the efficacy of the action plans, programmes and measures adopted;
   (b) to revise and amend any Annex to this Protocol, as appropriate;
   (c) to formulate and adopt action plans, programmes and measures in accordance with Articles 5, 7 and 15 of this Protocol;
   (d) to adopt, in accordance with Article 7 of this Protocol, common guidelines, standards or criteria, in any form decided upon by the Parties;
   (e) to make recommendations in accordance with Article 12, paragraph 2, of this Protocol;
   (f) to consider the reports submitted by the Parties under Article 13 of this Protocol;
   (g) to discharge such other functions as may be appropriate for the application of this Protocol.

Article 15 Adoption of action plans, programmes and measures
1. The meeting of the Parties shall adopt, by a two-thirds majority, the short-term and medium-term regional action plans and programmes containing measures and timetables for their implementation provided for in Article 5 of this Protocol.
2. Regional action plans and programmes as referred to in paragraph 1 shall be formulated by the Organization and considered and approved by the relevant technical

body of the Contracting Parties within one year at the latest of the entry into force of the amendments to this Protocol. Such regional action plans and programmes shall be put on the agenda for the subsequent meeting of the Parties for adoption. The same procedure shall be followed for any additional action plans and programmes.

3. The measures and timetables adopted in accordance with paragraph 1 of this Article shall be notified by the Secretariat to all the Parties. Such measures and timetables become binding on the one hundred and eightieth day following the day of notification for the Parties which have not notified the Secretariat of an objection within one hundred and seventy-nine days from the date of notification.

4. The Parties which have notified an objection in accordance with the preceding paragraph shall inform the meeting of the Parties of the provisions they intend to take, it being understood that these Parties may at any time give their consent to these measures or timetables.

Article 16 Final provisions

1. The provisions of the Convention relating to any Protocol shall apply with respect to this Protocol.

2. The rules of procedure and the financial rules adopted pursuant to Article 24 of the Convention shall apply with respect to this Protocol, unless the Parties to this Protocol agree otherwise.

3. This Protocol shall be open for signature, at Athens from 17 May 1980 to 16 June 1980, and at Madrid from 17 June 1980 to 16 May 1981, by any State invited to the Conference of Plenipotentiaries of the Coastal States of the Mediterranean Region for the Protection of the Mediterranean Sea against Pollution from Land-Based Sources held at Athens from 12 May to 17 May 1980. It shall also be open until the same dates for signature by the European Economic Community and by any similar regional economic grouping of which at least one member is a coastal State of the Mediterranean Sea Area and which exercises competence in fields covered by this Protocol.

4. This Protocol shall be subject to ratification, acceptance or approval. Instruments of ratification, acceptance or approval shall be deposited with the Government of Spain, which will assume the functions of Depositary.

5. As from 17 May 1981, this Protocol shall be open for accession by the States referred to in paragraph 3 above, by the European Economic Community and by any grouping referred to in that paragraph.

6. This Protocol shall enter into force on the thirtieth day following the deposit of at least six instruments of ratification, acceptance or approval of, or accession to, the Protocol by the Parties referred to in paragraph 3 of this Article.

IN WITNESS WHEREOF the undersigned, being duly authorized by their respective Governments, have signed this Protocol.

DONE at Athens on 17 May 1980 and amended at Syracuse on 7 March 1996 in a single copy in the Arabic, English, French and Spanish languages, the four texts being equally authoritative.

Protocol for the Protection of the Mediterranean Sea against Pollution Resulting from Exploration and Exploitation of the Continental Shelf and the Seabed and Its Subsoil (Offshore Protocol)

Done at Madrid, 14 October 1994; not yet in force
UNEP, Mediterranean Action Plan, *Convention for the Protection of the Marine Environment and the Coastal Region of the Mediterranean and its Protocols*, 2005, 105[1]

The Contracting Parties to the present Protocol,

Being Parties to the Convention for the Protection of the Mediterranean Sea against Pollution, adopted at Barcelona on 16 February 1976,

Bearing in mind Article 7 of the said Convention,

Bearing in mind the increase in the activities concerning exploration and exploitation of the Mediterranean seabed and its subsoil,

Recognizing that the pollution which may result therefrom represents a serious danger to the environment and to human beings,

Desirous of protecting and preserving the Mediterranean Sea from pollution resulting from exploration and exploitation activities,

Taking into account the Protocols related to the Convention for the Protection of the Mediterranean Sea against Pollution and, in particular, the Protocol concerning Cooperation in Combating Pollution of the Mediterranean Sea by Oil and Other Harmful Substances in Cases of Emergency, adopted at Barcelona on 16 February 1976, and the Protocol concerning Mediterranean Specially Protected Areas, adopted at Geneva on 3 April 1982,

Bearing in mind the relevant provisions of the United Nations Convention on the Law of the Sea, done at Montego Bay on 10 December 1982 and signed by many Contracting Parties,

Recognizing the differences in levels of development among the coastal States, and taking account of the economic and social imperatives of the developing countries,

Have agreed as follows:

SECTION I. GENERAL PROVISIONS

Article 1 Definitions

For the purposes of this Protocol:

(a) 'Convention' means the Convention for the Protection of the Mediterranean Sea against Pollution, adopted at Barcelona on 16 February 1976;

(b) 'Organization' means the body referred to in Article 17 of the Convention;

(c) 'Resources' means all mineral resources, whether solid, liquid or gaseous;

(d) 'Activities concerning exploration and/or exploitation of the resources in the Protocol Area' (hereinafter referred to as 'activities') means:

  (i) activities of scientific research concerning the resources of the seabed and its subsoil;

  (ii) exploration activities:

    – seismological activities; surveys of the seabed and its subsoil; sample taking;

    – exploration drilling;

---

[1] Annexes and Appendix omitted.

(iii)   exploitation activities:
- establishment of an installation for the purpose of recovering resources, and activities connected therewith;
- development drilling;
- recovery, treatment and storage;
- transportation to shore by pipeline and loading of ships;
- maintenance, repair and other ancillary operations;

(e)   'Pollution' is defined as in Article 2, paragraph (a), of the Convention;

(f)   'Installation' means any fixed or floating structure, and any integral part thereof, that is engaged in activities, including, in particular:
  (i)   fixed or mobile offshore drilling units;
  (ii)   fixed or floating production units including dynamically-positioned units;
  (iii) offshore storage facilities including ships used for this purpose;
  (iv)   offshore loading terminals and transport systems for the extracted products, such as submarine pipelines;
  (v)   apparatus attached to it and equipment for the reloading, processing, storage and disposal of substances removed from the seabed or its subsoil;

(g)   'Operator' means:
  (i)   any natural or juridical person who is authorized by the Party exercising jurisdiction over the area where the activities are undertaken (hereinafter referred to as the 'Contracting Party') in accordance with this Protocol to carry out activities and/or who carries out such activities; or
  (ii)   any person who does not hold an authorization within the meaning of this Protocol but is de facto in control of such activities;

(h)   'Safety zone' means a zone established around installations in conformity with the provisions of general international law and technical requirements, with appropriate markings to ensure the safety of both navigation and the installations;

(i)   'Wastes' means substances and materials of any kind, form or description resulting from activities covered by this Protocol which are disposed of or are intended for disposal or are required to be disposed of;

(j)   'Harmful or noxious substances and materials' means substances and materials of any kind, form or description, which might cause pollution, if introduced into the Protocol Area;

(k)   'Chemical Use Plan' means a plan drawn up by the operator of any offshore installation which shows:
  (i)   the chemicals which the operator intends to use in the operations;
  (ii)   the purpose or purposes for which the operator intends to use the chemicals;
  (iii) the maximum concentrations of the chemicals which the operator intends to use within any other substances, and maximum amounts intended to be used in any specified period;
  (iv)   the area within which the chemical may escape into the marine environment;

(l)   'Oil' means petroleum in any form including crude oil, fuel oil, oily sludge, oil refuse and refined products and, without limiting the generality of the foregoing, includes the substances listed in the Appendix to this Protocol;

(m)   'Oily mixture' means a mixture with any oil content;

(n)   'Sewage' means:
  (i)   drainage and other wastes from any form of toilets, urinals and water-closet scuppers;

      (ii)   drainage from medical premises (dispensary, sick bay, etc.) via wash basins, wash tubs and scuppers located in such premises;

      (iii) other waste waters when mixed with the drainages defined above;

(o)   'Garbage' means all kinds of food, domestic and operational waste generated during the normal operation of the installation and liable to be disposed of continuously or periodically, except those substances which are defined or listed elsewhere in this Protocol;

(p)   'Freshwater limit' means the place in water courses where, at low tides and in a period of low freshwater flow, there is an appreciable increase in salinity due to the presence of sea water.

Article 2 Geographical coverage

1.   The area to which this Protocol applies (referred to in this Protocol as the 'Protocol Area') shall be:

(a)   the Mediterranean Sea Area as defined in Article 1 of the Convention, including the continental shelf and the seabed and its subsoil;

(b)   waters, including the seabed and its subsoil, on the landward side of the baselines from which the breadth of the territorial sea is measured and extending, in the case of watercourses, up to the freshwater limit.

2.   Any of the Contracting Parties to this Protocol (referred to in this Protocol as 'the Parties') may also include in the Protocol area wetlands or coastal areas of their territory.

3.   Nothing in this Protocol, nor any act adopted on the basis of this Protocol, shall prejudice the rights of any State concerning the delimitation of the continental shelf.

Article 3 General undertakings

1.   The Parties shall take, individually or through bilateral or multilateral cooperation, all appropriate measures to prevent, abate, combat and control pollution in the Protocol Area resulting from activities, *inter alia* by ensuring that the best available techniques, environmentally effective and economically appropriate, are used for this purpose.

2.   The Parties shall ensure that all necessary measures are taken so that activities do not cause pollution.

SECTION II. AUTHORIZATION SYSTEM

Article 4 General principles

1.   All activities in the Protocol Area, including erection on site of installations, shall be subject to the prior written authorization for exploration or exploitation from the competent authority. Such authority, before granting the authorization, shall be satisfied that the installation has been constructed according to international standards and practice and that the operator has the technical competence and the financial capacity to carry out the activities. Such authorization shall be granted in accordance with the appropriate procedure, as defined by the competent authority.

2.   Authorization shall be refused if there are indications that the proposed activities are likely to cause significant adverse effects on the environment that could not be avoided by compliance with the conditions laid down in the authorization and referred to in Article 6, paragraph 3, of this Protocol.

3.   When considering approval of the siting of an installation, the Contracting Party shall ensure that no detrimental effects will be caused to existing facilities by such siting, in particular, to pipelines and cables.

Article 5 Requirements for authorizations

1. The Contracting Party shall prescribe that any application for authorization or for the renewal of an authorization is subject to the submission of the project by the candidate operator to the competent authority and that any such application must include, in particular, the following:

(a) a survey concerning the effects of the proposed activities on the environment; the competent authority may, in the light of the nature, scope, duration and technical methods employed in the activities and of the characteristics of the area, require that an environmental impact assessment be prepared in accordance with Annex IV to this Protocol;

(b) the precise definition of the geographical areas where the activity is envisaged, including safety zones;

(c) particulars of the professional and technical qualifications of the candidate operator and personnel on the installation, as well as of the composition of the crew;

(d) the safety measures as specified in Article 15;

(e) the operator's contingency plan as specified in Article 16;

(f) the monitoring procedures as specified in Article 19;

(g) the plans for removal of installations as specified in Article 20;

(h) precautions for specially protected areas as specified in Article 21;

(i) the insurance or other financial security to cover liability as prescribed in Article 27, paragraph 2 (b).

2. The competent authority may decide, for scientific research and exploration activities, to limit the scope of the requirements laid down in paragraph 1 of this Article, in the light of the nature, scope, duration and technical methods employed in the activities and of the characteristics of the area.

Article 6 Granting of authorizations

1. The authorizations referred to in Article 4 shall be granted only after examination by the competent authority of the requirements listed in Article 5 and Annex IV.

2. Each authorization shall specify the activities and the period of validity of the authorization, establish the geographical limits of the area subject to the authorization and specify the technical requirements and the authorized installations. The necessary safety zones shall be established at a later appropriate stage.

3. The authorization may impose conditions regarding measures, techniques or methods designed to reduce to the minimum risks of and damage due to pollution resulting from the activities.

4. The Parties shall notify the Organization as soon as possible of authorizations granted or renewed. The Organization shall keep a register of all the authorized installations in the Protocol Area.

Article 7 Sanctions

Each Party shall prescribe sanctions to be imposed for breach of obligations arising out of this Protocol, or for non-observance of the national laws or regulations implementing this Protocol, or for non-fulfilment of the specific conditions attached to the authorization.

SECTION III. WASTES AND HARMFUL OR NOXIOUS SUBSTANCES AND MATERIALS

Article 8 General Obligation

Without prejudice to other standards or obligations referred to in this Section, the Parties shall impose a general obligation upon operators to use the best available, environmentally effective and economically appropriate techniques and to observe internationally accepted standards regarding wastes, as well as the use, storage and discharge of harmful or noxious substances and materials, with a view to minimizing the risk of pollution.

Article 9 Harmful or noxious substances and materials

1. The use and storage of chemicals for the activities shall be approved by the competent authority, on the basis of the Chemical Use Plan.

2. The Contracting Party may regulate, limit or prohibit the use of chemicals for the activities in accordance with guidelines to be adopted by the Contracting Parties.

3. For the purpose of protecting the environment, the Parties shall ensure that each substance and material used for activities is accompanied by a compound description provided by the entity producing such substance or material.

4. The disposal into the Protocol Area of harmful or noxious substances and materials resulting from the activities covered by this Protocol and listed in Annex I to this Protocol is prohibited.

5. The disposal into the Protocol Area of harmful or noxious substances and materials resulting from the activities covered by this Protocol and listed in Annex II to this Protocol requires, in each case, a prior special permit from the competent authority.

6. The disposal into the Protocol Area of all other harmful or noxious substances and materials resulting from the activities covered by this Protocol and which might cause pollution requires a prior general permit from the competent authority.

7. The permits referred to in paragraphs 5 and 6 above shall be issued only after careful consideration of all the factors set forth in Annex III to this Protocol.

Article 10 Oil and oily mixtures and drilling fluids and cuttings

1. The Parties shall formulate and adopt common standards for the disposal of oil and oily mixtures from installations into the Protocol Area:

(a) such common standards shall be formulated in accordance with the provisions of Annex V, A;

(b) such common standards shall not be less restrictive than the following, in particular:

  (i) for machinery space drainage, a maximum oil content of 15 mg per litre whilst undiluted;

  (ii) for production water, a maximum oil content of 40 mg per litre as an average in any calendar month; the content shall not at any time exceed 100 mg per litre;

(c) the Parties shall determine by common agreement which method will be used to analyze the oil content.

2. The Parties shall formulate and adopt common standards for the use and disposal of drilling fluids and drill cuttings into the Protocol Area. Such common standards shall be formulated in accordance with the provisions of Annex V, B.

3. Each Party shall take appropriate measures to enforce the common standards adopted pursuant to this Article or to enforce more restrictive standards that it may have adopted.

Article 11 Sewage

1. The Contracting Party shall prohibit the discharge of sewage from installations permanently manned by 10 or more persons into the Protocol Area except in cases where:

(a)   the installation is discharging sewage after treatment as approved by the competent authority at a distance of at least four nautical miles from the nearest land or fixed fisheries installation, leaving the Contracting Party to decide on a case by case basis; or

(b)   the sewage is not treated, but the discharge is carried out in accordance with international rules and standards; or

(c)   the sewage has passed through an approved sewage treatment plant certified by the competent authority.

2. The Contracting Party shall impose stricter provisions, as appropriate, where deemed necessary, *inter alia* because of the regime of the currents in the area or proximity to any area referred to in Article 21.

3. The exceptions referred to in paragraph 1 shall not apply if the discharge produces visible floating solids or produces colouration, discolouration or opacity of the surrounding water.

4. If the sewage is mixed with wastes and harmful or noxious substances and materials having different disposal requirements, the more stringent requirements shall apply.

Article 12 Garbage

1. The Contracting Party shall prohibit the disposal into the Protocol Area of the following products and materials:

(a)   all plastics, including but not limited to synthetic ropes, synthetic fishing nets and plastic garbage bags;

(b)   all other non-biodegradable garbage, including paper products, rags, glass, metal, bottles, crockery, dunnage, lining and packing materials.

2. Disposal into the Protocol Area of food wastes shall take place as far away as possible from land, in accordance with international rules and standards.

3. If garbage is mixed with other discharges having different disposal or discharge requirements, the more stringent requirements shall apply.

Article 13 Reception facilities, instructions and sanctions

The Parties shall ensure that:

(a)   operators dispose satisfactorily of all wastes and harmful or noxious substances and materials in designated onshore reception facilities, except as otherwise authorized by the Protocol;

(b)   instructions are given to all personnel concerning proper means of disposal;

(c)   sanctions are imposed in respect of illegal disposals.

Article 14 Exceptions

1. The provisions of this Section shall not apply in case of:

(a)   *force majeure* and in particular for disposals:

(i)   to save human life,

(ii)   to ensure the safety of installations,

(iii) in case of damage to the installation or its equipment,

on condition that all reasonable precautions have been taken after the damage is discovered or after the disposal has been performed to reduce the negative effects.

(b)	the discharge into the sea of substances containing oil or harmful or noxious substances or materials which, subject to the prior approval of the competent authority, are being used for the purpose of combating specific pollution incidents in order to minimize the damage due to the pollution.

2.	However, the provisions of this Section shall apply in any case where the operator acted with the intent to cause damage or recklessly and with knowledge that damage will probably result.

3.	Disposals carried out in the circumstances referred to in paragraph 1 of this Article shall be reported immediately to the Organization and, either through the Organization or directly, to any Party or Parties likely to be affected, together with full details of the circumstances and of the nature and quantities of wastes or harmful or noxious substances or materials discharged.

SECTION IV. SAFEGUARDS

Article 15 Safety measures

1.	The Contracting Party within whose jurisdiction activities are envisaged or are being carried out shall ensure that safety measures are taken with regard to the design, construction, placement, equipment, marking, operation and maintenance of installations.

2.	The Contracting Party shall ensure that at all times the operator has on the installations adequate equipment and devices, maintained in good working order, for protecting human life, preventing and combating accidental pollution and facilitating prompt response to an emergency, in accordance with the best available environmentally effective and economically appropriate techniques and the provisions of the operator's contingency plan referred to in Article 16.

3.	The competent authority shall require a certificate of safety and fitness for the purpose (hereinafter referred to as 'certificate') issued by a recognized body to be submitted in respect of production platforms, mobile offshore drilling units, offshore storage facilities, offshore loading systems and pipelines and in respect of such other installations as may be specified by the Contracting Party.

4.	The Parties shall ensure through inspection that the activities are conducted by the operators in accordance with this Article.

Article 16 Contingency Planning

1.	In cases of emergency the Contracting Parties shall implement *mutatis mutandis* the provisions of the Protocol concerning Cooperation in Combating Pollution of the Mediterranean Sea by Oil and Other Harmful Substances in Cases of Emergency.

2.	Each Party shall require operators in charge of installations under its jurisdiction to have a contingency plan to combat accidental pollution, coordinated with the contingency plan of the Contracting Party established in accordance with the Protocol concerning Cooperation in Combating Pollution of the Mediterranean Sea by Oil and Other Harmful Substances in Cases of Emergency and approved in conformity with the procedures established by the competent authorities.

3.	Each Contracting Party shall establish coordination for the development and implementation of contingency plans. Such plans shall be established in accordance with guidelines adopted by the competent international organization. They shall, in particular, be in accordance with the provisions of Annex VII to this Protocol.

Article 17 Notification

Each Party shall require operators in charge of installations under its jurisdiction to report without delay to the competent authority:

    (a)   any event on their installation causing or likely to cause pollution in the Protocol Area;

    (b)   any observed event at sea causing or likely to cause pollution in the Protocol Area.

Article 18 Mutual assistance in cases of emergency

In cases of emergency, a Party requiring assistance in order to prevent, abate or combat pollution resulting from activities may request help from the other Parties, either directly or through the Regional Marine Pollution Emergency Response Centre for the Mediterranean Sea (REMPEC), which shall do their utmost to provide the assistance requested.

For this purpose, a Party which is also a Party to the Protocol concerning Cooperation in Combating Pollution of the Mediterranean Sea by Oil and Other Harmful Substances in Cases of Emergency shall apply the pertinent provisions of the said Protocol.

Article 19 Monitoring

1. The operator shall be required to measure, or to have measured by a qualified entity, expert in the matter, the effects of the activities on the environment in the light of the nature, scope, duration and technical methods employed in the activities and of the characteristics of the area and to report on them periodically or upon request by the competent authority for the purpose of an evaluation by such competent authority according to a procedure established by the competent authority in its authorization system.

2. The competent authority shall establish, where appropriate, a national monitoring system in order to be in a position to monitor regularly the installations and the impact of the activities on the environment, so as to ensure that the conditions attached to the grant of the authorization are being fulfilled.

Article 20 Removal of installations

1. The operator shall be required by the competent authority to remove any installation which is abandoned or disused, in order to ensure safety of navigation, taking into account the guidelines and standards adopted by the competent international organization. Such removal shall also have due regard to other legitimate uses of the sea, in particular fishing, the protection of the marine environment and the rights and duties of other Contracting Parties. Prior to such removal, the operator under its responsibility shall take all necessary measures to prevent spillage or leakage from the site of the activities.

2. The competent authority shall require the operator to remove abandoned or disused pipelines in accordance with paragraph 1 of this Article or to clean them inside and abandon them or to clean them inside and bury them so that they neither cause pollution, endanger navigation, hinder fishing, threaten the marine environment, nor interfere with other legitimate uses of the sea or with the rights and duties of other Contracting Parties. The competent authority shall ensure that appropriate publicity is given to the depth, position and dimensions of any buried pipeline and that such information is indicated on charts and notified to the Organization and other competent international organizations and the Parties.

3. The provisions of this Article apply also to installations disused or abandoned by any operator whose authorization may have been withdrawn or suspended in compliance with Article 7.

4. The competent authority may indicate eventual modifications to be made to the level of activities and to the measures for the protection of the marine environment which had initially been provided for.

5. The competent authority may regulate the cession or transfer of authorized activities to other persons.

6. Where the operator fails to comply with the provisions of this Article, the competent authority shall undertake, at the operator's expense, such action or actions as may be necessary to remedy the operator's failure to act.

Article 21 Specially Protected Areas

For the protection of the areas defined in the Protocol concerning Mediterranean Specially Protected Areas and any other area established by a Party and in furtherance of the goals stated therein, the Parties shall take special measures in conformity with international law, either individually or through multilateral or bilateral cooperation, to prevent, abate, combat and control pollution arising from activities in these areas. In addition to the measures referred to in the Protocol concerning Mediterranean Specially Protected Areas for the granting of authorization, such measures may include, *inter alia*:

    (a)   special restrictions or conditions when granting authorizations for such areas:

        (i)   the preparation and evaluation of environmental impact assessments;

        (ii) the elaboration of special provisions in such areas concerning monitoring, removal of installations and prohibition of any discharge.

    (b)   intensified exchange of information among operators, the competent authorities, Parties and the Organization regarding matters which may affect such areas.

SECTION V. COOPERATION

Article 22 Studies and research programmes

In conformity with Article 13 of the Convention, the Parties shall, where appropriate, cooperate in promoting studies and undertaking programmes of scientific and technological research for the purpose of developing new methods of:

    (a)   carrying out activities in a way that minimizes the risk of pollution;

    (b)   preventing, abating, combating and controlling pollution, especially in cases of emergency.

Article 23   International rules, standards and recommended practices and procedures

1. The Parties shall cooperate, either directly or through the Organization or other competent international organizations, in order to:

    (a)   establish appropriate scientific criteria for the formulation and elaboration of international rules, standards and recommended practices and procedures for achieving the aims of this Protocol;

    (b)   formulate and elaborate such international rules, standards and recommended practices and procedures;

    (c)   formulate and adopt guidelines in accordance with international practices and procedures to ensure observance of the provisions of Annex VI.

2. The Parties shall, as soon as possible, endeavour to harmonize their laws and regulations with the international rules, standards and recommended practices and procedures referred to in paragraph 1 of this Article.

3. The Parties shall endeavour, as far as possible, to exchange information relevant to their domestic policies, laws and regulations and the harmonization referred to in paragraph 2 of this Article.

Article 24 Scientific and technical assistance to developing countries

1. The Parties shall, directly or with the assistance of competent regional or other international organizations, cooperate with a view to formulating and, as far as possible, implementing programmes of assistance to developing countries, particularly in the fields of science, law, education and technology, in order to prevent, abate, combat and control pollution due to activities in the Protocol Area.

2. Technical assistance shall include, in particular, the training of scientific, legal and technical personnel, as well as the acquisition, utilization and production by those countries of appropriate equipment on advantageous terms to be agreed upon among the Parties concerned.

Article 25 Mutual information

The Parties shall inform one another directly or through the Organization of measures taken, of results achieved and, if the case arises, of difficulties encountered in the application of this Protocol. Procedures for the collection and submission of such information shall be determined at the meetings of the Parties.

Article 26 Transboundary pollution

1. Each Party shall take all measures necessary to ensure that activities under its jurisdiction are so conducted as not to cause pollution beyond the limits of its jurisdiction.

2. A Party within whose jurisdiction activities are being envisaged or carried out shall take into account any adverse environmental effects, without discrimination as to whether such effects are likely to occur within the limits of its jurisdiction or beyond such limits.

3. If a Party becomes aware of cases in which the marine environment is in imminent danger of being damaged, or has been damaged, by pollution, it shall immediately notify other Parties which in its opinion are likely to be affected by such damage, as well as the Regional Marine Pollution Emergency Response Centre for the Mediterranean Sea (REMPEC), and provide them with timely information that would enable them, where necessary, to take appropriate measures. REMPEC shall distribute the information immediately to all relevant Parties.

4. The Parties shall endeavour, in accordance with their legal systems and, where appropriate, on the basis of an agreement, to grant equal access to and treatment in administrative proceedings to persons in other States who may be affected by pollution or other adverse effects resulting from proposed or existing operations.

5. Where pollution originates in the territory of a State which is not a Contracting Party to this Protocol, any Contracting Party affected shall endeavour to cooperate with the said State so as to make possible the application of the Protocol.

Article 27 Liability and compensation

1. The Parties undertake to cooperate as soon as possible in formulating and adopting appropriate rules and procedures for the determination of liability and compensation for damage resulting from the activities dealt with in this Protocol, in conformity with Article 16 of the Convention.

2. Pending development of such procedures, each Party:
  (a) shall take all measures necessary to ensure that liability for damage caused by activities is imposed on operators, and they shall be required to pay prompt and adequate compensation;
  (b) shall take all measures necessary to ensure that operators shall have and maintain insurance cover or other financial security of such type and under such

terms as the Contracting Party shall specify in order to ensure compensation for damages caused by the activities covered by this Protocol.

SECTION VI. FINAL PROVISIONS

Article 28 Appointment of competent authorities

Each Contracting Party shall appoint one or more competent authorities to:
- (a) grant, renew and register the authorizations provided for in Section II of this Protocol;
- (b) issue and register the special and general permits referred to in Article 9 of this Protocol;
- (c) issue the permits referred to in Annex V to this Protocol;
- (d) approve the treatment system and certify the sewage treatment plant referred to in Article 11, paragraph 1, of this Protocol;
- (e) give the prior approval for exceptional discharges referred to in Article 14, paragraph 1 (b), of this Protocol;
- (f) carry out the duties regarding safety measures referred to in Article 15, paragraphs 3 and 4, of this Protocol;
- (g) perform the functions relating to contingency planning described in Article 16 and Annex VII to this Protocol;
- (h) establish monitoring procedures as provided in Article 19 of this Protocol;
- (i) supervise the removal operations of the installations as provided in Article 20 of this Protocol.

Article 29 Transitional measures

Each Party shall elaborate procedures and regulations regarding activities, whether authorized or not, initiated before the entry into force of this Protocol, to ensure their conformity, as far as practicable, with the provisions of this Protocol.

Article 30 Meetings

1. Ordinary meetings of the Parties shall take place in conjunction with ordinary meetings of the Contracting Parties to the Convention held pursuant to Article 18 of the Convention. The Parties may also hold extraordinary meetings in accordance with Article 18 of the Convention.

2. The functions of the meetings of the Parties to this Protocol shall be, *inter alia*:
- (a) to keep under review the implementation of this Protocol and to consider the efficacy of the measures adopted and the advisability of any other measures, in particular in the form of annexes and appendices;
- (b) to revise and amend any Annex or Appendix to this Protocol
- (c) to consider the information concerning authorizations granted or renewed in accordance with Section II of this Protocol;
- (d) to consider the information concerning the permits issued and approvals given in accordance with Section III of this Protocol;
- (e) to adopt the guidelines referred to in Article 9, paragraph 2, and Article 23, paragraph 1 (c), of this Protocol;
- (f) to consider the records of the contingency plans and means of intervention in emergencies adopted in accordance with Article 16 of this Protocol;
- (g) to establish criteria and formulate international rules, standards and recommended practices and procedures in accordance with Article 23, paragraph 1, of this Protocol, in whatever form the Parties may agree;

(h)   to facilitate the implementation of the policies and the achievement of the objectives referred to in Section V, in particular the harmonization of national and European Community legislation in accordance with Article 23, paragraph 2, of this Protocol;

(i)   to review progress made in the implementation of Article 27 of this Protocol;

(j)   to discharge such other functions as may be appropriate for the application of this Protocol.

Article 31 Relations with the Convention

1. The provisions of the Convention relating to any Protocol shall apply with respect to this Protocol.

2. The rules of procedure and the financial rules adopted pursuant to Article 24 of the Convention shall apply with respect to this Protocol, unless the Parties to this Protocol agree otherwise.

Article 32 Final clause

1. This Protocol shall be open for signature at Madrid from 14 October 1994 to 14 October 1995, by any State Party to the Convention invited to the Conference of Plenipotentiaries of the Coastal States of the Mediterranean Region on the Protocol for the Protection of the Mediterranean Sea against Pollution Resulting from Exploration and Exploitation of the Seabed and its Subsoil, held at Madrid on 13 and 14 October 1994. It shall also be open until the same dates for signature by the European Community and by any similar regional economic grouping of which at least one member is a coastal State of the Protocol Area and which exercises competence in fields covered by this Protocol in conformity with Article 30 of the Convention.

2. This Protocol shall be subject to ratification, acceptance or approval. Instruments of ratification, acceptance or approval shall be deposited with the Government of Spain, which will assume the functions of Depositary.

3. As from 15 October 1995, this Protocol shall be open for accession by the States referred to in paragraph 1 above, by the European Community and by any grouping referred to in that paragraph.

4. This Protocol shall enter into force on the thirtieth day following the date of deposit of at least six instruments of ratification, acceptance or approval of, or accession to, the Protocol by the Parties referred to in paragraph 1 of this Article.

IN WITNESS WHEREOF the undersigned, being duly authorized, have signed this Protocol.

Protocol concerning Specially Protected Areas and Biological Diversity in the Mediterranean (SPA and Biodiversity Protocol)

Done at Barcelona, 10 June 1995; entry into force, 12 December 1999
2102 UNTS 203 [Registration Number 36553][1]

The Contracting Parties to the present Protocol,

Being Parties to the Convention for the Protection of the Mediterranean Sea against Pollution, adopted at Barcelona on 16 February 1976,

Conscious of the profound impact of human activities on the state of the marine environment and the littoral and more generally on the ecosystems of areas having prevailing Mediterranean features,

Stressing the importance of protecting and, as appropriate, improving the state of the Mediterranean natural and cultural heritage, in particular through the establishment of specially protected areas and also by the protection and conservation of threatened species,

Considering the instruments adopted by the United Nations Conference on Environment and Development and particularly the Convention on Biological Diversity (Rio de Janeiro, 1992),

Conscious that when there is a threat of significant reduction or loss of biological diversity, lack of full scientific certainty should not be invoked as a reason for postponing measures to avoid or minimize such a threat,

Considering that all the Contracting Parties should cooperate to conserve, protect and restore the health and integrity of ecosystems and that they have, in this respect, common but differentiated responsibilities,

Have agreed as follows:

PART I. GENERAL PROVISIONS

Article 1 Definitions

For the purposes of this Protocol:

(a) 'Convention' means the Convention for the Protection of the Mediterranean Sea against Pollution, adopted at Barcelona on 16 February 1976 and amended at Barcelona in 1995;

(b) 'Biological diversity' means the variability among living organisms from all sources including, *inter alia*, terrestrial, marine and other aquatic ecosystems and the ecological complexes of which they are part; this includes diversity within species, between species and of ecosystems;

(c) 'Endangered species' means any species that is in danger of extinction throughout all or part of its range;

(d) 'Endemic species' means any species whose range is restricted to a limited geographical area;

---

[1] This Protocol replaced in the relations between the parties to both instruments the Protocol Concerning Mediterranean Specially Protected Areas which had been adopted in Geneva on 3 April 1980 and had entered into force on 23 March 1986 (1425 UNTS 161 [Registration Number 24079]). On 24 November 1996, the Meeting of Plenipotentiaries on the Annexes to the Protocol concerning Specially Protected Areas and Biological Diversity in the Mediterranean adopted three Annexes – Common Criteria for the Choice of Protected Marine and Coastal Areas that Could Be Included in the SPAMI List (Annex I), List of Endangered or Threatened Species (Annex II), List of Species Whose Exploitation Is Regulated (Annex III) – which are omitted.

(e) 'Threatened species' means any species that is likely to become extinct within the foreseeable future throughout all or part of its range and whose survival is unlikely if the factors causing numerical decline or habitat degradation continue to operate;

(f) 'Conservation status of a species' means the sum of the influences acting on the species that may affect its long-term distribution and abundance;

(g) 'Parties' means the Contracting Parties to this Protocol;

(h) 'Organization' means the organization referred to in Article 2 of the Convention;

(i) 'Centre' means the Regional Activity Centre for Specially Protected Areas.

Article 2 Geographical coverage

1. The area to which this Protocol applies shall be the area of the Mediterranean Sea as delimited in Article 1 of the Convention. It also includes:

– the seabed and its subsoil;

– the waters, the seabed and its subsoil on the landward side of the baseline from which the breadth of the territorial sea is measured and extending, in the case of watercourses, up to the freshwater limit;

– the terrestrial coastal areas designated by each of the Parties, including wetlands.

2. Nothing in this Protocol nor any act adopted on the basis of this Protocol shall prejudice the rights, the present and future claims or legal views of any State relating to the law of the sea, in particular, the nature and the extent of marine areas, the delimitation of marine areas between States with opposite or adjacent coasts, freedom of navigation on the high seas, the right and the modalities of passage through straits used for international navigation and the right of innocent passage in territorial seas, as well as the nature and extent of the jurisdiction of the coastal State, the flag State and the port State.

3. No act or activity undertaken on the basis of this Protocol shall constitute grounds for claiming, contending or disputing any claim to national sovereignty or jurisdiction.

Article 3 General obligations

1. Each Party shall take the necessary measures to:

(a) protect, preserve and manage in a sustainable and environmentally sound way areas of particular natural or cultural value, notably by the establishment of specially protected areas;

(b) protect, preserve and manage threatened or endangered species of flora and fauna.

2. The Parties shall cooperate, directly or through the competent international organizations, in the conservation and sustainable use of biological diversity in the area to which this Protocol applies.

3. The Parties shall identify and compile inventories of the components of biological diversity important for its conservation and sustainable use.

4. The Parties shall adopt strategies, plans and programmes for the conservation of biological diversity and the sustainable use of marine and coastal biological resources and shall integrate them into their relevant sectoral and intersectoral policies.

5. The Parties shall monitor the components of biological diversity referred to in paragraph 3 of this Article and shall identify processes and categories of activities which have or are likely to have a significant adverse impact on the conservation and sustainable use of biological diversity, and monitor their effects.

6.   Each Party shall apply the measures provided for in this Protocol without prejudice to the sovereignty or the jurisdiction of other Parties or other States. Any measures taken by a Party to enforce these measures shall be in accordance with international law.

PART II. PROTECTION OF AREAS

SECTION ONE - SPECIALLY PROTECTED AREAS

Article 4 Objectives

The objective of specially protected areas is to safeguard:

(a)   representative types of coastal and marine ecosystems of adequate size to ensure their long-term viability and to maintain their biological diversity;

(b)   habitats which are in danger of disappearing in their natural area of distribution in the Mediterranean or which have a reduced natural area of distribution as a consequence of their regression or on account of their intrinsically restricted area;

(c)   habitats critical to the survival, reproduction and recovery of endangered, threatened or endemic species of flora or fauna;

(d)   sites of particular importance because of their scientific, aesthetic, cultural or educational interest.

Article 5 Establishment of specially protected areas

1.   Each Party may establish specially protected areas in the marine and coastal zones subject to its sovereignty or jurisdiction.

2.   If a Party intends to establish, in an area subject to its sovereignty or national jurisdiction, a specially protected area contiguous to the frontier and to the limits of a zone subject to the sovereignty or national jurisdiction of another Party, the competent authorities of the two Parties shall endeavour to cooperate, with a view to reaching agreement on the measures to be taken and shall, *inter alia*, examine the possibility of the other Party establishing a corresponding specially protected area or adopting any other appropriate measures.

3.   If a Party intends to establish, in an area subject to its sovereignty or national jurisdiction, a specially protected area contiguous to the frontier and to the limits of a zone subject to the sovereignty or national jurisdiction of a State that is not a Party to this Protocol, the Party shall endeavour to cooperate with that State as referred to in the previous paragraph.

4.   If a State which is not party to this Protocol intends to establish a specially protected area contiguous to the frontier and to the limits of a zone subject to the sovereignty or national jurisdiction of a Party to this Protocol, the latter shall endeavour to cooperate with that State as referred to in paragraph 2.

Article 6 Protection Measures

The Parties, in conformity with international law and taking into account the characteristics of each specially protected area, shall take the protection measures required, in particular:

(a)   the strengthening of the application of the other Protocols to the Convention and of other relevant treaties to which they are Parties;

(b)   the prohibition of the dumping or discharge of wastes and other substances likely directly or indirectly to impair the integrity of the specially protected area;

(c)   the regulation of the passage of ships and any stopping or anchoring;

(d)   the regulation of the introduction of any species not indigenous to the specially protected area in question, or of genetically modified species, as well as the introduction or reintroduction of species which are or have been present in the specially protected area;

(e)   the regulation or prohibition of any activity involving the exploration or modification of the soil or the exploitation of the subsoil of the land part, the seabed or its subsoil;

(f)   the regulation of any scientific research activity;

(g)   the regulation or prohibition of fishing, hunting, taking of animals and harvesting of plants or their destruction, as well as trade in animals, parts of animals, plants, parts of plants, which originate in specially protected areas;

(h)   the regulation and if necessary the prohibition of any other activity or act likely to harm or disturb the species or that might endanger the state of conservation of the ecosystems or species or might impair the natural or cultural characteristics of the specially protected area;

(i)   any other measure aimed at safeguarding ecological and biological processes and the landscape.

Article 7 Planning and management

1.   The Parties shall, in accordance with the rules of international law, adopt planning, management, supervision and monitoring measures for the specially protected areas.

2.   Such measures should include for each specially protected area:

(a)   the development and adoption of a management plan that specifies the legal and institutional framework and the management and protection measures applicable;

(b)   the continuous monitoring of ecological processes, habitats, population dynamics, landscapes, as well as the impact of human activities;

(c)   the active involvement of local communities and populations, as appropriate, in the management of specially protected areas, including assistance to local inhabitants who might be affected by the establishment of such areas;

(d)   the adoption of mechanisms for financing the promotion and management of specially protected areas, as well as the development of activities which ensure that management is compatible with the objectives of such areas;

(e)   the regulation of activities compatible with the objectives for which the specially protected area was established and the terms of the related permits;

(f)   the training of managers and qualified technical personnel, as well as the development of an appropriate infrastructure.

3.   The Parties shall ensure that national contingency plans incorporate measures for responding to incidents that could cause damage or constitute a threat to the specially protected areas.

4.   When specially protected areas covering both land and marine areas have been established, the Parties shall endeavour to ensure the coordination of the administration and management of the specially protected area as a whole.

SECTION TWO - SPECIALLY PROTECTED AREAS OF MEDITERRANEAN IMPORTANCE

Article 8 Establishment of the list of specially protected areas of Mediterranean importance

1.   In order to promote cooperation in the management and conservation of natural areas, as well as in the protection of threatened species and their habitats, the Parties shall

draw up a 'List of Specially Protected Areas of Mediterranean Importance', hereinafter referred to as the 'SPAMI List'.

2. The SPAMI List may include sites which:
-   are of importance for conserving the components of biological diversity in the Mediterranean;
-   contain ecosystems specific to the Mediterranean area or the habitats of endangered species;
-   are of special interest at the scientific, aesthetic, cultural or educational levels.

3. The Parties agree:
(a) to recognize the particular importance of these areas for the Mediterranean;
(b) to comply with the measures applicable to the SPAMIs and not to authorize nor undertake any activities that might be contrary to the objectives for which the SPAMIs were established.

Article 9 Procedure for the establishment and listing of SPAMIs

1. SPAMIs may be established, following the procedure provided for in paragraph 2 to 4 of this Article, in:
(a) the marine and coastal zones subject to the sovereignty or jurisdiction of the Parties;
(b) zones partly or wholly on the high seas.

2. Proposals for inclusion in the List may be submitted:
(a) by the Party concerned, if the area is situated in a zone already delimited, over which it exercises sovereignty or jurisdiction;
(b) by two or more neighbouring Parties concerned if the area is situated, partly or wholly, on the high sea;
(c) by the neighbouring Parties concerned in areas where the limits of national sovereignty or jurisdiction have not yet been defined.

3. Parties making proposals for inclusion in the SPAMI List shall provide the Centre with an introductory report containing information on the area's geographical location, its physical and ecological characteristics, its legal status, its management plans and the means for their implementation, as well as a statement justifying its Mediterranean importance;
(a) where a proposal is formulated under subparagraphs 2 (b) and 2 (c) of this Article, the neighbouring Parties concerned shall consult each other with a view to ensuring the consistency of the proposed protection and management measures, as well as the means for their implementation;
(b) proposals made under paragraph 2 of this Article shall indicate the protection and management measures applicable to the area as well as the means of their implementation.

4. The procedure for inclusion of the proposed area in the List is the following:
(a) for each area, the proposal shall be submitted to the National Focal Points, which shall examine its conformity with the common guidelines and criteria adopted pursuant to Article 16;
(b) if a proposal made in accordance with subparagraph 2 (a) of this Article is consistent with the guidelines and common criteria, after assessment, the Organization shall inform the meeting of the Parties, which shall decide to include the area in the SPAMI List;
(c) if a proposal made in accordance with subparagraphs 2 (b) and 2 (c) of this Article is consistent with the guidelines and common criteria, the Centre shall transmit it to the Organization, which shall inform the meeting of the Parties.

The decision to include the area in the SPAMI list shall be taken by consensus by the Contracting Parties, which shall also approve the management measures applicable to the area.

5. The Parties which proposed the inclusion of the area in the List shall implement the protection and conservation measures specified in their proposals in accordance with paragraph 3 of this Article. The Contracting Parties undertake to observe the rules thus laid down. The Centre shall inform the competent international organizations of the List and of the measures taken in the SPAMIs.

6. The Parties may revise the SPAMI List. To this end, the Centre shall prepare a report.

Article 10 Changes in the status of SPAMIs

Changes in the delimitation or legal status of a SPAMI or the suppression of all or part of such an area shall not be decided upon unless there are important reasons for doing so, taking into account the need to safeguard the environment and comply with the obligations laid down in this Protocol and a procedure similar to that followed for the creation of the SPAMI and its inclusion in the List shall be observed.

PART III. PROTECTION AND CONSERVATION OF SPECIES

Article 11 National measures for the protection and conservation of species

1. The Parties shall manage species of flora and fauna with the aim of maintaining them in a favourable state of conservation.

2. The Parties shall, in the zones subject to their sovereignty or national jurisdiction, identify and compile lists of the endangered or threatened species of flora and fauna and accord protected status to such species. The Parties shall regulate and, where appropriate, prohibit activities having adverse effects on such species or their habitats, and carry out management, planning and other measures to ensure a favourable state of conservation of such species.

3. With respect to protected species of fauna, the Parties shall control and, where appropriate, prohibit:

(a) the taking, possession or killing (including, to the extent possible, the incidental taking, possession or killing), the commercial trade, the transport and the exhibition for commercial purposes of these species, their eggs, parts or products;

(b) to the extent possible, the disturbance of wild fauna, particularly during the period of breeding, incubation, hibernation or migration, as well as other periods of biological stress.

4. In addition to the measures specified in the previous paragraph, the Parties shall coordinate their efforts, through bilateral or multilateral action, including if necessary, agreements for the protection and recovery of migratory species whose range extends into the area to which this Protocol applies.

5. With respect to protected species of flora and their parts and products, the Parties shall regulate, and where appropriate, prohibit all forms of destruction and disturbance, including the picking, collecting, cutting, uprooting, possession of, commercial trade in, or transport and exhibition for commercial purposes of such species.

6. The Parties shall formulate and adopt measures and plans with regard to *ex situ* reproduction, in particular captive breeding, of protected fauna and propagation of protected flora.

7. The Parties shall endeavour, directly or through the Centre, to consult with range States that are not Parties to this Protocol, with a view to coordinating their efforts to manage and protect endangered or threatened species.

8. The Parties shall make provision, where possible, for the return of protected species exported or held illegally. Efforts should be made by Parties to reintroduce such specimens to their natural habitat.

Article 12   Cooperative measures for the protection and conservation of species

1. The Parties shall adopt cooperative measures to ensure the protection and conservation of the flora and fauna listed in the Annexes to this Protocol relating to the List of Endangered or Threatened Species and the List of Species whose Exploitation is Regulated.

2. The Parties shall ensure the maximum possible protection and recovery of the species of fauna and flora listed in the Annex relating to the List of Endangered or Threatened Species by adopting at the national level the measures provided for in paragraphs 3 and 5 of Article 11 of this Protocol.

3. The Parties shall prohibit the destruction of and damage to the habitat of species listed in the Annex relating to the List of Endangered or Threatened Species and shall formulate and implement action plans for their conservation or recovery. They shall continue to cooperate in implementing the relevant action plans already adopted.

4. The Parties, in cooperation with competent international organizations, shall take all appropriate measures to ensure the conservation of the species listed in the Annex relating to the List of Species whose Exploitation is Regulated while at the same time authorizing and regulating the exploitation of these species so as to ensure and maintain their favourable state of conservation.

5. When the range area of a threatened or endangered species extends to both sides of a national frontier or of the limit that separates the territories or the areas subject to the sovereignty or the national jurisdiction of two Parties to this Protocol, these Parties shall cooperate with a view to ensuring the protection and conservation and, if necessary, the recovery of such species.

6. Provided that no other satisfactory solutions are available and that the exemption does not harm the survival of the population or of any other species, the Parties may grant exemptions to the prohibitions prescribed for the protection of the species listed in the Annexes to this Protocol for scientific, educational or management purposes necessary to ensure the survival of the species or to prevent significant damage. Such exemptions shall be notified to the Contracting Parties.

Article 13 Introduction of non-indigenous or genetically modified species

1. The Parties shall take all appropriate measures to regulate the intentional or accidental introduction of non-indigenous or genetically modified species to the wild and prohibit those that may have harmful impacts on the ecosystems, habitats or species in the area to which this Protocol applies.

2. The Parties shall endeavour to implement all possible measures to eradicate species that have already been introduced when, after scientific assessment, it appears that such species cause or are likely to cause damage to ecosystems, habitats or species in the area to which this Protocol applies.

PART IV. PROVISIONS COMMON TO PROTECTED AREAS AND SPECIES

Article 14 Amendments to Annexes

1. The procedures for amendments to Annexes to this Protocol shall be those set forth in Article 23 of the Convention.

2. All proposed amendments submitted to the meeting of Contracting Parties shall have been the subject of prior evaluation by the meeting of National Focal Points.

Article 15 Inventories

Each Party shall compile comprehensive inventories of:

(a)   areas over which they exercise sovereignty or jurisdiction that contain rare or fragile ecosystems, that are reservoirs of biological diversity, that are important for threatened or endangered species;

(b)   species of fauna or flora that are endangered or threatened.

Article 16 Guidelines and common criteria

The Parties shall adopt:

(a)   common criteria for the choice of protected marine and coastal areas that could be included in the SPAMI List which shall be annexed to the Protocol;

(b)   common criteria for the inclusion of additional species in the Annexes;

(c)   guidelines for the establishment and management of specially protected areas.

The criteria and guidelines referred to in paragraphs (b) and (c) may be amended by the meeting of the Parties on the basis of a proposal made by one or more Parties.

Article 17 Environmental impact assessment

In the planning process leading to decisions on industrial and other projects and activities that could significantly affect protected areas and species and their habitats, the Parties shall evaluate and take into consideration the possible direct or indirect, immediate or long-term, impact, including the cumulative impact of the projects and activities being contemplated.

Article 18 Integration of traditional activities

1. In formulating protective measures, the Parties shall take into account the traditional subsistence and cultural activities of their local populations. They shall grant exemptions, as necessary, to meet such needs. No exemption which is allowed for this reason shall:

(a)   endanger either the maintenance of ecosystems protected under this Protocol or the biological processes contributing to the maintenance of those ecosystems;

(b)   cause either the extinction of, or a substantial reduction in, the number of individuals making up the populations or species of flora and fauna, in particular endangered, threatened, migratory or endemic species.

2. Parties which grant exemptions from the protection measures shall inform the Contracting Parties accordingly.

Article 19 Publicity, information, public awareness and education.

1. The Parties shall give appropriate publicity to the establishment of specially protected areas, their boundaries, applicable regulations, and to the designation of protected species, their habitats and applicable regulations.

2. The Parties shall endeavour to inform the public of the interest and value of specially protected areas and species, and of the scientific knowledge which may be

gained from the point of view of nature conservation and other points of view. Such information should have an appropriate place in education programmes. The Parties shall also endeavour to promote the participation of their public and their conservation organizations in measures that are necessary for the protection of the areas and species concerned, including environmental impact assessments.

Article 20 Scientific, technical and management research
1. The Parties shall encourage and develop scientific and technical research relating to the aims of this Protocol. They shall also encourage and develop research into the sustainable use of specially protected areas and the management of protected species.

2. The Parties shall consult, when necessary, among themselves and with competent international organizations with a view to identifying, planning and undertaking scientific and technical research and monitoring programmes necessary for the identification and monitoring of protected areas and species and assessing the effectiveness of measures taken to implement management and recovery plans.

3. The Parties shall exchange, directly or through the Centre, scientific and technical information concerning current and planned research and monitoring programmes and the results thereof. They shall, to the fullest extent possible, coordinate their research and monitoring programmes, and endeavour jointly to define or standardize their procedures.

4. In technical and scientific research, the Parties shall give priority to SPAMIs and species appearing in the Annexes to this Protocol.

Article 21 Mutual cooperation
1. The Parties shall, directly or with the assistance of the Centre or international organizations concerned, establish cooperation programmes to coordinate the establishment, conservation, planning and management of specially protected areas, as well as the selection, management and conservation of protected species. There shall be regular exchanges of information concerning the characteristics of protected areas and species, the experience acquired and the problems encountered.

2. The Parties shall, at the earliest opportunity, communicate any situation that might endanger the ecosystems of specially protected areas or the survival of protected species of flora and fauna to the other Parties, to the States that might be affected and to the Centre.

Article 22 Mutual assistance
1. The Parties shall cooperate, directly or with the assistance of the Centre or the international organizations concerned, in formulating, financing and implementing programmes of mutual assistance and assistance to developing countries that express a need for it with a view to implementing this Protocol.

2. These programmes shall include public environmental education, the training of scientific, technical and management personnel, scientific research, the acquisition, utilization, design and development of appropriate equipment, and transfer of technology on advantageous terms to be agreed among the Parties concerned.

3. The Parties shall, in matters of mutual assistance, give priority to the SPAMIs and species appearing in the Annexes to this Protocol.

Article 23 Reports of the Parties
The Parties shall submit to ordinary meetings of the Parties a report on the implementation of this Protocol, in particular on:
(a) the status and the state of the areas included in the SPAMI List;
(b) any changes in the delimitation or legal status of the SPAMIs and protected species;

(c)   possible exemptions allowed pursuant to Articles 12 and 18 of this Protocol.

PART V. INSTITUTIONAL PROVISIONS

Article 24 National Focal Points

Each Party shall designate a National Focal Point to serve as liaison with the Centre on the technical and scientific aspects of the implementation of this Protocol. The National Focal Points shall meet periodically to carry out the functions deriving from this Protocol.

Article 25 Coordination

1. The Organization shall be responsible for coordinating the implementation of this Protocol. For this purpose, it shall receive the support of the Centre, to which it may entrust the following functions:

(a)   assisting the Parties, in cooperation with the competent international, intergovernmental and non-governmental organizations, in:
  –   establishing and managing specially protected areas in the area to which this Protocol applies;
  –   conducting programmes of technical and scientific research as provided for in Article 20 of this Protocol;
  –   conducting the exchange of scientific and technical information among the Parties as provided for in Article 20 of this Protocol;
  –   preparing management plans for specially protected areas and species;
  –   developing cooperative programmes pursuant to Article 21 of this Protocol;
  –   preparing educational materials designed for various groups;

(b)   convening and organizing the meetings of the National Focal Points and providing them with secretariat services;

(c)   formulating recommendations on guidelines and common criteria pursuant to Article 16 of this Protocol;

(d)   creating and updating databases of specially protected areas, protected species and other matters relevant to this Protocol;

(e)   preparing reports and technical studies that may be required for the implementation of this Protocol;

(f)   elaborating and implementing the training programmes mentioned in Article 22, paragraph 2;

(g)   cooperating with regional and international governmental and non-governmental organizations concerned with the protection of areas and species, provided that the specificity of each organization and the need to avoid the duplication of activities are respected;

(h)   carrying out the functions assigned to it in the action plans adopted in the framework of this Protocol;

(i)   carrying out any other function assigned to it by the Parties.

Article 26 Meetings of the Parties

1. The ordinary meetings of the Parties to this Protocol shall be held in conjunction with the ordinary meetings of the Contracting Parties to the Convention held pursuant to Article 18 of the Convention. The Parties may also hold extraordinary meetings in conformity with that Article.

2. The meetings of the Parties to this Protocol are particularly aimed at:

(a) keeping under review the implementation of this Protocol;

(b) overseeing the work of the Organization and of the Centre relating to the implementation of this Protocol and providing policy guidance for their activities;

(c) considering the efficacy of the measures adopted for the management and protection of areas and species, and examining the need for other measures, in particular in the form of Annexes and amendments to this Protocol or to its Annexes;

(d) adopting the guidelines and common criteria provided for in Article 16 of this Protocol;

(e) considering reports transmitted by the Parties under Article 23 of this Protocol, as well as any other pertinent information which the Parties transmit through the Centre;

(f) making recommendations to the Parties on the measures to be adopted for the implementation of this Protocol;

(g) examining the recommendations of the meetings of the National Focal Points pursuant to Article 24 of this Protocol;

(h) deciding on the inclusion of an area in the SPAMI List in conformity with Article 9, paragraph 4, of this Protocol;

(i) examining any other matter relevant to this Protocol, as appropriate;

(j) discussing and evaluating the exemptions allowed by the Parties in conformity with Articles 12 and 18 of this Protocol.

PART VI. FINAL PROVISIONS

Article 27 Effect of the Protocol on domestic legislation

The provisions of this Protocol shall not affect the right of Parties to adopt relevant stricter domestic measures for the implementation of this Protocol.

Article 28 Relationship with third Parties

1. The Parties shall invite States that are not Parties to the Protocol and international organizations to cooperate in the implementation of this Protocol.

2. The Parties undertake to adopt appropriate measures, consistent with international law, to ensure that no one engages in any activity contrary to the principles or purposes of this Protocol.

Article 29 Signature

This Protocol shall be open for signature in Barcelona on 10 June 1995 and in Madrid from 11 June 1995 to 10 June 1996 by any Contracting Party to the Convention.

Article 30 Ratification, acceptance or approval

This Protocol shall be subject to ratification, acceptance or approval. Instruments of ratification, acceptance or approval shall be deposited with the Government of Spain, which will assume the functions of Depositary.

Article 31 Accession

As from 10 June 1996, this Protocol shall be open for accession by any State and regional economic grouping which is Party to the Convention.

Article 32 Entry into force

1. This Protocol shall enter into force on the thirtieth day following the deposit of the sixth instrument of ratification, acceptance or approval of, or accession to, the Protocol.

2. From the date of its entry into force, this Protocol shall replace the Protocol Concerning Mediterranean Specially Protected Areas of 1982, in the relationship among the Parties to both instruments.

IN WITNESS WHEREOF, the undersigned, being duly authorized, have signed this Protocol.

DONE at Barcelona, on 10 June 1995, in a single copy in the Arabic, English, French and Spanish languages, the four texts being equally authoritative, for signature by any Party to the Convention.

Protocol on the Prevention of Pollution of the Mediterranean Sea by Transboundary Movements of Hazardous Wastes and Their Disposal (Hazardous Wastes Protocol)

Done at Izmir, 1 October 1996; entry into force, 19 December 2007
UNEP, Mediterranean Action Plan, *Convention for the Protection of the Marine Environment and the Coastal Region of the Mediterranean and its Protocols*, 2005, 143[1]

The Contracting Parties to the present Protocol,

Being Parties to the Convention for the Protection of the Mediterranean Sea against Pollution, adopted at Barcelona on 16 February 1976 and amended on 10 June 1995,

Conscious of the danger threatening the environment of the Mediterranean Sea caused by the transboundary movements and disposal of hazardous wastes,

Convinced that the most effective way of protecting human health and the marine environment from the dangers posed by hazardous wastes is the reduction and elimination of their generation, for example through substitution and other clean production methods,

Recognizing the increased will for the prohibition of transboundary movements of hazardous wastes and their disposal in other States, especially in developing countries,

Taking into account the 1992 Rio Declaration on Environment and Development and especially Principle 14 which declares that States 'should effectively cooperate to discourage or prevent the relocation and transfer to other States of any activities or substances that cause severe environmental degradation or are found to be harmful to human health',

Aware of the growing international concern regarding the need to ensure that pollution originating in one State is not transferred to other States and, consistent with this objective, of the need to reduce transboundary movements of hazardous wastes to a minimum as far as possible, with the ultimate aim of phasing out such movements,

Recognizing also that any State has the sovereign right to ban the entry, transit or disposal of hazardous wastes in its territory,

Bearing in mind the relevant provisions of the United Nations Convention on the Law of the Sea of 1982,

---

[1] Annex I (Categories of Wastes Subject to this Protocol), Annex II (List of Hazardous Characteristics), Annex III (Disposal Operations), Annex IV (A) (Information to be Provided on Notification) and Annex IV (B) (Information to be Provided on the Movement Document) omitted.

Taking into account also the Basel Convention on the Control of Transboundary Movements of Hazardous Wastes and their Disposal, adopted on 22 March 1989, in particular Article 11, and decisions I/22, II/12 and III/1 adopted by the First, Second and Third Meetings respectively of the Conference of the Parties to the Basel Convention,

Taking into account further that many States, among them Contracting Parties to the Barcelona Convention, have taken legal measures and entered into international agreements consistent with the Basel Convention to ban transboundary movements of hazardous wastes, for example, the IVth ACP/EEC Convention signed in Lomé on 15 December 1989 by the European Economic Community and the African, Caribbean and Pacific Group of States, and the Bamako Convention on the Ban of the Import into Africa and the Control of Transboundary Movement and Management of Hazardous Wastes within Africa, adopted under the auspices of the Organization of African Unity on 30 January 1991,

Recognizing further the differences in levels of economic and legislative development among the various Mediterranean coastal States, and realizing that hazardous waste should not be allowed to be transported in order to take advantage of such economic or legislative disparities to the detriment of the environment and of the social well-being of developing countries,

Bearing in mind also the fact that the most effective way of dealing with the threats represented by wastes for human health and the environment consists in decreasing or even prohibiting the transfer of activities which generate hazardous wastes,
Have agreed as follows:

Article 1 Definitions

For the purposes of this Protocol:
(a) 'Convention' means the Convention for the Protection of the Mediterranean Sea against Pollution, adopted at Barcelona on 16 February 1976 and amended on 10 June 1995;
(b) A 'Party' means a Contracting Party to this Protocol in accordance with Article 29, paragraph 1, of the Convention;
(c) 'Wastes' means substances or objects which are disposed of or are intended to be disposed of or are required to be disposed of by the provisions of national law;
(d) 'Hazardous wastes' means wastes or categories of substances as specified in Article 3 of this Protocol;
(e) 'Disposal' means any operation specified in Annex III to this Protocol;
(f) 'Transboundary movement' means any movement of hazardous wastes from an area under the national jurisdiction of one State to or through an area under the national jurisdiction of another State or to or through an area not under the national jurisdiction of any State, provided at least two States are involved in the movement;
(g) 'Approved site or facility' means a site or facility for the disposal of hazardous wastes which is authorized or permitted to operate for this purpose by a relevant authority of the State where the site or facility is located;
(h) 'Competent authority' means one governmental authority designated by a Party to be responsible, within such geographical areas as the Party may think fit, for receiving the notification of a transboundary movement of hazardous waste, and any information related to it, and for responding to such a notification;
(i) 'Clean production methods' means those which reduce or avoid the generation of hazardous wastes in conformity with Articles 5 and 8 of this Protocol;

(j)   'Environmentally sound management' of hazardous wastes means taking all practicable steps to ensure that hazardous wastes are collected, transported and disposed of (including after-care of disposal sites) in a manner which will protect human health and the environment against the adverse effects which may result from such wastes;

(k)   'Area under the national jurisdiction of a State' means any land, marine area or airspace within which a State exercises administrative and regulatory responsibilities in accordance with international law in regard to the protection of human health or the environment;

(l)   'State of export' means a Party from which a transboundary movement of hazardous wastes is planned to be initiated or is initiated;

(m)   'State of import' means a Party to which a transboundary movement of hazardous wastes is planned or takes place for the purpose of disposal therein or for the purpose of loading prior to disposal in an area not under the national jurisdiction of any State;

(n)   'State of transit' means any State, other than the State of export or import, through which a movement of hazardous wastes is planned or takes place;

(o)   'Exporter' means any person under the jurisdiction of the State of export who arranges for hazardous wastes to be exported;

(p)   'Importer' means any person under the jurisdiction of the State of import who arranges for hazardous wastes to be imported;

(q)   'Generator' means any person whose activity produces hazardous wastes or, if that person is not known, the person who is in possession and/or control of those wastes;

(r)   'Disposer' means any person to whom hazardous wastes are shipped and who carries out the disposal of such wastes;

(s)   'Illegal traffic' means any transboundary movement of hazardous wastes as specified in Article 9;

(t)   'Person' means any natural or legal person;

(u)   'Developing countries' means those countries which are not Member States of the Organization for Economic Co-operation and Development (OECD);[2]

(v)   'Developed countries' means those countries which are Member States of the Organization for Economic Co-operation and Development (OECD);[3]

(w)   'Organization' means the body referred to in Article 2 (b) of the Convention.

Article 2 Protocol Area

The Protocol Area as referred to in this Protocol shall mean the area as defined in Article 1 of the Convention.

Article 3 Scope of the Protocol

1. This Protocol shall apply to:

(a)   wastes that belong to any category in Annex I to this Protocol;

(b)   wastes that are not covered under paragraph (a) above but are defined as, or are considered to be, hazardous wastes by the domestic legislation of the State of export, import or transit;

(c)   wastes that possess any of the characteristics contained in Annex II to this Protocol;

---

[2] Footnote in original: For the purpose of this Protocol, Monaco shall have the same rights and obligations as Member States of the OECD.

[3] Footnote in original: For the purpose of this Protocol, Monaco shall have the same rights and obligations as Member States of the OECD.

(d)   hazardous substances that have been banned or are expired, or whose registration has been cancelled or refused through government regulatory action in the country of manufacture or export for human health or environmental reasons, or have been voluntarily withdrawn or omitted from the government registration required for use in the country of manufacture or export.

2.   Wastes which derive from the normal operations of ships, the discharge of which is covered by another international instrument, are excluded from the scope of this Protocol.

3.   The generator, the exporter or the importer, depending on the circumstances, shall bear the responsibility for checking with the competent authorities of the State of export, import or transit that a particular waste, prior to its transboundary movement, is not subject to this Protocol.

Article 4 National definitions of hazardous wastes

1.   Each Party to the Convention shall, within six months of becoming a Party, inform the Organization of the wastes, other than those listed in Annex I to this Protocol, considered or defined as hazardous wastes under its national legislation, and of any requirements concerning transboundary movement procedures applicable to such wastes.

2.   Each Party shall subsequently inform the Organization of any significant changes in information it has provided pursuant to paragraph 1 of this Article.

3.   The Organization shall inform all Parties of the information it has received pursuant to paragraphs 1 and 2 of this Article.

4.   The Parties shall be responsible for making the information transmitted to them by the Organization under paragraph 3 of this Article available to their exporters.

Article 5 General obligations

1.   The Parties shall take all appropriate measures to prevent, abate and eliminate pollution of the Protocol area which can be caused by transboundary movements and disposal of hazardous wastes.

2.   The Parties shall take all appropriate measures to reduce to a minimum, and where possible eliminate, the generation of hazardous wastes.

3.   The Parties shall also take all appropriate measures to reduce to a minimum the transboundary movement of hazardous wastes, and if possible to eliminate such movement in the Mediterranean. To achieve this goal, Parties have the right individually or collectively to ban the import of hazardous wastes. Other Parties shall respect this sovereign decision and not permit the export of hazardous wastes to States which have prohibited their import.

4.   Subject to the specific provisions relating to the transboundary movement of hazardous wastes through the territorial sea of a State of transit, referred to in Article 6 paragraph 4 of this Protocol, all Parties shall take appropriate legal, administrative and other measures within the area under their jurisdiction to prohibit the export and transit of hazardous wastes to developing countries, and Parties which are not Member States of the European Community[4] shall prohibit all imports and transit of hazardous wastes.

5.   The Parties shall cooperate with other United Nations agencies, relevant international and regional organizations in order to prevent illegal traffic, and shall take appropriate measures to achieve this goal, including criminal punishment measures in accordance with their national legislation.

---

[4] Footnote in original: For the purposes of this Protocol, Monaco shall have the same rights and obligations as Member States of the European Community.

Article 6 Transboundary movement and notification procedures

In exceptional cases, unless otherwise prohibited, when hazardous wastes cannot be disposed of in an environmentally sound manner in the country in which they originated, transboundary movements of such wastes can be allowed if:

1. The special situation of the Mediterranean developing countries which do not have the technical capabilities nor the disposal facilities for the environmentally sound management of hazardous wastes is taken into consideration;

2. The competent authority of the State of import ensures that the hazardous waste is disposed of in an approved site or facility with the technical capacity for its environmentally sound disposal;

3. The transboundary movement of hazardous wastes only takes place with the prior written notification of the State of export as specified in Annex IV to this Protocol, and the prior written consent of the State(s) of import and the State(s) of transit. This paragraph does not apply to conditions of passage through the territorial sea, which are governed by paragraph 4 of this Article;

4. The transboundary movement of hazardous wastes through the territorial sea of a State of transit only takes place with the prior notification by the State of export to the State of transit, as specified in Annex IV to this Protocol. After reception of the notification, the State of transit brings to the attention of the State of export all the obligations relating to passage through its territorial sea in application of international law and the relevant provisions of its domestic legislation adopted in compliance with international law to protect the marine environment. Where necessary, the State of transit may take appropriate measures in accordance with international law. This procedure must be complied with within the delays provided for by the Basel Convention;

5. Every State involved in a transboundary movement ensures that such movement is consistent with international safety standards and financial guarantees, in particular the procedures and standards set out in the Basel Convention.

Article 7 Duty to reimport

The State of export shall reimport the hazardous wastes if the transboundary movement cannot be completed by reason of impossibility of performance of the contracts relating to the movement and disposal of the wastes. To this end, any State of transit shall not oppose, hinder or prevent the return of those wastes to the State of export after being properly informed by the State of export.

Article 8 Regional cooperation

1. In conformity with Article 13 of the Convention, the Parties shall cooperate as far as possible in scientific and technological fields related to pollution from hazardous wastes, particularly in the implementation and development of new methods for reducing and eliminating hazardous waste generated through clean production methods.

2. To this end, the Parties shall submit annual reports to the Organization regarding the hazardous wastes they generate and transfer within the Protocol area in order to enable the Organization to produce a hazardous waste audit.

3. The Parties shall cooperate in taking appropriate measures to implement the precautionary approach based on prevention of pollution problems arising from hazardous wastes and their transboundary movement and disposal. To this end, the Parties shall ensure that clean production methods are applied to production processes.

Article 9 Illegal traffic

1. For the purpose of this Protocol, any transboundary movement of hazardous wastes in contravention of this Protocol or of other rules of international law shall be deemed to be illegal traffic.

2. Each Party shall introduce appropriate national legislation to prevent and punish illegal traffic, including criminal penalties on all persons involved in such illegal activities.

3. In the case of illegal traffic due to the conduct of the generator or the exporter, the State of export shall ensure that the wastes in question are taken back by the exporter or the generator or, if necessary, by itself, into the State of export within 30 days from the time the illegal traffic has come to its attention and that appropriate legal action is taken against the contravenor(s).

4. In the case of illegal traffic due to the conduct of the importer or disposer, the State of import shall ensure that the wastes in question are eliminated according to environmentally sound methods by the importer within 30 days from the time the illegal traffic has come to the attention of the State of import; if not possible, the State of export shall ensure that the wastes are taken back by the exporter, the generator or, if necessary, by itself into the State of export. The competent authorities of the importing or exporting States shall ensure that legal proceedings according to this Protocol are taken against the contravenor(s).

5. In cases where the responsibility for the illegal traffic cannot be assigned either to the exporter or generator or to the importer or disposer, the Parties concerned or other Parties, as appropriate, shall ensure, through cooperation that the wastes in question are disposed of as soon as possible in an environmentally sound manner either in the State of export or the State of import or elsewhere as appropriate.

6. The Parties shall forward, as soon as possible, all information relating to illegal traffic to the Organization, which shall distribute the information to all Contracting Parties.

7. The Parties shall cooperate to ensure that no illegal traffic takes place. Upon request, the Organization shall assist Parties in their identification of cases of illegal traffic and shall circulate immediately to the Parties concerned any information it has received regarding illegal traffic.

8. The Organization shall undertake the necessary coordination with the Secretariat of the Basel Convention in relation to the effective prevention and monitoring of illegal traffic in hazardous wastes. Such coordination shall be mainly based on:

   (a) exchange of information on cases or alleged cases of illegal traffic in the Mediterranean and coordination of action to remedy such cases;

   (b) providing assistance in the field of capacity-building, including development of national legislation and of appropriate infrastructure in the Mediterranean States with a view to the prevention and penalization of illegal traffic in hazardous wastes;

   (c) the establishment of a mechanism to prevent and monitor illegal traffic in hazardous wastes in the Mediterranean.

Article 10 Assistance to developing countries

The Parties shall, directly or with the assistance of competent or other international organizations or bilaterally, cooperate with a view to formulating and implementing programmes of financial and technical assistance to developing countries for the implementation of this Protocol.

Article 11 Transmission of information

The Parties shall inform one another through the Organization of measures taken, of results achieved and, if the case arises, of difficulties encountered in the application of this Protocol. Procedures for the collection and distribution of such information shall be determined at the meetings of the Parties.

Article 12 Information to and participation of the public

1. In the exceptional cases in which transboundary movement of hazardous wastes is permitted under Article 6 of this Protocol, the Parties shall ensure that adequate information is made available to the public, transmitted through such channels as the Parties deem appropriate.

2. The State of export and the State of import shall, in accordance with the provisions of this Protocol and whenever possible and appropriate, give the public an opportunity to participate in relevant procedures with the aim of making known its views and concerns.

Article 13 Verification

1. Any Party which has reason to believe that another Party is acting or has acted in breach of its obligations under this Protocol informs the Organization thereof, and, in such an event, simultaneously and immediately informs, directly or through the Organization, the Party against whom the allegations are made.

2. The Organization shall carry out a verification of the substance of the allegation through consultation with the Parties concerned and submit a report thereon to the Parties.

Article 14 Liability and compensation

The Parties shall cooperate with a view to setting out, as soon as possible, appropriate guidelines for the evaluation of the damage, as well as rules and procedures in the field of liability and compensation for damage resulting from the transboundary movement and disposal of hazardous wastes.

Article 15 Meetings

1. Ordinary meetings of the Parties shall take place in conjunction with ordinary meetings of the Contracting Parties to the Convention held pursuant to Article 18 of the Convention. The Parties to this Protocol may also hold extraordinary meetings in conformity with Article 18 of the Convention.

2. The functions of the meetings of the Parties shall be, *inter alia*:

   (a) to keep under review the implementation of this Protocol, and consider any additional measures, including in the form of annexes;

   (b) to revise and amend this Protocol and any Annex thereto, as appropriate;

   (c) to formulate and adopt programmes, methods and measures in accordance with the relevant Articles of this Protocol;

   (d) to consider any information submitted by the Parties to the Organization or to the meetings of the Parties in accordance with the relevant Articles of this Protocol;

   (e) to perform such other functions as may be appropriate for the application of this Protocol.

Article 16 Adoption of additional programmes and measures

The meeting of the Parties shall adopt, by a two-thirds (2/3) majority, any additional programmes and measures for the prevention and elimination of pollution from transboundary movements of hazardous wastes and their disposal.

Article 17 Final clauses

1. The provisions of the Convention relating to any Protocol shall apply with respect to this Protocol.

2. The Rules of Procedure and the Financial Rules adopted pursuant to Article 24 of the Convention shall apply with respect to this Protocol, unless the Parties to this Protocol agree otherwise.

3. This Protocol shall be open for signature at Izmir on 1 October 1996, and at Madrid from 2 October 1996 to 1 October 1997 by any State Party to the Convention. It shall also be open on the same dates for signature by the European Community and by any similar regional economic grouping of which at least one member is a coastal State of the Protocol area and which exercises competence in the fields covered by this Protocol.

4. This Protocol shall be subject to ratification, acceptance or approval. Instruments of ratification, acceptance or approval shall be deposited with the Government of Spain, which will assume the functions of Depositary.

5. As from 2 October 1997, this Protocol shall be open for accession by the States referred to in paragraph 3 above, by the European Community and by any grouping referred to in that paragraph.

6. This Protocol shall enter into force on the thirtieth (30) day following the deposit of at least six (6) instruments of ratification, acceptance or approval of, or accession to, the Protocol by the Parties referred to in paragraph 3 of this Article.

IN WITNESS WHEREOF, the undersigned, being duly authorized by their respective governments, have signed this Protocol.

DONE at Izmir on this first day of October 1996 in a single copy in the Arabic, English, French, and Spanish languages, the four texts being equally authoritative.

Protocol Concerning Cooperation in Preventing Pollution from Ships and, in Cases of Emergency, Combating Pollution of the Mediterranean Sea (Prevention and Emergency Protocol)

Adopted inn Malta, 25 January 2002; entry into force, 17 March 2004
UNEP, Mediterranean Action Plan, *Convention for the Protection of the Marine Environment and the Coastal Region of the Mediterranean and its Protocols*, 2005, 33[1]

The Contracting Parties to the present Protocol,

Being Parties to the Convention for the Protection of the Mediterranean Sea against Pollution, adopted at Barcelona on 16 February 1976 and amended on 10 June 1995,

Desirous of implementing Articles 6 and 9 of the said Convention,

Recognizing that grave pollution of the sea by oil and hazardous and noxious substances or a threat thereof in the Mediterranean Sea Area involves a danger for the coastal States and the marine environment,

Considering that the cooperation of all the coastal States of the Mediterranean Sea is called for to prevent pollution from ships and to respond to pollution incidents, irrespective of their origin,

---

[1] This Protocol replaced in the relations between the parties to both instruments the Protocol Concerning Co-operation in Combating Pollution of the Mediterranean Sea by Oil and Other Harmful Substances in Cases of Emergency which had been adopted in Barcelona on 16 February 1976 and had entered into force on 12 February 1978 (1102 UNTS 122 [Registration Number 16908]).

Acknowledging the role of the International Maritime Organization and the importance of cooperating within the framework of this Organization, in particular in promoting the adoption and the development of international rules and standards to prevent, reduce and control pollution of the marine environment from ships,

Emphasizing the efforts made by the Mediterranean coastal States for the implementation of these international rules and standards,

Acknowledging also the contribution of the European Community to the implementation of international standards as regards maritime safety and the prevention of pollution from ships,

Recognizing also the importance of cooperation in the Mediterranean Sea Area in promoting the effective implementation of international regulations to prevent, reduce and control pollution of the marine environment from ships,

Recognizing further the importance of prompt and effective action at the national, subregional and regional levels in taking emergency measures to deal with pollution of the marine environment or a threat thereof,

Applying the precautionary principle, the polluter pays principle and the method of environmental impact assessment, and utilizing the best available techniques and the best environmental practices, as provided for in Article 4 of the Convention,

Bearing in mind the relevant provisions of the United Nations Convention on the Law of the Sea, done at Montego Bay on 10 December 1982, which is in force and to which many Mediterranean coastal States and the European Community are Parties,

Taking into account the international conventions dealing in particular with maritime safety, the prevention of pollution from ships, preparedness for and response to pollution incidents, and liability and compensation for pollution damage,

Wishing to further develop mutual assistance and cooperation in preventing and combating pollution,

Have agreed as follows:

Article 1   Definitions

For the purpose of this Protocol:

(a)   'Convention' means the Convention for the Protection of the Mediterranean Sea against Pollution, adopted at Barcelona on 16 February 1976 and amended on 10 June 1995;

(b)   'Pollution incident' means an occurrence or series of occurrences having the same origin, which results or may result in a discharge of oil and/or hazardous and noxious substances and which poses or may pose a threat to the marine environment, or to the coastline or related interests of one or more States, and which requires emergency action or other immediate response;

(c)   'Hazardous and noxious substances' means any substance other than oil which, if introduced into the marine environment, is likely to create hazards to human health, to harm living resources and marine life, to damage amenities or to interfere with other legitimate uses of the sea;

(d)   'Related interests' means the interests of a coastal State directly affected or threatened and concerning, among others:

(i)   maritime activities in coastal areas, in ports or estuaries, including fishing activities;

(ii)   the historical and tourist appeal of the area in question, including water sports and recreation;

(iii)   the health of the coastal population;

(iv)   the cultural, aesthetic, scientific and educational value of the area;

(v)   the conservation of biological diversity and the sustainable use of marine and coastal biological resources;

(e)   'International regulations' means regulations aimed at preventing, reducing and controlling pollution of the marine environment from ships as adopted, at the global level and in conformity with international law, under the aegis of United Nations specialized agencies, and in particular of the International Maritime Organization;

(f)   'Regional Centre' means the 'Regional Marine Pollution Emergency Response Centre for the Mediterranean Sea' (REMPEC), established by Resolution 7 adopted by the Conference of Plenipotentiaries of the Coastal States of the Mediterranean Region on the Protection of the Mediterranean Sea at Barcelona on 9 February 1976, which is administered by the International Maritime Organization and the United Nations Environment Programme, and the objectives and functions of which are defined by the Contracting Parties to the Convention.

Article 2 Protocol Area

The area to which the Protocol applies shall be the Mediterranean Sea Area as defined in Article 1 of the Convention.

Article 3 General provisions

1. The Parties shall cooperate:

(a)   to implement international regulations to prevent, reduce and control pollution of the marine environment from ships; and

(b)   to take all necessary measures in cases of pollution incidents.

2. In cooperating, the Parties should take into account as appropriate the participation of local authorities, non-governmental organizations and socio-economic actors.

3. Each Party shall apply this Protocol without prejudice to the sovereignty or the jurisdiction of other Parties or other States. Any measures taken by a Party to apply this Protocol shall be in accordance with international law.

Article 4 Contingency plans and other means of preventing and combating pollution incidents

1. The Parties shall endeavour to maintain and promote, either individually or through bilateral or multilateral cooperation, contingency plans and other means of preventing and combating pollution incidents. These means shall include, in particular, equipment, ships, aircraft and personnel prepared for operations in cases of emergency, the enactment, as appropriate, of relevant legislation, the development or strengthening of the capability to respond to a pollution incident and the designation of a national authority or authorities responsible for the implementation of this Protocol.

2. The Parties shall also take measures in conformity with international law to prevent the pollution of the Mediterranean Sea Area from ships in order to ensure the effective implementation in that Area of the relevant international conventions in their capacity as flag State, port State and coastal State, and their applicable legislation. They shall develop their national capacity as regards the implementation of those international conventions and may cooperate for their effective implementation through bilateral or multilateral agreements.

3. The Parties shall inform the Regional Centre every two years of the measures taken for the implementation of this Article. The Regional Centre shall present a report to the Parties on the basis of the information received.

Article 5 Monitoring

The Parties shall develop and apply, either individually or through bilateral or multilateral cooperation, monitoring activities covering the Mediterranean Sea Area in order to prevent, detect and combat pollution, and to ensure compliance with the applicable international regulations.

Article 6 Cooperation in recovery operations

In case of release or loss overboard of hazardous and noxious substances in packaged form, including those in freight containers, portable tanks, road and rail vehicles and shipborne barges, the Parties shall cooperate as far as practicable in the salvage of these packages and the recovery of such substances so as to prevent or reduce the danger to the marine and coastal environment.

Article 7 Dissemination and exchange of information

1.   Each Party undertakes to disseminate to the other Parties information concerning:
(a)   the competent national organization or authorities responsible for combating pollution of the sea by oil and hazardous and noxious substances;
(b)   the competent national authorities responsible for receiving reports of pollution of the sea by oil and hazardous and noxious substances and for dealing with matters concerning measures of assistance between Parties;
(c)   the national authorities entitled to act on behalf of the State in regard to measures of mutual assistance and cooperation between Parties;
(d)   the national organization or authorities responsible for the implementation of paragraph 2 of Article 4, in particular those responsible for the implementation of the international conventions concerned and other relevant applicable regulations, those responsible for port reception facilities and those responsible for the monitoring of discharges which are illegal under MARPOL 73/78;
(e)   its regulations and other matters which have a direct bearing on preparedness for and response to pollution of the sea by oil and hazardous and noxious substances;
(f)   new ways in which pollution of the sea by oil and hazardous and noxious substances may be avoided, new measures for combating pollution, new developments in the technology of conducting monitoring and the development of research programmes.

2.   The Parties which have agreed to exchange information directly shall communicate such information to the Regional Centre. The latter shall communicate this information to the other Parties and, on a basis of reciprocity, to coastal States of the Mediterranean Sea Area which are not Parties to this Protocol.

3.   Parties concluding bilateral or multilateral agreements within the framework of this Protocol shall inform the Regional Centre of such agreements, which shall communicate them to the other Parties.

Article 8   Communication of information and reports concerning pollution incidents

The Parties undertake to coordinate the utilization of the means of communication at their disposal in order to ensure, with the necessary speed and reliability, the reception, transmission and dissemination of all reports and urgent information concerning pollution incidents. The Regional Centre shall have the necessary means of communication to enable it to participate in this coordinated effort and, in particular, to fulfil the functions assigned to it by paragraph 2 of Article 12.

Article 9 Reporting procedure

1. Each Party shall issue instructions to masters or other persons having charge of ships flying its flag and to the pilots of aircraft registered in its territory to report by the most rapid and adequate channels in the circumstances, following reporting procedures to the extent required by, and in accordance with, the applicable provisions of the relevant international agreements, to the nearest coastal State and to this Party:

(a)   all incidents which result or may result in a discharge of oil or hazardous and noxious substances;

(b)   the presence, characteristics and extent of spillages of oil or hazardous and noxious substances, including hazardous and noxious substances in packaged form, observed at sea which pose or are likely to pose a threat to the marine environment or to the coast or related interests of one or more of the Parties.

2. Without prejudice to the provisions of Article 20 of the Protocol, each Party shall take appropriate measures with a view to ensuring that the master of every ship sailing in its territorial waters complies with the obligations under (a) and (b) of paragraph 1 and may request assistance from the Regional Centre in this respect. It shall inform the International Maritime Organization of the measures taken.

3. Each Party shall also issue instructions to persons having charge of sea ports or handling facilities under its jurisdiction to report to it, in accordance with applicable laws, all incidents which result or may result in a discharge of oil or hazardous and noxious substances.

4. In accordance with the relevant provisions of the Protocol for the Protection of the Mediterranean Sea against Pollution Resulting from Exploration and Exploitation of the Continental Shelf and the Seabed and its Subsoil, each Party shall issue instructions to persons having charge of offshore units under its jurisdiction to report to it by the most rapid and adequate channels in the circumstances, following reporting procedures it has prescribed, all incidents which result or may result in a discharge of oil or hazardous and noxious substances.

5. In paragraphs 1, 3 and 4 of this Article, the term 'incident' means an incident meeting the conditions described therein, whether or not it is a pollution incident.

6. The information collected in accordance with paragraphs 1, 3 and 4 shall be communicated
to the Regional Centre in the case of a pollution incident.

7. The information collected in accordance with paragraphs 1, 3 and 4 shall be immediately communicated to the other Parties likely to be affected by a pollution incident:

(a)   by the Party which has received the information, preferably directly or through the Regional Centre; or

(b)   by the Regional Centre.

In case of direct communication between Parties, these shall inform the Regional Centre of the measures taken, and the Centre shall communicate them to the other Parties.

8. The Parties shall use a mutually agreed standard form proposed by the Regional Centre for the reporting of pollution incidents as required under paragraphs 6 and 7 of this Article.

9. In consequence of the application of the provisions of paragraph 7, the Parties are not bound by the obligation laid down in Article 9, paragraph 2, of the Convention.

Article 10 Operational measures

1. Any Party faced with a pollution incident shall:

(a)   make the necessary assessments of the nature, extent and possible consequences of the pollution incident or, as the case may be, the type and approximate quantity of oil or hazardous and noxious substances and the direction and speed of drift of the spillage;

(b)   take every practicable measure to prevent, reduce and, to the fullest possible extent, eliminate the effects of the pollution incident;

(c)   immediately inform all Parties likely to be affected by the pollution incident of these assessments and of any action which it has taken or intends to take, and simultaneously provide the same information to the Regional Centre, which shall communicate it to all other Parties;

(d)   continue to observe the situation for as long as possible and report thereon in accordance with Article 9.

2.   Where action is taken to combat pollution originating from a ship, all possible measures shall be taken to safeguard:

(a)   human lives;

(b)   the ship itself; in doing so, damage to the environment in general shall be prevented or minimized.

Any Party which takes such action shall inform the International Maritime Organization either directly or through the Regional Centre.

Article 11   Emergency measures on board ships, on offshore installations and in ports

1.   Each Party shall take the necessary steps to ensure that ships flying its flag have on board a pollution emergency plan as required by, and in accordance with, the relevant international regulations.

2.   Each Party shall require masters of ships flying its flag, in case of a pollution incident, to follow the procedures described in the shipboard emergency plan and in particular to provide the proper authorities, at their request, with such detailed information about the ship and its cargo as is relevant to actions taken in pursuance of Article 9, and to cooperate with these authorities.

3.   Without prejudice to the provisions of Article 20 of the Protocol, each Party shall take appropriate measures with a view to ensuring that the master of every ship sailing in its territorial waters complies with the obligation under paragraph 2 and may request assistance from the Regional Centre in this respect. It shall inform the International Maritime Organization of the measures taken.

4.   Each Party shall require that authorities or operators in charge of sea ports and handling facilities under its jurisdiction as it deems appropriate have pollution emergency plans or similar arrangements that are coordinated with the national system established in accordance with Article 4 and approved in accordance with procedures established by the competent national authority.

5.   Each Party shall require operators in charge of offshore installations under its jurisdiction to have a contingency plan to combat any pollution incident, which is coordinated with the national system established in accordance with Article 4 and in accordance with the procedures established by the competent national authority.

Article 12   Assistance

1.   Any Party requiring assistance to deal with a pollution incident may call for assistance from other Parties, either directly or through the Regional Centre, starting with the Parties which appear likely to be affected by the pollution. This assistance may comprise, in particular, expert advice and the supply to or placing at the disposal of the

Party concerned of the required specialized personnel, products, equipment and nautical facilities. Parties so requested shall use their best endeavours to render this assistance.

2.   Where the Parties engaged in an operation to combat pollution cannot agree on the organization of the operation, the Regional Centre may, with the approval of all the Parties involved, coordinate the activity of the facilities put into operation by these Parties.

3.   In accordance with applicable international agreements, each Party shall take the necessary legal and administrative measures to facilitate:
   (a)   the arrival and utilization in and departure from its territory of ships, aircraft and other modes of transport engaged in responding to a pollution incident or transporting personnel, cargoes, materials and equipment required to deal with such an incident; and
   (b)   the expeditious movement into, through and out of its territory of the personnel, cargoes, materials and equipment referred to in subparagraph (a).

Article 13 Reimbursement of costs of assistance

1.   Unless an agreement concerning the financial arrangements governing actions of Parties to deal with pollution incidents has been concluded on a bilateral or multilateral basis prior to the pollution incident, Parties shall bear the costs of their respective action in dealing with pollution in accordance with paragraph 2.

2.   (a)   If the action was taken by one Party at the express request of another Party, the requesting Party shall reimburse to the assisting Party the costs of its action. If the request is cancelled, the requesting Party shall bear the costs already incurred or committed by the assisting Party;
   (b)   if the action was taken by a Party on its own initiative, that Party shall bear the cost of its action;
   (c)   the principles laid down in subparagraphs (a) and (b) above shall apply unless the Parties concerned otherwise agree in any individual case.

3.   Unless otherwise agreed, the costs of the action taken by a Party at the request of another Party shall be fairly calculated according to the law and current practice of the assisting Party concerning the reimbursement of such costs.

4.   The Party requesting assistance and the assisting Party shall, where appropriate, cooperate in concluding any action in response to a compensation claim. To that end, they shall give due consideration to existing legal regimes. Where the action thus concluded does not permit full compensation for expenses incurred in the assistance operation, the Party requesting assistance may ask the assisting Party to waive reimbursement of the expenses exceeding the sums compensated or to reduce the costs which have been calculated in accordance with paragraph 3. It may also request a postponement of the reimbursement of such costs. In considering such a request, assisting Parties shall give due consideration to the needs of developing countries.

5.   The provisions of this Article shall not be interpreted as in any way prejudicing the rights of Parties to recover from third parties the costs of actions taken to deal with pollution incidents under other applicable provisions and rules of national and international law applicable to one or to the other Party involved in the assistance.

Article 14 Port reception facilities

1.   The Parties shall individually, bilaterally or multilaterally take all necessary steps to ensure that reception facilities meeting the needs of ships are available in their ports and terminals. They shall ensure that these facilities are used efficiently without causing undue delay to ships. The Parties are invited to explore ways and means to charge reasonable costs for the use of these facilities.

2. The Parties shall also ensure the provision of adequate reception facilities for pleasure craft.

3. The Parties shall take all the necessary steps to ensure that reception facilities operate efficiently to limit any impact of their discharges to the marine environment.

4. The Parties shall take the necessary steps to provide ships using their ports with updated information relevant to the obligations arising from MARPOL 73/78 and from their legislation applicable in this field.

Article 15 Environmental risks of maritime traffic

In conformity with generally accepted international rules and standards and the global mandate of the International Maritime Organization, the Parties shall individually, bilaterally or multilaterally take the necessary steps to assess the environmental risks of the recognized routes used in maritime traffic and shall take the appropriate measures aimed at reducing the risks of accidents or the environmental consequences thereof.

Article 16 Reception of ships in distress in ports and places of refuge

The Parties shall define national, subregional or regional strategies concerning reception in places of refuge, including ports, of ships in distress presenting a threat to the marine environment. They shall cooperate to this end and inform the Regional Centre of the measures they have adopted.

Article 17 Subregional agreements

The Parties may negotiate, develop and maintain appropriate bilateral or multilateral subregional agreements in order to facilitate the implementation of this Protocol, or part of it. Upon request of the interested Parties, the Regional Centre shall assist them, within the framework of its functions, in the process of developing and implementing these subregional agreements.

Article 18 Meetings

1. Ordinary meetings of the Parties to this Protocol shall be held in conjunction with ordinary meetings of the Contracting Parties to the Convention, held pursuant to Article 18 of the Convention. The Parties to this Protocol may also hold extraordinary meetings as provided in Article 18 of the Convention.

2. It shall be the function of the meetings of the Parties to this Protocol, in particular:

(a) to examine and discuss reports from the Regional Centre on the implementation of this Protocol, and particularly of its Articles 4, 7 and 16;

(b) to formulate and adopt strategies, action plans and programmes for the implementation of this Protocol;

(c) to keep under review and consider the efficacy of these strategies, action plans and programmes, and the need to adopt any new strategies, action plans and programmes and to develop measures to that effect;

(d) to discharge such other functions as may be appropriate for the implementation of this Protocol.

Article 19 Relationship with the Convention

1. The provisions of the Convention relating to any Protocol shall apply with respect to the present Protocol.

2. The rules of procedure and the financial rules adopted pursuant to Article 24 of the Convention shall apply with respect to this Protocol, unless the Parties agree otherwise.

Article 20 Effect of the Protocol on domestic legislation
    In implementing the provisions of this Protocol, the right of Parties to adopt relevant stricter domestic measures or other measures in conformity with international law, in the matters covered by this Protocol, shall not be affected.

Article 21 Relations with third Parties
    The Parties shall, where appropriate, invite States that are not Parties to the Protocol and international organizations to cooperate in the implementation of the Protocol.

Article 22 Signature
    This Protocol shall be open for signature at Valletta, Malta, on 25 January 2002 and in Madrid from 26 January 2002 to 25 January 2003 by any Contracting Party to the Convention.

Article 23 Ratification, acceptance or approval
    This Protocol shall be subject to ratification, acceptance or approval. The instruments of ratification, acceptance or approval shall be deposited with the Government of Spain, which will assume the functions of Depositary.

Article 24 Accession
    As from 26 January 2003, this Protocol shall be open for accession by any Party to the Convention.

Article 25 Entry into force
    1. This Protocol shall enter into force on the thirtieth day following the deposit of the sixth instrument of ratification, acceptance, approval or accession.
    2. From the date of its entry into force, this Protocol shall replace the Protocol concerning Cooperation in Combating Pollution of the Mediterranean Sea by Oil and other Harmful Substances in Cases of Emergency of 1976 in the relations between the Parties to both instruments.

Protocol on Integrated Coastal Zone Management in the Mediterranean
(ICZM Protocol)

Done at Madrid, 21 January 2008; not yet in force

The Contracting Parties to the present Protocol,
    Being Parties to the Convention for the Protection of the Marine Environment and the Coastal Region of the Mediterranean, adopted at Barcelona on 16 February 1976, and amended on 10 June 1995,
    Desirous of implementing the obligations set out in Article 4, paragraphs 3(e) and 5, of the said Convention,
    Considering that the coastal zones of the Mediterranean Sea are the common natural and cultural heritage of the peoples of the Mediterranean and that they should be preserved and used judiciously for the benefit of present and future generations,

Concerned at the increase in anthropic pressure on the coastal zones of the Mediterranean Sea which is threatening their fragile nature and *desirous* of halting and reversing the process of coastal zone degradation and of significantly reducing the loss of biodiversity of coastal ecosystems,

Worried by the risks threatening coastal zones due to climate change, which is likely to result, *inter alia*, in a rise in sea level, and *aware* of the need to adopt sustainable measures to reduce the negative impact of natural phenomena,

Convinced that, as an irreplaceable ecological, economic and social resource, the planning and management of coastal zones with a view to their preservation and sustainable development requires a specific integrated approach at the level of the Mediterranean basin as a whole and of its coastal States, taking into account their diversity and in particular the specific needs of islands related to geomorphological characteristics,

Taking into account the United Nations Convention on the Law of the Sea, done at Montego Bay on 10 December 1982, the Convention on Wetlands of International Importance especially as Waterfowl Habitat, done at Ramsar on 2 February 1971, and the Convention on Biological Diversity, done at Rio de Janeiro on 5 June 1992, to which many Mediterranean coastal States and the European Community are Parties,

Concerned in particular to act in cooperation for the development of appropriate and integrated plans for coastal zone management pursuant to Article 4, paragraph 1(e), of the United Nations Framework Convention on Climate Change, done at New York on 9 May 1992,

Drawing on existing experience with integrated coastal zone management and the work of various organizations, including the European institutions,

Based upon the recommendations and work of the Mediterranean Commission on Sustainable Development and the recommendations of the Meetings of the Contracting Parties held in Tunis in 1997, Monaco in 2001, Catania in 2003, and Portoroz in 2005, and the Mediterranean Strategy for Sustainable Development adopted in Portoroz in 2005,

Resolved to strengthen at the Mediterranean level the efforts made by coastal States to ensure integrated coastal zone management,

Determined to stimulate national, regional and local initiatives through coordinated promotional action, cooperation and partnership with the various actors concerned with a view to promoting efficient governance for the purpose of integrated coastal zone management,

Desirous of ensuring that coherence is achieved with regard to integrated coastal zone management in the application of the Convention and its Protocols,

Have agreed as follows:

PART I
GENERAL PROVISIONS

Article 1 General obligations

In conformity with the Convention for the Protection of the Marine Environment and the Coastal Region of the Mediterranean and its Protocols, the Parties shall establish a common framework for the integrated management of the Mediterranean coastal zone and shall take the necessary measures to strengthen regional co-operation for this purpose.

Article 2 Definitions

For the purposes of this Protocol:

(a)   'Parties' means the Contracting Parties to this Protocol.

(b) 'Convention' means the Convention for the Protection of the Marine Environment and the Coastal Region of the Mediterranean, done at Barcelona on 16 February 1976, as amended on 10 June 1995.

(c) 'Organization' means the body referred to in Article 17 of the Convention.

(d) 'Centre' means the Priority Actions Programme Regional Activity Centre.

(e) 'Coastal zone' means the geomorphologic area either side of the seashore in which the interaction between the marine and land parts occurs in the form of complex ecological and resource systems made up of biotic and abiotic components coexisting and interacting with human communities and relevant socio-economic activities.

(f) 'Integrated coastal zone management' means a dynamic process for the sustainable management and use of coastal zones, taking into account at the same time the fragility of coastal ecosystems and landscapes, the diversity of activities and uses, their interactions, the maritime orientation of certain activities and uses and their impact on both the marine and land parts.

Article 3 Geographic coverage

1. The area to which the Protocol applies shall be the Mediterranean Sea area as defined in Article 1 of the Convention. The area is also defined by:

(a) the seaward limit of the coastal zone, which shall be the external limit of the territorial sea of Parties; and

(b) the landward limit of the coastal zone, which shall be the limit of the competent coastal units as defined by the Parties.

2. If, within the limits of its sovereignty, a Party establishes limits different from those envisaged in paragraph 1 of this Article, it shall communicate a declaration to the Depositary at the time of the deposit of its instrument of ratification, acceptance, approval of, or accession to this Protocol, or at any other subsequent time, in so far as:

(a) the seaward limit is less than the external limit of the territorial sea;

(b) the landward limit is different, either more or less, from the limits of the territory of coastal units as defined above , in order to apply, *inter alia*, the ecosystem approach and economic and social criteria and to consider the specific needs of islands related to geomorphological characteristics and to take into account the negative effects of climate change.

3. Each Party shall adopt or promote at the appropriate institutional level adequate actions to inform populations and any relevant actor of the geographical coverage of the present Protocol.

Article 4 Preservation of rights

1. Nothing in this Protocol nor any act adopted on the basis of this Protocol shall prejudice the rights, the present and future claims or legal views of any Party relating to the Law of the Sea, in particular the nature and the extent of marine areas, the delimitation of marine areas between States with opposite or adjacent coasts, the right and modalities of passage through straits used for international navigation and the right of innocent passage in territorial seas, as well as the nature and extent of the jurisdiction of the coastal State, the flag State or the port State.

2. No act or activity undertaken on the basis of this Protocol shall constitute grounds for claiming, contending or disputing any claim to national sovereignty or jurisdiction.

3. The provisions of this Protocol shall be without prejudice to stricter provisions respecting the protection and management of the coastal zone contained in other existing or future national or international instruments or programmes.

4.   Nothing in this Protocol shall prejudice national security and defence activities and facilities; however, each Party agrees that such activities and facilities should be operated or established, so far as is reasonable and practicable, in a manner consistent with this Protocol.

Article 5 Objectives of integrated coastal zone management

The objectives of integrated coastal zone management are to:

(a)   facilitate, through the rational planning of activities, the sustainable development of coastal zones by ensuring that the environment and landscapes are taken into account in harmony with economic, social and cultural development;

(b)   preserve coastal zones for the benefit of current and future generations;

(c)   ensure the sustainable use of natural resources, particularly with regard to water use;

(d)   ensure preservation of the integrity of coastal ecosystems, landscapes and geomorphology;

(e)   prevent and/or reduce the effects of natural hazards and in particular of climate change, which can be induced by natural or human activities;

(f)   achieve coherence between public and private initiatives and between all decisions by the public authorities, at the national, regional and local levels, which affect the use of the coastal zone.

Article 6 General principles of integrated coastal zone management

In implementing this Protocol, the Parties shall be guided by the following principles of integrated coastal zone management:

(a)   The biological wealth and the natural dynamics and functioning of the intertidal area and the complementary and interdependent nature of the marine part and the land part forming a single entity shall be taken particularly into account.

(b)   All elements relating to hydrological, geomorphological, climatic, ecological, socio- economic and cultural systems shall be taken into account in an integrated manner, so as not to exceed the carrying capacity of the coastal zone and to prevent the negative effects of natural disasters and of development.

(c)   The ecosystems approach to coastal planning and management shall be applied so as to ensure the sustainable development of coastal zones.

(d)   Appropriate governance allowing adequate and timely participation in a transparent decision-making process by local populations and stakeholders in civil society concerned with coastal zones shall be ensured.

(e)   Cross-sectorally organized institutional coordination of the various administrative services and regional and local authorities competent in coastal zones shall be required.

(f)   The formulation of land use strategies, plans and programmes covering urban development and socio-economic activities, as well as other relevant sectoral policies, shall be required.

(g)   The multiplicity and diversity of activities in coastal zones shall be taken into account, and priority shall be given, where necessary, to public services and activities requiring, in terms of use and location, the immediate proximity of the sea.

(h)   The allocation of uses throughout the entire coastal zone should be balanced, and unnecessary concentration and urban sprawl should be avoided.

(i)   Preliminary assessments shall be made of the risks associated with the various human activities and infrastructure so as to prevent and reduce their negative impact on coastal zones.

(j)   Damage to the coastal environment shall be prevented and, where it occurs, appropriate restoration shall be effected.

Article 7 Coordination

1. For the purposes of integrated coastal zone management, the Parties shall:

(a)   ensure institutional coordination, where necessary through appropriate bodies or mechanisms, in order to avoid sectoral approaches and facilitate comprehensive approaches;

(b)   organize appropriate coordination between the various authorities competent for both the marine and the land parts of coastal zones in the different administrative services, at the national, regional and local levels;

(c)   organize close coordination between national authorities and regional and local bodies in the field of coastal strategies, plans and programmes and in relation to the various authorizations for activities that may be achieved through joint consultative bodies or joint decision-making procedures.

2. Competent national, regional and local coastal zone authorities shall, insofar as practicable, work together to strengthen the coherence and effectiveness of the coastal strategies, plans and programmes established.

PART II
ELEMENTS OF INTEGRATED COASTAL ZONE MANAGEMENT

Article 8 Protection and sustainable use of the coastal zone

1. In conformity with the objectives and principles set out in Articles 5 and 6 of this Protocol, the Parties shall endeavour to ensure the sustainable use and management of coastal zones in order to preserve the coastal natural habitats, landscapes, natural resources and ecosystems, in compliance with international and regional legal instruments.

2. For this purpose, the Parties:

(a)   Shall establish in coastal zones, as from the highest winter waterline, a zone where construction is not allowed. Taking into account, *inter alia*, the areas directly and negatively affected by climate change and natural risks, this zone may not be less than 100 meters in width, subject to the provisions of subparagraph (b) below. Stricter national measures determining this width shall continue to apply.

(b)   May adapt, in a manner consistent with the objectives and principles of this Protocol, the provisions mentioned above:

1)   for projects of public interest;

2)   in areas having particular geographical or other local constraints, especially related to population density or social needs, where individual housing, urbanisation or development are provided for by national legal instruments.

(c)   Shall notify to the Organization their national legal instruments providing for the above adaptations.

3. The Parties shall also endeavour to ensure that their national legal instruments include criteria for sustainable use of the coastal zone. Such criteria, taking into account specific local conditions, shall include, *inter alia*, the following:

(a)   identifying and delimiting, outside protected areas, open areas in which urban development and other activities are restricted or, where necessary, prohibited;

(b)   limiting the linear extension of urban development and the creation of new transport infrastructure along the coast;

(c)   ensuring that environmental concerns are integrated into the rules for the management and use of the public maritime domain;

(d)   providing for freedom of access by the public to the sea and along the shore;

(e)   restricting or, where necessary, prohibiting the movement and parking of land vehicles, as well as the movement and anchoring of marine vessels, in fragile natural areas on land or at sea, including beaches and dunes.

Article 9 Economic activities

1.   In conformity with the objectives and principles set forth in Articles 5 and 6 of this Protocol, and taking into account the relevant provisions of the Barcelona Convention and its Protocols, the Parties shall:

(a)   accord specific attention to economic activities that require immediate proximity to the sea;

(b)   ensure that the various economic activities minimize the use of natural resources and take into account the needs of future generations;

(c)   ensure respect for integrated water resources management and environmentally sound waste management;

(d)   ensure that the coastal and maritime economy is adapted to the fragile nature of coastal zones and that resources of the sea are protected from pollution;

(e)   define indicators of the development of economic activities to ensure sustainable use of coastal zones and reduce pressures that exceed their carrying capacity;

(f)   promote codes of good practice among public authorities, economic actors and non- governmental organizations.

2.   In addition, with regard to the following economic activities, the Parties agree:

(a)   Agriculture and industry, to guarantee a high level of protection of the environment in the location and operation of agricultural and industrial activities so as to preserve coastal ecosystems and landscapes and prevent pollution of the sea, water, air and soil;

(b)   Fishing,
   (i)   to take into account the need to protect fishing areas in development projects;
   (ii)   to ensure that fishing practices are compatible with sustainable use of natural marine resources;

(c)   Aquaculture,
   (i)   to take into account the need to protect aquaculture and shellfish areas in development projects;
   (ii)   to regulate aquaculture by controlling the use of inputs and waste treatment;

(d)   Tourism, sporting and recreational activities,
   (i)   to encourage sustainable coastal tourism that preserves coastal ecosystems, natural resources, cultural heritage and landscapes;
   (ii)   to promote specific forms of coastal tourism, including cultural, rural and ecotourism, while respecting the traditions of local populations;
   (iii)   to regulate or, where necessary, prohibit the practice of various sporting and recreational activities, including recreational fishing and shellfish extraction;

(e)   Utilization of specific natural resources,
   (i)   to subject to prior authorization the excavation and extraction of minerals, including the use of seawater in desalination plants and stone exploitation;

      (ii)   to regulate the extraction of sand, including on the seabed and river sediments or prohibit it where it is likely to adversely affect the equilibrium of coastal ecosystems;

      (iii) to monitor coastal aquifers and dynamic areas of contact or interface between fresh and salt water, which may be adversely affected by the extraction of underground water or by discharges into the natural environment;

(f)   Infrastructure, energy facilities, ports and maritime works and structures, to subject such infrastructure, facilities, works and structures to authorization so that their negative impact on coastal ecosystems, landscapes and geomorphology is minimized or, where appropriate, compensated by non-financial measures;

(g)   Maritime activities, to conduct maritime activities in such a manner as to ensure the preservation of coastal ecosystems in conformity with the rules, standards and procedures of the relevant international conventions.

Article 10 Specific coastal ecosystems

The Parties shall take measures to protect the characteristics of certain specific coastal ecosystems, as follows:

1. Wetlands and estuaries

In addition to the creation of protected areas and with a view to preventing the disappearance of wetlands and estuaries, the Parties shall:

(a)   take into account in national coastal strategies and coastal plans and programmes and when issuing authorizations, the environmental, economic and social function of wetlands and estuaries;

(b)   take the necessary measures to regulate or, if necessary, prohibit activities that may have adverse effects on wetlands and estuaries;

(c)   undertake, to the extent possible, the restoration of degraded coastal wetlands with a view to reactivating their positive role in coastal environmental processes.

2. Marine habitats

The Parties, recognizing the need to protect marine areas hosting habitats and species of high conservation value, irrespective of their classification as protected areas, shall:

(a)   adopt measures to ensure the protection and conservation, through legislation, planning and management of marine and coastal areas, in particular of those hosting habitats and species of high conservation value;

(b)   undertake to promote regional and international cooperation for the implementation of common programmes on the protection of marine habitats.

3. Coastal forests and woods

The Parties shall adopt measures intended to preserve or develop coastal forests and woods located, in particular, outside specially protected areas.

4. Dunes

The Parties undertake to preserve and, where possible, rehabilitate in a sustainable manner dunes and bars.

Article 11 Coastal landscapes

1. The Parties, recognizing the specific aesthetic, natural and cultural value of coastal landscapes, irrespective of their classification as protected areas, shall adopt measures to ensure the protection of coastal landscapes through legislation, planning and management.

2. The Parties undertake to promote regional and international cooperation in the field of landscape protection, and in particular, the implementation, where appropriate, of joint actions for transboundary coastal landscapes.

Article 12 Islands

The Parties undertake to accord special protection to islands, including small islands, and for this purpose to:

(a) promote environmentally friendly activities in such areas and take special measures to ensure the participation of the inhabitants in the protection of coastal ecosystems based on their local customs and knowledge;

(b) take into account the specific characteristics of the island environment and the necessity to ensure interaction among islands in national coastal strategies, plans and programmes and management instruments, particularly in the fields of transport, tourism, fishing, waste and water.

Article 13 Cultural heritage

1. The Parties shall adopt, individually or collectively, all appropriate measures to preserve and protect the cultural, in particular archaeological and historical, heritage of coastal zones, including the underwater cultural heritage, in conformity with the applicable national and international instruments.

2. The Parties shall ensure that the preservation in situ of the cultural heritage of coastal zones is considered as the first option before any intervention directed at this heritage.

3. The Parties shall ensure in particular that elements of the underwater cultural heritage of coastal zones removed from the marine environment are conserved and managed in a manner safeguarding their long-term preservation and are not traded, sold, bought or bartered as commercial goods.

Article 14 Participation

1. With a view to ensuring efficient governance throughout the process of the integrated management of coastal zones, the Parties shall take the necessary measures to ensure the appropriate involvement in the phases of the formulation and implementation of coastal and marine strategies, plans and programmes or projects, as well as the issuing of the various authorizations, of the various stakeholders, including:

 – the territorial communities and public entities concerned;
 – economic operators;
 – non-governmental organizations;
 – social actors;
 – the public concerned.

Such participation shall involve *inter alia* consultative bodies, inquiries or public hearings, and may extend to partnerships.

2. With a view to ensuring such participation, the Parties shall provide information in an adequate, timely and effective manner.

3. Mediation or conciliation procedures and a right of administrative or legal recourse should be available to any stakeholder challenging decisions, acts or omissions, subject to the participation provisions established by the Parties with respect to plans, programmes or projects concerning the coastal zone.

Article 15 Awareness-raising, training, education and research

1. The Parties undertake to carry out, at the national, regional or local level, awareness- raising activities on integrated coastal zone management and to develop educational programmes, training and public education on this subject.

2. The Parties shall organize, directly, multilaterally or bilaterally, or with the assistance of the Organization, the Centre or the international organizations concerned, educational programmes, training and public education on integrated management of coastal zones with a view to ensuring their sustainable development.

3. The Parties shall provide for interdisciplinary scientific research on integrated coastal zone management and on the interaction between activities and their impacts on coastal zones. To this end, they should establish or support specialized research centres. The purpose of this research is, in particular, to further knowledge of integrated coastal zone management, to contribute to public information and to facilitate public and private decision-making.

PART III
INSTRUMENTS FOR INTEGRATED COASTAL ZONE MANAGEMENT

Article 16 Monitoring and observation mechanisms and networks

1. The Parties shall use and strengthen existing appropriate mechanisms for monitoring and observation, or create new ones if necessary. They shall also prepare and regularly update national inventories of coastal zones which should cover, to the extent possible, information on resources and activities, as well as on institutions, legislation and planning that may influence coastal zones.

2. In order to promote exchange of scientific experience, data and good practices, the Parties shall participate, at the appropriate administrative and scientific level, in a Mediterranean coastal zone network, in cooperation with the Organization.

3. With a view to facilitating the regular observation of the state and evolution of coastal zones, the Parties shall set out an agreed reference format and process to collect appropriate data in national inventories.

4. The Parties shall take all necessary means to ensure public access to the information derived from monitoring and observation mechanisms and networks.

Article 17 Mediterranean strategy for integrated coastal zone management

The Parties undertake to cooperate for the promotion of sustainable development and integrated management of coastal zones, taking into account the Mediterranean Strategy for Sustainable Development and complementing it where necessary. To this end, the Parties shall define, with the assistance of the Centre, a common regional framework for integrated coastal zone management in the Mediterranean to be implemented by means of appropriate regional action plans and other operational instruments, as well as through their national strategies.

Article 18 National coastal strategies, plans and programmes

1. Each Party shall further strengthen or formulate a national strategy for integrated coastal zone management and coastal implementation plans and programmes consistent with the common regional framework and in conformity with the integrated management objectives and principles of this Protocol and shall inform the Organization about the coordination mechanism in place for this strategy.

2. The national strategy, based on an analysis of the existing situation, shall set objectives, determine priorities with an indication of the reasons, identify coastal ecosystems needing management, as well as all relevant actors and processes, enumerate the measures to be taken and their cost as well as the institutional instruments and legal and financial means available, and set an implementation schedule.

3. Coastal plans and programmes, which may be self-standing or integrated in other plans and programmes, shall specify the orientations of the national strategy and implement it at an appropriate territorial level, determining, *inter alia* and where appropriate, the carrying capacities and conditions for the allocation and use of the respective marine and land parts of coastal zones.

4. The Parties shall define appropriate indicators in order to evaluate the effectiveness of integrated coastal zone management strategies, plans and programmes, as well as the progress of implementation of the Protocol.

Article 19 Environmental assessment

1. Taking into account the fragility of coastal zones, the Parties shall ensure that the process and related studies of environmental impact assessment for public and private projects likely to have significant environmental effects on the coastal zones, and in particular on their ecosystems, take into consideration the specific sensitivity of the environment and the inter-relationships between the marine and terrestrial parts of the coastal zone.

2. In accordance with the same criteria, the Parties shall formulate, as appropriate, a strategic environmental assessment of plans and programmes affecting the coastal zone.

3. The environmental assessments should take into consideration the cumulative impacts on the coastal zones, paying due attention, *inter alia,* to their carrying capacities.

Article 20 Land policy

1. For the purpose of promoting integrated coastal zone management, reducing economic pressures, maintaining open areas and allowing public access to the sea and along the shore, Parties shall adopt appropriate land policy instruments and measures, including the process of planning.

2. To this end, and in order to ensure the sustainable management of public and private land of the coastal zones, Parties may *inter alia* adopt mechanisms for the acquisition, cession, donation or transfer of land to the public domain and institute easements on properties.

Article 21 Economic, financial and fiscal instruments

For the implementation of national coastal strategies and coastal plans and programmes, Parties may take appropriate measures to adopt relevant economic, financial and/or fiscal instruments intended to support local, regional and national initiatives for the integrated management of coastal zones.

PART IV
RISKS AFFECTING THE COASTAL ZONE

Article 22 Natural hazards

Within the framework of national strategies for integrated coastal zone management, the Parties shall develop policies for the prevention of natural hazards. To this end, they shall undertake vulnerability and hazard assessments of coastal zones and take prevention, mitigation and adaptation measures to address the effects of natural disasters, in particular of climate change.

Article 23 Coastal erosion

1. In conformity with the objectives and principles set out in Articles 5 and 6 of this Protocol, the Parties, with a view to preventing and mitigating the negative impact of

coastal erosion more effectively, undertake to adopt the necessary measures to maintain or restore the natural capacity of the coast to adapt to changes, including those caused by the rise in sea levels.

2. The Parties, when considering new activities and works located in the coastal zone including marine structures and coastal defence works, shall take particular account of their negative effects on coastal erosion and the direct and indirect costs that may result. In respect of existing activities and structures, the Parties should adopt measures to minimize their effects on coastal erosion.

3. The Parties shall endeavour to anticipate the impacts of coastal erosion through the integrated management of activities, including adoption of special measures for coastal sediments and coastal works.

4. The Parties undertake to share scientific data that may improve knowledge on the state, development and impacts of coastal erosion.

Article 24 Response to natural disasters

1. The Parties undertake to promote international cooperation to respond to natural disasters, and to take all necessary measures to address in a timely manner their effects.

2. The Parties undertake to coordinate use of the equipment for detection, warning and communication at their disposal, making use of existing mechanisms and initiatives, to ensure the transmission as rapidly as possible of urgent information concerning major natural disasters. The Parties shall notify the Organization which national authorities are competent to issue and receive such information in the context of relevant international mechanisms.

3. The Parties undertake to promote mutual cooperation and cooperation among national, regional and local authorities, non-governmental organizations and other competent organizations for the provision on an urgent basis of humanitarian assistance in response to natural disasters affecting the coastal zones of the Mediterranean Sea.

PART V
INTERNATIONAL COOPERATION

Article 25 Training and research

1. The Parties undertake, directly or with the assistance of the Organization or the competent international organizations, to cooperate in the training of scientific, technical and administrative personnel in the field of integrated coastal zone management, particularly with a view to:

(a) identifying and strengthening capacities;
(b) developing scientific and technical research;
(c) promoting centres specialized in integrated coastal zone management;
(d) promoting training programmes for local professionals.

2. The Parties undertake, directly or with the assistance of the Organization or the competent international organizations, to promote scientific and technical research into integrated coastal zone management, particularly through the exchange of scientific and technical information and the coordination of their research programmes on themes of common interest.

Article 26 Scientific and technical assistance

For the purposes of integrated coastal zone management, the Parties undertake, directly or with the assistance of the Organization or the competent international organizations to cooperate for the provision of scientific and technical assistance, including access to environmentally sound technologies and their transfer, and other possible forms of assistance, to Parties requiring such assistance.

Article 27 Exchange of information and activities of common interest

1. The Parties undertake, directly or with the assistance of the Organization or the competent international organizations, to cooperate in the exchange of information on the use of the best environmental practices.

2. With the support of the Organization, the Parties shall in particular:

(a) define coastal management indicators, taking into account existing ones, and cooperate in the use of such indicators;

(b) establish and maintain up-to-date assessments of the use and management of coastal zones;

(c) carry out activities of common interest, such as demonstration projects of integrated coastal zone management.

Article 28 Transboundary cooperation

The Parties shall endeavour, directly or with the assistance of the Organization or the competent international organizations, bilaterally or multilaterally, to coordinate, where appropriate, their national coastal strategies, plans and programmes related to contiguous coastal zones. Relevant domestic administrative bodies shall be associated with such coordination.

Article 29 Transboundary environmental assessment

1. Within the framework of this Protocol, the Parties shall, before authorizing or approving plans, programmes and projects that are likely to have a significant adverse effect on the coastal zones of other Parties, cooperate by means of notification, exchange of information and consultation in assessing the environmental impacts of such plans, programmes and projects, taking into account Article 19 of this Protocol and Article 4, paragraph 3 (d) of the Convention.

2. To this end, the Parties undertake to cooperate in the formulation and adoption of appropriate guidelines for the determination of procedures for notification, exchange of information and consultation at all stages of the process.

3. The Parties may, where appropriate, enter into bilateral or multilateral agreements for the effective implementation of this Article.

PART VI
INSTITUTIONAL PROVISIONS

Article 30 Focal points

Each Party shall designate a Focal Point to serve as liaison with the Centre on the technical and scientific aspects of the implementation of this Protocol and to disseminate information at the national, regional and local level. The Focal Points shall meet periodically to carry out the functions deriving from this Protocol.

Article 31 Reports

The Parties shall submit to the ordinary Meetings of the Contracting Parties, reports on the implementation of this Protocol, in such form and at such intervals as these Meetings may determine, including the measures taken, their effectiveness and the problems encountered in their implementation.

Article 32 Institutional coordination

1. The Organization shall be responsible for coordinating the implementation of this Protocol. For this purpose, it shall receive the support of the Centre, to which it may entrust the following functions:

(a) to assist the Parties to define a common regional framework for integrated coastal zone management in the Mediterranean pursuant to Article 17;

(b) to prepare a regular report on the state and development of integrated coastal zone management in the Mediterranean Sea with a view to facilitating implementation of the Protocol;

(c) to exchange information and carry out activities of common interest pursuant to Article 27;

(d) upon request, to assist the Parties:

–   to participate in a Mediterranean coastal zone network pursuant to Article 16;

–   to prepare and implement their national strategies for integrated coastal zone management pursuant to Article 18;

–   to cooperate in training activities and in scientific and technical research programmes pursuant to Article 25;

–   to coordinate, when appropriate, the management of transboundary coastal zones pursuant to Article 28;

(e) to organize the meetings of the Focal Points pursuant to Article 30;

(f) to carry out any other function assigned to it by the Parties.

2. For the purposes of implementing this Protocol, the Parties, the Organization and the Centre may jointly establish cooperation with non-governmental organizations the activities of which are related to the Protocol.

Article 33 Meetings of the Parties

1. The ordinary meetings of the Parties to this Protocol shall be held in conjunction with the ordinary meetings of the Contracting Parties to the Convention held pursuant to Article 18 of the Convention. The Parties may also hold extraordinary meetings in conformity with that Article.

2. The functions of the meetings of the Parties to this Protocol shall be:

(a) to keep under review the implementation of this Protocol;

(b) to ensure that this Protocol is implemented in coordination and synergy with the other Protocols;

(c) to oversee the work of the Organization and of the Centre relating to the implementation of this Protocol and providing policy guidance for their activities;

(d) to consider the efficiency of the measures adopted for integrated coastal zone management and the need for other measures, in particular in the form of annexes or amendments to this Protocol;

(e) to make recommendations to the Parties on the measures to be adopted for the implementation of this Protocol;

(f) to examine the proposals made by the Meetings of Focal Points pursuant to Article 30 of this Protocol;

(g) to consider reports transmitted by the Parties and making appropriate recommendations pursuant to Article 26 of the Convention;

(h) to examine any other relevant information submitted through the Centre;

(i) to examine any other matter relevant to this Protocol, as appropriate.

PART VII
FINAL PROVISIONS

Article 34 Relationship with the Convention

1. The provisions of the Convention relating to any Protocol shall apply with respect to this Protocol.

2. The rules of procedure and the financial rules adopted pursuant to Article 24 of the Convention shall apply with respect to this Protocol, unless the Parties to this Protocol agree otherwise.

Article 35 Relations with third parties

1. The Parties shall invite, where appropriate, States that are not Parties to this Protocol and international organizations to cooperate in the implementation of this Protocol.

2. The Parties undertake to adopt appropriate measures, consistent with international law, to ensure that no one engages in any activity contrary to the principles and objectives of this Protocol.

Article 36 Signature

This Protocol shall be open for signature at Madrid, Spain, from 21 January 2008 to 20 January 2009 by any Contracting Party to the Convention.

Convention on Cooperation in the Northwest Atlantic Fisheries (NAFO Convention)

Done at Ottawa, 24 October 1978, and amended at Lisbon, 28 September 2007;
entry into force, 1 January 1979; amendment not yet in force
NAFO/GC Doc. 07/4[1]

The Contracting Parties,

Noting that the coastal States of the Northwest Atlantic have established exclusive economic zones consistent with the United Nations Convention on the Law of the Sea of 10 December 1982 and customary international law, within which they exercise sovereign rights for the purpose of exploring and exploiting, conserving and managing living resources;

Recalling the relevant provisions of the United Nations Convention on the Law of the Sea of 10 December 1982, the Agreement for the Implementation of the Provisions of the United Nations Convention on the Law of the Sea of 10 December 1982 relating to the Conservation and Management of Straddling Fish Stocks and Highly Migratory Fish Stocks of 4 August 1995, and the FAO Agreement to Promote Compliance with International Conservation and Management Measures by Fishing Vessels on the High Seas of 24 November 1993;

---

[1] On 28 September 2007, at the 29th annual meeting of the General Council of the Northwest Atlantic Fisheries Organization the 1978 Convention on Future Multilateral Cooperation in the Northwest Atlantic Fisheries (1135 UNTS 370 [Registration Number 17799]) was amended and renamed the Convention on Cooperation in the Northwest Atlantic Fisheries. The text reproduced is a consolidated version incorporating this amendment which largely replaces the old Convention. On 26 September 2008, the French text of the Convention was adopted paving the way for the start of the ratification process. Annex I (Scientific and Statistical Subareas, Divisions and Subdivisions) and Annex II (Rules Concerning the Ad Hoc Panel Procedure Pursuant to Article XV) omitted.

Taking into account the Code of Conduct for Responsible Fisheries adopted by the 28th Session of the Conference of the Food and Agriculture Organization of the United Nations on 31 October 1995 and related instruments adopted by the Food and Agriculture Organization of the United Nations;

Recognizing the economic and social benefits deriving from the sustainable use of fishery resources;

Desiring to promote the long term conservation and sustainable use of the fishery resources of the Northwest Atlantic;

Conscious of the need for international cooperation and consultation with respect to those fishery resources;

Mindful that effective conservation and management of these fishery resources should be based on the best available scientific advice and the precautionary approach;

Committed to apply an ecosystem approach to fisheries management in the Northwest Atlantic that includes safeguarding the marine environment, conserving its marine biodiversity, minimizing the risk of long term or irreversible adverse effects of fishing activities, and taking account of the relationship between all components of the ecosystem;

Further committed to conduct responsible fishing activities and to prevent, deter and eliminate IUU fishing;

Have agreed as follows:

Article I Use of Terms

For the purpose of this Convention:

(a) '1982 Convention' means the United Nations Convention on the Law of the Sea of 10 December 1982;

(b) '1995 Agreement' means the Agreement for the Implementation of the Provisions of the United Nations Convention on the Law of the Sea of 10 December 1982 relating to the Conservation and Management of Straddling Fish Stocks and Highly Migratory Fish Stocks of 4 August 1995;

(c) 'coastal State' means a Contracting Party having an exclusive economic zone within the Convention Area;

(d) 'Contracting Party' means

    (i) any State or regional economic integration organization which has consented to be bound by this Convention, and for which the Convention is in force; and

    (ii) this Convention applies *mutatis mutandis* to any entity referred to in Article 305, paragraph 1 c), d) and e) of the 1982 Convention, which is situated in the North Atlantic, and which becomes a Party to this Convention, and to that extent 'Contracting Party' refers to such entities.

(e) 'Convention Area', means the area to which this Convention applies, as described in Article IV paragraph 1;

(f) 'fishery resources' means all fish, molluscs and crustaceans within the Convention Area excluding:

    (i) sedentary species over which coastal States may exercise sovereign rights consistent with Article 77 of the 1982 Convention; and

    (ii) in so far as they are managed under other international treaties, anadromous and catadromous stocks and highly migratory species listed in Annex I of the 1982 Convention;

(g) 'fishing activities' means harvesting or processing fishery resources, or transhipping of fishery resources or products derived from fishery resources, or any other activity in preparation for, in support of, or related to the harvesting of fishery resources, including:

(i)   the actual or attempted searching for, catching or taking of fishery resources;

(ii) any activity that can reasonably be expected to result in locating, catching, taking, or harvesting of fishery resources for any purpose; and

(iii) any operation at sea in support of, or in preparation for, any activity described in this definition;

but does not include any operation related to emergencies involving the health and safety of crew members or the safety of a vessel;

(h)   'fishing vessel' means any vessel that is or has been engaged in fishing activities, and includes fish processing vessels and vessels engaged in transhipment or any other activity in preparation for or related to fishing activities, or in experimental or exploratory fishing activities;

(i)   'flag State' means:

(i)   a State or entity whose vessels are entitled to fly its flag; or

(ii) a regional economic integration organization in which vessels are entitled to fly the flag of a member State of that regional economic integration organization;

(j)   'IUU fishing' refers to the activities described in the International Plan of Action to Prevent, Deter and Eliminate Illegal, Unreported and Unregulated Fishing adopted by the Food and Agriculture Organization of the United Nations on 2 March 2001;

(k)   'living resources' means all living components of marine ecosystems;

(l)   'marine biological diversity' means the variability among living marine organisms and the ecological complexes of which they are part; this includes diversity within species, between species and of ecosystems;

(m)   'nationals' includes both natural and legal persons;

(n)   'port State' means any State receiving fishing vessels in its ports, offshore terminals or other installations for, *inter alia*, landing, transhipping, refuelling or re-supplying;

(o)   'regional economic integration organization' means a regional economic integration organization to which its member States have transferred competence over matters covered by this Convention, including the authority to make decisions binding on its member States in respect of those matters; and

(p)   'Regulatory Area' means that part of the Convention Area beyond areas under national jurisdiction.

Article II Objective

The objective of this Convention is to ensure the long term conservation and sustainable use of the fishery resources in the Convention Area and, in so doing, to safeguard the marine ecosystems in which these resources are found.

Article III General Principles

In giving effect to the objective of this Convention, Contracting Parties individually or collectively, as appropriate, shall:

(a)   promote the optimum utilization and long-term sustainability of fishery resources;

(b)   adopt measures based on the best scientific advice available to ensure that fishery resources are maintained at or restored to levels capable of producing maximum sustainable yield;

(c) apply the precautionary approach in accordance with Article 6 of the 1995 Agreement;

(d) take due account of the impact of fishing activities on other species and marine ecosystems and in doing so, adopt measures to minimize harmful impact on living resources and marine ecosystems;

(e) take due account of the need to preserve marine biological diversity;

(f) prevent or eliminate overfishing and excess fishing capacity, and ensure that levels of fishing effort do not exceed those commensurate with the sustainable use of the fishery resources;

(g) ensure that complete and accurate data concerning fishing activities within the Convention Area are collected and shared among them in a timely manner;

(h) ensure effective compliance with management measures and that sanctions for any infringements are adequate in severity; and

(i) take due account of the need to minimize pollution and waste originating from fishing vessels as well as minimize discards, catch by lost or abandoned gear, catch of species not subject to a directed fishery and impacts on associated or dependent species, in particular endangered species.

Article IV Area of Application

1. This Convention applies to the waters of the Northwest Atlantic Ocean north of 35°00′ N and west of a line extending due north from 35°00′ N and 42°00′ W to 59°00′ N, thence due west to 44°00′ W, and thence due north to the coast of Greenland, and the waters of the Gulf of St. Lawrence, Davis Strait and Baffin Bay south of 78°10′ N.

2. The Convention Area shall be divided into scientific and statistical subareas, divisions and subdivisions, the boundaries of which shall be as defined in Annex I to this Convention.

Article V The Organization

1. Contracting Parties hereby agree to establish, maintain and strengthen the Northwest Atlantic Fisheries Organization, hereinafter 'the Organization' that shall carry out the functions set out in this Convention in order to achieve the objective of this Convention.

2. The Organization shall consist of:

(a) a Commission;

(b) a Scientific Council; and

(c) a Secretariat.

3. The Organization shall have legal personality and shall enjoy in its relations with other international organizations and in the territories of the Contracting Parties such legal capacity as may be necessary to perform its functions and achieve its objective. The privileges and immunities which the Organization and its officers shall enjoy in the territory of a Contracting Party shall be subject to agreement between the Organization and the Contracting Party including, in particular, a headquarters agreement between the Organization and the host Contracting Party.

4. The Chairperson of the Commission shall serve as the President and principal representative of the Organization.

5. The President shall convene the annual meeting of the Organization at such time and place as the Commission may determine.

6. The headquarters of the Organization shall be in the Halifax Regional Municipality, Nova Scotia, Canada, or at such other place as may be decided by the Commission.

Article VI The Commission

1. Each Contracting Party shall be a member of the Commission and shall appoint one representative to the Commission who may be accompanied by alternative representatives, experts and advisers.

2. The Commission shall elect a Chairperson and a Vice-Chairperson for a term of two years. Each shall be eligible for re-election but shall not serve for more than four years in succession in the same capacity. The Chairperson and Vice-Chairperson shall not be representatives of the same Contracting Party.

3. Any Contracting Party may request a special meeting of the Commission. The Chairperson of the Commission shall thereupon convene such meeting at such time and place as the Chairperson may determine.

4. Unless otherwise provided, measures adopted by the Commission shall apply to the Regulatory Area.

5. The Commission shall:

(a) adopt and may amend the rules for the conduct of its meetings and for the exercise of its functions, including rules of procedure, financial regulations and other regulations;

(b) establish such subsidiary bodies as it considers desirable for the exercise of its functions and direct their activities;

(c) supervise the organizational, administrative, financial and other internal affairs of the Organization, including relations among its constituent bodies;

(d) appoint an Executive Secretary on such terms and conditions as it may determine;

(e) direct the external relations of the Organization;

(f) approve the budget of the Organization;

(g) adopt rules to provide for the participation of representatives of inter-governmental organizations, non-Contracting Parties and non-governmental organizations as observers at its meetings, as appropriate. Such rules shall not be unduly restrictive and shall provide for timely access to reports and records of the Commission;

(h) exercise such other functions and carry out such other activities consistent with this Convention as it may decide;

(i) guide the Scientific Council in identifying tasks and priorities for its work; and

(j) develop appropriate procedures in accordance with international law to assess the performance by Contracting Parties of their obligations pursuant to Articles X and XI.

6. The Commission shall, in collaboration with the Scientific Council:

(a) regularly review the status of fish stocks and identify actions required for their conservation and management;

(b) collect, analyze and disseminate relevant information;

(c) assess the impact of fishing activities and other human activities on living resources and their ecosystems;

(d) develop guidelines for the conduct of fishing activities for scientific purposes; and

(e) develop guidelines for the collection, submission, verification, access to and use of data.

7. The Commission may refer to the Scientific Council any question pertaining to the scientific basis for the decisions it may need to take concerning fishery resources, the impact of fishing activities on living resources, and the safeguarding of the ecosystem in which these resources are found.

8. In applying the principles set out in Article III, the Commission shall, in relation to the Regulatory Area adopt:

(a) conservation and management measures to achieve the objective of this Convention;

(b) conservation and management measures to minimize the impact of fishing activities on living resources and their ecosystems;

(c) total allowable catches and/or levels of fishing effort and determine the nature and extent of participation in fishing;

(d) measures for the conduct of fishing for scientific purposes as referred to in subparagraph 6(d);

(e) measures for the collection, submission, verification, access to and use of data as referred to in subparagraph 6(e), and

(f) measures to ensure adequate flag State performance.

9. The Commission shall adopt measures for appropriate cooperative mechanisms for effective monitoring, control, surveillance and enforcement of the conservation and management measures adopted by the Commission including:

(a) reciprocal rights of boarding and inspection by Contracting Parties within the Regulatory Area and flag State prosecution and sanctions on the basis of evidence resulting from such boardings and inspections;

(b) minimum standards for inspection of fishing vessels by Contracting Parties in ports where fishery resources or products derived from fishery resources originating in the Regulatory Area are landed;

(c) follow-up actions as provided for in Articles X, XI or XII on the basis of evidence resulting from such inspections; and

(d) without prejudice to any measures a Contracting Party may itself take in this regard, measures for the prevention, deterrence and elimination of IUU fishing.

10. The Commission may adopt measures on matters set out in paragraphs 8 and 9 concerning an area under national jurisdiction of a Contracting Party, provided that the coastal State in question so requests and the measure receives its affirmative vote.

11. (a) In exercising its functions pursuant to paragraph 8, the Commission shall seek to ensure consistency between:

(i) any measure that applies to a stock or group of stocks found both within the Regulatory Area and within an area under national jurisdiction of a coastal State, or any measure that would have an effect through species interrelationships on a stock or group of stocks found in whole or in part within an area under national jurisdiction of a coastal State; and

(ii) any actions taken by a coastal State for the management and conservation of that stock or group of stocks with respect to fishing activities conducted within the area under its national jurisdiction.

(b) The Commission and the appropriate coastal State shall accordingly promote the coordination of their respective measures and actions. Each coastal State shall keep the Commission informed of its actions for the purpose of this Article.

12. Measures adopted by the Commission for the allocation of fishing opportunities in the Regulatory Area shall take into account the interests of Contracting Parties whose vessels have traditionally fished within that area and the interests of the relevant coastal States. In the allocation of fishing opportunities from the Grand Bank and Flemish Cap, the Commission shall give special consideration to the Contracting Party whose coastal communities are primarily dependent on fishing activities for stocks related to these

fishing banks and which has undertaken extensive efforts to ensure the conservation of such stocks through international action, in particular, by providing surveillance and inspection of international fishing activities on these banks under an international scheme of joint enforcement.

13.   The Commission may develop procedures that allow for actions, including non-discriminatory trade-related measures, to be taken by Contracting Parties against any flag State or fishing entity whose fishing vessels engage in fishing activities that undermine the effectiveness of the conservation and management measures adopted by the Commission. Implementation by a Contracting Party of trade-related measures shall be consistent with its international obligations.

Article VII The Scientific Council

1.   Each Contracting Party shall be a member of the Scientific Council and may appoint representatives who may be accompanied at any of its meetings by alternates, experts and advisers.

2.   The Scientific Council shall elect a Chairperson and a Vice-Chairperson for a term of two years. Each shall be eligible for re-election but shall not serve for more than four years in succession in the same capacity.

3.   Any special meeting of the Scientific Council may be called by the Chairperson at his or her own initiative, upon the request of a coastal State, or upon the request of a Contracting Party with the concurrence of another Contracting Party at such time and place as the Chairperson may determine.

4.   The Scientific Council shall adopt, and amend as occasion may require, rules for the conduct of its meetings and for the exercise of its functions, including rules of procedure.

5.   The Scientific Council may establish such subsidiary bodies as it may consider necessary for the exercise of its functions.

6.   Election of officers, adoption or amendment of rules or other matters pertaining to the organization of work shall be by a majority of the votes of all Contracting Parties present and casting affirmative or negative votes. Each Contracting Party shall have one vote. No vote shall be taken in the absence of a quorum of at least two-thirds of the Contracting Parties.

7.   The Scientific Council shall adopt rules to provide for the participation of representatives of intergovernmental organizations, non Contracting Parties and non-governmental organizations as observers to its meetings, as appropriate. Such rules shall not be unduly restrictive and shall provide for timely access to reports and records of the Scientific Council.

8.   The Scientific Council shall consistent with the objective and principles of the Convention:

   (a)   provide a forum for consultation and cooperation among the Contracting Parties to study and exchange scientific information and views on fishing activities and the ecosystems in which they occur, and to study and appraise the current and future status of fishery resources including environmental and ecological factors affecting them;

   (b)   promote cooperation in scientific research among Contracting Parties to fill gaps in scientific knowledge;

   (c)   compile and maintain statistics and records;

   (d)   publish or disseminate reports, information and materials pertaining to the fishing activities in the Convention Area and their ecosystems; and

   (e)   provide scientific advice to the Commission as required by the Commission.

9. The Scientific Council may:

(a) on its own initiative provide such advice as may assist the Commission in the exercise of its functions;

(b) cooperate with any public or private organization sharing similar objectives; and

(c) request Contracting Parties to provide such statistical or scientific information as it may require for the exercise of its functions.

10. The Scientific Council shall provide scientific advice in response to any question referred to it by:

(a) the Commission pertaining to the scientific basis for the conservation and management of fishery resources and their ecosystems within the Regulatory Area, taking into account the terms of reference specified by the Commission in respect of that question; or

(b) a coastal State pertaining to the scientific basis for the conservation and management of fishery resources and their ecosystems within areas under the jurisdiction of that coastal State in the Convention Area.

11. The coastal State shall, in consultation with the Scientific Council, specify terms of reference for the consideration of any question it may refer to the Scientific Council. Such terms of reference shall include, *inter alia*:

(a) description of the fishing activities and area to be considered;

(b) where scientific estimates or predictions are sought, description of any relevant factors or assumptions to be taken into account; and

(c) where applicable, description of any objectives the coastal State is seeking to attain and an indication of whether specific advice or a range of options should be provided.

12. As a general rule, the Scientific Council shall provide its advice by consensus. Where consensus cannot be achieved, the Scientific Council shall set out in its report all views of its members.

13. All reports provided by the Scientific Council shall be published by the Secretariat.

Article VIII The Secretariat

1. The Secretariat shall provide services to the Commission, the Scientific Council and their subsidiary bodies to facilitate the exercise of their functions.

2. The chief administrative officer of the Secretariat shall be the Executive Secretary.

3. The employees of the Secretariat shall be appointed by the Executive Secretary in accordance with such rules and procedures as the Commission may adopt in consultation with the Scientific Council, as appropriate.

4. Subject to the general supervision of the Commission, the Executive Secretary shall have full authority over managing employees and employee-related issues of the Secretariat and shall perform such other duties and functions as the Commission may prescribe.

Article IX Budget

1. Each Contracting Party shall pay the expenses of its own delegation to any meetings held pursuant to this Convention.

2. The Commission shall establish the amount of the annual contributions due from each Contracting Party pursuant to the annual budget on the following basis:

(a) 10% of the budget shall be divided among the coastal States in proportion to their nominal catches in the Convention Area in the year ending two years before the beginning of the budget year;

(b)   30% of the budget shall be divided equally among all the Contracting Parties;

(c)   60% of the budget shall be divided among all Contracting Parties in proportion to their nominal catches in the Convention Area in the year ending two years before the beginning of the budget year; and

(d)   the annual contribution of any Contracting Party which has a population of less than 300,000 inhabitants shall be limited to a maximum of 12% of the total budget. When this contribution is so limited, the remaining part of the budget shall be divided among the other Contracting Parties in accordance with subparagraphs (a), (b) and (c).

The nominal catches referred to above shall be the reported catches of the fishery resources specified in the financial regulations adopted by the Commission pursuant to subparagraph 5 (a) of Article VI.

3.   The Executive Secretary shall notify each Contracting Party of the amount of its contribution due as calculated pursuant to paragraph 2, and as soon as possible thereafter, each Contracting Party shall pay its contribution to the Organization.

4.   Contributions shall be payable in the currency of the country in which the headquarters of the Organization is located.

5.   No later than sixty days before the annual meeting, the Executive Secretary shall submit the draft annual budget to each Contracting Party together with the schedule of contributions.

6.   A Contracting Party acceding to this Convention shall contribute in respect of the year it accedes an amount proportional to the number of complete months remaining in the year calculated from the day of its accession.

7.   Unless the Commission decides otherwise, a Contracting Party that has not fully paid its contributions for two consecutive years shall have its right of casting votes and presenting objections suspended until such time as it has discharged its financial obligations to the Organization.

8.   The financial affairs of the Organization shall be audited annually by external auditors to be selected by the Commission.

Article X Contracting Party Duties

1.   Each Contracting Party shall:

(a)   implement this Convention and any conservation and management measures or other obligations binding on it and regularly submit to the Commission a description of the steps it has taken to implement and comply with such measures or obligations including outcomes of proceedings referred to in Article XI, subparagraph 2 (e);

(b)   co-operate in furthering the objective of this Convention;

(c)   take all necessary actions to ensure the effectiveness of and to enforce the conservation and management measures adopted by the Commission;

(d)   collect and exchange scientific, technical, and statistical data and knowledge pertaining to living resources and their ecosystems in the Convention Area including complete and detailed information on commercial catches and fishing effort and take appropriate actions to verify the accuracy of such data;

(e)   perform biological sampling on commercial catches;

(f)   make such information as may be required by the Commission or Scientific Council available in a timely manner;

(g)   without prejudice to the jurisdiction of the flag State, to the greatest extent possible, take actions or cooperate with other Contracting Parties, to ensure that its nationals and fishing vessels owned or operated by its nationals conducting fishing activities comply with the provisions of this Convention and with the conservation and management measures adopted by the Commission; and

(h) without prejudice to the jurisdiction of the flag State, to the greatest extent possible, when provided with the relevant information, investigate immediately and fully and report promptly on actions it has taken in response to any alleged serious infringement by its nationals, or foreign flagged fishing vessels owned or operated by its nationals, of this Convention or any conservation and management measure adopted by the Commission.

2. Each coastal State Contracting Party shall regularly submit to the Commission a description of the actions, including enforcement actions, it has taken for the conservation and management of straddling stocks found in waters under its jurisdiction within the Convention Area.

Article XI Flag State Duties

1. Each Contracting Party shall ensure that fishing vessels entitled to fly its flag:

(a) comply with the provisions of this Convention and with the conservation and management measures adopted by the Commission and that such vessels do not engage in any activity that undermines the effectiveness of such measures;

(b) do not conduct unauthorized fishing activities within areas under national jurisdiction in the Convention Area; and

(c) do not engage in fishing activities in the Regulatory Area unless they have been authorized to do so by that Contracting Party.

2. Each Contracting Party shall:

(a) refrain from authorizing fishing vessels entitled to fly its flag to engage in fishing activities in the Regulatory Area unless it is able to exercise effectively its responsibilities in respect of such vessels pursuant to this Convention and consistent with international law;

(b) maintain a record of fishing vessels entitled to fly its flag it has authorized to fish for fishery resources in the Regulatory Area and ensure that such information as may be specified by the Commission is recorded therein;

(c) exchange the information contained in the record referred to in subparagraph (b) in accordance with such procedures as may be specified by the Commission;

(d) in accordance with procedures adopted by the Commission, investigate immediately and fully and report promptly on actions it has taken in response to an alleged infringement by a vessel entitled to fly its flag of measures adopted by the Commission; and

(e) in respect of an alleged infringement referred to in subparagraph (d) ensure that appropriate enforcement actions are taken without delay and that administrative or judicial proceedings are initiated in accordance with its laws.

3. Enforcement actions taken or sanctions applied pursuant to subparagraph 2 (e) shall be adequate in severity to be effective in securing compliance, discouraging further infringements and depriving offenders of the benefits accruing from their illegal activities.

Article XII Port State Duties

1. Actions taken by a port State Contracting Party pursuant to this Convention shall take full account of its rights and duties under international law to promote the effectiveness of conservation and management measures adopted by the Commission.

2. Each port State Contracting Party shall implement the measures concerning inspections in port adopted by the Commission.

3.   Nothing in this Article shall affect the sovereignty of a Contracting Party over ports in its territory.

Article XIII Decision Making of the Commission

1. As a general rule, decision-making within the Commission shall be by consensus. For the purposes of this Article, 'consensus' means the absence of any formal objection made at the time the decision was taken.

2. If the Chairperson considers that all efforts to reach consensus have been exhausted, decisions of the Commission shall, except where otherwise provided, be taken by two-thirds majority of the votes of all Contracting Parties present and casting affirmative or negative votes, provided that no vote shall be taken unless there is a quorum of at least two-thirds of the Contracting Parties. Each Contracting Party shall have one vote.

Article XIV Implementation of Commission Decisions

1. Each measure adopted by the Commission pursuant to Article VI, paragraphs 8 and 9 shall become binding on each Contracting Party in the following manner:

    (a)   the Executive Secretary shall within five working days of adoption transmit the measure to each Contracting Party specifying the date of transmittal for the purposes of paragraph 2; and

    (b)   subject to paragraph 2, unless otherwise specified in the measure, it shall become binding on each Contracting Party sixty days following the date of transmittal.

2. Where any Contracting Party presents an objection to a measure by delivering it to the Executive Secretary within sixty days of the date of transmittal specified pursuant to subparagraph 1(a), any other Contracting Party may similarly present an objection prior to the expiration of an additional twenty day period, or within fifteen days after the date of transmittal specified in the notification to the Contracting Parties of any objection presented within that additional twenty day period, whichever shall be later. The measure shall then become binding on each Contracting Party, except any that has presented an objection. If, however, at the end of such extended period or periods, objections have been presented and maintained by a majority of Contracting Parties, the measure shall not become binding, unless any or all of the Contracting Parties nevertheless agree as among themselves to be bound by it on an agreed date.

3. Any Contracting Party that has presented an objection may withdraw it at any time and the measure shall then become binding on it.

4.   (a)   Any time after the expiration of one year from the date on which a measure enters into force, any Contracting Party may notify the Executive Secretary of its intention not to be bound by the measure and, if that notification is not withdrawn, the measure shall cease to be binding on it at the end of one year from the date of receipt of such notification by the Executive Secretary.

    (b)   Any time after a measure has ceased to be binding on a Contracting Party pursuant to subparagraph (a), the measure shall cease to be binding on any other Contracting Party on the date the Executive Secretary receives notification of its intention not to be bound.

5. Any Contracting Party that has presented an objection to a measure pursuant to paragraph 2 or given notification of its intention not to be bound by a measure pursuant to paragraph 4 shall at the same time provide an explanation for its reasons for taking this action. This explanation shall specify whether it considers that the measure is inconsistent with the provisions of this Convention, or that the measure unjustifiably discriminates in form or fact against it. The explanation shall also include a declaration of the actions

it intends to take following the objection or -notification, including a description of the alternative measures it intends to take or has taken for conservation and management of the relevant fishery resources consistent with the objective of this Convention.

6. The Executive Secretary shall immediately notify each Contracting Party of:
   (a) the receipt or withdrawal of any objection pursuant to paragraph 2 or 3;
   (b) the date on which any measure becomes binding pursuant to paragraph 1;
   (c) the receipt of any notification pursuant to paragraph 4; and
   (d) each explanation and description of alternative measures received pursuant to paragraph 5.

7. Any Contracting Party that invokes the procedure set out in paragraphs 2, 4 or 5, may at the same time submit the matter to *ad hoc* panel proceedings. Annex II shall apply *mutatis mutandis*.

8. Where a Contracting Party does not submit the matter to *ad hoc* panel proceedings pursuant to paragraph 7, the Commission shall decide by simple majority mail vote, whether to submit that Contracting Party's explanation made pursuant to paragraph 5 to such proceedings. Where the Commission decides to submit the matter to such proceedings, Annex II shall apply *mutatis mutandis*.

9. Where, pursuant to paragraph 8, the Commission decides not to submit the matter to *ad hoc* panel proceedings, any Contracting Party may request a meeting of the Commission to review the measure adopted by the Commission and the explanation made pursuant to paragraph 5.

10. An *ad hoc* panel constituted pursuant to paragraph 7 or 8 shall review the explanation made pursuant to paragraph 5 and the measure to which it relates and make recommendations to the Commission on:
    (a) whether the explanation provided by the Contracting Party pursuant to paragraph 5 is well founded, and if so, whether the measure should accordingly be modified or rescinded, or where it finds that the explanation is not well founded, whether the measure should be maintained; and
    (b) whether the alternative measures set out in the explanation made by the Contracting Party pursuant to paragraph 5 are consistent with the objective of this Convention and preserve the respective rights of all Contracting Parties.

11. No later than thirty days following the termination of the *ad hoc* panel proceedings pursuant to this Article, the Commission shall meet to consider the recommendations of the *ad hoc* panel.

12. Where the procedures set out in paragraphs 7 to 11 have been concluded, any Contracting Party may invoke the dispute settlement procedures set out in Article XV.

Article XV Settlement of Disputes

1. Contracting Parties shall co-operate in order to prevent disputes.

2. Where a dispute arises between two or more Contracting Parties concerning the interpretation or application of this Convention, including the explanation referred to in Article XIV, paragraph 5, any actions taken by a Contracting Party following an objection presented pursuant to Article XIV, paragraph 2, or any notification made pursuant of Article XIV, paragraph 4, those Contracting Parties, hereinafter referred to as 'Contracting Parties to the dispute', shall seek to resolve their dispute by negotiation, inquiry, mediation, conciliation, arbitration, judicial settlement, *ad hoc* panel proceedings or other peaceful means of their choice.

3. Where a dispute concerns the interpretation or application of a measure adopted by the Commission pursuant to Article VI, paragraph 8 and 9, or matters related thereto, including the explanation referred to in Article XIV, paragraph 5, any actions taken by a

Contracting Party to the dispute following an objection presented pursuant to Article XIV, paragraph 2, or notification made pursuant to Article XIV, paragraph 4, the Contracting Parties to the dispute may submit the dispute to non binding *ad hoc* panel proceedings pursuant to Annex II.

4.   Where a dispute has been submitted to *ad hoc* panel proceedings, the *ad hoc* panel shall at the earliest opportunity confer with the Contracting Parties to the dispute with a view to resolving the dispute expeditiously. The *ad hoc* panel shall present a report to the Contracting Parties to the dispute and through the Executive Secretary to the other Contracting Parties. The report shall include any recommendations that the *ad hoc* panel considers appropriate to resolve the dispute.

5.   Where the Contracting Parties to the dispute accept the recommendations of the *ad hoc* panel, they shall within fourteen days of receipt of the report of the *ad hoc* panel notify all other Contracting Parties, through the Executive Secretary, of the actions they intend to take with a view to implementing the recommendations. Thereupon, the recommendations of the *ad hoc* panel may be referred for consideration by the Commission in accordance with its appropriate procedures.

6.   Where no settlement has been reached following the recommendations of the *ad hoc* panel, any of the Contracting Parties to the dispute may submit the dispute to compulsory proceedings entailing binding decisions pursuant to Section 2 of Part XV of the 1982 Convention or Part VIII of the 1995 Agreement.

7.   Where the Contracting Parties to a dispute have agreed to submit the dispute to *ad hoc* panel proceedings, they may at the same time agree to apply provisionally the relevant measure adopted by the Commission until the report of the *ad hoc* panel is presented unless they have settled the dispute by other means.

8.   Where the Contracting Parties to a dispute are unable to agree on any peaceful means referred to in paragraph 2 to resolve their dispute or are unable to otherwise reach a settlement, the dispute shall at the request of one of them, be submitted to compulsory proceedings entailing a binding decision pursuant to Part XV, Section 2, of the 1982 Convention or Part VIII of the 1995 Agreement.

9.   Where recourse is made to compulsory proceedings entailing binding decisions, the Contracting Parties to the dispute shall, unless they agree otherwise, provisionally apply any recommendation made by the *ad hoc* panel pursuant to paragraph 4 or, where applicable, pursuant to Article XIV, paragraph 10. They shall continue to apply such provisional measures or any arrangements of equivalent effect agreed between them until a court or tribunal having jurisdiction over the dispute prescribes provisional measures or renders a decision, or, until the expiration of the measure in question.

10.   The notification provisions of paragraph 5 shall apply *mutatis mutandis* with respect to provisional measures applied pursuant to paragraph 7 or prescribed pursuant to paragraph 9 or to any decision of a court or tribunal to which the dispute has been submitted.

11.   A court, tribunal or *ad hoc* panel to which a dispute has been submitted pursuant to this Article shall apply the relevant provisions of this Convention, the 1982 Convention, the 1995 Agreement, generally accepted standards for the conservation and management of living resources and other rules of international law not incompatible with this Convention with a view to attaining the objective of this Convention.

12.   Nothing in this Convention shall be argued or construed to prevent a Contracting Party to a dispute, as State Party to the 1982 Convention, from submitting the dispute to compulsory procedures entailing binding decisions against another State Party pursuant to Section 2 of Part XV of the 1982 Convention, or as State Party to the 1995 Agreement from submitting the dispute to compulsory procedures entailing binding decisions against another State Party pursuant to Article 30 of the 1995 Agreement.

Article XVI Co-operation with non-Contracting Parties

1. Where a vessel entitled to fly the flag of a non-Contracting Party engages in fishing activities in the Regulatory Area, the Commission shall request the flag State to cooperate fully with the Organization either by becoming a Contracting Party or by agreeing to apply the conservation and management measures adopted by the Commission.

2. Contracting Parties shall:
   (a) exchange information on fishing activities in the Regulatory Area by vessels entitled to fly the flag of any non-Contracting Party and on any action they have taken in response to such fishing activities;
   (b) take measures consistent with this Convention and international law to deter fishing activities of vessels entitled to fly the flag of any non-Contracting Party that undermine the effectiveness of the conservation and management measures adopted by the Commission;
   (c) advise any non-Contracting Party to this Convention of any fishing activity by its nationals or vessels entitled to fly its flag that undermine the effectiveness of the conservation and management measures adopted by the Commission; and
   (d) seek co-operation with any non-Contracting Party that has been identified as importing, exporting or re-exporting fishery products derived from fishing activities in the Convention Area.

Article XVII Co-operation with Other Organizations

The Organization shall:
   (a) cooperate, as appropriate, on matters of mutual interest, with the Food and Agriculture Organization of the United Nations, with other specialized agencies of the United Nations and with other relevant organizations;
   (b) seek to develop cooperative working relationships and may enter into agreements for this purpose with intergovernmental organizations that can contribute to its work and have competence for ensuring the long-term conservation and sustainable use of living resources and their ecosystems. It may invite such organizations to send observers to its meetings or those of any of its subsidiary bodies; it may also seek to participate in meetings of such organizations as appropriate; and
   (c) cooperate with other relevant regional fisheries management organizations taking note of their conservation and management measures.

Article XVIII Review

The Commission shall periodically initiate reviews and assessments of the adequacy of provisions of this Convention and, if necessary, propose means for strengthening their substance and methods of implementation in order to address any problems in attaining the objective of this Convention.

Article XIX Annexes

The Annexes shall form an integral part of this Convention and unless expressly provided otherwise, reference to this Convention includes reference to the Annexes.

Article XX Good Faith and Abuse of Rights

Contracting Parties shall fulfil in good faith the obligations assumed under this Convention and shall exercise the rights recognized in this Convention in a manner which would not constitute an abuse of right.

Article XXI Relation to Other Agreements

1. This Convention shall not alter the rights and obligations of Contracting Parties that arise from other Agreements compatible with this Convention and that do not affect the enjoyment by other Contracting Parties of their rights or the performance of their obligations under this Convention.

2. Nothing in this Convention shall prejudice the rights, jurisdiction and duties of Contracting Parties under the 1982 Convention or the 1995 Agreement. This Convention shall be interpreted and applied in the context of and in a manner consistent with the 1982 Convention and the 1995 Agreement.

Article XXII Amendments to the Convention

1. Any Contracting Party may propose amendments to this Convention to be considered and acted upon by the Commission at its annual meeting or at a special meeting. Any such proposal shall be sent to the Executive Secretary at least ninety days prior to the meeting at which it is proposed to be acted upon, and the Executive Secretary shall immediately transmit the proposal to each Contracting Party.

2. Adoption of a proposed amendment shall require a three-fourths majority of the votes of all Contracting Parties. The text of any amendment so adopted shall be transmitted by the Depositary to each Contracting Party.

3. An amendment shall take effect for all Contracting Parties one hundred and twenty days following the date of transmittal specified in the notification by the Depositary of receipt of written notification of approval by three-fourths of all Contracting Parties unless within ninety days of the date of transmittal specified in the notification by the Depositary of such receipt, any other Contracting Party notifies the Depositary that it objects to the amendment, in which case the amendment shall not take effect for any Contracting Party. Any Contracting Party that has objected to an amendment may at any time withdraw that objection. If all objections to an amendment that has been approved by three-fourths of all Contracting Parties are withdrawn, the amendment shall take effect for all Contracting Parties one hundred and twenty days following the date of transmittal specified in the notification by the Depositary, of receipt of the last withdrawal.

4. Any party that becomes a Contracting Party to the Convention after an amendment has been adopted in accordance with paragraph 2 shall be deemed to have approved that amendment.

5. The Depositary shall promptly notify all Contracting Parties of the receipt of notifications of approval of amendments, the receipt of notifications of objection or withdrawal of objections, and the entry into force of amendments.

6. Notwithstanding paragraphs 1 through 5, the Commission may by a two-thirds majority vote of all Contracting Parties:

    (a) taking into account the advice of the Scientific Council, if it considers it necessary for management purposes, divide the Regulatory Area into scientific and statistical subareas, regulatory divisions and subdivisions, as appropriate. The boundaries of any such subareas, divisions and subdivisions shall be set out in Annex I;

    (b) at the request of the Scientific Council, if it considers it necessary for management, scientific or statistical purposes, modify the boundaries of the scientific and statistical subareas, divisions and subdivisions set out in Annex I, provided that each coastal State affected concurs in such action.

Article XXIII

1. This Convention shall be open for signature at Ottawa until 31 December 1978, by the Parties represented at the Diplomatic Conference on the Future of Multilateral Cooperation in the Northwest Atlantic Fisheries, held at Ottawa from 11 to 21 October 1977. It shall thereafter be open for accession.

2. This Convention shall be subject to ratification, acceptance or approval by the Signatories and the instruments of ratification, acceptance or approval shall be deposited with the Government of Canada, referred to in this Convention as 'the Depositary'.

3. This Convention shall enter into force upon the first day of January following the deposit of instruments of ratification, acceptance or approval by not less than six Signatories, at least one of which exercises fisheries jurisdiction in waters forming part of the Convention Area.

4. Any party which has not signed this Convention may accede thereto by a notification in writing to the Depositary. Accessions received by the Depositary prior to the date of entry into force of this Convention shall become effective on the date this Convention enters into force. Accessions received by the Depositary after the date of entry into force of this Convention shall become effective on the date of receipt by the Depositary.

5. The Depositary shall inform all Signatories and all Contracting Parties of all ratifications, acceptances or approvals deposited and accessions received.

6. The Depositary shall convene the initial meeting of the Organization to be held not more than six months after the coming into force of the Convention, and shall communicate the provisional agenda to each Contracting Party not less than one month before the date of the meeting.

Article XXIV Denunciation

1. A Contracting Party may denounce this Convention by written notification to the Depositary on or before 30 June of any year. The denunciation shall take effect on 31 December of that same year. The Depositary shall without delay notify all other Contracting Parties.

2. Any other Contracting Party may thereupon by written notification to the Depositary no later than thirty days following notification pursuant to paragraph 1 also denounce the Convention with effect on 31 December of that year. The Depositary shall without delay notify all other Contracting Parties.

Article XXV Registration

1. The original of the present Convention shall be deposited with the Government of Canada, which shall communicate certified copies thereof to all the Signatories and to all the Contracting Parties.

2. The Depositary shall register the present Convention and any amendment thereof with the Secretariat of the United Nations.

IN WITNESS WHEREOF the undersigned, being duly authorized thereto, have signed this Convention.

DONE at Ottawa, this 24th day of October, 1978, in a single original, in the English and French languages, each text being equally authentic.

International Convention on Maritime Search and Rescue

Done at Hamburg, 27 April 1979; entry into force, 22 June 1985
1405 UNTS 119 [Registration Number 23489][1]

The Parties to the Convention,

Noting the great importance attached in several conventions to the rendering of assistance to persons in distress at sea and to the establishment by every coastal State of adequate and effective arrangements for coast watching and for search and rescue services,

Having considered Recommendation 40 adopted by the International Conference on Safety of Life at Sea, 1960, which recognizes the desirability of co-ordinating activities regarding safety on and over the sea among a number of inter-governmental organizations,

Desiring to develop and promote these activities by establishing an international maritime search and rescue plan responsible to the needs of maritime traffic for the rescue of persons in distress at sea,

Wishing to promote co-operation among search and rescue organizations around the world and among those participating in search and rescue operations at sea,

Have agreed as follows:

Article I General obligations under the Convention

The Parties undertake to adopt all legislative or other appropriate measures necessary to give full effect to the Convention and its Annex, which is an integral part of the Convention. Unless expressly provided otherwise, a reference to the Convention constitutes at the same time a reference to its Annex.

Article II Other treaties and interpretation

1. Nothing in the Convention shall prejudice the codification and development of the law of the sea by the United Nations Conference on the Law of the Sea convened pursuant to resolution 2750 (XXV) of the General Assembly of the United Nations nor the present or future claims and legal views of any State concerning the law of the sea and the nature and extent of coastal and flag State jurisdiction.

2. No provision of the Convention shall be construed as prejudicing obligations or rights of vessels provided for in other international instruments.

Article III Amendments

1. The Convention may be amended by either of the procedures specified in paragraphs (2) and (3) hereinafter.

2. Amendment after consideration within the Inter-Governmental Maritime Consultative Organization (hereinafter referred to as the Organization):

    (a)   Any amendment proposed by a Party and transmitted to the Secretary-General of the Organization (hereinafter referred to as the Secretary-General), or any amendment deemed necessary by the Secretary-General as a result of an amendment to a corresponding provision of Annex 12 to the Convention on International Civil Aviation, shall be circulated to all Members of the

---

[1] The Annex to the Convention was amended by Resolutions MSC.70(69), adopted on 18 May 1998, and MSC.155(78), adopted on 20 May 2004. The amendments entered into force on 1 July 1999 and 1 July 2006, respectively. The text of the Convention reproduced is a consolidated version incorporating the two amendments.

Organization and all Parties at least six months prior to its consideration by the Maritime Safety Committee of the Organization.

(b) Parties, whether or not Members of the Organization, shall be entitled to participate in the proceedings of the Maritime Safety Committee for the consideration and adoption of amendments.

(c) Amendments shall be adopted by a two-thirds majority of the Parties present and voting in the Maritime Safety Committee on condition that at least one third of the Parties shall be present at the time of adoption of the amendment.

(d) Amendments adopted in accordance with sub-paragraph (c) shall be communicated by the Secretary-General to all Parties for acceptance.

(e) An amendment to an Article or to paragraphs 2.1.4, 2.1.5, 2.1.7, 2.1.10, 3.1.2 or 3.1.3 of the Annex shall be deemed to have been accepted on the date on which the Secretary-General has received an instrument of acceptance from two thirds of the Parties.

(f) An amendment to the Annex other than to paragraphs 2.1.4, 2.1.5, 2.1.7, 2.1.10, 3.1.2 or 3.1.3 shall be deemed to have been accepted at the end of one year from the date on which it is communicated to the Parties for acceptance. However, if within such period of one year more than one third of the Parties notify the Secretary-General that they object to the amendment, it shall be deemed not to have been accepted.

(g) An amendment to an Article or to paragraphs 2.1.4, 2.1.5, 2.1.7, 2.1.10, 3.1.2 or 3.1.3 of the Annex shall enter into force:

  (i) with respect to those Parties which have accepted it, six months after the date on which it is deemed to have been accepted;

  (ii) with respect to those Parties which accept it after the condition mentioned in sub-paragraph (e) has been met and before the amendment enters into force, on the date of entry into force of the amendment;

  (iii) with respect to those Parties which accept it after the date on which the amendment enters into force, 30 days after the deposit of an instrument of acceptance.

(h) An amendment to the Annex other than to paragraphs 2.1.4, 2.1.5, 2.1.7, 2.1.10, 3.1.2 or 3.1.3 shall enter into force with respect to all Parties, except those which have objected to the amendment under sub-paragraph (f) and which have not withdrawn such objections, six months after the date on which it is deemed to have been accepted. However, before the date set for entry into force, any Party may give notice to the Secretary-General that it exempts itself from giving effect to that amendment for a period not longer than one year from the date of its entry into force, or for such longer period as may be determined by a two-thirds majority of the Parties present and voting in the Maritime Safety Committee at the time of the adoption of the amendment.

3. Amendment by a conference:

(a) Upon the request of a Party concurred in by at least one third of the Parties, the Organization shall convene a conference of Parties to consider amendments to the Convention. Proposed amendments shall be circulated by the Secretary-General to all Parties at least six months prior to their consideration by the conference.

(b) Amendments shall be adopted by such a conference by a two-thirds majority of the Parties present and voting, on condition that at least one third of the Parties shall be present at the time of adoption of the amendment. Amendments so adopted shall be communicated by the Secretary-General to all Parties for acceptance.

(c)   Unless the conference decides otherwise, the amendment shall be deemed to have been accepted and shall enter into force in accordance with the procedures specified in sub-paragraphs 2(e), 2(f), 2(g) and 2(h) respectively, provided that reference in sub-paragraph 2(h) to the Maritime Safety Committee expanded in accordance with sub-paragraph 2(b) shall be taken to mean reference to the conference.

4.   Any declaration of acceptance of, or objection to, an amendment or any notice given under sub-paragraph 2(h) shall be submitted in writing to the Secretary-General who shall inform all Parties of any such submission and the date of its receipt.

5.   The Secretary-General shall inform States of any amendments which enter into force, together with the date on which each such amendment enters into force.

Article IV Signature, ratification, acceptance approval and accession

1.   The Convention shall remain open for signature at the Headquarters of the Organization from 1 November 1979 until 31 October 1980 and shall thereafter remain open for accession. States may become Parties to the Convention by:

(a)   signature without reservation as to ratification, acceptance or approval; or

(b)   signature subject to ratification, acceptance or approval, followed by ratification, acceptance or approval; or

(c)   accession.

2.   Ratification, acceptance, approval or accession shall be effected by the deposit of an instrument to that effect with the Secretary-General.

3.   The Secretary-General shall inform States of any signature or of the deposit of any instrument of ratification, acceptance, approval or accession and the date of its deposit.

Article V Entry into force

1.   The Convention shall enter into force 12 months after the date on which 15 States have become Parties to it in accordance with Article IV.

2.   Entry into force for States which ratify, accept, approve or accede to the Convention in accordance with Article IV after the condition prescribed in paragraph (1) has been met and before the Convention enters into force, shall be on the date of entry into force of the Convention.

3.   Entry into force for States which ratify, accept, approve or accede to the Convention after the date on which the Convention enters into force shall be 30 days after the date of deposit of an instrument in accordance with Article IV.

4.   Any instrument of ratification, acceptance, approval or accession deposited after the date of entry into force of an amendment to the Convention in accordance with Article III shall apply to the Convention, as amended, and the Convention, as amended, shall enter into force for a State depositing such an instrument 30 days after the date of its deposit.

5.   The Secretary-General shall inform States of the date of entry into force of the Convention.

Article VI Denunciation

1.   The Convention may be denounced by any Party at any time after the expiry of five years from the date on which the Convention enters into force for that Party.

2.   Denunciation shall be effected by the deposit of an instrument of denunciation with the Secretary-General who shall notify States of any instrument of denunciation received and of the date of its receipt as well as the date on which such denunciation takes effect.

3.   A denunciation shall take effect one year, or such longer period as may be specified in the instrument of denunciation, after its receipt by the Secretary-General.

Article VII Deposit and registration

1. The Convention shall be deposited with the Secretary-General who shall transmit certified true copies thereof to States.

2. As soon as the Convention enters into force, the Secretary-General shall transmit the text thereof to the Secretary-General of the United Nations for registration and publication, in accordance with Article 102 of the Charter of the United Nations.

Article VIII Languages

The Convention is established in a single copy in the Chinese, English, French, Russian and Spanish languages, each text being equally authentic. Official translations in the Arabic, German and Italian languages shall be prepared and deposited with the signed original.

DONE at Hamburg this twenty-seventh day of April one thousand nine hundred and seventy-nine.

IN WITNESS WHEREOF the undersigned, being duly authorized by their respective Governments for the purpose, have signed the Convention.

ANNEX
CHAPTER 1. TERMS AND DEFINITIONS

1.1 'Shall' is used in the Annex to indicate a provision, the uniform application of which by all Parties is required in the interest of safety of life at sea.

1.2 'Should' is used in the Annex to indicate a provision, the uniform application of which by all Parties is recommended in the interest of safety of life at sea.

1.3 The terms listed below are used in the Annex with the following meanings:

.1 'Search'. An operation, normally co-ordinated by a rescue co-ordination centre or rescue sub-centre, using available personnel and facilities to locate persons in distress.

.2 'Rescue'. An operation to retrieve persons in distress, provide for their initial medical or other needs, and deliver them to a place of safety.

.3 'Search and rescue service'. The performance of distress monitoring, communication, co-ordination and search and rescue functions, including provision of medical advice, initial medical assistance, or medical evacuation, through the use of public and private resources including co-operating aircraft, vessels and other craft and installations.

.4 'Search and rescue region'. An area of defined dimensions associated with a rescue co-ordination centre within which search and rescue services are provided.

.5 'Rescue co-ordination centre'. A unit responsible for promoting efficient organization of search and rescue services and for co-ordinating the conduct of search and rescue operations within a search and rescue region.

.6 'Rescue sub-centre'. A unit subordinate to a rescue co-ordination centre established to complement the latter according to particular provisions of the responsible authorities.

.7 'Search and rescue facility'. Any mobile resource, including designated search and rescue units, used to conduct search and rescue operations.

.8 'Search and rescue unit'. A unit composed of trained personnel and provided with equipment suitable for the expeditious conduct of search and rescue operations.

.9   'Alerting post'. Any facility intended to serve as an intermediary between a person reporting an emergency and a rescue co-ordination centre or rescue sub-centre.

.10   'Emergency phase'. A generic term meaning, as the case may be, uncertainty phase, alert phase or distress phase.

.11   'Uncertainty phase'. A situation wherein uncertainty exists as to the safety of a person, a vessel or other craft.

.12   'Alert phase'. A situation wherein apprehension exists as to the safety of a person, a vessel or other craft.

.13   'Distress phase'. A situation wherein there is a reasonable certainty that a person, a vessel or other craft is threatened by grave and imminent danger and requires immediate assistance.

.14   'On-scene co-ordinator'. A person designated to co-ordinate search and rescue operations within a specified search area.

.15   'Secretary-General'. The Secretary-General of the International Maritime Organization.

CHAPTER 2. ORGANIZATION AND CO-ORDINATION

2.1 Arrangements for provision and co-ordination of search and rescue services

2.1.1   Parties shall, as they are able to so individually or in co-operation with other States and, as appropriate, with the Organization, participate in the development of search and rescue services to ensure that assistance is rendered to any person in distress at sea. On receiving information that any person is, or appears to be, in distress at sea, the responsible authorities of a Party shall take urgent steps to ensure that the necessary assistance is provided. The notion of a person in distress at sea also includes persons in need of assistance who have found refuge on a coast in a remote location within an ocean area inaccessible to any rescue facility other than as provided for in the Annex.

2.1.2   Parties shall, either individually or, if appropriate, in co-operation with other States, establish the following basic elements of a search and rescue service:

.1   legal framework;
.2   assignment of a responsible authority;
.3   organization of available resources;
.4   communication facilities;
.5   co-ordination and operational functions;
.6   processes to improve the service, including planning, domestic and international co-operative relationships and training.

Parties shall, as far as practicable, follow relevant standards and guidelines developed by the Organization.

2.1.3   To help ensure the provision of adequate shore-based communication infrastructure, efficient distress alert routeing, and proper operational co-ordination to effectively support search and rescue services, Parties shall individually or in co-operation with other States, ensure that sufficient search and rescue regions are established within each sea area in accordance with paragraphs 2.1.4 and 2.1.5. Such regions should be contiguous and, as far as practicable, not overlap.

2.1.4   Each search and rescue region shall be established by agreement among Parties concerned. The Secretary-General shall be notified of such agreements.

2.1.5   In case agreement on the exact dimensions of a search and rescue region is not reached by the Parties concerned, those Parties shall use their best endeavours to reach agreement upon appropriate arrangements under which the equivalent overall co-ordination of search and rescue services is provided in the area. The Secretary-General shall be notified of such arrangements.

2.1.6 Agreement on the regions or arrangements referred to in paragraphs 2.1.4 and 2.1.5 shall be recorded by the Parties concerned, or in written plans accepted by the Parties.

2.1.7 The delimitation of search and rescue regions is not related to and shall not prejudice the delimitation of any boundary between States.

2.1.8 Parties should seek to promote consistency, where applicable, between their maritime and aeronautical search and rescue services while considering the establishment of maritime search and rescue regions which shall be established in accordance with paragraph 2.1.4 or the reaching of agreement upon appropriate arrangements in accordance with paragraph 2.1.5.

2.1.9 Parties having accepted responsibility to provide search and rescue services for a specified area shall use search and rescue units and other available facilities for providing assistance to a person who, is or appears to be, in distress at sea.

2.1.10 Parties shall ensure that assistance be provided to any person in distress at sea. They shall do so regardless of the nationality or status of such a person or the circumstances in which that person is found.

2.1.11 Parties shall forward to the Secretary-General information on their search and rescue service, including the:

   .1   national authority responsible for the maritime search and rescue services;
   .2   location of the established rescue co-ordination centres or other centres providing search and rescue coordination, for the search and rescue region or regions and communications therein;
   .3   limits of their search and rescue region or regions and the coverage provided by their shore- based distress and safety communication facilities; and
   .4   principal types of available search and rescue units.

Parties shall with priority, update the information provided with respect to any alterations of importance. The Secretary-General shall transmit to all Parties the information received.

2.1.12 The Secretary-General shall notify all Parties of the agreements or arrangements referred to in paragraphs 2.1.4 and 2.1.5.

2.2 Development of national search and rescue services

2.2.1 Parties shall establish appropriate national procedures for overall development, co-ordination, and improvement of search and rescue services.

2.2.2 To support efficient search and rescue operations, Parties shall:
   .1   ensure the co-ordinated use of available facilities; and
   .2   establish close co-operation between services and organizations which may contribute to improve the search and rescue service in areas such as operations, planning, training, exercises and research and development.

2.3 Establishment of rescue co-ordination centres and rescue sub-centres

2.3.1 To meet the requirements of paragraph 2.2 Parties shall individually or in co-operation with other States establish rescue co-ordination centres for their search and rescue services and such rescue sub-centres as they consider appropriate.

2.3.2 Each rescue co-ordination centre and rescue sub-centre, established in accordance with paragraph 2.3.1, shall arrange for the receipt of distress alerts originating from within its search and rescue region. Every such centre shall also arrange for communications with persons in distress, with search and rescue facilities, and with other rescue co-ordination centres or rescue sub-centres.

2.3.3 Each rescue co-ordination centre shall be operational on a 24-hour basis and be constantly staffed by trained personnel having a working knowledge of the English language.

2.4 Co-ordination with aeronautical services

2.4.1 Parties shall ensure the closest practicable co-ordination between maritime and aeronautical services so as to provide for the most effective and efficient search and rescue services in and over their search and rescue regions.

2.4.2 Whenever practicable, each Party should establish joint rescue co-ordination centres and rescue sub-centres to serve both maritime and aeronautical purposes.

2.4.3 Whenever separate maritime and aeronautical rescue co-ordination centres or rescue sub-centres are established to serve the same area, the Party concerned shall ensure the closest practicable co-ordination between the centres or sub-centres.

2.4.4 Parties shall ensure as far as is possible the use of common procedures by search and rescue units established for maritime purposes and those established for aeronautical purposes.

2.5 Designation of search and rescue facilities

Parties shall identify all facilities able to participate in search and rescue operations, and may designate suitable facilities as search and rescue units.

2.6 Equipment of search and rescue units

2.6.1 Each search and rescue unit shall be provided with equipment appropriate to its task.

2.6.2 Containers and packages containing survival equipment for dropping to survivors should have the general nature of their contents indicated by markings in accordance with standards adopted by the Organization.

CHAPTER 3. CO-OPERATION BETWEEN STATES

3.1 Co-operation between States

3.1.1 Parties shall co-ordinate their search and rescue organizations and should, whenever necessary, co-ordinate search and rescue operations with those of neighbouring States.

3.1.2 Unless otherwise agreed between the States concerned, a Party should authorize, subject to applicable national laws, rules and regulations, immediate entry into or over its territorial sea or territory of rescue units of other Parties solely for the purpose of searching for the position of maritime casualties and rescuing the survivors of such casualties. In such cases, search and rescue operations shall, as far as practicable, be co-ordinated by the appropriate rescue co-ordination centre of the Party which has authorized entry, or such other authority as has been designated by that Party.

3.1.3 Unless otherwise agreed between the States concerned, the authorities of a Party which wishes its rescue units to enter into or over the territorial sea or territory of another Party solely for the purpose of searching for the position of maritime casualties and rescuing the survivors of such casualties, shall transmit a request, giving full details of the projected mission and the need for it, to the rescue co-ordination centre of that other Party, or to such other authority as has been designated by that Party.

3.1.4 The responsible authorities of Parties shall:

 .1 immediately acknowledge the receipt of such a request; and

 .2 as soon as possible indicate the conditions, if any, under which the projected mission may be undertaken.

3.1.5   Parties should enter into agreements with neighbouring States setting forth the conditions for entry of each other's rescue units into or over their respective territorial sea or territory. These agreements should also provide for expediting entry of such units with the least possible formalities.

3.1.6   Each Party should authorize its rescue co-ordination centres:

.1   to request from other rescue co-ordination centres such assistance, including vessels, aircraft, personnel or equipment, as may be needed;

.2   to grant any necessary permission for the entry of such vessels, aircraft, personnel or equipment into or over its territorial sea or territory; and

.3   to make the necessary arrangements with the appropriate customs, immigration, health or other authorities with a view to expediting such entry; and

.4   to make the necessary arrangements in co-operation with other RCCs to identify the most appropriate place(s) for disembarking persons found in distress at sea.

3.1.7   Each Party shall ensure its rescue co-ordination centres to provide, when requested, assistance to other rescue co-ordination centres, including assistance in the form of vessels, aircraft, personnel or equipment.

3.1.8   Parties should enter into agreements with other States, where appropriate, to strengthen search and rescue co-operation and co-ordination. Parties shall authorize their responsible authority to make operational plans and arrangements for search and rescue co-operation and co-ordination with responsible authorities of other States.

3.1.9   Parties shall co-ordinate and co-operate to ensure the masters of ships providing assistance by embarking persons in distress at sea are released from their obligations with minimum further deviation from the ships' intended voyage, provided that releasing the master of the ship from these obligations does not further endanger the safety of life at sea. The Party responsible for the search and rescue region in which such assistance is rendered shall exercise primary responsibility for ensuring such co-ordination and co-operation occurs, so that survivors assisted are disembarked from the assisting ship and delivered to a place of safety, taking into account the particular circumstances of the case and guidelines developed by the Organization. In these cases, the relevant Parties shall arrange for such disembarkation to be effected as soon as reasonably practicable.

CHAPTER 4. OPERATING PROCEDURES

4.1 Preparatory measures

4.1.1   Each rescue co-ordination centre and rescue sub-centre shall have available up-to-date information especially concerning search and rescue facilities and available communications relevant to search and rescue operations in its area.

4.1.2   Each rescue co-ordination centre and rescue sub-centre should have ready access to information regarding the position, course and speed of vessels within its area which may be able to provide assistance to persons, vessels or other craft in distress at sea, and regarding how to contact them. This information should either be kept in the rescue co-ordination centre, or be readily obtainable when necessary.

4.1.3   Each rescue co-ordination centre and rescue sub-centre shall have detailed plans of operation for the conduct of search and rescue operations. Where appropriate, these plans shall be developed jointly with the representatives of those who may assist in providing, or who may benefit from, the search and rescue services.

4.1.4   Rescue co-ordination centres or sub-centres shall be kept informed of the state of preparedness of search and rescue units.

4.2   Information concerning emergencies

4.2.1   Parties, either individually or in co-operation with other States, shall ensure that they are capable on a 24-hour basis of promptly and reliably receiving distress alerts from equipment used for this purpose within their search and rescue regions. Any alerting post receiving a distress alert shall:

.1   immediately relay the alert to the appropriate rescue co-ordination centre or sub-centre, and then assist with search and rescue communications as appropriate; and

.2   if practicable acknowledge the alert.

4.2.2   Parties shall, where appropriate, ensure that effective arrangements are in place for the registration of communication equipment and for responding to emergencies, to enable any rescue co-ordination centre or sub-centre to access pertinent registration information quickly.

4.2.3   Any authority or element of the search and rescue service having reason to believe that a person, a vessel or other craft is in a state of emergency shall forward as soon as possible all available information to the rescue co-ordination centre or rescue sub-centre concerned.

4.2.4   Rescue co-ordination centres and rescue sub-centres shall, immediately upon receipt of information concerning a person, a vessel, or other craft in a state of emergency, evaluate such information and determine the phase of emergency in accordance with paragraph 4.4, and the extent of operations required.

4.3   Initial action

Any search and rescue unit receiving information of a distress incident shall initially take immediate action if in the position to assist and shall, in any case without delay, notify the rescue co-ordination centre or rescue sub-centre in whose area the incident has occurred.

4.4   Emergency phases

To assist in determining the appropriate operating procedures, the following emergency phases shall be distinguished by the rescue co-ordination centre or sub-centre concerned:

.1   *Uncertainty phase:*

.1.1   when a person has been reported as missing, or a vessel or other craft is overdue; or

.1.2   when a person, a vessel or other craft has failed to make an expected position or safety report.

.2   *Alert phase:*

.2.1   when, following the uncertainty phase, attempts to establish contact with a person, a vessel or other craft have failed and inquiries addressed to other appropriate sources have been unsuccessful; or

.2.2   when information has been received indicating that the operating efficiency of a vessel or other craft is impaired, but not to the extent that a distress situation is likely.

.3   *Distress phase:*

.3.1   when positive information is received that a person, a vessel or other craft is in danger and in need of immediate assistance; or

.3.2   when, following the alert phase, further unsuccessful attempts to establish contact with a person, a vessel or other craft and more widespread unsuccessful inquiries point to the probability that a distress situation exists; or

.3.3   when information is received which indicates that the operating efficiency of a vessel or other craft has been impaired to the extent that a distress situation is likely.

4.5 Procedures to be followed by rescue co-ordination centres and rescue sub-centres during emergency phases

4.5.1 Upon the declaration of the uncertainty phase, the rescue co-ordination centre or rescue sub-centre, as appropriate, shall initiate inquiries to determine the safety of a person, a vessel or other craft, or shall declare the alert phase.

4.5.2 Upon the declaration of the alert phase, the rescue co-ordination centre or rescue sub-centre, as appropriate, shall extend the inquiries for the missing person, vessel or other craft, alert appropriate search and rescue services and initiate such action, as is necessary in the light of the circumstances of the particular case.

4.5.3 Upon the declaration of the distress phase, the rescue co-ordination centre or rescue sub-centre, as appropriate, shall proceed as prescribed in its plans of operation, as required by paragraph 4.1.

4.5.4 *Initiation of search and rescue operations when the position of the search object is unknown*

In the event of an emergency phase being declared for a search object whose position is unknown, the following shall apply:

.1 when an emergency phase exists, a rescue co-ordination centre or rescue sub-centre shall, unless it is aware that other centres are taking action, assume responsibility for initiating suitable action and confer with other centres with the objective of designating one centre to assume responsibility;

.2 unless otherwise decided by agreement between the centres concerned, the centre to be designated shall be the centre responsible for the area in which the search object was according to its last reported position; and

.3 after the declaration of the distress phase, the centre co-ordinating the search and rescue operations shall, as appropriate, inform other centres of all the circumstances of the emergency and of all subsequent developments.

4.5.5 *Passing information to persons, vessels, or other craft for which an emergency phase has been declared*

Whenever possible, the rescue co-ordination centre or rescue sub-centre responsible for search and rescue operations shall forward to the person, a vessel or other craft for which an emergency phase has been declared, information on the search and rescue operations it has initiated.

4.6 Co-ordination when two or more Parties are involved

For search and rescue operations involving more than one Party, each Party shall take appropriate action in accordance with the plans of operation referred to in paragraph 4.1 when so requested by the rescue co-ordination centre of the region.

4.7 On-scene co-ordination of search and rescue activities

4.7.1 The activities of search and rescue units and other facilities engaged in search and rescue operations shall be co-ordinated on-scene to ensure the most effective results.

4.7.2 When multiple facilities are about to engage in search and rescue operations, and the rescue co-ordination centre or rescue sub-centre considers it necessary, the most capable person should be designated as on-scene co-ordinator as early as practicable and preferably before the facilities arrive within the specified area of operation. Specific responsibilities shall be assigned to the on-scene co-ordinator taking into account the apparent capabilities of the on-scene coordinator and operational requirements.

4.7.3 If there is no responsible rescue co-ordination centre or, by any reason, the responsible rescue co-ordination centre is unable to co-ordinate the search and rescue mission, the facilities involved should designate an on-scene co-ordinator by mutual agreement.

4.8   Termination and suspension of search and rescue operations

4.8.1   Search and rescue operations shall continue, when practicable, until all reasonable hope of rescuing survivors has passed.

4.8.2   The responsible rescue co-ordination centre or rescue sub-centre concerned shall normally decide when to discontinue search and rescue operations. If no such centre is involved in co-ordinating the operations, the on-scene co-ordinator may take this decision.

4.8.3   When a rescue co-ordination centre or rescue sub-centre considers, on the basis of reliable information, that a search and rescue operation has been successful, or that the emergency no longer exists, it shall terminate the search and rescue operation and promptly so inform any authority, facility or service which has been activated or notified.

4.8.4   If a search and rescue operation on-scene becomes impracticable and the rescue co-ordination centre or rescue sub-centre concludes that survivors might still be alive, the centre may temporarily suspend the on-scene activities pending further developments, and shall promptly so inform any authority, facility or service which has been activated or notified. Information subsequently received shall be evaluated and search and rescue operations resumed when justified on the basis of such information.

4.8.5   The rescue co-ordination centre or rescue sub-centre concerned shall initiate the process of identifying the most appropriate place(s) for disembarking such persons found in distress at sea. It shall inform the ship or ships and other relevant parties concerned thereof.

CHAPTER 5. SHIP REPORTING SYSTEMS

5.1   General

5.1.1   Ship reporting systems may be established either individually by Parties or in co-operation with other States, where this is considered necessary, to facilitate search and rescue operations.

5.1.2   Parties contemplating the institution of a ship reporting system should take account of the relevant recommendations of the Organization. Parties should also consider whether existing reporting systems or other sources of ship position data can provide adequate information for the region, and seek to minimize unnecessary additional reports by ships, or the need for rescue co-ordination centres to check with multiple reporting systems to determine availability of ships to assist with search and rescue operations.

5.1.3   The ship reporting system should provide up-to-date information on the movements of vessels in order, in the event of a distress incident, to:

  .1   reduce the interval between the loss of contact with a vessel and the initiation of search and rescue operations in cases where no distress signal has been received;

  .2   permit rapid identification of vessels which may be called upon to provide assistance;

  .3   permit delineation of a search area of limited size in case the position of a person, a vessel or other craft in distress is unknown or uncertain; and

  .4   facilitate the provision of urgent medical assistance or advice.

5.2   Operational requirements

5.2.1   Ship reporting systems should satisfy the following requirements:

  .1   provision of information, including sailing plans and position reports, which would make it possible to determine the current and future positions of participating vessels;

  .2   maintenance of a shipping plot;

  .3   receipt of reports at appropriate intervals from participating vessels;

.4   simplicity in system design and operation; and

.5   use of internationally agreed standard ship reporting format and procedures.

5.3 Types of reports

5.3.1   A ship reporting system should incorporate the following types of ship reports in accordance with the recommendations of the Organization:

.1   Sailing plan;

.2   Position report; and

.3   Final report.

5.4 Use of systems

5.4.1   Parties should encourage all vessels to report their position when travelling in areas where arrangements have been made to collect information on positions for search and rescue purposes.

5.4.2   Parties recording information on the position of vessels should disseminate, so far as practicable, such information to other States when so requested for search and rescue purposes.

Paris Memorandum of Understanding on Port State Control

Done at Paris, 26 January 1982; entry into force, 1 July 1982
http://www.parismou.org/[1]

The Maritime Authorities of Belgium, Bulgaria, Canada, Croatia, Cyprus, Denmark, Estonia, Finland, France, Germany (Federal Republic of), Greece, Iceland, Ireland, Italy, Latvia, Lithuania, Malta, Netherlands, Norway, Poland, Portugal, Romania, Russian Federation, Slovenia, Spain, Sweden, United Kingdom of Great Britain and Northern Ireland hereinafter referred to as 'the Authorities',

Recalling the Final Declaration adopted on 2 December 1980 by the Regional European Conference on Maritime Safety which underlined the need to increase maritime safety and the protection of the marine environment and the importance of improving living and working conditions on board ship;

Noting with appreciation the progress achieved in these fields by the International Maritime Organization and the International Labour Organization;

Noting also the contribution of the European Union towards meeting the above mentioned objectives;

Mindful that the principal responsibility for the effective application of standards laid down in international instruments rests upon the authorities of the State whose flag a ship is entitled to fly;

Recognizing nevertheless that effective action by port States is required to prevent the operation of substandard ships;

Recognizing also the need to avoid distorting competition between ports;

---

[1] The text of the Memorandum has been amended several times since 1982. The 29th amendment was adopted on 10 May 2007 and entered into force on 1 July 2007. Annex 1 (Port State Control Procedures), Annex 2 (Procedures for Investigations under MARPOL 73/78), Annex 3 (Access Refusal Measures Concerning Certain Ships), Annex 4 (Information System of Inspections), Annex 5 (Publication of Information Related to Detentions and Inspections), Annex 6 (Qualitative Criteria for Adherence to the Memorandum in Accordance with 8.2 of the Memorandum) and Annex 7 (Minimum Criteria for Port State Control Officers) omitted.

Convinced of the necessity, for these purposes, of an improved and harmonized system of port State control and of strengthening co-operation and the exchange of information; Have reached the following understanding:

Section 1 Commitments

1.1   Each Authority will give effect to the provisions of the present Memorandum and the Annexes thereto, which constitute an integral part of the Memorandum.

1.2   Each Authority will maintain an effective system of port State control with a view to ensuring that, without discrimination as to flag, foreign merchant ships calling at a port of its State, or anchored off such a port, comply with the standards laid down in the relevant instruments as defined in section 2. Each Authority may also carry out controls on ships at off-shore installations.

1.3   Each Authority will achieve an annual total of inspections corresponding to 25% of the average number of individual foreign merchant ships, hereinafter referred to as 'ships', which entered the ports of its State during the three last calendar years for which statistics are available.

1.4   Each Authority will consult, cooperate and exchange information with the other Authorities in order to further the aims of the Memorandum.

1.5   Each Authority, or any other body, as the case may be, will establish an appropriate procedure for pilot services and port authorities to immediately inform the competent Authority of the port State, whenever they learn in the course of their normal duties that there are deficiencies which may prejudice the safety of the ship, or which may pose a threat of harm to the marine environment.

Section 2 Relevant instruments

2.1   For the purposes of the Memorandum 'relevant instruments' are the following instruments:

.1   the International Convention on Load Lines, 1966 (LOAD LINES 66);

.2   the Protocol of 1988 relating to the International Convention on Load Lines, 1966 (LL PROT 88);

.3   the International Convention for the Safety of Life at Sea, 1974 (SOLAS 74);

.4   the Protocol of 1978 relating to the International Convention for the Safety of Life at Sea, 1974 (SOLAS PROT 78);

.5   the Protocol of 1988 relating to the International Convention for the Safety of Life at Sea, 1974 (SOLAS PROT 88);

.6   the International Convention for the Prevention of Pollution from Ships, 1973, as modified by the Protocols of 1978 and 1997 relating thereto (MARPOL 73/78);

.7   the International Convention on Standards of Training, Certification and Watchkeeping for Seafarers, 1978 (STCW 78);

.8   the Convention on the International Regulations for Preventing Collisions at Sea, 1972 (COLREG 72);

.9   the International Convention on Tonnage Measurement of Ships, 1969 (TONNAGE 69);

.10   the Merchant Shipping (Minimum Standards) Convention, 1976 (ILO Convention No. 147) (ILO 147);

.11   the Protocol of 1996 to the Merchant Shipping (Minimum Standards) Convention, 1976 (ILO Convention No. 147) (ILO147 PROT 96);

.12   the International Convention on Civil Liability for Oil Pollution Damage, 1992.

2.2   With respect to ILO 147 and the ILO Protocol 1996, each Authority will apply the procedures referred to in section 7 of Annex 1 for the application of ILO publication 'Inspection of Labour Conditions on board Ship: Guide-lines for procedure'.

2.3   Each Authority will apply those relevant instruments which are in force and to which its State is a Party. In the case of amendments to a relevant instrument each Authority will apply those amendments which are in force and which its State has accepted. An instrument so amended will then be deemed to be the 'relevant instrument' for that Authority.

2.4   In applying a relevant instrument, the Authorities will ensure that no more favourable treatment is given to ships of non-Parties or to ships below convention size. The Authorities will thereby apply the procedures specified in section 3 of Annex 1.

Section 3 Inspection procedures, rectification and detention

3.1   In fulfilling their commitments the Authorities will carry out inspections, which will consist of a visit on board a ship in order to check the certificates and documents as referred to in section 2 of Annex 1. Furthermore the Authorities will satisfy themselves that the crew and the overall condition of the ship, including the engine room and accommodation and including hygienic conditions, meets generally accepted international rules and standards.

In the absence of valid certificates or documents or if there are clear grounds for believing that the condition of a ship or of its equipment, or its crew does not substantially meet the requirements of a relevant instrument, a more detailed inspection will be carried out, as referred to in section 5 of Annex 1. Examples of clear grounds are given in section 4 of Annex 1.

The Authorities will include control on compliance with on board operational requirements in their inspections.

3.2   The Authorities will ensure that an inspection in accordance with the provisions of section 3.1 is carried out on any ship not subject to expanded inspection with a target factor greater than 50 in the SIReNaC information system, provided that a period of at least one month has elapsed since the last inspection carried out in the region of the Memorandum.

3.3   A ship in one of the categories in section 8.2 of Annex 1, is liable to an expanded inspection after a period of twelve months since the last expanded inspection carried out in a port within the region of the Memorandum.

If such a ship is selected for inspection in accordance with section 3.6, an expanded inspection shall be carried out. However an inspection in accordance with section 3.1 may be carried out in the period between two expanded inspections.

The Authorities will ensure that an expanded inspection is carried out on a ship for which the inspection is indicated as mandatory by the SIReNaC system at its first port visited after a period of 12 months since the last expanded inspection.

3.4   In cases where, for operational reasons, an Authority is unable to carry out an inspection or an expanded inspection as referred to in sections 3.2 and 3.3 respectively, the Authority will, without delay, inform the SIReNaC system that such inspection did not take place.

3.5   Nothing in these procedures will be construed as restricting the powers of the Authorities to take measures within its jurisdiction in respect of any matter to which the relevant instruments relate.

3.6   In selecting for inspection ships other than those referred to in sections 3.2 and 3.3, the Authorities will determine the order of priority on the basis of the criteria indicated in section 1 of Annex 1.

3.7   The Authorities will seek to avoid inspecting ships which have been inspected by any of the other Authorities within the previous six months, unless they have clear grounds for inspection. The frequency of inspection does not apply to the ships referred to in 3.6 and in 3.2 in which case the Authorities will seek satisfaction whenever they will deem this appropriate.

3.8   Inspections will be carried out by properly qualified persons authorized for that purpose by the Authority concerned and acting under its responsibility, having regard in particular to Annex 7.

When the required professional expertise cannot be provided by the Authority, the port State control officer of that Authority may be assisted by any person with the required expertise. Port State control officers and the persons assisting them will have no commercial interest, either in the port of inspection or in the ships inspected, nor will port State control officers be employed by or undertake work on behalf of non-governmental organizations which issue statutory and classification certificates or which carry out the surveys necessary for the issue of those certificates to ships.

Each port State control officer will carry a personal document in the form of an identity card issued by his Authority in accordance with the national legislation, indicating that the port State control officer is authorized to carry out inspections.

3.9.1   Each Authority will endeavour to secure the rectification of all deficiencies detected. On the condition that all possible efforts have been made to rectify all deficiencies, other than those referred to in 3.10.1, the ship may be allowed to proceed to a port where any such deficiencies can be rectified.

3.9.2   In exceptional circumstances where, as a result of the initial control and a more detailed inspection, the overall condition of a ship and its equipment, also taking the crew and its living and working conditions into account, is found to be sub-standard, the Authority may suspend an inspection.

The suspension of the inspection may continue until the responsible parties have taken the steps necessary to ensure that the ship complies with the requirements of the relevant instruments.

Prior to suspending an inspection, the Authority must have recorded detainable deficiencies in the areas set out in 9.3.3 and 9.3.4 of Annex 1, as appropriate.

In cases where the ship is detained and an inspection is suspended, the Authority will as soon as possible notify the responsible parties. The notification will include information about the detention. Furthermore it will state that the inspection is suspended until the Authority has been informed that the ship complies with all relevant requirements.

3.10.1   In the case of deficiencies which are clearly hazardous to safety, health or the environment, the Authority will, except as provided in 3.11, ensure that the hazard is removed before the ship is allowed to proceed to sea. For this purpose appropriate action will be taken, which may include detention or a formal prohibition of a ship to continue an operation due to established deficiencies which, individually or together, would render the continued operation hazardous.

3.10.2   In the case of a detention, the Authority will immediately notify the flag State Administration in writing, which includes the report of inspection. Like wise, the classification society which has issued the class certificates and the recognized organization that has issued the relevant certificates on behalf of the flag State Administration will be notified, where appropriate. The parties above will also be notified in writing of the release of detention.

3.10.3   Where the ground for a detention is the result of accidental damage suffered on the ship's voyage to a port or during cargo operations, no detention order will be issued, provided that:

.1   due account has been given to the requirements contained in Regulation I/11(c) of SOLAS 74 regarding notification to the flag State Administration, the nominated surveyor or the recognized organization responsible for issuing the relevant certificate;

.2   prior to entering a port or immediately after a damage has occurred, the master or ship owner has submitted to the port State control authority details on the circumstances of the accident and the damage suffered and information about the required notification of the flag State Administration;

.3   appropriate remedial action, to the satisfaction of the Authority, is being taken by the ship; and

.4   the Authority has ensured, having been notified of the completion of the remedial action, that deficiencies which were clearly hazardous to safety, health or the environment have been rectified.

3.10.4   The following procedure is applicable in the absence of ISM certificates:

.1   Where the inspection reveals that the copy of the Document of Compliance or the Safety Management Certificate issued in accordance with the International Safety Management Code for the Safe Operation of Ships and for Pollution Prevention (ISM Code) are missing on board a vessel to which the ISM Code is applicable at the date of the inspection, the Authority will ensure that the vessel is detained.

.2   Notwithstanding the absence of the documentation referred to in 3.10.4.1, if the inspection finds no other deficiencies warranting detention the Authority may lift the detention order in order to avoid port congestion. Whenever such a decision is taken, the Authority will immediately inform all other Authorities thereof.

.3   The Authorities will take the measures necessary to ensure that all ships authorised to leave a port of their State under the circumstances referred to in 3.10.4.2 will be refused access to any port within the States, the Authorities of which are signatories to the Memorandum, except in the situations referred to in 3.12.3, until the owner or operator of the vessel has demonstrated, to the satisfaction of the Authority in whose State detention was ordered, that the ship has valid certificates issued in accordance with the ISM Code.

3.10.5   Access refusal measures concerning certain ships

.1   The Authorities will ensure that a ship in one of the categories of Annex 3, section A, is refused access to any port within the region of the Memorandum, except in the situations described in section 3.12.3 if the ship:

–   either flies the flag of a State appearing in the black list as published in the annual report of the MOU, and has been detained more than twice in the course of the preceding 24 months in ports within the region of the Memorandum;

–   or flies the flag of a State described as 'very high risk' or 'high risk' in the black list as published in the annual report of the MOU, and has been detained more than once in the course of the preceding 36 months in ports within the region of the Memorandum.

The refusal of access shall become applicable immediately the ship has been authorised to leave the port where it has been subject of a second or third detention as appropriate.

.2   For the purpose of paragraph 1, the Authorities will comply with the procedures laid down in Annex 3 section B.

3.11   Where deficiencies which caused a detention as referred to in 3.10.1 cannot be remedied in the port of inspection, the Authority may allow the ship concerned to proceed to the nearest appropriate repair yard available, as chosen by the master and the Authority, provided that the conditions determined by the competent authority of the flag State and agreed by the Authority are complied with. Such conditions, which may include discharging of cargo and/or temporary repairs, will ensure that the ship can proceed without risk to the safety and health of the passengers or crew, or risk to other ships, or without being an unreasonable threat of harm to the marine environment.

Where the decision to send a ship to a repair yard is due to a lack of compliance with IMO Resolution A.744(18), either with respect to ship's documentation or with respect to ship's structural failures and deficiencies, the Authority may require that the necessary thickness measurements are carried out in the port of detention before the ship is allowed to sail.

If the vessel is detained because it is not equipped with a functioning voyage data recorder system, when its use is compulsory, and this deficiency cannot be readily rectified in the port of detention, the competent authority may allow the ship to proceed to the nearest appropriate port where it shall be readily rectified or require that the deficiency is rectified within a maximum period of 30 days.

In such circumstances the Authority will notify the competent authority of the region State where the next port of call of the ship is situated, the parties mentioned in 3.10.2 and any other authority as appropriate. Notification to Authorities shall include the final report of inspection and the estimated place and time of arrival. Additional notification will be made by means of the SIReNaC system. The Authority receiving such notification will inform the notifying Authority of action taken.

3.12.1   The Authorities will take measures to ensure that:

.1   ships referred to in 3.10.1 or 3.11 which proceed to sea without complying with the conditions determined by the Authority in the port of inspection; or

.2   ships referred to in 3.11 which refuse to comply with the applicable requirements of the relevant instruments by not calling into the indicated repair yard;

will be refused access to any port within the States, the Authorities of which are signatories to the Memorandum, until the owner or operator has provided evidence to the satisfaction of the Authority where the ship was found defective, that the ship fully complies with all applicable requirements of the relevant instruments.

3.12.2   In the circumstances referred to in 3.12.1.1, the Authority where the ship was found defective will immediately alert all other Authorities.

In the circumstances referred to in 3.12.1.2, the Authority in whose State the repair yard lies will immediately alert all other Authorities.

Before denying entry, the Authority may request consultations with the flag State Administration of the ship concerned.

3.12.3   Notwithstanding the provisions of 3.12.1, access to a specific port may be permitted by the relevant authority of that port State in the event of force majeure or overriding safety considerations, or to reduce or minimize the risk of pollution, provided that adequate measures to the satisfaction of the competent authority of such State have been implemented by the owner, the operator or the master of the ship to ensure safe entry.

3.13   The provisions of 3.10.2 and 3.11 are without prejudice to the requirements of relevant instruments or procedures established by international organizations concerning notification and reporting procedures related to port State control.

3.14   The Authorities will ensure that, on the conclusion of an inspection, the master of the ship is provided with a report of inspection, giving the results of the inspection and details of any action taken.

3.15   Should any inspection referred to in 3.1 confirm or reveal deficiencies in relation to the requirements of a relevant instrument warranting the detention of a ship, all costs relating to the inspections in any normal accounting period will be covered by the shipowner or the operator or by his representative in the port State.

All costs relating to inspections carried out by the Authority under the provisions of 3.12.1 will be charged to the owner or the operator of the ship.

The detention will not be lifted until full payment has been made or a sufficient guarantee has been given for the reimbursement of the costs.

3.16   The owner or the operator of a ship or his representative in the State concerned will have a right of appeal against a detention decision or refusal of access taken by the Authority of that State. An appeal will not cause the detention or refusal of access to be suspended. The Authority will properly inform the master of a ship of the right of appeal.

3.17   Each Authority will take necessary measure in order to ensure that information listed in Annex 5 on ships inspected and ships detained is published at least every month.

3.18   When exercising control under the Memorandum, the Authorities will make all possible efforts to avoid unduly detaining or delaying a ship. Nothing in the Memorandum affects rights created by provisions of relevant instruments relating to compensation for undue detention or delay. In any instance of alleged undue detention or delay the burden of proof lies with the owner or operator of the ship.

Section 4 Provision of information

4.1   Each Authority will report on its inspections under the Memorandum and their results, in accordance with the procedures specified in Annex 4.

4.2   Information provided in accordance with the previous paragraph may be made available for publication in printed form or by electronic means in order to assist Authorities with the publications mentioned in section 3.17 as well as for other purposes in accordance with decisions of the Committee mentioned in section 6.

4.3   DSI, mentioned in Annex 4 and the Secretariat, mentioned in section 6.4 may facilitate the publication of data by providing data in any electronic or printed format derived unaltered from the information system mentioned in Annex 4.

4.4   When inspection or detention data contain information concerning private persons the Authorities undertake to ensure protection of the privacy of those persons in accordance with applicable international, European Community and national laws and regulations. This protection shall however not prevent the publication of the company of ships inspected or publication of the names of charterers involved.

Section 5 Operational violations

The Authorities will upon the request of another Authority, endeavour to secure evidence relating to suspected violations of the requirements on operational matters of Rule 10 of COLREG 72 and MARPOL 73/78. In case of suspected violations involving the discharge of harmful substances, an Authority will, upon the request of another Authority, visit in port the ship suspected of such a violation in order to obtain information and where appropriate to take a sample of any alleged pollutant. Procedures for investigations into contravention of discharge provisions are listed in Annex 2.

Section 6 Organization

6.1   A Committee will be established, composed of a representative of each of the Authorities and of the Commission of the European Communities. An advisor from each of the International Governmental Organizations, Observers and Associates will be invited to participate in the work of the Committee and any other meetings.

6.2   The Committee will meet once a year and at such other times as it may decide.

6.3   The Committee will:

.1   carry out the specific tasks assigned to it under the Memorandum;

.2   promote by all means necessary, including seminars for port State control officers, the harmonization of procedures and practices relating to the inspection, rectification, detention and the application of 2.4;

.3   develop and review guidelines and procedures for carrying out inspections under the Memorandum;

.4   develop and review procedures for the exchange of information;

.5   keep under review other matters relating to the operation and the effectiveness of the Memorandum.

6.4   A secretariat provided by the Netherlands' Ministry of Transport, Public Works and Water Management will be set up and will have its office in The Hague.

6.5   The secretariat, acting under the guidance of the Committee and within the limits of the resources made available to it, will:

.1   prepare meetings, circulate papers and provide such assistance as may be required to enable the Committee to carry out its functions;

.2   facilitate the exchange of information, carry out the procedures outlined in Annex 4 and prepare reports as may be necessary for the purposes of the Memorandum;

.3   carry out such other work as may be necessary to ensure the effective operation of the Memorandum.

Section 7 Amendments

7.1   Any Authority may propose amendments to the Memorandum.

7.2   In the case of proposed amendments to sections of the Memorandum the following procedure will apply:

.1   the proposed amendment will be submitted through the secretariat for consideration by the Committee;

.2   amendments will be adopted by a two-thirds majority of the representatives of the Authorities present and voting in the Committee. If so adopted an amendment will be communicated by the secretariat to the Authorities for acceptance;

.3   an amendment will be deemed to have been accepted either at the end of a period of six months after adoption by the representatives of the Authorities in the Committee or at the end of any different period determined unanimously by the representatives of the Authorities in the Committee at the time of adoption, unless within the relevant period an objection is communicated to the secretariat by an Authority;

.4   an amendment will take effect 60 days after it has been accepted or at the end of any different period determined unanimously by the representatives of the Authorities in the Committee.

7.3   In the case of proposed amendments to Annexes of the Memorandum the following procedure will apply:

.1   the proposed amendment will be submitted through the secretariat for consideration by the Authorities;

.2   the amendment will be deemed to have been accepted at the end of a period of three months from the date on which it has been communicated by the secretariat unless an Authority requests in writing that the amendment should be considered by the Committee. In the latter case the procedure specified in 7.2 will apply;

.3   the amendment will take effect 60 days after it has been accepted or at the end of any different period determined unanimously by the Authorities.

Section 8

8.1   The Memorandum is without prejudice to rights and obligations under any international Agreement.

8.2   A Maritime Authority of a European coastal State and a coastal State of the North Atlantic basin from North America to Europe, which complies with the criteria specified in Annex 6, may adhere to the Memorandum with the consent of all Authorities participating in the Memorandum.

8.3   When the Memorandum takes effect, it will supersede the 'Memorandum of Understanding between Certain Maritime Authorities on the Maintenance of Standards on Merchant Ships', signed at The Hague on 2 March 1978.

8.4   The Memorandum will take effect on 1 July 1982.

8.5   The English and French versions of the text of the Memorandum are equally authentic.

Signed at Paris in the English and French languages, this twenty-sixth day of January one thousand nine hundred and eighty-two.

The United Kingdom and Argentine Exclusion Zones Notices During the Falkland Islands Conflict

[I] Notice Issued by the British Government, 7 April 1982
UN Doc. S/14963, 10 April 1982

From 0400 Greenwich mean time on Monday 12 April 1982, a maritime exclusion zone will be established around the Falklands Islands. The outer limit of this zone is a circle of 200 nautical mile radius from latitude 51° 40′S, 59 30′W., which is approximately the centre of the Falkland Islands. From the time indicated, any Argentine warships and Argentine naval auxiliaries found within this zone will be treated as hostile and are liable to be attacked by British forces. This measure is without prejudice to the right of the United Kingdom to take whatever additional measures may be needed in exercise of its right to self-defence, under Article 51 of the United Nations Charter.

[II] Communique No. 19 of the Argentine Government,
Issued at 2330 on 7 April 1982 (330 on 8 April 1982 GMT)
BBC, SWB, Part 5, V/7000/I, 13 April 1982

The creation of the South Atlantic Theatre of Operations constitutes an important instrument for the defence of the national sovereignty in the vast area in which it will exercise its jurisdiction: 200 nautical miles from the coast of the mainland and around the recovered Malvinas, South Georgias and South Sandwich islands. Once the theatre is constituted, the military committee can at any time order the implementation of 'acts of self-defence' in face of situations that could endanger national security. Vice-Admiral Juan Jose Lombardo, Commander of Naval Operations, has been designated as Commander of the South Atlantic Theatre of Operations.

[III] Communication by the British Government to the
Government of Argentina, 23 April 1982
UN Doc. S/14997, 24 April 1982

In announcing the establishment of a maritime exclusion zone around the Falkland Islands, Her Majesty's Government made it clear that this measure was without prejudice to the right of the United Kingdom to take whatever additional measures may be needed in the exercise of its right of self-defence under Article 51 of the United Nations Charter. In this connection, Her Majesty's Government now wishes to make clear that any approach on the part of Argentine warships, including submarines, naval auxiliaries, or military aircraft which could amount to a threat to interfere with the mission of the British forces in the South Atlantic, will encounter the appropriate response. All Argentine aircraft including civil aircraft engaging in surveillance of these British forces will be regarded as hostile and are liable to be dealt with accordingly.

[IV] Announcement by the British Government, 28 April 1982
UN Doc. S/15006, 28 April 1982

From 1100 Greenwich mean time on 30 April 1982, a total exclusion zone will be established around Falklands Islands. The outer limit of the zone is the same as for the maritime exclusion zone established on Monday 12 April 1982, namely a circle of 200 nautical miles radius from latitude 51° 40′ south, 59° 30′ west. From the time indicated, the exclusion zone will apply not only to Argentine warships and Argentine naval auxiliaries but also to any other ship, whether naval or merchant vessel, which is operating in support of the illegal occupation of the Falkland Islands by Argentine forces. The exclusion zone will also apply to any aircraft, whether military or civil, which is operating in support of the illegal occupation. Any ship and any aircraft, whether military or civil, whether military or civil, which is found within this zone without due authority from the Ministry of Defence in London will be regarded as operating in support of the illegal occupation and will therefore be regarded as hostile and will be liable to be attacked by the British forces.

Also from the time indicated, Port Stanley Airport will be closed; and any aircraft on the ground in the Falkland Islands will be regarded as present in support of the illegal occupation and, accordingly, is liable to attack.

These measures are without prejudice to the right of the United Kingdom to take whatever additional measures may be needed in exercise of its right of self-defence, under Article 51 of the United Nations Charter.

[V] Communication by the British Government to the Government of Argentina
Delivered Through the Swiss Embassy on 29 April 1982
UN Doc. S/15016, 30 April 1982

In announcing the establishment of a total exclusion zone around the Falklands, Her Majesty's Government made it clear that this measure was without prejudice to the right of the United Kingdom to take whatever additional measures may be needed in exercise of its right to self-defence under Article 51 of the Charter of the United Nations. In this connexion, her Majesty's Government now wishes to make clear that all Argentine vessels, including merchant vessels, apparently engaging in surveillance of, or intelligence-gathering activities against, British forces in the South Atlantic will be regarded as hostile and are liable to be dealt with accordingly.

[VI] Communique No. 37 of the Argentine Government of 29 April 1982
BBC, SWB, Part 5, V/7016/I, 1 May 1982

The Military Junta reports that, in view of the receipt of an urgent message from the British authorities through the Swiss Embassy which reads: [Text of British communication above], the Military Junta resolves:

1. From today, all English ships, including merchant ships and fishing ships, navigating in Argentine waters within an area of 200 miles off the continental coast and off the coast of the Malvinas, South Georgia and South Sandwich islands, will be considered hostile and will therefore be treated accordingly.

2. From today, any British military or civilian aircraft that flies within Argentine air space will be considered hostile and will be treated accordingly.

3. The above measures are taken without prejudice to any other additional measures that might be taken in exercise of the right of legitimate defence under Article 51 of the UN Charter.

VII. Press Statement by the British Government, 7 May 1982
UKMIL 1982, BYBIL 53 (1982), 549

Her Majesty's Government has consistently made clear that the United Kingdom has the right to take whatever additional measures may be needed in exercise of its inherent right of self-defence under Article 51 of the United Nations Charter. Her Majesty's Government will take all necessary measures in the South Atlantic in the self-defence of British ships and aircraft engaged in operations and in re-supplying and reinforcing British forces in the South Atlantic. Because of the proximity of Argentine bases and the distances that hostile forces can cover undetected, particularly at night and in bad weather, Her Majesty's Government warns that any Argentine warship or military aircraft which are found more than 12 nautical miles from the Argentine coast will be regarded as hostile and are liable to be dealt with accordingly.

[VIII] Communique Nos. 40 and 41 of the Argentine Government of 11 May 1982
BBC, SWB, Part 5, V/7024/i, 12 May 1982

The military junta communicates that, in view of Great Britain's persistence in its aggressive attitude, as reflected, among other actions, in the restrictions that country intends to impose on Argentine maritime traffic in the South Atlantic, it invokes the right of self-defence under Article 51 of the UN Charter, and it has determined that any ship under the British flag sailing through the abovementioned zone and headed towards the area of operations, and/or presumably constituting a threat to national security should be considered as hostile and therefore treated accordingly.

The military junta, in view of Great Britain's persistence in its aggressive attitude, as reflected, among other actions, in the limitations that country intends to impose on the traffic of Argentine aircraft through South Atlantic airspace, invokes the right of self-defence under Article 51 of the UN Charter and has determined that all British aircraft flying in the above-mentioned airspace heading towards the area of operations and/or presumably posing a threat to national security should be considered as hostile and treated accordingly.

Agreement Concerning Interim Arrangements Relating to Polymetallic Nodules on the Deep Sea Bed between France, the Federal Republic of Germany, the United Kingdom and the United States

Done at Washington, 2 September 1982; entry into force, 2 September 1982
1871 UNTS 276 [Registration Number 31958][1]

The Parties to this Agreement:

Having regard to investments made in exploration, research and other pioneer activities relating to the polymetallic nodules of the deep sea bed;

Noting the adoption by the Third United Nations Conference on the Law of the Sea of a Convention on the Law of the Sea and of a Resolution Governing Preparatory Investment in Pioneer Activities Relating to Polymetallic Nodules prior to the entry into force of the Convention on the Law of the Sea, and the provision of that Resolution concerning resolution of conflicts among pioneer operators;

Recalling the interim character of legislation with respect to deep sea bed operations enacted by certain Parties;

Desiring to make appropriate provisions for avoiding overlaps in the areas claimed for future pioneer activities in the deep sea bed and to ensure that, during the interim period, such activities are carried out in an orderly and peaceful manner;

Emphasizing that this Agreement is without prejudice to the decisions of the Parties with respect to the Convention on Law of the Sea adopted by the Third United Nations Conference on the Law of the Sea;

Desiring also to avoid any discrimination among Parties in the implementation of this Agreement;

Desiring further to insure that adequate areas containing polymetallic nodules remain available for operations by other States and entities in conformity with international law;

Have agreed as follows:

1. The object of the present Agreement is to facilitate the identification and resolution of conflicts which may arise from the filing and processing of applications for authorizations made by Pre-Enactment Explorers (PEEs) on or before March 12, 1982 under legislation in respect of deep sea bed operations enacted by any of the Parties.

2. In the case of a conflict between the areas claimed in such applications, the Parties shall afford the applicants adequate opportunity, and shall encourage them, to resolve such conflict in a timely manner by voluntary procedures.

3. The Parties with whom applications for authorizations have been made by PEEs on or before March 12, 1982 shall follow the procedures set out in Part I of the Schedule hereto in respect of such applications.

4. The Parties shall consult together:

    (a) with a view to coordinating and reviewing implementation of this Agreement;

    (b) before issuing any authorization under their respective laws relating to deep sea bed operations;

    (c) in regard to consideration of any arrangement to facilitate mutual recognitions of such authorizations, it being understood that any such arrangement shall not enter into force before January 1, 1983;

---

[1] Appendix I (Arbitration Procedure) and Appendix II (Principles for Resolution of Conflicts) omitted.

(d)   before entering into any other bilateral or any multilateral arrangement between themselves or any arrangement with other States, with respect to deep sea bed operations.

5.   In the event that any of the Parties with whom applications for authorizations have been made by PEEs on or before March 12, 1982 enter into an agreement for the mutual recognition of authorizations granted under their respective laws in respect of deep sea bed operations, the Parties concerned shall apply the procedures and impose the requirements set out in Part II of the Schedule hereto.

6.   To the extent permissible under national law, a Party shall maintain the confidentiality of the coordinates of application areas and other proprietary or confidential commercial information received in confidence from any other Party in pursuance of cooperation under this Agreement in accordance with the principles set out in Part III of the Schedule hereto.

7.   The Parties shall settle any dispute arising from the interpretation or application of this Agreement by appropriate means. The Parties to the dispute shall consider the possibility of recourse to binding arbitration and, if they agree, shall have recourse to it.

8.   The Schedule hereto is an integral part of this Agreement and Part IV thereof shall apply for the interpretation of this Agreement.

9.   The Parties shall not enter into any supplementary international agreement inconsistent with this Agreement.

10. This Agreement may be amended by written agreement of all the Parties.

11. This Agreement shall enter into force upon signature.

12. After entry into force of this Agreement, additional States may be invited to accede to this Agreement at nay time with the consent of all Parties.

13. Any Party may denounce this Agreement on 30 days' notice to the Government of the United States of America, and in no case shall the denunciation have effect before January 3, 1983.

DONE at Washington this second day of September, 1982, in the English, German and French languages, all texts being equally authentic, in a single copy which shall be deposited in the archives of the Government of the United States of America, which will transmit a duly certified copy to each of the other signatory Governments.

THE SCHEDULE
PART I
APPLICATION PROCEDURES FOR PRE-ENACTMENT EXPLORERS

1.   Each Party as provided in paragraph 3 of the Agreement shall forthwith inform the other Parties of entities which have filed applications with it.

2.   Any application filed on or before March 12, 1982 shall be deemed to be filed on that date.

3.   Each Party shall with all dispatch determine whether:
(a)   each application filed with it fulfils its domestic requirements;
(b)   the applicant is a PEE with respect to the area applied for (an applicant filing on behalf of a PEE shall itself be deemed a PEE for that application);
(c)   the area is bounded by a continuous boundary;
(d)   the area is reasonably compact.

4.   Each Party shall:
(a)   notify the other Parties of the results of the initial processing under paragraph 3 above;

(b)   with the other Parties establish the final list of applications to which this Agreement applies;

(c)   inform the other Parties whether the applicant has applied for the same area, or substantially the same area, to one or more other Parties;

(d)   if the applicant agrees, inform the other Parties of the coordinates of the area specified in any application filed with it;

(e)   endeavor to determine the exact locations of any conflicts.

5.   No Party shall issue any authorization before January 3, 1983.

6.   Where it is informed of the relevant coordinates, each Party shall notify each of its applicants who is involved in a conflict that a conflict exists. Such notification shall include coordinates identifying the areas in conflict and the identity of each applicant with whom conflict has arisen.

7.   Each Party shall ensure that domestic conflicts are resolved pursuant to its respective domestic requirements. Upon agreement of the applicants, domestic conflicts may be resolved in accordance with the international conflict resolution procedures specified in the Schedule. The Parties shall enter into consultations if it appears that the resolution of a domestic conflict might affect the international conflict resolution procedures, or *vice versa*.

8.   (1)   Each Party shall accept amendments to applications to which this Agreement applies only if they:

    (a)   pertain to areas with respect to which the applicant is a PEE (the area applied for in an amendment need not be adjacent to the area applied for in the original application); and

    (b)   are made in order to resolve an existing conflict with respect to that application.

(2)   Each Party shall process any amendment filed pursuant to this paragraph in accordance with the procedures described in the foregoing provisions of this Part except that paragraphs 2, 3(c), 3(d), and 4(c) shall not apply to amendments.

(3)   Amendments filed under paragraph 8 of the Schedule shall be eligible for mutual recognition in accordance with the terms of an agreement entered into by any of the Parties pursuant to paragraph 5 of the Agreement.

PART II
CONFLICT RESOLUTION FOR PRE-ENACTMENT EXPLORERS

9.   (1)   Where there is an international conflict, the Parties shall use their good offices to assist the applicants to resolve the conflict by voluntary procedures.

(2)   If, within six months from the entry into force of an agreement between the Parties referred to in paragraph 5 of the Agreement, notwithstanding the good offices of the Parties, all applicants involved in an international conflict have not resolved that conflict, or are not parties to a written agreement submitting the conflict to a specified binding conflict resolution procedure, the conflict shall be resolved by binding arbitration in accordance with Appendices 1 and 2 if a Party so elects.

(3)   The procedures provided in the Appendices shall commence 10 days after a Party notifies the other Party or Parties of the decision to elect arbitration.

PART III
PRINCIPLES OF CONFIDENTIALITY

10.   In implementing the provisions of paragraph 6 of the Agreement, Parties shall apply the following principles:

(a)   The confidentiality of the coordinates of application areas shall be maintained until any conflict involving such area is resolved and the relevant authorization is issued, except on the basis of a demonstrated need to know and adequate assurances that the confidentiality of the information shall be maintained by the recipient;

(b)   The confidentiality of other proprietary or confidential commercial information shall be maintained in accordance with domestic law as long as such information retains its character as such.

PART IV DEFINITIONS

11.   In this Agreement:

(a)   'activities' means the undertakings, commitments of resources, investigations, findings, research, engineering development, and other activities relevant to the identification, discovery, and systematic analysis and evaluation of polymetallic nodules and to the determination of the technical and economic feasibility of exploitation;

(b)   'authorization' means any license, permit, or other authorization issued under the national law of a Party which authorizes the holder to engage in deep sea bed operations in a specified area or areas;

(c)   'conflict' means the existence of more than one application or amendment covered by this Agreement submitted by different applicants:

(1)   whether filed with the same Party or with more than one Party; and

(2)   in which the deep sea bed areas applied for overlap in whole or part, to the extent of the overlap;

'international conflict' means a conflict arising from applications or amendments filed with more than one Party;

'domestic conflict' means any other conflict;

(d)   a 'pre-enactment explorer' ('PEE') is an entity which was engaged, prior to the earliest date of enactment of domestic legislation by any Party, in deep sea bed polymetallic nodule exploration by substantial surveying activity with respect to the area applied for; and

(e)   'polymetallic nodules' means any deposit or accretion on or just below the surface of the deep sea bed consisting of nodules which contain manganese, nickel, cobalt, or copper.

United Nations Convention on the Law of the Sea

Done at Montego Bay, 10 December 1982; entry into force, 16 November 1994
1834 UNTS 397 [Registration Number 31363]

The States Parties to this Convention,

Prompted by the desire to settle, in a spirit of mutual understanding and co-operation, all issues relating to the law of the sea and aware of the historic significance of this Convention as an important contribution to the maintenance of peace, justice and progress for all peoples of the world,

Noting that developments since the United Nations Conferences on the Law of the Sea held at Geneva in 1958 and 1960 have accentuated the need for a new and generally acceptable Convention on the law of the sea,

Conscious that the problems of ocean space are closely interrelated and need to be considered as a whole,

Recognizing the desirability of establishing through this Convention, with due regard for the sovereignty of all States, a legal order for the seas and oceans which will facilitate international communication, and will promote the peaceful uses of the seas and oceans, the equitable and efficient utilization of their resources, the conservation of their living resources, and the study, protection and preservation of the marine environment,

Bearing in mind that the achievement of these goals will contribute to the realization of a just and equitable international economic order which takes into account the interests and needs of mankind as a whole and, in particular, the special interests and needs of developing countries, whether coastal or land-locked,

Desiring by this Convention to develop the principles embodied in resolution 2749 (XXV) of 17 December 1970 in which the General Assembly of the United Nations solemnly declared *inter alia* that the area of the sea-bed and ocean floor and the subsoil thereof, beyond the limits of national jurisdiction, as well as its resources, are the common heritage of mankind, the exploration and exploitation of which shall be carried out for the benefit of mankind as a whole, irrespective of the geographic allocation of States,

Believing that the codification and progressive development of the law of the sea achieved in this Convention will contribute to the strengthening of peace, security, co-operation and friendly relations among all nations in conformity with the principles of justice and equal rights and will promote the economic and social advancement of all peoples of the world, in accordance with the Purposes and Principles of the United Nations as set forth in the Charter,

Affirming that matters not regulated by this Convention continue to be governed by the rules and principles of general international law,

Have agreed as follows:

PART I
INTRODUCTION

Article 1 Use of terms and scope

1. For the purposes of this Convention:
    (1) 'Area' means the sea-bed and ocean floor and subsoil thereof, beyond the limits of national jurisdiction;
    (2) 'Authority' means the International Seabed Authority;

(3)   'activities in the Area' means all activities of exploration for, and exploitation of, the resources of the Area;

(4)   'pollution of the marine environment' means the introduction by man, directly or indirectly, of substances or energy into the marine environment, including estuaries, which results or is likely to result in such deleterious effects as harm to living resources and marine life, hazards to human health, hindrance to marine activities, including fishing and other legitimate uses of the sea, impairment of quality for use of sea water and reduction of amenities;

(5)   (a)   'dumping' means:

      (i)   any deliberate disposal of wastes or other matter from vessels, aircraft, platforms or other man-made structures at sea;

      (ii)   any deliberate disposal of vessels, aircraft, platforms or other man-made structures at sea;

    (b)   'dumping' does not include:

      (i)   the disposal of wastes or other matter incidental to, or derived from the normal operations of vessels, aircraft, platforms or other man-made structures at sea and their equipment, other than wastes or other matter transported by or to vessels, aircraft, platforms or other man-made structures at sea, operating for the purpose of disposal of such matter or derived from the treatment of such wastes or other matter on such vessels, aircraft, platforms or structures;

      (ii)   placement of matter for a purpose other than the mere disposal thereof, provided that such placement is not contrary to the aims of this Convention.

2.   (1)   'States Parties' means States which have consented to be bound by this Convention and for which this Convention is in force.

    (2)   This Convention applies *mutatis mutandis* to the entities referred to in article 305, paragraph l(b), (c), (d), (e) and (f), which become Parties to this Convention in accordance with the conditions relevant to each, and to that extent 'States Parties' refers to those entities.

PART II

TERRITORIAL SEA AND CONTIGUOUS ZONE

SECTION 1. GENERAL PROVISIONS

Article 2 Legal status of the territorial sea, of the air space over the territorial sea and of its bed and subsoil

1. The sovereignty of a coastal State extends, beyond its land territory and internal waters and, in the case of an archipelagic State, its archipelagic waters, to an adjacent belt of sea, described as the territorial sea.

2. This sovereignty extends to the air space over the territorial sea as well as to its bed and subsoil.

3. The sovereignty over the territorial sea is exercised subject to this Convention and to other rules of international law.

SECTION 2. LIMITS OF THE TERRITORIAL SEA

Article 4 Outer limit of the territorial sea

The outer limit of the territorial sea is the line every point of which is at a distance from the nearest point of the baseline equal to the breadth of the territorial sea.

Article 5 Normal baseline

Except where otherwise provided in this Convention, the normal baseline for measuring the breadth of the territorial sea is the low-water line along the coast as marked on large-scale charts officially recognized by the coastal State.

Article 6 Reefs

In the case of islands situated on atolls or of islands having fringing reefs, the baseline for measuring the breadth of the territorial sea is the seaward low-water line of the reef, as shown by the appropriate symbol on charts officially recognized by the coastal State.

Article 7 Straight baselines

1. In localities where the coastline is deeply indented and cut into, or if there is a fringe of islands along the coast in its immediate vicinity, the method of straight baselines joining appropriate points may be employed in drawing the baseline from which the breadth of the territorial sea is measured.

2. Where because of the presence of a delta and other natural conditions the coastline is highly unstable, the appropriate points may be selected along the furthest seaward extent of the low-water line and, notwithstanding subsequent regression of the low-water line, the straight baselines shall remain effective until changed by the coastal State in accordance with this Convention.

3. The drawing of straight baselines must not depart to any appreciable extent from the general direction of the coast, and the sea areas lying within the lines must be sufficiently closely linked to the land domain to be subject to the regime of internal waters.

4. Straight baselines shall not be drawn to and from low-tide elevations, unless lighthouses or similar installations which are permanently above sea level have been built on them or except in instances where the drawing of baselines to and from such elevations has received general international recognition.

5. Where the method of straight baselines is applicable under paragraph 1, account may be taken, in determining particular baselines, of economic interests peculiar to the region concerned, the reality and the importance of which are clearly evidenced by long usage.

6. The system of straight baselines may not be applied by a State in such a manner as to cut off the territorial sea of another State from the high seas or an exclusive economic zone.

Article 8 Internal waters

1. Except as provided in Part IV, waters on the landward side of the baseline of the territorial sea form part of the internal waters of the State.

2. Where the establishment of a straight baseline in accordance with the method set forth in article 7 has the effect of enclosing as internal waters areas which had not previously been considered as such, a right of innocent passage as provided in this Convention shall exist in those waters.

Article 9 Mouths of rivers

If a river flows directly into the sea, the baseline shall be a straight line across the mouth of the river between points on the low-water line of its banks.

Article 10 Bays

1. This article relates only to bays the coasts of which belong to a single State.

2. For the purposes of this Convention, a bay is a well-marked indentation whose penetration is in such proportion to the width of its mouth as to contain land-locked waters and constitute more than a mere curvature of the coast. An indentation shall not, however, be regarded as a bay unless its area is as large as, or larger than, that of the semi-circle whose diameter is a line drawn across the mouth of that indentation.

3. For the purpose of measurement, the area of an indentation is that lying between the low-water mark around the shore of the indentation and a line joining the low-water mark of its natural entrance points. Where, because of the presence of islands, an indentation has more than one mouth, the semi-circle shall be drawn on a line as long as the sum total of the lengths of the lines across the different mouths. Islands within an indentation shall be included as if they were part of the water area of the indentation.

4. If the distance between the low-water marks of the natural entrance points of a bay does not exceed 24 nautical miles, a closing line may be drawn between these two low-water marks, and the waters enclosed thereby shall be considered as internal waters.

5. Where the distance between the low-water marks of the natural entrance points of a bay exceeds 24 nautical miles, a straight baseline of 24 nautical miles shall be drawn within the bay in such a manner as to enclose the maximum area of water that is possible with a line of that length.

6. The foregoing provisions do not apply to so-called 'historic' bays, or in any case where the system of straight baselines provided for in article 7 is applied.

Article 11 Ports

For the purpose of delimiting the territorial sea, the outermost permanent harbour works which form an integral part of the harbour system are regarded as forming part of the coast. Off-shore installations and artificial islands shall not be considered as permanent harbour works.

Article 12 Roadsteads

Roadsteads which are normally used for the loading, unloading and anchoring of ships, and which would otherwise be situated wholly or partly outside the outer limit of the territorial sea, are included in the territorial sea.

Article 13 Low-tide elevations

1. A low-tide elevation is a naturally formed area of land which is surrounded by and above water at low tide but submerged at high tide. Where a low-tide elevation is situated wholly or partly at a distance not exceeding the breadth of the territorial sea from the mainland or an island, the low-water line on that elevation may be used as the baseline for measuring the breadth of the territorial sea.

2. Where a low-tide elevation is wholly situated at a distance exceeding the breadth of the territorial sea from the mainland or an island, it has no territorial sea of its own.

Article 14 Combination of methods for determining baselines

The coastal State may determine baselines in turn by any of the methods provided for in the foregoing articles to suit different conditions.

Article 15 Delimitation of the territorial sea between States with opposite or adjacent coasts

Where the coasts of two States are opposite or adjacent to each other, neither of the two States is entitled, failing agreement between them to the contrary, to extend its territorial sea beyond the median line every point of which is equidistant from the nearest points on the baselines from which the breadth of the territorial seas of each of the two States is measured. The above provision does not apply, however, where it is necessary by reason of historic title or other special circumstances to delimit the territorial seas of the two States in a way which is at variance therewith.

Article 16 Charts and lists of geographical coordinates

1. The baselines for measuring the breadth of the territorial sea determined in accordance with articles 7, 9 and 10, or the limits derived therefrom, and the lines of delimitation drawn in accordance with articles 12 and 15 shall be shown on charts of a scale or scales adequate for ascertaining their position. Alternatively, a list of geographical coordinates of points, specifying the geodetic datum, may be substituted.

2. The coastal State shall give due publicity to such charts or lists of geographical coordinates and shall deposit a copy of each such chart or list with the Secretary-General of the United Nations.

Section 3. Innocent Passage in the Territorial Sea

Subsection A. Rules Applicable to All Ships

Article 17 Right of innocent passage

Subject to this Convention, ships of all States, whether coastal or land-locked, enjoy the right of innocent passage through the territorial sea.

Article 18 Meaning of passage

1. Passage means navigation through the territorial sea for the purpose of:
   (a) traversing that sea without entering internal waters or calling at a roadstead or port facility outside internal waters; or
   (b) proceeding to or from internal waters or a call at such roadstead or port facility.

2. Passage shall be continuous and expeditious. However, passage includes stopping and anchoring, but only in so far as the same are incidental to ordinary navigation or are rendered necessary by force majeure or distress or for the purpose of rendering assistance to persons, ships or aircraft in danger or distress.

Article 19 Meaning of innocent passage

1. Passage is innocent so long as it is not prejudicial to the peace, good order or security of the coastal State. Such passage shall take place in conformity with this Convention and with other rules of international law.

2. Passage of a foreign ship shall be considered to be prejudicial to the peace, good order or security of the coastal State if in the territorial sea it engages in any of the following activities:
   (a) any threat or use of force against the sovereignty, territorial integrity or political independence of the coastal State, or in any other manner in violation of the principles of international law embodied in the Charter of the United Nations;
   (b) any exercise or practice with weapons of any kind;

   (c)   any act aimed at collecting information to the prejudice of the defence or security of the coastal State;

   (d)   any act of propaganda aimed at affecting the defence or security of the coastal State;

   (e)   the launching, landing or taking on board of any aircraft;

   (f)   the launching, landing or taking on board of any military device;

   (g)   the loading or unloading of any commodity, currency or person contrary to the customs, fiscal, immigration or sanitary laws and regulations of the coastal State;

   (h)   any act of wilful and serious pollution contrary to this Convention;

   (i)   any fishing activities;

   (j)   the carrying out of research or survey activities;

   (k)   any act aimed at interfering with any systems of communication or any other facilities or installations of the coastal State;

   (l)   any other activity not having a direct bearing on passage.

Article 20 Submarines and other underwater vehicles

In the territorial sea, submarines and other underwater vehicles are required to navigate on the surface and to show their flag.

Article 21 Laws and regulations of the coastal State relating to innocent passage

1. The coastal State may adopt laws and regulations, in conformity with the provisions of this Convention and other rules of international law, relating to innocent passage through the territorial sea, in respect of all or any of the following:

   (a)   the safety of navigation and the regulation of maritime traffic;

   (b)   the protection of navigational aids and facilities and other facilities or installations;

   (c)   the protection of cables and pipelines;

   (d)   the conservation of the living resources of the sea;

   (e)   the prevention of infringement of the fisheries laws and regulations of the coastal State;

   (f)   the preservation of the environment of the coastal State and the prevention, reduction and control of pollution thereof;

   (g)   marine scientific research and hydrographic surveys;

   (h)   the prevention of infringement of the customs, fiscal, immigration or sanitary laws and regulations of the coastal State.

2. Such laws and regulations shall not apply to the design, construction, manning or equipment of foreign ships unless they are giving effect to generally accepted international rules or standards.

3. The coastal State shall give due publicity to all such laws and regulations.

4. Foreign ships exercising the right of innocent passage through the territorial sea shall comply with all such laws and regulations and all generally accepted international regulations relating to the prevention of collisions at sea.

Article 22 Sea lanes and traffic separation schemes in the territorial sea

1. The coastal State may, where necessary having regard to the safety of navigation, require foreign ships exercising the right of innocent passage through its territorial sea to use such sea lanes and traffic separation schemes as it may designate or prescribe for the regulation of the passage of ships.

2. In particular, tankers, nuclear-powered ships and ships carrying nuclear or other inherently dangerous or noxious substances or materials may be required to confine their passage to such sea lanes.

3. In the designation of sea lanes and the prescription of traffic separation schemes under this article, the coastal State shall take into account:

(a)　the recommendations of the competent international organization;

(b)　any channels customarily used for international navigation;

(c)　the special characteristics of particular ships and channels; and

(d)　the density of traffic.

4. The coastal State shall clearly indicate such sea lanes and traffic separation schemes on charts to which due publicity shall be given.

Article 23　Foreign nuclear-powered ships and ships carrying nuclear or other inherently dangerous or noxious substances

Foreign nuclear-powered ships and ships carrying nuclear or other inherently dangerous or noxious substances shall, when exercising the right of innocent passage through the territorial sea, carry documents and observe special precautionary measures established for such ships by international agreements.

Article 24　Duties of the coastal State

1. The coastal State shall not hamper the innocent passage of foreign ships through the territorial sea except in accordance with this Convention. In particular, in the application of this Convention or of any laws or regulations adopted in conformity with this Convention, the coastal State shall not:

(a)　impose requirements on foreign ships which have the practical effect of denying or impairing the right of innocent passage; or

(b)　discriminate in form or in fact against the ships of any State or against ships carrying cargoes to, from or on behalf of any State.

2. The coastal State shall give appropriate publicity to any danger to navigation, of which it has knowledge, within its territorial sea.

Article 25　Rights of protection of the coastal State

1. The coastal State may take the necessary steps in its territorial sea to prevent passage which is not innocent.

2. In the case of ships proceeding to internal waters or a call at a port facility outside internal waters, the coastal State also has the right to take the necessary steps to prevent any breach of the conditions to which admission of those ships to internal waters or such a call is subject.

3. The coastal State may, without discrimination in form or in fact among foreign ships, suspend temporarily in specified areas of its territorial sea the innocent passage of foreign ships if such suspension is essential for the protection of its security, including weapons exercises. Such suspension shall take effect only after having been duly published.

Article 26　Charges which may be levied upon foreign ships

1. No charge may be levied upon foreign ships by reason only of their passage through the territorial sea.

2. Charges may be levied upon a foreign ship passing through the territorial sea as payment only for specific services rendered to the ship. These charges shall be levied without discrimination.

Subsection B. Rules Applicable to Merchant Ships and Government Ships
Operated for Commercial Purposes

Article 27 Criminal jurisdiction on board a foreign ship

1. The criminal jurisdiction of the coastal State should not be exercised on board a foreign ship passing through the territorial sea to arrest any person or to conduct any investigation in connection with any crime committed on board the ship during its passage, save only in the following cases:

(a)   if the consequences of the crime extend to the coastal State;

(b)   if the crime is of a kind to disturb the peace of the country or the good order of the territorial sea;

(c)   if the assistance of the local authorities has been requested by the master of the ship or by a diplomatic agent or consular officer of the flag State; or

(d)   if such measures are necessary for the suppression of illicit traffic in narcotic drugs or psychotropic substances.

2. The above provisions do not affect the right of the coastal State to take any steps authorized by its laws for the purpose of an arrest or investigation on board a foreign ship passing through the territorial sea after leaving internal waters.

3. In the cases provided for in paragraphs 1 and 2, the coastal State shall, if the master so requests, notify a diplomatic agent or consular officer of the flag State before taking any steps, and shall facilitate contact between such agent or officer and the ship's crew. In cases of emergency this notification may be communicated while the measures are being taken.

4. In considering whether or in what manner an arrest should be made, the local authorities shall have due regard to the interests of navigation.

5. Except as provided in Part XII or with respect to violations of laws and regulations adopted in accordance with Part V, the coastal State may not take any steps on board a foreign ship passing through the territorial sea to arrest any person or to conduct any investigation in connection with any crime committed before the ship entered the territorial sea, if the ship, proceeding from a foreign port, is only passing through the territorial sea without entering internal waters.

Article 28 Civil jurisdiction in relation to foreign ships

1. The coastal State should not stop or divert a foreign ship passing through the territorial sea for the purpose of exercising civil jurisdiction in relation to a person on board the ship.

2. The coastal State may not levy execution against or arrest the ship for the purpose of any civil proceedings, save only in respect of obligations or liabilities assumed or incurred by the ship itself in the course or for the purpose of its voyage through the waters of the coastal State.

3. Paragraph 2 is without prejudice to the right of the coastal State, in accordance with its laws, to levy execution against or to arrest, for the purpose of any civil proceedings, a foreign ship lying in the territorial sea, or passing through the territorial sea after leaving internal waters.

Subsection C. Rules Applicable to Warships and Other Government Ships
Operated for Non-Commercial Purposes

Article 29 Definition of warships

For the purposes of this Convention, 'warship' means a ship belonging to the armed forces of a State bearing the external marks distinguishing such ships of its nationality, under the command of an officer duly commissioned by the government of the State and whose name appears in the appropriate service list or its equivalent, and manned by a crew which is under regular armed forces discipline.

Article 30 Non-compliance by warships with the laws and regulations of the coastal State

If any warship does not comply with the laws and regulations of the coastal State concerning passage through the territorial sea and disregards any request for compliance therewith which is made to it, the coastal State may require it to leave the territorial sea immediately.

Article 31 Responsibility of the flag State for damage caused by a warship or other government ship operated for non-commercial purposes

The flag State shall bear international responsibility for any loss or damage to the coastal State resulting from the non-compliance by a warship or other government ship operated for non-commercial purposes with the laws and regulations of the coastal State concerning passage through the territorial sea or with the provisions of this Convention or other rules of international law.

Article 32 Immunities of warships and other government ships operated for non-commercial purposes

With such exceptions as are contained in subsection A and in articles 30 and 31, nothing in this Convention affects the immunities of warships and other government ships operated for non-commercial purposes.

SECTION 4. CONTINUOUS ZONE

Article 33 Contiguous zone

1. In a zone contiguous to its territorial sea, described as the contiguous zone, the coastal State may exercise the control necessary to:
    (a)   prevent infringement of its customs, fiscal, immigration or sanitary laws and regulations within its territory or territorial sea;
    (b)   punish infringement of the above laws and regulations committed within its territory or territorial sea.
2. The contiguous zone may riot extend beyond 24 nautical miles from the baselines from which the breadth of the territorial sea is measured.

PART III
STRAITS USED FOR INTERNATIONAL NAVIGATION

SECTION 1. GENERAL PROVISIONS

Article 34 Legal status of waters forming straits used for international navigation

1. The regime of passage through straits used for international navigation established in this Part shall not in other respects affect the legal status of the waters forming such straits or the exercise by the States bordering the straits of their sovereignty or jurisdiction over such waters and their air space, bed and subsoil.
2. The sovereignty or jurisdiction of the States bordering the straits is exercised subject to this Part and to other rules of international law.

Article 35 Scope of this Part

Nothing in this Part affects:

(a) any areas of internal waters within a strait, except where the establishment of a straight baseline in accordance with the method set forth in article 7 has the effect of enclosing as internal waters areas which had not previously been considered as such;

(b) the legal status of the waters beyond the territorial seas of States bordering straits as exclusive economic zones or high seas; or

(c) the legal regime in straits in which passage is regulated in whole or in part by long-standing international conventions in force specifically relating to such straits.

Article 36 High seas routes or routes through exclusive economic zones through straits used for international navigation

This Part does not apply to a strait used for international navigation if there exists through the strait a route through the high seas or through an exclusive economic zone of similar convenience with respect to navigational and hydrographical characteristics; in such routes, the other relevant Parts of this Convention, including the provisions regarding the freedoms of navigation and overflight, apply.

SECTION 2. TRANSIT PASSAGE

Article 37 Scope of this section

This section applies to straits which are used for international navigation between one part of the high seas or an exclusive economic zone and another part of the high seas or an exclusive economic zone.

Article 38 Right of transit passage

1. In straits referred to in article 37, all ships and aircraft enjoy the right of transit passage, which shall not be impeded; except that, if the strait is formed by an island of a State bordering the strait and its mainland, transit passage shall not apply if there exists seaward of the island a route through the high seas or through an exclusive economic zone of similar convenience with respect to navigational and hydrographical characteristics.

2. Transit passage means the exercise in accordance with this Part of the freedom of navigation and overflight solely for the purpose of continuous and expeditious transit of the strait between one part of the high seas or an exclusive economic zone and another part of the high seas or an exclusive economic zone. However, the requirement of continuous and expeditious transit does not preclude passage through the strait for the purpose of entering, leaving or returning from a State bordering the strait, subject to the conditions of entry to that State.

3. Any activity which is not an exercise of the right of transit passage through a strait remains subject to the other applicable provisions of this Convention.

Article 39 Duties of ships and aircraft during transit passage

1. Ships and aircraft, while exercising the right of transit passage, shall:

(a) proceed without delay through or over the strait;

(b) refrain from any threat or use of force against the sovereignty, territorial integrity or political independence of States bordering the strait, or in any other manner in violation of the principles of international law embodied in the Charter of the United Nations;

(c)   refrain from any activities other than those incident to their normal modes of continuous and expeditious transit unless rendered necessary by *force majeure* or by distress;

(d)   comply with other relevant provisions of this Part.

2.   Ships in transit passage shall:

(a)   comply with generally accepted international regulations, procedures and practices for safety at sea, including the International Regulations for Preventing Collisions at Sea;

(b)   comply with generally accepted international regulations, procedures and practices for the prevention, reduction and control of pollution from ships.

3.   Aircraft in transit passage shall:

(a)   observe the Rules of the Air established by the International Civil Aviation Organization as they apply to civil aircraft; state aircraft will normally comply with such safety measures and will at all times operate with due regard for the safety of navigation;

(b)   at all times monitor the radio frequency assigned by the competent internationally designated air traffic control authority or the appropriate international distress radio frequency.

Article 40 Research and survey activities

During transit passage, foreign ships, including marine scientific research and hydrographic survey ships, may not carry out any research or survey activities without the prior authorization of the States bordering straits.

Article 41 Sea lanes and traffic separation schemes in straits used for international navigation

1.   In conformity with this Part, States bordering straits may designate sea lanes and prescribe traffic separation schemes for navigation in straits where necessary to promote the safe passage of ships.

2.   Such States may, when circumstances require, and after giving due publicity thereto, substitute other sea lanes or traffic separation schemes for any sea lanes or traffic separation schemes previously designated or prescribed by them.

3.   Such sea lanes and traffic separation schemes shall conform to generally accepted international regulations.

4.   Before designating or substituting sea lanes or prescribing or substituting traffic separation schemes, States bordering straits shall refer proposals to the competent international organization with a view to their adoption. The organization may adopt only such sea lanes and traffic separation schemes as may be agreed with the States bordering the straits, after which the States may designate, prescribe or substitute them.

5.   In respect of a strait where sea lanes or traffic separation schemes through the waters of two or more States bordering the strait are being proposed, the States concerned shall cooperate in formulating proposals in consultation with the competent international organization.

6.   States bordering straits shall clearly indicate all sea lanes and traffic separation schemes designated or prescribed by them on charts to which due publicity shall be given.

7.   Ships in transit passage shall respect applicable sea lanes and traffic separation schemes established in accordance with this article.

Article 42   Laws and regulations of States bordering straits relating to transit passage

1.   Subject to the provisions of this section, States bordering straits may adopt laws and regulations relating to transit passage through straits, in respect of all or any of the following:

(a)   the safety of navigation and the regulation of maritime traffic, as provided in article 41;

(b)   the prevention, reduction and control of pollution, by giving effect to applicable international regulations regarding the discharge of oil, oily wastes and other noxious substances in the strait;

(c)   with respect to fishing vessels, the prevention of fishing, including the stowage of fishing gear;

(d)   the loading or unloading of any commodity, currency or person in contravention of the customs, fiscal, immigration or sanitary laws and regulations of States bordering straits.

2.   Such laws and regulations shall not discriminate in form or in fact among foreign ships or in their application have the practical effect of denying, hampering or impairing the right of transit passage as defined in this section.

3.   States bordering straits shall give due publicity to all such laws and regulations.

4.   Foreign ships exercising the right of transit passage shall comply with such laws and regulations.

5.   The flag State of a ship or the State of registry of an aircraft entitled to sovereign immunity which acts in a manner contrary to such laws and regulations or other provisions of this Part shall bear international responsibility for any loss or damage which results to States bordering straits.

Article 43   Navigational and safety aids and other improvements and the prevention, reduction and control of pollution

User States and States bordering a strait should by agreement cooperate:

(a)   in the establishment and maintenance in a strait of necessary navigational and safety aids or other improvements in aid of international navigation; and

(b)   for the prevention, reduction and control of pollution from ships.

Article 44   Duties of States bordering straits

States bordering straits shall not hamper transit passage and shall give appropriate publicity to any danger to navigation or overflight within or over the strait of which they have knowledge. There shall be no suspension of transit passage.

SECTION 3.   INNOCENT PASSAGE

Article 45   Innocent passage

1.   The regime of innocent passage, in accordance with Part II, section 3 shall apply in straits used for international navigation:

(a)   excluded from the application of the regime of transit passage under article 38, paragraph 1; or

(b)   between a part of the high seas or an exclusive economic zone and the territorial sea of a foreign State.

2.   There shall be no suspension of innocent passage through such straits.

PART IV
ARCHIPELAGIC STATES

Article 46 Use of terms
For the purposes of this Convention:
(a) 'archipelagic State' means a State constituted wholly by one or more archipelagos and may include other islands;
(b) 'archipelago' means a group of islands, including parts of islands, interconnecting waters and other natural features which are so closely interrelated that such islands, waters and other natural features form an intrinsic geographical, economic and political entity, or which historically have been regarded as such.

Article 47 Archipelagic baselines
1. An archipelagic State may draw straight archipelagic baselines joining the outermost points of the outermost islands and drying reefs of the archipelago provided that within such baselines are included the main islands and an area in which the ratio of the area of the water to the area of the land, including atolls, is between 1 to 1 and 9 to 1.

2. The length of such baselines shall not exceed 100 nautical miles, except that up to 3 per cent of the total number of baselines enclosing any archipelago may exceed that length, up to a maximum length of 125 nautical miles.

3. The drawing of such baselines shall not depart to any appreciable extent from the general configuration of the archipelago.

4. Such baselines shall not be drawn to and from low-tide elevations, unless lighthouses or similar installations which are permanently above sea level have been built on them or where a low-tide elevation is situated wholly or partly at a distance not exceeding the breadth of the territorial sea from the nearest island.

5. The system of such baselines shall not be applied by an archipelagic State in such a manner as to cut off from the high seas or the exclusive economic zone the territorial sea of another State.

6. If a part of the archipelagic waters of an archipelagic State lies between two parts of an immediately adjacent neighbouring State, existing rights and all other legitimate interests which the latter State has traditionally exercised in such waters and all rights stipulated by agreement between those States shall continue and be respected.

7. For the purpose of computing the ratio of water to land under paragraph 1, land areas may include waters lying within the fringing reefs of islands and atolls, including that part of a steep-sided oceanic plateau which is enclosed or nearly enclosed by a chain of limestone islands and drying reefs lying on the perimeter of the plateau.

8. The baselines drawn in accordance with this article shall be shown on charts of a scale or scales adequate for ascertaining their position. Alternatively, lists of geographical coordinates of points, specifying the geodetic datum, may be substituted.

9. The archipelagic State shall give due publicity to such charts or lists of geographical coordinates and shall deposit a copy of each such chart or list with the Secretary-General of the United Nations.

Article 48 Measurement of the breadth of the territorial sea, the contiguous zone, the exclusive economic zone and the continental shelf
The breadth of the territorial sea, the contiguous zone, the exclusive economic zone and the continental shelf shall be measured from archipelagic baselines drawn in accordance with article 47.

Article 49 Legal status of archipelagic waters, of the air space over archipelagic waters and of their bed and subsoil

1.   The sovereignty of an archipelagic State extends to the waters enclosed by the archipelagic baselines drawn in accordance with article 47, described as archipelagic waters, regardless of their depth or distance from the coast.

2.   This sovereignty extends to the air space over the archipelagic waters, as well as to their bed and subsoil, and the resources contained therein.

3.   This sovereignty is exercised subject to this Part.

4.   The regime of archipelagic sea lanes passage established in this Part shall not in other respects affect the status of the archipelagic waters, including the sea lanes, or the exercise by the archipelagic State of its sovereignty over such waters and their air space, bed and subsoil, and the resources contained therein.

Article 50 Delimitation of internal waters

Within its archipelagic waters, the archipelagic State may draw closing lines for the delimitation of internal waters, in accordance with articles 9, 10 and 11.

Article 51 Existing agreements, traditional fishing rights and existing submarine cables

1.   Without prejudice to article 49, an archipelagic State shall respect existing agreements with other States and shall recognize traditional fishing rights and other legitimate activities of the immediately adjacent neighbouring States in certain areas falling within archipelagic waters. The terms and conditions for the exercise of such rights and activities, including the nature, the extent and the areas to which they apply, shall, at the request of any of the States concerned, be regulated by bilateral agreements between them. Such rights shall not be transferred to or shared with third States or their nationals.

2.   An archipelagic State shall respect existing submarine cables laid by other States and passing through its waters without making a landfall. An archipelagic State shall permit the maintenance and replacement of such cables upon receiving due notice of their location and the intention to repair or replace them.

Article 52 Right of innocent passage

1.   Subject to article 53 and without prejudice to article 50, ships of all States enjoy the right of innocent passage through archipelagic waters, in accordance with Part II, section 3.

2.   The archipelagic State may, without discrimination in form or in fact among foreign ships, suspend temporarily in specified areas of its archipelagic waters the innocent passage of foreign ships if such suspension is essential for the protection of its security. Such suspension shall take effect only after having been duly published.

Article 53 Right of archipelagic sea lanes passage

1.   An archipelagic State may designate sea lanes and air routes thereabove, suitable for the continuous and expeditious passage of foreign ships and aircraft through or over its archipelagic waters and the adjacent territorial sea.

2.   All ships and aircraft enjoy the right of archipelagic sea lanes passage in such sea lanes and air routes.

3.   Archipelagic sea lanes passage means the exercise in accordance with this Convention of the rights of navigation and overflight in the normal mode solely for the purpose of continuous, expeditious and unobstructed transit between one part of the high seas or an exclusive economic zone and another part of the high seas or an exclusive economic zone.

4. Such sea lanes and air routes shall traverse the archipelagic waters and the adjacent territorial sea and shall include all normal passage routes used as routes for international navigation or overflight through or over archipelagic waters and, within such routes, so far as ships are concerned, all normal navigational channels, provided that duplication of routes of similar convenience between the same entry and exit points shall not be necessary.

5. Such sea lanes and air routes shall be defined by a series of continuous axis lines from the entry points of passage routes to the exit points. Ships and aircraft in archipelagic sea lanes passage shall not deviate more than 25 nautical miles to either side of such axis lines during passage, provided that such ships and aircraft shall not navigate closer to the coasts than 10 per cent of the distance between the nearest points on islands bordering the sea lane.

6. An archipelagic State which designates sea lanes under this article may also prescribe traffic separation schemes for the safe passage of ships through narrow channels in such sea lanes.

7. An archipelagic State may, when circumstances require, after giving due publicity thereto, substitute other sea lanes or traffic separation schemes for any sea lanes or traffic separation schemes previously designated or prescribed by it.

8. Such sea lanes and traffic separation schemes shall conform to generally accepted international regulations.

9. In designating or substituting sea lanes or prescribing or substituting traffic separation schemes, an archipelagic State shall refer proposals to the competent international organization with a view to their adoption. The organization may adopt only such sea lanes and traffic separation schemes as may be agreed with the archipelagic State, after which the archipelagic State may designate, prescribe or substitute them.

10. The archipelagic State shall clearly indicate the axis of the sea lanes and the traffic separation schemes designated or prescribed by it on charts to which due publicity shall be given.

11. Ships in archipelagic sea lanes passage shall respect applicable sea lanes and traffic separation schemes established in accordance with this article.

12. If an archipelagic State does not designate sea lanes or air routes, the right of archipelagic sea lanes passage may be exercised through the routes normally used for international navigation.

Article 54 Duties of ships and aircraft during their passage, research and survey activities, duties of the archipelagic State and laws and regulations of the archipelagic State relating to archipelagic sea lanes passage

Articles 39, 40, 42 and 44 apply *mutatis mutandis* to archipelagic sea lanes passage.

PART V

EXCLUSIVE ECONOMIC ZONE

Article 55 Specific legal regime of the exclusive economic zone

The exclusive economic zone is an area beyond and adjacent to the territorial sea, subject to the specific legal regime established in this Part, under which the rights and jurisdiction of the coastal State and the rights and freedoms of other States are governed by the relevant provisions of this Convention.

Article 56 Rights, jurisdiction and duties of the coastal State in the exclusive economic zone

1. In the exclusive economic zone, the coastal State has:
   (a) sovereign rights for the purpose of exploring and exploiting, conserving and managing the natural resources, whether living or non-living, of the waters superjacent to the seabed and of the sea-bed and its subsoil, and with regard to other activities for the economic exploitation and exploration of the zone, such as the production of energy from the water, currents and winds;
   (b) jurisdiction as provided for in the relevant provisions of this Convention with regard to:
      (i) the establishment and use of artificial islands, installations and structures;
      (ii) marine scientific research;
      (iii) the protection and preservation of the marine environment;
   (c) other rights and duties provided for in this Convention.

2. In exercising its rights and performing its duties under this Convention in the exclusive economic zone, the coastal State shall have due regard to the rights and duties of other States and shall act in a manner compatible with the provisions of this Convention.

3. The rights set out in this article with respect to the sea-bed and subsoil shall be exercised in accordance with Part VI.

Article 57 Breadth of the exclusive economic zone

The exclusive economic zone shall not extend beyond 200 nautical miles from the baselines from which the breadth of the territorial sea is measured.

Article 58 Rights and duties of other States in the exclusive economic zone

1. In the exclusive economic zone, all States, whether coastal or land-locked, enjoy, subject to the relevant provisions of this Convention, the freedoms referred to in article 87 of navigation and overflight and of the laying of submarine cables and pipelines, and other internationally lawful uses of the sea related to these freedoms, such as those associated with the operation of ships, aircraft and submarine cables and pipelines, and compatible with the other provisions of this Convention.

2. Articles 88 to 115 and other pertinent rules of international law apply to the exclusive economic zone in so far as they are not incompatible with this Part.

3. In exercising their rights and performing their duties under this Convention in the exclusive economic zone, States shall have due regard to the rights and duties of the coastal State and shall comply with the laws and regulations adopted by the coastal State in accordance with the provisions of this Convention and other rules of international law in so far as they are not incompatible with this Part.

Article 59 Basis for the resolution of conflicts regarding the attribution of rights and jurisdiction in the exclusive economic zone

In cases where this Convention does not attribute rights or jurisdiction to the coastal State or to other States within the exclusive economic zone, and a conflict arises between the interests of the coastal State and any other State or States, the conflict should be resolved on the basis of equity and in the light of all the relevant circumstances, taking into account the respective importance of the interests involved to the parties as well as to the international community as a whole.

Article 60 Artificial islands, installations and structures in the exclusive economic zone

1. In the exclusive economic zone, the coastal State shall have the exclusive right to construct and to authorize and regulate the construction, operation and use of:
    (a) artificial islands;
    (b) installations and structures for the purposes provided for in article 56 and other economic purposes;
    (c) installations and structures which may interfere with the exercise of the rights of the coastal State in the zone.

2. The coastal State shall have exclusive jurisdiction over such artificial islands, installations and structures, including jurisdiction with regard to customs, fiscal, health, safety and immigration laws and regulations.

3. Due notice must be given of the construction of such artificial islands, installations or structures, and permanent means for giving warning of their presence must be maintained. Any installations or structures which are abandoned or disused shall be removed to ensure safety of navigation, taking into account any generally accepted international standards established in this regard by the competent international organization. Such removal shall also have due regard to fishing, the protection of the marine environment and the rights and duties of other States. Appropriate publicity shall be given to the depth, position and dimensions of any installations or structures not entirely removed.

4. The coastal State may, where necessary, establish reasonable safety zones around such artificial islands, installations and structures in which it may take appropriate measures to ensure the safety both of navigation and of the artificial islands, installations and structures.

5. The breadth of the safety zones shall be determined by the coastal State, taking into account applicable international standards. Such zones shall be designed to ensure that they are reasonably related to the nature and function of the artificial islands, installations or structures, and shall not exceed a distance of 500 metres around them, measured from each point of their outer edge, except as authorized by generally accepted international standards or as recommended by the competent international organization. Due notice shall be given of the extent of safety zones.

6. All ships must respect these safety zones and shall comply with generally accepted international standards regarding navigation in the vicinity of artificial islands, installations, structures and safety zones.

7. Artificial islands, installations and structures and the safety zones around them may not be established where interference may be caused to the use of recognized sea lanes essential to international navigation.

8. Artificial islands, installations and structures do not possess the status of islands. They have no territorial sea of their own, and their presence does not affect the delimitation of the territorial sea, the exclusive economic zone or the continental shelf.

Article 61 Conservation of the living resources

1. The coastal State shall determine the allowable catch of the living resources in its exclusive economic zone.

2. The coastal State, taking into account the best scientific evidence available to it, shall ensure through proper conservation and management measures that the maintenance of the living resources in the exclusive economic zone is not endangered by over-exploitation. As appropriate, the coastal State and competent international organizations, whether subregional, regional or global, shall cooperate to this end.

3. Such measures shall also be designed to maintain or restore populations of harvested species at levels which can produce the maximum sustainable yield, as qualified by relevant environmental and economic factors, including the economic needs of coastal fishing communities and the special requirements of developing States, and taking into account fishing patterns, the interdependence of stocks and any generally recommended international minimum standards, whether subregional, regional or global.

4. In taking such measures the coastal State shall take into consideration the effects on species associated with or dependent upon harvested species with a view to maintaining or restoring populations of such associated or dependent species above levels at which their reproduction may become seriously threatened.

5. Available scientific information, catch and fishing effort statistics, and other data relevant to the conservation of fish stocks shall be contributed and exchanged on a regular basis through competent international organizations, whether subregional, regional or global, where appropriate and with participation by all States concerned, including States whose nationals are allowed to fish in the exclusive economic zone.

Article 62 Utilization of the living resources

1. The coastal State shall promote the objective of optimum utilization of the living resources in the exclusive economic zone without prejudice to article 61.

2. The coastal State shall determine its capacity to harvest the living resources of the exclusive economic zone. Where the coastal State does not have the capacity to harvest the entire allowable catch, it shall, through agreements or other arrangements and pursuant to the terms, conditions, laws and regulations referred to in paragraph 4, give other States access to the surplus of the allowable catch, having particular regard to the provisions of articles 69 and 70, especially in relation to the developing States mentioned therein.

3. In giving access to other States to its exclusive economic zone under this article, the coastal State shall take into account all relevant factors, including, *inter alia*, the significance of the living resources of the area to the economy of the coastal State concerned and its other national interests, the provisions of articles 69 and 70, the requirements of developing States in the subregion or region in harvesting part of the surplus and the need to minimize economic dislocation in States whose nationals have habitually fished in the zone or which have made substantial efforts in research and identification of stocks.

4. Nationals of other States fishing in the exclusive economic zone shall comply with the conservation measures and with the other terms and conditions established in the laws and regulations of the coastal State. These laws and regulations shall be consistent with this Convention and may relate, *inter alia*, to the following:

(a) licensing of fishermen, fishing vessels and equipment, including payment of fees and other forms of remuneration, which, in the case of developing coastal States, may consist of adequate compensation in the field of financing, equipment and technology relating to the fishing industry;

(b) determining the species which may be caught, and fixing quotas of catch, whether in relation to particular stocks or groups of stocks or catch per vessel over a period of time or to the catch by nationals of any State during a specified period;

(c) regulating seasons and areas of fishing, the types, sizes and amount of gear, and the types, sizes and number of fishing vessels that may be used;

(d) fixing the age and size of fish and other species that may be caught;

(e) specifying information required of fishing vessels, including catch and effort statistics and vessel position reports;

(f) requiring, under the authorization and control of the coastal State, the conduct of specified fisheries research programmes and regulating the conduct of such research, including the sampling of catches, disposition of samples and reporting of associated scientific data;

(g) the placing of observers or trainees on board such vessels by the coastal State;

(h) the landing of all or any part of the catch by such vessels in the ports of the coastal State;

(i) terms and conditions relating to joint ventures or other co-operative arrangements;

(j) requirements for the training of personnel and the transfer of fisheries technology, including enhancement of the coastal State's capability of undertaking fisheries research;

(k) enforcement procedures.

5. Coastal States shall give due notice of conservation and management laws and regulations.

Article 63 Stocks occurring within the exclusive economic zones of two or more coastal States or both within the exclusive economic zone and in an area beyond and adjacent to it

1. Where the same stock or stocks of associated species occur within the exclusive economic zones of two or more coastal States, these States shall seek, either directly or through appropriate subregional or regional organizations, to agree upon the measures necessary to co-ordinate and ensure the conservation and development of such stocks without prejudice to the other provisions of this Part.

2. Where the same stock or stocks of associated species occur both within the exclusive economic zone and in an area beyond and adjacent to the zone, the coastal State and the States fishing for such stocks in the adjacent area shall seek, either directly or through appropriate subregional or regional organizations, to agree upon the measures necessary for the conservation of these stocks in the adjacent area.

Article 64 Highly migratory species

1. The coastal State and other States whose nationals fish in the region for the highly migratory species listed in Annex I shall co-operate directly or through appropriate international organizations with a view to ensuring conservation and promoting the objective of optimum utilization of such species throughout the region, both within and beyond the exclusive economic zone. In regions for which no appropriate international organization exists, the coastal State and other States whose nationals harvest these species in the region shall co-operate to establish such an organization and participate in its work.

2. The provisions of paragraph 1 apply in addition to the other provisions of this Part.

Article 65 Marine mammals

Nothing in this Part restricts the right of a coastal State or the competence of an international organization, as appropriate, to prohibit, limit or regulate the exploitation of marine mammals more strictly than provided for in this Part. States shall co-operate with a view to the conservation of marine mammals and in the case of cetaceans shall in particular work through the appropriate international organizations for their conservation, management and study.

Article 66 Anadromous stocks

1. States in whose rivers anadromous stocks originate shall have the primary interest in and responsibility for such stocks.

2. The State of origin of anadromous stocks shall ensure their conservation by the establishment of appropriate regulatory measures for fishing in all waters landward of the outer limits of its exclusive economic zone and for fishing provided for in paragraph 3(b). The State of origin may, after consultations with the other States referred to in paragraphs 3 and 4 fishing these stocks, establish total allowable catches for stocks originating in its rivers.

3. (a) Fisheries for anadromous stocks shall be conducted only in waters landward of the outer limits of exclusive economic zones, except in cases where this provision would result in economic dislocation for a State other than the State of origin. With respect to such fishing beyond the outer limits of the exclusive economic zone, States concerned shall maintain consultations with a view to achieving agreement on terms and conditions of such fishing giving due regard to the conservation requirements and the needs of the State of origin in respect of these stocks.

   (b) The State of origin shall co-operate in minimizing economic dislocation in such other States fishing these stocks, taking into account the normal catch and the mode of operations of such States, and all the areas in which such fishing has occurred.

   (c) States referred to in subparagraph (b), participating by agreement with the State of origin in measures to renew anadromous stocks, particularly by expenditures for that purpose, shall be given special consideration by the State of origin in the harvesting of stocks originating in its rivers.

   (d) Enforcement of regulations regarding anadromous stocks beyond the exclusive economic zone shall be by agreement between the State of origin and the other States concerned.

4. In cases where anadromous stocks migrate into or through the waters landward of the outer limits of the exclusive economic zone of a State other than the State of origin, such State shall co-operate with the State of origin with regard to the conservation and management of such stocks.

5. The State of origin of anadromous stocks and other States fishing these stocks shall make arrangements for the implementation of the provisions of this article, where appropriate, through regional organizations.

Article 67 Catadromous species

1. A coastal State in whose waters catadromous species spend the greater part of their life cycle shall have responsibility for the management of these species and shall ensure the ingress and egress of migrating fish.

2. Harvesting of catadromous species shall be conducted only in waters landward of the outer limits of exclusive economic zones. When conducted in exclusive economic zones, harvesting shall be subject to this article and the other provisions of this Convention concerning fishing in these zones.

3. In cases where catadromous fish migrate through the exclusive economic zone of another State, whether as juvenile or maturing fish, the management, including harvesting, of such fish shall be regulated by agreement between the State mentioned in paragraph 1 and the other State concerned. Such agreement shall ensure the rational management of the species and take into account the responsibilities of the State mentioned in paragraph 1 for the maintenance of these species.

Article 68 Sedentary species
This Part does not apply to sedentary species as defined in article 77, paragraph 4.

Article 69 Right of land-locked States
1. Land-locked States shall have the right to participate, on an equitable basis, in the exploitation of an appropriate part of the surplus of the living resources of the exclusive economic zones of coastal States of the same subregion or region, taking into account the relevant economic and geographical circumstances of all the States concerned and in conformity with the provisions of this article and of articles 61 and 62.
2. The terms and modalities of such participation shall be established by the States concerned through bilateral, subregional or regional agreements taking into account, *inter alia*:
 (a) the need to avoid effects detrimental to fishing communities or fishing industries of the coastal State;
 (b) the extent to which the land-locked State, in accordance with the provisions of this article, is participating or is entitled to participate under existing bilateral, subregional or regional agreements in the exploitation of living resources of the exclusive economic zones of other coastal States;
 (c) the extent to which other land-locked States and geographically disadvantaged States are participating in the exploitation of the living resources of the exclusive economic zone of the coastal State and the consequent need to avoid a particular burden for any single coastal State or a part of it;
 (d) the nutritional needs of the populations of the respective States.
3. When the harvesting capacity of a coastal State approaches a point which would enable it to harvest the entire allowable catch of the living resources in its exclusive economic zone, the coastal State and other States concerned shall co-operate in the establishment of equitable arrangements on a bilateral, subregional or regional basis to allow for participation of developing land-locked States of the same subregion or region in the exploitation of the living resources of the exclusive economic zones of coastal States of the subregion or region, as may be appropriate in the circumstances and on terms satisfactory to all parties. In the implementation of this provision the factors mentioned in paragraph 2 shall also be taken into account.
4. Developed land-locked States shall, under the provisions of this article, be entitled to participate in the exploitation of living resources only in the exclusive economic zones of developed coastal States of the same subregion or region having regard to the extent to which the coastal State, in giving access to other States to the living resources of its exclusive economic zone, has taken into account the need to minimize detrimental effects on fishing communities and economic dislocation in States whose nationals have habitually fished in the zone.
5. The above provisions are without prejudice to arrangements agreed upon in subregions or regions where the coastal States may grant to land-locked States of the same subregion or region equal or preferential rights for the exploitation of the living resources in the exclusive economic zones.

Article 70 Right of geographically disadvantaged States
1. Geographically disadvantaged States shall have the right to participate, on an equitable basis, in the exploitation of an appropriate part of the surplus of the living resources of the exclusive economic zones of coastal States of the same subregion or region, taking into account the relevant economic and geographical circumstances of all the States concerned and in conformity with the provisions of this article and of articles 61 and 62.

2. For the purposes of this Part, 'geographically disadvantaged States' means coastal States, including States bordering enclosed or semi-enclosed seas, whose geographical situation makes them dependent upon the exploitation of the living resources of the exclusive economic zones of other States in the subregion or region for adequate supplies of fish for the nutritional purposes of their populations or parts thereof, and coastal States which can claim no exclusive economic zones of their own.

3. The terms and modalities of such participation shall be established by the States concerned through bilateral, subregional or regional agreements taking into account, *inter alia*:

(a) the need to avoid effects detrimental to fishing communities or fishing industries of the coastal State;

(b) the extent to which the geographically disadvantaged State, in accordance with the provisions of this article, is participating or is entitled to participate under existing bilateral, subregional or regional agreements in the exploitation of living resources of the exclusive economic zones of other coastal States;

(c) the extent to which other geographically disadvantaged States and land-locked States are participating in the exploitation of the living resources of the exclusive economic zone of the coastal State and the consequent need to avoid a particular burden for any single coastal State or a part of it;

(d) the nutritional needs of the populations of the respective States.

4. When the harvesting capacity of a coastal State approaches a point which would enable it to harvest the entire allowable catch of the living resources in its exclusive economic zone, the coastal State and other States concerned shall co-operate in the establishment of equitable arrangements on a bilateral, subregional or regional basis to allow for participation of developing geographically disadvantaged States of the same subregion or region in the exploitation of the living resources of the exclusive economic zones of coastal States of the subregion or region, as may be appropriate in the circumstances and on terms satisfactory to all parties. In the implementation of this provision the factors mentioned in paragraph 3 shall also be taken into account.

5. Developed geographically disadvantaged States shall, under the provisions of this article, be entitled to participate in the exploitation of living resources only in the exclusive economic zones of developed coastal States of the same subregion or region having regard to the extent to which the coastal State, in giving access to other States to the living resources of its exclusive economic zone, has taken into account the need to minimize detrimental effects on fishing communities and economic dislocation in States whose nationals have habitually fished in the zone.

6. The above provisions are without prejudice to arrangements agreed upon in subregions or regions where the coastal States may grant to geographically disadvantaged States of the same subregion or region equal or preferential rights for the exploitation of the living resources in the exclusive economic zones.

Article 71 Non-applicability of articles 69 and 70

The provisions of articles 69 and 70 do not apply in the case of a coastal State whose economy is overwhelmingly dependent on the exploitation of the living resources of its exclusive economic zone.

Article 72 Restrictions on transfer of rights

1. Rights provided under articles 69 and 70 to exploit living resources shall not be directly or indirectly transferred to third States or their nationals by lease or licence, by

establishing joint ventures or in any other manner which has the effect of such transfer unless otherwise agreed by the States concerned.

2. The foregoing provision does not preclude the States concerned from obtaining technical or financial assistance from third States or international organizations in order to facilitate the exercise of the rights pursuant to articles 69 and 70, provided that it does not have the effect referred to in paragraph 1.

Article 73 Enforcement of laws and regulations of the coastal State

1. The coastal State may, in the exercise of its sovereign rights to explore, exploit, conserve and manage the living resources in the exclusive economic zone, take such measures, including boarding, inspection, arrest and judicial proceedings, as may be necessary to ensure compliance with the laws and regulations adopted by it in conformity with this Convention.

2. Arrested vessels and their crews shall be promptly released upon the posting of reasonable bond or other security.

3. Coastal State penalties for violations of fisheries laws and regulations in the exclusive economic zone may not include imprisonment, in the absence of agreements to the contrary by the States concerned, or any other form of corporal punishment.

4. In cases of arrest or detention of foreign vessels the coastal State shall promptly notify the flag State, through appropriate channels, of the action taken and of any penalties subsequently imposed.

Article 74 Delimitation of the exclusive economic zone between States with opposite or adjacent coasts

1. The delimitation of the exclusive economic zone between States with opposite or adjacent coasts shall be effected by agreement on the basis of international law, as referred to in Article 38 of the Statute of the International Court of Justice, in order to achieve an equitable solution.

2. If no agreement can be reached within a reasonable period of time, the States concerned shall resort to the procedures provided for in Part XV.

3. Pending agreement as provided for in paragraph 1, the States concerned, in a spirit of understanding and co-operation, shall make every effort to enter into provisional arrangements of a practical nature and, during this transitional period, not to jeopardize or hamper the reaching of the final agreement. Such arrangements shall be without prejudice to the final delimitation.

4. Where there is an agreement in force between the States concerned, questions relating to the delimitation of the exclusive economic zone shall be determined in accordance with the provisions of that agreement.

Article 75 Charts and lists of geographical co-ordinates

1. Subject to this Part, the outer limit lines of the exclusive economic zone and the lines of delimitation drawn in accordance with article 74 shall be shown on charts of a scale or scales adequate for ascertaining their position. Where appropriate, lists of geographical coordinates of points, specifying the geodetic datum, may be substituted for such outer limit lines or lines of delimitation.

2. The coastal State shall give due publicity to such charts or lists of geographical coordinates and shall deposit a copy of each such chart or list with the Secretary-General of the United Nations.

PART VI
CONTINENTAL SHELF

Article 76 Definition of the continental shelf

1. The continental shelf of a coastal State comprises the sea-bed and subsoil of the submarine areas that extend beyond its territorial sea throughout the natural prolongation of its land territory to the outer edge of the continental margin, or to a distance of 200 nautical miles from the baselines from which the breadth of the territorial sea is measured where the outer edge of the continental margin does not extend up to that distance.

2. The continental shelf of a coastal State shall not extend beyond the limits provided for in paragraphs 4 to 6.

3. The continental margin comprises the submerged prolongation of the land mass of the coastal State, and consists of the sea-bed and subsoil of the shelf, the slope and the rise. It does not include the deep ocean floor with its oceanic ridges or the subsoil thereof.

4. (a) For the purposes of this Convention, the coastal State shall establish the outer edge of the continental margin wherever the margin extends beyond 200 nautical miles from the baselines from which the breadth of the territorial sea is measured, by either:[1]

   (i) a line delineated in accordance with paragraph 7 by reference to the outermost fixed points at each of which the thickness of sedimentary rocks is at least 1 per cent of the shortest distance from such point to the foot of the continental slope; or

   (ii) a line delineated in accordance with paragraph 7 by reference to fixed points not more than 60 nautical miles from the foot of the continental slope.

   (b) In the absence of evidence to the contrary, the foot of the continental slope shall be determined as the point of maximum change in the gradient at its base.

5. The fixed points comprising the line of the outer limits of the continental shelf on the sea-bed, drawn in accordance with paragraph 4 (a)(i) and (ii), either shall not exceed 350 nautical miles from the baselines from which the breadth of the territorial sea is

---

[1] See also the Statement of Understanding Concerning a Specific Method to Be Used in Establishing the Outer Edge of the Continental Margin (Annex II to the Final Act of the Third United Nations Conference on the Law of the Sea): *The Third United Nations Conference on the Law of the Sea,*

   Considering the special characteristics of a State's continental margin where:
(1) the average distance at which the 200 metre isobath occurs is not more than 20 nautical miles; (2) the greater proportion of the sedimentary rock of the continental margin lies beneath the rise; and

   Taking into account the inequity that would result to that State from the application to its continental margin of article 76 of the Convention, in that, the mathematical average of the thickness of sedimentary rock along a line established at the maximum distance permissible in accordance with the provisions of paragraph 4 (a) (i) and (ii) of that article as representing the entire outer edge of the continental margin would not be less than 3.5 kilometres; and that more than half of the margin would be excluded thereby;

   Recognizes that such State may, notwithstanding the provisions of article 76, establish the outer edge of its continental margin by straight lines not exceeding 60 nautical miles in length connecting fixed points, defined by latitude and longitude, at each of which the thickness of sedimentary rock is not less than 1 kilometre,

   Where a State establishes the outer edge of its continental margin by applying the method set forth in the preceding paragraph of this statement, this method may also be utilized by a neighbouring State for delineating the outer edge of its continental margin on a common geological feature, where its outer edge would lie on such feature on a line established at the maximum distance permissible in accordance with article 76, paragraph 4(a) (i) and (ii), along which the mathematical average of the thickness of sedimentary rock is not less than 3.5 kilometres,

   The Conference requests the Commission on the Limits of the Continental Shelf set up pursuant to Annex II of the Convention, to be governed by the terms of this Statement when making its recommendations on matters related to the establishment of the outer edge of the continental margin of these States in the southern part of the Bay of Bengal.

measured or shall not exceed 100 nautical miles from the 2,500 metre isobath, which is a line connecting the depth of 2,500 metres.

6.   Notwithstanding the provisions of paragraph 5, on submarine ridges, the outer limit of the continental shelf shall not exceed 350 nautical miles from the baselines from which the breadth of the territorial sea is measured. This paragraph does not apply to submarine elevations that are natural components of the continental margin, such as its plateaux, rises, caps, banks and spurs.

7.   The coastal State shall delineate the outer limits of its continental shelf, where that shelf extends beyond 200 nautical miles from the baselines from which the breadth of the territorial sea is measured, by straight lines not exceeding 60 nautical miles in length, connecting fixed points, defined by co-ordinates of latitude and longitude.

8.   Information on the limits of the continental shelf beyond 200 nautical miles from the baselines from which the breadth of the territorial sea is measured shall be submitted by the coastal State to the Commission on the Limits of the Continental Shelf set up under Annex II on the basis of equitable geographical representation. The Commission shall make recommendations to coastal States on matters related to the establishment of the outer limits of their continental shelf. The limits of the shelf established by a coastal State on the basis of these recommendations shall be final and binding.

9.   The coastal State shall deposit with the Secretary-General of the United Nations charts and relevant information, including geodetic data, permanently describing the outer limits of its continental shelf. The Secretary-General shall give due publicity thereto.

10.   The provisions of this article are without prejudice to the question of delimitation of the continental shelf between States with opposite or adjacent coasts.

Article 77   Rights of the coastal State over the continental shelf

1.   The coastal State exercises over the continental shelf sovereign rights for the purpose of exploring it and exploiting its natural resources.

2.   The rights referred to in paragraph 1 are exclusive in the sense that if the coastal State does not explore the continental shelf or exploit its natural resources, no one may undertake these activities without the express consent of the coastal State.

3.   The rights of the coastal State over the continental shelf do not depend on occupation, effective or notional, or on any express proclamation.

4.   The natural resources referred to in this Part consist of the mineral and other non-living resources of the sea-bed and subsoil together with living organisms belonging to sedentary species, that is to say, organisms which, at the harvestable stage, either are immobile on or under the seabed or are unable to move except in constant physical contact with the seabed or the subsoil.

Article 78   Legal status of the superjacent waters and air space and the rights and freedoms of other States

1.   The rights of the coastal State over the continental shelf do not affect the legal status of the superjacent waters or of the air space above those waters.

2.   The exercise of the rights of the coastal State over the continental shelf must not infringe or result in any unjustifiable interference with navigation and other rights and freedoms of other States as provided for in this Convention.

Article 79   Submarine cables and pipelines on the continental shelf

1.   All States are entitled to lay submarine cables and pipelines on the continental shelf, in accordance with the provisions of this article.

2. Subject to its right to take reasonable measures for the exploration of the continental shelf, the exploitation of its natural resources and the prevention, reduction and control of pollution from pipelines, the coastal State may not impede the laying or maintenance of such cables or pipelines.

3. The delineation of the course for the laying of such pipelines on the continental shelf is subject to the consent of the coastal State.

4. Nothing in this Part affects the right of the coastal State to establish conditions for cables or pipelines entering its territory or territorial sea, or its jurisdiction over cables and pipelines constructed or used in connection with the exploration of its continental shelf or exploitation of its resources or the operations of artificial islands, installations and structures under its jurisdiction.

5. When laying submarine cables or pipelines, States shall have due regard to cables or pipelines already in position. In particular, possibilities of repairing existing cables or pipelines shall not be prejudiced.

Article 80 Artificial islands, installations and structures on the continental shelf

Article 60 applies *mutatis mutandis* to artificial islands, installations and structures on the continental shelf.

Article 81 Drilling on the continental shelf

The coastal State shall have the exclusive right to authorize and regulate drilling on the continental shelf for all purposes.

Article 82 Payments and contributions with respect to the exploitation of the continental shelf beyond 200 nautical miles

1. The coastal State shall make payments or contributions in kind in respect of the exploitation of the non-living resources of the continental shelf beyond 200 nautical miles from the baselines from which the breadth of the territorial sea is measured.

2. The payments and contributions shall be made annually with respect to all production at a site after the first five years of production at that site. For the sixth year, the rate of payment or contribution shall be 1 per cent of the value or volume of production at the site. The rate shall increase by 1 per cent for each subsequent year until the twelfth year and shall remain at 7 per cent thereafter. Production does not include resources used in connection with exploitation.

3. A developing State which is a net importer of a mineral resource produced from its continental shelf is exempt from making such payments or contributions in respect of that mineral resource.

4. The payments or contributions shall be made through the Authority, which shall distribute them to States Parties to this Convention, on the basis of equitable sharing criteria, taking into account the interests and needs of developing States, particularly the least developed and the land-locked among them.

Article 83 Delimitation of the continental shelf between States with opposite or adjacent coasts

1. The delimitation of the continental shelf between States with opposite or adjacent coasts shall be effected by agreement on the basis of international law, as referred to in Article 38 of the Statute of the International Court of Justice, in order to achieve an equitable solution.

2. If no agreement can be reached within a reasonable period of time, the States concerned shall resort to the procedures provided for in Part XV.

3. Pending agreement as provided for in paragraph 1, the States concerned, in a spirit of understanding and co-operation, shall make every effort to enter into provisional arrangements of a practical nature and, during this transitional period, not to jeopardize or hamper the reaching of the final agreement. Such arrangements shall be without prejudice to the final delimitation.

4. Where there is an agreement in force between the States concerned, questions relating to the delimitation of the continental shelf shall be determined in accordance with the provisions of that agreement.

Article 84 Charts and lists of geographical coordinates

1. Subject to this Part, the outer limit lines of the continental shelf and the lines of delimitation drawn in accordance with article 83 shall be shown on charts of a scale or scales adequate for ascertaining their position. Where appropriate, lists of geographical coordinates of points, specifying the geodetic datum, may be substituted for such outer limit lines or lines of delimitation.

2. The coastal State shall give due publicity to such charts or lists of geographical coordinates and shall deposit a copy of each such chart or list with the Secretary-General of the United Nations and, in the case of those showing the outer limit lines of the continental shelf, with the Secretary-General of the Authority.

Article 85 Tunnelling

This Part does not prejudice the right of the coastal State to exploit the subsoil by means of tunnelling, irrespective of the depth of water above the subsoil.

PART VII
HIGH SEAS

SECTION 1. GENERAL PROVISIONS

Article 86 Application of the provisions of this Part

The provisions of this Part apply to all parts of the sea that are not included in the exclusive economic zone, in the territorial sea or in the internal waters of a State, or in the archipelagic waters of an archipelagic State. This article does not entail any abridgement of the freedoms enjoyed by all States in the exclusive economic zone in accordance with article 58.

Article 87 Freedom of the high seas

1. The high seas are open to all States, whether coastal or land-locked. Freedom of the high seas is exercised under the conditions laid down by this Convention and by other rules of international law. It comprises, *inter alia*, both for coastal and land-locked States:
  (a)   freedom of navigation;
  (b)   freedom of overflight;
  (c)   freedom to lay submarine cables and pipelines, subject to Part VI;
  (d)   freedom to construct artificial islands and other installations permitted under international law, subject to Part VI;
  (e)   freedom of fishing, subject to the conditions laid down in section 2;
  (f)   freedom of scientific research, subject to Parts VI and XIII.
2. These freedoms shall be exercised by all States with due regard for the interests of other States in their exercise of the freedom of the high seas, and also with due regard for the rights under this Convention with respect to activities in the Area.

Article 88 Reservation of the high seas for peaceful purposes

The high seas shall be reserved for peaceful purposes.

Article 89 Invalidity of claims of sovereignty over the high seas

No State may validly purport to subject any part of the high seas to its sovereignty.

Article 90 Right of navigation

Every State, whether coastal or land-locked, has the right to sail ships flying its flag on the high seas.

Article 91 Nationality of ships

1. Every State shall fix the conditions for the grant of its nationality to ships, for the registration of ships in its territory, and for the right to fly its flag. Ships have the nationality of the State whose flag they are entitled to fly. There must exist a genuine link between the State and the ship.

2. Every State shall issue to ships to which it has granted the right to fly its flag documents to that effect.

Article 92 Status of ships

1. Ships shall sail under the flag of one State only and, save in exceptional cases expressly provided for in international treaties or in this Convention, shall be subject to its exclusive jurisdiction on the high seas. A ship may not change its flag during a voyage or while in a port of call, save in the case of a real transfer of ownership or change of registry.

2. A ship which sails under the flags of two or more States, using them according to convenience, may not claim any of the nationalities in question with respect to any other State, and may be assimilated to a ship without nationality.

Article 93 Ships flying the flag of the United Nations, its specialized agencies and the International Atomic Energy Agency

The preceding articles do not prejudice the question of ships employed on the official service of the United Nations, its specialized agencies or the International Atomic Energy Agency, flying the flag of the organization.

Article 94 Duties of the flag State

1. Every State shall effectively exercise its jurisdiction and control in administrative, technical and social matters over ships flying its flag.

2. In particular every State shall:

(a) maintain a register of ships containing the names and particulars of ships flying its flag, except those which are excluded from generally accepted international regulations on account of their small size; and

(b) assume jurisdiction under its internal law over each ship flying its flag and its master, officers and crew in respect of administrative, technical and social matters concerning the ship.

3. Every State shall take such measures for ships flying its flag as are necessary to ensure safety at sea with regard, *inter alia*, to:

(a) the construction, equipment and seaworthiness of ships;

(b) the manning of ships, labour conditions and the training of crews, taking into account the applicable international instruments;

(c) the use of signals, the maintenance of communications and the prevention of collisions.

4. Such measures shall include those necessary to ensure:
(a) that each ship, before registration and thereafter at appropriate intervals, is surveyed by a qualified surveyor of ships, and has on board such charts, nautical publications and navigational equipment and instruments as are appropriate for the safe navigation of the ship;
(b) that each ship is in the charge of a master and officers who possess appropriate qualifications, in particular in seamanship, navigation, communications and marine engineering, and that the crew is appropriate in qualification and numbers for the type, size, machinery and equipment of the ship;
(c) that the master, officers and, to the extent appropriate, the crew are fully conversant with and required to observe the applicable international regulations concerning the safety of life at sea, the prevention of collisions, the prevention, reduction and control of marine pollution, and the maintenance of communications by radio.

5. In taking the measures called for in paragraphs 3 and 4 each State is required to conform to generally accepted international regulations, procedures and practices and to take any steps which may be necessary to secure their observance.

6. A State which has clear grounds to believe that proper jurisdiction and control with respect to a ship have not been exercised may report the facts to the flag State. Upon receiving such a report, the flag State shall investigate the matter and, if appropriate, take any action necessary to remedy the situation.

7. Each State shall cause an inquiry to be held by or before a suitably qualified person or persons into every marine casualty or incident of navigation on the high seas involving a ship flying its flag and causing loss of life or serious injury to nationals of another State or serious damage to ships or installations of another State or to the marine environment. The flag State and the other State shall co-operate in the conduct of any inquiry held by that other State into any such marine casualty or incident of navigation.

Article 95 Immunity of warships on the high seas
Warships on the high seas have complete immunity from the jurisdiction of any State other than the flag State.

Article 96 Immunity of ships used only on government non-commercial service
Ships owned or operated by a State and used only on government non-commercial service shall, on the high seas, have complete immunity from the jurisdiction of any State other than the flag State.

Article 97 Penal jurisdiction in matters of collision or any other incident of navigation
1. In the event of a collision or any other incident of navigation concerning a ship on the high seas, involving the penal or disciplinary responsibility of the master or of any other person in the service of the ship, no penal or disciplinary proceedings may be instituted against such person except before the judicial or administrative authorities either of the flag State or of the State of which such person is a national.

2. In disciplinary matters, the State which has issued a master's certificate or a certificate of competence or licence shall alone be competent, after due legal process, to pronounce the withdrawal of such certificates, even if the holder is not a national of the State which issued them.

3. No arrest or detention of the ship, even as a measure of investigation, shall be ordered by any authorities other than those of the flag State.

Article 98 Duty to render assistance

1. Every State shall require the master of a ship flying its flag, in so far as he can do so without serious danger to the ship, the crew or the passengers:

(a) to render assistance to any person found at sea in danger of being lost;

(b) to proceed with all possible speed to the rescue of persons in distress, if informed of their need of assistance, in so far as such action may reasonably be expected of him;

(c) after a collision, to render assistance to the other ship, its crew and its passengers and, where possible, to inform the other ship of the name of his own ship, its port of registry and the nearest port at which it will call.

2. Every coastal State shall promote the establishment, operation and maintenance of an adequate and effective search and rescue service regarding safety on and over the sea and, where circumstances so require, by way of mutual regional arrangements co-operate with neighbouring States for this purpose.

Article 99 Prohibition of the transport of slaves

Every State shall take effective measures to prevent and punish the transport of slaves in ships authorized to fly its flag and to prevent the unlawful use of its flag for that purpose. Any slave taking refuge on board any ship, whatever its flag, shall *ipso facto* be free.

Article 100 Duty to co-operate in the repression of piracy

All States shall co-operate to the fullest possible extent in the repression of piracy on the high seas or in any other place outside the jurisdiction of any State.

Article 101 Definition of piracy

Piracy consists of any of the following acts:

(a) any illegal acts of violence or detention, or any act of depredation, committed for private ends by the crew or the passengers of a private ship or a private aircraft, and directed:

(i) on the high seas, against another ship or aircraft, or against persons or property on board such ship or aircraft;

(ii) against a ship, aircraft, persons or property in a place outside the jurisdiction of any State;

(b) any act of voluntary participation in the operation of a ship or of an aircraft with knowledge of facts making it a pirate ship or aircraft;

(c) any act of inciting or of intentionally facilitating an act described in subparagraph (a) or (b).

Article 102 Piracy by a warship, government ship or government aircraft whose crew has mutinied

The acts of piracy, as defined in article 101, committed by a warship, government ship or government aircraft whose crew has mutinied and taken control of the ship or aircraft are assimilated to acts committed by a private ship or aircraft.

Article 103 Definition of a pirate ship or aircraft

A ship or aircraft is considered a pirate ship or aircraft if it is intended by the persons in dominant control to be used for the purpose of committing one of the acts referred to in article 101. The same applies if the ship or aircraft has been used to commit any such act, so long as it remains under the control of the persons guilty of that act.

Article 104 Retention or loss of the nationality of a pirate ship or aircraft

A ship or aircraft may retain its nationality although it has become a pirate ship or aircraft. The retention or loss of nationality is determined by the law of the State from which such nationality was derived.

Article 105 Seizure of a pirate ship or aircraft

On the high seas, or in any other place outside the jurisdiction of any State, every State may seize a pirate ship or aircraft, or a ship or aircraft taken by piracy and under the control of pirates, and arrest the persons and seize the property on board. The courts of the State which carried out the seizure may decide upon the penalties to be imposed, and may also determine the action to be taken with regard to the ships, aircraft or property, subject to the rights of third parties acting in good faith.

Article 106 Liability for seizure without adequate grounds

Where the seizure of a ship or aircraft on suspicion of piracy has been effected without adequate grounds, the State making the seizure shall be liable to the State the nationality of which is possessed by the ship or aircraft for any loss or damage caused by the seizure.

Article 107 Ships and aircraft which are entitled to seize on account of piracy

A seizure on account of piracy may be carried out only by warships or military aircraft, or other ships or aircraft clearly marked and identifiable as being on government service and authorized to that effect.

Article 108 Illicit traffic in narcotic drugs or psychotropic substances

1. All States shall cooperate in the suppression of illicit traffic in narcotic drugs and psychotropic substances engaged in by ships on the high seas contrary to international conventions.

2. Any State which has reasonable grounds for believing that a ship flying its flag is engaged in illicit traffic in narcotic drugs or psychotropic substances may request the co-operation of other States to suppress such traffic.

Article 109 Unauthorized broadcasting from the high seas

1. All States shall co-operate in the suppression of unauthorized broadcasting from the high seas.

2. For the purposes of this Convention, 'unauthorized broadcasting' means the transmission of sound radio or television broadcasts from a ship or installation on the high seas intended for reception by the general public contrary to international regulations, but excluding the transmission of distress calls.

3. Any person engaged in unauthorized broadcasting may be prosecuted before the court of:

    (a) the flag State of the ship;

    (b) the State of registry of the installation;

    (c) the State of which the person is a national;

    (d) any State where the transmissions can be received; or

    (e) any State where authorized radio communication is suffering interference.

4. On the high seas, a State having jurisdiction in accordance with paragraph 3 may, in conformity with article 110, arrest any person or ship engaged in unauthorized broadcasting and seize the broadcasting apparatus.

Article 110 Right of visit

1. Except where acts of interference derive from powers conferred by treaty, a warship which encounters on the high seas a foreign ship, other than a ship entitled to complete immunity in accordance with articles 95 and 96, is not justified in boarding it unless there is reasonable ground for suspecting that:

(a) the ship is engaged in piracy;

(b) the ship is engaged in the slave trade;

(c) the ship is engaged in unauthorized broadcasting and the flag State of the warship has jurisdiction under article 109;

(d) the ship is without nationality; or

(e) though flying a foreign flag or refusing to show its flag, the ship is, in reality, of the same nationality as the warship.

2. In the cases provided for in paragraph 1, the warship may proceed to verify the ship's right to fly its flag. To this end, it may send a boat under the command of an officer to the suspected ship. If suspicion remains after the documents have been checked, it may proceed to a further examination on board the ship, which must be carried out with all possible consideration.

3. If the suspicions prove to be unfounded, and provided that the ship boarded has not committed any act justifying them, it shall be compensated for any loss or damage that may have been sustained.

4. These provisions apply *mutatis mutandis* to military aircraft.

5. These provisions also apply to any other duly authorized ships or aircraft clearly marked and identifiable as being on government service.

Article 111 Right of hot pursuit

1. The hot pursuit of a foreign ship may be undertaken when the competent authorities of the coastal State have good reason to believe that the ship has violated the laws and regulations of that State. Such pursuit must be commenced when the foreign ship or one of its boats is within the internal waters, the archipelagic waters, the territorial sea or the contiguous zone of the pursuing State, and may only be continued outside the territorial sea or the contiguous zone if the pursuit has not been interrupted. It is not necessary that, at the time when the foreign ship within the territorial sea or the contiguous zone receives the order to stop, the ship giving the order should likewise be within the territorial sea or the contiguous zone. If the foreign ship is within a contiguous zone, as defined in article 33, the pursuit may only be undertaken if there has been a violation of the rights for the protection of which the zone was established.

2. The right of hot pursuit shall apply *mutatis mutandis* to violations in the exclusive economic zone or on the continental shelf, including safety zones around continental shelf installations, of the laws and regulations of the coastal State applicable in accordance with this Convention to the exclusive economic zone or the continental shelf, including such safety zones.

3. The right of hot pursuit ceases as soon as the ship pursued enters the territorial sea of its own State or of a third State.

4. Hot pursuit is not deemed to have begun unless the pursuing ship has satisfied itself by such practicable means as may be available that the ship pursued or one of its boats or other craft working as a team and using the ship pursued as a mother ship is within the limits of the territorial sea, or, as the case may be, within the contiguous zone or the exclusive economic zone or above the continental shelf. The pursuit may only be commenced after a visual or auditory signal to stop has been given at a distance which enables it to be seen or heard by the foreign ship.

5. The right of hot pursuit may be exercised only by warships or military aircraft, or other ships or aircraft clearly marked and identifiable as being on government service and authorized to that effect.

6. Where hot pursuit is effected by an aircraft:

(a) the provisions of paragraphs 1 to 4 shall apply *mutatis mutandis*;

(b) the aircraft giving the order to stop must itself actively pursue the ship until a ship or another aircraft of the coastal State, summoned by the aircraft, arrives to take over the pursuit, unless the aircraft is itself able to arrest the ship. It does not suffice to justify an arrest outside the territorial sea that the ship was merely sighted by the aircraft as an offender or suspected offender, if it was not both ordered to stop and pursued by the aircraft itself or other aircraft or ships which continue the pursuit without interruption.

7. The release of a ship arrested within the jurisdiction of a State and escorted to a port of that State for the purposes of an inquiry before the competent authorities may not be claimed solely on the ground that the ship, in the course of its voyage, was escorted across a portion of the exclusive economic zone or the high seas, if the circumstances rendered this necessary.

8. Where a ship has been stopped or arrested outside the territorial sea in circumstances which do not justify the exercise of the right of hot pursuit, it shall be compensated for any loss or damage that may have been thereby sustained.

Article 112 Right to lay submarine cables and pipelines

1. All States are entitled to lay submarine cables and pipelines on the bed of the high seas beyond the continental shelf.

2. Article 79, paragraph 5, applies to such cables and pipelines.

Article 113 Breaking or injury of a submarine cable or pipeline

Every State shall adopt the laws and regulations necessary to provide that the breaking or injury by a ship flying its flag or by a person subject to its jurisdiction of a submarine cable beneath the high seas done wilfully or through culpable negligence, in such a manner as to be liable to interrupt or obstruct telegraphic or telephonic communications, and similarly the breaking or injury of a submarine pipeline or high-voltage power cable, shall be a punishable offence. This provision shall apply also to conduct calculated or likely to result in such breaking or injury. However, it shall not apply to any break or injury caused by persons who acted merely with the legitimate object of saving their lives or their ships, after having taken all necessary precautions to avoid such break or injury.

Article 114 Breaking or injury by owners of a submarine cable or pipeline of another submarine cable or pipeline

Every State shall adopt the laws and regulations necessary to provide that, if persons subject to its jurisdiction who are the owners of a submarine cable or pipeline beneath the high seas, in laying or repairing that cable or pipeline, cause a break in or injury to another cable or pipeline, they shall bear the cost of the repairs.

Article 115 Indemnity for loss incurred in avoiding injury to a submarine cable or pipeline

Every State shall adopt the laws and regulations necessary to ensure that the owners of ships who can prove that they have sacrificed an anchor, a net or any other fishing gear, in order to avoid injuring a submarine cable or pipeline, shall be indemnified by the owner of the cable or pipeline, provided that the owner of the ship has taken all reasonable precautionary measures beforehand.

SECTION 2. CONSERVATION AND MANAGEMENT OF THE LIVING RESOURCES OF THE HIGH SEAS

Article 116 Right to fish on the high seas
All States have the right for their nationals to engage in fishing on the high seas subject to:
(a)   their treaty obligations;
(b)   the rights and duties as well as the interests of coastal States provided for, *inter alia*, in article 63, paragraph 2, and articles 64 to 67; and
(c)   the provisions of this section.

Article 117 Duty of States to adopt with respect to their nationals measures for the conservation of the living resources of the high seas
All States have the duty to take, or to co-operate with other States in taking, such measures for their respective nationals as may be necessary for the conservation of the living resources of the high seas.

Article 118 Co-operation of States in the conservation and management of living resources
States shall co-operate with each other in the conservation and management of living resources in the areas of the high seas. States whose nationals exploit identical living resources, or different living resources in the same area, shall enter into negotiations with a view to taking the measures necessary for the conservation of the living resources concerned. They shall, as appropriate, co-operate to establish subregional or regional fisheries organizations to this end.

Article 119 Conservation of the living resources of the high seas
1.   In determining the allowable catch and establishing other conservation measures for the living resources in the high seas, States shall:
(a)   take measures which are designed, on the best scientific evidence available to the States concerned, to maintain or restore populations of harvested species at levels which can produce the maximum sustainable yield, as qualified by relevant environmental and economic factors, including the special requirements of developing States, and taking into account fishing patterns, the interdependence of stocks and any generally recommended international minimum standards, whether subregional, regional or global;
(b)   take into consideration the effects on species associated with or dependent upon harvested species with a view to maintaining or restoring populations of such associated or dependent species above levels at which their reproduction may become seriously threatened.
2.   Available scientific information, catch and fishing effort statistics, and other data relevant to the conservation of fish stocks shall be contributed and exchanged on a regular basis through competent international organizations, whether subregional, regional or global, where appropriate and with participation by all States concerned.
3.   States concerned shall ensure that conservation measures and their implementation do not discriminate in form or in fact against the fishermen of any State.

Article 120 Marine mammals
Article 65 also applies to the conservation and management of marine mammals in the high seas.

PART VIII
REGIME OF ISLANDS

Article 121 Regime of islands

1. An island is a naturally formed area of land, surrounded by water, which is above water at high tide.

2. Except as provided for in paragraph 3, the territorial sea, the contiguous zone, the exclusive economic zone and the continental shelf of an island are determined in accordance with the provisions of this Convention applicable to other land territory.

3. Rocks which cannot sustain human habitation or economic life of their own shall have no exclusive economic zone or continental shelf.

PART IX
ENCLOSED OR SEMI-ENCLOSED SEAS

Article 122 Definition

For the purposes of this Convention, 'enclosed or semi-enclosed sea' means a gulf, basin or sea surrounded by two or more States and connected to another sea or the ocean by a narrow outlet or consisting entirely or primarily of the territorial seas and exclusive economic zones of two or more coastal States.

Article 123 Co-operation of States bordering enclosed or semi-enclosed seas

States bordering an enclosed or semi-enclosed sea should co-operate with each other in the exercise of their rights and in the performance of their duties under this Convention. To this end they shall endeavour, directly or through an appropriate regional organization:

(a) to co-ordinate the management, conservation, exploration and exploitation of the living resources of the sea;

(b) to co-ordinate the implementation of their rights and duties with respect to the protection and preservation of the marine environment;

(c) to co-ordinate their scientific research policies and undertake where appropriate joint programmes of scientific research in the area;

(d) to invite, as appropriate, other interested States or international organizations to co-operate with them in furtherance of the provisions of this article.

PART X
RIGHT OF ACCESS OF LAND-LOCKED STATES TO AND FROM THE SEA AND FREEDOM OF TRANSIT

Article 124 Use of terms

1. For the purposes of this Convention:

(a) 'land-locked State' means a State which has no sea-coast;

(b) 'transit State' means a State, with or without a sea-coast, situated between a land-locked State and the sea, through whose territory traffic in transit passes;

(c) 'traffic in transit' means transit of persons, baggage, goods and means of transport across the territory of one or more transit States, when the passage across such territory, with or without trans-shipment, warehousing, breaking bulk or change in the mode of transport, is only a portion of a complete journey which begins or terminates within the territory of the land-locked State;

(d) 'means of transport' means:

　　(i)　railway rolling stock, sea, lake and river craft and road vehicles;

　　(ii)　where local conditions so require, porters and pack animals.

2.　Land-locked States and transit States may, by agreement between them, include as means of transport pipelines and gas lines and means of transport other than those included in paragraph 1.

Article 125　Right of access to and from the sea and freedom of transit

1.　Land-locked States shall have the right of access to and from the sea for the purpose of exercising the rights provided for in this Convention including those relating to the freedom of the high seas and the common heritage of mankind. To this end, land-locked States shall enjoy freedom of transit through the territory of transit States by all means of transport.

2.　The terms and modalities for exercising freedom of transit shall be agreed between the land-locked States and transit States concerned through bilateral, subregional or regional agreements.

3.　Transit States, in the exercise of their full sovereignty over their territory, shall have the right to take all measures necessary to ensure that the rights and facilities provided for in this Part for land-locked States shall in no way infringe their legitimate interests.

Article 126　Exclusion of application of the most-favoured-nation clause

The provisions of this Convention, as well as special agreements relating to the exercise of the right of access to and from the sea, establishing rights and facilities on account of the special geographical position of land-locked States, are excluded from the application of the most-favoured-nation clause.

Article 127　Customs duties, taxes and other charges

1.　Traffic in transit shall not be subject to any customs duties, taxes or other charges except charges levied for specific services rendered in connection with such traffic.

2.　Means of transport in transit and other facilities provided for and used by land-locked States shall not be subject to taxes or charges higher than those levied for the use of means of transport of the transit State.

Article 128　Free zones and other customs facilities

For the convenience of traffic in transit, free zones or other customs facilities may be provided at the ports of entry and exit in the transit States, by agreement between those States and the land-locked States.

Article 129　Cooperation in the construction and improvement of means of transport

Where there are no means of transport in transit States to give effect to the freedom of transit or where the existing means, including the port installations and equipment, are inadequate in any respect, the transit States and land-locked States concerned may co-operate in constructing or improving them.

Article 130　Measures to avoid or eliminate delays or other difficulties of a technical nature in traffic in transit

1.　Transit States shall take all appropriate measures to avoid delays or other difficulties of a technical nature in traffic in transit.

2.　Should such delays or difficulties occur, the competent authorities of the transit States and land-locked States concerned shall cooperate towards their expeditious elimination.

Article 131 Equal treatment in maritime ports

Ships flying the flag of land-locked States shall enjoy treatment equal to that accorded to other foreign ships in maritime ports.

Article 132 Grant of greater transit facilities

This Convention does not entail in any way the withdrawal of transit facilities which are greater than those provided for in this Convention and which are agreed between States Parties to this Convention or granted by a State Party. This Convention also does not preclude such grant of greater facilities in the future.

PART XI
THE AREA

SECTION 1. GENERAL PROVISIONS

Article 133 Use of terms

For the purposes of this Part:
(a)   'resources' means all solid, liquid or gaseous mineral resources *in situ* in the Area at or beneath the sea-bed, including polymetallic nodules;
(b)   resources, when recovered from the Area, are referred to as 'minerals'.

Article 134 Scope of this Part

1.   This Part applies to the Area.
2.   Activities in the Area shall be governed by the provisions of this Part.
3.   The requirements concerning deposit of, and publicity to be given to, the charts or lists of geographical co-ordinates showing the limits referred to in article 1, paragraph 1(1), are set forth in Part VI.
4.   Nothing in this article affects the establishment of the outer limits of the continental shelf in accordance with Part VI or the validity of agreements relating to delimitation between States with opposite or adjacent coasts.

Article 135 Legal status of the superjacent waters and air space

Neither this Part nor any rights granted or exercised pursuant thereto shall affect the legal status of the waters superjacent to the Area or that of the air space above those waters.

SECTION 2. PRINCIPLES GOVERNING THE AREA

Article 136 Common heritage of mankind

The Area and its resources are the common heritage of mankind.

Article 137 Legal status of the Area and its resources

1.   No State shall claim or exercise sovereignty or sovereign rights over any part of the Area or its resources, nor shall any State or natural or juridical person appropriate any part thereof. No such claim or exercise of sovereignty or sovereign rights nor such appropriation shall be recognized.
2.   All rights in the resources of the Area are vested in mankind as a whole, on whose behalf the Authority shall act. These resources are not subject to alienation. The minerals recovered from the Area, however, may only be alienated in accordance with this Part and the rules, regulations and procedures of the Authority.

3. No State or natural or juridical person shall claim, acquire or exercise rights with respect to the minerals recovered from the Area except in accordance with this Part. Otherwise, no such claim, acquisition or exercise of such rights shall be recognized.

Article 138 General conduct of States in relation to the Area

The general conduct of States in relation to the Area shall be in accordance with the provisions of this Part, the principles embodied in the Charter of the United Nations and other rules of international law in the interests of maintaining peace and security and promoting international co-operation and mutual understanding.

Article 139 Responsibility to ensure compliance and liability for damage

1. States Parties shall have the responsibility to ensure that activities in the Area, whether carried out by States Parties, or state enterprises or natural or juridical persons which possess the nationality of States Parties or are effectively controlled by them or their nationals, shall be carried out in conformity with this Part. The same responsibility applies to international organizations for activities in the Area carried out by such organizations.

2. Without prejudice to the rules of international law and Annex III, article 22, damage caused by the failure of a State Party or international organization to carry out its responsibilities under this Part shall entail liability; States Parties or international organizations acting together shall bear joint and several liability. A State Party shall not however be liable for damage caused by any failure to comply with this Part by a person whom it has sponsored under article 153, paragraph 2(b), if the State Party has taken all necessary and appropriate measures to secure effective compliance under article 153, paragraph 4, and Annex III, article 4, paragraph 4.

3. States Parties that are members of international organizations shall take appropriate measures to ensure the implementation of this article with respect to such organizations.

Article 140 Benefit of mankind

1. Activities in the Area shall, as specifically provided for in this Part, be carried out for the benefit of mankind as a whole, irrespective of the geographical location of States, whether coastal or land-locked, and taking into particular consideration the interests and needs of developing States and of peoples who have not attained full independence or other self-governing status recognized by the United Nations in accordance with General Assembly resolution 1514 (XV) and other relevant General Assembly resolutions.

2. The Authority shall provide for the equitable sharing of financial and other economic benefits derived from activities in the Area through any appropriate mechanism, on a non-discriminatory basis, in accordance with article 160, paragraph 2(f)(i).

Article 141 Use of the Area exclusively for peaceful purposes

The Area shall be open to use exclusively for peaceful purposes by all States, whether coastal or land-locked, without discrimination and without prejudice to the other provisions of this Part.

Article 142 Rights and legitimate interests of coastal States

1. Activities in the Area, with respect to resource deposits in the Area which lie across limits of national jurisdiction, shall be conducted with due regard to the rights and legitimate interests of any coastal State across whose jurisdiction such deposits lie.

2. Consultations, including a system of prior notification, shall be maintained with the State concerned, with a view to avoiding infringement of such rights and interests. In cases where activities in the Area may result in the exploitation of resources lying within national jurisdiction, the prior consent of the coastal State concerned shall be required.

3. Neither this Part nor any rights granted or exercised pursuant thereto shall affect the rights of coastal States to take such measures consistent with the relevant provisions of Part XII as may be necessary to prevent, mitigate or eliminate grave and imminent danger to their coastline, or related interests from pollution or threat thereof or from other hazardous occurrences resulting from or caused by any activities in the Area.

Article 143 Marine scientific research

1. Marine scientific research in the Area shall be carried out exclusively for peaceful purposes and for the benefit of mankind as a whole, in accordance with Part XIII.

2. The Authority may carry out marine scientific research concerning the Area and its resources, and may enter into contracts for that purpose. The Authority shall promote and encourage the conduct of marine scientific research in the Area, and shall co-ordinate and disseminate the results of such research and analysis when available.

3. States Parties may carry out marine scientific research in the Area. States Parties shall promote international co-operation in marine scientific research in the Area by:

(a) participating in international programmes and encouraging co-operation in marine scientific research by personnel of different countries and of the Authority;

(b) ensuring that programmes are developed through the Authority or other international organizations as appropriate for the benefit of developing States and technologically less developed States with a view to:
(i) strengthening their research capabilities;
(ii) training their personnel and the personnel of the Authority in the techniques and applications of research;
(iii) fostering the employment of their qualified personnel in research in the Area;

(c) effectively disseminating the results of research and analysis when available, through the Authority or other international channels when appropriate.

Article 144 Transfer of technology[2]

1. The Authority shall take measures in accordance with this Convention:
(a) to acquire technology and scientific knowledge relating to activities in the Area; and
(b) to promote and encourage the transfer to developing States of such technology and scientific knowledge so that all States Parties benefit therefrom.

2. To this end the Authority and States Parties shall co-operate in promoting the transfer of technology and scientific knowledge relating to activities in the Area so that the Enterprise and all States Parties may benefit therefrom. In particular they shall initiate and promote:

(a) programmes for the transfer of technology to the Enterprise and to developing States with regard to activities in the Area, including, *inter alia*, facilitating the access of the Enterprise and of developing States to the relevant technology, under fair and reasonable terms and conditions;

(b) measures directed towards the advancement of the technology of the Enterprise and the domestic technology of developing States, particularly by providing opportunities to personnel from the Enterprise and from developing States for training in marine science and technology and for their full participation in activities in the Area.

---

[2] See also Implementation Agreement [Doc. 37], Annex, Section 5, para. 1.

Article 145 Protection of the marine environment

Necessary measures shall be taken in accordance with this Convention with respect to activities in the Area to ensure effective protection for the marine environment from harmful effects which may arise from such activities. To this end the Authority shall adopt appropriate rules, regulations and procedures for *inter alia*:

(a) the prevention, reduction and control of pollution and other hazards to the marine environment, including the coastline, and of interference with the ecological balance of the marine environment, particular attention being paid to the need for protection from harmful effects of such activities as drilling, dredging, excavation, disposal of waste, construction and operation or maintenance of installations, pipelines and other devices related to such activities;

(b) the protection and conservation of the natural resources of the Area and the prevention of damage to the flora and fauna of the marine environment.

Article 146 Protection of human life

With respect to activities in the Area, necessary measures shall be taken to ensure effective protection of human life. To this end the Authority shall adopt appropriate rules, regulations and procedures to supplement existing international law as embodied in relevant treaties.

Article 147 Accommodation of activities in the Area and in the marine environment

1. Activities in the Area shall be carried out with reasonable regard for other activities in the marine environment.

2. Installations used for carrying out activities in the Area shall be subject to the following conditions:

(a) such installations shall be erected, emplaced and removed solely in accordance with this Part and subject to the rules, regulations and procedures of the Authority. Due notice must be given of the erection, emplacement and removal of such installations, and permanent means for giving warning of their presence must be maintained;

(b) such installations may not be established where interference may be caused to the use of recognized sea lanes essential to international navigation or in areas of intense fishing activity;

(c) safety zones shall be established around such installations with appropriate markings to ensure the safety of both navigation and the installations. The configuration and location of such safety zones shall not be such as to form a belt impeding the lawful access of shipping to particular maritime zones or navigation along international sea lanes;

(d) such installations shall be used exclusively for peaceful purposes;

(e) such installations do not possess the status of islands. They have no territorial sea of their own, and their presence does not affect the delimitation of the territorial sea, the exclusive economic zone or the continental shelf.

3. Other activities in the marine environment shall be conducted with reasonable regard for activities in the Area.

Article 148 Participation of developing States in activities in the Area

The effective participation of developing States in activities in the Area shall be promoted as specifically provided for in this Part, having due regard to their special interests and needs, and in particular to the special need of the land-locked and geographically disadvantaged among them to overcome obstacles arising from their disadvantaged location, including remoteness from the Area and difficulty of access to and from it.

Article 149 Archaeological and historical objects

All objects of an archaeological and historical nature found in the Area shall be preserved or disposed of for the benefit of mankind as a whole, particular regard being paid to the preferential rights of the State or country of origin, or the State of cultural origin, or the State of historical and archaeological origin.

SECTION 3. DEVELOPMENT OF RESOURCES OF THE AREA

Article 150 Policies relating to activities in the Area

Activities in the Area shall, as specifically provided for in this Part, be carried out in such a manner as to foster healthy development of the world economy and balanced growth of international trade, and to promote international co-operation for the over-all development of all countries, especially developing States, and with a view to ensuring:

    (a)   the development of the resources of the Area;

    (b)   orderly, safe and rational management of the resources of the Area, including the efficient conduct of activities in the Area and, in accordance with sound principles of conservation, the avoidance of unnecessary waste;

    (c)   the expansion of opportunities for participation in such activities consistent in particular with articles 144 and 148;

    (d)   participation in revenues by the Authority and the transfer of technology to the Enterprise and developing States as provided for in this Convention;

    (e)   increased availability of the minerals derived from the Area as needed in conjunction with minerals derived from other sources, to ensure supplies to consumers of such minerals;

    (f)   the promotion of just and stable prices remunerative to producers and fair to consumers for minerals derived both from the Area and from other sources, and the promotion of long-term equilibrium between supply and demand;

    (g)   the enhancement of opportunities for all States Parties, irrespective of their social and economic systems or geographical location, to participate in the development of the resources of the Area and the prevention of monopolization of activities in the Area;

    (h)   the protection of developing countries from adverse effects on their economies or on their export earnings resulting from a reduction in the price of an affected mineral, or in the volume of exports of that mineral, to the extent that such reduction is caused by activities in the Area, as provided in article 151;

    (i)   the development of the common heritage for the benefit of mankind as a whole; and

    (j)   conditions of access to markets for the imports of minerals produced from the resources of the Area and for imports of commodities produced from such minerals shall not be more favourable than the most favourable applied to imports from other sources.

Article 151 Production policies[3]

    1.   (a)   Without prejudice to the objectives set forth in article 150 and for the purpose of implementing subparagraph (h) of that article, the Authority, acting through existing forums or such new arrangements or agreements as may be appropriate, in which all interested parties, including both producers and consumers, participate, shall take measures necessary to promote the growth, efficiency and stability of markets for those

---

[3] See also Implementation Agreement [Doc. 37], Annex, Sections 6 and 7.

commodities produced from the minerals derived from the Area, at prices remunerative to producers and fair to consumers. All States Parties shall cooperate to this end.

(b) The Authority shall have the right to participate in any commodity conference dealing with those commodities and in which all interested parties including both producers and consumers participate. The Authority shall have the right to become a party to any arrangement or agreement resulting from such conferences. Participation of the Authority in any organs established under those arrangements or agreements shall be in respect of production in the Area and in accordance with the relevant rules of those organs.

(c) The Authority shall carry out its obligations under the arrangements or agreements referred to in this paragraph in a manner which assures a uniform and non-discriminatory implementation in respect of all production in the Area of the minerals concerned. In doing so, the Authority shall act in a manner consistent with the terms of existing contracts and approved plans of work of the Enterprise.

2. (a) During the interim period specified in paragraph 3, commercial production shall not be undertaken pursuant to an approved plan of work until the operator has applied for and has been issued a production authorization by the Authority. Such production authorizations may not be applied for or issued more than five years prior to the planned commencement of commercial production under the plan of work unless, having regard to the nature and timing of project development, the rules, regulations and procedures of the Authority prescribe another period.

(b) In the application for the production authorization, the operator shall specify the annual quantity of nickel expected to be recovered under the approved plan of work. The application shall include a schedule of expenditures to be made by the operator after he has received the authorization which are reasonably calculated to allow him to begin commercial production on the date planned.

(c) For the purposes of subparagraphs (a) and (b), the Authority shall establish appropriate performance requirements in accordance with Annex III, article 17.

(d) The Authority shall issue a production authorization for the level of production applied for unless the sum of that level and the levels already authorized exceeds the nickel production ceiling, as calculated pursuant to paragraph 4 in the year of issuance of the authorization, during any year of planned production falling within the interim period.

(e) When issued, the production authorization and approved application shall become a part of the approved plan of work.

(f) If the operator's application for a production authorization is denied pursuant to subparagraph (d), the operator may apply again to the Authority at any time.

3. The interim period shall begin five years prior to 1 January of the year in which the earliest commercial production is planned to commence under an approved plan of work. If the earliest commercial production is delayed beyond the year originally planned, the beginning of the interim period and the production ceiling originally calculated shall be adjusted accordingly. The interim period shall last 25 years or until the end of the Review Conference referred to in article 155 or until the day when such new arrangements

or agreements as are referred to in paragraph 1 enter into force, whichever is earliest. The Authority shall resume the power provided in this article for the remainder of the interim period if the said arrangements or agreements should lapse or become ineffective for any reason whatsoever.

4. (a) The production ceiling for any year of the interim period shall be the sum of:

        (i) the difference between the trend line values for nickel consumption, as calculated pursuant to subparagraph (b), for the year immediately prior to the year of the earliest commercial production and the year immediately prior to the commencement of the interim period; and

        (ii) sixty per cent of the difference between the trend line values for nickel consumption, as calculated pursuant to subparagraph (b), for the year for which the production authorization is being applied for and the year immediately prior to the year of the earliest commercial production.

    (b) For the purposes of subparagraph (a):

        (i) trend line values used for computing the nickel production ceiling shall be those annual nickel consumption values on a trend line computed during the year in which a production authorization is issued. The trend line shall be derived from a linear regression of the logarithms of actual nickel consumption for the most recent 15-year period for which such data are available, time being the independent variable. This trend line shall be referred to as the original trend line;

        (ii) if the annual rate of increase of the original trend line is less than 3 per cent, then the trend line used to determine the quantities referred to in subparagraph (a) shall instead be one passing through the original trend line at the value for the first year of the relevant 15-year period, and increasing at 3 per cent annually; provided however that the production ceiling established for any year of the interim period may not in any case exceed the difference between the original trend line value for that year and the original trend line value for the year immediately prior to the commencement of the interim period.

5. The Authority shall reserve to the Enterprise for its initial production a quantity of 38,000 metric tonnes of nickel from the available production ceiling calculated pursuant to paragraph 4.

6. (a) An operator may in any year produce less than or up to 8 per cent more than the level of annual production of minerals from polymetallic nodules specified in his production authorization, provided that the over-all amount of production shall not exceed that specified in the authorization. Any excess over 8 per cent and up to 20 per cent in any year, or any excess in the first and subsequent years following two consecutive years in which excesses occur, shall be negotiated with the Authority, which may require the operator to obtain a supplementary production authorization to cover additional production.

    (b) Applications for such supplementary production authorizations shall be considered by the Authority only after all pending applications by operators who have not yet received production authorizations have been acted upon and due account has been taken of other likely applicants. The Authority shall be guided by the principle of not exceeding the total production allowed under the production ceiling in any year of the interim period. It shall not authorize the production under any plan of work of a quantity in excess of 46,500 metric tonnes of nickel per year.

7. The levels of production of other metals such as copper, cobalt and manganese extracted from the polymetallic nodules that are recovered pursuant to a production authorization should not be higher than those which would have been produced had the operator produced the maximum level of nickel from those nodules pursuant to this article. The Authority shall establish rules, regulations and procedures pursuant to Annex III, article 17, to implement this paragraph.

8. Rights and obligations relating to unfair economic practices under relevant multilateral trade agreements shall apply to the exploration for and exploitation of minerals from the Area. In the settlement of disputes arising under this provision, States Parties which are Parties to such multilateral trade agreements shall have recourse to the dispute settlement procedures of such agreements.

9. The Authority shall have the power to limit the level of production of minerals from the Area, other than minerals from polymetallic nodules, under such conditions and applying such methods as may be appropriate by adopting regulations in accordance with article 161, paragraph 8.

10. Upon the recommendation of the Council on the basis of advice from the Economic Planning Commission, the Assembly shall establish a system of compensation or take other measures of economic adjustment assistance including co-operation with specialized agencies and other international organizations to assist developing countries which suffer serious adverse effects on their export earnings or economies resulting from a reduction in the price of an affected mineral or in the volume of exports of that mineral, to the extent that such reduction is caused by activities in the Area. The Authority on request shall initiate studies on the problems of those States which are likely to be most seriously affected with a view to minimizing their difficulties and assisting them in their economic adjustment.

Article 152 Exercise of powers and functions by the Authority

1. The Authority shall avoid discrimination in the exercise of its powers and functions, including the granting of opportunities for activities in the Area.

2. Nevertheless, special consideration for developing States, including particular consideration for the land-locked and geographically disadvantaged among them, specifically provided for in this Part shall be permitted.

Article 153 System of exploration and exploitation

1. Activities in the Area shall be organized, carried out and controlled by the Authority on behalf of mankind as a whole in accordance with this article as well as other relevant provisions of this Part and the relevant Annexes, and the rules, regulations and procedures of the Authority.

2. Activities in the Area shall be carried out as prescribed in paragraph 3:

(a) by the Enterprise, and

(b) in association with the Authority by States Parties, or state enterprises or natural or juridical persons which possess the nationality of States Parties or are effectively controlled by them or their nationals, when sponsored by such States, or any group of the foregoing which meets the requirements provided in this Part and in Annex III.

3. Activities in the Area shall be carried out in accordance with a formal written plan of work drawn up in accordance with Annex III and approved by the Council after review by the Legal and Technical Commission. In the case of activities in the Area carried out

as authorized by the Authority by the entities specified in paragraph 2(b), the plan of work shall, in accordance with Annex III, article 3, be in the form of a contract. Such contracts may provide for joint arrangements in accordance with Annex III, article 11.[4]

4. The Authority shall exercise such control over activities in the Area as is necessary for the purpose of securing compliance with the relevant provisions of this Part and the Annexes relating thereto, and the rules, regulations and procedures of the Authority, and the plans of work approved in accordance with paragraph 3. States Parties shall assist the Authority by taking all measures necessary to ensure such compliance in accordance with article 139.

5. The Authority shall have the right to take at any time any measures provided for under this Part to ensure compliance with its provisions and the exercise of the functions of control and regulation assigned to it thereunder or under any contract. The Authority shall have the right to inspect all installations in the Area used in connection with activities in the Area.

6. A contract under paragraph 3 shall provide for security of tenure. Accordingly, the contract shall not be revised, suspended or terminated except in accordance with Annex III, articles 18 and 19.

Article 154 Periodic review

Every five years from the entry into force of this Convention, the Assembly shall undertake a general and systematic review of the manner in which the international regime of the Area established in this Convention has operated in practice. In the light of this review the Assembly may take, or recommend that other organs take, measures in accordance with the provisions and procedures of this Part and the Annexes relating thereto which will lead to the improvement of the operation of the regime.

Article 155 The Review Conference[5]

1. Fifteen years from 1 January of the year in which the earliest commercial production commences under an approved plan of work, the Assembly shall convene a conference for the review of those provisions of this Part and the relevant Annexes which govern the system of exploration and exploitation of the resources of the Area. The Review Conference shall consider in detail, in the light of the experience acquired during that period:

(a) whether the provisions of this Part which govern the system of exploration and exploitation of the resources of the Area have achieved their aims in all respects, including whether they have benefited mankind as a whole;

(b) whether, during the 15-year period, reserved areas have been exploited in an effective and balanced manner in comparison with non-reserved areas;

(c) whether the development and use of the Area and its resources have been undertaken in such a manner as to foster healthy development of the world economy and balanced growth of international trade;

(d) whether monopolization of activities in the Area has been prevented;

(e) whether the policies set forth in articles 150 and 151 have been fulfilled; and

(f) whether the system has resulted in the equitable sharing of benefits derived from activities in the Area, taking into particular consideration the interests and needs of the developing States.

2. The Review Conference shall ensure the maintenance of the principle of the common heritage of mankind, the international regime designed to ensure equitable

---

[4] See also Implementation Agreement [Doc. 37], Annex, Section 2, para. 4
[5] See also Implementation Agreement [Doc. 37], Annex, Section 4

exploitation of the resources of the Area for the benefit of all countries, especially the developing States, and an Authority to organize, conduct and control activities in the Area. It shall also ensure the maintenance of the principles laid down in this Part with regard to the exclusion of claims or exercise of sovereignty over any part of the Area, the rights of States and their general conduct in relation to the Area, and their participation in activities in the Area in conformity with this Convention, the prevention of monopolization of activities in the Area, the use of the Area exclusively for peaceful purposes, economic aspects of activities in the Area, marine scientific research, transfer of technology, protection of the marine environment, protection of human life, rights of coastal States, the legal status of the waters superjacent to the Area and that of the air space above those waters and accommodation between activities in the Area and other activities in the marine environment.

3. The decision-making procedure applicable at the Review Conference shall be the same as that applicable at the Third United Nations Conference on the Law of the Sea. The Conference shall make every effort to reach agreement on any amendments by way of consensus and there should be no voting on such matters until all efforts at achieving consensus have been exhausted.

4. If, five years after its commencement, the Review Conference has not reached agreement on the system of exploration and exploitation of the resources of the Area, it may decide during the ensuing 12 months, by a three-fourths majority of the States Parties, to adopt and submit to the States Parties for ratification or accession such amendments changing or modifying the system as it determines necessary and appropriate. Such amendments shall enter into force for all States Parties 12 months after the deposit of instruments of ratification or accession by three fourths of the States Parties.

5. Amendments adopted by the Review Conference pursuant to this article shall not affect rights acquired under existing contracts.

Section 4. The Authority[6]

Subsection A. General Provisions

Article 156 Establishment of the Authority[7]

1. There is hereby established the International Sea-bed Authority, which shall function in accordance with this Part.

2. All States Parties are *ipso facto* members of the Authority.

3. Observers at the Third United Nations Conference on the Law of the Sea who have signed the Final Act and who are not referred to in article 305, paragraph 1(c), (d), (e) or (f), shall have the right to participate in the Authority as observers, in accordance with its rules, regulations and procedures.

4. The seat of the Authority shall be in Jamaica.

5. The Authority may establish such regional centres or offices as it deems necessary for the exercise of its functions.

Article 157 Nature and fundamental principles of the Authority[8]

1. The Authority is the organization through which States Parties shall, in accordance with this Part, organize and control activities in the Area, particularly with a view to administering the resources of the Area.

---

[6] See also Implementation Agreement [Doc. 37], Annex, Section 1, para. 17.
[7] See also Implementation Agreement [Doc. 37], Annex, Section 1, para. 12.
[8] See also Implementation Agreement [Doc. 37], Annex, Section 1, para. 1.

2. The powers and functions of the Authority shall be those expressly conferred upon it by this Convention. The Authority shall have such incidental powers, consistent with this Convention, as are implicit in and necessary for the exercise of those powers and functions with respect to activities in the Area.

3. The Authority is based on the principle of the sovereign equality of all its members.

4. All members of the Authority shall fulfil in good faith the obligations assumed by them in accordance with this Part in order to ensure to all of them the rights and benefits resulting from membership.

Article 158 Organs of the Authority[9]

1. There are hereby established, as the principal organs of the Authority, an Assembly, a Council and a Secretariat.

2. There is hereby established the Enterprise, the organ through which the Authority shall carry out the functions referred to in article 170, paragraph 1.

3. Such subsidiary organs as may be found necessary may be established in accordance with this Part.

4. Each principal organ of the Authority and the Enterprise shall be responsible for exercising those powers and functions which are conferred upon it. In exercising such powers and functions each organ shall avoid taking any action which may derogate from or impede the exercise of specific powers and functions conferred upon another organ.

Subsection B. The Assembly[10]

Article 159 Composition, procedure and voting

1. The Assembly shall consist of all the members of the Authority. Each member shall have one representative in the Assembly, who may be accompanied by alternates and advisers.

2. The Assembly shall meet in regular annual sessions and in such special sessions as may be decided by the Assembly, or convened by the Secretary-General at the request of the Council or of a majority of the members of the Authority.

3. Sessions shall take place at the seat of the Authority unless otherwise decided by the Assembly.

4. The Assembly shall adopt its rules of procedure. At the beginning of each regular session, it shall elect its President and such other officers as may be required. They shall hold office until a new President and other officers are elected at the next regular session.

5. A majority of the members of the Assembly shall constitute a quorum.

6. Each member of the Assembly shall have one vote.

7. Decisions on questions of procedure, including decisions to convene special sessions of the Assembly, shall be taken by a majority of the members present and voting.

8. Decisions on questions of substance shall be taken by a two-thirds majority of the members present and voting, provided that such majority includes a majority of the members participating in the session. When the issue arises as to whether a question is one of substance or not, that question shall be treated as one of substance unless otherwise decided by the Assembly by the majority required for decisions on questions of substance.[11]

---

[9] See also Implementation Agreement [Doc. 37], Annex, Section 1, paras. 2-5.

[10] See also Implementation Agreement [Doc. 37], Annex, Section 3, para. 14.

[11] See also Implementation Agreement [Doc. 37], Annex, Section 3, paras. 2, 3, 4, 7.

9. When a question of substance comes up for voting for the first time, the President may, and shall, if requested by at least one fifth of the members of the Assembly, defer the issue of taking a vote on that question for a period not exceeding five calendar days. This rule may be applied only once to any question, and shall not be applied so as to defer the question beyond the end of the session.

10. Upon a written request addressed to the President and sponsored by at least one fourth of the members of the Authority for an advisory opinion on the conformity with this Convention of a proposal before the Assembly on any matter, the Assembly shall request the Sea-bed Disputes Chamber of the International Tribunal for the Law of the Sea to give an advisory opinion thereon and shall defer voting on that proposal pending receipt of the advisory opinion by the Chamber. If the advisory opinion is not received before the final week of the session in which it is requested, the Assembly shall decide when it will meet to vote upon the deferred proposal.

Article 160 Powers and functions

1. The Assembly, as the sole organ of the Authority consisting of all the members, shall be considered the supreme organ of the Authority to which the other principal organs shall be accountable as specifically provided for in this Convention. The Assembly shall have the power to establish general policies in conformity with the relevant provisions of this Convention on any question or matter within the competence of the Authority.[12]

2. In addition, the powers and functions of the Assembly shall be:

(a) to elect the members of the Council in accordance with article 161;

(b) to elect the Secretary-General from among the candidates proposed by the Council;

(c) to elect, upon the recommendation of the Council, the members of the Governing Board of the Enterprise and the Director-General of the Enterprise;

(d) to establish such subsidiary organs as it finds necessary for the exercise of its functions in accordance with this Part. In the composition of these subsidiary organs due account shall be taken of the principle of equitable geographical distribution and of special interests and the need for members qualified and competent in the relevant technical questions dealt with by such organs;

(e) to assess the contributions of members to the administrative budget of the Authority in accordance with an agreed scale of assessment based upon the scale used for the regular budget of the United Nations until the Authority shall have sufficient income from other sources to meet its administrative expenses;[13]

(f) (i) to consider and approve, upon the recommendation of the Council, the rules, regulations and procedures on the equitable sharing of financial and other economic benefits derived from activities in the Area and the payments and contributions made pursuant to article 82, taking into particular consideration the interests and needs of developing States and peoples who have not attained full independence or other self-governing status. If the Assembly does not approve the recommendations of the Council, the Assembly shall return them to the Council for reconsideration in the light of the views expressed by the Assembly;

(ii) to consider and approve the rules, regulations and procedures of the Authority, and any amendments thereto, provisionally adopted by the Council pursuant to article 162, paragraph 2 (o)(ii). These rules, regulations and procedures shall relate to prospecting, exploration

---

[12] See also Implementation Agreement [Doc. 37], Annex, Section 3, para. 1.
[13] See also Implementation Agreement [Doc. 37], Annex, Section 9, para. 7.

and exploitation in the Area, the financial management and internal administration of the Authority, and, upon the recommendation of the Governing Board of the Enterprise, to the transfer of funds from the Enterprise to the Authority;

(g)   to decide upon the equitable sharing of financial and other economic benefits derived from activities in the Area, consistent with this Convention and the rules, regulations and procedures of the Authority;

(h)   to consider and approve the proposed annual budget of the Authority submitted by the Council;

(i)   to examine periodic reports from the Council and from the Enterprise and special reports requested from the Council or any other organ of the Authority;

(j)   to initiate studies and make recommendations for the purpose of promoting international co-operation concerning activities in the Area and encouraging the progressive development of international law relating thereto and its codification;

(k)   to consider problems of a general nature in connection with activities in the Area arising in particular for developing States, as well as those problems for States in connection with activities in the Area that are due to their geographical location, particularly for land-locked and geographically disadvantaged States;

(l)   to establish, upon the recommendation of the Council, on the basis of advice from the Economic Planning Commission, a system of compensation or other measures of economic adjustment assistance as provided in article 151, paragraph 10;[14]

(m)   to suspend the exercise of rights and privileges of membership pursuant to article 185;

(n)   to discuss any question or matter within the competence of the Authority and to decide as to which organ of the Authority shall deal with any such question or matter not specifically entrusted to a particular organ, consistent with the distribution of powers and functions among the organs of the Authority.

Subsection C. The Council

Article 161 Composition, procedure and voting
   1.   The Council shall consist of 36 members of the Authority elected by the Assembly in the following order:

(a)   four members from among those States Parties which, during the last five years for which statistics are available, have either consumed more than 2 per cent of total world consumption or have had net imports of more than 2 per cent of total world imports of the commodities produced from the categories of minerals to be derived from the Area, and in any case one State from the Eastern European (Socialist) region, as well as the largest consumer;

(b)   four members from among the eight States Parties which have the largest investments in preparation for and in the conduct of activities in the Area, either directly or through their nationals, including at least one State from the Eastern European (Socialist) region;

(c)   four members from among States Parties which on the basis of production in areas under their jurisdiction are major net exporters of the categories of minerals to be derived from the Area, including at least two developing States whose exports of such minerals have a substantial bearing upon their economies;

---

[14] See also Implementation Agreement [Doc. 37], Annex, Section 7, para. 2.

(d)   six members from among developing States Parties, representing special interests. The special interests to be represented shall include those of States with large populations, States which are land-locked or geographically disadvantaged, States which are major importers of the categories of minerals to be derived from the Area, States which are potential producers of such minerals, and least developed States;

(e)   eighteen members elected according to the principle of ensuring an equitable geographical distribution of seats in the Council as a whole, provided that each geographical region shall have at least one member elected under this subparagraph. For this purpose, the geographical regions shall be Africa, Asia, Eastern European (Socialist), Latin America and Western European and Others.[15]

2.   In electing the members of the Council in accordance with paragraph 1, the Assembly shall ensure that:

(a)   land-locked and geographically disadvantaged States are represented to a degree which is reasonably proportionate to their representation in the Assembly;

(b)   coastal States, especially developing States, which do not qualify under paragraph 1(a), (b), (c) or (d) are represented to a degree which is reasonably proportionate to their representation in the Assembly;

(c)   each group of States Parties to be represented on the Council is represented by those members, if any, which are nominated by that group.

3.   Elections shall take place at regular sessions of the Assembly. Each member of the Council shall be elected for four years. At the first election, however, the term of one half of the members of each group referred to in paragraph 1 shall be two years.

4.   Members of the Council shall be eligible for re-election, but due regard should be paid to the desirability of rotation of membership.

5.   The Council shall function at the seat of the Authority, and shall meet as often as the business of the Authority may require, but not less than three times a year.

6.   A majority of the members of the Council shall constitute a quorum.

7.   Each member of the Council shall have one vote.

8.   (a)   Decisions on questions of procedure shall be taken by a majority of the members present and voting.

(b)   Decisions on questions of substance arising under the following provisions shall be taken by a two-thirds majority of the members present and voting, provided that such majority includes a majority of the members of the Council: article 162, paragraph 2, subparagraphs (f); (g); (h); (i); (n); (p); (v); article 191.[16]

(c)   Decisions on questions of substance arising under the following provisions shall be taken by a three-fourths majority of the members present and voting, provided that such majority includes a majority of the members of the Council: article 162, paragraph 1; article 162, paragraph 2, subparagraphs (a); (b); (c); (d); (e); (l); (q); (r); (s); (t); (u) in cases of non-compliance by a contractor or a sponsor; (w) provided that orders issued thereunder may be binding for not more than 30 days unless confirmed by a decision taken in accordance with subparagraph (d); article 162, paragraph 2, subparagraphs (x); (y); (z); article 163, paragraph 2; article 174, paragraph 3; Annex IV, article 11.[17]

---

[15] See also Implementation Agreement [Doc. 37], Annex, Section 3, paras. 16, 15, 9 and 10.
[16] See also Implementation Agreement [Doc. 37], Annex, Section 3, para. 8.
[17] See also Implementation Agreement [Doc. 37], Annex, Section 3, para. 8.

(d) Decisions on questions of substance arising under the following provisions shall be taken by consensus: article 162, paragraph 2(m) and (o); adoption of amendments to Part XI.

(e) For the purposes of subparagraphs (d), (f) and (g), 'consensus' means the absence of any formal objection. Within 14 days of the submission of a proposal to the Council, the President of the Council shall determine whether there would be a formal objection to the adoption of the proposal. If the President determines that there would be such an objection, the President shall establish and convene, within three days following such determination, a conciliation committee consisting of not more than nine members of the Council, with the President as chairman, for the purpose of reconciling the differences and producing a proposal which can be adopted by consensus. The committee shall work expeditiously and report to the Council within 14 days following its establishment. If the committee is unable to recommend a proposal which can be adopted by consensus, it shall set out in its report the grounds on which the proposal is being opposed.

(f) Decisions on questions not listed above which the Council is authorized to take by the rules, regulations and procedures of the Authority or otherwise shall be taken pursuant to the subparagraphs of this paragraph specified in the rules, regulations and procedures or, if not specified therein, then pursuant to the subparagraph determined by the Council if possible in advance, by consensus.

(g) When the issue arises as to whether a question is within subparagraph (a), (b), (c) or (d), the question shall be treated as being within the subparagraph requiring the higher or highest majority or consensus as the case may be, unless otherwise decided by the Council by the said majority or by consensus.[18]

9. The Council shall establish a procedure whereby a member of the Authority not represented on the Council may send a representative to attend a meeting of the Council when a request is made by such member, or a matter particularly affecting it is under consideration. Such a representative shall be entitled to participate in the deliberations but not to vote.

Article 162 Powers and functions

1. The Council is the executive organ of the Authority. The Council shall have the power to establish, in conformity with this Convention and the general policies established by the Assembly, the specific policies to be pursued by the Authority on any question or matter within the competence of the Authority.

2. In addition, the Council shall:

(a) supervise and co-ordinate the implementation of the provisions of this Part on all questions and matters within the competence of the Authority and invite the attention of the Assembly to cases of non-compliance;

(b) propose to the Assembly a list of candidates for the election of the Secretary-General;

(c) recommend to the Assembly candidates for the election of the members of the Governing Board of the Enterprise and the Director-General of the Enterprise;

(d) establish, as appropriate, and with due regard to economy and efficiency, such subsidiary organs as it finds necessary for the exercise of its functions in accord-

---

[18] See also Implementation Agreement [Doc. 37], Annex, Section 3, paras. 2, 5-7.

ance with this Part. In the composition of subsidiary organs, emphasis shall be placed on the need for members qualified and competent in relevant technical matters dealt with by those organs provided that due account shall be taken of the principle of equitable geographical distribution and of special interests;

(e)　adopt its rules of procedure including the method of selecting its president;

(f)　enter into agreements with the United Nations or other international organizations on behalf of the Authority and within its competence, subject to approval by the Assembly;

(g)　consider the reports of the Enterprise and transmit them to the Assembly with its recommendations;

(h)　present to the Assembly annual reports and such special reports as the Assembly may request;

(i)　issue directives to the Enterprise in accordance with article 170;

(j)　approve plans of work in accordance with Annex III, article 6. The Council shall act upon each plan of work within 60 days of its submission by the Legal and Technical Commission at a session of the Council in accordance with the following procedures:

　(i)　if the Commission recommends the approval of a plan of work, it shall be deemed to have been approved by the Council if no member of the Council submits in writing to the President within 14 days a specific objection alleging non-compliance with the requirements of Annex III, article 6. If there is an objection, the conciliation procedure set forth in article 161, paragraph 8(e), shall apply. If, at the end of the conciliation procedure, the objection is still maintained, the plan of work shall be deemed to have been approved by the Council unless the Council disapproves it by consensus among its members excluding any State or States making the application or sponsoring the applicant;

　(ii)　if the Commission recommends the disapproval of a plan of work or does not make a recommendation, the Council may approve the plan of work by a three-fourths majority of the members present and voting, provided that such majority includes a majority of the members participating in the session;[19]

(k)　approve plans of work submitted by the Enterprise in accordance with Annex IV, article 12, applying, *mutatis mutandis*, the procedures set forth in subparagraph (j);

(l)　exercise control over activities in the Area in accordance with article 153, paragraph 4, and the rules, regulations and procedures of the Authority;

(m)　take, upon the recommendation of the Economic Planning Commission, necessary and appropriate measures in accordance with article 150, subparagraph (h), to provide protection from the adverse economic effects specified therein;

(n)　make recommendations to the Assembly, on the basis of advice from the Economic Planning Commission, for a system of compensation or other measures of economic adjustment assistance as provided in article 151, paragraph 10;[20]

(o)　(i)　recommend to the Assembly rules, regulations and procedures on the equitable sharing of financial and other economic benefits derived from activities in the Area and the payments and contributions made pursuant to article 82, taking into particular consideration the interests and needs of

---

[19] See also Implementation Agreement [Doc. 37], Annex, Section 3, paras. 11 and 12.

[20] See also Implementation Agreement [Doc. 37], Annex, Section 7, para. 2.

the developing States and peoples who have not attained full independence or other self-governing status;

(ii) adopt and apply provisionally, pending approval by the Assembly, the rules, regulations and procedures of the Authority, and any amendments thereto, taking into account the recommendations of the Legal and Technical Commission or other subordinate organ concerned. These rules, regulations and procedures shall relate to prospecting, exploration and exploitation in the Area and the financial management and internal administration of the Authority. Priority shall be given to the adoption of rules, regulations and procedures for the exploration for and exploitation of polymetallic nodules. Rules, regulations and procedures for the exploration for and exploitation of any resource other than polymetallic nodules shall be adopted within three years from the date of a request to the Authority by any of its members to adopt such rules, regulations and procedures in respect of such resource. All rules, regulations and procedures shall remain in effect on a provisional basis until approved by the Assembly or until amended by the Council in the light of any views expressed by the Assembly;[21]

(p) review the collection of all payments to be made by or to the Authority in connection with operations pursuant to this Part;

(q) make the selection from among applicants for production authorizations pursuant to Annex III, article 7, where such selection is required by that provision;[22]

(r) submit the proposed annual budget of the Authority to the Assembly for its approval;

(s) make recommendations to the Assembly concerning policies on any question or matter within the competence of the Authority;

(t) make recommendations to the Assembly concerning suspension of the exercise of the rights and privileges of membership pursuant to article 185;

(u) institute proceedings on behalf of the Authority before the Sea-bed Disputes Chamber in cases of non-compliance;

(v) notify the Assembly upon a decision by the Sea-bed Disputes Chamber in proceedings instituted under subparagraph (u), and make any recommendations which it may find appropriate with respect to measures to be taken;

(w) issue emergency orders, which may include orders for the suspension or adjustment of operations, to prevent serious harm to the marine environment arising out of activities in the Area;

(x) disapprove areas for exploitation by contractors or the Enterprise in cases where substantial evidence indicates the risk of serious harm to the marine environment;

(y) establish a subsidiary organ for the elaboration of draft financial rules, regulations and procedures relating to:

(i) financial management in accordance with articles 171 to 175; and

(ii) financial arrangements in accordance with Annex III, article 13 and article 17, paragraph 1(c);[23]

(z) establish appropriate mechanisms for directing and supervising a staff of inspectors who shall inspect activities in the Area to determine whether this Part, the rules, regulations and procedures of the Authority, and the terms and conditions of any contract with the Authority are being complied with.

---

[21] See also Implementation Agreement [Doc. 37], Annex, Section 1, paras. 15 and 16.

[22] See also Implementation Agreement [Doc. 37], Annex, Section 6, para. 7.

[23] See also Implementation Agreement [Doc. 37], Annex, Section 9 and, in particular, para. 9.

Article 163 Organs of the Council

1.   There are hereby established the following organs of the Council:

(a)   an Economic Planning Commission;

(b)   a Legal and Technical Commission.

2.   Each Commission shall be composed of 15 members, elected by the Council from among the candidates nominated by the States Parties. However, if necessary, the Council may decide to increase the size of either Commission having due regard to economy and efficiency.

3.   Members of a Commission shall have appropriate qualifications in the area of competence of that Commission. States Parties shall nominate candidates of the highest standards of competence and integrity with qualifications in relevant fields so as to ensure the effective exercise of the functions of the Commissions.

4.   In the election of members of the Commissions, due account shall be taken of the need for equitable geographical distribution and the representation of special interests.

5.   No State Party may nominate more than one candidate for the same Commission. No person shall be elected to serve on more than one Commission.

6.   Members of the Commissions shall hold office for a term of five years. They shall be eligible for re-election for a further term.

7.   In the event of the death, incapacity or resignation of a member of a Commission prior to the expiration of the term of office, the Council shall elect for the remainder of the term, a member from the same geographical region or area of interest.

8.   Members of Commissions shall have no financial interest in any activity relating to exploration and exploitation in the Area. Subject to their responsibilities to the Commissions upon which they serve, they shall not disclose, even after the termination of their functions, any industrial secret, proprietary data which are transferred to the Authority in accordance with Annex III, article 14, or any other confidential information coming to their knowledge by reason of their duties for the Authority.

9.   Each Commission shall exercise its functions in accordance with such guidelines and directives as the Council may adopt.

10.   Each Commission shall formulate and submit to the Council for approval such rules and regulations as may be necessary for the efficient conduct of the Commission's functions.

11.   The decision-making procedures of the Commissions shall be established by the rules, regulations and procedures of the Authority. Recommendations to the Council shall, where necessary, be accompanied by a summary on the divergencies of opinion in the Commission.[24]

12.   Each Commission shall normally function at the seat of the Authority and shall meet as often as is required for the efficient exercise of its functions.

13.   In the exercise of its functions, each Commission may, where appropriate, consult another commission, any competent organ of the United Nations or of its specialized agencies or any international organizations with competence in the subject-matter of such consultation.

Article 164 The Economic Planning Commission

1.   Members of the Economic Planning Commission shall have appropriate qualifications such as those relevant to mining, management of mineral resource activities, international trade or international economics. The Council shall endeavour to ensure that the membership of the Commission reflects all appropriate qualifications. The Commission shall include at least two members from developing States whose exports

---

[24] See also Implementation Agreement [Doc. 37], Annex, Section 3, paras. 2 and 13.

of the categories of minerals to be derived from the Area have a substantial bearing upon their economies.[25]

2. The Commission shall:

(a) propose, upon the request of the Council, measures to implement decisions relating to activities in the Area taken in accordance with this Convention;

(b) review the trends of and the factors affecting supply, demand and prices of minerals which may be derived from the Area, bearing in mind the interests of both importing and exporting countries, and in particular of the developing States among them;

(c) examine any situation likely to lead to the adverse effects referred to in article 150, subparagraph (h), brought to its attention by the State Party or States Parties concerned, and make appropriate recommendations to the Council;

(d) propose to the Council for submission to the Assembly, as provided in article 151, paragraph 10, a system of compensation or other measures of economic adjustment assistance for developing States which suffer adverse effects caused by activities in the Area. The Commission shall make the recommendations to the Council that are necessary for the application of the system or other measures adopted by the Assembly in specific cases.[26]

Article 165 The Legal and Technical Commission

1. Members of the Legal and Technical Commission shall have appropriate qualifications such as those relevant to exploration for and exploitation and processing of mineral resources, oceanology, protection of the marine environment, or economic or legal matters relating to ocean mining and related fields of expertise. The Council shall endeavour to ensure that the membership of the Commission reflects all appropriate qualifications.

2. The Commission shall:

(a) make recommendations with regard to the exercise of the Authority's functions upon the request of the Council;

(b) review formal written plans of work for activities in the Area in accordance with article 153, paragraph 3, and submit appropriate recommendations to the Council. The Commission shall base its recommendations solely on the grounds stated in Annex III and shall report fully thereon to the Council;

(c) supervise, upon the request of the Council, activities in the Area, where appropriate, in consultation and collaboration with any entity carrying out such activities or State or States concerned and report to the Council;

(d) prepare assessments of the environmental implications of activities in the Area;

(e) make recommendations to the Council on the protection of the marine environment, taking into account the views of recognized experts in that field;

(f) formulate and submit to the Council the rules, regulations and procedures referred to in article 162, paragraph 2(o), taking into account all relevant factors including assessments of the environmental implications of activities in the Area;

(g) keep such rules, regulations and procedures under review and recommend to the Council from time to time such amendments thereto as it may deem necessary or desirable;

(h) make recommendations to the Council regarding the establishment of a monitoring programme to observe, measure, evaluate and analyse, by recognized scientific methods, on a regular basis, the risks or effects of

---

[25] See also Implementation Agreement [Doc. 37], Annex, Section 1, para. 4.
[26] See also Implementation Agreement [Doc. 37], Annex, Section 7, para. 2.

pollution of the marine environment resulting from activities in the Area, ensure that existing regulations are adequate and are complied with and co-ordinate the implementation of the monitoring programme approved by the Council;

(i)   recommend to the Council that proceedings be instituted on behalf of the Authority before the Sea-bed Disputes Chamber, in accordance with this Part and the relevant Annexes taking into account particularly article 187;

(j)   make recommendations to the Council with respect to measures to be taken, upon a decision by the Sea-bed Disputes Chamber in proceedings instituted in accordance with subparagraph (i);

(k)   make recommendations to the Council to issue emergency orders, which may include orders for the suspension or adjustment of operations, to prevent serious harm to the marine environment arising out of activities in the Area. Such recommendations shall be taken up by the Council on a priority basis;

(l)   make recommendations to the Council to disapprove areas for exploitation by contractors or the Enterprise in cases where substantial evidence indicates the risk of serious harm to the marine environment;

(m)   make recommendations to the Council regarding the direction and supervision of a staff of inspectors who shall inspect activities in the Area to determine whether the provisions of this Part, the rules, regulations and procedures of the Authority, and the terms and conditions of any contract with the Authority are being complied with;

(n)   calculate the production ceiling and issue production authorizations on behalf of the Authority pursuant to article 151, paragraphs 2 to 7, following any necessary selection among applicants for production authorizations by the Council in accordance with Annex III, article 7.[27]

3.   The members of the Commission shall, upon request by any State Party or other party concerned, be accompanied by a representative of such State or other party concerned when carrying out their function of supervision and inspection.

Subsection D. The Secretariat

Article 166 The Secretariat

1.   The Secretariat of the Authority shall comprise a Secretary-General and such staff as the Authority may require.

2.   The Secretary-General shall be elected for four years by the Assembly from among the candidates proposed by the Council and may be re-elected.

3.   The Secretary-General shall be the chief administrative officer of the Authority, and shall act in that capacity in all meetings of the Assembly, of the Council and of any subsidiary organ, and shall perform such other administrative functions as are entrusted to the Secretary-General by these organs.

4.   The Secretary-General shall make an annual report to the Assembly on the work of the Authority.

Article 167 The staff of the Authority

1.   The staff of the Authority shall consist of such qualified scientific and technical and other personnel as may be required to fulfil the administrative functions of the Authority.

2.   The paramount consideration in the recruitment and employment of the staff and in the determination of their conditions of service shall be the necessity of securing the highest standards of efficiency, competence and integrity. Subject to this consideration,

---

[27] See also Implementation Agreement [Doc. 37], Annex, Section 6, para. 7.

due regard shall be paid to the importance of recruiting the staff on as wide a geographical basis as possible.

3. The staff shall be appointed by the Secretary-General. The terms and conditions on which they shall be appointed, remunerated and dismissed shall be in accordance with the rules, regulations and procedures of the Authority.

Article 168 International character of the Secretariat

1. In the performance of their duties the Secretary-General and the staff shall not seek or receive instructions from any government or from any other source external to the Authority. They shall refrain from any action which might reflect on their position as international officials responsible only to the Authority. Each State Party undertakes to respect the exclusively international character of the responsibilities of the Secretary-General and the staff and not to seek to influence them in the discharge of their responsibilities. Any violation of responsibilities by a staff member shall be submitted to the appropriate administrative tribunal as provided in the rules, regulations and procedures of the Authority.

2. The Secretary-General and the staff shall have no financial interest in any activity relating to exploration and exploitation in the Area. Subject to their responsibilities to the Authority, they shall not disclose, even after the termination of their functions, any industrial secret, proprietary data which are transferred to the Authority in accordance with Annex III, article 14, or any other confidential information coming to their knowledge by reason of their employment with the Authority.

3. Violations of the obligations of a staff member of the Authority set forth in paragraph 2 shall, on the request of a State Party affected by such violation, or a natural or juridical person, sponsored by a State Party as provided in article 153, paragraph 2(b), and affected by such violation, be submitted by the Authority against the staff member concerned to a tribunal designated by the rules, regulations and procedures of the Authority. The Party affected shall have the right to take part in the proceedings. If the tribunal so recommends, the Secretary-General shall dismiss the staff member concerned.

4. The rules, regulations and procedures of the Authority shall contain such provisions as are necessary to implement this article.

Article 169 Consultation and co-operation with international and non-governmental organizations

1. The Secretary-General shall, on matters within the competence of the Authority, make suitable arrangements, with the approval of the Council, for consultation and co-operation with international and non-governmental organizations recognized by the Economic and Social Council of the United Nations.

2. Any organization with which the Secretary-General has entered into an arrangement under paragraph 1 may designate representatives to attend meetings of the organs of the Authority as observers in accordance with the rules of procedure of these organs. Procedures shall be established for obtaining the views of such organizations in appropriate cases.

3. The Secretary-General may distribute to States Parties written reports submitted by the non-governmental organizations referred to in paragraph 1 on subjects in which they have special competence and which are related to the work of the Authority.

Subsection E. The Enterprise

Article 170 The Enterprise[28]

1. The Enterprise shall be the organ of the Authority which shall carry out activities in the Area directly, pursuant to article 153, paragraph 2(a), as well as the transporting, processing and marketing of minerals recovered from the Area.

2. The Enterprise shall, within the framework of the international legal personality of the Authority, have such legal capacity as is provided for in the Statute set forth in Annex IV. The Enterprise shall act in accordance with this Convention and the rules, regulations and procedures of the Authority, as well as the general policies established by the Assembly, and shall be subject to the directives and control of the Council.

3. The Enterprise shall have its principal place of business at the seat of the Authority.

4. The Enterprise shall, in accordance with article 173, paragraph 2, and Annex IV, article 11, be provided with such funds as it may require to carry out its functions, and shall receive technology as provided in article 144 and other relevant provisions of this Convention.

Subsection F. Financial Arrangements of the Authority

Article 171 Funds of the Authority

The funds of the Authority shall include:

(a) assessed contributions made by members of the Authority in accordance with article 160, paragraph 2(e);

(b) funds received by the Authority pursuant to Annex III, article 13, in connection with activities in the Area;

(c) funds transferred from the Enterprise in accordance with Annex IV, article 10;

(d) funds borrowed pursuant to article 174;

(e) voluntary contributions made by members or other entities; and

(f) payments to a compensation fund, in accordance with article 151, paragraph 10, whose sources are to be recommended by the Economic Planning Commission.[29]

Article 172 Annual budget of the Authority[30]

The Secretary-General shall draft the proposed annual budget of the Authority and submit it to the Council. The Council shall consider the proposed annual budget and submit it to the Assembly, together with any recommendations thereon. The Assembly shall consider and approve the proposed annual budget in accordance with article 160, paragraph 2(h).

Article 173 Expenses of the Authority

1. The contributions referred to in article 171, subparagraph (a), shall be paid into a special account to meet the administrative expenses of the Authority until the Authority has sufficient funds from other sources to meet those expenses.

2. The administrative expenses of the Authority shall be a first call upon the funds of the Authority. Except for the assessed contributions referred to in article 171, subparagraph (a), the funds which remain after payment of administrative expenses may, *inter alia*:

---

[28] See also Implementation Agreement [Doc. 37], Annex, Section 2.

[29] See also Implementation Agreement [Doc. 37], Annex, Section 7, para. 2.

[30] See also Implementation Agreement [Doc. 37], Annex, Section 1, para. 14, and Section 9, para. 7.

(a) be shared in accordance with article 140 and article 160, paragraph 2(g);

(b) be used to provide the Enterprise with funds in accordance with article 170, paragraph 4;

(c) be used to compensate developing States in accordance with article 151, paragraph 10, and article 160, paragraph 2(l).[31]

Article 174 Borrowing power of the Authority

1. The Authority shall have the power to borrow funds.[32]

2. The Assembly shall prescribe the limits on the borrowing power of the Authority in the financial regulations adopted pursuant to article 160, paragraph 2(f).

3. The Council shall exercise the borrowing power of the Authority.

4. States Parties shall not be liable for the debts of the Authority.

Article 175 Annual audit

The records, books and accounts of the Authority, including its annual financial statements, shall be audited annually by an independent auditor appointed by the Assembly.

Subsection G. Legal Status, Privileges and Immunities

Article 176 Legal status

The Authority shall have international legal personality and such legal capacity as may be necessary for the exercise of its functions and the fulfilment of its purposes.

Article 177 Privileges and immunities

To enable the Authority to exercise its functions, it shall enjoy in the territory of each State Party the privileges and immunities set forth in this subsection. The privileges and immunities relating to the Enterprise shall be those set forth in Annex IV, article 13.

Article 178 Immunity from legal process

The Authority, its property and assets, shall enjoy immunity from legal process except to the extent that the Authority expressly waives this immunity in a particular case.

Article 179 Immunity from search and any form of seizure

The property and assets of the Authority, wherever located and by whomsoever held, shall be immune from search, requisition, confiscation, expropriation or any other form of seizure by executive or legislative action.

Article 180 Exemption from restrictions, regulations, controls and moratoria

The property and assets of the Authority shall be exempt from restrictions, regulations, controls and moratoria of any nature.

Article 181 Archives and official communications of the Authority

1. The archives of the Authority, wherever located, shall be inviolable.

2. Proprietary data, industrial secrets or similar information and personnel records shall not be placed in archives which are open to public inspection.

---

[31] See also Implementation Agreement [Doc. 37], Annex, Section 7, para. 2.

[32] See also Implementation Agreement [Doc. 37], Annex, Section 1, para. 14.

3. With regard to its official communications, the Authority shall be accorded by each State Party treatment no less favourable than that accorded by that State to other international organizations.

Article 182 Privileges and immunities of certain persons connected with the Authority

Representatives of States Parties attending meetings of the Assembly, the Council or organs of the Assembly or the Council, and the Secretary-General and staff of the Authority, shall enjoy in the territory of each State Party:

(a) immunity from legal process with respect to acts performed by them in the exercise of their functions, except to the extent that the State which they represent or the Authority, as appropriate, expressly waives this immunity in a particular case;

(b) if they are not nationals of that State Party, the same exemptions from immigration restrictions, alien registration requirements and national service obligations, the same facilities as regards exchange restrictions and the same treatment in respect of travelling facilities as are accorded by that State to the representatives, officials and employees of comparable rank of other States Parties.

Article 183 Exemption from taxes and customs duties

1. Within the scope of its official activities, the Authority, its assets and property, its income, and its operations and transactions, authorized by this Convention, shall be exempt from all direct taxation and goods imported or exported for its official use shall be exempt from all customs duties. The Authority shall not claim exemption from taxes which are no more than charges for services rendered.

2. When purchases of goods or services of substantial value necessary for the official activities of the Authority are made by or on behalf of the Authority, and when the price of such goods or services includes taxes or duties, appropriate measures shall, to the extent practicable, be taken by States Parties to grant exemption from such taxes or duties or provide for their reimbursement. Goods imported or purchased under an exemption provided for in this article shall not be sold or otherwise disposed of in the territory of the State Party which granted the exemption, except under conditions agreed with that State Party.

3. No tax shall be levied by States Parties on or in respect of salaries and emoluments paid or any other form of payment made by the Authority to the Secretary-General and staff of the Authority, as well as experts performing missions for the Authority, who are not their nationals.

Subsection H. Suspension of the Exercise of Rights and Privileges of Members

Article 184 Suspension of the exercise of voting rights

A State Party which is in arrears in the payment of its financial contributions to the Authority shall have no vote if the amount of its arrears equals or exceeds the amount of the contributions due from it for the preceding two full years. The Assembly may, nevertheless, permit such a member to vote if it is satisfied that the failure to pay is due to conditions beyond the control of the member.

Article 185 Suspension of exercise of rights and privileges of membership

1. A State Party which has grossly and persistently violated the provisions of this Part may be suspended from the exercise of the rights and privileges of membership by the Assembly upon the recommendation of the Council.

2. No action may be taken under paragraph 1 until the Seabed Disputes Chamber has found that a State Party has grossly and persistently violated the provisions of this Part.

SECTION 5. SETTLEMENT OF DISPUTES AND ADVISORY OPINIONS

Article 186 Sea-bed Disputes Chamber of the International Tribunal for the Law of the Sea

The establishment of the Sea-bed Disputes Chamber and the manner in which it shall exercise its jurisdiction shall be governed by the provisions of this section, of Part XV and of Annex VI.

Article 187 Jurisdiction of the Sea-bed Disputes Chamber

The Sea-bed Disputes Chamber shall have jurisdiction under this Part and the Annexes relating thereto in disputes with respect to activities in the Area falling within the following categories:

(a) disputes between States Parties concerning the interpretation or application of this Part and the Annexes relating thereto;

(b) disputes between a State Party and the Authority concerning:

   (i) acts or omissions of the Authority or of a State Party alleged to be in violation of this Part or the Annexes relating thereto or of rules, regulations and procedures of the Authority adopted in accordance therewith; or

   (ii) acts of the Authority alleged to be in excess of jurisdiction or a misuse of power;

(c) disputes between parties to a contract, being States Parties, the Authority or the Enterprise, state enterprises and natural or juridical persons referred to in article 153, paragraph 2(b), concerning:

   (i) the interpretation or application of a relevant contract or a plan of work; or

   (ii) acts or omissions of a party to the contract relating to activities in the Area and directed to the other party or directly affecting its legitimate interests;

(d) disputes between the Authority and a prospective contractor who has been sponsored by a State as provided in article 153, paragraph 2(b), and has duly fulfilled the conditions referred to in Annex III, article 4, paragraph 6, and article 13, paragraph 2, concerning the refusal of a contract or a legal issue arising in the negotiation of the contract;

(e) disputes between the Authority and a State Party, a state enterprise or a natural or juridical person sponsored by a State Party as provided for in article 153, paragraph 2(b), where it is alleged that the Authority has incurred liability as provided in Annex III, article 22;

(f) any other disputes for which the jurisdiction of the Chamber is specifically provided in this Convention.

Article 188 Submission of disputes to a special chamber of the International Tribunal for the Law of the Sea or an *ad hoc* chamber of the Sea-bed Disputes Chamber or to binding commercial arbitration

1. Disputes between States Parties referred to in article 187, subparagraph (a), may be submitted:

(a) at the request of the parties to the dispute, to a special chamber of the International Tribunal for the Law of the Sea to be formed in accordance with Annex VI, articles 15 and 17; or

(b) at the request of any party to the dispute, to an *ad hoc* chamber of the Sea-bed Disputes Chamber to be formed in accordance with Annex VI, article 36.

2. (a) Disputes concerning the interpretation or application of a contract referred to in article 187, subparagraph (c)(i), shall be submitted, at the request of any party to the dispute, to binding commercial arbitration, unless the parties otherwise agree. A commercial arbitral tribunal to which the dispute is submitted shall have no jurisdiction to decide any question of interpretation of this Convention. When the dispute also involves a question of the interpretation of Part XI and the Annexes relating thereto, with respect to activities in the Area, that question shall be referred to the Sea-bed Disputes Chamber for a ruling.

(b) If, at the commencement of or in the course of such arbitration, the arbitral tribunal determines, either at the request of any party to the dispute or *proprio motu*, that its decision depends upon a ruling of the Sea-bed Disputes Chamber, the arbitral tribunal shall refer such question to the Sea-bed Disputes Chamber for such ruling. The arbitral tribunal shall then proceed to render its award in conformity with the ruling of the Sea-bed Disputes Chamber.

(c) In the absence of a provision in the contract on the arbitration procedure to be applied in the dispute, the arbitration shall be conducted in accordance with the UNCITRAL Arbitration Rules or such other arbitration rules as may be prescribed in the rules, regulations and procedures of the Authority, unless the parties to the dispute otherwise agree.

Article 189 Limitation on jurisdiction with regard to decisions of the Authority

The Sea-bed Disputes Chamber shall have no jurisdiction with regard to the exercise by the Authority of its discretionary powers in accordance with this Part; in no case shall it substitute its discretion for that of the Authority. Without prejudice to article 191, in exercising its jurisdiction pursuant to article 187, the Sea-bed Disputes Chamber shall not pronounce itself on the question of whether any rules, regulations and procedures of the Authority are in conformity with this Convention, nor declare invalid any such rules, regulations and procedures. Its jurisdiction in this regard shall be confined to deciding claims that the application of any rules, regulations and procedures of the Authority in individual cases would be in conflict with the contractual obligations of the parties to the dispute or their obligations under this Convention, claims concerning excess of jurisdiction or misuse of power, and to claims for damages to be paid or other remedy to be given to the party concerned for the failure of the other party to comply with its contractual obligations or its obligations under this Convention.

Article 190 Participation and appearance of sponsoring States Parties in proceedings

1. If a natural or juridical person is a party to a dispute referred to in article 187, the sponsoring State shall be given notice thereof and shall have the right to participate in the proceedings by submitting written or oral statements.

2. If an action is brought against a State Party by a natural or juridical person sponsored by another State Party in a dispute referred to in article 187, subparagraph (c), the respondent State may request the State sponsoring that person to appear in the proceedings on behalf of that person. Failing such appearance, the respondent State may arrange to be represented by a juridical person of its nationality.

Article 191 Advisory opinions

The Sea-bed Disputes Chamber shall give advisory opinions at the request of the Assembly or the Council on legal questions arising within the scope of their activities. Such opinions shall be given as a matter of urgency.

PART XII
PROTECTION AND PRESERVATION OF THE MARINE ENVIRONMENT

SECTION 1. GENERAL PROVISIONS

Article 192 General obligation

States have the obligation to protect and preserve the marine environment.

Article 193 Sovereign right of States to exploit their natural resources

States have the sovereign right to exploit their natural resources pursuant to their environmental policies and in accordance with their duty to protect and preserve the marine environment.

Article 194 Measures to prevent, reduce and control pollution of the marine environment

1. States shall take, individually or jointly as appropriate, all measures consistent with this Convention that are necessary to prevent, reduce and control pollution of the marine environment from any source, using for this purpose the best practicable means at their disposal and in accordance with their capabilities, and they shall endeavour to harmonize their policies in this connection.

2. States shall take all measures necessary to ensure that activities under their jurisdiction or control are so conducted as not to cause damage by pollution to other States and their environment, and that pollution arising from incidents or activities under their jurisdiction or control does not spread beyond the areas where they exercise sovereign rights in accordance with this Convention.

3. The measures taken pursuant to this Part shall deal with all sources of pollution of the marine environment. These measures shall include, *inter alia*, those designed to minimize to the fullest possible extent:

(a) the release of toxic, harmful or noxious substances, especially those which are persistent, from land-based sources, from or through the atmosphere or by dumping;

(b) pollution from vessels, in particular measures for preventing accidents and dealing with emergencies, ensuring the safety of operations at sea, preventing intentional and unintentional discharges, and regulating the design, construction, equipment, operation and manning of vessels;

(c) pollution from installations and devices used in exploration or exploitation of the natural resources of the sea-bed and subsoil, in particular measures for preventing accidents and dealing with emergencies, ensuring the safety of operations at sea, and regulating the design, construction, equipment, operation and manning of such installations or devices;

(d) pollution from other installations and devices operating in the marine environment, in particular measures for preventing accidents and dealing with emergencies, ensuring the safety of operations at sea, and regulating the design, construction, equipment, operation and manning of such installations or devices.

4. In taking measures to prevent, reduce or control pollution of the marine environment, States shall refrain from unjustifiable interference with activities carried out by other States in the exercise of their rights and in pursuance of their duties in conformity with this Convention.

5. The measures taken in accordance with this Part shall include those necessary to protect and preserve rare or fragile ecosystems as well as the habitat of depleted, threatened or endangered species and other forms of marine life.

Article 195 Duty not to transfer damage or hazards or transform one type of pollution into another

In taking measures to prevent, reduce and control pollution of the marine environment, States shall act so as not to transfer, directly or indirectly, damage or hazards from one area to another or transform one type of pollution into another.

Article 196 Use of technologies or introduction of alien or new species

1. States shall take all measures necessary to prevent, reduce and control pollution of the marine environment resulting from the use of technologies under their jurisdiction or control, or the intentional or accidental introduction of species, alien or new, to a particular part of the marine environment, which may cause significant and harmful changes thereto.

2. This article does not affect the application of this Convention regarding the prevention, reduction and control of pollution of the marine environment.

SECTION 2. GLOBAL AND REGIONAL CO-OPERATION

Article 197 Co-operation on a global or regional basis

States shall co-operate on a global basis and, as appropriate, on a regional basis, directly or through competent international organizations, in formulating and elaborating international rules, standards and recommended practices and procedures consistent with this Convention, for the protection and preservation of the marine environment, taking into account characteristic regional features.

Article 198 Notification of imminent or actual damage

When a State becomes aware of cases in which the marine environment is in imminent danger of being damaged or has been damaged by pollution, it shall immediately notify other States it deems likely to be affected by such damage, as well as the competent international organizations.

Article 199 Contingency plans against pollution

In the cases referred to in article 198, States in the area affected, in accordance with their capabilities, and the competent international organizations shall co-operate, to the extent possible, in eliminating the effects of pollution and preventing or minimizing the damage. To this end, States shall jointly develop and promote contingency plans for responding to pollution incidents in the marine environment.

Article 200 Studies, research programmes and exchange of information and data

States shall co-operate, directly or through competent international organizations, for the purpose of promoting studies, undertaking programmes of scientific research and encouraging the exchange of information and data acquired about pollution of the marine environment. They shall endeavour to participate actively in regional and global programmes to acquire knowledge for the assessment of the nature and extent of pollution, exposure to it, and its pathways, risks and remedies.

Article 201 Scientific criteria for regulations

In the light of the information and data acquired pursuant to article 200, States shall co-operate, directly or through competent international organizations, in establishing appropriate scientific criteria for the formulation and elaboration of rules, standards and recommended practices and procedures for the prevention, reduction and control of pollution of the marine environment.

SECTION 3. TECHNICAL ASSISTANCE

Article 202 Scientific and technical assistance to developing States

States shall, directly or through competent international organizations:
   (a) promote programmes of scientific, educational, technical and other assistance to developing States for the protection and preservation of the marine environment and the prevention, reduction and control of marine pollution. Such assistance shall include, *inter alia*:
      (i) training of their scientific and technical personnel;
      (ii) facilitating their participation in relevant international programmes;
      (iii) supplying them with necessary equipment and facilities;
      (iv) enhancing their capacity to manufacture such equipment;
      (v) advice on and developing facilities for research, monitoring, educational and other programmes;
   (b) provide appropriate assistance, especially to developing States, for the minimization of the effects of major incidents which may cause serious pollution of the marine environment;
   (c) provide appropriate assistance, especially to developing States, concerning the preparation of environmental assessments.

Article 203 Preferential treatment for developing States

Developing States shall, for the purposes of prevention, reduction and control of pollution of the marine environment or minimization of its effects, be granted preference by international organizations in:
   (a) the allocation of appropriate funds and technical assistance; and
   (b) the utilization of their specialized services.

Article 204 Monitoring of the risks or effects of pollution

1. States shall, consistent with the rights of other States, endeavour, as far as practicable, directly or through the competent international organizations, to observe, measure, evaluate and analyse, by recognized scientific methods, the risks or effects of pollution of the marine environment.

2. In particular, States shall keep under surveillance the effects of any activities which they permit or in which they engage in order to determine whether these activities are likely to pollute the marine environment.

Article 205 Publication of reports

States shall publish reports of the results obtained pursuant to article 204 or provide such reports at appropriate intervals to the competent international organizations, which should make them available to all States.

Article 206 Assessment of potential effects of activities

When States have reasonable grounds for believing that planned activities under their jurisdiction or control may cause substantial pollution of or significant and harmful changes to the marine environment, they shall, as far as practicable, assess the potential effects of such activities on the marine environment and shall communicate reports of the results of such assessments in the manner provided in article 205.

SECTION 5. INTERNATIONAL RULES AND NATIONAL LEGISLATION TO PREVENT, REDUCE AND CONTROL POLLUTION OF THE MARINE ENVIRONMENT

Article 207 Pollution from land-based sources

1. States shall adopt laws and regulations to prevent, reduce and control pollution of the marine environment from land-based sources, including rivers, estuaries, pipelines and outfall structures, taking into account internationally agreed rules, standards and recommended practices and procedures.

2. States shall take other measures as may be necessary to prevent, reduce and control such pollution.

3. States shall endeavour to harmonize their policies in this connection at the appropriate regional level.

4. States, acting especially through competent international organizations or diplomatic conference, shall endeavour to establish global and regional rules, standards and recommended practices and procedures to prevent, reduce and control pollution of the marine environment from land-based sources, taking into account characteristic regional features, the economic capacity of developing States and their need for economic development. Such rules, standards and recommended practices and procedures shall be re-examined from time to time as necessary.

5. Laws, regulations, measures, rules, standards and recommended practices and procedures referred to in paragraphs 1, 2 and 4 shall include those designed to minimize, to the fullest extent possible, the release of toxic, harmful or noxious substances, especially those which are persistent, into the marine environment.

Article 208 Pollution from seabed activities subject to national jurisdiction

1. Coastal States shall adopt laws and regulations to prevent, reduce and control pollution of the marine environment arising from or in connection with sea-bed activities

subject to their jurisdiction and from artificial islands, installations and structures under their jurisdiction, pursuant to articles 60 and 80.

2.   States shall take other measures as may be necessary to prevent, reduce and control such pollution.

3.   Such laws, regulations and measures shall be no less effective than international rules, standards and recommended practices and procedures.

4.   States shall endeavour to harmonize their policies in this connection at the appropriate regional level.

5.   States, acting especially through competent international organizations or diplomatic conference, shall establish global and regional rules, standards and recommended practices and procedures to prevent, reduce and control pollution of the marine environment referred to in paragraph 1. Such rules, standards and recommended practices and procedures shall be re-examined from time to time as necessary.

Article 209   Pollution from activities in the Area

1.   International rules, regulations and procedures shall be established in accordance with Part XI to prevent, reduce and control pollution of the marine environment from activities in the Area. Such rules, regulations and procedures shall be re-examined from time to time as necessary.

2.   Subject to the relevant provisions of this section, States shall adopt laws and regulations to prevent, reduce and control pollution of the marine environment from activities in the Area undertaken by vessels, installations, structures and other devices flying their flag or of their registry or operating under their authority, as the case may be. The requirements of such laws and regulations shall be no less effective than the international rules, regulations and procedures referred to in paragraph 1.

Article 210   Pollution by dumping

1.   States shall adopt laws and regulations to prevent, reduce and control pollution of the marine environment by dumping.

2.   States shall take other measures as may be necessary to prevent, reduce and control such pollution.

3.   Such laws, regulations and measures shall ensure that dumping is not carried out without the permission of the competent authorities of States.

4.   States, acting especially through competent international organizations or diplomatic conference, shall endeavour to establish global and regional rules, standards and recommended practices and procedures to prevent, reduce and control such pollution. Such rules, standards and recommended practices and procedures shall be re-examined from time to time as necessary.

5.   Dumping within the territorial sea and the exclusive economic zone or onto the continental shelf shall not be carried out without the express prior approval of the coastal State, which has the right to permit, regulate and control such dumping after due consideration of the matter with other States which by reason of their geographical situation may be adversely affected thereby.

6.   National laws, regulations and measures shall be no less effective in preventing, reducing and controlling such pollution than the global rules and standards.

Article 211   Pollution from vessels

1.   States, acting through the competent international organization or general diplomatic conference, shall establish international rules and standards to prevent, reduce and control pollution of the marine environment from vessels and promote the adoption,

in the same manner, wherever appropriate, of routeing systems designed to minimize the threat of accidents which might cause pollution of the marine environment, including the coastline, and pollution damage to the related interests of coastal States. Such rules and standards shall, in the same manner, be re-examined from time to time as necessary.

2. States shall adopt laws and regulations for the prevention, reduction and control of pollution of the marine environment from vessels flying their flag or of their registry. Such laws and regulations shall at least have the same effect as that of generally accepted international rules and standards established through the competent international organization or general diplomatic conference.

3. States which establish particular requirements for the prevention, reduction and control of pollution of the marine environment as a condition for the entry of foreign vessels into their ports or internal waters or for a call at their off-shore terminals shall give due publicity to such requirements and shall communicate them to the competent international organization. Whenever such requirements are established in identical form by two or more coastal States in an endeavour to harmonize policy, the communication shall indicate which States are participating in such cooperative arrangements. Every State shall require the master of a vessel flying its flag or of its registry, when navigating within the territorial sea of a State participating in such co-operative arrangements, to furnish, upon the request of that State, information as to whether it is proceeding to a State of the same region participating in such cooperative arrangements and, if so, to indicate whether it complies with the port entry requirements of that State. This article is without prejudice to the continued exercise by a vessel of its right of innocent passage or to the application of article 25, paragraph 2.

4. Coastal States may, in the exercise of their sovereignty within their territorial sea, adopt laws and regulations for the prevention, reduction and control of marine pollution from foreign vessels, including vessels exercising the right of innocent passage. Such laws and regulations shall, in accordance with Part II, section 3, not hamper innocent passage of foreign vessels.

5. Coastal States, for the purpose of enforcement as provided for in section 6, may in respect of their exclusive economic zones adopt laws and regulations for the prevention, reduction and control of pollution from vessels conforming to and giving effect to generally accepted international rules and standards established through the competent international organization or general diplomatic conference.

6. (a) Where the international rules and standards referred to in paragraph 1 are inadequate to meet special circumstances and coastal States have reasonable grounds for believing that a particular, clearly defined area of their respective exclusive economic zones is an area where the adoption of special mandatory measures for the prevention of pollution from vessels is required for recognized technical reasons in relation to its oceanographical and ecological conditions, as well as its utilization or the protection of its resources and the particular character of its traffic, the coastal States, after appropriate consultations through the competent international organization with any other States concerned, may, for that area, direct a communication to that organization, submitting scientific and technical evidence in support and information on necessary reception facilities. Within 12 months after receiving such a communication, the organization shall determine whether the conditions in that area correspond to the requirements set out above. If the organization so determines, the coastal States may, for that area, adopt laws and regulations for the prevention, reduction and control of pollution

from vessels implementing such international rules and standards or navigational practices as are made applicable, through the organization, for special areas. These laws and regulations shall not become applicable to foreign vessels until 15 months after the submission of the communication to the organization.

(b) The coastal States shall publish the limits of any such particular, clearly defined area.

(c) If the coastal States intend to adopt additional laws and regulations for the same area for the prevention, reduction and control of pollution from vessels, they shall, when submitting the aforesaid communication, at the same time notify the organization thereof. Such additional laws and regulations may relate to discharges or navigational practices but shall not require foreign vessels to observe design, construction, manning or equipment standards other than generally accepted international rules and standards; they shall become applicable to foreign vessels 15 months after the submission of the communication to the organization, provided that the organization agrees within 12 months after the submission of the communication.

7. The international rules and standards referred to in this article should include *inter alia* those relating to prompt notification to coastal States, whose coastline or related interests may be affected by incidents, including maritime casualties, which involve discharges or probability of discharges.

Article 212 Pollution from or through the atmosphere

1. States shall adopt laws and regulations to prevent, reduce and control pollution of the marine environment from or through the atmosphere, applicable to the air space under their sovereignty and to vessels flying their flag or vessels or aircraft of their registry, taking into account internationally agreed rules, standards and recommended practices and procedures and the safety of air navigation.

2. States shall take other measures as may be necessary to prevent, reduce and control such pollution.

3. States, acting especially through competent international organizations or diplomatic conference, shall endeavour to establish global and regional rules, standards and recommended practices and procedures to prevent, reduce and control such pollution.

SECTION 6. ENFORCEMENT

Article 213 Enforcement with respect to pollution from land-based sources

States shall enforce their laws and regulations adopted in accordance with article 207 and shall adopt laws and regulations and take other measures necessary to implement applicable international rules and standards established through competent international organizations or diplomatic conference to prevent, reduce and control pollution of the marine environment from land-based sources.

Article 214 Enforcement with respect to pollution from sea-bed activities

States shall enforce their laws and regulations adopted in accordance with article 208 and shall adopt laws and regulations and take other measures necessary to implement applicable international rules and standards established through competent international organizations or diplomatic conference to prevent, reduce and control pollution of the marine environment arising from or in connection with sea-bed activities subject to their jurisdiction and from artificial islands, installations and structures under their jurisdiction, pursuant to articles 60 and 80.

Article 215 Enforcement with respect to pollution from activities in the Area

Enforcement of international rules, regulations and procedures established in accordance with Part XI to prevent, reduce and control pollution of the marine environment from activities in the Area shall be governed by that Part.

Article 216 Enforcement with respect to pollution by dumping

1. Laws and regulations adopted in accordance with this Convention and applicable international rules and standards established through competent international organizations or diplomatic conference for the prevention, reduction and control of pollution of the marine environment by dumping shall be enforced:

    (a)   by the coastal State with regard to dumping within its territorial sea or its exclusive economic zone or onto its continental shelf;

    (b)   by the flag State with regard to vessels flying its flag or vessels or aircraft of its registry;

    (c)   by any State with regard to acts of loading of wastes or other matter occurring within its territory or at its off-shore terminals.

2. No State shall be obliged by virtue of this article to institute proceedings when another State has already instituted proceedings in accordance with this article.

Article 217 Enforcement by flag States

1. States shall ensure compliance by vessels flying their flag or of their registry with applicable international rules and standards, established through the competent international organization or general diplomatic conference, and with their laws and regulations adopted in accordance with this Convention for the prevention, reduction and control of pollution of the marine environment from vessels and shall accordingly adopt laws and regulations and take other measures necessary for their implementation. Flag States shall provide for the effective enforcement of such rules, standards, laws and regulations, irrespective of where a violation occurs.

2. States shall, in particular, take appropriate measures in order to ensure that vessels flying their flag or of their registry are prohibited from sailing, until they can proceed to sea in compliance with the requirements of the international rules and standards referred to in paragraph 1, including requirements in respect of design, construction, equipment and manning of vessels.

3. States shall ensure that vessels flying their flag or of their registry carry on board certificates required by and issued pursuant to international rules and standards referred to in paragraph 1. States shall ensure that vessels flying their flag are periodically inspected in order to verify that such certificates are in conformity with the actual condition of the vessels. These certificates shall be accepted by other States as evidence of the condition of the vessels and shall be regarded as having the same force as certificates issued by them, unless there are clear grounds for believing that the condition of the vessel does not correspond substantially with the particulars of the certificates.

4. If a vessel commits a violation of rules and standards established through the competent international organization or general diplomatic conference, the flag State, without prejudice to articles 218, 220 and 228, shall provide for immediate investigation and where appropriate institute proceedings in respect of the alleged violation irrespective of where the violation occurred or where the pollution caused by such violation has occurred or has been spotted.

5. Flag States conducting an investigation of the violation may request the assistance of any other State whose co-operation could be useful in clarifying the circumstances of the case. States shall endeavour to meet appropriate requests of flag States.

6. States shall, at the written request of any State, investigate any violation alleged to have been committed by vessels flying their flag. If satisfied that sufficient evidence is available to enable proceedings to be brought in respect of the alleged violation, flag States shall without delay institute such proceedings in accordance with their laws.

7. Flag States shall promptly inform the requesting State and the competent international organization of the action taken and its outcome. Such information shall be available to all States.

8. Penalties provided for by the laws and regulations of States for vessels flying their flag shall be adequate in severity to discourage violations wherever they occur.

Article 218 Enforcement by port States

1. When a vessel is voluntarily within a port or at an off-shore terminal of a State, that State may undertake investigations and, where the evidence so warrants, institute proceedings in respect of any discharge from that vessel outside the internal waters, territorial sea or exclusive economic zone of that State in violation of applicable international rules and standards established through the competent international organization or general diplomatic conference.

2. No proceedings pursuant to paragraph 1 shall be instituted in respect of a discharge violation in the internal waters, territorial sea or exclusive economic zone of another State unless requested by that State, the flag State, or a State damaged or threatened by the discharge violation, or unless the violation has caused or is likely to cause pollution in the internal waters, territorial sea or exclusive economic zone of the State instituting the proceedings.

3. When a vessel is voluntarily within a port or at an off-shore terminal of a State, that State shall, as far as practicable, comply with requests from any State for investigation of a discharge violation referred to in paragraph 1, believed to have occurred in, caused, or threatened damage to the internal waters, territorial sea or exclusive economic zone of the requesting State. It shall likewise, as far as practicable, comply with requests from the flag State for investigation of such a violation, irrespective of where the violation occurred.

4. The records of the investigation carried out by a port State pursuant to this article shall be transmitted upon request to the flag State or to the coastal State. Any proceedings instituted by the port State on the basis of such an investigation may, subject to section 7, be suspended at the request of the coastal State when the violation has occurred within its internal waters, territorial sea or exclusive economic zone. The evidence and records of the case, together with any bond or other financial security posted with the authorities of the port State, shall in that event be transmitted to the coastal State. Such transmittal shall preclude the continuation of proceedings in the port State.

Article 219 Measures relating to seaworthiness of vessels to avoid pollution

Subject to section 7, States which, upon request or on their own initiative, have ascertained that a vessel within one of their ports or at one of their off-shore terminals is in violation of applicable international rules and standards relating to seaworthiness of vessels and thereby threatens damage to the marine environment shall, as far as practicable, take administrative measures to prevent the vessel from sailing. Such States may permit the vessel to proceed only to the nearest appropriate repair yard and, upon removal of the causes of the violation, shall permit the vessel to continue immediately.

Article 220 Enforcement by coastal States

1. When a vessel is voluntarily within a port or at an off-shore terminal of a State, that State may, subject to section 7, institute proceedings in respect of any violation of its laws and regulations adopted in accordance with this Convention or applicable international rules and standards for the prevention, reduction and control of pollution from vessels when the violation has occurred within the territorial sea or the exclusive economic zone of that State.

2. Where there are clear grounds for believing that a vessel navigating in the territorial sea of a State has, during its passage therein, violated laws and regulations of that State adopted in accordance with this Convention or applicable international rules and standards for the prevention, reduction and control of pollution from vessels, that State, without prejudice to the application of the relevant provisions of Part II, section 3, may undertake physical inspection of the vessel relating to the violation and may, where the evidence so warrants, institute proceedings, including detention of the vessel, in accordance with its laws, subject to the provisions of section 7.

3. Where there are clear grounds for believing that a vessel navigating in the exclusive economic zone or the territorial sea of a State has, in the exclusive economic zone, committed a violation of applicable international rules and standards for the prevention, reduction and control of pollution from vessels or laws and regulations of that State conforming and giving effect to such rules and standards, that State may require the vessel to give information regarding its identity and port of registry, its last and its next port of call and other relevant information required to establish whether a violation has occurred.

4. States shall adopt laws and regulations and take other measures so that vessels flying their flag comply with requests for information pursuant to paragraph 3.

5. Where there are clear grounds for believing that a vessel navigating in the exclusive economic zone or the territorial sea of a State has, in the exclusive economic zone, committed a violation referred to in paragraph 3 resulting in a substantial discharge causing or threatening significant pollution of the marine environment, that State may undertake physical inspection of the vessel for matters relating to the violation if the vessel has refused to give information or if the information supplied by the vessel is manifestly at variance with the evident factual situation and if the circumstances of the case justify such inspection.

6. Where there is clear objective evidence that a vessel navigating in the exclusive economic zone or the territorial sea of a State has, in the exclusive economic zone, committed a violation referred to in paragraph 3 resulting in a discharge causing major damage or threat of major damage to the coastline or related interests of the coastal State, or to any resources of its territorial sea or exclusive economic zone, that State may, subject to section 7, provided that the evidence so warrants, institute proceedings, including detention of the vessel, in accordance with its laws.

7. Notwithstanding the provisions of paragraph 6, whenever appropriate procedures have been established, either through the competent international organization or as otherwise agreed, whereby compliance with requirements for bonding or other appropriate financial security has been assured, the coastal State if bound by such procedures shall allow the vessel to proceed.

8. The provisions of paragraphs 3, 4, 5, 6 and 7 also apply in respect of national laws and regulations adopted pursuant to article 211, paragraph 6.

Article 221 Measures to avoid pollution arising from maritime casualties

1. Nothing in this Part shall prejudice the right of States, pursuant to international law, both customary and conventional, to take and enforce measures beyond the territorial sea proportionate to the actual or threatened damage to protect their coastline or related interests, including fishing, from pollution or threat of pollution following upon a maritime casualty or acts relating to such a casualty, which may reasonably be expected to result in major harmful consequences.

2. For the purposes of this article, 'maritime casualty' means a collision of vessels, stranding or other incident of navigation, or other occurrence on board a vessel or external to it resulting in material damage or imminent threat of material damage to a vessel or cargo.

Article 222 Enforcement with respect to pollution from or through the atmosphere

States shall enforce, within the air space under their sovereignty or with regard to vessels flying their flag or vessels or aircraft of their registry, their laws and regulations adopted in accordance with article 212, paragraph 1, and with other provisions of this Convention and shall adopt laws and regulations and take other measures necessary to implement applicable international rules and standards established through competent international organizations or diplomatic conference to prevent, reduce and control pollution of the marine environment from or through the atmosphere, in conformity with all relevant international rules and standards concerning the safety of air navigation.

Section 7. Safeguards

Article 223 Measures to facilitate proceedings

In proceedings instituted pursuant to this Part, States shall take measures to facilitate the hearing of witnesses and the admission of evidence submitted by authorities of another State, or by the competent international organization, and shall facilitate the attendance at such proceedings of official representatives of the competent international organization, the flag State and any State affected by pollution arising out of any violation. The official representatives attending such proceedings shall have such rights and duties as may be provided under national laws and regulations or international law.

Article 224 Exercise of powers of enforcement

The powers of enforcement against foreign vessels under this Part may only be exercised by officials or by warships, military aircraft, or other ships or aircraft clearly marked and identifiable as being on government service and authorized to that effect.

Article 225 Duty to avoid adverse consequences in the exercise of the powers of enforcement

In the exercise under this Convention of their powers of enforcement against foreign vessels, States shall not endanger the safety of navigation or otherwise create any hazard to a vessel, or bring it to an unsafe port or anchorage, or expose the marine environment to an unreasonable risk.

Article 226 Investigation of foreign vessels

1.   (a)   States shall not delay a foreign vessel longer than is essential for purposes of the investigations provided for in articles 216, 218 and 220. Any physical inspection of a foreign vessel shall be limited to an examination of such certificates, records or other documents as the vessel is required

to carry by generally accepted international rules and standards or of any similar documents which it is carrying; further physical inspection of the vessel may be undertaken only after such an examination and only when:

    (i)   there are clear grounds for believing that the condition of the vessel or its equipment does not correspond substantially with the particulars of those documents;

    (ii) the contents of such documents are not sufficient to confirm or verify a suspected violation; or

    (iii) the vessel is not carrying valid certificates and records.

  (b)   If the investigation indicates a violation of applicable laws and regulations or international rules and standards for the protection and preservation of the marine environment, release shall be made promptly subject to reasonable procedures such as bonding or other appropriate financial security.

  (c)   Without prejudice to applicable international rules and standards relating to the seaworthiness of vessels, the release of a vessel may, whenever it would present an unreasonable threat of damage to the marine environment, be refused or made conditional upon proceeding to the nearest appropriate repair yard. Where release has been refused or made conditional, the flag State of the vessel must be promptly notified, and may seek release of the vessel in accordance with Part XV.

2.   States shall co-operate to develop procedures for the avoidance of unnecessary physical inspection of vessels at sea.

Article 227 Non-discrimination with respect to foreign vessels

In exercising their rights and performing their duties under this Part, States shall not discriminate in form or in fact against vessels of any other State.

Article 228 Suspension and restrictions on institution of proceedings

1.   Proceedings to impose penalties in respect of any violation of applicable laws and regulations or international rules and standards relating to the prevention, reduction and control of pollution from vessels committed by a foreign vessel beyond the territorial sea of the State instituting proceedings shall be suspended upon the taking of proceedings to impose penalties in respect of corresponding charges by the flag State within six months of the date on which proceedings were first instituted, unless those proceedings relate to a case of major damage to the coastal State or the flag State in question has repeatedly disregarded its obligation to enforce effectively the applicable international rules and standards in respect of violations committed by its vessels. The flag State shall in due course make available to the State previously instituting proceedings a full dossier of the case and the records of the proceedings, whenever the flag State has requested the suspension of proceedings in accordance with this article. When proceedings instituted by the flag State have been brought to a conclusion, the suspended proceedings shall be terminated. Upon payment of costs incurred in respect of such proceedings, any bond posted or other financial security provided in connection with the suspended proceedings shall be released by the coastal State.

2.   Proceedings to impose penalties on foreign vessels shall not be instituted after the expiry of three years from the date on which the violation was committed, and shall not be taken by any State in the event of proceedings having been instituted by another State subject to the provisions set out in paragraph 1.

3. The provisions of this article are without prejudice to the right of the flag State to take any measures, including proceedings to impose penalties, according to its laws irrespective of prior proceedings by another State.

Article 229 Institution of civil proceedings

Nothing in this Convention affects the institution of civil proceedings in respect of any claim for loss or damage resulting from pollution of the marine environment.

Article 230 Monetary penalties and the observance of recognized rights of the accused

1. Monetary penalties only may be imposed with respect to violations of national laws and regulations or applicable international rules and standards for the prevention, reduction and control of pollution of the marine environment, committed by foreign vessels beyond the territorial sea.

2. Monetary penalties only may be imposed with respect to violations of national laws and regulations or applicable international rules and standards for the prevention, reduction and control of pollution of the marine environment, committed by foreign vessels in the territorial sea, except in the case of a wilful and serious act of pollution in the territorial sea.

3. In the conduct of proceedings in respect of such violations committed by a foreign vessel which may result in the imposition of penalties, recognized rights of the accused shall be observed.

Article 231 Notification to the flag State and other States concerned

States shall promptly notify the flag State and any other State concerned of any measures taken pursuant to section 6 against foreign vessels, and shall submit to the flag State all official reports concerning such measures. However, with respect to violations committed in the territorial sea, the foregoing obligations of the coastal State apply only to such measures as are taken in proceedings. The diplomatic agents or consular officers and where possible the maritime authority of the flag State, shall be immediately informed of any such measures taken pursuant to section 6 against foreign vessels.

Article 232 Liability of States arising from enforcement measures

States shall be liable for damage or loss attributable to them arising from measures taken pursuant to section 6 when such measures are unlawful or exceed those reasonably required in the light of available information. States shall provide for recourse in their courts for actions in respect of such damage or loss.

Article 233 Safeguards with respect to straits used for international navigation

Nothing in sections 5, 6 and 7 affects the legal regime of straits used for international navigation. However, if a foreign ship other than those referred to in section 10 has committed a violation of the laws and regulations referred to in article 42, paragraph 1(a) and (b), causing or threatening major damage to the marine environment of the straits, the States bordering the straits may take appropriate enforcement measures and if so shall respect *mutatis mutandis* the provisions of this section.

SECTION 8. ICE-COVERED AREAS

Article 234 Ice-covered areas

Coastal States have the right to adopt and enforce non-discriminatory laws and regulations for the prevention, reduction and control of marine pollution from vessels in ice-covered areas within the limits of the exclusive economic zone, where particularly severe climatic conditions and the presence of ice covering such areas for most of the year create obstructions or exceptional hazards to navigation, and pollution of the marine environment could cause major harm to or irreversible disturbance of the ecological balance. Such laws and regulations shall have due regard to navigation and the protection and preservation of the marine environment based on the best available scientific evidence.

SECTION 9. RESPONSIBILITY AND LIABILITY

Article 235 Responsibility and liability

1. States are responsible for the fulfilment of their international obligations concerning the protection and preservation of the marine environment. They shall be liable in accordance with international law.

2. States shall ensure that recourse is available in accordance with their legal systems for prompt and adequate compensation or other relief in respect of damage caused by pollution of the marine environment by natural or juridical persons under their jurisdiction.

3. With the objective of assuring prompt and adequate compensation in respect of all damage caused by pollution of the marine environment, States shall co-operate in the implementation of existing international law and the further development of international law relating to responsibility and liability for the assessment of and compensation for damage and the settlement of related disputes, as well as, where appropriate, development of criteria and procedures for payment of adequate compensation, such as compulsory insurance or compensation funds.

SECTION 10. SOVEREIGN IMMUNITY

Article 236 Sovereign immunity

The provisions of this Convention regarding the protection and preservation of the marine environment do not apply to any warship, naval auxiliary, other vessels or aircraft owned or operated by a State and used, for the time being, only on government non-commercial service. However, each State shall ensure, by the adoption of appropriate measures not impairing operations or operational capabilities of such vessels or aircraft owned or operated by it, that such vessels or aircraft act in a manner consistent, so far as is reasonable and practicable, with this Convention.

SECTION 11. OBLIGATIONS UNDER OTHER CONVENTIONS ON THE PROTECTION AND PRESERVATION OF THE MARINE ENVIRONMENT

Article 237 Obligations under other conventions on the protection and preservation of the marine environment

1. The provisions of this Part are without prejudice to the specific obligations assumed by States under special conventions and agreements concluded previously which relate to the protection and preservation of the marine environment and to agreements which may be concluded in furtherance of the general principles set forth in this Convention.

2. Specific obligations assumed by States under special conventions, with respect to the protection and preservation of the marine environment, should be carried out in a manner consistent with the general principles and objectives of this Convention.

PART XIII
MARINE SCIENTIFIC RESEARCH

SECTION 1. GENERAL PROVISIONS

Article 238 Right to conduct marine scientific research

All States, irrespective of their geographical location, and competent international organizations have the right to conduct marine scientific research subject to the rights and duties of other States as provided for in this Convention.

Article 239 Promotion of marine scientific research

States and competent international organizations shall promote and facilitate the development and conduct of marine scientific research in accordance with this Convention.

Article 240 General principles for the conduct of marine scientific research

In the conduct of marine scientific research the following principles shall apply:

(a) marine scientific research shall be conducted exclusively for peaceful purposes;

(b) marine scientific research shall be conducted with appropriate scientific methods and means compatible with this Convention;

(c) marine scientific research shall not unjustifiably interfere with other legitimate uses of the sea compatible with this Convention and shall be duly respected in the course of such uses;

(d) marine scientific research shall be conducted in compliance with all relevant regulations adopted in conformity with this Convention including those for the protection and preservation of the marine environment.

Article 241 Non-recognition of marine scientific research activities as the legal basis for claims

Marine scientific research activities shall not constitute the legal basis for any claim to any part of the marine environment or its resources.

SECTION 2. INTERNATIONAL CO-OPERATION

Article 242 Promotion of international co-operation

1. States and competent international organizations shall, in accordance with the principle of respect for sovereignty and jurisdiction and on the basis of mutual benefit, promote international co-operation in marine scientific research for peaceful purposes.

2. In this context, without prejudice to the rights and duties of States under this Convention, a State, in the application of this Part, shall provide, as appropriate, other States with a reasonable opportunity to obtain from it, or with its co-operation, information necessary to prevent and control damage to the health and safety of persons and to the marine environment.

Article 243 Creation of favourable conditions

States and competent international organizations shall co-operate, through the conclusion of bilateral and multilateral agreements, to create favourable conditions for the conduct of marine scientific research in the marine environment and to integrate the efforts of scientists in studying the essence of phenomena and processes occurring in the marine environment and the interrelations between them.

Article 244 Publication and dissemination of information and knowledge

1. States and competent international organizations shall, in accordance with this Convention, make available by publication and dissemination through appropriate channels information on proposed major programmes and their objectives as well as knowledge resulting from marine scientific research.

2. For this purpose, States, both individually and in cooperation with other States and with competent international organizations, shall actively promote the flow of scientific data and information and the transfer of knowledge resulting from marine scientific research, especially to developing States, as well as the strengthening of the autonomous marine scientific research capabilities of developing States through, *inter alia*, programmes to provide adequate education and training of their technical and scientific personnel.

SECTION 3. CONDUCT AND PROMOTION OF MARINE SCIENTIFIC RESEARCH

Article 245 Marine scientific research in the territorial sea

Coastal States, in the exercise of their sovereignty, have the exclusive right to regulate, authorize and conduct marine scientific research in their territorial sea. Marine scientific research therein shall be conducted only with the express consent of and under the conditions set forth by the coastal State.

Article 246 Marine scientific research in the exclusive economic zone and on the continental shelf

1. Coastal States, in the exercise of their jurisdiction, have the right to regulate, authorize and conduct marine scientific research in their exclusive economic zone and on their continental shelf in accordance with the relevant provisions of this Convention.

2. Marine scientific research in the exclusive economic zone and on the continental shelf shall be conducted with the consent of the coastal State.

3. Coastal States shall, in normal circumstances, grant their consent for marine scientific research projects by other States or competent international organizations in their exclusive economic zone or on their continental shelf to be carried out in accordance with this Convention exclusively for peaceful purposes and in order to increase scientific knowledge of the marine environment for the benefit of all mankind. To this end, coastal States shall establish rules and procedures ensuring that such consent will not be delayed or denied unreasonably.

4. For the purposes of applying paragraph 3, normal circumstances may exist in spite of the absence of diplomatic relations between the coastal State and the researching State.

5. Coastal States may however in their discretion withhold their consent to the conduct of a marine scientific research project of another State or competent international organization in the exclusive economic zone or on the continental shelf of the coastal State if that project:

   (a)   is of direct significance for the exploration and exploitation of natural resources, whether living or non-living;

   (b)   involves drilling into the continental shelf, the use of explosives or the introduction of harmful substances into the marine environment;

(c) involves the construction, operation or use of artificial islands, installations and structures referred to in articles 60 and 80;

(d) contains information communicated pursuant to article 248 regarding the nature and objectives of the project which is inaccurate or if the researching State or competent international organization has outstanding obligations to the coastal State from a prior research project.

6. Notwithstanding the provisions of paragraph 5, coastal States may not exercise their discretion to withhold consent under subparagraph (a) of that paragraph in respect of marine scientific research projects to be undertaken in accordance with the provisions of this Part on the continental shelf, beyond 200 nautical miles from the baselines from which the breadth of the territorial sea is measured, outside those specific areas which coastal States may at any time publicly designate as areas in which exploitation or detailed exploratory operations focused on those areas are occurring or will occur within a reasonable period of time. Coastal States shall give reasonable notice of the designation of such areas, as well as any modifications thereto, but shall not be obliged to give details of the operations therein.

7. The provisions of paragraph 6 are without prejudice to the rights of coastal States over the continental shelf as established in article 77.

8. Marine scientific research activities referred to in this article shall not unjustifiably interfere with activities undertaken by coastal States in the exercise of their sovereign rights and jurisdiction provided for in this Convention.

Article 247 Marine scientific research projects undertaken by or under the auspices of international organizations

A coastal State which is a member of or has a bilateral agreement with an international organization, and in whose exclusive economic zone or on whose continental shelf that organization wants to carry out a marine scientific research project, directly or under its auspices, shall be deemed to have authorized the project to be carried out in conformity with the agreed specifications if that State approved the detailed project when the decision was made by the organization for the undertaking of the project, or is willing to participate in it, and has not expressed any objection within four months of notification of the project by the organization to the coastal State.

Article 248 Duty to provide information to the coastal State

States and competent international organizations which intend to undertake marine scientific research in the exclusive economic zone or on the continental shelf of a coastal State shall, not less than six months in advance of the expected starting date of the marine scientific research project, provide that State with a full description of:

(a) the nature and objectives of the project;

(b) the method and means to be used, including name, tonnage, type and class of vessels and a description of scientific equipment;

(c) the precise geographical areas in which the project is to be conducted;

(d) the expected date of first appearance and final departure of the research vessels, or deployment of the equipment and its removal, as appropriate;

(e) the name of the sponsoring institution, its director, and the person in charge of the project; and

(f) the extent to which it is considered that the coastal State should be able to participate or to be represented in the project.

Article 249 Duty to comply with certain conditions

1. States and competent international organizations when undertaking marine scientific research in the exclusive economic zone or on the continental shelf of a coastal State shall comply with the following conditions:

(a) ensure the right of the coastal State, if it so desires, to participate or be represented in the marine scientific research project, especially on board research vessels and other craft or scientific research installations, when practicable, without payment of any remuneration to the scientists of the coastal State and without obligation to contribute towards the costs of the project;

(b) provide the coastal State, at its request, with preliminary reports, as soon as practicable, and with the final results and conclusions after the completion of the research;

(c) undertake to provide access for the coastal State, at its request, to all data and samples derived from the marine scientific research project and likewise to furnish it with data which may be copied and samples which may be divided without detriment to their scientific value;

(d) if requested, provide the coastal State with an assessment of such data, samples and research results or provide assistance in their assessment or interpretation;

(e) ensure, subject to paragraph 2, that the research results are made internationally available through appropriate national or international channels, as soon as practicable;

(f) inform the coastal State immediately of any major change in the research programme;

(g) unless otherwise agreed, remove the scientific research installations or equipment once the research is completed.

2. This article is without prejudice to the conditions established by the laws and regulations of the coastal State for the exercise of its discretion to grant or withhold consent pursuant to article 246, paragraph 5, including requiring prior agreement for making internationally available the research results of a project of direct significance for the exploration and exploitation of natural resources.

Article 250 Communications concerning marine scientific research projects

Communications concerning the marine scientific research projects shall be made through appropriate official channels, unless otherwise agreed.

Article 251 General criteria and guidelines

States shall seek to promote through competent international organizations the establishment of general criteria and guidelines to assist States in ascertaining the nature and implications of marine scientific research.

Article 252 Implied consent

States or competent international organizations may proceed with a marine scientific research project six months after the date upon which the information required pursuant to article 248 was provided to the coastal State unless within four months of the receipt of the communication containing such information the coastal State has informed the State or organization conducting the research that:

(a) it has withheld its consent under the provisions of article 246; or

(b) the information given by that State or competent international organization regarding the nature or objectives of the project does not conform to the manifestly evident facts; or

(c)   it requires supplementary information relevant to conditions and the information provided for under articles 248 and 249; or

(d)   outstanding obligations exist with respect to a previous marine scientific research project carried out by that State or organization, with regard to conditions established in article 249.

Article 253 Suspension or cessation of marine scientific research activities

1. A coastal State shall have the right to require the suspension of any marine scientific research activities in progress within its exclusive economic zone or on its continental shelf if:

(a)   the research activities are not being conducted in accordance with the information communicated as provided under article 248 upon which the consent of the coastal State was based; or

(b)   the State or competent international organization conducting the research activities fails to comply with the provisions of article 249 concerning the rights of the coastal State with respect to the marine scientific research project.

2. A coastal State shall have the right to require the cessation of any marine scientific research activities in case of any non-compliance with the provisions of article 248 which amounts to a major change in the research project or the research activities.

3. A coastal State may also require cessation of marine scientific research activities if any of the situations contemplated in paragraph 1 are not rectified within a reasonable period of time.

4. Following notification by the coastal State of its decision to order suspension or cessation, States or competent international organizations authorized to conduct marine scientific research activities shall terminate the research activities that are the subject of such a notification.

5. An order of suspension under paragraph 1 shall be lifted by the coastal State and the marine scientific research activities allowed to continue once the researching State or competent international organization has complied with the conditions required under articles 248 and 249.

Article 254 Rights of neighbouring land-locked and geographically disadvantaged States

1. States and competent international organizations which have submitted to a coastal State a project to undertake marine scientific research referred to in article 246, paragraph 3, shall give notice to the neighbouring land-locked and geographically disadvantaged States of the proposed research project, and shall notify the coastal State thereof.

2. After the consent has been given for the proposed marine scientific research project by the coastal State concerned, in accordance with article 246 and other relevant provisions of this Convention, States and competent international organizations undertaking such a project shall provide to the neighbouring land-locked and geographically disadvantaged States, at their request and when appropriate, relevant information as specified in article 248 and article 249, paragraph 1(f).

3. The neighbouring land-locked and geographically disadvantaged States referred to above shall, at their request, be given the opportunity to participate, whenever feasible, in the proposed marine scientific research project through qualified experts appointed by them and not objected to by the coastal State, in accordance with the conditions agreed for the project, in conformity with the provisions of this Convention, between the coastal State concerned and the State or competent international organizations conducting the marine scientific research.

4.   States and competent international organizations referred to in paragraph 1 shall provide to the above-mentioned land-locked and geographically disadvantaged States, at their request, the information and assistance specified in article 249, paragraph 1(d), subject to the provisions of article 249, paragraph 2.

Article 255   Measures to facilitate marine scientific research and assist research vessels

States shall endeavour to adopt reasonable rules, regulations and procedures to promote and facilitate marine scientific research conducted in accordance with this Convention beyond their territorial sea and, as appropriate, to facilitate, subject to the provisions of their laws and regulations, access to their harbours and promote assistance for marine scientific research vessels which comply with the relevant provisions of this Part.

Article 256   Marine scientific research in the Area

All States, irrespective of their geographical location, and competent international organizations have the right, in conformity with the provisions of Part XI, to conduct marine scientific research in the Area.

Article 257   Marine scientific research in the water column beyond the exclusive economic zone

All States, irrespective of their geographical location, and competent international organizations have the right, in conformity with this Convention, to conduct marine scientific research in the water column beyond the limits of the exclusive economic zone.

SECTION 4.   SCIENTIFIC RESEARCH INSTALLATIONS OR EQUIPMENT IN THE
MARINE ENVIRONMENT

Article 258   Deployment and use

The deployment and use of any type of scientific research installations or equipment in any area of the marine environment shall be subject to the same conditions as are prescribed in this Convention for the conduct of marine scientific research in any such area.

Article 259   Legal status

The installations or equipment referred to in this section do not possess the status of islands. They have no territorial sea of their own, and their presence does not affect the delimitation of the territorial sea, the exclusive economic zone or the continental shelf.

Article 260   Safety zones

Safety zones of a reasonable breadth not exceeding a distance of 500 metres may be created around scientific research installations in accordance with the relevant provisions of this Convention. All States shall ensure that such safety zones are respected by their vessels.

Article 261   Non-interference with shipping routes

The deployment and use of any type of scientific research installations or equipment shall not constitute an obstacle to established international shipping routes.

Article 262 Identification markings and warning signals

Installations or equipment referred to in this section shall bear identification markings indicating the State of registry or the international organization to which they belong and shall have adequate internationally agreed warning signals to ensure safety at sea and the safety of air navigation, taking into account rules and standards established by competent international organizations.

SECTION 5. RESPONSIBILITY AND LIABILITY

Article 263 Responsibility and liability

1. States and competent international organizations shall be responsible for ensuring that marine scientific research, whether undertaken by them or on their behalf, is conducted in accordance with this Convention.

2. States and competent international organizations shall be responsible and liable for the measures they take in contravention of this Convention in respect of marine scientific research conducted by other States, their natural or juridical persons or by competent international organizations, and shall provide compensation for damage resulting from such measures.

3. States and competent international organizations shall be responsible and liable pursuant to article 235 for damage caused by pollution of the marine environment arising out of marine scientific research undertaken by them or on their behalf.

SECTION 6. SETTLEMENT OF DISPUTES AND INTERIM MEASURES

Article 264 Settlement of disputes

Disputes concerning the interpretation or application of the provisions of this Convention with regard to marine scientific research shall be settled in accordance with Part XV, sections 2 and 3.

Article 265 Interim measures

Pending settlement of a dispute in accordance with Part XV, sections 2 and 3, the State or competent international organization authorized to conduct a marine scientific research project shall not allow research activities to commence or continue without the express consent of the coastal State concerned.

PART XIV
DEVELOPMENT AND TRANSFER OF MARINE TECHNOLOGY

SECTION 1. GENERAL PROVISIONS

Article 266 Promotion of the development and transfer of marine technology

1. States, directly or through competent international organizations, shall co-operate in accordance with their capabilities to promote actively the development and transfer of marine science and marine technology on fair and reasonable terms and conditions.

2. States shall promote the development of the marine scientific and technological capacity of States which may need and request technical assistance in this field, particularly developing States, including land-locked and geographically disadvantaged States, with regard to the exploration, exploitation, conservation and management of marine resources, the protection and preservation of the marine environment, marine scientific research and other activities in the marine environment compatible with this

Convention, with a view to accelerating the social and economic development of the developing States.

3. States shall endeavour to foster favourable economic and legal conditions for the transfer of marine technology for the benefit of all parties concerned on an equitable basis.

Article 267 Protection of legitimate interests

States, in promoting co-operation pursuant to article 266, shall have due regard for all legitimate interests including, *inter alia*, the rights and duties of holders, suppliers and recipients of marine technology.

Article 268 Basic objectives

States, directly or through competent international organizations, shall promote:
(a)   the acquisition, evaluation and dissemination of marine technological knowledge and facilitate access to such information and data;
(b)   the development of appropriate marine technology;
(c)   the development of the necessary technological infrastructure to facilitate the transfer of marine technology;
(d)   the development of human resources through training and education of nationals of developing States and countries and especially the nationals of the least developed among them;
(e)   international co-operation at all levels, particularly at the regional, subregional and bilateral levels.

Article 269 Measures to achieve the basic objectives

In order to achieve the objectives referred to in article 268, States, directly or through competent international organizations, shall endeavour, *inter alia*, to:
(a)   establish programmes of technical co-operation for the effective transfer of all kinds of marine technology to States which may need and request technical assistance in this field, particularly the developing land-locked and geographically disadvantaged States, as well as other developing States which have not been able either to establish or develop their own technological capacity in marine science and in the exploration and exploitation of marine resources or to develop the infrastructure of such technology;
(b)   promote favourable conditions for the conclusion of agreements, contracts and other similar arrangements, under equitable and reasonable conditions;
(c)   hold conferences, seminars and symposia on scientific and technological subjects, in particular on policies and methods for the transfer of marine technology;
(d)   promote the exchange of scientists and of technological and other experts;
(e)   undertake projects and promote joint ventures and other forms of bilateral and multilateral co-operation.

SECTION 2. INTERNATIONAL CO-OPERATION

Article 270 Ways and means of international co-operation

International co-operation for the development and transfer of marine technology shall be carried out, where feasible and appropriate, through existing bilateral, regional or multilateral programmes, and also through expanded and new programmes in order to facilitate marine scientific research, the transfer of marine technology, particularly in new fields, and appropriate international funding for ocean research and development.

Article 271 Guidelines, criteria and standards

States, directly or through competent international organizations, shall promote the establishment of generally accepted guidelines, criteria and standards for the transfer of marine technology on a bilateral basis or within the framework of international organizations and other fora, taking into account, in particular, the interests and needs of developing States.

Article 272 Co-ordination of international programmes

In the field of transfer of marine technology, States shall endeavour to ensure that competent international organizations co-ordinate their activities, including any regional or global programmes, taking into account the interests and needs of developing States, particularly land-locked and geographically disadvantaged States.

Article 273 Co-operation with international organizations and the Authority

States shall co-operate actively with competent international organizations and the Authority to encourage and facilitate the transfer to developing States, their nationals and the Enterprise of skills and marine technology with regard to activities in the Area.

Article 274 Objectives of the Authority

Subject to all legitimate interests including, *inter alia*, the rights and duties of holders, suppliers and recipients of technology, the Authority, with regard to activities in the Area, shall ensure that:

(a) on the basis of the principle of equitable geographical distribution, nationals of developing States, whether coastal, land-locked or geographically disadvantaged, shall be taken on for the purposes of training as members of the managerial, research and technical staff constituted for its undertakings;

(b) the technical documentation on the relevant equipment, machinery, devices and processes is made available to all States, in particular developing States which may need and request technical assistance in this field;

(c) adequate provision is made by the Authority to facilitate the acquisition of technical assistance in the field of marine technology by States which may need and request it, in particular developing States, and the acquisition by their nationals of the necessary skills and know-how, including professional training;

(d) States which may need and request technical assistance in this field, in particular developing States, are assisted in the acquisition of necessary equipment, processes, plant and other technical know-how through any financial arrangements provided for in this Convention.

SECTION 3. NATIONAL AND REGIONAL MARINE SCIENTIFIC AND TECHNOLOGICAL CENTRES

Article 275 Establishment of national centres

1. States, directly or through competent international organizations and the Authority, shall promote the establishment, particularly in developing coastal States, of national marine scientific and technological research centres and the strengthening of existing national centres, in order to stimulate and advance the conduct of marine scientific research by developing coastal States and to enhance their national capabilities to utilize and preserve their marine resources for their economic benefit.

2. States, through competent international organizations and the Authority, shall give adequate support to facilitate the establishment and strengthening of such national centres so as to provide for advanced training facilities and necessary equipment, skills

and know-how as well as technical experts to such States which may need and request such assistance.

Article 276 Establishment of regional centres

1. States, in co-ordination with the competent international organizations, the Authority and national marine scientific and technological research institutions, shall promote the establishment of regional marine scientific and technological research centres, particularly in developing States, in order to stimulate and advance the conduct of marine scientific research by developing States and foster the transfer of marine technology.

2. All States of a region shall co-operate with the regional centres therein to ensure the more effective achievement of their objectives.

Article 277 Functions of regional centres

The functions of such regional centres shall include, *inter alia*:

(a) training and educational programmes at all levels on various aspects of marine scientific and technological research, particularly marine biology, including conservation and management of living resources, oceanography, hydrography, engineering, geological exploration of the sea-bed, mining and desalination technologies;

(b) management studies;

(c) study programmes related to the protection and preservation of the marine environment and the prevention, reduction and control of pollution;

(d) organization of regional conferences, seminars and symposia;

(e) acquisition and processing of marine scientific and technological data and information;

(f) prompt dissemination of results of marine scientific and technological research in readily available publications;

(g) publicizing national policies with regard to the transfer of marine technology and systematic comparative study of those policies;

(h) compilation and systematization of information on the marketing of technology and on contracts and other arrangements concerning patents;

(i) technical co-operation with other States of the region.

SECTION 4. CO-OPERATION AMONG INTERNATIONAL ORGANIZATIONS

Article 278 Co-operation among international organizations

The competent international organizations referred to in this Part and in Part XIII shall take all appropriate measures to ensure, either directly or in close co-operation among themselves, the effective discharge of their functions and responsibilities under this Part.

PART XV
SETTLEMENT OF DISPUTES

SECTION 1. GENERAL PROVISIONS

Article 279 Obligation to settle disputes by peaceful means

States Parties shall settle any dispute between them concerning the interpretation or application of this Convention by peaceful means in accordance with Article 2, paragraph 3, of the Charter of the United Nations and, to this end, shall seek a solution by the means indicated in Article 33, paragraph 1, of the Charter.

Article 280 Settlement of disputes by any peaceful means chosen by the parties

Nothing in this Part impairs the right of any States Parties to agree at any time to settle a dispute between them concerning the interpretation or application of this Convention by any peaceful means of their own choice.

Article 281 Procedure where no settlement has been reached by the parties

1. If the States Parties which are parties to a dispute concerning the interpretation or application of this Convention have agreed to seek settlement of the dispute by a peaceful means of their own choice, the procedures provided for in this Part apply only where no settlement has been reached by recourse to such means and the agreement between the parties does not exclude any further procedure.

2. If the parties have also agreed on a time-limit, paragraph 1 applies only upon the expiration of that time-limit.

Article 282 Obligations under general, regional or bilateral agreements

If the States Parties which are parties to a dispute concerning the interpretation or application of this Convention have agreed, through a general, regional or bilateral agreement or otherwise, that such dispute shall, at the request of any party to the dispute, be submitted to a procedure that entails a binding decision, that procedure shall apply in lieu of the procedures provided for in this Part, unless the parties to the dispute otherwise agree.

Article 283 Obligation to exchange views

1. When a dispute arises between States Parties concerning the interpretation or application of this Convention, the parties to the dispute shall proceed expeditiously to an exchange of views regarding its settlement by negotiation or other peaceful means.

2. The parties shall also proceed expeditiously to an exchange of views where a procedure for the settlement of such a dispute has been terminated without a settlement or where a settlement has been reached and the circumstances require consultation regarding the manner of implementing the settlement.

Article 284 Conciliation

1. A State Party which is a party to a dispute concerning the interpretation or application of this Convention may invite the other party or parties to submit the dispute to conciliation in accordance with the procedure under Annex V, section 1, or another conciliation procedure.

2. If the invitation is accepted and if the parties agree upon the conciliation procedure to be applied, any party may submit the dispute to that procedure.

3. If the invitation is not accepted or the parties do not agree upon the procedure, the conciliation proceedings shall be deemed to be terminated.

4. Unless the parties otherwise agree, when a dispute has been submitted to conciliation, the proceedings may be terminated only in accordance with the agreed conciliation procedure.

Article 285 Application of this section to disputes submitted pursuant to Part XI

This section applies to any dispute which pursuant to Part XI, section 5, is to be settled in accordance with procedures provided for in this Part. If an entity other than a State Party is a party to such a dispute, this section applies *mutatis mutandis*.

SECTION 2. COMPULSORY PROCEDURES ENTAILING BINDING DECISIONS

Article 286 Application of procedures under this section

Subject to section 3, any dispute concerning the interpretation or application of this Convention shall, where no settlement has been reached by recourse to section 1, be submitted at the request of any party to the dispute to the court or tribunal having jurisdiction under this section.

Article 287 Choice of procedure

1. When signing, ratifying or acceding to this Convention or at any time thereafter, a State shall be free to choose, by means of a written declaration, one or more of the following means for the settlement of disputes concerning the interpretation or application of this Convention:

    (a) the International Tribunal for the Law of the Sea established in accordance with Annex VI;

    (b) the International Court of Justice;

    (c) an arbitral tribunal constituted in accordance with Annex VII;

    (d) a special arbitral tribunal constituted in accordance with Annex VIII for one or more of the categories of disputes specified therein.

2. A declaration made under paragraph 1 shall not affect or be affected by the obligation of a State Party to accept the jurisdiction of the Sea-bed Disputes Chamber of the International Tribunal for the Law of the Sea to the extent and in the manner provided for in Part XI, section 5.

3. A State Party, which is a party to a dispute not covered by a declaration in force, shall be deemed to have accepted arbitration in accordance with Annex VII.

4. If the parties to a dispute have accepted the same procedure for the settlement of the dispute, it may be submitted only to that procedure, unless the parties otherwise agree.

5. If the parties to a dispute have not accepted the same procedure for the settlement of the dispute, it may be submitted only to arbitration in accordance with Annex VII, unless the parties otherwise agree.

6. A declaration made under paragraph 1 shall remain in force until three months after notice of revocation has been deposited with the Secretary-General of the United Nations.

7. A new declaration, a notice of revocation or the expiry of a declaration does not in any way affect proceedings pending before a court or tribunal having jurisdiction under this article, unless the parties otherwise agree.

8. Declarations and notices referred to in this article shall be deposited with the Secretary-General of the United Nations, who shall transmit copies thereof to the States Parties.

Article 288 Jurisdiction

1. A court or tribunal referred to in article 287 shall have jurisdiction over any dispute concerning the interpretation or application of this Convention which is submitted to it in accordance with this Part.

2. A court or tribunal referred to in article 287 shall also have jurisdiction over any dispute concerning the interpretation or application of an international agreement related to the purposes of this Convention, which is submitted to it in accordance with the agreement.

3. The Sea-bed Disputes Chamber of the International Tribunal for the Law of the Sea established in accordance with Annex VI, and any other chamber or arbitral tribunal

referred to in Part XI, section 5, shall have jurisdiction in any matter which is submitted to it in accordance therewith.

4. In the event of a dispute as to whether a court or tribunal has jurisdiction, the matter shall be settled by decision of that court or tribunal.

Article 289 Experts

In any dispute involving scientific or technical matters, a court or tribunal exercising jurisdiction under this section may, at the request of a party or *proprio motu*, select in consultation with the parties no fewer than two scientific or technical experts chosen preferably from the relevant list prepared in accordance with Annex VIII, article 2, to sit with the court or tribunal but without the right to vote.

Article 290 Provisional measures

1. If a dispute has been duly submitted to a court or tribunal which considers that *prima facie* it has jurisdiction under this Part or Part XI, section 5, the court or tribunal may prescribe any provisional measures which it considers appropriate under the circumstances to preserve the respective rights of the parties to the dispute or to prevent serious harm to the marine environment, pending the final decision.

2. Provisional measures may be modified or revoked as soon as the circumstances justifying them have changed or ceased to exist.

3. Provisional measures may be prescribed, modified or revoked under this article only at the request of a party to the dispute and after the parties have been given an opportunity to be heard.

4. The court or tribunal shall forthwith give notice to the parties to the dispute, and to such other States Parties as it considers appropriate, of the prescription, modification or revocation of provisional measures.

5. Pending the constitution of an arbitral tribunal to which a dispute is being submitted under this section, any court or tribunal agreed upon by the parties or, failing such agreement within two weeks from the date of the request for provisional measures, the International Tribunal for the Law of the Sea or, with respect to activities in the Area, the Sea-bed Disputes Chamber, may prescribe, modify or revoke provisional measures in accordance with this article if it considers that *prima facie* the tribunal which is to be constituted would have jurisdiction and that the urgency of the situation so requires. Once constituted, the tribunal to which the dispute has been submitted may modify, revoke or affirm those provisional measures, acting in conformity with paragraphs 1 to 4.

6. The parties to the dispute shall comply promptly with any provisional measures prescribed under this article.

Article 291 Access

1. All the dispute settlement procedures specified in this Part shall be open to States Parties.

2. The dispute settlement procedures specified in this Part shall be open to entities other than States Parties only as specifically provided for in this Convention.

Article 292 Prompt release of vessels and crews

1. Where the authorities of a State Party have detained a vessel flying the flag of another State Party and it is alleged that the detaining State has not complied with the provisions of this Convention for the prompt release of the vessel or its crew upon the posting of a reasonable bond or other financial security, the question of release from detention may be submitted to any court or tribunal agreed upon by the parties or, failing

such agreement within 10 days from the time of detention, to a court or tribunal accepted by the detaining State under article 287 or to the International Tribunal for the Law of the Sea, unless the parties otherwise agree.

2.   The application for release may be made only by or on behalf of the flag State of the vessel.

3.   The court or tribunal shall deal without delay with the application for release and shall deal only with the question of release, without prejudice to the merits of any case before the appropriate domestic forum against the vessel, its owner or its crew. The authorities of the detaining State remain competent to release the vessel or its crew at any time.

4.   Upon the posting of the bond or other financial security determined by the court or tribunal, the authorities of the detaining State shall comply promptly with the decision of the court or tribunal concerning the release of the vessel or its crew.

Article 293 Applicable law

1.   A court or tribunal having jurisdiction under this section shall apply this Convention and other rules of international law not incompatible with this Convention.

2.   Paragraph 1 does not prejudice the power of the court or tribunal having jurisdiction under this section to decide a case *ex aequo et bono*, if the parties so agree.

Article 294 Preliminary proceedings

1.   A court or tribunal provided for in article 287 to which an application is made in respect of a dispute referred to in article 297 shall determine at the request of a party, or may determine *proprio motu*, whether the claim constitutes an abuse of legal process or whether *prima facie* it is well founded. If the court or tribunal determines that the claim constitutes an abuse of legal process or is *prima facie* unfounded, it shall take no further action in the case.

2.   Upon receipt of the application, the court or tribunal shall immediately notify the other party or parties of the application, and shall fix a reasonable time-limit within which they may request it to make a determination in accordance with paragraph 1.

3.   Nothing in this article affects the right of any party to a dispute to make preliminary objections in accordance with the applicable rules of procedure.

Article 295 Exhaustion of local remedies

Any dispute between States Parties concerning the interpretation or application of this Convention may be submitted to the procedures provided for in this section only after local remedies have been exhausted where this is required by international law.

Article 296 Finality and binding force of decisions

1.   Any decision rendered by a court or tribunal having jurisdiction under this section shall be final and shall be complied with by all the parties to the dispute.

2.   Any such decision shall have no binding force except between the parties and in respect of that particular dispute.

SECTION 3. LIMITATIONS AND EXCEPTIONS TO APPLICABILITY OF SECTION 2

Article 297 Limitations on applicability of section 2

1.   Disputes concerning the interpretation or application of this Convention with regard to the exercise by a coastal State of its sovereign rights or jurisdiction provided for in this Convention shall be subject to the procedures provided for in section 2 in the following cases:

(a) when it is alleged that a coastal State has acted in contravention of the provisions of this Convention in regard to the freedoms and rights of navigation, overflight or the laying of submarine cables and pipelines, or in regard to other internationally lawful uses of the sea specified in article 58;

(b) when it is alleged that a State in exercising the aforementioned freedoms, rights or uses has acted in contravention of this Convention or of laws or regulations adopted by the coastal State in conformity with this Convention and other rules of international law not incompatible with this Convention; or

(c) when it is alleged that a coastal State has acted in contravention of specified international rules and standards for the protection and preservation of the marine environment which are applicable to the coastal State and which have been established by this Convention or through a competent international organization or diplomatic conference in accordance with this Convention.

2. (a) Disputes concerning the interpretation or application of the provisions of this Convention with regard to marine scientific research shall be settled in accordance with section 2, except that the coastal State shall not be obliged to accept the submission to such settlement of any dispute arising out of:

    (i) the exercise by the coastal State of a right or discretion in accordance with article 246; or

    (ii) a decision by the coastal State to order suspension or cessation of a research project in accordance with article 253.

(b) A dispute arising from an allegation by the researching State that with respect to a specific project the coastal State is not exercising its rights under articles 246 and 253 in a manner compatible with this Convention shall be submitted, at the request of either party, to conciliation under Annex V, section 2, provided that the conciliation commission shall not call in question the exercise by the coastal State of its discretion to designate specific areas as referred to in article 246, paragraph 6, or of its discretion to withhold consent in accordance with article 246, paragraph 5.

3. (a) Disputes concerning the interpretation or application of the provisions of this Convention with regard to fisheries shall be settled in accordance with section 2, except that the coastal State shall not be obliged to accept the submission to such settlement of any dispute relating to its sovereign rights with respect to the living resources in the exclusive economic zone or their exercise, including its discretionary powers for determining the allowable catch, its harvesting capacity, the allocation of surpluses to other States and the terms and conditions established in its conservation and management laws and regulations.

(b) Where no settlement has been reached by recourse to section 1 of this Part, a dispute shall be submitted to conciliation under Annex V, section 2, at the request of any party to the dispute, when it is alleged that:

    (i) a coastal State has manifestly failed to comply with its obligations to ensure through proper conservation and management measures that the maintenance of the living resources in the exclusive economic zone is not seriously endangered;

    (ii) a coastal State has arbitrarily refused to determine, at the request of another State, the allowable catch and its capacity to harvest living resources with respect to stocks which that other State is interested in fishing; or

    (iii) a coastal State has arbitrarily refused to allocate to any State, under articles 62, 69 and 70 and under the terms and conditions established by the coastal State consistent with this Convention, the whole or part of the surplus it has declared to exist.

(c) In no case shall the conciliation commission substitute its discretion for that of the coastal State.

(d) The report of the conciliation commission shall be communicated to the appropriate international organizations.

(e) In negotiating agreements pursuant to articles 69 and 70, States Parties, unless they otherwise agree, shall include a clause on measures which they shall take in order to minimize the possibility of a disagreement concerning the interpretation or application of the agreement, and on how they should proceed if a disagreement nevertheless arises.

Article 298 Optional exceptions to applicability of section 2

1. When signing, ratifying or acceding to this Convention or at any time thereafter, a State may, without prejudice to the obligations arising under section 1, declare in writing that it does not accept any one or more of the procedures provided for in section 2 with respect to one or more of the following categories of disputes:

(a) (i) disputes concerning the interpretation or application of articles 15, 74 and 83 relating to sea boundary delimitations, or those involving historic bays or titles, provided that a State having made such a declaration shall, when such a dispute arises subsequent to the entry into force of this Convention and where no agreement within a reasonable period of time is reached in negotiations between the parties, at the request of any party to the dispute, accept submission of the matter to conciliation under Annex V, section 2; and provided further that any dispute that necessarily involves the concurrent consideration of any unsettled dispute concerning sovereignty or other rights over continental or insular land territory shall be excluded from such submission;

(ii) after the conciliation commission has presented its report, which shall state the reasons on which it is based, the parties shall negotiate an agreement on the basis of that report; if these negotiations do not result in an agreement, the parties shall, by mutual consent, submit the question to one of the procedures provided for in section 2, unless the parties otherwise agree;

(iii) this subparagraph does not apply to any sea boundary dispute finally settled by an arrangement between the parties, or to any such dispute which is to be settled in accordance with a bilateral or multilateral agreement binding upon those parties;

(b) disputes concerning military activities, including military activities by government vessels and aircraft engaged in non-commercial service, and disputes concerning law enforcement activities in regard to the exercise of sovereign rights or jurisdiction excluded from the jurisdiction of a court or tribunal under article 297, paragraph 2 or 3;

(c) disputes in respect of which the Security Council of the United Nations is exercising the functions assigned to it by the Charter of the United Nations, unless the Security Council decides to remove the matter from its agenda or calls upon the parties to settle it by the means provided for in this Convention.

2. A State Party which has made a declaration under paragraph 1 may at any time withdraw it, or agree to submit a dispute excluded by such declaration to any procedure specified in this Convention.

3. A State Party which has made a declaration under paragraph 1 shall not be entitled to submit any dispute falling within the excepted category of disputes to any procedure in this Convention as against another State Party, without the consent of that party.

4. If one of the States Parties has made a declaration under paragraph 1(a), any other State Party may submit any dispute falling within an excepted category against the declarant party to the procedure specified in such declaration.

5. A new declaration, or the withdrawal of a declaration, does not in any way affect proceedings pending before a court or tribunal in accordance with this article, unless the parties otherwise agree.

6. Declarations and notices of withdrawal of declarations under this article shall be deposited with the Secretary-General of the United Nations, who shall transmit copies thereof to the States Parties.

Article 299 Right of the parties to agree upon a procedure

1. A dispute excluded under article 297 or excepted by a declaration made under article 298 from the dispute settlement procedures provided for in section 2 may be submitted to such procedures only by agreement of the parties to the dispute.

2. Nothing in this section impairs the right of the parties to the dispute to agree to some other procedure for the settlement of such dispute or to reach an amicable settlement.

PART XVI

GENERAL PROVISIONS

Article 300 Good faith and abuse of rights

States Parties shall fulfil in good faith the obligations assumed under this Convention and shall exercise the rights, jurisdiction and freedoms recognized in this Convention in a manner which would not constitute an abuse of right.

Article 301 Peaceful uses of the seas

In exercising their rights and performing their duties under this Convention, States Parties shall refrain from any threat or use of force against the territorial integrity or political independence of any State, or in any other manner inconsistent with the principles of international law embodied in the Charter of the United Nations.

Article 302 Disclosure of information

Without prejudice to the right of a State Party to resort to the procedures for the settlement of disputes provided for in this Convention, nothing in this Convention shall be deemed to require a State Party, in the fulfilment of its obligations under this Convention, to supply information the disclosure of which is contrary to the essential interests of its security.

Article 303 Archaeological and historical objects found at sea

1. States have the duty to protect objects of an archaeological and historical nature found at sea and shall co-operate for this purpose.

2. In order to control traffic in such objects, the coastal State may, in applying article 33, presume that their removal from the sea-bed in the zone referred to in that article without its approval would result in an infringement within its territory or territorial sea of the laws and regulations referred to in that article.

3. Nothing in this article affects the rights of identifiable owners, the law of salvage or other rules of admiralty, or laws and practices with respect to cultural exchanges.

4. This article is without prejudice to other international agreements and rules of international law regarding the protection of objects of an archaeological and historical nature.

Article 304 Responsibility and liability for damage

The provisions of this Convention regarding responsibility and liability for damage are without prejudice to the application of existing rules and the development of further rules regarding responsibility and liability under international law.

PART XVII

FINAL PROVISIONS

Article 305 Signature

1. This Convention shall be open for signature by:
    (a) all States;
    (b) Namibia, represented by the United Nations Council for Namibia;
    (c) all self-governing associated States which have chosen that status in an act of self-determination supervised and approved by the United Nations in accordance with General Assembly resolution 1514 (XV) and which have competence over the matters governed by this Convention, including the competence to enter into treaties in respect of those matters;
    (d) all self-governing associated States which, in accordance with their respective instruments of association, have competence over the matters governed by this Convention, including the competence to enter into treaties in respect of those matters;
    (e) all territories which enjoy full internal self-government, recognized as such by the United Nations, but have not attained full independence in accordance with General Assembly resolution 1514 (XV) and which have competence over the matters governed by this Convention, including the competence to enter into treaties in respect of those matters;
    (f) international organizations, in accordance with Annex IX.
2. This Convention shall remain open for signature until 9 December 1984 at the Ministry of Foreign Affairs of Jamaica and also, from 1 July 1983 until 9 December 1984, at United Nations Headquarters in New York.

Article 306 Ratification and formal confirmation

This Convention is subject to ratification by States and the other entities referred to in article 305, paragraph l(b), (c), (d) and (e), and to formal confirmation, in accordance with Annex IX, by the entities referred to in article 305, paragraph l(f). The instruments of ratification and of formal confirmation shall be deposited with the Secretary-General of the United Nations.

Article 307 Accession

This Convention shall remain open for accession by States and the other entities referred to in article 305. Accession by the entities referred to in article 305, paragraph l(f), shall be in accordance with Annex IX. The instruments of accession shall be deposited with the Secretary-General of the United Nations.

Article 308 Entry into force

1. This Convention shall enter into force 12 months after the date of deposit of the sixtieth instrument of ratification or accession.
2. For each State ratifying or acceding to this Convention after the deposit of the sixtieth instrument of ratification or accession, the Convention shall enter into force on the thirtieth day following the deposit of its instrument of ratification or accession, subject to paragraph 1.

3. The Assembly of the Authority shall meet on the date of entry into force of this Convention and shall elect the Council of the Authority. The first Council shall be constituted in a manner consistent with the purpose of article 161 if the provisions of that article cannot be strictly applied.

4. The rules, regulations and procedures drafted by the Preparatory Commission shall apply provisionally pending their formal adoption by the Authority in accordance with Part XI.

5. The Authority and its organs shall act in accordance with resolution II of the Third United Nations Conference on the Law of the Sea relating to preparatory investment and with decisions of the Preparatory Commission taken pursuant to that resolution.

Article 309 Reservations and exceptions

No reservations or exceptions may be made to this Convention unless expressly permitted by other articles of this Convention.

Article 310 Declarations and statements

Article 309 does not preclude a State, when signing, ratifying or acceding to this Convention, from making declarations or statements, however phrased or named, with a view, *inter alia*, to the harmonization of its laws and regulations with the provisions of this Convention, provided that such declarations or statements do not purport to exclude or to modify the legal effect of the provisions of this Convention in their application to that State.

Article 311 Relation to other conventions and international agreements

1. This Convention shall prevail, as between States Parties, over the Geneva Conventions on the Law of the Sea of 29 April 1958.

2. This Convention shall not alter the rights and obligations of States Parties which arise from other agreements compatible with this Convention and which do not affect the enjoyment by other States Parties of their rights or the performance of their obligations under this Convention.

3. Two or more States Parties may conclude agreements modifying or suspending the operation of provisions of this Convention, applicable solely to the relations between them, provided that such agreements do not relate to a provision derogation from which is incompatible with the effective execution of the object and purpose of this Convention, and provided further that such agreements shall not affect the application of the basic principles embodied herein, and that the provisions of such agreements do not affect the enjoyment by other States Parties of their rights or the performance of their obligations under this Convention.

4. States Parties intending to conclude an agreement referred to in paragraph 3 shall notify the other States Parties through the depositary of this Convention of their intention to conclude the agreement and of the modification or suspension for which it provides.

5. This article does not affect international agreements expressly permitted or preserved by other articles of this Convention.

6. States Parties agree that there shall be no amendments to the basic principle relating to the common heritage of mankind set forth in article 136 and that they shall not be party to any agreement in derogation thereof.

Article 312 Amendment

1. After the expiry of a period of 10 years from the date of entry into force of this Convention, a State Party may, by written communication addressed to the Secretary-General of the United Nations, propose specific amendments to this Convention, other

than those relating to activities in the Area, and request the convening of a conference to consider such proposed amendments. The Secretary-General shall circulate such communication to all States Parties. If, within 12 months from the date of the circulation of the communication, not less than one half of the States Parties reply favourably to the request, the Secretary-General shall convene the conference.

2. The decision-making procedure applicable at the amendment conference shall be the same as that applicable at the Third United Nations Conference on the Law of the Sea unless otherwise decided by the conference. The conference should make every effort to reach agreement on any amendments by way of consensus and there should be no voting on them until all efforts at consensus have been exhausted.

Article 313 Amendment by simplified procedure

1. A State Party may, by written communication addressed to the Secretary-General of the United Nations, propose an amendment to this Convention, other than an amendment relating to activities in the Area, to be adopted by the simplified procedure set forth in this article without convening a conference. The Secretary-General shall circulate the communication to all States Parties.

2. If, within a period of 12 months from the date of the circulation of the communication, a State Party objects to the proposed amendment or to the proposal for its adoption by the simplified procedure, the amendment shall be considered rejected. The Secretary-General shall immediately notify all States Parties accordingly.

3. If, 12 months from the date of the circulation of the communication, no State Party has objected to the proposed amendment or to the proposal for its adoption by the simplified procedure, the proposed amendment shall be considered adopted. The Secretary-General shall notify all States Parties that the proposed amendment has been adopted.

Article 314 Amendments to the provisions of this Convention relating exclusively to activities in the Area

1. A State Party may, by written communication addressed to the Secretary-General of the Authority, propose an amendment to the provisions of this Convention relating exclusively to activities in the Area, including Annex VI, section 4. The Secretary-General shall circulate such communication to all States Parties. The proposed amendment shall be subject to approval by the Assembly following its approval by the Council. Representatives of States Parties in those organs shall have full powers to consider and approve the proposed amendment. The proposed amendment as approved by the Council and the Assembly shall be considered adopted.

2. Before approving any amendment under paragraph 1, the Council and the Assembly shall ensure that it does not prejudice the system of exploration for and exploitation of the resources of the Area, pending the Review Conference in accordance with article 155.

Article 315 Signature, ratification of, accession to and authentic texts of amendments

1. Once adopted, amendments to this Convention shall be open for signature by States Parties for 12 months from the date of adoption, at United Nations Headquarters in New York, unless otherwise provided in the amendment itself.

2. Articles 306, 307 and 320 apply to all amendments to this Convention.

Article 316 Entry into force of amendments

1. Amendments to this Convention, other than those referred to in paragraph 5, shall enter into force for the States Parties ratifying or acceding to them on the thirtieth day

following the deposit of instruments of ratification or accession by two thirds of the States Parties or by 60 States Parties, whichever is greater. Such amendments shall not affect the enjoyment by other States Parties of their rights or the performance of their obligations under this Convention.

2. An amendment may provide that a larger number of ratifications or accessions shall be required for its entry into force than are required by this article.

3. For each State Party ratifying or acceding to an amendment referred to in paragraph 1 after the deposit of the required number of instruments of ratification or accession, the amendment shall enter into force on the thirtieth day following the deposit of its instrument of ratification or accession.

4. A State which becomes a Party to this Convention after the entry into force of an amendment in accordance with paragraph 1 shall, failing an expression of a different intention by that State:

(a) be considered as a Party to this Convention as so amended; and

(b) be considered as a Party to the unamended Convention in relation to any State Party not bound by the amendment.

5. Any amendment relating exclusively to activities in the Area and any amendment to Annex VI shall enter into force for all States Parties one year following the deposit of instruments of ratification or accession by three fourths of the States Parties.

6. A State which becomes a Party to this Convention after the entry into force of amendments in accordance with paragraph 5 shall be considered as a Party to this Convention as so amended.

Article 317 Denunciation

1. A State Party may, by written notification addressed to the Secretary-General of the United Nations, denounce this Convention and may indicate its reasons. Failure to indicate reasons shall not affect the validity of the denunciation. The denunciation shall take effect one year after the date of receipt of the notification, unless the notification specifies a later date.

2. A State shall not be discharged by reason of the denunciation from the financial and contractual obligations which accrued while it was a Party to this Convention, nor shall the denunciation affect any right, obligation or legal situation of that State created through the execution of this Convention prior to its termination for that State.

3. The denunciation shall not in any way affect the duty of any State Party to fulfil any obligation embodied in this Convention to which it would be subject under international law independently of this Convention.

Article 318 Status of Annexes

The Annexes form an integral part of this Convention and, unless expressly provided otherwise, a reference to this Convention or to one of its Parts includes a reference to the Annexes relating thereto.

Article 319 Depositary

1. The Secretary-General of the United Nations shall be the depositary of this Convention and amendments thereto.

2. In addition to his functions as depositary, the Secretary-General shall:

(a) report to all States Parties, the Authority and competent international organizations on issues of a general nature that have arisen with respect to this Convention;

(b) notify the Authority of ratifications and formal confirmations of and accessions to this Convention and amendments thereto, as well as of denunciations of this Convention;

(c)   notify States Parties of agreements in accordance with article 311, paragraph 4;

(d)   circulate amendments adopted in accordance with this Convention to States Parties for ratification or accession;

(e)   convene necessary meetings of States Parties in accordance with this Convention.

3.   (a)   The Secretary-General shall also transmit to the observers referred to in article 156:

(i)   reports referred to in paragraph 2(a);

(ii)   notifications referred to in paragraph 2(b) and (c); and

(iii)   texts of amendments referred to in paragraph 2(d), for their information.

(b)   The Secretary-General shall also invite those observers to participate as observers at meetings of States Parties referred to in paragraph 2(e).

Article 320 Authentic texts

The original of this Convention, of which the Arabic, Chinese, English, French, Russian and Spanish texts are equally authentic, shall, subject to article 305, paragraph 2, be deposited with the Secretary-General of the United Nations.

IN WITNESS WHEREOF, the undersigned Plenipotentiaries, being duly authorized thereto, have signed this Convention.

DONE at Montego Bay, this tenth day of December, one thousand nine hundred and eighty-two.

ANNEX I
HIGHLY MIGRATORY SPECIES

1.   Albacore tuna: *Thunnus alalunga*.

2.   Bluefin tuna: *Thunnus thynnus*.

3.   Bigeye tuna: *Thunnus obesus*.

4.   Skipjack tuna: *Katsuwonus pelamis*.

5.   Yellowfin tuna: *Thunnus albacares*.

6.   Blackfin tuna: *Thunnus atlanticus*.

7.   Little tuna: *Euthynnus alletteratus*; *Euthynnus affinis*.

8.   Southern bluefin tuna: *Thunnus maccoyii*.

9.   Frigate mackerel: *Auxis thazard*; *Auxis rochei*.

10.   Pomfrets: Family *Bramidae*.

11.   Marlins: *Tetrapturus angustirostris*; *Tetrapturus belone*; *Tetrapturus pfluegeri*; *Tetrapturus albidus*; *Tetrapturus audax*; *Tetrapturus georgei*; *Makaira mazara*; *Makaira indica*; *Makaira nigricans*.

12.   Sail-fishes: *Istiophorus platypterus*; *Istiophorus albicans*.

13.   Swordfish: *Xiphias gladius*.

14.   Sauries: *Scomberesox saurus*; *Cololabis saira*; *Cololabis adocetus*; *Scomberesox saurus scombroides*.

15.   Dolphin: *Coryphaena hippurus*; *Coryphaena equiselis*.

16.   Oceanic sharks: *Hexanchus griseus*; *Cetorhinus maximus*; Family *Alopiidae*; *Rhincodon typus*; Family *Carcharhinidae*; Family *Sphyrnidae*; Family *Isurida*.

17.   Cetaceans: Family *Physeteridae*; Family *Balaenopteridae*; Family *Balaenidae*; Family *Eschrichtiidae*; Family *Monodontidae*; Family *Ziphiidae*; Family *Delphinidae*.

ANNEX II
COMMISSION ON THE LIMITS OF THE CONTINENTAL SHELF

Article 1
In accordance with the provisions of article 76, a Commission on the Limits of the Continental Shelf beyond 200 nautical miles shall be established in conformity with the following articles.

Article 2
1. The Commission shall consist of 21 members who shall be experts in the field of geology, geophysics or hydrography, elected by States Parties to this Convention from among their nationals, having due regard to the need to ensure equitable geographical representation, who shall serve in their personal capacities.

2. The initial election shall be held as soon as possible but in any case within 18 months after the date of entry into force of this Convention. At least three months before the date of each election, the Secretary-General of the United Nations shall address a letter to the States Parties, inviting the submission of nominations, after appropriate regional consultations, within three months. The Secretary-General shall prepare a list in alphabetical order of all persons thus nominated and shall submit it to all the States Parties.

3. Elections of the members of the Commission shall be held at a meeting of States Parties convened by the Secretary-General at United Nations Headquarters. At that meeting, for which two thirds of the States Parties shall constitute a quorum, the persons elected to the Commission shall be those nominees who obtain a two-thirds majority of the votes of the representatives of States Parties present and voting. Not less than three members shall be elected from each geographical region.

4. The members of the Commission shall be elected for a term of five years. They shall be eligible for re-election.

5. The State Party which submitted the nomination of a member of the Commission shall defray the expenses of that member while in performance of Commission duties. The coastal State concerned shall defray the expenses incurred in respect of the advice referred to in article 3, paragraph 1(b), of this Annex. The secretariat of the Commission shall be provided by the Secretary-General of the United Nations.

Article 3
1. The functions of the Commission shall be:
(a)   to consider the data and other material submitted by coastal States concerning the outer limits of the continental shelf in areas where those limits extend beyond 200 nautical miles, and to make recommendations in accordance with article 76 and the Statement of Understanding adopted on 29 August 1980 by the Third United Nations Conference on the Law of the Sea;
(b)   to provide scientific and technical advice, if requested by the coastal State concerned during the preparation of the data referred to in subparagraph (a).

2. The Commission may co-operate, to the extent considered necessary and useful, with the Intergovernmental Oceanographic Commission of UNESCO, the International Hydrographic Organization and other competent international organizations with a view to exchanging scientific and technical information which might be of assistance in discharging the Commission's responsibilities.

Article 4
Where a coastal State intends to establish, in accordance with article 76, the outer limits of its continental shelf beyond 200 nautical miles, it shall submit particulars of

such limits to the Commission along with supporting scientific and technical data as soon as possible but in any case within 10 years of the entry into force of this Convention for that State. The coastal State shall at the same time give the names of any Commission members who have provided it with scientific and technical advice.

Article 5

Unless the Commission decides otherwise, the Commission shall function by way of sub-commissions composed of seven members, appointed in a balanced manner taking into account the specific elements of each submission by a coastal State. Nationals of the coastal State making the submission who are members of the Commission and any Commission member who has assisted a coastal State by providing scientific and technical advice with respect to the delineation shall not be a member of the sub-commission dealing with that submission but has the right to participate as a member in the proceedings of the Commission concerning the said submission. The coastal State which has made a submission to the Commission may send its representatives to participate in the relevant proceedings without the right to vote.

Article 6

1. The sub-commission shall submit its recommendations to the Commission.

2. Approval by the Commission of the recommendations of the sub-commission shall be by a majority of two thirds of Commission members present and voting.

3. The recommendations of the Commission shall be submitted in writing to the coastal State which made the submission and to the Secretary-General of the United Nations.

Article 7

Coastal States shall establish the outer limits of the continental shelf in conformity with the provisions of article 76, paragraph 8, and in accordance with the appropriate national procedures.

Article 8

In the case of disagreement by the coastal State with the recommendations of the Commission, the coastal State shall, within a reasonable time, make a revised or new submission to the Commission.

Article 9

The actions of the Commission shall not prejudice matters relating to delimitation of boundaries between States with opposite or adjacent coasts.

ANNEX III
BASIC CONDITIONS OF PROSPECTING, EXPLORATION AND EXPLOITATION

Article 1 Title to minerals

Title to minerals shall pass upon recovery in accordance with this Convention.

Article 2 Prospecting

1. (a) The Authority shall encourage prospecting in the Area.

    (b) Prospecting shall be conducted only after the Authority has received a satisfactory written undertaking that the proposed prospector will comply with this Convention and the relevant rules, regulations and procedures of the Authority concerning cooperation in the training programmes referred to in articles 143 and 144 and the protection of the marine environment, and will accept verification by the Authority of compliance therewith. The proposed prospector shall, at the same time, notify the Authority of the approximate area or areas in which prospecting is to be conducted.

(c) Prospecting may be conducted simultaneously by more than one prospector in the same area or areas.

2. Prospecting shall not confer on the prospector any rights with respect to resources. A prospector may, however, recover a reasonable quantity of minerals to be used for testing.

Article 3 Exploration and exploitation

1. The Enterprise, States Parties, and the other entities referred to in article 153, paragraph 2(b), may apply to the Authority for approval of plans of work for activities in the Area.

2. The Enterprise may apply with respect to any part of the Area, but applications by others with respect to reserved areas are subject to the additional requirements of article 9 of this Annex.

3. Exploration and exploitation shall be carried out only in areas specified in plans of work referred to in article 153, paragraph 3, and approved by the Authority in accordance with this Convention and the relevant rules, regulations and procedures of the Authority.

4. Every approved plan of work shall:

(a) be in conformity with this Convention and the rules, regulations and procedures of the Authority;

(b) provide for control by the Authority of activities in the Area in accordance with article 153, paragraph 4;

(c) confer on the operator, in accordance with the rules, regulations and procedures of the Authority, the exclusive right to explore for and exploit the specified categories of resources in the area covered by the plan of work. If, however, the applicant presents for approval a plan of work covering only the stage of exploration or the stage of exploitation, the approved plan of work shall confer such exclusive right with respect to that stage only.

5. Upon its approval by the Authority, every plan of work, except those presented by the Enterprise, shall be in the form of a contract concluded between the Authority and the applicant or applicants.[1]

Article 4 Qualifications of applicants

1. Applicants, other than the Enterprise, shall be qualified if they have the nationality or control and sponsorship required by article 153, paragraph 2(b), and if they follow the procedures and meet the qualification standards set forth in the rules, regulations and procedures of the Authority.

2. Except as provided in paragraph 6, such qualification standards shall relate to the financial and technical capabilities of the applicant and his performance under any previous contracts with the Authority.

3. Each applicant shall be sponsored by the State Party of which it is a national unless the applicant has more than one nationality, as in the case of a partnership or consortium of entities from several States, in which event all States Parties involved shall sponsor the application, or unless the applicant is effectively controlled by another State Party or its nationals, in which event both States Parties shall sponsor the application. The criteria and procedures for implementation of the sponsorship requirements shall be set forth in the rules, regulations and procedures of the Authority.

---

[1] See also Implementation Agreement [Doc. 37], Annex, Section 2, para. 4.

4.   The sponsoring State or States shall, pursuant to article 139, have the responsibility to ensure, within their legal systems, that a contractor so sponsored shall carry out activities in the Area in conformity with the terms of its contract and its obligations under this Convention. A sponsoring State shall not, however, be liable for damage caused by any failure of a contractor sponsored by it to comply with its obligations if that State Party has adopted laws and regulations and taken administrative measures which are, within the framework of its legal system, reasonably appropriate for securing compliance by persons under its jurisdiction.

5.   The procedures for assessing the qualifications of States Parties which are applicants shall take into account their character as States.

6.   The qualification standards shall require that every applicant, without exception, shall as part of his application undertake:

(a)   to accept as enforceable and comply with the applicable obligations created by the provisions of Part XI, the rules, regulations and procedures of the Authority, the decisions of the organs of the Authority and terms of his contracts with the Authority;

(b)   to accept control by the Authority of activities in the Area, as authorized by this Convention;

(c)   to provide the Authority with a written assurance that his obligations under the contract will be fulfilled in good faith;

(d)   to comply with the provisions on the transfer of technology set forth in article 5 of this Annex.

Article 5 Transfer of technology[2]

1.   When submitting a plan of work, every applicant shall make available to the Authority a general description of the equipment and methods to be used in carrying out activities in the Area, and other relevant non-proprietary information about the characteristics of such technology and information as to where such technology is available.

2.   Every operator shall inform the Authority of revisions in the description and information made available pursuant to paragraph 1 whenever a substantial technological change or innovation is introduced.

3.   Every contract for carrying out activities in the Area shall contain the following undertakings by the contractor:

(a)   to make available to the Enterprise on fair and reasonable commercial terms and conditions, whenever the Authority so requests, the technology which he uses in carrying out activities in the Area under the contract, which the contractor is legally entitled to transfer. This shall be done by means of licences or other appropriate arrangements which the contractor shall negotiate with the Enterprise and which shall be set forth in a specific agreement supplementary to the contract. This undertaking may be invoked only if the Enterprise finds that it is unable to obtain the same or equally efficient and useful technology on the open market on fair and reasonable commercial terms and conditions;

(b)   to obtain a written assurance from the owner of any technology used in carrying out activities in the Area under the contract, which is not generally available on the open market and which is not covered by subparagraph (a), that the owner will, whenever the Authority so requests, make that technology available to the Enterprise under licence or other appropriate arrangements and on fair and reasonable commercial terms and conditions, to the same extent as made available to the contractor. If this assurance is not obtained, the technology in question shall not be used by the contractor in carrying out activities in the Area;

---

[2] See also Implementation Agreement [Doc. 37], Annex, Section 5, para. 2.

(c)   to acquire from the owner by means of an enforceable contract, upon the request of the Enterprise and if it is possible to do so without substantial cost to the contractor, the legal right to transfer to the Enterprise any technology used by the contractor, in carrying out activities in the Area under the contract, which the contractor is otherwise not legally entitled to transfer and which is not generally available on the open market. In cases where there is a substantial corporate relationship between the contractor and the owner of the technology, the closeness of this relationship and the degree of control or influence shall be relevant to the determination whether all feasible measures have been taken to acquire such a right. In cases where the contractor exercises effective control over the owner, failure to acquire from the owner the legal right shall be considered relevant to the contractor's qualification for any subsequent application for approval of a plan of work;

(d)   to facilitate, upon the request of the Enterprise, the acquisition by the Enterprise of any technology covered by subparagraph (b), under licence or other appropriate arrangements and on fair and reasonable commercial terms and conditions, if the Enterprise decides to negotiate directly with the owner of the technology;

(e)   to take the same measures as are prescribed in subparagraphs (a), (b), (c) and (d) for the benefit of a developing State or group of developing States which has applied for a contract under article 9 of this Annex, provided that these measures shall be limited to the exploitation of the part of the area proposed by the contractor which has been reserved pursuant to article 8 of this Annex and provided that activities under the contract sought by the developing State or group of developing States would not involve transfer of technology to a third State or the nationals of a third State. The obligation under this provision shall only apply with respect to any given contractor where technology has not been requested by the Enterprise or transferred by that contractor to the Enterprise.

4.   Disputes concerning undertakings required by paragraph 3, like other provisions of the contracts, shall be subject to compulsory settlement in accordance with Part XI and, in cases of violation of these undertakings, suspension or termination of the contract or monetary penalties may be ordered in accordance with article 18 of this Annex. Disputes as to whether offers made by the contractor are within the range of fair and reasonable commercial terms and conditions may be submitted by either party to binding commercial arbitration in accordance with the UNCITRAL Arbitration Rules or such other arbitration rules as may be prescribed in the rules, regulations and procedures of the Authority. If the finding is that the offer made by the contractor is not within the range of fair and reasonable commercial terms and conditions, the contractor shall be given 45 days to revise his offer to bring it within that range before the Authority takes any action in accordance with article 18 of this Annex.

5.   If the Enterprise is unable to obtain on fair and reasonable commercial terms and conditions appropriate technology to enable it to commence in a timely manner the recovery and processing of minerals from the Area, either the Council or the Assembly may convene a group of States Parties composed of those which are engaged in activities in the Area, those which have sponsored entities which are engaged in activities in the Area and other States Parties having access to such technology. This group shall consult together and shall take effective measures to ensure that such technology is made available to the Enterprise on fair and reasonable commercial terms and conditions. Each such State Party shall take all feasible measures to this end within its own legal system.

6.   In the case of joint ventures with the Enterprise, transfer of technology will be in accordance with the terms of the joint venture agreement.

7. The undertakings required by paragraph 3 shall be included in each contract for the carrying out of activities in the Area until 10 years after the commencement of commercial production by the Enterprise, and may be invoked during that period.

8. For the purposes of this article, 'technology' means the specialized equipment and technical know-how, including manuals, designs, operating instructions, training and technical advice and assistance, necessary to assemble, maintain and operate a viable system and the legal right to use these items for that purpose on a non-exclusive basis.

Article 6 Approval of plans of work

1. Six months after the entry into force of this Convention, and thereafter each fourth month, the Authority shall take up for consideration proposed plans of work.

2. When considering an application for approval of a plan of work in the form of a contract, the Authority shall first ascertain whether:

   (a) the applicant has complied with the procedures established for applications in accordance with article 4 of this Annex and has given the Authority the undertakings and assurances required by that article. In cases of non-compliance with these procedures or in the absence of any of these undertakings and assurances, the applicant shall be given 45 days to remedy these defects;

   (b) the applicant possesses the requisite qualifications provided for in article 4 of this Annex.

3. All proposed plans of work shall be taken up in the order in which they are received. The proposed plans of work shall comply with and be governed by the relevant provisions of this Convention and the rules, regulations and procedures of the Authority, including those on operational requirements, financial contributions and the undertakings concerning the transfer of technology. If the proposed plans of work conform to these requirements, the Authority shall approve them provided that they are in accordance with the uniform and non-discriminatory requirements set forth in the rules, regulations and procedures of the Authority, unless:

   (a) part or all of the area covered by the proposed plan of work is included in an approved plan of work or a previously submitted proposed plan of work which has not yet been finally acted on by the Authority;

   (b) part or all of the area covered by the proposed plan of work is disapproved by the Authority pursuant to article 162, paragraph 2(x); or

   (c) the proposed plan of work has been submitted or sponsored by a State Party which already holds:

      (i) plans of work for exploration and exploitation of polymetallic nodules in non-reserved areas that, together with either part of the area covered by the application for a plan of work, exceed in size 30 per cent of a circular area of 400,000 square kilometres surrounding the centre of either part of the area covered by the proposed plan of work;

      (ii) plans of work for the exploration and exploitation of polymetallic nodules in non-reserved areas which, taken together, constitute 2 per cent of the total seabed area which is not reserved or disapproved for exploitation pursuant to article 162, paragraph (2)(x).

4. For the purpose of the standard set forth in paragraph 3(c), a plan of work submitted by a partnership or consortium shall be counted on a *pro rata* basis among the sponsoring States Parties involved in accordance with article 4, paragraph 3, of this Annex. The Authority may approve plans of work covered by paragraph 3(c) if it determines that such approval would not permit a State Party or entities sponsored by it to monopolize the conduct of activities in the Area or to preclude other States Parties from activities in the Area.

5. Notwithstanding paragraph 3(a), after the end of the interim period specified in article 151, paragraph 3, the Authority may adopt by means of rules, regulations and procedures other procedures and criteria consistent with this Convention for deciding which applicants shall have plans of work approved in cases of selection among applicants for a proposed area. These procedures and criteria shall ensure approval of plans of work on an equitable and non-discriminatory basis.[3]

Article 7 Selection among applicants for production authorizations[4]

1. Six months after the entry into force of this Convention, and thereafter each fourth month, the Authority shall take up for consideration applications for production authorizations submitted during the immediately preceding period. The Authority shall issue the authorizations applied for if all such applications can be approved without exceeding the production limitation or contravening the obligations of the Authority under a commodity agreement or arrangement to which it has become a party, as provided in article 151.

2. When a selection must be made among applicants for production authorizations because of the production limitation set forth in article 151, paragraphs 2 to 7, or because of the obligations of the Authority under a commodity agreement or arrangement to which it has become a party, as provided for in article 151, paragraph 1, the Authority shall make the selection on the basis of objective and non-discriminatory standards set forth in its rules, regulations and procedures.

3. In the application of paragraph 2, the Authority shall give priority to those applicants which:
    (a) give better assurance of performance, taking into account their financial and technical qualifications and their performance, if any, under previously approved plans of work;
    (b) provide earlier prospective financial benefits to the Authority, taking into account when commercial production is scheduled to begin;
    (c) have already invested the most resources and effort in prospecting or exploration.

4. Applicants which are not selected in any period shall have priority in subsequent periods until they receive a production authorization.

5. Selection shall be made taking into account the need to enhance opportunities for all States Parties, irrespective of their social and economic systems or geographical locations so as to avoid discrimination against any State or system, to participate in activities in the Area and to prevent monopolization of those activities.

6. Whenever fewer reserved areas than non-reserved areas are under exploitation, applications for production authorizations with respect to reserved areas shall have priority.

7. The decisions referred to in this article shall be taken as soon as possible after the close of each period.

Article 8 Reservation of areas[5]

Each application, other than those submitted by the Enterprise or by any other entities for reserved areas, shall cover a total area, which need not be a single continuous area, sufficiently large and of sufficient estimated commercial value to allow two mining operations. The applicant shall indicate the co-ordinates dividing the area into two parts of equal estimated commercial value and submit all the data obtained by him with respect to both parts. Without prejudice to the powers of the Authority pursuant to article 17 of this

---

[3] See also Implementation Agreement [Doc. 37], Annex, Section 6, para. 7.

[4] See also Implementation Agreement [Doc. 37], Annex, Section 6, para. 7, and Section 1, paras. 6-11.

[5] See also Implementation Agreement [Doc. 37], Annex, Section 1, para. 10.

Annex, the data to be submitted concerning polymetallic nodules shall relate to mapping, sampling, the abundance of nodules, and their metal content. Within 45 days of receiving such data, the Authority shall designate which part is to be reserved solely for the conduct of activities by the Authority through the Enterprise or in association with developing States. This designation may be deferred for a further period of 45 days if the Authority requests an independent expert to assess whether all data required by this article has been submitted. The area designated shall become a reserved area as soon as the plan of work for the non-reserved area is approved and the contract is signed.

Article 9 Activities in reserved areas[6]
1. The Enterprise shall be given an opportunity to decide whether it intends to carry out activities in each reserved area. This decision may be taken at any time, unless a notification pursuant to paragraph 4 is received by the Authority, in which event the Enterprise shall take its decision within a reasonable time. The Enterprise may decide to exploit such areas in joint ventures with the interested State or entity.
2. The Enterprise may conclude contracts for the execution of part of its activities in accordance with Annex IV, article 12. It may also enter into joint ventures for the conduct of such activities with any entities which are eligible to carry out activities in the Area pursuant to article 153, paragraph 2(b). When considering such joint ventures, the Enterprise shall offer to States Parties which are developing States and their nationals the opportunity of effective participation.
3. The Authority may prescribe, in its rules, regulations and procedures, substantive and procedural requirements and conditions with respect to such contracts and joint ventures.
4. Any State Party which is a developing State or any natural or juridical person sponsored by it and effectively controlled by it or by other developing State which is a qualified applicant, or any group of the foregoing, may notify the Authority that it wishes to submit a plan of work pursuant to article 6 of this Annex with respect to a reserved area. The plan of work shall be considered if the Enterprise decides, pursuant to paragraph 1, that it does not intend to carry out activities in that area.

Article 10 Preference and priority among applicants[7]
An operator who has an approved plan of work for exploration only, as provided in article 3, paragraph 4(c), of this Annex shall have a preference and a priority among applicants for a plan of work covering exploitation of the same area and resources. However, such preference or priority may be withdrawn if the operator's performance has not been satisfactory.

Article 11 Joint arrangements
1. Contracts may provide for joint arrangements between the contractor and the Authority through the Enterprise, in the form of joint ventures or production sharing, as well as any other form of joint arrangement, which shall have the same protection against revision, suspension or termination as contracts with the Authority.
2. Contractors entering into such joint arrangements with the Enterprise may receive financial incentives as provided for in article 13 of this Annex.
3. Partners in joint ventures with the Enterprise shall be liable for the payments required by article 13 of this Annex to the extent of their share in the joint ventures, subject to financial incentives as provided for in that article.

---

[6] See also Implementation Agreement [Doc. 37], Annex, Section 2, para. 5.
[7] See also Implementation Agreement [Doc. 37], Annex, Section 1, para. 13.

Article 12 Activities carried out by the Enterprise[8]

1. Activities in the Area carried out by the Enterprise pursuant to article 153, paragraph 2(a), shall be governed by Part XI, the rules, regulations and procedures of the Authority and its relevant decisions.

2. Any plan of work submitted by the Enterprise shall be accompanied by evidence supporting its financial and technical capabilities.

Article 13 Financial terms of contracts[9]

1. In adopting rules, regulations and procedures concerning the financial terms of a contract between the Authority and the entities referred to in article 153, paragraph 2(b), and in negotiating those financial terms in accordance with Part XI and those rules, regulations and procedures, the Authority shall be guided by the following objectives:

(a) to ensure optimum revenues for the Authority from the proceeds of commercial production;

(b) to attract investments and technology to the exploration and exploitation of the Area;

(c) to ensure equality of financial treatment and comparable financial obligations for contractors;

(d) to provide incentives on a uniform and non-discriminatory basis for contractors to undertake joint arrangements with the Enterprise and developing States or their nationals, to stimulate the transfer of technology thereto, and to train the personnel of the Authority and of developing States;

(e) to enable the Enterprise to engage in seabed mining effectively at the same time as the entities referred to in article 153, paragraph 2(b); and

(f) to ensure that, as a result of the financial incentives provided to contractors under paragraph 14, under the terms of contracts reviewed in accordance with article 19 of this Annex or under the provisions of article 11 of this Annex with respect to joint ventures, contractors are not subsidized so as to be given an artificial competitive advantage with respect to land-based miners.

2. A fee shall be levied for the administrative cost of processing an application for approval of a plan of work in the form of a contract and shall be fixed at an amount of $US 500,000 per application. The amount of the fee shall be reviewed from time to time by the Council in order to ensure that it covers the administrative cost incurred. If such administrative cost incurred by the Authority in processing an application is less than the fixed amount, the Authority shall refund the difference to the applicant.

3. A contractor shall pay an annual fixed fee of $US 1 million from the date of entry into force of the contract. If the approved date of commencement of commercial production is postponed because of a delay in issuing the production authorization, in accordance with article 151, the annual fixed fee shall be waived for the period of postponement. From the date of commencement of commercial production, the contractor shall pay either the production charge or the annual fixed fee, whichever is greater.

4. Within a year of the date of commencement of commercial production, in conformity with paragraph 3, a contractor shall choose to make his financial contribution to the Authority by either:

(a) paying a production charge only; or

(b) paying a combination of a production charge and a share of net proceeds.

5. (a) If a contractor chooses to make his financial contribution to the Authority by paying a production charge only, it shall be fixed at a percentage of the market value of the processed metals produced from the polymetallic

---

[8] See also Implementation Agreement [Doc. 37], Annex, Section 2, para. 4.
[9] See also Implementation Agreement [Doc. 37], Annex, Section 8.

nodules recovered from the area covered by the contract. This percentage shall be fixed as follows:

    (i)   years 1-10 of commercial production: 5 per cent

    (ii) years 11 to the end of commercial production: 12 per cent

  (b) The said market value shall be the product of the quantity of the processed metals produced from the polymetallic nodules extracted from the area covered by the contract and the average price for those metals during the relevant accounting year, as defined in paragraphs 7 and 8.

  6. If a contractor chooses to make his financial contribution to the Authority by paying a combination of a production charge and a share of net proceeds, such payments shall be determined as follows:

  (a) The production charge shall be fixed at a percentage of the market value, determined in accordance with subparagraph (b), of the processed metals produced from the polymetallic nodules recovered from the area covered by the contract. This percentage shall be fixed as follows:

    (i)   first period of commercial production: 2 per cent

    (ii) second period of commercial production: 4 per cent

    If, in the second period of commercial production, as defined in subparagraph (d), the return on investment in any accounting year as defined in subparagraph (m) falls below 15 per cent as a result of the payment of the production charge at 4 per cent, the production charge shall be 2 per cent instead of 4 per cent in that accounting year.

  (b) The said market value shall be the product of the quantity of the processed metals produced from the polymetallic nodules recovered from the area covered by the contract and the average price for those metals during the relevant accounting year as defined in paragraphs 7 and 8.

  (c) (i) The Authority's share of net proceeds shall be taken out of that portion of the contractor's net proceeds which is attributable to the mining of the resources of the area covered by the contract, referred to hereinafter as attributable net proceeds.

    (ii) The Authority's share of attributable net proceeds shall be determined in accordance with the following incremental schedule:

Portion of attributable net proceeds	Share of the Authority	
	First period of commercial production	Second period of commercial production
The portion representing a return on investment which is greater than 0 per cent, but less than 10 per cent	35 per cent	40 per cent
That portion representing a return on investment which is 10 per cent or greater, but less and 20 per cent	42.5 per cent	50 per cent
That portion representing a return on investment which is 20 per cent or greater	50 per cent	70 per cent

  (d) (i) The first period of commercial production referred to in subparagraphs (a) and (c) shall commence in the first accounting year of commercial production and terminate in the accounting year in which the contractor's development costs with interest on the unrecovered portion thereof are fully recovered by his cash surplus, as follows:

In the first accounting year during which development costs are incurred, unrecovered development costs shall equal the development costs less cash surplus in that year. In each subsequent accounting year, unrecovered development costs shall equal the unrecovered development costs at the end of the preceding accounting year, plus interest thereon at the rate of 10 per cent per annum, plus development costs incurred in the current accounting year and less contractor's cash surplus in the current accounting year. The accounting year in which unrecovered development costs become zero for the first time shall be the accounting year in which the contractor's development costs with interest on the unrecovered portion thereof are fully recovered by his cash surplus. The contractor's cash surplus in any accounting year shall be his gross proceeds less his operating costs and less his payments to the Authority under subparagraph (c).

(ii) The second period of commercial production shall commence in the accounting year following the termination of the first period of commercial production and shall continue until the end of the contract.

(e) 'Attributable net proceeds' means the product of the contractor's net proceeds and the ratio of the development costs in the mining sector to the contractor's development costs. If the contractor engages in mining, transporting polymetallic nodules and production primarily of three processed metals, namely, cobalt, copper and nickel, the amount of attributable net proceeds shall not be less than 25 per cent of the contractor's net proceeds. Subject to subparagraph (n), in all other cases, including those where the contractor engages in mining, transporting polymetallic nodules, and production primarily of four processed metals, namely, cobalt, copper, manganese and nickel, the Authority may, in its rules, regulations and procedures, prescribe appropriate floors which shall bear the same relationship to each case as the 25 per cent floor does to the three-metal case.

(f) 'Contractor's net proceeds' means the contractor's gross proceeds less his operating costs and less the recovery of his development costs as set out in subparagraph (j).

(g) (i) If the contractor engages in mining, transporting polymetallic nodules and production of processed metals, 'contractor's gross proceeds' means the gross revenues from the sale of the processed metals and any other monies deemed reasonably attributable to operations under the contract in accordance with the financial rules, regulations and procedures of the Authority.

(ii) In all cases other than those specified in subparagraphs (g)(i) and (n)(iii), 'contractor's gross proceeds' means the gross revenues from the sale of the semi-processed metals from the polymetallic nodules recovered from the area covered by the contract, and any other monies deemed reasonably attributable to operations under the contract in accordance with the financial rules, regulations and procedures of the Authority.

(h) 'Contractor's development costs' means:
(i) all expenditures incurred prior to the commencement of commercial production which are directly related to the development of the productive capacity of the area covered by the contract and the activities related thereto for operations under the contract in all cases other than that specified in subparagraph (n), in conformity with generally recognized accounting principles, including, *inter alia*, costs of machinery, equipment, ships,

processing plant, construction, buildings, land, roads, prospecting and exploration of the area covered by the contract, research and development, interest, required leases, licences and fees; and

(ii) expenditures similar to those set forth in (i) above incurred subsequent to the commencement of commercial production and necessary to carry out the plan of work, except those chargeable to operating costs.

(i) The proceeds from the disposal of capital assets and the market value of those capital assets which are no longer required for operations under the contract and which are not sold shall be deducted from the contractor's development costs during the relevant accounting year. When these deductions exceed the contractor's development costs the excess shall be added to the contractor's gross proceeds.

(j) The contractor's development costs incurred prior to the commencement of commercial production referred to in subparagraphs (h)(i) and (n)(iv) shall be recovered in 10 equal annual instalments from the date of commencement of commercial production. The contractor's development costs incurred subsequent to the commencement of commercial production referred to in subparagraphs (h)(ii) and (n)(iv) shall be recovered in 10 or fewer equal annual instalments so as to ensure their complete recovery by the end of the contract.

(k) 'Contractor's operating costs' means all expenditures incurred after the commencement of commercial production in the operation of the productive capacity of the area covered by the contract and the activities related thereto for operations under the contract, in conformity with generally recognized accounting principles, including, *inter alia*, the annual fixed fee or the production charge, whichever is greater, expenditures for wages, salaries, employee benefits, materials, services, transporting, processing and marketing costs, interest, utilities, preservation of the marine environment, overhead and administrative costs specifically related to operations under the contract, and any net operating losses carried forward or backward as specified herein. Net operating losses may be carried forward for two consecutive years except in the last two years of the contract in which case they may be carried backward to the two preceding years.

(l) If the contractor engages in mining, transporting of polymetallic nodules, and production of processed and semi-processed metals, 'development costs of the mining sector' means the portion of the contractor's development costs which is directly related to the mining of the resources of the area covered by the contract, in conformity with generally recognized accounting principles, and the financial rules, regulations and procedures of the Authority, including, *inter alia*, application fee, annual fixed fee and, where applicable, costs of prospecting and exploration of the area covered by the contract, and a portion of research and development costs.

(m) 'Return on investment' in any accounting year means the ratio of attributable net proceeds in that year to the development costs of the mining sector. For the purpose of computing this ratio the development costs of the mining sector shall include expenditures on new or replacement equipment in the mining sector less the original cost of the equipment replaced.

(n) If the contractor engages in mining only:

(i) 'attributable net proceeds' means the whole of the contractor's net proceeds;

(ii) 'contractor's net proceeds' shall be as defined in subparagraph (f);

(iii) 'contractor's gross proceeds' means the gross revenues from the sale of the polymetallic nodules, and any other monies deemed reasonably attributable to operations under the contract in accordance with the financial rules, regulations and procedures of the Authority;

(iv) 'contractor's development costs' means all expenditures incurred prior to the commencement of commercial production as set forth in subparagraph (h)(i), and all expenditures incurred subsequent to the commencement of commercial production as set forth in subparagraph (h)(ii), which are directly related to the mining of the resources of the area covered by the contract, in conformity with generally recognized accounting principles;

(v) 'contractor's operating costs' means the contractor's operating costs as in subparagraph (k) which are directly related to the mining of the resources of the area covered by the contract in conformity with generally recognized accounting principles;

(vi) 'return on investment' in any accounting year means the ratio of the contractor's net proceeds in that year to the contractor's development costs. For the purpose of computing this ratio, the contractor's development costs shall include expenditures on new or replacement equipment less the original cost of the equipment replaced.

(o) The costs referred to in subparagraphs (h), (k), (l) and (n) in respect of interest paid by the contractor shall be allowed to the extent that, in all the circumstances, the Authority approves, pursuant to article 4, paragraph 1, of this Annex, the debt-equity ratio and the rates of interest as reasonable, having regard to existing commercial practice.

(p) The costs referred to in this paragraph shall not be interpreted as including payments of corporate income taxes or similar charges levied by States in respect of the operations of the contractor.

7. (a) 'Processed metals', referred to in paragraphs 5 and 6, means the metals in the most basic form in which they are customarily traded on international terminal markets. For this purpose, the Authority shall specify, in its financial rules, regulations and procedures, the relevant international terminal market. For the metals which are not traded on such markets, 'processed metals' means the metals in the most basic form in which they are customarily traded in representative arm's length transactions.

(b) If the Authority cannot otherwise determine the quantity of the processed metals produced from the polymetallic nodules recovered from the area covered by the contract referred to in paragraphs 5(b) and 6(b), the quantity shall be determined on the basis of the metal content of the nodules, processing recovery efficiency and other relevant factors, in accordance with the rules, regulations and procedures of the Authority and in conformity with generally recognized accounting principles.

8. If an international terminal market provides a representative pricing mechanism for processed metals, polymetallic nodules and semi-processed metals from the nodules, the average price on that market shall be used. In all other cases, the Authority shall, after consulting the contractor, determine a fair price for the said products in accordance with paragraph 9.

9. (a) All costs, expenditures, proceeds and revenues and all determinations of price and value referred to in this article shall be the result of free market or arm's length transactions. In the absence thereof, they shall be determined by the Authority, after consulting the contractor, as though they were the result of free market or arm's length transactions, taking into account relevant transactions in other markets.

(b) In order to ensure compliance with and enforcement of the provisions of this paragraph, the Authority shall be guided by the principles adopted for, and the interpretation given to, arm's length transactions by the Commission on Transnational Corporations of the United Nations, the Group of Experts on Tax Treaties between Developing and Developed Countries and other international organizations, and shall, in its rules, regulations and procedures, specify uniform and internationally acceptable accounting rules and procedures, and the means of selection by the contractor of certified independent accountants acceptable to the Authority for the purpose of carrying out auditing in compliance with those rules, regulations and procedures.

10. The contractor shall make available to the accountants, in accordance with the financial rules, regulations and procedures of the Authority, such financial data as are required to determine compliance with this article.

11. All costs, expenditures, proceeds and revenues, and all prices and values referred to in this article, shall be determined in accordance with generally recognized accounting principles and the financial rules, regulations and procedures of the Authority.

12. Payments to the Authority under paragraphs 5 and 6 shall be made in freely usable currencies or currencies which are freely available and effectively usable on the major foreign exchange markets or, at the contractor's option, in the equivalents of processed metals at market value. The market value shall be determined in accordance with paragraph 5(b). The freely usable currencies and currencies which are freely available and effectively usable on the major foreign exchange markets shall be defined in the rules, regulations and procedures of the Authority in accordance with prevailing international monetary practice.

13. All financial obligations of the contractor to the Authority, as well as all his fees, costs, expenditures, proceeds and revenues referred to in this article, shall be adjusted by expressing them in constant terms relative to a base year.

14. The Authority may, taking into account any recommendations of the Economic Planning Commission and the Legal and Technical Commission, adopt rules, regulations and procedures that provide for incentives, on a uniform and non-discriminatory basis, to contractors to further the objectives set out in paragraph 1.

15. In the event of a dispute between the Authority and a contractor over the interpretation or application of the financial terms of a contract, either party may submit the dispute to binding commercial arbitration, unless both parties agree to settle the dispute by other means, in accordance with article 188, paragraph 2.

Article 14 Transfer of data

1. The operator shall transfer to the Authority, in accordance with its rules, regulations and procedures and the terms and conditions of the plan of work, at time intervals determined by the Authority all data which are both necessary for and relevant to the effective exercise of the powers and functions of the principal organs of the Authority in respect of the area covered by the plan of work.

2. Transferred data in respect of the area covered by the plan of work, deemed proprietary, may only be used for the purposes set forth in this article. Data necessary for the formulation by the Authority of rules, regulations and procedures concerning protection of the marine environment and safety, other than equipment design data, shall not be deemed proprietary.

3. Data transferred to the Authority by prospectors, applicants for contracts or contractors, deemed proprietary, shall not be disclosed by the Authority to the Enterprise or to anyone external to the Authority, but data on the reserved areas may be disclosed to the Enterprise. Such data transferred by such persons to the Enterprise shall not be disclosed by the Enterprise to the Authority or to anyone external to the Authority.

Article 15 Training programmes

The contractor shall draw up practical programmes for the training of personnel of the Authority and developing States, including the participation of such personnel in all activities in the Area which are covered by the contract, in accordance with article 144, paragraph 2.

Article 16 Exclusive right to explore and exploit

The Authority shall, pursuant to Part XI and its rules, regulations and procedures, accord the operator the exclusive right to explore and exploit the area covered by the plan of work in respect of a specified category of resources and shall ensure that no other entity operates in the same area for a different category of resources in a manner which might interfere with the operations of the operator. The operator shall have security of tenure in accordance with article 153, paragraph 6.

Article 17 Rules, regulations and procedures of the Authority[10]

1. The Authority shall adopt and uniformly apply rules, regulations and procedures in accordance with article 160, paragraph 2(f)(ii), and article 162, paragraph 2(o)(ii), for the exercise of its functions as set forth in Part XI on, *inter alia*, the following matters:

    (a) administrative procedures relating to prospecting, exploration and exploitation in the Area;

    (b) operations:

        (i)   size of area;

        (ii)   duration of operations;

        (iii) performance requirements including assurances pursuant to article 4, paragraph 6(c), of this Annex;

        (iv) categories of resources;

        (v)   renunciation of areas;

        (vi) progress reports;

        (vii) submission of data;

        (viii)inspection and supervision of operations;

        (ix) prevention of interference with other activities in the marine environment;

        (x)   transfer of rights and obligations by a contractor;

        (xi) procedures for transfer of technology to developing States in accordance with article 144 and for their direct participation;

        (xii) mining standards and practices, including those relating to operational safety, conservation of the resources and the protection of the marine environment;

        (xiii)definition of commercial production;

        (xiv)qualification standards for applicants;

    (c) financial matters:

        (i)   establishment of uniform and non-discriminatory costing and accounting rules and the method of selection of auditors;

        (ii)   apportionment of proceeds of operations;

        (iii) the incentives referred to in article 13 of this Annex;

    (d) implementation of decisions taken pursuant to article 151, paragraph 10, and article 164, paragraph 2(d).

2. Rules, regulations and procedures on the following items shall fully reflect the objective criteria set out below:

---

[10] See also Implementation Agreement [Doc. 37], Annex, Section 1, para. 5.

(a) Size of areas:

The Authority shall determine the appropriate size of areas for exploration which may be up to twice as large as those for exploitation in order to permit intensive exploration operations. The size of area shall be calculated to satisfy the requirements of article 8 of this Annex on reservation of areas as well as stated production requirements consistent with article 151 in accordance with the terms of the contract taking into account the state of the art of technology then available for sea-bed mining and the relevant physical characteristics of the areas. Areas shall be neither smaller nor larger than are necessary to satisfy this objective.

(b) Duration of operations:

(i) Prospecting shall be without time-limit;

(ii) Exploration should be of sufficient duration to permit a thorough survey of the specific area, the design and construction of mining equipment for the area and the design and construction of small and medium-size processing plants for the purpose of testing mining and processing systems;

(iii) The duration of exploitation should be related to the economic life of the mining project, taking into consideration such factors as the depletion of the ore, the useful life of mining equipment and processing facilities and commercial viability. Exploitation should be of sufficient duration to permit commercial extraction of minerals of the area and should include a reasonable time period for construction of commercial-scale mining and processing systems, during which period commercial production should not be required. The total duration of exploitation, however, should also be short enough to give the Authority an opportunity to amend the terms and conditions of the plan of work at the time it considers renewal in accordance with rules, regulations and procedures which it has adopted subsequent to approving the plan of work.

(c) Performance requirements:

The Authority shall require that during the exploration stage periodic expenditures be made by the operator which are reasonably related to the size of the area covered by the plan of work and the expenditures which would be expected of a *bona fide* operator who intended to bring the area into commercial production within the time-limits established by the Authority. The required expenditures should not be established at a level which would discourage prospective operators with less costly technology than is prevalently in use. The Authority shall establish a maximum time interval, after the exploration stage is completed and the exploitation stage begins, to achieve commercial production. To determine this interval, the Authority should take into consideration that construction of large-scale mining and processing systems cannot be initiated until after the termination of the exploration stage and the commencement of the exploitation stage. Accordingly, the interval to bring an area into commercial production should take into account the time necessary for this construction after the completion of the exploration stage and reasonable allowance should be made for unavoidable delays in the construction schedule. Once commercial production is achieved, the Authority shall within reasonable limits and taking into consideration all relevant factors require the operator to maintain commercial production throughout the period of the plan of work.

(d) Categories of resources:

In determining the category of resources in respect of which a plan of work may be approved, the Authority shall give emphasis *inter alia* to the following characteristics:

(i)   that certain resources require the use of similar mining methods; and

(ii)   that some resources can be developed simultaneously without undue inter-
       ference between operators developing different resources in the same area.

Nothing in this subparagraph shall preclude the Authority from approving a
plan of work with respect to more than one category of resources in the same
area to the same applicant.

(e) Renunciation of areas:

The operator shall have the right at any time to renounce without penalty the
whole or part of his rights in the area covered by a plan of work.

(f) Protection of the marine environment:

Rules, regulations and procedures shall be drawn up in order to secure effective
protection of the marine environment from harmful effects directly resulting
from activities in the Area or from shipboard processing immediately above
a mine site of minerals derived from that mine site, taking into account the
extent to which such harmful effects may directly result from drilling, dredging,
coring and excavation and from disposal, dumping and discharge into the
marine environment of sediment, wastes or other effluents.

(g) Commercial production:

Commercial production shall be deemed to have begun if an operator engages
in sustained large-scale recovery operations which yield a quantity of materials
sufficient to indicate clearly that the principal purpose is large-scale production
rather than production intended for information gathering, analysis or the testing
of equipment or plant.

Article 18 Penalties

1. A contractor's rights under the contract may be suspended or terminated only in
the following cases:

(a)   if, in spite of warnings by the Authority, the contractor has conducted his
      activities in such a way as to result in serious, persistent and wilful violations
      of the fundamental terms of the contract, Part XI and the rules, regulations and
      procedures of the Authority; or

(b)   if the contractor has failed to comply with a final binding decision of the dispute
      settlement body applicable to him.

2. In the case of any violation of the contract not covered by paragraph 1(a), or in
lieu of suspension or termination under paragraph 1(a), the Authority may impose upon
the contractor monetary penalties proportionate to the seriousness of the violation.

3. Except for emergency orders under article 162, paragraph 2(w), the Authority
may not execute a decision involving monetary penalties, suspension or termination until
the contractor has been accorded a reasonable opportunity to exhaust the judicial remedies
available to him pursuant to Part XI, section 5.

Article 19 Revision of contract

1. When circumstances have arisen or are likely to arise which, in the opinion of
either party, would render the contract inequitable or make it impracticable or impossible
to achieve the objectives set out in the contract or in Part XI, the parties shall enter into
negotiations to revise it accordingly.

2. Any contract entered into in accordance with article 153, paragraph 3, may be
revised only with the consent of the parties.

Article 20 Transfer of rights and obligations

The rights and obligations arising under a contract may be transferred only with the
consent of the Authority, and in accordance with its rules, regulations and procedures.

The Authority shall not unreasonably withhold consent to the transfer if the proposed transferee is in all respects a qualified applicant and assumes all of the obligations of the transferor and if the transfer does not confer to the transferee a plan of work, the approval of which would be forbidden by article 6, paragraph 3(c), of this Annex.

Article 21 Applicable law

1. The contract shall be governed by the terms of the contract, the rules, regulations and procedures of the Authority, Part XI and other rules of international law not incompatible with this Convention.

2. Any final decision rendered by a court or tribunal having jurisdiction under this Convention relating to the rights and obligations of the Authority and of the contractor shall be enforceable in the territory of each State Party.

3. No State Party may impose conditions on a contractor that are inconsistent with Part XI. However, the application by a State Party to contractors sponsored by it, or to ships flying its flag, of environmental or other laws and regulations more stringent than those in the rules, regulations and procedures of the Authority adopted pursuant to article 17, paragraph 2(f), of this Annex shall not be deemed inconsistent with Part XI.

Article 22 Responsibility

The contractor shall have responsibility or liability for any damage arising out of wrongful acts in the conduct of its operations, account being taken of contributory acts or omissions by the Authority. Similarly, the Authority shall have responsibility or liability for any damage arising out of wrongful acts in the exercise of its powers and functions, including violations under article 168, paragraph 2, account being taken of contributory acts or omissions by the contractor. Liability in every case shall be for the actual amount of damage.

ANNEX IV
STATUTE OF THE ENTERPRISE[1]

Article 1 Purposes

1. The Enterprise is the organ of the Authority which shall carry out activities in the Area directly, pursuant to article 153, paragraph 2(a), as well as the transporting, processing and marketing of minerals recovered from the Area.

2. In carrying out its purposes and in the exercise of its functions, the Enterprise shall act in accordance with this Convention and the rules, regulations and procedures of the Authority.

3. In developing the resources of the Area pursuant to paragraph 1, the Enterprise shall, subject to this Convention, operate in accordance with sound commercial principles.

Article 2 Relationship to the Authority

1. Pursuant to article 170, the Enterprise shall act in accordance with the general policies of the Assembly and the directives of the Council.

2. Subject to paragraph 1, the Enterprise shall enjoy autonomy in the conduct of its operations.

3. Nothing in this Convention shall make the Enterprise liable for the acts or obligations of the Authority, or make the Authority liable for the acts or obligations of the Enterprise.

---

[1] See also Implementation Agreement [Doc. 37], Annex, Section 2.

Article 3 Limitation of liability

Without prejudice to article 11, paragraph 3, of this Annex, no member of the Authority shall be liable by reason only of its membership for the acts or obligations of the Enterprise.

Article 4 Structure

The Enterprise shall have a Governing Board, a Director-General and the staff necessary for the exercise of its functions.

Article 5 Governing Board

1. The Governing Board shall be composed of 15 members elected by the Assembly in accordance with article 160, paragraph 2(c). In the election of the members of the Board, due regard shall be paid to the principle of equitable geographical distribution. In submitting nominations of candidates for election to the Board, members of the Authority shall bear in mind the need to nominate candidates of the highest standard of competence, with qualifications in relevant fields, so as to ensure the viability and success of the Enterprise.

2. Members of the Board shall be elected for four years and may be re-elected; and due regard shall be paid to the principle of rotation of membership.

3. Members of the Board shall continue in office until their successors are elected. If the office of a member of the Board becomes vacant, the Assembly shall, in accordance with article 160, paragraph 2(c), elect a new member for the remainder of his predecessor's term.

4. Members of the Board shall act in their personal capacity. In the performance of their duties they shall not seek or receive instructions from any government or from any other source. Each member of the Authority shall respect the independent character of the members of the Board and shall refrain from all attempts to influence any of them in the discharge of their duties.

5. Each member of the Board shall receive remuneration to be paid out of the funds of the Enterprise. The amount of remuneration shall be fixed by the Assembly, upon the recommendation of the Council.

6. The Board shall normally function at the principal office of the Enterprise and shall meet as often as the business of the Enterprise may require.

7. Two thirds of the members of the Board shall constitute a quorum.

8. Each member of the Board shall have one vote. All matters before the Board shall be decided by a majority of its members. If a member has a conflict of interest on a matter before the Board he shall refrain from voting on that matter.

9. Any member of the Authority may ask the Board for information in respect of its operations which particularly affect that member. The Board shall endeavour to provide such information.

Article 6 Powers and functions of the Governing Board

The Governing Board shall direct the operations of the Enterprise. Subject to this Convention, the Governing Board shall exercise the powers necessary to fulfil the purposes of the Enterprise, including powers:

(a) to elect a Chairman from among its members;

(b) to adopt its rules of procedure;

(c) to draw up and submit formal written plans of work to the Council in accordance with article 153, paragraph 3, and article 162, paragraph 2(j);[2]

(d) to develop plans of work and programmes for carrying out the activities specified in article 170;

---

[2] See also Implementation Agreement [Doc. 37], Annex, Section 3, para. 11(b).

(e) to prepare and submit to the Council applications for production authorizations in accordance with article 151, paragraphs 2 to 7;[3]

(f) to authorize negotiations concerning the acquisition of technology, including those provided for in Annex III, article 5, paragraph 3(a), (c) and (d), and to approve the results of those negotiations;[4]

(g) to establish terms and conditions, and to authorize negotiations, concerning joint ventures and other forms of joint arrangements referred to in Annex III, articles 9 and 11, and to approve the results of such negotiations;

(h) to recommend to the Assembly what portion of the net income of the Enterprise should be retained as its reserves in accordance with article 160, paragraph 2(f), and article 10 of this Annex;

(i) to approve the annual budget of the Enterprise;

(j) to authorize the procurement of goods and services in accordance with article 12, paragraph 3, of this Annex;

(k) to submit an annual report to the Council in accordance with article 9 of this Annex;

(l) to submit to the Council for the approval of the Assembly draft rules in respect of the organization, management, appointment and dismissal of the staff of the Enterprise and to adopt regulations to give effect to such rules;

(m) to borrow funds and to furnish such collateral or other security as it may determine in accordance with article 11, paragraph 2, of this Annex;

(n) to enter into any legal proceedings, agreements and transactions and to take any other actions in accordance with article 13 of this Annex;

(o) to delegate, subject to the approval of the Council, any non-discretionary powers to the Director-General and to its committees.

Article 7 Director-General and staff of the Enterprise

1. The Assembly shall, upon the recommendation of the Council and the nomination of the Governing Board, elect the Director-General of the Enterprise who shall not be a member of the Board. The Director-General shall hold office for a fixed term, not exceeding five years, and may be re-elected for further terms.

2. The Director-General shall be the legal representative and chief executive of the Enterprise and shall be directly responsible to the Board for the conduct of the operations of the Enterprise. He shall be responsible for the organization, management, appointment and dismissal of the staff of the Enterprise in accordance with the rules and regulations referred to in article 6, subparagraph (l), of this Annex. He shall participate, without the right to vote, in the meetings of the Board and may participate, without the right to vote, in the meetings of the Assembly and the Council when these organs are dealing with matters concerning the Enterprise.

3. The paramount consideration in the recruitment and employment of the staff and in the determination of their conditions of service shall be the necessity of securing the highest standards of efficiency and of technical competence. Subject to this consideration, due regard shall be paid to the importance of recruiting the staff on an equitable geographical basis.

4. In the performance of their duties the Director-General and the staff shall not seek or receive instructions from any government or from any other source external to the Enterprise. They shall refrain from any action which might reflect on their position as international officials of the Enterprise responsible only to the Enterprise. Each State Party

---

[3] See also Implementation Agreement [Doc. 37], Annex, Section 6, para. 7.
[4] See also Implementation Agreement [Doc. 37], Annex, Section 5, para. 2.

undertakes to respect the exclusively international character of the responsibilities of the Director-General and the staff and not to seek to influence them in the discharge of their responsibilities.

5. The responsibilities set forth in article 168, paragraph 2, are equally applicable to the staff of the Enterprise.

Article 8 Location

The Enterprise shall have its principal office at the seat of the Authority. The Enterprise may establish other offices and facilities in the territory of any State Party with the consent of that State Party.

Article 9 Reports and financial statements

1. The Enterprise shall, not later than three months after the end of each financial year, submit to the Council for its consideration an annual report containing an audited statement of its accounts and shall transmit to the Council at appropriate intervals a summary statement of its financial position and a profit and loss statement showing the results of its operations.

2. The Enterprise shall publish its annual report and such other reports as it finds appropriate.

3. All reports and financial statements referred to in this article shall be distributed to the members of the Authority.

Article 10 Allocation of net income

1. Subject to paragraph 3, the Enterprise shall make payments to the Authority under Annex III, article 13, or their equivalent.

2. The Assembly shall, upon the recommendation of the Governing Board, determine what portion of the net income of the Enterprise shall be retained as reserves of the Enterprise. The remainder shall be transferred to the Authority.

3. During an initial period required for the Enterprise to become self-supporting, which shall not exceed 10 years from the commencement of commercial production by it, the Assembly shall exempt the Enterprise from the payments referred to in paragraph 1, and shall leave all of the net income of the Enterprise in its reserves.

Article 11 Finances

1. The funds of the Enterprise shall include:
   (a)   amounts received from the Authority in accordance with article 173, paragraph 2(b);
   (b)   voluntary contributions made by States Parties for the purpose of financing activities of the Enterprise;
   (c)   amounts borrowed by the Enterprise in accordance with paragraphs 2 and 3;
   (d)   income of the Enterprise from its operations;
   (e)   other funds made available to the Enterprise to enable it to commence operations as soon as possible and to carry out its functions.
2.   (a)   The Enterprise shall have the power to borrow funds and to furnish such collateral or other security as it may determine. Before making a public sale of its obligations in the financial markets or currency of a State Party, the Enterprise shall obtain the approval of that State Party. The total amount of borrowings shall be approved by the Council upon the recommendation of the Governing Board.

  (b) States Parties shall make every reasonable effort to support applications by the Enterprise for loans on capital markets and from international financial institutions.

3. (a) The Enterprise shall be provided with the funds necessary to explore and exploit one mine site, and to transport, process and market the minerals recovered therefrom and the nickel, copper, cobalt and manganese obtained, and to meet its initial administrative expenses. The amount of the said funds, and the criteria and factors for its adjustment, shall be included by the Preparatory Commission in the draft rules, regulations and procedures of the Authority.[5]

  (b) All States Parties shall make available to the Enterprise an amount equivalent to one half of the funds referred to in subparagraph (a) by way of long-term interest-free loans in accordance with the scale of assessments for the United Nations regular budget in force at the time when the assessments are made, adjusted to take into account the States which are not members of the United Nations. Debts incurred by the Enterprise in raising the other half of the funds shall be guaranteed by all States Parties in accordance with the same scale.

  (c) If the sum of the financial contributions of States Parties is less than the funds to be provided to the Enterprise under subparagraph (a), the Assembly shall, at its first session, consider the extent of the shortfall and adopt by consensus measures for dealing with this shortfall, taking into account the obligation of States Parties under subparagraphs (a) and (b) and any recommendations of the Preparatory Commission.

  (d) (i) Each State Party shall, within 60 days after the entry into force of this Convention, or within 30 days after the deposit of its instrument of ratification or accession, whichever is later, deposit with the Enterprise irrevocable, non-negotiable, non-interest-bearing promissory notes in the amount of the share of such State Party of interest-free loans pursuant to subparagraph (b).

    (ii) The Board shall prepare, at the earliest practicable date after this Convention enters into force, and thereafter at annual or other appropriate intervals, a schedule of the magnitude and timing of its requirements for the funding of its administrative expenses and for activities carried out by the Enterprise in accordance with article 170 and article 12 of this Annex.

    (iii) The States Parties shall, thereupon, be notified by the Enterprise, through the Authority, of their respective shares of the funds in accordance with subparagraph (b), required for such expenses. The Enterprise shall encash such amounts of the promissory notes as may be required to meet the expenditure referred to in the schedule with respect to interest-free loans.

    (iv) States Parties shall, upon receipt of the notification, make available their respective shares of debt guarantees for the Enterprise in accordance with subparagraph (b).

  (e) (i) If the Enterprise so requests, State Parties may provide debt guarantees in addition to those provided in accordance with the scale referred to in subparagraph (b).

---

[5] See also Implementation Agreement [Doc. 37], Annex, Section 2, para. 3.

(ii) In lieu of debt guarantees, a State Party may make a voluntary contribution to the Enterprise in an amount equivalent to that portion of the debts which it would otherwise be liable to guarantee.

(f) Repayment of the interest-bearing loans shall have priority over the repayment of the interest-free loans. Repayment of interest-free loans shall be in accordance with a schedule adopted by the Assembly, upon the recommendation of the Council and the advice of the Board. In the exercise of this function the Board shall be guided by the relevant provisions of the rules, regulations and procedures of the Authority, which shall take into account the paramount importance of ensuring the effective functioning of the Enterprise and, in particular, ensuring its financial independence.

(g) Funds made available to the Enterprise shall be in freely usable currencies or currencies which are freely available and effectively usable in the major foreign exchange markets. These currencies shall be defined in the rules, regulations and procedures of the Authority in accordance with prevailing international monetary practice. Except as provided in paragraph 2, no State Party shall maintain or impose restrictions on the holding, use or exchange by the Enterprise of these funds.

(h) 'Debt guarantee' means a promise of a State Party to creditors of the Enterprise to pay, *pro rata* in accordance with the appropriate scale, the financial obligations of the Enterprise covered by the guarantee following notice by the creditors to the State Party of a default by the Enterprise. Procedures for the payment of those obligations shall be in conformity with the rules, regulations and procedures of the Authority.

4. The funds, assets and expenses of the Enterprise shall be kept separate from those of the Authority. This article shall not prevent the Enterprise from making arrangements with the Authority regarding facilities, personnel and services and arrangements for reimbursement of administrative expenses paid by either on behalf of the other.

5. The records, books and accounts of the Enterprise, including its annual financial statements, shall be audited annually by an independent auditor appointed by the Council.

Article 12 Operations

1. The Enterprise shall propose to the Council projects for carrying out activities in accordance with article 170. Such proposals shall include a formal written plan of work for activities in the Area in accordance with article 153, paragraph 3, and all such other information and data as may be required from time to time for its appraisal by the Legal and Technical Commission and approval by the Council.

2. Upon approval by the Council, the Enterprise shall execute the project on the basis of the formal written plan of work referred to in paragraph 1.

3. (a) If the Enterprise does not possess the goods and services required for its operations it may procure them. For that purpose, it shall issue invitations to tender and award contracts to bidders offering the best combination of quality, price and delivery time.

(b) If there is more than one bid offering such a combination, the contract shall be awarded in accordance with:

(i) the principle of non-discrimination on the basis of political or other considerations not relevant to the carrying out of operations with due diligence and efficiency; and

(ii) guidelines approved by the Council with regard to the preferences to be accorded to goods and services originating in developing States, including the land-locked and geographically disadvantaged among them.

(c) The Governing Board may adopt rules determining the special circumstances in which the requirement of invitations to bid may, in the best interests of the Enterprise, be dispensed with.

4. The Enterprise shall have title to all minerals and processed substances produced by it.

5. The Enterprise shall sell its products on a non-discriminatory basis. It shall not give non-commercial discounts.

6. Without prejudice to any general or special power conferred on the Enterprise under any other provision of this Convention, the Enterprise shall exercise such powers incidental to its business as shall be necessary.

7. The Enterprise shall not interfere in the political affairs of any State Party; nor shall it be influenced in its decisions by the political character of the State Party concerned. Only commercial considerations shall be relevant to its decisions, and these considerations shall be weighed impartially in order to carry out the purposes specified in article 1 of this Annex.

Article 13 Legal status, privileges and immunities

1. To enable the Enterprise to exercise its functions, the status, privileges and immunities set forth in this article shall be accorded to the Enterprise in the territories of States Parties. To give effect to this principle the Enterprise and States Parties may, where necessary, enter into special agreements.

2. The Enterprise shall have such legal capacity as is necessary for the exercise of its functions and the fulfilment of its purposes and, in particular, the capacity:

(a) to enter into contracts, joint arrangements or other arrangements, including agreements with States and international organizations;

(b) to acquire, lease, hold and dispose of immovable and movable property;

(c) to be a party to legal proceedings.

3. (a) Actions may be brought against the Enterprise only in a court of competent jurisdiction in the territory of a State Party in which the Enterprise:

(i) has an office or facility;

(ii) has appointed an agent for the purpose of accepting service or notice of process;

(iii) has entered into a contract for goods or services;

(iv) has issued securities; or

(v) is otherwise engaged in commercial activity.

(b) The property and assets of the Enterprise, wherever located and by whomsoever held, shall be immune from all forms of seizure, attachment or execution before the delivery of final judgment against the Enterprise.

4. (a) The property and assets of the Enterprise, wherever located and by whomsoever held, shall be immune from requisition, confiscation, expropriation or any other form of seizure by executive or legislative action.

(b) The property and assets of the Enterprise, wherever located and by whomsoever held, shall be free from discriminatory restrictions, regulations, controls and moratoria of any nature.

(c) The Enterprise and its employees shall respect local laws and regulations in any State or territory in which the Enterprise or its employees may do business or otherwise act.

(d)   States Parties shall ensure that the Enterprise enjoys all rights, privileges and immunities accorded by them to entities conducting commercial activities in their territories. These rights, privileges and immunities shall be accorded to the Enterprise on no less favourable a basis than that on which they are accorded to entities engaged in similar commercial activities. If special privileges are provided by States Parties for developing States or their commercial entities, the Enterprise shall enjoy those privileges on a similarly preferential basis.

(e)   States Parties may provide special incentives, rights, privileges and immunities to the Enterprise without the obligation to provide such incentives, rights, privileges and immunities to other commercial entities.

5.   The Enterprise shall negotiate with the host countries in which its offices and facilities are located for exemption from direct and indirect taxation.

6.   Each State Party shall take such action as is necessary for giving effect in terms of its own law to the principles set forth in this Annex and shall inform the Enterprise of the specific action which it has taken.

7.   The Enterprise may waive any of the privileges and immunities conferred under this article or in the special agreements referred to in paragraph 1 to such extent and upon such conditions as it may determine.

ANNEX V
CONCILIATION

SECTION 1. CONCILIATION PROCEDURE PURSUANT TO SECTION 1 OF PART XV

Article 1 Institution of proceedings

If the parties to a dispute have agreed, in accordance with article 284, to submit it to conciliation under this section, any such party may institute the proceedings by written notification addressed to the other party or parties to the dispute.

Article 2 List of conciliators

A list of conciliators shall be drawn up and maintained by the Secretary-General of the United Nations. Every State Party shall be entitled to nominate four conciliators, each of whom shall be a person enjoying the highest reputation for fairness, competence and integrity. The names of the persons so nominated shall constitute the list. If at any time the conciliators nominated by a State Party in the list so constituted shall be fewer than four, that State Party shall be entitled to make further nominations as necessary. The name of a conciliator shall remain on the list until withdrawn by the State Party which made the nomination, provided that such conciliator shall continue to serve on any conciliation commission to which that conciliator has been appointed until the completion of the proceedings before that commission.

Article 3 Constitution of conciliation commission

The conciliation commission shall, unless the parties otherwise agree, be constituted as follows:

(a)   Subject to subparagraph (g), the conciliation commission shall consist of five members.

(b)   The party instituting the proceedings shall appoint two conciliators to be chosen preferably from the list referred to in article 2 of this Annex, one of whom may be its national, unless the parties otherwise agree. Such appointments shall be included in the notification referred to in article 1 of this Annex.

(c)   The other party to the dispute shall appoint two conciliators in the manner set forth in subparagraph (b) within 21 days of receipt of the notification referred to in article 1 of this Annex. If the appointments are not made within that period, the party instituting the proceedings may, within one week of the expiration of that period, either terminate the proceedings by notification addressed to the other party or request the Secretary-General of the United Nations to make the appointments in accordance with subparagraph (e).

(d)   Within 30 days after all four conciliators have been appointed, they shall appoint a fifth conciliator chosen from the list referred to in article 2 of this Annex, who shall be chairman. If the appointment is not made within that period, either party may, within one week of the expiration of that period, request the Secretary-General of the United Nations to make the appointment in accordance with subparagraph (e).

(e)   Within 30 days of the receipt of a request under subparagraph (c) or (d), the Secretary-General of the United Nations shall make the necessary appointments from the list referred to in article 2 of this Annex in consultation with the parties to the dispute.

(f)   Any vacancy shall be filled in the manner prescribed for the initial appointment.

(g)   Two or more parties which determine by agreement that they are in the same interest shall appoint two conciliators jointly. Where two or more parties have separate interests or there is a disagreement as to whether they are of the same interest, they shall appoint conciliators separately.

(h)   In disputes involving more than two parties having separate interests, or where there is disagreement as to whether they are of the same interest, the parties shall apply subparagraphs (a) to (f) in so far as possible.

Article 4 Procedure

The conciliation commission shall, unless the parties otherwise agree, determine its own procedure. The commission may, with the consent of the parties to the dispute, invite any State Party to submit to it its views orally or in writing. Decisions of the commission regarding procedural matters, the report and recommendations shall be made by a majority vote of its members.

Article 5 Amicable settlement

The commission may draw the attention of the parties to any measures which might facilitate an amicable settlement of the dispute.

Article 6 Functions of the commission

The commission shall hear the parties, examine their claims and objections, and make proposals to the parties with a view to reaching an amicable settlement.

Article 7 Report

1.   The commission shall report within 12 months of its constitution. Its report shall record any agreements reached and, failing agreement, its conclusions on all questions of fact or law relevant to the matter in dispute and such recommendations as the commission may deem appropriate for an amicable settlement. The report shall be deposited with the Secretary-General of the United Nations and shall immediately be transmitted by him to the parties to the dispute.

2.   The report of the commission, including its conclusions or recommendations, shall not be binding upon the parties.

Article 8 Termination

The conciliation proceedings are terminated when a settlement has been reached, when the parties have accepted or one party has rejected the recommendations of the report by written notification addressed to the Secretary-General of the United Nations, or when a period of three months has expired from the date of transmission of the report to the parties.

Article 9 Fees and expenses

The fees and expenses of the commission shall be borne by the parties to the dispute.

Article 10 Right of parties to modify procedure

The parties to the dispute may by agreement applicable solely to that dispute modify any provision of this Annex.

SECTION 2. COMPULSORY SUBMISSION TO CONCILIATION PROCEDURE
PURSUANT TO SECTION 3 OF PART XV

Article 11 Institution of proceedings

1. Any party to a dispute which, in accordance with Part XV, section 3, may be submitted to conciliation under this section, may institute the proceedings by written notification addressed to the other party or parties to the dispute.

2. Any party to the dispute, notified under paragraph 1, shall be obliged to submit to such proceedings.

Article 12 Failure to reply or to submit to conciliation

The failure of a party or parties to the dispute to reply to notification of institution of proceedings or to submit to such proceedings shall not constitute a bar to the proceedings.

Article 13 Competence

A disagreement as to whether a conciliation commission acting under this section has competence shall be decided by the commission.

Article 14 Application of section 1

Articles 2 to 10 of section 1 of this Annex apply subject to this section.

ANNEX VI
STATUTE OF THE INTERNATIONAL TRIBUNAL FOR THE LAW OF THE SEA

Article 1 General provisions

1. The International Tribunal for the Law of the Sea is constituted and shall function in accordance with the provisions of this Convention and this Statute.

2. The seat of the Tribunal shall be in the Free and Hanseatic City of Hamburg in the Federal Republic of Germany.

3. The Tribunal may sit and exercise its functions elsewhere whenever it considers this desirable.

4. A reference of a dispute to the Tribunal shall be governed by the provisions of Parts XI and XV.

SECTION 1. ORGANIZATION OF THE TRIBUNAL

Article 2 Composition

1. The Tribunal shall be composed of a body of 21 independent members, elected from among persons enjoying the highest reputation for fairness and integrity and of recognized competence in the field of the law of the sea.

2. In the Tribunal as a whole the representation of the principal legal systems of the world and equitable geographical distribution shall be assured.

Article 3 Membership

1. No two members of the Tribunal may be nationals of the same State. A person who for the purposes of membership in the Tribunal could be regarded as a national of more than one State shall be deemed to be a national of the one in which he ordinarily exercises civil and political rights.

2. There shall be no fewer than three members from each geographical group as established by the General Assembly of the United Nations.

Article 4 Nominations and elections

1. Each State Party may nominate not more than two persons having the qualifications prescribed in article 2 of this Annex. The members of the Tribunal shall be elected from the list of persons thus nominated.

2. At least three months before the date of the election, the Secretary-General of the United Nations in the case of the first election and the Registrar of the Tribunal in the case of subsequent elections shall address a written invitation to the States Parties to submit their nominations for members of the Tribunal within two months. He shall prepare a list in alphabetical order of all the persons thus nominated, with an indication of the States Parties which have nominated them, and shall submit it to the States Parties before the seventh day of the last month before the date of each election.

3. The first election shall be held within six months of the date of entry into force of this Convention.

4. The members of the Tribunal shall be elected by secret ballot. Elections shall be held at a meeting of the States Parties convened by the Secretary-General of the United Nations in the case of the first election and by a procedure agreed to by the States Parties in the case of subsequent elections. Two thirds of the States Parties shall constitute a quorum at that meeting. The persons elected to the Tribunal shall be those nominees who obtain the largest number of votes and a two-thirds majority of the States Parties present and voting, provided that such majority includes a majority of the States Parties.

Article 5 Term of office

1. The members of the Tribunal shall be elected for nine years and may be re-elected; provided, however, that of the members elected at the first election, the terms of seven members shall expire at the end of three years and the terms of seven more members shall expire at the end of six years.

2. The members of the Tribunal whose terms are to expire at the end of the above-mentioned initial periods of three and six years shall be chosen by lot to be drawn by the Secretary-General of the United Nations immediately after the first election.

3. The members of the Tribunal shall continue to discharge their duties until their places have been filled. Though replaced, they shall finish any proceedings which they may have begun before the date of their replacement.

4.   In the case of the resignation of a member of the Tribunal, the letter of resignation shall be addressed to the President of the Tribunal. The place becomes vacant on the receipt of that letter.

Article 6 Vacancies

1.   Vacancies shall be filled by the same method as that laid down for the first election, subject to the following provision: the Registrar shall, within one month of the occurrence of the vacancy, proceed to issue the invitations provided for in article 4 of this Annex, and the date of the election shall be fixed by the President of the Tribunal after consultation with the States Parties.

2.   A member of the Tribunal elected to replace a member whose term of office has not expired shall hold office for the remainder of his predecessor's term.

Article 7 Incompatible activities

1.   No member of the Tribunal may exercise any political or administrative function, or associate actively with or be financially interested in any of the operations of any enterprise concerned with the exploration for or exploitation of the resources of the sea or the sea-bed or other commercial use of the sea or the sea-bed.

2.   No member of the Tribunal may act as agent, counsel or advocate in any case.

3.   Any doubt on these points shall be resolved by decision of the majority of the other members of the Tribunal present.

Article 8 Conditions relating to participation of members in a particular case

1.   No member of the Tribunal may participate in the decision of any case in which he has previously taken part as agent, counsel or advocate for one of the parties, or as a member of a national or international court or tribunal, or in any other capacity.

2.   If, for some special reason, a member of the Tribunal considers that he should not take part in the decision of a particular case, he shall so inform the President of the Tribunal.

3.   If the President considers that for some special reason one of the members of the Tribunal should not sit in a particular case, he shall give him notice accordingly.

4.   Any doubt on these points shall be resolved by decision of the majority of the other members of the Tribunal present.

Article 9 Consequence of ceasing to fulfil required conditions

If, in the unanimous opinion of the other members of the Tribunal, a member has ceased to fulfil the required conditions, the President of the Tribunal shall declare the seat vacant.

Article 10 Privileges and immunities

The members of the Tribunal, when engaged on the business of the Tribunal, shall enjoy diplomatic privileges and immunities.

Article 11 Solemn declaration by members

Every member of the Tribunal shall, before taking up his duties, make a solemn declaration in open session that he will exercise his powers impartially and conscientiously.

Article 12 President, Vice-President and Registrar

1.   The Tribunal shall elect its President and Vice-President for three years; they may be re-elected.

2. The Tribunal shall appoint its Registrar and may provide for the appointment of such other officers as may be necessary.

3. The President and the Registrar shall reside at the seat of the Tribunal.

Article 13 Quorum

1. All available members of the Tribunal shall sit; a quorum of 11 elected members shall be required to constitute the Tribunal.

2. Subject to article 17 of this Annex, the Tribunal shall determine which members are available to constitute the Tribunal for the consideration of a particular dispute, having regard to the effective functioning of the chambers as provided for in articles 14 and 15 of this Annex.

3. All disputes and applications submitted to the Tribunal shall be heard and determined by the Tribunal, unless article 14 of this Annex applies, or the parties request that it shall be dealt with in accordance with article 15 of this Annex.

Article 14 Sea-bed Disputes Chamber

A Sea-bed Disputes Chamber shall be established in accordance with the provisions of section 4 of this Annex. Its jurisdiction, powers and functions shall be as provided for in Part XI, section 5.

Article 15 Special chambers

1. The Tribunal may form such chambers, composed of three or more of its elected members, as it considers necessary for dealing with particular categories of disputes.

2. The Tribunal shall form a chamber for dealing with a particular dispute submitted to it if the parties so request. The composition of such a chamber shall be determined by the Tribunal with the approval of the parties.

3. With a view to the speedy dispatch of business, the Tribunal shall form annually a chamber composed of five of its elected members which may hear and determine disputes by summary procedure. Two alternative members shall be selected for the purpose of replacing members who are unable to participate in a particular proceeding.

4. Disputes shall be heard and determined by the chambers provided for in this article if the parties so request.

5. A judgment given by any of the chambers provided for in this article and in article 14 of this Annex shall be considered as rendered by the Tribunal.

Article 16 Rules of the Tribunal

The Tribunal shall frame rules for carrying out its functions. In particular it shall lay down rules of procedure.

Article 17 Nationality of members

1. Members of the Tribunal of the nationality of any of the parties to a dispute shall retain their right to participate as members of the Tribunal.

2. If the Tribunal, when hearing a dispute, includes upon the bench a member of the nationality of one of the parties, any other party may choose a person to participate as a member of the Tribunal.

3. If the Tribunal, when hearing a dispute, does not include upon the bench a member of the nationality of the parties, each of those parties may choose a person to participate as a member of the Tribunal.

4. This article applies to the chambers referred to in articles 14 and 15 of this Annex. In such cases, the President, in consultation with the parties, shall request specified

members of the Tribunal forming the chamber, as many as necessary, to give place to the members of the Tribunal of the nationality of the parties concerned, and, failing such, or if they are unable to be present, to the members specially chosen by the parties.

5. Should there be several parties in the same interest, they shall, for the purpose of the preceding provisions, be considered as one party only. Any doubt on this point shall be settled by the decision of the Tribunal.

6. Members chosen in accordance with paragraphs 2, 3 and 4 shall fulfil the conditions required by articles 2, 8 and 11 of this Annex. They shall participate in the decision on terms of complete equality with their colleagues.

Article 18 Remuneration of members

1. Each elected member of the Tribunal shall receive an annual allowance and, for each day on which he exercises his functions, a special allowance, provided that in any year the total sum payable to any member as special allowance shall not exceed the amount of the annual allowance.

2. The President shall receive a special annual allowance.

3. The Vice-President shall receive a special allowance for each day on which he acts as President.

4. The members chosen under article 17 of this Annex, other than elected members of the Tribunal, shall receive compensation for each day on which they exercise their functions.

5. The salaries, allowances and compensation shall be determined from time to time at meetings of the States Parties, taking into account the workload of the Tribunal. They may not be decreased during the term of office.

6. The salary of the Registrar shall be determined at meetings of the States Parties, on the proposal of the Tribunal.

7. Regulations adopted at meetings of the States Parties shall determine the conditions under which retirement pensions may be given to members of the Tribunal and to the Registrar, and the conditions under which members of the Tribunal and Registrar shall have their travelling expenses refunded.

8. The salaries, allowances, and compensation shall be free of all taxation.

Article 19 Expenses of the Tribunal

1. The expenses of the Tribunal shall be borne by the States Parties and by the Authority on such terms and in such a manner as shall be decided at meetings of the States Parties.

2. When an entity other than a State Party or the Authority is a party to a case submitted to it, the Tribunal shall fix the amount which that party is to contribute towards the expenses of the Tribunal.

SECTION 2. COMPETENCE

Article 20 Access to the Tribunal

1. The Tribunal shall be open to States Parties.

2. The Tribunal shall be open to entities other than States Parties in any case expressly provided for in Part XI or in any case submitted pursuant to any other agreement conferring jurisdiction on the Tribunal which is accepted by all the parties to that case.

Article 21 Jurisdiction

The jurisdiction of the Tribunal comprises all disputes and all applications submitted to it in accordance with this Convention and all matters specifically provided for in any other agreement which confers jurisdiction on the Tribunal.

Article 22 Reference of disputes subject to other agreements

If all the parties to a treaty or convention already in force and concerning the subject-matter covered by this Convention so agree, any disputes concerning the interpretation or application of such treaty or convention may, in accordance with such agreement, be submitted to the Tribunal.

Article 23 Applicable law

The Tribunal shall decide all disputes and applications in accordance with article 293.

SECTION 3. PROCEDURE

Article 24 Institution of proceedings

1. Disputes are submitted to the Tribunal, as the case may be, either by notification of a special agreement or by written application, addressed to the Registrar. In either case, the subject of the dispute and the parties shall be indicated.

2. The Registrar shall forthwith notify the special agreement or the application to all concerned.

3. The Registrar shall also notify all States Parties.

Article 25 Provisional measures

1. In accordance with article 290, the Tribunal and its Sea-bed Disputes Chamber shall have the power to prescribe provisional measures.

2. If the Tribunal is not in session or a sufficient number of members is not available to constitute a quorum, the provisional measures shall be prescribed by the chamber of summary procedure formed under article 15, paragraph 3, of this Annex. Notwithstanding article 15, paragraph 4, of this Annex, such provisional measures may be adopted at the request of any party to the dispute. They shall be subject to review and revision by the Tribunal.

Article 26 Hearing

1. The hearing shall be under the control of the President or, if he is unable to preside, of the Vice-President. If neither is able to preside, the senior judge present of the Tribunal shall preside.

2. The hearing shall be public, unless the Tribunal decides otherwise or unless the parties demand that the public be not admitted.

Article 27 Conduct of case

The Tribunal shall make orders for the conduct of the case, decide the form and time in which each party must conclude its arguments, and make all arrangements connected with the taking of evidence.

Article 28 Default

When one of the parties does not appear before the Tribunal or fails to defend its case, the other party may request the Tribunal to continue the proceedings and make its decision. Absence of a party or failure of a party to defend its case shall not constitute a bar to the proceedings. Before making its decision, the Tribunal must satisfy itself not only that it has jurisdiction over the dispute, but also that the claim is well founded in fact and law.

Article 29 Majority for decision

1.   All questions shall be decided by a majority of the members of the Tribunal who are present.

2.   In the event of an equality of votes, the President or the member of the Tribunal who acts in his place shall have a casting vote.

Article 30 Judgment

1.   The judgment shall state the reasons on which it is based.

2.   It shall contain the names of the members of the Tribunal who have taken part in the decision.

3.   If the judgment does not represent in whole or in part the unanimous opinion of the members of the Tribunal, any member shall be entitled to deliver a separate opinion.

4.   The judgment shall be signed by the President and by the Registrar. It shall be read in open court, due notice having been given to the parties to the dispute.

Article 31 Request to intervene

1.   Should a State Party consider that it has an interest of a legal nature which may be affected by the decision in any dispute, it may submit a request to the Tribunal to be permitted to intervene.

2.   It shall be for the Tribunal to decide upon this request.

3.   If a request to intervene is granted, the decision of the Tribunal in respect of the dispute shall be binding upon the intervening State Party in so far as it relates to matters in respect of which that State Party intervened.

Article 32 Right to intervene in cases of interpretation or application

1.   Whenever the interpretation or application of this Convention is in question, the Registrar shall notify all States Parties forthwith.

2.   Whenever pursuant to article 21 or 22 of this Annex the interpretation or application of an international agreement is in question, the Registrar shall notify all the parties to the agreement.

3.   Every party referred to in paragraphs 1 and 2 has the right to intervene in the proceedings; if it uses this right, the interpretation given by the judgment will be equally binding upon it.

Article 33 Finality and binding force of decisions

1.   The decision of the Tribunal is final and shall be complied with by all the parties to the dispute.

2.   The decision shall have no binding force except between the parties in respect of that particular dispute.

3.   In the event of dispute as to the meaning or scope of the decision, the Tribunal shall construe it upon the request of any party.

Article 34 Costs

Unless otherwise decided by the Tribunal, each party shall bear its own costs.

SECTION 4. SEA-BED DISPUTES CHAMBER

Article 35 Composition

1. The Sea-bed Disputes Chamber referred to in article 14 of this Annex shall be composed of 11 members, selected by a majority of the elected members of the Tribunal from among them.

2. In the selection of the members of the Chamber, the representation of the principal legal systems of the world and equitable geographical distribution shall be assured. The Assembly of the Authority may adopt recommendations of a general nature relating to such representation and distribution.

3. The members of the Chamber shall be selected every three years and may be selected for a second term.

4. The Chamber shall elect its President from among its members, who shall serve for the term for which the Chamber has been selected.

5. If any proceedings are still pending at the end of any three-year period for which the Chamber has been selected, the Chamber shall complete the proceedings in its original composition.

6. If a vacancy occurs in the Chamber, the Tribunal shall select a successor from among its elected members, who shall hold office for the remainder of his predecessor's term.

7. A quorum of seven of the members selected by the Tribunal shall be required to constitute the Chamber.

Article 36 *Ad hoc* chambers

1. The Sea-bed Disputes Chamber shall form an *ad hoc* chamber, composed of three of its members, for dealing with a particular dispute submitted to it in accordance with article 188, paragraph 1(b). The composition of such a chamber shall be determined by the Sea-bed Disputes Chamber with the approval of the parties.

2. If the parties do not agree on the composition of an *ad hoc* chamber, each party to the dispute shall appoint one member, and the third member shall be appointed by them in agreement. If they disagree, or if any party fails to make an appointment, the President of the Sea-bed Disputes Chamber shall promptly make the appointment or appointments from among its members, after consultation with the parties.

3. Members of the *ad hoc* chamber must not be in the service of, or nationals of, any of the parties to the dispute.

Article 37 Access

The Chamber shall be open to the States Parties, the Authority and the other entities referred to in Part XI, section 5.

Article 38 Applicable law

In addition to the provisions of article 293, the Chamber shall apply:
(a) the rules, regulations and procedures of the Authority adopted in accordance with this Convention; and
(b) the terms of contracts concerning activities in the Area in matters relating to those contracts.

Article 39 Enforcement of decisions of the Chamber

The decisions of the Chamber shall be enforceable in the territories of the States Parties in the same manner as judgments or orders of the highest court of the State Party in whose territory the enforcement is sought.

Article 40 Applicability of other sections of this Annex

1. The other sections of this Annex which are not incompatible with this section apply to the Chamber.

2. In the exercise of its functions relating to advisory opinions, the Chamber shall be guided by the provisions of this Annex relating to procedure before the Tribunal to the extent to which it recognizes them to be applicable.

Section 5. Amendments

Article 4l Amendments

1. Amendments to this Annex, other than amendments to section 4, may be adopted only in accordance with article 313 or by consensus at a conference convened in accordance with this Convention.

2. Amendments to section 4 may be adopted only in accordance with article 314.

3. The Tribunal may propose such amendments to this Statute as it may consider necessary, by written communications to the States Parties for their consideration in conformity with paragraphs 1 and 2.

ANNEX VII

ARBITRATION

Article 1 Institution of proceedings

Subject to the provisions of Part XV, any party to a dispute may submit the dispute to the arbitral procedure provided for in this Annex by written notification addressed to the other party or parties to the dispute. The notification shall be accompanied by a statement of the claim and the grounds on which it is based.

Article 2 List of arbitrators

1. A list of arbitrators shall be drawn up and maintained by the Secretary-General of the United Nations. Every State Party shall be entitled to nominate four arbitrators, each of whom shall be a person experienced in maritime affairs and enjoying the highest reputation for fairness, competence and integrity. The names of the persons so nominated shall constitute the list.

2. If at any time the arbitrators nominated by a State Party in the list so constituted shall be fewer than four, that State Party shall be entitled to make further nominations as necessary.

3. The name of an arbitrator shall remain on the list until withdrawn by the State Party which made the nomination, provided that such arbitrator shall continue to serve on any arbitral tribunal to which that arbitrator has been appointed until the completion of the proceedings before that arbitral tribunal.

Article 3 Constitution of arbitral tribunal

For the purpose of proceedings under this Annex, the arbitral tribunal shall, unless the parties otherwise agree, be constituted as follows:

(a) Subject to subparagraph (g), the arbitral tribunal shall consist of five members.

(b) The party instituting the proceedings shall appoint one member to be chosen preferably from the list referred to in article 2 of this Annex, who may be its national. The appointment shall be included in the notification referred to in article 1 of this Annex.

(c) The other party to the dispute shall, within 30 days of receipt of the notification referred to in article 1 of this Annex, appoint one member to be chosen preferably from the list, who may be its national. If the appointment is not made within that period, the party instituting the proceedings may, within two weeks of the expiration of that period, request that the appointment be made in accordance with subparagraph (e).

(d) The other three members shall be appointed by agreement between the parties. They shall be chosen preferably from the list and shall be nationals of third States unless the parties otherwise agree. The parties to the dispute shall appoint the President of the arbitral tribunal from among those three members. If, within 60 days of receipt of the notification referred to in article 1 of this Annex, the parties are unable to reach agreement on the appointment of one or more of the members of the tribunal to be appointed by agreement, or on the appointment of the President, the remaining appointment or appointments shall be made in accordance with subparagraph (e), at the request of a party to the dispute. Such request shall be made within two weeks of the expiration of the aforementioned 60-day period.

(e) Unless the parties agree that any appointment under subparagraphs (c) and (d) be made by a person or a third State chosen by the parties, the President of the International Tribunal for the Law of the Sea shall make the necessary appointments. If the President is unable to act under this subparagraph or is a national of one of the parties to the dispute, the appointment shall be made by the next senior member of the International Tribunal for the Law of the Sea who is available and is not a national of one of the parties. The appointments referred to in this subparagraph shall be made from the list referred to in article 2 of this Annex within a period of 30 days of the receipt of the request and in consultation with the parties. The members so appointed shall be of different nationalities and may not be in the service of, ordinarily resident in the territory of, or nationals of, any of the parties to the dispute.

(f) Any vacancy shall be filled in the manner prescribed for the initial appointment.

(g) Parties in the same interest shall appoint one member of the tribunal jointly by agreement. Where there are several parties having separate interests or where there is disagreement as to whether they are of the same interest, each of them shall appoint one member of the tribunal. The number of members of the tribunal appointed separately by the parties shall always be smaller by one than the number of members of the tribunal to be appointed jointly by the parties.

(h) In disputes involving more than two parties, the provisions of subparagraphs (a) to (f) shall apply to the maximum extent possible.

Article 4 Functions of arbitral tribunal

An arbitral tribunal constituted under article 3 of this Annex shall function in accordance with this Annex and the other provisions of this Convention.

Article 5 Procedure

Unless the parties to the dispute otherwise agree, the arbitral tribunal shall determine its own procedure, assuring to each party a full opportunity to be heard and to present its case.

Article 6 Duties of parties to a dispute

The parties to the dispute shall facilitate the work of the arbitral tribunal and, in particular, in accordance with their law and using all means at their disposal, shall:

(a)   provide it with all relevant documents, facilities and information; and
(b)   enable it when necessary to call witnesses or experts and receive their evidence and to visit the localities to which the case relates.

Article 7 Expenses

Unless the arbitral tribunal decides otherwise because of the particular circumstances of the case, the expenses of the tribunal, including the remuneration of its members, shall be borne by the parties to the dispute in equal shares.

Article 8 Required majority for decisions

Decisions of the arbitral tribunal shall be taken by a majority vote of its members. The absence or abstention of less than half of the members shall not constitute a bar to the tribunal reaching a decision. In the event of an equality of votes, the President shall have a casting vote.

Article 9 Default of appearance

If one of the parties to the dispute does not appear before the arbitral tribunal or fails to defend its case, the other party may request the tribunal to continue the proceedings and to make its award. Absence of a party or failure of a party to defend its case shall not constitute a bar to the proceedings. Before making its award, the arbitral tribunal must satisfy itself not only that it has jurisdiction over the dispute but also that the claim is well founded in fact and law.

Article 10 Award

The award of the arbitral tribunal shall be confined to the subject-matter of the dispute and state the reasons on which it is based. It shall contain the names of the members who have participated and the date of the award. Any member of the tribunal may attach a separate or dissenting opinion to the award.

Article 11 Finality of award

The award shall be final and without appeal, unless the parties to the dispute have agreed in advance to an appellate procedure. It shall be complied with by the parties to the dispute.

Article 12 Interpretation or implementation of award

1. Any controversy which may arise between the parties to the dispute as regards the interpretation or manner of implementation of the award may be submitted by either party for decision to the arbitral tribunal which made the award. For this purpose, any vacancy in the tribunal shall be filled in the manner provided for in the original appointments of the members of the tribunal.

2. Any such controversy may be submitted to another court or tribunal under article 287 by agreement of all the parties to the dispute.

Article 13 Application to entities other than States Parties

The provisions of this Annex shall apply *mutatis mutandis* to any dispute involving entities other than States Parties.

ANNEX VIII
SPECIAL ARBITRATION

Article 1 Institution of proceedings

Subject to Part XV, any party to a dispute concerning the interpretation or application of the articles of this Convention relating to (1) fisheries, (2) protection and preservation of the marine environment, (3) marine scientific research, or (4) navigation, including pollution from vessels and by dumping, may submit the dispute to the special arbitral procedure provided for in this Annex by written notification addressed to the other party or parties to the dispute. The notification shall be accompanied by a statement of the claim and the grounds on which it is based.

Article 2 Lists of experts

1. A list of experts shall be established and maintained in respect of each of the fields of (1) fisheries, (2) protection and preservation of the marine environment, (3) marine scientific research, and (4) navigation, including pollution from vessels and by dumping.

2. The lists of experts shall be drawn up and maintained, in the field of fisheries by the Food and Agriculture Organization of the United Nations, in the field of protection and preservation of the marine environment by the United Nations Environment Programme, in the field of marine scientific research by the Intergovernmental Oceanographic Commission, in the field of navigation, including pollution from vessels and by dumping, by the International Maritime Organization, or in each case by the appropriate subsidiary body concerned to which such organization, programme or commission has delegated this function.

3. Every State Party shall be entitled to nominate two experts in each field whose competence in the legal, scientific or technical aspects of such field is established and generally recognized and who enjoy the highest reputation for fairness and integrity. The names of the persons so nominated in each field shall constitute the appropriate list.

4. If at any time the experts nominated by a State Party in the list so constituted shall be fewer than two, that State Party shall be entitled to make further nominations as necessary.

5. The name of an expert shall remain on the list until withdrawn by the State Party which made the nomination, provided that such expert shall continue to serve on any special arbitral tribunal to which that expert has been appointed until the completion of the proceedings before that special arbitral tribunal.

Article 3 Constitution of special arbitral tribunal

For the purpose of proceedings under this Annex, the special arbitral tribunal shall, unless the parties otherwise agree, be constituted as follows:

(a) Subject to subparagraph (g), the special arbitral tribunal shall consist of five members.

(b) The party instituting the proceedings shall appoint two members to be chosen preferably from the appropriate list or lists referred to in article 2 of this Annex relating to the matters in dispute, one of whom may be its national. The appointments shall be included in the notification referred to in article 1 of this Annex.

(c) The other party to the dispute shall, within 30 days of receipt of the notification referred to in article 1 of this Annex, appoint two members to be chosen preferably from the appropriate list or lists relating to the matters in dispute, one of whom may be its national. If the appointments are not made within that period, the party instituting the proceedings may, within two weeks of the expiration of that period, request that the appointments be made in accordance with subparagraph (e).

(d) The parties to the dispute shall by agreement appoint the President of the special arbitral tribunal, chosen preferably from the appropriate list, who shall be a national of a third State, unless the parties otherwise agree. If, within 30 days of receipt of the notification referred to in article 1 of this Annex, the parties are unable to reach agreement on the appointment of the President, the appointment shall be made in accordance with subparagraph (e), at the request of a party to the dispute. Such request shall be made within two weeks of the expiration of the aforementioned 30-day period.

(e) Unless the parties agree that the appointment be made by a person or a third State chosen by the parties, the Secretary-General of the United Nations shall make the necessary appointments within 30 days of receipt of a request under subparagraphs (c) and (d). The appointments referred to in this subparagraph shall be made from the appropriate list or lists of experts referred to in article 2 of this Annex and in consultation with the parties to the dispute and the appropriate international organization. The members so appointed shall be of different nationalities and may not be in the service of, ordinarily resident in the territory of, or nationals of, any of the parties to the dispute.

(f) Any vacancy shall be filled in the manner prescribed for the initial appointment.

(g) Parties in the same interest shall appoint two members of the tribunal jointly by agreement. Where there are several parties having separate interests or where there is disagreement as to whether they are of the same interest, each of them shall appoint one member of the tribunal.

(h) In disputes involving more than two parties, the provisions of subparagraphs (a) to (f) shall apply to the maximum extent possible.

Article 4 General provisions

Annex VII, articles 4 to 13, apply *mutatis mutandis* to the special arbitration proceedings in accordance with this Annex.

Article 5 Fact finding

1. The parties to a dispute concerning the interpretation or application of the provisions of this Convention relating to (1) fisheries, (2) protection and preservation of the marine environment, (3) marine scientific research, or (4) navigation, including pollution from vessels and by dumping, may at any time agree to request a special arbitral tribunal constituted in accordance with article 3 of this Annex to carry out an inquiry and establish the facts giving rise to the dispute.

2. Unless the parties otherwise agree, the findings of fact of the special arbitral tribunal acting in accordance with paragraph 1, shall be considered as conclusive as between the parties.

3. If all the parties to the dispute so request, the special arbitral tribunal may formulate recommendations which, without having the force of a decision, shall only constitute the basis for a review by the parties of the questions giving rise to the dispute.

4. Subject to paragraph 2, the special arbitral tribunal shall act in accordance with the provisions of this Annex, unless the parties otherwise agree.

ANNEX IX
PARTICIPATION BY INTERNATIONAL ORGANIZATIONS

Article 1 Use of terms

For the purposes of article 305 and of this Annex, 'international organization' means an intergovernmental organization constituted by States to which its member States have transferred competence over matters governed by this Convention, including the competence to enter into treaties in respect of those matters.

Article 2 Signature

An international organization may sign this Convention if a majority of its member States are signatories of this Convention. At the time of signature an international organization shall make a declaration specifying the matters governed by this Convention in respect of which competence has been transferred to that organization by its member States which are signatories, and the nature and extent of that competence.

Article 3 Formal confirmation and accession

1. An international organization may deposit its instrument of formal confirmation or of accession if a majority of its member States deposit or have deposited their instruments of ratification or accession.

2. The instruments deposited by the international organization shall contain the undertakings and declarations required by articles 4 and 5 of this Annex.

Article 4 Extent of participation and rights and obligations

1. The instrument of formal confirmation or of accession of an international organization shall contain an undertaking to accept the rights and obligations of States under this Convention in respect of matters relating to which competence has been transferred to it by its member States which are Parties to this Convention.

2. An international organization shall be a Party to this Convention to the extent that it has competence in accordance with the declarations, communications of information or notifications referred to in article 5 of this Annex.

3. Such an international organization shall exercise the rights and perform the obligations which its member States which are Parties would otherwise have under this Convention, on matters relating to which competence has been transferred to it by those member States. The member States of that international organization shall not exercise competence which they have transferred to it.

4. Participation of such an international organization shall in no case entail an increase of the representation to which its member States which are States Parties would otherwise be entitled, including rights in decision-making.

5. Participation of such an international organization shall in no case confer any rights under this Convention on member States of the organization which are not States Parties to this Convention.

6. In the event of a conflict between the obligations of an international organization under this Convention and its obligations under the agreement establishing the organization or any acts relating to it, the obligations under this Convention shall prevail.

Article 5 Declarations, notifications and communications

1. The instrument of formal confirmation or of accession of an international organization shall contain a declaration specifying the matters governed by this Convention in respect of which competence has been transferred to the organization by its member States which are Parties to this Convention.

2. A member State of an international organization shall, at the time it ratifies or accedes to this Convention or at the time when the organization deposits its instrument of formal confirmation or of accession, whichever is later, make a declaration specifying the matters governed by this Convention in respect of which it has transferred competence to the organization.

3. States Parties which are member States of an international organization which is a Party to this Convention shall be presumed to have competence over all matters governed by this Convention in respect of which transfers of competence to the organization have not been specifically declared, notified or communicated by those States under this article.

4. The international organization and its member States which are States Parties shall promptly notify the depositary of this Convention of any changes to the distribution of competence, including new transfers of competence, specified in the declarations under paragraphs 1 and 2.

5. Any State Party may request an international organization and its member States which are States Parties to provide information as to which, as between the organization and its member States, has competence in respect of any specific question which has arisen. The organization and the member States concerned shall provide this information within a reasonable time. The international organization and the member States may also, on their own initiative, provide this information.

6. Declarations, notifications and communications of information under this article shall specify the nature and extent of the competence transferred.

Article 6 Responsibility and liability

1. Parties which have competence under article 5 of this Annex shall have responsibility for failure to comply with obligations or for any other violation of this Convention.

2. Any State Party may request an international organization or its member States which are States Parties for information as to who has responsibility in respect of any specific matter. The organization and the member States concerned shall provide this information. Failure to provide this information within a reasonable time or the provision of contradictory information shall result in joint and several liability.

Article 7 Settlement of disputes

1. At the time of deposit of its instrument of formal confirmation or of accession, or at any time thereafter, an international organization shall be free to choose, by means of a written declaration, one or more of the means for the settlement of disputes concerning the interpretation or application of this Convention, referred to in article 287, paragraph 1(a), (c) or (d).

2. Part XV applies *mutatis mutandis* to any dispute between Parties to this Convention, one or more of which are international organizations.

3. When an international organization and one or more of its member States are joint parties to a dispute, or parties in the same interest, the organization shall be deemed to have accepted the same procedures for the settlement of disputes as the member States; when, however, a member State has chosen only the International Court of Justice under article 287, the organization and the member State concerned shall be deemed to have accepted arbitration in accordance with Annex VII, unless the parties to the dispute otherwise agree.

Article 8 Applicability of Part XVII

Part XVII applies *mutatis mutandis* to an international organization, except in respect of the following:

(a) the instrument of formal confirmation or of accession of an international organization shall not be taken into account in the application of article 308, paragraph 1;

(b) (i) an international organization shall have exclusive capacity with respect to the application of articles 312 to 315, to the extent that it has competence under article 5 of this Annex over the entire subject-matter of the amendment;

(ii) the instrument of formal confirmation or of accession of an international organization to an amendment, the entire subject-matter over which the international organization has competence under article 5 of this Annex, shall be considered to be the instrument of ratification or accession of each of the member States which are States Parties, for the purposes of applying article 316, paragraphs 1, 2 and 3;

(iii) the instrument of formal confirmation or of accession of the international organization shall not be taken into account in the application of article 316, paragraphs 1 and 2, with regard to all other amendments;

(c) (i) an international organization may not denounce this Convention in accordance with article 317 if any of its member States is a State Party and if it continues to fulfil the qualifications specified in article 1 of this Annex;

(ii) an international organization shall denounce this Convention when none of its member States is a State Party or if the international organization no longer fulfils the qualifications specified in article 1 of this Annex. Such denunciation shall take effect immediately.

Agreement Relating to the Implementation of Part XI of the United Nations Convention of the Law of the Sea of 10 December 1982

Done at New York, 28 July 1994; entry into force, 28 July 1996
1836 UNTS 42 [Registration Number 31364]

The States Parties to this Agreement,

Recognizing the important contribution of the United Nations Convention on the Law of the Sea of 10 December 1982 (hereinafter referred to as 'the Convention') to the maintenance of peace, justice and progress for all peoples of the world,

Reaffirming that the seabed and ocean floor and subsoil thereof, beyond the limits of national jurisdiction (hereinafter referred to as 'the Area'), as well as the resources of the Area, are the common heritage of mankind,

Mindful of the importance of the Convention for the protection and preservation of the marine environment and of the growing concern for the global environment,

Having considered the report of the Secretary-General of the United Nations on the results of the informal consultations among States held from 1990 to 1994 on outstanding issues relating to Part XI and related provisions of the Convention (hereinafter referred to as 'Part XI'),

Noting the political and economic changes, including market-oriented approaches, affecting the implementation of Part XI,

Wishing to facilitate universal participation in the Convention,

Considering that an agreement relating to the implementation of Part XI would best meet that objective,

Have agreed as follows:

Article 1 Implementation of Part XI

1. The States Parties to this Agreement undertake to implement Part XI in accordance with this Agreement.

2. The Annex forms an integral part of this Agreement.

Article 2 Relationship between this Agreement and Part XI

1. The provisions of this Agreement and Part XI shall be interpreted and applied together as a single instrument. In the event of any inconsistency between this Agreement and Part XI, the provisions of this Agreement shall prevail.

2. Articles 309 to 319 of the Convention shall apply to this Agreement as they apply to the Convention.

Article 3 Signature

This Agreement shall remain open for signature at United Nations Headquarters by the States and entities referred to in article 305, paragraph 1 (a), (c), (d), (e) and (f), of the Convention for 12 months from the date of its adoption.

Article 4 Consent to be bound

1. After the adoption of this Agreement, any instrument of ratification or formal confirmation of or accession to the Convention shall also represent consent to be bound by this Agreement.

2. No State or entity may establish its consent to be bound by this Agreement unless it has previously established or establishes at the same time its consent to be bound by the Convention.

3. A State or entity referred to in article 3 may express its consent to be bound by this Agreement by:

(a) Signature not subject to ratification, formal confirmation or the procedure set out in article 5;

(b) Signature subject to ratification or formal confirmation, followed by ratification or formal confirmation;

(c) Signature subject to the procedure set out in article 5; or

(d) Accession.

4. Formal confirmation by the entities referred to in article 305, paragraph 1 (f), of the Convention shall be in accordance with Annex IX of the Convention.

5. The instruments of ratification, formal confirmation or accession shall be deposited with the Secretary-General of the United Nations.

Article 5 Simplified procedure

1. A State or entity which has deposited before the date of the adoption of this Agreement an instrument of ratification or formal confirmation of or accession to the Convention and which has signed this Agreement in accordance with article 4, paragraph 3 (c), shall be considered to have established its consent to be bound by this Agreement 12 months after the date of its adoption, unless that State or entity notifies the depositary in writing before that date that it is not availing itself of the simplified procedure set out in this article.

2. In the event of such notification, consent to be bound by this Agreement shall be established in accordance with article 4, paragraph 3 (b).

Article 6 Entry into force

1. This Agreement shall enter into force 30 days after the date on which 40 States have established their consent to be bound in accordance with articles 4 and 5, provided that such States include at least seven of the States referred to in paragraph 1 (a) of resolution II of the Third United Nations Conference on the Law of the Sea (hereinafter referred to as 'resolution II') and that at least five of those States are developed States. If these conditions for entry into force are fulfilled before 16 November 1994, this Agreement shall enter into force on 16 November 1994.

2. For each State or entity establishing its consent to be bound by this Agreement after the requirements set out in paragraph 1 have been fulfilled, this Agreement shall enter into force on the thirtieth day following the date of establishment of its consent to be bound.

Article 7 Provisional application

1. If on 16 November 1994 this Agreement has not entered into force, it shall be applied provisionally pending its entry into force by:

(a) States which have consented to its adoption in the General Assembly of the United Nations, except any such State which before 16 November 1994 notifies the depositary in writing either that it will not so apply this Agreement or that it will consent to such application only upon subsequent signature or notification in writing;

(b) States and entities which sign this Agreement, except any such State or entity which notifies the depositary in writing at the time of signature that it will not so apply this Agreement;

(c) States and entities which consent to its provisional application by so notifying the depositary in writing;

(d) States which accede to this Agreement.

2. All such States and entities shall apply this Agreement provisionally in accordance with their national or internal laws and regulations, with effect from 16 November 1994 or the date of signature, notification of consent or accession, if later.

3. Provisional application shall terminate upon the date of entry into force of this Agreement. In any event, provisional application shall terminate on 16 November 1998 if at that date the requirement in article 6, paragraph 1, of consent to be bound by this Agreement by at least seven of the States (of which at least five must be developed States) referred to in paragraph 1 (a) of resolution II has not been fulfilled.

Article 8 States Parties

1. For the purposes of this Agreement, 'States Parties' means States which have consented to be bound by this Agreement and for which this Agreement is in force.

2. This Agreement applies *mutatis mutandis* to the entities referred to in article 305, paragraph 1 (c), (d), (e) and (f), of the Convention which become Parties to this Agreement in accordance with the conditions relevant to each, and to that extent 'States Parties' refers to those entities.

Article 9 Depositary

The Secretary-General of the United Nations shall be the depositary of this Agreement.

Article 10 Authentic texts

The original of this Agreement, of which the Arabic, Chinese, English, French, Russian and Spanish texts are equally authentic, shall be deposited with the Secretary-General of the United Nations.

In witness whereof, the undersigned Plenipotentiaries, being duly authorized thereto, have signed this Agreement.

Done at New York, this twenty-eighth day of July, one thousand nine hundred and ninety-four.

ANNEX

Section 1. Costs to States Parties and Institutional Arrangements

1. The International Seabed Authority (hereinafter referred to as 'the Authority') is the organization through which States Parties to the Convention shall, in accordance with the regime for the Area established in Part XI and this Agreement, organize and control activities in the Area, particularly with a view to administering the resources of the Area. The powers and functions of the Authority shall be those expressly conferred upon it by the Convention. The Authority shall have such incidental powers, consistent with the Convention, as are implicit in, and necessary for, the exercise of those powers and functions with respect to activities in the Area.

2. In order to minimize costs to States Parties, all organs and subsidiary bodies to be established under the Convention and this Agreement shall be cost-effective. This principle shall also apply to the frequency, duration and scheduling of meetings.

3. The setting up and the functioning of the organs and subsidiary bodies of the Authority shall be based on an evolutionary approach, taking into account the functional needs of the organs and subsidiary bodies concerned in order that they may discharge effectively their respective responsibilities at various stages of the development of activities in the Area.

4. The early functions of the Authority upon entry into force of the Convention shall be carried out by the Assembly, the Council, the Secretariat, the Legal and Technical Commission and the Finance Committee. The functions of the Economic Planning Commission shall be performed by the Legal and Technical Commission until such time as the Council decides otherwise or until the approval of the first plan of work for exploitation.

5. Between the entry into force of the Convention and the approval of the first plan of work for exploitation, the Authority shall concentrate on:
   (a) Processing of applications for approval of plans of work for exploration in accordance with Part XI and this Agreement;
   (b) Implementation of decisions of the Preparatory Commission for the International Seabed Authority and for the International Tribunal for the Law of the Sea (hereinafter referred to as 'the Preparatory Commission') relating to the registered pioneer investors and their certifying States, including their rights and obligations, in accordance with article 308, paragraph 5, of the Convention and resolution II, paragraph 13;
   (c) Monitoring of compliance with plans of work for exploration approved in the form of contracts;
   (d) Monitoring and review of trends and developments relating to deep seabed mining activities, including regular analysis of world metal market conditions and metal prices, trends and prospects;
   (e) Study of the potential impact of mineral production from the Area on the economies of developing land-based producers of those minerals which are likely to be most seriously affected, with a view to minimizing their difficulties and assisting them in their economic adjustment, taking into account the work done in this regard by the Preparatory Commission;

(f) Adoption of rules, regulations and procedures necessary for the conduct of activities in the Area as they progress. Notwithstanding the provisions of Annex III, article 17, paragraph 2 (b) and (c), of the Convention, such rules, regulations and procedures shall take into account the terms of this Agreement, the prolonged delay in commercial deep seabed mining and the likely pace of activities in the Area;

(g) Adoption of rules, regulations and procedures incorporating applicable standards for the protection and preservation of the marine environment;

(h) Promotion and encouragement of the conduct of marine scientific research with respect to activities in the Area and the collection and dissemination of the results of such research and analysis, when available, with particular emphasis on research related to the environmental impact of activities in the Area;

(i) Acquisition of scientific knowledge and monitoring of the development of marine technology relevant to activities in the Area, in particular technology relating to the protection and preservation of the marine environment;

(j) Assessment of available data relating to prospecting and exploration;

(k) Timely elaboration of rules, regulations and procedures for exploitation, including those relating to the protection and preservation of the marine environment.

6. (a) An application for approval of a plan of work for exploration shall be considered by the Council following the receipt of a recommendation on the application from the Legal and Technical Commission. The processing of an application for approval of a plan of work for exploration shall be in accordance with the provisions of the Convention, including Annex III thereof, and this Agreement, and subject to the following:

  (i) A plan of work for exploration submitted on behalf of a State or entity, or any component of such entity, referred to in resolution II, paragraph 1 (a) (ii) or (iii), other than a registered pioneer investor, which had already undertaken substantial activities in the Area prior to the entry into force of the Convention, or its successor in interest, shall be considered to have met the financial and technical qualifications necessary for approval of a plan of work if the sponsoring State or States certify that the applicant has expended an amount equivalent to at least US$ 30 million in research and exploration activities and has expended no less than 10 per cent of that amount in the location, survey and evaluation of the area referred to in the plan of work. If the plan of work otherwise satisfies the requirements of the Convention and any rules, regulations and procedures adopted pursuant thereto, it shall be approved by the Council in the form of a contract. The provisions of section 3, paragraph 11, of this Annex shall be interpreted and applied accordingly;

  (ii) Notwithstanding the provisions of resolution II, paragraph 8 (a), a registered pioneer investor may request approval of a plan of work for exploration within 36 months of the entry into force of the Convention. The plan of work for exploration shall consist of documents, reports and other data submitted to the Preparatory Commission both before and after registration and shall be accompanied by a certificate of compliance, consisting of a factual report describing the status of fulfilment of obligations under the pioneer investor regime, issued by the Preparatory Commission in accordance with resolution II, paragraph 11 (a). Such a plan of work shall be considered to be approved. Such an approved plan of work shall be in the form of a contract concluded between the Authority and the registered pioneer investor in accordance with Part XI and this Agreement. The fee of US$ 250,000 paid pursuant to resolution II, paragraph 7 (a), shall be deemed to be the fee relating to the exploration phase pursuant to section 8, paragraph 3, of this Annex. Section 3, paragraph 11, of this Annex shall be interpreted and applied accordingly;

(iii)   In accordance with the principle of non-discrimination, a contract with a State or entity or any component of such entity referred to in subparagraph (a) (i) shall include arrangements which shall be similar to and no less favourable than those agreed with any registered pioneer investor referred to in subparagraph (a) (ii). If any of the States or entities or any components of such entities referred to in subparagraph (a) (i) are granted more favourable arrangements, the Council shall make similar and no less favourable arrangements with regard to the rights and obligations assumed by the registered pioneer investors referred to in subparagraph (a) (ii), provided that such arrangements do not affect or prejudice the interests of the Authority;

(iv)   A State sponsoring an application for a plan of work pursuant to the provisions of subparagraph (a) (i) or (ii) may be a State Party or a State which is applying this Agreement provisionally in accordance with article 7, or a State which is a member of the Authority on a provisional basis in accordance with paragraph 12;

(v)   Resolution II, paragraph 8 (c), shall be interpreted and applied in accordance with subparagraph (a) (iv).

(b)   The approval of a plan of work for exploration shall be in accordance with article 153, paragraph 3, of the Convention.

7.   An application for approval of a plan of work shall be accompanied by an assessment of the potential environmental impacts of the proposed activities and by a description of a programme for oceanographic and baseline environmental studies in accordance with the rules, regulations and procedures adopted by the Authority.

8.   An application for approval of a plan of work for exploration, subject to paragraph 6 (a) (i) or (ii), shall be processed in accordance with the procedures set out in section 3, paragraph 11, of this Annex.

9.   A plan of work for exploration shall be approved for a period of 15 years. Upon the expiration of a plan of work for exploration, the contractor shall apply for a plan of work for exploitation unless the contractor has already done so or has obtained an extension for the plan of work for exploration. Contractors may apply for such extensions for periods of not more than five years each. Such extensions shall be approved if the contractor has made efforts in good faith to comply with the requirements of the plan of work but for reasons beyond the contractor's control has been unable to complete the necessary preparatory work for proceeding to the exploitation stage or if the prevailing economic circumstances do not justify proceeding to the exploitation stage.

10.   Designation of a reserved area for the Authority in accordance with Annex III, article 8, of the Convention shall take place in connection with approval of an application for a plan of work for exploration or approval of an application for a plan of work for exploration and exploitation.

11.   Notwithstanding the provisions of paragraph 9, an approved plan of work for exploration which is sponsored by at least one State provisionally applying this Agreement shall terminate if such a State ceases to apply this Agreement provisionally and has not

become a member on a provisional basis in accordance with paragraph 12 or has not become a State Party.

12.　Upon the entry into force of this Agreement, States and entities referred to in article 3 of this Agreement which have been applying it provisionally in accordance with article 7 and for which it is not in force may continue to be members of the Authority on a provisional basis pending its entry into force for such States and entities, in accordance with the following subparagraphs:

(a)　If this Agreement enters into force before 16 November 1996, such States and entities shall be entitled to continue to participate as members of the Authority on a provisional basis upon notification to the depositary of the Agreement by such a State or entity of its intention to participate as a member on a provisional basis. Such membership shall terminate either on 16 November 1996 or upon the entry into force of this Agreement and the Convention for such member, whichever is earlier. The Council may, upon the request of the State or entity concerned, extend such membership beyond 16 November 1996 for a further period or periods not exceeding a total of two years provided that the Council is satisfied that the State or entity concerned has been making efforts in good faith to become a party to the Agreement and the Convention;

(b)　If this Agreement enters into force after 15 November 1996, such States and entities may request the Council to grant continued membership in the Authority on a provisional basis for a period or periods not extending beyond 16 November 1998. The Council shall grant such membership with effect from the date of the request if it is satisfied that the State or entity has been making efforts in good faith to become a party to the Agreement and the Convention;

(c)　States and entities which are members of the Authority on a provisional basis in accordance with subparagraph (a) or (b) shall apply the terms of Part XI and this Agreement in accordance with their national or internal laws, regulations and annual budgetary appropriations and shall have the same rights and obligations as other members, including:

(i)　The obligation to contribute to the administrative budget of the Authority in accordance with the scale of assessed contributions;

(ii)　The right to sponsor an application for approval of a plan of work for exploration. In the case of entities whose components are natural or juridical persons possessing the nationality of more than one State, a plan of work for exploration shall not be approved unless all the States whose natural or juridical persons comprise those entities are States Parties or members on a provisional basis;

(d)　Notwithstanding the provisions of paragraph 9, an approved plan of work in the form of a contract for exploration which was sponsored pursuant to subparagraph (c) (ii) by a State which was a member on a provisional basis shall terminate if such membership ceases and the State or entity has not become a State Party;

(e)　If such a member has failed to make its assessed contributions or otherwise failed to comply with its obligations in accordance with this paragraph, its membership on a provisional basis shall be terminated.

13.　The reference in Annex III, article 10, of the Convention to performance which has not been satisfactory shall be interpreted to mean that the contractor has failed to comply with the requirements of an approved plan of work in spite of a written warning or warnings from the Authority to the contractor to comply therewith.

14.　The Authority shall have its own budget. Until the end of the year following the year during which this Agreement enters into force, the administrative expenses of the Authority shall be met through the budget of the United Nations. Thereafter, the administrative expenses of the Authority shall be met by assessed contributions of its members, including any members on a provisional basis, in accordance with articles 171, subparagraph (a), and 173 of the Convention and this Agreement, until the Authority has sufficient funds from other sources to meet those expenses. The Authority shall not exercise the power referred to in article 174, paragraph 1, of the Convention to borrow funds to finance its administrative budget.

15.   The Authority shall elaborate and adopt, in accordance with article 162, paragraph 2 (o) (ii), of the Convention, rules, regulations and procedures based on the principles contained in sections 2, 5, 6, 7 and 8 of this Annex, as well as any additional rules, regulations and procedures necessary to facilitate the approval of plans of work for exploration or exploitation, in accordance with the following subparagraphs:

(a)   The Council may undertake such elaboration any time it deems that all or any of such rules, regulations or procedures are required for the conduct of activities in the Area, or when it determines that commercial exploitation is imminent, or at the request of a State whose national intends to apply for approval of a plan of work for exploitation;

(b)   If a request is made by a State referred to in subparagraph (a) the Council shall, in accordance with article 162, paragraph 2 (o), of the Convention, complete the adoption of such rules, regulations and procedures within two years of the request;

(c)   If the Council has not completed the elaboration of the rules, regulations and procedures relating to exploitation within the prescribed time and an application for approval of a plan of work for exploitation is pending, it shall none the less consider and provisionally approve such plan of work based on the provisions of the Convention and any rules, regulations and procedures that the Council may have adopted provisionally, or on the basis of the norms contained in the Convention and the terms and principles contained in this Annex as well as the principle of non-discrimination among contractors.

16.   The draft rules, regulations and procedures and any recommendations relating to the provisions of Part XI, as contained in the reports and recommendations of the Preparatory Commission, shall be taken into account by the Authority in the adoption of rules, regulations and procedures in accordance with Part XI and this Agreement.

17.   The relevant provisions of Part XI, section 4, of the Convention shall be interpreted and applied in accordance with this Agreement.

SECTION 2. THE ENTERPRISE

1.   The Secretariat of the Authority shall perform the functions of the Enterprise until it begins to operate independently of the Secretariat. The Secretary-General of the Authority shall appoint from within the staff of the Authority an interim Director-General to oversee the performance of these functions by the Secretariat.

These functions shall be:

(a)   Monitoring and review of trends and developments relating to deep seabed mining activities, including regular analysis of world metal market conditions and metal prices, trends and prospects;

(b)   Assessment of the results of the conduct of marine scientific research with respect to activities in the Area, with particular emphasis on research related to the environmental impact of activities in the Area;

(c)   Assessment of available data relating to prospecting and exploration, including the criteria for such activities;

(d)   Assessment of technological developments relevant to activities in the Area, in particular technology relating to the protection and preservation of the marine environment;

(e)   Evaluation of information and data relating to areas reserved for the Authority;

(f)   Assessment of approaches to joint-venture operations;

(g)   Collection of information on the availability of trained manpower;

(h)   Study of managerial policy options for the administration of the Enterprise at different stages of its operations.

2.   The Enterprise shall conduct its initial deep seabed mining operations through joint ventures. Upon the approval of a plan of work for exploitation for an entity other than the Enterprise, or upon receipt by the Council of an application for a joint-venture operation with the Enterprise, the Council shall take up the issue of the functioning of the Enterprise independently of the Secretariat of the Authority. If joint-venture operations with the Enterprise accord with sound commercial principles, the Council shall issue a directive pursuant to article 170, paragraph 2, of the Convention providing for such independent functioning.

3.   The obligation of States Parties to fund one mine site of the Enterprise as provided for in Annex IV, article 11, paragraph 3, of the Convention shall not apply and States Parties shall be under no obligation to finance any of the operations in any mine site of the Enterprise or under its joint-venture arrangements.

4.   The obligations applicable to contractors shall apply to the Enterprise. Notwithstanding the provisions of article 153, paragraph 3, and Annex III, article 3, paragraph 5, of the Convention, a plan of work for the Enterprise upon its approval shall be in the form of a contract concluded between the Authority and the Enterprise.

5.   A contractor which has contributed a particular area to the Authority as a reserved area has the right of first refusal to enter into a joint-venture arrangement with the Enterprise for exploration and exploitation of that area. If the Enterprise does not submit an application for a plan of work for activities in respect of such a reserved area within 15 years of the commencement of its functions independent of the Secretariat of the Authority or within 15 years of the date on which that area is reserved for the Authority, whichever is the later, the contractor which contributed the area shall be entitled to apply for a plan of work for that area provided it offers in good faith to include the Enterprise as a joint-venture partner.

6.   Article 170, paragraph 4, Annex IV and other provisions of the Convention relating to the Enterprise shall be interpreted and applied in accordance with this section.

Section 3. Decision-Making

1.   The general policies of the Authority shall be established by the Assembly in collaboration with the Council.

2.   As a general rule, decision-making in the organs of the Authority should be by consensus.

3.   If all efforts to reach a decision by consensus have been exhausted, decisions by voting in the Assembly on questions of procedure shall be taken by a majority of members present and voting, and decisions on questions of substance shall be taken by a two-thirds majority of members present and voting, as provided for in article 159, paragraph 8, of the Convention.

4.   Decisions of the Assembly on any matter for which the Council also has competence or on any administrative, budgetary or financial matter shall be based on the recommendations of the Council. If the Assembly does not accept the recommendation of the Council on any matter, it shall return the matter to the Council for further consideration. The Council shall reconsider the matter in the light of the views expressed by the Assembly.

5. If all efforts to reach a decision by consensus have been exhausted, decisions by voting in the Council on questions of procedure shall be taken by a majority of members present and voting, and decisions on questions of substance, except where the Convention provides for decisions by consensus in the Council, shall be taken by a two-thirds majority of members present and voting, provided that such decisions are not opposed by a majority in any one of the chambers referred to in paragraph 9. In taking decisions the Council shall seek to promote the interests of all the members of the Authority.

6. The Council may defer the taking of a decision in order to facilitate further negotiation whenever it appears that all efforts at achieving consensus on a question have not been exhausted.

7. Decisions by the Assembly or the Council having financial or budgetary implications shall be based on the recommendations of the Finance Committee.

8. The provisions of article 161, paragraph 8 (b) and (c), of the Convention shall not apply.

9. (a) Each group of States elected under paragraph 15 (a) to (c) shall be treated as a chamber for the purposes of voting in the Council. The developing States elected under paragraph 15(d) and (e) shall be treated as a single chamber for the purposes of voting in the Council.

(b) Before electing the members of the Council, the Assembly shall establish lists of countries fulfilling the criteria for membership in the groups of States in paragraph 15 (a) to (d). If a State fulfils the criteria for membership in more than one group, it may only be proposed by one group for election to the Council and it shall represent only that group in voting in the Council.

10. Each group of States in paragraph 15 (a) to (d) shall be represented in the Council by those members nominated by that group. Each group shall nominate only as many candidates as the number of seats required to be filled by that group. When the number of potential candidates in each of the groups referred to in paragraph 15 (a) to (e) exceeds the number of seats available in each of those respective groups, as a general rule, the principle of rotation shall apply. States members of each of those groups shall determine how this principle shall apply in those groups.

11. (a) The Council shall approve a recommendation by the Legal and Technical Commission for approval of a plan of work unless by a two-thirds majority of its members present and voting, including a majority of members present and voting in each of the chambers of the Council, the Council decides to disapprove a plan of work. If the Council does not take a decision on a recommendation for approval of a plan of work within a prescribed period, the recommendation shall be deemed to have been approved by the Council at the end of that period. The prescribed period shall normally be 60 days unless the Council decides to provide for a longer period. If the Commission recommends the disapproval of a plan of work or does not make a recommendation, the Council may nevertheless approve the plan of work in accordance with its rules of procedure for decision-making on questions of substance.

(b) The provisions of article 162, paragraph 2 (j), of the Convention shall not apply.

12. Where a dispute arises relating to the disapproval of a plan of work, such dispute shall be submitted to the dispute settlement procedures set out in the Convention.

13. Decisions by voting in the Legal and Technical Commission shall be by a majority of members present and voting.

14. Part XI, section 4, subsections B and C, of the Convention shall be interpreted and applied in accordance with this section.

15. The Council shall consist of 36 members of the Authority elected by the Assembly in the following order:

(a) Four members from among those States Parties which, during the last five years for which statistics are available, have either consumed more than 2 per cent in value terms of total world consumption or have had net imports of more than 2 per cent in value terms of total world imports of the commodities produced from the categories of minerals to be derived from the Area, provided that the four members shall include one State from the Eastern European region having the largest economy in that region in terms of gross domestic product and the State, on the date of entry into force of the Convention, having the largest economy in terms of gross domestic product, if such States wish to be represented in this group;

(b) Four members from among the eight States Parties which have made the largest investments in preparation for and in the conduct of activities in the Area, either directly or through their nationals;

(c) Four members from among States Parties which, on the basis of production in areas under their jurisdiction, are major net exporters of the categories of minerals to be derived from the Area, including at least two developing States whose exports of such minerals have a substantial bearing upon their economies;

(d) Six members from among developing States Parties, representing special interests. The special interests to be represented shall include those of States with large populations, States which are land-locked or geographically disadvantaged, island States, States which are major importers of the categories of minerals to be derived from the Area, States which are potential producers of such minerals and least developed States;

(e) Eighteen members elected according to the principle of ensuring an equitable geographical distribution of seats in the Council as a whole, provided that each geographical region shall have at least one member elected under this subparagraph. For this purpose, the geographical regions shall be Africa, Asia, Eastern Europe, Latin America and the Caribbean and Western Europe and Others.

16. The provisions of article 161, paragraph 1, of the Convention shall not apply.

SECTION 4. REVIEW CONFERENCE

The provisions relating to the Review Conference in article 155, paragraphs 1, 3 and 4, of the Convention shall not apply. Notwithstanding the provisions of article 314, paragraph 2, of the Convention, the Assembly, on the recommendation of the Council, may undertake at any time a review of the matters referred to in article 155, paragraph 1, of the Convention. Amendments relating to this Agreement and Part XI shall be subject to the procedures contained in articles 314, 315 and 316 of the Convention, provided that the principles, regime and other terms referred to in article 155, paragraph 2, of the Convention shall be maintained and the rights referred to in paragraph 5 of that article shall not be affected.

SECTION 5. TRANSFER OF TECHNOLOGY

1. In addition to the provisions of article 144 of the Convention, transfer of technology for the purposes of Part XI shall be governed by the following principles:

(a) The Enterprise, and developing States wishing to obtain deep seabed mining technology, shall seek to obtain such technology on fair and reasonable commercial terms and conditions on the open market, or through joint-venture arrangements;

(b) If the Enterprise or developing States are unable to obtain deep seabed mining technology, the Authority may request all or any of the contractors and their respective sponsoring State or States to cooperate with it in facilitating the acquisition of deep seabed mining technology by the Enterprise or its joint venture, or by a developing State or States seeking to acquire such technology on fair and reasonable commercial terms and conditions, consistent with the effective protection of intellectual property rights. States Parties undertake to cooperate fully and effectively with the Authority for this purpose and to ensure that contractors sponsored by them also cooperate fully with the Authority;

(c) As a general rule, States Parties shall promote international technical and scientific cooperation with regard to activities in the Area either between the parties concerned or by developing training, technical assistance and scientific cooperation programmes in marine science and technology and the protection and preservation of the marine environment.

2. The provisions of Annex III, article 5, of the Convention shall not apply.

Section 6. Production Policy

1. The production policy of the Authority shall be based on the following principles:

(a) Development of the resources of the Area shall take place in accordance with sound commercial principles;

(b) The provisions of the General Agreement on Tariffs and Trade, its relevant codes and successor or superseding agreements shall apply with respect to activities in the Area;

(c) In particular, there shall be no subsidization of activities in the Area except as may be permitted under the agreements referred to in subparagraph (b). Subsidization for the purpose of these principles shall be defined in terms of the agreements referred to in subparagraph (b);

(d) There shall be no discrimination between minerals derived from the Area and from other sources. There shall be no preferential access to markets for such minerals or for imports of commodities produced from such minerals, in particular:

  (i) By the use of tariff or non-tariff barriers; and

  (ii) Given by States Parties to such minerals or commodities produced by their state enterprises or by natural or juridical persons which possess their nationality or are controlled by them or their nationals;

(e) The plan of work for exploitation approved by the Authority in respect of each mining area shall indicate an anticipated production schedule which shall include the estimated maximum amounts of minerals that would be produced per year under the plan of work;

(f) The following shall apply to the settlement of disputes concerning the provisions of the agreements referred to in subparagraph (b):

  (i) Where the States Parties concerned are parties to such agreements, they shall have recourse to the dispute settlement procedures of those agreements;

  (ii) Where one or more of the States Parties concerned are not parties to such agreements, they shall have recourse to the dispute settlement procedures set out in the Convention;

(g) In circumstances where a determination is made under the agreements referred to in subparagraph (b) that a State Party has engaged in subsidization which is prohibited or has resulted in adverse effects on the interests of another State Party and appropriate steps have not been taken by the relevant State Party or States Parties, a State Party may request the Council to take appropriate measures.

2. The principles contained in paragraph 1 shall not affect the rights and obligations under any provision of the agreements referred to in paragraph 1(b), as well as the relevant free trade and customs union agreements, in relations between States Parties which are parties to such agreements.

3. The acceptance by a contractor of subsidies other than those which may be permitted under the agreements referred to in paragraph 1 (b) shall constitute a violation of the fundamental terms of the contract forming a plan of work for the carrying out of activities in the Area.

4. Any State Party which has reason to believe that there has been a breach of the requirements of paragraphs 1 (b) to (d) or 3 may initiate dispute settlement procedures in conformity with paragraph 1 (f) or (g).

5. A State Party may at any time bring to the attention of the Council activities which in its view are inconsistent with the requirements of paragraph 1 (b) to (d).

6. The Authority shall develop rules, regulations and procedures which ensure the implementation of the provisions of this section, including relevant rules, regulations and procedures governing the approval of plans of work.

7. The provisions of article 151, paragraphs 1 to 7 and 9, article 162, paragraph 2 (q), article 165, paragraph 2 (n), and Annex III, article 6, paragraph 5, and article 7, of the Convention shall not apply.

SECTION 7. ECONOMIC ASSISTANCE

1. The policy of the Authority of assisting developing countries which suffer serious adverse effects on their export earnings or economies resulting from a reduction in the price of an affected mineral or in the volume of exports of that mineral, to the extent that such reduction is caused by activities in the Area, shall be based on the following principles:

(a) The Authority shall establish an economic assistance fund from a portion of the funds of the Authority which exceeds those necessary to cover the administrative expenses of the Authority. The amount set aside for this purpose shall be determined by the Council from time to time, upon the recommendation of the Finance Committee. Only funds from payments received from contractors, including the Enterprise, and voluntary contributions shall be used for the establishment of the economic assistance fund;

(b) Developing land-based producer States whose economies have been determined to be seriously affected by the production of minerals from the deep seabed shall be assisted from the economic assistance fund of the Authority;

(c) The Authority shall provide assistance from the fund to affected developing land-based producer States, where appropriate, in cooperation with existing global or regional development institutions which have the infrastructure and expertise to carry out such assistance programmes;

(d) The extent and period of such assistance shall be determined on a case-by-case basis. In doing so, due consideration shall be given to the nature and magnitude of the problems encountered by affected developing land-based producer States.

2. Article 151, paragraph 10, of the Convention shall be implemented by means of measures of economic assistance referred to in paragraph 1. Article 160, paragraph 2 (l), article 162, paragraph 2 (n), article 164, paragraph 2 (d), article 171, subparagraph (f), and article 173, paragraph 2 (c), of the Convention shall be interpreted accordingly.

SECTION 8. FINANCIAL TERMS OF CONTRACTS

1. The following principles shall provide the basis for establishing rules, regulations and procedures for financial terms of contracts:

(a)   The system of payments to the Authority shall be fair both to the contractor and to the Authority and shall provide adequate means of determining compliance by the contractor with such system;

(b)   The rates of payments under the system shall be within the range of those prevailing in respect of land-based mining of the same or similar minerals in order to avoid giving deep seabed miners an artificial competitive advantage or imposing on them a competitive disadvantage;

(c)   The system should not be complicated and should not impose major administrative costs on the Authority or on a contractor. Consideration should be given to the adoption of a royalty system or a combination of a royalty and profit-sharing system. If alternative systems are decided upon, the contractor has the right to choose the system applicable to its contract. Any subsequent change in choice between alternative systems, however, shall be made by agreement between the Authority and the contractor;

(d)   An annual fixed fee shall be payable from the date of commencement of commercial production. This fee may be credited against other payments due under the system adopted in accordance with subparagraph (c). The amount of the fee shall be established by the Council;

(e)   The system of payments may be revised periodically in the light of changing circumstances. Any changes shall be applied in a non-discriminatory manner. Such changes may apply to existing contracts only at the election of the contractor. Any subsequent change in choice between alternative systems shall be made by agreement between the Authority and the contractor;

(f)   Disputes concerning the interpretation or application of the rules and regulations based on these principles shall be subject to the dispute settlement procedures set out in the Convention.

2. The provisions of Annex III, article 13, paragraphs 3 to 10, of the Convention shall not apply.

3. With regard to the implementation of Annex III, article 13, paragraph 2, of the Convention, the fee for processing applications for approval of a plan of work limited to one phase, either the exploration phase or the exploitation phase, shall be US$ 250,000.

SECTION 9. THE FINANCE COMMITTEE

1. There is hereby established a Finance Committee. The Committee shall be composed of 15 members with appropriate qualifications relevant to financial matters. States Parties shall nominate candidates of the highest standards of competence and integrity.

2. No two members of the Finance Committee shall be nationals of the same State Party.

3. Members of the Finance Committee shall be elected by the Assembly and due account shall be taken of the need for equitable geographical distribution and the representation of special interests. Each group of States referred to in section 3, paragraph 15 (a), (b), (c) and (d), of this Annex shall be represented on the Committee by at least one member. Until the Authority has sufficient funds other than assessed contributions to meet its administrative expenses, the membership of the Committee shall include representatives of the five largest financial contributors to the administrative budget of the

Authority. Thereafter, the election of one member from each group shall be on the basis of nomination by the members of the respective group, without prejudice to the possibility of further members being elected from each group.

4. Members of the Finance Committee shall hold office for a term of five years. They shall be eligible for re-election for a further term.

5. In the event of the death, incapacity or resignation of a member of the Finance Committee prior to the expiration of the term of office, the Assembly shall elect for the remainder of the term a member from the same geographical region or group of States.

6. Members of the Finance Committee shall have no financial interest in any activity relating to matters upon which the Committee has the responsibility to make recommendations. They shall not disclose, even after the termination of their functions, any confidential information coming to their knowledge by reason of their duties for the Authority.

7. Decisions by the Assembly and the Council on the following issues shall take into account recommendations of the Finance Committee:

(a) Draft financial rules, regulations and procedures of the organs of the Authority and the financial management and internal financial administration of the Authority;

(b) Assessment of contributions of members to the administrative budget of the Authority in accordance with article 160, paragraph 2 (e), of the Convention;

(c) All relevant financial matters, including the proposed annual budget prepared by the Secretary-General of the Authority in accordance with article 172 of the Convention and the financial aspects of the implementation of the programmes of work of the Secretariat;

(d) The administrative budget;

(e) Financial obligations of States Parties arising from the implementation of this Agreement and Part XI as well as the administrative and budgetary implications of proposals and recommendations involving expenditure from the funds of the Authority;

(f) Rules, regulations and procedures on the equitable sharing of financial and other economic benefits derived from activities in the Area and the decisions to be made thereon.

8. Decisions in the Finance Committee on questions of procedure shall be taken by a majority of members present and voting. Decisions on questions of substance shall be taken by consensus.

9. The requirement of article 162, paragraph 2 (y), of the Convention to establish a subsidiary organ to deal with financial matters shall be deemed to have been fulfilled by the establishment of the Finance Committee in accordance with this section.

Provisional Understanding Regarding Deep Seabed Matters between Belgium, France, the Federal Republic of Germany, Italy, Japan, the Netherlands, the United Kingdom and the United States

Done at Geneva, 3 August 1984; entry into force, 2 September 1984
1409 UNTS 464 [Registration Number 23601]

1. (1) No Party shall issue an authorization in respect of an application, or seek registration, for an area included:

       (a)   Within an area which is covered in another application filed in conformity with the agreements for voluntary conflict resolution reached 18 May 1983 and 15 December 1983 and being still under consideration by another Party;

       (b)   Within an area claimed in any other application which has been filed in conformity with national law and this Agreement,

           (i)   Prior to the signature of this Agreement, or

           (ii)   Earlier than the application or request for registration in question, and which is still under consideration by another Party; or

       (c)   Within an authorization granted by another Party in conformity with this Agreement.

   (2)   No Party shall itself engage in deep seabed operations in an area for which, in accordance with this paragraph, it shall not issue an authorization or seek registration.

2.   The Parties shall, as far as possible, process applications without delay. To this end, each Party shall, with reasonable dispatch, make an initial examination of each application to determine whether it complies with requirements for minimum content of applications under its national law, and thereafter determine the applicant's eligibility for the issuance of an authorization.

3.   Each Party shall immediately notify the other Parties of each application for an authorization which it accepts, including applications already received, and of each amendment to such an application. Each Party shall also immediately notify the other Parties after it has taken action subsequently with respect to an application or any action with respect to an authorization.

4.   No Party shall authorize, or itself engage in, exploitation of the hard mineral resources of the deep seabed before 1 January 1988.

5.   (1)   The Parties shall consult together:

       (a)   Prior to the issuance of any authorization or before themselves engaging in deep seabed operations or seeking registration for an area;

       (b)   With regard to any arrangements between one or more Parties and another State or States for the avoidance of overlapping in deep seabed operations;

       (c)   With regard to relevant legal provisions and any modification thereof; and

       (d)   Generally with a view to coordinating and reviewing the implementation of this Agreement.

   (2)   The relevant Parties shall consult together in the event that two or more applications are filed simultaneously.

6.   (1)   To the extent permissible under national law, a Party shall maintain the confidentiality of the coordinates of application areas and other proprietary or confidential commercial information received in confidence from any other Party in pursuance of cooperation in regard to deep seabed operations. In particular:

       (a)   The confidentiality of the coordinates of application areas shall be maintained until any overlap involving such an area is resolved and the relevant authorization is issued; and

       (b)   The confidentiality of other proprietary or confidential commercial information shall be maintained in accordance with national law as long as such information retains its character as such.

(2) Denunciation or other action by a Party pursuant to paragraph 14 of this Agreement shall not affect the Parties' obligations under this paragraph.

7. (1) The rights and interests of an applicant or of the grantee of an authorization may be transferred, in whole or in part, consistent with national law. Subject to national law, the rights, interests, and obligations of the transferee shall be as set forth in an agreement between the transferor and the transferee.

(2) For the purposes of this Agreement, the transferee is deemed to stand in the same position as that of the transferor for his rights and interests including the right of priority to the extent those rights and interests represent in whole or in part the original rights and interests of the transferor.

8. The Parties shall seek consistency in their application requirements and operating standards.

9. The Parties shall implement this Agreement in accordance with relevant national laws and regulations.

10. The Parties shall settle any dispute arising from the interpretation or application of this Agreement by appropriate means. The Parties to the dispute shall consider the possibility of recourse to binding arbitration and, if they agree, shall have recourse to it.

11. This Agreement, which includes Appendices I and II, may be amended only by written agreement of all Parties.

12. (1) This Agreement shall enter into force 30 days after signature.

(2) A Party which has not adopted the necessary legal provisions for the issue of authorization may, by a declaration relating to its signature of this Agreement, limit the application of this Agreement to the parts thereof other than those relating to the issue of authorizations. Where such a Party adopts legal provisions which, in the view of the other Parties, are similar in aims and effects to their own legal provisions, the first mentioned Party shall notify all other Parties that it accepts fully the provisions of this Agreement. Such a Party may also declare that, upon signature, that, for constitutional reasons, this Agreement shall become effective for it only after notification to all other Parties.

13. After entry into force of this Agreement additional States may, with the consent of all Parties, be invited to accede to this Agreement.

14. (1) A Party may denounce this Agreement by written notice to all other Parties, subject to the provisions of paragraph 6. Such denunciation shall become effective 180 days from the date of the latest receipt of such notice.

(2) A Party may, for good cause related to the implementation of this Agreement, after consultation, serve written notice on another Party, that from a date not less than 90 days thereafter, it will cease to give effect to paragraph 1 of this Agreement in respect of such other Party. The rights and obligation of these two Parties towards the other Parties remain unaffected by such notice.

(3) Subsequent to such notice referred to in sub-paragraphs (1) and (2), the Parties concerned shall seek, to the extent possible, to mitigate adverse effects resulting therefrom.

15. This Agreement is without prejudice to, nor does it affect, the positions of the Parties, or any obligations assumed by any of the Parties, in respect of the United Nations Convention on the Law of the Sea.

DONE at Geneva on 3 August 1984, in eight copies in the English, French, German, Italian, Japanese Netherlands language, each of which shall be equally authentic.

United Nations Convention against Illicit Traffic in Narcotic Drugs and Psychotropic Substances

Done at Vienna, 20 December 1988; entry into force, 11 November 1990
1582 UNTS 165 [Registration Number 27627][1]

The Parties to this Convention,

Deeply concerned by the magnitude of and rising trend in the illicit production of, demand for and traffic in narcotic drugs and psychotropic substances, which pose a serious threat to the health and welfare of human beings and adversely affect the economic, cultural and political foundations of society,

Deeply concerned also by the steadily increasing inroads into various social groups made by illicit traffic in narcotic drugs and psychotropic substances, and particularly by the fact that children are used in many parts of the world as an illicit drug consumers market and for purposes of illicit production, distribution and trade in narcotic drugs and psychotropic substances, which entails a danger of incalculable gravity,

Recognizing the links between illicit traffic and other related organized criminal activities which undermine the legitimate economies and threaten the stability, security and sovereignty of States,

Recognizing also that illicit traffic is an international criminal activity, the suppression of which demands urgent attention and the highest priority,

Aware that illicit traffic generates large financial profits and wealth enabling transnational criminal organizations to penetrate, contaminate and corrupt the structures of government, legitimate commercial and financial business, and society at all its levels,

Determined to deprive persons engaged in illicit traffic of the proceeds of their criminal activities and thereby eliminate their main incentive for so doing,

Desiring to eliminate the root causes of the problem of abuse of narcotic drugs and psychotropic substances, including the illicit demand for such drugs and substances and the enormous profits derived from illicit traffic,

Considering that measures are necessary to monitor certain substances, including precursors, chemicals and solvents, which are used in the manufacture of narcotic drugs and psychotropic substances, the ready availability of which has led to an increase in the clandestine manufacture of such drugs and substances,

Determined to improve international co-operation in the suppression of illicit traffic by sea,

Recognizing that eradication of illicit traffic is a collective responsibility of all States and that, to that end, co-ordinated action within the framework of international co-operation is necessary,

Acknowledging the competence of the United Nations in the field of control of narcotic drugs and psychotropic substances and desirous that the international organs concerned with such control should be within the framework of that Organization,

Reaffirming the guiding principles of existing treaties in the field of narcotic drugs and psychotropic substances and the system of control which they embody,

Recognizing the need to reinforce and supplement the measures provided in the Single Convention on Narcotic Drugs, 1961, that Convention as amended by the 1972 Protocol Amending the Single Convention on Narcotic Drugs, 1961, and the 1971 Convention on Psychotropic Substances, in order to counter the magnitude and extent of illicit traffic and its grave consequences,

---

[1] Articles 1, 3, 5-16, 18-34 omitted.

Recognizing also the importance of strengthening and enhancing effective legal means for international co-operation in criminal matters for suppressing the international criminal activities of illicit traffic,

Desiring to conclude a comprehensive, effective and operative international convention that is directed specifically against illicit traffic and that considers the various aspects of the problem as a whole, in particular those aspects not envisaged in the existing treaties in the field of narcotic drugs and psychotropic substances,

Hereby agree as follows:

Article 2 Scope of the Convention

1. The purpose of this Convention is to promote co-operation among the Parties so that they may address more effectively the various aspects of illicit traffic in narcotic drugs and psychotropic substances having an international dimension. In carrying out their obligations under the Convention, the Parties shall take necessary measures, including legislative and administrative measures, in conformity with the fundamental provisions of their respective domestic legislative systems.

2. The Parties shall carry out their obligations under this Convention in a manner consistent with the principles of sovereign equality and territorial integrity of States and that of non-intervention in the domestic affairs of other States.

3. A Party shall not undertake in the territory of another Party the exercise of jurisdiction and performance of functions which are exclusively reserved for the authorities of that other Party by its domestic law.

Article 4 Jurisdiction

1. Each Party:
   (a) Shall take such measures as may be necessary to establish its jurisdiction over the offences it has established in accordance with article 3, paragraph 1, when:
      (i) The offence is committed in its territory;
      (ii) The offence is committed on board a vessel flying its flag or an aircraft which is registered under its laws at the time the offence is committed;
   (b) May take such measures as may be necessary to establish its jurisdiction over the offences it has established in accordance with article 3, paragraph 1, when:
      (i) The offence is committed by one of its nationals or by a person who has his habitual residence in its territory;
      (ii) The offence is committed on board a vessel concerning which that Party has been authorized to take appropriate action pursuant to article 17, provided that such jurisdiction shall be exercised only on the basis of agreements or arrangements referred to in paragraphs 4 and 9 of that article;
      (iii) The offence is one of those established in accordance with article 3, paragraph 1, subparagraph (c) (iv), and is committed outside its territory with a view to the commission, within its territory, of an offence established in accordance with article 3, paragraph 1.

2. Each Party:
   (a) Shall also take such measures as may be necessary to establish its jurisdiction over the offences it has established in accordance with article 3, paragraph 1, when the alleged offender is present in its territory and it does not extradite him to another Party on the ground:
      (i) That the offence has been committed in its territory or on board a vessel flying its flag or an aircraft which was registered under its law at the time the offence was committed; or

(ii)   That the offence has been committed by one of its nationals;

(b)   May also take such measures as may be necessary to establish its jurisdiction over the offences it has established in accordance with article 3, paragraph 1, when the alleged offender is present in its territory and it does not extradite him to another Party.

3.   This Convention does not exclude the exercise of any criminal jurisdiction established by a Party in accordance with its domestic law.

Article 17 Illicit traffic by sea

1.   The Parties shall co-operate to the fullest extent possible to suppress illicit traffic by sea, in conformity with the international law of the sea.

2.   A Party which has reasonable grounds to suspect that a vessel flying its flag or not displaying a flag or marks of registry is engaged in illicit traffic may request the assistance of other Parties in suppressing its use for that purpose. The Parties so requested shall render such assistance within the means available to them.

3.   A Party which has reasonable grounds to suspect that a vessel exercising freedom of navigation in accordance with international law and flying the flag or displaying marks of registry of another Party is engaged in illicit traffic may so notify the flag State, request confirmation of registry and, if confirmed, request authorization from the flag State to take appropriate measures in regard to that vessel.

4.   In accordance with paragraph 3 or in accordance with treaties in force between them or in accordance with any agreement or arrangement otherwise reached between those Parties, the flag State may authorize the requesting State to, *inter alia*:

(a)   Board the vessel;

(b)   Search the vessel;

(c)   If evidence of involvement in illicit traffic is found, take appropriate action with respect to the vessel, persons and cargo on board.

5.   Where action is taken pursuant to this article, the Parties concerned shall take due account of the need not to endanger the safety of life at sea, the security of the vessel and the cargo or to prejudice the commercial and legal interests of the flag State or any other interested State.

6.   The flag State may, consistent with its obligations in paragraph 1 of this article, subject its authorization to conditions to be mutually agreed between it and the requesting Party, including conditions relating to responsibility.

7.   For the purposes of paragraphs 3 and 4 of this article, a Party shall respond expeditiously to a request from another Party to determine whether a vessel that is flying its flag is entitled to do so, and to requests for authorization made pursuant to paragraph 3. At the time of becoming a Party to this Convention, each Party shall designate an authority or, when necessary, authorities to receive and respond to such requests. Such designation shall be notified through the Secretary-General to all other Parties within one month of the designation.

8.   A Party which has taken any action in accordance with this article shall promptly inform the flag State concerned of the results of that action.

9.   The Parties shall consider entering into bilateral or regional agreements or arrangements to carry out, or to enhance the effectiveness of, the provisions of this article.

10.   Action pursuant to paragraph 4 of this article shall be carried out only by warships or military aircraft, or other ships or aircraft clearly marked and identifiable as being on government service and authorized to that effect.

11.   Any action taken in accordance with this article shall take due account of the need not to interfere with or affect the rights and obligations and the exercise of jurisdiction of coastal States in accordance with the international law of the sea.

IN WITNESS WHEREOF the undersigned, being duly authorized thereto, have signed this Convention.

DONE at Vienna, in one original, this twentieth day of December one thousand nine hundred and eighty-eight.

International Convention on Salvage

Done at London, 28 April 1989; entry into force, 14 July 1996
1953 UNTS 194 [Registration Number 33479]

The State Parties to the present Convention,

Recognizing the desirability of determining by agreement uniform international rules regarding salvage operations,

Noting that substantial developments, in particular the increased concern for the protection of the environment, have demonstrated the need to review the international rules presently contained in the Convention for the Unification of Certain Rules of Law relating to Assistance and Salvage at Sea, done at Brussels, 23 September 1910,

Conscious of the major contribution which efficient and timely salvage operations can make to the safety of vessels and other property in danger and to the protection of the environment,

Convinced of the need to ensure that adequate incentives are available to persons who undertake salvage operations in respect of vessels and other property in danger,

Have agreed as follows:

CHAPTER I - GENERAL PROVISIONS

Article 1   Definitions

For the purpose of this Convention:

(a)   'Salvage operation' means any act or activity undertaken to assist a vessel or any other property in danger in navigable waters or in any other waters whatsoever.

(b)   'Vessel' means any ship or craft, or any structure capable of navigation.

(c)   'Property' means any property not permanently and intentionally attached to the shoreline and includes freight at risk.

(d)   'Damage to the environment' means substantial physical damage to human health or to marine life or resources in coastal or inland waters or areas adjacent thereto, caused by pollution, contamination, fire, explosion or similar major incidents.

(e)   'Payment' means any reward, remuneration or compensation due under this Convention.

(f)   'Organization' means the International Maritime Organization.

(g)   'Secretary-General' means the Secretary-General of the Organization.

Article 2   Application of the Convention

This Convention shall apply whenever judicial or arbitral proceedings relating to matters dealt with in this Convention are brought in a State Party.

Article 3　Platforms and drilling units

This Convention shall not apply to fixed or floating platforms or to mobile offshore drilling units when such platforms or units are on location engaged in the exploration, exploitation or production of sea-bed mineral resources.

Article 4　State-owned vessels

1.　Without prejudice to article 5, this Convention shall not apply to warships or other non-commercial vessels owned or operated by a State and entitled, at the time of salvage operations, to sovereign immunity under generally recognized principles of international law unless that State decides otherwise.

2.　Where a State Party decides to apply the Convention to its warships or other vessels described in paragraph 1, it shall notify the Secretary-General thereof specifying the terms and conditions of such application.

Article 5　Salvage operations controlled by public authorities

1.　This Convention shall not affect any provisions of national law or any international convention relating to salvage operations by or under the control of public authorities.

2.　Nevertheless, salvors carrying out such salvage operations shall be entitled to avail themselves of the rights and remedies provided for in this Convention in respect of salvage operations.

3.　The extent to which a public authority under a duty to perform salvage operations may avail itself of the rights and remedies provided for in this Convention shall be determined by the law of the State where such authority is situated.

Article 6　Salvage contracts

1.　This Convention shall apply to any salvage operations save to the extent that a contract otherwise provides expressly or by implication.

2.　The master shall have the authority to conclude contracts for salvage operations on behalf of the owner of the vessel. The master or the owner of the vessel shall have the authority to conclude such contracts on behalf of the owner of the property on board the vessel.

3.　Nothing in this article shall affect the application of article 7 nor duties to prevent or minimize damage to the environment.

Article 7　Annulment and modification of contracts

A contract or any terms thereof may be annulled or modified if:
- (a)　the contract has been entered into under undue influence or the influence of danger and its terms are inequitable; or
- (b)　the payment under the contract is in an excessive degree too large or too small for the services actually rendered.

CHAPTER II - PERFORMANCE OF SALVAGE OPERATIONS

Article 8　Duties of the salvor and of the owner and master

1.　The salvor shall owe a duty to the owner of the vessel or other property in danger:
- (a)　to carry out the salvage operations with due care;
- (b)　in performing the duty specified in subparagraph (a), to exercise due care to prevent or minimize damage to the environment;
- (c)　whenever circumstances reasonably require, to seek assistance from other salvors; and

(d)   to accept the intervention of other salvors when reasonably requested to do so by the owner or master of the vessel or other property in danger; provided however that the amount of his reward shall not be prejudiced should it be found that such a request was unreasonable.

2.   The owner and master of the vessel or the owner of other property in danger shall owe a duty to the salvor:

(a)   to co-operate fully with him during the course of the salvage operations;

(b)   in so doing, to exercise due care to prevent or minimize damage to the environment; and

(c)   when the vessel or other property has been brought to a place of safety, to accept redelivery when reasonably requested by the salvor to do so.

Article 9 Rights of coastal States

Nothing in this Convention shall affect the right of the coastal State concerned to take measures in accordance with generally recognized principles of international law to protect its coastline or related interests from pollution or the threat of pollution following upon a maritime casualty or acts relating to such a casualty which may reasonably be expected to result in major harmful consequences, including the right of a coastal State to give directions in relation to salvage operations.

Article 10 Duty to render assistance

1.   Every master is bound, so far as he can do so without serious danger to his vessel and persons thereon, to render assistance to any person in danger of being lost at sea.

2.   The States Parties shall adopt the measures necessary to enforce the duty set out in paragraph 1.

3.   The owner of the vessel shall incur no liability for a breach of the duty of the master under paragraph 1.

Article 11 Co-operation

A State Party shall, whenever regulating or deciding upon matters relating to salvage operations such as admittance to ports of vessels in distress or the provision of facilities to salvors, take into account the need for co-operation between salvors, other interested parties and public authorities in order to ensure the efficient and successful performance of salvage operations for the purpose of saving life or property in danger as well as preventing damage to the environment in general.

CHAPTER III - RIGHTS OF SALVORS

Article 12 Conditions for reward

1.   Salvage operations which have had a useful result give right to a reward.

2.   Except as otherwise provided, no payment is due under this Convention if the salvage operations have had no useful result.

3.   This chapter shall apply, notwithstanding that the salved vessel and the vessel undertaking the salvage operations belong to the same owner.

Article 13 Criteria for fixing the reward

1.   The reward shall be fixed with a view to encouraging salvage operations, taking into account the following criteria without regard to the order in which they are presented below:

(a)   the salved value of the vessel and other property;

(b)   the skill and efforts of the salvors in preventing or minimizing damage to the environment;

(c)   the measure of success obtained by the salvor;

(d)   the nature and degree of the danger;

(e)   the skill and efforts of the salvors in salving the vessel, other property and life;

(f)   the time used and expenses and losses incurred by the salvors;

(g)   the risk of liability and other risks run by the salvors or their equipment;

(h)   the promptness of the services rendered;

(i)   the availability and use of vessels or other equipment intended for salvage operations;

(j)   the state of readiness and efficiency of the salvor's equipment and the value thereof.

2.   Payment of a reward fixed according to paragraph 1 shall be made by all of the vessel and other property interests in proportion to their respective salved values. However, a State Party may in its national law provide that the payment of a reward has to be made by one of these interests, subject to a right of recourse of this interest against the other interests for their respective shares. Nothing in this article shall prevent any right of defence.

3.   The rewards, exclusive of any interest and recoverable legal costs that may be payable thereon, shall not exceed the salved value of the vessel and other property.

Article 14   Special compensation

1.   If the salvor has carried out salvage operations in respect of a vessel which by itself or its cargo threatened damage to the environment and has failed to earn a reward under article 13 at least equivalent to the special compensation assessable in accordance with this article, he shall be entitled to special compensation from the owner of that vessel equivalent to his expenses as herein defined.

2.   If, in the circumstances set out in paragraph 1, the salvor by his salvage operations has prevented or minimized damage to the environment, the special compensation payable by the owner to the salvor under paragraph 1 may be increased up to a maximum of 30% of the expenses incurred by the salvor. However, the tribunal, if it deems it fair and just to do so and bearing in mind the relevant criteria set out in article 13, paragraph 1, may increase such special compensation further, but in no event shall the total increase be more than 100% of the expenses incurred by the salvor.

3.   Salvor's expenses for the purpose of paragraphs 1 and 2 means the out-of-pocket expenses reasonably incurred by the salvor in the salvage operation and a fair rate for equipment and personnel actually and reasonably used in the salvage operation, taking into consideration the criteria set out in article 13, paragraph 1(h), (i) and (j).

4.   The total special compensation under this article shall be paid only if and to the extent that such compensation is greater than any reward recoverable by the salvor under article 13.

5.   If the salvor has been negligent and has thereby failed to prevent or minimize damage to the environment, he may be deprived of the whole or part of any special compensation due under this article.

6.   Nothing in this article shall affect any right of recourse on the part of the owner of the vessel.

Article 15   Apportionment between salvors

1.   The apportionment of a reward under article 13 between salvors shall be made on the basis of the criteria contained in that article.

2.   The apportionment between the owner, master and other persons in the service of each salving vessel shall be determined by the law of the flag of that vessel. If the salvage has not been carried out from a vessel, the apportionment shall be determined by the law governing the contract between the salvor and his servants.

Article 16 Salvage of persons

1. No remuneration is due from persons whose lives are saved, but nothing in this article shall affect the provisions of national law on this subject.

2. A salvor of human life, who has taken part in the services rendered on the occasion of the accident giving rise to salvage, is entitled to a fair share of the payment awarded to the salvor for salving the vessel or other property or preventing or minimizing damage to the environment.

Article 17 Services rendered under existing contracts

No payment is due under the provisions of this Convention unless the services rendered exceed what can be reasonably considered as due performance of a contract entered into before the danger arose.

Article 18 The effect of salvor's misconduct

A salvor may be deprived of the whole or part of the payment due under this Convention to the extent that the salvage operations have become necessary or more difficult because of fault or neglect on his part or if the salvor has been guilty of fraud or other dishonest conduct.

Article 19 Prohibition of salvage operations

Services rendered notwithstanding the express and reasonable prohibition of the owner or master of the vessel or the owner of any other property in danger which is not and has not been on board the vessel shall not give rise to payment under this Convention.

CHAPTER IV - CLAIMS AND ACTIONS

Article 20 Maritime lien

1. Nothing in this Convention shall affect the salvor's maritime lien under any international convention or national law.

2. The salvor may not enforce his maritime lien when satisfactory security for his claim, including interest and costs, has been duly tendered or provided.

Article 21 Duty to provide security

1. Upon the request of the salvor a person liable for a payment due under this Convention shall provide satisfactory security for the claim, including interest and costs of the salvor.

2. Without prejudice to paragraph 1, the owner of the salved vessel shall use his best endeavours to ensure that the owners of the cargo provide satisfactory security for the claims against them including interest and costs before the cargo is released.

3. The salved vessel and other property shall not, without the consent of the salvor, be removed from the port or place at which they first arrive after the completion of the salvage operations until satisfactory security has been put up for the salvor's claim against the relevant vessel or property.

Article 22 Interim payment

1. The tribunal having jurisdiction over the claim of the salvor may, by interim decision, order that the salvor shall be paid on account such amount as seems fair and just, and on such terms including terms as to security where appropriate, as may be fair and just according to the circumstances of the case.

2. In the event of an interim payment under this article the security provided under article 21 shall be reduced accordingly.

Article 23 Limitation of actions

1. Any action relating to payment under this Convention shall be time-barred if judicial or arbitral proceedings have not been instituted within a period of two years. The limitation period commences on the day on which the salvage operations are terminated.

2. The person against whom a claim is made at any time during the running of the limitation period extend that period by a declaration to the claimant. This period may in the like manner be further extended.

3. An action for indemnity by a person liable may be instituted even after the expiration of the limitation period provided for in the preceding paragraphs, if brought within the time allowed by the law of the State where proceedings are instituted.

Article 24 Interest

The right of the salvor to interest on any payment due under this Convention shall be determined according to the law of the State in which the tribunal seized of the case is situated.

Article 25 State-owned cargoes

Unless the State owner consents, no provision of this Convention shall be used as a basis for the seizure, arrest or detention by any legal process of, nor for any proceedings *in rem* against, non-commercial cargoes owned by a State and entitled, at the time of the salvage operations, to sovereign immunity under generally recognized principles of international law.

Article 26 Humanitarian cargoes

No provision of this Convention shall be used as a basis for the seizure, arrest or detention of humanitarian cargoes donated by a State, if such State has agreed to pay for salvage services rendered in respect of such humanitarian cargoes.

Article 27 Publication of arbitral awards

States Parties shall encourage, as far as possible and with the consent of the parties, the publication of arbitral awards made in salvage cases.

CHAPTER V - FINAL CLAUSES

Article 28 Signature, ratification, acceptance, approval and accession

1. This Convention shall be open for signature at the Headquarters of the Organization from 1 July 1989 to 30 June 1990 and shall thereafter remain open for accession.

2. States may express their consent to be bound by this Convention by:

(a) signature without reservation as to ratification, acceptance or approval; or

(b) signature subject to ratification, acceptance or approval, followed by ratification, acceptance of approval; or

(c) accession.

3. Ratification, acceptance, approval or accession shall be effected by the deposit of an instrument to that effect with the Secretary-General.

Article 29 Entry into force

1. This Convention shall enter into force one year after the date on which 15 States have expressed their consent to be bound by it.

2. For a State which expresses its consent to be bound by this Convention after the conditions for entry into force thereof have been met, such consent shall take effect one year after the date of expression of such consent.

Article 30 Reservations

1. Any State may, at the time of signature, ratification, acceptance, approval or accession, reserve the right not to apply the provisions of this Convention:
  (a) when the salvage operation takes place in inland waters and all vessels involved are of inland navigation;
  (b) when the salvage operations take place in inland waters and no vessel is involved;
  (c) when all interested parties are nationals of that State;
  (d) when the property involved is maritime cultural property of prehistoric, archaeological or historic interest and is situated on the sea-bed.

2. Reservations made at the time of signature are subject to confirmation upon ratification, acceptance or approval.

3. Any State which has made a reservation to this Convention may withdraw it at any time by means of a notification addressed to the Secretary-General. Such withdrawal shall take effect on the date the notification is received. If the notification states that the withdrawal of a reservation is to take effect on a date specified therein, and such date is later than the date the notification is received by the Secretary-General, the withdrawal shall take effect on such later date.

Article 31 Denunciation

1. This Convention may be denounced by any State Party at any time after the expiry of one year from the date on which this Convention enters into force for that State.

2. Denunciation shall be effected by the deposit of an instrument of denunciation with the Secretary-General.

3. A denunciation shall take effect one year, or such longer period as may be specified in the instrument of denunciation, after the receipt of the instrument of denunciation by the Secretary-General.

Article 32 Revision and amendment

1. A conference for the purpose of revising or amending this Convention may be convened by the Organization.

2. The Secretary-General shall convene a conference of the States Parties to this Convention for revising or amending the Convention, at the request of eight States Parties, or one fourth of the States Parties, whichever is the higher figure.

3. Any consent to be bound by this Convention expressed after the date of entry into force of an amendment to this Convention shall be deemed to apply to the Convention as amended.

Article 33 Depositary

1. This Convention shall be deposited with the Secretary-General.

2. The Secretary-General shall:
  (a) inform all States which have signed this Convention or acceded thereto, and all Members of the Organization, of:
    (i)   each new signature or deposit of an instrument of ratification, acceptance, approval or accession together with the date thereof;
    (ii) the date of the entry into force of this Convention;
    (iii) the deposit of any instrument of denunciation of this Convention together with the date on which it received and the date on which the denunciation takes effect;
    (iv) any amendment adopted in conformity with article 32;

(v)   the receipt of any reservation, declaration or notification made under this Convention;

(b)   transmit certified true copies of this Convention to all States which have signed this Convention or acceded thereto.

3.   As soon as this Convention enters into force, a certified true copy thereof shall be transmitted by the Depositary to the Secretary-General of the United Nations for registration and publication in accordance with Article 102 of the Charter of the United Nations.

Article 34 Languages

This Convention is established in a single original in the Arabic, Chinese, English, French, Russian and Spanish languages, each text being equally authentic.

IN WITNESS WHEREOF the undersigned being duly authorized by their respective Governments for that purpose have signed this Convention.

DONE at London this twenty-eighth day of April one thousand nine hundred and eighty-nine.

Guidelines and Standards for the Removal of Offshore Installations and Structures on the Continental Shelf and in the Exclusive Economic Zone

IMO Resolution A.672(16), adopted on 19 October 1989

1.   General removal requirement

1.1   Abandoned or disused offshore installations or structures on any continental shelf or in any exclusive economic zone are required to be removed, except where non-removal or partial removal is consistent with the following guidelines and standards.

1.2   The coastal State having jurisdiction over the installation or structure should ensure that it is removed in whole or in part in conformity with these guidelines and standards once it is no longer serving the primary purpose for which it was originally designed and installed, or serving a subsequent new use, or where no other reasonable justification cited in these guidelines and standards exists for allowing the installation or structure or parts thereof to remain on the sea-bed. Such removal should be performed as soon as reasonably practicable after abandonment or permanent disuse of such installation or structure.

1.3   Notification of such non-removal or partial removal should be forwarded to the Organization.

1.4   Nothing in these guidelines and standards is intended to preclude a coastal State from imposing more stringent removal requirements for existing or future installations or structures on its continental shelf or in its exclusive economic zone.

2.   Guidelines

2.1   The decision to allow an offshore installation, structure, or parts thereof, to remain on the sea-bed should be based, in particular, on a case-by-case evaluation, by the coastal State with jurisdiction over the installation or structure, of the following matters:

.1   any potential effect on the safety of surface or subsurface navigation, or of other uses of the sea;

.2   the rate of deterioration of the material and its present and possible future effect on the marine environment;

.3   the potential effect on the marine environment, including living resources;

.4   the risk that the material will shift from its position at some future time;

.5   the costs, technical feasibility, and risks of injury to personnel associated with removal of the installation or structure; and

.6   the determination of a new use or other reasonable justification for allowing the installation or structure or parts thereof to remain on the sea-bed.

2.2 The determination of any potential effect on safety of surface or subsurface navigation or of other uses of the sea should be based on: the number, type and draught of vessels expected to transit the area in the foreseeable future; the cargoes being carried in the area; the tide, current, general hydrographic conditions and potentially extreme climatic conditions; the proximity of designated or customary sea lanes and port access routes; the aids to navigation in the vicinity; the location of commercial fishing areas; the width of the available navigable fairway; and whether the area is an approach to or in straits used for international navigation or routes used for international navigation through archipelagic waters.

2.3 The determination of any potential effect on the marine environment should be based upon scientific evidence taking into account: the effect on water quality; geological and hydrographic characteristics; the presence of endangered or threatened species; existing habitat types; local fishery resources; and the potential for pollution or contamination of the site by residual products from, or deterioration of, the offshore installation or structure.

2.4 The process for allowing an offshore installation or structure, or parts thereof, to remain on the sea-bed should also include the following actions by the coastal State with jurisdiction over the installation or structure: special official authorization identifying the conditions under which an installation or structure, or parts thereof, will be allowed to remain on the sea-bed; the drawing up of a specific plan, adopted by the coastal State, to monitor the accumulation and deterioration of material left on the sea-bed to ensure there is no subsequent adverse impact on navigation, other uses of the sea or the marine environment; advance notice to mariners as to the specific position, dimensions, surveyed depth and markings of any installations or structures not entirely removed from the sea-bed; and advance notice to appropriate hydrographic services to allow for timely revision of nautical charts.

3.   Standards

The following standards should be taken into account when a decision is made regarding the removal of an offshore installation or structure.

3.1 All abandoned or disused installations or structures standing in less than 75 m of water and weighing less than 4,000 tonnes in air, excluding the deck and superstructure, should be entirely removed.

3.2 All abandoned or disused installations or structures emplaced on the sea-bed on or after 1 January 1998, standing in less than 100 m of water and weighing less than 4,000 tonnes in air, excluding the deck and superstructure, should be entirely removed.

3.3 Removal should be performed in such a way as to cause no significant adverse effects upon navigation or the marine environment. Installations should continue to be marked in accordance with IALA recommendations prior to the completion of any partial or complete removal that may be required. Details of the position and dimensions of any installations remaining after the removal operations should be promptly passed to the relevant national authorities and to one of the world charting hydrographic authorities. The means of removal or partial removal should not cause a significant adverse effect on living resources of the marine environment, especially threatened and endangered species.

3.4   The coastal State may determine that the installation or structure may be left wholly or partially in place where:

.1   an existing installation or structure, including one referred to in paragraphs 3.1 or 3.2, or a part thereof, will serve a new use if permitted to remain wholly or partially in place on the sea-bed (such as enhancement of a living resource); or

.2   an existing installation or structure, other than one referred to in paragraphs 3.1 and 3.2, or part thereof, can be left there without causing unjustifiable interference with other uses of the sea.

3.5   Notwithstanding the requirements of paragraphs 3.1 and 3.2, where entire removal is not technically feasible or would involve extreme cost, or an unacceptable risk to personnel or the marine environment, the coastal State may determine that it need not be entirely removed.

3.6   Any abandoned or disused installation or structure, or part thereof, which projects above the surface of the sea should be adequately maintained to prevent structural failure. In cases of partial removal referred to in paragraphs 3.4.2 or 3.5, an unobstructed water column sufficient to ensure safety of navigation, but not less than 55 m, should be provided above any partially removed installation or structure which does not project above the surface of the sea.

3.7   Installations or structures which no longer serve the primary purpose for which they were originally designed or installed and are located in approaches to or in straits used for international navigation or routes used for international navigation through archipelagic waters, in customary deep-draught sea lanes, or in, or immediately adjacent to, routeing systems which have been adopted by the Organization should be entirely removed and should not be subject to any exceptions.

3.8   The coastal State should ensure that the position, surveyed depth and dimensions of material from any installation or structure which has not been entirely removed from the sea-bed are indicated on nautical charts and that any remains are, where necessary, properly marked with aids to navigation. The coastal State should also ensure that advance notice of at least 120 days is issued to advise mariners and appropriate hydrographic services of the change in the status of the installation or structure.

3.9   Prior to giving consent to the partial removal of any installation or structure, the coastal State should satisfy itself that any remaining materials will remain on location on the sea-bed and not move under the influence of waves, tides, currents, storms or other foreseeable natural causes so as to cause a hazard to navigation.

3.10 The coastal State should identify the party responsible for maintaining the aids to navigation, if they are deemed necessary to mark the position of any obstruction to navigation, and for monitoring the condition of remaining material. The coastal State should also ensure that the responsible party conducts periodic monitoring, as necessary, to ensure continued compliance with these guidelines and standards.

3.11 The coastal State should ensure that legal title to installations and structures which have not been entirely removed from the sea-bed is unambiguous and that responsibility for maintenance and the financial ability to assume liability for future damages are clearly established.

3.12 Where living resources can be enhanced by the placement on the sea-bed of material from removed installations or structures (e.g. to create an artificial reef), such material should be located well away from customary traffic lanes, taking into account these guidelines and standards and other relevant standards for the maintenance of maritime safety.

3.13 On or after 1 January 1998, no installation or structure should be placed on any continental shelf or in any exclusive economic zone unless the design and construction of the installation or structure is such that entire removal upon abandonment or permanent disuse would be feasible.

3.14 Unless otherwise stated, these standards should be applied to existing as well as future installations or structures.

USA-USSR Joint Statement on the Uniform Interpretation of Rules of International Law Governing Innocent Passage

Done at Jackson Hole, Wyoming, 23 September 1989
(1989) 14 LOSB 13[1]

1. The relevant rules of international law governing innocent passage of ships in the territorial sea are stated in the 1982 United National Convention on Law of the Sea (Convention of 1982), particularly in Part II, Section 3.

2. All ships, including warships, regardless of cargo, armament or means of propulsion, enjoy the right of innocent passage through the territorial sea in accordance with international law, for which neither prior notification nor authorization is required.

3. Article 19 of the Convention of 1982 sets out in paragraph 2 an exhaustive list of activities that would render passage not innocent. A ship passing through the territorial sea that does not engage in any of those activities is in innocent passage.

4. A coastal State which questions whether the particular passage of a ship through its territorial sea is innocent shall inform the ship of the reason why it questions the innocence of the passage, and provide the ship an opportunity to clarify its intentions or correct its conduct in a reasonably short period of time.

5. Ships exercising the right of innocent passage shall comply with all laws and regulations of the coastal State adopted in conformity with relevant rules of international law as reflected in Articles 21, 22, 23 and 25 of the Convention of 1982. These include the laws and regulations requiring ships exercising the right of innocent passage through its territorial sea to use such sea lanes and traffic separation schemes as it may prescribe where needed to protect safety of navigation. In areas where no such sea lanes or traffic separation schemes have been prescribed, ships nevertheless enjoy the right of innocent passage.

6. Such laws and regulations of the coastal State may not have the practical effect of denying or impairing the exercise of the right of innocent passage as set forth in Article 24 of the Convention of 1982.

7. If a warship engages in conduct which violates such law or regulations or renders its passage not innocent and does not take corrective action upon request, the coastal State may require it to leave the territorial sea, as set forth in Article 30 of the Convention of 1982. In such case the warship shall do so immediately.

---

[1] The Statement was introduced as follows: Since 1986, representatives of the United States of America and the Union of Soviet Socialist Republics have been conducting friendly and constructive discussions of certain international legal aspects of traditional uses of the oceans, in particular, navigation.

The Governments are guided by the provisions of the 1982 United Nations Convention on the Law of the Sea, which, with respect to traditional uses of the oceans, generally constitute international law and practice and balance fairly the interests of all States. They recognize the need to encourage all States to harmonize their internal laws, regulations and practices with those provisions.

The Governments consider it useful to issue the attached Uniform Interpretation of the Rules of International Law Governing Innocent Passage. Both Governments have agreed to take the necessary steps to conform their internal laws, regulations and practices with this understanding of the rules.

8.   Without prejudice to the exercise of rights of coastal and flag States, all differences which may arise regarding a particular case of passage of ships through the territorial sea shall be settled through diplomatic channels or other agreed means.

UN Security Council Resolution 665 (1990)

UN Doc. S/RES/665 (1990) of 25 August 1990

The Security Council,

Recalling its resolutions 660 (1990), 661 (1990), 662 (1990) and 664 (1990) and demanding their full and immediate implementation,

Having decided in resolution 661 (1990) to impose economic sanctions under Chapter VII of the Charter of the United Nations,

Determined to bring an end to the occupation of Kuwait by Iraq which imperils the existence of a Member State and to restore the legitimate authority, and the sovereignty, independence and territorial integrity of Kuwait which requires the speedy implementation of the above resolutions,

Deploring the loss of innocent life stemming from the Iraqi invasion of Kuwait and determined to prevent further such losses,

Gravely alarmed that Iraq continues to refuse to comply with resolutions 660 (1990), 661 (1990), 662 (1990) and 664 (1990) and in particular at the conduct of the Government of Iraq in using Iraqi flag vessels to export oil,

1.   *Calls upon* those Member States co-operating with the Government of Kuwait which are deploying maritime forces to the area to use such measures commensurate to the specific circumstances as may be necessary under the authority of the Security Council to halt all inward and outward maritime shipping in order to inspect and verify their cargoes and destinations and to ensure strict implementation of the provisions related to such shipping laid down in resolution 661 (1990);

2.   *Invites* Member States accordingly to co-operate as may be necessary to ensure compliance with the provisions of resolution 661 (1990) with maximum use of political and diplomatic measures, in accordance with paragraph 1 above;

3.   *Requests* all States to provide in accordance with the Charter such assistance as may be required by the States referred to in paragraph 1 of this resolution;

4.   *Further requests* the States concerned to co-ordinate their actions in pursuit of the above paragraphs of this resolution using as appropriate mechanisms of the Military Staff Committee and after consultation with the Secretary-General to submit reports to the Security Council and its Committee established under resolution 661 (1990) to facilitate the monitoring of the implementation of this resolution;

5.   *Decides* to remain actively seized of the matter.

Arrangement between the Government of the United States and the Government of Panama for Support and Assistance from the US Coast Guard for the National Maritime Service of the Ministry of Government and Justice

Signed at Panama, 18 March 1991; entry into force, 18 March 1991
2212 UNTS 8 [Registration Number 39296]

Referring to the recent discussions between representatives of our two Governments concerning the desire of the United States of America to provide assistance to the Republic of Panama in training members of the National Maritime Service (SMN) of the Ministry of Government and Justice and providing for conducting bilateral police operations within the territorial waters of the Republic of Panama, to stop illegal activities, such as the international trafficking of drugs, illegal fishing and transportation of contraband;

The Government of the United States of America and the Government of the Republic of Panama agree to the following with regard to the conduct of bilateral operations under the framework of this arrangement:

1. The US Coast Guard shall provide appropriate patrol vessels to support and assist vessels of the Republic of Panama, in order that Panamanian officers from the National Maritime Service (SMN) of the Ministry of Government and Justice, empowered to enforce pertinent Panamanian laws within waters under Panamanian jurisdiction, may effectively exercise their power and authority over said area of the national territory.

2. The Ministry of Government and Justice desires the cooperation of the US Coast Guard, so that the US Coast Guard may provide training, vessels and operational support during the bilateral operations with the National Maritime Service (SMN).

3. The National Maritime Service (SMN) of the Ministry of Government and Justice shall exercise Panamanian jurisdiction during the bilateral operations. The US Coast Guard shall only provide assistance and training, and shall not exercise any form of jurisdiction over those vessels while operating in Panamanian territorial waters under the present arrangement.

4. The bilateral operations shall consist of Panamanian vessels operating at all times in company with an equal number of vessels of the US Coast Guard. The vessels of the US Coast Guard shall not patrol Panamanian territorial waters independently. However, the vessels of the US Coast Guard may transit Panamanian territorial waters for purpose related to logistics, maintenance, or while said vessels are in transit to or from the Republic of Panama or otherwise in connection with the exercise of innocent passage.

5. The vessels of the US Coast Guard, while patrolling by virtue of this arrangement with Panamanian vessels, shall carry on board at least two Panamanian officials from the National Maritime Service (SMN) empowered to enforce pertinent Panamanian laws within the Panamanian territorial waters. One of these officials shall be in charge of directing the operation. These officials must exercise the functions granted to them by Panamanian laws in order that all Panamanian and foreign vessels within Panamanian territorial waters comply with all measures established by Panamanian law. These officials shall conduct the operation in coordination with the officer of the US Coast Guard in tactical control of the vessel of the US Coast Guard.

6. During each bilateral patrol, the vessel of the US Coast Guard shall display, prominently, the flag of the Republic of Panama, and the same shall be flown from the main mast of all vessels participating in the bilateral patrols. When operating at night, the

Panamanian flag shall be illuminated during boardings as necessary to ensure recognitions of Panamanian jurisdiction.

7. Actual boardings of Panamanian or foreign vessels encountered during bilateral operations within the territorial waters of Panama shall only be conducted by the Panamanian personnel empowered to enforce pertinent Panamanian laws. The personnel of the US Coast Guard shall only provide assistance during the boarding from the vessels of the US Coast Guard and from their small boats.

8. Only Panamanian law enforcement officials from the National Maritime Service (SMN), empowered to enforce pertinent Panamanian laws within Panamanian territorial waters shall conduct communications for domestic law enforcement purposes with respect to vessels located in Panamanian territorial waters. The Republic of Panama shall ensure that its vessels are adequately equipped with communications equipment which will enable its vessels to effectively communicate with each other and the US Coast Guard during the bilateral patrol operations.

9. Actual details of this bilateral operation shall be coordinated between the National Maritime Service (SMN) of the Ministry of Government and Justice and the designated operational commander of the vessels of the US Coast Guard. These individuals shall prepare an operations plan which specifies the details of each phase of the bilateral operation. Each patrol shall be conducted in accordance with the bilateral operations plan. This bilateral operations plan may be amended as necessary by such individuals in order to improve the nature of the bilateral operations. Such amendments shall be formulated in accordance with the framework of this arrangement.

10. Representatives of each Government shall meet at the request of either one to consider any matter which they may deem appropriate regarding the implementation of this arrangement.

11. Bilateral operations pursuant to this arrangement shall commence on a date mutually agreed upon between the National Maritime Service (SMN), of the Ministry of Government and Justice and the US Coast Guard, after notification to the Government of the United States of America by the Republic of Panama that Panamanian vessels have been made ready to conduct bilateral operations in accordance with this arrangement. This notification shall be provided in order to give the US Coast Guard sufficient time to set up logistical, maintenance, communications, and security arrangements in order to properly support the operation of its vessels.

12. Nothing in this arrangement and no acts taken pursuant to this arrangement shall prejudice in any manner the respective positions of either the Government of the United States of America or the Government of the Republic of Panama, regarding any matter relating to the international law of the sea.

This arrangement shall enter into force upon signature. This arrangement shall remain in force until terminated by either Government giving one month's advance notification in writing to the other Government. It shall continue to apply after termination with respect to any administrative or judicial proceedings arising out of action taken pursuant to this arrangement.

Done at Panamá, R.P., in duplicate, in the English and Spanish languages, both texts being equally authentic, this eighteenth day of March, 1991.

Supplementary Arrangement between the Government of the United States of America and the Government of the Republic of Panama for Support and Assistance from the United States Coast Guard for the National Maritime Service of the Ministry of Government and Justice

Signed at Panama, 5 February 2002; entry into force, 5 February 2002
http://www.state.gov/t/isn/trty/32859.htm

The Government of the United States of America and the Government of the Republic Panama (hereinafter, 'the Parties');

Bearing in mind that the Arrangement between the Government of the United States of America and the Government of Panama for support and assistance from the United States Coast Guard for the National Maritime Service of the Ministry of Government and Justice, signed at Panama, March 18, 1991 (hereinafter, 'the Arrangement'), establishes a program for conducting bilateral maritime police operations within the territorial waters of Panama to stop illegal activities, such as the international trafficking of drugs, illegal fishing and transportation of contraband;

Whereas the transnational character of illicit traffic by sea and by air in narcotics and related offenses gives rise to the need for major international cooperation in the suppression thereof, which is recognized in the 1961 Single Convention on Narcotic Drugs and its 1972 Protocol, in the 1971 Convention on Psychotropic Substances, in the 1988 United Nations Convention Against Illicit Traffic in Narcotic Drugs and Psychotropic Substances (hereinafter, 'the 1988 Convention'), and in the 1982 United Nations Convention on the Law of the Sea (hereinafter, 'the Law of the Sea Convention');

Recalling that Article 17 of the 1988 Convention provides, *inter alia*, that the Parties shall consider entering into bilateral and regional agreements to carry out, or to enhance the effectiveness of, the provisions of Article 17;

Desiring to promote greater and resolute cooperation between the Parties to combat illicit traffic by sea and by air in narcotics and related offenses;

Recalling the Treaty between the Parties on Mutual Assistance in Criminal Matters, with annexes and appendices, signed at Panama, April 11, 1991, that enables more effective cooperation between the Parties in the investigation, prosecution and suppression of serious crimes, such as narcotic trafficking;

Recalling further the Inter-American Convention against the illicit manufacturing of and trafficking in firearms, ammunition, explosives and other related materials, signed by Panama and the United States, on November 14, 1997; and

Recalling the annual programs of counter-narcotics assistance provided by the Government of the United States of America to the Government of Panama;
Have agreed as follows:

Article I Purpose and scope

The Parties shall continue to cooperate in combating illicit traffic by sea and air in narcotics and related offenses to the fullest extent possible, consistent with available law enforcement resources and priorities related thereto.

Article II Definitions

For the purposes of this Supplementary Arrangement, unless the context otherwise requires:

(a)   'illicit traffic' has the same meaning as in Article 1(m) of the 1988 Convention and includes illicit traffic by air.

(b)   'illicit traffic' also includes other illegal activities prohibited by international law, including other international conventions to which both States are party, but only to the extent enforcement pursuant to this Supplementary Arrangement is authorized by the laws of both Parties.

(c)   'territory, waters and airspace of a Party' means:

    (i)   For the Republic of Panama: the territory under the sovereignty of Panama, those waters within 12 nautical miles of Panamanian territory, and the airspace over Panamanian territory and waters.

    (ii)   For the Government of the United States of America: the Commonwealth of Puerto Rico, the United States Virgin Islands, Navassa Island and other territories and possessions in the Caribbean Sea over which the United States exercises sovereignty, those waters within 12 nautical miles of United States territory, and the airspace over such United States territory and waters.

(d)   'continental territory' means the mainland territory of Panama situated within Panama's boundaries with bordering States and between its maritime coasts.

(e)   'contiguous zone' has the same meaning as in Article 33 of the Law of the Sea Convention.

(f)   'international waters' means all parts of the sea not included in the territorial sea and internal waters of a State.

(g)   'international airspace' means the airspace situated over international waters.

(h)   'law enforcement authority' means, for the Government of Panama, the National Maritime Service (hereinafter, 'SMN') and National Air Service, (hereinafter, 'SAN'), agencies of the Ministry of Government and Justice of Panama, and for the Government of the United States of America, the United States Coast Guard, an agency of the US Department of Transportation.

(i)   'law enforcement vessels' means armed and unarmed vessels belonging to the SMN and vessels of the United States Coast Guard, aboard which law enforcement officials are embarked, clearly marked and identifiable as being on government non-commercial service and authorized to that effect, including any boat or aircraft embarked on such vessels.

(j)   'law enforcement aircraft' means aircraft belonging to the SAN and SMN, and aircraft of the United States Coast Guard, clearly marked and identifiable as being on government non-commercial service and authorized to that effect.

(k)   'technical support vessels and aircraft' means vessels and aircraft of a Party, clearly marked and identifiable as being on government non-commercial service and authorized to that effect, which, though not belonging to its law enforcement authority, may be temporarily under its authority and control for the achievement of the purposes of this Supplementary Arrangement or which, though not under its temporary authority and control, support law enforcement officials, vessels and aircraft in the performance of their functions and responsibilities under this Supplementary Arrangement.

(l)   'technical support vessels and aircraft of third States' means vessels and aircraft of States other than the Parties, clearly marked and identifiable as being on government non-commercial service and authorized to that effect, with which the Republic of Panama or the United States of America has agreements or arrangements for combating illicit traffic, and which, when they are under the temporary authority and control of a law enforcement official of one of the Parties, may be authorized by agreement of the Parties, to be afforded the status of 'technical support vessels' or 'technical support aircraft' of the Party to which the law enforcement officials belong, and therefore be authorized to engage in operations under the terms and conditions of this Supplementary Arrangement.

(m) 'law enforcement officials' means, for the Government of Panama, uniformed members of the SMN and SAN, and for the Government of the United States of America, uniformed members of the United States Coast Guard.

(n) 'designated auxiliary personnel' means personnel of a Party who, while not law enforcement officials, support the law enforcement officials of that Party in the operations under this Supplementary Arrangement.

(o) 'Shiprider Program' means the program of activities agreed upon for the performance of shipboarding pursuant to this Supplementary Arrangement.

(p) 'shiprider' means a law enforcement official of one Party authorized to embark on a law enforcement vessel or aircraft of the other Party and to exercise the authority and control and perform the functions set out in this Supplementary Arrangement.

(q) 'Shiprider Program Coordinator' means the law enforcement official of a Party designated to organize its program activities with the other Party.

(r) 'Liaison Office' means the point of contact designated by the Parties as responsible for guaranteeing communication between the law enforcement authorities of the Parties.

(s) 'liaison official' means a law enforcement official of a Party, who may or may not be embarked on a vessel or aircraft of that Party, who has been designated to perform the functions of the Liaison Office of that Party.

(t) 'suspect vessel or aircraft' means a vessel or aircraft used for commercial or private purposes in respect of which there are reasonable grounds to suspect it is engaged in illicit traffic.

Article III Designated auxiliary personnel

1. The Parties, by mutual agreement, shall define the number and functions of auxiliary personnel designated to lend technical support to the law enforcement officials and to the vessels and aircraft participating in the maritime and/or air operations, depending on their needs.

2. When the functions these personnel routinely perform are unrelated to the operation of such vessels and aircraft, the other Party shall be given advance notice of the nature of the technical support functions such personnel are to carry out.

3. The designated auxiliary personnel shall not have the powers conferred by this Supplementary Arrangement on law enforcement officials, and their actions shall be limited to providing the technical support described in the notice of their functions given to the other Party.

4. Nevertheless, in emergencies and under exceptional circumstances, the designated auxiliary personnel of one Party may be requested by a shiprider of the other Party to support the law enforcement officials in enforcing the law.

5. In any case, these designated auxiliary personnel shall be subject to the same requirements the Parties have defined for the other participants in the Shiprider Program.

Article IV Shiprider program

1. The Parties shall establish a joint law enforcement Shiprider Program between their respective law enforcement authorities. Each Party shall designate a Coordinator to organize its program activities and to identify the types of vessels and officials involved in the Program to the other Party.

2. Each Party shall designate shipriders who, subject to its laws and policies and to the provisions this Supplemental Arrangement, shall embark on law enforcement vessels and aircraft of the other Party and exercise authority and control, in appropriate circumstances, to:

(a) search suspect vessels, seize property, detain persons, and authorize the use of force, including the use of weapons in accordance with the terms of Article XVII of this Supplementary Arrangement;

(b) authorize vessels or aircraft of the other Party aboard which they are embarked to pursue suspect vessels or aircraft in the waters and airspace of the Party they represent;

(c) authorize law enforcement vessels of the other Party aboard which they are embarked to patrol the waters of the Party they represent, for purposes of this Supplementary Arrangement;

(d) authorize the law enforcement aircraft of the other Party aboard which they are embarked to overfly, for purposes of this Supplementary Arrangement, the airspace of the Party they represent;

(e) enforce the laws of their respective countries in the waters and in the airspace over the waters of the Party they represent or seaward therefrom in exercise of the right of hot pursuit in accordance with international law of the sea; and

(f) request and authorize the law enforcement officials of the other Party to assist in the enforcement of the laws of the Party they represent.

3. The implementation of this Program shall not result in additional operating costs to the Party providing a shiprider to the other Party. Each Party shall assume the normal costs associated with the payment of its officials assigned to this Program.

4. Each Party shall endeavor to designate shipriders and liaison officials fluent in the language of the other Party.

Article V Assistance in law enforcement

1. When a shiprider is embarked on the other Party's law enforcement vessel, and the enforcement action being carried out is pursuant to paragraph 2 of Article IV, any law enforcement measure, including any boarding, search or seizure of property, any detention of a person, and any use of force pursuant to this Supplementary Arrangement, whether or not involving weapons, shall be carried out by the shiprider in accordance with the laws and regulations of the shiprider's Government.

2. Law enforcement officials of the other Party's law enforcement vessel and, in emergencies and under exceptional circumstances, designated auxiliary personnel of the other Party, may assist in any such action if expressly requested to do so by the shiprider and only within the limits of such request and in the manner requested. Such request may only be made, agreed to, and acted upon in accordance with the applicable laws and policies of both Parties.

3. Such law enforcement officials and designated auxiliary personnel may use force in self-defense, in accordance with the terms of Article XVII of this Supplementary Arrangement.

4. The assistance requested may not be contrary to the laws or policies of the Party of which this assistance is requested.

Article VI Law enforcement in the waters of a Party and in the airspace over such waters

1. The law enforcement authority of each Party is authorized to provide the other Party operational support and technical assistance in the suppression of illicit traffic in the waters of a Party and the airspace over such waters, by means of sea and air police

operations involving law enforcement vessels or aircraft with embarked shipriders designated in accordance with this Supplementary Arrangement.

2. The law enforcement authorities of both Parties shall endeavor to exchange operational information on the detection and location of suspect vessels or aircraft and to make best efforts to communicate with each other.

3. If a law enforcement vessel or aircraft of a Party ('the first Party') detects a suspect vessel or aircraft located in or entering the waters or airspace of the other Party, or the airspace over such waters, the first Party shall promptly notify the other Party.

4. In the event that the suspect vessel or aircraft is entering the waters or airspace of the other Party, and the law enforcement vessel or aircraft of the first Party does not have on board a shiprider of the other Party, the vessel or aircraft of the first Party may proceed as follows:

(a) It may pursue the suspect vessel into the waters of the other Party, in order to stop and secure the suspect vessel while awaiting the arrival of the law enforcement officials of the other Party, who shall conduct the search and assume jurisdiction of the suspect vessel, its cargo and persons on board;

(b) At the request of the law enforcement authority of the other Party, law enforcement officials of the first Party may search the suspect vessel, its cargo and persons on board, and if evidence of illicit traffic is found, detain the vessel pending instructions from the law enforcement authority of the other Party; and

(c) It may engage in pursuit of the suspect aircraft in the airspace of the other Party, in order to maintain contact and relay to the suspect aircraft the instructions of the aviation authority of the other Party.

5. In the event that the suspect vessel or aircraft is located in the waters or airspace of the other Party, and the law enforcement vessel or aircraft of the first Party does not have on board a shiprider of the other Party, the vessel or aircraft of the first Party may proceed as follows:

(a) upon receipt of authorization from the law enforcement authority of the other Party, it may enter the waters of the other Party, in order to investigate, stop and secure the suspect vessel and persons on board while awaiting the arrival of the law enforcement officials of the other Party, who shall conduct the search and assume jurisdiction of the suspect vessel, its cargo and persons onboard;

(b) at the request of the law enforcement authority of the other Party, law enforcement officials of the first Party may search the suspect vessel, and if evidence of illicit traffic is found, detain the vessel pending instructions from the law enforcement authority of the other Party; and

(c) upon receipt of authorization from the law enforcement authority of the other Party, it may pursue of the suspect aircraft in the airspace of the other Party, in order to maintain contact and relay to the suspect aircraft the instructions of the aviation authority of the other Party.

6. Each Party may permit, after notification to and coordination with appropriate officials, on the occasions and for the time necessary for the proper performance of the operations required under this Supplementary Arrangement:

(a) the temporary mooring of law enforcement vessels of the other Party at national ports in accordance with international norms for the purpose of resupplying fuel and provisions, medical assistance, minor repairs, weather and other logistics and related purposes;

(b) entry of additional law enforcement officials of the other Party; and

(c) entry of suspect vessels not flying the flag of either Party escorted from waters seaward of either Party's territorial sea by law enforcement officials of the other Party.

7. The Government of Panama may permit, after notification to and coordination with appropriate officials, on the occasions and for the time necessary for the proper performance of the operations required under this Supplementary Arrangement, the escort of persons, other than Panamanian nationals, from suspect vessels escorted by United States law enforcement officials through and exiting out of Panamanian territory.

Article VII Overflight operations for suppression of illicit traffic

1. Each Party ('the first Party') authorizes the law enforcement aircraft and the technical support aircraft of the other Party, in accordance with Articles IV, V, and VI(1) of this Supplementary Arrangement, to overfly its waters, observing the laws, policies, and instructions of the civil aviation authority of the first Party.

2. For overflight of continental territory by technical support aircraft pursuant to Article VIII, the Parties shall agree upon an embarkation and disembarkation program for shipriders of the other Party at the air facilities from which these operations are to be conducted.

3. The civil aviation authority of the first Party may deny, in specific instances, the overflight of the first Party's waters or territory, even in cases of pursuit of suspect aircraft, if it deems that such overflight endangers the safety of air navigation or the life or safety of third parties.

4. In the interest of flight safety, the law enforcement officials aboard these aircraft shall observe the following procedures:
   (a) identify the aircraft and provide notification of its entry into and departure from the air traffic control zone assigned to the appropriate civil aviation authority;
   (b) maintain open and ongoing communication with the civil aviation authority of the other Party;
   (c) observe the air navigation regulations and practices stipulated by the ICAO and international law; and
   (d) follow the flight safety instructions of the civil aviation authority of the other Party.

5. Subject to the laws of each Party, the aircraft may relay the orders of the competent authorities to suspect aircraft to land in the territory of the other Party.

6. Each Party may permit, after notification to and coordination with appropriate officials, on the occasions and for the time necessary for the proper performance of the operations required under this Supplementary Arrangement, law enforcement aircraft operated by the other Party to:
   (a) land and temporarily remain at international airports in accordance with international norms for the purposes of resupplying fuel and provisions, medical assistance, minor repairs, weather, and other logistics and related purposes; and
   (b) disembark and embark law enforcement officials of the other Party, including additional law enforcement officials.

7. The Government of Panama may permit, after notification to and coordination with appropriate officials, on the occasions and for the time necessary for the proper performance of the operations required under this Supplementary Arrangement, United States law enforcement aircraft to disembark, embark and depart out of Panamanian territory with persons referred to in Article VI (7).

Article VIII Law enforcement from technical support flights

The Parties agree that:
   (a) the collection of law enforcement information from technical support flights over the continental territory of a Party provided for under this Supplementary

Arrangement may take place only in the presence of and with authorization from the shiprider of the Party over whose territory the flights take place;

(b)   both parties shall have total and unrestricted access to this material at all times;

(c)   the law enforcement information obtained in these operations shall be classified in accordance with the laws and policy of the Party collecting the information, shall be supplied to the other Party under the appropriate laws and policies, and shall be used only for the purposes provided for in this Supplementary Arrangement; and

(d)   the law enforcement information collected under this Supplementary Arrangement may not be communicated to third parties without the prior express consent of the Party in whose jurisdiction they were collected.

Article IX Air pursuit

This Supplementary Arrangement authorizes the pursuit for the purposes of and in accordance with its provisions, by law enforcement aircraft and technical support aircraft of one Party of suspect aircraft in or into the airspace over waters of the other Party and in or into the airspace over the continental territory of the other Party.

Article X Operations in international waters

1.   Whenever the law enforcement officials of one Party ('the requesting Party') encounter a suspect vessel flying the flag of or claiming to be registered in the other Party ('the requested Party') located seaward of any State's territorial sea, the requesting Party may request that the Liaison Office designated by the requested Party:

(a)   confirm the claim of registry in or the right to fly the flag of the requested Party; and

(b)   if such claim is confirmed:

    (i)   authorize the boarding and search of the suspect vessel, cargo and the persons found on board by law enforcement officials of the requesting Party; and

    (ii)   if evidence of illicit traffic is found, authorize the law enforcement officials of the requesting Party to detain the vessel, cargo and persons on board pending instructions from the law enforcement authorities of the requested Party as to the exercise of jurisdiction in accordance with Article XI of this Supplementary Arrangement.

2.   Each request should contain the name of the suspect vessel, the basis for the suspicion, the registration number, home port, the port of origin and destination, and any other identifying information. If a request is conveyed orally, the requesting Party shall confirm the request in writing as soon as possible.

3.   If the registration or the right to fly its flag is verified, the requested Party may:

(a)   decide to conduct the boarding and search with its own law enforcement officials;

(b)   authorize the boarding and search by the law enforcement officials of the requesting Party;

(c)   decide to conduct the boarding and search together with the requesting Party; or

(d)   deny permission to board and search.

4.   The requested Party shall answer requests made for the verification of registry or right to fly its flag within two (2) hours of the receipt of such requests.

5.   If the registration or the right to fly its flag is not verified within the two (2) hours, the requested Party may:

(a)   nevertheless authorize the boarding and search by the law enforcement officials of the requesting Party; or

(b)   refute the claim of the suspect vessel to registration or the right to fly its flag under its laws.

6.   If there is no response from the requested Party within two (2) hours of its receipt of the request, the requesting Party will be deemed to have been authorized to board the suspect vessel for the purpose of inspecting the vessel's documents, questioning the persons on board, and searching the vessel to determine if it is engaged in illicit traffic.

7.   Notwithstanding the foregoing paragraphs of this Article, this Supplementary Arrangement authorizes the law enforcement officials of one Party ('the first Party') to board suspect vessels claiming to be registered in the other Party that are not flying the flag of the other Party, not displaying any marks of its registration, and claiming to have no documentation on board the vessel, for the purpose of locating and examining the vessel's documentation. If documentation is located, the foregoing paragraphs of this Article apply. If no evidence of registration or nationality is found, the first Party may assimilate the vessel to a ship without nationality in accordance with international law.

8.   The authorization to board, search and detain includes the authority to use force in accordance with Article XVII of this Supplementary Arrangement.

9.   Except as expressly provided herein, this Supplementary Arrangement does not apply to or limit boardings of vessels, conducted by either Party in accordance with international law, seaward of any State's territorial sea, whether based, *inter alia*, on the right of visit, the rendering of assistance to persons, vessels, and property in distress or peril, the consent of the vessel master, or an authorization from the flag State to take law enforcement action.

Article XI Jurisdiction over vessels or aircraft detained

1.   As provided in Article 2(3) of the 1988 Convention, neither Party shall undertake in the territory of the other Party the exercise of jurisdiction and performance of functions that are exclusively reserved to the authorities of that other Party by its domestic law.

2.   In all cases arising in a Party's waters, or concerning vessels registered in or flying the flag of a Party seaward of any State's territorial sea, that Party ('the first Party') shall have the right to exercise jurisdiction over a detained vessel, cargo and/or persons on board (including seizure, forfeiture, arrest, and prosecution), provided, however, the first Party may, subject to its Constitution and laws, waive its right to exercise jurisdiction and authorize the enforcement of the other Party's law against the vessel, cargo and/or persons on board. The first Party has the right to exercise jurisdiction over aircraft that have landed in its territory and aboard which evidence of illicit traffic has been found.

3.   In cases arising in the contiguous zone of a Party, not involving suspect vessels fleeing from the waters of that Party or suspect vessels flying the flag of or registered in that Party, in which both Parties have the authority to exercise jurisdiction to prosecute, the Party which conducts the boarding and search shall have the right to exercise jurisdiction.

4.   If the evidence so warrants, the other Party may request that the first Party waive jurisdiction. Instructions as to the exercise of jurisdiction pursuant to this Supplementary Arrangement shall be given without delay.

5.   A waiver of jurisdiction may be granted verbally, but as soon as possible, it shall be recorded in a written note from the competent authority and be processed through the diplomatic authorities, without prejudice to the immediate exercise of jurisdiction over the suspect vessel by the other Party.

6.   Failure by the first Party to waive jurisdiction shall not be interpreted as authorization for the other Party to assume jurisdiction.

7. In no case shall such authorizations be understood to cover the boarding or inspection of vessels of a flag other than that of the first Party; in such case, the other Party shall proceed in accordance with the rules of international law.

Article XII Liaison Office

Each Party shall identify to the other Party the Liaison Office and liaison officials responsible for communicating with its national authorities competent to receive and act on notifications under Articles III, IV, VI, VII, XIV and XVI, for processing requests under Article X for verification of registration and the right to fly its flag and authority to board, search and detain suspect vessels, and for instructions as to the exercise of jurisdiction under Article XI, in addition to any other communication necessary for the implementation of this Supplementary Arrangement.

Article XIII Suspect vessels and aircraft

Operations to suppress illicit traffic pursuant to this Supplementary Arrangement shall be carried out only against suspect vessels and aircraft, including vessels and aircraft without nationality.

Article XIV Notification of results of shipboardings and actions taken

1. Each Party shall promptly notify the other Party of the results of any boarding and search of the vessels of the other Party conducted pursuant to this Supplementary Arrangement.

2. Each Party, consistent with its laws, shall report in a timely manner to the other Party on the status of all investigations, prosecutions and judicial proceedings resulting from enforcement action taken pursuant to this Supplementary Arrangement where evidence of illicit traffic was found.

Article XV Conduct of law enforcement

1. Each Party shall ensure that its law enforcement officials, when conducting boardings, searches and air intercept activities pursuant to this Supplementary Arrangement, act in accordance with its applicable national laws and policies and with international law and accepted international practices.

2. In particular, while carrying out boarding and search activities pursuant to this Supplementary Arrangement, the Parties shall take due account of the need not to endanger the safety of life at sea, the security of the suspect vessel and its cargo, or to prejudice the commercial and legal interests of the flag State or any other interested State; and shall observe the norms of courtesy, respect and consideration for the persons on board the suspect vessel. While conducting air intercept activities pursuant to this Supplementary Arrangement, the Parties shall not endanger the lives of persons on board and the safety of civil aircraft.

3. Boardings and searches pursuant to this Supplementary Arrangement shall be carried out by law enforcement officials from law enforcement ships or aircraft, or from technical support vessels of a Party or of third States, and, in emergencies and under exceptional circumstances, may be assisted by designated auxiliary personnel from technical support vessels or aircraft of a Party or of third States.

4. When conducting boardings and searches law enforcement officials may carry regulation weapons.

5. Law enforcement vessels of a Party operating with the authorization of the other Party pursuant to this Supplementary Arrangement shall, during such operations, also fly, in the case of the United States of America, the Panamanian flag, and in the case of Panama, the United States Coast Guard ensign.

Article XVI Identification of technical support vessels and aircraft

Prior to entry into the territory, waters or airspace of a Party, the law enforcement authority of the other Party shall furnish information on the technical support vessels and aircraft it will need for the conduct of the operations provided for in this Supplementary Arrangement, the type of service and support they will provide, their technical features, and the approximate period of time they will remain within the territory, waters or airspace of the other Party.

Article XVII Use of force

1. All uses of force by a Party pursuant to this Supplementary Arrangement shall be in strict accordance with applicable laws and policies of that Party and shall in all cases be the minimum reasonably necessary under the circumstances, except that neither Party shall use force against civil aircraft in flight.

2. Nothing in this Supplementary Arrangement shall impair the exercise of the inherent right of self-defense by law enforcement or other officials of the Parties.

Article XVIII Exchange and knowledge of laws and policies of the Parties

1. To facilitate implementation of this Supplementary Arrangement, each Party shall ensure that the other Party is fully informed of its respective applicable laws and policies, particularly those pertaining to the use of force.

2. Each Party shall ensure that all of its law enforcement officials acting pursuant to this Supplementary Arrangement are knowledgeable of the applicable laws and policies of both Parties.

Article XIX Disposition of seized property

1. Assets seized in consequence of any operation undertaken pursuant to this Supplementary Arrangement shall be disposed of in accordance with the laws of the Party exercising jurisdiction in accordance with Article XI of this Supplementary Arrangement.

2. To the extent permitted by its laws and upon such terms as it deems appropriate, the seizing Party may, in any case, transfer forfeited assets or proceeds of their sale to the other Party. Each transfer generally will reflect the contribution of the other Party to facilitating or effecting the forfeiture of such assets or proceeds.

Article XX Technical assistance

The law enforcement authority of one Party (the 'first Party') may request, and the law enforcement authority of the other Party may authorize, law enforcement officials of the other Party to provide technical assistance, such as specialized assistance in the conduct of search of suspect vessels, to law enforcement officials of the first Party for the boarding and search of suspect vessels located in the territory or waters of the first Party.

Article XXI Follow-up and evaluation

1. The Parties shall hold an annual meeting for the purpose of evaluating and following up on the implementation of this Supplementary Arrangement.

2. For the same purpose, either Party may invite, with sufficient advance notice, the other Party to special meetings.

Article XXII Consultations and dispute settlement

1. In case a question arises in connection with implementation of this Supplementary Arrangement, either Party may request consultations with the other Party to resolve the matter.

2. The Parties undertake to settle by consultation any disputes that arise from the implementation of this Supplemental Arrangement.

Article XXIII Claims

1. Any claim for damages, injury or loss resulting from an operation carried out under this Supplemental Arrangement shall be examined by the Party whose authorities conducted the operation.

2. If responsibility is established, the claim shall be resolved in favor of the claimant by that Party, in accordance with the domestic law of that Party, and in a manner consistent with international law, including paragraph 3 of Article 110 of the Law of the Sea Convention.

3. Neither Party thereby waives any rights it may have under international law to raise a claim with the other Party through diplomatic channels.

Article XXIV Miscellaneous provisions

Nothing in this Supplementary Arrangement:

(a) precludes the Parties from otherwise agreeing on operations or other forms of cooperation to suppress illicit traffic;

(b) supersedes any bilateral or multilateral agreement or other cooperative mechanism concluded by the Parties for the suppression of illicit traffic;

(c) is intended to alter the rights and privileges due any individual in any legal proceeding; and

(d) prejudices in any manner the positions of either Party regarding the international law of the sea or legal status of the Gulf of Panama.

Article XXV Entry into force

This Supplementary Arrangement shall enter into force upon signature.

Article XXVI Termination

1. This Supplementary Arrangement may be terminated at any time by either Party upon written notification to the other Party through the diplomatic channel.

2. Such termination shall take effect six months from the date of notification.

Article XXVII Continuation of actions taken

This Supplementary Arrangement shall continue to apply after termination with respect to any administrative or judicial proceedings arising out of actions taken pursuant to this Arrangement.

In witness whereof, the undersigned, being duly authorized by their respective Governments, have signed this Supplementary Arrangement.

Done at Panama City, Republic of Panama, this fifth day of February, 2002, in the English and Spanish languages, each text being duly authentic.

Amendment to the Supplementary Arrangement Between the Government of the United States of America and the Government of the Republic of Panama to the Arrangement Between the Government of the United States of America and the Government of Panama for Support and Assistance from the United States Coast Guard for the National Maritime Service of the Ministry of Government and Justice

Done at Washington, 12 May 2004; entry into force, 1 December 2004
http://www.state.gov/t/isn/trty/32858.htm

The Government of the United States of America and the Government of the Republic of Panama (hereinafter 'the Parties'):

Bearing in mind that the Arrangement between the Government of the United States of America and the Government of Panama for Support and Assistance from the United States Coast Guard for the National Maritime Service of the Ministry of Government and Justice, signed at Panama, March 18, 1991 (hereinafter 'the Arrangement'), and the Supplementary Arrangement between the Government of the United States of America and the Government of the Republic of Panama to the Arrangement between the Government of the United States of America and the Government of Panama for Support and Assistance from the United States Coast Guard for the National Maritime Service of the Ministry of Government and Justice, signed at Panama, February 5, 2002 (hereinafter 'the Supplementary Arrangement'), establish a program for conducting bilateral maritime law enforcement operations to stop illegal activities, such as the international trafficking of drugs, illegal fishing and transportation of contraband;

Deeply concerned about the proliferation of weapons of mass destruction (WMD), their delivery systems, and related materials, particularly by sea, as well as the risk that these may fall into the hands of terrorists;

Recalling the January 31, 1992, United Nations Security Council Presidential Statement that proliferation of all WMD constitutes a threat to international peace and security, and underlines the need for Member States of the United Nations to prevent proliferation;

Recalling also United Nations Security Council Resolution 1373 of September 28, 2001, which, *inter alia*, noted with concern the close connection between international terrorism and illegal movement of nuclear, chemical, biological and other potentially deadly materials, and in this regard emphasized the need to enhance coordination of efforts on national, subregional, regional and international levels in order to strengthen a global response to this serious challenge and threat to international security, and called upon States to find ways of intensifying and accelerating the exchange of operational information, especially regarding the threat posed by the possession of weapons of mass destruction by terrorist groups;

Recalling further the Convention on the Prohibition of the Development, Production, Stockpiling and Use of Chemical Weapons and on their Destruction, done at Paris, January 13, 1993; the Treaty on Non-Proliferation of Nuclear Weapons, done at Washington, London and Moscow, July 1, 1968; and the Convention on the Prohibition of the Development, Production and Stockpiling of Bacteriological (Biological) and Toxin Weapons and on their Destruction, done at Washington, London and Moscow, April 10, 1972;

Acknowledging the widespread consensus that proliferation and terrorism seriously threaten international peace and security;

Convinced that trafficking in WMD, their delivery systems, and related materials by States and non-state actors of proliferation concern must be stopped;

Inspired by the Statement of Interdiction Principles for the Proliferation Security Initiative, Paris, September 4, 2003;

Reaffirming the importance of the customary international law of the sea, as reflected in the 1982 United Nations Convention on the Law of the Sea; and

Desiring to amend the Supplementary Arrangement in order to enhance cooperation between the Parties to prevent illicit traffic involving proliferation by sea of WMD, their delivery systems, and related materials to or from States and non-state actors of proliferation concern;

Have agreed to amend the Supplementary Arrangement as follows:

Article I

1. Paragraph (b) of Article II of the Supplementary Arrangement, Definitions, is amended to read:

'(b) "illicit traffic" also includes proliferation by sea and other illegal activities prohibited by international law, including other international conventions to which both States are party, but only to the extent enforcement pursuant to this Supplementary Arrangement is authorized by the laws of both Parties.'

2. The following paragraphs (u) through (y) are added to Article II of the Supplementary Arrangement, Definitions, as follows:

'(u) "Proliferation by sea" means the transportation by ship of weapons of mass destruction, their delivery systems, and related materials to or from States and non-state actors of proliferation concern.

(v) "Weapons of mass destruction (WMD)" means nuclear, chemical, biological and radiological weapons.

(w) "Related materials" means materials, equipment and technology, of whatever nature or type, that are related to and destined for use in the development, production, utilization or delivery of WMD.

(x) "Items of proliferation concern" means WMD, their delivery systems, and related materials.

(y) "States and non-state actors of proliferation concern" means those countries or entities that should be subject to interdiction activities because they are or are believed to be engaged in: (1) efforts to develop or acquire WMD or their delivery systems; or (2) transfers (either selling, receiving, or facilitating) of items of proliferation concern.'

3. Paragraph 3 of Article III of the Supplementary Arrangement, Designated Auxiliary Personnel, is amended to read:

'3. Except as provided in paragraph 3 of Article XV, the designated auxiliary personnel shall not have the powers conferred by this Supplementary Arrangement on law enforcement officials, and their actions shall be limited to providing the technical support described in the notice of their functions given to the other Party.'

4. Paragraph 3 of Article XV of the Supplementary Arrangement, Conduct of Law Enforcement Officials, is amended to read:

'3. Boardings and searches pursuant to this Supplementary Arrangement shall be carried out by law enforcement officials from law enforcement ships or aircraft, or from technical support vessels of a Party or of third States, and, in emergencies and under exceptional circumstances, may be assisted by designated auxiliary personnel from technical support vessels or aircraft of a Party or of third States. However, when law enforcement officials are not readily available, boardings and searches undertaken pursuant to Article X of this Supplementary Arrangement to suppress proliferation by sea may, upon advance notice to the other Party, also be carried out by designated auxiliary personnel. These personnel shall in such cases be subject to the provisions in this Supplementary Arrangement governing the conduct and operations of law enforcement officials.'

Article II

1. The Parties agree that the Government of the Republic of Panama may extend, *mutatis mutandis*, all rights under the Supplementary Arrangement as amended by the present Amendment concerning vessels suspected of proliferation by sea, claiming its nationality and located seaward of any State's territorial sea, to such third States as it may deem appropriate, on the understanding that such third States shall likewise comply with all conditions set forth in the present Amendment and with those provisions of the Supplementary Arrangement agreed between the Government of the Republic of Panama and the third States for the exercise of such rights. Further, the Government of the Republic of Panama and such third States shall identify Liaison Offices and liaison officials in accordance with Article XII of the Supplementary Arrangement.

2. Such third States shall enjoy rights and be subject to all conditions governing their exercise as set forth in paragraph 1 of this Article, effective on the date of notification by the third State to the Government of the Republic of Panama that it will comply with the conditions for the exercise of those rights.

3. Such rights may be modified by written agreement between the Government of the Republic of Panama and the third State and shall be effective on the date agreed by the Government of the Republic of Panama and the third State.

4. Such rights shall be revocable by the Government of the Republic of Panama or the third State by written notification. Such rights shall be revoked, and the conditions governing their exercise shall cease to apply, effective on the date of such notification.

Article III

1. The Parties shall apply this Amendment provisionally from the date of its signature. This Amendment shall enter into force on the date that the Government of the United States of America notifies the Government of the Republic of Panama that its necessary internal procedures have been completed, and shall remain in force concurrent with the Supplementary Arrangement.

2. Either Party may discontinue provisional application at any time. Each Party shall notify the other Party immediately of any constraints or limitations on provisional application, of any changes to such constraints or limitations, and upon discontinuance of provisional application.

IN WITNESS WHEREOF, the undersigned, being duly authorized by their respective Governments, have signed this Amendment.

DONE AT Washington, this 12th day of May, 2004, in duplicate, in the English and Spanish languages, both texts being equally authentic.

UN General Assembly Resolution 46/215
Large-Scale Pelagic Drift-Net Fishing and Its Impact on the Living Marine Resources of the World's Oceans and Seas

UN Doc. A/RES/46/215 (1991) of 20 December 1991

The General Assembly,

Recalling its resolutions 44/225 and 45/197, concerning large-scale pelagic drift-net fishing and its impact on the living marine resources of the world's oceans and seas, including enclosed and semi-enclosed seas, which took into account the concerns of the developing countries and were adopted by consensus on 22 December 1989 and 21 December 1990, respectively,

Also recalling, in particular, that the General Assembly recommended that all members of the international community agree to certain measures specified in the operative paragraphs of resolution 44/225,

Further recalling the relevant principles elaborated in the United Nations Convention on the Law of the Sea, which are referred to in the seventh to tenth preambular paragraphs of resolution 44/225,

Expressing deep concern about reports of expansion of large-scale pelagic drift-net fishing activities on the high seas in contravention of resolutions 44/225 and 45/197, including attempts to expand large-scale pelagic drift-net fishing in the high seas areas of the Indian Ocean,

Commending the unilateral, regional and international efforts that have been undertaken by members of the international community and international organizations to implement and support the objectives of resolutions 44/225 and 45/197,

Noting that at the Twenty-second South Pacific Forum, held at Palikir on 29 and 30 July 1991, the heads of Government reaffirmed their opposition to large-scale pelagic drift-net fishing, and in this regard, *inter alia*, welcomed the entry into force on 17 May 1991 of the Convention for the Prohibition of Fishing with Long Drift-nets in the South Pacific,

Recalling the Castries Declaration, in which the Authority of the Organization of Eastern Caribbean States resolved to establish a regional regime for the regulation and management of the pelagic resources in the Lesser Antilles region that would outlaw the use of drift-nets and called upon other States in the region to cooperate in this regard,

Welcoming the actions taken that have resulted in the cessation of all large-scale pelagic drift-net fishing activities in the South Pacific in advance of the date stipulated in paragraph 4 (b) of resolution 44/225 for the termination of such activities,

Also welcoming the decision of other members of the international community to cease large-scale pelagic drift-net fishing on the high seas,

Commending the efforts of many members of the international community to compile data on large-scale pelagic drift-net fishing and to submit their findings to the Secretary-General,

Noting the contributions to the report of the Secretary-General made by some members of the international community and by intergovernmental and non-governmental organizations,

Noting also the significant concerns expressed by members of the international community and competent regional fisheries bodies regarding the impact of large-scale pelagic drift-net fishing on the marine environment,

Noting further that, in accordance with paragraph 3 of resolution 44/225, some members of the international community have reviewed the best available scientific data on the impact of large-scale pelagic drift-net fishing and have failed to conclude that this practice has no adverse impact which threatens the conservation and sustainable management of living marine resources,

Noting that the grounds for concerns expressed in resolutions 44/225 and 45/197 about the unacceptable impact of large-scale pelagic drift-net fishing have been confirmed and that evidence has not demonstrated that the impact can be fully prevented,

Recognizing that a moratorium on large-scale pelagic drift-net fishing is required, notwithstanding that it will have adverse socio-economic effects on the communities involved in high seas pelagic drift-net fishing operations,

1.   *Recalls* its resolutions 44/225 and 45/197;

2.   *Commends* the efforts jointly to collect statistically sound data regarding large-scale pelagic drift-net fishing in the North Pacific Ocean, which were reviewed at the meeting of scientists held at Sidney, Canada, in June 1991, and presented at the symposium on the high seas drift-net fisheries in the North Pacific Ocean, held at Tokyo in November 1991 under the auspices of the International North Pacific Fisheries Commission;

3.   *Calls upon* all members of the international community to implement resolutions 44/225 and 45/197 by, *inter alia*, taking the following actions:

    (a)   Beginning on 1 January 1992, reduce fishing effort in existing large-scale pelagic high seas drift-net fisheries by, *inter alia*, reducing the number of vessels involved, the length of the nets and the area of operation, so as to achieve, by 30 June 1992, a 50 per cent reduction in fishing effort;

    (b)   Continue to ensure that the areas of operation of large-scale pelagic high seas drift-net fishing are not expanded and, beginning on 1 January 1992, are further reduced in accordance with paragraph 3 (a) of the present resolution;

    (c)   Ensure that a global moratorium on all large-scale pelagic drift-net fishing is fully implemented on the high seas of the world's oceans and seas, including enclosed seas and semi-enclosed seas, by 31 December 1992;

4.   *Reaffirms* the importance it attaches to compliance with the present resolution and encourages all members of the international community to take measures, individually and collectively, to prevent large-scale pelagic drift-net fishing operations on the high seas of the world's oceans and seas, including enclosed seas and semi-enclosed seas;

5.   *Requests* the Secretary-General to bring the present resolution to the attention of all members of the international community, intergovernmental and non-governmental organizations and well-established scientific institutions with expertise in relation to living marine resources;

6.   *Requests* the members and organizations referred to above to submit to the Secretary-General information concerning activities or conduct inconsistent with the terms of the present resolution;

7.   *Also requests* the Secretary-General to submit to the General Assembly at its forty-seventh session a report on the implementation of the present resolution.

Agenda 21, Chapter 17
Protection of the Oceans, All Kinds of Seas, Including Enclosed and Semi-Enclosed Seas, and Coastal Areas and the Protection, Rational Use and Development of Their Living Resources

A/CONF.151/26 (Vol. II), 13 August 1992

INTRODUCTION

17.1 The marine environment – including the oceans and all seas and adjacent coastal areas – forms an integrated whole that is an essential component of the global life-support system and a positive asset that presents opportunities for sustainable development. International law, as reflected in the provisions of the United Nations Convention on the Law of the Sea,[1] referred to in this chapter of Agenda, sets forth rights and obligations of States and provides the international basis upon which to pursue the protection and sustainable development of the marine and coastal environment and its resources. This requires new approaches to marine and coastal area management and development, at the national, subregional, regional and global levels, approaches that are integrated in content and are precautionary and anticipatory in ambit, as reflected in the following programme areas:[2]

(a) Integrated management and sustainable development of coastal areas, including exclusive economic zones;

(b) Marine environmental protection;

(c) Sustainable use and conservation of marine living resources of the high seas;

(d) Sustainable use and conservation of marine living resources under national jurisdiction;

(e) Addressing critical uncertainties for the management of the marine environment and climate change;

(f) Strengthening international, including regional, cooperation and coordination;

(g) Sustainable development of small islands.

17.2. The implementation by developing countries of the activities set forth below shall be commensurate with their individual technological and financial capacities and priorities in allocating resources for development needs and ultimately depends on the technology transfer and financial resources required and made available to them.

---

[1] Footnotes in original: (1) References to the United Nations Convention on the Law of the Sea in this chapter of Agenda 21 do not prejudice the position of any State with respect to signature, ratification of or accession to the Convention. (2)References to the United Nations Convention on the Law of the Sea in this chapter of Agenda 21 do not prejudice the position of States which view the Convention as having a unified character.

[2] Footnote in original: (3) Nothing in the programme areas of this chapter should be interpreted as prejudicing the rights of the States involved in a dispute of sovereignty or in the delimitation of the maritime areas concerned.

PROGRAMME AREAS

A. Integrated Management and Sustainable Development of Coastal and Marine Areas, Including Exclusive Economic Zones

Basis for action

17.3.   The coastal area contains diverse and productive habitats important for human settlements, development and local subsistence. More than half the world's population lives within 60 km of the shoreline, and this could rise to three quarters by the year 2020. Many of the world's poor are crowded in coastal areas. Coastal resources are vital for many local communities and indigenous people. The exclusive economic zone (EEZ) is also an important marine area where the States manage the development and conservation of natural resources for the benefit of their people. For small island States or countries, these are the areas most available for development activities.

17.4.   Despite national, subregional, regional and global efforts, current approaches to the management of marine and coastal resources have not always proved capable of achieving sustainable development, and coastal resources and the coastal environment are being rapidly degraded and eroded in many parts of the world.

Objectives

17.5.   Coastal States commit themselves to integrated management and sustainable development of coastal areas and the marine environment under their national jurisdiction. To this end, it is necessary to, *inter alia*:

(a)   Provide for an integrated policy and decision-making process, including all involved sectors, to promote compatibility and a balance of uses;

(b)   Identify existing and projected uses of coastal areas and their interactions;

(c)   Concentrate on well-defined issues concerning coastal management;

(d)   Apply preventive and precautionary approaches in project planning and implementation, including prior assessment and systematic observation of the impacts of major projects;

(e)   Promote the development and application of methods, such as national resource and environmental accounting, that reflect changes in value resulting from uses of coastal and marine areas, including pollution, marine erosion, loss of resources and habitat destruction;

(f)   Provide access, as far as possible, for concerned individuals, groups and organizations to relevant information and opportunities for consultation and participation in planning and decision-making at appropriate levels.

Activities

(a)   Management-related activities

17.6.   Each coastal State should consider establishing, or where necessary strengthening, appropriate coordinating mechanisms (such as a high-level policy planning body) for integrated management and sustainable development of coastal and marine areas and their resources, at both the local and national levels. Such mechanisms should include consultation, as appropriate, with the academic and private sectors, non-governmental organizations, local communities, resource user groups, and indigenous people. Such national coordinating mechanisms could provide, *inter alia*, for:

(a)   Preparation and implementation of land and water use and siting policies;

(b)   Implementation of integrated coastal and marine management and sustainable development plans and programmes at appropriate levels;

(c) Preparation of coastal profiles identifying critical areas, including eroded zones, physical processes, development patterns, user conflicts and specific priorities for management;

(d) Prior environmental impact assessment, systematic observation and follow-up of major projects, including the systematic incorporation of results in decision-making;

(e) Contingency plans for human induced and natural disasters, including likely effects of potential climate change and sea level rise, as well as contingency plans for degradation and pollution of anthropogenic origin, including spills of oil and other materials;

(f) Improvement of coastal human settlements, especially in housing, drinking water and treatment and disposal of sewage, solid wastes and industrial effluents;

(g) Periodic assessment of the impacts of external factors and phenomena to ensure that the objectives of integrated management and sustainable development of coastal areas and the marine environment are met;

(h) Conservation and restoration of altered critical habitats;

(i) Integration of sectoral programmes on sustainable development for settlements, agriculture, tourism, fishing, ports and industries affecting the coastal area;

(j) Infrastructure adaptation and alternative employment;

(k) Human resource development and training;

(l) Public education, awareness and information programmes;

(m) Promoting environmentally sound technology and sustainable practices;

(n) Development and simultaneous implementation of environmental quality criteria.

17.7. Coastal States, with the support of international organizations, upon request, should undertake measures to maintain biological diversity and productivity of marine species and habitats under national jurisdiction. *Inter alia*, these measures might include: surveys of marine biodiversity, inventories of endangered species and critical coastal and marine habitats; establishment and management of protected areas; and support of scientific research and dissemination of its results.

(b) Data and information

17.8. Coastal States, where necessary, should improve their capacity to collect, analyse, assess and use information for sustainable use of resources, including environmental impacts of activities affecting the coastal and marine areas. Information for management purposes should receive priority support in view of the intensity and magnitude of the changes occurring in the coastal and marine areas. To this end, it is necessary to, *inter alia*:

(a) Develop and maintain databases for assessment and management of coastal areas and all seas and their resources;

(b) Develop socio-economic and environmental indicators;

(c) Conduct regular environmental assessment of the state of the environment of coastal and marine areas;

(d) Prepare and maintain profiles of coastal area resources, activities, uses, habitats and protected areas based on the criteria of sustainable development;

(e) Exchange information and data.

17.9. Cooperation with developing countries, and, where applicable, subregional and regional mechanisms, should be strengthened to improve their capacities to achieve the above.

(c) International and regional cooperation and coordination

17.10. The role of international cooperation and coordination on a bilateral basis and, where applicable, within a subregional, interregional, regional or global framework, is to support and supplement national efforts of coastal States to promote integrated management and sustainable development of coastal and marine areas.

17.11. States should cooperate, as appropriate, in the preparation of national guidelines for integrated coastal zone management and development, drawing on existing experience. A global conference to exchange experience in the field could be held before 1994.

Means of implementation
(a) Financing and cost evaluation

17.12. The Conference secretariat has estimated the average total annual cost (1993-2000) of implementing the activities of this programme to be about $6 billion including about $50 million from the international community on grant or concessional terms. These are indicative and order-of-magnitude estimates only and have not been reviewed by Governments. Actual costs and financial terms, including any that are non-concessional, will depend upon, *inter alia*, the specific strategies and programmes Governments decide upon for implementation.

(b) Scientific and technological means

17.13. States should cooperate in the development of necessary coastal systematic observation, research and information management systems. They should provide access to and transfer environmentally safe technologies and methodologies for sustainable development of coastal and marine areas to developing countries. They should also develop technologies and endogenous scientific and technological capacities.

17.14. International organizations, whether subregional, regional or global, as appropriate, should support coastal States, upon request, in these efforts, as indicated above, devoting special attention to developing countries.

(c) Human resource development

17.15. Coastal States should promote and facilitate the organization of education and training in integrated coastal and marine management and sustainable development for scientists, technologists, managers (including community-based managers) and users, leaders, indigenous peoples, fisherfolk, women and youth, among others. Management and development, as well as environmental protection concerns and local planning issues, should be incorporated in educational curricula and public awareness campaigns, with due regard to traditional ecological knowledge and socio-cultural values.

17.16. International organizations, whether subregional, regional or global, as appropriate, should support coastal States, upon request, in the areas indicated above, devoting special attention to developing countries.

(d) Capacity-building

17.17. Full cooperation should be extended, upon request, to coastal States in their capacity-building efforts and, where appropriate, capacity-building should be included in bilateral and multilateral development cooperation. Coastal States may consider, *inter alia*:

    (a) Ensuring capacity-building at the local level;

    (b) Consulting on coastal and marine issues with local administrations, the business community, the academic sector, resource user groups and the general public;

    (c) Coordinating sectoral programmes while building capacity;

(d) Identifying existing and potential capabilities, facilities and needs for human resources development and scientific and technological infrastructure;

(e) Developing scientific and technological means and research;

(f) Promoting and facilitating human resource development and education;

(g) Supporting 'centres of excellence' in integrated coastal and marine resource management;

(h) Supporting pilot demonstration programmes and projects in integrated coastal and marine management.

B. Marine Environmental Protection

Basis for action

17.18. Degradation of the marine environment can result from a wide range of sources. Land-based sources contribute 70 per cent of marine pollution, while maritime transport and dumping-at-sea activities contribute 10 per cent each. The contaminants that pose the greatest threat to the marine environment are, in variable order of importance and depending on differing national or regional situations, sewage, nutrients, synthetic organic compounds, sediments, litter and plastics, metals, radionuclides, oil/hydrocarbons and polycyclic aromatic hydrocarbons (PAHs). Many of the polluting substances originating from land-based sources are of particular concern to the marine environment since they exhibit at the same time toxicity, persistence and bioaccumulation in the food chain. There is currently no global scheme to address marine pollution from land-based sources.

17.19. Degradation of the marine environment can also result from a wide range of activities on land. Human settlements, land use, construction of coastal infrastructure, agriculture, forestry, urban development, tourism and industry can affect the marine environment. Coastal erosion and siltation are of particular concern.

17.20. Marine pollution is also caused by shipping and sea-based activities. Approximately 600,000 tons of oil enter the oceans each year as a result of normal shipping operations, accidents and illegal discharges. With respect to offshore oil and gas activities, currently machinery space discharges are regulated internationally and six regional conventions to control platform discharges have been under consideration. The nature and extent of environmental impacts from offshore oil exploration and production activities generally account for a very small proportion of marine pollution.

17.21. A precautionary and anticipatory rather than a reactive approach is necessary to prevent the degradation of the marine environment. This requires, *inter alia*, the adoption of precautionary measures, environmental impact assessments, clean production techniques, recycling, waste audits and minimization, construction and/or improvement of sewage treatment facilities, quality management criteria for the proper handling of hazardous substances, and a comprehensive approach to damaging impacts from air, land and water. Any management framework must include the improvement of coastal human settlements and the integrated management and development of coastal areas.

Objectives

17.22. States, in accordance with the provisions of the United Nations Convention on the Law of the Sea on protection and preservation of the marine environment, commit themselves, in accordance with their policies, priorities and resources, to prevent, reduce and control degradation of the marine environment so as to maintain and improve its life-support and productive capacities. To this end, it is necessary to:

(a) Apply preventive, precautionary and anticipatory approaches so as to avoid degradation of the marine environment, as well as to reduce the risk of long-term or irreversible adverse effects upon it;

(b) Ensure prior assessment of activities that may have significant adverse impacts upon the marine environment;

(c) Integrate protection of the marine environment into relevant general environmental, social and economic development policies;

(d) Develop economic incentives, where appropriate, to apply clean technologies and other means consistent with the internalization of environmental costs, such as the polluter pays principle, so as to avoid degradation of the marine environment;

(e) Improve the living standards of coastal populations, particularly in developing countries, so as to contribute to reducing the degradation of the coastal and marine environment.

17.23. States agree that provision of additional financial resources, through appropriate international mechanisms, as well as access to cleaner technologies and relevant research, would be necessary to support action by developing countries to implement this commitment.

Activities

(a) Management-related activities

Prevention, reduction and control of degradation of the marine environment from land-based activities.

17.24. In carrying out their commitment to deal with degradation of the marine environment from land-based activities, States should take action at the national level and, where appropriate, at the regional and subregional levels, in concert with action to implement programme area A, and should take account of the Montreal Guidelines for the Protection of the Marine Environment from Land-Based Sources.

17.25. To this end, States, with the support of the relevant international environmental, scientific, technical and financial organizations, should cooperate, *inter alia*, to:

(a) Consider updating, strengthening and extending the Montreal Guidelines, as appropriate;

(b) Assess the effectiveness of existing regional agreements and action plans, where appropriate, with a view to identifying means of strengthening action, where necessary, to prevent, reduce and control marine degradation caused by land-based activities;

(c) Initiate and promote the development of new regional agreements, where appropriate;

(d) Develop means of providing guidance on technologies to deal with the major types of pollution of the marine environment from land-based sources, according to the best scientific evidence;

(e) Develop policy guidance for relevant global funding mechanisms;

(f) Identify additional steps requiring international cooperation.

17.26. The UNEP Governing Council is invited to convene, as soon as practicable, an intergovernmental meeting on protection of the marine environment from land-based activities.

17.27. As concerns sewage, priority actions to be considered by States may include:

(a) Incorporating sewage concerns when formulating or reviewing coastal development plans, including human settlement plans;

(b) Building and maintaining sewage treatment facilities in accordance with national policies and capacities and international cooperation available;

(c) Locating coastal outfalls so as to maintain an acceptable level of environmental quality and to avoid exposing shell fisheries, water intakes and bathing areas to pathogens;

(d) Promoting environmentally sound co-treatments of domestic and compatible industrial effluents, with the introduction, where practicable, of controls on the entry of effluents that are not compatible with the system;

(e) Promoting primary treatment of municipal sewage discharged to rivers, estuaries and the sea, or other solutions appropriate to specific sites;

(f) Establishing and improving local, national, subregional and regional, as necessary, regulatory and monitoring programmes to control effluent discharge, using minimum sewage effluent guidelines and water quality criteria and giving due consideration to the characteristics of receiving bodies and the volume and type of pollutants.

17.28. As concerns other sources of pollution, priority actions to be considered by States may include:

(a) Establishing or improving, as necessary, regulatory and monitoring programmes to control effluent discharges and emissions, including the development and application of control and recycling technologies;

(b) Promoting risk and environmental impact assessments to help ensure an acceptable level of environmental quality;

(c) Promoting assessment and cooperation at the regional level, where appropriate, with respect to the input of point source pollutants from new installations;

(d) Eliminating the emission or discharge of organohalogen compounds that threaten to accumulate to dangerous levels in the marine environment;

(e) Reducing the emission or discharge of other synthetic organic compounds that threaten to accumulate to dangerous levels in the marine environment;

(f) Promoting controls over anthropogenic inputs of nitrogen and phosphorus that enter coastal waters where such problems as eutrophication threaten the marine environment or its resources;

(g) Cooperating with developing countries, through financial and technological support, to maximize the best practicable control and reduction of substances and wastes that are toxic, persistent or liable to bio-accumulate and to establish environmentally sound land-based waste disposal alternatives to sea dumping;

(h) Cooperating in the development and implementation of environmentally sound land-use techniques and practices to reduce run-off to water-courses and estuaries which would cause pollution or degradation of the marine environment;

(i) Promoting the use of environmentally less harmful pesticides and fertilizers and alternative methods for pest control, and considering the prohibition of those found to be environmentally unsound;

(j) Adopting new initiatives at national, subregional and regional levels for controlling the input of non-point source pollutants, which require broad changes in sewage and waste management, agricultural practices, mining, construction and transportation.

17.29. As concerns physical destruction of coastal and marine areas causing degradation of the marine environment, priority actions should include control and prevention of coastal erosion and siltation due to anthropogenic factors related to, *inter alia*, land-use and construction techniques and practices. Watershed management practices should be promoted so as to prevent, control and reduce degradation of the marine environment.

Prevention, reduction and control of degradation of the marine environment from sea-based activities

17.30. States, acting individually, bilaterally, regionally or multilaterally and within the framework of IMO and other relevant international organizations, whether subregional, regional or global, as appropriate, should assess the need for additional measures to address degradation of the marine environment:

(a) From shipping, by:

(i) Supporting wider ratification and implementation of relevant shipping conventions and protocols;

(ii) Facilitating the processes in (i), providing support to individual States upon request to help them overcome the obstacles identified by them;

(iii) Cooperating in monitoring marine pollution from ships, especially from illegal discharges (e.g., aerial surveillance), and enforcing MARPOL discharge, provisions more rigorously;

(iv) Assessing the state of pollution caused by ships in particularly sensitive areas identified by IMO and taking action to implement applicable measures, where necessary, within such areas to ensure compliance with generally accepted international regulations;

(v) Taking action to ensure respect of areas designated by coastal States, within their exclusive economic zones, consistent with international law, in order to protect and preserve rare or fragile ecosystems, such as coral reefs and mangroves;

(vi) Considering the adoption of appropriate rules on ballast water discharge to prevent the spread of non-indigenous organisms;

(vii) Promoting navigational safety by adequate charting of coasts and ship-routing, as appropriate;

(viii) Assessing the need for stricter international regulations to further reduce the risk of accidents and pollution from cargo ships (including bulk carriers);

(ix) Encouraging IMO and IAEA to work together to complete consideration of a code on the carriage of irradiated nuclear fuel in flasks on board ships;

(x) Revising and updating the IMO Code of Safety for Nuclear Merchant Ships and considering how best to implement a revised code;

(xi) Supporting the ongoing activity within IMO regarding development of appropriate measures for reducing air pollution from ships;

(xii) Supporting the ongoing activity within IMO regarding the development of an international regime governing the transportation of hazardous and noxious substances carried by ships and further considering whether the compensation funds similar to the ones established under the Fund Convention would be appropriate in respect of pollution damage caused by substances other than oil;

(b) From dumping, by:

(i) Supporting wider ratification, implementation and participation in relevant Conventions on dumping at sea, including early conclusion of a future strategy for the London Dumping Convention;

(ii) Encouraging the London Dumping Convention parties to take appropriate steps to stop ocean dumping and incineration of hazardous substances;

(c) From offshore oil and gas platforms, by assessing existing regulatory measures to address discharges, emissions and safety and assessing the need for additional measures;

(d) From ports, by facilitating establishment of port reception facilities for the collection of oily and chemical residues and garbage from ships, especially in MARPOL special areas, and promoting the establishment of smaller scale facilities in marinas and fishing harbours.

17.31. IMO and as appropriate, other competent United Nations organizations, when requested by the States concerned, should assess, where appropriate, the state of marine pollution in areas of congested shipping, such as heavily used international straits, with a view to ensuring compliance with generally accepted international regulations, particularly those related to illegal discharges from ships, in accordance with the provisions of Part III of the United Nations Convention on the Law of the Sea.

17.32. States should take measures to reduce water pollution caused by organotin compounds used in anti-fouling paints.

17.33. States should consider ratifying the Convention on Oil Pollution Preparedness, Response and Cooperation, which addresses, *inter alia*, the development of contingency plans on the national and international level, as appropriate, including provision of oil-spill response material and training of personnel, including its possible extension to chemical spill response.

17.34. States should intensify international cooperation to strengthen or establish, where necessary, regional oil/chemical-spill response centres and/or, as appropriate, mechanisms in cooperation with relevant subregional, regional or global intergovernmental organizations and, where appropriate, industry-based organizations.

(b) Data and information

17.35. States should, as appropriate, and in accordance with the means at their disposal and with due regard for their technical and scientific capacity and resources, make systematic observations on the state of the marine environment. To this end, States should, as appropriate, consider:

(a) Establishing systematic observation systems to measure marine environmental quality, including causes and effects of marine degradation, as a basis for management;

(b) Regularly exchanging information on marine degradation caused by land-based and sea-based activities and on actions to prevent, control and reduce such degradation;

(c) Supporting and expanding international programmes for systematic observations such as the mussel watch programme, building on existing facilities with special attention to developing countries;

(d) Establishing a clearing-house on marine pollution control information, including processes and technologies to address marine pollution control and to support their transfer to developing countries and other countries with demonstrated needs;

(e) Establishing a global profile and database providing information on the sources, types, amounts and effects of pollutants reaching the marine environment from land-based activities in coastal areas and sea-based sources;

(f) Allocating adequate funding for capacity-building and training programmes to ensure the full participation of developing countries, in particular, in any international scheme under the organs and organizations of the United Nations system for the collection, analysis and use of data and information.

Means of implementation

(a) Financing and cost evaluation

17.36. The Conference secretariat has estimated the average total annual cost (1993-2000) of implementing the activities of this programme to be about $200 million from the international community on grant or concessional terms. These are indicative and order-of-magnitude estimates only and have not been reviewed by Governments. Actual costs and financial terms, including any that are non-concessional, will depend upon, *inter alia*, the specific strategies and programmes Governments decide upon for implementation.

(b) Scientific and technological means

17.37. National, subregional and regional action programmes will, where appropriate, require technology transfer, in conformity with chapter 34, and financial resources, particularly where developing countries are concerned, including:

(a) Assistance to industries in identifying and adopting clean production or cost-effective pollution control technologies;

(b) Planning development and application of low-cost and low-maintenance sewage installation and treatment technologies for developing countries;

(c) Equipment of laboratories to observe systematically human and other impacts on the marine environment;

(d) Identification of appropriate oil- and chemical-spill control materials, including low-cost locally available materials and techniques, suitable for pollution emergencies in developing countries;

(e) Study of the use of persistent organohalogens that are liable to accumulate in the marine environment to identify those that cannot be adequately controlled and to provide a basis for a decision on a time schedule for phasing them out as soon as practicable;

(f) Establishment of a clearing-house for information on marine pollution control, including processes and technologies to address marine pollution control, and support for their transfer to developing and other countries with demonstrated needs.

(c) Human resource development

17.38. States individually or in cooperation with each other and with the support of international organizations, whether subregional, regional or global, as appropriate, should:

(a) Provide training for critical personnel required for the adequate protection of the marine environment as identified by training needs' surveys at the national, regional or subregional levels;

(b) Promote the introduction of marine environmental protection topics into the curriculum of marine studies programmes;

(c) Establish training courses for oil- and chemical-spill response personnel, in cooperation, where appropriate, with the oil and chemical industries;

(d) Conduct workshops on environmental aspects of port operations and development;

(e) Strengthen and provide secure financing for new and existing specialized international centres of professional maritime education;

(f) States should, through bilateral and multilateral cooperation, support and supplement the national efforts of developing countries as regards human resource development in relation to prevention and reduction of degradation of the marine environment.

(d) Capacity-building

17.39. National planning and coordinating bodies should be given the capacity and authority to review all land-based activities and sources of pollution for their impacts on the marine environment and to propose appropriate control measures.

17.40. Research facilities should be strengthened or, where appropriate, developed in developing countries for systematic observation of marine pollution, environmental impact assessment and development of control recommendations and should be managed and staffed by local experts.

17.41. Special arrangements will be needed to provide adequate financial and technical resources to assist developing countries in preventing and solving problems associated with activities that threaten the marine environment.

17.42. An international funding mechanism should be created for the application of appropriate sewage treatment technologies and building sewage treatment facilities, including grants or concessional loans from international agencies and appropriate regional funds, replenished at least in part on a revolving basis by user fees.

17.43. In carrying out these programme activities, particular attention needs to be given to the problems of developing countries that would bear an unequal burden because of their lack of facilities, expertise or technical capacities.

C. SUSTAINABLE USE AND CONSERVATION OF MARINE LIVING RESOURCES OF THE HIGH SEAS

Basis for action

17.44. Over the last decade, fisheries on the high seas have considerably expanded and currently represent approximately 5 per cent of total world landings. The provisions of the United Nations Convention on the Law of the Sea on the marine living resources of the high seas sets forth rights and obligations of States with respect to conservation and utilization of those resources.

17.45. However, management of high seas fisheries, including the adoption, monitoring and enforcement of effective conservation measures, is inadequate in many areas and some resources are overutilized. There are problems of unregulated fishing, overcapitalization, excessive fleet size, vessel reflagging to escape controls, insufficiently selective gear, unreliable databases and lack of sufficient cooperation between States. Action by States whose nationals and vessels fish on the high seas, as well as cooperation at the bilateral, subregional, regional and global levels, is essential particularly for highly migratory species and straddling stocks. Such action and cooperation should address inadequacies in fishing practices, as well as in biological knowledge, fisheries statistics and improvement of systems for handling data. Emphasis should also be on multi-species management and other approaches that take into account the relationships among species, especially in addressing depleted species, but also in identifying the potential of underutilized or unutilized populations.

Objectives

17.46. States commit themselves to the conservation and sustainable use of marine living resources on the high seas. To this end, it is necessary to:

(a) Develop and increase the potential of marine living resources to meet human nutritional needs, as well as social, economic and development goals;

(b) Maintain or restore populations of marine species at levels that can produce the maximum sustainable yield as qualified by relevant environmental and economic factors, taking into consideration relationships among species;

(c) Promote the development and use of selective fishing gear and practices that minimize waste in the catch of target species and minimize by-catch of non-target species;

(d) Ensure effective monitoring and enforcement with respect to fishing activities;

(e) Protect and restore endangered marine species;

(f) Preserve habitats and other ecologically sensitive areas;

(g) Promote scientific research with respect to the marine living resources in the high seas.

17.47. Nothing in paragraph 17.46 above restricts the right of a State or the competence of an international organization, as appropriate, to prohibit, limit or regulate the exploitation of marine mammals on the high seas more strictly than provided for in that paragraph. States shall cooperate with a view to the conservation of marine mammals and, in the case of cetaceans, shall in particular work through the appropriate international organizations for their conservation, management and study.

17.48. The ability of developing countries to fulfil the above objectives is dependent upon their capabilities, including the financial, scientific and technological means at their disposal. Adequate financial, scientific and technological cooperation should be provided to support action by them to implement these objectives.

Activities

(a) Management-related activities

17.49. States should take effective action, including bilateral and multilateral cooperation, where appropriate at the subregional, regional and global levels, to ensure that high seas fisheries are managed in accordance with the provisions of the United Nations Convention on the Law of the Sea. In particular, they should:

(a) Give full effect to these provisions with regard to fisheries populations whose ranges lie both within and beyond exclusive economic zones (straddling stocks);

(b) Give full effect to these provisions with regard to highly migratory species;

(c) Negotiate, where appropriate, international agreements for the effective management and conservation of fishery stocks;

(d) Define and identify appropriate management units;

(e) States should convene, as soon as possible, an intergovernmental conference under United Nations auspices, taking into account relevant activities at the subregional, regional and global levels, with a view to promoting effective implementation of the provisions of the United Nations

(f) Convention on the Law of the Sea on straddling fish stocks and highly migratory fish stocks. The conference, drawing, *inter alia*, on scientific and technical studies by FAO, should identify and assess existing problems related to the conservation and management of such fish stocks, and consider means of improving cooperation on fisheries among States, and formulate appropriate recommendations. The work and the results of the conference should be fully consistent with the provisions of the United Nations Convention on the Law of the Sea, in particular the rights and obligations of coastal States and States fishing on the high seas.

17.50. States should ensure that fishing activities by vessels flying their flags on the high seas take place in a manner so as to minimize incidental catch.

17.51. States should take effective action consistent with international law to monitor and control fishing activities by vessels flying their flags on the high seas to ensure compliance with applicable conservation and management rules, including full, detailed, accurate and timely reporting of catches and effort.

17.52. States should take effective action, consistent with international law, to deter reflagging of vessels by their nationals as a means of avoiding compliance with applicable conservation and management rules for fishing activities on the high seas.

17.53. States should prohibit dynamiting, poisoning and other comparable destructive fishing practices.

17.54. States should fully implement General Assembly resolution 46/215 on large-scale pelagic drift-net fishing.

17.55. States should take measures to increase the availability of marine living resources as human food by reducing wastage, post-harvest losses and discards, and improving techniques of processing, distribution and transportation.

(b)   Data and information

17.56. States, with the support of international organizations, whether subregional, regional or global, as appropriate, should cooperate to:

(a)   Promote enhanced collection of data necessary for the conservation and Sustainable use of the marine living resources of the high seas;

(b)   Exchange on a regular basis up-to-date data and information adequate for fisheries assessment;

(c)   Develop and share analytical and predictive tools, such as stock assessment and bioeconomic models;

(d)   Establish or expand appropriate monitoring and assessment programmes.

(c)   International and regional cooperation and coordination

17.57. States, through bilateral and multilateral cooperation and within the framework of subregional and regional fisheries bodies, as appropriate, and with the support of other international intergovernmental agencies, should assess high seas resource potentials and develop profiles of all stocks (target and non-target).

17.58. States should, where and as appropriate, ensure adequate coordination and cooperation in enclosed and semi-enclosed seas and between subregional, regional and global intergovernmental fisheries bodies.

17.59. Effective cooperation within existing subregional, regional or global fisheries bodies should be encouraged. Where such organizations do not exist, States should, as appropriate, cooperate to establish such organizations.

17.60. States with an interest in a high seas fishery regulated by an existing subregional and/or regional high seas fisheries organization of which they are not members should be encouraged to join that organization, where appropriate.

17.61. States recognize:

(a)   The responsibility of the International Whaling Commission for the conservation and management of whale stocks and the regulation of whaling pursuant to the 1946 International Convention for the Regulation of Whaling;

(b)   The work of the International Whaling Commission Scientific Committee in carrying out studies of large whales in particular, as well as of other cetaceans;

(c)   The work of other organizations, such as the Inter-American Tropical Tuna Commission and the Agreement on Small Cetaceans in the Baltic and North Sea under the Bonn Convention, in the conservation, management and study of cetaceans and other marine mammals.

17.62. States should cooperate for the conservation, management and study of cetaceans.

Means of implementation

(a) Financing and cost evaluation

17.63. The Conference secretariat has estimated the average total annual cost (1993-2000) of implementing the activities of this programme to be about $12 million from the international community on grant or concessional terms. These are indicative and order-of-magnitude estimates only and have not been reviewed by Governments. Actual costs and financial terms, including any that are non-concessional, will depend upon, *inter alia*, the specific strategies and programmes Governments decide upon for implementation.

(b) Scientific and technological means

17.64. States, with the support of relevant international organizations, where necessary, should develop collaborative technical and research programmes to improve understanding of the life cycles and migrations of species found on the high seas, including identifying critical areas and life stages.

17.65. States, with the support of relevant international organizations, whether subregional, regional or global, as appropriate, should:

(a) Develop databases on the high seas marine living resources and fisheries;

(b) Collect and correlate marine environmental data with high seas marine living resources data, including the impacts of regional and global changes brought about by natural causes and by human activities;

(c) Cooperate in coordinating research programmes to provide the knowledge necessary to manage high seas resources.

(c) Human resource development

17.66. Human resource development at the national level should be targeted at both development and management of high seas resources, including training in high seas fishing techniques and in high seas resource assessment, strengthening cadres of personnel to deal with high seas resource management and conservation and related environmental issues, and training observers and inspectors to be placed on fishing vessels.

(d) Capacity-building

17.67. States, with the support, where appropriate, of relevant international organizations, whether subregional, regional or global, should cooperate to develop or upgrade systems and institutional structures for monitoring, control and surveillance, as well as the research capacity for assessment of marine living resource populations.

17.68. Special support, including cooperation among States, will be needed to enhance the capacities of developing countries in the areas of data and information, scientific and technological means, and human resource development in order to participate effectively in the conservation and sustainable utilization of high seas marine living resources.

D. Sustainable Use and Conservation of Marine Living Resources under National Jurisdiction

Basis for action

17.69. Marine fisheries yield 80 to 90 million tons of fish and shellfish per year, 95 per cent of which is taken from waters under national jurisdiction. Yields have increased nearly fivefold over the past four decades. The provisions of the United Nations Convention on the Law of the Sea on marine living resources of the exclusive economic zone and other areas under national jurisdiction set forth rights and obligations of States with respect to conservation and utilization of those resources.

17.70. Marine living resources provide an important source of protein in many countries and their use is often of major importance to local communities and indigenous people. Such resources provide food and livelihoods to millions of people and, if sustainably utilized, offer increased potential to meet nutritional and social needs, particularly in developing countries. To realize this potential requires improved knowledge and identification of marine living resource stocks, particularly of underutilized and unutilized stocks and species, use of new technologies, better handling and processing facilities to avoid wastage, and improved quality and training of skilled personnel to manage and conserve effectively the marine living resources of the exclusive economic zone and other areas under national jurisdiction. Emphasis should also be on multi-species management and other approaches that take into account the relationships among species.

17.71. Fisheries in many areas under national jurisdiction face mounting problems, including local overfishing, unauthorized incursions by foreign fleets, ecosystem degradation, overcapitalization and excessive fleet sizes, underevaluation of catch, insufficiently selective gear, unreliable databases, and increasing competition between artisanal and large-scale fishing, and between fishing and other types of activities.

17.72. Problems extend beyond fisheries. Coral reefs and other marine and coastal habitats, such as mangroves and estuaries, are among the most highly diverse, integrated and productive of the Earth's ecosystems. They often serve important ecological functions, provide coastal protection, and are critical resources for food, energy, tourism and economic development. In many parts of the world, such marine and coastal systems are under stress or are threatened from a variety of sources, both human and natural.

Objectives

17.73. Coastal States, particularly developing countries and States whose economies are overwhelmingly dependent on the exploitation of the marine living resources of their exclusive economic zones, should obtain the full social and economic benefits from sustainable utilization of marine living resources within their exclusive economic zones and other areas under national jurisdiction.

17.74. States commit themselves to the conservation and sustainable use of marine living resources under national jurisdiction. To this end, it is necessary to:

(a) Develop and increase the potential of marine living resources to meet human nutritional needs, as well as social, economic and development goals;

(b) Take into account traditional knowledge and interests of local communities, small-scale artisanal fisheries and indigenous people in development and management programmes;

(c) Maintain or restore populations of marine species at levels that can produce the maximum sustainable yield as qualified by relevant environmental and economic factors, taking into consideration relationships among species;

(d) Promote the development and use of selective fishing gear and practices that minimize waste in the catch of target species and minimize by-catch of non-target species;

(e) Protect and restore endangered marine species;

(f) Preserve rare or fragile ecosystems, as well as habitats and other ecologically sensitive areas.

17.75. Nothing in paragraph 17.74 above restricts the right of a coastal State or the competence of an international organization, as appropriate, to prohibit, limit or regulate the exploitation of marine mammals more strictly than provided for in that paragraph. States shall cooperate with a view to the conservation of marine mammals and in the case of cetaceans shall in particular work through the appropriate international organizations for their conservation, management and study.

17.76. The ability of developing countries to fulfil the above objectives is dependent upon their capabilities, including the financial, scientific and technological means at their disposal. Adequate financial, scientific and technological cooperation should be provided to support action by them to implement these objectives.

Activities
(a)   Management-related activities
17.77. States should ensure that marine living resources of the exclusive economic zone and other areas under national jurisdiction are conserved and managed in accordance with the provisions of the United Nations Convention on the Law of the Sea.

17.78. States, in implementing the provisions of the United Nations Convention on the Law of the Sea, should address the issues of straddling stocks and highly migratory species, and, taking fully into account the objective set out in paragraph 17.73, access to the surplus of allowable catches.

17.79. Coastal States, individually or through bilateral and/or multilateral cooperation and with the support, as appropriate of international organizations, whether subregional, regional or global, should *inter alia*:

(a)   Assess the potential of marine living resources, including underutilized or unutilized stocks and species, by developing inventories, where necessary, for their conservation and sustainable use;

(b)   Implement strategies for the sustainable use of marine living resources, taking into account the special needs and interests of small-scale artisanal fisheries, local communities and indigenous people to meet human nutritional and other development needs;

(c)   Implement, in particular in developing countries, mechanisms to develop mariculture, aquaculture and small-scale, deep-sea and oceanic fisheries within areas under national jurisdiction where assessments show that marine living resources are potentially available;

(d)   Strengthen their legal and regulatory frameworks, where appropriate, including management, enforcement and surveillance capabilities, to regulate activities related to the above strategies;

(e)   Take measures to increase the availability of marine living resources as human food by reducing wastage, post-harvest losses and discards, and improving techniques of processing, distribution and transportation;

(f)   Develop and promote the use of environmentally sound technology under criteria compatible with the sustainable use of marine living resources, including assessment of the environmental impact of major new fishery practices;

(g)   Enhance the productivity and utilization of their marine living resources for food and income.

17.80. Coastal States should explore the scope for expanding recreational and tourist activities based on marine living resources, including those for providing alternative sources of income. Such activities should be compatible with conservation and sustainable development policies and plans.

17.81. Coastal States should support the sustainability of small-scale artisanal fisheries. To this end, they should, as appropriate:

(a)   Integrate small-scale artisanal fisheries development in marine and coastal planning, taking into account the interests and, where appropriate, encouraging representation of fishermen, small-scale fisherworkers, women, local communities and indigenous people;

(b) Recognize the rights of small-scale fishworkers and the special situation of indigenous people and local communities, including their rights to utilization and protection of their habitats on a sustainable basis;

(c) Develop systems for the acquisition and recording of traditional knowledge concerning marine living resources and environment and promote the incorporation of such knowledge into management systems.

17.82. Coastal States should ensure that, in the negotiation and implementation of international agreements on the development or conservation of marine living resources, the interests of local communities and indigenous people are taken into account, in particular their right to subsistence.

17.83. Coastal States, with the support, as appropriate, of international organizations should conduct analyses of the potential for aquaculture in marine and coastal areas under national jurisdiction and apply appropriate safeguards as to the introduction of new species.

17.84. States should prohibit dynamiting, poisoning and other comparable destructive fishing practices.

17.85. States should identify marine ecosystems exhibiting high levels of biodiversity and productivity and other critical habitat areas and should provide necessary limitations on use in these areas, through, *inter alia*, designation of protected areas. Priority should be accorded, as appropriate, to:

(a) Coral reef ecosystems;

(b) Estuaries;

(c) Temperate and tropical wetlands, including mangroves;

(d) Seagrass beds;

(e) Other spawning and nursery areas.

(b) Data and information

17.86. States, individually or through bilateral and multilateral cooperation and with the support, as appropriate, of international organizations, whether subregional, regional or global, should:

(a) Promote enhanced collection and exchange of data necessary for the conservation and sustainable use of the marine living resources under national jurisdiction;

(b) Exchange on a regular basis up-to-date data and information necessary for fisheries assessment;

(c) Develop and share analytical and predictive tools, such as stock assessment and bioeconomic models;

(d) Establish or expand appropriate monitoring and assessment programmes;

(e) Complete or update marine biodiversity, marine living resource and critical habitat profiles of exclusive economic zones and other areas under national jurisdiction, taking account of changes in the environment brought about by natural causes and human activities.

(c) International and regional cooperation and coordination

17.87. States, through bilateral and multilateral cooperation, and with the support of relevant United Nations and other international organizations, should cooperate to:

(a) Develop financial and technical cooperation to enhance the capacities of developing countries in small-scale and oceanic fisheries, as well as in coastal aquaculture and mariculture;

(b) Promote the contribution of marine living resources to eliminate malnutrition and to achieve food self-sufficiency in developing countries, *inter alia*, by minimizing post-harvest losses and managing stocks for guaranteed sustainable yields;

(c) Develop agreed criteria for the use of selective fishing gear and practices to minimize waste in the catch of target species and minimize by-catch of non-target species;

(d) Promote seafood quality, including through national quality assurance systems for seafood, in order to promote access to markets, improve consumer confidence and maximize economic returns.

17.88. States should, where and as appropriate, ensure adequate coordination and cooperation in enclosed and semi-enclosed seas and between subregional, regional and global intergovernmental fisheries bodies.

17.89. States recognize:

(a) The responsibility of the International Whaling Commission for the conservation and management of whale stocks and the regulation of whaling pursuant to the 1946 International Convention for the Regulation of Whaling;

(b) The work of the International Whaling Commission Scientific Committee in carrying out studies of large whales in particular, as well as of other cetaceans;

(c) The work of other organizations, such as the Inter-American Tropical Tuna Commission and the Agreement on Small Cetaceans in the Baltic and North Sea under the Bonn Convention, in the conservation, management and study of cetaceans and other marine mammals.

17.90. States should cooperate for the conservation, management and study of cetaceans.

Means of implementation

(a) Financing and cost evaluation

17.91. The Conference secretariat has estimated the average total annual cost (1993-2000) of implementing the activities of this programme to be about $6 billion, including about $60 million from the international community on grant or concessional terms. These are indicative and order-of-magnitude estimates only and have not been reviewed by Governments. Actual costs will depend upon, *inter alia*, the specific strategies and programmes Governments decide upon for implementation.

(b) Scientific and technological means

17.92. States, with the support of relevant intergovernmental organizations, as appropriate, should:

(a) Provide for the transfer of environmentally sound technologies to develop fisheries, aquaculture and mariculture, particularly to developing countries;

(b) Accord special attention to mechanisms for transferring resource information and improved fishing and aquaculture technologies to fishing communities at the local level;

(c) Promote the study, scientific assessment and use of appropriate traditional management systems;

(d) Consider observing, as appropriate, the FAO/ICES Code of Practice for Consideration of Transfer and Introduction of Marine and Freshwater Organisms;

(e) Promote scientific research on marine areas of particular importance for marine living resources, such as areas of high diversity, endemism and productivity and migratory stopover points.

(c) Human resource development

17.93. States individually, or through bilateral and multilateral cooperation and with the support of relevant international organizations, whether subregional, regional or global, as appropriate, should encourage and provide support for developing countries, *inter alia*, to:

(a) Expand multidisciplinary education, training and research on marine living resources, particularly in the social and economic sciences;

(b) Create training opportunities at national and regional levels to support artisanal (including subsistence) fisheries, to develop small-scale use of marine living resources and to encourage equitable participation of local communities, small-scale fish workers, women and indigenous people;

(c) Introduce topics relating to the importance of marine living resources in educational curricula at all levels.

(d) Capacity-building

17.94. Coastal States, with the support of relevant subregional, regional and global agencies, where appropriate, should:

(a) Develop research capacities for assessment of marine living resource populations and monitoring;

(b) Provide support to local fishing communities, in particular those that rely on fishing for subsistence, indigenous people and women, including, as appropriate, the technical and financial assistance to organize, maintain, exchange and improve traditional knowledge of marine living resources and fishing techniques, and upgrade knowledge on marine ecosystems;

(c) Establish sustainable aquaculture development strategies, including environmental management in support of rural fish-farming communities;

(d) Develop and strengthen, where the need may arise, institutions capable of implementing the objectives and activities related to the conservation and management of marine living resources.

17.95. Special support, including cooperation among States, will be needed to enhance the capacities of developing countries in the areas of data and information, scientific and technological means and human resource development in order to enable them to participate effectively in the conservation and sustainable use of marine living resources under national jurisdiction.

E. Addressing Critical Uncertainties for the Management of the Marine Environment and Climate Change

Basis for action

17.96. The marine environment is vulnerable and sensitive to climate and atmospheric changes. Rational use and development of coastal areas, all seas and marine resources, as well as conservation of the marine environment, requires the ability to determine the present state of these systems and to predict future conditions. The high degree of uncertainty in present information inhibits effective management and limits the ability to make predictions and assess environmental change. Systematic collection of data on marine environmental parameters will be needed to apply integrated management approaches and to predict effects of global climate change and of atmospheric phenomena, such as ozone depletion, on living marine resources and the marine environment. In order to determine the role of the oceans and all seas in driving global systems and to predict natural and human-induced changes in marine and coastal environments, the mechanisms to collect, synthesize and disseminate information from research and systematic observation activities need to be restructured and reinforced considerably.

17.97. There are many uncertainties about climate change and particularly about sealevel rise. Small increases in sealevel have the potential of causing significant damage to small islands and low-lying coasts. Response strategies should be based on sound data. A long-term cooperative research commitment is needed to provide the data required for global climate models and to reduce uncertainty. Meanwhile, precautionary measures should be undertaken to diminish the risks and effects, particularly on small islands and on low-lying and coastal areas of the world.

17.98. Increased ultraviolet radiation derived from ozone depletion has been reported in some areas of the world. An assessment of its effects in the marine environment is needed to reduce uncertainty and to provide a basis for action.

Objectives

17.99. States, in accordance with provisions of the United Nations Convention on the Law of the Sea on marine scientific research, commit themselves to improve the understanding of the marine environment and its role on global processes. To this end, it is necessary to:

(a) Promote scientific research on and systematic observation of the marine environment within the limits of national jurisdiction and high seas, including interactions with atmospheric phenomena, such as ozone depletion;

(b) Promote exchange of data and information resulting from scientific research and systematic observation and from traditional ecological knowledge and ensure its availability to policy makers and the public at the national level;

(c) Cooperate with a view to the development of standard inter-calibrated procedures, measuring techniques, data storage and management capabilities for scientific research on and systematic observation of the marine environment.

Activities

(a) Management-related activities

17.100. States should consider, *inter alia*:

(a) Coordinating national and regional observation programmes for coastal and near-shore phenomena related to climate change and for research parameters essential for marine and coastal management in all regions;

(b) Providing improved forecasts of marine conditions for the safety of inhabitants of coastal areas and for the efficiency of maritime operations;

(c) Cooperating with a view to adopting special measures to cope with and adapt to potential climate change and sealevel rise, including the development of globally accepted methodologies for coastal vulnerability assessment, modelling and response strategies particularly for priority areas, such as small islands and low-lying and critical coastal areas;

(d) Identifying ongoing and planned programmes of systematic observation of the marine environment, with a view to integrating activities and establishing priorities to address critical uncertainties for oceans and all seas;

(e) Initiating a programme of research to determine the marine biological effects of increased levels of ultraviolet rays due to the depletion of the stratospheric ozone layer and to evaluate the possible effects.

17.101. Recognizing the important role that oceans and all seas play in attenuating potential climate change, IOC and other relevant competent United Nations bodies, with the support of countries having the resources and expertise, should carry out analysis, assessments and systematic observation of the role of oceans as a carbon sink.

(b) Data and information

17.102.   States should consider, *inter alia*:

(a)   Increasing international cooperation particularly with a view to strengthening national scientific and technological capabilities for analysing, assessing and predicting global climate and environmental change;

(b)   Supporting the role of the IOC in cooperation with WMO, UNEP and other international organizations in the collection, analysis and distribution of data and information from the oceans and all seas, including as appropriate, through the Global Ocean Observing System, giving special attention to the need for IOC to develop fully the strategy for providing training and technical assistance for developing countries through its Training, Education and Mutual Assistance (TEMA) programme;

(c)   Creating national multisectoral information bases, covering the results of research and systematic observation programmes;

(d)   Linking these databases to existing data and information services and mechanisms, such as World Weather Watch and Earthwatch;

(e)   Cooperating with a view to the exchange of data and information and its storage and archiving through the world and regional data centres;

(f)   Cooperating to ensure full participation of developing countries, in particular, in any international scheme under the organs and organizations of the United Nations system for the collection, analysis and use of data and information.

(c) International and regional cooperation and coordination

17.103.   States should consider bilaterally and multilaterally and in cooperation with international organizations, whether subregional, regional, interregional or global, where appropriate:

(a)   Providing technical cooperation in developing the capacity of coastal and island States for marine research and systematic observation and for using its results;

(b)   Strengthening existing national institutions and creating, where necessary, international analysis and prediction mechanisms in order to prepare and exchange regional and global oceanographic analyses and forecasts and to provide facilities for international research and training at national, subregional and regional levels, where applicable.

17.104.   In recognition of the value of Antarctica as an area for the conduct of scientific research, in particular research essential to understanding the global environment, States carrying out such research activities in Antarctica should, as provided for in Article III of the Antarctic Treaty, continue to:

(a)   Ensure that data and information resulting from such research are freely available to the international community;

(b)   Enhance access of the international scientific community and specialized agencies of the United Nations to such data and information, including the encouragement of periodic seminars and symposia.

17.105.   States should strengthen high-level inter-agency, subregional, regional and global coordination, as appropriate, and review mechanisms to develop and integrate systematic observation networks. This would include:

(a)   Review of existing regional and global databases;

(b)   Mechanisms to develop comparable and compatible techniques, validate methodologies and measurements, organize regular scientific reviews, develop options for corrective measures, agree on formats for presentation and storage, and communicate the information gathered to potential users;

(c)   Systematic observation of coastal habitats and sealevel changes, inventories of marine pollution sources and reviews of fisheries statistics;

(d)   Organization of periodic assessments of ocean and all seas and coastal area status and trends.

17.106.   International cooperation, through relevant organizations within the United Nations system, should support countries to develop and integrate regional systematic long-term observation programmes, when applicable, into the Regional Seas Programmes in a coordinated fashion to implement, where appropriate, subregional, regional and global observing systems based on the principle of exchange of data. One aim should be the predicting of the effects of climate-related emergencies on existing coastal physical and socio-economic infrastructure.

17.107.   Based on the results of research on the effects of the additional ultraviolet radiation reaching the Earth's surface, in the fields of human health, agriculture and marine environment, States and international organizations should consider taking appropriate remedial measures.

Means of implementation
(a)   Financing and cost evaluation

17.108.   The Conference secretariat has estimated the average total annual cost (1993-2000) of implementing the activities of this programme to be about $750 million, including about $480 million from the international community on grant or concessional terms. These are indicative and order-of-magnitude estimates only and have not been reviewed by Governments. Actual costs and financial terms, including any that are non-concessional, will depend upon, *inter alia*, the specific strategies and programmes Governments decide upon for implementation.

17.109.   Developed countries should provide the financing for the further development and implementation of the Global Ocean Observing System.

(b)   Scientific and technological means

17.110.   To address critical uncertainties through systematic coastal and marine observations and research, coastal States should cooperate in the development of procedures that allow for comparable analysis and soundness of data. They should also cooperate on a subregional and regional basis, through existing programmes where applicable, share infrastructure and expensive and sophisticated equipment, develop quality assurance procedures and develop human resources jointly. Special attention should be given to transfer of scientific and technological knowledge and means to support States, particularly developing countries, in the development of endogenous capabilities.

17.111.   International organizations should support, when requested, coastal countries in implementing research projects on the effects of additional ultraviolet radiation.

(c)   Human resource development

17.112.   States, individually or through bilateral and multilateral cooperation and with the support, as appropriate, of international organizations whether subregional, regional or global, should develop and implement comprehensive programmes, particularly in developing countries, for a broad and coherent approach to meeting their core human resource needs in the marine sciences.

(d) Capacity-building

17.113. States should strengthen or establish as necessary, national scientific and technological oceanographic commissions or equivalent bodies to develop, support and coordinate marine science activities and work closely with international organizations.

17.114. States should use existing subregional and regional mechanisms, where applicable, to develop knowledge of the marine environment, exchange information, organize systematic observations and assessments, and make the most effective use of scientists, facilities and equipment. They should also cooperate in the promotion of endogenous research capabilities in developing countries.

F. STRENGTHENING INTERNATIONAL, INCLUDING REGIONAL, COOPERATION AND COORDINATION

Basis for action

17.115. It is recognized that the role of international cooperation is to support and supplement national efforts. Implementation of strategies and activities under the programme areas relative to marine and coastal areas and seas requires effective institutional arrangements at national, subregional, regional and global levels, as appropriate. There are numerous national and international, including regional, institutions, both within and outside the United Nations system, with competence in marine issues, and there is a need to improve coordination and strengthen links among them. It is also important to ensure that an integrated and multisectoral approach to marine issues is pursued at all levels.

Objectives

17.116. States commit themselves, in accordance with their policies, priorities and resources, to promote institutional arrangements necessary to support the implementation of the programme areas in this chapter. To this end, it is necessary, as appropriate, to:

(a) Integrate relevant sectoral activities addressing environment and development in marine and coastal areas at national, subregional, regional and global levels, as appropriate;

(b) Promote effective information exchange and, where appropriate, institutional linkages between bilateral and multilateral national, regional, subregional and interregional institutions dealing with environment and development in marine and coastal areas;

(c) Promote within the United Nations system, regular intergovernmental review and consideration of environment and development issues with respect to marine and coastal areas;

(d) Promote the effective operation of coordinating mechanisms for the components of the United Nations system dealing with issues of environment and development in marine and coastal areas, as well as links with relevant international development bodies.

Activities

(a) Management-related activities

Global

17.117. The General Assembly should provide for regular consideration, within the United Nations system, at the intergovernmental level of general marine and coastal issues, including environment and development matters, and should request the Secretary-General and executive heads of United Nations agencies and organizations to:

(a) Strengthen coordination and develop improved arrangements among the relevant United Nations organizations with major marine and coastal responsibilities, including their subregional and regional components;

(b) Strengthen coordination between those organizations and other United Nations organizations, institutions and specialized agencies dealing with development, trade and other related economic issues, as appropriate;

(c) Improve representation of United Nations agencies dealing with the marine environment in United Nations system-wide coordination efforts;

(d) Promote, where necessary, greater collaboration between the United Nations agencies and subregional and regional coastal and marine programmes;

(e) Develop a centralized system to provide for information on legislation and advice on implementation of legal agreements on marine environmental and development issues.

17.118.   States recognize that environmental policies should deal with the root causes of environmental degradation, thus preventing environmental measures from resulting in unnecessary restrictions to trade. Trade policy measures for environmental purposes should not constitute a means of arbitrary or unjustifiable discrimination or a disguised restriction on international trade. Unilateral actions to deal with environmental challenges outside the jurisdiction of the importing country should be avoided. Environmental measures addressing international environmental problems should, as far as possible, be based on an international consensus. Domestic measures targeted to achieve certain environmental objectives may need trade measures to render them effective. Should trade policy measures be found necessary for the enforcement of environmental policies, certain principles and rules should apply. These could include, *inter alia*, the principle of non-discrimination; the principle that the trade measure chosen should be the least trade-restrictive necessary to achieve the objectives; an obligation to ensure transparency in the use of trade measures related to the environment and to provide adequate notification of national regulations; and the need to give consideration to the special conditions and development requirements of developing countries as they move towards internationally agreed environmental objectives

Subregional and regional

17.119.   States should consider, as appropriate:

(a) Strengthening, and extending where necessary, intergovernmental regional cooperation, the Regional Seas Programmes of UNEP, regional and subregional fisheries organizations and regional commissions;

(b) Introduce, where necessary, coordination among relevant United Nations and other multilateral organizations at the subregional and regional levels, including consideration of co-location of their staff;

(c) Arrange for periodic intraregional consultations;

(d) Facilitate access to and use of expertise and technology through relevant national bodies to subregional and regional centres and networks, such as the Regional Centres for Marine Technology.

(b) Data and information

17.120.   States should, where appropriate:

(a) Promote exchange of information on marine and coastal issues;

(b) Strengthen the capacity of international organizations to handle information and support the development of national, subregional and regional data and information systems, where appropriate. This could also include networks linking countries with comparable environmental problems;

(c) Further develop existing international mechanisms such as Earthwatch and GESAMP.

Means of implementation

(a) Financing and cost evaluation

17.121.   The Conference secretariat has estimated the average total annual cost (1993-2000) of implementing the activities of this programme to be about $50 million from the international community on grant or concessional terms. These are indicative and order-of-magnitude estimates only and have not been reviewed by Governments. Actual costs and financial terms, including any that are non-concessional, will depend upon, *inter alia*, the specific strategies and programmes Governments decide upon for implementation.

(b) Scientific and technological means, human resource development and capacity-building

17.122.   The means of implementation outlined in the other programme areas on marine and coastal issues, under the sections on Scientific and technological means, human resource development and capacity-building are entirely relevant for this programme area as well. Additionally, States should, through international cooperation, develop a comprehensive programme for meeting the core human resource needs in marine sciences at all levels.

G. SUSTAINABLE DEVELOPMENT OF SMALL ISLANDS

Basis for action

17.123.   Small island developing States, and islands supporting small communities are a special case both for environment and development. They are ecologically fragile and vulnerable. Their small size, limited resources, geographic dispersion and isolation from markets, place them at a disadvantage economically and prevent economies of scale. For small island developing States the ocean and coastal environment is of strategic importance and constitutes a valuable development resource.

17.124.   Their geographic isolation has resulted in their habitation of a comparatively large number of unique species of flora and fauna, giving them a very high share of global biodiversity. They also have rich and diverse cultures with special adaptations to island environments and knowledge of the sound management of island resources.

17.125.   Small island developing States have all the environmental problems and challenges of the coastal zone concentrated in a limited land area. They are considered extremely vulnerable to global warming and sealevel rise, with certain small low-lying islands facing the increasing threat of the loss of their entire national territories. Most tropical islands are also now experiencing the more immediate impacts of increasing frequency of cyclones, storms and hurricanes associated with climate change. These are causing major set-backs to their socio-economic development.

17.126.   Because small island development options are limited, there are special challenges to planning for and implementing sustainable development. Small island developing States will be constrained in meeting these challenges without the cooperation and assistance of the international community.

Objectives

17.127.   States commit themselves to addressing the problems of sustainable development of small island developing States. To this end, it is necessary:

(a) To adopt and implement plans and programmes to support the sustainable development and utilization of their marine and coastal resources, including meeting essential human needs, maintaining biodiversity and improving the quality of life for island people;

(b) To adopt measures which will enable small island developing States to cope effectively, creatively and sustainably with environmental change and to mitigate impacts and reduce the threats posed to marine and coastal resources.

Activities
(a) Management-related activities

17.128. Small island developing States, with the assistance as appropriate of the international community and on the basis of existing work of national and international organizations, should:

(a) Study the special environmental and developmental characteristics of small islands, producing an environmental profile and inventory of their natural resources, critical marine habitats and biodiversity;

(b) Develop techniques for determining and monitoring the carrying capacity of small islands under different development assumptions and resource constraints;

(c) Prepare medium- and long-term plans for sustainable development that emphasize multiple use of resources, integrate environmental considerations with economic and sectoral planning and policies, define measures for maintaining cultural and biological diversity and conserve endangered species and critical marine habitats;

(d) Adapt coastal area management techniques, such as planning, siting and environmental impact assessments, using Geographical Information Systems (GIS), suitable to the special characteristics of small islands, taking into account the traditional and cultural values of indigenous people of island countries;

(e) Review the existing institutional arrangements and identify and undertake appropriate institutional reforms essential to the effective implementation of sustainable development plans, including intersectoral coordination and community participation in the planning process;

(f) Implement sustainable development plans, including the review and modification of existing unsustainable policies and practices;

(g) Based on precautionary and anticipatory approaches, design and implement rational response strategies to address the environmental, social and economic impacts of climate change and sealevel rise, and prepare appropriate contingency plans;

(h) Promote environmentally sound technology for sustainable development within small island developing States and identify technologies that should be excluded because of their threats to essential island ecosystems.

(b) Data and information

17.129. Additional information on the geographic, environmental, cultural and socio-economic characteristics of islands should be compiled and assessed to assist in the planning process. Existing island databases should be expanded and geographic information systems developed and adapted to suit the special characteristics of islands.

(c) International and regional cooperation and coordination

17.130. Small island developing States, with the support, as appropriate, of international organizations, whether subregional, regional or global, should develop and strengthen inter-island, regional and interregional cooperation and information exchange, including periodic regional and global meetings on sustainable development of small island developing States with the first global conference on the sustainable development of small island developing States, to be held in 1993.

17.131. International organizations, whether subregional, regional or global, must recognize the special development requirements of small island developing States and give adequate priority in the provision of assistance, particularly with respect to the development and implementation of sustainable development plans.

Means of implementation

(a) Financing and cost evaluation

17.132. The Conference secretariat has estimated the average total annual cost (1993-2000) of implementing the activities of this programme to be about $130 million, including about $50 million from the international community on grant or concessional terms. These are indicative and order-of-magnitude estimates only and have not been reviewed by Governments. Actual costs and financial terms, including any that are non-concessional, will depend upon, *inter alia*, the specific strategies and programmes Governments decide upon for implementation.

(b) Scientific and technical means

17.133. Centres for the development and diffusion of scientific information and advice on technical means and technologies appropriate to small island developing States, especially with reference to the management of the coastal zone, the exclusive economic zone and marine resources, should be established or strengthened, as appropriate, on a regional basis.

(c) Human resource development

17.134. Since populations of small island developing States cannot maintain all necessary specializations, training for integrated coastal management and development should aim to produce cadres of managers or scientists, engineers and coastal planners able to integrate the many factors that need to be considered in integrated coastal management. Resource users should be prepared to execute both management and protection functions and to apply the polluter pays principle and support the training of their personnel. Educational systems should be modified to meet these needs and special training programmes developed in integrated island management and development. Local planning should be integrated in educational curricula of all levels and public awareness campaigns developed with the assistance of non-governmental organizations and indigenous coastal populations.

(d) Capacity-building

17.135. The total capacity of small island developing States will always be limited. Existing capacity must therefore be restructured to meet efficiently the immediate needs for sustainable development and integrated management. At the same time, adequate and appropriate assistance from the international community must be directed at strengthening the full range of human resources needed on a continuous basis to implement sustainable development plans.

17.136. New technologies that can increase the output and range of capability of the limited human resources should be employed to increase the capacity of very small populations to meet their needs. The development and application of traditional knowledge to improve the capacity of countries to implement sustainable development should be fostered.

Convention on the Protection of the Marine Environment of the Baltic Sea Area (Helsinki Convention)

Done at Helsinki, 9 April 1992; entry into force, 17 January 2000
2099 UNTS 197 [Registration Number 36495][1]

The Contracting Parties,

Conscious of the indispensable values of the marine environment of the Baltic Sea Area, its exceptional hydrographic and ecological characteristics and the sensitivity of its living resources to changes in the environment;

Bearing in mind the historical and present economic, social and cultural values of the Baltic Sea Area for the well-being and development of the peoples of that region;

Noting with deep concern the still ongoing pollution of the Baltic Sea Area;

Declaring their firm determination to assure the ecological restoration of the Baltic Sea, ensuring the possibility of self-regeneration of the marine environment and preservation of its ecological balance;

Recognizing that the protection and enhancement of the marine environment of the Baltic Sea Area are tasks that cannot effectively be accomplished by national efforts alone but by close regional co-operation and other appropriate international measures;

Appreciating the achievements in environmental protection within the framework of the 1974 Convention on the Protection of the Marine Environment of the Baltic Sea Area, and the role of the Baltic Marine Environment Protection Commission therein;

Recalling the pertinent provisions and principles of the 1972 Declaration of the Stockholm Conference on the Human Environment and the 1975 Final Act of the Conference on Security and Co-operation in Europe (CSCE);

Desiring to enhance co-operation with competent regional organizations such as the International Baltic Sea Fishery Commission established by the 1973 Gdansk Convention on Fishing and Conservation of the Living Resources in the Baltic Sea and the Belts;

Welcoming the Baltic Sea Declaration by the Baltic and other interested States, the European Economic Community and co-operating international financial institutions assembled at Ronneby in 1990, and the Joint Comprehensive Programme aimed at a joint action plan in order to restore the Baltic Sea Area to a sound ecological balance;

Conscious of the importance of transparency and public awareness as well as the work by non-governmental organizations for successful protection of the Baltic Sea Area;

Welcoming the improved opportunities for closer co-operation which have been opened by the recent political developments in Europe on the basis of peaceful co-operation and mutual understanding;

Determined to embody developments in international environmental policy and environmental law into a new Convention to extend, strengthen and modernize the legal regime for the protection of the Marine Environment of the Baltic Sea Area;

Have agreed as follows:

---

[1] The seven Annexes of the Convention were amended by the Helsinki Commission in 2000, 2001, 2003 and 2007. The latest amendments entered into force on 15 November 2008. The text of the Annexes reproduced is a consolidated version incorporating these amendments. Annex I (Harmful Substances), Annex II (Criteria for the use of Best Environmental Practice and Best Available Technology), Annex III (Criteria and measures concerning the prevention of pollution from land-based sources), Annex V (Exemptions from the general prohibition of dumping of waste and other matter in the Baltic Sea Area) and Annex VII (Response to pollution incidents) omitted.

Article 1 Convention Area

This Convention shall apply to the Baltic Sea Area. For the purposes of this Convention the 'Baltic Sea Area' shall be the Baltic Sea and the entrance to the Baltic Sea bounded by the parallel of the Skaw in the Skagerrak at 57° 44.43′N. It includes the internal waters, i.e., for the purpose of this Convention waters on the landward side of the base lines from which the breadth of the territorial sea is measured up to the landward limit according to the designation by the Contracting Parties.

A Contracting Party shall, at the time of the deposit of the instrument of ratification, approval or accession inform the Depositary of the designation of its internal waters for the purposes of this Convention.

Article 2 Definitions

For the purposes of this Convention:

1. 'Pollution' means introduction by man, directly or indirectly, of substances or energy into the sea, including estuaries, which are liable to create hazards to human health, to harm living resources and marine ecosystems, to cause hindrance to legitimate uses of the sea including fishing, to impair the quality for use of sea water, and to lead to a reduction of amenities;

2. 'Pollution from land-based sources' means pollution of the sea by point or diffuse inputs from all sources on land reaching the sea waterborne, airborne or directly from the coast. It includes pollution from any deliberate disposal under the seabed with access from land by tunnel, pipeline or other means;

3. 'Ship' means a vessel of any type whatsoever operating in the marine environment and includes hydrofoil boats, air-cushion vehicles, submersibles, floating craft and fixed or floating platforms;

4. (a) 'Dumping' means:

    (i) any deliberate disposal at sea or into the seabed of wastes or other matter from ships, other man-made structures at sea or aircraft;

    (ii) any deliberate disposal at sea of ships, other man-made structures at sea or aircraft;

   (b) 'Dumping' does not include:

    (i) the disposal at sea of wastes or other matter incidental to, or derived from the normal operations of ships, other man-made structures at sea or aircraft and their equipment, other than wastes or other matter transported by or to ships, other man-made structures at sea or aircraft, operating for the purpose of disposal of such matter or derived from the treatment of such wastes or other matter on such ships, structures or aircraft;

    (ii) placement of matter for a purpose other than the mere disposal thereof, provided that such placement is not contrary to the aims of the present Convention;

5. 'Incineration' means the deliberate combustion of wastes or other matter at sea for the purpose of their thermal destruction. Activities incidental to the normal operation of ships or other man-made structures are excluded from the scope of this definition;

6. 'Oil' means petroleum in any form including crude oil, fuel oil, sludge, oil refuse and refined products;

7. 'Harmful substance' means any substance, which, if introduced into the sea, is liable to cause pollution;

8. 'Hazardous substance' means any harmful substance which due to its intrinsic properties is persistent, toxic or liable to bio-accumulate;

9. 'Pollution incident' means an occurrence or series of occurrences having the same origin, which results or may result in a discharge of oil or other harmful substances and which poses or may pose a threat to the marine environment of the Baltic Sea or to the coastline or related interests of one or more Contracting Parties, and which requires emergency actions or other immediate response;

10. 'Regional economic integration organization' means any organization constituted by sovereign states, to which their member states have transferred competence in respect of matters governed by this Convention, including the competence to enter into international agreements in respect of these matters;

11. The 'Commission' means the Baltic Marine Environment Protection Commission referred to in Article 19.

Article 3 Fundamental principles and obligations

1. The Contracting Parties shall individually or jointly take all appropriate legislative, administrative or other relevant measures to prevent and eliminate pollution in order to promote the ecological restoration of the Baltic Sea Area and the preservation of its ecological balance.

2. The Contracting Parties shall apply the precautionary principle, i.e., to take preventive measures when there is reason to assume that substances or energy introduced, directly or indirectly, into the marine environment may create hazards to human health, harm living resources and marine ecosystems, damage amenities or interfere with other legitimate uses of the sea even when there is no conclusive evidence of a causal relationship between inputs and their alleged effects.

3. In order to prevent and eliminate pollution of the Baltic Sea Area the Contracting Parties shall promote the use of Best Environmental Practice and Best Available Technology. If the reduction of inputs, resulting from the use of Best Environmental Practice and Best Available Technology, as described in Annex II, does not lead to environmentally acceptable results, additional measures shall be applied.

4. The Contracting Parties shall apply the polluter-pays principle.

5. The Contracting Parties shall ensure that measurements and calculations of emissions from point sources to water and air and of inputs from diffuse sources to water and air are carried out in a scientifically appropriate manner in order to assess the state of the marine environment of the Baltic Sea Area and ascertain the implementation of this Convention.

6. The Contracting Parties shall use their best endeavours to ensure that the implementation of this Convention does not cause transboundary pollution in areas outside the Baltic Sea Area. Furthermore, the relevant measures shall not lead either to unacceptable environmental strains on air quality and the atmosphere or on waters, soil and ground water, to unacceptably harmful or increasing waste disposal, or to increased risks to human health.

Article 4 Application

1. This Convention shall apply to the protection of the marine environment of the Baltic Sea Area which comprises the water-body and the seabed including their living resources and other forms of marine life.

2. Without prejudice to its sovereignty each Contracting Party shall implement the provisions of this Convention within its territorial sea and its internal waters through its national authorities.

3. This Convention shall not apply to any warship, naval auxiliary, military aircraft or other ship and aircraft owned or operated by a state and used, for the time being, only on government non-commercial service.

However, each Contracting Party shall ensure, by the adoption of appropriate measures not impairing the operations or operational capabilities of such ships and aircraft owned or operated by it, that such ships and aircraft act in a manner consistent, so far as is reasonable and practicable, with this Convention.

Article 5 Harmful substances

The Contracting Parties undertake to prevent and eliminate pollution of the marine environment of the Baltic Sea Area caused by harmful substances from all sources, according to the provisions of this Convention and, to this end, to implement the procedures and measures of Annex I.

Article 6 Principles and obligations concerning pollution from land-based sources

1. The Contracting Parties undertake to prevent and eliminate pollution of the Baltic Sea Area from land-based sources by using, *inter alia*, Best Environmental Practice for all sources and Best Available Technology for point sources. The relevant measures to this end shall be taken by each Contracting Party in the catchment area of the Baltic Sea without prejudice to its sovereignty.

2. The Contracting Parties shall implement the procedures and measures set out in Annex III. To this end they shall, *inter alia*, as appropriate co-operate in the development and adoption of specific programmes, guidelines, standards or regulations concerning emissions and inputs to water and air, environmental quality, and products containing harmful substances and materials and the use thereof.

3. Harmful substances from point sources shall not, except in negligible quantities, be introduced directly or indirectly into the marine environment of the Baltic Sea Area, without a prior special permit, which may be periodically reviewed, issued by the appropriate national authority in accordance with the principles contained in Annex III, Regulation 3. The Contracting Parties shall ensure that authorized emissions to water and air are monitored and controlled.

4. If the input from a watercourse, flowing through the territories of two or more Contracting Parties or forming a boundary between them, is liable to cause pollution of the marine environment of the Baltic Sea Area, the Contracting Parties concerned shall jointly and, if possible, in co-operation with a third state interested or concerned, take appropriate measures in order to prevent and eliminate such pollution.

Article 7 Environmental impact assessment

1. Whenever an environmental impact assessment of a proposed activity that is likely to cause a significant adverse impact on the marine environment of the Baltic Sea Area is required by international law or supra-national regulations applicable to the Contracting Party of origin, that Contracting Party shall notify the Commission and any Contracting Party which may be affected by a transboundary impact on the Baltic Sea Area.

2. The Contracting Party of origin shall enter into consultations with any Contracting Party which is likely to be affected by such transboundary impact, whenever consultations are required by international law or supra-national regulations applicable to the Contracting Party of origin.

3. Where two or more Contracting Parties share transboundary waters within the catchment area of the Baltic Sea, these Parties shall cooperate to ensure that potential impacts on the marine environment of the Baltic Sea Area are fully investigated within the environmental impact assessment referred to in paragraph 1 of this Article. The Contracting Parties concerned shall jointly take appropriate measures in order to prevent and eliminate pollution including cumulative deleterious effects.

Article 8 Prevention of pollution from ships

1. In order to protect the Baltic Sea Area from pollution from ships, the Contracting Parties shall take measures as set out in Annex IV.

2. The Contracting Parties shall develop and apply uniform requirements for the provision of reception facilities for ship-generated wastes, taking into account, *inter alia*, the special needs of passenger ships operating in the Baltic Sea Area.

Article 9 Pleasure craft

The Contracting Parties shall, in addition to implementing those provisions of this Convention which can appropriately be applied to pleasure craft, take special measures in order to abate harmful effects on the marine environment of the Baltic Sea Area caused by pleasure craft activities. The measures shall, *inter alia*, deal with air pollution, noise and hydrodynamic effects as well as with adequate reception facilities for wastes from pleasure craft.

Article 10 Prohibition of incineration

1. The Contracting Parties shall prohibit incineration in the Baltic Sea Area.

2. Each Contracting Party undertakes to ensure compliance with the provisions of this Article by ships:

   (a)   Registered in its territory or flying its flag;

   (b)   Loading, within its territory or territorial sea, matter which is to be incinerated; or

   (c)   Believed to be engaged in incineration within its internal waters and territorial sea.

3. In case of suspected incineration the Contracting Parties shall co-operate in investigating the matter in accordance with Regulation 2 of Annex IV.

Article 11 Prevention of dumping

1. The Contracting Parties shall, subject to exemptions set forth in paragraphs 2 and 4 of this Article, prohibit dumping in the Baltic Sea Area.

2. Dumping of dredged material shall be subject to a prior special permit issued by the appropriate national authority in accordance with the provisions of Annex V.

3. Each Contracting Party undertakes to ensure compliance with the provisions of this Article by ships and aircraft:

   (a)   Registered in its territory or flying its flag;

   (b)   Loading, within its territory or territorial sea, matter which is to be dumped; or

   (c)   Believed to be engaged in dumping within its internal waters and territorial sea.

4. The provisions of this Article shall not apply when the safety of human life or of a ship or aircraft at sea is threatened by the complete destruction or total loss of the ship or aircraft, or in any case which constitutes a danger to human life, if dumping appears to be the only way of averting the threat and if there is every probability that the damage consequent upon such dumping will be less than would otherwise occur. Such dumping shall be so conducted as to minimize the likelihood of damage to human or marine life.

5. Dumping made under the provisions of paragraph 4 of this Article shall be reported and dealt with in accordance with Annex VII and shall be reported forthwith to the Commission in accordance with the provisions of Regulation 4 of Annex V.

6. In case of dumping suspected to be in contravention of the provisions of this Article the Contracting Parties shall co-operate in investigating the matter in accordance with Regulation 2 of Annex IV.

Article 12 Exploration and exploitation of the seabed and its subsoil

1. Each Contracting Party shall take all measures in order to prevent pollution of the marine environment of the Baltic Sea Area resulting from exploration or exploitation

of its part of the seabed and the subsoil thereof or from any associated activities thereon as well as to ensure that adequate preparedness is maintained for immediate response actions against pollution incidents caused by such activities.

2. In order to prevent and eliminate pollution from such activities the Contracting Parties undertake to implement the procedures and measures set out in Annex VI, as far as they are applicable.

Article 13 Notification and consultation on pollution incidents

1. Whenever a pollution incident in the territory of a Contracting Party is likely to cause pollution to the marine environment of the Baltic Sea Area outside its territory and adjacent maritime area in which it exercises sovereign rights and jurisdiction according to international law, this Contracting Party shall notify without delay such Contracting Parties whose interests are affected or likely to be affected.

2. Whenever deemed necessary by the Contracting Parties referred to in paragraph 1, consultations should take place with a view to preventing, reducing and controlling such pollution.

3. Paragraphs 1 and 2 shall also apply in cases where a Contracting Party has sustained such pollution from the territory of a third state.

Article 14 Co-operation in combatting marine pollution

The Contracting Parties shall individually and jointly take, as set out in Annex VII, all appropriate measures to maintain adequate ability and to respond to pollution incidents in order to eliminate or minimize the consequences of these incidents to the marine environment of the Baltic Sea Area.

Article 15 Nature conservation and biodiversity

The Contracting Parties shall individually and jointly take all appropriate measures with respect to the Baltic Sea Area and its coastal ecosystems influenced by the Baltic Sea to conserve natural habitats and biological diversity and to protect ecological processes. Such measures shall also be taken in order to ensure the sustainable use of natural resources within the Baltic Sea Area. To this end, the Contracting Parties shall aim at adopting subsequent instruments containing appropriate guidelines and criteria.

Article 16 Reporting and exchange of information

1. The Contracting Parties shall report to the Commission at regular intervals on:
   (a) The legal, regulatory, or other measures taken for the implementation of the provisions of this Convention, of its Annexes and of recommendations adopted thereunder;
   (b) The effectiveness of the measures taken to implement the provisions referred to in sub-paragraph (a) of this paragraph; and
   (c) Problems encountered in the implementation of the provisions referred to in sub-paragraph (a) of this paragraph.

2. On the request of a Contracting Party or of the Commission, the Contracting Parties shall provide information on discharge permits, emission data or data on environmental quality, as far as available.

Article 17 Information to the public

1. The Contracting Parties shall ensure that information is made available to the public on the condition of the Baltic Sea and the waters in its catchment area, measures taken or planned to be taken to prevent and eliminate pollution and the effectiveness of those measures. For this purpose, the Contracting Parties shall ensure that the following information is made available to the public:

(a)   Permits issued and the conditions required to be met;

(b)   Results of water and effluent sampling carried out for the purposes of monitoring and assessment, as well as results of checking compliance with water-quality objectives or permit conditions; and

(c)   Water-quality objectives.

2.   Each Contracting Party shall ensure that this information shall be available to the public at all reasonable times and shall provide members of the public with reasonable facilities for obtaining, on payment of reasonable charges, copies of entries in its registers.

Article 18 Protection of information

1.   The provisions of this Convention shall not affect the right or obligation of any Contracting Party under its national law and applicable supra-national regulation to protect information related to intellectual property including industrial and commercial secrecy or national security and the confidentiality of personal data.

2.   If a Contracting Party nevertheless decides to supply such protected information to another Contracting Party, the Party receiving such protected information shall respect the confidentiality of the information received and the conditions under which it is supplied, and shall use that information only for the purposes for which it was supplied.

Article 19 Commission

1.   The Baltic Marine Environment Protection Commission, referred to as 'the Commission', is established for the purposes of this Convention.

2.   The Baltic Marine Environment Protection Commission, established pursuant to the Convention on the Protection of the Marine Environment of the Baltic Sea Area of 1974, shall be the Commission.

3.   The chairmanship of the Commission shall be given to each Contracting Party in turn in alphabetical order of the names of the Contracting Parties in the English language. The Chairman shall serve for a period of two years, and cannot during the period of chairmanship serve as a representative of the Contracting Party holding the chairmanship.

Should the chairman fail to complete his term, the Contracting Party holding the chairmanship shall nominate a successor to remain in office until the term of that Contracting Party expires.

4.   Meetings of the Commission shall be held at least once a year upon convocation by the Chairman. Extraordinary meetings shall, upon the request of any Contracting Party endorsed by another Contracting Party, be convened by the Chairman to be held as soon as possible, however, not later than ninety days after the date of submission of the request.

5.   Unless otherwise provided under this Convention, the Commission shall take its decisions unanimously.

Article 20 The duties of the Commission

1.   The duties of the Commission shall be:

(a)   To keep the implementation of this Convention under continuous observation;

(b)   To make recommendations on measures relating to the purposes of this Convention;

(c)   To keep under review the contents of this Convention including its Annexes and to recommend to the Contracting Parties such amendments to this Convention including its Annexes as may be required including changes in the lists of substances and materials as well as the adoption of new Annexes;

(d)   To define pollution control criteria, objectives for the reduction of pollution, and objectives concerning measures, particularly those described in Annex III;

(e) To promote in close co-operation with appropriate governmental bodies, taking into consideration sub-paragraph (f) of this Article, additional measures to protect the marine environment of the Baltic Sea Area and for this purpose:
   (i) To receive, process, summarize and disseminate relevant scientific, technological and statistical information from available sources; and
   (ii) To promote scientific and technological research; and
(f) To seek, when appropriate, the services of competent regional and other international organizations to collaborate in scientific and technological research as well as other relevant activities pertinent to the objectives of this Convention.

2. The Commission may assume such other functions as it deems appropriate to further the purposes of this Convention.

Article 21 Administrative provisions for the Commission

1. The working language of the Commission shall be English.
2. The Commission shall adopt its Rules of Procedure.
3. The office of the Commission, known as 'the Secretariat', shall be in Helsinki.
4. The Commission shall appoint an Executive Secretary and make provisions for the appointment of such other personnel as may be necessary, and determine the duties, terms and conditions of service of the Executive Secretary.
5. The Executive Secretary shall be the chief administrative official of the Commission and shall perform the functions that are necessary for the administration of this Convention, the work of the Commission and other tasks entrusted to the Executive Secretary by the Commission and its Rules of Procedure.

Article 22 Financial provisions for the Commission

1. The Commission shall adopt its Financial Rules.
2. The Commission shall adopt an annual or biennial budget of proposed expenditures and consider budget estimates for the fiscal period following thereafter.
3. The total amount of the budget, including any supplementary budget adopted by the Commission shall be contributed by the Contracting Parties other than the European Economic Community, in equal parts, unless unanimously decided otherwise by the Commission.
4. The European Economic Community shall contribute no more than 2.5% of the administrative costs to the budget.
5. Each Contracting Party shall pay the expenses related to the participation in the Commission of its representatives, experts and advisers.

Article 23 Right to vote

1. Except as provided for in paragraph 2 of this Article, each Contracting Party shall have one vote in the Commission.
2. The European Economic Community and any other regional economic integration organization, in matters within their competence, shall exercise their right to vote with a number of votes equal to the number of their member states which are Contracting Parties to this Convention. Such organizations shall not exercise their right to vote if their member states exercise theirs, and *vice versa*.

Article 24 Scientific and technological co-operation

1. The Contracting Parties undertake directly, or when appropriate through competent regional or other international organizations, to co-operate in the fields of science, technology and other research, and to exchange data and other scientific information for

the purposes of this Convention. In order to facilitate research and monitoring activities in the Baltic Sea Area the Contracting Parties undertake to harmonize their policies with respect to permission procedures for conducting such activities.

2. Without prejudice to Article 4, paragraph 2 of this Convention the Contracting Parties undertake directly, or when appropriate, through competent regional or other international organizations, to promote studies and to undertake, support or contribute to programmes aimed at developing methods assessing the nature and extent of pollution, pathways, exposures, risks and remedies in the Baltic Sea Area. In particular, the Contracting Parties undertake to develop alternative methods of treatment, disposal and elimination of such matter and substances that are likely to cause pollution of the marine environment of the Baltic Sea Area.

3. Without prejudice to Article 4, paragraph 2 of this Convention the Contracting Parties undertake directly, or when appropriate through competent regional or other international organizations, and, on the basis of the information and data acquired pursuant to paragraphs 1 and 2 of this Article, to co-operate in developing inter-comparable observation methods, in performing baseline studies and in establishing complementary or joint programmes for monitoring.

4. The organization and scope of work connected with the implementation of tasks referred to in the preceding paragraphs should primarily be outlined by the Commission.

Article 25 Responsibility for damage

The Contracting Parties undertake jointly to develop and accept rules concerning responsibility for damage resulting from acts or omissions in contravention of this Convention, including, *inter alia*, limits of responsibility, criteria and procedures for the determination of liability and available remedies.

Article 26 Settlement of disputes

1. In case of a dispute between Contracting Parties as to the interpretation or application of this Convention, they should seek a solution by negotiation. If the Parties concerned cannot reach agreement they should seek the good offices of or jointly request mediation by a third Contracting Party, a qualified international organization or a qualified person.

2. If the Parties concerned have not been able to resolve their dispute through negotiation or have been unable to agree on measures as described above, such disputes shall be, upon common agreement, submitted to an *ad hoc* arbitration tribunal, to a permanent arbitration tribunal, or to the International Court of Justice.

Article 27 Safeguard of certain freedoms

Nothing in this Convention shall be construed as infringing upon the freedom of navigation, fishing, marine scientific research and other legitimate uses of the high seas, as well as upon the right of innocent passage through the territorial sea.

Article 28 Status of Annexes

The Annexes attached to this Convention form an integral part of this Convention.

Article 29 Relation to other Conventions

The provisions of this Convention shall be without prejudice to the rights and obligations of the Contracting Parties under existing and future treaties which further and develop the general principles of the Law of the Sea underlying this Convention and, in particular, provisions concerning the prevention of pollution of the marine environment.

Article 30 Conference for the revision or amendment of the Convention

A conference for the purpose of a general revision of or an amendment to this Convention may be convened with the consent of the Contracting Parties or at the request of the Commission.

Article 31 Amendments to the Articles of the Convention

1. Each Contracting Party may propose amendments to the Articles of this Convention. Any such proposed amendment shall be submitted to the Depositary and communicated by it to all Contracting Parties, which shall inform the Depositary of either their acceptance or rejection of the amendment as soon as possible after receipt of the communication.

A proposed amendment shall, at the request of a Contracting Party, be considered in the Commission. In such a case Article 19 paragraph 4 shall apply. If an amendment is adopted by the Commission, the procedure in paragraph 2 of this Article shall apply.

2. The Commission may recommend amendments to the Articles of this Convention. Any such recommended amendment shall be submitted to the Depositary and communicated by it to all Contracting Parties, which shall notify the Depositary of either their acceptance or rejection of the amendment as soon as possible after receipt of the communication.

3. The amendment shall enter into force ninety days after the Depositary has received notifications of acceptance of that amendment from all Contracting Parties.

Article 32 Amendments to the Annexes and the adoption of Annexes

1. Any amendment to the Annexes proposed by a Contracting Party shall be communicated to the other Contracting Parties by the Depositary and considered in the Commission. If adopted by the Commission, the amendment shall be communicated to the Contracting Parties and recommended for acceptance.

2. Any amendment to the Annexes recommended by the Commission shall be communicated to the Contracting Parties by the Depositary and recommended for acceptance.

3. Such amendment shall be deemed to have been accepted at the end of a period determined by the Commission unless within that period any one of the Contracting Parties has, by written notification to the Depositary, objected to the amendment. The accepted amendment shall enter into force on a date determined by the Commission.

The period determined by the Commission shall be prolonged for an additional period of six months and the date of entry into force of the amendment postponed accordingly, if, in exceptional cases, any Contracting Party informs the Depositary before the expiration of the period determined by the Commission that, although it intends to accept the amendment, the constitutional requirements for such an acceptance are not yet fulfilled.

4. An Annex to this Convention may be adopted in accordance with the provisions of this Article.

Article 33 Reservations

1. The provisions of this Convention shall not be subject to reservations.

2. The provision of paragraph 1 of this Article does not prevent a Contracting Party from suspending for a period not exceeding one year the application of an Annex of this Convention or part thereof or an amendment thereto after the Annex in question or the amendment thereto has entered into force. Any Contracting Party to the 1974 Convention on the Protection of the Marine Environment of the Baltic Sea Area, which upon the entry into force of this Convention, suspends the application of an Annex or part thereof, shall apply the corresponding Annex or part thereof to the 1974 Convention for the period of suspension.

3. If after the entry into force of this Convention a Contracting Party invokes the provisions of paragraph 2 of this Article it shall inform the other Contracting Parties, at the time of the adoption by the Commission of an amendment to an Annex, or a new Annex, of those provisions which will be suspended in accordance with paragraph 2 of this Article.

Article 34 Signature

This Convention shall be open for signature in Helsinki from 9 April 1992 until 9 October 1992 by States and by the European Economic Community participating in the Diplomatic Conference on the Protection of the Marine Environment of the Baltic Sea Area held in Helsinki on 9 April 1992.

Article 35 Ratification, approval and accession

1. This Convention shall be subject to ratification or approval.

2. This Convention shall, after its entry into force, be open for accession by any other State or regional economic integration organization interested in fulfilling the aims and purposes of this Convention, provided that this State or organization is invited by all the Contracting Parties. In the case of limited competence of a regional economic integration organization, the terms and conditions of its participation may be agreed upon between the Commission and the interested organization.

3. The instruments of ratification, approval or accession shall be deposited with the Depositary.

4. The European Economic Community and any other regional economic integration organization which becomes a Contracting Party to this Convention shall in matters within their competence, on their own behalf, exercise the rights and fulfill the responsibilities which this Convention attributes to their member states. In such cases, the member states of these organizations shall not be entitled to exercise such rights individually.

Article 36 Entry into force

1. This Convention shall enter into force two months after the deposit of the instruments of ratification or approval by all signatory States bordering the Baltic Sea and by the European Economic Community.

2. For each State which ratifies or approves this Convention before or after the deposit of the last instrument of ratification or approval referred to in paragraph 1 of this Article, this Convention shall enter into force two months after the date of deposit by such State of its instrument of ratification or approval or on the date of the entry into force of this Convention, whichever is the latest date.

3. For each acceding State or regional economic integration organization this Convention shall enter into force two months after the date of deposit by such State or regional economic integration organization of its instrument of accession.

4. Upon entry into force of this Convention the Convention on the Protection of the Marine Environment of the Baltic Sea Area, signed in Helsinki on 22 March 1974 as amended, shall cease to apply.

5. Notwithstanding paragraph 4 of this Article, amendments to the annexes of the said Convention adopted by the Contracting Parties to the said Convention between the signing of this Convention and its entry into force, shall continue to apply until the corresponding annexes of this Convention have been amended accordingly.

6. Notwithstanding paragraph 4 of this Article, recommendations and decisions adopted under the said Convention shall continue to be applicable to the extent that they are compatible with, or not explicitly terminated by this Convention or any decision adopted thereunder.

Article 37 Withdrawal

1. At any time after the expiry of five years from the date of entry into force of this Convention any Contracting Party may, by giving written notification to the Depositary, withdraw from this Convention. The withdrawal shall take effect for such Contracting Party on the thirtieth day of June of the year which follows the year in which the Depositary was notified of the withdrawal.

2. In case of notification of withdrawal by a Contracting Party the Depositary shall convene a meeting of the Contracting Parties for the purpose of considering the effect of the withdrawal.

Article 38 Depositary

The Government of Finland, acting as Depositary, shall:

(a) Notify all Contracting Parties and the Executive Secretary of:
  (i)   The signatures;
  (ii) The deposit of any instrument of ratification, approval or accession;
  (iii) Any date of entry into force of this Convention;
  (iv) Any proposed or recommended amendment to any Article or Annex or the adoption of a new Annex as well as the date on which such amendment or new Annex enters into force;
  (v)   Any notification, and the date of its receipt, under Articles 31 and 32;
  (vi) Any notification of withdrawal and the date on which such withdrawal takes effect;
  (vii) Any other act or notification relating to this Convention;
(b) Transmit certified copies of this Convention to acceding States and regional economic integration organizations.

IN WITNESS WHEREOF the undersigned, being duly authorized thereto, have signed this Convention.

DONE at Helsinki, this ninth day of April one thousand nine hundred and ninety two in a single authentic copy in the English language which shall be deposited with the Government of Finland. The Government of Finland shall transmit certified copies to all Signatories.

ANNEX IV
PREVENTION OF POLLUTION FROM SHIPS[1]

Regulation 1 Co-operation

The Contracting Parties shall, in matters concerning the protection of the Baltic Sea Area from pollution by ships, co-operate:

(a) Within the International Maritime Organization, in particular in promoting the development of international rules, based, *inter alia*, on the fundamental principles and obligations of this Convention which also includes the promotion of the use of Best Available Technology and Best Environmental Practice as defined in Annex II;
(b) In the effective and harmonized implementation of rules adopted by the International Maritime Organization.

Regulation 2 Assistance in investigations

The Contracting Parties shall, without prejudice to Article 4, paragraph 3 of this Convention, assist each other as appropriate in investigating violations of the existing legislation on antipollution measures, which have occurred or are suspected to have

---

[1] Regulations 5, 8, 9 and 11 omitted.

occurred within the Baltic Sea Area. This assistance may include but is not limited to inspection by the competent authorities of oil record books, cargo record books, log books and engine log books and taking oil samples for analytical identification purposes.

Regulation 3 Definitions

For the purposes of this Annex:

1. 'Administration' means the Government of the Contracting Party under whose authority the ship is operating. With respect to a ship entitled to fly a flag of any State, the Administration is the Government of that State. With respect to fixed or floating platforms engaged in exploration and exploitation of the sea-bed and subsoil thereof adjacent to the coast over which the coastal State exercises sovereign rights for the purposes of exploration and exploitation of their natural resources, the Administration is the Government of the coastal State concerned.

2. (a) 'Discharge', in relation to harmful substances or effluents containing such substances, means any release howsoever caused from a ship and includes any escape, disposal, spilling, leaking, pumping, emitting or emptying;

   (b) 'Discharge' does not include:

   (i) Dumping within the meaning of the Convention on the Prevention of Marine Pollution by Dumping of Wastes and Other Matter done at London on 29 December 1972; or

   (ii) Release of harmful substances directly arising from the exploration, exploitation and associated off-shore processing of sea-bed mineral resources; or

   (iii) Release of harmful substances for purposes of legitimate scientific research into pollution abatement or control.

3. The term 'from the nearest land' means from the baseline from which the territorial sea of the territory in question is established in accordance with international law.

4. The term 'jurisdiction' shall be interpreted in accordance with international law in force at the time of application or interpretation of this Annex.

5. The term 'MARPOL 73/78' means the International Convention for the Prevention of Pollution from Ships, 1973, as modified by the Protocol of 1978 relating thereto.

Regulation 4 Application of the Annexes of MARPOL 73/78

1. The Contracting Parties shall apply the provisions of Annexes I-V of MARPOL 73/78.

2. At the entry into force of the revised Regulation 13G[2] of Annex I to MARPOL 73/78 the Contracting Parties:

   (a) Shall amend the conditions under which ships are permitted to fly their flags so as not to allow the operation of ships which may not comply with the requirements of Regulation 13F[3] in accordance with Regulation 13G(4);

   (b) Shall refrain from making use of the provisions of either paragraph (5)(a) or paragraph (5)(b) of Regulation 13G and thus will not allow ships entitled to fly their flag to which paragraph (5)(a) and (5)(b) may be applied to continue operating beyond the date specified in Regulation 13G(4); and

   (c) Shall make use, as from 1 January 2015, of the provisions of paragraph 8(b) of Regulation 13G for the purpose of denying entry into their ports or offshore terminals of ships which have been permitted, on the basis of the provisions of paragraph (5)(a) or (5)(b) of Regulation 13G, to continue operating beyond the anniversary of the date of their delivery in 2015;

---

[2] Regulation 13G has been renumbered Regulation 20, see above, Doc. 21.
[3] Regulation 13F has been renumbered Regulation 21, see above, Doc. 21.

(d)   May under exceptional circumstances allow an individual ship not complying with Regulation 13F in accordance with Regulation 13G(4), to enter their ports or offshore terminals, when:

–   an oil tanker is in difficulty and in search of a safe haven or of a place of refuge,

–   an unloaded oil tanker is proceeding to a port of repair.

3. As from 1 January 2004 the Contracting Parties shall:

(a)   Apply the provisions for discharge of sewage as stated in Regulation 11, paragraphs 1 and 3 of the revised Annex IV of MARPOL 73/78; and

(b)   Ensure the provision of facilities at ports and terminals for the reception of sewage as stated in Regulation 12, paragraph 1 of the revised Annex IV of MARPOL 73/78.

Regulation 6 Mandatory discharge of all wastes to a port reception facility

A.   Definitions

For the purpose of this Regulation:

1. 'Ship-generated wastes' means all residues generated during the service of the ship, including oily residues from engine room spaces, sewage, and garbage as defined in Annex V of MARPOL 73/78, cargo associated waste including but not limited to loading/unloading excess and spillage, dunnage, shoring, pallets, lining and packing materials, plywood, paper, cardboard, wire and steel strapping;

2. 'Cargo residues' means the remnants of any cargo material on board in cargo holds which remain for disposal after unloading procedures are completed.

B.   Discharge of wastes to a port reception facility

Before leaving port ships shall discharge all ship-generated wastes, which are not allowed to be discharged into the sea in the Baltic Sea Area in accordance with MARPOL 73/78 and this Convention, to a port reception facility. Before leaving port all cargo residues shall be discharged to a port reception facility in accordance with the requirements of MARPOL 73/78.

C.   Exemptions

1. Exemptions may be granted by the Administration from mandatory discharge of all wastes to a port reception facility taking into account the need for special arrangements for, e.g., passenger ferries engaged in short voyages. The Administration shall inform the Helsinki Commission on the issued exemptions.

2. In case of inadequate reception facilities ships shall have the right to properly stow and keep wastes on board for delivery to next adequate port reception facility. The Port Authority or the Operator shall provide a ship with a document informing on inadequacy of reception facilities.

3. A ship should be allowed to keep on board minor amounts of wastes which are unreasonable to discharge to port reception facilities.

Regulation 7 Incineration of ship-generated wastes on board ships

A.   Definition

For the purpose of this Regulation 'incineration of ship-generated wastes on board ships' means the deliberate combustion of ship-generated wastes, incidental to the normal operation of ships, for the purpose of thermal destruction of such wastes.

B.   Prohibition

The Contracting Parties shall prohibit any incineration of ship-generated wastes on board ships, irrespective of their nationality, operating in their territorial seas.

Regulation 10 Port State control

The Contracting Parties shall carry out port State control on the basis of either the 1982 Paris Memorandum of Understanding on Port State Control or the Council Directive 95/21/EC of 19 June 1995, as amended, concerning the enforcement, in respect of shipping using Community ports and sailing in the waters under the jurisdiction of the Member States, of international standards for ship safety, pollution prevention and shipboard living and working conditions (port State control).

Regulation 12 Places of refuge

The Contracting Parties:

(a)   Shall, following-up the work of EC and IMO, draw up plans to accommodate, in the waters under their jurisdiction, ships in distress in order to ensure that ships in distress may immediately go to a place of refuge subject to authorisation by the competent authority; and

(b)   Shall exchange details on plans for accommodating ships in distress.

ANNEX VI
PREVENTION OF POLLUTION FROM OFFSHORE ACTIVITIES

Regulation 1 Definitions

For the purposes of this Annex:

1.   'Offshore activity' means any exploration and exploitation of oil and gas by a fixed or floating offshore installation or structure including all associated activities thereon;

2.   'Offshore unit' means any fixed or floating offshore installation or structure engaged in gas or oil exploration, exploitation or production activities, or loading or unloading of oil;

3.   'Exploration' includes any drilling activity but not seismic investigations;

4.   'Exploitation' includes any production, well testing or stimulation activity.

Regulation 2 Use of Best Available Technology and Best Environmental Practice

The Contracting Parties undertake to prevent and eliminate pollution from offshore activities by using the principles of Best Available Technology and Best Environmental Practice as defined in Annex II.

Regulation 3 Environmental impact assessment and monitoring

1.   An environmental impact assessment shall be made before an offshore activity is permitted to start. In case of exploitation referred to in Regulation 5 the outcome of this assessment shall be notified to the Commission before the offshore activity is permitted to start.

2.   In connection with the environmental impact assessment the environmental sensitivity of the sea area around a proposed offshore unit should be assessed with respect to the following:

(a)   The importance of the area for birds and marine mammals;

(b)   The importance of the area as fishing or spawning grounds for fish and shellfish, and for aquaculture;

(c)   The recreational importance of the area;

(d)   The composition of the sediment measured as: grain size distribution, dry matter, ignition loss, total hydrocarbon content, and Ba, Cr, Pb, Cu, Hg and Cd content;

(e)   The abundance and diversity of benthic fauna and the content of selected aliphatic and aromatic hydrocarbons.

3. In order to monitor the consequent effects of the exploration phase of the offshore activity studies, at least those referred to in sub-paragraph (d) above, shall be carried out before and after the operation.

4. In order to monitor the consequent effects of the exploitation phase of the offshore activity studies, at least those referred to in sub-paragraphs (d) and (e) above, shall be carried out before the operation, at annual intervals during the operation, and after the operation has been concluded.

Regulation 4 Discharges on the exploration phase

1. The use of oil-based drilling mud or muds containing other harmful substances shall be restricted to cases where it is necessary for geological, technical or safety reasons and only after prior authorization by the appropriate national authority. In such cases appropriate measures shall be taken and appropriate installations provided in order to prevent the discharge of such muds into the marine environment.

2. Oil-based drilling muds and cuttings arising from the use of oil-based drilling muds should not be discharged in the Baltic Sea Area but taken ashore for final treatment or disposal in an environmentally acceptable manner.

3. The discharge of water-based mud and cuttings shall be subject to authorization by the appropriate national authority. Before authorization the content of the water-based mud must be proven to be of low toxicity.

4. The discharge of cuttings arising from the use of water based drilling mud shall not be permitted in specifically sensitive parts of the Baltic Sea Area such as confined or shallow areas with limited water exchange and areas characterized by rare, valuable or particularly fragile ecosystems.

Regulation 5 Discharges on the exploitation phase

In addition to the provisions of Annex IV the following provisions shall apply to discharges:

(a) All chemicals and materials shall be taken ashore and may be discharged only exceptionally after obtaining permission from the appropriate national authority in each individual operation;

(b) The discharge of production water and displacement water is prohibited unless its oil content is proven to be less than 15 mg/I measured by the methods of analysis and sampling to be adopted by the Commission;

(c) If compliance with this limit value cannot be achieved by the use of Best Environmental Practice and Best Available Technology the appropriate national authority may require adequate additional measures to prevent possible pollution of the marine environment of the Baltic Sea Area and allow, if necessary, a higher limit value which shall, however, be as low as possible and in no case exceed 40 mg/I; the oil content shall be measured as provided in sub-paragraph (b) above.

(d) The permitted discharge shall not, in any case, create any unacceptable effects on the marine environment;

(e) In order to benefit from the future development in cleaning and production technology, discharge permits shall be regularly reviewed by the appropriate national authority and the discharge limits shall be revised accordingly.

Regulation 6 Reporting procedure

Each Contracting Party shall require that the operator or any other person having charge of the offshore unit shall report in accordance with the provisions of Regulation 5.1 of Annex VII of this Convention.

Regulation 7 Contingency planning

Each offshore unit shall have a pollution emergency plan approved in accordance with the procedure established by the appropriate national authority. The plan shall contain information on alarm and communication systems, organization of response measures, a list of prepositioned equipment and a description of the measures to be taken in different types of pollution incidents.

Regulation 8 Disused offshore units

The Contracting Parties shall ensure that abandoned, disused offshore units and accidentally wrecked offshore units are entirely removed and brought ashore under the responsibility of the owner and that disused drilling wells are plugged.

Regulation 9 Exchange of information

The Contracting Parties shall continuously exchange information through the Commission on the location and nature of all planned or accomplished offshore activities and on the nature and amounts of discharges as well as on contingency measures that are undertaken.

Convention for the Protection of the Marine Environment of the North-East Atlantic (OSPAR Convention)

Done at 22 September 1992, entry into force, 25 March 1998
(1993) 23 LOSB 32[1]

The Contracting Parties,

Recognising that the marine environment and the fauna and flora which it supports are of vital importance to all nations;

Recognising the inherent worth of the marine environment of the North-East Atlantic and the necessity for providing coordinated protection for it;

Recognising that concerted action at national, regional and global levels is essential to prevent and eliminate marine pollution and to achieve sustainable management of the maritime area, that is, the management of human activities in such a manner that the marine ecosystem will continue to sustain the legitimate uses of the sea and will continue to meet the needs of present and future generations;

Mindful that the ecological equilibrium and the legitimate uses of the sea are threatened by pollution;

Considering the recommendations of the United Nations Conference on the Human Environment, held in Stockholm in June 1972;

Considering also the results of the United Nations Conference on the Environment and Development held in Rio de Janeiro in June 1992;

---

[1] The Convention was amended in 1998 by adding Annex V. In 2007, a new subparagraph (f) was added to Article 3 (2) of Annex II and new paragraphs 3 and 4 were added to Article 3 of Annex III. The 2007 amendments are not yet in force. The text reproduced is a consolidated version incorporating all amendments. Annex I on the prevention and elimination of pollution from land-based sources and Annex IV on the assessment of the quality of the marine environment as well as Appendixes 1 (criteria for the definition of practices and techniques mentioned in paragraph 3(b)(i) of Article 2 of the Convention), 2 (criteria mentioned in paragraph 2 of article 1 of annex I and in paragraph 2 of Article 2 of Annex III) and 3 (criteria for identifying human activities for the purpose of Annex V) omitted.

Recalling the relevant provisions of customary international law reflected in Part XII of the United Nations Law of the Sea Convention and, in particular, Article 197 on global and regional cooperation for the protection and preservation of the marine environment;

Considering that the common interests of States concerned with the same marine area should induce them to cooperate at regional or sub-regional levels;

Recalling the positive results obtained within the context of the Convention for the prevention of marine pollution by dumping from ships and aircraft signed in Oslo on 15th February 1972, as amended by the protocols of 2nd March 1983 and 5th December 1989, and the Convention for the prevention of marine pollution from land-based sources signed in Paris on 4th June 1974, as amended by the protocol of 26th March 1986;

Convinced that further international action to prevent and eliminate pollution of the sea should be taken without delay, as part of progressive and coherent measures to protect the marine environment;

Recognising that it may be desirable to adopt, on the regional level, more stringent measures with respect to the prevention and elimination of pollution of the marine environment or with respect to the protection of the marine environment against the adverse effects of human activities than are provided for in international conventions or agreements with a global scope;

Recognising that questions relating to the management of fisheries are appropriately regulated under international and regional agreements dealing specifically with such questions;

Considering that the present Oslo and Paris Conventions do not adequately control some of the many sources of pollution, and that it is therefore justifiable to replace them with the present Convention, which addresses all sources of pollution of the marine environment and the adverse effects of human activities upon it, takes into account the precautionary principle and strengthens regional cooperation;

Have agreed as follows:

Article 1 Definitions

For the purposes of the Convention:

(a) 'Maritime area' means the internal waters and the territorial seas of the Contracting Parties, the sea beyond and adjacent to the territorial sea under the jurisdiction of the coastal state to the extent recognised by international law, and the high seas, including the bed of all those waters and its sub-soil, situated within the following limits:

(i) those parts of the Atlantic and Arctic Oceans and their dependent seas which lie north of 36° north latitude and between 42° west longitude and 51° east longitude, but excluding:

(1) the Baltic Sea and the Belts lying to the south and east of lines drawn from Hasenore Head to Gniben Point, from Korshage to Spodsbjerg and from Gilbjerg Head to Kullen,

(2) the Mediterranean Sea and its dependent seas as far as the point of intersection of the parallel of 36° north latitude and the meridian of 5° 36′ west longitude;

(ii) that part of the Atlantic Ocean north of 59° north latitude and between 44° west longitude and 42° west longitude.

(b) 'Internal waters' means the waters on the landward side of the baselines from which the breadth of the territorial sea is measured, extending in the case of watercourses up to the freshwater limit.

(c) 'Freshwater limit' means the place in a watercourse where, at low tide and in a period of low freshwater flow, there is an appreciable increase in salinity due to the presence of seawater.

(d) 'Pollution' means the introduction by man, directly or indirectly, of substances or energy into the maritime area which results, or is likely to result, in hazards to human health, harm to living resources and marine ecosystems, damage to amenities or interference with other legitimate uses of the sea.

(e) 'Land-based sources' means point and diffuse sources on land from which substances or energy reach the maritime area by water, through the air, or directly from the coast. It includes sources associated with any deliberate disposal under the sea-bed made accessible from land by tunnel, pipeline or other means and sources associated with man-made structures placed, in the maritime area under the jurisdiction of a Contracting Party, other than for the purpose of offshore activities.

(f) 'Dumping' means:
   (i)   any deliberate disposal in the maritime area of wastes or other matter
         (1) from vessels or aircraft;
         (2) from offshore installations;
   (ii) any deliberate disposal in the maritime area of
         (1) vessels or aircraft;
         (2) offshore installations and offshore pipelines.

(g) 'Dumping' does not include:
   (i)   the disposal in accordance with the International Convention for the Prevention of Pollution from Ships, 1973, as modified by the Protocol of 1978 relating thereto, or other applicable international law, of wastes or other matter incidental to, or derived from, the normal operations of vessels or aircraft or offshore installations other than wastes or other matter transported by or to vessels or aircraft or offshore installations for the purpose of disposal of such wastes or other matter or derived from the treatment of such wastes or other matter on such vessels or aircraft or offshore installations;
   (ii) placement of matter for a purpose other than the mere disposal thereof, provided that, if the placement is for a purpose other than that for which the matter was originally designed or constructed, it is in accordance with the relevant provisions of the Convention; and
   (iii) for the purposes of Annex III, the leaving wholly or partly in place of a disused offshore installation or disused offshore pipeline, provided that any such operation takes place in accordance with any relevant provision of the Convention and with other relevant international law.

(h) 'Incineration' means any deliberate combustion of wastes or other matter in the maritime area for the purpose of their thermal destruction.

(i) 'Incineration' does not include the thermal destruction of wastes or other matter in accordance with applicable international law incidental to, or derived from the normal operation of vessels or aircraft, or offshore installations other than the thermal destruction of wastes or other matter on vessels or aircraft or offshore installations operating for the purpose of such thermal destruction.

(j) 'Offshore activities' means activities carried out in the maritime area for the purposes of the exploration, appraisal or exploitation of liquid and gaseous hydrocarbons.

(k) 'Offshore sources' means offshore installations and offshore pipelines from which substances or energy reach the maritime area.

(l) 'Offshore installation' means any man-made structure, plant or vessel or parts thereof, whether floating or fixed to the seabed, placed within the maritime area for the purpose of offshore activities.

(m) 'Offshore pipeline' means any pipeline which has been placed in the maritime area for the purpose of offshore activities.

(n) 'Vessels or aircraft' means waterborne or airborne craft of any type whatsoever, their parts and other fittings. This expression includes air-cushion craft, floating craft whether self-propelled or not, and other man-made structures in the maritime area and their equipment, but excludes offshore installations and offshore pipelines.

(o) 'Wastes or other matter' does not include:
  (i) human remains;
  (ii) offshore installations;
  (iii) offshore pipelines;
  (iv) unprocessed fish and fish offal discarded from fishing vessels.

(p) 'Convention' means, unless the text otherwise indicates, the Convention for the Protection of the Marine Environment of the North-East Atlantic, its Annexes and Appendices.

(q) 'Oslo Convention' means the Convention for the Prevention of Marine Pollution by Dumping from Ships and Aircraft signed in Oslo on 15th February 1972, as amended by the protocols of 2nd March 1983 and 5th December 1989.

(r) 'Paris Convention' means the Convention for the Prevention of Marine Pollution from Land-based Sources, signed in Paris on 4th June 1974, as amended by the protocol of 26th March 1986.

(s) 'Regional economic integration organisation' means an organisation constituted by sovereign States of a given region which has competence in respect of matters governed by the Convention and has been duly authorised, in accordance with its internal procedures, to sign, ratify, accept, approve or accede to the Convention.

Article 2 General obligations

1. (a) The Contracting Parties shall, in accordance with the provisions of the Convention, take all possible steps to prevent and eliminate pollution and shall take the necessary measures to protect the maritime area against the adverse effects of human activities so as to safeguard human health and to conserve marine ecosystems and, when practicable, restore marine areas which have been adversely affected.

   (b) To this end Contracting Parties shall, individually and jointly, adopt pro-grammes and measures and shall harmonise their policies and strategies.

2. The Contracting Parties shall apply:

(a) the precautionary principle, by virtue of which preventive measures are to be taken when there are reasonable grounds for concern that substances or energy introduced, directly or indirectly, into the marine environment may bring about hazards to human health, harm living resources and marine ecosystems, damage amenities or interfere with other legitimate uses of the sea, even when there is no conclusive evidence of a causal relationship between the inputs and the effects;

(b) the polluter pays principle, by virtue of which the costs of pollution prevention, control and reduction measures are to be borne by the polluter.

3. (a) In implementing the Convention, Contracting Parties shall adopt programmes and measures which contain, where appropriate, time-limits for their completion and which take full account of the use of the latest technological developments and practices designed to prevent and eliminate pollution fully.

(b) To this end they shall:

(i) taking into account the criteria set forth in Appendix 1, define with respect to programmes and measures the application of, *inter alia*,

(1) best available techniques

(2) best environmental practice

including, where appropriate, clean technology;

(ii) in carrying out such programmes and measures, ensure the application of best available techniques and best environmental practice as so defined, including, where appropriate, clean technology.

4. The Contracting Parties shall apply the measures they adopt in such a way as to prevent an increase in pollution of the sea outside the maritime area or in other parts of the environment.

5. No provision of the Convention shall be interpreted as preventing the Contracting Parties from taking, individually or jointly, more stringent measures with respect to the prevention and elimination of pollution of the maritime area or with respect to the protection of the maritime area against the adverse effects of human activities.

Article 3 Pollution from land-based sources

The Contracting Parties shall take, individually and jointly, all possible steps to prevent and eliminate pollution from land-based sources in accordance with the provisions of the Convention, in particular as provided for in Annex I.

Article 4 Pollution by dumping or incineration

The Contracting Parties shall take, individually and jointly, all possible steps to prevent and eliminate pollution by dumping or incineration of wastes or other matter in accordance with the provisions of the Convention, in particular as provided for in Annex II.

Article 5 Pollution from offshore sources

The Contracting Parties shall take, individually and jointly, all possible steps to prevent and eliminate pollution from offshore sources in accordance with the provisions of the Convention, in particular as provided for in Annex III.

Article 6 Assessment of the quality of the marine environment

The Contracting Parties shall, in accordance with the provisions of the Convention, in particular as provided for in Annex IV:

(a) undertake and publish at regular intervals joint assessments of the quality status of the marine environment and of its development, for the maritime area or for regions or sub-regions thereof;

(b) include in such assessments both an evaluation of the effectiveness of the measures taken and planned for the protection of the marine environment and the identification of priorities for action.

Article 7 Pollution from other sources

The Contracting Parties shall cooperate with a view to adopting Annexes, in addition to the Annexes mentioned in Articles 3, 4, 5 and 6 above, prescribing measures, procedures and standards to protect the maritime area against pollution from other sources, to the extent that such pollution is not already the subject of effective measures agreed by other international organisations or prescribed by other international conventions.

Article 8 Scientific and technical research

1. To further the aims of the Convention, the Contracting Parties shall establish complementary or joint programmes of scientific or technical research and, in accordance with a standard procedure, to transmit to the Commission:

  (a) the results of such complementary, joint or other relevant research;

  (b) details of other relevant programmes of scientific and technical research.

2. In so doing, the Contracting Parties shall have regard to the work carried out, in these fields, by the appropriate international organisations and agencies.

Article 9 Access to information

1. The Contracting Parties shall ensure that their competent authorities are required to make available the information described in paragraph 2 of this Article to any natural or legal person, in response to any reasonable request, without that person's [sic] having to prove an interest, without unreasonable charges, as soon as possible and at the latest within two months.

2. The information referred to in paragraph 1 of this Article is any available information in written, visual, aural or data-base form on the state of the maritime area, on activities or measures adversely affecting or likely to affect it and on activities or measures introduced in accordance with the Convention.

3. The provisions of this Article shall not affect the right of Contracting Parties, in accordance with their national legal systems and applicable international regulations, to provide for a request for such information to be refused where it affects:

  (a) the confidentiality of the proceedings of public authorities, international relations and national defence;

  (b) public security;

  (c) matters which are, or have been, *sub judice*, or under enquiry (including disciplinary enquiries), or which are the subject of preliminary investigation proceedings;

  (d) commercial and industrial confidentiality, including intellectual property;

  (e) the confidentiality of personal data and/or files;

  (f) material supplied by a third party without that party being under a legal obligation to do so;

  (g) material, the disclosure of which would make it more likely that the environment to which such material related would be damaged.

4. The reasons for a refusal to provide the information requested must be given.

Article 10 Commission

1. A Commission, made up of representatives of each of the Contracting Parties, is hereby established. The Commission shall meet at regular intervals and at any time when, due to special circumstances, it is so decided in accordance with the Rules of Procedure.

2. It shall be the duty of the Commission:

  (a) to supervise the implementation of the Convention;

  (b) generally to review the condition of the maritime area, the effectiveness of the measures being adopted, the priorities and the need for any additional or different measures;

  (c) to draw up, in accordance with the General Obligations of the Convention, programmes and measures for the prevention and elimination of pollution and for the control of activities which may, directly or indirectly, adversely affect the maritime area; such programmes and measure [sic] may, when appropriate, include economic instruments;

(d)   to establish at regular intervals its programme of work;

(e)   to set up such subsidiary bodies as it considers necessary and to define their terms of reference;

(f)   to consider and, where appropriate, adopt proposals for the amendment of the Convention in accordance with Articles 15, 16, 17, 18, 19 and 27;

(g)   to discharge the functions conferred by Articles 21 and 23 and such other functions as may be appropriate under the terms of the Convention;

3. To these ends the Commission may, *inter alia,* adopt decisions and recommendations in accordance with Article 13.

4. The Commission shall draw up its Rules of Procedure which shall be adopted by unanimous vote of the Contracting Parties.

5. The Commission shall draw up its Financial Regulations which shall be adopted by unanimous vote of the Contracting Parties.

Article 11 Observers

1. The Commission may, by unanimous vote of the Contracting Parties, decide to admit as an observer:

(a)   any State which is not a Contracting Party to the Convention;

(b)   any international governmental or any non-governmental organisation the activities of which are related to the Convention.

2. Such observers may participate in meetings of the Commission but without the right to vote and may present to the Commission any information or reports relevant to the objectives of the Convention.

3. The conditions for the admission and the participation of observers shall be set in the Rules of Procedure of the Commission.

Article 12 Secretariat

1. A permanent Secretariat is hereby established.

2. The Commission shall appoint an Executive Secretary and determine the duties of that post and the terms and conditions upon which it is to be held.

3. The Executive Secretary shall perform the functions that are necessary for the administration of the Convention and for the work of the Commission as well as the other tasks entrusted to the Executive Secretary by the Commission in accordance with its Rules of Procedure and its Financial Regulations.

Article 13 Decisions and recommendations

1. Decisions and recommendations shall be adopted by unanimous vote of the Contracting Parties. Should unanimity not be attainable, and unless otherwise provided in the Convention, the Commission may nonetheless adopt decisions or recommendations by a three-quarters majority vote of the Contracting Parties.

2. A decision shall be binding on the expiry of a period of two hundred days after its adoption for those Contracting Parties that voted for it and have not within that period notified the Executive Secretary in writing that they are unable to accept the decision, provided that at the expiry of that period three-quarters of the Contracting Parties have either voted for the decision and not withdrawn their acceptance or notified the Executive Secretary in writing that they are able to accept the decision. Such a decision shall become binding on any other Contracting Party which has notified the Executive Secretary in

writing that it is able to accept the decision from the moment of that notification or after the expiry of a period of two hundred days after the adoption of the decision, whichever is later.

3. A notification under paragraph 2 of this Article to the Executive Secretary may indicate that a Contracting Party is unable to accept a decision insofar as it relates to one or more of its dependent or autonomous territories to which the Convention applies.

4. All decisions adopted by the Commission shall, where appropriate, contain provisions specifying the timetable by which the decision shall be implemented.

5. Recommendations shall have no binding force.

6. Decisions concerning any Annex or Appendix shall be taken only by the Contracting Parties bound by the Annex or Appendix concerned.

Article 14 Status of Annexes and Appendices

1. The Annexes and Appendices form an integral part of the Convention.

2. The Appendices shall be of a scientific, technical or administrative nature.

Article 15 Amendment of the Convention

1. Without prejudice to the provisions of paragraph 2 of Article 27 and to specific provisions applicable to the adoption or amendment of Annexes or Appendices, an amendment to the Convention shall be governed by the present Article.

2. Any Contracting Party may propose an amendment to the Convention. The text of the proposed amendment shall be communicated to the Contracting Parties by the Executive Secretary of the Commission at least six months before the meeting of the Commission at which it is proposed for adoption. The Executive Secretary shall also communicate the proposed amendment to the signatories to the Convention for information.

3. The Commission shall adopt the amendment by unanimous vote of the Contracting Parties.

4. The adopted amendment shall be submitted by the Depositary Government to the Contracting Parties for ratification, acceptance or approval. Ratification, acceptance or approval of the amendment shall be notified to the Depositary Government in writing.

5. The amendment shall enter into force for those Contracting Parties which have ratified, accepted or approved it on the thirtieth day after receipt by the Depositary Government of notification of its ratification, acceptance or approval by at least seven Contracting Parties. Thereafter the amendment shall enter into force for any other Contracting Party on the thirtieth day after that Contracting Party has deposited its instrument of ratification, acceptance or approval of the amendment.

Article 16 Adoption of Annexes

The provisions of Article 15 relating to the amendment of the Convention shall also apply to the proposal, adoption and entry into force of an Annex to the Convention, except that the Commission shall adopt any Annex referred to in Article 7 by a three-quarters majority vote of the Contracting Parties.

Article 17 Amendment of Annexes

1. The provisions of Article 15 relating to the amendment of the Convention shall also apply to an amendment to an Annex to the Convention, except that the Commission shall adopt amendments to any Annex referred to in Articles 3, 4, 5, 6 or 7 by a three-quarters majority vote of the Contracting Parties bound by that Annex.

2. If the amendment of an Annex is related to an amendment to the Convention, the amendment of the Annex shall be governed by the same provisions as apply to the amendment to the Convention.

Article 18 Adoption of Appendices

1. If a proposed Appendix is related to an amendment to the Convention or an Annex, proposed for adoption in accordance with Article 15 or Article 17, the proposal, adoption and entry into force of that Appendix shall be governed by the same provisions as apply to the proposal, adoption and entry into force of that amendment.

2. If a proposed Appendix is related to an Annex to the Convention, proposed for adoption in accordance with Article 16, the proposal, adoption and entry into force of that Appendix shall be governed by the same provisions as apply to the proposal, adoption and entry into force of that Annex.

Article 19 Amendment of Appendices

1. Any Contracting Party bound by an Appendix may propose an amendment to that Appendix. The text of the proposed amendment shall be communicated to all Contracting Parties to the Convention by the Executive Secretary of the Commission as provided for in paragraph 2 of Article 15.

2. The Commission shall adopt the amendment to an Appendix by a three-quarters majority vote of the Contracting Parties bound by that Appendix.

3. An amendment to an Appendix shall enter into force on the expiry of a period of two hundred days after its adoption for those Contracting Parties which are bound by that Appendix and have not within that period notified the Depositary Government in writing that they are unable to accept that amendment, provided that at the expiry of that period three-quarters of the Contracting Parties bound by that Appendix have either voted for the amendment and not withdrawn their acceptance or have notified the Depositary Government in writing that they are able to accept the amendment.

4. A notification under paragraph 3 of this Article to the Depositary Government may indicate that a Contracting Party is unable to accept the amendment insofar as it relates to one or more of its dependent or autonomous territories to which the Convention applies.

5. An amendment to an Appendix shall become binding on any other Contracting Party bound by the Appendix which has notified the Depositary Government in writing that it is able to accept the amendment from the moment of that notification or after the expiry of a period of two hundred days after the adoption of the amendment, whichever is later.

6. The Depositary Government shall without delay notify all Contracting Parties of any such notification received.

7. If the amendment of an Appendix is related to an amendment to the Convention or an Annex, the amendment of the Appendix shall be governed by the same provisions as apply to the amendment to the Convention or that Annex.

Article 20 Right to vote

1. Each Contracting Party shall have one vote in the Commission.

2. Notwithstanding the provisions of paragraph 1 of this Article, the European Economic Community and other regional economic integration organisations, within the areas of their competence, are entitled to a number of votes equal to the number of their Member States which are Contracting Parties to the Convention. Those organisations shall not exercise their right to vote in cases where their Member States exercise theirs and conversely.

Article 21 Transboundary pollution

1. When pollution originating from a Contracting Party is likely to prejudice the interests of one or more of the other Contracting Parties to the Convention, the Contracting Parties concerned shall enter into consultation, at the request of any one of them, with a view to negotiating a cooperation agreement.

2. At the request of any Contracting Party concerned, the Commission shall consider the question and may make recommendations with a view to reaching a satisfactory solution.

3. An agreement referred to in paragraph 1 of this Article may, *inter alia,* define the areas to which it shall apply, the quality objectives to be achieved and the methods for achieving these objectives, including methods for the application of appropriate standards and the scientific and technical information to be collected.

4. The Contracting Parties signatory to such an agreement shall, through the medium of the Commission, inform the other Contracting Parties of its purport and of the progress made in putting it into effect.

Article 22 Reporting to the Commission

The Contracting Parties shall report to the Commission at regular intervals on:

(a) the legal, regulatory, or other measures taken by them for the implementation of the provisions of the Convention and of decisions and recommendations adopted thereunder, including in particular measures taken to prevent and punish conduct in contravention of those provisions;

(b) the effectiveness of the measures referred to in subparagraph (a) of this Article;

(c) problems encountered in the implementation of the provisions referred to in subparagraph (a) of this Article.

Article 23 Compliance

The Commission shall:

(a) on the basis of the periodical reports referred to in Article 22 and any other report submitted by the Contracting Parties, assess their compliance with the Convention and the decisions and recommendations adopted thereunder;

(b) when appropriate, decide upon and call for steps to bring about full compliance with the Convention, and decisions adopted thereunder, and promote the implementation of recommendations, including measures to assist a Contracting Party to carry out its obligations.

Article 24 Regionalisation

The Commission may decide that any decision or recommendation adopted by it shall apply to all, or a specified part, of the maritime area and may provide for different timetables to be applied, having regard to the differences between ecological and economic conditions in the various regions and sub-regions covered by the Convention.

Article 25 Signature

The Convention shall be open for signature at Paris from 22nd September 1992 to 30th June 1993 by:

(a) the Contracting Parties to the Oslo Convention or the Paris Convention;

(b) any other coastal State bordering the maritime area;

(c) any State located upstream on watercourses reaching the maritime area;

(d) any regional economic integration organisation having as a member at least one State to which any of the subparagraphs (a) to (c) of this Article applies.

Article 26 Ratification, acceptance or approval

The Convention shall be subject to ratification, acceptance or approval. The instruments of ratification, acceptance or approval shall be deposited with the Government of the French Republic.

Article 27 Accessions

1. After 30th June 1993, the Convention shall be open for accession by the States and regional economic integration organisations referred to in Article 25.

2. The Contracting Parties may unanimously invite States or regional economic integration organisations not referred to in Article 25 to accede to the Convention. In the case of such an accession, the definition of the maritime area shall, if necessary, be amended by a decision of the Commission adopted by unanimous vote of the Contracting Parties. Any such amendment shall enter into force after unanimous approval of all the Contracting Parties on the thirtieth day after the receipt of the last notification by the Depositary Government.

3. Any such accession shall relate to the Convention including any Annex and any Appendix that have been adopted at the date of such accession, except when the instrument of accession contains an express declaration of non-acceptance of one or several Annexes other than Annexes I, II, III and IV.

4. The instruments of accession shall be deposited with the Government of the French Republic.

Article 28 Reservations

No reservation to the Convention may be made.

Article 29 Entry into force

1. The Convention shall enter into force on the thirtieth day following the date on which all Contracting Parties to the Oslo Convention and all Contracting Parties to the Paris Convention have deposited their instrument of ratification, acceptance, approval or accession.

2. For any State or regional economic integration organisation not referred to in paragraph 1 of this Article, the Convention shall enter into force in accordance with paragraph 1 of this Article, or on the thirtieth day following the date of the deposit of the instrument of ratification, acceptance, approval or accession by that State or regional economic integration organisations, whichever is later.

Article 30 Withdrawal

1. At any time after the expiry of two years from the date of entry into force of the Convention for a Contracting Party, that Contracting Party may withdraw from the Convention by notification in writing to the Depositary Government.

2. Except as may be otherwise provided in an Annex other than Annexes I to IV to the Convention, any Contracting Party may at any time after the expiry of two years from the date of entry into force of such Annex for that Contracting Party withdraw from such Annex by notification in writing to the Depositary Government.

3. Any withdrawal referred to in paragraphs 1 and 2 of this Article shall take effect one year after the date on which the notification of that withdrawal is received by the Depositary Government.

Article 31 Replacement of the Oslo and Paris Conventions

1. Upon its entry into force, the Convention shall replace the Oslo and Paris Conventions as between the Contracting Parties.

2. Notwithstanding paragraph 1 of this Article, decisions, recommendations and all other agreements adopted under the Oslo Convention or the Paris Convention shall continue to be applicable, unaltered in their legal nature, to the extent that they are compatible with, or not explicitly terminated by, the Convention, any decisions or, in the case of existing recommendations, any recommendations adopted thereunder.

Article 32 Settlement of disputes

1. Any disputes between Contracting Parties relating to the interpretation or application of the Convention, which cannot be settled otherwise by the Contracting Parties concerned, for instance by means of inquiry or conciliation within the Commission, shall at the request of any of those Contracting Parties, be submitted to arbitration under the conditions laid down in this Article.

2. Unless the parties to the dispute decide otherwise, the procedure of the arbitration referred to in paragraph 1 of this Article shall be in accordance with paragraphs 3 to 10 of this Article.

3. (a) At the request addressed by one Contracting Party to another Contracting Party in accordance with paragraph 1 of this Article, an arbitral tribunal shall be constituted. The request for arbitration shall state the subject matter of the application including in particular the Articles of the Convention, the interpretation or application of which is in dispute.

   (b) The applicant party shall inform the Commission that it has requested the setting up of an arbitral tribunal, stating the name of the other party to the dispute and the Articles of the Convention the interpretation or application of which, in its opinion, is in dispute. The Commission shall forward the information thus received to all Contracting Parties to the Convention.

4. The arbitral tribunal shall consist of three members: each of the parties to the dispute shall appoint an arbitrator; the two arbitrators so appointed shall designate by common agreement the third arbitrator who shall be the chairman of the tribunal. The latter shall not be a national of one of the parties to the dispute, nor have his usual place of residence in the territory of one of these parties, nor be employed by any of them, nor have dealt with the case in any other capacity.

5. (a) If the chairman of the arbitral tribunal has not been designated within two months of the appointment of the second arbitrator, the President of the International Court of Justice shall, at the request of either party, designate him within a further two months' period.

   (b) If one of the parties to the dispute does not appoint an arbitrator within two months of receipt of the request, the other party may inform the President of the International Court of Justice who shall designate the chairman of the arbitral tribunal within a further two months' period. Upon designation, the chairman of the arbitral tribunal shall request the party which has not appointed an arbitrator to do so within two months. After such period, he shall inform the President of the International Court of Justice who shall make this appointment within a further two months' period.

6. (a) The arbitral tribunal shall decide according to the rules of international law and, in particular, those of the Convention.

   (b) Any arbitral tribunal constituted under the provisions of this Article shall draw up its own rules of procedure.

   (c) In the event of a dispute as to whether the arbitral tribunal has jurisdiction, the matter shall be decided by the decision of the arbitral tribunal.

7. (a) The decisions of the arbitral tribunal, both on procedure and on substance, shall be taken by majority voting of its members.

   (b) The arbitral tribunal may take all appropriate measures in order to establish the facts. It may, at the request of one of the parties, recommend essential interim measures of protection.

   (c) If two or more arbitral tribunals constituted under the provisions of this Article are seized of requests with identical or similar subjects, they may inform themselves of the procedures for establishing the facts and take them into account as far as possible.

(d) The parties to the dispute shall provide all facilities necessary for the effective conduct of the proceedings.

(e) The absence or default of a party to the dispute shall not constitute an impediment to the proceedings.

8. Unless the arbitral tribunal determines otherwise because of the particular circumstances of the case, the expenses of the tribunal, including the remuneration of its members, shall be borne by the parties to the dispute in equal shares. The tribunal shall keep a record of all its expenses, and shall furnish a final statement thereof to the parties.

9. Any Contracting Party that has an interest of a legal nature in the subject matter of the dispute which may be affected by the decision in the case, may intervene in the proceedings with the consent of the tribunal.

10. (a) The award of the arbitral tribunal shall be accompanied by a statement of reasons. It shall be final and binding upon the parties to the dispute.

(b) Any dispute which may arise between the parties concerning the interpretation or execution of the award may be submitted by either party to the arbitral tribunal which made the award or, if the latter cannot be seized thereof, to another arbitral tribunal constituted for this purpose in the same manner as the first.

Article 33 Duties of the Depositary Government

The Depositary Government shall inform the Contracting Parties and the signatories to the Convention:

(a) of the deposit of instruments of ratification, acceptance, approval or accession, of declarations of non-acceptance and of notifications of withdrawal in accordance with Articles 26, 27 and 30;

(b) of the date on which the Convention comes into force in accordance with Article 29;

(c) of the receipt of notifications of acceptance, of the deposit of instruments of ratification, acceptance, approval or accession and of the entry into force of amendments to the Convention and of the adoption and amendment of Annexes or Appendices, in accordance with Articles 15, 16, 17, 18 and 19.

Article 34 Original text

The original of the Convention, of which the French and English texts shall be equally authentic, shall be deposited with the Government of the French Republic which shall send certified copies thereof to the Contracting Parties and the signatories to the Convention and shall deposit a certified copy with the Secretary General of the United Nations for registration and publication in accordance with Article 102 of the United Nations Charter.

IN WITNESS WHEREOF, the undersigned, being duly authorised by their respective Governments, have signed this Convention.

DONE at Paris, on the twenty-second day of September 1992

ANNEX II
ON THE PREVENTION AND ELIMINATION OF POLLUTION BY DUMPING OR INCINERATION

Article 1

This Annex shall not apply to any deliberate disposal in the maritime area of:

(a) wastes or other matter from offshore installations;

(b) offshore installations and offshore pipelines.

Article 2

Incineration is prohibited.

Article 3

1. The dumping of all wastes or other matter is prohibited, except for those wastes or other matter listed in paragraphs 2 and 3 of this Article.

2. The list referred to in paragraph 1 of this Article is as follows:

(a) dredged material;

(b) inert materials of natural origin, that is solid, chemically unprocessed geological material the chemical constituents of which are unlikely to be released into the marine environment;

(c) sewage sludge until 31st December 1998;

(d) fish waste from industrial fish processing operations;

(e) vessels or aircraft until, at the latest, 31st December 2004.

(f) carbon dioxide streams from carbon dioxide capture processes for storage, provided:

  i. disposal is into a sub-soil geological formation;

  ii. the streams consist overwhelmingly of carbon dioxide. They may contain incidental associated substances derived from the source material and the capture, transport and storage processes used;

  iii. no wastes or other matter are added for the purpose of disposing of those wastes or other matter;

  iv. they are intended to be retained in these formations permanently and will not lead to significant adverse consequences for the marine environment, human health and other legitimate uses of the maritime area.

3. (a) The dumping of low and intermediate level radioactive substances, including wastes, is prohibited.

  (b) [...]

  (c) [...].[1]

Article 4

1. The Contracting Parties shall ensure that:

(a) no wastes or other matter listed in paragraph 2 of Article 3 of this Annex shall be dumped without authorisation by their competent authorities, or regulation;

(b) such authorisation or regulation is in accordance with the relevant applicable criteria, guidelines and procedures adopted by the Commission in accordance with Article 6 of this Annex;

(c) with the aim of avoiding situations in which the same dumping operation is authorised or regulated by more than one Contracting Party, their competent authorities shall, as appropriate, consult before granting an authorisation or applying regulation.

2. Any authorisation or regulation under paragraph 1 of this Article shall not permit the dumping of vessels or aircraft containing substances which result or are likely to result in hazards to human health, harm to living resources and marine ecosystems, damage to amenities or interference with other legitimate uses of the sea.

---

[1] After the entry into force of OSPAR Decision 98/2 on Dumping Radioactive Waste on 9 February 1999, para. 3 (b) and (c), ceased to have effect.

3. Each Contracting Party shall keep, and report to the Commission records of the nature and the quantities of wastes or other matter dumped in accordance with paragraph 1 of this Article, and of the dates, places and methods of dumping.

Article 5

No placement of matter in the maritime area for a purpose other than that for which it was originally designed or constructed shall take place without authorisation or regulation by the competent authority of the relevant Contracting Party. Such authorisation or regulation shall be in accordance with the relevant applicable criteria, guidelines and procedures adopted by the Commission in accordance with Article 6 of this Annex. This provision shall not be taken to permit the dumping of wastes or other matter otherwise prohibited under this Annex.

Article 6

For the purposes of this Annex, it shall, *inter alia,* be the duty of the Commission to draw up and adopt criteria, guidelines and procedures relating to the dumping of wastes or other matter listed in paragraph 2 of Article 3, and to the placement of matter referred to in Article 5, of this Annex, with a view to preventing and eliminating pollution.

Article 7

The provisions of this Annex concerning dumping shall not apply in case of *force majeure,* due to stress of weather or any other cause, when the safety of human life or of a vessel or aircraft is threatened. Such dumping shall be so conducted as to minimise the likelihood of damage to human or marine life and shall immediately be reported to the Commission, together with full details of the circumstances and of the nature and quantities of the wastes or other matter dumped.

Article 8

The Contracting Parties shall take appropriate measures, both individually and within relevant international organisations, to prevent and eliminate pollution resulting from the abandonment of vessels or aircraft in the maritime area caused by accidents. In the absence of relevant guidance from such international organisations, the measures taken by individual Contracting Parties should be based on such guidelines as the Commission may adopt.

Article 9

In an emergency, if a Contracting Party considers that wastes or other matter the dumping of which is prohibited under this Annex cannot be disposed of on land without unacceptable danger or damage, it shall forthwith consult other Contracting Parties with a view to finding the most satisfactory methods of storage or the most satisfactory means of destruction or disposal under the prevailing circumstances. The Contracting Party shall inform the Commission of the steps adopted following this consultation. The Contracting Parties pledge themselves to assist one another in such situations.

Article 10

1. Each Contracting Party shall ensure compliance with the provisions of this Annex:
(a)   by vessels or aircraft registered in its territory;
(b)   by vessels or aircraft loading in its territory the wastes or other matter which are to be dumped or incinerated;
(c)   by vessels or aircraft believed to be engaged in dumping or incineration within its internal waters or within its territorial sea or within that part of the sea beyond

and adjacent to the territorial sea under the jurisdiction of the coastal state to the extent recognised by international law.

2. Each Contracting Party shall issue instructions to its maritime inspection vessels and aircraft and to other appropriate services to report to its authorities any incidents or conditions in the maritime area which give rise to suspicions that dumping in contravention of the provisions of the present Annex has occurred or is about to occur. Any Contracting Party whose authorities receive such a report shall, if it considers it appropriate, accordingly inform any other Contracting Party concerned.

3. Nothing in this Annex shall abridge the sovereign immunity to which certain vessels are entitled under international law.

ANNEX III
ON THE PREVENTION AND ELIMINATION OF POLLUTION
FROM OFFSHORE SOURCES

Article 1

This Annex shall not apply to any deliberate disposal in the maritime area of:
  (a)   wastes or other matter from vessels or aircraft;
  (b)   vessels or aircraft.

Article 2

1. When adopting programmes and measures for the purpose of this Annex, the Contracting Parties shall require, either individually or jointly, the use of:
  (a)   best available techniques
  (b)   best environmental practice
  including, where appropriate, clean technology.

2. When setting priorities and in assessing the nature and extent of the programmes and measures and their time scales, the Contracting Parties shall use the criteria given in Appendix 2.

Article 3

1. Any dumping of wastes or other matter from offshore installations is prohibited.

2. This prohibition does not relate to discharges or emissions from offshore sources.

3. The prohibition referred to in paragraph 1 of this Article does not apply to carbon dioxide streams from carbon dioxide capture processes for storage, provided:
  (a)   disposal is into a sub-soil geological formation;
  (b)   the streams consist overwhelmingly of carbon dioxide. They may contain incidental associated substances derived from the source material and the capture, transport and storage processes used;
  (c)   no wastes or other matter are added for the purpose of disposing of those wastes or other matter;
  (d)   they are intended to be retained in these formations permanently and will not lead to significant adverse consequences for the marine environment, human health and other legitimate uses of the maritime area.

4. The Contracting Parties shall ensure that no streams referred to in paragraph 3 shall be disposed of in sub-soil geological formations without authorisation or regulation by their competent authorities. Such authorisation or regulation shall, in particular, implement the relevant applicable decisions, recommendations and all other agreements adopted under the Convention.

Article 4

1. The use on, or the discharge or emission from, offshore sources of substances which may reach and affect the maritime area shall be strictly subject to authorisation or regulation by the competent authorities of the Contracting Parties. Such authorisation or regulation shall, in particular, implement the relevant applicable decisions, recommendations and all other agreements adopted under the Convention.

2. The competent authorities of the Contracting Parties shall provide for a system of monitoring and inspection to assess compliance with authorisation or regulation as provided for in paragraph 1 of Article 4 of this Annex.

Article 5

1. No disused offshore installation or disused offshore pipeline shall be dumped and no disused offshore installation shall be left wholly or partly in place in the maritime area without a permit issued by the competent authority of the relevant Contracting Party on a case-by-case basis. The Contracting Parties shall ensure that their authorities, when granting such permits, shall implement the relevant applicable decisions, recommendations and all other agreements adopted under the Convention.

2. No such permit shall be issued if the disused offshore installation or disused offshore pipeline contains substances which result or are likely to result in hazards to human health, harm to living resources and marine ecosystems, damage to amenities or interference with other legitimate uses of the sea.

3. Any Contracting Party which intends to take the decision to issue a permit for the dumping of a disused offshore installation or a disused offshore pipeline placed in the maritime area after 1 January 1998 shall, through the medium of the Commission, inform the other Contracting Parties of its reasons for accepting such dumping, in order to make consultation possible.

4. Each Contracting Party shall keep, and report to the Commission, records of the disused offshore installations and disused offshore pipelines dumped and of the disused offshore installations left in place in accordance with the provisions of this Article, and of the dates, places and methods of dumping.

Article 6

Articles 3 and 5 of this Annex shall not apply in case of *force majeure,* due to stress of weather or any other cause, when the safety of human life or of an offshore installation is threatened. Such dumping shall be so conducted as to minimise the likelihood of damage to human or marine life and shall immediately be reported to the Commission, together with full details of the circumstances and of the nature and quantities of the matter dumped.

Article 7

The Contracting Parties shall take appropriate measures, both individually and within relevant international organisations, to prevent and eliminate pollution resulting from the abandonment of offshore installations in the maritime area caused by accidents. In the absence of relevant guidance from such international organisations, the measures taken by individual Contracting Parties should be based on such guidelines as the Commission may adopt.

Article 8

No placement of a disused offshore installation or a disused offshore pipeline in the maritime area for a purpose other than that for which it was originally designed or constructed shall take place without authorisation or regulation by the competent authority of the relevant Contracting Party. Such authorisation or regulation shall be in accordance with the relevant applicable criteria, guidelines and procedures adopted by the Commission in accordance with subparagraph (d) of Article 10 of this Annex. This provision shall not be taken to permit the dumping of disused offshore installations or disused offshore pipelines in contravention of the provisions of this Annex.

Article 9

1. Each Contracting Party shall issue instructions to its maritime inspection vessels and aircraft and to other appropriate services to report to its authorities any incidents or conditions in the maritime area which give rise to suspicions that a contravention of the provisions of the present Annex has occurred or is about to occur. Any Contracting Party whose authorities receive such a report shall, if it considers it appropriate, accordingly inform any other Contracting Party concerned.

2. Nothing in this Annex shall abridge the sovereign immunity to which certain vessels are entitled under international law.

Article 10

For the purposes of this Annex, it shall, *inter alia,* be the duty of the Commission:
  (a) to collect information about substances which are used in offshore activities and, on the basis of that information, to agree lists of substances for the purposes of paragraph 1 of Article 4 of this Annex;
  (b) to list substances which are toxic, persistent and liable to bioaccumulate and to draw up plans for the reduction and phasing out of their use on, or discharge from, offshore sources;
  (c) to draw up criteria, guidelines and procedures for the prevention of pollution from dumping of disused offshore installations and of disused offshore pipelines, and the leaving in place of offshore installations, in the maritime area;
  (d) to draw up criteria, guidelines and procedures relating to the placement of disused offshore installations and disused offshore pipelines referred to in Article 8 of this Annex, with a view to preventing and eliminating pollution.

ANNEX V
ON THE PROTECTION AND CONSERVATION OF THE ECOSYSTEMS
AND BIOLOGICAL DIVERSITY OF THE MARITIME AREA[1]

Article 1

For the purposes of this Annex and of Appendix 3 the definitions of 'biological diversity', 'ecosystem' and 'habitat' are those contained in the Convention on Biological Diversity of 5 June 1992.

---

[1] The resolution passed by the first Ministerial Meeting of the OSPAR Commission at Sintra, Portugal, in 1998, adopting Annex V, reads:
  Recalling the welcome in the Final Declaration of the Ministerial Meeting of the Oslo and Paris Commissions, 21-22 September 1992, for the possibility under the 1992 OSPAR Convention of addressing matters relating to the protection of the marine environment other than those relating to the prevention and elimination of pollution, and for the possibility of taking any necessary measures on these matters by the adoption of new Annexes to that Convention in the future;
  Recalling the Recitals of the 1992 OSPAR Convention;
  Recalling Article 16 and 18 of that Convention, which provide the procedure for the proposal, adoption and entry into force of new Annexes and of new Appendixes to that Convention;
  Recalling the United Nations Convention on the Law of the Sea, in particular the provisions relating to navigation and the exploitation of natural resources; *(Cont.)*

Article 2

In fulfilling their obligation under the Convention to take, individually and jointly, the necessary measures to protect the maritime area against the adverse effects of human activities so as to safeguard human health and to conserve marine ecosystems and, when practicable, restore marine areas which have been adversely affected, as well as their obligation under the Convention on Biological Diversity of 5 June 1992 to develop strategies, plans or programmes for the conservation and sustainable use of biological diversity, Contracting Parties shall:

(a) take the necessary measures to protect and conserve the ecosystems and the biological diversity of the maritime area, and to restore, where practicable, marine areas which have been adversely affected; and

(b) cooperate in adopting programmes and measures for those purposes for the control of the human activities identified by the application of the criteria in Appendix.

Article 3

1. For the purposes of this Annex, it shall *inter alia* be the duty of the Commission:

(a) to draw up programmes and measures for the control of the human activities identified by the application of the criteria in Appendix 3;

(b) in doing so:

 (i) to collect and review information on such activities and their effects on ecosystems and biological diversity;

 (ii) to develop means, consistent with international law, for instituting protective, conservation, restorative or precautionary measures related to specific areas or sites or related to particular species or habitats;

 (iii) subject to Article 4 of this Annex, to consider aspects of national strategies and guidelines on the sustainable use of components of biological diversity of the maritime area as they affect the various regions and sub-regions of that area;

 (iv) subject to Article 4 of this Annex, to aim for the application of an integrated ecosystem approach.

(c) also in doing so, to take account of programmes and measures adopted by Contracting Parties for the protection and conservation of ecosystems within waters under their sovereignty or jurisdiction.

Recalling the provisions of other global and regional agreements on the protection and conservation of marine ecosystems and biological diversity;

Recalling the importance of coordination and harmonisation of work in different forums for the protection of marine species and their habitats;

Recalling the significant differences which exist between:

(a)   the ecological conditions of the maritime area;

(b) the impacts of human activities affecting these conditions;

in the different regions and sub-regions covered by the 1992 OSPAR Convention;

Recalling the fact that certain Contracting Parties are not coastal states bordering the maritime area;

The Contracting Parties to the Convention for the Protection of the Marine Environment of the North-East Atlantic adopt Annex V and Appendix 3 to the Convention

And further decide that:

(a) programmes or measures under this new Annex shall avoid duplicating action which is already prescribed by other international conventions and the subject of appropriate measures agreed by other international organisations; and

(b) before a programme or measure is adopted under this new Annex, consideration shall be given to whether action could be taken more appropriately under some other international convention or arrangement.

2. In the adoption of such programmes and measures, due consideration shall be given to the question whether any particular programme or measure should apply to all, or a specified part, of the maritime area.

Article 4

1. In accordance with the penultimate recital of the Convention, no programme or measure concerning a question relating to the management of fisheries shall be adopted under this Annex. However where the Commission considers that action is desirable in relation to such a question, it shall draw that question to the attention of the authority or international body competent for that question. Where action within the competence of the Commission is desirable to complement or support action by those authorities or bodies, the Commission shall endeavour to cooperate with them.

2. Where the Commission considers that action under this Annex is desirable in relation to a question concerning maritime transport, it shall draw that question to the attention of the International Maritime Organisation. The Contracting Parties who are members of the International Maritime Organisation shall endeavour to cooperate within that Organisation in order to achieve an appropriate response, including in relevant cases that Organisation's agreement to regional or local action, taking account of any guidelines developed by that Organisation on the designation of special areas, the identification of particularly sensitive areas or other matters.

OSPAR Decision 98/3 on the Disposal of Disused Offshore Installations

Adopted by the Ministerial Meeting of the OSPAR Commission, 23 July 1998;
entry into force, 9 February 1999
OSPAR 98/14/1-E, Annex 33[1]

Recalling the Convention for the Protection of the Marine Environment of the North East Atlantic, in particular Articles 2 and 5 of that Convention,

Recalling the relevant provisions of the United Nations Convention on the Law of the Sea,

Recognising that an increasing number of offshore installations in the maritime area are approaching the end of their operational life-time,

Affirming that the disposal of such installations should be governed by the precautionary principle, which takes account of potential effects on the environment,

Recognising that reuse, recycling or final disposal on land will generally be the preferred option for the decommissioning of offshore installations in the maritime area,

Acknowledging that the national legal and administrative systems of the relevant Contracting Parties need to make adequate provision for establishing and satisfying legal liabilities in respect of disused offshore installations,

The Contracting Parties to the Convention for the Protection of the Marine Environment of the North East Atlantic decide that

Definitions

1. For the purposes of this Decision,

---

[1] Annex 1 (Categories of disused offshore installations where derogations may be considered), 2 (Framework fo the assessment of proposals for the disposal at sea of disused offshore installations), 3 (Consultation procedure) and 4 (Permit conditions and reports) omitted.

'concrete installation' means a disused offshore installation constructed wholly or mainly of concrete;

'disused offshore installation' means an offshore installation, which is neither

- a. serving the purpose of offshore activities for which it was originally placed within the maritime area, nor
- b. serving another legitimate purpose in the maritime area authorised or regulated by the competent authority of the relevant Contracting Party;

but does not include:

- c. any part of an offshore installation which is located below the surface of the sea-bed, or
- d. any concrete anchor-base associated with a floating installation which does not, and is not likely to, result in interference with other legitimate uses of the sea; 'relevant Contracting Party' means the Contracting Party, which has jurisdiction over the offshore installation in question; 'steel installation' means a disused offshore installation, which is constructed wholly or mainly of steel; 'topsides' means those parts of an entire offshore installation which are not part of the substructure and includes modular support frames and decks where their removal would not endanger the structural stability of the substructure; 'footings' means those parts of a steel installation which:
    - (i) are below the highest point of the piles which connect the installation to the sea bed;
    - (ii) in the case of an installation built without piling, form the foundation of the installation and contain amounts of cement grouting similar to those found in footings as defined in sub-paragraph 3(a); or
    - (iii) are so closely connected to the parts mentioned in subparagraphs (i) and (ii) of this definition as to present major engineering problems in severing them from those parts.

Programmes and Measures

2. The dumping, and the leaving wholly or partly in place, of disused offshore installations within the maritime area is prohibited.

3. By way of derogation from paragraph 2, if the competent authority of the relevant Contracting Party is satisfied that an assessment in accordance with Annex 2 shows that there are significant reasons why an alternative disposal mentioned below is preferable to reuse or recycling or final disposal on land, it may issue a permit for

- a. all or part of the footings of a steel installation in a category listed in Annex 1, placed in the maritime area before 9 February 1999, to be left in place;
- b. a concrete installation in a category listed in Annex 1 or constituting a concrete anchor base, to be dumped or left wholly or partly in place;
- c. any other disused offshore installation to be dumped or left wholly or partly in place, when exceptional and unforeseen circumstances resulting from structural damage or deterioration, or from some other cause presenting equivalent difficulties, can be demonstrated.

4. Before a decision is taken to issue a permit under paragraph 3, the relevant Contracting Party shall first consult the other Contracting Parties in accordance with Annex 3.

5. Any permit for a disused offshore installation to be dumped or permanently left wholly or partly in place shall accord with the requirements of Annex 4.

6. Contracting Parties shall report to the Commission by 31 December 1999 and every 2 years thereafter, relevant information on the offshore installations within their

jurisdiction including, when appropriate, information on their disposal for inclusion in the inventory to be maintained by the Commission.

7. In the light of experience in decommissioning offshore installations, in particular those in categories listed in Annex 1, and in the light of relevant research and exchange of information, the Commission shall endeavour to achieve unanimous support for amendments to that Annex in order to reduce the scope of possible derogations under paragraph 3. The preparation of such amendments shall be considered by the Commission at its meeting in 2003 and at regular intervals thereafter.

Entry into force

8. This Decision enters into force on 9 February 1999, and shall then replace Decision 95/1 of the Oslo Commission concerning the Disposal of Offshore Installations.

Implementation Reports

9. If any Contracting Party decides to issue a permit for a disused offshore installation to be dumped or left wholly or partly in place within the maritime area, it shall submit to the Commission at the time of the issue of the permit a report in accordance with paragraph 3 of Annex 4.

10. If any disused offshore installation is dumped or left wholly or partly in place within the maritime area, the relevant Contracting Party shall submit to the Commission, within six months of the disposal, a report in accordance with paragraph 4 of Annex 4.

OSPAR Decision 2007/1 to Prohibit the Storage of Carbon Dioxide Streams in the Water Column or on the Sea-bed

Adopted by the Ministerial Meeting of the OSPAR Commission, 29 June 2007;
entry into force, 15 January 2008
OSPAR 07/24/1-E, Annex 5

Recalling the general obligations in Article 2 of the Convention for the Protection of the Marine Environment of the North-East Atlantic;

Being seriously concerned by the implications for the marine environment of climate change and ocean acidification due to elevated concentrations of carbon dioxide in the atmosphere;

Emphasising the need to further develop renewable and low carbon forms of energy generation and use;

Recognising that carbon dioxide capture and storage is one of a portfolio of options to reduce levels of atmospheric carbon dioxide, and that it represents an important interim supplement to measures for the reduction or prevention of carbon dioxide emissions and should not be considered as a substitute for such measures;

Noting that, since the adoption of the Convention, developments in technology have made it possible to capture carbon dioxide from industrial and energy-related sources, transport it and inject it into geological formations for long-term isolation from the atmosphere and the sea;

Having agreed to amend Annexes II and III to the Convention to facilitate the long-term safe storage of carbon dioxide streams in geological formations and *noting* that regulating such activity is within the scope of the Convention;

Convinced that carbon dioxide storage in the water column or on the sea-bed is not a sustainable storage option, is likely to result in harm to living resources and marine ecosystems and is thus neither a viable solution with regard to mitigating climate change nor compatible with the aims of the Convention;

Concerned that in international fora ocean storage of carbon dioxide in the water column or on the seabed is nevertheless still under consideration;

Noting Article 1(g)(i) which excludes from the definition of dumping the disposal of wastes or other matter incidental to, or derived from, the normal operations of vessels or aircraft as defined in Article 1(n) or offshore installations as defined in Article 1(l);

Noting further Article 1(g)(ii) which excludes from the definition of dumping the placement of matter for a purpose other than the mere disposal thereof;

The Contracting Parties to the Convention for the Protection of the Marine Environment of the North-East Atlantic decide that:

The placement[1] of carbon dioxide streams in the water column or on the seabed is prohibited, unless it results from normal operations as described in Article 1(g)(i) of the Convention or is for a purpose other than the mere disposal thereof as described in Article 1(g)(ii) of the Convention and is in accordance with the relevant provisions of the Convention.

This Decision enters into force on 15 January 2008.

OSPAR Decision 2007/2 on the Storage of Carbon Dioxide Streams in Geological Formations

Adopted by the Ministerial Meeting of the OSPAR Commission, 29 June 2007;
entry into force, 15 January 2008
OSPAR 07/24/1-E, Annex 6

Recalling the general obligations in Article 2 of the Convention for the Protection of the Marine Environment of the North-East Atlantic;

Recalling Article 21 of the Convention on procedures for consultation between Contracting Parties;

Recalling also the adoption of the amendments of Annex II and Annex III to the OSPAR Convention relating to the storage of carbon dioxide streams in geological formations;

Emphasising the need for the storage of carbon dioxide streams to be environmentally safe and to ensure net reductions of carbon dioxide emissions;

Recalling that carbon dioxide capture and storage is not a mandatory obligation for the Contracting Parties to the Convention but an option which the individual Contracting Parties can choose to allow the use of;

Recognising the need for authorisation or regulation by the competent authorities of the Contracting Parties to effectively control the storage of carbon dioxide streams in geological formations;

Recognising that guidance on the storage of carbon dioxide streams in geological formations will contribute to the short-term and long-term protection of the maritime area;

Welcoming the finalisation of the OSPAR Guidelines for Risk Assessment and Management of Storage of CO_2 Streams in Geological Formations;

---

[1] Footnote in original: For the purpose of this Decision, the term 'placement' encompasses the term 'disposal'.

Being aware of the fact that scientific knowledge of the environmental risks of storage of carbon dioxide streams in geological formations is in development and that the Guidelines for Risk Assessment and Management of Storage of Carbon Dioxide Streams in Geological Formations, including the Framework for Risk Assessment and Management, will be evaluated and reviewed as this knowledge progresses;

The Contracting Parties to the Convention for the Protection of the Marine Environment of the North-East Atlantic *decide*:

1. Definitions

1.1 For the purpose of this Decision:

'geological formations' means geological formations in the sub-soil of the OSPAR maritime area, including sub-seabed geological formations;

'carbon dioxide streams' means those streams that consist overwhelmingly of carbon dioxide from carbon dioxide capture processes for storage in geological formations in the sub-soil of the OSPAR maritime area. Provided that no wastes or other matter are added for the purpose of disposing of those wastes or other matter, the carbon dioxide streams may contain incidental associated substances derived from the source material and the capture, transport and storage processes used;

'operator' means companies operating or controlling the operations of installations used for the process of capture and storage of carbon dioxide streams in geological formations.

2. Purpose and scope

2.1 The purpose of the Decision is that by application of the OSPAR Guidelines for Risk Assessment and Management of Storage of CO_2 Streams in Geological Formations, authorities shall ensure that carbon dioxide streams, which are stored in geological formations, are intended to be retained in these formations permanently and will not lead to significant adverse consequences for the marine environment, human health and other legitimate uses of the maritime area.

This Decision shall be applied to any regulatory action, such as the granting of permits or approvals by the competent authorities concerning the storage of carbon dioxide streams in geological formations.

3. Programmes and Measures

3.1 The storage in geological formations of carbon dioxide streams from carbon dioxide capture processes shall not be permitted by Contracting Parties without authorisation or regulation by their competent authorities. Any authorisation or regulation shall be in accordance with the OSPAR Guidelines for Risk Assessment and Management of Storage of CO_2 Streams in Geological Formations, as updated from time to time. A decision to grant a permit or approval shall only be made if a full risk assessment and management process has been completed to the satisfaction of the competent authority and that the storage will not lead to significant adverse consequences for the marine environment, human health and other legitimate uses of the maritime area.

3.2 The provisions of the permit or approval shall ensure the avoidance of significant adverse effects on the marine environment, bearing in mind that the ultimate objective is permanent containment of CO_2 streams in geological formations. Any permit or approval issued shall contain at least:

1. a description of the operation, including injection rates;
2. the planned types, amounts and sources of the CO_2 streams, including incidental associated substances, to be stored in the geological formation;

3.   the location of the injection facility;

4.   characteristics of the geological formations;

5.   the methods of transport of the CO_2 stream;

6.   a risk management plan that includes:

  i.   monitoring and reporting requirements;

  ii.   mitigation and remediation options including the pre-closure phases; and

  iii. a requirement for a site closure plan, including a description of post-closure monitoring and mitigation and remediation options; monitoring shall continue until there is confirmation that the probability of any future adverse environmental effects has been reduced to an insignificant level.

3.3   Permits or approvals shall be reviewed at regular intervals, taking into account the results of monitoring programmes and their objectives.

3.4   Contracting Parties shall also encourage operators to make publicly available plans for the storage of carbon dioxide streams in geological formations and subsequent progress reports on the realization and performance of the various phases of those activities throughout the life cycle of the project.

3.5   The competent authorities shall require reports, including post-closure reports on the results of the risk assessment and management process from the operator. The data from these reports shall be made available to the Commission.

3.6   Sufficient stakeholder involvement shall be ensured in the process of risk assessment and management as to ensure completeness in the assessment process.

4.   Entry into Force

4.1   This Decision enters into force, in respect of storage in accordance with Annex I to the Convention, on 15 January 2008 and, in respect of storage in accordance with Annexes II and III, from the date of entry into force of the amendments of those Annexes.

5.   Implementation Report

5.1   A Contracting Party that issues a permit for the storage of carbon dioxide streams in geological formations shall notify the Executive Secretary. The Executive Secretary shall send copies of the notification to all Contracting Parties.

5.2   Subsequent to the notification of a permit, the Contracting Party shall report to the next meeting of the appropriate OSPAR subsidiary body on the implementation of this Decision using, to the extent possible, the format as set out in Appendix 1.[2] Subsequent implementation reports shall be made annually.

Agreement to Promote Compliance with International Conservation and Management Measures by Fishing Vessels on the High Seas

Done at Rome, 24 November 1993; entry into force, 24 April 2003
2221 UNTS 120 [Registration Number 39486]

The Parties to this Agreement,

Recognizing that all States have the right for their nationals to engage in fishing on the high seas, subject to the relevant rules of international law, as reflected in the United Nations Convention on the Law of the Sea,

---

[2] Appendix 1 omitted.

Further recognizing that, under international law as reflected in the United Nations Convention on the Law of the Sea, all States have the duty to take, or to cooperate with other States in taking, such measures for their respective nationals as may be necessary for the conservation of the living resources of the high seas,

Acknowledging the right and interest of all States to develop their fishing sectors in accordance with their national policies, and the need to promote cooperation with developing countries to enhance their capabilities to fulfil their obligations under this Agreement,

Recalling that Agenda 21, adopted by the United Nations Conference on Environment and Development, calls upon States to take effective action, consistent with international law, to deter reflagging of vessels by their nationals as a means of avoiding compliance with applicable conservation and management rules for fishing activities on the high seas,

Further recalling that the Declaration of Cancun, adopted by the International Conference on Responsible Fishing, also calls on States to take action in this respect,

Bearing in mind that under Agenda 21, States commit themselves to the conservation and sustainable use of marine living resources on the high seas,

Calling upon States which do not participate in global, regional or subregional fisheries organizations or arrangements to join or, as appropriate, to enter into understandings with such organizations or with parties to such organizations or arrangements with a view to achieving compliance with international conservation and management measures,

Conscious of the duties of every State to exercise effectively its jurisdiction and control over vessels flying its flag, including fishing vessels and vessels engaged in the transhipment of fish,

Mindful that the practice of flagging or reflagging fishing vessels as a means of avoiding compliance with international conservation and management measures for living marine resources, and the failure of flag States to fulfil their responsibilities with respect to fishing vessels entitled to fly their flag, are among the factors that seriously undermine the effectiveness of such measures,

Realizing that the objective of this Agreement can be achieved through specifying flag States' responsibility in respect of fishing vessels entitled to fly their flags and operating on the high seas, including the authorization by the flag State of such operations, as well as through strengthened international cooperation and increased transparency through the exchange of information on high seas fishing,

Noting that this Agreement will form an integral part of the International Code of Conduct for Responsible Fishing called for in the Declaration of Cancun,

Desiring to conclude an international agreement within the framework of the Food and Agriculture Organization of the United Nations, hereinafter referred to as FAO, under Article XIV of the FAO Constitution,

Have agreed as follows:

Article I Definitions

For the purposes of this Agreement:

(a) 'fishing vessel' means any vessel used or intended for use for the purposes of the commercial exploitation of living marine resources, including mother ships and any other vessels directly engaged in such fishing operations;

(b) 'international conservation and management measures' means measures to conserve or manage one or more species of living marine resources that are adopted and applied in accordance with the relevant rules of international law as reflected in the 1982 United Nations Convention on the Law of the Sea. Such measures may be adopted either by global, regional or subregional fisheries organizations, subject to the rights and obligations of their members, or by treaties or other international agreements;

(c) 'length' means

(i) for any fishing vessel built after 18 July 1982, 96 percent of the total length on a waterline at 85 percent of the least moulded depth measured from the top of the keel, or the length from the foreside of the stem to the axis of the rudder stock on that waterline, if that be greater. In ships designed with a rake of keel the waterline on which this length is measured shall be parallel to the designed waterline;

(ii) for any fishing vessel built before 18 July 1982, registered length as entered on the national register or other record of vessels;

(d) 'record of fishing vessels' means a record of fishing vessels in which are recorded pertinent details of the fishing vessel. It may constitute a separate record for fishing vessels or form part of a general record of vessels;

(e) 'regional economic integration organization' means a regional economic integration organization to which its Member States have transferred competence over matters covered by this Agreement, including the authority to make decisions binding on its Member States in respect of those matters;

(f) 'vessels entitled to fly its flag' and 'vessels entitled to fly the flag of a State', includes vessels entitled to fly the flag of a Member State of a regional economic integration organization.

Article II Application

1. Subject to the following paragraphs of this Article, this Agreement shall apply to all fishing vessels that are used or intended for fishing on the high seas.

2. A Party may exempt fishing vessels of less than 24 metres in length entitled to fly its flag from the application of this Agreement unless the Party determines that such an exemption would undermine the object and purpose of this Agreement, provided that such exemptions:

(a) shall not be granted in respect of fishing vessels operating in fishing regions referred to in paragraph 3 below, other than fishing vessels that are entitled to fly the flag of a coastal State of that fishing region; and

(b) shall not apply to the obligations undertaken by a Party under paragraph 1 of Article III, or paragraph 7 of Article VI of this Agreement.

3. Without prejudice to the provisions of paragraph 2 above, in any fishing region where bordering coastal States have not yet declared exclusive economic zones, or equivalent zones of national jurisdiction over fisheries, such coastal States as are Parties to this Agreement may agree, either directly or through appropriate regional fisheries organizations, to establish a minimum length of fishing vessels below which this Agreement shall not apply in respect of fishing vessels flying the flag of any such coastal State and operating exclusively in such fishing region.

Article III Flag State responsibility

1. (a) Each Party shall take such measures as may be necessary to ensure that fishing vessels entitled to fly its flag do not engage in any activity that undermines the effectiveness of international conservation and management measures.

(b) In the event that a Party has, pursuant to paragraph 2 of Article II, granted an exemption for fishing vessels of less than 24 metres in length entitled to fly its flag from the application of other provisions of this Agreement, such Party shall nevertheless take effective measures in respect of any such fishing vessel that undermines the effectiveness of international conservation and management measures. These measures shall be such as to ensure that the fishing vessel ceases to engage in activities that undermine the effectiveness of the international conservation and management measures.

2. In particular, no Party shall allow any fishing vessel entitled to fly its flag to be used for fishing on the high seas unless it has been authorized to be so used by the appropriate authority or authorities of that Party. A fishing vessel so authorized shall fish in accordance with the conditions of the authorization.

3. No Party shall authorize any fishing vessel entitled to fly its flag to be used for fishing on the high seas unless the Party is satisfied that it is able, taking into account the links that exist between it and the fishing vessel concerned, to exercise effectively its responsibilities under this Agreement in respect of that fishing vessel.

4. Where a fishing vessel that has been authorized to be used for fishing on the high seas by a Party ceases to be entitled to fly the flag of that Party, the authorization to fish on the high seas shall be deemed to have been cancelled.

5.   (a) No Party shall authorize any fishing vessel previously registered in the territory of another Party that has undermined the effectiveness of international conservation and management measures to be used for fishing on the high seas, unless it is satisfied that

      (i)   any period of suspension by another Party of an authorization for such fishing vessel to be used for fishing on the high seas has expired; and

      (ii) no authorization for such fishing vessel to be used for fishing on the high seas has been withdrawn by another Party within the last three years.

  (b) The provisions of subparagraph (a) above shall also apply in respect of fishing vessels previously registered in the territory of a State which is not a Party to this Agreement, provided that sufficient information is available to the Party concerned on the circumstances in which the authorization to fish was suspended or withdrawn.

  (c) The provisions of subparagraphs (a) and (b) shall not apply where the ownership of the fishing vessel has subsequently changed, and the new owner has provided sufficient evidence demonstrating that the previous owner or operator has no further legal, beneficial or financial interest in, or control of, the fishing vessel.

  (d) Notwithstanding the provisions of subparagraphs (a) and (b) above, a Party may authorize a fishing vessel, to which those subparagraphs would otherwise apply, to be used for fishing on the high seas, where the Party concerned, after having taken into account all relevant facts, including the circumstances in which the fishing authorization has been withdrawn by the other Party or State, has determined that to grant an authorization to use the vessel for fishing on the high seas would not undermine the object and purpose of this Agreement.

6. Each Party shall ensure that all fishing vessels entitled to fly its flag that it has entered in the record maintained under Article IV are marked in such a way that they can be readily identified in accordance with generally accepted standards, such as the FAO Standard Specifications for the Marking and Identification of Fishing Vessels.

7. Each Party shall ensure that each fishing vessel entitled to fly its flag shall provide it with such information on its operations as may be necessary to enable the Party to fulfil its obligations under this Agreement, including in particular information pertaining to the area of its fishing operations and to its catches and landings.

8. Each Party shall take enforcement measures in respect of fishing vessels entitled to fly its flag which act in contravention of the provisions of this Agreement, including, where appropriate, making the contravention of such provisions an offence under national legislation. Sanctions applicable in respect of such contraventions shall be of sufficient gravity as to be effective in securing compliance with the requirements of this Agreement and to deprive offenders of the benefits accruing from their illegal activities. Such sanctions shall, for serious offences, include refusal, suspension or withdrawal of the authorization to fish on the high seas.

Article IV Records of fishing vessels

Each Party shall, for the purposes of this Agreement, maintain a record of fishing vessels entitled to fly its flag and authorized to be used for fishing on the high seas, and shall take such measures as may be necessary to ensure that all such fishing vessels are entered in that record.

Article V International cooperation

1. The Parties shall cooperate as appropriate in the implementation of this Agreement, and shall, in particular, exchange information, including evidentiary material, relating to activities of fishing vessels in order to assist the flag State in identifying those fishing vessels flying its flag reported to have engaged in activities undermining international conservation and management measures, so as to fulfil its obligations under Article 3.

2. When a fishing vessel is voluntarily in the port of a Party other than its flag State, that Party, where it has reasonable grounds for believing that the fishing vessel has been used for an activity that undermines the effectiveness of international conservation and management measures, shall promptly notify the flag State accordingly. Parties may make arrangements regarding the undertaking by port States of such investigatory measures as may be considered necessary to establish whether the fishing vessel has indeed been used contrary to the provisions of this Agreement.

3. The Parties shall, when and as appropriate, enter into cooperative agreements or arrangements of mutual assistance on a global, regional, subregional or bilateral basis so as to promote the achievement of the objectives of this Agreement.

Article VI Exchange of information

1. Each Party shall make readily available to FAO the following information with respect to each fishing vessel entered in the record required to be maintained under Article IV:

    (a) name of fishing vessel, registration number, previous names (if known), and port of registry;

    (b) previous flag (if any);

    (c) International Radio Call Sign (if any);

    (d) name and address of owner or owners;

    (e) where and when built;

    (f) type of vessel;

    (g) length.

2. Each Party shall, to the extent practicable, make available to FAO the following additional information with respect to each fishing vessel entered in the record required to be maintained under Article IV:

    (a)   name and address of operator (manager) or operators (managers) (if any);

    (b)   type of fishing method or methods;

    (c)   moulded depth;

    (d)   beam;

    (e)   gross register tonnage;

    (f)   power of main engine or engines.

    3.   Each Party shall promptly notify to FAO any modifications to the information listed in paragraphs 1 and 2 of this Article.

    4.   FAO shall circulate periodically the information provided under paragraphs 1, 2, and 3 of this Article to all Parties, and, on request, individually to any Party. FAO shall also, subject to any restrictions imposed by the Party concerned regarding the distribution of information, provide such information on request individually to any global, regional or subregional fisheries organization.

    5.   Each Party shall also promptly inform FAO of –

    (a)   any additions to the record;

    (b)   any deletions from the record by reason of –

        (i)   the voluntary relinquishment or non-renewal of the fishing authorization by the fishing vessel owner or operator;

        (ii)   the withdrawal of the fishing authorization issued in respect of the fishing vessel under paragraph 8 of Article III;

        (iii)   the fact that the fishing vessel concerned is no longer entitled to fly its flag;

        (iv)   the scrapping, decommissioning or loss of the fishing vessel concerned; or

        (v)   any other reason.

    6.   Where information is given to FAO under paragraph 5 (b) above, the Party concerned shall specify which of the reasons listed in that paragraph is applicable.

    7.   Each Party shall inform FAO of –

    (a)   any exemption it has granted under paragraph 2 of Article II, the number and type of fishing vessel involved and the geographical areas in which such fishing vessels operate; and

    (b)   any agreement reached under paragraph 3 of Article II.

    8.   (a)   Each Party shall report promptly to FAO all relevant information regarding any activities of fishing vessels flying its flag that undermine the effectiveness of international conservation and management measures, including the identity of the fishing vessel or vessels involved and measures imposed by the Party in respect of such activities. Reports on measures imposed by a Party may be subject to such limitations as may be required by national legislation with respect to confidentiality, including, in particular, confidentiality regarding measures that are not yet final.

        (b)   Each Party, where it has reasonable grounds to believe that a fishing vessel not entitled to fly its flag has engaged in any activity that undermines the effectiveness of international conservation and management measures, shall draw this to the attention of the flag State concerned and may, as appropriate, draw it to the attention of FAO. It shall provide the flag State with full supporting evidence and may provide FAO with a summary of such evidence. FAO shall not circulate such information until such time as the flag State has had an opportunity to comment on the allegation and evidence submitted, or to object as the case may be.

    9.   Each Party shall inform FAO of any cases where the Party, pursuant to paragraph 5 (d) of Article III, has granted an authorization notwithstanding the provisions of paragraph

5 (a) or 5 (b) of Article III. The information shall include pertinent data permitting the identification of the fishing vessel and the owner or operator and, as appropriate, any other information relevant to the Party's decision.

10.   FAO shall circulate promptly the information provided under paragraphs 5, 6, 7, 8 and 9 of this Article to all Parties, and, on request, individually to any Party. FAO shall also, subject to any restrictions imposed by the Party concerned regarding the distribution of information, provide such information promptly on request individually to any global, regional or subregional fisheries organization.

11.   The Parties shall exchange information relating to the implementation of this Agreement, including through FAO and other appropriate global, regional and subregional fisheries organizations.

Article VII Cooperation with developing countries

The Parties shall cooperate, at a global, regional, subregional or bilateral level, and, as appropriate, with the support of FAO and other international or regional organizations, to provide assistance, including technical assistance, to Parties that are developing countries in order to assist them in fulfilling their obligations under this Agreement.

Article VIII Non-Parties

1.   The Parties shall encourage any State not party to this Agreement to accept this Agreement and shall encourage any non-Party to adopt laws and regulations consistent with the provisions of this Agreement.

2.   The Parties shall cooperate in a manner consistent with this Agreement and with international law to the end that fishing vessels entitled to fly the flags of non-Parties do not engage in activities that undermine the effectiveness of international conservation and management measures.

3.   The Parties shall exchange information amongst themselves, either directly or through FAO, with respect to activities of fishing vessels flying the flags of non-Parties that undermine the effectiveness of international conservation and management measures.

Article IX Settlement of disputes

1.   Any Party may seek consultations with any other Party or Parties on any dispute with regard to the interpretation or application of the provisions of this Agreement with a view to reaching a mutually satisfactory solution as soon as possible.

2.   In the event that the dispute is not resolved through these consultations within a reasonable period of time, the Parties in question shall consult among themselves as soon as possible with a view to having the dispute settled by negotiation, inquiry, mediation, conciliation, arbitration, judicial settlement or other peaceful means of their own choice.

3.   Any dispute of this character not so resolved shall, with the consent of all Parties to the dispute, be referred for settlement to the International Court of Justice, to the International Tribunal for the Law of the Sea upon entry into force of the 1982 United Nations Convention on the Law of the Sea or to arbitration. In the case of failure to reach agreement on referral to the International Court of Justice, to the International Tribunal for the Law of the Sea or to arbitration, the Parties shall continue to consult and cooperate with a view to reaching settlement of the dispute in accordance with the rules of international law relating to the conservation of living marine resources.

Article X Acceptance

1.   This Agreement shall be open to acceptance by any Member or Associate Member of FAO, and to any non-member State that is a Member of the United Nations, or of any

of the specialized agencies of the United Nations or of the International Atomic Energy Agency.

2. Acceptance of this Agreement shall be effected by the deposit of an instrument of acceptance with the Director-General of FAO, hereinafter referred to as the Director-General.

3. The Director-General shall inform all Parties, all Members and Associate Members of FAO and the Secretary-General of the United Nations of all instruments of acceptance received.

4. When a regional economic integration organization becomes a Party to this Agreement, such regional economic integration organization shall, in accordance with the provisions of Article II.7 of the FAO Constitution, as appropriate, notify such modifications or clarifications to its declaration of competence submitted under Article II.5 of the FAO Constitution as may be necessary in light of its acceptance of this Agreement. Any Party to this Agreement may, at any time, request a regional economic integration organization that is a Party to this Agreement to provide information as to which, as between the regional economic integration organization and its Member States, is responsible for the implementation of any particular matter covered by this Agreement. The regional economic integration organization shall provide this information within a reasonable time.

Article XI Entry into Force

1. This Agreement shall enter into force as from the date of receipt by the Director-General of the twenty-fifth instrument of acceptance.

2. For the purpose of this Article, an instrument deposited by a regional economic integration organization shall not be counted as additional to those deposited by Member States of such an organization.

Article XII Reservations

Acceptance of this Agreement may be made subject to reservations which shall become effective only upon unanimous acceptance by all Parties to this Agreement. The Director-General shall notify forthwith all Parties of any reservation. Parties not having replied within three months from the date of the notification shall be deemed to have accepted the reservation. Failing such acceptance, the State or regional economic integration organization making the reservation shall not become a Party to this Agreement.

Article XIII Amendments

1. Any proposal by a Party for the amendment of this Agreement shall be communicated to the Director-General.

2. Any proposed amendment of this Agreement received by the Director-General from a Party shall be presented to a regular or special session of the Conference for approval and, if the amendment involves important technical changes or imposes additional obligations on the Parties, it shall be considered by an advisory committee of specialists convened by FAO prior to the Conference.

3. Notice of any proposed amendment of this Agreement shall be transmitted to the Parties by the Director-General not later than the time when the agenda of the session of the Conference at which the matter is to be considered is dispatched.

4. Any such proposed amendment of this Agreement shall require the approval of the Conference and shall come into force as from the thirtieth day after acceptance by two-thirds of the Parties. Amendments involving new obligations for Parties, however, shall come into force in respect of each Party only on acceptance by it and as from the thirtieth day after such acceptance. Any amendment shall be deemed to involve new obligations

for Parties unless the Conference, in approving the amendment, decides otherwise by consensus.

5. The instruments of acceptance of amendments involving new obligations shall be deposited with the Director-General, who shall inform all Parties of the receipt of acceptance and the entry into force of amendments.

6. For the purpose of this Article, an instrument deposited by a regional economic integration organization shall not be counted as additional to those deposited by Member States of such an organization.

Article XIV Withdrawal

Any Party may withdraw from this Agreement at any time after the expiry of two years from the date upon which the Agreement entered into force with respect to that Party, by giving written notice of such withdrawal to the Director-General who shall immediately inform all the Parties and the Members and Associate Members of FAO of such withdrawal. Withdrawal shall become effective at the end of the calendar year following that in which the notice of withdrawal has been received by the Director-General.

Article XV Duties of the Depositary

The Director-General shall be the Depositary of this Agreement. The Depositary shall:

(a)   send certified copies of this Agreement to each Member and Associate Member of FAO and to such non-member States as may become Party to this Agreement;

(b)   arrange for the registration of this Agreement, upon its entry into force, with the Secretariat of the United Nations in accordance with Article 102 of the Charter of the United Nations;

(c)   inform each Member and Associate Member of FAO and any non-member States as may become Party to this Agreement of:

(i)   instruments of acceptance deposited in accordance with Article X;

(ii)   the date of entry into force of this Agreement in accordance with Article XI;

(iii) proposals for and the entry into force of amendments to this Agreement in accordance with Article XIII;

(iv) withdrawals from this Agreement pursuant to Article XIV.

Article XVI Authentic Texts

The Arabic, Chinese, English, French, and Spanish texts of this Agreement are equally authentic.

Convention for the Conservation of Southern Bluefin Tuna

Done at Canberra, 10 May 1993; entry into force, 20 May 1994
1819 UNTS 360 [Registration Number 31155]

The Parties to this Convention:

Considering their mutual interest in southern bluefin tuna;

Recalling that Australia, Japan and New Zealand have already taken certain measures for the conservation and management of southern bluefin tuna;

Paying due regard to the rights and obligations of the Parties under relevant principles of international law;

Noting the adoption of the United Nations Convention on the Law of the Sea in 1982;

Noting that States have established exclusive economic or fishery zones within which they exercise, in accordance with international law, sovereign rights or jurisdiction for the purposes of exploring and exploiting, conserving and managing the living resources;

Recognising that southern bluefin tuna is a highly migratory species which migrates through such zones;

Noting that the coastal States through whose exclusive economic or fishery zones southern bluefin tuna migrates exercise sovereign rights within such zones for the purpose of exploring and exploiting, conserving and managing the living resources including southern bluefin tuna;

Acknowledging the importance of scientific research for the conservation and management of southern bluefin tuna and the importance of collecting scientific information relating to southern bluefin tuna and ecologically related species;

Recognising that it is essential that they cooperate to ensure the conservation and optimum utilisation of southern bluefin tuna;

Have agreed as follows:

Article 1

This Convention shall apply to southern bluefin tuna (*Thunnus maccoyii*).

Article 2

For the purposes of this Convention:

(a) 'ecologically related species' means living marine species which are associated with southern bluefin tuna, including but not restricted to both predators and prey of southern bluefin tuna;

(b) 'fishing' means:

(i) the catching, taking or harvesting of fish, or any other activity which can reasonably be expected to result in the catching, taking or harvesting of fish; or

(ii) any operation at sea in preparation for or in direct support of any activity described in sub-paragraph (i) above.

Article 3

The objective of this Convention is to ensure, through appropriate management, the conservation and optimum utilisation of southern bluefin tuna.

Article 4

Nothing in this Convention nor any measures adopted pursuant to it shall be deemed to prejudice the positions or views of any Party with respect to its rights and obligations under treaties and other international agreements to which it is party or its positions or views with respect to the law of the sea.

Article 5

1. Each Party shall take all action necessary to ensure the enforcement of this Convention and compliance with measures which become binding under paragraph 7 of Article 8.

2.   The Parties shall expeditiously provide to the Commission for the Conservation of Southern Bluefin Tuna scientific information, fishing catch and effort statistics and other data relevant to the conservation of southern bluefin tuna and, as appropriate, ecologically related species.

3.   The Parties shall cooperate in collection and direct exchange, when appropriate, of fisheries data, biological samples and other information relevant for scientific research on southern bluefin tuna and ecologically related species.

4.   The Parties shall cooperate in the exchange of information regarding any fishing for southern bluefin tuna by nationals, residents and vessels of any State or entity not party to this Convention.

Article 6

1.   The Parties hereby establish and agree to maintain the Commission for the Conservation of Southern Bluefin Tuna (hereinafter referred to as 'the Commission').

2.   Each Party shall be represented on the Commission by not more than three delegates who may be accompanied by experts and advisers.

3.   The Commission shall hold an annual meeting before 1 August each year or at such other time as it may determine.

4.   At each annual meeting the Commission shall elect from among the delegates a Chair and a Vice-Chair. The Chair and the Vice-Chair shall be elected from different Parties and shall remain in office until the election of their successors at the next annual meeting. A delegate, when acting as Chair, shall not vote.

5.   Special meetings of the Commission shall be convened by the Chair at the request of a Party supported by at least two other Parties.

6.   A special meeting may consider any matter of relevance to this Convention.

7.   Two-thirds of the Parties shall constitute a quorum.

8.   The rules of procedure of the Commission and other internal administrative regulations as may be necessary to carry out its functions shall be decided upon at the first meeting of the Commission and may be amended by the Commission as occasion may require.

9.   The Commission shall have legal personality and shall enjoy in its relations with other international organisations and in the territories of the Parties such legal capacity as may be necessary to perform its functions and achieve its ends. The immunities and privileges which the Commission and its officers shall enjoy in the territory of a Party shall be subject to agreement between the Commission and the Party concerned.

10.   The Commission shall determine the location of its headquarters at such time as a Secretariat is established pursuant to paragraph 1 of Article 10.

11.   The official languages of the Commission shall be Japanese and English. Proposals and data may be submitted to the Commission in either language.

Article 7

Each Party shall have one vote in the Commission. Decisions of the Commission shall be taken by a unanimous vote of the Parties present at the Commission meeting.

Article 8

1.   The Commission shall collect and accumulate information described below:
(a)   scientific information, statistical data and other information relating to southern bluefin tuna and ecologically related species;
(b)   information relating to laws, regulations and administrative measures on southern bluefin tuna fisheries;

(c)   any other information relating to southern bluefin tuna.

2.   The Commission shall consider matters described below:

(a)   interpretation or implementation of this Convention and measures adopted pursuant to it;

(b)   regulatory measures for conservation, management and optimum utilisation of southern bluefin tuna;

(c)   matters which shall be reported by the Scientific Committee prescribed in Article 9;

(d)   matters which may be entrusted to the Scientific Committee prescribed in Article 9;

(e)   matters which may be entrusted to the Secretariat prescribed in Article 10;

(f)   other activities necessary to carry out the provisions of this Convention.

3.   For the conservation, management and optimum utilisation of southern bluefin tuna:

(a)   the Commission shall decide upon a total allowable catch and its allocation among the Parties unless the Commission decides upon other appropriate measures on the basis of the report and recommendations of the Scientific Committee referred to in paragraph 2(c) and (d) of Article 9; and

(b)   the Commission may, if necessary, decide upon other additional measures.

4.   In deciding upon allocations among the Parties under paragraph 3 above the Commission shall consider:

(a)   relevant scientific evidence;

(b)   the need for orderly and sustainable development of southern bluefin tuna fisheries;

(c)   the interests of Parties through whose exclusive economic or fishery zones southern bluefin tuna migrates;

(d)   the interests of Parties whose vessels engage in fishing for southern bluefin tuna including those which have historically engaged in such fishing and those which have southern bluefin tuna fisheries under development;

(e)   the contribution of each Party to conservation and enhancement of, and scientific research on, southern bluefin tuna;

(f)   any other factors which the Commission deems appropriate.

5.   The Commission may decide upon recommendations to the Parties in order to further the attainment of the objective of this Convention.

6.   In deciding upon measures under paragraph 3 above and recommendations under paragraph 5 above, the Commission shall take full account of the report and recommendations of the Scientific Committee under paragraph 2(c) and (d) of Article 9.

7.   All measures decided upon under paragraph 3 above shall be binding on the Parties.

8.   The Commission shall notify all Parties promptly of measures and recommendations decided upon by the Commission.

9.   The Commission shall develop, at the earliest possible time and consistent with international law, systems to monitor all fishing activities related to southern bluefin tuna in order to enhance scientific knowledge necessary for conservation and management of southern bluefin tuna and in order to achieve effective implementation of this Convention and measures adopted pursuant to it.

10.   The Commission may establish such subsidiary bodies as it considers desirable for the exercise of its duties and functions.

Article 9

1. The Parties hereby establish the Scientific Committee as an advisory body to the Commission.

2. The Scientific Committee shall:

(a)   assess and analyse the status and trends of the population of southern bluefin tuna;

(b)   coordinate research and studies of southern bluefin tuna;

(c)   report to the Commission its findings or conclusions, including consensus, majority and minority views, on the status of the southern bluefin tuna stock and, where appropriate, of ecologically related species;

(d)   make recommendations, as appropriate, to the Commission by consensus on matters concerning the conservation, management and optimum utilisation of southern bluefin tuna;

(e)   consider any matter referred to it by the Commission.

3. A meeting of the Scientific Committee shall be held prior to the annual meeting of the Commission. A special meeting of the Scientific Committee shall be called at any time at the request of a Party provided that such request is supported by at least two other Parties.

4. The Scientific Committee shall adopt and amend as necessary its rules of procedure. The rules and any amendments thereto shall be approved by the Commission.

5.   (a)   Each Party shall be a member of the Scientific Committee and shall appoint to the Committee a representative with suitable scientific qualifications who maybe accompanied by alternates, experts and advisers.

(b)   The Scientific Committee shall elect a Chair and a Vice-Chair. The Chair and the Vice-Chair shall be elected from different Parties.

Article 10

1. The Commission may establish a Secretariat consisting of an Executive Secretary to be appointed by the Commission and appropriate staff on conditions as may be determined by the Commission. The staff shall be appointed by the Executive Secretary.

2. Until such time as a Secretariat is established, the Chair of the Commission shall nominate from within his or her Government an official to act as Secretary to the Commission to perform the secretariat functions set out in paragraph 3 below for a term of one year. At each annual meeting of the Commission, the Chair shall advise the Parties of the name and address of the Secretary.

3. The Secretariat functions shall be prescribed by the Commission, and shall include the following:

(a)   receiving and transmitting the Commission's official communications;

(b)   facilitating the collection of data necessary to accomplish the objective of this Convention;

(c)   preparing administrative and other reports for the Commission and the Scientific Committee.

Article 11

1. The Commission shall decide upon an annual budget.

2. The contributions to the annual budget from each Party shall be calculated on the following basis:

(a)   30% of the budget shall be divided equally among all the Parties; and

(b)   70% of the budget shall be divided in proportion to the nominal catches of southern bluefin tuna among all the Parties.

3. Notwithstanding the provisions of Article 7, any Party that has not paid its contributions for two consecutive years shall not enjoy the right to participate in the

decision-making process in the Commission until it has fulfilled its obligations, unless the Commission decides otherwise.

4. The Commission shall decide upon, and amend as occasion may require, financial regulations for the conduct of the Commission and for the exercise of its functions.

5. Each Party shall meet its own expenses arising from attendance at meetings of the Commission and of the Scientific Committee.

Article 12

The Commission shall collaborate with other inter-governmental organisations which have related objectives, *inter alia*, to obtain the best available information including scientific information to further the attainment of the objective of this Convention and shall seek to avoid duplication with respect to their work. The Commission may make arrangements with such inter-governmental organisations to these ends.

Article 13

With a view to furthering the attainment of the objective of this Convention, the Parties shall cooperate with each other to encourage accession by any State to this Convention where the Commission considers this to be desirable.

Article 14

1. The Commission may invite any State or entity not party to this Convention, whose nationals, residents or fishing vessels harvest southern bluefin tuna, and any coastal State through whose exclusive economic or fishery zone southern bluefin tuna migrates, to send observers to meetings of the Commission and of the Scientific Committee.

2. The Commission may invite inter-governmental or, on request, non-governmental organisations having special competence concerning southern bluefin tuna to send observers to meetings of the Commission.

Article 15

1. The Parties agree to invite the attention of any State or entity not party to this Convention to any matter relating to the fishing activities of its nationals, residents or vessels which could affect the attainment of the objective of this Convention.

2. Each Party shall encourage its nationals not to associate with the southern bluefin tuna fishery of any State or entity not party to this Convention, where such association could affect adversely the attainment of the objective of this Convention.

3. Each Party shall take appropriate measures aimed at preventing vessels registered under its laws and regulations from transferring their registration for the purpose of avoiding compliance with the provisions of this Convention or measures adopted pursuant to it.

4. The Parties shall cooperate in taking appropriate action, consistent with international law and their respective domestic laws, to deter fishing activities for southern bluefin tuna by nationals, residents or vessels of any State or entity not party to this Convention where such activity could affect adversely the attainment of the objective of this Convention.

Article 16

1. If any dispute arises between two or more of the Parties concerning the interpretation or implementation of this Convention, those Parties shall consult among themselves with a view to having the dispute resolved by negotiation, inquiry, mediation, conciliation, arbitration, judicial settlement or other peaceful means of their own choice.

2.   Any dispute of this character not so resolved shall, with the consent in each case of all parties to the dispute, be referred for settlement to the International Court of Justice or to arbitration; but failure to reach agreement on reference to the International Court of Justice or to arbitration shall not absolve parties to the dispute from the responsibility of continuing to seek to resolve it by any of the various peaceful means referred to in paragraph 1 above.

3.   In cases where the dispute is referred to arbitration, the arbitral tribunal shall be constituted as provided in the Annex to this Convention.[1] The Annex forms an integral part of this Convention.

Article 17

1.   This Convention shall be open for signature by Australia, Japan and New Zealand.

2.   This Convention is subject to ratification, acceptance or approval by these three States in accordance with their respective internal legal procedures, and will enter into force on the date of deposit of the third instrument of ratification, acceptance or approval.

Article 18

After the entry into force of this Convention, any other State, whose vessels engage in fishing for southern bluefin tuna, or any other coastal State through whose exclusive economic or fishery zone southern bluefin tuna migrates, may accede to it. This Convention shall become effective for any such other State on the date of deposit of that State's instrument of accession.

Article 19

Reservations may not be made with respect to any of the provisions of this Convention.

Article 20

Any Party may withdraw from this Convention twelve months after the date on which it formally notifies the Depositary of its intention to withdraw.

Article 21

1.   Any Party may at any time propose an amendment to this Convention.

2.   If one-third of the Parties request a meeting to discuss a proposed amendment the Depositary shall call such a meeting.

3.   An amendment shall enter into force when the Depositary has received instruments of ratification, acceptance or approval thereof from all the Parties.

Article 22

1.   The original of this Convention shall be deposited with the Government of Australia, which shall be the Depositary. The Depositary shall transmit certified copies thereof to all other Signatories and acceding States.

2.   This Convention shall be registered by the Depositary pursuant to Article 102 of the Charter of the United Nations.

IN WITNESS WHEREOF the undersigned, being duly authorised thereto, have signed this Convention.

DONE AT Canberra on the tenth day of May 1993, in a single original, in the English and Japanese languages, each text being equally authentic.

---

[1] Annex omitted.

Agreement for the Implementation of the Provisions of the United Nations Convention on the Law of the Sea of 10 December 1982 Relating to the Conservation and Management of Straddling Fish Stocks and Highly Migratory Fish Stocks

Done at New York, 4 December 1995; entry into force, 11 December 2001
2167 UNTS 88 [Registration Number 37924]

The States Parties to this Agreement,

Recalling the relevant provisions of the United Nations Convention on the Law of the Sea of 10 December 1982,

Determined to ensure the long-term conservation and sustainable use of straddling fish stocks and highly migratory fish stocks,

Resolved to improve cooperation between States to that end,

Calling for more effective enforcement by flag States, port States and coastal States of the conservation and management measures adopted for such stocks,

Seeking to address in particular the problems identified in chapter 17, programme area C, of Agenda 21 adopted by the United Nations Conference on Environment and Development, namely, that the management of high seas fisheries is inadequate in many areas and that some resources are overutilized; noting that there are problems of unregulated fishing, over-capitalization, excessive fleet size, vessel reflagging to escape controls, insufficiently selective gear, unreliable databases and lack of sufficient cooperation between States,

Committing themselves to responsible fisheries,

Conscious of the need to avoid adverse impacts on the marine environment, preserve biodiversity, maintain the integrity of marine ecosystems and minimize the risk of long-term or irreversible effects of fishing operations,

Recognizing the need for specific assistance, including financial, scientific and technological assistance, in order that developing States can participate effectively in the conservation, management and sustainable use of straddling fish stocks and highly migratory fish stocks,

Convinced that an agreement for the implementation of the relevant provisions of the Convention would best serve these purposes and contribute to the maintenance of international peace and security,

Affirming that matters not regulated by the Convention or by this Agreement continue to be governed by the rules and principles of general international law,

Have agreed as follows:

PART I
GENERAL PROVISIONS

Article 1 Use of terms and scope
1. For the purposes of this Agreement:
   (a) 'Convention' means the United Nations Convention on the Law of the Sea of 10 December 1982;
   (b) 'conservation and management measures' means measures to conserve and manage one or more species of living marine resources that are adopted and applied consistent with the relevant rules of international law as reflected in the Convention and this Agreement;

    (c)   'fish' includes molluscs and crustaceans except those belonging to sedentary species as defined in article 77 of the Convention; and

    (d)   'arrangement' means a cooperative mechanism established in accordance with the Convention and this Agreement by two or more States for the purpose, *inter alia*, of establishing conservation and management measures in a subregion or region for one or more straddling fish stocks or highly migratory fish stocks.

2.   (a)   'States Parties' means States which have consented to be bound by this Agreement and for which the Agreement is in force.

    (b)   This Agreement applies *mutatis mutandis*:

        (i)   to any entity referred to in article 305, paragraph 1 (c), (d) and (e), of the Convention and

        (ii)   subject to article 47, to any entity referred to as an 'international organization' in Annex IX, article 1, of the Convention which becomes a Party to this Agreement, and to that extent 'States Parties' refers to those entities.

3.   This Agreement applies *mutatis mutandis* to other fishing entities whose vessels fish on the high seas.

Article 2 Objective

The objective of this Agreement is to ensure the long-term conservation and sustainable use of straddling fish stocks and highly migratory fish stocks through effective implementation of the relevant provisions of the Convention.

Article 3 Application

1.   Unless otherwise provided, this Agreement applies to the conservation and management of straddling fish stocks and highly migratory fish stocks beyond areas under national jurisdiction, except that articles 6 and 7 apply also to the conservation and management of such stocks within areas under national jurisdiction, subject to the different legal regimes that apply within areas under national jurisdiction and in areas beyond national jurisdiction as provided for in the Convention.

2.   In the exercise of its sovereign rights for the purpose of exploring and exploiting, conserving and managing straddling fish stocks and highly migratory fish stocks within areas under national jurisdiction, the coastal State shall apply *mutatis mutandis* the general principles enumerated in article 5.

3.   States shall give due consideration to the respective capacities of developing States to apply articles 5, 6 and 7 within areas under national jurisdiction and their need for assistance as provided for in this Agreement. To this end, Part VII applies *mutatis mutandis* in respect of areas under national jurisdiction.

Article 4 Relationship between this Agreement and the Convention

Nothing in this Agreement shall prejudice the rights, jurisdiction and duties of States under the Convention. This Agreement shall be interpreted and applied in the context of and in a manner consistent with the Convention.

PART II
CONSERVATION AND MANAGEMENT OF STRADDLING FISH STOCKS AND HIGHLY MIGRATORY FISH STOCKS

Article 5 General principles

In order to conserve and manage straddling fish stocks and highly migratory fish stocks, coastal States and States fishing on the high seas shall, in giving effect to their duty to cooperate in accordance with the Convention:

(a) adopt measures to ensure long-term sustainability of straddling fish stocks and highly migratory fish stocks and promote the objective of their optimum utilization;

(b) ensure that such measures are based on the best scientific evidence available and are designed to maintain or restore stocks at levels capable of producing maximum sustainable yield, as qualified by relevant environmental and economic factors, including the special requirements of developing States, and taking into account fishing patterns, the interdependence of stocks and any generally recommended international minimum standards, whether subregional, regional or global;

(c) apply the precautionary approach in accordance with article 6;

(d) assess the impacts of fishing, other human activities and environmental factors on target stocks and species belonging to the same ecosystem or associated with or dependent upon the target stocks;

(e) adopt, where necessary, conservation and management measures for species belonging to the same ecosystem or associated with or dependent upon the target stocks, with a view to maintaining or restoring populations of such species above levels at which their reproduction may become seriously threatened;

(f) minimize pollution, waste, discards, catch by lost or abandoned gear, catch of non-target species, both fish and non-fish species, (hereinafter referred to as non-target species) and impacts on associated or dependent species, in particular endangered species, through measures including, to the extent practicable, the development and use of selective, environmentally safe and cost-effective fishing gear and techniques;

(g) protect biodiversity in the marine environment;

(h) take measures to prevent or eliminate overfishing and excess fishing capacity and to ensure that levels of fishing effort do not exceed those commensurate with the sustainable use of fishery resources;

(i) take into account the interests of artisanal and subsistence fishers;

(j) collect and share, in a timely manner, complete and accurate data concerning fishing activities on, *inter alia*, vessel position, catch of target and non-target species and fishing effort, as set out in Annex I, as well as information from national and international research programmes;

(k) promote and conduct scientific research and develop appropriate technologies in support of fishery conservation and management; and

(l) implement and enforce conservation and management measures through effective monitoring, control and surveillance.

Article 6 Application of the precautionary approach

1. States shall apply the precautionary approach widely to conservation, management and exploitation of straddling fish stocks and highly migratory fish stocks in order to protect the living marine resources and preserve the marine environment.

2. States shall be more cautious when information is uncertain, unreliable or inadequate. The absence of adequate scientific information shall not be used as a reason for postponing or failing to take conservation and management measures.

3. In implementing the precautionary approach, States shall:

(a) improve decision-making for fishery resource conservation and management by obtaining and sharing the best scientific information available and implementing improved techniques for dealing with risk and uncertainty;

(b) apply the guidelines set out in Annex II and determine, on the basis of the best scientific information available, stock-specific reference points and the action to be taken if they are exceeded;

(c) take into account, *inter alia*, uncertainties relating to the size and productivity of the stocks, reference points, stock condition in relation to such reference points, levels and distribution of fishing mortality and the impact of fishing activities on non-target and associated or dependent species, as well as existing and predicted oceanic, environmental and socio-economic conditions; and

(d) develop data collection and research programmes to assess the impact of fishing on non-target and associated or dependent species and their environment, and adopt plans which are necessary to ensure the conservation of such species and to protect habitats of special concern.

4. States shall take measures to ensure that, when reference points are approached, they will not be exceeded. In the event that they are exceeded, States shall, without delay, take the action determined under paragraph 3 (b) to restore the stocks.

5. Where the status of target stocks or non-target or associated or dependent species is of concern, States shall subject such stocks and species to enhanced monitoring in order to review their status and the efficacy of conservation and management measures. They shall revise those measures regularly in the light of new information.

6. For new or exploratory fisheries, States shall adopt as soon as possible cautious conservation and management measures, including, *inter alia*, catch limits and effort limits. Such measures shall remain in force until there are sufficient data to allow assessment of the impact of the fisheries on the long-term sustainability of the stocks, whereupon conservation and management measures based on that assessment shall be implemented. The latter measures shall, if appropriate, allow for the gradual development of the fisheries.

7. If a natural phenomenon has a significant adverse impact on the status of straddling fish stocks or highly migratory fish stocks, States shall adopt conservation and management measures on an emergency basis to ensure that fishing activity does not exacerbate such adverse impact. States shall also adopt such measures on an emergency basis where fishing activity presents a serious threat to the sustainability of such stocks. Measures taken on an emergency basis shall be temporary and shall be based on the best scientific evidence available.

Article 7 Compatibility of conservation and management measures

1. Without prejudice to the sovereign rights of coastal States for the purpose of exploring and exploiting, conserving and managing the living marine resources within areas under national jurisdiction as provided for in the Convention, and the right of all States for their nationals to engage in fishing on the high seas in accordance with the Convention:

(a) with respect to straddling fish stocks, the relevant coastal States and the States whose nationals fish for such stocks in the adjacent high seas area shall seek, either directly or through the appropriate mechanisms for cooperation provided for in Part III, to agree upon the measures necessary for the conservation of these stocks in the adjacent high seas area;

(b)   with respect to highly migratory fish stocks, the relevant coastal States and other States whose nationals fish for such stocks in the region shall cooperate, either directly or through the appropriate mechanisms for cooperation provided for in Part III, with a view to ensuring conservation and promoting the objective of optimum utilization of such stocks throughout the region, both within and beyond the areas under national jurisdiction.

2.   Conservation and management measures established for the high seas and those adopted for areas under national jurisdiction shall be compatible in order to ensure conservation and management of the straddling fish stocks and highly migratory fish stocks in their entirety. To this end, coastal States and States fishing on the high seas have a duty to cooperate for the purpose of achieving compatible measures in respect of such stocks. In determining compatible conservation and management measures, States shall:

(a)   take into account the conservation and management measures adopted and applied in accordance with article 61 of the Convention in respect of the same stocks by coastal States within areas under national jurisdiction and ensure that measures established in respect of such stocks for the high seas do not undermine the effectiveness of such measures;

(b)   take into account previously agreed measures established and applied for the high seas in accordance with the Convention in respect of the same stocks by relevant coastal States and States fishing on the high seas;

(c)   take into account previously agreed measures established and applied in accordance with the Convention in respect of the same stocks by a subregional or regional fisheries management organization or arrangement;

(d)   take into account the biological unity and other biological characteristics of the stocks and the relationships between the distribution of the stocks, the fisheries and the geographical particularities of the region concerned, including the extent to which the stocks occur and are fished in areas under national jurisdiction;

(e)   take into account the respective dependence of the coastal States and the States fishing on the high seas on the stocks concerned; and

(f)   ensure that such measures do not result in harmful impact on the living marine resources as a whole.

3.   In giving effect to their duty to cooperate, States shall make every effort to agree on compatible conservation and management measures within a reasonable period of time.

4.   If no agreement can be reached within a reasonable period of time, any of the States concerned may invoke the procedures for the settlement of disputes provided for in Part VIII.

5.   Pending agreement on compatible conservation and management measures, the States concerned, in a spirit of understanding and cooperation, shall make every effort to enter into provisional arrangements of a practical nature. In the event that they are unable to agree on such arrangements, any of the States concerned may, for the purpose of obtaining provisional measures, submit the dispute to a court or tribunal in accordance with the procedures for the settlement of disputes provided for in Part VIII.

6.   Provisional arrangements or measures entered into or prescribed pursuant to paragraph 5 shall take into account the provisions of this Part, shall have due regard to the rights and obligations of all States concerned, shall not jeopardize or hamper the reaching of final agreement on compatible conservation and management measures and shall be without prejudice to the final outcome of any dispute settlement procedure.

7. Coastal States shall regularly inform States fishing on the high seas in the subregion or region, either directly or through appropriate subregional or regional fisheries management organizations or arrangements, or through other appropriate means, of the measures they have adopted for straddling fish stocks and highly migratory fish stocks within areas under their national jurisdiction.

8. States fishing on the high seas shall regularly inform other interested States, either directly or through appropriate subregional or regional fisheries management organizations or arrangements, or through other appropriate means, of the measures they have adopted for regulating the activities of vessels flying their flag which fish for such stocks on the high seas.

PART III

MECHANISMS FOR INTERNATIONAL COOPERATION CONCERNING STRADDLING FISH STOCKS AND HIGHLY MIGRATORY FISH STOCKS

Article 8 Cooperation for conservation and management
1. Coastal States and States fishing on the high seas shall, in accordance with the Convention, pursue cooperation in relation to straddling fish stocks and highly migratory fish stocks either directly or through appropriate subregional or regional fisheries management organizations or arrangements, taking into account the specific characteristics of the subregion or region, to ensure effective conservation and management of such stocks.

2. States shall enter into consultations in good faith and without delay, particularly where there is evidence that the straddling fish stocks and highly migratory fish stocks concerned may be under threat of over-exploitation or where a new fishery is being developed for such stocks. To this end, consultations may be initiated at the request of any interested State with a view to establishing appropriate arrangements to ensure conservation and management of the stocks. Pending agreement on such arrangements, States shall observe the provisions of this Agreement and shall act in good faith and with due regard to the rights, interests and duties of other States.

3. Where a subregional or regional fisheries management organization or arrangement has the competence to establish conservation and management measures for particular straddling fish stocks or highly migratory fish stocks, States fishing for the stocks on the high seas and relevant coastal States shall give effect to their duty to cooperate by becoming members of such organization or participants in such arrangement, or by agreeing to apply the conservation and management measures established by such organization or arrangement. States having a real interest in the fisheries concerned may become members of such organization or participants in such arrangement. The terms of participation in such organization or arrangement shall not preclude such States from membership or participation; nor shall they be applied in a manner which discriminates against any State or group of States having a real interest in the fisheries concerned.

4. Only those States which are members of such an organization or participants in such an arrangement, or which agree to apply the conservation and management measures established by such organization or arrangement, shall have access to the fishery resources to which those measures apply.

5. Where there is no subregional or regional fisheries management organization or arrangement to establish conservation and management measures for a particular straddling fish stock or highly migratory fish stock, relevant coastal States and States fishing on the high seas for such stock in the subregion or region shall cooperate to establish such an organization or enter into other appropriate arrangements to ensure conservation and management of such stock and shall participate in the work of the organization or arrangement.

6. Any State intending to propose that action be taken by an intergovernmental organization having competence with respect to living resources should, where such action would have a significant effect on conservation and management measures already established by a competent subregional or regional fisheries management organization or arrangement, consult through that organization or arrangement with its members or participants. To the extent practicable, such consultation should take place prior to the submission of the proposal to the intergovernmental organization.

Article 9 Subregional and regional fisheries management organizations and arrangements

1. In establishing subregional or regional fisheries management organizations or in entering into subregional or regional fisheries management arrangements for straddling fish stocks and highly migratory fish stocks, States shall agree, *inter alia*, on:
   (a) the stocks to which conservation and management measures apply, taking into account the biological characteristics of the stocks concerned and the nature of the fisheries involved;
   (b) the area of application, taking into account article 7, paragraph 1, and the characteristics of the subregion or region, including socio-economic, geographical and environmental factors;
   (c) the relationship between the work of the new organization or arrangement and the role, objectives and operations of any relevant existing fisheries management organizations or arrangements; and
   (d) the mechanisms by which the organization or arrangement will obtain scientific advice and review the status of the stocks, including, where appropriate, the establishment of a scientific advisory body.

2. States cooperating in the formation of a subregional or regional fisheries management organization or arrangement shall inform other States which they are aware have a real interest in the work of the proposed organization or arrangement of such cooperation.

Article 10 Functions of subregional and regional fisheries management organizations and arrangements

In fulfilling their obligation to cooperate through subregional or regional fisheries management organizations or arrangements, States shall:
   (a) agree on and comply with conservation and management measures to ensure the long-term sustainability of straddling fish stocks and highly migratory fish stocks;
   (b) agree, as appropriate, on participatory rights such as allocations of allowable catch or levels of fishing effort;
   (c) adopt and apply any generally recommended international minimum standards for the responsible conduct of fishing operations;
   (d) obtain and evaluate scientific advice, review the status of the stocks and assess the impact of fishing on non-target and associated or dependent species;
   (e) agree on standards for collection, reporting, verification and exchange of data on fisheries for the stocks;
   (f) compile and disseminate accurate and complete statistical data, as described in Annex I, to ensure that the best scientific evidence is available, while maintaining confidentiality where appropriate;
   (g) promote and conduct scientific assessments of the stocks and relevant research and disseminate the results thereof;

(h)   establish appropriate cooperative mechanisms for effective monitoring, control, surveillance and enforcement;

(i)   agree on means by which the fishing interests of new members of the organization or new participants in the arrangement will be accommodated;

(j)   agree on decision-making procedures which facilitate the adoption of conservation and management measures in a timely and effective manner;

(k)   promote the peaceful settlement of disputes in accordance with Part VIII;

(l)   ensure the full cooperation of their relevant national agencies and industries in implementing the recommendations and decisions of the organization or arrangement; and

(m)   give due publicity to the conservation and management measures established by the organization or arrangement.

Article 11 New members or participants

In determining the nature and extent of participatory rights for new members of a subregional or regional fisheries management organization, or for new participants in a subregional or regional fisheries management arrangement, States shall take into account, *inter alia*:

(a)   the status of the straddling fish stocks and highly migratory fish stocks and the existing level of fishing effort in the fishery;

(b)   the respective interests, fishing patterns and fishing practices of new and existing members or participants;

(c)   the respective contributions of new and existing members or participants to conservation and management of the stocks, to the collection and provision of accurate data and to the conduct of scientific research on the stocks;

(d)   the needs of coastal fishing communities which are dependent mainly on fishing for the stocks;

(e)   the needs of coastal States whose economies are overwhelmingly dependent on the exploitation of living marine resources; and

(f)   the interests of developing States from the subregion or region in whose areas of national jurisdiction the stocks also occur.

Article 12 Transparency in activities of subregional and regional fisheries management organizations and arrangements

1.   States shall provide for transparency in the decision-making process and other activities of subregional and regional fisheries management organizations and arrangements.

2.   Representatives from other intergovernmental organizations and representatives from non-governmental organizations concerned with straddling fish stocks and highly migratory fish stocks shall be afforded the opportunity to take part in meetings of subregional and regional fisheries management organizations and arrangements as observers or otherwise, as appropriate, in accordance with the procedures of the organization or arrangement concerned. Such procedures shall not be unduly restrictive in this respect. Such intergovernmental organizations and non-governmental organizations shall have timely access to the records and reports of such organizations and arrangements, subject to the procedural rules on access to them.

Article 13 Strengthening of existing organizations and arrangements

States shall cooperate to strengthen existing subregional and regional fisheries management organizations and arrangements in order to improve their effectiveness in establishing and implementing conservation and management measures for straddling fish stocks and highly migratory fish stocks.

Article 14   Collection and provision of information and cooperation in scientific research

1. States shall ensure that fishing vessels flying their flag provide such information as may be necessary in order to fulfil their obligations under this Agreement. To this end, States shall in accordance with Annex I:

(a)   collect and exchange scientific, technical and statistical data with respect to fisheries for straddling fish stocks and highly migratory fish stocks;

(b)   ensure that data are collected in sufficient detail to facilitate effective stock assessment and are provided in a timely manner to fulfil the requirements of subregional or regional fisheries management organizations or arrangements; and

(c)   take appropriate measures to verify the accuracy of such data.

2. States shall cooperate, either directly or through subregional or regional fisheries management organizations or arrangements:

(a)   to agree on the specification of data and the format in which they are to be provided to such organizations or arrangements, taking into account the nature of the stocks and the fisheries for those stocks; and

(b)   to develop and share analytical techniques and stock assessment methodologies to improve measures for the conservation and management of straddling fish stocks and highly migratory fish stocks.

3. Consistent with Part XIII of the Convention, States shall cooperate, either directly or through competent international organizations, to strengthen scientific research capacity in the field of fisheries and promote scientific research related to the conservation and management of straddling fish stocks and highly migratory fish stocks for the benefit of all. To this end, a State or the competent international organization conducting such research beyond areas under national jurisdiction shall actively promote the publication and dissemination to any interested States of the results of that research and information relating to its objectives and methods and, to the extent practicable, shall facilitate the participation of scientists from those States in such research.

Article 15   Enclosed and semi-enclosed seas

In implementing this Agreement in an enclosed or semi-enclosed sea, States shall take into account the natural characteristics of that sea and shall also act in a manner consistent with Part IX of the Convention and other relevant provisions thereof.

Article 16   Areas of high seas surrounded entirely by an area under the national jurisdiction of a single State

1. States fishing for straddling fish stocks and highly migratory fish stocks in an area of the high seas surrounded entirely by an area under the national jurisdiction of a single State and the latter State shall cooperate to establish conservation and management measures in respect of those stocks in the high seas area. Having regard to the natural characteristics of the area, States shall pay special attention to the establishment of compatible conservation and management measures for such stocks pursuant to article 7. Measures taken in respect of the high seas shall take into account the rights, duties and interests of the coastal State under the Convention, shall be based on the best scientific evidence available and shall also take into account any conservation and management measures adopted and applied in respect of the same stocks in accordance with article 61

of the Convention by the coastal State in the area under national jurisdiction. States shall also agree on measures for monitoring, control, surveillance and enforcement to ensure compliance with the conservation and management measures in respect of the high seas.

2. Pursuant to article 8, States shall act in good faith and make every effort to agree without delay on conservation and management measures to be applied in the carrying out of fishing operations in the area referred to in paragraph 1. If, within a reasonable period of time, the fishing States concerned and the coastal State are unable to agree on such measures, they shall, having regard to paragraph 1, apply article 7, paragraphs 4, 5 and 6, relating to provisional arrangements or measures. Pending the establishment of such provisional arrangements or measures, the States concerned shall take measures in respect of vessels flying their flag in order that they not engage in fisheries which could undermine the stocks concerned.

PART IV
NON-MEMBERS AND NON-PARTICIPANTS

Article 17 Non-members of organizations and non-participants in arrangements

1. A State which is not a member of a subregional or regional fisheries management organization or is not a participant in a subregional or regional fisheries management arrangement, and which does not otherwise agree to apply the conservation and management measures established by such organization or arrangement, is not discharged from the obligation to cooperate, in accordance with the Convention and this Agreement, in the conservation and management of the relevant straddling fish stocks and highly migratory fish stocks.

2. Such State shall not authorize vessels flying its flag to engage in fishing operations for the straddling fish stocks or highly migratory fish stocks which are subject to the conservation and management measures established by such organization or arrangement.

3. States which are members of a subregional or regional fisheries management organization or participants in a subregional or regional fisheries management arrangement shall, individually or jointly, request the fishing entities referred to in article 1, paragraph 3, which have fishing vessels in the relevant area to cooperate fully with such organization or arrangement in implementing the conservation and management measures it has established, with a view to having such measures applied de facto as extensively as possible to fishing activities in the relevant area. Such fishing entities shall enjoy benefits from participation in the fishery commensurate with their commitment to comply with conservation and management measures in respect of the stocks.

4. States which are members of such organization or participants in such arrangement shall exchange information with respect to the activities of fishing vessels flying the flags of States which are neither members of the organization nor participants in the arrangement and which are engaged in fishing operations for the relevant stocks. They shall take measures consistent with this Agreement and international law to deter activities of such vessels which undermine the effectiveness of subregional or regional conservation and management measures.

PART V
DUTIES OF THE FLAG STATE

Article 18 Duties of the flag State

1. A State whose vessels fish on the high seas shall take such measures as may be necessary to ensure that vessels flying its flag comply with subregional and regional

conservation and management measures and that such vessels do not engage in any activity which undermines the effectiveness of such measures.

2. A State shall authorize the use of vessels flying its flag for fishing on the high seas only where it is able to exercise effectively its responsibilities in respect of such vessels under the Convention and this Agreement.

3. Measures to be taken by a State in respect of vessels flying its flag shall include:

(a) control of such vessels on the high seas by means of fishing licences, authorizations or permits, in accordance with any applicable procedures agreed at the subregional, regional or global level;

(b) establishment of regulations:

(i) to apply terms and conditions to the licence, authorization or permit sufficient to fulfil any subregional, regional or global obligations of the flag State;

(ii) to prohibit fishing on the high seas by vessels which are not duly licensed or authorized to fish, or fishing on the high seas by vessels otherwise than in accordance with the terms and conditions of a licence, authorization or permit;

(iii) to require vessels fishing on the high seas to carry the licence, authorization or permit on board at all times and to produce it on demand for inspection by a duly authorized person; and

(iv) to ensure that vessels flying its flag do not conduct unauthorized fishing within areas under the national jurisdiction of other States;

(c) establishment of a national record of fishing vessels authorized to fish on the high seas and provision of access to the information contained in that record on request by directly interested States, taking into account any national laws of the flag State regarding the release of such information;

(d) requirements for marking of fishing vessels and fishing gear for identification in accordance with uniform and internationally recognizable vessel and gear marking systems, such as the Food and Agriculture Organization of the United Nations Standard Specifications for the Marking and Identification of Fishing Vessels;

(e) requirements for recording and timely reporting of vessel position, catch of target and non-target species, fishing effort and other relevant fisheries data in accordance with subregional, regional and global standards for collection of such data;

(f) requirements for verifying the catch of target and non-target species through such means as observer programmes, inspection schemes, unloading reports, supervision of transshipment and monitoring of landed catches and market statistics;

(g) monitoring, control and surveillance of such vessels, their fishing operations and related activities by, *inter alia*:

(i) the implementation of national inspection schemes and subregional and regional schemes for cooperation in enforcement pursuant to articles 21 and 22, including requirements for such vessels to permit access by duly authorized inspectors from other States;

(ii) the implementation of national observer programmes and subregional and regional observer programmes in which the flag State is a participant, including requirements for such vessels to permit access by observers from other States to carry out the functions agreed under the programmes; and

    (iii) the development and implementation of vessel monitoring systems, including, as appropriate, satellite transmitter systems, in accordance with any national programmes and those which have been subregionally, regionally or globally agreed among the States concerned;

  (h) regulation of transshipment on the high seas to ensure that the effectiveness of conservation and management measures is not undermined; and

  (i) regulation of fishing activities to ensure compliance with subregional, regional or global measures, including those aimed at minimizing catches of non-target species.

  4. Where there is a subregionally, regionally or globally agreed system of monitoring, control and surveillance in effect, States shall ensure that the measures they impose on vessels flying their flag are compatible with that system.

PART VI

COMPLIANCE AND ENFORCEMENT

Article 19 Compliance and enforcement by the flag State

  1. A State shall ensure compliance by vessels flying its flag with subregional and regional conservation and management measures for straddling fish stocks and highly migratory fish stocks. To this end, that State shall:

  (a) enforce such measures irrespective of where violations occur;

  (b) investigate immediately and fully any alleged violation of subregional or regional conservation and management measures, which may include the physical inspection of the vessels concerned, and report promptly to the State alleging the violation and the relevant subregional or regional organization or arrangement on the progress and outcome of the investigation;

  (c) require any vessel flying its flag to give information to the investigating authority regarding vessel position, catches, fishing gear, fishing operations and related activities in the area of an alleged violation;

  (d) if satisfied that sufficient evidence is available in respect of an alleged violation, refer the case to its authorities with a view to instituting proceedings without delay in accordance with its laws and, where appropriate, detain the vessel concerned; and

  (e) ensure that, where it has been established, in accordance with its laws, a vessel has been involved in the commission of a serious violation of such measures, the vessel does not engage in fishing operations on the high seas until such time as all outstanding sanctions imposed by the flag State in respect of the violation have been complied with.

  2. All investigations and judicial proceedings shall be carried out expeditiously. Sanctions applicable in respect of violations shall be adequate in severity to be effective in securing compliance and to discourage violations wherever they occur and shall deprive offenders of the benefits accruing from their illegal activities. Measures applicable in respect of masters and other officers of fishing vessels shall include provisions which may permit, *inter alia*, refusal, withdrawal or suspension of authorizations to serve as masters or officers on such vessels.

Article 20 International cooperation in enforcement

  1. States shall cooperate, either directly or through subregional or regional fisheries management organizations or arrangements, to ensure compliance with and enforcement of subregional and regional conservation and management measures for straddling fish stocks and highly migratory fish stocks.

2. A flag State conducting an investigation of an alleged violation of conservation and management measures for straddling fish stocks or highly migratory fish stocks may request the assistance of any other State whose cooperation may be useful in the conduct of that investigation. All States shall endeavour to meet reasonable requests made by a flag State in connection with such investigations.

3. A flag State may undertake such investigations directly, in cooperation with other interested States or through the relevant subregional or regional fisheries management organization or arrangement. Information on the progress and outcome of the investigations shall be provided to all States having an interest in, or affected by, the alleged violation.

4. States shall assist each other in identifying vessels reported to have engaged in activities undermining the effectiveness of subregional, regional or global conservation and management measures.

5. States shall, to the extent permitted by national laws and regulations, establish arrangements for making available to prosecuting authorities in other States evidence relating to alleged violations of such measures.

6. Where there are reasonable grounds for believing that a vessel on the high seas has been engaged in unauthorized fishing within an area under the jurisdiction of a coastal State, the flag State of that vessel, at the request of the coastal State concerned, shall immediately and fully investigate the matter. The flag State shall cooperate with the coastal State in taking appropriate enforcement action in such cases and may authorize the relevant authorities of the coastal State to board and inspect the vessel on the high seas. This paragraph is without prejudice to article 111 of the Convention.

7. States Parties which are members of a subregional or regional fisheries management organization or participants in a subregional or regional fisheries management arrangement may take action in accordance with international law, including through recourse to subregional or regional procedures established for this purpose, to deter vessels which have engaged in activities which undermine the effectiveness of or otherwise violate the conservation and management measures established by that organization or arrangement from fishing on the high seas in the subregion or region until such time as appropriate action is taken by the flag State.

Article 21 Subregional and regional cooperation in enforcement
1. In any high seas area covered by a subregional or regional fisheries management organization or arrangement, a State Party which is a member of such organization or a participant in such arrangement may, through its duly authorized inspectors, board and inspect, in accordance with paragraph 2, fishing vessels flying the flag of another State Party to this Agreement, whether or not such State Party is also a member of the organization or a participant in the arrangement, for the purpose of ensuring compliance with conservation and management measures for straddling fish stocks and highly migratory fish stocks established by that organization or arrangement.

2. States shall establish, through subregional or regional fisheries management organizations or arrangements, procedures for boarding and inspection pursuant to paragraph 1, as well as procedures to implement other provisions of this article. Such procedures shall be consistent with this article and the basic procedures set out in article 22 and shall not discriminate against non-members of the organization or non-participants in the arrangement. Boarding and inspection as well as any subsequent enforcement action shall be conducted in accordance with such procedures. States shall give due publicity to procedures established pursuant to this paragraph.

3. If, within two years of the adoption of this Agreement, any organization or arrangement has not established such procedures, boarding and inspection pursuant to

paragraph 1, as well as any subsequent enforcement action, shall, pending the establishment of such procedures, be conducted in accordance with this article and the basic procedures set out in article 22.

4. Prior to taking action under this article, inspecting States shall, either directly or through the relevant subregional or regional fisheries management organization or arrangement, inform all States whose vessels fish on the high seas in the subregion or region of the form of identification issued to their duly authorized inspectors. The vessels used for boarding and inspection shall be clearly marked and identifiable as being on government service. At the time of becoming a Party to this Agreement, a State shall designate an appropriate authority to receive notifications pursuant to this article and shall give due publicity of such designation through the relevant subregional or regional fisheries management organization or arrangement.

5. Where, following a boarding and inspection, there are clear grounds for believing that a vessel has engaged in any activity contrary to the conservation and management measures referred to in paragraph 1, the inspecting State shall, where appropriate, secure evidence and shall promptly notify the flag State of the alleged violation.

6. The flag State shall respond to the notification referred to in paragraph 5 within three working days of its receipt, or such other period as may be prescribed in procedures established in accordance with paragraph 2, and shall either:

    (a)   fulfil, without delay, its obligations under article 19 to investigate and, if evidence so warrants, take enforcement action with respect to the vessel, in which case it shall promptly inform the inspecting State of the results of the investigation and of any enforcement action taken; or

    (b)   authorize the inspecting State to investigate.

7. Where the flag State authorizes the inspecting State to investigate an alleged violation, the inspecting State shall, without delay, communicate the results of that investigation to the flag State. The flag State shall, if evidence so warrants, fulfil its obligations to take enforcement action with respect to the vessel. Alternatively, the flag State may authorize the inspecting State to take such enforcement action as the flag State may specify with respect to the vessel, consistent with the rights and obligations of the flag State under this Agreement.

8. Where, following boarding and inspection, there are clear grounds for believing that a vessel has committed a serious violation, and the flag State has either failed to respond or failed to take action as required under paragraphs 6 or 7, the inspectors may remain on board and secure evidence and may require the master to assist in further investigation including, where appropriate, by bringing the vessel without delay to the nearest appropriate port, or to such other port as may be specified in procedures established in accordance with paragraph 2. The inspecting State shall immediately inform the flag State of the name of the port to which the vessel is to proceed. The inspecting State and the flag State and, as appropriate, the port State shall take all necessary steps to ensure the well-being of the crew regardless of their nationality.

9. The inspecting State shall inform the flag State and the relevant organization or the participants in the relevant arrangement of the results of any further investigation.

10. The inspecting State shall require its inspectors to observe generally accepted international regulations, procedures and practices relating to the safety of the vessel and the crew, minimize interference with fishing operations and, to the extent practicable, avoid action which would adversely affect the quality of the catch on board. The inspecting State shall ensure that boarding and inspection is not conducted in a manner that would constitute harassment of any fishing vessel.

11. For the purposes of this article, a serious violation means:

(a) fishing without a valid licence, authorization or permit issued by the flag State in accordance with article 18, paragraph 3 (a);

(b) failing to maintain accurate records of catch and catch-related data, as required by the relevant subregional or regional fisheries management organization or arrangement, or serious misreporting of catch, contrary to the catch reporting requirements of such organization or arrangement;

(c) fishing in a closed area, fishing during a closed season or fishing without, or after attainment of, a quota established by the relevant subregional or regional fisheries management organization or arrangement;

(d) directed fishing for a stock which is subject to a moratorium or for which fishing is prohibited;

(e) using prohibited fishing gear;

(f) falsifying or concealing the markings, identity or registration of a fishing vessel;

(g) concealing, tampering with or disposing of evidence relating to an investigation;

(h) multiple violations which together constitute a serious disregard of conservation and management measures; or

(i) such other violations as may be specified in procedures established by the relevant subregional or regional fisheries management organization or arrangement.

12. Notwithstanding the other provisions of this article, the flag State may, at any time, take action to fulfil its obligations under article 19 with respect to an alleged violation. Where the vessel is under the direction of the inspecting State, the inspecting State shall, at the request of the flag State, release the vessel to the flag State along with full information on the progress and outcome of its investigation.

13. This article is without prejudice to the right of the flag State to take any measures, including proceedings to impose penalties, according to its laws.

14. This article applies *mutatis mutandis* to boarding and inspection by a State Party which is a member of a subregional or regional fisheries management organization or a participant in a subregional or regional fisheries management arrangement and which has clear grounds for believing that a fishing vessel flying the flag of another State Party has engaged in any activity contrary to relevant conservation and management measures referred to in paragraph 1 in the high seas area covered by such organization or arrangement, and such vessel has subsequently, during the same fishing trip, entered into an area under the national jurisdiction of the inspecting State.

15. Where a subregional or regional fisheries management organization or arrangement has established an alternative mechanism which effectively discharges the obligation under this Agreement of its members or participants to ensure compliance with the conservation and management measures established by the organization or arrangement, members of such organization or participants in such arrangement may agree to limit the application of paragraph 1 as between themselves in respect of the conservation and management measures which have been established in the relevant high seas area.

16. Action taken by States other than the flag State in respect of vessels having engaged in activities contrary to subregional or regional conservation and management measures shall be proportionate to the seriousness of the violation.

17. Where there are reasonable grounds for suspecting that a fishing vessel on the high seas is without nationality, a State may board and inspect the vessel. Where evidence so warrants, the State may take such action as may be appropriate in accordance with international law.

18.   States shall be liable for damage or loss attributable to them arising from action taken pursuant to this article when such action is unlawful or exceeds that reasonably required in the light of available information to implement the provisions of this article.

Article 22   Basic procedures for boarding and inspection pursuant to article 21

1.   The inspecting State shall ensure that its duly authorized inspectors:

(a)   present credentials to the master of the vessel and produce a copy of the text of the relevant conservation and management measures or rules and regulations in force in the high seas area in question pursuant to those measures;

(b)   initiate notice to the flag State at the time of the boarding and inspection;

(c)   do not interfere with the master's ability to communicate with the authorities of the flag State during the boarding and inspection;

(d)   provide a copy of a report on the boarding and inspection to the master and to the authorities of the flag State, noting therein any objection or statement which the master wishes to have included in the report;

(e)   promptly leave the vessel following completion of the inspection if they find no evidence of a serious violation; and

(f)   avoid the use of force except when and to the degree necessary to ensure the safety of the inspectors and where the inspectors are obstructed in the execution of their duties. The degree of force used shall not exceed that reasonably required in the circumstances.

2.   The duly authorized inspectors of an inspecting State shall have the authority to inspect the vessel, its licence, gear, equipment, records, facilities, fish and fish products and any relevant documents necessary to verify compliance with the relevant conservation and management measures.

3.   The flag State shall ensure that vessel masters:

(a)   accept and facilitate prompt and safe boarding by the inspectors;

(b)   cooperate with and assist in the inspection of the vessel conducted pursuant to these procedures;

(c)   do not obstruct, intimidate or interfere with the inspectors in the performance of their duties;

(d)   allow the inspectors to communicate with the authorities of the flag State and the inspecting State during the boarding and inspection;

(e)   provide reasonable facilities, including, where appropriate, food and accommodation, to the inspectors; and

(f)   facilitate safe disembarkation by the inspectors.

4.   In the event that the master of a vessel refuses to accept boarding and inspection in accordance with this article and article 21, the flag State shall, except in circumstances where, in accordance with generally accepted international regulations, procedures and practices relating to safety at sea, it is necessary to delay the boarding and inspection, direct the master of the vessel to submit immediately to boarding and inspection and, if the master does not comply with such direction, shall suspend the vessel's authorization to fish and order the vessel to return immediately to port. The flag State shall advise the inspecting State of the action it has taken when the circumstances referred to in this paragraph arise.

Article 23   Measures taken by a port State

1.   A port State has the right and the duty to take measures, in accordance with international law, to promote the effectiveness of subregional, regional and global conservation and management measures. When taking such measures a port State shall not discriminate in form or in fact against the vessels of any State.

2. A port State may, *inter alia*, inspect documents, fishing gear and catch on board fishing vessels, when such vessels are voluntarily in its ports or at its offshore terminals.

3. States may adopt regulations empowering the relevant national authorities to prohibit landings and transshipments where it has been established that the catch has been taken in a manner which undermines the effectiveness of subregional, regional or global conservation and management measures on the high seas.

4. Nothing in this article affects the exercise by States of their sovereignty over ports in their territory in accordance with international law.

PART VII
REQUIREMENTS OF DEVELOPING STATES

Article 24 Recognition of the special requirements of developing States

1. States shall give full recognition to the special requirements of developing States in relation to conservation and management of straddling fish stocks and highly migratory fish stocks and development of fisheries for such stocks. To this end, States shall, either directly or through the United Nations Development Programme, the Food and Agriculture Organization of the United Nations and other specialized agencies, the Global Environment Facility, the Commission on Sustainable Development and other appropriate international and regional organizations and bodies, provide assistance to developing States.

2. In giving effect to the duty to cooperate in the establishment of conservation and management measures for straddling fish stocks and highly migratory fish stocks, States shall take into account the special requirements of developing States, in particular:

(a)   the vulnerability of developing States which are dependent on the exploitation of living marine resources, including for meeting the nutritional requirements of their populations or parts thereof;

(b)   the need to avoid adverse impacts on, and ensure access to fisheries by, subsistence, small-scale and artisanal fishers and women fishworkers, as well as indigenous people in developing States, particularly small island developing States; and

(c)   the need to ensure that such measures do not result in transferring, directly or indirectly, a disproportionate burden of conservation action onto developing States.

Article 25 Forms of cooperation with developing States

1. States shall cooperate, either directly or through subregional, regional or global organizations:

(a)   to enhance the ability of developing States, in particular the least-developed among them and small island developing States, to conserve and manage straddling fish stocks and highly migratory fish stocks and to develop their own fisheries for such stocks;

(b)   to assist developing States, in particular the least-developed among them and small island developing States, to enable them to participate in high seas fisheries for such stocks, including facilitating access to such fisheries subject to articles 5 and 11; and

(c)   to facilitate the participation of developing States in subregional and regional fisheries management organizations and arrangements.

2. Cooperation with developing States for the purposes set out in this article shall include the provision of financial assistance, assistance relating to human resources development, technical assistance, transfer of technology, including through joint venture arrangements, and advisory and consultative services.

3. Such assistance shall, *inter alia*, be directed specifically towards:
(a) improved conservation and management of straddling fish stocks and highly migratory fish stocks through collection, reporting, verification, exchange and analysis of fisheries data and related information;
(b) stock assessment and scientific research; and
(c) monitoring, control, surveillance, compliance and enforcement, including training and capacity-building at the local level, development and funding of national and regional observer programmes and access to technology and equipment.

Article 26 Special assistance in the implementation of this Agreement

1. States shall cooperate to establish special funds to assist developing States in the implementation of this Agreement, including assisting developing States to meet the costs involved in any proceedings for the settlement of disputes to which they may be parties.

2. States and international organizations should assist developing States in establishing new subregional or regional fisheries management organizations or arrangements, or in strengthening existing organizations or arrangements, for the conservation and management of straddling fish stocks and highly migratory fish stocks.

PART VIII
PEACEFUL SETTLEMENT OF DISPUTES

Article 27 Obligation to settle disputes by peaceful means

States have the obligation to settle their disputes by negotiation, inquiry, mediation, conciliation, arbitration, judicial settlement, resort to regional agencies or arrangements, or other peaceful means of their own choice.

Article 28 Prevention of disputes

States shall cooperate in order to prevent disputes. To this end, States shall agree on efficient and expeditious decision-making procedures within subregional and regional fisheries management organizations and arrangements and shall strengthen existing decision-making procedures as necessary.

Article 29 Disputes of a technical nature

Where a dispute concerns a matter of a technical nature, the States concerned may refer the dispute to an *ad hoc* expert panel established by them. The panel shall confer with the States concerned and shall endeavour to resolve the dispute expeditiously without recourse to binding procedures for the settlement of disputes.

Article 30 Procedures for the settlement of disputes

1. The provisions relating to the settlement of disputes set out in Part XV of the Convention apply *mutatis mutandis* to any dispute between States Parties to this Agreement concerning the interpretation or application of this Agreement, whether or not they are also Parties to the Convention.

2. The provisions relating to the settlement of disputes set out in Part XV of the Convention apply *mutatis mutandis* to any dispute between States Parties to this Agreement concerning the interpretation or application of a subregional, regional or global fisheries agreement relating to straddling fish stocks or highly migratory fish stocks to which they are parties, including any dispute concerning the conservation and management of such stocks, whether or not they are also Parties to the Convention.

3. Any procedure accepted by a State Party to this Agreement and the Convention pursuant to article 287 of the Convention shall apply to the settlement of disputes under this Part, unless that State Party, when signing, ratifying or acceding to this Agreement, or at any time thereafter, has accepted another procedure pursuant to article 287 for the settlement of disputes under this Part.

4. A State Party to this Agreement which is not a Party to the Convention, when signing, ratifying or acceding to this Agreement, or at any time thereafter, shall be free to choose, by means of a written declaration, one or more of the means set out in article 287, paragraph 1, of the Convention for the settlement of disputes under this Part. Article 287 shall apply to such a declaration, as well as to any dispute to which such State is a party which is not covered by a declaration in force. For the purposes of conciliation and arbitration in accordance with Annexes V, VII and VIII to the Convention, such State shall be entitled to nominate conciliators, arbitrators and experts to be included in the lists referred to in Annex V, article 2, Annex VII, article 2, and Annex VIII, article 2, for the settlement of disputes under this Part.

5. Any court or tribunal to which a dispute has been submitted under this Part shall apply the relevant provisions of the Convention, of this Agreement and of any relevant subregional, regional or global fisheries agreement, as well as generally accepted standards for the conservation and management of living marine resources and other rules of international law not incompatible with the Convention, with a view to ensuring the conservation of the straddling fish stocks and highly migratory fish stocks concerned.

Article 31 Provisional measures

1. Pending the settlement of a dispute in accordance with this Part, the parties to the dispute shall make every effort to enter into provisional arrangements of a practical nature.

2. Without prejudice to article 290 of the Convention, the court or tribunal to which the dispute has been submitted under this Part may prescribe any provisional measures which it considers appropriate under the circumstances to preserve the respective rights of the parties to the dispute or to prevent damage to the stocks in question, as well as in the circumstances referred to in article 7, paragraph 5, and article 16, paragraph 2.

3. A State Party to this Agreement which is not a Party to the Convention may declare that, notwithstanding article 290, paragraph 5, of the Convention, the International Tribunal for the Law of the Sea shall not be entitled to prescribe, modify or revoke provisional measures without the agreement of such State.

Article 32 Limitations on applicability of procedures for the settlement of disputes

Article 297, paragraph 3, of the Convention applies also to this Agreement.

PART IX
NON-PARTIES TO THIS AGREEMENT

Article 33 Non-parties to this Agreement

1. States Parties shall encourage non-parties to this Agreement to become parties thereto and to adopt laws and regulations consistent with its provisions.

2. States Parties shall take measures consistent with this Agreement and international law to deter the activities of vessels flying the flag of non-parties which undermine the effective implementation of this Agreement.

PART X
GOOD FAITH AND ABUSE OF RIGHTS

Article 34 Good faith and abuse of rights

States Parties shall fulfil in good faith the obligations assumed under this Agreement and shall exercise the rights recognized in this Agreement in a manner which would not constitute an abuse of right.

PART XI
RESPONSIBILITY AND LIABILITY

Article 35 Responsibility and liability

States Parties are liable in accordance with international law for damage or loss attributable to them in regard to this Agreement.

PART XII
REVIEW CONFERENCE

Article 36 Review conference

1. Four years after the date of entry into force of this Agreement, the Secretary-General of the United Nations shall convene a conference with a view to assessing the effectiveness of this Agreement in securing the conservation and management of straddling fish stocks and highly migratory fish stocks. The Secretary-General shall invite to the conference all States Parties and those States and entities which are entitled to become parties to this Agreement as well as those intergovernmental and non-governmental organizations entitled to participate as observers.

2. The conference shall review and assess the adequacy of the provisions of this Agreement and, if necessary, propose means of strengthening the substance and methods of implementation of those provisions in order better to address any continuing problems in the conservation and management of straddling fish stocks and highly migratory fish stocks.

PART XIII
FINAL PROVISIONS

Article 37 Signature

This Agreement shall be open for signature by all States and the other entities referred to in article 1, paragraph 2 (b), and shall remain open for signature at United Nations Headquarters for twelve months from the fourth of December 1995.

Article 38 Ratification

This Agreement is subject to ratification by States and the other entities referred to in article 1, paragraph 2 (b). The instruments of ratification shall be deposited with the Secretary-General of the United Nations.

Article 39 Accession

This Agreement shall remain open for accession by States and the other entities referred to in article 1, paragraph 2 (b). The instruments of accession shall be deposited with the Secretary-General of the United Nations.

Article 40 Entry into force

1. This Agreement shall enter into force 30 days after the date of deposit of the thirtieth instrument of ratification or accession.

2. For each State or entity which ratifies the Agreement or accedes thereto after the deposit of the thirtieth instrument of ratification or accession, this Agreement shall enter into force on the thirtieth day following the deposit of its instrument of ratification or accession.

Article 41 Provisional application

1. This Agreement shall be applied provisionally by a State or entity which consents to its provisional application by so notifying the depositary in writing. Such provisional application shall become effective from the date of receipt of the notification.

2. Provisional application by a State or entity shall terminate upon the entry into force of this Agreement for that State or entity or upon notification by that State or entity to the depositary in writing of its intention to terminate provisional application.

Article 42 Reservations and exceptions

No reservations or exceptions may be made to this Agreement.

Article 43 Declarations and statements

Article 42 does not preclude a State or entity, when signing, ratifying or acceding to this Agreement, from making declarations or statements, however phrased or named, with a view, *inter alia*, to the harmonization of its laws and regulations with the provisions of this Agreement, provided that such declarations or statements do not purport to exclude or to modify the legal effect of the provisions of this Agreement in their application to that State or entity.

Article 44 Relation to other agreements

1. This Agreement shall not alter the rights and obligations of States Parties which arise from other agreements compatible with this Agreement and which do not affect the enjoyment by other States Parties of their rights or the performance of their obligations under this Agreement.

2. Two or more States Parties may conclude agreements modifying or suspending the operation of provisions of this Agreement, applicable solely to the relations between them, provided that such agreements do not relate to a provision derogation from which is incompatible with the effective execution of the object and purpose of this Agreement, and provided further that such agreements shall not affect the application of the basic principles embodied herein, and that the provisions of such agreements do not affect the enjoyment by other States Parties of their rights or the performance of their obligations under this Agreement.

3. States Parties intending to conclude an agreement referred to in paragraph 2 shall notify the other States Parties through the depositary of this Agreement of their intention to conclude the agreement and of the modification or suspension for which it provides.

Article 45 Amendment

1. A State Party may, by written communication addressed to the Secretary-General of the United Nations, propose amendments to this Agreement and request the convening of a conference to consider such proposed amendments. The Secretary-General shall circulate such communication to all States Parties. If, within six months from the date of the circulation of the communication, not less than one half of the States Parties reply favourably to the request, the Secretary-General shall convene the conference.

2. The decision-making procedure applicable at the amendment conference convened pursuant to paragraph 1 shall be the same as that applicable at the United Nations Conference on Straddling Fish Stocks and Highly Migratory Fish Stocks, unless otherwise decided by the conference. The conference should make every effort to reach agreement on any amendments by way of consensus and there should be no voting on them until all efforts at consensus have been exhausted.

3. Once adopted, amendments to this Agreement shall be open for signature at United Nations Headquarters by States Parties for twelve months from the date of adoption, unless otherwise provided in the amendment itself.

4. Articles 38, 39, 47 and 50 apply to all amendments to this Agreement.

5. Amendments to this Agreement shall enter into force for the States Parties ratifying or acceding to them on the thirtieth day following the deposit of instruments of ratification or accession by two thirds of the States Parties. Thereafter, for each State Party ratifying or acceding to an amendment after the deposit of the required number of such instruments, the amendment shall enter into force on the thirtieth day following the deposit of its instrument of ratification or accession.

6. An amendment may provide that a smaller or a larger number of ratifications or accessions shall be required for its entry into force than are required by this article.

7. A State which becomes a Party to this Agreement after the entry into force of amendments in accordance with paragraph 5 shall, failing an expression of a different intention by that State:

(a) be considered as a Party to this Agreement as so amended; and

(b) be considered as a Party to the unamended Agreement in relation to any State Party not bound by the amendment.

Article 46 Denunciation

1. A State Party may, by written notification addressed to the Secretary-General of the United Nations, denounce this Agreement and may indicate its reasons. Failure to indicate reasons shall not affect the validity of the denunciation. The denunciation shall take effect one year after the date of receipt of the notification, unless the notification specifies a later date.

2. The denunciation shall not in any way affect the duty of any State Party to fulfil any obligation embodied in this Agreement to which it would be subject under international law independently of this Agreement.

Article 47 Participation by international organizations

1. In cases where an international organization referred to in Annex IX, article 1, of the Convention does not have competence over all the matters governed by this Agreement, Annex IX to the Convention shall apply *mutatis mutandis* to participation by such international organization in this Agreement, except that the following provisions of that Annex shall not apply:

(a) article 2, first sentence; and

(b) article 3, paragraph 1.

2. In cases where an international organization referred to in Annex IX, article 1, of the Convention has competence over all the matters governed by this Agreement, the following provisions shall apply to participation by such international organization in this Agreement:

(a) at the time of signature or accession, such international organization shall make a declaration stating:

(i)   that it has competence over all the matters governed by this Agreement;

    (ii) that, for this reason, its member States shall not become States Parties, except in respect of their territories for which the international organization has no responsibility; and

    (iii) that it accepts the rights and obligations of States under this Agreement;

(b) participation of such an international organization shall in no case confer any rights under this Agreement on member States of the international organization;

(c) in the event of a conflict between the obligations of an international organization under this Agreement and its obligations under the agreement establishing the international organization or any acts relating to it, the obligations under this Agreement shall prevail.

Article 48 Annexes

1. The Annexes form an integral part of this Agreement and, unless expressly provided otherwise, a reference to this Agreement or to one of its Parts includes a reference to the Annexes relating thereto.

2. The Annexes may be revised from time to time by States Parties. Such revisions shall be based on scientific and technical considerations. Notwithstanding the provisions of article 45, if a revision to an Annex is adopted by consensus at a meeting of States Parties, it shall be incorporated in this Agreement and shall take effect from the date of its adoption or from such other date as may be specified in the revision. If a revision to an Annex is not adopted by consensus at such a meeting, the amendment procedures set out in article 45 shall apply.

Article 49 Depositary

The Secretary-General of the United Nations shall be the depositary of this Agreement and any amendments or revisions thereto.

Article 50 Authentic texts

The Arabic, Chinese, English, French, Russian and Spanish texts of this Agreement are equally authentic.

IN WITNESS WHEREOF, the undersigned Plenipotentiaries, being duly authorized thereto, have signed this Agreement.

OPENED FOR SIGNATURE at New York, this fourth day of December, one thousand nine hundred and ninety-five, in a single original, in the Arabic, Chinese, English, French, Russian and Spanish languages.

ANNEX I
STANDARD REQUIREMENTS FOR THE COLLECTION AND SHARING OF DATA

Article 1 General principles

1. The timely collection, compilation and analysis of data are fundamental to the effective conservation and management of straddling fish stocks and highly migratory fish stocks. To this end, data from fisheries for these stocks on the high seas and those in areas under national jurisdiction are required and should be collected and compiled in such a way as to enable statistically meaningful analysis for the purposes of fishery resource conservation and management. These data include catch and fishing effort statistics and other fishery-related information, such as vessel-related and other data for standardizing fishing effort. Data collected should also include information on non-target and associated or dependent species. All data should be verified to ensure accuracy. Confidentiality of

non-aggregated data shall be maintained. The dissemination of such data shall be subject to the terms on which they have been provided.

2. Assistance, including training as well as financial and technical assistance, shall be provided to developing States in order to build capacity in the field of conservation and management of living marine resources. Assistance should focus on enhancing capacity to implement data collection and verification, observer programmes, data analysis and research projects supporting stock assessments. The fullest possible involvement of developing State scientists and managers in conservation and management of straddling fish stocks and highly migratory fish stocks should be promoted.

Article 2 Principles of data collection, compilation and exchange

The following general principles should be considered in defining the parameters for collection, compilation and exchange of data from fishing operations for straddling fish stocks and highly migratory fish stocks:

(a)   States should ensure that data are collected from vessels flying their flag on fishing activities according to the operational characteristics of each fishing method (e.g., each individual tow for trawl, each set for long-line and purse-seine, each school fished for pole-and-line and each day fished for troll) and in sufficient detail to facilitate effective stock assessment;

(b)   States should ensure that fishery data are verified through an appropriate system;

(c)   States should compile fishery-related and other supporting scientific data and provide them in an agreed format and in a timely manner to the relevant subregional or regional fisheries management organization or arrangement where one exists. Otherwise, States should cooperate to exchange data either directly or through such other cooperative mechanisms as may be agreed among them;

(d)   States should agree, within the framework of subregional or regional fisheries management organizations or arrangements, or otherwise, on the specification of data and the format in which they are to be provided, in accordance with this Annex and taking into account the nature of the stocks and the fisheries for those stocks in the region. Such organizations or arrangements should request non-members or non-participants to provide data concerning relevant fishing activities by vessels flying their flag;

(e)   such organizations or arrangements shall compile data and make them available in a timely manner and in an agreed format to all interested States under the terms and conditions established by the organization or arrangement; and

(f)   scientists of the flag State and from the relevant subregional or regional fisheries management organization or arrangement should analyse the data separately or jointly, as appropriate.

Article 3 Basic fishery data

1. States shall collect and make available to the relevant subregional or regional fisheries management organization or arrangement the following types of data in sufficient detail to facilitate effective stock assessment in accordance with agreed procedures:

(a)   time series of catch and effort statistics by fishery and fleet;

(b)   total catch in number, nominal weight, or both, by species (both target and non-target) as is appropriate to each fishery. [Nominal weight is defined by the Food and Agriculture Organization of the United Nations as the live-weight equivalent of the landings];

(c) discard statistics, including estimates where necessary, reported as number or nominal weight by species, as is appropriate to each fishery;

(d) effort statistics appropriate to each fishing method; and

(e) fishing location, date and time fished and other statistics on fishing operations as appropriate.

2. States shall also collect where appropriate and provide to the relevant subregional or regional fisheries management organization or arrangement information to support stock assessment, including:

(a) composition of the catch according to length, weight and sex;

(b) other biological information supporting stock assessments, such as information on age, growth, recruitment, distribution and stock identity; and

(c) other relevant research, including surveys of abundance, biomass surveys, hydro-acoustic surveys, research on environmental factors affecting stock abundance, and oceanographic and ecological studies.

Article 4 Vessel data and information

1. States should collect the following types of vessel-related data for standardizing fleet composition and vessel fishing power and for converting between different measures of effort in the analysis of catch and effort data:

(a) vessel identification, flag and port of registry;

(b) vessel type;

(c) vessel specifications (e.g., material of construction, date built, registered length, gross registered tonnage, power of main engines, hold capacity and catch storage methods); and

(d) fishing gear description (e.g., types, gear specifications and quantity).

2. The flag State will collect the following information:

(a) navigation and position fixing aids;

(b) communication equipment and international radio call sign; and

(c) crew size.

Article 5 Reporting

A State shall ensure that vessels flying its flag send to its national fisheries administration and, where agreed, to the relevant subregional or regional fisheries management organization or arrangement, logbook data on catch and effort, including data on fishing operations on the high seas, at sufficiently frequent intervals to meet national requirements and regional and international obligations. Such data shall be transmitted, where necessary, by radio, telex, facsimile or satellite transmission or by other means.

Article 6 Data verification

States or, as appropriate, subregional or regional fisheries management organizations or arrangements should establish mechanisms for verifying fishery data, such as:

(a) position verification through vessel monitoring systems;

(b) scientific observer programmes to monitor catch, effort, catch composition (target and non-target) and other details of fishing operations;

(c) vessel trip, landing and transshipment reports; and

(d) port sampling.

Article 7 Data exchange

1. Data collected by flag States must be shared with other flag States and relevant coastal States through appropriate subregional or regional fisheries management

organizations or arrangements. Such organizations or arrangements shall compile data and make them available in a timely manner and in an agreed format to all interested States under the terms and conditions established by the organization or arrangement, while maintaining confidentiality of non-aggregated data, and should, to the extent feasible, develop database systems which provide efficient access to data.

2. At the global level, collection and dissemination of data should be effected through the Food and Agriculture Organization of the United Nations. Where a subregional or regional fisheries management organization or arrangement does not exist, that organization may also do the same at the subregional or regional level by arrangement with the States concerned.

ANNEX II
GUIDELINES FOR THE APPLICATION OF PRECAUTIONARY REFERENCE POINTS IN CONSERVATION AND MANAGEMENT OF STRADDLING FISH STOCKS AND HIGHLY MIGRATORY FISH STOCKS

1. A precautionary reference point is an estimated value derived through an agreed scientific procedure, which corresponds to the state of the resource and of the fishery, and which can be used as a guide for fisheries management.

2. Two types of precautionary reference points should be used: conservation, or limit, reference points and management, or target, reference points. Limit reference points set boundaries which are intended to constrain harvesting within safe biological limits within which the stocks can produce maximum sustainable yield. Target reference points are intended to meet management objectives.

3. Precautionary reference points should be stock-specific to account, *inter alia*, for the reproductive capacity, the resilience of each stock and the characteristics of fisheries exploiting the stock, as well as other sources of mortality and major sources of uncertainty.

4. Management strategies shall seek to maintain or restore populations of harvested stocks, and where necessary associated or dependent species, at levels consistent with previously agreed precautionary reference points. Such reference points shall be used to trigger pre-agreed conservation and management action. Management strategies shall include measures which can be implemented when precautionary reference points are approached.

5. Fishery management strategies shall ensure that the risk of exceeding limit reference points is very low. If a stock falls below a limit reference point or is at risk of falling below such a reference point, conservation and management action should be initiated to facilitate stock recovery. Fishery management strategies shall ensure that target reference points are not exceeded on average.

6. When information for determining reference points for a fishery is poor or absent, provisional reference points shall be set. Provisional reference points may be established by analogy to similar and better-known stocks. In such situations, the fishery shall be subject to enhanced monitoring so as to enable revision of provisional reference points as improved information becomes available.

7. The fishing mortality rate which generates maximum sustainable yield should be regarded as a minimum standard for limit reference points. For stocks which are not overfished, fishery management strategies shall ensure that fishing mortality does not exceed that which corresponds to maximum sustainable yield, and that the biomass does not fall below a predefined threshold. For overfished stocks, the biomass which would produce maximum sustainable yield can serve as a rebuilding target.

Agreement on Illicit Traffic by Sea, Implementing Article 17 of the United Nations Convention against Illicit Traffic in Narcotic Drugs and Psychotropic Substances

Done at Strasbourg, 31 January 1995; entry into force, 1 May 2000
2136 UNTS 81 [Registration Number 37251]

The member States of the Council of Europe, having expressed their consent to be bound by the United Nations Convention against Illicit Traffic in Narcotic Drugs and Psychotropic Substances, done at Vienna on 20 December 1988, hereinafter referred to as 'The Vienna Convention',

Considering that the aim of the Council of Europe is to achieve a greater unity between its members;

Convinced of the need to pursue a common criminal policy aimed at the protection of society;

Considering that the fight against serious crime, which has become an increasingly international problem, calls for close co-operation on an international scale;

Desiring to increase their co-operation to the fullest possible extent in the suppression of illicit traffic in narcotic drugs and psychotropic substances by sea, in conformity with the international law of the sea and in full respect of the principle of right of freedom of navigation;

Considering, therefore, that Article 17 of the Vienna Convention should be supplemented by a regional agreement to carry out, and to enhance the effectiveness of, the provisions of that article,

Have agreed as follows:

CHAPTER I - DEFINITIONS

Article 1 Definitions

For the purposes of this Agreement:

a. 'Intervening State' means a State Party which has requested or proposes to request authorisation from another Party to take action under this Agreement in relation to a vessel flying the flag or displaying the marks of registry of that other State Party;

b. 'Preferential jurisdiction' means, in relation to a flag State having concurrent jurisdiction over a relevant offence with another State, the right to exercise its jurisdiction on a priority basis, to the exclusion of the other State's jurisdiction over the offence;

c. 'Relevant offence' means any offence of the kind described in Article 3, paragraph 1, of the Vienna Convention;

d. 'Vessel' means a ship or any other floating craft of any description, including hovercraft and submersible craft.

CHAPTER II - INTERNATIONAL CO-OPERATION

Article 2 General Principles

1. The Parties shall co-operate to the fullest extent possible to suppress illicit traffic in narcotic drugs and psychotropic substances by sea, in conformity with the international law of the sea.

2. In the implementation of this Agreement the Parties shall endeavour to ensure that their actions maximise the effectiveness of law enforcement measures against illicit traffic in narcotic drugs and psychotropic substances by sea.

3. Any action taken in pursuance of this Agreement shall take due account of the need not to interfere with or affect the rights and obligations of and the exercise of jurisdiction by costal States, in accordance with the international law of the sea.

4. Nothing in this Agreement shall be so construed as to infringe the principle of *non bis in idem*, as applied in national law.

5. The Parties recognise the value of gathering and exchanging information concerning vessels, cargo and facts, whenever they consider that such exchange of information could assist a Party in the suppression of illicit traffic in narcotic drugs and psychotropic substances by sea.

6. Nothing in this Agreement affects the immunities of warships and other government vessels operated for non-commercial purposes.

Article 3 Jurisdiction

1. Each Party shall take such measures as may be necessary to establish its jurisdiction over the relevant offences when the offence is committed on board a vessel flying its flag.

2. For the purposes of applying this Agreement, each Party shall take such measures as may be necessary to establish its jurisdiction over the relevant offences committed on board a vessel flying the flag or displaying the marks of registry or bearing any other indication of nationality of any other Party to this Agreement. Such jurisdiction shall be exercised only in conformity with this Agreement.

3. For the purposes of applying this Agreement, each Party shall take such measures as may be necessary to establish its jurisdiction over the relevant offences committed on board a vessel which is without nationality, or which is assimilated to a vessel without nationality under international law.

4. The flag State has preferential jurisdiction over any relevant offence committed on board its vessel.

5. Each State may, at the time of signature or when depositing its instrument of ratification, acceptance, approval, or accession, or at any later date, by a declaration addressed to the Secretary General of the Council of Europe, inform the other Parties to the agreement of the criteria it intends to apply in respect of the exercise of the jurisdiction established pursuant to paragraph 2 of this article.

6. Any State which does not have in service warships, military aircraft or other government ships or aircraft operated for non-commercial purposes, which would enable it to become an intervening State under this Agreement may, at the time of signature or when depositing its instrument of ratification, acceptance, approval or accession, by a declaration addressed to the Secretary General of the Council of Europe declare that it will not apply paragraphs 2 and 3 of this Article. A State which has made such a declaration is under the obligation to withdraw it when the circumstances justifying the reservation no longer exist.

Article 4 Assistance to flag States

1. A Party which has reasonable grounds to suspect that a vessel flying its flag is engaged in or being used for the commission of a relevant offence, may request the assistance of other Parties in suppressing its use for that purpose. The Parties so requested shall render such assistance within the means available to them.

2. In making its request, the flag State may, *inter alia*, authorise the requested Party, subject to any conditions or limitations which may be imposed, to take some or all of the actions specified in this Agreement.

3. When the requested Party agrees to act upon the authorisation of the flag State given to it in accordance with paragraph 2, the provisions of this Agreement in respect of the rights and obligations of the intervening State and the flag State shall, where appropriate and unless otherwise specified, apply to the requested and requesting Party, respectively.

Article 5 Vessels without nationality

1. A Party which has reasonable grounds to suspect that a vessel without nationality, or assimilated to a vessel without nationality under international law, is engaged in or being used for the commission of a relevant offence, shall inform such other Parties as appear most closely affected and may request the assistance of any such Party in suppressing its use for that purpose. The Party so requested shall render such assistance within the means available to it.

2. Where a Party, having received information in accordance with paragraph 1, takes action it shall be for that Party to determine what actions are appropriate and to exercise its jurisdiction over any relevant offences which may have been committed by any persons on board the vessel.

3. Any Party which has taken action under this article shall communicate as soon as possible to the Party which has provided information, or made a request for assistance, the results of any action taken in respect of the vessel and any persons on board.

SECTION 2. AUTHORISATION PROCEDURES

Article 6 Basic rules on authorisation

Where the intervening State has reasonable grounds to suspect that a vessel, which is flying the flag or displaying the marks of registry of another Party or bears any other indications of nationality of the vessel, is engaged in or being used for the commission of a relevant offence, the intervening State may request the authorisation of the flag State to stop and board the vessel in waters beyond the territorial sea of any Party, and to take some or all of the other actions specified in this Agreement. No such actions may be taken by virtue of this Agreement, without the authorisation of the flag State.

Article 7 Decision on the request for authorisation

The flag State shall immediately acknowledge receipt of a request for authorisation under Article 6 and shall communicate a decision thereon as soon as possible and, wherever practicable, within four hours of receipt of the request.

Article 8 Conditions

1. If the flag State grants the request, such authorisation may be made subject to conditions or limitations. Such conditions or limitations may, in particular, provide that the flag State's express authorisation be given before any specified steps are taken by the intervening State.

2. Each State may, at the time of signature or when depositing its instrument of ratification, acceptance, approval or accession, by declaration addressed to the Secretary General of the Council of Europe declare that, when acting as an intervening State, it may subject its intervention to the condition that persons having its nationality who are surrendered to the flag State under Article 15 and there convicted of a relevant offence, shall have the possibility to be transferred to the intervening State to serve the sentence imposed.

SECTION 3. RULES GOVERNING ACTION

Article 9 Authorised actions
1. Having received the authorisation of the flag State, and subject to the conditions or limitations, if any, made under Article 8, paragraph 1, the intervening State may take the following actions:

   i.   a.   stop and board the vessel;

          b.   establish effective control of the vessel and over any person thereon;

          c.   take any action provided for in sub-paragraph ii of this article which is considered necessary to establish whether a relevant offence has been committed and to secure any evidence thereof;

          d.   require the vessel and any persons thereon to be taken into the territory of the intervening State and detain the vessel there for the purpose of carrying out further investigations;

   ii.   and, having established effective control of the vessel:

          a.   search the vessel, anyone on it and anything in it, including its cargo;

          b.   open or require the opening of any containers, and test or take samples of anything on the vessel;

          c.   require any person on the vessel to give information concerning himself or anything on the vessel;

          d.   require the production of documents, books or records relating to the vessel or any persons or objects on it, and make photographs or copies or anything the production of which the competent authorities have the power to require;

          e.   seize, secure and protect any evidence or material discovered on the vessel.

2. Any action taken under paragraph 1 of this article shall be without prejudice to any right existing under the law of the intervening State of suspected persons not to incriminate themselves.

Article 10 Enforcement measures
1. Where, as a result of action taken under Article 9, the intervening State has evidence that a relevant offence has been committed which would be sufficient under its laws to justify its either arresting the persons concerned or detaining the vessel, or both, it may so proceed.

2. The intervening State shall, without delay, notify the flag State of steps taken under paragraph 1 above.

3. The vessel shall not be detained for a period longer than that which is strictly necessary to complete the investigations into relevant offences. Where there are reasonable grounds to suspect that the owners of the vessel are directly involved in a relevant offence, the vessel and its cargo may be further detained on completion of the investigation. Persons not suspected of any relevant offence and objects not required as evidence shall be released.

4. Notwithstanding the provisions of the preceding paragraph, the intervening State and the flag State may agree with a third State, Party to this Agreement, that the vessel may be taken to the territory of that third State and, once the vessel is in that territory, the third State shall be treated for the purposes of this Agreement as an intervening State.

Article 11 Execution of action

1. Actions taken under Articles 9 and 10 shall be governed by the law of the intervening State.

2. Actions under Article 9, paragraph 1 a, b and d, shall be carried out only by warships or military aircraft, or by other ships or aircraft clearly marked and identifiable as being on government service and authorised to that effect.

3.   a.   An official of the intervening State may not be prosecuted in the flag State for any act performed in the exercise of his functions. In such a case, the official shall be liable to prosecution in the intervening State as if the elements constituting the offence had been committed within the jurisdiction of that State.

      b.   In any proceedings instituted in the flag State, offences committed against an official of the intervening State with respect to actions carried out under Articles 9 and 10 shall be treated as if they had been committed against an official of the flag State.

4. The master of a vessel which has been boarded in accordance with this Agreement shall be entitled to communicate with the authorities of the vessel's flag State as well as with the owners or operators of the vessel for the purpose of notifying them that the vessel has been boarded. However, the authorities of the intervening State may prevent or delay any communication with the owners or operators of the vessel if they have reasonable grounds for believing that such communication would obstruct the investigations into a relevant offence.

Article 12 Operational safeguards

1. In the application of this Agreement, the Parties concerned shall take due account of the need not to endanger the safety of life at sea, the security of the vessel and cargo and not to prejudice any commercial or legal interest. In particular, they shall take into account:

    a.   the dangers involved in boarding a vessel at sea, and give consideration to whether this could be more safely done at the vessel's next port of call;

    b.   the need to minimise any interference with the legitimate commercial activities of a vessel;

    c.   the need to avoid unduly detaining or delaying a vessel;

    d.   the need to restrict the use of force to the minimum necessary to ensure compliance with the instructions of the intervening State.

2. The use of firearms against, or on, the vessel shall be reported as soon as possible to the flag State.

3. The death, or injury, of any person aboard the vessel shall be reported as soon as possible to the flag State. The authorities of the intervening State shall fully co-operate with the authorities of the flag State in any investigation the flag State may hold into any such death or injury.

SECTION 4. RULES GOVERNING THE EXERCISE OF JURISDICTION

Article 13 Evidence of offences

1. To enable the flag State to decide whether to exercise its preferential jurisdiction in accordance with the provisions of Article 14, the intervening State shall without delay transmit to the flag State a summary of the evidence of any offences discovered as a result of action taken pursuant to Article 9. The flag State shall acknowledge receipt of the summary forthwith.

2. If the intervening State discovers evidence which leads it to believe that offences outside the scope of this Agreement may have been committed, or that suspect persons not involved in relevant offences are on board the vessel, it shall notify the flag State. Where appropriate, the Parties involved shall consult.

3. The provisions of this Agreement shall be so construed as to permit the intervening State to take measures, including the detention of persons, other than those aimed at the investigation and prosecution of relevant offences, only when:

   a. the flag State gives its express consent; or
   b. such measures are aimed at the investigation and prosecution of an offence committed after the person has been taken into the territory of the intervening State.

Article 14 Exercise of preferential jurisdiction

1. A flag State wishing to exercise its preferential jurisdiction shall do so in accordance with the provisions of this article.

2. It shall notify the intervening State to this effect as soon as possible and at the latest within fourteen days from the receipt of the summary of evidence pursuant to Article 13. If the flag State fails to do this, it shall be deemed to have waived the exercise of its preferential jurisdiction.

3. Where the flag State has notified the intervening State that it exercises its preferential jurisdiction, the exercise of the jurisdiction of the intervening State shall be suspended, save for the purpose of surrendering persons, vessels, cargoes and evidence in accordance with this Agreement.

4. The flag State shall submit the case forthwith to its competent authorities for the purpose of prosecution.

5. Measures taken by the intervening State against the vessel and persons on board may be deemed to have been taken as part of the procedure of the flag State.

Article 15 Surrender of vessels, cargoes, persons and evidence

1. Where the flag State has notified the intervening State of its intention to exercise its preferential jurisdiction, and if the flag State so requests, the persons arrested, the vessel, the cargo and the evidence seized shall be surrendered to that State in accordance with the provisions of this Agreement.

2. The request for the surrender of arrested persons shall be supported by, in respect of each person, the original or a certified copy of the warrant of arrest or other order having the same effect, issued by a judicial authority in accordance with the procedure prescribed by the law of the flag State.

3. The Parties shall use their best endeavours to expedite the surrender of persons, vessels, cargoes and evidence.

4. Nothing in this Agreement shall be so construed as to deprive any detained person of his right under the law of intervening State to have the lawfulness of his detention reviewed by a court of that State, in accordance with procedures established by its national law.

5. Instead of requesting the surrender of the detained persons or of the vessel, the flag State may request their immediate release. Where this request has been made, the intervening State shall release them forthwith.

Article 16 Capital punishment

If any offence for which the flag State decides to exercise its preferential jurisdiction in accordance with Article 14 is punishable by death under the law of that State, and if in respect of such an offence the death penalty is not provided by the law of the intervening State or is not normally carried out, the surrender of any person may be refused unless the flag State gives such assurances as the intervening State considers sufficient that the death penalty will not be carried out.

SECTION 5. PROCEDURAL AND OTHER GENERAL RULES

Article 17 Competent authorities

1. Each Party shall designate an authority, which shall be responsible for sending and answering requests under Articles 6 and 7 of this Agreement. So far as is practicable, each Party shall make arrangements so that this authority may receive and respond to the requests at any hour of any day or night.

2. The Parties shall furthermore designate a central authority which shall be responsible for the notification of the exercise of preferential jurisdiction under Article 14 and for all other communications or notifications under this Agreement.

3. Each Party shall, at the time of signature or when depositing its instrument of ratification, acceptance, approval or accession, communicate to the Secretary General of the Council of Europe the names and addresses of the authorities designated in pursuance of this article, together with any other information facilitating communication under this Agreement. Any subsequent change with respect to the name, address or other relevant information concerning such authorities shall likewise be communicated to the Secretary General.

Article 18 Communication between designated authorities

1. The authorities designated under Article 17 shall communicate directly with one another.

2. Where, for any reason, direct communication is not practicable, Parties may agree to use the communication channels of ICPO-Interpol or of the Customs Co-operation Council.

Article 19 Form of request and languages

1. All communications under Articles 5 to 16 shall be made in writing. Modern means of telecommunications, such as telefax, may be used.

2. Subject to the provisions of paragraph 3 of this article, translations of the requests, other communications and supporting documents shall not be required.

3. At the time of signature or when depositing its instrument of ratification, acceptance, approval or accession, any Party may communicate to the Secretary General of the Council of Europe a declaration that it reserves the right to require that requests, other communications and supporting documents sent to it, be made in or accompanied by a translation into its own language or into one of the official languages of the Council of Europe or into such one of these languages as it shall indicate. It may on that occasion declare its readiness to accept translations in any other language as it may specify. The other Parties may apply the reciprocity rule.

Article 20 Authentication and legalisation

Documents transmitted in application of this Agreement shall be exempt from all authentication and legalisation formalities.

Article 21 Content of request

A request under Article 6 shall specify:

a. the authority making the request and the authority carrying out the investigations or proceedings;

b. details of the vessel concerned, including, as far as possible, its name, a description of the vessel, any marks of registry or other signs indicating nationality, as well as its location, together with a request for confirmation that the vessel has the nationality of the requested Party;

c. details of the suspected offences, together with the grounds for suspicion;

d. the action it is proposed to take and an assurance that such action would be taken if the vessel concerned had been flying the flag of the intervening State.

Article 22 Information for owners and masters of vessels

Each Party shall take such measures as may be necessary to inform the owners and masters of vessels flying their flag that States Parties to this Agreement may be granted the authority to board vessels beyond the territorial sea of any Party for the purposes specified in this Agreement and to inform them in particular of the obligation to comply with instructions given by a boarding party from an intervening State exercising that authority.

Article 23 Restriction of use

The flag State may make the authorisation referred to in Article 6 subject to the condition that the information or evidence obtained will not, without its prior consent, be used or transmitted by the authorities of the intervening State in respect of investigations or proceedings other than those relating to relevant offences.

Article 24 Confidentiality

The Parties concerned shall, if this is not contrary to the basic principles of their national law, keep confidential any evidence and information provided by another Party in pursuance of this Agreement, except to the extent that its disclosure is necessary for the application of the Agreement or for any investigations or proceedings.

Section 6. Costs and Damages

Article 25 Costs

1. Unless otherwise agreed by the Parties concerned, the cost of carrying out any action under Articles 9 and 10 shall be borne by the intervening State, and the cost of carrying out action under Articles 4 and 5 shall normally be borne by the Party which renders assistance.

2. Where the flag State has exercised its preferential jurisdiction in accordance with Article 14, the cost of returning the vessel and of transporting suspected persons and evidence shall be borne by it.

Article 26 Damages

1. If, in the process of taking action pursuant to Articles 9 and 10 above, any person, whether natural or legal, suffers loss, damage or injury as a result of negligence or some

other fault attributable to the intervening State, it shall be liable to pay compensation in respect thereof.

2. Where the action is taken in a manner which is not justified by the terms of this Agreement, the intervening State shall be liable to pay compensation for any resulting loss, damage or injury. The intervening State shall also be liable to pay compensation for any such loss, damage or injury, if the suspicions prove to be unfounded and provided that the vessel boarded, the operator or the crew have not committed any act justifying them.

3. Liability for any damage resulting from action under Article 4 shall rest with the requesting State, which may seek compensation from the requested State where the damage was a result of negligence or some other fault attributable to that State.

CHAPTER III - FINAL PROVISIONS

Article 27 Signature and entry into force

1. This Agreement shall be open for signature by the member States of the Council of Europe which have already expressed their consent to be bound by the Vienna Convention. They may express their consent to be bound by this Agreement by:

    a. signature without reservation as to ratification, acceptance or approval; or

    b. signature subject to ratification, acceptance or approval, followed by ratification, acceptance or approval.

2. Instruments of ratification, acceptance or approval shall be deposited with the Secretary General of the Council of Europe.

3. This Agreement shall enter into force on the first day of the month following the expiry of a period of three months after the date on which three member States of the Council of Europe have expressed their consent to be bound by the Agreement in accordance with the provisions of paragraph 1.

4. In respect of any signatory State which subsequently expresses its consent to be bound by it, the Agreement shall enter into force on the first day of the month following the expiry of a period of three months after the date of its consent to be bound by the Agreement in accordance with the provisions of paragraph 1.

Article 28 Accession

1. After the entry into force of this Agreement, the Committee of Ministers of the Council of Europe, after consulting the Contracting States to the Agreement, may invite any State which is not a member of the Council but which has expressed its consent to be bound by the Vienna Convention to accede to this Agreement, by a decision taken by the majority provided for in Article 20.d of the Statute of the Council of Europe and by the unanimous vote of the representatives of the Contracting States entitled to sit on the Committee.

2. In respect of any acceding State, the Agreement shall enter into force on the first day of the month following the expiry of a period of three months after the date of deposit of the instrument of accession with the Secretary General of the Council of Europe.

Article 29 Territorial application

1. Any State may, at the time of signature or when depositing its instrument of ratification, acceptance, approval or accession, specify the territory or territories in respect of which its consent to be bound to this Agreement shall apply.

2. Any State may, at any later date, by a declaration addressed to the Secretary General of the Council of Europe, extend its consent to be bound by the present Agreement to any other territory specified in the declaration. In respect of such territory the Agreement shall enter into force on the first day of the month following the expiry of a period of three months after the date of receipt of such declaration by the Secretary General.

3. In respect of any territory subject to a declaration under paragraphs 1 and 2 above, authorities may be designated under Article 17, paragraphs 1 and 2.

4. Any declaration made under the preceding paragraphs may, in respect of any territory specified in such declaration, be withdrawn by a notification addressed to the Secretary General. The withdrawal shall become effective on the first day of the month following the expiry of a period of three months after the date of receipt of such notification by the Secretary General.

Article 30 Relationship to other conventions and agreements

1. This Agreement shall not affect rights and undertakings derived from the Vienna Convention or from any international multilateral conventions concerning special matters.

2. The Parties to the Agreement may conclude bilateral or multilateral agreements with one another on the matters dealt with in this Agreement, for the purpose of supplementing or strengthening its provisions or facilitating the application of the principles embodied in it and in Article 17 of the Vienna Convention.

3. If two or more Parties have already concluded an agreement or treaty in respect of a subject dealt with in this Agreement or have otherwise established their relations in respect of that subject, they may agree to apply that agreement or treaty or to regulate those relations accordingly, in lieu of the present Agreement, if it facilitates international co-operation.

Article 31 Reservations

1. Any State may, at the time of signature or when depositing its instrument of ratification, acceptance, approval or accession, declare that it avails itself of one or more of the reservations provided for in Article 3, paragraph 6, Article 19, paragraph 3 and Article 34, paragraph 5. No other reservation may be made.

2. Any State which has made a reservation under the preceding paragraph may wholly or partly withdraw it by means of a notification addressed to the Secretary General of the Council of Europe. The withdrawal shall take effect on the date of receipt of such notification by the Secretary General.

3. A Party which has made a reservation in respect of a provision of this Agreement may not claim the application of that provision by any other Party. It may, however, if its reservation is partial or conditional, claim the application of that provision in so far as it has itself accepted it.

Article 32 Monitoring committee

1. After the entry into force of the present Agreement, a monitoring committee of experts representing the Parties shall be convened at the request of a Party to the Agreement by the Secretary General of the Council of Europe.

2. The monitoring committee shall review the working of the Agreement and make appropriate suggestions to secure its efficient operation.

3. The monitoring committee may decide its own procedural rules.

4. The monitoring committee may decide to invite States not Parties to the Agreement as well as international organisations or bodies, as appropriate, to its meetings.

5. Each Party send every second year a report on the operation of the Agreement to the Secretary General of the Council of Europe in such form and manner as may be decided by the monitoring committee or the European Committee on Crime Problems. The monitoring committee may decide to circulate the information supplied or a report thereon to the Parties and to such international organisations or bodies as it deems appropriate.

Article 33 Amendments

1. Amendments to this Agreement may be proposed by any Party, and shall be communicated by the Secretary General of the Council of Europe to the member States of the Council of Europe and to every non-member State which has acceded to or has been invited to accede to the Agreement in accordance with the provisions of Article 28.

2. Any amendment proposed by a Party shall be communicated to the European Committee on Crime Problems, which shall submit to the Committee of Ministers its opinion on the proposed amendment.

3. The Committee of Ministers shall consider the proposed amendment and the opinion submitted by the European Committee on Crime Problems, and may adopt the amendment.

4. The text of any amendment adopted by the Committee of Ministers in accordance with paragraph 3 of this article shall be forwarded to the Parties for acceptance.

5. Any amendment adopted in accordance with paragraph 3 of this article shall come into force on the thirtieth day after all the Parties have informed the Secretary General of their acceptance thereof.

Article 34 Settlement of disputes

1. The European Committee on Crime Problems of the Council of Europe shall be kept informed of the interpretation and application of this Agreement.

2. In case of a dispute between Parties as to the interpretation or application of this Agreement, the Parties shall seek a settlement of the dispute through negotiation or any other peaceful means of their choice, including submission of the dispute to the European Committee on Crime Problems, to an arbitral tribunal whose decisions shall be binding upon the Parties, mediation, conciliation or judicial process, as agreed upon by the Parties concerned.

3. Any State may, at the time of signature or when depositing its instrument of ratification, acceptance, approval or accession, or on any later date, by a declaration addressed to the Secretary General of the Council of Europe, declare that, in respect of any dispute concerning the interpretation or application of this Agreement, it recognises as compulsory, without prior agreement, and subject to reciprocity, the submission of the dispute to arbitration in accordance with the procedure set out in the appendix to this Agreement.[1]

4. Any dispute which has not been settled in accordance with paragraphs 2 or 3 of this article shall be referred, at the request of any one of the parties to the dispute, to the International Court of Justice for decision.

5. Any State may, at the time of signature or when depositing its instrument of ratification, acceptance, approval or accession, by a declaration addressed to the Secretary General of the Council of Europe, declare that it does not consider itself bound by paragraph 4 of this article.

6. Any Party having made a declaration in accordance with paragraphs 3 or 5 of this article may at any time withdraw the declaration by notification to the Secretary General of the Council of Europe.

Article 35 Denunciation

1. Any Party may, at any time, denounce this Agreement by means of a notification addressed to the Secretary General of the Council of Europe.

---

[1] Appendix omitted.

2. Such denunciation shall become effective on the first day of the month following the expiry of a period of three months after the date of receipt of the notification by the Secretary General.

3. The present Agreement shall, however, continue to remain effective in respect of any actions or proceedings based on applications or requests made during the period of its validity in respect of the denouncing Party.

Article 36 Notifications

The Secretary General of the Council of Europe shall notify the member States of the Council, any State which has acceded to this Agreement and the Secretary General of the United Nations of:

a.   any signature;

b.   the deposit of any instrument of ratification, acceptance, approval or accession;

c.   the name of any authority and any other information communicated pursuant to Article 17;

d.   any reservation made in accordance with Article 31, paragraph 1;

e.   the date of entry into force of this Agreement in accordance with Articles 27 and 28;

f.   any request made under Article 32, paragraph 1, and the date of any meeting convened under that paragraph;

g.   any declaration made under Article 3, paragraphs 5 and 6, Article 8, paragraph 2, Article 19, paragraph 3 and Article 34, paragraphs 3 and 5;

h.   any other act, notification or communication relating to this Agreement.

IN WITNESS WHEREOF the undersigned, being duly authorised thereto, have signed this Agreement.

DONE at Strasbourg, this 31st day of January 1995, in English and in French, both texts being equally authentic, in a single copy which shall be deposited in the archives of the Council of Europe. The Secretary General of the Council of Europe shall transmit certified copies to each member State of the Council of Europe and to any State invited to accede to this Agreement.

Code of Conduct for Responsible Fisheries

Adopted by the Twenty-eighth Session of the FAO Conference on 31 October 1995
FAO, *Code of Conduct for Responsible Fisheries*, 1995[1]

Introduction

Fisheries, including aquaculture, provide a vital source of food, employment, recreation, trade and economic well being for people throughout the world, both for present and future generations and should therefore be conducted in a responsible manner. This Code sets out principles and international standards of behaviour for responsible practices with a view to ensuring the effective conservation, management and development of living aquatic resources, with due respect for the ecosystem and biodiversity. The Code recognises the nutritional, economic, social, environmental and cultural importance of fisheries, and the interests of all those concerned with the fishery sector. The Code takes

---

[1] Preface as well as Annex 1 (Background to the Origin and Elaboration of the Code) and Annex 2 (Resolution adopting the Code of Conduct for Responsible Fisheries) omitted.

into account the biological characteristics of the resources and their environment and the interests of consumers and other users. States and all those involved in fisheries are encouraged to apply the Code and give effect to it.

Article 1 Nature and scope of the Code

1.1 This Code is voluntary. However, certain parts of it are based on relevant rules of international law, including those reflected in the United Nations Convention on the Law of the Sea of 10 December 1982.[2] The Code also contains provisions that may be or have already been given binding effect by means of other obligatory legal instruments amongst the Parties, such as the Agreement to Promote Compliance with International Conservation and Management Measures by Fishing Vessels on the High Seas, 1993, which, according to FAO Conference resolution 15/93, paragraph 3, forms an integral part of the Code.

1.2 The Code is global in scope, and is directed toward members and non-members of FAO, fishing entities, subregional, regional and global organizations, whether governmental or non-governmental, and all persons concerned with the conservation of fishery resources and management and development of fisheries, such as fishers, those engaged in processing and marketing of fish and fishery products and other users of the aquatic environment in relation to fisheries.

1.3 The Code provides principles and standards applicable to the conservation, management and development of all fisheries. It also covers the capture, processing and trade of fish and fishery products, fishing operations, aquaculture, fisheries research and the integration of fisheries into coastal area management.

1.4 In this Code, the reference to States includes the European Community in matters within its competence, and the term fisheries applies equally to capture fisheries and aquaculture.

Article 2 Objectives of the Code

The objectives of the Code are to:

a) establish principles, in accordance with the relevant rules of international law, for responsible fishing and fisheries activities, taking into account all their relevant biological, technological, economic, social, environmental and commercial aspects;

b) establish principles and criteria for the elaboration and implementation of national policies for responsible conservation of fisheries resources and fisheries management and development;

c) serve as an instrument of reference to help States to establish or to improve the legal and institutional framework required for the exercise of responsible fisheries and in the formulation and implementation of appropriate measures;

d) provide guidance which may be used where appropriate in the formulation and implementation of international agreements and other legal instruments, both binding and voluntary;

e) facilitate and promote technical, financial and other cooperation in conservation of fisheries resources and fisheries management and development;

f) promote the contribution of fisheries to food security and food quality, giving priority to the nutritional needs of local communities;

g) promote protection of living aquatic resources and their environments and coastal areas;

---

[2] Footnote in original: References in this Code to the United Nations Convention on the Law of the Sea, 1982, or to other international agreements do not prejudice the position of any State with respect to signature, ratification or accession to the Convention or with respect to such other agreements.

h) promote the trade of fish and fishery products in conformity with relevant international rules and avoid the use of measures that constitute hidden barriers to such trade;

i) promote research on fisheries as well as on associated ecosystems and relevant environmental factors; and

j) provide standards of conduct for all persons involved in the fisheries sector.

Article 3 Relationship with other international instruments

3.1 The Code is to be interpreted and applied in conformity with the relevant rules of international law, as reflected in the United Nations Convention on the Law of the Sea, 1982. Nothing in this Code prejudices the rights, jurisdiction and duties of States under international law as reflected in the Convention.

3.2 The Code is also to be interpreted and applied:

a) in a manner consistent with the relevant provisions of the Agreement for the Implementation of the Provisions of the United Nations Convention on the Law of the Sea of 10 December 1982 Relating to the Conservation and Management of Straddling Fish Stocks and Highly Migratory Fish Stocks;

b) in accordance with other applicable rules of international law, including the respective obligations of States pursuant to international agreements to which they are party; and

c) in the light of the 1992 Declaration of Cancun, the 1992 Rio Declaration on Environment and Development, and Agenda 21 adopted by the United Nations Conference on Environment and Development (UNCED), in particular Chapter 17 of Agenda 21, and other relevant declarations and international instruments.

Article 4 Implementation, monitoring and updating

4.1 All members and non-members of FAO, fishing entities and relevant subregional, regional and global organizations, whether governmental or non-governmental, and all persons concerned with the conservation, management and utilization of fisheries resources and trade in fish and fishery products should collaborate in the fulfilment and implementation of the objectives and principles contained in this Code.

4.2 FAO, in accordance with its role within the United Nations system, will monitor the application and implementation of the Code and its effects on fisheries and the Secretariat will report accordingly to the Committee on Fisheries (COFI). All States, whether members or non-members of FAO, as well as relevant international organizations, whether governmental or non-governmental should actively cooperate with FAO in this work.

4.3 FAO, through its competent bodies, may revise the Code, taking into account developments in fisheries as well as reports to COFI on the implementation of the Code.

4.4 States and international organizations, whether governmental or non-governmental, should promote the understanding of the Code among those involved in fisheries, including, where practicable, by the introduction of schemes which would promote voluntary acceptance of the Code and its effective application.

Article 5 Special requirements of developing countries

5.1 The capacity of developing countries to implement the recommendations of this Code should be duly taken into account.

5.2 In order to achieve the objectives of this Code and to support its effective implementation, countries, relevant international organizations, whether governmental or non-governmental, and financial institutions should give full recognition to the special circumstances and requirements of developing countries, including in particular the least-developed among them, and small island developing countries. States, relevant intergovernmental and non-governmental organizations and financial institutions should work for the adoption of measures to address the needs of developing countries, especially in the areas of financial and technical assistance, technology transfer, training and scientific cooperation and in enhancing their ability to develop their own fisheries as well as to participate in high seas fisheries, including access to such fisheries.

Article 6 General principles

6.1   States and users of living aquatic resources should conserve aquatic ecosystems. The right to fish carries with it the obligation to do so in a responsible manner so as to ensure effective conservation and management of the living aquatic resources.

6.2   Fisheries management should promote the maintenance of the quality, diversity and availability of fishery resources in sufficient quantities for present and future generations in the context of food security, poverty alleviation and sustainable development. Management measures should not only ensure the conservation of target species but also of species belonging to the same ecosystem or associated with or dependent upon the target species.

6.3   States should prevent overfishing and excess fishing capacity and should implement management measures to ensure that fishing effort is commensurate with the productive capacity of the fishery resources and their sustainable utilization. States should take measures to rehabilitate populations as far as possible and when appropriate.

6.4   Conservation and management decisions for fisheries should be based on the best scientific evidence available, also taking into account traditional knowledge of the resources and their habitat, as well as relevant environmental, economic and social factors. States should assign priority to undertake research and data collection in order to improve scientific and technical knowledge of fisheries including their interaction with the ecosystem. In recognizing the transboundary nature of many aquatic ecosystems, States should encourage bilateral and multilateral cooperation in research, as appropriate.

6.5   States and subregional and regional fisheries management organizations should apply a precautionary approach widely to conservation, management and exploitation of living aquatic resources in order to protect them and preserve the aquatic environment, taking account of the best scientific evidence available. The absence of adequate scientific information should not be used as a reason for postponing or failing to take measures to conserve target species, associated or dependent species and non-target species and their environment.

6.6   Selective and environmentally safe fishing gear and practices should be further developed and applied, to the extent practicable, in order to maintain biodiversity and to conserve the population structure and aquatic ecosystems and protect fish quality. Where proper selective and environmentally safe fishing gear and practices exist, they should be recognized and accorded a priority in establishing conservation and management measures for fisheries. States and users of aquatic ecosystems should minimize waste, catch of non-target species, both fish and non-fish species, and impacts on associated or dependent species.

6.7   The harvesting, handling, processing and distribution of fish and fishery products should be carried out in a manner which will maintain the nutritional value, quality and safety of the products, reduce waste and minimize negative impacts on the environment.

6.8   All critical fisheries habitats in marine and fresh water ecosystems, such as wetlands, mangroves, reefs, lagoons, nursery and spawning areas, should be protected and rehabilitated as far as possible and where necessary. Particular effort should be made to protect such habitats from destruction, degradation, pollution and other significant impacts resulting from human activities that threaten the health and viability of the fishery resources.

6.9 States should ensure that their fisheries interests, including the need for conservation of the resources, are taken into account in the multiple uses of the coastal zone and are integrated into coastal area management, planning and development.

6.10 Within their respective competences and in accordance with international law, including within the framework of subregional or regional fisheries conservation and management organizations or arrangements, States should ensure compliance with and enforcement of conservation and management measures and establish effective mechanisms, as appropriate, to monitor and control the activities of fishing vessels and fishing support vessels.

6.11 States authorizing fishing and fishing support vessels to fly their flags should exercise effective control over those vessels so as to ensure the proper application of this Code. They should ensure that the activities of such vessels do not undermine the effectiveness of conservation and management measures taken in accordance with international law and adopted at the national, subregional, regional or global levels. States should also ensure that vessels flying their flags fulfil their obligations concerning the collection and provision of data relating to their fishing activities.

6.12 States should, within their respective competences and in accordance with international law, cooperate at subregional, regional and global levels through fisheries management organizations, other international agreements or other arrangements to promote conservation and management, ensure responsible fishing and ensure effective conservation and protection of living aquatic resources throughout their range of distribution, taking into account the need for compatible measures in areas within and beyond national jurisdiction.

6.13 States should, to the extent permitted by national laws and regulations, ensure that decision making processes are transparent and achieve timely solutions to urgent matters. States, in accordance with appropriate procedures, should facilitate consultation and the effective participation of industry, fishworkers, environmental and other interested organizations in decision making with respect to the development of laws and policies related to fisheries management, development, international lending and aid.

6.14 International trade in fish and fishery products should be conducted in accordance with the principles, rights and obligations established in the World Trade Organization (WTO) Agreement and other relevant international agreements. States should ensure that their policies, programmes and practices related to trade in fish and fishery products do not result in obstacles to this trade, environmental degradation or negative social, including nutritional, impacts.

6.15 States should cooperate in order to prevent disputes. All disputes relating to fishing activities and practices should be resolved in a timely, peaceful and cooperative manner, in accordance with applicable international agreements or as may otherwise be agreed between the parties. Pending settlement of a dispute, the States concerned should make every effort to enter into provisional arrangements of a practical nature which should be without prejudice to the final outcome of any dispute settlement procedure.

6.16 States, recognising the paramount importance to fishers and fishfarmers of understanding the conservation and management of the fishery resources on which they depend, should promote awareness of responsible fisheries through education and training. They should ensure that fishers and fishfarmers are involved in the policy formulation and implementation process, also with a view to facilitating the implementation of the Code.

6.17 States should ensure that fishing facilities and equipment as well as all fisheries activities allow for safe, healthy and fair working and living conditions and meet internationally agreed standards adopted by relevant international organizations.

6.18 Recognizing the important contributions of artisanal and small-scale fisheries to employment, income and food security, States should appropriately protect the rights of fishers and fishworkers, particularly those engaged in subsistence, small-scale and artisanal fisheries, to a secure and just livelihood, as well as preferential access, where appropriate, to traditional fishing grounds and resources in the waters under their national jurisdiction.

6.19 States should consider aquaculture, including culture-based fisheries, as a means to promote diversification of income and diet. In so doing, States should ensure that resources are used responsibly and adverse impacts on the environment and on local communities are minimized.

Article 7 Fisheries management
7.1 General

7.1.1 States and all those engaged in fisheries management should, through an appropriate policy, legal and institutional framework, adopt measures for the long-term conservation and sustainable use of fisheries resources. Conservation and management measures, whether at local, national, subregional or regional levels, should be based on the best scientific evidence available and be designed to ensure the long-term sustainability of fishery resources at levels which promote the objective of their optimum utilization and maintain their availability for present and future generations; short term considerations should not compromise these objectives.

7.1.2 Within areas under national jurisdiction, States should seek to identify relevant domestic parties having a legitimate interest in the use and management of fisheries resources and establish arrangements for consulting them to gain their collaboration in achieving responsible fisheries.

7.1.3 For transboundary fish stocks, straddling fish stocks, highly migratory fish stocks and high seas fish stocks, where these are exploited by two or more States, the States concerned, including the relevant coastal States in the case of straddling and highly migratory stocks, should cooperate to ensure effective conservation and management of the resources. This should be achieved, where appropriate, through the establishment of a bilateral, subregional or regional fisheries organization or arrangement.

7.1.4 A subregional or regional fisheries management organization or arrangement should include representatives of States in whose jurisdictions the resources occur, as well as representatives from States which have a real interest in the fisheries on the resources outside national jurisdictions. Where a subregional or regional fisheries management organization or arrangement exists and has the competence to establish conservation and management measures, those States should cooperate by becoming a member of such organization or a participant in such arrangement, and actively participate in its work.

7.1.5 A State which is not a member of a subregional or regional fisheries management organization or is not a participant in a subregional or regional fisheries management arrangement should nevertheless cooperate, in accordance with relevant international agreements and international law, in the conservation and management of the relevant fisheries resources by giving effect to any conservation and management measures adopted by such organization or arrangement.

7.1.6 Representatives from relevant organizations, both governmental and non-governmental, concerned with fisheries should be afforded the opportunity to take part in meetings of subregional and regional fisheries management organizations and arrangements as observers or otherwise, as appropriate, in accordance with the procedures of the organization or arrangement concerned. Such representatives should be given timely access to the records and reports of such meetings, subject to the procedural rules on access to them.

7.1.7   States should establish, within their respective competences and capacities, effective mechanisms for fisheries monitoring, surveillance, control and enforcement to ensure compliance with their conservation and management measures, as well as those adopted by subregional or regional organizations or arrangements.

7.1.8   States should take measures to prevent or eliminate excess fishing capacity and should ensure that levels of fishing effort are commensurate with the sustainable use of fishery resources as a means of ensuring the effectiveness of conservation and management measures.

7.1.9   States and subregional or regional fisheries management organizations and arrangements should ensure transparency in the mechanisms for fisheries management and in the related decision-making process.

7.1.10   States and subregional or regional fisheries management organizations and arrangements should give due publicity to conservation and management measures and ensure that laws, regulations and other legal rules governing their implementation are effectively disseminated. The bases and purposes of such measures should be explained to users of the resource in order to facilitate their application and thus gain increased support in the implementation of such measures.

7.2 Management objectives

7.2.1   Recognizing that long-term sustainable use of fisheries resources is the overriding objective of conservation and management, States and subregional or regional fisheries management organizations and arrangements should, *inter alia*, adopt appropriate measures, based on the best scientific evidence available, which are designed to maintain or restore stocks at levels capable of producing maximum sustainable yield, as qualified by relevant environmental and economic factors, including the special requirements of developing countries.

7.2.2   Such measures should provide *inter alia* that:

a)   excess fishing capacity is avoided and exploitation of the stocks remains economically viable;

b)   the economic conditions under which fishing industries operate promote responsible fisheries;

c)   the interests of fishers, including those engaged in subsistence, small-scale and artisanal fisheries, are taken into account;

d)   biodiversity of aquatic habitats and ecosystems is conserved and endangered species are protected;

e)   depleted stocks are allowed to recover or, where appropriate, are actively restored;

f)   adverse environmental impacts on the resources from human activities are assessed and, where appropriate, corrected; and

g)   pollution, waste, discards, catch by lost or abandoned gear, catch of non-target species, both fish and non-fish species, and impacts on associated or dependent species are minimized, through measures including, to the extent practicable, the development and use of selective, environmentally safe and cost-effective fishing gear and techniques.

7.2.3   States should assess the impacts of environmental factors on target stocks and species belonging to the same ecosystem or associated with or dependent upon the target stocks, and assess the relationship among the populations in the ecosystem.

7.3 Management framework and procedures

7.3.1   To be effective, fisheries management should be concerned with the whole stock unit over its entire area of distribution and take into account previously agreed management measures established and applied in the same region, all removals and the biological unity and other biological characteristics of the stock. The best scientific evidence available should be used to determine, *inter alia*, the area of distribution of the resource and the area through which it migrates during its life cycle.

7.3.2   In order to conserve and manage transboundary fish stocks, straddling fish stocks, highly migratory fish stocks and high seas fish stocks throughout their range, conservation and management measures established for such stocks in accordance with the respective competences of relevant States or, where appropriate, through subregional and regional fisheries management organizations and arrangements, should be compatible. Compatibility should be achieved in a manner consistent with the rights, competences and interests of the States concerned.

7.3.3   Long-term management objectives should be translated into management actions, formulated as a fishery management plan or other management framework.

7.3.4   States and, where appropriate, subregional or regional fisheries management organizations and arrangements should foster and promote international cooperation and coordination in all matters related to fisheries, including information gathering and exchange, fisheries research, management and development.

7.3.5   States seeking to take any action through a non-fishery organization which may affect the conservation and management measures taken by a competent subregional or regional fisheries management organization or arrangement should consult with the latter, in advance to the extent practicable, and take its views into account.

7.4 Data gathering and management advice

7.4.1   When considering the adoption of conservation and management measures, the best scientific evidence available should be taken into account in order to evaluate the current state of the fishery resources and the possible impact of the proposed measures on the resources.

7.4.2   Research in support of fishery conservation and management should be promoted, including research on the resources and on the effects of climatic, environmental and socio-economic factors. The results of such research should be disseminated to interested parties.

7.4.3   Studies should be promoted which provide an understanding of the costs, benefits and effects of alternative management options designed to rationalize fishing, in particular, options relating to excess fishing capacity and excessive levels of fishing effort.

7.4.4   States should ensure that timely, complete and reliable statistics on catch and fishing effort are collected and maintained in accordance with applicable international standards and practices and in sufficient detail to allow sound statistical analysis. Such data should be updated regularly and verified through an appropriate system. States should compile and disseminate such data in a manner consistent with any applicable confidentiality requirements.

7.4.5   In order to ensure sustainable management of fisheries and to enable social and economic objectives to be achieved, sufficient knowledge of social, economic and institutional factors should be developed through data gathering, analysis and research.

7.4.6   States should compile fishery-related and other supporting scientific data relating to fish stocks covered by subregional or regional fisheries management organizations or arrangements in an internationally agreed format and provide them in a timely manner to the organization or arrangement. In cases of stocks which occur in the jurisdiction of more than one State and for which there is no such organization or arrangement, the States concerned should agree on a mechanism for cooperation to compile and exchange such data.

7.4.7   Subregional or regional fisheries management organizations or arrangements should compile data and make them available, in a manner consistent with any applicable confidentiality requirements, in a timely manner and in an agreed format to all members of these organizations and other interested parties in accordance with agreed procedures.

7.5 Precautionary approach

7.5.1   States should apply the precautionary approach widely to conservation, management and exploitation of living aquatic resources in order to protect them and preserve the aquatic environment. The absence of adequate scientific information should not be used as a reason for postponing or failing to take conservation and management measures.

7.5.2   In implementing the precautionary approach, States should take into account, *inter alia*, uncertainties relating to the size and productivity of the stocks, reference points, stock condition in relation to such reference points, levels and distribution of fishing mortality and the impact of fishing activities, including discards, on non-target and associated or dependent species, as well as environmental and socio-economic conditions.

7.5.3   States and subregional or regional fisheries management organizations and arrangements should, on the basis of the best scientific evidence available, *inter alia*, determine:

a)   stock specific target reference points, and, at the same time, the action to be taken if they are exceeded; and

b)   stock-specific limit reference points, and, at the same time, the action to be taken if they are exceeded; when a limit reference point is approached, measures should be taken to ensure that it will not be exceeded.

7.5.4   In the case of new or exploratory fisheries, States should adopt as soon as possible cautious conservation and management measures, including, *inter alia*, catch limits and effort limits. Such measures should remain in force until there are sufficient data to allow assessment of the impact of the fisheries on the long-term sustainability of the stocks, whereupon conservation and management measures based on that assessment should be implemented. The latter measures should, if appropriate, allow for the gradual development of the fisheries.

7.5.5   If a natural phenomenon has a significant adverse impact on the status of living aquatic resources, States should adopt conservation and management measures on an emergency basis to ensure that fishing activity does not exacerbate such adverse impact. States should also adopt such measures on an emergency basis where fishing activity presents a serious threat to the sustainability of such resources. Measures taken on an emergency basis should be temporary and should be based on the best scientific evidence available.

7.6 Management measures

7.6.1   States should ensure that the level of fishing permitted is commensurate with the state of fisheries resources.

7.6.2   States should adopt measures to ensure that no vessel be allowed to fish unless so authorized, in a manner consistent with international law for the high seas or in conformity with national legislation within areas of national jurisdiction.

7.6.3   Where excess fishing capacity exists, mechanisms should be established to reduce capacity to levels commensurate with the sustainable use of fisheries resources so as to ensure that fishers operate under economic conditions that promote responsible fisheries. Such mechanisms should include monitoring the capacity of fishing fleets.

7.6.4   The performance of all existing fishing gear, methods and practices should be examined and measures taken to ensure that fishing gear, methods and practices which are not consistent with responsible fishing are phased out and replaced with more acceptable alternatives. In this process, particular attention should be given to the impact of such measures on fishing communities, including their ability to exploit the resource.

7.6.5   States and fisheries management organizations and arrangements should regulate fishing in such a way as to avoid the risk of conflict among fishers using different vessels, gear and fishing methods.

7.6.6   When deciding on the use, conservation and management of fisheries resources, due recognition should be given, as appropriate, in accordance with national laws and regulations, to the traditional practices, needs and interests of indigenous people and local fishing communities which are highly dependent on fishery resources for their livelihood.

7.6.7   In the evaluation of alternative conservation and management measures, their cost-effectiveness and social impact should be considered.

7.6.8   The efficacy of conservation and management measures and their possible interactions should be kept under continuous review. Such measures should, as appropriate, be revised or abolished in the light of new information.

7.6.9   States should take appropriate measures to minimize waste, discards, catch by lost or abandoned gear, catch of non-target species, both fish and non-fish species, and negative impacts on associated or dependent species, in particular endangered species. Where appropriate, such measures may include technical measures related to fish size, mesh size or gear, discards, closed seasons and areas and zones reserved for selected fisheries, particularly artisanal fisheries. Such measures should be applied, where appropriate, to protect juveniles and spawners. States and subregional or regional fisheries management organizations and arrangements should promote, to the extent practicable, the development and use of selective, environmentally safe and cost effective gear and techniques.

7.6.10   States and subregional and regional fisheries management organizations and arrangements, in the framework of their respective competences, should introduce measures for depleted resources and those resources threatened with depletion that facilitate the sustained recovery of such stocks. They should make every effort to ensure that resources and habitats critical to the well-being of such resources which have been adversely affected by fishing or other human activities are restored.

7.7   Implementation

7.7.1   States should ensure that an effective legal and administrative framework at the local and national level, as appropriate, is established for fisheries resource conservation and fisheries management.

7.7.2   States should ensure that laws and regulations provide for sanctions applicable in respect of violations which are adequate in severity to be effective, including sanctions which allow for the refusal, withdrawal or suspension of authorizations to fish in the event of non-compliance with conservation and management measures in force.

7.7.3   States, in conformity with their national laws, should implement effective fisheries monitoring, control, surveillance and law enforcement measures including, where appropriate, observer programmes, inspection schemes and vessel monitoring systems. Such measures should be promoted and, where appropriate, implemented by subregional or regional fisheries management organizations and arrangements in accordance with procedures agreed by such organizations or arrangements.

7.7.4   States and subregional or regional fisheries management organizations and arrangements, as appropriate, should agree on the means by which the activities of such organizations and arrangements will be financed, bearing in mind, *inter alia*, the relative benefits derived from the fishery and the differing capacities of countries to provide financial and other contributions. Where appropriate, and when possible, such organizations and arrangements should aim to recover the costs of fisheries conservation, management and research.

7.7.5   States which are members of or participants in subregional or regional fisheries management organizations or arrangements should implement internationally agreed measures adopted in the framework of such organizations or arrangements and consistent with international law to deter the activities of vessels flying the flag of non-members or non-participants which engage in activities which undermine the effectiveness of conservation and management measures established by such organizations or arrangements.

7.8 Financial institutions

7.8.1   Without prejudice to relevant international agreements, States should encourage banks and financial institutions not to require, as a condition of a loan or mortgage, fishing vessels or fishing support vessels to be flagged in a jurisdiction other than that of the State of beneficial ownership where such a requirement would have the effect of increasing the likelihood of non-compliance with international conservation and management measures.

Article 8 Fishing operations

8.1 Duties of all States

8.1.1   States should ensure that only fishing operations allowed by them are conducted within waters under their jurisdiction and that these operations are carried out in a responsible manner.

8.1.2   States should maintain a record, updated at regular intervals, on all authorizations to fish issued by them.

8.1.3   States should maintain, in accordance with recognized international standards and practices, statistical data, updated at regular intervals, on all fishing operations allowed by them.

8.1.4   States should, in accordance with international law, within the framework of subregional or regional fisheries management organizations or arrangements, cooperate to establish systems for monitoring, control, surveillance and enforcement of applicable measures with respect to fishing operations and related activities in waters outside their national jurisdiction.

8.1.5   States should ensure that health and safety standards are adopted for everyone employed in fishing operations. Such standards should be not less than the minimum requirements of relevant international agreements on conditions of work and service.

8.1.6   States should make arrangements individually, together with other States or with the appropriate international organization to integrate fishing operations into maritime search and rescue systems.

8.1.7   States should enhance through education and training programmes the education and skills of fishers and, where appropriate, their professional qualifications. Such programmes should take into account agreed international standards and guidelines.

8.1.8   States should, as appropriate, maintain records of fishers which should, whenever possible, contain information on their service and qualifications, including certificates of competency, in accordance with their national laws.

8.1.9   States should ensure that measures applicable in respect of masters and other officers charged with an offence relating to the operation of fishing vessels should include provisions which may permit, *inter alia*, refusal, withdrawal or suspension of authorizations to serve as masters or officers of a fishing vessel.

8.1.10   States, with the assistance of relevant international organizations, should endeavour to ensure through education and training that all those engaged in fishing operations be given information on the most important provisions of this Code, as well as provisions of relevant international conventions and applicable environmental and other standards that are essential to ensure responsible fishing operations.

8.2   Flag State duties

8.2.1   Flag States should maintain records of fishing vessels entitled to fly their flag and authorized to be used for fishing and should indicate in such records details of the vessels, their ownership and authorization to fish.

8.2.2   Flag States should ensure that no fishing vessels entitled to fly their flag fish on the high seas or in waters under the jurisdiction of other States unless such vessels have been issued with a Certificate of Registry and have been authorized to fish by the competent authorities. Such vessels should carry on board the Certificate of Registry and their authorization to fish.

8.2.3   Fishing vessels authorized to fish on the high seas or in waters under the jurisdiction of a State other than the flag State, should be marked in accordance with uniform and internationally recognizable vessel marking systems such as the FAO Standard Specifications and Guidelines for Marking and Identification of Fishing Vessels.

8.2.4   Fishing gear should be marked in accordance with national legislation in order that the owner of the gear can be identified. Gear marking requirements should take into account uniform and internationally recognizable gear marking systems.

8.2.5   Flag States should ensure compliance with appropriate safety requirements for fishing vessels and fishers in accordance with international conventions, internationally agreed codes of practice and voluntary guidelines. States should adopt appropriate safety requirements for all small vessels not covered by such international conventions, codes of practice or voluntary guidelines.

8.2.6   States not party to the Agreement to Promote Compliance with International Conservation and Management Measures by Vessels Fishing in the High Seas should be encouraged to accept the Agreement and to adopt laws and regulations consistent with the provisions of the Agreement.

8.2.7   Flag States should take enforcement measures in respect of fishing vessels entitled to fly their flag which have been found by them to have contravened applicable conservation and management measures, including, where appropriate, making the contravention of such measures an offence under national legislation. Sanctions applicable in respect of violations should be adequate in severity to be effective in securing compliance and to discourage violations wherever they occur and should deprive offenders of the benefits accruing from their illegal activities. Such sanctions may, for serious violations, include provisions for the refusal, withdrawal or suspension of the authorization to fish.

8.2.8   Flag States should promote access to insurance coverage by owners and charterers of fishing vessels. Owners or charterers of fishing vessels should carry sufficient insurance cover to protect the crew of such vessels and their interests, to indemnify third parties against loss or damage and to protect their own interests.

8.2.9   Flag States should ensure that crew members are entitled to repatriation, taking account of the principles laid down in the 'Repatriation of Seafarers Convention (Revised), 1987, (No.166)'.

8.2.10   In the event of an accident to a fishing vessel or persons on board a fishing vessel, the flag State of the fishing vessel concerned should provide details of the accident to the State of any foreign national on board the vessel involved in the accident. Such information should also, where practicable, be communicated to the International Maritime Organization.

8.3 Port State duties

8.3.1   Port States should take, through procedures established in their national legislation, in accordance with international law, including applicable international agreements or arrangements, such measures as are necessary to achieve and to assist other States in achieving the objectives of this Code, and should make known to other States details of regulations and measures they have established for this purpose. When taking such measures a port State should not discriminate in form or in fact against the vessels of any other State.

8.3.2   Port States should provide such assistance to flag States as is appropriate, in accordance with the national laws of the port State and international law, when a fishing vessel is voluntarily in a port or at an offshore terminal of the port State and the flag State of the vessel requests the port State for assistance in respect of non-compliance with subregional, regional or global conservation and management measures or with internationally agreed minimum standards for the prevention of pollution and for safety, health and conditions of work on board fishing vessels.

8.4 Fishing activities

8.4.1   States should ensure that fishing is conducted with due regard to the safety of human life and the International Maritime Organization International Regulations for Preventing Collisions at Sea, as well as International Maritime Organization requirements relating to the organization of marine traffic, protection of the marine environment and the prevention of damage to or loss of fishing gear.

8.4.2   States should prohibit dynamiting, poisoning and other comparable destructive fishing practices.

8.4.3   States should make every effort to ensure that documentation with regard to fishing operations, retained catch of fish and non-fish species and, as regards discards, the information required for stock assessment as decided by relevant management bodies, is collected and forwarded systematically to those bodies. States should, as far as possible, establish programmes, such as observer and inspection schemes, in order to promote compliance with applicable measures.

8.4.4   States should promote the adoption of appropriate technology, taking into account economic conditions, for the best use and care of the retained catch.

8.4.5   States, with relevant groups from industry, should encourage the development and implementation of technologies and operational methods that reduce discards. The use of fishing gear and practices that lead to the discarding of catch should be discouraged and the use of fishing gear and practices that increase survival rates of escaping fish should be promoted.

8.4.6   States should cooperate to develop and apply technologies, materials and operational methods that minimize the loss of fishing gear and the ghost fishing effects of lost or abandoned fishing gear.

8.4.7   States should ensure that assessments of the implications of habitat disturbance are carried out prior to the introduction on a commercial scale of new fishing gear, methods and operations to an area.

8.4.8   Research on the environmental and social impacts of fishing gear and, in particular, on the impact of such gear on biodiversity and coastal fishing communities should be promoted.

8.5 Fishing gear selectivity

8.5.1   States should require that fishing gear, methods and practices, to the extent practicable, are sufficiently selective so as to minimize waste, discards, catch of non-target species, both fish and non-fish species, and impacts on associated or dependent species and that the intent of related regulations is not circumvented by technical devices. In this regard, fishers should cooperate in the development of selective fishing gear and methods. States should ensure that information on new developments and requirements is made available to all fishers.

8.5.2   In order to improve selectivity, States should, when drawing up their laws and regulations, take into account the range of selective fishing gear, methods and strategies available to the industry.

8.5.3   States and relevant institutions should collaborate in developing standard methodologies for research into fishing gear selectivity, fishing methods and strategies.

8.5.4   International cooperation should be encouraged with respect to research programmes for fishing gear selectivity, and fishing methods and strategies, dissemination of the results of such research programmes and the transfer of technology.

8.6   Energy optimization

8.6.1   States should promote the development of appropriate standards and guidelines which would lead to the more efficient use of energy in harvesting and post-harvest activities within the fisheries sector.

8.6.2   States should promote the development and transfer of technology in relation to energy optimization within the fisheries sector and, in particular, encourage owners, charterers and managers of fishing vessels to fit energy optimization devices to their vessels.

8.7   Protection of the aquatic environment

8.7.1   States should introduce and enforce laws and regulations based on the International Convention for the Prevention of Pollution from Ships, 1973, as modified by the Protocol of 1978 relating thereto (MARPOL 73/78).

8.7.2   Owners, charterers and managers of fishing vessels should ensure that their vessels are fitted with appropriate equipment as required by MARPOL 73/78 and should consider fitting a shipboard compactor or incinerator to relevant classes of vessels in order to treat garbage and other shipboard wastes generated during the vessel's normal service.

8.7.3   Owners, charterers and managers of fishing vessels should minimize the taking aboard of potential garbage through proper provisioning practices.

8.7.4   The crew of fishing vessels should be conversant with proper shipboard procedures in order to ensure discharges do not exceed the levels set by MARPOL 73/78. Such procedures should, as a minimum, include the disposal of oily waste and the handling and storage of shipboard garbage.

8.8   Protection of the atmosphere

8.8.1   States should adopt relevant standards and guidelines which would include provisions for the reduction of dangerous substances in exhaust gas emissions.

8.8.2   Owners, charterers and managers of fishing vessels should ensure that their vessels are fitted with equipment to reduce emissions of ozone depleting substances. The responsible crew members of fishing vessels should be conversant with the proper running and maintenance of machinery on board.

8.8.3   Competent authorities should make provision for the phasing out of the use of chlorofluorocarbons (CFCs) and transitional substances such as hydrochlorofluorocarbons (HCFCs) in the refrigeration systems of fishing vessels and should ensure that the shipbuilding industry and those engaged in the fishing industry are informed of and comply with such provisions.

8.8.4   Owners or managers of fishing vessels should take appropriate action to refit existing vessels with alternative refrigerants to CFCs and HCFCs and alternatives to Halons in fire fighting installations. Such alternatives should be used in specifications for all new fishing vessels.

8.8.5   States and owners, charterers and managers of fishing vessels as well as fishers should follow international guidelines for the disposal of CFCs, HCFCs and Halons.

8.9   Harbours and landing places for fishing vessels

8.9.1   States should take into account, *inter alia*, the following in the design and construction of harbours and landing places:

a)   safe havens for fishing vessels and adequate servicing facilities for vessels, vendors and buyers are provided;

b)   adequate freshwater supplies and sanitation arrangements should be provided;

c)   waste disposal systems should be introduced, including for the disposal of oil, oily water and fishing gear;

d)   pollution from fisheries activities and external sources should be minimized; and

e)   arrangements should be made to combat the effects of erosion and siltation.

8.9.2   States should establish an institutional framework for the selection or improvement of sites for harbours for fishing vessels which allows for consultation among the authorities responsible for coastal area management.

8.10 Abandonment of structures and other materials

8.10.1   States should ensure that the standards and guidelines for the removal of redundant offshore structures issued by the International Maritime Organization are followed. States should also ensure that the competent fisheries authorities are consulted prior to decisions being made on the abandonment of structures and other materials by the relevant authorities.

8.11 Artificial reefs and fish aggregation devices

8.11.1   States, where appropriate, should develop policies for increasing stock populations and enhancing fishing opportunities through the use of artificial structures, placed with due regard to the safety of navigation, on or above the seabed or at the surface. Research into the use of such structures, including the impacts on living marine resources and the environment, should be promoted.

8.11.2   States should ensure that, when selecting the materials to be used in the creation of artificial reefs as well as when selecting the geographical location of such artificial reefs, the provisions of relevant international conventions concerning the environment and safety of navigation are observed.

8.11.3   States should, within the framework of coastal area management plans, establish management systems for artificial reefs and fish aggregation devices. Such management systems should require approval for the construction and deployment of such reefs and devices and should take into account the interests of fishers, including artisanal and subsistence fishers.

8.11.4   States should ensure that the authorities responsible for maintaining cartographic records and charts for the purpose of navigation, as well as relevant environmental authorities, are informed prior to the placement or removal of artificial reefs or fish aggregation devices.

Article 9 Aquaculture development

9.1   Responsible development of aquaculture, including culture-based fisheries, in areas under national jurisdiction

9.1.1   States should establish, maintain and develop an appropriate legal and administrative framework which facilitates the development of responsible aquaculture.

9.1.2   States should promote responsible development and management of aquaculture, including an advance evaluation of the effects of aquaculture development on genetic diversity and ecosystem integrity, based on the best available scientific information.

9.1.3   States should produce and regularly update aquaculture development strategies and plans, as required, to ensure that aquaculture development is ecologically sustainable and to allow the rational use of resources shared by aquaculture and other activities.

9.1.4   States should ensure that the livelihoods of local communities, and their access to fishing grounds, are not negatively affected by aquaculture developments.

9.1.5   States should establish effective procedures specific to aquaculture to undertake appropriate environmental assessment and monitoring with the aim of minimizing adverse ecological changes and related economic and social consequences resulting from water extraction, land use, discharge of effluents, use of drugs and chemicals, and other aquaculture activities.

9.2   Responsible development of aquaculture including culture-based fisheries within transboundary aquatic ecosystems

9.2.1   States should protect transboundary aquatic ecosystems by supporting responsible aquaculture practices within their national jurisdiction and by cooperation in the promotion of sustainable aquaculture practices.

9.2.2   States should, with due respect to their neighbouring States, and in accordance with international law, ensure responsible choice of species, siting and management of aquaculture activities which could affect transboundary aquatic ecosystems.

9.2.3   States should consult with their neighbouring States, as appropriate, before introducing non-indigenous species into transboundary aquatic ecosystems.

9.2.4   States should establish appropriate mechanisms, such as databases and information networks to collect, share and disseminate data related to their aquaculture activities to facilitate cooperation on planning for aquaculture development at the national, subregional, regional and global level.

9.2.5   States should cooperate in the development of appropriate mechanisms, when required, to monitor the impacts of inputs used in aquaculture.

9.3   Use of aquatic genetic resources for the purposes of aquaculture including culture-based fisheries

9.3.1   States should conserve genetic diversity and maintain integrity of aquatic communities and ecosystems by appropriate management. In particular, efforts should be undertaken to minimize the harmful effects of introducing non-native species or genetically altered stocks used for aquaculture including culture-based fisheries into waters, especially where there is a significant potential for the spread of such non-native species or genetically altered stocks into waters under the jurisdiction of other States as well as waters under the jurisdiction of the State of origin. States should, whenever possible, promote steps to minimize adverse genetic, disease and other effects of escaped farmed fish on wild stocks.

9.3.2   States should cooperate in the elaboration, adoption and implementation of international codes of practice and procedures for introductions and transfers of aquatic organisms.

9.3.3   States should, in order to minimize risks of disease transfer and other adverse effects on wild and cultured stocks, encourage adoption of appropriate practices in the genetic improvement of broodstocks, the introduction of non-native species, and in the production, sale and transport of eggs, larvae or fry, broodstock or other live materials. States should facilitate the preparation and implementation of appropriate national codes of practice and procedures to this effect.

9.3.4   States should promote the use of appropriate procedures for the selection of broodstock and the production of eggs, larvae and fry.

9.3.5   States should, where appropriate, promote research and, when feasible, the development of culture techniques for endangered species to protect, rehabilitate and enhance their stocks, taking into account the critical need to conserve genetic diversity of endangered species.

9.4   Responsible aquaculture at the production level

9.4.1   States should promote responsible aquaculture practices in support of rural communities, producer organizations and fish farmers.

9.4.2   States should promote active participation of fishfarmers and their communities in the development of responsible aquaculture management practices.

9.4.3   States should promote efforts which improve selection and use of appropriate feeds, feed additives and fertilizers, including manures.

9.4.4   States should promote effective farm and fish health management practices favouring hygienic measures and vaccines. Safe, effective and minimal use of therapeutants, hormones and drugs, antibiotics and other disease control chemicals should be ensured.

9.4.5   States should regulate the use of chemical inputs in aquaculture which are hazardous to human health and the environment.

9.4.6   States should require that the disposal of wastes such as offal, sludge, dead or diseased fish, excess veterinary drugs and other hazardous chemical inputs does not constitute a hazard to human health and the environment.

9.4.7   States should ensure the food safety of aquaculture products and promote efforts which maintain product quality and improve their value through particular care before and during harvesting and on-site processing and in storage and transport of the products.

Article 10 Integration of fisheries into costal area management

10.1 Institutional framework

10.1.1   States should ensure that an appropriate policy, legal and institutional framework is adopted to achieve the sustainable and integrated use of the resources, taking into account the fragility of coastal ecosystems and the finite nature of their natural resources and the needs of coastal communities.

10.1.2   In view of the multiple uses of the coastal area, States should ensure that representatives of the fisheries sector and fishing communities are consulted in the decision-making processes and involved in other activities related to coastal area management planning and development.

10.1.3   States should develop, as appropriate, institutional and legal frameworks in order to determine the possible uses of coastal resources and to govern access to them taking into account the rights of coastal fishing communities and their customary practices to the extent compatible with sustainable development.

10.1.4   States should facilitate the adoption of fisheries practices that avoid conflict among fisheries resources users and between them and other users of the coastal area.

10.1.5   States should promote the establishment of procedures and mechanisms at the appropriate administrative level to settle conflicts which arise within the fisheries sector and between fisheries resource users and other users of the coastal area.

10.2 Policy measures

10.2.1   States should promote the creation of public awareness of the need for the protection and management of coastal resources and the participation in the management process by those affected.

10.2.2   In order to assist decision-making on the allocation and use of coastal resources, States should promote the assessment of their respective value taking into account economic, social and cultural factors.

10.2.3   In setting policies for the management of coastal areas, States should take due account of the risks and uncertainties involved.

10.2.4   States, in accordance with their capacities, should establish or promote the establishment of systems to monitor the coastal environment as part of the coastal management process using physical, chemical, biological, economic and social parameters.

10.2.5   States should promote multi-disciplinary research in support of coastal area management, in particular on its environmental, biological, economic, social, legal and institutional aspects.

10.3 Regional cooperation

10.3.1   States with neighbouring coastal areas should cooperate with one another to facilitate the sustainable use of coastal resources and the conservation of the environment.

10.3.2   In the case of activities that may have an adverse transboundary environmental effect on coastal areas, States should:

a)   provide timely information and, if possible, prior notification to potentially affected States; and

b)   consult with those States as early as possible.

10.3.3   States should cooperate at the subregional and regional level in order to improve coastal area management.

10.4 Implementation

10.4.1   States should establish mechanisms for cooperation and coordination among national authorities involved in planning, development, conservation and management of coastal areas.

10.4.2   States should ensure that the authority or authorities representing the fisheries sector in the coastal management process have the appropriate technical capacities and financial resources.

Article 11 Post-harvest practices and trade

11.1 Responsible fish utilization

11.1.1   States should adopt appropriate measures to ensure the right of consumers to safe, wholesome and unadulterated fish and fishery products.

11.1.2   States should establish and maintain effective national safety and quality assurance systems to protect consumer health and prevent commercial fraud.

11.1.3   States should set minimum standards for safety and quality assurance and make sure that these standards are effectively applied throughout the industry. They should promote the implementation of quality standards agreed within the context of the FAO/WHO Codex Alimentarius Commission and other relevant organizations or arrangements.

11.1.4   States should cooperate to achieve harmonization, or mutual recognition, or both, of national sanitary measures and certification programmes as appropriate and explore possibilities for the establishment of mutually recognized control and certification agencies.

11.1.5   States should give due consideration to the economic and social role of the post-harvest fisheries sector when formulating national policies for the sustainable development and utilization of fishery resources.

11.1.6   States and relevant organizations should sponsor research in fish technology and quality assurance and support projects to improve post-harvest handling of fish, taking into account the economic, social, environmental and nutritional impact of such projects.

11.1.7   States, noting the existence of different production methods, should through cooperation and by facilitating the development and transfer of appropriate technologies, ensure that processing, transporting and storage methods are environmentally sound.

11.1.8   States should encourage those involved in fish processing, distribution and marketing to:

a)   reduce post-harvest losses and waste;

b)   improve the use of by-catch to the extent that this is consistent with responsible fisheries management practices; and

c)   use the resources, especially water and energy, in particular wood, in an environmentally sound manner.

11.1.9   States should encourage the use of fish for human consumption and promote consumption of fish whenever appropriate.

11.1.10 States should cooperate in order to facilitate the production of value-added products by developing countries.

11.1.11 States should ensure that international and domestic trade in fish and fishery products accords with sound conservation and management practices through improving the identification of the origin of fish and fishery products traded.

11.1.12 States should ensure that environmental effects of post-harvest activities are considered in the development of related laws, regulations and policies without creating any market distortions.

11.2 Responsible international trade

11.2.1   The provisions of this Code should be interpreted and applied in accordance with the principles, rights and obligations established in the World Trade Organization (WTO) Agreement.

11.2.2   International trade in fish and fishery products should not compromise the sustainable development of fisheries and responsible utilization of living aquatic resources.

11.2.3   States should ensure that measures affecting international trade in fish and fishery products are transparent, based, when applicable, on scientific evidence, and are in accordance with internationally agreed rules.

11.2.4   Fish trade measures adopted by States to protect human or animal life or health, the interests of consumers or the environment, should not be discriminatory and should be in accordance with internationally agreed trade rules, in particular the principles, rights and obligations established in the Agreement on the Application of Sanitary and Phytosanitary Measures and the Agreement on Technical Barriers to Trade of the WTO.

11.2.5   States should further liberalize trade in fish and fishery products and eliminate barriers and distortions to trade such as duties, quotas and non-tariff barriers in accordance with the principles, rights and obligations of the WTO Agreement.

11.2.6   States should not directly or indirectly create unnecessary or hidden barriers to trade which limit the consumer's freedom of choice of supplier or that restrict market access.

11.2.7   States should not condition access to markets to access to resources. This principle does not preclude the possibility of fishing agreements between States which include provisions referring to access to resources, trade and access to markets, transfer of technology, scientific research, training and other relevant elements.

11.2.8   States should not link access to markets to the purchase of specific technology or sale of other products.

11.2.9   States should cooperate in complying with relevant international agreements regulating trade in endangered species.

11.2.10 States should develop international agreements for trade in live specimens where there is a risk of environmental damage in importing or exporting States.

11.2.11 States should cooperate to promote adherence to, and effective implementation of relevant international standards for trade in fish and fishery products and living aquatic resource conservation.

11.2.12 States should not undermine conservation measures for living aquatic resources in order to gain trade or investment benefits.

11.2.13 States should cooperate to develop internationally acceptable rules or standards for trade in fish and fishery products in accordance with the principles, rights, and obligations established in the WTO Agreement.

11.2.14 States should cooperate with each other and actively participate in relevant regional and multilateral fora, such as the WTO, in order to ensure equitable, non-discriminatory trade in fish and fishery products as well as wide adherence to multilaterally agreed fishery conservation measures.

11.2.15 States, aid agencies, multilateral development banks and other relevant international organizations should ensure that their policies and practices related to the promotion of international fish trade and export production do not result in environmental degradation or adversely impact the nutritional rights and needs of people for whom fish is critical to their health and well being and for whom other comparable sources of food are not readily available or affordable.

11.3 Laws and regulations relating to fish trade

11.3.1 Laws, regulations and administrative procedures applicable to international trade in fish and fishery products should be transparent, as simple as possible, comprehensible and, when appropriate, based on scientific evidence.

11.3.2 States, in accordance with their national laws, should facilitate appropriate consultation with and participation of industry as well as environmental and consumer groups in the development and implementation of laws and regulations related to trade in fish and fishery products.

11.3.3 States should simplify their laws, regulations and administrative procedures applicable to trade in fish and fishery products without jeopardizing their effectiveness.

11.3.4 When a State introduces changes to its legal requirements affecting trade in fish and fishery products with other States, sufficient information and time should be given to allow the States and producers affected to introduce, as appropriate, the changes needed in their processes and procedures. In this connection, consultation with affected States on the time frame for implementation of the changes would be desirable. Due consideration should be given to requests from developing countries for temporary derogations from obligations.

11.3.5 States should periodically review laws and regulations applicable to international trade in fish and fishery products in order to determine whether the conditions which gave rise to their introduction continue to exist.

11.3.6 States should harmonize as far as possible the standards applicable to international trade in fish and fishery products in accordance with relevant internationally recognized provisions.

11.3.7 States should collect, disseminate and exchange timely, accurate and pertinent statistical information on international trade in fish and fishery products through relevant national institutions and international organizations.

11.3.8 States should promptly notify interested States, WTO and other appropriate international organizations on the development of and changes to laws, regulations and administrative procedures applicable to international trade in fish and fishery products.

Article 12 Fisheries research

12.1 States should recognize that responsible fisheries requires the availability of a sound scientific basis to assist fisheries managers and other interested parties in making decisions. Therefore, States should ensure that appropriate research is conducted into all aspects of fisheries including biology, ecology, technology, environmental science, economics, social science, aquaculture and nutritional science. States should ensure the availability of research facilities and provide appropriate training, staffing and institution building to conduct the research, taking into account the special needs of developing countries.

12.2 States should establish an appropriate institutional framework to determine the applied research which is required and its proper use.

12.3 States should ensure that data generated by research are analyzed, that the results of such analyses are published, respecting confidentiality where appropriate, and distributed in a timely and readily understood fashion, in order that the best scientific evidence is made available as a contribution to fisheries conservation, management and development. In the absence of adequate scientific information, appropriate research should be initiated as soon as possible.

12.4 States should collect reliable and accurate data which are required to assess the status of fisheries and ecosystems, including data on bycatch, discards and waste. Where appropriate, this data should be provided, at an appropriate time and level of aggregation, to relevant States and subregional, regional and global fisheries organizations.

12.5 States should be able to monitor and assess the state of the stocks under their jurisdiction, including the impacts of ecosystem changes resulting from fishing pressure, pollution or habitat alteration. They should also establish the research capacity necessary to assess the effects of climate or environment change on fish stocks and aquatic ecosystems.

12.6 States should support and strengthen national research capabilities to meet acknowledged scientific standards.

12.7 States, as appropriate in cooperation with relevant international organizations, should encourage research to ensure optimum utilization of fishery resources and stimulate the research required to support national policies related to fish as food.

12.8 States should conduct research into, and monitor, human food supplies from aquatic sources and the environment from which they are taken and ensure that there is no adverse health impact on consumers. The results of such research should be made publicly available.

12.9 States should ensure that the economic, social, marketing and institutional aspects of fisheries are adequately researched and that comparable data are generated for ongoing monitoring, analysis and policy formulation.

12.10 States should carry out studies on the selectivity of fishing gear, the environmental impact of fishing gear on target species and on the behaviour of target and non-target species in relation to such fishing gear as an aid for management decisions and with a view to minimizing non-utilized catches as well as safeguarding the biodiversity of ecosystems and the aquatic habitat.

12.11 States should ensure that before the commercial introduction of new types of gear, a scientific evaluation of their impact on the fisheries and ecosystems where they will be used should be undertaken. The effects of such gear introductions should be monitored.

12.12 States should investigate and document traditional fisheries knowledge and technologies, in particular those applied to small-scale fisheries, in order to assess their application to sustainable fisheries conservation, management and development.

12.13   States should promote the use of research results as a basis for the setting of management objectives, reference points and performance criteria, as well as for ensuring adequate linkages between applied research and fisheries management.

12.14   States conducting scientific research activities in waters under the jurisdiction of another State should ensure that their vessels comply with the laws and regulations of that State and international law.

12.15   States should promote the adoption of uniform guidelines governing fisheries research conducted on the high seas.

12.16   States should, where appropriate, support the establishment of mechanisms, including, *inter alia*, the adoption of uniform guidelines, to facilitate research at the subregional or regional level and should encourage the sharing of the results of such research with other regions.

12.17   States, either directly or with the support of relevant international organizations, should develop collaborative technical and research programmes to improve understanding of the biology, environment and status of transboundary aquatic stocks.

12.18   States and relevant international organizations should promote and enhance the research capacities of developing countries, *inter alia*, in the areas of data collection and analysis, information, science and technology, human resource development and provision of research facilities, in order for them to participate effectively in the conservation, management and sustainable use of living aquatic resources.

12.19   Competent international organizations should, where appropriate, render technical and financial support to States upon request and when engaged in research investigations aimed at evaluating stocks which have been previously unfished or very lightly fished.

12.20   Relevant technical and financial international organizations should, upon request, support States in their research efforts, devoting special attention to developing countries, in particular the least-developed among them and small island developing countries.

Council Directive 95/21/EC of 19 June 1995 on
Port State Control of Shipping

Entry into force, 27 July 1995;
deadline for transposition in the Member States, 30 June 1996
Official Journal L 157, 7 July 1995, 1[1]

The Council of the European Union,
　　Having regard to the Treaty establishing the European Community, and in particular Article 84 (2) thereof,
　　Having regard to the proposal from the Commission,
　　Having regard to the opinion of the Economic and Social Committee,
　　Acting in accordance with Article 189c of the Treaty,

---

[1] The Directive was amended by Council Directive 98/25/EC of 27 April 1998 (OJ L 133, 7 May 1998, 19), Commission Directive 98/42/EC of 19 June 1998 (OJ L 184, 27 June 1998, 40), Commission Directive 1999/97/EC of 13 December 1999 (OJ L 331, 23 December 1999, 67), Directive 2001/106/EC of the European Parliament and of the Council of 19 December 2001 (OJ L 19, 22 January 2002, 17), and Directive 2002/84/EC of the European Parliament and of the Council of 5 November 2002 (OJ L 324, 29 November 2002, 53). The text reproduced is a consolidated version incorporating these amendments. All footnotes as well as Annexes II-V, VII-X and XII omitted.

Whereas the Community is seriously concerned about shipping casualties and pollution of the seas and coastlines of the Member States;

Whereas the Community is equally concerned about on-board living and working conditions;

Whereas the Council, at its meeting on 25 January 1993, adopted conclusions that urged the Community and the Member States to ensure more effective application and enforcement of adequate international maritime safety and environment protection standards and to implement the new measures when adopted;

Whereas, in its resolution of 8 June 1993 on a common policy on safe seas, the Council urged the Commission to submit as soon as possible to the Council suggestions for specific action and formal proposals concerning criteria for the inspection of ships, including the harmonization of detention rules, and including the possibility of publication of the results of the inspections and refusal of access to Community ports;

Whereas safety, pollution prevention and shipboard living and working conditions may be effectively enhanced through a drastic reduction of substandard ships from Community waters, by strictly applying international Conventions, codes and resolutions;

Whereas monitoring the compliance of ships with the international standards for safety, pollution prevention and shipboard living and working conditions should rest primarily with the flag State; whereas, however, there is a serious failure on the part of an increasing number of flag States to implement and enforce international standards; whereas henceforth the monitoring of compliance with the international standards for safety, pollution prevention and shipboard living and working conditions has also to be ensured by the port State;

Whereas a harmonized approach to the effective enforcement of these international standards by the Member States in respect of ships sailing in the waters under their jurisdiction and using their ports will avoid distortions of competition;

Whereas a framework in Community law for harmonizing inspection procedures is fundamental to ensuring the homogeneous application of the principles of shipping safety and prevention of pollution which lie at the heart of Community transport and environment policies;

Whereas pollution of the seas is by nature a trans-boundary phenomenon; whereas, in accordance with the principle of subsidiarity, the development of the means of taking preventive action in this field as regards the seas adjacent to the Member States is best done at Community level, since Member States cannot take adequate and effective action in isolation;

Whereas the adoption of a Council Directive is the appropriate procedure for laying down the legal framework and the harmonized rules and criteria for port State control;

Whereas advantage should be taken of the experience gained during the operation of the Paris Memorandum of Understanding (MOU) on Port State Control (PSC), signed in Paris on 26 January 1982;

Whereas the inspection by each Member State of at least 25% of the number of individual foreign ships which enter its ports in a given year in practice means that a large number of ships operating within the Community area at any given time have undergone an inspection;

Whereas further efforts should be made to develop a better targeting system;

Whereas the rules and procedures for port-State inspections, including criteria for the detention of ships, must be harmonized to ensure consistent effectiveness in all ports, which would also drastically reduce the selective use of certain ports of destination to avoid the net of proper control;

Whereas the casualty, detention and deficiency statistics published in the Commission's communication entitled 'A common policy on safe seas' and in the annual report of the MOU show that certain categories of ships need to be subject to an expanded inspection;

Whereas non-compliance with the provisions of the relevant Conventions must be rectified; whereas ships which are required to take corrective action must, where the deficiencies in compliance are clearly hazardous to safety, health or the environment, be detained until such time as the non-compliance has been rectified;

Whereas a right of appeal should be made available against decisions for detention taken by the competent authorities, in order to prevent unreasonable decisions which are liable to cause undue detention and delay;

Whereas the facilities in the port of inspection may be such that the competent authority will be obliged to authorize the ship to proceed to an appropriate repair yard, provided that the conditions for the transfer are complied with; whereas non-complying ships would continue to pose a threat to safety, health or the environment and to enjoy commercial advantages by not being upgraded in accordance with the relevant provisions of the Conventions and should therefore be refused access to all ports in the Community;

Whereas there are circumstances where a ship which has been refused access to ports within the Community has to be granted permission to enter; whereas under such circumstances the ship should only be permitted access to a specific port if all precautions are taken to ensure it safe entry;

Whereas, given the complexity of the requirements of the Conventions as regards a ship's construction, equipment and manning, the severe consequences of the decisions taken by the inspectors, and the necessity for the inspectors to take completely impartial decisions, inspections must be carried out only by inspectors who are duly authorized public service employees or other such persons, and highly knowledgeable and experienced;

Whereas pilots and port authorities may be able to provide useful information on the deficiencies of such ships and crews;

Whereas cooperation between the competent authorities of the Member States and other authorities or organizations is necessary to ensure an effective follow-up with regard to ships with deficiencies which have been permitted to proceed and for the exchange of information about ships in port;

Whereas the information system called Sirenac E established under the MOU provides a large amount of the additional information needed for the application of this Directive;

Whereas publication of information concerning ships which do not comply with international standards on safety, health and protection of the marine environment, may be an effective deterrent discouraging shippers to use such ships, and an incentive to their owners to take corrective action without being compelled to do so;

Whereas all costs of inspecting ships which warrant detention should be borne by the owner or the operator;

Whereas for the purposes of implementing this Directive use should be made of the Committee set up pursuant to Article 12 of Council Directive 93/75/EEC of 13 September 1993 concerning minimum requirements for vessels bound for or leaving Community ports and carrying dangerous or polluting goods in order to assist the Commission with the task of adapting Member States' inspection obligations on the basis of experience gained, taking into account developments in the MOU, and also adopting the Annexes as necessary in the light of amendments to the Conventions, Protocols, codes and resolutions of relevant international bodies and to the MOU,

Has adopted this Directive:

Article 1 Purpose

The purpose of this Directive is to help drastically to reduce substandard shipping in the waters under the jurisdiction of Member States by:

- increasing compliance with international and relevant Community legislation on maritime safety, protection of the marine environment and living and working conditions on board ships of all flags,
- establishing common criteria for control of ships by the port State and harmonizing procedures on inspection and detention, taking proper account of the commitments made by the maritime authorities of the Member States under the Paris Memorandum of Understanding on Port State Control (MOU).

Article 2 Definitions

For the purpose of this Directive including its Annexes:

1. '*Conventions*' means:
- the International Convention on Load Lines, 1966 (LL 66),
- the International Convention for the Safety of Life at Sea, 1974 (SOLAS 74),
- the International Convention for the Prevention of Pollution from Ships, 1973, and the 1978 Protocol relating thereto (Marpol 73/78),
- the International Convention on Standards of Training, Certification and Watchkeeping for Seafarers, 1978 (STCW 78),
- the Convention on the International Regulations for Preventing Collisions at Sea, 1972 (Colreg 72),
- the International Convention on Tonnage Measurement of Ships, 1969 (ITC 69),
- the Merchant Shipping (Minimum Standards) Convention, 1976 (ILO No 147),
- the International Convention on Civil Liability for Oil Pollution Damage, 1992 (CLC 92),

together with the Protocols and amendments to these Conventions and related codes of mandatory status, in its up-to-date version.

2. '*MOU*' means the Memorandum of Understanding on Port State Control, signed in Paris on 26 January 1982, in its up-to date version.

3. '*Ship*' means any seagoing vessel to which one or more of the Conventions apply, flying a flag other than that of the port State.

4. '*Off-shore installation*' means a fixed or floating platform operating on or over the continental shelf of a Member State.

5. '*Inspector*' means a public-sector employee or other person, duly authorized by the competent authority of a Member State to carry out port-State control inspections, and responsible to that competent authority.

6. '*Inspection*' means a visit on board a ship in order to check both the validity of the relevant certificates and other documents and the condition of the ship, its equipment and crew, as well as the living and working conditions of the crew.

7. '*More detailed inspection*' means an inspection where the ship, its equipment and crew as a whole or, as appropriate, parts thereof are subjected, in the circumstances specified in Article 6(3), to an indepth inspection covering the ship's construction, equipment, manning, living and working conditions and compliance with onboard operational procedures.

8. '*Expanded inspection*' means an inspection as specified in Article 7.

9. '*Detention*' means the formal prohibition of a ship to proceed to sea due to established deficiencies which, individually or together, make the ship unseaworthy.

10. '*Stoppage of an operation*' means a formal prohibition of a ship to continue an operation due to established deficiencies which, individually or together, would render the continued operation hazardous.

Article 3 Scope
1. This Directive applies to any ship and its crew:
- calling at a port of a Member State or at an off-shore installation, or
- anchored off such a port or such an installation.

Nothing in this Article shall affect the rights of intervention available to a Member State under the relevant international Conventions.

2. In case of ships of a gross tonnage below 500, Member States shall apply those requirements of a relevant Convention which are applicable and shall, to the extent that a Convention does not apply, take such action as may be necessary to ensure that the ships concerned are not clearly hazardous to safety, health or the environment. In their application of this paragraph, Member States shall be guided by Annex 1 to the MOU.

3. When inspecting a ship flying the flag of a State which is not a party to a Convention, Member States shall ensure that the treatment given to such ship and its crew is no more favourable than that given to a ship flying the flag of a State which is a party to that Convention.

4. Fishing vessels, ships of war, naval auxiliaries, wooden ships of a primitive build, government ships used for non-commercial purposes and pleasure yachts not engaged in trade shall be excluded from the scope of this Directive.

Article 4 Inspection body
Member States shall maintain appropriate national maritime administrations with the requisite number of staff, in particular qualified inspectors, hereinafter called 'competent authorities', for the inspection of ships and shall take whatever measures are appropriate to ensure that their competent authorities perform their duties as laid down in this Directive.

Article 5 Inspection commitments
1. The total number of inspections of the ships referred to in paragraph (2) and Article 7 to be carried out annually by the competent authority of each Member State shall correspond to at least 25% of the average annual number of individual ships which entered its ports, calculated on the basis of the three most recent calendar years for which statistics are available.

2. (a) The competent authority shall, subject to the provisions of Article 7a, ensure that an inspection in accordance with Article 6 is carried out on any ship not subject to an expanded inspection with a target factor greater than 50 in the Sirenac information system, provided that a period of at least one month has elapsed since the last inspection carried out in a port in the MOU region.

(b) In selecting other ships for inspection, the competent authorities shall determine the order of priority as follows:
- the first ships to be selected for inspection shall be those listed in Annex I, Part I, irrespective of their target factor,
- the ships listed in Annex I, Part II shall be selected in decreasing order, depending on the order of priority resulting from the value of their target factor ranges as referred to in the Sirenac information system.

3. Member States shall refrain from inspecting ships which have been inspected by any Member State within the previous six months, provided that:
- the ship is not listed in Annex I,
- no deficiencies have been reported, following a previous inspection,

- no clear grounds exist for carrying out an inspection,
- the ship is not covered by paragraph 2(a).

4. The provisions of paragraph 3 shall not apply to any of the operational controls specifically provided for in the Conventions.

5. The Member States and the Commission shall cooperate in seeking to develop priorities and practices which will enable ships likely to be defective to be targeted more effectively.

Any consequent amendment of this Article, except to the figure of 25% in paragraph 1, shall be made under the provisions of Article 19.

Article 6 Inspection procedure

1. The competent authority shall ensure that the inspector shall as a minimum:
    (a) check the certificates and documents listed in Annex II, to the extent applicable;
    (b) satisfy himself of the overall condition of the ship, including the engine room and accommodation and including hygienic conditions.

2. The inspector may examine all relevant certificates and documents, other than those listed in Annex II, which are required to be carried on board in accordance with the Conventions.

3. Whenever there are clear grounds for believing, after the inspection referred to in paragraphs 1 and 2, that the condition of a ship or of its equipment or crew does not substantially meet the relevant requirements of a Convention, a more detailed inspection shall be carried out, including further checking of compliance with on-board operational requirements.

'Clear grounds' exist when the inspector finds evidence which in his professional judgement warrants a more detailed inspection of the ship, its equipment or its crew.

Examples of 'clear grounds' are set out in Annex III.

4. The relevant procedures and guidelines for the control of ships specified in Annex IV shall also be observed.

Article 7 Mandatory expanded inspection of certain ships

1. A ship in one of the categories in Annex V, section A, is liable to an expanded inspection after a period of 12 months since the last expanded inspection carried out in a port of a State signatory of the MOU.

2. If such a ship is selected for inspection in accordance with Article 5(2)(b), an expanded inspection shall be carried out. However an inspection in accordance with Article 6 may be carried out in the period between two expanded inspections.

3. (a) The operator or master of a ship to which paragraph 1 applies shall communicate all the information listed in Annex V, section B, to the competent authority of the Member State of each port visited after a period of 12 months since the last expanded inspection. This information shall be provided at least three days before the expected time of arrival in the port or before leaving the previous port if the voyage is expected to take fewer than three days.
    (b) Any ship not complying with subparagraph (a) shall be subject to an expanded inspection at the port of destination.

4. Member States shall, subject to Article 7a, ensure that an expanded inspection is carried out on a ship to which paragraph 3 applies and which has a target factor of 7 or more at its first port visited after a period of 12 months since the last expanded inspection.

In cases where the Member States are unable to increase their capacity in time to carry out all the additional inspections required, particularly because of problems connected with the recruitment and training of inspectors, they shall be allowed until 1 January 2003 to build up their inspection service gradually. This period may be extended by six months for the port of Rotterdam. The Commission shall notify the Member States and the European Parliament of any such extension.

5. Expanded inspection shall be carried out in accordance with the procedures in Annex V, section C.

6. Where there is a risk that an amendment or draft amendment to the MOU may weaken the scope of the obligation for expanded inspection under this Article, the Commission shall submit without delay to the Committee established by Article 18, draft measures with a view to reintroducing target factor values complying with the objectives of this Directive.

Article 7a Procedure in case certain ships cannot be inspected

1. In cases where, for operational reasons, a Member State is unable to carry out an inspection of a ship with a target factor of more than 50 as referred to in Article 5(2)(a) or a mandatory expanded inspection as referred to in Article 7(4), the Member State shall, without delay, inform the Sirenac system that such inspection did not take place.

2. Such cases shall be notified, at intervals of six months, to the Commission together with the reasons for not inspecting the ships concerned.

3. During any calendar year, such non-inspections shall not exceed 5 % of the average annual number of individual ships eligible for the inspections referred to in paragraph 1 calling at the ports of the Member State, calculated on the basis of the three most recent calendar years for which statistics are available.

4. Ships referred to in paragraph 1 shall be subject to an inspection, as provided for in Article 5(2)(a) or a mandatory expanded inspection as referred to in Article 7(4), as appropriate, in the next port of call in the Community.

5. By 22 July 2008 the figure of 5 % referred to in paragraph 3 shall be amended on the basis of an assessment by the Commission, if it is considered appropriate, in accordance with the procedure laid down in Article 19.

Article 7b Access refusal measures concerning certain ships

1. A Member State shall ensure that a ship in one of the categories of Annex XI, section A, is refused access to its ports, except in the situations described in Article 11(6), if the ship: either

- flies the flag of a State appearing in the black list as published in the annual report of the MOU, and
- has been detained more than twice in the course of the preceding 24 months in a port of a State signatory of the MOU,

or

- flies the flag of a State described as 'very high risk' or 'high risk' in the black list as published in the annual report of the MOU, and
- has been detained more than once in the course of the preceding 36 months in a port of a State signatory of the MOU.

The refusal of access shall become applicable immediately the ship has been authorised to leave the port where it has been the subject of a second or third detention as appropriate.

2. For the purposes of paragraph 1, Member States shall comply with the procedures laid down in Annex XI, section B.

3. The Commission shall publish every six months the information relating to ships that have been refused access to Community ports in application of this Article.

Article 8 Report of inspection to the master

On completion of an inspection, a more detailed inspection or an expanded inspection, the inspector shall draw up a report in accordance with Annex IX. A copy of the inspection report shall be provided to the ship's master.

Article 9 Rectification and detention

1. The competent authority shall be satisfied that any deficiencies confirmed or revealed by the inspection referred to in Article 5(2) and Article 7 are or will be rectified in accordance with the Conventions.

2. In the case of deficiencies which are clearly hazardous to safety, health or the environment, the competent authority of the port State where the ship is being inspected shall ensure that the ship is detained, or the operation in the course of which the deficiencies have been revealed is stopped. The detention order or stoppage of an operation shall not be lifted until the hazard is removed or until such authority establishes that the ship can, subject to any necessary conditions, proceed to sea or the operation be resumed without risk to the safety and health of passengers or crew, or risk to other ships, or without there being an unreasonable threat of harm to the marine environment.

3. When exercising his professional judgment as to whether or not a ship should be detained, the inspector shall apply the criteria set out in Annex VI. In this respect, the ship shall be detained, if not equipped with a functioning voyage data recorder system, when its use is compulsory in accordance with Annex XII. If this deficiency cannot be readily rectified in the port of detention, the competent authority may allow the ship to proceed to the nearest appropriate port where it shall be readily rectified or require that the deficiency is rectified within a maximum period of 30 days. For these purposes, the procedures laid down in Article 11 shall apply.

4. In exceptional circumstances, where the overall condition of a ship is obviously substandard, the competent authority may suspend the inspection of that ship until the responsible parties have taken the steps necessary to ensure that it complies with the relevant requirements of the Conventions.

5. In the event that the inspections referred to in Article 5(2) and Article 7 give rise to detention, the competent authority shall immediately inform, in writing and including the report of inspection, the administration of the State whose flag the ship is entitled to fly (hereinafter called 'flag administration') or, when this is not possible, the Consul or, in his absence, the nearest diplomatic representative of that State, of all the circumstances in which intervention was deemed necessary. In addition, nominated surveyors or recognised organisations responsible for the issue of class certificates or certificates issued on behalf of the flag State in accordance with the international conventions shall also be notified where relevant.

6. The provisions of this Directive shall be without prejudice to the additional requirements of the Conventions concerning notification and reporting procedures related to port State control.

7. When exercising port State control under this Directive, all possible efforts shall be made to avoid a ship being unduly detained or delayed. If a ship is unduly detained or delayed, the owner or operator shall be entitled to compensation for any loss or damage suffered. In any instance of alleged undue detention or delay the burden of proof shall lie with the owner or operator of the ship.

Article 9a Procedure applicable in the absence of ISM certificates

1. Where the inspection reveals that the copy of the document of compliance or the safety management certificate issued in accordance with the International management code for the safe operation of ships and for pollution prevention (ISM Code) are missing on board a vessel to which, within the Community, the ISM Code is applicable at the date of the inspection, the competent authority shall ensure that the vessel is detained.

2. Notwithstanding the absence of the documentation referred to in paragraph 1, if the inspection finds no other deficiencies warranting detention the competent authority may lift the detention order in order to avoid port congestion. Whenever such a decision is taken, the competent authority shall immediately inform the competent authorities of the other Member States thereof.

3. Member States shall take the measures necessary to ensure that all ships authorised to leave a port in a Member State under the circumstances referred to in paragraph 2 shall be refused access to all ports in the Community, except in the situations referred to in Article 11(6), until the owner or operator of the vessel has demonstrated, to the satisfaction of the competent authority of the Member State in which detention was ordered, that the ship has valid certificates issued in accordance with the ISM Code. Where deficiencies as referred to in Article 9(2) are found and cannot be rectified in the port of detention, the relevant provisions of Article 11 shall also apply.

Article 10 Right of appeal

1. The owner or the operator of a ship or his representative in the Member State shall have a right of appeal against a detention decision or refusal of access taken by the competent authority. An appeal shall not cause the detention or refusal of access to be suspended.

2. Member States shall establish and maintain appropriate procedures for this purpose in accordance with their national legislation.

3. The competent authority shall properly inform the master of a ship referred to in paragraph 1 of the right of appeal.

Article 11 Follow-up to inspections and detention

1. Where deficiencies as referred to in Article 9(2) cannot be rectified in the port of inspection, the competent authority of that Member State may allow the ship concerned to proceed to the nearest appropriate repair yard available, as chosen by the master and the authorities concerned, provided that the conditions determined by the competent authority of the flag State and agreed by that Member State are complied with. Such conditions shall ensure that the ship can proceed without risk to the safety and health of passengers or crew, or risk to other ships, or without there being an unreasonable threat of harm to the marine environment.

2. In the circumstances referred to in paragraph 1, the competent authority of the Member State in the port of inspection shall notify the competent authority of the State where the repair yard is situated, the parties mentioned in Article 9(5) and any other authority as appropriate of all the conditions for the voyage.

3. The notification of the parties referred to in paragraph 2 shall be in accordance with Annex 2 to the MOU.

The competent authority of a Member State receiving such notification shall inform the notifying authority of the action taken.

4. Member States shall take measures to ensure that ships referred to in paragraph 1 which proceed to sea:

    (i)   without complying with the conditions determined by the competent authority of any Member State in the port of inspection; or

(ii)   which refuse to comply with the applicable requirements of the Conventions by not calling into the indicated repair yard;

shall be refused access to any port within the Community, until the owner or operator has provided evidence to the satisfaction of the competent authority of the Member State where the ship was found defective that the ship fully complies with all applicable requirements of the Conventions.

5.   In the circumstances referred to in paragraph 4(i), the competent authority of the Member State where the ship was found defective shall immediately alert the competent authorities of all the other Member States.

In the circumstances referred to in paragraph 4(ii), the competent authority of the Member State in which the repair yard lies shall immediately alert the competent authorities of all the other Member States.

Before denying entry, the Member State may request consultations with the flag administration of the ship concerned.

6.   Notwithstanding the provisions of paragraph 4, access to a specific port may be permitted by the relevant authority of that port State in the event of *force majeure* or overriding safety considerations, or to reduce or minimize the risk of pollution or to have deficiencies rectified, provided adequate measures to the satisfaction of the competent authority of such Member State have been implemented by the owner, the operator or the master of the ship to ensure safe entry.

Article 12 Professional profile of inspectors

1.   The inspections shall be carried out only by inspectors who fulfil the qualification criteria specified in Annex VII.

2.   When the required professional expertise cannot be provided by the competent authority of the port State, the inspector of that competent authority may be assisted by any person with the required expertise.

3.   The inspectors carrying out port State control and the persons assisting them shall have no commercial interest either in the port of inspection or in the ships inspected, nor shall the inspectors be employed by or undertake work on behalf of non-governmental organizations which issue statutory and classification certificates or which carry out the surveys necessary for the issue of those certificates to ships.

4.   Each inspector shall carry a personal document in the form of an identity card issued by his competent authority in accordance with the national legislation, indicating that the inspector is authorized to carry out inspections.

A common model for such an identity card shall be established in accordance with the procedure in Article 19.

Article 13 Reports from pilots and port authorities

1.   Pilots of Member States, engaged in berthing or unberthing ships or engaged on ships bound for a port within a Member State, shall immediately inform the competent authority of the port State or the coastal State, as appropriate, whenever they learn in the course of their normal duties that there are deficiencies which may prejudice the safe navigation of the ship, or which may pose a threat of harm to the marine environment.

2.   If port authorities, when exercising their normal duties, learn that a ship within their port has deficiencies which may prejudice the safety of the ship or poses an unreasonable threat of harm to the marine environment, such authority shall immediately inform the competent authority of the port State concerned.

Article 14 Cooperation

1. Each Member State shall make provision for cooperation between its competent authority, its port authorities and other relevant authorities or commercial organizations to ensure that its competent authority can obtain all relevant information on ships calling at its ports.

2. Member States shall maintain provisions for the exchange of information and cooperation between their competent authority and the competent authorities of all other Member States and maintain the established operational link between their competent authority, the Commission and the Sirenac information system set up in St Malo, France.

For the purposes of carrying out the inspections referred to in Article 5(2) and Article 7, inspectors shall consult the public and private databases relating to ship inspection accessible through the Equasis information system.

3. The information referred to in paragraph 2 shall be that specified in Annex 4 to the MOU, and that required to comply with Article 15 of this Directive.

Article 15 Release of information

1. The competent authority of each Member State shall take necessary measures in order to ensure that information listed in Annex VIII, Part I, concerning ships which have been detained in, or which are subject to refusal of access to, a port of this Member State during the previous month, is published at least every month.

2. The information listed in Annex VIII, Parts I and II, and the information on changes, suspensions and withdrawals of class referred to in Article 15(3) of Directive 94/57/EC, shall be available in the Sirenac system. It shall be made public through the Equasis information system, as soon as possible after the inspection has been completed or the detention has been lifted.

3. Member States and the Commission shall cooperate in order to establish the appropriate technical arrangements referred to in paragraph 2.

4. Where appropriate, the Sirenac information system is amended in order to implement the abovementioned requirements.

5. The provisions of this Article do not affect national legislation on liability.

Article 16 Reimbursement of costs

1. Should the inspections referred to in Articles 6 and 7 confirm or reveal deficiencies in relation to the requirements of a Convention warranting the detention of a ship, all costs relating to the inspections in any normal accounting period shall be covered by the shipowner or the operator or by his representative in the port State.

2. All costs relating to inspections carried out by the competent authority of a Member State under the provisions of Article 11(4) shall be charged to the owner or operator of the ship.

2a. In the case of detention of a vessel for deficiencies or lack of valid certificates as laid down in Article 9 and Annex VI, all costs relating to the detention in port shall be borne by the owner or operator of the ship.

3. The detention shall not be lifted until full payment has been made or a sufficient guarantee has been given for the reimbursement of the costs.

Article 17 Data to monitor implementation

Member States shall provide the Commission with the information listed in Annex X at the intervals stated therein in that Annex.

Article 18 Regulatory Committee

1. The Commission shall be assisted by the Committee on Safe Seas and the Prevention of Pollution from Ships (COSS) created by Article 3 of Regulation (EC) No 2099/2002 of the European Parliament and of the Council of 5 November 2002 establishing a Committee on Safe Seas and the Prevention of Pollution from Ships (COSS).

2. Where reference is made to this paragraph, Articles 5 and 7 of Decision 1999/468/ EC shall apply, having regard to the provisions of Article 8 thereof.

The period laid down in Article 5(6) of Decision 1999/468/EC shall be set at three months.

3. The Committee shall adopt its rules of procedure.

Article 19 Amendment procedure

This Directive may, without broadening its scope, be amended in accordance with the procedure laid down in Article 18(2), in order to:

(a)   adapt the obligations referred to in Article 5, except the figure of 25 % referred to in paragraph 1 thereof, in Articles 6, 7, 7a, 7b, 8, 15 and 17, and in the Annexes to which these Articles refer, on the basis of the experience gained from the implementation of this Directive and taking into account developments in the MOU.

(b)   adapt the Annexes in order to take into account amendments which have entered into force to the Conventions, Protocols, codes and resolutions of relevant international organizations and to the MOU.

(c)   update, in Article 2(1), the list of international conventions which are relevant for the purposes of this Directive.

The amendments to the international instruments referred to in Article 2 may be excluded from the scope of this Directive, pursuant to Article 5 of Regulation (EC) No 2099/2002.

Article 19a Penalties

Member States shall lay down a system of penalties for the breach of national provisions adopted pursuant to this Directive and shall take all the measures necessary to ensure that those penalties are applied. The penalties thus provided shall be effective, proportionate and dissuasive.

Article 20 Implementation

1. Member States shall adopt the laws, regulations and administrative provisions necessary to implement this Directive not later than 30 June 1996 and shall forthwith inform the Commission thereof.

2. When Member States adopt these measures, they shall contain a reference to this Directive or shall be accompanied by such reference on the occasion of their official publication. The methods of making such a reference shall be laid down by Member States.

3. Member States shall communicate to the Commission the text of the provisions of national law which they have adopted in the field governed by this Directive.

4. In addition, the Commission shall inform the European Parliament and the Council on a regular basis of progress in the implementation of the Directive within the Member States.

Article 21

This Directive shall enter into force on the 20th day following that of its publication.

Article 22
This Directive is addressed to the Member States.

ANNEX I
SHIPS TO BE CONSIDERED FOR PRIORITY INSPECTION
(as referred to in Article 5(2))

I.   Overriding factors
Regardless of the value of the target factor, the following ships shall be considered as an overriding priority for inspection.

1.   Ships which have been reported by pilots or port authorities as having deficiencies which may prejudice their safe navigation (pursuant to Directive 93/75/EEC and Article 13 of this Directive).

2.   Ships which have failed to comply with the obligations laid down in Directive 93/75/EEC.

3.   Ships which have been the subject of a report or notification by another Member State.

4.   Ships which have been the subject of a report or complaint by the master, a crew member, or any person or organization with a legitimate interest in the safe operation of the ship, shipboard living and working conditions or the prevention of pollution, unless the Member State concerned deems the report or complaint to be manifestly unfounded; the identity of the person lodging the report or complaint must not be revealed to the master or the shipowner of the ship concerned.

5.   Ships which have been:
—   involved in a collision, grounding or stranding on their way to the port,
—   accused of an alleged violation of the provisions on discharge of harmful substances or effluents,
—   manoeuvred in an erratic or unsafe manner whereby routing measures, adopted by the IMO, or safe navigation practices and procedures have not been followed, or
—   otherwise operated in such a manner as to pose a danger to persons, property or the environment.

6.   Ships which have been suspended or withdrawn from their class for safety reasons in the course of the preceding six months.

II. Overall targeting factor
The following ships shall be considered as priority for inspection.

1.   Ships visiting a port of a Member State for the first time or after an absence of 12 months or more. In applying these criteria Member States shall also take into account those inspections which have been carried out by members of the MOU. In the absence of appropriate data for this purpose, Member States shall rely upon the available Sirenac data and inspect those ships which have not been registered in the Sirenac following the entry into force of that database on 1 January 1993.

2.   Ships not inspected by any Member State within the previous six months.

3.   Ships whose statutory certificates on the ship's construction and equipment, issued in accordance with the conventions, and the classification certificates, have been issued by organisations which are not recognised under the terms of Council Directive 94/57/EC.

4.   Ships flying the flag of a State appearing in the black list as published in the annual report of the MOU.

5. Ships which have been permitted to leave the port of a Member State on certain conditions, such as:
  (a) deficiencies to be rectified before departure;
  (b) deficiencies to be rectified at the next port of call;
  (c) deficiencies to be rectified within 14 days;
  (d) deficiencies for which other conditions have been specified.
If ship-related action has been taken and all deficiencies have been rectified, this is taken into account.

6. Ships for which deficiencies have been recorded during a previous inspection, according to the number of deficiencies.

7. Ships which have been detained in a previous port.

8. Ships flying the flag of a country which has not ratified all relevant international conventions referred to in Article 2 of this Directive.

9. Ships classed with classification society with deficiency ratio above average.

10. Ships of the categories referred to in Annex V(A).

11. Ships above 13 years old.

In determining the order of priority for the inspection of the ships listed above, the competent authority shall take into account the overall target factor displayed on the Sirenac information system, according to Annex I, Section I, of the MOU. A higher target factor is indicative of a higher priority. The overall target factor is the sum of the applicable target factor values as defined within the framework of the MOU. Items 5, 6 and 7 shall only apply to inspections carried out in the last 12 months. The overall target factor shall not be less than the sum of the values established for items 3, 4, 8, 9, 10 and 11.

However, for the purpose of Article 7.4, the overall target factor shall not take into account item 10.

ANNEX VI
CRITERIA FOR DETENTION OF A SHIP
(as referred to in Article 9 (3))

Introduction

Before determining whether deficiencies found during an inspection warrant detention of the ship involved, the inspector must apply the criteria mentioned below in sections 1 and 2.

Section 3 includes examples of deficiencies that may for themselves warrant detention of the ship involved (see Article 9 (3)).

Where the ground for detention is the result of accidental damage suffered on the ship's voyage to a port, no detention order shall be issued, provided that:
  1. due account has been given to the requirements contained in Regulation I/11(c) of SOLAS 74 regarding notification to the flag State administration, the nominated surveyor or the recognised organisation responsible for issuing the relevant certificate;
  2. prior to entering a port, the master or shipowner has submitted to the port State control authority details on the circumstances of the accident and the damage suffered and information about the required notification of the flag State administration;
  3. appropriate remedial action, to the satisfaction of the Authority, is being taken by the ship; and
  4. the authority has ensured, having been notified of the completion of the remedial action, that deficiencies which were clearly hazardous to safety, health or the environment have been rectified.

1. Main criteria

When exercising his professional judgement as to whether or not a ship should be detained the inspector must apply the following criteria:

Timing:

Ships which are unsafe to proceed to sea must be detained upon the first inspection irrespective of how much time the ship will stay in port.

Criterion:

The ship is detained if its deficiencies are sufficiently serious to merit an inspector returning to satisfy himself that they have been rectified before the ship sails.

The need for the inspector to return to the ship is a measure of the seriousness of the deficiencies. However, it does not impose such an obligation for every case. It implies that the authority must verify one way or another, preferably by a further visit, that the deficiencies have been rectified before departure.

2. Application of main criteria

When deciding whether the deficiencies found in a ship are sufficiently serious to merit detention the inspector must assess whether:

1. the ship has relevant, valid documentation;
2. the ship has the crew required in the Minimum Safe Manning Document.

During inspection the inspector must further assess whether the ship and/or crew is able to:

3. navigate safely throughout the forthcoming voyage;
4. safely handle, carry and monitor the condition of the cargo throughout the forthcoming voyage;
5. operate the engine room safely throughout the forthcoming voyage;
6. maintain proper propulsion and steering throughout the forthcoming voyage;
7. fight fires effectively in any part of the ship if necessary during the forthcoming voyage;
8. abandon ship speedily and safely and effect rescue if necessary during the forthcoming voyage;
9. prevent pollution of the environment throughout the forthcoming voyage;
10. maintain adequate stability throughout the forthcoming voyage;
11. maintain adequate watertight integrity throughout the forthcoming voyage;
12. communicate in distress situations if necessary during the forthcoming voyage;
13. provide safe and healthy conditions on board throughout the forthcoming voyage;
14. provide the maximum of information in case of accident.

If the answer to any of these assessments is negative, taking into account all deficiencies found, the ship must be strongly considered for detention. A combination of deficiencies of a less serious nature may also warrant the detention of the ship.

3. To assist the inspector in the use of these guidelines, there follows a list of deficiencies, grouped under relevant conventions and/or codes, which are considered of such a serious nature that they may warrant the detention of the ship involved. This list is not intended to be exhaustive. However, the detainable deficiencies in the area of STCW 78 listed under item 3.8 below are the only grounds for detention under this Convention.

3.1. General

The lack of valid certificates and documents as required by the relevant instruments. However, ships flying the flag of States not party to a Convention (relevant instrument) or not having implemented another relevant instrument, are not entitled to carry the certificates provided for by the Convention or other relevant instrument. Therefore, absence of the required certificates should not by itself constitute reason to detain these ships; however, in applying the 'no more favourable treatment' clause, substantial compliance with the provisions is required before the ship sails. [...].[1]

ANNEX XI

A. CATEGORIES OF SHIPS SUBJECT TO REFUSAL OF ACCESS
TOCOMMUNITY PORTS (as referred to in Article 7b(1))

1.   Gas and chemical tankers.
2.   Bulk carriers.
3.   Oil tankers.
4.   Passenger ships.

B. PROCEDURES RELATING TO REFUSAL OF ACCESS TO COMMUNITY
PORTS (as referred to in Article 7b(2))

1. If the conditions described in Article 7b are met, the competent authority of the port in which the ship is detained for the second or third time, as appropriate, must inform the captain and the owner or the operator of the ship in writing of the access refusal order served on the ship.

The competent authority must also inform the flag State administration, the classification society concerned, the other Member States, the Commission, the Centre administratif des affaires maritimes and the MOU Secretariat.

The access refusal order will take effect as soon as the ship has been authorised to leave the port after the deficiencies leading to the detention have been remedied.

2. In order to have the access refusal order lifted, the owner or the operator must address a formal request to the competent authority of the Member State that imposed the access refusal order. This request must be accompanied by a certificate from the flag State administration showing that the ship fully conforms to the applicable provisions of the international conventions. The request for the lifting of the access refusal order must also be accompanied, where appropriate, by a certificate from the classification society which has the ship in class showing that the ship conforms to the class standards stipulated by that society.

3. The access refusal order may only be lifted following a re-inspection of the ship at an agreed port by inspectors of the competent authority of the Member State that imposed the access refusal order and if evidence is provided to the satisfaction of this Member State that the vessel fully complies with the applicable requirements of the International Conventions.

If the agreed port is located within the Community, the competent authority of the Member State of the port of destination may, with the agreement of the competent authority of the Member State that imposed the access refusal order, authorise the ship to proceed to the port of destination in question, for the sole purpose of verifying that the ship meets the conditions specified in paragraph 2.

---

[1] There follows a list of detainable deficiencies in the areas of the Solas Convention, IBC Code, IGC Code, Load Lines Convention, Marpol Convention, Annex I and II, STCW Convention, ILO Conventions, and of areas which may not warrant a detention, but where e.g. cargo operations have to be suspended. Both have been omitted.

The re-inspection shall consist of an expanded inspection that must cover at least the relevant items of Annex V, section C.

All costs of this expanded inspection will be borne by the owner or the operator.

4. If the results of the expanded inspection satisfy the Member State in accordance with paragraph 2, the access refusal order must be lifted. The owner or the operator of the ship must be informed thereof in writing.

The competent authority must also notify its decision in writing to the flag State administration, the classification society concerned, the other Member States, the Commission, the Centre administratif des affaires maritimes and the MOU Secretariat.

5. Information relating to ships that have been refused access to Community ports must be made available in the Sirenac system and published in conformity with the provisions of Article 15 and of Annex VIII.

Rules of Procedure of the Commission on the Limits of the Continental Shelf

Adopted at the 2nd Session of the CLCS, 12 September 1997
CLCS/40/Rev.1, 17 April 2008[1]

I. INTRODUCTION

Rule 1 Use of terms
For the purposes of these Rules:

'Convention' means the 1982 United Nations Convention on the Law of the Sea;

'Statement of Understanding' means the Statement of Understanding adopted on 29 August 1980 by the Third United Nations Conference on the Law of the Sea and contained in Annex II to its Final Act;

'Guidelines' means the Scientific and Technical Guidelines of the Commission on the Limits of the Continental Shelf, unless otherwise specified;

'Commission' means the Commission on the Limits of the Continental Shelf, established in accordance with article 76, paragraph 8, and Annex II to the Convention;

'Secretary-General' means the Secretary-General of the United Nations, unless otherwise specified;

'Secretariat' means the Secretariat of the United Nations;

'States Parties' means States Parties to the Convention;

'Meeting of States Parties' means a meeting of States Parties to the Convention convened in accordance with the relevant provisions of the Convention.

---

[1] The Rules of Procedure were first adopted at the 2nd Session of the CLCS on 12 September 1997 (CLCS/4, 17 September 1997, 2, para. 10). Annexes I and II to the present Rules were adopted by the Commission at its 4th Session, held from 31 August to 4 September 1998. Annex III was adopted by the Commission at its 13th Session, held from 26 to 30 April 2004, and replaced the modus operandi of the Commission (CLCS/L.3, 12 September 1997) and the internal procedure of the sub-commission of the CLCS (CLCS/L.12, 25 May 2001). Following the adoption of Annex III and of the amendments to several rules on 30 April 2004, the CLCS requested its Secretariat to reissue the Rules of Procedure as a new consolidated document, incorporating what had originally been three separate documents into a single document (CLCS/40, 30 April 2004). Document CLCS/40/Rev.1, 17 April 2008, contains the latest version of the Rules of Procedure, embodying amendments and additions adopted by the Commission (CLCS/58, 25 April 2008, 9, para. 40). Footnotes omitted.

II. SESSIONS AND MEETINGS

Rule 2 Sessions and meetings

1. The Commission shall hold sessions at least once a year and as often as is required for the effective performance of its functions under the Convention, in particular, to consider submissions by coastal States and to make recommendations thereon. A session may include several meetings of the Commission and its subcommissions.

2. Taking into account financial considerations that may influence the frequency of its sessions, the Commission shall be convened:

(a) At the request of the Chairperson of the Commission;

(b) At the request of a majority of the members of the Commission;

(c) At the request of the Secretary-General; or

(d) By a decision of the Commission.

Rule 3 Notification of opening date of session

The Secretary-General shall notify the members of the Commission of the date, place and duration of a session as soon as possible, but no later than sixty days in advance of its opening date. Any coastal State whose submission is to be considered at the session shall also be notified.

Rule 4 Venue

1. Sessions of the Commission and its subcommissions shall normally be held at United Nations Headquarters in New York.

2. Another venue for an entire session, or any part thereof, may be designated by the Commission in consultation with any coastal State which made a submission to be considered at that session and with the Secretary-General, subject to the requirements established by the United Nations that no additional costs are directly or indirectly incurred by the United Nations.

Rule 5 Agenda

1. The provisional agenda of each session shall be prepared by the Secretary-General in consultation with the Chairperson of the Commission.

2. The Secretary-General shall transmit the provisional agenda to the members of the Commission together with the notification referred to in rule 3 and with the names of any members of the Commission who have provided any coastal State concerned with scientific and technical advice.

3. The Commission may include in its agenda any other item relevant to the effective performance of its functions.

4. The Commission shall adopt the agenda at the beginning of the session.

5. During a session, the Commission may revise the agenda.

III. MEMBERS OF THE COMMISSION

Rule 6 Members

The Commission shall consist of the members elected pursuant to article 2 of Annex II to the Convention.

Rule 7 Term of office

1. In accordance with article 2, paragraph 4, of Annex II to the Convention, the members of the Commission shall be elected for a term of five years and they shall be eligible for re-election.

2. The members of the Commission elected at the first election shall begin their term of office on the date of the first meeting of the Commission.

3. The term of office of the members of the Commission elected at subsequent elections shall begin on the day after the date of expiry of the term of office of the members of the Commission whom they replace.

4. The absence of a member of the Commission during two consecutive sessions of the Commission without justification shall be brought to the attention of the Meeting of States Parties.

Rule 8 By-elections

If a member of the Commission dies or resigns or for any other cause can no longer perform his or her duties, the Meeting of States Parties shall elect a member for the remainder of the predecessor's term. Such by-elections shall be carried out in accordance with article 76 and Annex II to the Convention.

Rule 9 Expenses of members

In accordance with article 2, paragraph 5, of Annex II to the Convention:

(a) The State Party which submitted the nomination of a member of the Commission shall defray the expenses of that member while in performance of Commission duties;

(b) The coastal States requesting the scientific and technical advice referred to in article 3, paragraph 1 (b), of Annex II to the Convention shall defray the expenses incurred in respect of this advice.

Rule 10 Solemn declaration

Before assuming his or her duties, each member of the Commission shall make the following solemn declaration in the Commission:

'I solemnly declare that I will perform my duties as a member of the Commission on the Limits of the Continental Shelf honourably, faithfully, impartially and conscientiously.'

Rule 11 Duty to act independently

In the performance of their duties, members of the Commission shall not seek or receive instructions from any Government or from any other authority external to the Commission. They shall refrain from any action which might reflect negatively on their position as members of the Commission.

IV. OFFICERS

Rule 12 Elections

The Commission shall elect from among its members a Chairperson and four Vice-Chairpersons, and shall give due regard to the equitable geographical representation and rotation of the Office of the Chairperson among the five regions. In doing so, the Commission shall also take into account those regional groups whose members have already been elected to that office.

Rule 13 Term of office

The officers of the Commission shall be elected for a term of two and a half years. They shall be eligible for re-election.

Rule 14 Acting Chairperson

1. If the Chairperson is absent from a session, or any part thereof, the Commission shall designate one of the Vice-Chairpersons to act in his or her place.

2. A Vice-Chairperson acting as Chairperson shall have the same powers and duties as the Chairperson.

Rule 15 Replacement of officers

If any of the officers of the Commission ceases to be, or declares his or her inability to continue serving as, a member of the Commission, or for any reason is no longer able to act as an officer, a new officer shall be elected for the unexpired term of his or her predecessor.

V. SECRETARIAT

Rule 16 Duties of the Secretary-General

1. The Secretary-General shall act in that capacity in all sessions of the Commission and meetings of its subcommissions and any subsidiary bodies which it may establish. The Secretary-General may designate a member of the Secretariat to participate on his or her behalf.

2. The Secretary-General shall be responsible for making the arrangements related to the sessions of the Commission and meetings of its subcommissions and any subsidiary bodies which it may establish and shall provide and direct the staff required for such sessions and meetings.

3. The Secretariat shall perform all work that the Commission may require for the effective performance of its functions.

Rule 17 Statements by the Secretary-General and members of the Secretariat

The Secretary-General or any member of the Secretariat designated by him or her may make oral or written statements at any meeting of the Commission and of its subcommissions.

Rule 18 Financial implications of proposals

Before any proposal that involves expenditures is approved by the Commission, the Secretary-General shall prepare and circulate to the members of the Commission, as early as possible, an estimate of the cost involved in the proposal. The Chairperson shall draw the attention of members to this estimate and invite discussion on it when the proposal is considered by the Commission or any subsidiary body.

VI. LANGUAGES

Rule 19 Official and working languages

1. The official and working languages of the Commission shall be Arabic, Chinese, English, French, Russian and Spanish.

2. In the absence of objections by any member, the Commission may decide not to use some of its official and working languages for any particular meeting, taking into account the language preferences of the members of the Commission participating at that meeting and of any coastal State whose submission is under consideration.

Rule 20 Interpretation

Subject to rule 19, paragraph 2, speeches made in any of the languages of the Commission shall be interpreted into the other languages.

Rule 21 Interpretation from a language other than the languages of the Commission

Oral statements may be made in a language other than the languages of the Commission, provided the person making the statement arranges for interpretation into one of the languages of the Commission. Interpretation into the other languages of the Commission may be based on the interpretation given in the first such language.

Rule 22 Languages of documents of the Commission

Documents of the Commission shall be issued in the languages of the Commission, unless otherwise decided by the Commission. The languages of the recommendations of the Commission shall be in accordance with rule 53, paragraph 3.

VII. PUBLIC AND PRIVATE MEETINGS

Rule 23 Public and private meetings

The meetings of the Commission, its subcommissions and subsidiary bodies shall be held in private, unless the Commission decides otherwise.

VIII. CONDUCT OF BUSINESS

Rule 24 Quorum

Two thirds of the members of the Commission, subcommission or subsidiary body shall constitute a quorum.

Rule 25 Powers of the Chairperson

1. In addition to exercising the powers conferred upon him or her elsewhere by these Rules, the Chairperson shall declare the opening and closing of each session and meeting of the Commission, direct the discussion, ensure observance of these Rules, accord the right to speak, put questions to the vote and announce decisions. The Chairperson shall rule on points of order and, subject to these Rules, shall have complete control over the proceedings and over the maintenance of order thereat. He or she may propose to the Commission the limitation of time to be allowed to speakers, the limitation of the number of times each representative may speak on any question, the closure of the list of speakers, the adjournment or closure of the debate and the suspension or adjournment of a meeting.

2. The Chairperson, in the exercise of his or her functions, remains under the authority of the Commission.

Rule 26 Points of order

During the discussion of any matter, a member may at any time raise a point of order, which shall be immediately decided by the Chairperson in accordance with the present Rules. Any appeal against the ruling of the Chairperson shall be immediately put to the vote, and the ruling of the Chairperson shall stand unless overruled by a majority of the members present and voting. A member may not, in raising a point of order, speak on the substance of the matter under discussion.

Rule 27 Time limits on speakers

The Commission may limit the time allowed to each speaker on any question. When debate is limited and a speaker exceeds the allotted time, the Chairperson shall call the speaker to order without delay.

Rule 28 Closure of debate

During the discussion of any matter, a member may move the closure of the debate on the item under discussion, whether or not any other member has signified a wish to speak. Permission to speak on the closure of the debate shall be accorded only to the member who proposed the motion, and to one member who opposes it and one member who favours it, after which the motion shall be immediately put to the vote.

Rule 29 Adjournment of debate

During the discussion of any matter, a member may move the adjournment of the debate on the item under discussion. Permission to speak on the adjournment of the debate shall be accorded only to the member who proposed the motion, and to one member who opposes it and one member who favours it, after which the motion shall be immediately put to the vote.

Rule 30 Suspension or adjournment of the meeting

During the discussion of any matter, a member may move the suspension or adjournment of the meeting. No discussion on such motions shall be permitted, and they shall be immediately put to the vote.

Rule 31 Order of motions

The motions indicated below shall have precedence in the following order over all proposals or other motions before the meeting:
(a)   To suspend the meeting;
(b)   To adjourn the meeting;
(c)   To adjourn the debate on the question under discussion; and
(d)   To close the debate on the question under discussion.

Rule 32 Submission of proposals by members of the Commission

Proposals by members of the Commission shall be submitted in writing to the Chairperson of the Commission and copies thereof shall be circulated to all members of the Commission by the Secretariat.

Rule 33 Decisions on competence

Any motion calling for a decision on the competence of the Commission to adopt a proposal submitted to it shall be put to the vote before a decision is taken on the proposal in question.

Rule 34 Reconsideration of proposals by members of the Commission

When a proposal has been adopted or rejected, it may not be reconsidered unless the Commission, by a two-thirds majority of the members present and voting, so decides. Permission to speak on a motion to reconsider shall be accorded only to two speakers opposing reconsideration, after which the motion shall be immediately put to the vote.

IX. VOTING

Rule 35 General agreement

1. The Commission, its subcommissions and subsidiary bodies shall make their best endeavours to ensure that their work is accomplished by general agreement.

2. Accordingly, the Commission, its subcommissions and subsidiary bodies shall make every effort to reach agreement on substantive matters by way of consensus and there shall be no voting on such matters until all efforts to achieve consensus have been exhausted.

Rule 36 Voting rights

Each member of the Commission shall have one vote.

Rule 37 Majority required

1. Subject to rule 35, decisions of the Commission, subcommission or subsidiary body on all matters of substance shall be taken by a two-thirds majority of the members present and voting. For the Commission, this shall include the establishment of subcommissions, the approval of the recommendations prepared by a subcommission, requests for advice by specialists, cooperation with competent international organizations, as well as the amendment of the existing and the adoption of new Rules and other regulations, guidelines and annexes to these Rules.

2. Except as otherwise provided in these Rules, decisions of the Commission on all matters of procedure shall be taken by a majority of the members present and voting.

3. If the question arises whether a matter is one of procedure or of substance, the Chairperson of the Commission shall rule on the question. Any appeal against this ruling shall be put to the vote immediately, and the Chairperson's ruling shall stand unless overruled by a majority of the members present and voting.

4. If a vote is equally divided on a matter other than the election of officers, which is regulated by rule 40, paragraph 4, the proposal or motion shall be regarded as rejected.

5. For the purpose of these Rules, the phrase 'members present and voting' means members casting an affirmative or negative vote. Members who abstain from voting shall be regarded as not voting.

Rule 38 Method of voting

The Commission shall normally vote by a show of hands, except as provided for in rule 40.

Rule 39 Conduct during voting

After the Chairperson has announced the commencement of voting, no member shall interrupt the voting except on a point of order raised in connection with the process of voting.

Rule 40 Election of officers

1. All elections shall be held by secret ballot unless, in the absence of any objection, the Commission decides to proceed without taking a ballot when there is an agreed candidate or slate.

2. A single ballot shall be taken in respect of all places to be filled at one time under the same conditions. Those candidates, in a number not exceeding the number of places to be filled, obtaining a majority of the votes cast and the largest number of votes, shall be elected.

3. If the number of candidates obtaining such a majority is less than the number of places to be filled, additional ballots shall be held to fill the remaining places, the voting being restricted to the candidates obtaining the greatest number of votes in the previous ballot to a number not more than twice the places remaining to be filled.

4. If a tie vote between two or more candidates persists for two successive ballots, a decision, by lot drawn by the Chairperson, shall be taken as to which candidate shall be chosen.

Rule 41 Announcement of the outcome of a voting and of the election of the officers

The Chairperson shall announce the outcome of any voting and, in the case of elections pursuant to rule 40, the names of the officers who have been elected.

X. SUBCOMISSIONS AND OTHER SUBSIDIARY BODIES

Rule 42 Subcommissions

1. If, in accordance with article 5 of Annex II to the Convention, the Commission decides to establish a subcommission for the consideration of a submission, it shall:

(a) Identify any members of the Commission who are defined as ineligible, in accordance with article 5 of Annex II to the Convention, i.e. nationals of the coastal State making the submission and members who have assisted the coastal State by providing scientific and technical advice with respect to the delineation;

(b) Identify any members of the Commission who may, for other reasons, be perceived to have a conflict of interest regarding the submission, e.g., members who are nationals of a State which may have a dispute or unresolved border with the submitting State;

(c) Through informal consultations among the members of the Commission, nominate candidates for the subcommission other than those identified in subparagraph (a), taking into account the factors regarding the members identified in paragraph (b), and the specific elements of the submission as well as, to the extent possible, the need to ensure a scientific and geographical balance; and

(d) Appoint from among the nominated candidates seven members of the subcommission.

2. The term of a subcommission shall extend from the time of its appointment to the time that the submitting coastal State deposits, in accordance with article 76, paragraph 9, of the Convention, the charts and relevant information, including geodetic data, regarding the outer limits for that part of the continental shelf for which the submission was originally made.

3. A member of the Commission can be appointed to be a member of more than one subcommission. Members of the Commission identified under subparagraph 1 (a) have the right to participate as members in the proceedings of the Commission concerning the said submission. Such members, by prior consultation and agreement within the subcommission, may be invited to participate in the proceedings of the subcommission on specific issues concerning the said submission without the right to vote.

Rule 43 Other subsidiary bodies

The Commission may establish such other subsidiary bodies composed of its members as may be required for the effective performance of its functions.

Rule 44 Conduct of business

1. Each subcommission or other subsidiary body established by the Commission shall elect its own Chairperson and two Vice-Chairpersons, and report the results of the election to the Commission.

2. The present Rules apply *mutatis mutandis* to the conduct of business of the subcommissions and other subsidiary bodies.

Rule 44*bis* **Interaction among members of the Commission**

1. The submissions made by coastal States area available for examination by all members of the Commission. Practical mechanisms to consider the material and ensure its confidentiality if necessary shall be arranged with the assistance of the Secretariat.

2. Additional presentations, written materials and data submitted by the coastal State, and any written communications provided by the subcommission, are available for the consideration of members of the Commission.

3. Members of the Commission may discuss among them any matters relating to any part of any submission notwithstanding the fact that the subcommission has the mandate to examine the submission and to prepare draft recommendations for the consideration of the Commission through private deliberations.

4. The sessions of the subcommission shall be held in private in accordance with paragraph 4.2 of annex II to the Rules of Procedure. No records of the oral deliberations and personal notes distributed among members of the subcommission shall be disclosed to other members of the Commission who are not members of the subcommission.

XI. SUBMISSION BY A COASTAL STATE

Rule 45 Submission by a coastal State

In accordance with article 4 of Annex II to the Convention:

(a) Where a coastal State intends to establish the outer limits of its continental shelf beyond 200 nautical miles from the baselines from which the breadth of the territorial sea is measured, it shall submit particulars of such limits to the Commission along with supporting scientific and technical data as soon as possible, but in any case within ten years of the entry into force of the Convention for that State. In the case of a State Party for which the Convention entered into force before 13 May 1999, it is understood, in accordance with the 'Decision regarding the date of commencement of the ten-year period for making submissions to the Commission on the Limits of the Continental Shelf set out in article 4 of Annex II to the United Nations Convention on the Law of the Sea' (SPLOS/72 of 29 May 2001), that the ten-year time period referred to in article 4 of Annex II to the Convention shall be taken to have commenced on 13 May 1999.

(b) The coastal State shall at the same time give the names of any Commission members who have provided it with scientific and technical advice.

Rule 46 Submissions in case of a dispute between States with opposite or adjacent coasts or in other cases of unresolved land or maritime disputes

1. In case there is a dispute in the delimitation of the continental shelf between opposite or adjacent States or in other cases of unresolved land or maritime disputes, submissions may be made and shall be considered in accordance with Annex I to these Rules.

2. The actions of the Commission shall not prejudice matters relating to the delimitation of boundaries between States.

Rule 47   Form and language of submission

1. A submission shall conform to the requirements established by the Commission.

2. A submission, as well as its annexes, attachments and other supporting material, shall be made in one of the official languages of the Commission. If made in an official language other than English, it shall be translated by the Secretariat into English. In order to enable the Secretary-General to make public the proposed outer limits pursuant to the submission, as envisaged in rule 50, the executive summary of the submission shall be translated expeditiously, given the time frame required for such translation by the rules of the Secretariat. Taking into account the volume and complexity of the main body and supporting scientific and technical data of the submission, a reasonable time should be allowed for the completion of the translation of the full submission, including its annexes and charts, and the conversion of the data, if necessary, before the Commission shall meet for consideration of the submission.

Rule 48   Recording of the submission

1. Each submission shall be recorded by the Secretary-General upon receipt.

2. The record shall contain the date of receipt of the submission, a list of attachments and annexes thereto and the date of entry into force of the Convention for the coastal State which made the submission.

Rule 49   Acknowledgement of the receipt of the submission

The Secretary-General shall promptly acknowledge by letter to the submitting State the receipt of its submission and attachments and annexes thereto, specifying the date of receipt.

Rule 50   Notification of the receipt of a submission and publication of the proposed outer limits of the continental shelf related to the submission

The Secretary-General shall, through the appropriate channels, promptly notify the Commission and all States Members of the United Nations, including States Parties to the Convention, of the receipt of the submission, and make public the executive summary including all charts and coordinates referred to in paragraph 9.1.4 of the Guidelines and contained in that summary, upon completion of the translation of the executive summary referred to in rule 47, paragraph 3.

Rule 51   Consideration of the submission

1. Upon receipt of a submission by the Secretary-General, the consideration of that submission shall be included in the provisional agenda of the next ordinary session of the Commission prepared in accordance with rule 5 and paragraph 2 of annex III, provided that that session, as convened in accordance with rule 2, is held not earlier than three months after the date of the publication by the Secretary-General of the executive summary including all charts and coordinates referred to in rule 50.

2. If the next ordinary session of the Commission is not scheduled within a reasonable time, the Chairperson of the Commission may, upon the notification by the Secretary-General of the receipt of the submission in accordance with rule 50, request an additional session to be convened in accordance with rule 2, within a suitable time for the purpose of considering the submission.

3. The submission shall be considered in accordance with the rules on confidentiality contained in annex II to these Rules.

4. Unless it decides otherwise, the Commission shall establish a subcommission in accordance with rule 42 for the consideration of each submission.

4*bis*.   Unless the Commission decides otherwise, only three subcommissions shall function simultaneously while considering submissions.

4*ter*.   Submissions shall be queued in the order they are received. The submission next in line shall be taken for consideration by a subcommission only after one of the three working subcommissions presents its recommendations to the Commission.

5. The recommendations prepared by the subcommission shall be submitted in writing to the Chairperson of the Commission.

Rule 52 Attendance by the coastal State at the consideration of its submission

The Commission shall, through the Secretary-General, notify the coastal State which has made a submission, no later than sixty days prior to the opening date of the session, of the date and place at which its submission will be first considered. The coastal State shall, in accordance with article 5 of Annex II to the Convention, be invited to send its representatives to participate, without the right to vote, in the relevant proceedings of the Commission pursuant to section VI of annex III to these Rules.

Rule 53 Recommendations of the Commission

1. The Commission shall consider and approve or amend the recommendations prepared by the subcommission following their submission by the subcommission. Unless the Commission decides otherwise, the recommendations drafted by the subcommission shall be considered by the Commission during the next session following their submission by the subcommission. Sufficient time shall be allowed to the members of the Commission to consider the submission and the recommendations in each case.

2. The recommendations of the Commission based on the recommendations prepared by the subcommission shall be approved in accordance with rule 35 and rule 37, paragraph 1.

3. The recommendations of the Commission on matters related to the establishment of the outer limits of the continental shelf shall be submitted in writing to the coastal State which made the submission and to the Secretary-General, in accordance with article 6, paragraph 3, of Annex II to the Convention. For this purpose the Chairperson of the Commission shall transmit to the Secretariat two copies of the recommendations, one to be submitted to the coastal State, and one to remain in the custody of the Secretary-General. If the submission was not originally made in English, the recommendations shall be translated by the Secretariat into the official language in which the submission was originally made. The translation shall be transmitted to the coastal State together with the original English text of the recommendations.

4. In the case of disagreement by the coastal State with the recommendations of the Commission, the coastal State shall, in accordance with article 8 of Annex II to the Convention, make a revised or new submission to the Commission within a reasonable time.

5. The outer limits of the continental shelf established by a coastal State on the basis of the recommendations of the Commission shall be final and binding, in accordance with article 76, paragraph 8, of the Convention.

Rule 54 Deposit and publicity of the limits of the continental shelf

1. The coastal State shall, in accordance with article 76, paragraph 9, and article 84 of the Convention, deposit with the Secretary-General of the United Nations and the Secretary-General of the International Seabed Authority charts and relevant information, including geodetic data permanently describing the outer limits of its continental shelf.

2. Pursuant to article 84 of the Convention, in the case of delimitation of the continental shelf between States with opposite or adjacent coasts, charts and/or coordinates describing the lines of delimitation drawn in accordance with article 83 of the Convention shall be deposited with the Secretary-General of the United Nations.

3. Upon giving due publicity to the charts and relevant information, including geodetic data, permanently describing the outer limits of the continental shelf deposited by the coastal State in accordance with article 76, paragraph 9, of the Convention, the Secretary-General shall give due publicity also to the recommendations of the Commission which in the view of the Commission are related to those limits.

XII. ADVICE TO COASTAL STATE

Rule 55 Advice to a coastal State

1. A coastal State may request scientific and technical advice from the Commission, in accordance with article 3, paragraph 1 (b), of Annex II to the Convention.

2. The Commission shall elect a standing subsidiary body composed of five of its members, which will prepare with respect to each request a list of proposed members who may provide advice taking into consideration the technical and scientific nature of each request. The list shall contain a copy of the curriculum vitae containing details of the scientific education and experience of each proposed member. The preparation of this list may take into consideration an explicit request made by a coastal State for the advice of any member of the Commission.

3. The maximum number of members of the Commission who may provide advice to a coastal State in support of a submission shall not exceed three.

4. The dates and terms of advice shall be determined by agreement between the selected members of the Commission and the coastal State.

5. The members selected to provide technical and scientific advice to the coastal State shall submit to the Commission a report outlining their activities.

XIII. COOPERATION WITH COMPETENT INTERNATIONAL ORGANIZATIONS

Rule 56 Cooperation with competent international organizations

The procedure for cooperation referred to in article 3, paragraph 2, of Annex II to the Convention shall be decided by the Commission on a case-by-case basis.

XIV. ADVICE BY SPECIALISTS

Rule 57 Advice by specialists

1. The Commission may, to the extent considered necessary and useful, consult specialists in any field relevant to the work of the Commission.

2. The Commission shall decide in each case the way in which such consultations may be conducted.

XV. ADOPTION OF OTHER REGULATIONS, GUIDELINES AND ANNEXES TO THE RULES OF PROCEDURE

Rule 58 Adoption of other regulations, guidelines and annexes to the Rules of Procedure

1. Subject to rules 35 and 37, the Commission may adopt such regulations, guidelines and annexes to the present Rules as are required for the effective performance of its functions.

2.   The annexes form an integral part of these Rules, and a reference to the Rules or any part thereof includes a reference to the annexes relating thereto.

XVI. AMENDMENTS TO THE RULES OF PROCEDURE

Rule 59 Amendments to the Rules of Procedure

Subject to rules 35 and 37, the Commission may amend the present Rules and the annexes thereto as well as other regulations and guidelines.

ANNEX I
SUBMISSIONS IN CASE OF A DISPUTE BETWEEN STATES WITH OPPOSITE OR ADJACENT COASTS OR IN OTHER CASES OF UNRESOLVED LAND OR MARITIME DISPUTES

1.   The Commission recognizes that the competence with respect to matters regarding disputes which may arise in connection with the establishment of the outer limits of the continental shelf rests with States.

2.   In case there is a dispute in the delimitation of the continental shelf between opposite or adjacent States, or in other cases of unresolved land or maritime disputes, related to the submission, the Commission shall be:

    (a)   Informed of such disputes by the coastal States making the submission; and

    (b)   Assured by the coastal States making the submission to the extent possible that the submission will not prejudice matters relating to the delimitation of boundaries between States.

3.   A submission may be made by a coastal State for a portion of its continental shelf in order not to prejudice questions relating to the delimitation of boundaries between States in any other portion or portions of the continental shelf for which a submission may be made later, notwithstanding the provisions regarding the ten-year period established by article 4 of Annex II to the Convention.

4.   Joint or separate submissions to the Commission requesting the Commission to make recommendations with respect to delineation may be made by two or more coastal States by agreement:

    (a)   Without regard to the delimitation of boundaries between those States; or

    (b)   With an indication, by means of geodetic coordinates, of the extent to which a submission is without prejudice to the matters relating to the delimitation of boundaries with another or other States Parties to this Agreement.

5.   (a)   In cases where a land or maritime dispute exists, the Commission shall not consider and qualify a submission made by any of the States concerned in the dispute. However, the Commission may consider one or more submissions in the areas under dispute with prior consent given by all States that are parties to such a dispute.

    (b)   The submissions made before the Commission and the recommendations approved by the Commission thereon shall not prejudice the position of States which are parties to a land or maritime dispute.

6.   The Commission may request a State making a submission to cooperate with it in order not to prejudice matters relating to the delimitation of boundaries between opposite or adjacent States.

ANNEX II
CONFIDENTIALITY

1. Safe custody of the submission
The Secretary-General shall ensure the safe custody of the submission and the attachments and annexes thereto at United Nations Headquarters in New York until such time as they are required by the Commission.

2. Classification as confidential of data and information by the coastal State
1. The coastal State making a submission may classify as confidential any data and other material, not otherwise publicly available, that it submits in accordance with rule 45. In dealing with such classified material and in the exercise of all their other functions, the members of the Commission shall enjoy the privileges and immunities as experts on mission for the United Nations in accordance with article VI of the Convention on the Privileges and Immunities of the United Nations.

2. Confidential material so classified by the coastal State shall be submitted in accordance with rule 47, paragraph 2, to the Chairperson of the Commission in a separate sealed package, with a list of the material included therein.

3. Confidential material so classified by the coastal State shall remain confidential after the consideration of the submission is concluded unless decided otherwise by the Commission with the written consent of the coastal State concerned.

3. Access to confidential data and information
1. Save with the consent of the coastal State making the submission, access to confidential material shall be in accordance with the procedures set out in this rule and shall be confined to:
    (a) The members of the Commission; and
    (b) The Secretary-General and other members of the Secretariat designated for that purpose.

2. Access to confidential material shall only be given by the Secretary-General at the request of the Chairperson of the Commission and of the chairpersons of the relevant subcommissions.

3. Access to confidential material submitted by the coastal State or States shall be given by the Secretary-General through the chairpersons to the members of the Commission or the relevant subcommissions that have been established to consider the submission.

4. All confidential material forwarded with the submission shall be consulted in the room designated for that purpose and only in the presence of the Secretary-General or one of his or her staff members designated for that purpose.

5. Whenever confidential material is consulted, the name of the person who has authorized access and the time and date of such consultation shall be recorded in the register maintained for that purpose by the Secretary-General or one of his or her designated staff members. The member consulting the confidential material and the staff member present during the consultation shall print their names clearly and sign the entry.

6. Confidential material shall not be copied, duplicated or reproduced in any manner without the written authorization of the coastal State that submitted it.

4. Duty to preserve confidentiality
1. The deliberations of the Commission and subcommissions on all submissions made in accordance with article 76, paragraph 8, of the Convention shall take place in private and remain confidential.

2. Only members of the subcommission and, if necessary, specialists appointed in accordance with rule 57 shall take part in the subcommission deliberations on submissions. The Secretary and other members of the staff of the Secretariat as may be required shall be present. No other person shall be present except by permission of the subcommission.

3. Any records of the Commission and subcommission deliberations on all submissions shall contain only the title or nature of the subjects or matters discussed and the results of any vote taken. They shall not contain any details of the discussions or the views expressed, provided, however, that any member is entitled to require that a statement made by him be inserted in the records.

4. The members of the Commission shall not disclose, also after they cease to be members, any confidential information coming to their knowledge by reason of their duties in relation to the Commission.

5. The duty of the members of the Commission not to disclose confidential information constitutes an obligation in respect of the individual's membership in the Commission.

5. Enforcement of rules on confidentiality

1. The Commission shall elect a standing Committee on Confidentiality composed of five of its members to deal with issues of confidentiality. In case of an alleged breach of confidentiality by a member of the Commission, the Commission may institute appropriate proceedings. In such cases, the Committee on Confidentiality shall establish an investigating body consisting of three or five of its members. The work of the investigating body shall be conducted in strict confidentiality and shall follow established procedures with regard to due process. Having completed its examination of the case, the investigating body shall prepare a report on its findings. The report shall contain the following:

(a) The allegations of a breach of confidentiality;

(b) The statement of the member of the Commission concerned;

(c) A synopsis of the evidence and the evaluation of it by the investigating body;

(d) The findings, indicating which of the allegations, if any, appear to be supported by the evidence;

(e) The conclusions reached by the investigating body; and

(f) Dissenting or separate opinions, if any.

2. The report shall be presented by the Chairperson of the Committee on Confidentiality to the Commission. The Commission shall inform the Meeting of States Parties of the allegations and the results of the investigation, together with its recommendations.

3. The Secretary-General shall provide the Commission with all necessary assistance in enforcing the rules concerning confidentiality.

6. Cessation of confidentiality

The charts and relevant information, including geodetic data, describing the outer limits of the continental shelf, which are deposited by the coastal State with the Secretary-General and which are to be given due publicity by the Secretary-General in accordance with article 76, paragraph 9, of the Convention, shall cease to be classified as confidential, if they had been so classified earlier, upon their receipt by the Secretary-General.

7. Return of confidential data and information to the coastal State

Any and all confidential material submitted by the coastal State, other than materials subject to the provisions of paragraph 6 of this annex, shall be returned to the coastal State upon its request at any time, and in any event after receipt by the Secretary-General of the charts and relevant information, including geodetic data, referred to in paragraph 6 of this annex.

ANNEX III
MODUS OPERANDI FOR THE CONSIDERATION OF A SUBMISSION MADE TO THE COMMISSION ON THE LIMITS OF THE CONTINENTAL SHELF[1]

I. SUBMISSION BY A COASTAL STATE

1.   Format and number of copies of the submission
1. In accordance with paragraphs 9.1.3, 9.1.4, 9.1.5 and 9.1.6 of the Guidelines, the submission shall contain three separate parts: an executive summary, a main analytical and descriptive part (main body), and a part containing all data referred to in the analytical and descriptive part (supporting scientific and technical data).

2. If the submission is made in hard copy only, it shall be made in accordance with paragraph 9.1.3 of the Guidelines, i.e. the submission shall consist of the following number of copies: 22 copies of the executive summary, 8 copies of the main analytical and descriptive part, and 2 copies of the part containing all data referred to in the analytical and descriptive part. Notwithstanding the requirement of paragraph 9.1.3 of the Guidelines, the submission shall be made with a sufficient number of both hard copies and electronic copies for the Commission and the Secretariat as follows:

	Hard copy	*Electronic copy*
Executive summary	22	2
Main body	8	2
All supporting data	2[a]	2

[a] Where feasible. Some data, for example, multibeam bathymetric soundings, would not be expected to be provided in hard copy.

One electronic copy should be made in a secure unalterable format (e.g. locked pdf file), and should be certified by the coastal State to be identical to the hard copy version; the other electronic copy should be open. In the case of any discrepancies between the secure electronic copy and the hard copy of the submission, the latter will be deemed to be the primary source, unless the coastal State indicates otherwise. Any additional data or material submitted by the coastal State during the course of the examination of the corresponding submission by the Commission should be provided with two hard copies and two electronic copies.

II. ORGANIZATION OF THE WORK OF THE COMMISSION

2.   Agenda items related to the submission
Upon notification that a submission has been received and made public in accordance with rule 50, and after a period of at least three months following the date of publication, in accordance with rule 51, paragraph 1, the Commission shall convene its session with the following items on the provisional agenda prepared in accordance with rule 5 and rule 51, paragraph 1:

---

[1] Part VII (Summary flow chart of the procedures concerning a submission made to the Commission) omitted.

(a) Presentation of the submission by coastal State representatives, to include the following subjects:

(i) Charts indicating the proposed limits;

(ii) The provisions of article 76 of the Convention which were applied, and the location of the foot of the continental slope;

(iii) Names of members of the Commission who have assisted the coastal State by providing scientific and technical advice with respect to the delineation;

(iv) Information regarding any disputes related to the submission; and

(v) Comments on any note verbale from other States regarding the data reflected in the executive summary including all charts and coordinates as made public by the Secretary-General in accordance with rule 50.

(b) Consideration of any information regarding any disputes related to the submission, and decisions in accordance with rule 46 and Annex I to these Rules as to whether to proceed with the consideration of the submission, or part thereof, or not. The Commission may defer these decisions to a subcommission in accordance with paragraph 7.

(c) Consideration of how to proceed with the further work of the Commission, inter alia, by way of a subcommission, in accordance with article 5 of Annex II to the Convention.

III. INITIAL EXAMINATION OF THE SUBMISSION

3.   Format and completeness of the submission

The subcommission shall examine whether the format of the submission is in compliance with the requirements set out in paragraph 1, and shall ensure that all necessary information has been included in the submission. If it is deemed necessary, the subcommission may request the coastal State to correct the format and/or to provide any necessary additional information, in a timely manner.

4.   Working language of the subcommissions

In recognition of the size and complexity of the submission, the resources and the time-constraints involved in the translation, and the timely consideration of the submission by the Commission, the working language of the subcommission shall be English.

5.   Preliminary analysis of the submission

1. The subcommission shall undertake a preliminary analysis of the submission in accordance with article 76 of the Convention and the Guidelines in order to determine:

(a) If the test of appurtenance is satisfied by the coastal State;

(b) Which portions of the outer limits of the continental shelf are determined by each of the formulae and constraint lines provided for in article 76 of the Convention and the Statement of Understanding;

(bbis) Whether appropriate combinations of foot of the continental slope points and constraint lines have been used;

(c) If the construction of the outer limits contains straight lines not longer than 60 M;

(d) If the subcommission intends to recommend that the advice of specialists, in accordance with rule 57, or that the cooperation of relevant international organizations, in accordance with rule 56, be sought; and

(e) The estimated time required by the subcommission to review all the data and prepare its recommendations for the Commission.

2. At the stage of the examination and consideration of a submission by the subcommission:

    (a)   The full content of the submission of any State is available at any time for examination by all members of the Commission. Practical ways to view the material should be agreed with the Secretariat;

    (b)   The meetings of the subcommission shall be held in private in accordance with paragraph 4.2 of annex II to these Rules. No records of the oral deliberations in the subcommission meetings, which shall be taken in conformity with paragraph 4.3 of annex II to these Rules, may be disclosed to anyone outside the subcommission;

    (c)   The written communications between a subcommission and the coastal State shall be made available to all members of the Commission;

    (d)   All members of the Commission may freely discuss between them any matters related to any submission, notwithstanding the fact that it is the prerogative and responsibility of the subcommission, through private deliberations, to carry out the examination of a submission on behalf of the Commission and to prepare the final recommendations for consideration by the Commission.

6.   Clarifications

1. The subcommission shall determine whether there are any matters to be clarified by the coastal State.

2. If necessary, the Chairperson of the subcommission shall, through the Secretariat, request clarification from the representatives of the coastal State on those matters. Clarifications should be sought in the form of written questions and answers and translated by the Secretariat, if necessary, into the language in which the submission was made. If the delegation of experts from the coastal State is available at United Nations Headquarters in New York, the written communication should be combined with consultations between the national experts and members of the subcommission at meetings arranged by the Secretariat.

3. The coastal State may provide additional clarification to the subcommission on any matters relating to the submission. Clarifications can be provided in the form of presentations and/or additional materials submitted through the Secretariat.

7.   Disputes related to a submission

The subcommission shall examine all information regarding any disputes related to the submission, in accordance with rule 46. If necessary, the subcommission shall take action based on the procedures in annex I to these Rules.

8.   Notification to the Commission

1. The initial examination shall be completed within a period of not more than one week, after which the subcommission shall notify the Commission of the estimated time and possible advice it might need in order to complete the review of the submission and prepare recommendations thereon for the Commission.

2. The Commission or the subcommission, through the Secretariat, shall notify the coastal State of the preliminary timetable for the examination of the submission by the subcommission.

IV. MAIN SCIENTIFIC AND TECHNICAL EXAMINATION OF THE SUBMISSION

9.   Examination of the submission

1. The subcommission shall conduct an examination of the submission based on the Guidelines in order to evaluate the following, where applicable:

(a)   The data and methodology employed by the coastal State, or coastal States in the case of joint submissions, to determine the location of the foot of the continental slope;

(b)   The methodology used to determine the formula line at a distance of 60 M from the foot of the continental slope;

(c)   The data and methodology used to determine the formula line delineated by reference to the outermost fixed points at each of which the thickness of sedimentary rocks is at least 1 per cent of the shortest distance from such point to the foot of the continental slope, or not less than 1 kilometre in the cases in which the Statement of Understanding applies;

(d)   The data and methodology employed in the determination of the 2,500- metre isobath;

(e)   The methodology used to determine the constraint line at a distance of 100 M from the 2,500-metre isobath;

(f)   The data and methodology used to determine the constraint line at a distance of 350 M from the baselines from which the breadth of the territorial sea is measured;

(g)   The construction of the formulae line as the outer envelope of the two formulae;

(h)   The construction of the constraint line as the outer envelope of the two constraints;

(i)   The construction of the inner envelope of the formulae and constraint lines;

(j)   The delineation of the outer limit of the continental shelf by means of straight lines not longer than 60 M with a view to ensuring that only the portion of the seabed that satisfies all the provisions of article 76 of the Convention and the Statement of Understanding is enclosed;

(k)   The estimates of the uncertainties in the methods applied, with a view to identifying the main source(s) of such uncertainties and their effect on the submission; and, in all cases,

(l)   That the data submitted are sufficient in terms of quantity and quality to justify the proposed limits.

2. The subcommission shall operate through working sessions of suitable duration in the designated facilities at United Nations Headquarters in New York. In addition, the subcommission may decide to assign further work to its members on specific parts of the submission in intersessional periods.

10.   Additional data, information or advice

1. At any stage of the examination, should the subcommission arrive at the conclusion that there is a need for additional data, information or clarifications, its Chairperson shall request the coastal State to provide such data or information or to make clarifications. Such a request, articulated in precise technical terms, shall be transmitted through the Secretariat. If necessary, the Secretariat will translate the request and questions. The data, information or clarifications requested shall be provided within a time period agreed upon between the coastal State and the subcommission.

2. If necessary, the subcommission may request the advice of other members of the Commission and/or, on behalf of the Commission, request the advice of a specialist in

accordance with rule 57, and/or the cooperation of relevant international organizations, in accordance with rule 56.

3. At an advanced stage during the examination of the submission, the subcommission shall invite the delegation of the coastal State to one or several meetings at which it shall provide a comprehensive presentation of its views and general conclusions arising from the examination of part or all of the submission.

4. The coastal State shall have the opportunity to respond to the presentations of the subcommission during the same session, and/or at a later stage, in a format and schedule determined by agreement between the delegation and the subcommission. Printed and electronic copies of the written materials presented by the subcommission and the delegation of the coastal State shall be made available to one another through the Secretariat.

5. Following the meeting(s) with the delegation of the coastal State, the subcommission shall proceed to prepare its recommendations to be submitted to the Commission for its consideration in accordance with these Rules.

V. RECOMMENDATIONS PREPARED BY THE SUBCOMMISSION

11. Formulation of the recommendations

1. The recommendations prepared by the subcommission shall be in accordance with article 76 of the Convention, the Statement of Understanding, these Rules and the Guidelines.

2. The recommendations prepared by the subcommission shall focus on the data and other material submitted by the coastal States in support of the establishment of the outer limits of their continental shelf.

3. The recommendations prepared by the subcommission shall include a summary thereof, and such summary shall not contain information which might be of a confidential nature and/or which might violate the proprietary rights of the coastal State over the data and information provided in the submission. The Secretary- General shall make public the summary of the recommendations upon their approval by the Commission.

12. Drafting of the recommendations

1. The subcommission may appoint one of its members to produce, after consultation with the other members, a first draft of the recommendations. Each member shall produce notes to be considered for the preparation of the draft.

2. The subcommission may prepare an 'Outline of the recommendations prepared by the subcommission' containing the agreed format, contents and main conclusions at an appropriate time. Based on this outline and under the coordination and supervision of an appointed member, each member of the subcommission may be assigned the task of drafting various parts of the recommendations during intersessional periods.

3. At the next session of the subcommission, the combined draft, consolidated by an appointed member, shall be examined by the subcommission at a first reading. Any member who wishes to modify the draft may propose amendments in writing.

4. If the submission contains sufficient data and other material upon which the outer limits of the continental shelf are based, the recommendations shall include the rationale on which such recommendations are based.

5. If the submission contains sufficient data and other material supporting outer limits of the continental shelf which would be different from those proposed in the submission, the recommendations shall contain the rationale on which the recommended outer limits are based.

6. If the submission does not contain sufficient data and other material upon which the outer limits of the continental shelf could be based, the recommendations shall include provisions regarding the additional data and other material that may be needed to support the preparation of a revised or new submission in accordance with the Guidelines.

13. Adoption of the recommendations by the subcommission

1. Pursuant to rule 35, the subcommission shall make its best endeavours to ensure that its work is accomplished by general agreement. Accordingly, the subcommission shall make every effort to reach agreement on recommendations by way of consensus. There shall be no voting on such matters until all efforts to achieve consensus have been exhausted.

2. Should it prove impossible to achieve consensus, the subcommission shall proceed to vote according to rules 36 to 39.

14. Submission of the recommendations prepared by the subcommission to the Commission

The recommendations prepared by the subcommission shall be submitted in writing to the Chairperson of the Commission in accordance with rule 51, paragraph 45, through the Secretariat.

VI. PARTICIPATION BY COASTAL STATE REPRESENTATIVES IN THE PROCEEDINGS

15. Definition of relevant proceedings

1. Representatives of the submitting coastal State can participate in the relevant proceedings of the Commission, in accordance with rule 52. For this purpose, the Commission, taking into consideration the particulars of each submission, will identify the proceedings deemed relevant for the participation of the representatives of the submitting coastal State. The Commission understands that there are three proceedings deemed relevant for all submissions:

   (a) The meeting at which, in accordance with paragraph 2 (a) of section II, coastal State representatives make a presentation to the Commission concerning the submission;

   (b) Meetings at which the subcommission invites the representatives of the coastal State for consultation; and

   (c) Meetings at which the representatives of the coastal State wish to provide additional clarification to the subcommission on any matters relating to the submission, including those referred to in paragraph 10.4.

1 bis. After the subcommission presents its recommendations to the Commission, and before the Commission considers and adopts the recommendations, the coastal State may make a presentation on any matter related to its submission to the plenary of the Commission, if it so chooses. For that presentation, the coastal State may be allowed up to half a day. The coastal State and the Commission shall not engage in discussion on the submission or its recommendations at that meeting. After the presentation made by the coastal State, the Commission shall consider the recommendations in private, without the participation of the representatives of the coastal State.

Rules of the International Tribunal for the Law of the Sea

Adopted by the Tribunal on 28 October 1997
ITLOS/8, 17 March 2009[1]

PART I - USE OF TERMS

Article 1

For the purposes of these Rules:

(a) 'Convention' means the United Nations Convention on the Law of the Sea of 10 December 1982, together with the Agreement of 28 July 1994 relating to the implementation of Part XI of the Convention;

(b) 'Statute' means the Statute of the International Tribunal for the Law of the Sea, Annex VI to the Convention;

(c) 'States Parties' has the meaning set out in article 1, paragraph 2, of the Convention and includes, for the purposes of Part XI of the Convention, States and entities which are members of the Authority on a provisional basis in accordance with section 1, paragraph 12, of the Annex to the Agreement relating to the implementation of Part XI;

(d) 'international organization' has the meaning set out in Annex IX, article 1, to the Convention, unless otherwise specified;

(e) 'Member' means an elected judge;

(f) 'judge' means a Member as well as a judge *ad hoc;*

(g) 'judge *ad hoc*' means a person chosen under article 17 of the Statute for the purposes of a particular case;

(h) 'Authority' means the International Seabed Authority;

(i) 'certified copy' means a copy of a document bearing an attestation by or on behalf of the custodian of the original or the party submitting it that it is a true and accurate copy thereof.

PART II - ORGANIZATION

SECTION A. THE TRIBUNAL

Subsection 1. The Members

Article 2

1. The term of office of Members elected at a triennial election shall begin to run from 1 October following the date of the election.

2. The term of office of a Member elected to replace a Member whose term of office has not expired shall run from the date of the election for the remainder of that term.

Article 3

The Members, in the exercise of their functions, are of equal status, irrespective of age, priority of election or length of service.

---

[1] The Rules of the International Tribunal for the law of the Sea were amended on 15 March and 21 September 2001, and on 17 March 2009. The text reproduced is a consolidated version of the Rules as amended.

Article 4

1. The Members shall, except as provided in paragraphs 3 and 4, take precedence according to the date on which their respective terms of office began.

2. Members whose terms of office began on the same date shall take precedence in relation to one another according to seniority of age.

3. A Member who is re-elected to a new term of office which is continuous with his previous term shall retain his precedence.

4. The President and the Vice-President of the Tribunal, while holding these offices, shall take precedence over the other Members.

5. The Member who, in accordance with the foregoing paragraphs, takes precedence next after the President and the Vice-President of the Tribunal is in these Rules designated the 'Senior Member'. If that Member is unable to act, the Member who is next after him in precedence and able to act is considered as Senior Member.

Article 5

1. The solemn declaration to be made by every Member in accordance with article 11 of the Statute shall be as follows:

'I solemnly declare that I will perform my duties and exercise my powers as judge honourably, faithfully, impartially and conscientiously'.

2. This declaration shall be made at the first public sitting at which the Member is present. Such sitting shall be held as soon as practicable after his term of office begins and, if necessary, a special sitting shall be held for the purpose.

3. A Member who is re-elected shall make a new declaration only if his new term is not continuous with his previous one.

Article 6

1. In the case of the resignation of a Member, the letter of resignation shall be addressed to the President of the Tribunal. The place becomes vacant on the receipt of the letter.

2. In the case of the resignation of the President of the Tribunal, the letter of resignation shall be addressed to the Vice-President of the Tribunal or, failing him, the Senior Member. The place becomes vacant on the receipt of the letter.

Article 7

In any case in which the application of article 9 of the Statute is under consideration, the Member concerned shall be so informed by the President of the Tribunal or, if the circumstances so require, by the Vice-President of the Tribunal, in a written statement which shall include the grounds therefor and any relevant evidence. He shall subsequently, at a private meeting of the Tribunal specially convened for the purpose, be afforded an opportunity of making a statement, of furnishing any information or explanations he wishes to give and of supplying answers, orally or in writing, to any questions put to him. The Member concerned may be assisted or represented by counsel or any other person of his choice. At a further private meeting, at which the Member concerned shall not be present, the matter shall be discussed; each Member shall state his opinion, and if requested a vote shall be taken.

Subsection 2. Judges ad hoc

Article 8

1. Judges *ad hoc* shall participate in the case in which they sit on terms of complete equality with the other judges.

2. Judges *ad hoc* shall take precedence after the Members and in order of seniority of age.

3. In the case of the resignation of a judge *ad hoc*, the letter of resignation shall be addressed to the President of the Tribunal. The place becomes vacant on the receipt of the letter.

Article 9

1. The solemn declaration to be made by every judge *ad hoc* in accordance with articles 11 and 17, paragraph 6, of the Statute shall be as set out in article 5, paragraph 1, of these Rules.

2. This declaration shall be made at a public sitting in the case in which the judge *ad hoc* is participating.

3. Judges *ad hoc* shall make the declaration in relation to each case in which they are participating.

Subsection 3. President and Vice-President

Article 10

1. The term of office of the President and that of the Vice-President of the Tribunal shall begin to run from the date on which the term of office of the Members elected at a triennial election begins.

2. The elections of the President and the Vice-President of the Tribunal shall be held on that date or shortly thereafter. The former President, if still a Member, shall continue to exercise the functions of President of the Tribunal until the election to this position has taken place.

Article 11

1. If, on the date of the election to the presidency, the former President of the Tribunal is still a Member, he shall conduct the election. If he has ceased to be a Member, or is unable to act, the election shall be conducted by the Member exercising the functions of the presidency.

2. The election shall take place by secret ballot, after the presiding Member has declared the number of affirmative votes necessary for election; there shall be no nominations. The Member obtaining the votes of the majority of the Members composing the Tribunal at the time of the election shall be declared elected and shall enter forthwith upon his functions.

3. The new President of the Tribunal shall conduct the election of the Vice-President of the Tribunal either at the same or at the following meeting. Paragraph 2 applies to this election.

Article 12

1. The President of the Tribunal shall preside at all meetings of the Tribunal. He shall direct the work and supervise the administration of the Tribunal.

2. He shall represent the Tribunal in its relations with States and other entities.

Article 13

1. In the event of a vacancy in the presidency or of the inability of the President of the Tribunal to exercise the functions of the presidency, these shall be exercised by the Vice-President of the Tribunal or, failing him, by the Senior Member.

2. When the President of the Tribunal is precluded by a provision of the Statute or of these Rules either from sitting or from presiding in a particular case, he shall continue to exercise the functions of the presidency for all purposes save in respect of that case.

3. The President of the Tribunal shall take the measures necessary in order to ensure the continuous exercise of the functions of the presidency at the seat of the Tribunal. In the event of his absence, he may, so far as is compatible with the Statute and these Rules, arrange for these functions to be exercised by the Vice-President of the Tribunal or, failing him, by the Senior Member.

4. If the President of the Tribunal decides to resign the presidency, he shall communicate his decision in writing to the Tribunal through the Vice-President of the Tribunal or, failing him, the Senior Member. If the Vice-President of the Tribunal decides to resign the vice-presidency, he shall communicate his decision in writing to the President of the Tribunal.

Article 14

If a vacancy in the presidency or the vice-presidency occurs before the date when the current term is due to expire, the Tribunal shall decide whether or not the vacancy shall be filled during the remainder of the term.

Subsection 4. *Experts appointed under article 289 of the Convention*

Article 15

1. A request by a party for the selection by the Tribunal of scientific or technical experts under article 289 of the Convention shall, as a general rule, be made not later than the closure of the written proceedings. The Tribunal may consider a later request made prior to the closure of the oral proceedings, if appropriate in the circumstances of the case.

2. When the Tribunal decides to select experts, at the request of a party or *proprio motu*, it shall select such experts upon the proposal of the President of the Tribunal, who shall consult the parties before making such a proposal.

3. Experts shall be independent and enjoy the highest reputation for fairness, competence and integrity. An expert in a field mentioned in Annex VIII, article 2, to the Convention shall be chosen preferably from the relevant list prepared in accordance with that annex.

4. This article applies *mutatis mutandis* to any chamber and its President.

5. Before entering upon their duties, such experts shall make the following solemn declaration at a public sitting:

'I solemnly declare that I will perform my duties as an expert honourably, impartially and conscientiously and that I will faithfully observe all the provisions of the Statute and of the Rules of the Tribunal'.

Subsection 5. *The composition of the Tribunal for particular cases*

Article 16

1. No Member who is a national of a party in a case, a national of a State member of an international organization which is a party in a case or a national of a sponsoring State

of an entity other than a State which is a party in a case, shall exercise the functions of the presidency in respect of the case.

2. The Member who is presiding in a case on the date on which the Tribunal meets in accordance with article 68 shall continue to preside in that case until completion of the current phase of the case, notwithstanding the election in the meantime of a new President or Vice-President of the Tribunal. If he should become unable to act, the presidency for the case shall be determined in accordance with article 13 and on the basis of the composition of the Tribunal on the date on which it met in accordance with article 68.

Article 17

Members who have been replaced following the expiration of their terms of office shall continue to sit in a case until the completion of any phase in respect of which the Tribunal has met in accordance with article 68.

Article 18

1. Whenever doubt arises on any point in article 8 of the Statute, the President of the Tribunal shall inform the other Members. The Member concerned shall be afforded an opportunity of furnishing any information or explanations.

2. If a party desires to bring to the attention of the Tribunal facts which it considers to be of possible relevance to the application of article 8 of the Statute, but which it believes may not be known to the Tribunal, that party shall communicate confidentially such facts to the President of the Tribunal in writing.

Article 19

1. If a party intends to choose a judge *ad hoc* in a case, it shall notify the Tribunal of its intention as soon as possible. It shall inform the Tribunal of the name, nationality and brief biographical details of the person chosen, preferably at the same time but in any event not later than two months before the time-limit fixed for the filing of the counter-memorial. The judge *ad hoc* may be of a nationality other than that of the party which chooses him.

2. If a party proposes to abstain from choosing a judge *ad hoc*, on condition of a like abstention by the other party, it shall so notify the Tribunal, which shall inform the other party. If the other party thereafter gives notice of its intention to choose, or chooses, a judge *ad hoc*, the time-limit for the party which had previously abstained from choosing a judge may be extended up to 30 days by the President of the Tribunal.

3. A copy of any notification relating to the choice of a judge *ad hoc* shall be communicated by the Registrar to the other party, which shall be requested to furnish, within a time-limit not exceeding 30 days to be fixed by the President of the Tribunal, such observations as it may wish to make. If within the said time-limit no objection is raised by the other party, and if none appears to the Tribunal itself, the parties shall be so informed. In the event of any objection or doubt, the matter shall be decided by the Tribunal, if necessary after hearing the parties.

4. A judge *ad hoc* who becomes unable to sit may be replaced.

5. If the Tribunal finds that the reasons for the participation of a judge *ad hoc* no longer exist, that judge shall cease to sit on the bench.

Article 20

1. If the Tribunal finds that two or more parties are in the same interest and are therefore to be considered as one party only, and that there is no Member of the nationality of any one of these parties upon the bench, the Tribunal shall fix a time-limit within which they may jointly choose a judge *ad hoc*.

2. Should any party among those found by the Tribunal to be in the same interest allege the existence of a separate interest of its own or put forward any other objection, the matter shall be decided by the Tribunal, if necessary after hearing the parties.

Article 21

1. If a Member having the nationality of one of the parties is or becomes unable to sit in any phase of a case, that party is entitled to choose a judge *ad hoc* within a time-limit to be fixed by the Tribunal, or by the President of the Tribunal if the Tribunal is not sitting.

2. Parties in the same interest shall be deemed not to have a Member of one of their nationalities upon the bench if every Member having one of their nationalities is or becomes unable to sit in any phase of the case.

3. If a Member having the nationality of one of the parties becomes able to sit not later than the closure of the written proceedings in that phase of the case, that Member shall resume the seat on the bench in the case.

Article 22

1. An entity other than a State may choose a judge *ad hoc* only if:

(a) one of the other parties is a State Party and there is upon the bench a judge of its nationality or, where such party is an international organization, there is upon the bench a judge of the nationality of one of its member States or the State Party has itself chosen a judge *ad hoc*; or

(b) there is upon the bench a judge of the nationality of the sponsoring State of one of the other parties.

2. However, an international organization or a natural or juridical person or state enterprise is not entitled to choose a judge *ad hoc* if there is upon the bench a judge of the nationality of one of the member States of the international organization or a judge of the nationality of the sponsoring State of such natural or juridical person or state enterprise.

3. Where an international organization is a party to a case and there is upon the bench a judge of the nationality of a member State of the organization, the other party may choose a judge *ad hoc*.

4. Where two or more judges on the bench are nationals of member States of the international organization concerned or of the sponsoring States of a party, the President may, after consulting the parties, request one or more of such judges to withdraw from the bench.

SECTION B. THE SEABED DISPUTES CHAMBER

Subsection 1. The members and judges ad hoc

Article 23

The members of the Seabed Disputes Chamber shall be selected following each triennial election to the Tribunal as soon as possible after the term of office of Members elected at such election begins. The term of office of members of the Chamber shall begin to run from the date of their selection. The term of office of members selected at the first selection shall expire on 30 September 1999; the terms of office of members selected at subsequent triennial selections shall expire on 30 September every three years thereafter. Members of the Chamber who remain on the Tribunal after the expiry of their term of office shall continue to serve on the Chamber until the next selection.

Article 24

The President of the Chamber, while holding that office, takes precedence over the other members of the Chamber. The other members take precedence according to their precedence in the Tribunal in the case where the President and Vice-President of the Tribunal are not exercising the functions of those offices.

Article 25

Articles 8 and 9 apply *mutatis mutandis* to the judges *ad hoc* of the Chamber.

Subsection 2. The presidency

Article 26

1. The Chamber shall elect its President by secret ballot and by a majority vote of its members.

2. The President shall preside at all meetings of the Chamber.

3. In the event of a vacancy in the presidency or of the inability of the President of the Chamber to exercise the functions of the presidency, these shall be exercised by the member of the Chamber who is senior in precedence and able to act.

4. In other respects, articles 10 to 14 apply *mutatis mutandis*.

Subsection 3. Ad hoc chambers of the Seabed Disputes Chamber

Article 27

1. Any request for the formation of an *ad hoc* chamber of the Seabed Disputes Chamber in accordance with article 188, paragraph 1 (b), of the Convention shall be made within three months from the date of the institution of proceedings.

2. If, within a time-limit fixed by the President of the Seabed Disputes Chamber, the parties do not agree on the composition of the chamber, the President shall establish time limits for the parties to make the necessary appointments.

SECTION C. SPECIAL CHAMBERS

Article 28

1. The Chamber of Summary Procedure shall be composed of the President and Vice-President of the Tribunal, acting ex officio, and three other Members. In addition, two Members shall be selected to act as alternates.

2. The members and alternates of the Chamber shall be selected by the Tribunal upon the proposal of the President of the Tribunal.

3. The selection of members and alternates of the Chamber shall be made as soon as possible after 1 October in each year. The members of the Chamber and the alternates shall enter upon their functions on their selection and serve until 30 September of the following year. Members of the Chamber and alternates who remain on the Tribunal after that date shall continue to serve on the Chamber until the next selection.

4. If a member of the Chamber is unable, for whatever reason, to sit in a given case, that member shall be replaced for the purposes of that case by the senior in precedence of the two alternates.

5. If a member of the Chamber resigns or otherwise ceases to be a member, the place of that member shall be taken by the senior in precedence of the two alternates, who shall thereupon become a full member of the Chamber and be replaced by the selection of another alternate.

6. The quorum for meetings of the Chamber is three members.

Article 29

1. Whenever the Tribunal decides to form a standing special chamber provided for in article 15, paragraph 1, of the Statute, it shall determine the particular category of disputes for which it is formed, the number of its members, the period for which they will serve, the date when they will enter upon their duties and the quorum for meetings.

2. The members of such chamber shall be selected by the Tribunal upon the proposal of the President of the Tribunal from among the Members, having regard to any special knowledge, expertise or previous experience which any of the Members may have in relation to the category of disputes the chamber deals with.

3. The Tribunal may decide to dissolve a standing special chamber. The chamber shall finish any cases pending before it.

Article 30

1. A request for the formation of a special chamber to deal with a particular dispute, as provided for in article 15, paragraph 2, of the Statute, shall be made within two months from the date of the institution of proceedings. Upon receipt of a request made by one party, the President of the Tribunal shall ascertain whether the other party assents.

2. When the parties have agreed, the President of the Tribunal shall ascertain their views regarding the composition of the chamber and shall report to the Tribunal accordingly.

3. The Tribunal shall determine, with the approval of the parties, the Members who are to constitute the chamber. The same procedure shall be followed in filling any vacancy. The Tribunal shall also determine the quorum for meetings of the chamber.

4. Members of a chamber formed under this article who have been replaced, in accordance with article 5 of the Statute, following the expiration of their terms of office, shall continue to sit in all phases of the case, whatever the stage it has then reached.

Article 31

1. If a chamber when formed includes the President of the Tribunal, the President shall preside over the chamber. If it does not include the President but includes the Vice-President, the Vice-President shall preside. In any other event, the chamber shall elect its own President by secret ballot and by a majority of votes of its members. The member who, under this paragraph, presides over the chamber at the time of its formation shall continue to preside so long as he remains a member of that chamber.

2. Subject to paragraph 3, the President of a chamber shall exercise, in relation to cases being dealt with by that chamber and from the time it begins dealing with the case, the functions of the President of the Tribunal in relation to cases before the Tribunal.

3. The President of the Tribunal shall take such steps as may be necessary to give effect to article 17, paragraph 4, of the Statute.

4. If the President of a chamber is prevented from sitting or acting as President of the chamber, the functions of the presidency of the chamber shall be assumed by the member of the chamber who is the senior in precedence and able to act.

SECTION D. THE REGISTRY

Article 32

1. The Tribunal shall elect its Registrar by secret ballot from among candidates nominated by Members. The Registrar shall be elected for a term of five years and may be reelected.

2. The President of the Tribunal shall give notice of a vacancy or impending vacancy to Members, either forthwith upon the vacancy arising or, where the vacancy will arise on the expiration of the term of office of the Registrar, not less than three months prior thereto. The President of the Tribunal shall fix a date for the closure of the list of candidates so as to enable nominations and information concerning the candidates to be received in sufficient time.

3. Nominations shall be accompanied by the relevant information concerning the candidates, in particular information as to age, nationality, present occupation, academic and other qualifications, knowledge of languages and any previous experience in law, especially the law of the sea, diplomacy or the work of international organizations.

4. The candidate obtaining the votes of the majority of the Members composing the Tribunal at the time of the election shall be declared elected.

Article 33

The Tribunal shall elect a Deputy Registrar; it may also elect an Assistant Registrar. Article 32 applies to their election and terms of office.

Article 34

Before taking up their duties, the Registrar, the Deputy Registrar and the Assistant Registrar shall make the following solemn declaration at a meeting of the Tribunal:

'I solemnly declare that I will perform my duties as Registrar (Deputy Registrar or Assistant Registrar as the case may be) of the International Tribunal for the Law of the Sea in all loyalty, discretion and good conscience and that I will faithfully observe all the provisions of the Statute and of the Rules of the Tribunal'.

Article 35

1. The staff of the Registry, other than the Registrar, the Deputy Registrar and the Assistant Registrar, shall be appointed by the Tribunal on proposals submitted by the Registrar. Appointments to such posts as the Tribunal shall determine may, however, be made by the Registrar with the approval of the President of the Tribunal.

2. The paramount consideration in the recruitment and employment of the staff and in the determination of the conditions of service shall be the necessity of securing the highest standards of efficiency, competence and integrity. Due regard shall be paid to the importance of recruiting the staff on as wide a geographical basis as possible.

3. Before taking up their duties, the staff shall make the following solemn declaration before the President of the Tribunal, the Registrar being present:

'I solemnly declare that I will perform my duties as an official of the International Tribunal for the Law of the Sea in all loyalty, discretion and good conscience and that I will faithfully observe all the provisions of the Statute and of the Rules of the Tribunal'.

Article 36

1. The Registrar, in the discharge of his functions, shall:
(a) be the regular channel of communications to and from the Tribunal and in particular shall effect all communications, notifications and transmission of documents required by the Convention, the Statute, these Rules or any other relevant international agreement and ensure that the date of dispatch and receipt thereof may be readily verified;
(b) keep, under the supervision of the President of the Tribunal, and in such form as may be laid down by the Tribunal, a List of cases, entered and numbered in the

order in which the documents instituting proceedings or requesting an advisory opinion are receivedin the Registry;

(c) keep copies of declarations and notices of revocation or withdrawal thereof deposited with the Secretary-General of the United Nations under articles 287 and 298 of the Convention or Annex IX, article 7, to the Convention;

(d) keep copies of agreements conferring jurisdiction on the Tribunal;

(e) keep notifications received under article 110, paragraph 2;

(f) transmit to the parties certified copies of pleadings and annexes upon receipt thereof in the Registry;

(g) communicate to the Government of the State in which the Tribunal or a chamber is sitting, or is to sit, and any other Governments which may be concerned, the necessary information as to the persons from time to time entitled, under the Statute and the relevant agreements, to privileges, immunities or facilities;

(h) be present in person or represented by the Deputy Registrar, the Assistant Registrar or in their absence by a senior official of the Registry designated by him, at meetings of the Tribunal, and of the chambers, and be responsible for preparing records of such meetings;

(i) make arrangements for such provision or verification of translations and interpretations into the Tribunal's official languages as the Tribunal may require;

(j) sign all judgments, advisory opinions and orders of the Tribunal and the records referred to in subparagraph (h);

(k) be responsible for the reproduction, printing and publication of the Tribunal's judgments, advisory opinions and orders, the pleadings and statements and the minutes of public sittings in cases and of such other documents as the Tribunal may direct to be published;

(l) be responsible for all administrative work and in particular for the accounts and financial administration in accordance with the financial procedures of the Tribunal;

(m) deal with inquiries concerning the Tribunal and its work;

(n) assist in maintaining relations between the Tribunal and the Authority, the International Court of Justice and the other organs of the United Nations, its related agencies, the arbitral and special arbitral tribunals referred to in article 287 of the Convention and international bodies and conferences concerned with the codification and progressive development of international law, in particular the law of the sea;

(o) ensure that information concerning the Tribunal and its activities is accessible to Governments, the highest national courts of justice, professional and learned societies, legal faculties and schools of law and public information media;

(p) have custody of the seals and stamps of the Tribunal, of the archives of the Tribunal and of such other archives as may be entrusted to the Tribunal.

2. The Tribunal may at any time entrust additional functions to the Registrar.

3. In the discharge of his functions the Registrar shall be responsible to the Tribunal.

Article 37

1. The Deputy Registrar shall assist the Registrar, act as Registrar in the latter's absence and, in the event of the office becoming vacant, exercise the functions of Registrar until the office has been filled.

2. If the Registrar, the Deputy Registrar and the Assistant Registrar are unable to carry out the duties of Registrar, the President of the Tribunal shall appoint an official of

the Registry to discharge those duties for such time as may be necessary. If the three offices are vacant at the same time, the President, after consulting the Members, shall appoint an official of the Registry to discharge the duties of Registrar pending an election to that office.

Article 38

1. The Registry consists of the Registrar, the Deputy Registrar, the Assistant Registrar and such other staff as required for the efficient discharge of its functions.

2. The Tribunal shall determine the organization of the Registry and shall for this purpose request the Registrar to make proposals.

3. Instructions for the Registry shall be drawn up by the Registrar and approved by the Tribunal.

4. The staff of the Registry shall be subject to Staff Regulations drawn up by the Registrar and approved by the Tribunal.

Article 39

1. The Registrar may resign from office with two months' notice tendered in writing to the President of the Tribunal. The Deputy Registrar and the Assistant Registrar may resign from office with one month's notice tendered in writing to the President of the Tribunal through the Registrar.

2. The Registrar may be removed from office only if, in the opinion of two thirds of the Members, he has either committed a serious breach of his duties or become permanently incapacitated from exercising his functions. Before a decision to remove him is taken under this paragraph, he shall be informed by the President of the Tribunal of the action contemplated, in a written statement which shall include the grounds therefor and any relevant evidence. When the action contemplated concerns permanent incapacity, relevant medical information shall be included. The Registrar shall subsequently, at a private meeting of the Tribunal, be afforded an opportunity of making a statement, of furnishing any information or explanations he wishes to give and of supplying answers, orally or in writing, to any questions put to him. He may be assisted or represented at such meeting by counsel or any other person of his choice.

3. The Deputy Registrar and the Assistant Registrar may be removed from office only on the same grounds and by the same procedure as specified in paragraph 2.

SECTION E. INTERNAL FUNCTIONING OF THE TRIBUNAL

Article 40

The internal judicial practice of the Tribunal shall, subject to the Convention, the Statute and these Rules, be governed by any resolutions on the subject adopted by the Tribunal.

Article 41

1. The quorum specified by article 13, paragraph 1, of the Statute applies to all meetings of the Tribunal. The quorum specified in article 35, paragraph 7, of the Statute applies to all meetings of the Seabed Disputes Chamber. The quorum specified for a special chamber applies to all meetings of that chamber.

2. Members shall hold themselves permanently available to exercise their functions and shall attend all such meetings, unless they are absent on leave as provided for in paragraph 4 or prevented from attending by illness or for other serious reasons duly explained to the President of the Tribunal, who shall inform the Tribunal.

3. Judges *ad hoc* are likewise bound to hold themselves at the disposal of the Tribunal and to attend all meetings held in the case in which they are participating unless they are prevented from attending by illness or for other serious reasons duly explained to the President of the Tribunal, who shall inform the Tribunal. They shall not be taken into account for the calculation of the quorum.

4. The Tribunal shall fix the dates and duration of the judicial vacations and the periods and conditions of leave to be accorded to individual Members, having regard in both cases to the state of the List of cases and to the requirements of its current work.

5. Subject to the same considerations, the Tribunal shall observe the public holidays customary at the place where the Tribunal is sitting.

6. In case of urgency the President of the Tribunal may convene the Tribunal at any time.

Article 42

1. The deliberations of the Tribunal shall take place in private and remain secret. The Tribunal may, however, at any time decide in respect of its deliberations on other than judicial matters to publish or allow publication of any part of them.

2. Only judges and any experts appointed in accordance with article 289 of the Convention take part in the Tribunal's judicial deliberations. The Registrar, or his Deputy, and other members of the staff of the Registry as may be required shall be present. No other person shall be present except by permission of the Tribunal.

3. The records of the Tribunal's judicial deliberations shall contain only the title or nature of the subjects or matters discussed and the results of any vote taken. They shall not contain any details of the discussions nor the views expressed, provided however that any judge is entitled to require that a statement made by him be inserted in the records.

SECTION F. OFFICIAL LANGUAGES

Article 43

The official languages of the Tribunal are English and French.

PART III - PROCEDURE

SECTION A. GENERAL PROVISIONS

Article 44

1. The proceedings consist of two parts: written and oral.

2. The written proceedings shall consist of the communication to the Tribunal and to the parties of memorials, counter-memorials and, if the Tribunal so authorizes, replies and rejoinders, as well as all documents in support.

3. The oral proceedings shall consist of the hearing by the Tribunal of agents, counsel, advocates, witnesses and experts.

Article 45

In every case submitted to the Tribunal, the President shall ascertain the views of the parties with regard to questions of procedure. For this purpose, he may summon the agents of the parties to meet him as soon as possible after their appointment and whenever necessary thereafter, or use other appropriate means of communication.

Article 46

Time-limits for the completion of steps in the proceedings may be fixed by assigning a specified period but shall always indicate definite dates. Such time-limits shall be as short as the character of the case permits.

Article 47

The Tribunal may at any time direct that the proceedings in two or more cases be joined. It may also direct that the written or oral proceedings, including the calling of witnesses, be in common; or the Tribunal may, without effecting any formal joinder, direct common action in any of these respects.

Article 48

The parties may jointly propose particular modifications or additions to the Rules contained in this Part, which may be applied by the Tribunal or by a chamber if the Tribunal or the chamber considers them appropriate in the circumstances of the case.

Article 49

The proceedings before the Tribunal shall be conducted without unnecessary delay or expense.

Article 50

The Tribunal may issue guidelines consistent with these Rules concerning any aspect of its proceedings, including the length, format and presentation of written and oral pleadings and the use of electronic means of communication.

Article 51

All communications to the Tribunal under these Rules shall be addressed to the Registrar unless otherwise stated. Any request made by a party shall likewise be addressed to the Registrar unless made in open court in the course of the oral proceedings.

Article 52

1. All communications to the parties shall be sent to their agents.

2. The communications to a party before it has appointed an agent and to an entity other than a party shall be sent as follows:

   (a) in the case of a State, the Tribunal shall direct all communications to its Government;

   (b) in the case of the International Seabed Authority or the Enterprise, any international organization and any other intergovernmental organization, the Tribunal shall direct all communications to the competent body or executive head of such organization at its headquarters location;

   (c) in the case of state enterprises or natural or juridical persons referred to in article 153, paragraph 2 (b), of the Convention, the Tribunal shall direct all communications through the Government of the sponsoring or certifying State, as the case may be;

   (d) in the case of a group of States, state enterprises or natural or juridical persons referred to in article 153, paragraph 2 (b), of the Convention, the Tribunal shall direct all communications to each member of the group according to subparagraphs (a) and (c) above;

   (e) in the case of other natural or juridical persons, the Tribunal shall direct all communications through the Government of the State in whose territory the communication has to be received.

3. The same provisions apply whenever steps are to be taken to procure evidence on the spot.

Article 53

1. The parties shall be represented by agents.

2. The parties may have the assistance of counsel or advocates before the Tribunal.

SECTION B. PROCEEDINGS BEFORE THE TRIBUNAL

Subsection 1. Institution of proceedings

Article 54

1. When proceedings before the Tribunal are instituted by means of an application, the application shall indicate the party making it, the party against which the claim is brought and the subject of the dispute.

2. The application shall specify as far as possible the legal grounds upon which the jurisdiction of the Tribunal is said to be based; it shall also specify the precise nature of the claim, together with a succinct statement of the facts and grounds on which the claim is based.

3. The original of the application shall be signed by the agent of the party submitting it or by the diplomatic representative of that party in the country in which the Tribunal has its seat or by some other duly authorized person. If the application bears the signature of someone other than such diplomatic representative, the signature must be authenticated by the latter or by the competent governmental authority.

4. The Registrar shall forthwith transmit to the respondent a certified copy of the application.

5. When the applicant proposes to found the jurisdiction of the Tribunal upon a consent thereto yet to be given or manifested by the party against which the application is made, the application shall be transmitted to that party. It shall not however be entered in the List of cases, nor any action be taken in the proceedings, unless and until the party against which such application is made consents to the jurisdiction of the Tribunal for the purposes of the case.

Article 55

1. When proceedings are brought before the Tribunal by the notification of a special agreement, the notification may be effected by the parties jointly or by any one or more of them. If the notification is not a joint one, a certified copy of it shall forthwith be communicated by the Registrar to any other party.

2. In each case the notification shall be accompanied by an original or certified copy of the special agreement. The notification shall also, insofar as this is not already apparent from the agreement, indicate the precise subject of the dispute and identify the parties to it.

Article 56

1. Except in the circumstances contemplated by article 54, paragraph 5, all steps on behalf of the parties after proceedings have been instituted shall be taken by agents. Agents shall have an address for service at the seat of the Tribunal or in the capital of the country where the seat is located, to which all communications concerning the case are to be sent.

2. When proceedings are instituted by means of an application, the name of the agent for the applicant shall be stated. The respondent, upon receipt of the certified copy

of the application, or as soon as possible thereafter, shall inform the Tribunal of the name of its agent.

3. When proceedings are brought by notification of a special agreement, the party or parties making the notification shall state the name of its agent or the names of their agents, as the case may be. Any other party to the special agreement, upon receiving from the Registrar a certified copy of such notification, or as soon as possible thereafter, shall inform the Tribunal of the name of its agent if it has not already done so.

Article 57

1. Whenever proceedings are instituted on the basis of an agreement other than the Convention, the application or the notification shall be accompanied by a certified copy of the agreement in question.

2. In a dispute to which an international organization is a party, the Tribunal may, at the request of any other party or *proprio motu*, request the international organization to provide, within a reasonable time, information as to which, as between the organization and its member States, has competence in respect of any specific question which has arisen. If the Tribunal considers it necessary, it may suspend the proceedings until it receives such information.

Article 58

In the event of a dispute as to whether the Tribunal has jurisdiction, the matter shall be decided by the Tribunal.

Subsection 2. The written proceedings

Article 59

1. In the light of the views of the parties ascertained by the President of the Tribunal, the Tribunal shall make the necessary orders to determine, *inter alia*, the number and the order of filing of the pleadings and the time-limits within which they must be filed. The time-limits for each pleading shall not exceed six months.

2. The Tribunal may at the request of a party extend any time-limit or decide that any step taken after the expiration of the time-limit fixed therefor shall be considered as valid. It may not do so, however, unless it is satisfied that there is adequate justification for the request. In either case the other party shall be given an opportunity to state its views within a time-limit to be fixed by the Tribunal.

3. If the Tribunal is not sitting, its powers under this article may be exercised by the President of the Tribunal, but without prejudice to any subsequent decision of the Tribunal.

Article 60

1. The pleadings in a case begun by means of an application shall consist, in the following order, of: a memorial by the applicant and a counter-memorial by the respondent.

2. The Tribunal may authorize or direct that there shall be a reply by the applicant and a rejoinder by the respondent if the parties are so agreed or if the Tribunal decides, at the request of a party or *proprio motu*, that these pleadings are necessary.

Article 61

1. In a case begun by the notification of a special agreement, the number and order of the pleadings shall be governed by the provisions of the agreement, unless the Tribunal, after ascertaining the views of the parties, decides otherwise.

2. If the special agreement contains no such provision, and if the parties have not subsequently agreed on the number and order of pleadings, they shall each file a memorial and counter-memorial, within the same time-limits.

3. The Tribunal shall not authorize the presentation of replies and rejoinders unless it finds them to be necessary.

Article 62

1. A memorial shall contain: a statement of the relevant facts, a statement of law and the submissions.

2. A counter-memorial shall contain: an admission or denial of the facts stated in the memorial; any additional facts, if necessary; observations concerning the statement of law in the memorial; a statement of law in answer thereto; and the submissions.

3. A reply and rejoinder shall not merely repeat the parties' contentions, but shall be directed to bringing out the issues that still divide them.

4. Every pleading shall set out the party's submissions at the relevant stage of the case, distinctly from the arguments presented, or shall confirm the submissions previously made.

Article 63

1. There shall be annexed to the original of every pleading certified copies of any relevant documents adduced in support of the contentions contained in the pleading. Parties need not annex or certify copies of documents which have been published and are readily available to the Tribunal and the other party.

2. If only parts of a document are relevant, only such extracts as are necessary for the purpose of the pleading in question or for identifying the document need be annexed. A copy of the whole document shall be filed in the Registry, unless it has been published and is readily available to the Tribunal and the other party.

3. A list of all documents annexed to a pleading shall be furnished at the time the pleading is filed.

Article 64

1. The parties shall submit any pleading or any part of a pleading in one or both of the official languages.

2. A party may use a language other than one of the official languages for its pleadings. A translation into one of the official languages, certified as accurate by the party submitting it, shall be submitted together with the original of each pleading.

3. When a document annexed to a pleading is not in one of the official languages, it shall be accompanied by a translation into one of these languages certified as accurate by the party submitting it. The translation may be confined to part of an annex, or to extracts therefrom, but in this case it must be accompanied by an explanatory note indicating what passages are translated. The Tribunal may, however, require a more extensive or a complete translation to be furnished.

4. When a language other than one of the official languages is chosen by the parties and that language is an official language of the United Nations, the decision of the Tribunal shall, at the request of any party, be translated into that official language of the United Nations at no cost for the parties.

Article 65

1. The original of every pleading shall be signed by the agent and filed in the Registry. It shall be accompanied by a certified copy of the pleading, any document annexed thereto

and any translations, for communication to the other party. It shall also be accompanied by the number of additional copies required by the Registry; further copies may be required should the need arise later.

2. All pleadings shall be dated. When a pleading has to be filed by a certain date, it is the date of receipt of the pleading in the Registry which will be regarded by the Tribunal as the material date.

3. If the Registrar arranges for the reproduction of a pleading at the request of a party, the text must be supplied in sufficient time to enable the pleading to be filed in the Registry before expiration of any time-limit which may apply to it. The reproduction is done under the responsibility of the party in question.

4. The correction of a slip or error in any document which has been filed may be made at any time with the consent of the other party or by leave of the President of the Tribunal. Any correction so effected shall be notified to the other party in the same manner as the pleading to which it relates.

Article 66

A certified copy of every pleading and any document annexed thereto produced by one party shall be communicated by the Registrar to the other party upon receipt.

Article 67

1. Copies of the pleadings and documents annexed thereto shall, as soon as possible after their filing, be made available by the Tribunal to a State or other entity entitled to appear before the Tribunal and which has asked to be furnished with such copies. However, if the party submitting the memorial so requests, the Tribunal shall make the memorial available at the same time as the counter-memorial.

2. Copies of the pleadings and documents annexed thereto shall be made accessible to the public on the opening of the oral proceedings, or earlier if the Tribunal or the President if the Tribunal is not sitting so decides after ascertaining the views of the parties.

3. However, the Tribunal, or the President if the Tribunal is not sitting, may, at the request of a party, and after ascertaining the views of the other party, decide otherwise than as set out in this article.

Subsection 3. Initial deliberations

Article 68

After the closure of the written proceedings and prior to the opening of the oral proceedings, the Tribunal shall meet in private to enable judges to exchange views concerning the written pleadings and the conduct of the case.

Subsection 4. Oral proceedings

Article 69

1. Upon the closure of the written proceedings, the date for the opening of the oral proceedings shall be fixed by the Tribunal. Such date shall fall within a period of six months from the closure of the written proceedings unless the Tribunal is satisfied that there is adequate justification for deciding otherwise. The Tribunal may also decide, when necessary, that the opening or the continuance of the oral proceedings be postponed.

2. When fixing the date for the opening of the oral proceedings or postponing the opening or continuance of such proceedings, the Tribunal shall have regard to:

(a) the need to hold the hearing without unnecessary delay;

(b)   the priority required by articles 90 and 112;

(c)   any special circumstances, including the urgency of the case or other cases on the List of cases; and

(d)   the views expressed by the parties.

3.   When the Tribunal is not sitting, its powers under this article shall be exercised by the President.

Article 70

The Tribunal may, if it considers it desirable, decide pursuant to article 1, paragraph 3, of the Statute that all or part of the further proceedings in a case shall be held at a place other than the seat of the Tribunal. Before so deciding, it shall ascertain the views of the parties.

Article 71

1.   After the closure of the written proceedings, no further documents may be submitted to the Tribunal by either party except with the consent of the other party or as provided in paragraph 2. The other party shall be held to have given its consent if it does not lodge an objection to the production of the document within 15 days of receiving it.

2.   In the event of objection, the Tribunal, after hearing the parties, may authorize production of the document if it considers production necessary.

3.   The party desiring to produce a new document shall file the original or a certified copy thereof, together with the number of copies required by the Registry, which shall be responsible for communicating it to the other party and shall inform the Tribunal.

4.   If a new document is produced under paragraph 1 or 2, the other party shall have an opportunity of commenting upon it and of submitting documents in support of its comments.

5.   No reference may be made during the oral proceedings to the contents of any document which has not been produced as part of the written proceedings or in accordance with this article, unless the document is part of a publication readily available to the Tribunal and the other party.

6.   The application of this article shall not in itself constitute a ground for delaying the opening or the course of the oral proceedings.

Article 72

Without prejudice to the provisions of these Rules concerning the production of documents, each party shall communicate to the Registrar, in sufficient time before the opening of the oral proceedings, information regarding any evidence which it intends to produce or which it intends to request the Tribunal to obtain. This communication shall contain a list of the surnames, first names, nationalities, descriptions and places of residence of the witnesses and experts whom the party intends to call, with indications of the point or points to which their evidence will be directed. A certified copy of the communication shall also be furnished for transmission to the other party.

Article 73

1.   The Tribunal shall determine whether the parties should present their arguments before or after the production of the evidence; the parties shall, however, retain the right to comment on the evidence given.

2.   The Tribunal, after ascertaining the views of the parties, shall determine the order in which the parties will be heard, the method of handling the evidence and examining any witnesses and experts and the number of counsel and advocates to be heard on behalf of each party.

Article 74

The hearing shall, in accordance with article 26, paragraph 2, of the Statute, be public, unless the Tribunal decides otherwise or unless the parties request that the public be not admitted. Such a decision or request may concern either the whole or part of the hearing, and may be made at any time.

Article 75

1. The oral statements made on behalf of each party shall be as succinct as possible within the limits of what is requisite for the adequate presentation of that party's contentions at the hearing. Accordingly, they shall be directed to the issues that still divide the parties, and shall not go over the whole ground covered by the pleadings or merely repeat the facts and arguments these contain.

2. At the conclusion of the last statement made by a party at the hearing, its agent, without recapitulation of the arguments, shall read that party's final submissions. A copy of the written text of these, signed by the agent, shall be communicated to the Tribunal and transmitted to the other party.

Article 76

1. The Tribunal may at any time prior to or during the hearing indicate any points or issues which it would like the parties specially to address, or on which it considers that there has been sufficient argument.

2. The Tribunal may, during the hearing, put questions to the agents, counsel and advocates, and may ask them for explanations.

3. Each judge has a similar right to put questions, but before exercising it he should make his intention known to the President of the Tribunal.

4. The agents, counsel and advocates may answer either immediately or within a time limit fixed by the President of the Tribunal.

Article 77

1. The Tribunal may at any time call upon the parties to produce such evidence or to give such explanations as the Tribunal may consider to be necessary for the elucidation of any aspect of the matters in issue, or may itself seek other information for this purpose.

2. The Tribunal may, if necessary, arrange for the attendance of a witness or expert to give evidence in the proceedings.

Article 78

1. The parties may call any witnesses or experts appearing on the list communicated to the Tribunal pursuant to article 72. If at any time during the hearing a party wishes to call a witness or expert whose name was not included in that list, it shall make a request therefor to the Tribunal and inform the other party, and shall supply the information required by article 72. The witness or expert may be called either if the other party raises no objection or, in the event of objection, if the Tribunal so authorizes after hearing the other party.

2. The Tribunal may, at the request of a party or *proprio motu*, decide that a witness or expert be examined otherwise than before the Tribunal itself. The President of the Tribunal shall take the necessary steps to implement such a decision.

Article 79

Unless on account of special circumstances the Tribunal decides on a different form of words,

(a) every witness shall make the following solemn declaration before giving any evidence:

'I solemnly declare upon my honour and conscience that I will speak the truth, the whole truth and nothing but the truth';

(b) every expert shall make the following solemn declaration before making any statement:

'I solemnly declare upon my honour and conscience that I will speak the truth, the whole truth and nothing but the truth, and that my statement will be in accordance with my sincere belief'.

Article 80

Witnesses and experts shall, under the control of the President of the Tribunal, be examined by the agents, counsel or advocates of the parties starting with the party calling the witness or expert. Questions may be put to them by the President of the Tribunal and by the judges. Before testifying, witnesses and experts other than those appointed under article 289 of the Convention shall remain out of court.

Article 81

The Tribunal may at any time decide, at the request of a party or *proprio motu*, to exercise its functions with regard to the obtaining of evidence at a place or locality to which the case relates, subject to such conditions as the Tribunal may decide upon after ascertaining the views of the parties. The necessary arrangements shall be made in accordance with article 52.

Article 82

1. If the Tribunal considers it necessary to arrange for an inquiry or an expert opinion, it shall, after hearing the parties, issue an order to this effect, defining the subject of the inquiry or expert opinion, stating the number and mode of appointment of the persons to hold the inquiry or of the experts and laying down the procedure to be followed. Where appropriate, the Tribunal shall require persons appointed to carry out an inquiry, or to give an expert opinion, to make a solemn declaration.

2. Every report or record of an inquiry and every expert opinion shall be communicated to the parties, which shall be given the opportunity of commenting upon it.

Article 83

Witnesses and experts who appear at the instance of the Tribunal under article 77, paragraph 2, and persons appointed by the Tribunal under article 82, paragraph 1, to carry out an inquiry or to give an expert opinion, shall, where appropriate, be paid out of the funds of the Tribunal.

Article 84

1. The Tribunal may, at any time prior to the closure of the oral proceedings, at the request of a party or *proprio motu,* request an appropriate intergovernmental organization to furnish information relevant to a case before it. The Tribunal, after consulting the chief administrative officer of the organization concerned, shall decide whether such information shall be presented to it orally or in writing and fix the time-limits for its presentation.

2. When such an intergovernmental organization sees fit to furnish, on its own initiative, information relevant to a case before the Tribunal, it shall do so in the form of a memorial to be filed in the Registry before the closure of the written proceedings. The

Tribunal may require such information to be supplemented, either orally or in writing, in the form of answers to any questions which it may see fit to formulate, and also authorize the parties to comment, either orally or in writing, on the information thus furnished.

3. Whenever the construction of the constituent instrument of such an intergovernmental organization or of an international convention adopted thereunder is in question in a case before the Tribunal, the Registrar shall, on the instructions of the Tribunal, or of the President if the Tribunal is not sitting, so notify the intergovernmental organization concerned and shall communicate to it copies of all the written proceedings. The Tribunal, or the President if the Tribunal is not sitting, may, as from the date on which the Registrar has communicated copies of the written proceedings and after consulting the chief administrative officer of the intergovernmental organization concerned, fix a time-limit within which the organization may submit to the Tribunal its observations in writing. These observations shall be communicated to the parties and may be discussed by them and by the representative of the said organization during the oral proceedings.

4. In the foregoing paragraphs, 'intergovernmental organization' means an intergovernmental organization other than any organization which is a party or intervenes in the case concerned.

Article 85

1. Unless the Tribunal decides otherwise, all speeches and statements made and evidence given at the hearing in one of the official languages of the Tribunal shall be interpreted into the other official language. If they are made or given in any other language, they shall be interpreted into the two official languages of the Tribunal.

2. Whenever a language other than an official language is used, the necessary arrangements for interpretation into one of the official languages shall be made by the party concerned. The Registrar shall make arrangements for the verification of the interpretation provided by a party at the expense of that party. In the case of witnesses or experts who appear at the instance of the Tribunal, arrangements for interpretation shall be made by the Registrar.

3. A party on behalf of which speeches or statements are to be made, or evidence is to be given, in a language which is not one of the official languages of the Tribunal shall so notify the Registrar in sufficient time for the necessary arrangements to be made, including verification.

4. Before entering upon their duties in the case, interpreters provided by a party shall make the following solemn declaration:

'I solemnly declare upon my honour and conscience that my interpretation will be faithful and complete'.

Article 86

1. Minutes shall be made of each hearing. For this purpose, a verbatim record shall be made by the Registrar of every hearing, in the official language or languages of the Tribunal used during the hearing. When another language is used, the verbatim record shall be prepared in one of the official languages of the Tribunal.

2. In order to prepare such a verbatim record, the party on behalf of which speeches or statements are made in a language which is not one of the official languages shall supply to the Registry in advance a text thereof in one of the official languages.

3. The transcript of the verbatim record shall be preceded by the names of the judges present, and those of the agents, counsel and advocates of the parties.

4. Copies of the transcript shall be circulated to the judges sitting in the case and to the parties. The latter may, under the supervision of the Tribunal, correct the transcripts of

speeches and statements made on their behalf, but in no case may such corrections affect the meaning and scope thereof. The judges may likewise make corrections in the transcript of anything they have said.

5. Witnesses and experts shall be shown that part of the transcript which relates to the evidence given or the statements made by them, and may correct it in like manner as the parties.

6. One certified copy of the corrected transcript, signed by the President of the Tribunal and the Registrar, shall constitute the authentic minutes of the hearing. The minutes of public hearings shall be printed and published by the Tribunal.

Article 87

Any written reply by a party to a question put under article 76 or any evidence or explanation supplied by a party under article 77 received by the Tribunal after the closure of the oral proceedings shall be communicated to the other party, which shall be given the opportunity of commenting upon it. The oral proceedings may be reopened for that purpose, if necessary.

Article 88

1. When, subject to the control of the Tribunal, the agents, counsel and advocates have completed their presentation of the case, the President of the Tribunal shall declare the oral proceedings closed. The agents shall remain at the disposal of the Tribunal.

2. The Tribunal shall withdraw to consider the judgment.

SECTION C. INCIDENTAL PROCEEDINGS

Subsection 1. Provisional measures

Article 89

1. A party may submit a request for the prescription of provisional measures under article 290, paragraph 1, of the Convention at any time during the course of the proceedings in a dispute submitted to the Tribunal.

2. Pending the constitution of an arbitral tribunal to which a dispute is being submitted, a party may submit a request for the prescription of provisional measures under article 290, paragraph 5, of the Convention:

   (a)   at any time if the parties have so agreed;
   (b)   at any time after two weeks from the notification to the other party of a request for provisional measures if the parties have not agreed that such measures may be prescribed by another court or tribunal.

3. The request shall be in writing and specify the measures requested, the reasons therefor and the possible consequences, if it is not granted, for the preservation of the respective rights of the parties or for the prevention of serious harm to the marine environment.

4. A request for the prescription of provisional measures under article 290, paragraph 5, of the Convention shall also indicate the legal grounds upon which the arbitral tribunal which is to be constituted would have jurisdiction and the urgency of the situation. A certified copy of the notification or of any other document instituting the proceedings before the arbitral tribunal shall be annexed to the request.

5. When a request for provisional measures has been made, the Tribunal may prescribe measures different in whole or in part from those requested and indicate the parties which are to take or to comply with each measure.

Article 90

1. Subject to article 112, paragraph 1, a request for the prescription of provisional measures has priority over all other proceedings before the Tribunal.

2. The Tribunal, or the President if the Tribunal is not sitting, shall fix the earliest possible date for a hearing.

3. The Tribunal shall take into account any observations that may be presented to it by a party before the closure of the hearing.

4. Pending the meeting of the Tribunal, the President of the Tribunal may call upon the parties to act in such a way as will enable any order the Tribunal may make on the request for provisional measures to have its appropriate effects.

Article 91

1. If the President of the Tribunal ascertains that at the date fixed for the hearing referred to in article 90, paragraph 2, a sufficient number of Members will not be available to constitute a quorum, the Chamber of Summary Procedure shall be convened to carry out the functions of the Tribunal with respect to the prescription of provisional measures.

2. The Tribunal shall review or revise provisional measures prescribed by the Chamber of Summary Procedure at the written request of a party within 15 days of the prescription of the measures. The Tribunal may also at any time decide *proprio motu* to review or revise the measures.

Article 92

The rejection of a request for the prescription of provisional measures shall not prevent the party which made it from making a fresh request in the same case based on new facts.

Article 93

A party may request the modification or revocation of provisional measures. The request shall be submitted in writing and shall specify the change in, or disappearance of, the circumstances considered to be relevant. Before taking any decision on the request, the Tribunal shall afford the parties an opportunity of presenting their observations on the subject.

Article 94

Any provisional measures prescribed by the Tribunal or any modification or revocation thereof shall forthwith be notified to the parties and to such other States Parties as the Tribunal considers appropriate in each case.

Article 95

1. Each party shall inform the Tribunal as soon as possible as to its compliance with any provisional measures the Tribunal has prescribed. In particular, each party shall submit an initial report upon the steps it has taken or proposes to take in order to ensure prompt compliance with the measures prescribed.

2. The Tribunal may request further information from the parties on any matter connected with the implementation of any provisional measures it has prescribed.

Subsection 2. Preliminary proceedings

Article 96

1. When an application is made in respect of a dispute referred to in article 297 of the Convention, the Tribunal shall determine at the request of the respondent or may

determine *proprio motu*, in accordance with article 294 of the Convention, whether the claim constitutes an abuse of legal process or whether *prima facie* it is well founded.

2. The Registrar, when transmitting an application to the respondent under article 54, paragraph 4, shall notify the respondent of the time-limit fixed by the President of the Tribunal for requesting a determination under article 294 of the Convention.

3. The Tribunal may also decide, within two months from the date of an application, to exercise *proprio motu* its power under article 294, paragraph 1, of the Convention.

4. The request by the respondent for a determination under article 294 of the Convention shall be in writing and shall indicate the grounds for a determination by the Tribunal that:

(a)   the application is made in respect of a dispute referred to in article 297 of the Convention; and

(b)   the claim constitutes an abuse of legal process or is *prima facie* unfounded.

5. Upon receipt of such a request or *proprio motu*, the Tribunal, or the President if the Tribunal is not sitting, shall fix a time-limit not exceeding 60 days within which the parties may present their written observations and submissions. The proceedings on the merits shall be suspended.

6. Unless the Tribunal decides otherwise, the further proceedings shall be oral.

7. The written observations and submissions referred to in paragraph 5, and the statements and evidence presented at the hearings contemplated by paragraph 6, shall be confined to those matters which are relevant to the determination of whether the claim constitutes an abuse of legal process or is *prima facie* unfounded, and of whether the application is made in respect of a dispute referred to in article 297 of the Convention. The Tribunal may, however, request the parties to argue all questions of law and fact, and to adduce all evidence, bearing on the issue.

8. The Tribunal shall make its determination in the form of a judgment.

Subsection 3. Preliminary objections

Article 97

1. Any objection to the jurisdiction of the Tribunal or to the admissibility of the application, or other objection the decision upon which is requested before any further proceedings on the merits, shall be made in writing within 90 days from the institution of proceedings.

2. The preliminary objection shall set out the facts and the law on which the objection is based, as well as the submissions.

3. Upon receipt by the Registry of a preliminary objection, the proceedings on the merits shall be suspended and the Tribunal, or the President if the Tribunal is not sitting, shall fix a time-limit not exceeding 60 days within which the other party may present its written observations and submissions. It shall fix a further time-limit not exceeding 60 days from the receipt of such observations and submissions within which the objecting party may present its written observations and submissions in reply. Copies of documents in support shall be annexed to such statements and evidence which it is proposed to produce shall be mentioned.

4. Unless the Tribunal decides otherwise, the further proceedings shall be oral.

5. The written observations and submissions referred to in paragraph 3, and the statements and evidence presented at the hearings contemplated by paragraph 4, shall be confined to those matters which are relevant to the objection. Whenever necessary, however, the Tribunal may request the parties to argue all questions of law and fact and to adduce all evidence bearing on the issue.

6. The Tribunal shall give its decision in the form of a judgment, by which it shall uphold the objection or reject it or declare that the objection does not possess, in the circumstances of the case, an exclusively preliminary character. If the Tribunal rejects the objection or declares that it does not possess an exclusively preliminary character, it shall fix time-limits for the further proceedings.

7. The Tribunal shall give effect to any agreement between the parties that an objection submitted under paragraph 1 be heard and determined within the framework of the merits.

Subsection 4. Counter-claims

Article 98

1. A party may present a counter-claim provided that it is directly connected with the subject-matter of the claim of the other party and that it comes within the jurisdiction of the Tribunal.

2. A counter-claim shall be made in the counter-memorial of the party presenting it and shall appear as part of the submissions of that party.

3. In the event of doubt as to the connection between the question presented by way of counter-claim and the subject-matter of the claim of the other party the Tribunal shall, after hearing the parties, decide whether or not the question thus presented shall be joined to the original proceedings.

Subsection 5. Intervention

Article 99

1. An application for permission to intervene under the terms of article 31 of the Statute shall be filed not later than 30 days after the counter-memorial becomes available under article 67, paragraph 1, of these Rules. In exceptional circumstances, an application submitted at a later stage may however be admitted.

2. The application shall be signed in the manner provided for in article 54, paragraph 3, and state the name and address of an agent. It shall specify the case to which it relates and shall set out:

  (a) the interest of a legal nature which the State Party applying to intervene considers may be affected by the decision in that case;

  (b) the precise object of the intervention.

3. Permission to intervene under the terms of article 31 of the Statute may be granted irrespective of the choice made by the applicant under article 287 of the Convention.

4. The application shall contain a list of the documents in support, copies of which documents shall be annexed.

Article 100

1. A State Party or an entity other than a State Party referred to in article 32, paragraphs 1 and 2, of the Statute which desires to avail itself of the right of intervention conferred upon it by article 32, paragraph 3, of the Statute shall file a declaration to that effect. The declaration shall be filed not later than 30 days after the counter-memorial becomes available under article 67, paragraph 1, of these Rules. In exceptional circumstances, a declaration submitted at a later stage may, however, be admitted.

2. The declaration shall be signed in the manner provided for in article 54, paragraph 3, and state the name and address of an agent. It shall specify the case to which it relates and shall:

   (a)   identify the particular provisions of the Convention or of the international agreement the interpretation or application of which the declaring party considers to be in question;

   (b)   set out the interpretation or application of those provisions for which it contends;

   (c)   list the documents in support, copies of which documents shall be annexed.

Article 101

1. Certified copies of the application for permission to intervene under article 31 of the Statute, or of the declaration of intervention under article 32 of the Statute, shall be communicated forthwith to the parties to the case, which shall be invited to furnish their written observations within a time-limit to be fixed by the Tribunal or by the President if the Tribunal is not sitting.

2. The Registrar shall also transmit copies to: (a) States Parties; (b) any other parties which have to be notified under article 32, paragraph 2, of the Statute; (c) the Secretary-General of the United Nations; (d) the Secretary-General of the Authority when the proceedings are before the Seabed Disputes Chamber.

Article 102

1. The Tribunal shall decide whether an application for permission to intervene under article 31 of the Statute should be granted or whether an intervention under article 32 of the Statute is admissible as a matter of priority unless in view of the circumstances of the case the Tribunal determines otherwise.

2. If, within the time-limit fixed under article 101, an objection is filed to an application for permission to intervene, or to the admissibility of a declaration of intervention, the Tribunal shall hear the State Party or entity other than a State Party seeking to intervene and the parties before deciding.

Article 103

1. If an application for permission to intervene under article 31 of the Statute is granted, the intervening State Party shall be supplied with copies of the pleadings and documents annexed and shall be entitled to submit a written statement within a time-limit to be fixed by the Tribunal. A further time-limit shall be fixed within which the parties may, if they so desire, furnish their written observations on that statement prior to the oral proceedings. If the Tribunal is not sitting, these time-limits shall be fixed by the President.

2. The time-limits fixed according to paragraph 1 shall, so far as possible, coincide with those already fixed for the pleadings in the case.

3. The intervening State Party shall be entitled, in the course of the oral proceedings, to submit its observations with respect to the subject-matter of the intervention.

4. The intervening State Party shall not be entitled to choose a judge *ad hoc* or to object to an agreement to discontinue the proceedings under article 105, paragraph 1.

Article 104

1. If an intervention under article 32 of the Statute is admitted, the intervenor shall be supplied with copies of the pleadings and documents annexed and shall be entitled, within a time-limit to be fixed by the Tribunal, or the President if the Tribunal is not sitting, to submit its written observations on the subject-matter of the intervention.

2. These observations shall be communicated to the parties and to any other State Party or entity other than a State Party admitted to intervene. The intervenor shall be

entitled, in the course of the oral proceedings, to submit its observations with respect to the subject-matter of the intervention.

3. The intervenor shall not be entitled to choose a judge *ad hoc* or to object to an agreement to discontinue the proceedings under article 105, paragraph 1.

Subsection 6. Discontinuance

Article 105

1. If at any time before the final judgment on the merits has been delivered the parties, either jointly or separately, notify the Tribunal in writing that they have agreed to discontinue the proceedings, the Tribunal shall make an order recording the discontinuance and directing the Registrar to remove the case from the List of cases.

2. If the parties have agreed to discontinue the proceedings in consequence of having reached a settlement of the dispute and if they so desire, the Tribunal shall record this fact in the order for the removal of the case from the List, or indicate in, or annex to, the order the terms of the settlement.

3. If the Tribunal is not sitting, any order under this article may be made by the President.

Article 106

1. If, in the course of proceedings instituted by means of an application, the applicant informs the Tribunal in writing that it is not going on with the proceedings, and if, at the date on which this communication is received by the Registry, the respondent has not yet taken any step in the proceedings, the Tribunal shall make an order officially recording the discontinuance of the proceedings and directing the removal of the case from the List of cases. A copy of this order shall be sent by the Registrar to the respondent.

2. If, at the time when the notice of discontinuance is received, the respondent has already taken some step in the proceedings, the Tribunal shall fix a time-limit within which the respondent may state whether it opposes the discontinuance of the proceedings. If no objection is made to the discontinuance before the expiration of the time-limit, acquiescence will be presumed and the Tribunal shall make an order recording the discontinuance of the proceedings and directing the Registrar to remove the case from the List of cases. If objection is made, the proceedings shall continue.

3. If the Tribunal is not sitting, its powers under this article may be exercised by the President.

SECTION D. PROCEEDINGS BEFORE SPECIAL CHAMBERS

Article 107

Proceedings before the special chambers mentioned in article 15 of the Statute shall, subject to the provisions of the Convention, the Statute and these Rules relating specifically to the special chambers, be governed by the Rules applicable in contentious cases before the Tribunal.

Article 108

1. When it is desired that a case should be dealt with by one of the chambers which has been formed in accordance with article 15, paragraph 1 or 3, of the Statute, a request to this effect shall either be made in the document instituting the proceedings or accompany it. Effect shall be given to the request if the parties are in agreement.

2. Upon receipt by the Registry of this request, the President of the Tribunal shall communicate it to the members of the chamber concerned.

3. Effect shall be given to a request that a case be brought before a chamber to be formed in accordance with article 15, paragraph 2, of the Statute as soon as the chamber has been formed in accordance with article 30 of these Rules.

4. The President of the Tribunal shall convene the chamber at the earliest date compatible with the requirements of the procedure.

Article 109

1. Written proceedings in a case before a chamber shall consist of a single pleading by each party. The time-limits concerning the filing of written pleadings shall be fixed by the chamber, or its President if the chamber is not sitting.

2. The chamber may authorize or direct the filing of further pleadings if the parties are so agreed, or if the chamber decides, *proprio motu* or at the request of one of the parties, that such pleadings are necessary.

3. Oral proceedings shall take place unless the parties agree to dispense with them and the chamber consents. Even when no oral proceedings take place, the chamber may call upon the parties to supply information or furnish explanations orally.

SECTION E. PROMPT RELEASE OF VESSELS AND CREWS

Article 110

1. An application for the release of a vessel or its crew from detention may be made in accordance with article 292 of the Convention by or on behalf of the flag State of the vessel.

2. A State Party may at any time notify the Tribunal of:

(a) the State authorities competent to authorize persons to make applications on its behalf under article 292 of the Convention;

(b) the name and address of any person who is authorized to make an application on its behalf;

(c) the office designated to receive notice of an application for the release of a vessel or its crew and the most expeditious means for delivery of documents to that office;

(d) any clarification, modification or withdrawal of such notification.

3. An application on behalf of a flag State shall be accompanied by an authorization under paragraph 2, if such authorization has not been previously submitted to the Tribunal, as well as by documents stating that the person submitting the application is the person named in the authorization. It shall also contain a certification that a copy of the application and all supporting documentation has been delivered to the flag State.

Article 111

1. The application shall contain a succinct statement of the facts and legal grounds upon which the application is based.

2. The statement of facts shall:

(a) specify the time and place of detention of the vessel and the present location of the vessel and crew, if known;

(b) contain relevant information concerning the vessel and crew including, where appropriate, the name, flag and the port or place of registration of the vessel and its tonnage, cargo capacity and data relevant to the determination of its value, the name and address of the vessel owner and operator and particulars regarding its crew;

(c) specify the amount, nature and terms of the bond or other financial security that may have been imposed by the detaining State and the extent to which such requirements have been complied with;

(d) contain any further information the applicant considers relevant to the determination of the amount of a reasonable bond or other financial security and to any other issue in the proceedings.

3. Supporting documents shall be annexed to the application.

4. A certified copy of the application shall forthwith be transmitted by the Registrar to the detaining State, which may submit a statement in response with supporting documents annexed, to be filed as soon as possible but not later than 96 hours before the hearing referred to in article 112, paragraph 3.

5. The Tribunal may, at any time, require further information to be provided in a supplementary statement.

6. The further proceedings relating to the application shall be oral.

Article 112

1. The Tribunal shall give priority to applications for release of vessels or crews over all other proceedings before the Tribunal. However, if the Tribunal is seized of an application for release of a vessel or its crew and of a request for the prescription of provisional measures, it shall take the necessary measures to ensure that both the application and the request are dealt with without delay.

2. If the applicant has so requested in the application, the application shall be dealt with by the Chamber of Summary Procedure, provided that, within five days of the receipt of notice of the application, the detaining State notifies the Tribunal that it concurs with the request.

3. The Tribunal, or the President if the Tribunal is not sitting, shall fix the earliest possible date, within a period of 15 days commencing with the first working day following the date on which the application is received, for a hearing at which each of the parties shall be accorded, unless otherwise decided, one day to present its evidence and arguments.

4. The decision of the Tribunal shall be in the form of a judgment. The judgment shall be adopted as soon as possible and shall be read at a public sitting of the Tribunal to be held not later than 14 days after the closure of the hearing. The parties shall be notified of the date of the sitting.

Article 113

1. The Tribunal shall in its judgment determine in each case in accordance with article 292 of the Convention whether or not the allegation made by the applicant that the detaining State has not complied with a provision of the Convention for the prompt release of the vessel or the crew upon the posting of a reasonable bond or other financial security is well-founded.

2. If the Tribunal decides that the allegation is well-founded, it shall determine the amount, nature and form of the bond or financial security to be posted for the release of the vessel or the crew.

3. Unless the parties agree otherwise, the Tribunal shall determine whether the bond or other financial security shall be posted with the Registrar or the detaining State.

Article 114

1. If the bond or other financial security has been posted with the Registrar, the detaining State shall be promptly notified thereof.

2. The Registrar shall endorse or transmit the bond or other financial security to the detaining State to the extent that it is required to satisfy the final judgment, award or decision of the competent authority of the detaining State.

3. The bond or other financial security shall be endorsed or transmitted, to the extent that it is not required to satisfy the final judgment, award or decision, to the party at whose request the bond or other financial security is issued.

SECTION F. PROCEEDINGS IN CONTENTIOUS CASES BEFORE THE SEABED DISPUTES CHAMBER

Article 115

Proceedings in contentious cases before the Seabed Disputes Chamber and its *ad hoc* chambers shall, subject to the provisions of the Convention, the Statute and these Rules relating specifically to the Seabed Disputes Chamber and its *ad hoc* chambers, be governed by the Rules applicable in contentious cases before the Tribunal.

Article 116

Articles 117 to 121 apply to proceedings in all disputes before the Chamber with the exception of disputes exclusively between States Parties and between States Parties and the Authority.

Article 117

When proceedings before the Chamber are instituted by means of an application, the application shall indicate:

(a) the name of the applicant and, where the applicant is a natural or juridical person, the permanent residence or address or registered office address thereof;

(b) the name of the respondent and, where the respondent is a natural or juridical person, the permanent residence or address or registered office address thereof;

(c) the sponsoring State, in any case where the applicant is a natural or juridical person or a state enterprise;

(d) the sponsoring State of the respondent, in any case where the party against which the claim is brought is a natural or juridical person or state enterprise;

(e) an address for service at the seat of the Tribunal;

(f) the subject of the dispute and the legal grounds on which jurisdiction is said to be based; the precise nature of the claim, together with a statement of the facts and legal grounds on which the claim is based;

(g) the decision or measure sought by the applicant;

(h) the evidence on which the application is founded.

Article 118

1. The application shall be served on the respondent. The application shall also be served on the sponsoring State in any case where the applicant or respondent is a natural or juridical person or a state enterprise.

2. Within two months after service of the application, the respondent shall lodge a defence, stating:

(a) the name of the respondent and, where the respondent is a natural or juridical person, the permanent residence or address or registered office address thereof;

(b) an address for service at the seat of the Tribunal;

(c) the matters in issue between the parties and the facts and legal grounds on which the defence is based;

(d)   the decision or measure sought by the respondent;

(e)   the evidence on which the defence is founded.

3. At the request of the respondent, the President of the Chamber may extend the time limit referred to in paragraph 2, if satisfied that there is adequate justification for the request.

Article 119

1. Within two months after service of the application in accordance with article 118, paragraph 1, where the respondent is a State Party in a case brought by a natural or juridical person sponsored by another State Party in a dispute referred to in article 187, subparagraph (c), of the Convention, the respondent State may make an application in accordance with article 190, paragraph 2, of the Convention for the sponsoring State of the applicant to appear in the proceedings on behalf of the applicant.

2. Notice of an application under paragraph 1 shall be communicated to the applicant and its sponsoring State. If, within a time-limit fixed by the President of the Chamber, the sponsoring State does not indicate it will appear in the proceedings on behalf of the applicant, the respondent State may designate a juridical person of its nationality to represent it.

3. Within two months after service of the application in accordance with article 118, paragraph 1, on the sponsoring State of a party, such State may give written notice of its intention to submit written or oral statements in accordance with article 190, paragraph 1, of the Convention.

4. Upon receipt of such a notice, the President of the Chamber shall fix the time-limit within which the sponsoring State may submit its written statements. The sponsoring State shall be notified of such time-limit. It shall also be notified of the date of the hearing. The written statements shall be communicated to the parties and to any other sponsoring State of a party.

5. At the request of the respondent or a sponsoring State, the President of the Chamber may extend a time-limit referred to in this article, if satisfied that there is adequate justification for the request.

Article 120

1. When proceedings are brought before the Chamber by the notification of a special agreement, the notification shall indicate:

(a)   the parties to the case and any sponsoring States of the parties;

(b)   the subject of the dispute and the precise nature of the claims of the parties, together with a statement of the facts and legal grounds on which the claims are based;

(c)   the decisions or measures sought by the parties;

(d)   the evidence on which the claims are founded.

2. The notification shall also provide information regarding participation and appearance in the proceedings by sponsoring States Parties in accordance with article 190 of the Convention.

Article 121

1. The Chamber may authorize or direct the filing of further pleadings if the parties are so agreed or the Chamber decides, *proprio motu* or at the request of a party, that these pleadings are necessary.

2. The President of the Chamber shall fix the time-limits within which these pleadings are to be filed.

Article 122

Proceedings by the Council on behalf of the Authority under article 185, paragraph 2, of the Convention shall be instituted by means of an application in accordance with article 162, paragraph 2 (u), of the Convention. The application shall be accompanied by a certified copy of the decision or resolution of the Council upon which it is based and the full records of all discussions within the Authority on the matter.

Article 123

1. When a commercial arbitral tribunal, pursuant to article 188, paragraph 2, of the Convention, refers to the Chamber a question of interpretation of Part XI of the Convention and the annexes relating thereto upon which its decision depends, the document submitting the question to the Chamber shall contain a precise statement of the question and be accompanied by all relevant information and documents.

2. Upon receipt of the document, the President of the Chamber shall fix a time-limit not exceeding three months within which the parties to the proceedings before the arbitral tribunal and the States Parties may submit their written observations on the question. The parties to the proceedings and the States Parties shall be notified of the time-limit. The States Parties shall be informed of the contents of the submission.

3. The President of the Chamber shall fix a date for a hearing if, within one month from the expiration of the time-limit for submitting written observations, a party to the proceedings before the arbitral tribunal or a State Party gives written notice of its intention to submit oral observations.

4. The Chamber shall give its ruling in the form of a judgment.

SECTION G. JUDGMENTS, INTERPRETATION AND REVISION

Subsection 1. Judgments

Article 124

1. When the Tribunal has completed its deliberations and adopted its judgment, the parties shall be notified of the date on which it will be read.

2. The judgment shall be read at a public sitting of the Tribunal and shall become binding on the parties on the day of the reading.

Article 125

1. The judgment, which shall state whether it is given by the Tribunal or by a chamber, shall contain:
   (a) the date on which it is read;
   (b) the names of the judges participating in it;
   (c) the names of the parties;
   (d) the names of the agents, counsel and advocates of the parties;
   (e) the names of the experts, if any, appointed under article 289 of the Convention;
   (f) a summary of the proceedings;
   (g) the submissions of the parties;
   (h) a statement of the facts;
   (i) the reasons of law on which it is based;
   (j) the operative provisions of the judgment;
   (k) the decision, if any, in regard to costs;
   (l) the number and names of the judges constituting the majority and those constituting the minority, on each operative provision;

(m) a statement as to the text of the judgment which is authoritative.

2. Any judge may attach a separate or dissenting opinion to the judgment; a judge may record concurrence or dissent without stating reasons in the form of a declaration. The same applies to orders.

3. One copy of the judgment, signed by the President and by the Registrar and sealed, shall be placed in the archives of the Tribunal and other copies shall be transmitted to each party. Copies shall be sent to:

(a) States Parties;

(b) the Secretary-General of the United Nations;

(c) the Secretary-General of the Authority;

(d) in a case submitted under an agreement other than the Convention, the parties to such agreement.

Subsection 2. Requests for the interpretation or revision of a judgment

Article 126

1. In the event of dispute as to the meaning or scope of a judgment, any party may make a request for its interpretation.

2. A request for the interpretation of a judgment may be made either by an application or by the notification of a special agreement to that effect between the parties; the precise point or points in dispute as to the meaning or scope of the judgment shall be indicated.

3. If the request for interpretation is made by an application, the requesting party's contentions shall be set out therein, and the other party shall be entitled to file written observations thereon within a time-limit fixed by the Tribunal or by the President if the Tribunal is not sitting.

4. Whether the request is made by an application or by notification of a special agreement, the Tribunal may, if necessary, afford the parties the opportunity of furnishing further written or oral explanations.

Article 127

1. A request for revision of a judgment may be made only when it is based upon the discovery of some fact of such a nature as to be a decisive factor, which fact was, when the judgment was given, unknown to the Tribunal and also to the party requesting revision, always provided that such ignorance was not due to negligence. Such request must be made at the latest within six months of the discovery of the new fact and before the lapse of ten years from the date of the judgment.

2. The proceedings for revision shall be opened by a decision of the Tribunal in the form of a judgment expressly recording the existence of the new fact, recognizing that it has such a character as to lay the case open to revision, and declaring the application admissible on this ground.

Article 128

1. A request for the revision of a judgment shall be made by an application containing the particulars necessary to show that the conditions specified in article 127, paragraph 1, are fulfilled. Any document in support of the application shall be annexed to it.

2. The other party shall be entitled to file written observations on the admissibility of the application within a time-limit fixed by the Tribunal or by the President if the Tribunal is not sitting. These observations shall be communicated to the party making the application.

3. The Tribunal, before giving its judgment on the admissibility of the application, may afford the parties a further opportunity of presenting their views thereon.

4. If the Tribunal decides to make the admission of the proceedings in revision conditional on previous compliance with the judgment, it shall make an order accordingly.

5. If the Tribunal finds that the application is admissible it shall fix time-limits for such further proceedings on the merits of the application as, after ascertaining the views of the parties, it considers necessary.

Article 129

1. If the judgment to be revised or to be interpreted was given by the Tribunal, the request for its revision or interpretation shall be dealt with by the Tribunal.

2. If the judgment was given by a chamber, the request for its revision or interpretation shall, if possible, be dealt with by that chamber. If that is not possible, the request shall be dealt with by a chamber composed in conformity with the relevant provisions of the Statute and these Rules. If, according to the Statute and these Rules, the composition of the chamber requires the approval of the parties which cannot be obtained within time-limits fixed by the Tribunal, the request shall be dealt with by the Tribunal.

3. The decision on a request for interpretation or revision of a judgment shall be given in the form of a judgment.

SECTION H. ADVISORY PROCEEDINGS

Article 130

1. In the exercise of its functions relating to advisory opinions, the Seabed Disputes Chamber shall apply this section and be guided, to the extent to which it recognizes them to be applicable, by the provisions of the Statute and of these Rules applicable in contentious cases.

2. The Chamber shall consider whether the request for an advisory opinion relates to a legal question pending between two or more parties. When the Chamber so determines, article 17 of the Statute applies, as well as the provisions of these Rules concerning the application of that article.

Article 131

1. A request for an advisory opinion on a legal question arising within the scope of the activities of the Assembly or the Council of the Authority shall contain a precise statement of the question. It shall be accompanied by all documents likely to throw light upon the question.

2. The documents shall be transmitted to the Chamber at the same time as the request or as soon as possible thereafter in the number of copies required by the Registry.

Article 132

If the request for an advisory opinion states that the question necessitates an urgent answer the Chamber shall take all appropriate steps to accelerate the procedure.

Article 133

1. The Registrar shall forthwith give notice of the request for an advisory opinion to all States Parties.

2. The Chamber, or its President if the Chamber is not sitting, shall identify the intergovernmental organizations which are likely to be able to furnish information on the question. The Registrar shall give notice of the request to such organizations.

3. States Parties and the organizations referred to in paragraph 2 shall be invited to present written statements on the question within a time-limit fixed by the Chamber or its President if the Chamber is not sitting. Such statements shall be communicated to States Parties and organizations which have made written statements. The Chamber, or its President if the Chamber is not sitting, may fix a further time-limit within which such States Parties and organizations may present written statements on the statements made.

4. The Chamber, or its President if the Chamber is not sitting, shall decide whether oral proceedings shall be held and, if so, fix the date for the opening of such proceedings. States Parties and the organizations referred to in paragraph 2 shall be invited to make oral statements at the proceedings.

Article 134

The written statements and documents annexed shall be made accessible to the public as soon as possible after they have been presented to the Chamber.

Article 135

1. When the Chamber has completed its deliberations and adopted its advisory opinion, the opinion shall be read at a public sitting of the Chamber.

2. The advisory opinion shall contain:
(a)   the date on which it is delivered;
(b)   the names of the judges participating in it;
(c)   the question or questions on which the advisory opinion of the Chamber is requested;
(d)   a summary of the proceedings;
(e)   a statement of the facts;
(f)   the reasons of law on which it is based;
(g)   the reply to the question or questions put to the Chamber;
(h)   the number and names of the judges constituting the majority and those constituting the minority, on each question put to the Chamber;
(i)   a statement as to the text of the opinion which is authoritative.

3. Any judge may attach a separate or dissenting opinion to the advisory opinion of the Chamber; a judge may record concurrence or dissent without stating reasons in the form of a declaration.

Article 136

The Registrar shall inform the Secretary-General of the Authority as to the date and the time fixed for the public sitting to be held for the reading of the opinion. He shall also inform the States Parties and the intergovernmental organizations immediately concerned.

Article 137

One copy of the advisory opinion, signed by the President and by the Registrar and sealed, shall be placed in the archives of the Tribunal, others shall be sent to the Secretary-General of the Authority and to the Secretary-General of the United Nations. Copies shall besent to the States Parties and the intergovernmental organizations immediately concerned.

Article 138

1. The Tribunal may give an advisory opinion on a legal question if an international agreement related to the purposes of the Convention specifically provides for the submission to the Tribunal of a request for such an opinion.

2. A request for an advisory opinion shall be transmitted to the Tribunal by whatever body is authorized by or in accordance with the agreement to make the request to the Tribunal.

3. The Tribunal shall apply *mutatis mutandis* articles 130 to 137.

Regulations on Prospecting and Exploration for Polymetallic Nodules in the Area

Adopted by the Assembly of the International Seabed Authority on 13 July 2000
ISBA/6/A/18, 4 October 2000[1]

PREAMBLE

In accordance with the United Nations Convention on the Law of the Sea ('the Convention'), the seabed and ocean floor and the subsoil thereof beyond the limits of national jurisdiction, as well as its resources, are the common heritage of mankind, the exploration and exploitation of which shall be carried out for the benefit of mankind as a whole, on whose behalf the International Seabed Authority acts. The objective of this first set of Regulations is to provide for prospecting and exploration for polymetallic nodules.

PART I
INTRODUCTION

Regulation 1 Use of terms and scope

1. Terms used in the Convention shall have the same meaning in these Regulations.

2. In accordance with the Agreement relating to the Implementation of Part XI of the United Nations Convention on the Law of the Sea of 10 December 1982 ('the Agreement'), the provisions of the Agreement and Part XI of the United Nations Convention on the Law of the Sea of 10 December 1982 shall be interpreted and applied together as a single instrument. These Regulations and references in these Regulations to the Convention are to be interpreted and applied accordingly.

3. For the purposes of these Regulations:

    (a) 'Exploitation' means the recovery for commercial purposes of polymetallic nodules in the Area and the extraction of minerals therefrom, including the construction and operation of mining, processing and transportation systems, for the production and marketing of metals;

    (b) 'Exploration' means searching for deposits of polymetallic nodules in the Area with exclusive rights, the analysis of such deposits, the testing of collecting systems and equipment, processing facilities and transportation systems, and the carrying out of studies of the environmental, technical, economic, commercial and other appropriate factors that must be taken into account in exploitation;

---

[1] Annex 1 (Notification of intention to engage in prospecting), Annex 2 (Application for approval of a plan of work for exploration to obtain a contract), Annex 3 (Contract for exploration) and Annex 4 (Standard clauses of exploration contract) omitted.

(c) 'Marine environment' includes the physical, chemical, geological and biological components, conditions and factors which interact and determine the productivity, state, condition and quality of the marine ecosystem, the waters of the seas and oceans and the airspace above those waters, as well as the seabed and ocean floor and subsoil thereof;

(d) 'Polymetallic nodules' means one of the resources of the Area consisting of any deposit or accretion of nodules, on or just below the surface of the deep seabed, which contain manganese, nickel, cobalt and copper;

(e) 'Prospecting' means the search for deposits of polymetallic nodules in the Area, including estimation of the composition, sizes and distributions of polymetallic nodule deposits and their economic values, without any exclusive rights;

(f) 'Serious harm to the marine environment' means any effect from activities in the Area on the marine environment which represents a significant adverse change in the marine environment determined according to the rules, regulations and procedures adopted by the Authority on the basis of internationally recognized standards and practices.

4. These Regulations shall not in any way affect the freedom of scientific research, pursuant to article 87 of the Convention, or the right to conduct marine scientific research in the Area pursuant to articles 143 and 256 of the Convention. Nothing in these Regulations shall be construed in such a way as to restrict the exercise by States of the freedom of the high seas as reflected in article 87 of the Convention.

5. These Regulations may be supplemented by further rules, regulations and procedures, in particular on the protection and preservation of the marine environment. These Regulations shall be subject to the provisions of the Convention and the Agreement and other rules of international law not incompatible with the Convention.

PART II
PROSPECTING

Regulation 2 Prospecting

1. Prospecting shall be conducted in accordance with the Convention and these Regulations and may commence only after the prospector has been informed by the Secretary-General that its notification has been recorded pursuant to regulation 4, paragraph 2.

2. Prospecting shall not be undertaken if substantial evidence indicates the risk of serious harm to the marine environment.

3. Prospecting shall not be undertaken in an area covered by an approved plan of work for exploration for polymetallic nodules or in a reserved area; nor may there be prospecting in an area which the Council has disapproved for exploitation because of the risk of serious harm to the marine environment.

4. Prospecting shall not confer on the prospector any rights with respect to resources. A prospector may, however, recover a reasonable quantity of minerals, being the quantity necessary for testing, and not for commercial use.

5. There shall be no time limit on prospecting except that prospecting in a particular area shall cease upon written notification to the prospector by the Secretary-General that a plan of work for exploration has been approved with regard to that area.

6. Prospecting may be conducted simultaneously by more than one prospector in the same area or areas.

Regulation 3 Notification of prospecting

1. A proposed prospector shall notify the Authority of its intention to engage in prospecting.

2. Each notification of prospecting shall be in the form prescribed in Annex 1 to these Regulations, addressed to the Secretary-General, and shall conform to the requirements of these Regulations.

3. Each notification shall be submitted:

(a) In the case of a State, by the authority designated for that purpose by it;

(b) In the case of an entity, by its designated representative; and

(c) In the case of the Enterprise, by its competent authority.

4. Each notification shall be in one of the languages of the Authority and shall contain:

(a) The name, nationality and address of the proposed prospector and its designated representative;

(b) The coordinates of the broad area or areas within which prospecting is to be conducted, in accordance with the most recent generally accepted international standard used by the Authority;

(c) A general description of the prospecting programme, including the proposed date of commencement and its approximate duration;

(d) A satisfactory written undertaking that the proposed prospector will:

(i) Comply with the Convention and the relevant rules, regulations and procedures of the Authority concerning:

   a. Cooperation in the training programmes in connection with marine scientific research and transfer of technology referred to in articles 143 and 144 of the Convention; and

   b. Protection and preservation of the marine environment; and

(ii) Accept verification by the Authority of compliance there with.

Regulation 4 Consideration of notifications

1. The Secretary-General shall acknowledge in writing receipt of each notification submitted under regulation 3, specifying the date of receipt.

2. The Secretary-General shall review and act on the notification within 45 days of its receipt. If the notification conforms with the requirements of the Convention and these Regulations, the Secretary-General shall record the particulars of the notification in a register maintained for that purpose and shall inform the prospector in writing that the notification has been so recorded.

3. The Secretary-General shall, within 45 days of receipt of the notification, inform the proposed prospector in writing if the notification includes any part of an area included in an approved plan of work for exploration or exploitation of any category of resources, or any part of a reserved area, or any part of an area which has been disapproved by the Council for exploitation because of the risk of serious harm to the marine environment, or if the written undertaking is not satisfactory, and shall provide the proposed prospector with a written statement of reasons. In such cases, the proposed prospector may, within 90 days, submit an amended notification. The Secretary-General shall, within 45 days, review and act upon such amended notification.

4. A prospector shall inform the Secretary-General in writing of any change in the information contained in the notification.

5. The Secretary-General shall not release any particulars contained in the notification except with the written consent of the prospector. The Secretary-General shall, however,

from time to time inform all members of the Authority of the identity of prospectors and the general areas in which prospecting is being conducted.

Regulation 5 Annual report

1. A prospector shall, within 90 days of the end of each calendar year, submit a report to the Authority on the status of prospecting. Such reports shall be submitted by the Secretary-General to the Legal and Technical Commission. Each such report shall contain:

(a)   A general description of the status of prospecting and of the results obtained; and

(b)   Information on compliance with the undertakings referred to in regulation 3, paragraph (4) (d).

2. If the prospector intends to claim expenditures for prospecting as part of the development costs incurred prior to the commencement of commercial production, the prospector shall submit an annual statement, in conformity with internationally accepted accounting principles and certified by a duly qualified firm of public accountants, of the actual and direct expenditures incurred by the prospector in carrying out prospecting.

Regulation 6 Confidentiality of data and information from prospecting contained in the annual report

1. The Secretary-General shall ensure the confidentiality of all data and information contained in the reports submitted under regulation 5 in accordance with the provisions of regulations 35 and 36.

2. The Secretary-General may, at any time, with the consent of the prospector concerned, release data and information relating to prospecting in an area in respect of which a notification has been submitted. If the Secretary-General determines that the prospector no longer exists or cannot be located, the Secretary-General may release such data and information.

Regulation 7   Notification of incidents causing serious harm to the marine environment

A prospector shall immediately notify the Secretary-General in writing, using the most effective means, of any incident arising from prospecting which causes serious harm to the marine environment. Upon receipt of such notification the Secretary-General shall act in a manner consistent with regulation 32.

Regulation 8 Objects of an archaeological or historical nature

A prospector shall immediately notify the Secretary-General in writing of any finding in the Area of an object of an archaeological or historical nature and its location. The Secretary-General shall transmit such information to the Director-General of the United Nations Educational, Scientific and Cultural Organization.

PART III
APPLICATIONS FOR APPROVAL OF PLANS OF WORK
FOR EXPLORATION IN THE FORM OF CONTRACTS

SECTION 1 GENERAL PROVISIONS

Regulation 9 General

Subject to the provisions of the Convention, the following may apply to the Authority for approval of plans of work for exploration:

(a)   The Enterprise, on its own behalf or in a joint arrangement;

(b)   States Parties, state enterprises or natural or juridical persons which possess the nationality of States Parties or are effectively controlled by them or their nationals, when sponsored by such States, or any group of the foregoing which meets the requirements of these Regulations.[2]

SECTION 2 CONTENT OF APPLICATIONS

Regulation 10 Form of applications

1.   Each application for approval of a plan of work for exploration shall be in the form prescribed in Annex 2 to these Regulations, shall be addressed to the Secretary-General, and shall conform to the requirements of these Regulations.[3]

2.   Each application shall be submitted:

(a)   In the case of a State Party, by the authority designated for that purpose by it;

(b)   In the case of an entity, by its designated representative or the authority designated for that purpose by the sponsoring State or States; and

(c)   In the case of the Enterprise, by its competent authority.

3.   Each application by a state enterprise or one of the entities referred to in subparagraph (b) of regulation 9 shall also contain:

(a)   Sufficient information to determine the nationality of the applicant or the identity of the State or States by which, or by whose nationals, the applicant is effectively controlled; and

(b)   The principal place of business or domicile and, if applicable, place of registration of the applicant.

4.   Each application submitted by a partnership or consortium of entities shall contain the required information in respect of each member of the partnership or consortium.

Regulation 11 Certificate of sponsorship

1.   Each application by a state enterprise or one of the entities referred to in subparagraph (b) of regulation 9 shall be accompanied by a certificate of sponsorship issued by the State of which it is a national or by which or by whose nationals it is

---

[2] Footnote in original: A request by a registered pioneer investor for approval of a plan of work for exploration under paragraph 6 (a) (ii) of section 1 of the annex to the Agreement shall be submitted within 36 months of the entry into force of the Convention.

[3] Footnote in original: A request by a registered pioneer investor for approval of a plan of work for exploration under paragraph 6 (a) (ii) of section 1 of the annex to the Agreement shall consist of documents, reports and other data submitted to the Preparatory Commission both before and after registration and shall be accompanied by a certificate of compliance, consisting of a factual report describing the status of fulfilment of obligations under the registered pioneer investor regime, issued by the Preparatory Commission in accordance with resolution II, paragraph 11(a). The registered pioneer investor shall, where such information has not already been provided, update the information, using, as far as possible, the provisions of regulation 18 as a guide, and submit its programme of activities for the immediate future, including a general assessment of the potential environmental impacts of the proposed activities.

effectively controlled.[4] If the applicant has more than one nationality, as in the case of a partnership or consortium of entities from more than one State, each State involved shall issue a certificate of sponsorship.

2.   Where the applicant has the nationality of one State but is effectively controlled by another State or its nationals, each State involved shall issue a certificate of sponsorship.

3.   Each certificate of sponsorship shall be duly signed on behalf of the State by which it is submitted and shall contain:

(a)   The name of the applicant;

(b)   The name of the sponsoring State;

(c)   A statement that the applicant is:

(i)   A national of the sponsoring State; or

(ii)   Subject to the effective control of the sponsoring State or its nationals;

(d)   A statement by the sponsoring State that it sponsors the applicant;

(e)   The date of deposit by the sponsoring State of its instrument of ratification of, or accession or succession to, the Convention;

(f)   A declaration that the sponsoring State assumes responsibility in accordance with article 139, article 153, paragraph 4, and Annex III, article 4, paragraph 4, of the Convention.

4.   States or entities in a joint arrangement with the Enterprise shall also comply with this regulation.

Regulation 12 Financial and technical capabilities

1.   Each application for approval of a plan of work for exploration shall contain specific and sufficient information to enable the Council to determine whether the applicant is financially and technically capable of carrying out the proposed plan of work for exploration and of fulfilling its financial obligations to the Authority.[5]

2.   An application for approval of a plan of work for exploration submitted on behalf of a State or entity, or any component of such entity, referred to in resolution II, paragraph 1 (a) (ii) or (iii), other than a registered pioneer investor, which has already undertaken substantial activities in the Area prior to the entry into force of the Convention, or its successor in interest, shall be considered to have met the financial and technical qualifications necessary for approval of a plan of work for exploration if the sponsoring State or States certify that the applicant has expended an amount equivalent to at least US$ 30 million in research and exploration activities and has expended no less than 10 per cent of that amount in the location, survey and evaluation of the area referred to in the plan of work for exploration.

3.   An application for approval of a plan of work for exploration by the Enterprise shall include a statement by its competent authority certifying that the Enterprise has the necessary financial resources to meet the estimated costs of the proposed plan of work for exploration.

4.   An application for approval of a plan of work for exploration by a State or a state enterprise, other than a registered pioneer investor or an entity referred to in resolution II, paragraph 1 (a) (ii) or (iii), shall include a statement by the State or the sponsoring State certifying that the applicant has the necessary financial resources to meet the estimated costs of the proposed plan of work for exploration.

---

[4] Footnote in original: In the case of a request by a registered pioneer investor for approval of a plan of work for exploration, the certifying State or States at the time of registration or their successors shall be deemed to be the sponsoring State or States provided such State or States are States Parties to the Convention or are provisional members of the Authority at the time of the request.

[5] Footnote in original: A registered pioneer investor requesting approval of a plan of work for exploration under paragraph 6 (a) (ii) of section 1 of the annex to the Agreement shall be considered to have satisfied the financial and technical qualifications necessary for approval of a plan of work.

5. An application for approval of a plan of work for exploration by an entity, other than a registered pioneer investor or an entity referred to in resolution II, paragraph 1 (a) (ii) or (iii), shall include copies of its audited financial statements, including balance sheets and profit-and-loss statements, for the most recent three years, in conformity with internationally accepted accounting principles and certified by a duly qualified firm of public accountants; and

(a) If the applicant is a newly organized entity and a certified balance sheet is not available, a pro forma balance sheet certified by an appropriate official of the applicant;

(b) If the applicant is a subsidiary of another entity, copies of such financial statements of that entity and a statement from that entity, in conformity with internationally accepted accounting principles and certified by a duly qualified firm of public accountants, that the applicant will have the financial resources to carry out the plan of work for exploration;

(c) If the applicant is controlled by a State or a state enterprise, a statement from the State or state enterprise certifying that the applicant will have the financial resources to carry out the plan of work for exploration.

6. Where an applicant referred to in paragraph 5 intends to finance the proposed plan of work for exploration by borrowings, its application shall include the amount of such borrowings, the repayment period and the interest rate.

7. Except as provided for in paragraph 2, all applications shall include:

(a) A general description of the applicant's previous experience, knowledge, skills, technical qualifications and expertise relevant to the proposed plan of work for exploration;

(b) A general description of the equipment and methods expected to be used in carrying out the proposed plan of work for exploration and other relevant nonproprietary information about the characteristics of such technology; and

(c) A general description of the applicant's financial and technical capability to respond to any incident or activity which causes serious harm to the marine environment.

8. Where the applicant is a partnership or consortium of entities in a joint arrangement, each member of the partnership or consortium shall provide the information required by this regulation.

Regulation 13 Previous contracts with the Authority

Where the applicant or, in the case of an application by a partnership or consortium of entities in a joint arrangement, any member of the partnership or consortium, has previously been awarded any contract with the Authority, the application shall include:

(a) The date of the previous contract or contracts;

(b) The dates, reference numbers and titles of each report submitted to the Authority in connection with the contract or contracts; and

(c) The date of termination of the contract or contracts, if applicable.

Regulation 14 Undertakings

Each applicant, including the Enterprise, shall, as part of its application for approval of a plan of work for exploration, provide a written undertaking to the Authority that it will:

(a) Accept as enforceable and comply with the applicable obligations created by the provisions of the Convention and the rules, regulations and procedures of the Authority, the decisions of the relevant organs of the Authority and the terms of its contracts with the Authority;

(b)   Accept control by the Authority of activities in the Area, as authorized by the Convention; and

(c)   Provide the Authority with a written assurance that its obligations under the contract will be fulfilled in good faith.[6]

Regulation 15 Total area covered by the application

Each application for approval of a plan of work for exploration shall define the boundaries of the area under application by a list of coordinates in accordance with the most recent generally accepted international standard used by the Authority. Applications other than those under regulation 17 shall cover a total are a, which need not be a single continuous area, sufficiently large and of sufficient estimated commercial value to allow two mining operations. The applicant shall indicate the coordinates dividing the area into two parts of equal estimated commercial value. The area to be allocated to the applicant shall be subject to the provisions of regulation 25.

Regulation 16 Data and information to be submitted before the designation of a reserved area

1.   Each application shall contain sufficient data and information, as prescribed in Section II of Annex 2 to these Regulations, with respect to the area under application to enable the Council, on the recommendation of the Legal and Technical Commission, to designate a reserved area based on the estimated commercial value of each part. Such data and information shall consist of data available to the applicant with respect to both parts of the area under application, including the data used to determine their commercial value.

2.   The Council, on the basis of the data and information submitted by the applicant pursuant to Section II of Annex 2 to these Regulations, if found satisfactory, and taking into account the recommendation of the Legal and Technical Commission, shall designate the part of the area under application which is to be a reserved area. The area so designated shall become a reserved area as soon as the plan of work for exploration for the non-reserved area is approved and the contract is signed. If the Council determines that additional information, consistent with these Regulations and Annex 2, is needed to designate the reserved area, it shall refer the matter back to the Commission for further consideration, specifying the additional information required.

3.   Once the plan of work for exploration is approved and a contract has been issued, the data and information transferred to the Authority by the applicant in respect of the reserved area may be disclosed by the Authority in accordance with article 14, paragraph 3, of Annex III to the Convention.

Regulation 17 Applications for approval of plans of work with respect to a reserved area

1.   Any State which is a developing State or any natural or juridical person sponsored by it and effectively controlled by it or by any other developing State, or any group of the foregoing, may notify the Authority that it wishes to submit a plan of work for exploration with respect to a reserved area. The Secretary-General shall forward such notification to the Enterprise, which shall inform the Secretary-General in writing within six months whether or not it intends to carry out activities in that area. If the Enterprise intends to carry out activities in that area, it shall, pursuant to paragraph 4, also inform in writing the contractor whose application for approval of a plan of work for exploration originally included that area.

---

[6] Footnote in original: Such undertaking shall also be provided by a registered pioneer investor requesting approval of a plan of work for exploration under paragraph 6 (a) (ii) of section 1 of the annex to the Agreement.

2. An application for approval of a plan of work for exploration in respect of a reserved area may be submitted at any time after such an area becomes available following a decision by the Enterprise that it does not intend to carry out activities in that area or where the Enterprise has not, within six months of the notification by the Secretary-General, either taken a decision on whether it intends to carry out activities in that area or notified the Secretary-General in writing that it is engaged in discussions regarding a potential joint venture. In the latter instance, the Enterprise shall have one year from the date of such notification in which to decide whether to conduct activities in that area.

3. If the Enterprise or a developing State or one of the entities referred to in paragraph 1 does not submit an application for approval of a plan of work for exploration for activities in a reserved area within 15 years of the commencement by the Enterprise of its functions independent of the Secretariat of the Authority or within 15 years of the date on which that area is reserved for the Authority, whichever is the later, the contractor whose application for approval of a plan of work for exploration originally included that area shall be entitled to apply for a plan of work for exploration for that area provided it offers in good faith to include the Enterprise as a joint-venture partner.

4. A contractor has the right of first refusal to enter into a joint venture arrangement with the Enterprise for exploration of the area which was included in its application for approval of a plan of work for exploration and which was designated by the Council as a reserved area.

Regulation 18 Data and information to be submitted for approval of the plan of work for exploration[7]

After the Council has designated the reserved area, the applicant, if it has not already done so, shall submit, with a view to receiving approval of the plan of work for exploration in the form of a contract, the following information:

(a) A general description and a schedule of the proposed exploration programme, including the programme of activities for the immediate five-year period, such as studies to be undertaken in respect of the environmental, technical, economic and other appropriate factors that must be taken into account in exploration;

(b) A description of the programme for oceanographic and environmental baseline studies in accordance with these Regulations and any environmental rules, regulations and procedures established by the Authority that would enable an assessment of the potential environmental impact of the proposed exploration activities, taking into account any recommendations issued by the Legal and Technical Commission;

(c) A preliminary assessment of the possible impact of the proposed exploration activities on the marine environment;

(d) A description of proposed measures for the prevention, reduction and control of pollution and other hazards, as well as possible impacts, to the marine environment;

(e) Data necessary for the Council to make the determination it is required to make in accordance with regulation 12, paragraph 1; and

(f) A schedule of anticipated yearly expenditures in respect of the programme of activities for the immediate five-year period.

---

[7] Footnote in original: In the case of a request by a registered pioneer investor for approval of a plan of work for exploration under paragraph 6 (a) (ii) of section 1 of the annex to the Agreement, this regulation shall be implemented in the light of regulation 10.

SECTION 3 FEES

Regulation 19 Fee for applications

1. The fee for processing applications for approval of a plan of work for exploration shall be US\$ 250,000 or its equivalent in a freely convertible currency. The fee shall be paid to the Authority by the applicant at the time of submitting an application.[8]

2. The amount of the fee shall be reviewed from time to time by the Council in order to ensure that it covers the administrative costs incurred by the Authority in processing the application.

3. If the administrative costs incurred by the Authority in processing the application are less than the fixed amount, the Authority shall refund the difference to the applicant.

SECTION 4 PROCESSING OF APPLICATIONS

Regulation 20 Receipt, acknowledgement and safe custody of applications

1. The Secretary-General shall:

(a) Acknowledge in writing receipt of every application for approval of a plan of work for exploration submitted under this Part, specifying the date of receipt;

(b) Place the application together with the attachments and annexes thereto in safe custody and ensure the confidentiality of all confidential data and information contained in the application; and

(c) Notify the members of the Authority of the receipt of such application and circulate to them information of a general nature which is not confidential regarding the application.

Regulation 21 Consideration by the Legal and Technical Commission[9]

1. Upon receipt of an application for approval of a plan of work for exploration, the Secretary-General shall notify the members of the Legal and Technical Commission and place consideration of the application as an item on the agenda for the next meeting of the Commission.

2. The Commission shall examine applications in the order in which they are received.

3. The Commission shall determine if the applicant:

---

[8] Footnote in original: In the case of a registered pioneer investor requesting approval for a plan of work for exploration under paragraph 6 (a) (ii) of section 1 of the annex to the Agreement, the fee of US\$ 250,000 paid pursuant to resolution II, paragraph 7 (a), shall be deemed to be the fee referred to under paragraph 1 relating to the exploration phase.

[9] Footnote in original: In the case of a request by a registered pioneer investor for approval of a plan of work for exploration under paragraph 6 (a) (ii) of section 1 of the annex to the Agreement, the Secretary-General shall ascertain whether:

(a) The documents, reports and other data submitted to the Preparatory Commission both before and after registration are available;

(b) The certificate of compliance, consisting of a factual report describing the status of fulfilment of obligations under the registered pioneer investor regime, issued by the Preparatory Commission in accordance with resolution II, paragraph 11 (a), has been produced;

(c) The registered pioneer investor has updated the information provided in the documents, reports and other data submitted to the Preparatory Commission both before and after registration and has submitted its programme of activities for the immediate future, including a general assessment of the potential environmental impacts of the proposed activities; and

(d) The registered pioneer investor has given the undertakings and assurances specified in regulation 14.

If the Secretary-General informs the Commission that the provisions of (a), (b), (c) and (d) have been satisfied by a registered pioneer investor, the Commission shall recommend approval of the plan of work.

(a) Has complied with the provisions of these Regulations;

(b) Has given the undertakings and assurances specified in regulation 14;

(c) Possesses the financial and technical capability to carry out the proposed plan of work for exploration; and

(d) Has satisfactorily discharged its obligations in relation to any previous contract with the Authority.

4. The Commission shall, in accordance with the requirements set forth in these Regulations and its procedures, determine whether the proposed plan of work for exploration will:

(a) Provide for effective protection of human health and safety;

(b) Provide for effective protection and preservation of the marine environment;

(c) Ensure that installations are not established where interference may be caused to the use of recognized sea lanes essential to international navigation or in areas of intense fishing activity.

5. If the Commission makes the determinations specified in paragraph 3 and determines that the proposed plan of work for exploration meets the requirements of paragraph 4, the Commission shall recommend approval of the plan of work for exploration to the Council.

6. The Commission shall not recommend approval of the plan of work for exploration if part or all of the area covered by the proposed plan of work for exploration is included in:

(a) A plan of work for exploration approved by the Council for polymetallic nodules; or

(b) A plan of work approved by the Council for exploration for or exploitation of other resources if such proposed plan of work for exploration for polymetallic nodules might cause undue interference with activities under such an approved plan of work for such other resources; or

(c) An area disapproved for exploitation by the Council in cases where substantial evidence indicates the risk of serious harm to the marine environment; or

(d) If the proposed plan of work for exploration has been submitted or sponsored by a State that already holds:

(i) Plans of work for exploration and exploitation or exploitation only in non-reserved areas that, together with either part of the area covered by the application, exceed in size 30 per cent of a circular area of 400,000 square kilometres surrounding the centre of either part of the area covered by the proposed plan of work;

(ii) Plans of work for exploration and exploitation or exploitation only in non-reserved areas which, taken together, constitute 2 per cent of that part of the Area which is not reserved or disapproved for exploitation pursuant to article 162, paragraph (2) (x), of the Convention.

7. Except in the case of applications by the Enterprise, on its own behalf or in a joint venture, and applications under regulation 17, the Commission shall not recommend approval of the plan of work for exploration if part or all of the area covered by the proposed plan of work for exploration is included in a reserved area or an area designated by the Council to be a reserved area.

8. If the Commission finds that an application does not comply with these Regulations, it shall notify the applicant in writing, through the Secretary-General, indicating the reasons. The applicant may, within 45 days of such notification, amend its application. If the Commission after further consideration is of the view that it should not recommend approval of the plan of work for exploration, it shall so inform the applicant and provide the applicant with a further opportunity to make representations within 30

days of such information. The Commission shall consider any such representations made by the applicant in preparing its report and recommendation to the Council.

9. In considering a proposed plan of work for exploration, the Commission shall have regard to the principles, policies and objectives relating to activities in the Area as provided for in Part XI and Annex III of the Convention and the Agreement.

10. The Commission shall consider applications expeditiously and shall submit its report and recommendations to the Council on the designation of the areas and on the plan of work for exploration at the first possible opportunity, taking into account the schedule of meetings of the Authority.

11. In discharging its duties, the Commission shall apply these Regulations and the rules, regulations and procedures of the Authority in a uniform and nondiscriminatory manner.

Regulation 22 Consideration and approval of plans of work for exploration by the Council[10]

The Council shall consider the reports and recommendations of the Commission relating to approval of plans of work for exploration in accordance with paragraphs 11 and 12 of section 3 of the annex to the Agreement.

PART IV
CONTRACTS FOR EXPLORATION

Regulation 23 The contract

1. After a plan of work for exploration has been approved by the Council, it shall be prepared in the form of a contract between the Authority and the applicant as prescribed in Annex 3 to these Regulations. Each contract shall incorporate the standard clauses set out in Annex 4 in effect at the date of entry into force of the contract.

2. The contract shall be signed by the Secretary-General on behalf of the Authority and by the applicant. The Secretary-General shall notify all members of the Authority in writing of the conclusion of each contract.

3. In accordance with the principle of non-discrimination, a contract with a State or entity or any component of such entity referred to in paragraph 6 (a) (i) of section 1 of the annex to the Agreement shall include arrangements that shall be similar to and no less favourable than those agreed with any registered pioneer investor. If any of the States or entities or any components of such entities referred to in paragraph 6 (a) (i) of section 1 of the annex to the Agreement are granted more favourable arrangements, the Council shall make similar and no less favourable arrangements with regard to the rights and obligations assumed by the registered pioneer investors provided that such arrangements do not affect or prejudice the interests of the Authority.

Regulation 24 Rights of the contractor

1. The contractor shall have the exclusive right to explore an area covered by a plan of work for exploration in respect of polymetallic nodules. The Authority shall ensure that no other entity operates in the same area for resources other than polymetallic nodules in a manner that might interfere with the operations of the contractor.

2. A contractor who has an approved plan of work for exploration only shall have a preference and a priority among applicants submitting plans of work for exploitation of

---

[10] Footnote in original: In the case of a request by a registered pioneer investor for approval of a plan of work for exploration under paragraph 6 (a) (ii) of section 1 of the Agreement, once the Commission recommends approval of the plan of work and submits its recommendation to the Council, the plan of work shall be considered approved by the Council in accordance with paragraph 6 (a) (ii) of section 1 of the annex to the Agreement.

the same area and resources. Such preference or priority may be withdrawn by the Council if the contractor has failed to comply with the requirements of its approved plan of work for exploration within the time period specified in a written notice or notices from the Council to the contractor indicating which requirements have not been complied with by the contractor. The time period specified in any such notice shall not be unreasonable. The contractor shall be accorded a reasonable opportunity to be heard before the withdrawal of such preference or priority becomes final. The Council shall provide the reasons for its proposed withdrawal of preference or priority and shall consider any contractor's response. The decision of the Council shall take account of that response and shall be based on substantial evidence.

3. A withdrawal of preference or priority shall not become effective until the contractor has been accorded a reasonable opportunity to exhaust the judicial remedies available to it pursuant to Part XI, section 5, of the Convention.

Regulation 25 Size of area and relinquishment

1. The total area allocated to the contractor under the contract shall not exceed 150,000 square kilometres. The contractor shall relinquish portions of the area allocated to it to revert to the Area, in accordance with the following schedule:

   (a) 20 per cent of the area allocated by the end of the third year from the date of the contract;

   (b) An additional 10 per cent of the area allocated by the end of the fifth year from the date of the contract; and

   (c) An additional 20 per cent of the area allocated or such larger amount as would exceed the exploitation area decided upon by the Authority, after eight years from the date of the contract, provided that a contractor shall not be required to relinquish any portion of such area when the total area allocated to it does not exceed 75,000 square kilometres.

2. In the case of a registered pioneer investor, the contract shall take into account the schedule of relinquishment, where applicable, in accordance with the terms of its registration as a registered pioneer investor.

3. The Council may, at the request of the contractor, and on the recommendation of the Commission, in exceptional circumstances, defer the schedule of relinquishment. Such exceptional circumstances shall be determined by the Council and shall include, *inter alia*, consideration of prevailing economic circumstances or other unforeseen exceptional circumstances arising in connection with the operational activities of the Contractor.

Regulation 26 Duration of contracts

1. A plan of work for exploration shall be approved for a period of 15 years. Upon expiration of a plan of work for exploration, the contractor shall apply for a plan of work for exploitation unless the contractor has already done so, has obtained an extension for the plan of work for exploration or decides to renounce its rights in the area covered by the plan of work for exploration.

2. Not later than six months before the expiration of a plan of work for exploration, a contractor may apply for extensions for the plan of work for exploration for periods of not more than five years each. Such extensions shall be approved by the Council, on the recommendation of the Commission, if the contractor has made efforts in good faith to comply with the requirements of the plan of work but for reasons beyond the contractor's control has been unable to complete the necessary preparatory work for proceeding to the exploitation stage or if the prevailing economic circumstances do not justify proceeding to the exploitation stage.

Regulation 27 Training

1. Pursuant to article 15 of Annex III to the Convention, each contract shall include as a schedule a practical programme for the training of personnel of the Authority and developing States and drawn up by the contractor in cooperation with the Authority and the sponsoring State or States. Training programmes shall focus on training in the conduct of exploration, and shall provide for full participation by such personnel in all activities covered by the contract. Such training programmes may be revised and developed from time to time as necessary by mutual agreement.

2. In the case of a registered pioneer investor, the contract shall take into account the training provided in accordance with the terms of its registration as a registered pioneer investor.

Regulation 28   Periodic review of the implementation of the plan of work for exploration

1. The contractor and the Secretary-General shall jointly undertake a periodic review of the implementation of the plan of work for exploration at intervals of five years. The Secretary-General may request the contractor to submit such additional data and information as may be necessary for the purposes of the review.

2. In the light of the review, the contractor shall indicate its programme of activities for the following five-year period, making such adjustments to its previous programme of activities as are necessary.

3. The Secretary-General shall report on the review to the Commission and to the Council. The Secretary-General shall indicate in the report whether any observations transmitted to him by States Parties to the Convention concerning the manner in which the contractor has discharged its obligations under these Regulations relating to the protection and preservation of the marine environment were taken into account in the review.

Regulation 29 Termination of sponsorship

1. Each contractor shall have the required sponsorship throughout the period of the contract.

2. If a State terminates its sponsorship it shall promptly notify the Secretary-General in writing. The sponsoring State should also inform the Secretary-General of the reasons for terminating its sponsorship. Termination of sponsorship shall take effect six months after the date of receipt of the notification by the Secretary-General, unless the notification specifies a later date.

3. In the event of termination of sponsorship the contractor shall, within the period referred to in paragraph 2, obtain another sponsor. Such sponsor shall submit a certificate of sponsorship in accordance with regulation 11. Failure to obtain a sponsor within the required period shall result in the termination of the contract.

4. A sponsoring State shall not be discharged by reason of the termination of its sponsorship from any obligations accrued while it was a sponsoring State, nor shall such termination affect any legal rights and obligations created during such sponsorship.

5. The Secretary-General shall notify the members of the Authority of the termination or change of sponsorship.

Regulation 30 Responsibility and liability

Responsibility and liability of the contractor and of the Authority shall be in accordance with the Convention. The contractor shall continue to have responsibility for any damage arising out of wrongful acts in the conduct of its operations, in particular damage to the marine environment, after the completion of the exploration phase.

PART V
PROTECTION AND PRESERVATION OF THE MARINE ENVIRONMENT

Regulation 31 Protection and preservation of the marine environment

1. The Authority shall, in accordance with the Convention and the Agreement, establish and keep under periodic review environmental rules, regulations and procedures to ensure effective protection for the marine environment from harmful effects which may arise from activities in the Area.

2. In order to ensure effective protection for the marine environment from harmful effects which may arise from activities in the Area, the Authority and sponsoring States shall apply a precautionary approach, as reflected in principle 15 of the Rio Declaration, to such activities. The Legal and Technical Commission shall make recommendations to the Council on the implementation of this paragraph.

3. Pursuant to article 145 of the Convention and paragraph 2 of this regulation, each contractor shall take necessary measures to prevent, reduce and control pollution and other hazards to the marine environment arising from its activities in the Area as far as reasonably possible using the best technology available to it.

4. Each contract shall require the contractor to gather environmental baseline data and to establish environmental baselines, taking into account any recommendations issued by the Legal and Technical Commission pursuant to regulation 38, against which to assess the likely effects of its programme of activities under the plan of work for exploration on the marine environment and a programme to monitor and report on such effects. The recommendations issued by the Commission may, *inter alia*, list those exploration activities which may be considered to have no potential for causing harmful effects on the marine environment. The contractor shall cooperate with the Authority and the sponsoring State or States in the establishment and implementation of such monitoring programme.

5. The contractor shall report annually in writing to the Secretary-General on the implementation and results of the monitoring programme referred to in paragraph 4 and shall submit data and information, taking into account any recommendations issued by the Commission pursuant to regulation 38. The Secretary-General shall transmit such reports to the Commission for its consideration pursuant to article 165 of the Convention.

6. Contractors, sponsoring States and other interested States or entities shall cooperate with the Authority in the establishment and implementation of programmes for monitoring and evaluating the impacts of deep seabed mining on the marine environment.

7. If the Contractor applies for exploitation rights, it shall propose areas to be set aside and used exclusively as impact reference zones and preservation reference zones. 'Impact reference zones' means areas to be used for assessing the effect of each contractor's activities in the Area on the marine environment and which are representative of the environmental characteristics of the Area. 'Preservation reference zones' means areas in which no mining shall occur to ensure representative and stable biota of the seabed in order to assess any changes in the flora and fauna of the marine environment.

Regulation 32 Emergency orders

1. When the Secretary-General has been notified by a contractor or otherwise becomes aware of an incident resulting from or caused by a contractor's activities in the Area that has caused, or is likely to cause, serious harm to the marine environment, the Secretary-General shall issue a general notification of the incident, shall notify in writing the contractor and the sponsoring State or States, and shall report immediately to the Legal and Technical Commission and to the Council. A copy of the report shall be circulated to

all members of the Authority, to competent international organizations and to concerned subregional, regional and global organizations and bodies. The Secretary-General shall monitor developments with respect to all such incidents and shall report on them as appropriate to the Commission and to the Council.

2. Pending any action by the Council, the Secretary-General shall take such immediate measures of a temporary nature as are practical and reasonable in the circumstances to prevent, contain and minimize serious harm to the marine environment. Such temporary measures shall remain in effect for no longer than 90 days, or until the Council decides what measures, if any, to take pursuant to paragraph 5 of this regulation, whichever is the earlier.

3. After having received the report of the Secretary-General, the Commission shall determine, based on the evidence provided to it and taking into account the measures already taken by the contractor, which measures are necessary to respond effectively to the incident in order to prevent, contain and minimize the serious harm, and shall make its recommendations to the Council.

4. The Council shall consider the recommendations of the Commission.

5. The Council, taking into account the recommendations of the Commission and any information provided by the Contractor, may issue emergency orders, which may include orders for the suspension or adjustment of operations, as may be reasonably necessary to prevent, contain and minimize serious harm to the marine environment arising out of activities in the Area.

6. If a contractor does not promptly comply with an emergency order to prevent serious harm to the marine environment arising out of its activities in the Area, the Council shall take by itself or through arrangements with others on its behalf, such practical measures as are necessary to prevent, contain and minimize any such serious harm to the marine environment.

7. In order to enable the Council, when necessary, to take immediately the practical measures to prevent, contain and minimize serious harm to the marine environment referred to in paragraph 6, the contractor, prior to the commencement of testing of collecting systems and processing operations, will provide the Council with a guarantee of its financial and technical capability to comply promptly with emergency orders or to assure that the Council can take such emergency measures. If the contractor does not provide the Council with such a guarantee, the sponsoring State or States shall, in response to a request by the Secretary-General and pursuant to articles 139 and 235 of the Convention, take necessary measures to ensure that the contractor provides such a guarantee or shall take measures to ensure that assistance is provided to the Authority in the discharge of its responsibilities under paragraph 6.[11]

Regulation 33 Rights of coastal States

1. Nothing in these Regulations shall affect the rights of coastal States in accordance with article 142 and other relevant provisions of the Convention.

2. Any coastal State which has grounds for believing that any activity in the Area by a contractor is likely to cause serious harm to the marine environment under its jurisdiction or sovereignty may notify the Secretary-General in writing of the grounds upon which such belief is based. The Secretary-General shall provide the Contractor and its sponsoring State or States with a reasonable opportunity to examine the evidence, if any, provided by the coastal State as the basis for its belief. The contractor and its sponsoring State or States may submit their observations thereon to the Secretary-General within a reasonable time.

---

[11] Footnote in original: See ISBA/6/C/12 (Decision of the Council relating to the regulations on prospecting and exploration for polymetallic nodules in the Area).

3. If there are clear grounds for believing that serious harm to the marine environment is likely to occur, the Secretary-General shall act in accordance with regulation 32 and, if necessary, shall take immediate measures of a temporary nature as provided for in paragraph 2 of regulation 32.

Regulation 34 Objects of an archaeological or historical nature

The contractor shall immediately notify the Secretary-General in writing of any finding in the exploration area of an object of an archaeological or historical nature and its location. The Secretary-General shall transmit such information to the Director-General of the United Nations Educational, Scientific and Cultural Organization. Following the finding of any such object of an archaeological or historical nature in the exploration area, the contractor shall take all reasonable measures to avoid disturbing such object.

PART VI

CONFIDENTIALITY

Regulation 35 Proprietary data and information and confidentiality

1. Data and information submitted or transferred to the Authority or to any person participating in any activity or programme of the Authority pursuant to these Regulations or a contract issued under these Regulations, and designated by the contractor, in consultation with the Secretary-General, as being of a confidential nature, shall be considered confidential unless it is data and information which:

   (a)   Is generally known or publicly available from other sources;
   (b)   Has been previously made available by the owner to others without an obligation concerning its confidentiality; or
   (c)   Is already in the possession of the Authority with no obligation concerning its confidentiality.

2. Confidential data and information may only be used by the Secretary-General and staff of the Secretariat, as authorized by the Secretary-General, and by the members of the Legal and Technical Commission as necessary for and relevant to the effective exercise of their powers and functions. The Secretary-General shall authorize access to such data and information only for limited use in connection with the functions and duties of the staff of the Secretariat and the functions and duties of the Legal and Technical Commission.

3. Ten years after the date of submission of confidential data and information to the Authority or the expiration of the contract for exploration, whichever is the later, and every five years thereafter, the Secretary-General and the contractor shall review such data and information to determine whether they should remain confidential. Such data and information shall remain confidential if the contractor establishes that there would be a substantial risk of serious and unfair economic prejudice if the data and information were to be released. No such data and information shall be released until the contractor has been accorded a reasonable opportunity to exhaust the judicial remedies available to it pursuant to Part XI, section 5, of the Convention.

4. If, at any time following the expiration of the contract for exploration, the contractor enters into a contract for exploitation in respect of any part of the exploration area, confidential data and information relating to that part of the area shall remain confidential in accordance with the contract for exploitation.

5. The contractor may at any time waive confidentiality of data and information.

Regulation 36 Procedures to ensure confidentiality

1. The Secretary-General shall be responsible for maintaining the confidentiality of all confidential data and information and shall not, except with the prior written consent of the contractor, release such data and information to any person external to the Authority. To ensure the confidentiality of such data and information, the Secretary-General shall establish procedures, consistent with the provisions of the Convention, governing the handling of confidential information by members of the Secretariat, members of the Legal and Technical Commission and any other person participating in any activity or programme of the Authority. Such procedures shall include:

    (a) Maintenance of confidential data and information in secure facilities and development of security procedures to prevent unauthorized access to or removal of such data and information;

    (b) Development and maintenance of a classification, log and inventory system of all written data and information received, including its type and source and routing from the time of receipt until final disposition.

2. A person who is authorized pursuant to these Regulations to have access to confidential data and information shall not disclose such data and information except as permitted under the Convention and these Regulations. The Secretary-General shall require any person who is authorized to have access to confidential data and information to make a written declaration witnessed by the Secretary-General or his or her authorized representative to the effect that the person so authorized:

    (a) Acknowledges his or her legal obligation under the Convention and these Regulations with respect to the non-disclosure of confidential data and information;

    (b) Agrees to comply with the applicable regulations and procedures established to ensure the confidentiality of such data and information.

3. The Legal and Technical Commission shall protect the confidentiality of confidential data and information submitted to it pursuant to these Regulations or a contract issued under these Regulations. In accordance with the provisions of article 163, paragraph 8, of the Convention, members of the Commission shall not disclose, even after the termination of their functions, any industrial secret, proprietary data which are transferred to the Authority in accordance with Annex III, article 14, of the Convention, or any other confidential information coming to their knowledge by reason of their duties for the Authority.

4. The Secretary-General and staff of the Authority shall not disclose, even after the termination of their functions with the Authority, any industrial secret, proprietary data which are transferred to the Authority in accordance with Annex III, article 14, of the Convention, or any other confidential information coming to their knowledge by reason of their employment with the Authority.

5. Taking into account the responsibility and liability of the Authority pursuant to Annex III, article 22, of the Convention, the Authority may take such action as may be appropriate against any person who, by reason of his or her duties for the Authority, has access to any confidential data and information and who is in breach of the obligations relating to confidentiality contained in the Convention and these Regulations.

PART VII

GENERAL PROCEDURES

Regulation 37 Notice and general procedures

1. Any application, request, notice, report, consent, approval, waiver, direction or instruction hereunder shall be made by the Secretary-General or by the designated

representative of the prospector, applicant or contractor, as the case may be, in writing. Service shall be by hand, or by telex, facsimile or registered airmail to the Secretary-General at the headquarters of the Authority or to the designated representative.

2. Delivery by hand shall be effective when made. Delivery by telex shall be deemed to be effective on the business day following the day when the 'answer back' appears on the sender's telex machine. Delivery by facsimile shall be effective when the 'transmit confirmation report' confirming the transmission to the recipient's published facsimile number is received by the transmitter. Delivery by registered airmail shall be deemed to be effective 21 days after posting.

3. Notice to the designated representative of the prospector, applicant or contractor shall constitute effective notice to the prospector, applicant or contractor for all purposes under these Regulations, and the designated representative shall be the agent of the prospector, applicant or contractor for the service of process or notification in any proceeding of any court or tribunal having jurisdiction.

4. Notice to the Secretary-General shall constitute effective notice to the Authority for all purposes under these Regulations, and the Secretary-General shall be the Authority's agent for the service of process or notification in any proceeding of any court or tribunal having jurisdiction.

Regulation 38 Recommendations for the guidance of contractors

1. The Legal and Technical Commission may from time to time issue recommendations of a technical or administrative nature for the guidance of contractors to assist them in the implementation of the rules, regulations and procedures of the Authority.

2. The full text of such recommendations shall be reported to the Council. Should the Council find that a recommendation is inconsistent with the intent and purpose of these Regulations, it may request that the recommendation be modified or withdrawn.

PART VIII
SETTLEMENT OF DISPUTES

Regulation 39 Disputes

1. Disputes concerning the interpretation or application of these Regulations shall be settled in accordance with Part XI, section 5, of the Convention.

2. Any final decision rendered by a court or tribunal having jurisdiction under the Convention relating to the rights and obligations of the Authority and of the Contractor shall be enforceable in the territory of each State Party to the Convention.

PART IX
RESOURCES OTHER THAN POLYMETALLIC NODULES

Regulation 40 Resources other than polymetallic nodules

If a prospector or contractor finds resources in the Area other than polymetallic nodules, the prospecting and exploration for and exploitation of such resources shall be subject to the rules, regulations and procedures of the Authority relating to such resources in accordance with the Convention and the Agreement.

Convention on the Conservation and Management of Highly Migratory Fish Stocks in the Western and Central Pacific Ocean

Done at Honolulu, 5 September 2000; entry into force, 19 June 2004
(2001) 45 LOSB 79[1]

The Contracting Parties to this Convention,

Determined to ensure the long-term conservation and sustainable use, in particular for human food consumption, of highly migratory fish stocks in the western and central Pacific Ocean for present and future generations,

Recalling the relevant provisions of the United Nations Convention on the Law of the Sea of 10 December 1982 and the Agreement for the Implementation of the Provisions of the United Nations Convention on the Law of the Sea of 10 December 1982 relating to the Conservation and Management of Straddling Fish Stocks and Highly Migratory Fish Stocks,

Recognizing that, under the 1982 Convention and the Agreement, coastal States and States fishing in the region shall cooperate with a view to ensuring conservation and promoting the objective of optimum utilization of highly migratory fish stocks throughout their range,

Mindful that effective conservation and management measures require the application of the precautionary approach and the best scientific information available,

Conscious of the need to avoid adverse impacts on the marine environment, preserve biodiversity, maintain the integrity of marine ecosystems and minimize the risk of long-term or irreversible effects of fishing operations,

Recognizing the ecological and geographical vulnerability of the small island developing States, territories and possessions in the region, their economic and social dependence on highly migratory fish stocks, and their need for specific assistance, including financial, scientific and technological assistance, to allow them to participate effectively in the conservation, management and sustainable use of the highly migratory fish stocks,

Further recognizing that smaller island developing States have unique needs which require special attention and consideration in the provision of financial, scientific and technological assistance,

Acknowledging that compatible, effective and binding conservation and management measures can be achieved only through cooperation between coastal States and States fishing in the region,

Convinced that effective conservation and management of the highly migratory fish stocks of the western and central Pacific Ocean in their entirety may best be achieved through the establishment of a regional Commission,

Have agreed as follows:

PART I
GENERAL PROVISIONS

Article 1 Use of terms

For the purposes of this Convention:

(a)   '1982 Convention' means the United Nations Convention on the Law of the Sea of 10 December 1982;

---

[1] Annex II (Review Panel) and Annex IV (Information Requirements) omitted.

(b) 'Agreement' means the Agreement for the Implementation of the Provisions of the United Nations Convention on the Law of the Sea of 10 December 1982 relating to the Conservation and Management of Straddling Fish Stocks and Highly Migratory Fish Stocks;

(c) 'Commission' means the Commission for the Conservation and Management of Highly Migratory Fish Stocks in the Western and Central Pacific Ocean established in accordance with this Convention;

(d) 'fishing' means:

(i) searching for, catching, taking or harvesting fish;

(ii) attempting to search for, catch, take or harvest fish;

(iii) engaging in any other activity which can reasonably be expected to result in the locating, catching, taking or harvesting of fish for any purpose;

(iv) placing, searching for or recovering fish aggregating devices or associated electronic equipment such as radio beacons;

(v) any operations at sea directly in support of, or in preparation for, any activity described in subparagraphs (i) to (iv), including transhipment;

(vi) use of any other vessel, vehicle, aircraft or hovercraft, for any activity described in subparagraphs (i) to (v) except for emergencies involving the health and safety of the crew or the safety of a vessel;

(e) 'fishing vessel' means any vessel used or intended for use for the purpose of fishing, including support ships, carrier vessels and any other vessel directly involved in such fishing operations;

(f) 'highly migratory fish stocks' means all fish stocks of the species listed in Annex 1 of the 1982 Convention occurring in the Convention Area, and such other species of fish as the Commission may determine;

(g) 'regional economic integration organization' means a regional economic integration organization to which its member States have transferred competence over matters covered by this Convention, including the authority to make decisions binding on its member States in respect of those matters;

(h) 'transhipment' means the unloading of all or any of the fish on board a fishing vessel to another fishing vessel either at sea or in port.

Article 2 Objective

The objective of this Convention is to ensure, through effective management, the long-term conservation and sustainable use of highly migratory fish stocks in the western and central Pacific Ocean in accordance with the 1982 Convention and the Agreement.

Article 3 Area of application

1. Subject to article 4, the area of competence of the Commission (hereinafter referred to as 'the Convention Area') comprises all waters of the Pacific Ocean bounded to the south and to the east by the following line:

From the south coast of Australia due south along the 141° meridian of east longitude to its intersection with the 55° parallel of south latitude; thence due east along the 55° parallel of south latitude to its intersection with the 150° meridian of east longitude; thence due south along the 150° meridian of east longitude to its intersection with the 60° parallel of south latitude; thence due east along the 60° parallel of south latitude to its intersection with the 130° meridian of west longitude; thence due north along the 130° meridian of west longitude to its intersection with the 4° parallel of south latitude; thence due west along the 4° parallel of south latitude to its intersection with the 150° meridian of west longitude; thence due north along the 150° meridian of west longitude.

2. Nothing in this Convention shall constitute recognition of the claims or positions of any of the members of the Commission concerning the legal status and extent of waters and zones claimed by any such members.

3. This Convention applies to all stocks of highly migratory fish within the Convention Area except sauries. Conservation and management measures under this Convention shall be applied throughout the range of the stocks, or to specific areas within the Convention Area, as determined by the Commission.

Article 4 Relationship between this Convention and the 1982 Convention

Nothing in this Convention shall prejudice the rights, jurisdiction and duties of States under the 1982 Convention and the Agreement. This Convention shall be interpreted and applied in the context of and in a manner consistent with the 1982 Convention and the Agreement.

PART II
CONSERVATION AND MANAGEMENT OF HIGHLY MIGRATORY FISH STOCKS

Article 5 Principles and measures for conservation and management

In order to conserve and manage highly migratory fish stocks in the Convention Area in their entirety, the members of the Commission shall, in giving effect to their duty to cooperate in accordance with the 1982 Convention, the Agreement and this Convention:

(a)   adopt measures to ensure long-term sustainability of highly migratory fish stocks in the Convention Area and promote the objective of their optimum utilization;

(b)   ensure that such measures are based on the best scientific evidence available and are designed to maintain or restore stocks at levels capable of producing maximum sustainable yield, as qualified by relevant environmental and economic factors, including the special requirements of developing States in the Convention Area, particularly small island developing States, and taking into account fishing patterns, the interdependence of stocks and any generally recommended international minimum standards, whether subregional, regional or global;

(c)   apply the precautionary approach in accordance with this Convention and all relevant internationally agreed standards and recommended practices and procedures;

(d)   assess the impacts of fishing, other human activities and environmental factors on target stocks, non-target species, and species belonging to the same ecosystem or dependent upon or associated with the target stocks;

(e)   adopt measures to minimize waste, discards, catch by lost or abandoned gear, pollution originating from fishing vessels, catch of non-target species, both fish and non-fish species, (hereinafter referred to as non-target species) and impacts on associated or dependent species, in particular endangered species and promote the development and use of selective, environmentally safe and cost-effective fishing gear and techniques;

(f)   protect biodiversity in the marine environment;

(g)   take measures to prevent or eliminate over-fishing and excess fishing capacity and to ensure that levels of fishing effort do not exceed those commensurate with the sustainable use of fishery resources;

(h)   take into account the interests of artisanal and subsistence fishers;

(i)   collect and share, in a timely manner, complete and accurate data concerning fishing activities on, *inter alia*, vessel position, catch of target and non-target species and fishing effort, as well as information from national and international research programmes; and

(j)   implement and enforce conservation and management measures through effective monitoring, control and surveillance.

Article 6   Application of the precautionary approach

1.   In applying the precautionary approach, the members of the Commission shall:

(a)   apply the guidelines set out in Annex II of the Agreement, which shall form an integral part of this Convention, and determine, on the basis of the best scientific information available, stock-specific reference points and the action to be taken if they are exceeded;

(b)   take into account, *inter alia*, uncertainties relating to the size and productivity of the stocks, reference points, stock condition in relation to such reference points, levels and distributions of fishing mortality and the impact of fishing activities on non-target and associated or dependent species, as well as existing and predicted oceanic, environmental and socio-economic conditions; and

(c)   develop data collection and research programmes to assess the impact of fishing on non-target and associated or dependent species and their environment, and adopt plans where necessary to ensure the conservation of such species and to protect habitats of special concern.

2.   Members of the Commission shall be more cautious when information is uncertain, unreliable or inadequate. The absence of adequate scientific information shall not be used as a reason for postponing or failing to take conservation and management measures.

3.   Members of the Commission shall take measures to ensure that, when reference points are approached, they will not be exceeded. In the event they are exceeded, members of the Commission shall, without delay, take the action determined under paragraph 1(a) to restore the stocks.

4.   Where the status of target stocks or non-target or associated or dependent species is of concern, members of the Commission shall subject such stocks and species to enhanced monitoring in order to review their status and the efficacy of conservation and management measures. They shall revise those measures regularly in the light of new information.

5.   For new or exploratory fisheries, members of the Commission shall adopt as soon as possible cautious conservation and management measures, including, *inter alia*, catch limits and effort limits. Such measures shall remain in force until there are sufficient data to allow assessment of the impact of the fisheries on the long-term sustainability of the stocks, whereupon conservation and management measures based on that assessment shall be implemented. The latter measures shall, if appropriate, allow for the gradual development of the fisheries.

6.   If a natural phenomenon has a significant adverse impact on the status of highly migratory fish stocks, members of the Commission shall adopt conservation and management measures on an emergency basis to ensure that fishing activity does not exacerbate such adverse impacts. Members of the Commission shall also adopt such measures on an emergency basis where fishing activity presents a serious threat to the sustainability of such stocks. Measures taken on an emergency basis shall be temporary and shall be based on the best scientific information available.

Article 7 Implementation of principles in areas under national jurisdiction

1. The principles and measures for conservation and management enumerated in article 5 shall be applied by coastal States within areas under national jurisdiction in the Convention Area in the exercise of their sovereign rights for the purpose of exploring and exploiting, conserving and managing highly migratory fish stocks.

2. The members of the Commission shall give due consideration to the respective capacities of developing coastal States, in particular small island developing States, in the Convention Area to apply the provisions of articles 5 and 6 within areas under national jurisdiction and their need for assistance as provided for in this Convention.

Article 8 Compatibility of conservation and management measures

1. Conservation and management measures established for the high seas and those adopted for areas under national jurisdiction shall be compatible in order to ensure conservation and management of highly migratory fish stocks in their entirety. To this end, the members of the Commission have a duty to cooperate for the purpose of achieving compatible measures in respect of such stocks.

2. In establishing compatible conservation and management measures for highly migratory fish stocks in the Convention Area, the Commission shall:

(a) take into account the biological unity and other biological characteristics of the stocks and the relationships between the distribution of the stocks, the fisheries and the geographical particularities of the region concerned, including the extent to which the stocks occur and are fished in areas under national jurisdiction;

(b) take into account:

   (i) the conservation and management measures adopted and applied in accordance with article 61 of the 1982 Convention in respect of the same stocks by coastal States within areas under national jurisdiction and ensure that measures established in respect of such stocks for the Convention Area as a whole do not undermine the effectiveness of such measures;

   (ii) previously agreed measures established and applied in respect of the same stocks for the high seas which form part of the Convention Area by relevant coastal States and States fishing on the high seas in accordance with the 1982 Convention and the Agreement;

(c) take into account previously agreed measures established and applied in accordance with the 1982 Convention and the Agreement in respect of the same stocks by a subregional or regional fisheries management organization or arrangement;

(d) take into account the respective dependence of the coastal States and the States fishing on the high seas on the stocks concerned; and

(e) ensure that such measures do not result in harmful impact on the living marine resources as a whole.

3. The coastal State shall ensure that the measures adopted and applied by it to highly migratory fish stocks within areas under its national jurisdiction do not undermine the effectiveness of measures adopted by the Commission under this Convention in respect of the same stocks.

4. Where there are areas of high seas in the Convention Area entirely surrounded by the exclusive economic zones of members of the Commission, the Commission shall, in giving effect to this article, pay special attention to ensuring compatibility between conservation and management measures established for such high seas areas and those established in respect of the same stocks in accordance with article 61 of the 1982 Convention by the surrounding coastal States in areas under national jurisdiction.

PART III
COMMISSION FOR THE CONSERVATION AND MANAGEMENT OF HIGHLY
MIGRATORY FISH STOCKS IN THE WESTERN AND CENTRAL PACIFIC OCEAN

SECTION 1. GENERAL PROVISIONS

Article 9 Establishment of the Commission

1. There is hereby established the Commission for the Conservation and Management of Highly Migratory Fish Stocks in the Western and Central Pacific Ocean, which shall function in accordance with the provisions of this Convention.

2. A fishing entity referred to in the Agreement, which has agreed to be bound by the regime established by this Convention in accordance with the provisions of Annex I, may participate in the work, including decision-making, of the Commission in accordance with the provisions of this article and Annex I.

3. The Commission shall hold an annual meeting. The Commission shall hold such other meetings as may be necessary to carry out its functions under this Convention.

4. The Commission shall elect a chairman and a vice-chairman from among the Contracting Parties, who shall be of different nationalities. They shall be elected for a period of two years and shall be eligible for re-election. The chairman and vice-chairman shall remain in office until the election of their successors.

5. The principle of cost-effectiveness shall apply to the frequency, duration and scheduling of meetings of the Commission and its subsidiary bodies. The Commission may, where appropriate, enter into contractual arrangements with relevant institutions to provide expert services necessary for the efficient functioning of the Commission and to enable it to carry out effectively its responsibilities under this Convention.

6. The Commission shall have international legal personality and such legal capacity as may be necessary to perform its functions and achieve its objectives. The privileges and immunities which the Commission and its officers shall enjoy in the territory of a Contracting Party shall be determined by agreement between the Commission and the member concerned.

7. The Contracting Parties shall determine the location of the headquarters of the Commission and shall appoint its Executive Director.

8. The Commission shall adopt, and amend as required, by consensus, rules of procedure for the conduct of its meetings, including meetings of its subsidiary bodies, and for the efficient exercise of its functions.

Article 10 Functions of the Commission

1. Without prejudice to the sovereign rights of coastal States for the purpose of exploring and exploiting, conserving and managing highly migratory fish stocks within areas under national jurisdiction, the functions of the Commission shall be to:

(a) determine the total allowable catch or total level of fishing effort within the Convention Area for such highly migratory fish stocks as the Commission may decide and adopt such other conservation and management measures and recommendations as may be necessary to ensure the long-term sustainability of such stocks;

(b) promote cooperation and coordination between members of the Commission to ensure that conservation and management measures for highly migratory fish stocks in areas under national jurisdiction and measures for the same stocks on the high seas are compatible;

(c)   adopt, where necessary, conservation and management measures and recommendations for non-target species and species dependent on or associated with the target stocks, with a view to maintaining or restoring populations of such species above levels at which their reproduction may become seriously threatened;

(d)   adopt standards for collection, verification and for the timely exchange and reporting of data on fisheries for highly migratory fish stocks in the Convention Area in accordance with Annex I of the Agreement, which shall form an integral part of this Convention;

(e)   compile and disseminate accurate and complete statistical data to ensure that the best scientific information is available, while maintaining confidentiality, where appropriate;

(f)   obtain and evaluate scientific advice, review the status of stocks, promote the conduct of relevant scientific research and disseminate the results thereof;

(g)   develop, where necessary, criteria for the allocation of the total allowable catch or the total level of fishing effort for highly migratory fish stocks in the Convention Area;

(h)   adopt generally recommended international minimum standards for the responsible conduct of fishing operations;

(i)   establish appropriate cooperative mechanisms for effective monitoring, control, surveillance and enforcement, including a vessel monitoring system;

(j)   obtain and evaluate economic and other fisheries-related data and information relevant to the work of the Commission;

(k)   agree on means by which the fishing interests of any new member of the Commission may be accommodated;

(l)   adopt its rules of procedure and financial regulations and such other internal administrative regulations as may be necessary to carry out its functions;

(m)   consider and approve the proposed budget of the Commission;

(n)   promote the peaceful settlement of disputes; and

(o)   discuss any question or matter within the competence of the Commission and adopt any measures or recommendations necessary for achieving the objective of this Convention.

2.   In giving effect to paragraph 1, the Commission may adopt measures relating to, *inter alia*:

(a)   the quantity of any species or stocks which may be caught;

(b)   the level of fishing effort;

(c)   limitations of fishing capacity, including measures relating to fishing vessel numbers, types and sizes;

(d)   the areas and periods in which fishing may occur;

(e)   the size of fish of any species which may be taken;

(f)   the fishing gear and technology which may be used; and

(g)   particular subregions or regions.

3.   In developing criteria for allocation of the total allowable catch or the total level of fishing effort the Commission shall take into account, *inter alia*:

(a)   the status of the stocks and the existing level of fishing effort in the fishery;

(b)   the respective interests, past and present fishing patterns and fishing practices of participants in the fishery and the extent of the catch being utilized for domestic consumption;

(c)   the historic catch in an area;

(d)   the needs of small island developing States, and territories and possessions, in the Convention Area whose economies, food supplies and livelihoods are overwhelmingly dependent on the exploitation of marine living resources;

(e)   the respective contributions of participants to conservation and management of the stocks, including the provision by them of accurate data and their contribution to the conduct of scientific research in the Convention Area;

(f)   the record of compliance by the participants with conservation and management measures;

(g)   the needs of coastal communities which are dependent mainly on fishing for the stocks;

(h)   the special circumstances of a State which is surrounded by the exclusive economic zones of other States and has a limited exclusive economic zone of its own;

(i)   the geographical situation of a small island developing State which is made up of non-contiguous groups of islands having a distinct economic and cultural identity of their own but which are separated by areas of high seas;

(j)   the fishing interests and aspirations of coastal States, particularly small island developing States, and territories and possessions, in whose areas of national jurisdiction the stocks also occur.

4. The Commission may adopt decisions relating to the allocation of the total allowable catch or the total level of fishing effort. Such decisions, including decisions relating to the exclusion of vessel types, shall be taken by consensus.

5. The Commission shall take into account the reports and any recommendations of the Scientific Committee and the Technical and Compliance Committee on matters within their respective areas of competence.

6. The Commission shall promptly notify all members of the measures and recommendations decided upon by the Commission and shall give due publicity to the conservation and management measures adopted by it.

Article 11 Subsidiary bodies of the Commission

1. There are hereby established as subsidiary bodies to the Commission a Scientific Committee and a Technical and Compliance Committee to provide advice and recommendations to the Commission on matters within their respective areas of competence.

2. Each member of the Commission shall be entitled to appoint one representative to each Committee who may be accompanied by other experts and advisers. Such representatives shall have appropriate qualifications or relevant experience in the area of competence of the Committee.

3. Each Committee shall meet as often as is required for the efficient exercise of its functions, provided that each Committee shall, in any event, meet prior to the annual meeting of the Commission and shall report to the annual meeting the results of its deliberations.

4. Each Committee shall make every effort to adopt its reports by consensus. If every effort to achieve consensus has failed, the report shall indicate the majority and minority views and may include the differing views of the representatives of the members on all or any part of the report.

5. In the exercise of their functions, each Committee may, where appropriate, consult any other fisheries management, technical or scientific organization with competence in the subject matter of such consultation and may seek expert advice as required on an *ad hoc* basis.

6. The Commission may establish such other subsidiary bodies as it deems necessary for the exercise of its functions, including working groups for the purpose of examining technical issues relating to particular species or stocks and reporting thereon to the Commission.

7. The Commission shall establish a committee to make recommendations on the implementation of such conservation and management measures as may be adopted by the Commission for the area north of the 20° parallel of north latitude and on the formulation of such measures in respect of stocks which occur mostly in this area. The committee shall include the members situated in such area and those fishing in the area. Any member of the Commission not represented on the committee may send a representative to participate in the deliberations of the committee as an observer. Any extraordinary cost incurred for the work of the committee shall be borne by the members of the committee. The committee shall adopt recommendations to the Commission by consensus. In adopting measures in relation to particular stocks and species in such area, the decision of the Commission shall be based on any recommendations of the committee. Such recommendations shall be consistent with the general policies and measures adopted by the Commission in respect of the stocks or species in question and with the principles and measures for conservation and management set out in this Convention. If the Commission, in accordance with the rules of procedure for decision-making on matters of substance, does not accept the recommendation of the committee on any matter, it shall return the matter to the committee for further consideration. The committee shall reconsider the matter in the light of the views expressed by the Commission.

SECTION 2. SCIENTIFIC INFORMATION AND ADVICE

Article 12 Functions of the Scientific Committee

1. The Scientific Committee is established to ensure that the Commission obtains for its consideration the best scientific information available.

2. The functions of the Committee shall be to:

(a) recommend to the Commission a research plan, including specific issues and items to be addressed by the scientific experts or by other organizations or individuals, as appropriate, and identify data needs and coordinate activities that meet those needs;

(b) review the assessments, analyses, other work and recommendations prepared for the Commission by the scientific experts prior to consideration of such recommendations by the Commission and provide information, advice and comments thereon, as necessary;

(c) encourage and promote cooperation in scientific research, taking into account the provisions of article 246 of the 1982 Convention, in order to improve information on highly migratory fish stocks, non-target species, and species belonging to the same ecosystem or associated with or dependent upon such stocks in the Convention Area;

(d) review the results of research and analyses of target stocks or non-target or associated or dependent species in the Convention Area;

(e) report to the Commission its findings or conclusions on the status of target stocks or non-target or associated or dependent species in the Convention Area;

(f) in consultation with the Technical and Compliance Committee, recommend to the Commission the priorities and objectives of the regional observer programme and assess the results of that programme;

(g)　make reports and recommendations to the Commission as directed, or on its own initiative, on matters concerning the conservation and management of and research on target stocks or non-target or associated or dependent species in the Convention Area; and

(h)　perform such other functions and tasks as may be requested by or assigned to it by the Commission.

3.　The Committee shall exercise its functions in accordance with such guidelines and directives as the Commission may adopt.

4.　The representatives of the Oceanic Fisheries Programme of the Pacific Community and the Inter-American Tropical Tuna Commission, or their successor organizations, shall be invited to participate in the work of the Committee. The Committee may also invite other organizations or individuals with scientific expertise in matters related to the work of the Commission to participate in its meetings.

Article 13　Scientific services

1.　The Commission, taking into account any recommendation of the Scientific Committee, may engage the services of scientific experts to provide information and advice on the fishery resources covered by this Convention and related matters that may be relevant to the conservation and management of those resources. The Commission may enter into administrative and financial arrangements to utilize scientific services for this purpose. In this regard, and in order to carry out its functions in a cost-effective manner, the Commission shall, to the greatest extent possible, utilize the services of existing regional organizations and shall consult, as appropriate, with any other fisheries management, technical or scientific organization with expertise in matters related to the work of the Commission.

2.　The scientific experts may, as directed by the Commission:

(a)　conduct scientific research and analyses in support of the work of the Commission;

(b)　develop and recommend to the Commission and the Scientific Committee stock-specific reference points for the species of principal interest to the Commission;

(c)　assess the status of stocks against the reference points established by the Commission;

(d)　provide the Commission and the Scientific Committee with reports on the results of their scientific work, advice and recommendations in support of the formulation of conservation and management measures and other relevant matters; and

(e)　perform such other functions and tasks as may be required.

3.　In carrying out their work, the scientific experts may:

(a)　undertake the collection, compilation and dissemination of fisheries data according to agreed principles and procedures established by the Commission, including procedures and policies relating to the confidentiality, disclosure and publication of data;

(b)　conduct assessments of highly migratory fish stocks, non-target species, and species belonging to the same ecosystem or associated with or dependent upon such stocks, within the Convention Area;

(c)　assess the impacts of fishing, other human activities and environmental factors on target stocks and species belonging to the same ecosystem or dependent upon or associated with the target stocks;

(d)　assess the potential effects of proposed changes in the methods or levels of fishing and of proposed conservation and management measures; and

(e)   investigate such other scientific matters as may be referred to them by the Commission.

4.   The Commission may make appropriate arrangements for periodic peer review of scientific information and advice provided to the Commission by the scientific experts.

5.   The reports and recommendations of the scientific experts shall be provided to the Scientific Committee and to the Commission.

SECTION 3.   THE TECHNICAL AND COMPLIANCE COMMITTEE

Article 14   Functions of the Technical and Compliance Committee

1.   The functions of the Technical and Compliance Committee shall be to:

(a)   provide the Commission with information, technical advice and recommendations relating to the implementation of, and compliance with, conservation and management measures;

(b)   monitor and review compliance with conservation and management measures adopted by the Commission and make such recommendations to the Commission as may be necessary; and

(c)   review the implementation of cooperative measures for monitoring, control, surveillance and enforcement adopted by the Commission and make such recommendations to the Commission as may be necessary.

2.   In carrying out its functions, the Committee shall:

(a)   provide a forum for exchange of information concerning the means by which they are applying the conservation and management measures adopted by the Commission on the high seas and complementary measures in waters under national jurisdiction;

(b)   receive reports from each member of the Commission relating to measures taken to monitor, investigate and penalize violations of provisions of this Convention and measures adopted pursuant thereto;

(c)   in consultation with the Scientific Committee, recommend to the Commission the priorities and objectives of the regional observer programme, when established, and assess the results of that programme;

(d)   consider and investigate such other matters as may be referred to it by the Commission, including developing and reviewing measures to provide for the verification and validation of fisheries data;

(e)   make recommendations to the Commission on technical matters such as fishing vessel and gear markings;

(f)   in consultation with the Scientific Committee, make recommendations to the Commission on the fishing gear and technology which may be used;

(g)   report to the Commission its findings or conclusions on the extent of compliance with conservation and management measures; and

(h)   make recommendations to the Commission on matters relating to monitoring, control, surveillance and enforcement.

3.   The Committee may establish, with the approval of the Commission, such subsidiary bodies as may be necessary for the performance of its functions.

4.   The Committee shall exercise its functions in accordance with such guidelines and directives as the Commission may adopt.

SECTION 4. THE SECRETARIAT

Article 15 The Secretariat

1. The Commission may establish a permanent Secretariat consisting of an Executive Director and such other staff as the Commission may require.

2. The Executive Director shall be appointed for a term of four years and may be re-appointed for a further term of four years.

3. The Executive Director shall be the chief administrative officer of the Commission, and shall act in that capacity in all the meetings of the Commission and of any subsidiary body, and shall perform such other administrative functions as are entrusted to the Executive Director by the Commission.

4. The Secretariat functions shall include the following:

   (a)   receiving and transmitting the Commission's official communications;

   (b)   facilitating the compilation and dissemination of data necessary to accomplish the objective of this Convention;

   (c)   preparing administrative and other reports for the Commission and the Scientific and Technical and Compliance Committees;

   (d)   administering agreed arrangements for monitoring, control and surveillance and the provision of scientific advice;

   (e)   publishing the decisions of and promoting the activities of the Commission and its subsidiary bodies; and

   (f)   treasury, personnel and other administrative functions.

5. In order to minimize costs to the members of the Commission, the Secretariat to be established under this Convention shall be cost effective. The setting up and the functioning of the Secretariat shall, where appropriate, take into account the capacity of existing regional institutions to perform certain technical secretariat functions.

Article 16 The staff of the Commission

1. The staff of the Commission shall consist of such qualified scientific and technical and other personnel as may be required to fulfil the functions of the Commission. The staff shall be appointed by the Executive Director.

2. The paramount consideration in the recruitment and employment of the staff shall be the necessity of securing the highest standards of efficiency, competence and integrity. Subject to this consideration, due regard shall be paid to the importance of recruiting the staff on an equitable basis between the members of the Commission with a view to ensuring a broad-based Secretariat.

SECTION 5. FINANCIAL ARRANGEMENTS OF THE COMMISSION

Article 17 Funds of the Commission

1. The funds of the Commission shall include:

   (a)   assessed contributions in accordance with article 18, paragraph 2;

   (b)   voluntary contributions;

   (c)   the fund referred to in article 30, paragraph 3; and

   (d)   any other funds which the Commission may receive.

2. The Commission shall adopt, and amend as required, by consensus, financial regulations for the administration of the Commission and for the exercise of its functions.

Article 18 Budget of the Commission

1. The Executive Director shall draft the proposed budget of the Commission and submit it to the Commission. The proposed budget shall indicate which of the administrative expenses of the Commission are to be financed from the assessed contributions referred to in article 17, paragraph 1 (a), and which such expenses are to be financed from funds received pursuant to article 17, paragraphs 1 (b), (c) and (d). The Commission shall adopt the budget by consensus. If the Commission is unable to adopt a decision on the budget, the level of contributions to the administrative budget of the Commission shall be determined in accordance with the budget for the preceding year for the purposes of meeting the administrative expenses of the Commission for the following year until such time as a new budget can be adopted by consensus.

2. The amount of the contribution to the budget shall be determined in accordance with a scheme which the Commission shall adopt, and amend as required, by consensus. In adopting the scheme, due consideration shall be given to each member being assessed an equal basic fee, a fee based upon national wealth, reflecting the state of development of the member concerned and its ability to pay, and a variable fee. The variable fee shall be based, *inter alia*, on the total catch taken within exclusive economic zones and in areas beyond national jurisdiction in the Convention Area of such species as may be specified by the Commission, provided that a discount factor shall be applied to the catch taken in the exclusive economic zone of a member of the Commission which is a developing State or territory by vessels flying the flag of that member. The scheme adopted by the Commission shall be set out in the financial regulations of the Commission.

3. If a contributor is in arrears in the payment of its financial contributions to the Commission it shall not participate in the taking of decisions by the Commission if the amount of its arrears equals or exceeds the amount of the contributions due from it for the preceding two full years. Interest shall be payable on such unpaid contributions at such rate as may be determined by the Commission in its financial regulations. The Commission may, nevertheless, waive such interest payments and permit such a member to vote if it is satisfied that the failure to pay is due to conditions beyond the control of the member.

Article 19 Annual audit

The records, books and accounts of the Commission, including its annual financial statement, shall be audited annually by an independent auditor appointed by the Commission.

SECTION 6. DECISION-MAKING

Article 20 Decision-making

1. As a general rule, decision-making in the Commission shall be by consensus. For the purposes of this article, 'consensus' means the absence of any formal objection made at the time the decision was taken.

2. Except where this Convention expressly provides that a decision shall be made by consensus, if all efforts to reach a decision by consensus have been exhausted, decisions by voting on questions of procedure shall be taken by a majority of those present and voting. Decisions on questions of substance shall be taken by a three-fourths majority of those present and voting provided that such majority includes a three-fourths majority of the members of the South Pacific Forum Fisheries Agency present and voting and a three-fourths majority of non-members of the South Pacific Forum Fisheries Agency present and voting and provided further that in no circumstances shall a proposal be defeated by two or fewer votes in either chamber. When the issue arises as to whether a question is

one of substance or not, that question shall be treated as one of substance unless otherwise decided by the Commission by consensus or by the majority required for decisions on questions of substance.

3. If it appears to the Chairman that all efforts to reach a decision by consensus have been exhausted, the Chairman shall fix a time during that session of the Commission for taking the decision by a vote. At the request of any representative, the Commission may, by a majority of those present and voting, defer the taking of a decision until such time during the same session as the Commission may decide. At that time, the Commission shall take a vote on the deferred question. This rule may be applied only once to any question.

4. Where this Convention expressly provides that a decision on a proposal shall be taken by consensus and the Chairman determines that there would be an objection to such proposal, the Commission may appoint a conciliator for the purpose of reconciling the differences in order to achieve consensus on the matter.

5. Subject to paragraphs 6 and 7, a decision adopted by the Commission shall become binding 60 days after the date of its adoption.

6. A member which has voted against a decision or which was absent during the meeting at which the decision was made may, within 30 days of the adoption of the decision by the Commission, seek a review of the decision by a review panel constituted in accordance with the procedures set out in Annex II to this Convention on the grounds that:

(a) the decision is inconsistent with the provisions of this Convention, the Agreement or the 1982 Convention; or

(b) the decision unjustifiably discriminates in form or in fact against the member concerned.

7. Pending the findings and recommendations of the review panel and any action required by the Commission, no member of the Commission shall be required to give effect to the decision in question.

8. If the review panel finds that the decision of the Commission need not be modified, amended or revoked, the decision shall become binding 30 days from the date of communication by the Executive Director of the findings and recommendations of the review panel.

9. If the review panel recommends to the Commission that the decision be modified, amended or revoked, the Commission shall, at its next annual meeting, modify or amend its decision in order to conform with the findings and recommendations of the review panel or it may decide to revoke the decision, provided that, if so requested in writing by a majority of the members, a special meeting of the Commission shall be convened within 60 days of the date of communication of the findings and recommendations of the review panel.

SECTION 7. TRANSPARENCY AND COOPERATION WITH OTHER ORGANIZATIONS

Article 21 Transparency

The Commission shall promote transparency in its decision-making processes and other activities. Representatives from intergovernmental organizations and non-governmental organizations concerned with matters relevant to the implementation of this Convention shall be afforded the opportunity to participate in the meetings of the Commission and its subsidiary bodies as observers or otherwise as appropriate. The rules of procedure of the Commission shall provide for such participation. The procedures shall not be unduly restrictive in this respect. Such intergovernmental organizations and non-governmental organizations shall be given timely access to pertinent information subject to the rules and procedures which the Commission may adopt.

Article 22   Cooperation with other organizations

1.   The Commission shall cooperate, as appropriate, with the Food and Agriculture Organization of the United Nations and with other specialized agencies and bodies of the United Nations on matters of mutual interest.

2.   The Commission shall make suitable arrangements for consultation, cooperation and collaboration with other relevant intergovernmental organizations, particularly those which have related objectives and which can contribute to the attainment of the objective of this Convention, such as the Commission for the Conservation of Antarctic Marine Living Resources, the Commission for the Conservation of Southern Bluefin Tuna, the Indian Ocean Tuna Commission and the Inter-American Tropical Tuna Commission.

3.   Where the Convention Area overlaps with an area under regulation by another fisheries management organization, the Commission shall cooperate with such other organization in order to avoid the duplication of measures in respect of species in that area which are regulated by both organizations.

4.   The Commission shall cooperate with the Inter-American Tropical Tuna Commission to ensure that the objective set out in article 2 of this Convention is reached. To that end, the Commission shall initiate consultation with the Inter-American Tropical Tuna Commission with a view to reaching agreement on a consistent set of conservation and management measures, including measures relating to monitoring, control and surveillance, for fish stocks that occur in the Convention Areas of both organizations.

5.   The Commission may enter into relationship agreements with the organizations referred to in this article and with other organizations as may be appropriate, such as the Pacific Community and the South Pacific Forum Fisheries Agency, with a view to obtaining the best available scientific and other fisheries-related information to further the attainment of the objective of this Convention and to minimize duplication with respect to their work.

6.   Any organization with which the Commission has entered into an arrangement or agreement under paragraphs 1, 2 and 5 may designate representatives to attend meetings of the Commission as observers in accordance with the rules of procedure of the Commission. Procedures shall be established for obtaining the views of such organizations in appropriate cases.

PART IV
OBLIGATIONS OF MEMBERS OF THE COMMISSION

Article 23   Obligations of members of the Commission

1.   Each member of the Commission shall promptly implement the provisions of this Convention and any conservation, management and other measures or matters which may be agreed pursuant to this Convention from time to time and shall cooperate in furthering the objective of this Convention.

2.   Each member of the Commission shall:

(a)   provide annually to the Commission statistical, biological and other data and information in accordance with Annex I of the Agreement and, in addition, such data and information as the Commission may require;

(b)   provide to the Commission in the manner and at such intervals as may be required by the Commission, information concerning its fishing activities in the Convention Area, including fishing areas and fishing vessels in order to facilitate the compilation of reliable catch and effort statistics; and

(c) provide to the Commission at such intervals as may be required information on steps taken to implement the conservation and management measures adopted by the Commission.

3. The members of the Commission shall keep the Commission informed of the measures they have adopted for the conservation and management of highly migratory fish stocks in areas within the Convention Area under their national jurisdiction. The Commission shall circulate periodically such information to all members.

4. Each member of the Commission shall keep the Commission informed of the measures it has adopted for regulating the activities of fishing vessels flying its flag which fish in the Convention Area. The Commission shall circulate periodically such information to all members.

5. Each member of the Commission shall, to the greatest extent possible, take measures to ensure that its nationals, and fishing vessels owned or controlled by its nationals fishing in the Convention Area, comply with the provisions of this Convention. To this end, members of the Commission may enter into agreements with States whose flags such vessels are flying to facilitate such enforcement. Each member of the Commission shall, to the greatest extent possible, at the request of any other member, and when provided with the relevant information, investigate any alleged violation by its nationals, or fishing vessels owned or controlled by its nationals, of the provisions of this Convention or any conservation and management measure adopted by the Commission. A report on the progress of the investigation, including details of any action taken or proposed to be taken in relation to the alleged violation, shall be provided to the member making the request and to the Commission as soon as practicable and in any case within two months of such request and a report on the outcome of the investigation shall be provided when the investigation is completed.

PART V
DUTIES OF THE FLAG STATE

Article 24 Flag State duties

1. Each member of the Commission shall take such measures as may be necessary to ensure that:

(a) fishing vessels flying its flag comply with the provisions of this Convention and the conservation and management measures adopted pursuant hereto and that such vessels do not engage in any activity which undermine the effectiveness of such measures; and

(b) fishing vessels flying its flag do not conduct unauthorized fishing within areas under the national jurisdiction of any Contracting Party.

2. No member of the Commission shall allow any fishing vessel entitled to fly its flag to be used for fishing for highly migratory fish stocks in the Convention Area beyond areas of national jurisdiction unless it has been authorized to do so by the appropriate authority or authorities of that member. A member of the Commission shall authorize the use of vessels flying its flag for fishing in the Convention Area beyond areas of national jurisdiction only where it is able to exercise effectively its responsibilities in respect of such vessels under the 1982 Convention, the Agreement and this Convention.

3. It shall be a condition of every authorization issued by a member of the Commission that the fishing vessel in respect of which the authorization is issued:

(a) conducts fishing within areas under the national jurisdiction of other States only where the fishing vessel holds any licence, permit or authorization that may be required by such other State; and

(b)   is operated on the high seas in the Convention Area in accordance with the requirements of Annex III, the requirements of which shall also be established as a general obligation of all vessels operating pursuant to this Convention.

4.   Each member of the Commission shall, for the purposes of effective implementation of this Convention, maintain a record of fishing vessels entitled to fly its flag and authorized to be used for fishing in the Convention Area beyond its area of national jurisdiction, and shall ensure that all such fishing vessels are entered in that record.

5.   Each member of the Commission shall provide annually to the Commission, in accordance with such procedures as may be agreed by the Commission, the information set out in Annex IV to this Convention with respect to each fishing vessel entered in the record required to be maintained under paragraph 4 and shall promptly notify the Commission of any modifications to such information.

6.   Each member of the Commission shall also promptly inform the Commission of:

(a)   any additions to the record;

(b)   any deletions from the record by reason of:

(i)   the voluntary relinquishment or non-renewal of the fishing authorization by the fishing vessel owner or operator;

(ii)   the withdrawal of the fishing authorization issued in respect of the fishing vessel under paragraph 2;

(iii)   the fact that the fishing vessel concerned is no longer entitled to fly its flag;

(iv)   the scrapping, decommissioning or loss of the fishing vessel concerned; and

(v)   any other reason, specifying which of the reasons listed above is applicable.

7.   The Commission shall maintain its own record, based on the information provided to it pursuant to paragraphs 5 and 6, of fishing vessels referred to in paragraph 4. The Commission shall circulate periodically the information contained in such record to all members of the Commission, and, on request, individually to any member.

8.   Each member of the Commission shall require its fishing vessels that fish for highly migratory fish stocks on the high seas in the Convention Area to use near real-time satellite position-fixing transmitters while in such areas. The standards, specifications and procedures for the use of such transmitters shall be established by the Commission, which shall operate a vessel monitoring system for all vessels that fish for highly migratory fish stocks on the high seas in the Convention Area. In establishing such standards, specifications and procedures, the Commission shall take into account the characteristics of traditional fishing vessels from developing States. The Commission, directly, and simultaneously with the flag State where the flag State so requires, or through such other organization designated by the Commission, shall receive information from the vessel monitoring system in accordance with the procedures adopted by the Commission. The procedures adopted by the Commission shall include appropriate measures to protect the confidentiality of information received through the vessel monitoring system. Any member of the Commission may request that waters under its national jurisdiction be included within the area covered by such vessel monitoring system.

9.   Each member of the Commission shall require its fishing vessels that fish in the Convention Area in areas under the national jurisdiction of another member to operate near real-time satellite position-fixing transmitters in accordance with the standards, specification and procedures to be determined by the coastal State.

10.   The members of the Commission shall cooperate to ensure compatibility between national and high seas vessel monitoring systems.

PART VI
COMPLIANCE AND ENFORCEMENT

Article 25 Compliance and enforcement

1. Each member of the Commission shall enforce the provisions of this Convention and any conservation and management measures issued by the Commission.

2. Each member of the Commission shall, at the request of any other member, and when provided with the relevant information, investigate fully any alleged violation by fishing vessels flying its flag of the provisions of this Convention or any conservation and management measure adopted by the Commission. A report on the progress of the investigation, including details of any action taken or proposed to be taken in relation to the alleged violation, shall be provided to the member making the request and to the Commission as soon as practicable and in any case within two months of such request and a report on the outcome of the investigation shall be provided when the investigation is completed.

3. Each member of the Commission shall, if satisfied that sufficient evidence is available in respect of an alleged violation by a fishing vessel flying its flag, refer the case to its authorities with a view to instituting proceedings without delay in accordance with its laws and, where appropriate, detain the vessel concerned.

4. Each member of the Commission shall ensure that, where it has been established, in accordance with its laws, that a fishing vessel flying its flag has been involved in the commission of a serious violation of the provisions of this Convention or of any conservation and management measures adopted by the Commission, the vessel concerned ceases fishing activities and does not engage in such activities in the Convention Area until such time as all outstanding sanctions imposed by the flag State in respect of the violation have been complied with. Where the vessel concerned has conducted unauthorized fishing within areas under the national jurisdiction of any coastal State Party to this Convention, the flag State shall, in accordance with its laws, ensure that the vessel complies promptly with any sanctions which may be imposed by such coastal State in accordance with its national laws and regulations or shall impose appropriate sanctions in accordance with paragraph 7. For the purposes of this article, a serious violation shall include any of the violations specified in article 21, paragraphs 11 (a) to (h) of the Agreement and such other violations as may be determined by the Commission.

5. Each member of the Commission shall, to the extent permitted by its national laws and regulations, establish arrangements for making available to prosecuting authorities of other members evidence relating to alleged violations.

6. Where there are reasonable grounds for believing that a fishing vessel on the high seas has engaged in unauthorized fishing within an area under the national jurisdiction of a member of the Commission, the flag State of that vessel, at the request of the member concerned, shall immediately and fully investigate the matter. The flag State shall cooperate with the member concerned in taking appropriate enforcement action in such cases and may authorize the relevant authorities of such member to board and inspect the vessel on the high seas. This paragraph is without prejudice to article 111 of the 1982 Convention.

7. All investigations and judicial proceedings shall be carried out expeditiously. Sanctions applicable in respect of violations shall be adequate in severity to be effective in securing compliance and to discourage violations wherever they occur and shall deprive offenders of the benefits accruing from their illegal activities. Measures applicable in respect of masters and other officers of fishing vessels shall include provisions which may permit, *inter alia*, refusal, withdrawal or suspension of authorizations to serve as masters or officers on such vessels.

8. Each member shall transmit to the Commission an annual statement of compliance measures, including imposition of sanctions for any violations, it has taken in accordance with this article.

9. The provisions of this article are without prejudice to:

(a)   the rights of any of the members of the Commission in accordance with their national laws and regulations relating to fisheries, including the right to impose appropriate sanctions on the vessel concerned in respect of violations occurring within areas under national jurisdiction in accordance with such national laws and regulations; and

(b)   the rights of any of the members of the Commission in relation to any provision relating to compliance and enforcement contained in any relevant bilateral or multilateral fisheries access agreement not inconsistent with the provisions of this Convention, the Agreement or the 1982 Convention.

10. Each member of the Commission, where it has reasonable grounds for believing that a fishing vessel flying the flag of another State has engaged in any activity that undermines the effectiveness of conservation and management measures adopted for the Convention Area, shall draw this to the attention of the flag State concerned and may, as appropriate, draw the matter to the attention of the Commission. To the extent permitted by its national laws and regulations it shall provide the flag State with full supporting evidence and may provide the Commission with a summary of such evidence. The Commission shall not circulate such information until such time as the flag State has had an opportunity to comment, within a reasonable time, on the allegation and evidence submitted, or to object as the case may be.

11. The members of the Commission may take action in accordance with the Agreement and international law, including through procedures adopted by the Commission for this purpose, to deter fishing vessels which have engaged in activities which undermine the effectiveness of or otherwise violate the conservation and management measures adopted by the Commission from fishing in the Convention Area until such time as appropriate action is taken by the flag State.

12. The Commission, when necessary, shall develop procedures which allow for non-discriminatory trade measures to be taken, consistent with the international obligations of the members of the Commission, on any species regulated by the Commission, against any State or entity whose fishing vessels fish in a manner which undermines the effectiveness of the conservation and management measures adopted by the Commission.

Article 26 Boarding and inspection

1. For the purposes of ensuring compliance with conservation and management measures, the Commission shall establish procedures for boarding and inspection of fishing vessels on the high seas in the Convention Area. All vessels used for boarding and inspection of fishing vessels on the high seas in the Convention Area shall be clearly marked and identifiable as being on government service and authorized to undertake high seas boarding and inspection in accordance with this Convention.

2. If, within two years of the entry into force of this Convention, the Commission is not able to agree on such procedures, or on an alternative mechanism which effectively discharges the obligations of the members of the Commission under the Agreement and this Convention to ensure compliance with the conservation and management measures established by the Commission, articles 21 and 22 of the Agreement shall be applied, subject to paragraph 3, as if they were part of this Convention and boarding and inspection of fishing vessels in the Convention Area, as well as any subsequent enforcement action, shall be conducted in accordance with the procedures set out therein and such additional

practical procedures as the Commission may decide are necessary for the implementation of articles 21 and 22 of the Agreement.

3. Each member of the Commission shall ensure that fishing vessels flying its flag accept boarding by duly authorized inspectors in accordance with such procedures. Such duly authorized inspectors shall comply with the procedures for boarding and inspection.

Article 27 Measures taken by a port State

1. A port State has the right and the duty to take measures, in accordance with international law, to promote the effectiveness of subregional, regional and global conservation and management measures. When taking such measures a port State shall not discriminate in form or in fact against the fishing vessels of any State.

2. Whenever a fishing vessel of a member of the Commission voluntarily enters a port or offshore terminal of another member, the port State may, *inter alia*, inspect documents, fishing gear and catch on board such fishing vessel.

3. Members of the Commission may adopt regulations empowering the relevant national authorities to prohibit landings and transhipments where it has been established that the catch has been taken in a manner which undermines the effectiveness of conservation and management measures adopted by the Commission.

4. Nothing in this article affects the exercise by Contracting Parties of their sovereignty over ports in their territory in accordance with international law.

PART VII
REGIONAL OBSERVER PROGRAMME AND REGULATION OF TRANSHIPMENT

Article 28 Regional observer programme

1. The Commission shall develop a regional observer programme to collect verified catch data, other scientific data and additional information related to the fishery from the Convention Area and to monitor the implementation of the conservation and management measures adopted by the Commission.

2. The observer programme shall be coordinated by the Secretariat of the Commission, and shall be organized in a flexible manner which takes into account the nature of the fishery and other relevant factors. In this regard, the Commission may enter into contracts for the provision of the regional observer programme.

3. The regional observer programme shall consist of independent and impartial observers authorized by the Secretariat of the Commission. The programme should be coordinated, to the maximum extent possible, with other regional, subregional and national observer programmes.

4. Each member of the Commission shall ensure that fishing vessels flying its flag in the Convention Area, except for vessels that operate exclusively within waters under the national jurisdiction of the flag State, are prepared to accept an observer from the regional observer programme, if required by the Commission.

5. The provisions of paragraph 4 shall apply to vessels fishing exclusively on the high seas in the Convention Area, vessels fishing on the high seas and in waters under the jurisdiction of one or more coastal States, and vessels fishing in waters under the jurisdiction of two or more coastal States. When a vessel is operating on the same fishing trip both in waters under the national jurisdiction of its flag State and in the adjacent high seas, an observer placed under the regional observer programme shall not undertake any of the activities specified in paragraph 6 (e) when the vessel is in waters under the national jurisdiction of its flag State, unless the flag State of the vessel agrees otherwise.

6. The regional observer programme shall operate in accordance with the following guidelines and under the conditions set out in article 3 of Annex III of this Convention:

(a)   the programme shall provide a sufficient level of coverage to ensure that the Commission receives appropriate data and information on catch levels and related matters within the Convention Area, taking into account the characteristics of the fisheries;

(b)   each member of the Commission shall be entitled to have its nationals included in the programme as observers;

(c)   observers shall be trained and certified in accordance with uniform procedures to be approved by the Commission;

(d)   observers shall not unduly interfere with the lawful operations of the vessel and, in carrying out their functions, they shall give due consideration to the operational requirements of the vessel and shall communicate regularly with the captain or master for this purpose;

(e)   the activities of observers shall include collecting catch data and other scientific data, monitoring the implementation of conservation and management measures adopted by the Commission and reporting of their findings in accordance with procedures to be developed by the Commission;

(f)   the programme shall be cost effective, shall avoid duplication with existing regional, subregional and national observer programmes, and shall, to the extent practicable, seek to minimize disruption to the operations of vessels fishing in the Convention Area;

(g)   a reasonable period of notice of the placement of an observer shall be given.

7. The Commission shall develop further procedures and guidelines for the operation of the regional observer programme, including:

(a)   to ensure the security of non-aggregated data and other information which the Commission deems to be of a confidential nature;

(b)   for the dissemination of data and information collected by observers to the members of the Commission;

(c)   for boarding of observers which clearly define the rights and responsibilities of the captain or master of the vessel and the crew when an observer is on board a vessel, as well as the rights and responsibilities of observers in the performance of their duties.

8. The Commission shall determine the manner in which the costs of the observer programme would be defrayed.

Article 29 Transhipment

1. In order to support efforts to ensure accurate reporting of catches, the members of the Commission shall encourage their fishing vessels, to the extent practicable, to conduct transhipment in port. A member may designate one or more of its ports as transhipment ports for the purposes of this Convention, and the Commission shall circulate periodically to all members a list of such designated ports.

2. Transhipment at a port or in an area within waters under the national jurisdiction of a member of the Commission shall take place in accordance with applicable national laws.

3. The Commission shall develop procedures to obtain and verify data on the quantity and species transhipped both in port and at sea in the Convention Area and procedures to determine when transhipment covered by this Convention has been completed.

4. Transhipment at sea in the Convention Area beyond areas under national jurisdiction shall take place only in accordance with the terms and conditions set out

in article 4 of Annex III to this Convention, and any procedures established by the Commission pursuant to paragraph 3 of this article. Such procedures shall take into account the characteristics of the fishery concerned.

5. Notwithstanding paragraph 4 above, and subject to specific exemptions which the Commission adopts in order to reflect existing operations, transhipment at sea by purse-seine vessels operating within the Convention Area shall be prohibited.

PART VIII
REQUIREMENTS OF DEVELOPING STATES

Article 30 Recognition of the special requirements of developing States

1. The Commission shall give full recognition to the special requirements of developing States Parties to this Convention, in particular small island developing States, and of territories and possessions, in relation to conservation and management of highly migratory fish stocks in the Convention Area and development of fisheries for such stocks.

2. In giving effect to the duty to cooperate in the establishment of conservation and management measures for highly migratory fish stocks, the Commission shall take into account the special requirements of developing States Parties, in particular small island developing States, and of territories and possessions, in particular:

(a) the vulnerability of developing States Parties, in particular small island developing States, which are dependent on the exploitation of marine living resources, including for meeting the nutritional requirements of their populations or parts thereof;

(b) the need to avoid adverse impacts on, and ensure access to fisheries by, subsistence, small-scale and artisanal fishers and fishworkers, as well as indigenous people in developing States Parties, particularly small island developing States Parties, and territories and possessions; and

(c) the need to ensure that such measures do not result in transferring, directly or indirectly, a disproportionate burden of conservation action onto developing States Parties, and territories and possessions.

3. The Commission shall establish a fund to facilitate the effective participation of developing States Parties, particularly small island developing States, and, where appropriate, territories and possessions, in the work of the Commission, including its meetings and those of its subsidiary bodies. The financial regulations of the Commission shall include guidelines for the administration of the fund and criteria for eligibility for assistance.

4. Cooperation with developing States, and territories and possessions, for the purposes set out in this article may include the provision of financial assistance, assistance relating to human resources development, technical assistance, transfer of technology, including through joint venture arrangements, and advisory and consultative services. Such assistance shall, *inter alia*, be directed towards:

(a) improved conservation and management of highly migratory fish stocks through collection, reporting, verification, exchange and analysis of fisheries data and related information;

(b) stock assessment and scientific research; and

(c) monitoring, control, surveillance, compliance and enforcement, including training and capacity-building at the local level, development and funding of national and regional observer programmes and access to technology and equipment.

PART IX
PEACEFUL SETTLEMENT OF DISPUTES

Article 31 Procedures for the settlement of disputes

The provisions relating to the settlement of disputes set out in Part VIII of the Agreement apply, *mutatis mutandis*, to any dispute between members of the Commission, whether or not they are also Parties to the Agreement.

PART X
NON-PARTIES TO THIS CONVENTION

Article 32 Non-parties to this Convention

1. Each member of the Commission shall take measures consistent with this Convention, the Agreement and international law to deter the activities of vessels flying the flags of non-parties to this Convention which undermine the effectiveness of conservation and management measures adopted by the Commission.

2. The members of the Commission shall exchange information on the activities of fishing vessels flying the flags of non-parties to this Convention which are engaged in fishing operations in the Convention Area.

3. The Commission shall draw the attention of any State which is not a Party to this Convention to any activity undertaken by its nationals or vessels flying its flag which, in the opinion of the Commission, affects the implementation of the objective of this Convention.

4. The members of the Commission shall, individually or jointly, request non-parties to this Convention whose vessels fish in the Convention Area to cooperate fully in the implementation of conservation and management measures adopted by the Commission with a view to ensuring that such measures are applied to all fishing activities in the Convention Area. Such cooperating non-parties to this Convention shall enjoy benefits from participation in the fishery commensurate with their commitment to comply with, and their record of compliance with, conservation and management measures in respect of the relevant stocks.

5. Non-parties to this Convention, may, upon request and subject to the concurrence of the members of the Commission and to the rules of procedure relating to the granting of observer status, be invited to attend meetings of the Commission as observers.

PART XI
GOOD FAITH AND ABUSE OF RIGHTS

Article 33 Good faith and abuse of rights

The obligations assumed under this Convention shall be fulfilled in good faith and the rights recognized in this Convention shall be exercised in a manner which would not constitute an abuse of right.

PART XII
FINAL PROVISIONS

Article 34 Signature, ratification, acceptance, approval

1. This Convention shall be open for signature by Australia, Canada, China, Cook Islands, Federated States of Micronesia, Fiji Islands, France, Indonesia, Japan, Republic of Kiribati, Republic of the Marshall Islands, Republic of Nauru, New Zealand, Niue,

Republic of Palau, Independent State of Papua New Guinea, Republic of the Philippines, Republic of Korea, Independent State of Samoa, Solomon Islands, Kingdom of Tonga, Tuvalu, United Kingdom of Great Britain and Northern Ireland in respect of Pitcairn, Henderson, Ducie and Oeno Islands, United States of America and Republic of Vanuatu and shall remain open for signature for twelve months from the fifth day of September 2000.

2. This Convention is subject to ratification, acceptance or approval by the signatories.

3. Instruments of ratification, acceptance or approval shall be deposited with the depositary.

4. Each Contracting Party shall be a member of the Commission established by this Convention.

Article 35 Accession

1. This Convention shall remain open for accession by the States referred to in article 34, paragraph 1, and by any entity referred to in article 305, paragraph 1, subparagraphs (c), (d) and (e) of the 1982 Convention which is situated in the Convention Area.

2. After the entry into force of this Convention, the Contracting Parties may, by consensus, invite other States and regional economic integration organizations, whose nationals and fishing vessels wish to conduct fishing for highly migratory fish stocks in the Convention Area to accede to this Convention.

3. Instruments of accession shall be deposited with the depositary.

Article 36 Entry into force

1. This Convention shall enter into force 30 days after the deposit of instruments of ratification, acceptance, approval or accession by:
   (a) three States situated north of the 20° parallel of north latitude; and
   (b) seven States situated south of the 20° parallel of north latitude.

2. If, within three years of its adoption, this Convention has not been ratified by three of the States referred to in paragraph 1 (a), this Convention shall enter into force six months after the deposit of the thirteenth instrument of ratification, acceptance, approval or accession or in accordance with paragraph 1, whichever is the earlier.

3. For each State, entity referred to in article 305, paragraph 1, subparagraphs (c), (d) and (e) of the 1982 Convention which is situated in the Convention Area, or regional economic integration organization which ratifies, formally confirms, accepts or approves the Convention or accedes thereto after the entry into force of this Convention, this Convention shall enter into force on the thirtieth day following the deposit of its instrument of ratification, formal confirmation, acceptance, approval or accession.

Article 37 Reservations and exceptions

No reservations or exceptions may be made to this Convention.

Article 38 Declarations and statements

Article 37 does not preclude a State, entity referred to in article 305, paragraph 1, subparagraphs (c), (d) and (e) of the 1982 Convention which is situated in the Convention Area, or regional economic integration organization, when signing, ratifying or acceding to this Convention, from making declarations or statements, however phrased or named, with a view, *inter alia*, to the harmonization of its laws and regulations with the provisions of this Convention, provided that such declarations or statements do not purport to exclude or to modify the legal effect of the provisions of this Convention in their application to that State, entity or regional economic integration organization.

Article 39 Relation to other agreements

This Convention shall not alter the rights and obligations of Contracting Parties, and fishing entities referred to in article 9, paragraph 2, which arise from other agreements compatible with this Convention and which do not affect the enjoyment by other Contracting Parties of their rights or the performance of their obligations under this Convention.

Article 40 Amendment

1. Any member of the Commission may propose amendments to this Convention to be considered by the Commission. Any such proposal shall be made by written communication addressed to the Executive Director at least 60 days before the meeting of the Commission at which it is to be considered. The Executive Director shall promptly circulate such communication to all members of the Commission.

2. Amendments to this Convention shall be considered at the annual meeting of the Commission unless a majority of the members request a special meeting to consider the proposed amendment. A special meeting may be convened on not less than 60 days notice. Amendments to this Convention shall be adopted by consensus. The text of any amendment adopted by the Commission shall be transmitted promptly by the Executive Director to all members of the Commission.

3. Amendments to this Convention shall enter into force for the Contracting Parties ratifying or acceding to them on the thirtieth day following the deposit of instruments of ratification or accession by a majority of Contracting Parties. Thereafter, for each Contracting Party ratifying or acceding to an amendment after the deposit of the required number of such instruments, the amendment shall enter into force on the thirtieth day following the deposit of its instrument of ratification or accession.

Article 41 Annexes

1. The Annexes form an integral part of this Convention and, unless expressly provided otherwise, a reference to this Convention or to one of its Parts includes a reference to the Annexes relating thereto.

2. The Annexes to this Convention may be revised from time to time and any member of the Commission may propose revisions to an Annex. Notwithstanding the provisions of article 40, if a revision to an Annex is adopted by consensus at a meeting of the Commission, it shall be incorporated in this Convention and shall take effect from the date of its adoption or from such other date as may be specified in the revision.

Article 42 Withdrawal

1. A Contracting Party may, by written notification addressed to the depositary, withdraw from this Convention and may indicate its reasons. Failure to indicate reasons shall not affect the validity of the withdrawal. The withdrawal shall take effect one year after the date of receipt of the notification, unless the notification specifies a later date.

2. Withdrawal from this Convention by a Contracting Party shall not affect the financial obligations of such member incurred prior to its withdrawal becoming effective.

3. Withdrawal from this Convention by a Contracting Party shall not in any way affect the duty of such member to fulfil any obligation embodied in this Convention to which it would be subject under international law independently of this Convention.

Article 43 Participation by territories

1. The Commission and its subsidiary bodies shall be open to participation, with the appropriate authorization of the Contracting Party having responsibility for its international affairs, to each of the following:

- American Samoa
- French Polynesia
- Guam
- New Caledonia
- Northern Mariana Islands
- Tokelau
- Wallis and Futuna

2. The nature and extent of such participation shall be provided for by the Contracting Parties in separate rules of procedure of the Commission, taking into account international law, the distribution of competence on matters covered by this Convention and the evolution in the capacity of such territory to exercise rights and responsibilities under this Convention.

3. Notwithstanding paragraph 2, all such participants shall be entitled to participate fully in the work of the Commission, including the right to be present and to speak at the meetings of the Commission and its subsidiary bodies. In the performance of its functions, and in taking decisions, the Commission shall take into account the interests of all participants.

Article 44 Depositary

The Government of New Zealand shall be the depositary of this Convention and any amendments or revisions thereto. The depositary shall register this Convention with the Secretary-General of the United Nations in accordance with article 102 of the Charter of the United Nations.

IN WITNESS WHEREOF, the undersigned Plenipotentiaries, being duly authorized thereto, have signed this Convention.

DONE at Honolulu this fifth day of September, two thousand, in a single original.

ANNEX I. FISHING ENTITIES

1. After the entry into force of this Convention, any fishing entity whose vessels fish for highly migratory fish stocks in the Convention Area, may, by a written instrument delivered to the depositary, agree to be bound by the regime established by this Convention. Such agreement shall become effective thirty days following the delivery of the instrument. Any such fishing entity may withdraw such agreement by written notification addressed to the depositary. The withdrawal shall take effect one year after the date of receipt of the notification, unless the notification specifies a later date.

2. Such fishing entity shall participate in the work of the Commission, including decision-making, and shall comply with the obligations under this Convention. References thereto by the Commission or members of the Commission include, for the purposes of this Convention, such fishing entity as well as Contracting Parties.

3. If a dispute concerning the interpretation or application of this Convention involving a fishing entity cannot be settled by agreement between the parties to the dispute, the dispute shall, at the request of either party to the dispute, be submitted to final and binding arbitration in accordance with the relevant rules of the Permanent Court of Arbitration.

4. The provisions of this Annex relating to participation by fishing entities are solely for the purposes of this Convention.

ANNEX III. TERMS AND CONDITIONS FOR FISHING

Article 1 Introductory

The operator of every fishing vessel authorized to be used for fishing in the Convention Area shall comply with the following terms and conditions at all times when the vessel is in the Convention Area. Such terms and conditions shall apply in addition to any terms and conditions which may apply to the vessel in areas under the national jurisdiction of a member of the Commission by reason of a licence issued by such member or pursuant to a bilateral or multilateral fisheries agreement. For the purposes of this Annex, 'operator' means any person who is in charge of, directs or controls a fishing vessel, including the owner, master or charterer.

Article 2 Compliance with national laws

The operator of the vessel shall comply with the applicable national laws of each coastal State Party to this Convention in whose jurisdiction it enters and shall be responsible for the compliance by the vessel and its crew with such laws and the vessel shall be operated in accordance with such laws.

Article 3 Obligations of the operator in respect of observers

1. The operator and each member of the crew shall allow and assist any person identified as an observer under the regional observer programme to:
    (a) embark at a place and time agreed to;
    (b) have full access to and use of all facilities and equipment on board which the observer may determine is necessary to carry out his or her duties, including full access to the bridge, fish on board, and areas which may be used to hold, process, weigh and store fish, and full access to the vessel's records including its logs and documentation for the purpose of records inspection and copying, reasonable access to navigational equipment, charts and radios, and reasonable access to other information relating to fishing;
    (c) remove samples;
    (d) disembark at an agreed place and time; and
    (e) carry out all duties safely.

2. The operator or any crew member shall not assault, obstruct, resist, delay, refuse boarding to, intimidate or interfere with observers in the performance of their duties.

3. The operator shall provide the observer, while on board the vessel, at no expense to the observer or the observer's government, with food, accommodation and medical facilities of a reasonable standard equivalent to those normally available to an officer on board the vessel.

Article 4 Regulation of transhipment

1. The operator shall comply with any procedures established by the Commission to verify the quantity and species transhipped, and any additional procedures and measures established by the Commission with respect to transhipment in the Convention Area.

2. The operator shall allow and assist any person authorized by the Commission or by the member of the Commission in whose designated port or area a transhipment takes place to have full access to and use of facilities and equipment which such authorized person may determine is necessary to carry out his or her duties, including full access to the bridge, fish on board and areas which may be used to hold, process, weigh and store fish, and full access to the vessel's records, including its log and documentation for the purpose of inspection and photocopying. The operator shall also allow and assist any such

authorized person to remove samples and gather any other information required to fully monitor the activity. The operator or any member of the crew shall not assault, obstruct, resist, delay, refuse boarding to, intimidate or interfere with any such authorized person in the performance of such person's duties. Every effort should be made to ensure that any disruption to fishing operations is minimized during inspections of transhipments.

Article 5 Reporting

The operator shall record and report vessel position, catch of target and non-target species, fishing effort and other relevant fisheries data in accordance with the standards for collection of such data set out in Annex I of the Agreement.

Article 6 Enforcement

1. The authorization issued by the flag State of the vessel and, if applicable, any licence issued by a coastal State Party to this Convention, or a duly certified copy, facsimile or telex confirmation thereof, shall be carried on board the vessel at all times and produced at the request of an authorized enforcement official of any member of the Commission.

2. The master and each member of the crew of the vessel shall immediately comply with every instruction and direction given by an authorized and identified officer of a member of the Commission, including to stop, to move to a safe location, and to facilitate safe boarding and inspection of the vessel, its licence, gear, equipment, records, facilities, fish and fish products. Such boarding and inspection shall be conducted as much as possible in a manner so as not to interfere unduly with the lawful operation of the vessel. The operator and each member of the crew shall facilitate and assist in any action by an authorized officer and shall not assault, obstruct, resist, delay, refuse boarding to, intimidate or interfere with an authorized officer in the performance of his or her duties.

3. The vessel shall be marked and identified in accordance with the FAO Standard Specifications for the Marking and Identification of Fishing Vessels or such alternative standard as may be adopted by the Commission. At all times when the vessel is in the Convention Area, all parts of such markings shall be clear, distinct and uncovered.

4. The operator shall ensure the continuous monitoring of the international distress and calling frequency 2182 khz (HF) or the international safety and calling frequency 156.8 Mhz (channel 16, VHF-FM) to facilitate communication with the fisheries management, surveillance and enforcement authorities of the members of the Commission.

5. The operator shall ensure that a recent and up to date copy of the International Code of Signals (INTERCO) is on board and accessible at all times.

6. At all times when the vessel is navigating through an area under the national jurisdiction of a member of the Commission in which it does not have a licence to fish, and at all times when the vessel is navigating on the high seas in the Convention Area and has not been authorized by its flag State to fish on the high seas, all fishing equipment on board the vessel shall be stowed or secured in such a manner that it is not readily available to be used for fishing.

Protocol against the Smuggling of Migrants by Land, Sea and Air, Supplementing the United Nations Convention against Transnational Organized Crime

Adopted by General Assembly resolution, 15 November 2000;
entry into force, 28 January 2004
UN Doc. A/RES/55/25 (2000) of 15 November 2000, Annex III[1]

The States Parties to this Protocol,

Declaring that effective action to prevent and combat the smuggling of migrants by land, sea and air requires a comprehensive international approach, including cooperation, the exchange of information and other appropriate measures, including socio-economic measures, at the national, regional and international levels,

Recalling General Assembly resolution 54/212 of 22 December 1999, in which the Assembly urged Member States and the United Nations system to strengthen international cooperation in the area of international migration and development in order to address the root causes of migration, especially those related to poverty, and to maximize the benefits of international migration to those concerned, and encouraged, where relevant, interregional, regional and subregional mechanisms to continue to address the question of migration and development,

Convinced of the need to provide migrants with humane treatment and full protection of their rights,

Taking into account the fact that, despite work undertaken in other international forums, there is no universal instrument that addresses all aspects of smuggling of migrants and other related issues,

Concerned at the significant increase in the activities of organized criminal groups in smuggling of migrants and other related criminal activities set forth in this Protocol, which bring great harm to the States concerned,

Also concerned that the smuggling of migrants can endanger the lives or security of the migrants involved,

Recalling General Assembly resolution 53/111 of 9 December 1998, in which the Assembly decided to establish an open-ended intergovernmental ad hoc committee for the purpose of elaborating a comprehensive international convention against transnational organized crime and of discussing the elaboration of, inter alia, an international instrument addressing illegal trafficking in and transporting of migrants, including by sea,

Convinced that supplementing the United Nations Convention against Transnational Organized Crime with an international instrument against the smuggling of migrants by land, sea and air will be useful in preventing and combating that crime,

Have agreed as follows:

I. GENERAL PROVISIONS

Article 1   Relation with the United Nations Convention against Transnational Organized Crime

1. This Protocol supplements the United Nations Convention against Transnational Organized Crime. It shall be interpreted together with the Convention.

2. The provisions of the Convention shall apply, mutatis mutandis, to this Protocol unless otherwise provided herein.

---

[1] Articles 4-6, 10-25 omitted.

3. The offences established in accordance with article 6 of this Protocol shall be regarded as offences established in accordance with the Convention.

Article 2 Statement of purpose

The purpose of this Protocol is to prevent and combat the smuggling of migrants, as well as to promote cooperation among States Parties to that end, while protecting the rights of smuggled migrants.

Article 3 Use of terms

For the purposes of this Protocol:

(a) 'Smuggling of migrants' shall mean the procurement, in order to obtain, directly or indirectly, a financial or other material benefit, of the illegal entry of a person into a State Party of which the person is not a national or a permanent resident;

(b) 'Illegal entry' shall mean crossing borders without complying with the necessary requirements for legal entry into the receiving State;

(c) 'Fraudulent travel or identity document' shall mean any travel or identity document:

(i) That has been falsely made or altered in some material way by anyone other than a person or agency lawfully authorized to make or issue the travel or identity document on behalf of a State; or

(ii) That has been improperly issued or obtained through misrepresentation, corruption or duress or in any other unlawful manner; or

(iii) That is being used by a person other than the rightful holder;

(d) 'Vessel' shall mean any type of water craft, including non-displacement craft and seaplanes, used or capable of being used as a means of transportation on water, except a warship, naval auxiliary or other vessel owned or operated by a Government and used, for the time being, only on government non-commercial service.

II. SMUGGLING OF MIGRANTS BY SEA

Article 7 Cooperation

States Parties shall cooperate to the fullest extent possible to prevent and suppress the smuggling of migrants by sea, in accordance with the international law of the sea.

Article 8 Measures against the smuggling of migrants by sea

1. A State Party that has reasonable grounds to suspect that a vessel that is flying its flag or claiming its registry, that is without nationality or that, though flying a foreign flag or refusing to show a flag, is in reality of the nationality of the State Party concerned is engaged in the smuggling of migrants by sea may request the assistance of other States Parties in suppressing the use of the vessel for that purpose. The States Parties so requested shall render such assistance to the extent possible within their means.

2. A State Party that has reasonable grounds to suspect that a vessel exercising freedom of navigation in accordance with international law and flying the flag or displaying the marks of registry of another State Party is engaged in the smuggling of migrants by sea may so notify the flag State, request confirmation of registry and, if confirmed, request authorization from the flag State to take appropriate measures with regard to that vessel. The flag State may authorize the requesting State, inter alia:

(a)   To board the vessel;

(b)   To search the vessel; and

(c)   If evidence is found that the vessel is engaged in the smuggling of migrants by sea, to take appropriate measures with respect to the vessel and persons and cargo on board, as authorized by the flag State.

3.   A State Party that has taken any measure in accordance with paragraph 2 of this article shall promptly inform the flag State concerned of the results of that measure.

4.   A State Party shall respond expeditiously to a request from another State Party to determine whether a vessel that is claiming its registry or flying its flag is entitled to do so and to a request for authorization made in accordance with paragraph 2 of this article.

5.   A flag State may, consistent with article 7 of this Protocol, subject its authorization to conditions to be agreed by it and the requesting State, including conditions relating to responsibility and the extent of effective measures to be taken. A State Party shall take no additional measures without the express authorization of the flag State, except those necessary to relieve imminent danger to the lives of persons or those which derive from relevant bilateral or multilateral agreements.

6.   Each State Party shall designate an authority or, where necessary, authorities to receive and respond to requests for assistance, for confirmation of registry or of the right of a vessel to fly its flag and for authorization to take appropriate measures. Such designation shall be notified through the Secretary-General to all other States Parties within one month of the designation.

7.   A State Party that has reasonable grounds to suspect that a vessel is engaged in the smuggling of migrants by sea and is without nationality or may be assimilated to a vessel without nationality may board and search the vessel. If evidence confirming the suspicion is found, that State Party shall take appropriate measures in accordance with relevant domestic and international law.

Article 9 Safeguard clauses

1.   Where a State Party takes measures against a vessel in accordance with article 8 of this Protocol, it shall:

(a)   Ensure the safety and humane treatment of the persons on board;

(b)   Take due account of the need not to endanger the security of the vessel or its cargo;

(c)   Take due account of the need not to prejudice the commercial or legal interests of the flag State or any other interested State;

(d)   Ensure, within available means, that any measure taken with regard to the vessel is environmentally sound.

2.   Where the grounds for measures taken pursuant to article 8 of this Protocol prove to be unfounded, the vessel shall be compensated for any loss or damage that may have been sustained, provided that the vessel has not committed any act justifying the measures taken.

3.   Any measure taken, adopted or implemented in accordance with this chapter shall take due account of the need not to interfere with or to affect:

(a)   The rights and obligations and the exercise of jurisdiction of coastal States in accordance with the international law of the sea; or

(b)   The authority of the flag State to exercise jurisdiction and control in administrative, technical and social matters involving the vessel.

4.   Any measure taken at sea pursuant to this chapter shall be carried out only by warships or military aircraft, or by other ships or aircraft clearly marked and identifiable as being on government service and authorized to that effect.

Convention on the Protection of the Underwater Cultural Heritage

Done at Paris, 2 November 2001; entry into force, 2 January 2009
(2002) 48 LOSB 29

The General Conference of the United Nations Educational, Scientific and Cultural Organization, meeting in Paris from 15 October to 3 November 2001, at its 31st session,

Acknowledging the importance of underwater cultural heritage as an integral part of the cultural heritage of humanity and a particularly important element in the history of peoples, nations, and their relations with each other concerning their common heritage,

Realizing the importance of protecting and preserving the underwater cultural heritage and that responsibility therefor rests with all States,

Noting growing public interest in and public appreciation of underwater cultural heritage,

Convinced of the importance of research, information and education to the protection and preservation of underwater cultural heritage,

Convinced of the public's right to enjoy the educational and recreational benefits of responsible non-intrusive access to *in situ* underwater cultural heritage, and of the value of public education to contribute to awareness, appreciation and protection of that heritage,

Aware of the fact that underwater cultural heritage is threatened by unauthorized activities directed at it, and of the need for stronger measures to prevent such activities,

Conscious of the need to respond appropriately to the possible negative impact on underwater cultural heritage of legitimate activities that may incidentally affect it,

Deeply concerned by the increasing commercial exploitation of underwater cultural heritage, and in particular by certain activities aimed at the sale, acquisition or barter of underwater cultural heritage,

Aware of the availability of advanced technology that enhances discovery of and access to underwater cultural heritage,

Believing that cooperation among States, international organizations, scientific institutions, professional organizations, archaeologists, divers, other interested parties and the public at large is essential for the protection of underwater cultural heritage,

Considering that survey, excavation and protection of underwater cultural heritage necessitate the availability and application of special scientific methods and the use of suitable techniques and equipment as well as a high degree of professional specialization, all of which indicate a need for uniform governing criteria,

Realizing the need to codify and progressively develop rules relating to the protection and preservation of underwater cultural heritage in conformity with international law and practice, including the UNESCO Convention on the Means of Prohibiting and Preventing the Illicit Import, Export and Transfer of Ownership of Cultural Property of 14 November 1970, the UNESCO Convention for the Protection of the World Cultural and Natural Heritage of 16 November 1972 and the United Nations Convention on the Law of the Sea of 10 December 1982,

Committed to improving the effectiveness of measures at international, regional and national levels for the preservation *in situ* or, if necessary for scientific or protective purposes, the careful recovery of underwater cultural heritage,

Having decided at its twenty-ninth session that this question should be made the subject of an international convention,

Adopts this second day of November 2001 this Convention.

Article 1 Definitions

For the purposes of this Convention:

1.   (a) 'Underwater cultural heritage' means all traces of human existence having a cultural, historical or archaeological character which have been partially or totally under water, periodically or continuously, for at least 100 years such as:

(i)   sites, structures, buildings, artefacts and human remains, together with their archaeological and natural context;

(ii)   vessels, aircraft, other vehicles or any part thereof, their cargo or other contents, together with their archeological and natural context; and

(iii) objects of prehistoric character.

(b) Pipelines and cables placed on the seabed shall not be considered as underwater cultural heritage.

(c) Installations other than pipelines and cables, placed on the seabed and still in use, shall not be considered as underwater cultural heritage.

2.   (a) 'States Parties' means States which have consented to be bound by this Convention and for which this Convention is in force.

(b) This Convention applies *mutatis mutandis* to those territories referred to in Article 26, paragraph 2(b), which become Parties to this Convention in accordance with the conditions set out in that paragraph, and to that extent 'States Parties' refers to those territories.

3. 'UNESCO' means the United Nations Educational, Scientific and Cultural Organization.

4. 'Director-General' means the Director-General of UNESCO.

5. 'Area' means the seabed and ocean floor and subsoil thereof, beyond the limits of national jurisdiction.

6. 'Activities directed at underwater cultural heritage' means activities having underwater cultural heritage as their primary object and which may, directly or indirectly, physically disturb or otherwise damage underwater cultural heritage.

7. 'Activities incidentally affecting underwater cultural heritage' means activities which, despite not having underwater cultural heritage as their primary object or one of their objects, may physically disturb or otherwise damage underwater cultural heritage.

8. 'State vessels and aircraft' means warships, and other vessels or aircraft that were owned or operated by a State and used, at the time of sinking, only for government non-commercial purposes, that are identified as such and that meet the definition of underwater cultural heritage.

9. 'Rules' means the Rules concerning activities directed at underwater cultural heritage, as referred to in Article 33 of this Convention.

Article 2 Objectives and general principles

1. This Convention aims to ensure and strengthen the protection of underwater cultural heritage.

2. States Parties shall cooperate in the protection of underwater cultural heritage.

3. States Parties shall preserve underwater cultural heritage for the benefit of humanity in conformity with the provisions of this Convention.

4. States Parties shall, individually or jointly as appropriate, take all appropriate measures in conformity with this Convention and with international law that are necessary to protect underwater cultural heritage, using for this purpose the best practicable means at their disposal and in accordance with their capabilities.

5. The preservation *in situ* of underwater cultural heritage shall be considered as the first option before allowing or engaging in any activities directed at this heritage.

6. Recovered underwater cultural heritage shall be deposited, conserved and managed in a manner that ensures its long-term preservation.

7. Underwater cultural heritage shall not be commercially exploited.

8. Consistent with State practice and international law, including the United Nations Convention on the Law of the Sea, nothing in this Convention shall be interpreted as modifying the rules of international law and State practice pertaining to sovereign immunities, nor any State's rights with respect to its State vessels and aircraft.

9. States Parties shall ensure that proper respect is given to all human remains located in maritime waters.

10. Responsible non-intrusive access to observe or document *in situ* underwater cultural heritage shall be encouraged to create public awareness, appreciation, and protection of the heritage except where such access is incompatible with its protection and management.

11. No act or activity undertaken on the basis of this Convention shall constitute grounds for claiming, contending or disputing any claim to national sovereignty or jurisdiction.

Article 3 Relationship between this Convention and the United Nations Convention on the Law of the Sea

Nothing in this Convention shall prejudice the rights, jurisdiction and duties of States under international law, including the United Nations Convention on the Law of the Sea. This Convention shall be interpreted and applied in the context of and in a manner consistent with international law, including the United Nations Convention on the Law of the Sea.

Article 4 Relationship to law of salvage and law of finds

Any activity relating to underwater cultural heritage to which this Convention applies shall not be subject to the law of salvage or law of finds, unless it:

(a) is authorized by the competent authorities, and

(b) is in full conformity with this Convention, and

(c) ensures that any recovery of the underwater cultural heritage achieves its maximum protection.

Article 5 Activities incidentally affecting underwater cultural heritage

Each State Party shall use the best practicable means at its disposal to prevent or mitigate any adverse effects that might arise from activities under its jurisdiction incidentally affecting underwater cultural heritage.

Article 6 Bilateral, regional or other multilateral agreements

1. States Parties are encouraged to enter into bilateral, regional or other multilateral agreements or develop existing agreements, for the preservation of underwater cultural heritage. All such agreements shall be in full conformity with the provisions of this Convention and shall not dilute its universal character. States may, in such agreements, adopt rules and regulations which would ensure better protection of underwater cultural heritage than those adopted in this Convention.

2. The Parties to such bilateral, regional or other multilateral agreements may invite States with a verifiable link, especially a cultural, historical or archaeological link, to the underwater cultural heritage concerned to join such agreements.

3. This Convention shall not alter the rights and obligations of States Parties regarding the protection of sunken vessels, arising from other bilateral, regional or other multilateral agreements concluded before its adoption, and, in particular, those that are in conformity with the purposes of this Convention.

Article 7 Underwater cultural heritage in internal waters, archipelagic waters and territorial sea

1. States Parties, in the exercise of their sovereignty, have the exclusive right to regulate and authorize activities directed at underwater cultural heritage in their internal waters, archipelagic waters and territorial sea.

2. Without prejudice to other international agreements and rules of international law regarding the protection of underwater cultural heritage, States Parties shall require that the Rules be applied to activities directed at underwater cultural heritage in their internal waters, archipelagic waters and territorial sea.

3. Within their archipelagic waters and territorial sea, in the exercise of their sovereignty and in recognition of general practice among States, States Parties, with a view to cooperating on the best methods of protecting State vessels and aircraft, should inform the flag State Party to this Convention and, if applicable, other States with a verifiable link, especially a cultural, historical or archaeological link, with respect to the discovery of such identifiable State vessels and aircraft.

Article 8 Underwater cultural heritage in the contiguous zone

Without prejudice to and in addition to Articles 9 and 10, and in accordance with Article 303, paragraph 2, of the United Nations Convention on the Law of the Sea, States Parties may regulate and authorize activities directed at underwater cultural heritage within their contiguous zone. In so doing, they shall require that the Rules be applied.

Article 9 Reporting and notification in the exclusive economic zone and on the continental shelf

1. All States Parties have a responsibility to protect underwater cultural heritage in the exclusive economic zone and on the continental shelf in conformity with this Convention.

Accordingly:

(a) a State Party shall require that when its national, or a vessel flying its flag, discovers or intends to engage in activities directed at underwater cultural heritage located in its exclusive economic zone or on its continental shelf, the national or the master of the vessel shall report such discovery or activity to it;

(b) in the exclusive economic zone or on the continental shelf of another State Party:

(i)   State Parties shall require the national or the master of the vessel to report such discovery or activity to them and to that other State Party;

(ii) alternatively, a State Party shall require the national or master of the vessel to report such discovery or activity to it and shall ensure the rapid and effective transmission of such reports to all other States Parties.

2. On depositing its instrument of ratification, acceptance, approval or accession, a State Party shall declare the manner in which reports will be transmitted under paragraph 1(b) of this Article.

3. A State Party shall notify the Director-General of discoveries or activities reported to it under paragraph 1 of this Article.

4. The Director-General shall promptly make available to all States Parties any information notified to him under paragraph 3 of this Article.

5. Any State Party may declare to the State Party in whose exclusive economic zone or on whose continental shelf the underwater cultural heritage is located its interest in being consulted on how to ensure the effective protection of that underwater cultural heritage. Such declaration shall be based on a verifiable link, especially a cultural, historical or archaeological link, to the underwater cultural heritage concerned.

Article 10 Protection of underwater cultural heritage in the exclusive economic zone and on the continental shelf

1. No authorization shall be granted for an activity directed at underwater cultural heritage located in the exclusive economic zone or on the continental shelf except in conformity with the provisions of this Article.

2. A State Party in whose exclusive economic zone or on whose continental shelf underwater cultural heritage is located has the right to prohibit or authorize any activity directed at such heritage to prevent interference with its sovereign rights or jurisdiction as provided for by international law including the United Nations Convention on the Law of the Sea.

3. Where there is a discovery of underwater cultural heritage or it is intended that activity shall be directed at underwater cultural heritage in a State Party's exclusive economic zone or on its continental shelf, that State Party shall:

    (a) consult all other States Parties which have declared an interest under Article 9, paragraph 5, on how best to protect the underwater cultural heritage;

    (b) coordinate such consultations as 'Coordinating State', unless it expressly declares that it does not wish to do so, in which case the States Parties which have declared interest under Article 9, paragraph 5, shall appoint a Coordinating State.

4. Without prejudice to the duty of all States Parties to protect underwater cultural heritage by way of all practicable measures taken in accordance with international law to prevent immediate danger to the underwater cultural heritage, including looting, the Coordinating State may take all practicable measures, and/or issue any necessary authorizations in conformity with this Convention and, if necessary prior to consultations, to prevent any immediate danger to the underwater cultural heritage, whether arising from human activities or any other cause, including looting. In taking such measures assistance may be requested from other States Parties.

5. The Coordinating State:

    (a) shall implement measures of protection which have been agreed by the consulting States, which include the Coordinating State, unless the consulting States, which include the Coordinating State, agree that another State Party shall implement those measures;

    (b) shall issue all necessary authorizations for such agreed measures in conformity with the Rules, unless the consulting States, which include the Coordinating State, agree that another State Party shall issue those authorizations;

    (c) may conduct any necessary preliminary research on the underwater cultural heritage and shall issue all necessary authorizations therefore, and shall promptly inform the Director-General of the results, who in turn will make such information promptly available to other States Parties.

6. In coordinating consultations, taking measures, conducting preliminary research and/or issuing authorizations pursuant to this Article, the Coordinating State shall act on behalf of the States Parties as a whole and not in its own interest. Any such action shall not in itself constitute a basis for the assertion of any preferential or jurisdictional rights not provided for in international law, including the United Nations Convention on the Law of the Sea.

7. Subject to the provisions of paragraphs 2 and 4 of this Article, no activity directed at State vessels and aircraft shall be conducted without the agreement of the flag State and the collaboration of the Coordinating State.

Article 11 Reporting and notification in the Area

1. States Parties have a responsibility to protect underwater cultural heritage in the Area in conformity with this Convention and Article 149 of the United Nations Convention on the Law of the Sea. Accordingly when a national, or a vessel flying the flag of a State Party, discovers or intends to engage in activities directed at underwater cultural heritage located in the Area, that State Party shall require its national, or the master of the vessel, to report such discovery or activity to it.

2. States Parties shall notify the Director-General and the Secretary-General of the International Seabed Authority of such discoveries or activities reported to them.

3. The Director-General shall promptly make available to all States Parties any such information supplied by States Parties.

4. Any State Party may declare to the Director-General its interest in being consulted on how to ensure the effective protection of that underwater cultural heritage. Such declaration shall be based on a verifiable link to the underwater cultural heritage concerned, particular regard being paid to the preferential rights of States of cultural, historical or archaeological origin.

Article 12 Protection of underwater cultural heritage in the Area

1. No authorization shall be granted for any activity directed at underwater cultural heritage located in the Area except in conformity with the provisions of this Article.

2. The Director-General shall invite all States Parties which have declared an interest under Article 11, paragraph 4, to consult on how best to protect the underwater cultural heritage, and to appoint a State Party to coordinate such consultations as the 'Coordinating State'. The Director-General shall also invite the International Seabed Authority to participate in such consultations.

3. All States Parties may take all practicable measures in conformity with this Convention, if necessary prior to consultations, to prevent any immediate danger to the underwater cultural heritage, whether arising from human activity or any other cause including looting.

4. The Coordinating State shall:

(a)   implement measures of protection which have been agreed by the consulting States, which include the Coordinating State, unless the consulting States, which include the Coordinating State, agree that another State Party shall implement those measures; and

(b)   issue all necessary authorizations for such agreed measures, in conformity with this Convention, unless the consulting States, which include the Coordinating State, agree that another State Party shall issue those authorizations.

5. The Coordinating State may conduct any necessary preliminary research on the underwater cultural heritage and shall issue all necessary authorizations therefore, and shall promptly inform the Director-General of the results, who in turn shall make such information available to other States Parties.

6. In coordinating consultations, taking measures, conducting preliminary research, and/or issuing authorizations pursuant to this Article, the Coordinating State shall act for the benefit of humanity as a whole, on behalf of all States Parties. Particular regard shall be paid to the preferential rights of States of cultural, historical or archaeological origin in respect of the underwater cultural heritage concerned.

7. No State Party shall undertake or authorize activities directed at State vessels and aircraft in the Area without the consent of the flag State.

Article 13 Sovereign immunity

Warships and other government ships or military aircraft with sovereign immunity, operated for non-commercial purposes, undertaking their normal mode of operations, and not engaged in activities directed at underwater cultural heritage, shall not be obliged to report discoveries of underwater cultural heritage under Articles 9, 10, 11 and 12 of this Convention. However States Parties shall ensure, by the adoption of appropriate measures not impairing the operations or operational capabilities of their warships or other government ships or military aircraft with sovereign immunity operated for non-commercial purposes, that they comply, as far as is reasonable and practicable, with Articles 9, 10, 11 and 12 of this Convention.

Article 14 Control of entry into the territory, dealing and possession

States Parties shall take measures to prevent the entry into their territory, the dealing in, or the possession of, underwater cultural heritage illicitly exported and/or recovered, where recovery was contrary to this Convention.

Article 15 Non-use of areas under the jurisdiction of States Parties

States Parties shall take measures to prohibit the use of their territory, including their maritime ports, as well as artificial islands, installations and structures under their exclusive jurisdiction or control, in support of any activity directed at underwater cultural heritage which is not in conformity with this Convention.

Article 16 Measures relating to nationals and vessels

States Parties shall take all practicable measures to ensure that their nationals and vessels flying their flag do not engage in any activity directed at underwater cultural heritage in a manner not in conformity with this Convention.

Article 17 Sanctions

1. Each State Party shall impose sanctions for violations of measures it has taken to implement this Convention.

2. Sanctions applicable in respect of violations shall be adequate in severity to be effective in securing compliance with this Convention and to discourage violations wherever they occur and shall deprive offenders of the benefit deriving from their illegal activities.

3. States Parties shall cooperate to ensure enforcement of sanctions imposed under this Article.

Article 18 Seizure and disposition of underwater cultural heritage

1. Each State Party shall take measures providing for the seizure of underwater cultural heritage in its territory that has been recovered in a manner not in conformity with this Convention.

2. Each State Party shall record, protect and take all reasonable measures to stabilize underwater cultural heritage seized under this Convention.

3. Each State Party shall notify the Director-General and any other State with a verifiable link, especially a cultural, historical or archaeological link, to the underwater cultural heritage concerned of any seizure of underwater cultural heritage that it has made under this Convention.

4. A State Party which has seized underwater cultural heritage shall ensure that its disposition be for the public benefit, taking into account the need for conservation and research; the need for reassembly of a dispersed collection; the need for public access, exhibition and education; and the interests of any State with a verifiable link, especially a cultural, historical or archaeological link, in respect of the underwater cultural heritage concerned.

Article 19 Cooperation and information-sharing

1. States Parties shall cooperate and assist each other in the protection and management of underwater cultural heritage under this Convention, including, where practicable, collaborating in the investigation, excavation, documentation, conservation, study and presentation of such heritage.

2. To the extent compatible with the purposes of this Convention, each State Party undertakes to share information with other States Parties concerning underwater cultural heritage, including discovery of heritage, location of heritage, heritage excavated or recovered contrary to this Convention or otherwise in violation of international law, pertinent scientific methodology and technology, and legal developments relating to such heritage.

3. Information shared between States Parties, or between UNESCO and States Parties, regarding the discovery or location of underwater cultural heritage shall, to the extent compatible with their national legislation, be kept confidential and reserved to competent authorities of States Parties as long as the disclosure of such information might endanger or otherwise put at risk the preservation of such underwater cultural heritage.

4. Each State Party shall take all practicable measures to disseminate information, including where feasible through appropriate international databases, about underwater cultural heritage excavated or recovered contrary to this Convention or otherwise in violation of international law.

Article 20 Public awareness

Each State Party shall take all practicable measures to raise public awareness regarding the value and significance of underwater cultural heritage and the importance of protecting it under this Convention.

Article 21 Training in underwater archaeology

States Parties shall cooperate in the provision of training in underwater archaeology, in techniques for the conservation of underwater cultural heritage and, on agreed terms, in the transfer of technology relating to underwater cultural heritage.

Article 22 Competent authorities

1. In order to ensure the proper implementation of this Convention, States Parties shall establish competent authorities or reinforce the existing ones where appropriate, with the aim of providing for the establishment, maintenance and updating of an inventory of underwater cultural heritage, the effective protection, conservation, presentation and management of underwater cultural heritage, as well as research and education.

2. States Parties shall communicate to the Director-General the names and addresses of their competent authorities relating to underwater cultural heritage.

Article 23 Meetings of State Parties

1. The Director-General shall convene a Meeting of States Parties within one year of the entry into force of this Convention and thereafter at least once every two years.

At the request of a majority of States Parties, the Director-General shall convene an Extraordinary Meeting of States Parties.

2. The Meeting of States Parties shall decide on its functions and responsibilities.

3. The Meeting of States Parties shall adopt its own Rules of Procedure.

4. The Meeting of States Parties may establish a Scientific and Technical Advisory Body composed of experts nominated by the States Parties with due regard to the principle of equitable geographical distribution and the desirability of a gender balance.

5. The Scientific and Technical Advisory Body shall appropriately assist the Meeting of States Parties in questions of a scientific or technical nature regarding the implementation of the Rules.

Article 24 Secretariat for this Convention

1. The Director-General shall be responsible for the functions of the Secretariat for this Convention.

2. The duties of the Secretariat shall include:

(a) organizing Meetings of States Parties as provided for in Article 23, paragraph 1; and

(b) assisting States Parties in implementing the decisions of the Meetings of States Parties.

Article 25 Peaceful settlement of disputes

1. Any dispute between two or more States Parties concerning the interpretation or application of this Convention shall be subject to negotiations in good faith or other peaceful means of settlement of their own choice.

2. If those negotiations do not settle the dispute within a reasonable period of time, it may be submitted to UNESCO for mediation, by agreement between the States Parties concerned.

3. If mediation is not undertaken or if there is no settlement by mediation, the provisions relating to the settlement of disputes set out in Part XV of the United Nations Convention on the Law of the Sea apply *mutatis mutandis* to any dispute between States Parties to this Convention concerning the interpretation or application of this Convention, whether or not they are also Parties to the United Nations Convention on the Law of the Sea.

4. Any procedure chosen by a State Party to this Convention and to the United Nations Convention on the Law of the Sea pursuant to Article 287 of the latter shall apply to the settlement of disputes under this Article, unless that State Party, when ratifying, accepting, approving or acceding to this Convention, or at any time thereafter, chooses another procedure pursuant to Article 287 for the purpose of the settlement of disputes arising out of this Convention.

5. A State Party to this Convention which is not a Party to the United Nations Convention on the Law of the Sea, when ratifying, accepting, approving or acceding to this Convention or at any time thereafter shall be free to choose, by means of a written declaration, one or more of the means set out in Article 287, paragraph 1, of the United Nations Convention on the Law of the Sea for the purpose of settlement of disputes under this Article. Article 287 shall apply to such a declaration, as well as to any dispute to which such State is party, which is not covered by a declaration in force. For the purpose of conciliation and arbitration, in accordance with Annexes V and VII of the United Nations Convention on the Law of the Sea, such State shall be entitled to nominate conciliators and arbitrators to be included in the lists referred to in Annex V, Article 2, and Annex VII, Article 2, for the settlement of disputes arising out of this Convention.

Article 26 Ratification, acceptance, approval or accession

1. This Convention shall be subject to ratification, acceptance or approval by Member States of UNESCO.

2. This Convention shall be subject to accession:

(a) by States that are not members of UNESCO but are members of the United Nations or of a specialized agency within the United Nations system or of the International Atomic Energy Agency, as well as by States Parties to the Statute of the International Court of Justice and any other State invited to accede to this Convention by the General Conference of UNESCO;

(b) by territories which enjoy full internal self-government, recognized as such by the United Nations, but have not attained full independence in accordance with General Assembly resolution 1514 (XV) and which have competence over the matters governed by this Convention, including the competence to enter into treaties in respect of those matters.

3. The instruments of ratification, acceptance, approval or accession shall be deposited with the Director-General.

Article 27 Entry into force

This Convention shall enter into force three months after the date of the deposit of the twentieth instrument referred to in Article 26, but solely with respect to the twenty States or territories that have so deposited their instruments. It shall enter into force for each other State or territory three months after the date on which that State or territory has deposited its instrument.

Article 28 Declaration as to inland waters

When ratifying, accepting, approving or acceding to this Convention or at any time thereafter, any State or territory may declare that the Rules shall apply to inland waters not of a maritime character.

Article 29 Limitations to geographical scope

At the time of ratifying, accepting, approving or acceding to this Convention, a State or territory may make a declaration to the depositary that this Convention shall not be applicable to specific parts of its territory, internal waters, archipelagic waters or territorial sea, and shall identify therein the reasons for such declaration. Such State shall, to the extent practicable and as quickly as possible, promote conditions under which this Convention will apply to the areas specified in its declaration, and to that end shall also withdraw its declaration in whole or in part as soon as that has been achieved.

Article 30 Reservations

With the exception of Article 29, no reservations may be made to this Convention.

Article 31 Amendments

1. A State Party may, by written communication addressed to the Director-General, propose amendments to this Convention. The Director-General shall circulate such communication to all States Parties. If, within six months from the date of the circulation of the communication, not less than one half of the States Parties reply favourably to the request, the Director-General shall present such proposal to the next Meeting of States Parties for discussion and possible adoption.

2. Amendments shall be adopted by a two-thirds majority of States Parties present and voting.

3. Once adopted, amendments to this Convention shall be subject to ratification, acceptance, approval or accession by the States Parties.

4. Amendments shall enter into force, but solely with respect to the States Parties that have ratified, accepted, approved or acceded to them, three months after the deposit of the instruments referred to in paragraph 3 of this Article by two thirds of the States Parties. Thereafter, for each State or territory that ratifies, accepts, approves or accedes to it, the amendment shall enter into force three months after the date of deposit by that Party of its instrument of ratification, acceptance, approval or accession.

5. A State or territory which becomes a Party to this Convention after the entry into force of amendments in conformity with paragraph 4 of this Article shall, failing an expression of different intention by that State or territory, be considered:

(a)   as a Party to this Convention as so amended; and

(b)   as a Party to the unamended Convention in relation to any State Party not bound by the amendment.

Article 32 Denunciation

1. A State Party may, by written notification addressed to the Director-General, denounce this Convention.

2. The denunciation shall take effect twelve months after the date of receipt of the notification, unless the notification specifies a later date.

3. The denunciation shall not in any way affect the duty of any State Party to fulfil any obligation embodied in this Convention to which it would be subject under international law independently of this Convention.

Article 33 The Rules

The Rules annexed to this Convention form an integral part of it and, unless expressly provided otherwise, a reference to this Convention includes a reference to the Rules.

Article 34 Registration with the United Nations

In conformity with Article 102 of the Charter of the United Nations, this Convention shall be registered with the Secretariat of the United Nations at the request of the Director-General.

Article 35 Authoritative texts

This Convention has been drawn up in Arabic, Chinese, English, French, Russian and Spanish, the six texts being equally authoritative.

ANNEX
RULES CONCERNING ACTIVITIES DIRECTED AT
UNDERWATER CULTURAL HERITAGE

I. GENERAL PRINCIPLES

Rule 1.   The protection of underwater cultural heritage through *in situ* preservation shall be considered as the first option. Accordingly, activities directed at underwater cultural heritage shall be authorized in a manner consistent with the protection of that heritage, and subject to that requirement may be authorized for the purpose of making a significant contribution to protection or knowledge or enhancement of underwater cultural heritage.

Rule 2.   The commercial exploitation of underwater cultural heritage for trade or speculation or its irretrievable dispersal is fundamentally incompatible with the protection and proper management of underwater cultural heritage. Underwater cultural heritage shall not be traded, sold, bought or bartered as commercial goods.

This Rule cannot be interpreted as preventing:

(a) the provision of professional archaeological services or necessary services incidental thereto whose nature and purpose are in full conformity with this Convention and are subject to the authorization of the competent authorities;

(b) the deposition of underwater cultural heritage, recovered in the course of a research project in conformity with this Convention, provided such deposition does not prejudice the scientific or cultural interest or integrity of the recovered material or result in its irretrievable dispersal; is in accordance with the provisions of Rules 33 and 34; and is subject to the authorization of the competent authorities.

Rule 3.   Activities directed at underwater cultural heritage shall not adversely affect the underwater cultural heritage more than is necessary for the objectives of the project.

Rule 4.   Activities directed at underwater cultural heritage must use nondestructive techniques and survey methods in preference to recovery of objects. If excavation or recovery is necessary for the purpose of scientific studies or for the ultimate protection of the underwater cultural heritage, the methods and techniques used must be as non-destructive as possible and contribute to the preservation of the remains.

Rule 5.   Activities directed at underwater cultural heritage shall avoid the unnecessary disturbance of human remains or venerated sites.

Rule 6.   Activities directed at underwater cultural heritage shall be strictly regulated to ensure proper recording of cultural, historical and archaeological information.

Rule 7.   Public access to *in situ* underwater cultural heritage shall be promoted, except where such access is incompatible with protection and management.

Rule 8.   International cooperation in the conduct of activities directed at underwater cultural heritage shall be encouraged in order to further the effective exchange or use of archaeologists and other relevant professionals.

II. PROJECT DESIGN

Rule 9.   Prior to any activity directed at underwater cultural heritage, a project design for the activity shall be developed and submitted to the competent authorities for authorization and appropriate peer review.

Rule 10.   The project design shall include:

(a) an evaluation of previous or preliminary studies;

(b) the project statement and objectives;

(c) the methodology to be used and the techniques to be employed;

(d) the anticipated funding;

(e) an expected timetable for completion of the project;

(f) the composition of the team and the qualifications, responsibilities and experience of each team member;

(g) plans for post-fieldwork analysis and other activities;

(h) a conservation programme for artefacts and the site in close cooperation with the competent authorities;

(i) a site management and maintenance policy for the whole duration of the project;

(j)   a documentation programme;
(k)   a safety policy;
(l)   an environmental policy;
(m)   arrangements for collaboration with museums and other institutions, in particular scientific institutions;
(n)   report preparation;
(o)   deposition of archives, including underwater cultural heritage removed; and
(p)   a programme for publication.

Rule 11.   Activities directed at underwater cultural heritage shall be carried out in accordance with the project design approved by the competent authorities.

Rule 12.   Where unexpected discoveries are made or circumstances change, the project design shall be reviewed and amended with the approval of the competent authorities.

Rule 13.   In cases of urgency or chance discoveries, activities directed at the underwater cultural heritage, including conservation measures or activities for a period of short duration, in particular site stabilization, may be authorized in the absence of a project design in order to protect the underwater cultural heritage.

III. PRELIMINARY WORK

Rule 14.   The preliminary work referred to in Rule 10 (a) shall include an assessment that evaluates the significance and vulnerability of the underwater cultural heritage and the surrounding natural environment to damage by the proposed project, and the potential to obtain data that would meet the project objectives.

Rule 15.   The assessment shall also include background studies of available historical and archaeological evidence, the archaeological and environmental characteristics of the site, and the consequences of any potential intrusion for the long-term stability of the underwater cultural heritage affected by the activities.

IV. PROJECT OBJECTIVE, METHODOLOGY AND TECHNIQUES

Rule 16.   The methodology shall comply with the project objectives, and the techniques employed shall be as non-intrusive as possible.

V. FUNDING

Rule 17.   Except in cases of emergency to protect underwater cultural heritage, an adequate funding base shall be assured in advance of any activity, sufficient to complete all stages of the project design, including conservation, documentation and curation of recovered artefacts, and report preparation and dissemination.

Rule 18.   The project design shall demonstrate an ability, such as by securing a bond, to fund the project through to completion.

Rule 19.   The project design shall include a contingency plan that will ensure conservation of underwater cultural heritage and supporting documentation in the event of any interruption of anticipated funding.

VI. PROJECT DURATION – TIMETABLE

Rule 20.   An adequate timetable shall be developed to assure in advance of any activity directed at underwater cultural heritage the completion of all stages of the project design, including conservation, documentation and curation of recovered underwater cultural heritage, as well as report preparation and dissemination.

Rule 21. The project design shall include a contingency plan that will ensure conservation of underwater cultural heritage and supporting documentation in the event of any interruption or termination of the project.

VII. COMPETENCE AND QUALIFICATIONS

Rule 22. Activities directed at underwater cultural heritage shall only be undertaken under the direction and control of, and in the regular presence of, a qualified underwater archaeologist with scientific competence appropriate to the project.

Rule 23. All persons on the project team shall be qualified and have demonstrated competence appropriate to their roles in the project.

VIII. CONSERVATION AND SITE MANAGEMENT

Rule 24. The conservation programme shall provide for the treatment of the archaeological remains during the activities directed at underwater cultural heritage, during transit and in the long term. Conservation shall be carried out in accordance with current professional standards.

Rule 25. The site management programme shall provide for the protection and management *in situ* of underwater cultural heritage, in the course of and upon termination of fieldwork. The programme shall include public information, reasonable provision for site stabilization, monitoring, and protection against interference.

IX. DOCUMENTATION

Rule 26. The documentation programme shall set out thorough documentation including a progress report of activities directed at underwater cultural heritage, in accordance with current professional standards of archaeological documentation.

Rule 27. Documentation shall include, at a minimum, a comprehensive record of the site, including the provenance of underwater cultural heritage moved or removed in the course of the activities directed at underwater cultural heritage, field notes, plans, drawings, sections, and photographs or recording in other media.

X. SAFETY

Rule 28. A safety policy shall be prepared that is adequate to ensure the safety and health of the project team and third parties and that is in conformity with any applicable statutory and professional requirements.

XI. ENVIRONMENT

Rule 29. An environmental policy shall be prepared that is adequate to ensure that the seabed and marine life are not unduly disturbed.

XII. REPORTING

Rule 30. Interim and final reports shall be made available according to the timetable set out in the project design, and deposited in relevant public records.

Rule 31. Reports shall include:
(a)   an account of the objectives;
(b)   an account of the methods and techniques employed;
(c)   an account of the results achieved;
(d)   basic graphic and photographic documentation on all phases of the activity;
(e)   recommendations concerning conservation and curation of the site and of any underwater cultural heritage removed; and
(f)   recommendations for future activities.

XIII. CURATION OF PROJECT ARCHIVES

Rule 32. Arrangements for curation of the project archives shall be agreed to before any activity commences, and shall be set out in the project design.

Rule 33. The project archives, including any underwater cultural heritage removed and a copy of all supporting documentation shall, as far as possible, be kept together and intact as a collection in a manner that is available for professional and public access as well as for the curation of the archives. This should be done as rapidly as possible and in any case not later than ten years from the completion of the project, in so far as may be compatible with conservation of the underwater cultural heritage.

Rule 34. The project archives shall be managed according to international professional standards, and subject to the authorization of the competent authorities.

XIV. DISSEMINATION

Rule 35. Projects shall provide for public education and popular presentation of the project results where appropriate.

Rule 36. A final synthesis of a project shall be:
(a)   made public as soon as possible, having regard to the complexity of the project and the confidential or sensitive nature of the information; and
(b)   deposited in relevant public records.

Convention on the Conservation and Management of Fishery Resources in the South-East Atlantic Ocean

Done at Windhoek, 20 April 2001; entry into force, 13 April 2003
2221 UNTS 191 [Registration Number 39489][1]

The Contracting Parties to this Convention,

Committed to ensuring the long term conservation and sustainable use of all living marine resources in the South-East Atlantic Ocean, and to safeguarding the environment and marine ecosystems in which the resources occur;

Recognising the urgent and constant need for effective conservation and management of the fishery resources in the high seas of the South-East Atlantic Ocean;

Recognising the relevant provisions of the United Nations Convention on the Law of the Sea of 10 December 1982; the Agreement for the Implementation of the Provisions of the United Nations Convention on the Law of the Sea of 10 December 1982 relating to the Conservation and Management of Straddling Fish Stocks and Highly Migratory Fish

---

[1] Annex on Interim Arrangements omitted.

Stocks, 1995; and taking into account the FAO Agreement to Promote Compliance with International Conservation and Management Measures by Fishing Vessels on the High Seas,1993 and the FAO Code of Conduct for Responsible Fisheries, 1995;

Recognising the duties of States to cooperate with each other in the conservation and management of living resources in the South-East Atlantic Ocean;

Dedicated to exercising and implementing the precautionary approach in the management of fishery resources, in line with the principles set out in the Agreement for the Implementation of the Provisions of the United Nations Convention on the Law of the Sea of 10 December 1982 relating to the Conservation and Management of Straddling Fish Stocks and Highly Migratory Fish Stocks, 1995, and with the FAO Code of Conduct for Responsible Fisheries, 1995;

Recognising that the long term conservation and sustainable use of high seas fishery resources require cooperation among States through appropriate subregional or regional organisations which agree upon the measures necessary for this purpose;

Committed to responsible fisheries;

Noting that the coastal States have established areas of national jurisdiction in accordance with the United Nations Convention on the Law of the Sea of 10 December 1982, and general principles of international law within which they exercise sovereign rights for the purpose of exploring and exploiting, conserving and managing living marine resources;

Desiring cooperation with the coastal States and with all other States and Organisations having a real interest in the fishery resources of the South-East Atlantic Ocean to ensure compatible conservation and management measures;

Recognising economic and geographical considerations and the special requirements of developing States, and their coastal communities, for equitable benefit from living marine resources;

Calling upon States which are not Contracting Parties to this Convention, and which do not otherwise agree to apply the conservation and management measures adopted under this Convention, not to authorise vessels flying their flags to engage in fishing for the resources which are the subject of this Convention;

Convinced that the establishment of an organisation for the long term conservation and sustainable use of the fishery resources in the South-East Atlantic Ocean would best serve these purposes;

Bearing in mind that the achievements of the above will contribute to the realisation of a just and equitable economic order in the interests of all humankind, and in particular the special interests and needs of developing States,

Have agreed as follows:

Article 1 Use of terms

For the purposes of this Convention:

(a) '1982 Convention' means the United Nations Convention on the Law of the Sea of 10 December 1982;

(b) '1995 Agreement' means the Agreement for the Implementation of the Provisions of the United Nations Convention on the Law of the Sea of 10 December 1982 relating to the Conservation and Management of Straddling Fish Stocks and Highly Migratory Fish Stocks, 1995;

(c) 'Coastal State' means any Contracting Party with waters under national jurisdiction which are adjacent to the Convention Area;

(d) 'Commission' means the South-East Atlantic Fisheries Commission established pursuant to article 5;

(e) 'Contracting Party' means any State or regional economic integration organisation which has consented to be bound by this Convention, and for which the Convention is in force;

(f) 'Control measure' means any decision or action adopted by the Commission regarding observation, inspection, compliance and enforcement pursuant to article 16;

(g) 'Fisheries management organisation' means any intergovernmental organisation which has competence to take regulatory measures in relation to living marine resources;

(h) 'Fishing' means:

    (i) the actual or attempted searching for, catching, taking or harvesting of fishery resources;

    (ii) engaging in any activity which can reasonably be expected to result in the locating, catching, taking or harvesting of fishery resources for any purpose including scientific research;

    (iii) placing, searching for or recovering any aggregating device for fishery resources or associated equipment including radio beacons;

    (iv) any operation at sea in support of, or in preparation for, any activity described in this definition, except for any operation in emergencies involving the health and safety of crew members or the safety of a vessel; or

    (v) the use of an aircraft in relation to any activity described in this definition except for flights in emergencies involving the health or safety of crew members or the safety of a vessel;

(i) 'Fishing entity' means any fishing entity referred to in article I paragraph 3 of the 1995 Agreement;

(j) 'Fishing vessel' means any vessel used or intended for use for the purposes of the commercial exploitation of fishery resources, including mother ships, any other vessels directly engaged in such fishing operations, and vessels engaged in transshipment;

(k) 'Fishing research vessel' means any vessel engaged in fishing, as defined in point (h), for scientific research purposes, including permanent research vessels or vessels normally engaged in commercial fishing operations, or fishing support activities;

(l) 'Fishery resources' means resources of fish, molluscs, crustaceans and other sedentary species within the Convention Area, excluding:

    (i) sedentary species subject to the fishery jurisdiction of coastal States pursuant to article 77 paragraph 4 of the 1982 Convention; and

    (ii) highly migratory species listed in Annex I of the 1982 Convention;

(m) 'Flag State' means, unless otherwise indicated:

    (i) a state whose vessels are entitled to fly its flag; or

    (ii) a regional economic integration organisation in which vessels are entitled to fly the flag of a member State of that regional economic integration organisation.

(n) 'Living marine resources' means all living components of marine ecosystems, including seabirds;

(o) 'Regional economic integration organisation' unless otherwise specified, means a regional economic integration organisation to which all its member States have transferred competence over matters covered by this Convention, including the authority to make decisions binding on its member States in respect of those matters; and

(p) 'Transshipment' means unloading of all or any of the fishery resources on board a fishing vessel to another fishing vessel either at sea or in port without the products having been recorded by a port State as landed.

Article 2 Objective

The objective of this Convention is to ensure the long-term conservation and sustainable use of the fishery resources in the Convention Area through the effective implementation of this Convention.

Article 3 General principles

In giving effect to the objective of this Convention, the Contracting Parties, where appropriate through the Organisation, shall, in particular:

(a) adopt measures, based on the best scientific evidence available, to ensure the long term conservation and sustainable use of the fishery resources to which this Convention applies;

(b) apply the precautionary approach in accordance with article 7;

(c) apply the provisions of this Convention relating to fishery resources, taking due account of the impact of fishing operations on ecologically related species such as seabirds, cetaceans, seals and marine turtles;

(d) adopt, where necessary, conservation and management measures for species belonging to the same ecosystem as, or associated with or dependent upon, the harvested fishery resources;

(e) ensure that fishery practices and management measures take due account of the need to minimise harmful impacts on living marine resources as a whole; and

(f) protect biodiversity in the marine environment.

Article 4 Geographical application

Except as otherwise provided, this Convention applies within the Convention Area, being all waters beyond areas of national jurisdiction in the area bounded by a line joining the following points along parallels of latitude and meridians of longitude:

– beginning at the outer limit of waters under national jurisdiction at a point 6° South, thence due west along the 6° South parallel to the meridian 10° West, thence due north along the 10° West meridian to the equator, thence due west along the equator to the meridian 20° West, thence due south along the 20° West meridian to a parallel 50° South, thence due east along the 50° South parallel to the meridian 30° East, thence due north along the 30° East meridian to the coast of the African continent.

Article 5 The Organisation

1. The Contracting Parties hereby establish and agree to maintain the South-East Atlantic Fisheries Organisation, herein 'the Organisation'.

2. The Organisation shall comprise:

(a) the Commission;

(b) the Compliance and Scientific Committees, as subsidiary bodies, and any other subsidiary bodies that the Commission shall establish from time to time to assist in meeting the objective of this Convention; and

(c) the Secretariat.

3. The Organisation shall have legal personality and shall enjoy in the territory of each of the Contracting Parties such legal capacity as may be necessary to perform its functions and achieve the objective of this Convention. The privileges and immunities to be enjoyed by the Organisation and its staff in the territory of a Contracting Party shall be determined by agreement between the Organisation and the Contracting Party concerned.

4. The official languages of the Organisation shall be English and Portuguese.

5. The headquarters of the Organisation shall be established in Namibia.

Article 6 The Commission

1. Each Contracting Party shall be a member of the Commission.

2. Each member shall appoint one representative to the Commission who may be accompanied by alternate representatives and advisers.

3. The functions of the Commission shall be to:

(a) identify conservation and management needs;

(b) formulate and adopt conservation and management measures;

(c) determine total allowable catches and/or levels of fishing effort, taking into account total fishing mortality, including of non-target species;

(d) determine the nature and extent of participation in fishing;

(e) keep under review the status of stocks and gather, analyse and disseminate relevant information on stocks;

(f) encourage, promote and, where appropriate by agreement, coordinate scientific research on fishery resources within the Convention Area and in adjacent waters under national jurisdiction;

(g) manage stocks on the basis of the precautionary approach to be developed in accordance with article 7;

(h) establish appropriate cooperative mechanisms for effective monitoring, control, surveillance and enforcement;

(i) adopt measures concerning control and enforcement within the Convention Area;

(j) develop measures for the conduct of fishing for scientific research purposes;

(k) develop rules for the collection, submission, verification of, access to and use of data;

(l) compile and disseminate accurate and complete statistical data to ensure that the best scientific advice is available, while maintaining confidentiality, where appropriate;

(m) direct the Compliance and Scientific Committees, other subsidiary bodies, and the Secretariat;

(n) approve the budget of the Organisation; and

(o) carry out such other activities as may be necessary to fulfil its functions.

4. The Commission shall adopt its rules of procedure.

5. The Commission shall adopt measures, in accordance with international law, to promote compliance by vessels flying the flag of non-parties to this Convention with measures agreed by the Commission.

6. The Commission shall take full account of the recommendations and advice from the Scientific and Compliance Committees in formulating its decisions. The Commission shall, in particular, take full account of the biological unity and other biological characteristics of the stocks.

7. The Commission shall publish its conservation and management and control measures which are in force, and, as far as practicable, shall maintain records of other conservation and management measures in force in the Convention Area.

8. The measures referred to in paragraph 3 may include the following:

(a) the quantity of any species which may be caught;

(b) the areas and periods in which fishing may occur;

(c) the size and sex of any species which may be taken;

(d) the fishing gear and technology which may be used;

(e)   the level of fishing effort, including vessel numbers, types and sizes, which may be used;

(f)   the designation of regions and sub-regions;

(g)   other measures regulating fisheries with the objective of protecting any species; and

(h)   other measures the Commission considers necessary to meet the objective of this Convention.

9.   Conservation and management and control measures adopted by the Commission in accordance with this Convention shall become effective in accordance with Article 23.

10.   Taking account of Articles 116-119 of the 1982 Convention, the Commission may draw the attention of any State or fishing entity which is a non-party to this Convention to any activity which in the opinion of the Commission affects implementation of the objective of this Convention.

11.   The Commission shall draw the attention of all Contracting Parties to any activity which in the opinion of the Commission undermines:

(a)   the implementation by a Contracting Party of the objective of this Convention, or the compliance of that Contracting Party with its obligations under this Convention; or

(b)   the compliance of that Contracting Party with its obligations under this Convention.

12.   The Commission shall take account of measures established by other organisations which affect living marine resources in the Convention Area, and, without prejudice to the objective of this Convention, shall seek to ensure consistency with such measures.

13.   If the Commission determines that a Contracting Party has ceased to participate in the work of the Organisation, the Commission shall consult with the Contracting Party concerned and may take a decision to address the matter, as it deems appropriate.

Article 7 Application of the precautionary approach

1.   The Commission shall apply the precautionary approach widely to conservation and management and exploitation of fishery resources in order to protect those resources and preserve the marine environment.

2.   The Commission shall be more cautious when information is uncertain, unreliable or inadequate. The absence of adequate scientific information shall not be used as a reason for postponing or failing to take conservation and management measures.

3.   In implementing this article, the Commission shall take cognisance of best international practices regarding the application of the precautionary approach, including Annex II of the 1995 Agreement and the FAO Code of Conduct for Responsible Fisheries, 1995.

Article 8 Meetings of the Commission

1.   The Commission shall hold an annual meeting and any other meetings as deemed necessary.

2.   The first meeting of the Commission shall be held within three months of the entry into force of this Convention, provided that among the Contracting Parties there are at least two States conducting fishing activities in the Convention Area. The first meeting shall, in any event, be held within six months of the entry into force of the Convention. The Government of Namibia shall consult with the Contracting Parties regarding the first Commission meeting. The provisional agenda shall be communicated to each signatory and Contracting Party not less than one month before the date of the meeting.

3. The first meeting of the Commission shall, *inter alia*, give priority consideration to the costs associated with implementation of the Annex by the Secretariat and measures to fulfil the functions of the Commission set out in article 6.3 (k) and (l).

4. The first meeting of the Commission shall be held at the headquarters of the Organisation. Thereafter, meetings of the Commission shall be held at the headquarters, unless the Commission decides otherwise.

5. The Commission shall elect from among the representatives of the Contracting Parties a chairperson and vice chairperson, each of whom shall serve for a term of two years and shall be eligible for re-election for one additional term of two years. The first chairperson shall be elected at the first meeting of the Commission for an initial term of three years. The chairperson and vice chairperson shall not be representatives of the same Contracting Party.

6. The Commission shall adopt rules of procedure to govern the participation of representatives from non-Parties to this Convention as observers.

7. The Commission shall adopt rules of procedure to govern the participation of representatives from inter-governmental organisations as observers.

8. Representatives from non-governmental organisations concerned with the stocks found in the Convention Area shall be given the opportunity to participate as observers in the meetings of the Organisation, subject to rules adopted by the Commission.

9. The Commission shall adopt rules to govern such participation and to provide for transparency in the activities of the Organisation. The rules shall not be unduly restrictive in this respect and shall provide for timely access to records and reports of the Organisation, subject to the procedural rules on access to them. The Commission shall adopt such rules of procedure as soon as possible.

10. The Contracting Parties may decide, by consensus, to invite representatives from non-parties to this Convention and from intergovernmental organisations to participate as observers until the rules regarding such participation are adopted by the Commission.

Article 9 The Compliance Committee

1. Each Contracting Party shall be entitled to appoint one representative to the Compliance Committee who may be accompanied by alternate representatives and advisers.

2. Unless otherwise decided by the Commission, the functions of the Compliance Committee shall be to provide the Commission with information, advice and recommendations on the implementation of, and compliance with, conservation and management measures.

3. In performing its functions, the Compliance Committee shall conduct activities as the Commission may direct and shall:
  (a) coordinate compliance activities undertaken by or on behalf of the Organisation;
  (b) coordinate with the Scientific Committee on matters of common concern; and
  (c) perform such other tasks as directed by the Commission.

4. The Compliance Committee shall meet as deemed necessary by the Commission.

5. The Compliance Committee shall adopt, and amend as necessary, rules of procedure for the conduct of its meetings and the exercise of its functions. The rules and any amendments thereto shall be approved by the Commission. The rules shall include procedures for the presentation of minority reports.

6. The Compliance Committee may establish, with the approval of the Commission, such subsidiary bodies as are necessary for the performance of its functions.

Article 10 The Scientific Committee

1. Each Contracting Party shall be entitled to appoint one representative to the Scientific Committee who may be accompanied by alternate representatives and advisers.

2. The Scientific Committee may seek expert advice as required on an *ad hoc* basis.

3. The functions of the Scientific Committee shall be to provide the Commission with scientific advice and recommendations for the formulation of conservation and management measures for fishery resources covered by this Convention, and to encourage and promote cooperation in scientific research in order to improve knowledge of the living marine resources of the Convention Area.

4. In performing its functions, the Scientific Committee shall conduct such activities as the Commission may direct and shall:

   (a)   consult, cooperate and encourage the collection, study and exchange of information relevant to the living marine resources of the Convention Area;

   (b)   establish criteria and methods to be used in determining conservation and management measures;

   (c)   assess the status and trends of relevant populations of living marine resources;

   (d)   analyse data on the direct and indirect effects of fishing and other human activities on populations of fishery resources;

   (e)   assess the potential effects of proposed changes in the methods or levels of fishing and of proposed conservation and management measures; and

   (f)   transmit reports and recommendations to the Commission as directed, or on its own initiative, regarding conservation and management measures and research.

5. In carrying out its functions, the Scientific Committee shall seek to take into consideration the work of other fisheries management organisations, as well as other technical and scientific bodies.

6. The first meeting of the Scientific Committee shall be held within three months of the first meeting of the Commission.

7. The Scientific Committee shall adopt, and amend as necessary, rules of procedure for the conduct of its meetings and the exercise of its functions. The rules and any amendments thereto shall be approved by the Commission. The rules shall include procedures for the presentation of minority reports.

8. The Scientific Committee may establish, with the approval of the Commission, such subsidiary bodies as are necessary for the performance of its functions.

Article 11 The Secretariat

1. The Commission shall appoint an Executive Secretary according to such procedures and on such terms and conditions as the Commission may determine.

2. The Executive Secretary shall be appointed for a term of four years and may be reappointed for one additional term not exceeding four years.

3. The Commission shall authorise such staff for the Secretariat as may be necessary and the Executive Secretary shall appoint, direct and supervise such staff according to staff regulations approved by the Commission.

4. The Executive Secretary and the Secretariat shall perform the functions delegated to them by the Commission.

Article 12 Finance and budget

1. At each annual meeting, the Commission shall adopt the Organisation's budget. In determining the size of the budget, the Commission shall give due consideration to the principle of cost effectiveness.

2. A draft budget for the Organisation's next financial year shall be prepared by the Executive Secretary and submitted to the Contracting Parties at least 60 days before the annual meeting of the Commission.

3. Each Contracting Party shall contribute to the budget. The contribution by each Contracting Party shall be according to a combination of an equal basic fee, and a fee based on the total catch in the Convention Area of species covered by the Convention. The Commission shall adopt and amend the proportion in which these contributions are applied taking into account the economic status of each Contracting Party. For Contracting Parties with territory adjoining the Convention Area, this shall be the economic status of that territory.

4. For the first three years following the Convention's entry into force, or a shorter period as decided by the Commission, the contribution of each Contracting Party shall be equal.

5. The Commission may request and accept financial contributions and other forms of assistance from organisations, individuals and other sources for purposes connected with the fulfilment of its functions.

6. The financial activities of the Organisation, including the proportion of contributions referred to in paragraph 3, shall be conducted in accordance with Financial Regulations adopted by the Commission and shall be subject to an annual audit by independent auditors appointed by the Commission.

7. Each Contracting Party shall meet its own expenses arising from attendance at meetings of the bodies of the Organisation.

8. Unless otherwise decided by the Commission, a Contracting Party that is in arrears with its payment of any monies owing to the Organisation by more than two years:

    (a) shall not participate in the taking of any decisions by the Commission; and

    (b) may not notify non-acceptance of any measure adopted by the Commission until it has paid all monies owing by it to the Organisation.

Article 13 Contracting Party obligations

1. Each Contracting Party shall, in respect of its activities within the Convention Area:

    (a) collect and exchange scientific, technical and statistical data with respect to fisheries resources covered by this Convention;

    (b) ensure that data are collected in sufficient detail to facilitate effective stock assessment and are provided in a timely manner to fulfil the requirements of the Commission;

    (c) take appropriate measures to verify the accuracy of such data;

    (d) provide annually to the Organisation such statistical, biological and other data and information as the Commission may require;

    (e) provide to the Organisation in the manner and at such intervals as may be required by the Commission, information concerning its fishing activities, including fishing areas and fishing vessels in order to facilitate the compilation of reliable catch and effort statistics; and

    (f) provide to the Commission at such intervals as it may require information on steps taken to implement the conservation and management measures adopted by the Commission.

2. Each coastal State shall, in respect of activities that occur in its area of national jurisdiction relating to straddling stocks of fishery resources, provide to the Organisation data required in accordance with paragraph 1.

3. Each Contracting Party shall promptly implement this Convention and any conservation, management and other measures or matters which may be agreed by the Commission.

4. Each Contracting Party shall take appropriate measures, in accordance with the measures adopted by the Commission and international law, in order to ensure the effectiveness of the measures adopted by the Commission.

5. Each Contracting Party shall transmit to the Commission an annual statement of implementing and compliance measures, including imposition of sanctions for any violations, it has taken in accordance with this Article.

6.   (a) Without prejudice to the primacy of the responsibility of the flag State, each Contracting Party shall, to the greatest extent possible, take measures, or cooperate, to ensure that its nationals fishing in the Convention Area and its industries comply with the provisions of this Convention. Each Contracting Party shall, on a regular basis, inform the Commission of such measures taken.

     (b) Fishing opportunities granted to the Contracting Parties by the Commission shall be exercised exclusively by vessels flying the flag of Contracting Parties.

7. Each coastal State shall regularly inform the Organisation of the measures they have adopted for fishery resources within areas of water under their national jurisdiction adjacent to the Convention Area.

8. Each Contracting Party shall fulfil in good faith the obligations assumed under this Convention and shall exercise the rights recognised in this Convention in a manner which would not constitute an abuse of rights.

Article 14 Flag State duties

1. Each Contracting Party shall take such measures as may be necessary to ensure that vessels flying its flag comply with the conservation and management and control measures adopted by the Commission and that they do not engage in any activities which undermine the effectiveness of such measures.

2. Each Contracting Party shall authorise the use of vessels flying its flag for fishing in the Convention Area only where it is able to exercise effectively its responsibilities in respect of such vessels under this Convention.

3. Each Contracting Party shall take appropriate measures in respect of vessels flying its flag which are in accordance with measures adopted by the Commission and which give effect thereto, and which take account of existing international practices. These measures shall include, *inter alia*:

    (a) measures to ensure that a flag State investigates immediately and reports fully on actions taken in response to an alleged violation by a vessel flying its flag of measures adopted by the Commission;

    (b) control of such vessels in the Convention Area by means of fishing authorisation;

    (c) establishment of a national record of fishing vessels authorised to fish in the Convention Area and provision for sharing this information with the Commission on a regular basis;

    (d) requirements for marking of fishing vessels and fishing gear for identification;

(e)   requirements for recording and timely reporting of vessel position, catch of target and non-target species, catch landed, catch transhipped, fishing effort and other relevant fisheries data;

(f)   regulation of transhipment to ensure that the effectiveness of conservation and management measures is not undermined;

(g)   measures to permit access by observers from other Contracting Parties to carry out functions as agreed by the Commission; and

(h)   measures to require the use of a vessel monitoring system as agreed by the Commission.

4.   Each Contracting Party shall ensure that vessels flying its flag do not undermine measures agreed by the Commission through unauthorised fishing within areas adjacent to the Convention Area on stocks occurring in the Convention Area and the adjacent area.

Article 15 Port State duties and measures taken by a port State

1.   Measures taken by a port State in accordance with this Convention shall take full account of the right and the duty of a port State to take measures, in accordance with international law, to promote the effectiveness of subregional, regional and global conservation and management measures.

2.   Each Contracting Party shall, in accordance with measures agreed by the Commission, *inter alia*, inspect documents, fishing gear and catch on board fishing vessels, when such vessels are voluntarily in its ports or at its offshore terminals.

3.   Each Contracting Party shall, in accordance with measures agreed by the Commission, adopt regulations in accordance with international law to prohibit landings and transshipments by vessels flying the flag of non-parties to this Convention where it has been established that the catch of a stock covered by this Convention has been taken in a manner which undermines the effectiveness of conservation and management measures adopted by the Commission.

4.   In the event that a port State considers that there has been a violation by a Contracting Party vessel of a conservation and management or control measure adopted by the Commission, the port State shall draw this to the attention of the flag State concerned and, as appropriate, the Commission. The port State shall provide the flag State and the Commission with full documentation of the matter, including any record of inspection. In such cases, the flag State shall transmit to the Commission details of actions it has taken in respect of the matter.

5.   Nothing in this article affects the exercise by States of their sovereignty over ports in their territory in accordance with international law.

6.   All measures taken under this article shall be taken in accordance with international law.

Article 16 Observation, inspection, compliance and enforcement

1.   The Contracting Parties, through the Commission, shall establish a system of observation, inspection, compliance and enforcement, hereafter 'the System', to strengthen the effective exercise of flag State responsibility by Contracting Parties for fishing vessels and fishing research vessels flying their flags in the Convention Area. The major purpose of the System is to ensure that Contracting Parties effectively discharge their obligations under this Convention and, where applicable, under the 1995 Agreement, in order to ensure compliance with the conservation and management measures agreed by the Commission.

2.   In establishing the System, the Commission shall be guided, *inter alia*, by the following principles:

(a) fostering of cooperation among Contracting Parties to ensure effective implementation of the System;

(b) a System which is impartial and non-discriminatory in nature;

(c) verification of compliance with conservation and management measures agreed by the Commission; and

(d) prompt action on reports of infringements in contravention of measures agreed by the Commission.

3. In applying these principles the System shall, *inter alia*, comprise the following elements:

(a) control measures, including the authorisation of vessels to fish, the marking of vessels and fishing gear, the recording of fishing activities, and the near-to-real time reporting of vessel movements and activities by means such as satellite surveillance;

(b) an inspection programme, both at sea and in port, including procedures for boarding and inspection of vessels, on a reciprocal basis;

(c) an observer programme based on common standards for the conduct of observation, including, *inter alia*, arrangements for the placing of observers by a Contracting Party on vessels flying the flag of another Contracting Party with the consent of that Party; an appropriate level of coverage for different sizes and types of fishing vessels and fishery research vessels; and measures for reporting by observers of information regarding apparent violations of conservation and management measures, taking into account the need to ensure the safety of observers; and

(d) procedures for the follow-up on infringements detected under the System, including standards of investigation, reporting procedures, notification of proceedings and sanctions, and other enforcement actions.

4. The System shall have a multilateral and integrated character.

5. In order to strengthen the effective exercise of flag State responsibility by Contracting Parties for fishing vessels and fishery research vessels flying their flags in the Convention Area, the interim arrangements set out in the Annex, which forms an integral part of this Convention, shall apply upon entry into force of this Convention and remain in force until the establishment of the System or until the Commission decides otherwise.

6. If, within two years of the entry into force of this Convention, the Commission has not established the System, the Commission shall, at the request of any Contracting Party, give urgent consideration to adoption of boarding and inspection procedures in order to strengthen the effective discharge by Contracting Parties of their obligations under this Convention and where applicable, under the 1995 Agreement. A special meeting of the Commission may be convened for this purpose.

Article 17 Decision making

1. Decisions of the Commission on matters of substance shall be taken by consensus of the Contracting Parties present. The question of whether a matter is one of substance shall be treated as a matter of substance.

2. Decisions on matters other than those referred to in paragraph 1 shall be taken by a simple majority of the Contracting Parties present and voting.

3. In the taking of decisions pursuant to this Convention, a regional economic integration organisation shall have only one vote.

Article 18 Cooperation with other organisations
　1. The Organisation shall cooperate, as appropriate, with the Food and Agriculture Organisation of the United Nations and with other specialised agencies and organisations on matters of mutual interest.
　2. The Organisation shall seek to develop cooperative working relationships with other inter-governmental organisations which can contribute to their work and which have an interest in ensuring the long-term conservation and sustainable use of living marine resources in the Convention Area.
　3. The Commission may enter into agreements with the organisations referred to in this article and with other organisations as may be appropriate. The Commission may invite such organisations to send observers to its meetings, or to the meetings of any subsidiary bodies of the Organisation.
　4. In the application of Articles 2 and 3 of this Convention to fishery resources, the Organisation shall cooperate with other relevant fisheries management organisations and take account of their conservation and management measures applicable in the region.

Article 19 Compatibility of conservation and management measures
　1. The Contracting Parties recognise the need to ensure compatibility of conservation and management measures adopted for straddling fish stocks on the high seas and in areas under national jurisdiction. To this end, the Contracting Parties have a duty to cooperate for the purposes of achieving compatible measures in respect of such stocks of fisheries resources as occur in the Convention area and in areas under the jurisdiction of any Contracting Party. The appropriate Contracting Party and the Commission shall accordingly promote the compatibility of such measures. This compatibility shall be ensured in such a way which does not undermine measures established in accordance with Articles 61 and 119 of the 1982 Convention.
　2. For the purpose of paragraph 1, the coastal States and the Commission shall develop and agree on standards for reporting and exchanging data on fisheries for the stocks concerned as well as statistical data on the status of the stocks.
　3. Each Contracting Party shall keep the Commission informed of its measures and decisions taken in accordance with this Article.

Article 20 Fishing opportunities
　1. In determining the nature and extent of participatory rights in fishing opportunities, the Commission shall take into account, *inter alia*:
　(a)　the state of fishery resources including other living marine resources and existing levels of fishing effort, taking into account the advice and recommendations of the Scientific Committee;
　(b)　respective interests, past and present fishing patterns, including catches, and practices in the Convention Area;
　(c)　the stage of development of a fishery;
　(d)　the interests of developing States in whose areas of national jurisdiction the stocks also occur;
　(e)　contributions to conservation and management of fishery resources in the Convention Area, including the provision of information, the conduct of research and steps taken to establish cooperative mechanisms for effective monitoring, control, surveillance and enforcement;
　(f)　contributions to new or exploratory fisheries, taking account of the principles set out in article 6.6 of the 1995 Agreement;

(g)   the needs of coastal fishing communities which are dependent mainly on fishing for the stocks in the South-East Atlantic; and

(h)   the needs of coastal States whose economies are overwhelmingly dependent on the exploitation of fishery resources.

2.   In applying the provisions of paragraph 1, the Commission may, *inter alia* :

(a)   designate annual quota allocations or effort limitations for Contracting Parties;

(b)   allocate catch quantities for exploration and scientific research; and

(c)   set aside fishing opportunities for non-parties to this Convention, if necessary.

3.   The Commission shall, subject to agreed rules, review quota allocations, effort limitations and participation in fishing opportunities of Contracting Parties taking into account the information, advice and recommendations on the implementation of, and compliance with, conservation and management measures by Contracting Parties.

Article 21 Recognition of the special requirements of developing States in the region

1.   The Contracting Parties shall give full recognition to the special requirements of developing States in the region in relation to conservation and management of fishery resources and the development of such resources.

2.   In giving effect to the duty to cooperate in the establishment of conservation and management measures for stocks covered by this Convention, the Contracting Parties shall take into account the special requirements of such developing States, in particular:

(a)   the vulnerability of developing States in regions which are dependent on the exploitation of living marine resources, including for meeting the nutritional requirements of their populations or parts thereof;

(b)   the need to avoid adverse impacts on, and ensure access to fisheries by, subsistence, small-scale and artisanal fishers and women fishworkers; and

(c)   the need to ensure that such measures do not result in transferring, directly or indirectly, a disproportionate burden of conservation action onto developing States in the region.

3.   The Contracting Parties shall cooperate through the Commission and other subregional or regional organisations involved in the management of fishery resources:

(a)   to enhance the ability of developing States in the region to conserve and manage fishery resources and to develop their own fisheries for such resources; and

(b)   to assist developing States in the region which may fish for fishery resources, to enable them to participate in fisheries for such resources, including facilitating access in accordance with this Convention.

4.   Cooperation with developing States in the region for the purposes set out in this article shall include the provision of financial assistance, assistance relating to human resources development, technical assistance, transfer of technology, and activities directed specifically towards:

(a)   improved conservation and management of the fishery resources covered by this Convention through collection, reporting, verification, exchange and analysis of fisheries data and related information;

(b)   stock assessment and scientific research; and

(c)   monitoring, control, surveillance, compliance and enforcement, including training and capacity-building at the local level, development and funding of national and regional observer programmes and access to technology and equipment.

Article 22 Non-Parties to this Convention

1. The Contracting Parties shall, either directly or through the Commission, request non-parties to this Convention whose vessels fish in the Convention Area to cooperate fully with the Organisation either by becoming party to the Convention or by agreeing to apply the conservation and management measures adopted by the Commission with a view to ensuring that such measures are applied to all fishing activities in the Convention Area. Such non-parties to this Convention shall enjoy benefits from participation in the fishery commensurate with their commitment to comply with conservation and management measures in respect of the relevant stocks.

2. Contracting Parties may exchange information between each other or through the Commission on, and shall inform the Commission of activities of, fishing vessels flying the flags of the non-parties to this Convention which are engaged in fishing operations in the Convention Area, and of any action taken in response to fishing by non-parties to this Convention. The Commission shall share information on such activities with other appropriate regional or subregional organisations and arrangements.

3. The Contracting Parties may, either directly or through the Commission, take measures, which are consistent with international law, and which they deem necessary and appropriate, to deter fishing activities by fishing vessels of non-parties to this Convention which undermine the effectiveness of conservation and management measures adopted by the Commission.

4. The Contracting Parties shall, individually or jointly, request fishing entities which have fishing vessels in the Convention Area to cooperate fully with the organisation in implementing conservation and management measures, with a view to having such measures applied de facto as extensively as possible to fishing activities in the Convention Area. Such fishing entities shall enjoy benefits from participation in the fishery commensurate with their commitment to comply with conservation and management measures in respect of the stocks.

5. The Commission may invite non-parties to this Convention to send observers to its meetings, or to the meetings of any subsidiary bodies of the Organisation.

Article 23 Implementation

1. Conservation and management and control measures adopted by the Commission shall become binding on the Contracting Parties in the following manner:

    (a)   the Executive Secretary shall notify promptly in writing all Contracting Parties of such a measure following its adoption by the Commission;

    (b)   the measure shall become binding upon all Contracting Parties 60 days after notification by the Secretariat of the measure's adoption by the Commission, pursuant to subparagraph (a), unless otherwise specified in the measure;

    (c)   if a Contracting Party, within 60 days following the notification specified in subparagraph (a), notifies the Commission that it is unable to accept a measure, that measure shall not, to the extent stated, be binding upon that Contracting Party; however, the measure shall remain binding on all other Contracting Parties unless the Commission decides otherwise;

    (d)   any Contracting Party which makes a notification under subparagraph (c) shall at the same time provide a written explanation of its reasons for making the notification and, where appropriate, its proposals for alternative measures which the Contracting Party is going to implement. The explanation shall specify *inter alia* whether the basis for the notification is that:

        (i)   the Contracting Party considers that the measure is inconsistent with the provisions of this Convention;

(ii)   the Contracting Party cannot practicably comply with the measure;

(iii)   the measure unjustifiably discriminates in form or in fact against the Contracting Party; or

(iv)   other special circumstances apply;

(e)   the Executive Secretary shall promptly circulate to all Contracting Parties details of any notification and explanation received in accordance with subparagraphs (c) and (d);

(f)   in the event that any Contracting Party invokes the procedure set out in subparagraphs (c) and (d), the Commission shall meet at the request of any other Contracting Party to review the measure. At the time of such a meeting and within 30 days following the meeting, any Contracting Party shall have the right to notify the Commission that it is no longer able to accept the measure, in which case that Contracting Party shall no longer be bound by the measure; and

(g)   pending the conclusions of a review meeting called in accordance with subparagraph (f), any Contracting Party may request an *ad hoc* expert panel established in accordance with article 24 to make recommendations on any interim measures following the invocation of the procedures pursuant to subparagraphs (c) and (d) which may be necessary in respect of the measure to be reviewed. Subject to paragraph 3, such interim measures shall be binding on all Contracting Parties if all Contracting Parties (other than those who have indicated that they are unable to accept the measure, pursuant to subparagraphs (c) and (d)) agree that the long term sustainability of the stocks covered by this Convention will be undermined in the absence of such measures.

2. Any Contracting Party which invokes the procedure set out in paragraph 1 may at any time withdraw its notification of non-acceptance and become bound by the measure immediately if it is already in effect or at such time as it may come into effect under this article.

3. This article is without prejudice to the right of any Contracting Party to invoke the dispute settlement procedures set out in article 24 in respect of a dispute concerning the interpretation or application of this Convention, in the event that all other methods to settle the dispute, including the procedures set out in this article, have been exhausted.

Article 24 Dispute settlement

1. The Contracting Parties shall cooperate in order to prevent disputes.

2. If any dispute arises between two or more Contracting Parties concerning the interpretation or implementation of this Convention, those Contracting Parties shall consult among themselves with a view to resolving the dispute, or to having the dispute resolved by negotiation, inquiry, mediation, conciliation, arbitration, judicial settlement or other peaceful means of their own choice.

3. In cases where a dispute between two or more Contracting Parties is of a technical nature, and the Contracting Parties are unable to resolve the dispute among themselves, they may refer the dispute to an *ad hoc* expert panel established in accordance with procedures adopted by the Commission at its first meeting. The panel shall confer with the Contracting Parties concerned and shall endeavour to resolve the dispute expeditiously without recourse to binding procedures for the settlement of disputes.

4. Where a dispute is not referred for settlement within a reasonable time of the consultations referred to in paragraph 2, or where a dispute is not resolved by recourse to other means referred to in this article within a reasonable time, such dispute shall, at the request of any party to the dispute, be submitted for binding decision in accordance with

procedures for the settlement of disputes provided in Part XV of the 1982 Convention or, where the dispute concerns one or more straddling stocks, by provisions set out in Part VIII of the 1995 Agreement. The relevant part of the 1982 Convention and the 1995 Agreement shall apply whether or not the parties to the dispute are also Parties to these instruments.

5. A court, tribunal or panel to which any dispute has been submitted under this article shall apply the relevant provisions of this Convention, of the 1982 Convention, of the 1995 Agreement, as well as generally accepted standards for the conservation and management of living marine resources and other rules of international law, compatible with the 1982 Convention and the 1995 Agreement, with a view to ensuring the conservation of the fish stocks concerned.

Article 25 Signature, ratification, acceptance and approval

1. This Convention shall be open for signature on 20 April 2001, in Windhoek, Namibia, and subsequently at the head-quarters of the Food and Agriculture Organisation of the United Nations for one year from its adoption on 20 April 2001 by all States and regional economic integration organisations participating in the Conference on the South-East Atlantic Fisheries Organisation held on 20 April 2001 and by all States and regional economic integration organisations whose vessels fish, or have fished in the Convention Area, for fishery resources covered by this Convention, in the four years preceding the adoption of the Convention.

2. This Convention shall be subject to ratification, acceptance or approval by the States and regional economic integration organisations referred to in paragraph 1. The instruments of ratification, acceptance or approval shall be deposited with the Director-General of the Food and Agriculture Organisation of the United Nations, hereafter 'the Depositary '.

Article 26 Accession

1. This Convention shall be open for accession by coastal States, and by all other States and regional economic integration organisations whose vessels fish in the Convention Area for fishery resources covered by this Convention.

2. This Convention shall be open for accession by regional economic integration organisations, other than that regional economic integration organisation that qualifies as a Contracting Party under article 25,which include among their member States one or more States which have transferred, in whole or in part, competence over matters covered by this Convention. The accession of such regional economic integration organisations shall be the subject of consultations within the Commission concerning the conditions for participation in the work of the Commission.

3. Instruments of accession shall be deposited with the Depositary. Accessions received by the Depositary prior to the date of entry into force of this Convention shall become effective 30 days after the date on which this Convention enters into force.

Article 27 Entry into force

This Convention shall enter into force 60 days after the date of deposit with the Depositary of the third instrument of ratification, accession, acceptance or approval at least one of which has been deposited by a coastal State. For each State or regional economic integration organisation which, subsequent to the date of entry into force of this Convention, deposits an instrument of ratification or accession, this Convention shall enter into force on the thirtieth day following such deposit.

Article 28 Reservations and exceptions

No reservations or exceptions may be made to this Convention.

Article 29 Declarations and statements

Article 28 does not preclude a State or regional economic integration organisation, when signing, ratifying or acceding to this Convention, from making declarations or statements, however phrased or named, with a view, *inter alia*, to the harmonisation of its laws and regulations with the provisions of this Agreement, provided that such declarations or statements do not purport to exclude or to modify the legal effect of the provisions of this Convention in their application to that State or regional economic integration organisation.

Article 30 Relation to other agreements

This Convention shall not alter the rights and obligations of Contracting Parties which arise from the 1982 Convention and other agreements compatible with the 1982 Convention and which do not affect the enjoyment by other Contracting Parties of their rights or the performance of their obligations under this Convention.

Article 31 Maritime claims

Nothing in this Convention shall constitute recognition of the claims or positions of any of the Contracting Parties concerning the legal status and extent of waters and zones claimed by any such Contracting Party.

Article 32 Amendment

1. Any Contracting Party may at any time propose amendments to this Convention.

2. Any proposed amendment shall be notified in writing to the Executive Secretary at least 90 days prior to the meeting at which it is proposed to be considered, and the Executive Secretary shall promptly transmit the proposal to all Contracting Parties. Proposed amendments to the Convention shall be considered at the annual meeting of the Commission, unless a majority of the Contracting Parties request a special meeting to discuss the proposed amendment. A special meeting may be convened on not less than 90 days' notice.

3. The text of any amendment adopted by the Commission shall be transmitted promptly by the Executive Secretary to all Contracting Parties.

4. An amendment shall enter into force on the thirtieth day following the deposit of instruments of ratification, acceptance or approval thereof from all Contracting Parties.

Article 33 Withdrawal

1. A Contracting Party may, by written notification addressed to the Depositary, withdraw from this Convention and may indicate its reasons. Failure to indicate reasons shall not affect the validity of the withdrawal. The withdrawal shall take effect one year after the date of receipt of the notification by the Depositary, unless the notification specifies a later date.

2. Withdrawal from this Convention by any Contracting Party shall not affect its financial obligations under this Convention incurred prior to its withdrawal becoming effective.

Article 34 Registration

1. The Director-General of the Food and Agriculture Organisation of the United Nations shall be the Depositary of this Convention, and any amendments or revisions thereto. The Depositary shall:

   (a) send certified copies of this Convention to each signatory to this Convention and to all Contracting Parties;

   (b) arrange for the registration of this Convention, upon its entry into force, with the Secretary-General of the United Nations in accordance with article 102 of the Charter of the United Nations;

   (c) inform each signatory to this Convention and all Contracting Parties of:

       (i) instruments of ratification, accession, acceptance and approval deposited in accordance with Articles 25 and 26 respectively;

       (ii) the date of entry into force of the Convention in accordance with Article 27;

       (iii) the entry into force of amendments to this Convention in accordance with Article 32;

       (iv) withdrawals from this Convention pursuant to Article 33.

2. The language of communication for the functions of the Depositary shall be English.

Article 35 Authentic texts

The English and Portuguese texts of this Convention are equally authentic.

IN WITNESS WHEREOF the undersigned, being duly authorised thereto, have signed this Convention in the English and Portuguese languages.

DONE at Windhoek, Namibia, 20 April 2001, in a single original in the English and Portuguese languages.

International Plan of Action to Prevent, Deter and Eliminate Illegal, Unreported and Unregulated Fishing

Adopted by consensus at the 24th Session of the FAO Committee on Fisheries on 2 March 2001 and endorsed by the 120th of the FAO Council on 23 June 2001
FAO, *International Plan of Action to Prevent, Deter and Eliminate Illegal, Unreported and Unregulated Fishing,* 2001

I. INTRODUCTION

1. In the context of the Code of Conduct for Responsible Fisheries and its overall objective of sustainable fisheries, the issue of illegal, unreported and unregulated (IUU) fishing in world fisheries is of serious and increasing concern. IUU fishing undermines efforts to conserve and manage fish stocks in all capture fisheries. When confronted with IUU fishing, national and regional fisheries management organizations can fail to achieve management goals. This situation leads to the loss of both short and long-term social and economic opportunities and to negative effects on food security and environmental protection. IUU fishing can lead to the collapse of a fishery or seriously impair efforts to rebuild stocks that have already been depleted. Existing international instruments addressing IUU fishing have not been effective due to a lack of political will, priority, capacity and resources to ratify or accede to and implement them.

2. The Twenty-third Session of the FAO Committee on Fisheries (COFI) in February 1999 addressed the need to prevent, deter and eliminate IUU fishing. The Committee

was concerned about information presented indicating increases in IUU fishing, including fishing vessels flying 'flags of convenience'. Shortly afterwards, an FAO Ministerial Meeting on Fisheries in March 1999 declared that, without prejudice to the rights and obligations of States under international law, FAO 'will develop a global plan of action to deal effectively with all forms of illegal, unregulated and unreported fishing including fishing vessels flying 'flags of convenience' through coordinated efforts by States, FAO, relevant regional fisheries management bodies and other relevant international agencies such as the International Maritime Organization (IMO), as provided in Article IV of the Code of Conduct.' The Government of Australia, in cooperation with FAO, organized an Expert Consultation on Illegal, Unreported and Unregulated Fishing in Sydney, Australia, from 15 to 19 May 2000. Subsequently, an FAO Technical Consultation on Illegal, Unreported and Unregulated Fishing was held in Rome from 2 to 6 October 2000 and a further Technical Consultation was held in Rome from 22 to 23 February 2001. The draft International Plan of Action to Prevent, Deter and Eliminate Illegal, Unreported and Unregulated Fishing was adopted by the Consultation on 23 February 2001 with a request that the report be submitted to the Twenty-fourth Session of COFI for consideration and eventual adoption. COFI approved the International Plan of Action, by consensus, on 2 March 2001. In doing so, the Committee urged all Members to take the necessary steps to effectively implement the International Plan of Action.

II. NATURE AND SCOPE OF IUU FISHING AND THE INTERNATIONAL PLAN OF ACTION

3. In this document:
3.1 Illegal fishing refers to activities:
    3.1.1 conducted by national or foreign vessels in waters under the jurisdiction of a State, without the permission of that State, or in contravention of its laws and regulations;
    3.1.2 conducted by vessels flying the flag of States that are parties to a relevant regional fisheries management organization but operate in contravention of the conservation and management measures adopted by that organization and by which the States are bound, or relevant provisions of the applicable international law; or
    3.1.3 in violation of national laws or international obligations, including those undertaken by cooperating States to a relevant regional fisheries management organization.
3.2 Unreported fishing refers to fishing activities:
    3.2.1 which have not been reported, or have been misreported, to the relevant national authority, in contravention of national laws and regulations; or
    3.2.2 undertaken in the area of competence of a relevant regional fisheries management organization which have not been reported or have been misreported, in contravention of the reporting procedures of that organization.
3.3 Unregulated fishing refers to fishing activities:
    3.3.1 in the area of application of a relevant regional fisheries management organization that are conducted by vessels without nationality, or by those flying the flag of a State not party to that organization, or by a fishing entity, in a manner that is not consistent with or contravenes the conservation and management measures of that organization; or

      3.3.2 in areas or for fish stocks in relation to which there are no applicable conservation or management measures and where such fishing activities are conducted in a manner inconsistent with State responsibilities for the conservation of living marine resources under international law.

  3.4 Notwithstanding paragraph 3.3, certain unregulated fishing may take place in a manner which is not in violation of applicable international law, and may not require the application of measures envisaged under the International Plan of Action (IPOA).

4. The IPOA is voluntary. It has been elaborated within the framework of the FAO Code of Conduct for Responsible Fisheries as envisaged by Article 2 (d).

5. The FAO Code of Conduct for Responsible Fisheries, in particular Articles 1.1, 1.2, 3.1, and 3.2 applies to the interpretation and application of this IPOA and its relationship with other international instruments. The IPOA is also directed as appropriate towards fishing entities as referred to in the Code of Conduct. The IPOA responds to fisheries specific issues and nothing in it prejudices the positions of States in other fora.

6. In this document:

    a. the reference to States includes regional economic integration organizations in matters within their competence;

    b. the term 'regional' includes sub-regional, as appropriate;

    c. the term 'regional fisheries management organization' means an intergovernmental fisheries organization or arrangement, as appropriate, that has the competence to establish fishery conservation and management measures;

    d. the term 'conservation and management measures' means measures to conserve one or more species of living marine resources that are adopted and applied consistent with the relevant rules of international law;

    e. the term '1982 UN Convention' refers to the United Nations Convention on the Law of the Sea of 10 December 1982;

    f. the term '1993 FAO Compliance Agreement' refers to the Agreement to Promote Compliance with International Conservation and Management Measures by Fishing Vessels on the High Seas, approved by the FAO Conference on 24 November 1993;

    g. the term '1995 UN Fish Stocks Agreement' refers to the Agreement for the Implementation of the United Nations Convention on the Law of the Sea of 10 December 1982 relating to the Conservation and Management of Straddling Fish Stocks and Highly Migratory Fish Stocks; and

    h. the term 'Code of Conduct' refers to the FAO Code of Conduct for Responsible Fisheries.

7. This document is a further commitment by all States to implement the Code of Conduct.

III. OBJECTIVE AND PRINCIPLES

8. The objective of the IPOA is to prevent, deter and eliminate IUU fishing by providing all States with comprehensive, effective and transparent measures by which to act, including through appropriate regional fisheries management organizations established in accordance with international law.

9. The IPOA to prevent, deter and eliminate IUU fishing incorporates the following principles and strategies. Due consideration should be given to the special requirements of developing countries in accordance with Article 5 of the Code of Conduct.

9.1   *Participation and coordination*: To be fully effective, the IPOA should be implemented by all States either directly, in cooperation with other States, or indirectly through relevant regional fisheries management organizations or through FAO and other appropriate international organizations. An important element in successful implementation will be close and effective coordination and consultation, and the sharing of information to reduce the incidence of IUU fishing, among States and relevant regional and global organizations. The full participation of stakeholders in combating IUU fishing, including industry, fishing communities, and non-governmental organizations, should be encouraged.

9.2   *Phased implementation*: Measures to prevent, deter and eliminate IUU fishing should be based on the earliest possible phased implementation of national plans of action, and regional and global action in accordance with the IPOA.

9.3   *Comprehensive and integrated approach*: Measures to prevent, deter and eliminate IUU fishing should address factors affecting all capture fisheries. In taking such an approach, States should embrace measures building on the primary responsibility of the flag State and using all available jurisdiction in accordance with international law, including port State measures, coastal State measures, market-related measures and measures to ensure that nationals do not support or engage in IUU fishing. States are encouraged to use all these measures, where appropriate, and to cooperate in order to ensure that measures are applied in an integrated manner. The action plan should address all economic, social and environmental impacts of IUU fishing.

9.4   *Conservation*: Measures to prevent, deter and eliminate IUU fishing should be consistent with the conservation and long-term sustainable use of fish stocks and the protection of the environment.

9.5   *Transparency*: The IPOA should be implemented in a transparent manner in accordance with Article 6.13 of the Code of Conduct.

9.6   *Non-discrimination*: The IPOA should be developed and applied without discrimination in form or in fact against any State or its fishing vessels.

IV. IMPLEMENTATION OF MEASURES TO PREVENT, DETER AND ELIMINATE IUU FISHING

ALL STATE RESPONSIBILITIES

International Instruments

10.   States should give full effect to relevant norms of international law, in particular as reflected in the 1982 UN Convention, in order to prevent, deter and eliminate IUU fishing.

11.   States are encouraged, as a matter of priority, to ratify, accept or accede to, as appropriate, the 1982 UN Convention, the 1995 UN Fish Stocks Agreement and the 1993 FAO Compliance Agreement. Those States that have not ratified, accepted or acceded to these relevant international instruments should not act in a manner inconsistent with these instruments.

12.   States should implement fully and effectively all relevant international fisheries instruments which they have ratified, accepted or acceded to.

13.   Nothing in the IPOA affects, or should be interpreted as affecting, the rights and obligations of States under international law. Nothing in the IPOA affects, or should be interpreted as affecting, the rights and obligations contained in the 1995 UN Fish

Stocks Agreement and the 1993 FAO Compliance Agreement, for States parties to those instruments.

14. States should fully and effectively implement the Code of Conduct and its associated International Plans of Action.

15. States whose nationals fish on the high seas in fisheries not regulated by a relevant regional fisheries management organization should fully implement their obligations under Part VII of the 1982 UN Convention to take measures with respect to their nationals as may be necessary for the conservation of the living resources of the high seas.

National Legislation
Legislation

16. National legislation should address in an effective manner all aspects of IUU fishing.

17. National legislation should address, *inter alia*, evidentiary standards and admissibility including, as appropriate, the use of electronic evidence and new technologies.

State control over nationals

18. In the light of relevant provisions of the 1982 UN Convention, and without prejudice to the primary responsibility of the flag State on the high seas, each State should, to the greatest extent possible, take measures or cooperate to ensure that nationals subject to their jurisdiction do not support or engage in IUU fishing. All States should cooperate to identify those nationals who are the operators or beneficial owners of vessels involved in IUU fishing.

19. States should discourage their nationals from flagging fishing vessels under the jurisdiction of a State that does not meet its flag State responsibilities.

Vessels without nationality

20. States should take measures consistent with international law in relation to vessels without nationality on the high seas involved in IUU fishing.

Sanctions

21. States should ensure that sanctions for IUU fishing by vessels and, to the greatest extent possible, nationals under its jurisdiction are of sufficient severity to effectively prevent, deter and eliminate IUU fishing and to deprive offenders of the benefits accruing from such fishing. This may include the adoption of a civil sanction regime based on an administrative penalty scheme. States should ensure the consistent and transparent application of sanctions.

Non cooperating States

22. All possible steps should be taken, consistent with international law, to prevent, deter and eliminate the activities of non-cooperating States to a relevant regional fisheries management organization which engage in IUU fishing.

Economic incentives

23. States should, to the extent possible in their national law, avoid conferring economic support, including subsidies, to companies, vessels or persons that are involved in IUU fishing.

Monitoring, control and surveillance

24.   States should undertake comprehensive and effective monitoring, control and surveillance (MCS) of fishing from its commencement, through the point of landing, to final destination, including by:

24.1   developing and implementing schemes for access to waters and resources, including authorization schemes for vessels;

24.2   maintaining records of all vessels and their current owners and operators authorized to undertake fishing subject to their jurisdiction;

24.3   implementing, where appropriate, a vessel monitoring system (VMS), in accordance with the relevant national, regional or international standards, including the requirement for vessels under their jurisdiction to carry VMS on board;

24.4   implementing, where appropriate, observer programmes in accordance with relevant national, regional or international standards, including the requirement for vessels under their jurisdiction to carry observers on board;

24.5   providing training and education to all persons involved in MCS operations;

24.6   planning, funding and undertaking MCS operations in a manner that will maximize their ability to prevent, deter and eliminate IUU fishing;

24.7   promoting industry knowledge and understanding of the need for, and their cooperative participation in, MCS activities to prevent, deter and eliminate IUU fishing;

24.8   promoting knowledge and understanding of MCS issues within national judicial systems;

24.9   establishing and maintaining systems for the acquisition, storage and dissemination of MCS data, taking into account applicable confidentiality requirements;

24.10   ensuring effective implementation of national and, where appropriate, internationally agreed boarding and inspection regimes consistent with international law, recognizing the rights and obligations of masters and of inspection officers, and noting that such regimes are provided for in certain international agreements, such as the 1995 UN Fish Stocks Agreement, and only apply to the parties to those agreements.

National Plans of Action

25.   States should develop and implement, as soon as possible but not later than three years after the adoption of the IPOA, national plans of action to further achieve the objectives of the IPOA and give full effect to its provisions as an integral part of their fisheries management programmes and budgets. These plans should also include, as appropriate, actions to implement initiatives adopted by relevant regional fisheries management organizations to prevent, deter and eliminate IUU fishing. In doing so, States should encourage the full participation and engagement of all interested stakeholders, including industry, fishing communities and non-governmental organizations.

26.   At least every four years after the adoption of their national plans of action, States should review the implementation of these plans for the purpose of identifying cost-effective strategies to increase their effectiveness and to take into account their reporting obligations to FAO under Part VI of the IPOA.

27.   States should ensure that national efforts to prevent, deter and eliminate IUU fishing are internally coordinated.

Cooperation between States

28.   States should coordinate their activities and cooperate directly, and as appropriate through relevant regional fisheries management organizations, in preventing, deterring and eliminating IUU fishing. In particular, States should:

28.1   exchange data or information, preferably in standardized format, from records of vessels authorized by them to fish, in a manner consistent with any applicable confidentiality requirements;

28.2   cooperate in effective acquisition, management and verification of all relevant data and information from fishing;

28.3   allow and enable their respective MCS practitioners or enforcement personnel to cooperate in the investigation of IUU fishing, and to this end States should collect and maintain data and information relating to such fishing;

28.4   cooperate in transferring expertise and technology;

28.5   cooperate to make policies and measures compatible;

28.6   develop cooperative mechanisms that allow, *inter alia*, rapid responses to IUU fishing; and

28.7   cooperate in monitoring, control and surveillance, including through international agreements.

29.   In the light of Article VI of the 1993 FAO Compliance Agreement, flag States should make available to FAO and, as appropriate, to other States and relevant regional or international organizations, information about vessels deleted from their records or whose authorization to fish has been cancelled and to the extent possible, the reasons therefor.

30.   In order to facilitate cooperation and exchange of information, each State and regional or international organization should nominate and publicize initial formal contact points.

31.   Flag States should consider entering into agreements or arrangements with other States and otherwise cooperate for the enforcement of applicable laws and conservation and management measures or provisions adopted at a national, regional or global level.

Publicity

32.   States should publicize widely, including through cooperation with other States, full details of IUU fishing and actions taken to eliminate it, in a manner consistent with any applicable confidentiality requirements.

Technical Capacity and Resources

33.   States should endeavour to make available the technical capacity and resources which are needed to implement the IPOA. This should include, where appropriate, the establishment of special funds at the national, regional or global level. In this respect, international cooperation should play an important role.

FLAG STATE RESPONSIBILITIES

Fishing Vessel Registration

34.   States should ensure that fishing vessels entitled to fly their flag do not engage in or support IUU fishing.

35.   A flag State should ensure, before it registers a fishing vessel, that it can exercise its responsibility to ensure that the vessel does not engage in IUU fishing.

36.   Flag States should avoid flagging vessels with a history of non-compliance except where:

36.1 the ownership of the vessel has subsequently changed and the new owner has provided sufficient evidence demonstrating that the previous owner or operator has no further legal, beneficial or financial interest in, or control of, the vessel; or

36.2 having taken into account all relevant facts, the flag State determines that flagging the vessel would not result in IUU fishing.

37. All States involved in a chartering arrangement, including flag States and other States that accept such an arrangement, should, within the limits of their respective jurisdictions, take measures to ensure that chartered vessels do not engage in IUU fishing.

38. Flag States should deter vessels from reflagging for the purposes of non-compliance with conservation and management measures or provisions adopted at a national, regional or global level. To the extent practicable, the actions and standards flag States adopt should be uniform to avoid creating incentives for vessel owners to reflag their vessels to other States.

39. States should take all practicable steps, including denial to a vessel of an authorization to fish and the entitlement to fly that State's flag, to prevent 'flag hopping'; that is to say, the practice of repeated and rapid changes of a vessel's flag for the purposes of circumventing conservation and management measures or provisions adopted at a national, regional or global level or of facilitating non-compliance with such measures or provisions.

40. Although the functions of registration of a vessel and issuing of an authorization to fish are separate, flag States should consider conducting these functions in a manner which ensures each gives appropriate consideration to the other. Flag States should ensure appropriate links between the operation of their vessel registers and the record those States keep of their fishing vessels. Where such functions are not undertaken by one agency, States should ensure sufficient cooperation and information sharing between the agencies responsible for those functions.

41. A Flag State should consider making its decision to register a fishing vessel conditional upon its being prepared to provide to the vessel an authorization to fish in waters under its jurisdiction, or on the high seas, or conditional upon an authorization to fish being issued by a coastal State to the vessel when it is under the control of that flag State.

Record of Fishing Vessels

42. Each flag State should maintain a record of fishing vessels entitled to fly its flag. Each flag State's record of fishing vessels should include, for vessels authorized to fish on the high seas, all the information set out in paragraphs 1 and 2 of Article VI of the 1993 FAO Compliance Agreement, and may also include, *inter alia*:

42.1 the previous names, if any and if known;

42.2 name, address and nationality of the natural or legal person in whose name the vessel is registered;

42.3 name, street address, mailing address and nationality of the natural or legal persons responsible for managing the operations of the vessel;

42.4 name, street address, mailing address and nationality of natural or legal persons with beneficial ownership of the vessel;

42.5 name and ownership history of the vessel, and, where this is known, the history of non-compliance by that vessel, in accordance with national laws, with conservation and management measures or provisions adopted at a national, regional or global level; and

42.6   vessel dimensions, and where appropriate, a photograph, taken at the time of registration or at the conclusion of any more recent structural alterations, showing a side profile view of the vessel.

43.   Flag States may also require the inclusion of the information in paragraph 42 in their record of fishing vessels that are not authorized to fish on the high seas.

Authorization to Fish

44.   States should adopt measures to ensure that no vessel be allowed to fish unless so authorized, in a manner consistent with international law for the high seas, in particular the rights and duties set out in articles 116 and 117 of the 1982 UN Convention, or in conformity with national legislation within areas of national jurisdiction.

45.   A flag State should ensure that each of the vessels entitled to fly its flag fishing in waters outside its sovereignty or jurisdiction holds a valid authorization to fish issued by that flag State. Where a coastal State issues an authorization to fish to a vessel, that coastal State should ensure that no fishing in its waters occurs without an authorization to fish issued by the flag State of the vessel.

46.   Vessels should have an authorization to fish and where required carry it on board. Each State's authorization should include, but need not be limited to:

46.1   the name of the vessel, and, where appropriate, the natural or legal person authorized to fish;

46.2   the areas, scope and duration of the authorization to fish; and

46.3   the species, fishing gear authorized, and where appropriate, other applicable management measures.

47.   Conditions under which an authorization is issued may also include, where required:

47.1   vessel monitoring systems;

47.2   catch reporting conditions, such as:

47.2.1   time series of catch and effort statistics by vessel;

47.2.2   total catch in number, nominal weight, or both, by species (both target and non-target) as is appropriate to each fishery period (nominal weight is defined as the live weight equivalent of the catch);

47.2.3   discard statistics, including estimates where necessary, reported as number or nominal weight by species, as is appropriate to each fishery;

47.2.4   effort statistics appropriate to each fishing method; and

47.2.5   fishing location, date and time fished and other statistics on fishing operations.

47.3   reporting and other conditions for transshipping, where transshipping is permitted;

47.4   observer coverage;

47.5   maintenance of fishing and related log books;

47.6   navigational equipment to ensure compliance with boundaries and in relation to restricted areas;

47.7   compliance with applicable international conventions and national laws and regulations in relation to maritime safety, protection of the marine environment, and conservation and management measures or provisions adopted at a national, regional or global level;

47.8   marking of its fishing vessels in accordance with internationally recognized standards, such as the FAO Standard Specification and Guidelines for the Marking and Identification of Fishing Vessels. Vessels' fishing gear should similarly be marked in accordance with internationally recognized standards;

47.9 where appropriate, compliance with other aspects of fisheries arrangements applicable to the flag State; and

47.10 the vessel having a unique, internationally recognized identification number, wherever possible, that enables it to be identified regardless of changes in registration or name over time.

48. Flag States should ensure that their fishing, transport and support vessels do not support or engage in IUU fishing. To this end, flag States should ensure that none of their vessels re-supply fishing vessels engaged in such activities or transship fish to or from these vessels. This paragraph is without prejudice to the taking of appropriate action, as necessary, for humanitarian purposes, including the safety of crew members.

49. Flag States should ensure that, to the greatest extent possible, all of their fishing, transport and support vessels involved in transshipment at sea have a prior authorization to transship issued by the flag State, and report to the national fisheries administration or other designated institution:

49.1 the date and location of all of their transshipments of fish at sea;

49.2 the weight by species and catch area of the catch transshipped;

49.3 the name, registration, flag and other information related to the identification of the vessels involved in the transshipment; and

49.4 the port of landing of the transshipped catch.

50. Flag States should make information from catch and transshipment reports available, aggregated according to areas and species, in a full, timely and regular manner and, as appropriate, to relevant national, regional and international organizations, including FAO, taking into account applicable confidentiality requirements.

Coastal State Measures

51. In the exercise of the sovereign rights of coastal States for exploring and exploiting, conserving and managing the living marine resources under their jurisdiction, in conformity with the 1982 UN Convention and international law, each coastal State should implement measures to prevent, deter and eliminate IUU fishing in the exclusive economic zone. Among the measures which the coastal State should consider, consistent with national legislation and international law, and to the extent practicable and appropriate, are:

51.1 effective monitoring, control and surveillance of fishing activities in the exclusive economic zone;

51.2 cooperation and exchange of information with other States, where appropriate, including neighbouring coastal States and with regional fisheries management organizations;

51.3 to ensure that no vessel undertakes fishing activities within its waters without a valid authorization to fish issued by that coastal State;

51.4 to ensure that an authorization to fish is issued only if the vessel concerned is entered on a record of vessels;

51.5 to ensure that each vessel fishing in its waters maintains a logbook recording its fishing activities where appropriate;

51.6 to ensure that at-sea transshipment and processing of fish and fish products in coastal State waters are authorized by that coastal State, or conducted in conformity with appropriate management regulations;

51.7　regulation of fishing access to its waters in a manner which will help to prevent, deter and eliminate IUU fishing; and

51.8　avoiding licensing a vessel to fish in its waters if that particular vessel has a history of IUU fishing, taking into account the provisions of paragraph 36.

PORT STATE MEASURES

52.　States should use measures, in accordance with international law, for port State control of fishing vessels in order to prevent, deter and eliminate IUU fishing. Such measures should be implemented in a fair, transparent and non-discriminatory manner.

53.　When used in paragraphs 52 to 64, port access means admission for foreign fishing vessels to ports or offshore terminals for the purpose of, *inter alia*, refuelling, re-supplying, transshipping and landing, without prejudice to the sovereignty of a coastal State in accordance with its national law and article 25.2 of the 1982 UN Convention and other relevant international law.

54.　Notwithstanding paragraphs 52, 53 and 55; a vessel should be provided port access, in accordance with international law, for reasons of *force majeure* or distress or for rendering assistance to persons, ships or aircraft in danger or distress.

55.　Prior to allowing a vessel port access, States should require fishing vessels and vessels involved in fishing related activities seeking permission to enter their ports to provide reasonable advance notice of their entry into port, a copy of their authorization to fish, details of their fishing trip and quantities of fish on board, with due regard to confidentiality requirements, in order to ascertain whether the vessel may have engaged in, or supported, IUU fishing.

56.　Where a port State has clear evidence that a vessel having been granted access to its ports has engaged in IUU fishing activity, the port State should not allow the vessel to land or transship fish in its ports, and should report the matter to the flag State of the vessel.

57.　States should publicize ports to which foreign flagged vessels may be permitted admission and should ensure that these ports have the capacity to conduct inspections.

58.　In the exercise of their right to inspect fishing vessels, port States should collect the following information and remit it to the flag State and, where appropriate, the relevant regional fisheries management organization:

58.1　the flag State of the vessel and identification details;

58.2　name, nationality, and qualifications of the master and the fishing master;

58.3　fishing gear;

58.4　catch on board, including origin, species, form, and quantity;

58.5　where appropriate, other information required by relevant regional fisheries management organizations or other international agreements; and

58.6　total landed and transshipped catch.

59.　If, in the course of an inspection, it is found that there are reasonable grounds to suspect that the vessel has engaged in or supported IUU fishing in areas beyond the jurisdiction of the port State, the port State should, in addition to any other actions it may take consistent with international law, immediately report the matter to the flag State of the vessel and, where appropriate, the relevant coastal States and regional fisheries management organization. The port State may take other action with the consent of, or upon the request of, the flag State.

60.　In applying paragraphs 58 and 59, States should safeguard the confidentiality of information collected, in accordance with their national laws.

61.   States should establish and publicize a national strategy and procedures for port State control of vessels involved in fishing and related activities, including training, technical support, qualification requirements and general operating guidelines for port State control officers. States should also consider capacity-building needs in the development and implementation of this strategy.

62.   States should cooperate, as appropriate, bilaterally, multilaterally and within relevant regional fisheries management organizations, to develop compatible measures for port State control of fishing vessels. Such measures should deal with the information to be collected by port States, procedures for information collection, and measures for dealing with suspected infringements by the vessel of measures adopted under these national, regional or international systems.

63.   States should consider developing within relevant regional fisheries management organizations port State measures building on the presumption that fishing vessels entitled to fly the flag of States not parties to a regional fisheries management organization and which have not agreed to cooperate with that regional fisheries management organization, which are identified as being engaged in fishing activities in the area of that particular organization, may be engaging in IUU fishing. Such port State measures may prohibit landings and transshipment of catch unless the identified vessel can establish that the catch was taken in a manner consistent with those conservation and management measures. The identification of the vessels by the regional fisheries management organization should be made through agreed procedures in a fair, transparent and non-discriminatory manner.

64.   States should enhance cooperation, including by the flow of relevant information, among and between relevant regional fisheries management organizations and States on port State controls.

INTERNATIONALLY AGREED MARKET-RELATED MEASURES

65.   The measures in paragraphs 66 to 76 are to be implemented in a manner which recognizes the right of States to trade in fish and fishery products harvested in a sustainable manner and should be interpreted and applied in accordance with the principles, rights and obligations established in the World Trade Organisation, and implemented in a fair, transparent and non-discriminatory manner.

66.   States should take all steps necessary, consistent with international law, to prevent fish caught by vessels identified by the relevant regional fisheries management organization to have been engaged in IUU fishing being traded or imported into their territories. The identification of the vessels by the regional fisheries management organization should be made through agreed procedures in a fair, transparent and non-discriminatory manner. Trade-related measures should be adopted and implemented in accordance with international law, including principles, rights and obligations established in WTO Agreements, and implemented in a fair, transparent and non-discriminatory manner. Trade-related measures should only be used in exceptional circumstances, where other measures have proven unsuccessful to prevent, deter and eliminate IUU fishing, and only after prior consultation with interested States. Unilateral trade-related measures should be avoided.

67.   States should ensure that measures on international trade in fish and fishery products are transparent, based on scientific evidence, where applicable, and are in accordance with internationally agreed rules.

68.   States should cooperate, including through relevant global and regional fisheries management organizations, to adopt appropriate multilaterally agreed trade-related measures, consistent with the WTO, that may be necessary to prevent, deter

and eliminate IUU fishing for specific fish stocks or species. Multilateral trade-related measures envisaged in regional fisheries management organizations may be used to support cooperative efforts to ensure that trade in specific fish and fish products does not in any way encourage IUU fishing or otherwise undermine the effectiveness of conservation and management measures which are consistent with the 1982 UN Convention.

69. Trade-related measures to reduce or eliminate trade in fish and fish products derived from IUU fishing could include the adoption of multilateral catch documentation and certification requirements, as well as other appropriate multilaterally-agreed measures such as import and export controls or prohibitions. Such measures should be adopted in a fair, transparent and non-discriminatory manner. When such measures are adopted, States should support their consistent and effective implementation.

70. Stock or species-specific trade-related measures may be necessary to reduce or eliminate the economic incentive for vessels to engage in IUU fishing.

71. States should take steps to improve the transparency of their markets to allow the traceability of fish or fish products.

72. States, when requested by an interested State, should assist any State in deterring trade in fish and fish products illegally harvested in its jurisdiction. Assistance should be given in accordance with terms agreed by both States and fully respecting the jurisdiction of the State requesting assistance.

73. States should take measures to ensure that their importers, transshippers, buyers, consumers, equipment suppliers, bankers, insurers, other services suppliers and the public are aware of the detrimental effects of doing business with vessels identified as engaged in IUU fishing, whether by the State under whose jurisdiction the vessel is operating or by the relevant regional fisheries management organizations in accordance with its agreed procedures, and should consider measures to deter such business. Such measures could include, to the extent possible under national law, legislation that makes it a violation to conduct such business or to trade in fish or fish products derived from IUU fishing. All identifications of vessels engaged in IUU fishing should be made in a fair, transparent and non-discriminatory manner.

74. States should take measures to ensure that their fishers are aware of the detrimental effects of doing business with importers, transshippers, buyers, consumers, equipment suppliers, bankers, insurers and other services suppliers identified as doing business with vessels identified as engaged in IUU fishing, whether by the State under whose jurisdiction the vessel is operating or by the relevant regional fisheries management organization in accordance with its agreed procedures, and should consider measures to deter such business. Such measures could include, to the extent possible under national law, legislation that makes it a violation to conduct such business or to trade in fish or fish products derived from IUU fishing. All identifications of vessels engaged in IUU fishing should be made in a fair, transparent and non-discriminatory manner.

75. States should work towards using the Harmonized Commodity Description and Coding System for fish and fisheries products in order to help promote the implementation of the IPOA.

76. Certification and documentation requirements should be standardized to the extent feasible, and electronic schemes developed where possible, to ensure their effectiveness, reduce opportunities for fraud, and avoid unnecessary burdens on trade.

RESEARCH

77. States should encourage scientific research on methods of identifying fish species from samples of processed products. FAO should facilitate the establishment of

a network of databases of genetic and other markers used to identify fish species from processed product, including the ability to identify the stock of origin where possible.

REGIONAL FISHERIES MANAGEMENT ORGANIZATIONS

78.   States should ensure compliance with and enforcement of policies and measures having a bearing on IUU fishing which are adopted by any relevant regional fisheries management organization and by which they are bound. States should cooperate in the establishment of such organizations in regions where none currently exist.

79.   As the cooperation of all relevant States is important for the success of measures taken by relevant regional fisheries management organizations to prevent, deter and eliminate IUU fishing, States which are not members of a relevant regional fisheries management organization are not discharged from their obligation to cooperate, in accordance with their international obligations, with that regional fisheries management organization. To that end, States should give effect to their duty to cooperate by agreeing to apply the conservation and management measures established by that regional fisheries management organization, or by adopting measures consistent with those conservation and management measures, and should ensure that vessels entitled to fly their flag do not undermine such measures.

80.   States, acting through relevant regional fisheries management organizations, should take action to strengthen and develop innovative ways, in conformity with international law, to prevent. deter, and eliminate IUU fishing. Consideration should be given to including the following measures:

80.1   institutional strengthening, as appropriate, of relevant regional fisheries management organizations with a view to enhancing their capacity to prevent, deter and eliminate IUU fishing;

80.2   development of compliance measures in conformity with international law;

80.3   development and implementation of comprehensive arrangements for mandatory reporting;

80.4   establishment of and cooperation in the exchange of information on vessels engaged in or supporting IUU fishing;

80.5   development and maintenance of records of vessels fishing in the area of competence of a relevant regional fisheries management organization, including both those authorized to fish and those engaged in or supporting IUU fishing;

80.6   development of methods of compiling and using trade information to monitor IUU fishing;

80.7   development of MCS, including promoting for implementation by its members in their respective jurisdictions, unless otherwise provided for in an international agreement, real time catch and vessel monitoring systems, other new technologies, monitoring of landings, port control, and inspections and regulation of transshipment, as appropriate;

80.8   development within a regional fisheries management organization, where appropriate, of boarding and inspection regimes consistent with international law, recognizing the rights and obligations of masters and inspection officers;

80.9   development of observer programmes;

80.10   where appropriate, market-related measures in accordance with the IPOA;

80.11 definition of circumstances in which vessels will be presumed to have engaged in or to have supported IUU fishing;

80.12 development of education and public awareness programmes;

80.13 development of action plans; and

80.14 where agreed by their members, examination of chartering arrangements, if there is concern that these may result in IUU fishing.

81. States, acting through relevant regional fisheries management organizations, should compile and make available on a timely basis, and at least on an annual basis, to other regional fisheries management organizations and to FAO, information relevant to the prevention, deterrence and elimination of IUU fishing, including:

81.1 estimates of the extent, magnitude and character of IUU activities in the area of competence of the regional fisheries management organization;

81.2 details of measures taken to deter, prevent and eliminate IUU fishing;

81.3 records of vessels authorized to fish, as appropriate; and

81.4 records of vessels engaged in IUU fishing.

82. Objectives of institutional and policy strengthening in relevant regional fisheries management organizations in relation to IUU fishing should include enabling regional fisheries management organizations to:

82.1 determine policy objectives regarding IUU fishing, both for internal purposes and co-ordination with other regional fisheries management organizations;

82.2 strengthen institutional mechanisms as appropriate, including mandate, functions, finance, decision making, reporting or information requirements and enforcement schemes, for the optimum implementation of policies in relation to IUU fishing;

82.3 regularize coordination with institutional mechanisms of other regional fisheries management organizations as far as possible in relation to IUU fishing, in particular information, enforcement and trade aspects; and

82.4 ensure timely and effective implementation of policies and measures internally, and in cooperation with other regional fisheries management organizations and relevant regional and international organizations.

83. States, acting through relevant regional fisheries management organizations, should encourage non-contracting parties with a real interest in the fishery concerned to join those organizations and to participate fully in their work. Where this is not possible, the regional fisheries management organizations should encourage and facilitate the participation and cooperation of non-contracting parties, in accordance with applicable international agreements and international law, in the conservation and management of the relevant fisheries resources and in the implementation of measures adopted by the relevant organizations. Regional fisheries management organizations should address the issue of access to the resource in order to foster cooperation and enhance sustainability in the fishery, in accordance with international law. States, acting through relevant regional fisheries management organizations, should also assist, as necessary, non-contracting parties in the implementation of paragraphs 78 and 79 of the IPOA.

84. When a State fails to ensure that fishing vessels entitled to fly its flag, or, to the greatest extent possible, its nationals, do not engage in IUU fishing activities that affect the fish stocks covered by a relevant regional fisheries management organization, the member States, acting through the organization, should draw the problem to the attention of that State. If the problem is not rectified, members of the organization may agree to adopt appropriate measures, through agreed procedures, in accordance with international law.

V. SPECIAL REQUIREMENTS OF DEVELOPING COUNTRIES

85.   States, with the support of FAO and relevant international financial institutions and mechanisms, where appropriate, should cooperate to support training and capacity building and consider providing financial, technical and other assistance to developing countries, including in particular the least developed among them and small island developing States, so that they can more fully meet their commitments under the IPOA and obligations under international law, including their duties as flag States and port States. Such assistance should be directed in particular to help such States in the development and implementation of national plans of action in accordance with paragraph 25.

86.   States, with the support of FAO and relevant international financial institutions and mechanisms, where appropriate, should cooperate to enable:

86.1   review and revision of national legislation and regional regulatory frameworks;

86.2   the improvement and harmonization of fisheries and related data collection;

86.3   the strengthening of regional institutions; and

86.4   the strengthening and enhancement of integrated MCS systems, including satellite monitoring systems.

VI. REPORTING

87.   States and regional fisheries management organizations should report to FAO on progress with the elaboration and implementation of their plans to prevent, deter and eliminate IUU fishing as part of their biennial reporting to FAO on the Code of Conduct. These reports should be published by FAO in a timely manner.

VII. ROLE OF FAO

88.   FAO will, as and to the extent directed by its Conference, collect all relevant information and data that might serve as a basis for further analysis aimed at identifying factors and causes contributing to IUU fishing such as, *inter alia*, a lack of input and output management controls, unsustainable fishery management methods and subsidies that contribute to IUU fishing.

89.   FAO will, as and to the extent directed by its Conference, support development and implementation of national and regional plans to prevent, deter and eliminate IUU fishing through specific, in-country technical assistance projects with Regular Programme funds and through the use of extra-budgetary funds made available to the Organization for this purpose.

90.   FAO should, in collaboration with other relevant international organizations, in particular IMO, further investigate the issue of IUU fishing.

91.   FAO should convene an Expert Consultation on the implementation of paragraph 76 of the IPOA.

92.   FAO should investigate the benefits of establishing and maintaining regional and global databases, including but not limited to, information as provided for in Article VI of the 1993 FAO Compliance Agreement.

93.   The FAO Committee on Fisheries will, based on a detailed analysis by the Secretariat, biennially evaluate the progress towards the implementation of the IPOA.

Guidelines for the Designation of Special Areas under MARPOL 73/78

IMO Resolution A.927(22), adopted on 29 November 2001

1 Introduction

1.1 The purpose of these guidelines is to provide guidance to Contracting Parties to the International Convention for the Prevention of Pollution from Ships, 1973, as modified by the Protocol of 1978 relating thereto (MARPOL 73/78) in the formulation and submission of applications for the designation of Special Areas under Annexes I, II and V to the Convention. These Guidelines also ensure that all interests – those of the coastal State, flag State, and the environmental and shipping communities – are thoroughly considered on the basis of relevant scientific, technical, economic, and environmental information and provide for the assessment of such applications by IMO. Contracting Parties should also review and comply with the applicable provisions of Annexes I, II, and V to the Convention in addition to these Guidelines.

2 Environmental Protection for Special Areas under MARPOL 73/78
General

2.1 MARPOL 73/78, in Annexes I, II and V, defines certain sea areas as Special Areas in relation to the type of pollution covered by each Annex. A Special Area is defined as 'a sea area where for recognized technical reasons in relation to its oceanographical and ecological conditions and to the particular character of its traffic, the adoption of special mandatory methods for the prevention of sea pollution by oil, noxious liquid substances, or garbage, as applicable, is required.' Under the Convention, these Special Areas are provided with a higher level of protection than other areas of the sea.

2.2 A Special Area may encompass the maritime zones of several States, or even an entire enclosed or semi-enclosed area. Special Area designation should be made on the basis of the criteria and characteristics listed in paragraphs 2.3 to 2.6 to avoid the proliferation of such areas.

Criteria for the designation of a Special Area

2.3 The criteria which must be satisfied for an area to be given Special Area status are grouped into the following categories:
- – oceanographic conditions;
- – ecological conditions; and
- – vessel traffic characteristics.

Generally, information on each category should be provided in a proposal for designation. Additional information that does not fall within these categories may also be considered.

Oceanographic conditions

2.4 The area possesses oceanographic conditions which may cause the concentration or retention of harmful substances in the waters or sediments of the area, including:
.1 particular circulation patterns (e.g. convergence zones and gyres) or temperature and salinity stratification;
.2 long residence time caused by low flushing rates;
.3 extreme ice state; and
.4 adverse wind conditions.

Ecological conditions

2.5   Conditions indicating that protection of the area from harmful substances is needed to preserve:

.1   depleted, threatened or endangered marine species;

.2   areas of high natural productivity (such as fronts, upwelling areas, gyres);

.3   spawning, breeding and nursery areas for important marine species and areas representing migratory routes for sea-birds and marine mammals;

.4   rare or fragile ecosystems such as coral reefs, mangroves, seagrass beds and wetlands; and

.5   critical habitats for marine resources including fish stocks and/or areas of critical importance for the support of large marine ecosystems.

Vessel traffic characteristics

2.6   The sea area is used by ships to an extent that the discharge of harmful substances by ships when operating in accordance with the requirements of MARPOL 73/78 for areas other than Special Areas would be unacceptable in the light of the existing oceanographic and ecological conditions in the area.

Implementation

2.7   The requirements of a Special Area designation can only become effective when adequate reception facilities are provided for ships in accordance with the provisions of MARPOL 73/78.

Other considerations

2.8   The threat to amenities posed by the discharge of harmful substances from ships operating in accordance with the MARPOL 73/78 requirements for areas other than Special Areas may strengthen the argument for designating an area a Special Area.

2.9   The extent to which the condition of a sea area is influenced by other sources of pollution such as pollution from land-based sources, dumping of wastes and dredged materials, as well as atmospheric deposition should be taken into account. Proposals would be strengthened if measures are being, or will be, taken to prevent, reduce and control pollution of the marine environment by these sources of pollution.

2.10 Consideration should be given to the extent to which a management regime is used in managing the area. Proposals for designation of a Special Area would be strengthened if measures are being taken to manage the area's resources.

3 Procedures for the designation of a Special Area

3.1   A proposal to designate a given sea area as a Special Area should be submitted to the Marine Environment Protection Committee (MEPC) for its consideration in accordance with the rules adopted by IMO for submission of papers.

3.2   A proposal to designate a sea area as a Special Area should contain:

.1   a draft amendment to MARPOL 73/78 as the formal basis for the designation; and

.2   a background document setting forth all the relevant information to explain the need for a designation.

3.3   The background document should contain the following information:

.1   a definition of the area proposed for designation, including its precise geographical co-ordinates. A reference chart is essential.

.2   an indication of the type of Special Area proposed. Proposals may be made simultaneously with respect to Annexes I, II and V of MARPOL 73/78, but proposals for each Annex should be presented and evaluated separately.

.3   a general description of the area, including information regarding:
- – oceanography
- – ecological characteristics
- – social and economic value
- – scientific and cultural significance
- – environmental pressures from ship-generated pollution
- – other environmental pressures
- – measures already taken to protect the area.

This general description may be supported by annexes containing more detailed material, or by references to readily available documentation.

.4   an analysis of how the sea area in question fulfils the criteria for the designation of Special Areas set out in paragraphs 2.3 to 2.6.

.5   information on the availability of adequate reception facilities in the proposed Special Area.

3.4   The formal amendment procedure applicable to proposals for the designation of Special Areas is set out in article 16 of MARPOL 73/78.

Detailed discharge requirements

3.5   For detailed requirements relating to discharges under Annexes I, II and V to MARPOL 73/78, please refer to the latest version of the Convention in force.

ASEAN-China Declaration on the Conduct of Parties in the South China Sea

Signed during the 8th ASEAN Summit in Phnom Penh, 4 November 2002
(2003) 2 *Chinese JIL* 418

The Government of the Member States of ASEAN and the Government of the People's Republic of China,

Reaffirming their determination to consolidate and develop the friendship and cooperation existing between their people and governments with the view to promoting a 21st century-oriented partnership of good neighbourliness and mutual trust;

Cognizant of the need to promote a peaceful, friendly and harmonious environment in the South China Sea between ASEAN and China for the enhancement of peace, stability, economic growth and prosperity in the region;

Committed to enhancing the principles and objectives of the 1997 Joint Statement of the Meeting of the Heads of State/Government of the Members States of ASEAN and President of the People's Republic of China;

Desiring to enhance favourable conditions for a peaceful and durable solution of differences and disputes among countries concerned;

Hereby declare the following:

1. The Parties reaffirm their commitment to the purposes and principles of the Charter of the United Nations, the 1982 UN Convention on the Law of the Sea, the Treaty of Amity and Cooperation in the Southeast Asia, the Five Principles of Peaceful Coexistence, and other universally recognized principles of international law which shall serve as the basic norms governing state-to-state relations;

2. The Parties are committed to exploring ways for building trust and confidence in accordance with the above-mentioned principles and on the basis of equality and mutual respect;

3. The Parties reaffirm their respect for and commitment to the freedom of navigation in and overflight above the South China Sea as provided for by the universally recognized principles of international law, including the 1982 UN Convention on the Law of the Sea;

4. The Parties concerned undertake to resolve their territorial and jurisdictional disputes by peaceful means, without resorting to the threat or use of force, through friendly consultations and negotiations by sovereign states directly concerned, in accordance with universally recognized principles of international law, including the 1982 UN Convention on the Law of the Sea;

5. The Parties undertake to exercise self-restraint in the conduct of activities that would complicate or escalate disputes and affect peace and stability including, among others, refraining from action of inhabiting on the presently uninhabited islands, reefs, shoals, cays, and other features and to handle their differences in a constructive manner.

6. Pending the peaceful settlement of territorial and jurisdictional disputes, the Parties concerned undertake to intensify efforts to seek ways, in the spirit of cooperation and understanding, to build trust and confidence between and among them, including:
    a.   holding dialogues and exchanges of views as appropriate between their defense and military officials;
    b.   ensuring just and humane treatment of all persons who are either in danger or in distress;.
    c.   notifying, on a voluntary basis, other Parties concerned of any impending joint/combined military exercise; and
    d.   exchanging, on a voluntary basis, relevant information.

7. Pending a comprehensive and durable settlement of the disputes, the Parties concerned may explore or undertake cooperative activities. These may include the following:
    a.   marine environmental protection;
    b.   marine scientific research;
    c.   safety of navigation and communication at sea;
    d.   search and rescue operations; and
    e.   combating transnational crime, including, but not limited to trafficking in illicit drugs, piracy and armed robbery at sea, and illegal traffic in arms.

The modalities, scope and locations, in respect of bilateral and multilateral cooperation, their should be agreed upon by the Parties concerned prior to their actual implementation.

8. The Parties concerned stand ready to continue their consultations and dialogues concerning relevant issues, through modalities to be agreed by them, including regular consultations on the observance of this Declaration, for the purpose of promoting good neighborliness and transparency, establishing harmony, mutual understanding and cooperation, and facilitating peaceful resolution of disputes among them;

9. The Parties undertake to respect the provisions of this Declaration and take actions consistent therewith;

10. The Parties encourage other countries to respect the principles contained in this Declaration;

11. The Parties concerned reaffirm that the adoption of a code of conduct in the South China Sea would further promote peace and stability in the region and agree to work, on the basis of consensus, towards the eventual attainment of this objective.

Done on the Fourth of November in the Year Two Thousand and Two in Phnom Penh, the Kingdom of Cambodia.

Timor Sea Treaty between the Government of East Timor and the Government of Australia

Done at Dili, 20 May 2002; entry into force, 2 April 2003
2258 UNTS 4 [Registration Number 40222][1]

The Government of Australia and the Government of East Timor,

Conscious of the importance of promoting East Timor's economic development;

Aware of the need to maintain security of investment for existing and planned petroleum activities in an area of seabed between East Timor and Australia;

Recognising the benefits that will flow to both East Timor and Australia by providing a continuing basis for petroleum activities in area of seabed between East Timor and Australia to proceed as planned;

Emphasising the importance of developing petroleum resources in a way that minimizes damage to the natural environment, that is economically sustainable, promotes further investment and contributes to the long-term development of East Timor and Australia;

Convinced that the development of the resources in accordance with this Treaty will provide a firm foundation for continuing and strengthening the friendly relations between East Timor and Australia;

Taking into account the United Nations Convention on the Law of the Sea done at Montego Bay on 10 December 1982, which provides in Article 83 that the delimitation of the continental shelf between States with opposite or adjacent coasts shall be effected by agreement on the basis of international law in order to achieve an equitable solution;

Taking further into account, in the absence of delimitation, the further obligation for States to make every effort, in a spirit of understanding and co-operation, to enter into provisional arrangements of a practical nature which do not prejudice a final determination of the seabed delimitation;

Noting the desirability of East Timor and Australia entering into a Treaty providing for the continued development of the petroleum resources in an area of seabed between East Timor and Australia;

Have agreed as follows:

Article 1 Definitions

For the purposes of this Treaty:

(a) 'Treaty' means this Treaty, including Annexes A-G and any Annexes subsequently agreed between East Timor and Australia.

(b) 'contractor' means a corporation or corporations which enter into a contract with the Designated Authority and which is registered as a contractor under the Petroleum Mining Code.

(c) 'criminal law' means any law in force in East Timor and Australia, whether substantive or procedural, that makes provision for or in relation to offences or for or in relation to the investigation or prosecution of offences or the punishment of offenders, including the carrying out of a penalty imposed by a court. For this purpose, 'investigation'

---

[1] Annex A (Designation and Description of the JPDA), Annex B (Dispute Resolution Procedure), Annex C (Powers and Functions of the Designated Authority), Annex D (Powers and Functions of the Joint Commission), Annex E (Unitisation of Greater Sunrise), Annex F (Fiscal Scheme for Certain Petroleum Deposits), and Annex G (Taxation Code for the Avoidance of Double Taxation and the Prevention of Fiscal Evasion in Respect of Activities Connected with the Joint Petroleum Development Area) omitted.

includes entry to an installation or structure in the JPDA, the exercise of powers of search and questioning and the apprehension of a suspected offender.

(d) 'Designated Authority' means the Designated Authority established in Article 6 of this Treaty.

(e) 'fiscal scheme' means a royalty, a Production Sharing Contract, or other scheme for determining Australia's and East Timor's share of petroleum or revenue from petroleum activities and does not include taxes referred to in Article 5 (b) of this Treaty.

(f) 'initially processed' means processing of petroleum to a point where it is ready for off-take from the production facility and may include such processes as the removal of water, volatiles and other impurities.

(g) 'Joint Commission' means the East Timor-Australia Joint Commission established in Article 6 of this Treaty.

(h) 'JPDA' means the Joint Petroleum Development Area established in Article 3 of this Treaty.

(i) 'Ministerial Council' means the East Timor-Australia Ministerial Council established in Article 6 of this Treaty.

(j) 'petroleum' means:

i. any naturally occurring hydrocarbon, whether in a gaseous, liquid, or solid state;

ii. any naturally occurring mixture of hydrocarbons, whether in a gaseous, liquid or solid state; or

iii. any naturally occurring mixture of one or more hydrocarbons, whether in a gaseous, liquid or solid state, as well as other substances produced in association with such hydrocarbons;

and includes any petroleum as defined by sub-paragraphs (i), (ii) or (iii) that has been returned to a natural reservoir.

(k) 'petroleum activities' means all activities undertaken to produce petroleum, authorised or contemplated under a contract, permit or licence, and includes exploration, development, initial processing, production, transportation and marketing, as well as the planning and preparation for such activities.

(l) 'Petroleum Mining Code' means the Code referred to in Article 7 of this Treaty.

(m) 'petroleum project' means petroleum activities taking place in a specified area within the JPDA.

(n) 'petroleum produced' means initially processed petroleum extracted from a reservoir through petroleum activities.

(o) 'Production Sharing Contract' means a contract between the Designated Authority and a limited liability corporation or entity with limited liability under which production from a specified area of the JPDA is shared between the parties to the contract.

(p) 'reservoir' means an accumulation of petroleum in a geological unit limited by rock, water or other substances without pressure communication through liquid or gas to another accumulation of petroleum.

(q) 'taxation code' means the code referred to in Article 13 (b) of this Treaty.

Article 2 Without prejudice

(a) This Treaty gives effect to international law as reflected in the United Nations Convention on the Law of the Sea done at Montego Bay on 10 December 1982 which under Article 83 requires States with opposite or adjacent coasts to make every effort to enter into provisional arrangements of a practical nature pending agreement on the final delimitation of the continental shelf between them in a manner consistent with international law. This Treaty is intended to adhere to such obligation.

(b)   Nothing contained in this Treaty and no acts taking place while this Treaty is in force shall be interpreted as prejudicing or affecting East Timor's or Australia's position on or rights relating to a seabed delimitation or their respective seabed entitlements.

Article 3   Joint Petroleum Development Area

(a)   The Joint Petroleum Development Area (JPDA) is established. It is the area in the Timor Sea contained within the lines described in Annex A.

(b)   East Timor and Australia shall jointly control, manage and facilitate the exploration, development and exploitation of the petroleum resources of the JPDA for the benefit of the peoples of East Timor and Australia.

(c)   Petroleum activities conducted in the JPDA shall be carried out pursuant to a contract between the Designated Authority and a limited liability corporation or entity with limited liability specifically established for the sole purpose of the contract. This provision shall also apply to the successors or assignees of such corporations.

(d)   East Timor and Australia shall make it an offence for any person to conduct petroleum activities in the JPDA otherwise than in accordance with this Treaty.

Article 4   Sharing of petroleum production

(a)   East Timor and Australia shall have title to all petroleum produced in the JPDA. Of the petroleum produced in the JPDA, ninety (90) percent shall belong to East Timor and ten (10) percent shall belong to Australia.

(b)   To the extent that fees referred to in Article 6(b)(vi) and other income are inadequate to cover the expenditure of the Designated Authority in relation to this Treaty, that expenditure shall be borne in the same proportion as set out in paragraph (a).

Article 5   Fiscal arrangements and taxes

Fiscal arrangements and taxes shall be dealt with in the following manner:

(a)   Unless a fiscal scheme is otherwise provided for in this Treaty:

i.   East Timor and Australia shall make every possible effort to agree on a joint fiscal scheme for each petroleum project in the JPDA.

ii.   If East Timor and Australia fail to reach agreement on a joint fiscal scheme referred to in sub-paragraph (i), they shall jointly appoint an independent expert to recommend an appropriate joint fiscal scheme to apply to the petroleum project concerned.

iii.   If either East Timor or Australia does not agree to the joint fiscal scheme recommended by the independent expert, East Timor and Australia may each separately impose their own fiscal scheme on their proportion of the production of the project as calculated in accordance with the formula contained in Article 4 of this Treaty.

iv.   If East Timor and Australia agree on a joint fiscal scheme pursuant to this Article, neither Australia nor East Timor may during the life of the project vary that scheme except by mutual agreement between East Timor and Australia.

(b)   Consistent with the formula contained in Article 4 of this Treaty, East Timor and Australia may, in accordance with their respective laws and the taxation code, impose taxes on their share of the revenue from petroleum activities in the JPDA and relating to activities referred to in Article 13 of this Treaty.

Article 6 Regulatory bodies

(a)   A three-tiered joint administrative structure consisting of a Designated Authority, a Joint Commission and a Ministerial Council is established.

(b)   Designated Authority:

i.   For the first three years after this Treaty enters into force, or for a different period of time if agreed to jointly by East Timor and Australia, the Joint Commission shall designate the Designated Authority.

ii.   After the period specified in sub-paragraph (i), the Designated Authority shall be the East Timor Government Ministry responsible for petroleum activities or, if so decided by the Ministry, an East Timor statutory authority.

iii. For the period specified in sub-paragraph (i), the Designated Authority has juridical personality and such legal capacities under the law of both East Timor and Australia as are necessary for the exercise of its powers and the performance of its functions. In particular, the Designated Authority shall have the capacity to contract, to acquire and dispose of movable and immovable property and to institute and be party to legal proceedings.

iv.   The Designated Authority shall be responsible to the Joint Commission and shall carry out the day-to-day regulation and management of petroleum activities.

v.   A non-exclusive listing of more detailed powers and functions of the Designated Authority is set out in Annex C. The Annexes to this Treaty may identify other additional detailed powers and functions of the Designated Authority. The Designated Authority also has such other powers and functions as may be conferred upon it by the Joint Commission.

vi.   The Designated Authority shall be financed from fees collected under the Petroleum Mining Code.

vii. For the period specified in sub-paragraph (i), the Designated Authority shall be exempt from the following existing taxes:

(1)   in East Timor, the income tax imposed under the law of East Timor;

(2)   in Australia, the income tax imposed under the federal law of Australia; as well as any identical or substantially similar taxes which are imposed after the date of signature of this Treaty in addition to, or in place of, the existing taxes.

viii. For the period specified in sub-paragraph (i), personnel of the Designated Authority:

(1)   shall be exempt from taxation of salaries, allowances and other emoluments paid to them by the Designated Authority in connection with their service with the Designated Authority other than taxation under the law of East Timor or Australia in which they are deemed to be resident for taxation purposes; and

(2)   shall, at the time of first taking up the post with the Designated Authority located in either East Timor or Australia in which they are not resident, be exempt from customs duties and other such charges (except payments for services) in respect of imports of furniture and other household and personal effects in their ownership or possession or already ordered by them and intended for their personal use or for their establishment; such goods shall be imported within six months of an officer's first entry but in exceptional circumstances an extension of time shall be granted by the Government of East Timor or the Government of Australia; goods which have been acquired or imported by officers and to which exemptions under this sub-paragraph apply shall not be given away, sold, lent or hired out, or

otherwise disposed of except under conditions agreed in advance with the Government of East Timor or the Government of Australia depending on in which country the officer is located.

(c)   Joint Commission:

i.   The Joint Commission shall consist of commissioners appointed by East Timor and Australia. There shall be one more commissioner appointed by East Timor than by Australia. The Joint Commission shall establish policies and regulations relating to petroleum activities in the JPDA and shall oversee the work of the Designated Authority.

ii.   A non-exclusive listing of more detailed powers and functions of the Joint Commission is set out in Annex D. The Annexes to this Treaty may identify other additional detailed powers and functions of the Joint Commission.

iii. Except as provided for in Article 8(c), the commissioners of either East Timor or Australia may at any time refer a matter to the Ministerial Council for resolution.

iv.   The Joint Commission shall meet annually or as may be required. Its meetings shall be chaired by a member nominated by East Timor and Australia on an alternate basis.

(d)   Ministerial Council:

i.   The Ministerial Council shall consist of an equal number of Ministers from East Timor and Australia. It shall consider any matter relating to the operation of this Treaty that is referred to it by either East Timor or Australia. It shall also consider any matter referred to in sub-paragraph (c) (iii).

ii.   In the event the Ministerial Council is unable to resolve a matter, either East Timor or Australia may invoke the dispute resolution procedure set out in Annex B.

iii. The Ministerial Council shall meet at the request of either East Timor or Australia or at the request of the Joint Commission.

iv.   Unless otherwise agreed between East Timor and Australia, meetings of the Ministerial Council where at least one member representing Australia and one member representing East Timor are physically present shall be held alternately in East Timor and Australia. Its meetings shall be chaired by a representative of East Timor or Australia on an alternate basis.

v.   The Ministerial Council may, if it so chooses, permit members to participate in a particular meeting, or all meetings, by telephone, closed circuit television or any other means of electronic communication, and a member who so participates is to be regarded as being present at the meeting. A meeting may be held solely by means of electronic communication.

(e)   Commissioners of the Joint Commission and personnel of the Designated Authority shall have no financial interest in any activity relating to exploration for and exploitation of petroleum resources in the JPDA.

Article 7 Petroleum Mining Code

(a)   East Timor and Australia shall negotiate an agreed Petroleum Mining Code which shall govern the exploration, development and exploitation of petroleum within the JPDA, as well as the export of petroleum from the JPDA.

(b)   In the event East Timor and Australia are unable to conclude a Petroleum Mining Code by the date of entry into force of this Treaty, the Joint Commission shall in its inaugural meeting adopt an interim code to remain in effect until a Petroleum Mining Code is adopted in accordance with paragraph (a).

Article 8 Pipelines

(a)   The construction and operation of a pipeline within the JPDA for the purposes of exporting petroleum from the JPDA shall be subject to the approval of the Joint Commission. East Timor and Australia shall consult on the terms and conditions of pipelines exporting petroleum from the JPDA to the point of landing.

(b)   A pipeline landing in East Timor shall be under the jurisdiction of East Timor. A pipeline landing in Australia shall be under the jurisdiction of Australia.

(c)   In the event a pipeline is constructed from the JPDA to the territory of either East Timor or Australia, the country where the pipeline lands may not object to or impede decisions of the Joint Commission regarding a pipeline to the other country. Notwithstanding Article 6(c)(iii), the Ministerial Council may not review or change any such decisions.

(d)   Paragraph (c) shall not apply where the effect of constructing a pipeline from the JPDA to the other country would cause the supply of gas to be withheld from a limited liability corporation or limited liability entity which has obtained consent under this Treaty to obtain gas from a project in the JPDA for contracts to supply gas for a specified period of time.

(e)   Neither East Timor nor Australia may object to, nor in any way impede, a proposal to use floating gas to liquids processing and off-take in the JPDA on a commercial basis where such proposal shall produce higher revenues to East Timor and Australia from royalties and taxes earned from activities conducted within the JPDA than would be earned if gas were transported by pipeline.

(f)   Paragraph (e) shall not apply where the effect of floating gas to liquids processing and off-take in the JPDA would cause the supply of gas to be withheld from a limited liability corporation or limited liability entity which has obtained consent under this Treaty to obtain gas from the JPDA for contracts to supply gas for a specified period of time.

(g)   Petroleum from the JPDA and from fields which straddle the boundaries of the JPDA shall at all times have priority of carriage along any pipeline carrying petroleum from and within the JPDA.

(h)   There shall be open access to pipelines for petroleum from the JPDA. The open access arrangements shall be in accordance with good international regulatory practice. If East Timor has jurisdiction over the pipeline, it shall consult with Australia over access to the pipeline. If Australia has jurisdiction over the pipeline, it shall consult with East Timor over access to the pipeline.

Article 9 Unitisation

(a)   Any reservoir of petroleum that extends across the boundary of the JPDA shall be treated as a single entity for management and development purposes.

(b)   East Timor and Australia shall work expeditiously and in good faith to reach agreement on the manner in which the deposit will be most effectively exploited and on the equitable sharing of the benefits arising from such exploitation.

Article 10 Marine environment

(a)   East Timor and Australia shall co-operate to protect the marine environment of the JPDA so as to prevent and minimise pollution and other environmental harm from petroleum activities. Special efforts shall be made to protect marine animals including marine mammals, seabirds, fish and coral. East Timor and Australia shall consult as to the best means to protect the marine environment of the JPDA from the harmful consequences of petroleum activities.

(b) Where pollution of the marine environment occurring in the JPDA spreads beyond the JPDA, East Timor and Australia shall co-operate in taking action to prevent, mitigate and eliminate such pollution.

(c) The Designated Authority shall issue regulations to protect the marine environment in the JPDA. It shall establish a contingency plan for combating pollution from petroleum activities in the JPDA.

(d) Limited liability corporations or limited liability entities shall be liable for damage or expenses incurred as a result of pollution of the marine environment arising out of petroleum activities within the JPDA in accordance with:

i. their contract, licence or permit or other form of authority issued pursuant to this Treaty; and

ii. the law of the jurisdiction (East Timor or Australia) in which the claim is brought.

Article 11 Employment

(a) East Timor and Australia shall:

i. take appropriate measures with due regard to occupational health and safety requirements to ensure that preference is given in employment in the JPDA to nationals or permanent residents of East Timor; and

ii. facilitate, as a matter of priority, training and employment opportunities for East Timorese nationals and permanent residents.

(b) Australia shall expedite and facilitate processing of applications for visas through its Diplomatic Mission in Dili by East Timorese nationals and permanent residents employed by limited liability corporations or limited liability entities in Australia associated with petroleum activities in the JPDA.

Article 12 Health and safety for workers

The Designated Authority shall develop, and limited liability corporations or limited liability entities shall apply, occupational health and safety standards and procedures for persons employed on structures in the JPDA that are no less effective than those standards and procedures that would apply to persons employed on similar structures in East Timor and Australia. The Designated Authority may adopt, consistent with this Article, standards and procedures taking into account an existing system established under the law of either East Timor or Australia.

Article 13 Application of taxation law

(a) For the purposes of taxation law related directly or indirectly to:

i. the exploration for or the exploitation of petroleum in the JPDA; or

ii. acts, matters, circumstances and things touching, concerning arising out of or connected with such exploration and exploitation the JPDA shall be deemed to be, and treated by, East Timor and Australia, as part of that country.

(b) The taxation code to provide relief from double taxation relating to petroleum activities is set out in Annex G.

(c) The taxation code contains its own dispute resolution mechanism. Article 23 of this Treaty shall not apply to disputes covered by that mechanism.

Article 14 Criminal jurisdiction

(a) A national or permanent resident of East Timor or Australia shall be subject to the criminal law of that country in respect of acts or omissions occurring in the JPDA connected with or arising out of exploration for and exploitation of petroleum resources, provided that a permanent resident of East Timor or Australia who is a national of the other country shall be subject to the criminal law of the latter country.

(b) Subject to paragraph (d), a national of a third state, not being a permanent resident of either East Timor or Australia, shall be subject to the criminal law of both East Timor and Australia in respect of acts or omissions occurring in the JPDA connected with or arising out of petroleum activities. Such a person shall not be subject to criminal proceedings under the law of either East Timor or Australia if he or she has already been tried and discharged or acquitted by a competent tribunal or already undergone punishment for the same act or omission under the law of the other country or where the competent authorities of one country, in accordance with its law, have decided in the public interest to refrain from prosecuting the person for that act or omission.

(c) In cases referred to in paragraph (b), East Timor and Australia shall, as and when necessary, consult each other to determine which criminal law is to be applied, taking into account the nationality of the victim and the interests of the country most affected by the alleged offence.

(d) The criminal law of the flag state shall apply in relation to acts or omissions on board vessels including seismic or drill vessels in, or aircraft in flight over, the JPDA.

(e) East Timor and Australia shall provide assistance to and co-operate with each other, including through agreements or arrangements as appropriate, for the purposes of enforcement of criminal law under this Article, including the obtaining of evidence and information.

(f) Both East Timor and Australia recognise the interest of the other country where a victim of an alleged offence is a national of that other country and shall keep that other country informed, to the extent permitted by its law, of action being taken with regard to the alleged offence.

(g) East Timor and Australia may make arrangements permitting officials of one country to assist in the enforcement of the criminal law of the other country. Where such assistance involves the detention of a person who under paragraph (a) is subject to the jurisdiction of the other country that detention may only continue until it is practicable to hand the person over to the relevant officials of that other country.

Article 15 Customs, quarantine and migration

(a) East Timor and Australia may, subject to paragraphs (c), (e), (f) and (g), apply customs, migration and quarantine laws to persons, equipment and goods entering its territory from, or leaving its territory for, the JPDA. East Timor and Australia may adopt arrangements to facilitate such entry and departure.

(b) Limited liability corporations or other limited liability entities shall ensure, unless otherwise authorised by East Timor or Australia, that persons, equipment and goods do not enter structures in the JPDA without first entering East Timor or Australia, and that their employees and the employees of their subcontractors are authorised by the Designated Authority to enter the JPDA.

(c) Either country may request consultations with the other country in relation to the entry of particular persons, equipment and goods to structures in the JPDA aimed at controlling the movement of such persons, equipment or goods.

(d) Nothing in this Article prejudices the right of either East Timor or Australia to apply customs, migration and quarantine controls to persons, equipment and goods entering the JPDA without the authority of either country. East Timor and Australia may adopt arrangements to co-ordinate the exercise of such rights.

(e) Goods and equipment entering the JPDA for purposes related to petroleum activities shall not be subject to customs duties.

(f)   Goods and equipment leaving or in transit through either East Timor or Australia for the purpose of entering the JPDA for purposes related to petroleum activities shall not be subject to customs duties.

(g)   Goods and equipment leaving the JPDA for the purpose of being permanently transferred to a part of either East Timor or Australia may be subject to customs duties of that country.

Article 16   Hydrographic and seismic surveys

(a)   East Timor and Australia shall have the right to carry out hydrographic surveys to facilitate petroleum activities in the JPDA. East Timor and Australia shall co-operate on:

i.   the conduct of such surveys, including the provision of necessary on-shore facilities; and

ii.   exchanging hydrographic information relevant to petroleum activities in the JPDA.

(b)   For the purposes of this Treaty, East Timor and Australia shall co-operate in facilitating the conduct of seismic surveys in the JPDA, including in the provision of necessary on-shore facilities.

Article 17   Petroleum industry vessel – safety, operating standards and crewing

Except as otherwise provided in this Treaty, vessels of the nationality of East Timor or Australia engaged in petroleum activities in the JPDA shall be subject to the law of their nationality in relation to safety and operating standards and crewing regulations. Vessels with the nationality of other countries shall apply the law of East Timor or Australia depending on whose ports they operate, in relation to safety and operating standards, and crewing regulations. Such vessels that enter the JPDA and do not operate out of either East Timor or Australia under the law of both East Timor or Australia shall be subject to the relevant international safety and operating standards.

Article 18   Surveillance

(a)   For the purposes of this Treaty, East Timor and Australia shall have the right to carry out surveillance activities in the JPDA.

(b)   East Timor and Australia shall co-operate on and co-ordinate any surveillance activities carried out in accordance with paragraph (a).

(c)   East Timor and Australia shall exchange information derived from any surveillance activities carried out in accordance with paragraph (a).

Article 19   Security measures

(a)   East Timor and Australia shall exchange information on likely threats to, or security incidents relating to, exploration for and exploitation of petroleum resources in the JPDA.

(b)   East Timor and Australia shall make arrangements for responding to security incidents in the JPDA.

Article 20   Search and rescue

East Timor and Australia shall, at the request of the Designated Authority and consistent with this Treaty, co-operate on and assist with search and rescue operations in the JPDA taking into account generally accepted international rules, regulations and procedures established through competent international organisations.

Article 21 Air traffic services

East Timor and Australia shall, in consultation with the Designated Authority or at itsrequest, and consistent with this Treaty, co-operate in relation to the operation of air services, the provision of air traffic services and air accident investigations, within the JPDA, in accordance with national laws applicable to flights to and within the JPDA, recognizing established international rules, regulations and procedures where these have been adopted by East Timor and Australia.

Article 22 Duration of the Treaty

This Treaty shall be in force until there is a permanent seabed delimitation between East Timor and Australia or for thirty years from the date of its entry into force, whichever is sooner. This Treaty may be renewed by agreement between East Timor and Australia. Petroleum activities of limited liability corporations or other limited liability entities entered into under the terms of the Treaty shall continue even if the Treaty is no longer in force under conditions equivalent to those in place under the Treaty.

Article 23 Settlement of Disputes

(a)   With the exception of disputes falling within the scope of the taxation code referred to in Article 13(b) of this Treaty and which shall be settled in accordance with that code, any dispute concerning the interpretation or application of this Treaty shall, as far as possible, be settled by consultation or negotiation.

(b)   Any dispute which is not settled in the manner set out in paragraph (a) and any unresolved matter relating to the operation of this Treaty under Article 6(d)(ii) shall, at the request of either East Timor or Australia, be submitted to an arbitral tribunal in accordance with the procedure set out in Annex B.

Article 24 Amendment

This Treaty may be amended at any time by written agreement between East Timor and Australia.

Article 25 Entry into force

(a)   This Treaty shall enter into force upon the day on which East Timor and Australia have notified each other in writing that their respective requirements for entry into force of this Treaty have been complied with.

(b)   Upon entry into force, the Treaty will be taken to have effect and all of its provisions will apply and be taken to have applied on and from the date of signature.

IN WITNESS WHEREOF the undersigned, being duly authorised thereto by their respective Governments, have signed this Treaty.

DONE at Dili, on this twentieth day of May, Two thousand and two in two originals in the English language.

Treaty between the Government of Australia and the Government of the Democratic Republic of Timor-Leste on Certain Maritime Arrangements in the Timor Sea

Done at Sydney, 12 January 2006; entry into force, 23 February 2007
[2007] ATS 12[1]

The Government of Australia and the Government of the Democratic Republic of Timor-Leste (hereinafter each referred to as 'Party' or both as 'Parties')

Conscious of their geographic proximity, friendship and developing economic relationship;

Noting that the Parties have not yet delimited their maritime boundaries;

Taking into account the United Nations Convention on the Law of the Sea done at Montego Bay on 10 December 1982 and, in particular, Articles 74 and 83 which provide that the delimitation of the exclusive economic zone and continental shelf between States with opposite or adjacent coasts shall be effected by agreement on the basis of international law in order to achieve an equitable solution;

Further taking into account, in the absence of delimitation, the obligation for States to make every effort in a spirit of understanding and cooperation to enter into provisional arrangements of a practical nature which are without prejudice to the final determination;

Recognising the benefits that will flow to both Australia and Timor-Leste by providing a long-term basis for petroleum activities in the area of seabed between Australia and Timor-Leste;

Emphasising the importance of developing and managing the living and non-living resources of the Timor Sea in an economically and environmentally sustainable manner, and the importance of promoting investment and long-term development in Australia and Timor-Leste;

Convinced that the long-term development of the resources, in accordance with this Treaty, the Timor Sea Treaty and the Sunrise IUA will provide a firm foundation for continuing and strengthening the friendly relations between Australia and Timor-Leste;

Fully committed to maintaining, renewing and further strengthening the mutual respect, friendship and cooperation between Australia and Timor-Leste;

Mindful of the interests which Australia and Timor-Leste share as immediate neighbours and in a spirit of cooperation, friendship and goodwill; and

Convinced that this Treaty will contribute to the strengthening of relations between the two countries;

Agree as follows:

Article 1 Definitions
For the purposes of this Treaty:

1. 'AUD' means the Australian Dollar;

2. 'JPDA' means the Joint Petroleum Development Area established by Article 3 of the Timor Sea Treaty;

3. 'LIBOR' means the British Bankers' Association fixing of the one (1) month London Interbank Offer Rate for USD;

4. 'period of this Treaty' means the period of the duration of this Treaty referred to in Article 12;

---

[1] Annex I (Assessment Procedure) and Annex II (Line Referred to in Article 8) omitted.

5. 'petroleum' means:

(a)   any naturally occurring hydrocarbon, whether in a gaseous, liquid or solid state;

(b)   any naturally occurring mixture of hydrocarbons, whether in a gaseous, liquid or solid state; or

(c)   any naturally occurring mixture of one or more hydrocarbons, whether in a gaseous, liquid or solid state, as well as other substances produced in association with such hydrocarbons;

including any petroleum as defined by sub-paragraphs (a), (b) or (c) of this paragraph that has been returned to a natural reservoir;

6.   'petroleum activities' means all activities undertaken to produce petroleum;

7.   'quarter' means the three months ending March, June, September and December;

8.   'Sunrise IUA' means the Agreement between the Government of Australia and the Government of the Democratic Republic of Timor-Leste relating to the Unitisation of the Sunrise and Troubadour Fields, done at Dili on 6 March 2003;

9.   'the 1982 Convention' means the United Nations Convention on the Law of the Sea, done at Montego Bay on 10 December 1982;

10.   'Timor Sea Treaty' means the Timor Sea Treaty between the Government of East Timor and the Government of Australia, done at Dili on 20 May 2002;

11.   'Unit Area' means the area described in Annex I of the Sunrise IUA;

12.   'Upstream' means the petroleum activities and facilities prior to the 'valuation point' as defined in the Sunrise IUA;

13.   'USD' means the United States Dollar; and

14.   Unless the context otherwise requires, terms which are not defined in this Treaty, but that are defined in the Timor Sea Treaty or the Sunrise IUA, shall have the same meaning in this Treaty as in the Timor Sea Treaty or the Sunrise IUA.

Article 2 Without prejudice

1.   Nothing contained in this Treaty shall be interpreted as:

(a)   prejudicing or affecting Timor-Leste's or Australia's legal position on, or legal rights relating to, the delimitation of their respective maritime boundaries;

(b)   a renunciation of any right or claim relating to the whole or any part of the Timor Sea; or

(c)   recognition or affirmation of any right or claim of the other Party to the whole or any part of the Timor Sea.

2.   No act or activities taking place as a result of, and no law entering into force by virtue of, this Treaty or the operation thereof, may be relied upon as a basis for asserting, supporting, denying or furthering the legal position of either Party with respect to maritime boundary claims, jurisdiction or rights concerning the whole or any part of the Timor Sea.

Article 3 Duration of the Timor Sea Treaty

The text of Article 22 of the Timor Sea Treaty relating to the duration of that Treaty is replaced by the following:

'This Treaty shall be in force for the duration of the Treaty between the Government of Australia and the Government of the Democratic Republic of Timor-Leste on Certain Maritime Arrangements in the Timor Sea. This Treaty may be renewed by agreement between Australia and East Timor. Petroleum activities of limited liability corporations or other limited liability entities entered into under the terms of the Treaty shall continue even if the Treaty is no longer in force under conditions equivalent to those in place under the Treaty.'

Article 4 Moratorium

1. Neither Australia nor Timor-Leste shall assert, pursue or further by any means in relation to the other Party its claims to sovereign rights and jurisdiction and maritime boundaries for the period of this Treaty.

2. Paragraph 1 of this Article does not prevent a Party from continuing activities (including the regulation and authorisation of existing and new activities) in areas in which its domestic legislation on 19 May 2002 authorised the granting of permission for conducting activities in relation to petroleum or other resources of the seabed and subsoil.

3. Notwithstanding paragraph 2 of this Article, the JPDA will continue to be governed by the terms of the Timor Sea Treaty and associated instruments.

4. Notwithstanding any other bilateral or multilateral agreement binding on the Parties, or any declaration made by either Party pursuant to any such agreement, neither Party shall commence or pursue any proceedings against the other Party before any court, tribunal or other dispute settlement mechanism that would raise or result in, either directly or indirectly, issues or findings of relevance to maritime boundaries or delimitation in the Timor Sea.

5. Any court, tribunal or other dispute settlement body hearing proceedings involving the Parties shall not consider, make comment on, nor make findings that would raise or result in, either directly or indirectly, issues or findings of relevance to maritime boundaries or delimitation in the Timor Sea. Any such comment or finding shall be of no effect, and shall not be relied upon, or cited, by the Parties at any time.

6. Neither Party shall raise or pursue in any international organisation matters that are, directly or indirectly, relevant to maritime boundaries or delimitation in the Timor Sea.

7. The Parties shall not be under an obligation to negotiate permanent maritime boundaries for the period of this Treaty.

Article 5 Division of revenues from the Unit Area

1. The Parties shall share equally revenue derived directly from the production of that petroleum lying within the Unit Area in so far as the revenue relates to the upstream exploitation of that petroleum.

2. The value of petroleum upstream shall be determined on the basis of arm's length principles.

3. The Australian revenue component means taxation revenue collected from:
    (a)   the petroleum resource rent tax;
    (b)   company tax (including capital gains tax); and
    (c)   first tranche petroleum and profit petroleum pursuant to the Timor Sea Treaty;
    or subsequent taxes of a similar nature.

4. The Australian revenue component shall be determined as follows:
    (a)   Revenue relating to the petroleum resource rent tax is the actual revenue collected each quarter adjusted:
        (i)   to include expenditures related to the petroleum activities undertaken within the Unit Area transferred out of this project and to exclude expenditures not related to the petroleum activities undertaken within the Unit Area transferred into this project; and

      (ii)   in the anticipated last 5 years of the project's life, to include estimated closing down costs (subject to reconciliation against actual closing down costs once the project has closed down).

(b)   Revenue relating to company tax is the actual revenue collected each quarter adjusted to determine the company tax position of the entity's upstream operations relating to the petroleum activities undertaken within the Unit Area.

(c)   The adjustment referred to in sub-paragraph (b) of this paragraph is based on:

      (i)   allocating direct revenues and direct deductible non-interest expenses between the upstream operations in the Unit Area and other operations of the entity;

      (ii)   allocating indirect revenues and indirect deductible non-interest expenses between the upstream operations in the Unit Area and the other operations of the entity in the same proportions as direct revenues and direct deductible expenses respectively; and

      (iii)   allocating deductible interest expenses between the upstream operations in the Unit Area and the other operations of the entity in the same proportion as the final allocation of deductible non-interest expenses.

(d)   Revenue relating to first tranche petroleum and profit petroleum is the actual revenue collected each quarter.

5.   The Timor-Leste revenue component means taxation revenue collected from first tranche petroleum, profit petroleum and all profit-based income taxes calculated and levied by annual assessment pursuant to the Timor Sea Treaty, or subsequent taxes of a similar nature, but excludes Value Added Tax or income tax withheld monthly or similar taxes, or subsequent taxes of a similar nature.

6.   The Timor-Leste revenue component shall be determined based on actual revenue collected each quarter.

7.   Each Party shall notify the other Party of the revenue amount (in domestic currency terms) relating to the quarter on the first working day in both Australia and Timor-Leste on or after 90 days following the end of that quarter.

8.   Australia's revenue amount in USD terms shall be:

(a)   determined on the first business day in both Sydney and Dili on or after 20 days following the notification referred to in paragraph 7 of this Article; and

(b)   based on the simple average of the USD/AUD exchange rate published by the Reserve Bank of Australia at 4.00 pm (Australian Eastern Standard Time) on that day, the two preceding days, and the two subsequent days.

9.   Australia shall make a payment in USD to Timor-Leste equivalent to half the aggregate of the Australian revenue component (in USD terms) and the Timor-Leste revenue component, less the Timor-Leste revenue component (in USD terms), on the first business day in both Sydney and Dili on or after 30 days following notification referred to in paragraph 7 of this Article.

10.   In the event that Timor-Leste's revenue component exceeds Australia's revenue component in USD terms in a particular quarter, Timor-Leste shall not make a payment to Australia, and subsequent quarterly payments by Australia to Timor-Leste shall be adjusted to take account of the earlier payment not made by Timor-Leste.

11.   Australia and Timor-Leste shall inform each other expeditiously of changes in their respective taxation policies and laws that may impact on the revenue derived directly from the production of petroleum in the Unit Area. Where one Party notifies the other that it considers that a change in the taxation laws of the other Party is likely to have a serious impact on the revenue to be received by the first Party:

(a) the Parties shall, as a matter of urgency, consult with a view to resolving the matter; and

(b) where the Parties are unable to resolve the matter pursuant to sub-paragraph (a) of this paragraph within a reasonable period, the matter shall be referred immediately to the Maritime Commission established in Article 9.

12. The Parties agree that during the period of this Treaty, the totality of financial payments from one Party to another concerning or relating to the exploration and exploitation of maritime areas between Australia and Timor-Leste are defined by the treaties and agreements referred to in paragraph 1 of Article 7 and such agreed associated documentation relating to those treaties and agreements that exists at the time of the entry into force of this Treaty, and neither Party shall seek additional payments.

13. The Parties shall establish procedures for the implementation of paragraphs 1 to 10 of this Article.

Article 6 Assessor

1. Either Party may request the appointment of an assessor to review adjustments used to calculate any one or more of the revenues referred to in paragraphs 3 and 5 of Article 5.

2. The Parties shall, within 30 days of a request being made to appoint an assessor, seek to reach agreement on the appointment of such an assessor. If, within this period, no agreement has been reached, the procedures for appointment specified in Annex I shall be followed.

3. The assessor shall act in accordance with the terms of Annex I.

4. The assessor's conclusions shall be implemented by the Parties unless the Parties agree otherwise.

5. Where adjustments are made to previous payments as the result of a review by an assessor, interest will be added, calculated as follows: [...][2]

Article 7 Petroleum resources

1. The applicable obligations and rights as between Australia and Timor-Leste governing the exploration and exploitation of petroleum resources during the period of this Treaty are those contained in:

(a) this Treaty;

(b) the Timor Sea Treaty;

(c) the Sunrise IUA; and

(d) any future agreement between Australia and Timor-Leste as referred to in Article 9 of the Timor Sea Treaty.

2. Except as otherwise provided for in this Treaty, nothing contained in this Treaty, and no actions taken pursuant to it, shall be interpreted as amending or revoking any terms of the Timor Sea Treaty or the Sunrise IUA.

Article 8 Water column jurisdiction

1. For the period of this Treaty:

(a) Australia will continue to exercise jurisdiction in relation to the water column, and sovereign rights over the resources of the water column, south of the line described in Annex II;

(b) Timor-Leste will continue to exercise jurisdiction in relation to the water column, and sovereign rights over the resources of the water column, north of the line described in Annex II; and

---

[2] Interest formula omitted.

(c)   the jurisdiction referred to in sub-paragraph (b) of this paragraph shall be exercised in a manner that does not unduly inhibit petroleum activities within the JPDA.

2.   Where the same stock or stocks of associated species straddle the line described in Annex II, Timor-Leste and Australia shall seek, either directly or through appropriate subregional or regional fisheries management organisations, to agree upon the measures necessary to co-ordinate and ensure the conservation and development of such stocks.

3.   Timor-Leste and Australia shall make every effort to pursue cooperation in relation to highly migratory fish stocks, as defined in Annex 1 to the 1982 Convention, either directly or through appropriate subregional or regional fisheries management organisations, to ensure effective conservation and management of such stocks.

Article 9 Timor-Leste/Australia Maritime Commission

1.   There is hereby established a Timor-Leste/Australia Maritime Commission ('Commission'), which shall constitute a focal point for bilateral consultations with regard to maritime matters of interest to the Parties.

2.   The Commission shall comprise one Minister each appointed by the Parties, or such other representative of the Governments of Australia and Timor-Leste as appointed respectively by the Parties.

3.   The Commission shall:
(a)   review the status of maritime boundary arrangements;
(b)   consult on maritime security, including the security of petroleum facilities and infrastructures;
(c)   consult on issues relating to the marine environment and its protection;
(d)   consult on the management of natural resources (renewable and non-renewable), and promote sustainable management strategies; and
(e)   consult on other maritime matters as appropriate as agreed by the Parties.

4.   The Commission shall meet at least annually.

5.   The proceedings in the Commission shall be without prejudice to the contents of this Treaty, and of any legislation, acts and activities thereunder.

Article 10 Re-apportionment of unit petroleum under the Sunrise IUA

Notwithstanding Article 8 of the Sunrise IUA, the Parties agree that there shall be no re-determination of the apportionment ratio referred to in that article during the period of this Treaty.

Article 11 Dispute settlement

Any disputes about the interpretation or application of this Treaty shall be settled by consultation or negotiation.

Article 12 Period of this Treaty

1.   Subject to paragraphs 2, 3 and 4 of this Article, this Treaty shall remain in force until the date 50 years after its entry into force, or until the date five years after the exploitation of the Unit Area ceases, whichever occurs earlier.

2.   If:
(a)   a development plan for the Unit Area has not been approved in accordance with paragraph 1 of Article 12 of the Sunrise IUA within six years after the date of entry into force of this Treaty; or
(b)   production of petroleum from the Unit Area has not commenced within ten years after the date of entry into force of this Treaty;

either Party may notify the other Party in writing that it wishes to terminate this Treaty, in which case the Treaty shall cease to be in force three calendar months after such notice is given.

3. Should petroleum production take place in the Unit Area subsequent to the termination of this Treaty pursuant to paragraph 2 of this Article, all the terms of this Treaty shall come back into force and operate from the date of commencement of production.

4. The following provisions of this Treaty shall survive termination of this Treaty, and the Parties shall continue to be bound by them after termination:

    (a)   Article 2;

    (b)   the second sentence of paragraph 5 of Article 4;

    (c)   paragraph 3 of this Article; and

    (d)   this paragraph.

5. The period of this Treaty referred to in paragraph 1 of this Article may be extended by agreement in writing between the Parties.

Article 13 Entry into Force

This Treaty shall enter into force on the day on which the Government of Australia and the Government of the Democratic Republic of Timor-Leste have notified each other, in writing, that their respective requirements for the entry into force of this Treaty have been complied with.

IN WITNESS WHEREOF the undersigned, being duly authorised thereto by their respective Governments, have signed this Treaty.

DONE at Sydney, on this twelfth day of January, Two thousand and six.

Agreement Concerning Co-operation in Suppressing Illicit Maritime and Air Trafficking in Narcotic Drugs and Psychotropic Substances in the Caribbean Area

Done at San José, 10 April 2003; not yet in force

FCO, *Agreement Concerning Co-operation in Suppressing Illicit Maritime and Air Trafficking in Narcotic Drugs and Psychotropic Substances in the Caribbean Area, 2003*, 2005, 47

The Parties to this Agreement,

Bearing in mind the complex nature of the problem of illicit maritime narcotics traffic in the Caribbean area;

Desiring to increase their co-operation to the fullest extent in the suppression of illicit traffic in narcotic drugs and psychotropic substances by sea in accordance with international law of the sea, respecting freedom of navigation and overflight;

Recognising that the Parties to this Agreement are also Parties to the *1988 United Nations Convention Against Illicit Traffic in Narcotic Drugs and Psychotropic Substances* (hereinafter, 'the 1988 Convention');

Having regard to the urgent need for international co-operation in suppressing illicit traffic by sea, which is recognised in the 1988 Convention;

Recalling that the 1988 Convention requires Parties to consider entering into bilateral or regional agreements or arrangements to carry out, or enhance the effectiveness of the provisions of Article 17 of that Convention;

Recalling further that some of the Parties have consented to be bound by the 1996 Treaty Establishing the Regional Security System, the 1989 Memorandum of Understanding Regarding Mutual Assistance and Co-operation for the Prevention and Repression of Customs Offences in the Caribbean Zone, which established the Caribbean Customs Law Enforcement Council, and the 1982 United Nations Convention on the Law of the Sea;

Recognising that the nature of illicit traffic urgently requires the Parties to foster regional and sub-regional co-operation;

Desiring to promote greater co-operation among the Parties, and thereby enhance their effectiveness in combating illicit traffic by and over the sea in the Caribbean area, in a manner consistent with the principles of sovereign equality and territorial integrity of States including non-intervention in the domestic affairs of other States;

Recalling that the Regional Meeting on Drug Control Co-ordination and Co-operation in the Caribbean held in Barbados in 1996 recommended the elaboration of a Regional Maritime Agreement;

Have agreed as follows:

NATURE AND SCOPE OF AGREEMENT

Article 1 Definitions
In this Agreement:
a. 'illicit traffic' has the same meaning as that term is defined in the 1988 *United Nations Convention Against Illicit Traffic in Narcotic Drugs and Psychotropic Substances* (hereinafter, 'the 1988 Convention').

b. 'competent national authority' means the authority or authorities designated pursuant to paragraph 7 of Article 17 of the 1988 Convention or what has been otherwise notified to the Depositary.

c. 'law enforcement authority' means the competent law enforcement entity or entities identified to the Depositary by each Party which has responsibility for carrying out the maritime or air law enforcement functions of that Party pursuant to this Agreement.

d. 'law enforcement officials' means the uniformed and other clearly identifiable members of the law enforcement authority of each Party.

e. 'law enforcement vessels' means vessels clearly marked and identifiable as being on government service, used for law enforcement purposes and duly authorised to that effect, including any boat and aircraft embarked on such vessels, aboard which law enforcement officials are embarked.

f. 'law enforcement aircraft' means aircraft clearly marked and identifiable as being on government service, used for law enforcement purposes and duly authorised to that effect, aboard which law enforcement officials are embarked.

g. 'aircraft in support of law enforcement operations' means aircraft clearly marked and identifiable as being on government service of one Party, providing assistance to a law enforcement aircraft or vessel of that Party, in a law enforcement operation.

h. 'waters of a Party' means the territorial sea and the archipelagic waters of that Party.

i. 'air space of a Party' means the air space over the territory (continental and insular) and waters of that Party.

j. 'Caribbean area' means the Gulf of Mexico, the Caribbean Sea and the Atlantic Ocean west of longitude 45-degrees West, north of latitude 0-degrees (the

Equator) and south of latitude 30-degrees North, with the exception of the territorial sea of States not Party to this Agreement.

k. 'suspect aircraft' means any aircraft in respect of which there are reasonable grounds to suspect that it is engaged in illicit traffic.

l. 'suspect vessel' means any vessel in respect of which there are reasonable grounds to suspect that it is engaged in illicit traffic.

Article 2 Objectives

The Parties shall co-operate to the fullest extent possible in combating illicit maritime and air traffic in and over the waters of the Caribbean area, consistent with available law enforcement resources of the Parties and related priorities, in conformity with the international law of the sea and applicable agreements, with a view to ensuring that suspect vessels and suspect aircraft are detected, identified, continuously monitored, and where evidence of involvement in illicit traffic is found, suspect vessels are detained for appropriate law enforcement action by the responsible law enforcement authorities.

Article 3 Regional and sub-regional co-operation

1. The Parties shall take the steps necessary within available resources to meet the objectives of this Agreement, including, on a cost-effective basis, the enhancement of regional and sub-regional institutional capabilities and the co-ordination and implementation of co-operation.

2. In order to meet the objectives of this Agreement, each Party is encouraged to co-operate closely with the other Parties, consistent with the relevant provisions of the 1988 Convention.

3. The Parties shall co-operate, directly or through competent international, regional or sub-regional organisations, to assist and support States party to this Agreement in need of such assistance and support, to the extent possible, through programmes of technical co-operation on suppression of illicit traffic. The Parties may undertake, directly or through competent international, regional or sub-regional organisations, to provide assistance to such States for the purpose of augmenting and strengthening the infrastructure needed for effective control and prevention of illicit traffic.

4. In order to enable Parties to better fulfil their obligations under this Agreement, they are encouraged to request and provide operational and technical assistance from and to each other.

Article 4 Facilitation of co-operation

1. Each Party is encouraged to accelerate the authorisations for law enforcement vessels and law enforcement aircraft, aircraft in support of law enforcement operations, and law enforcement officials of the other Parties to enter its waters, air space, ports and airports in order to carry out the objectives of this Agreement, in accordance with its provisions.

2. The Parties shall facilitate effective co-ordination between their law enforcement authorities and promote the exchange of law enforcement officials and other experts, including, where appropriate, the posting of liaison officers.

3. The Parties shall facilitate effective co-ordination among their civil aviation and law enforcement authorities to enable rapid verification of aircraft registrations and flight plans.

4. The Parties shall assist one another to plan and implement training of law enforcement officials in the conduct of maritime law enforcement operations covered in this Agreement, including combined operations and boarding, searching and detention of vessels.

MARITIME AND AIR LAW ENFORCEMENT OPERATIONS

Article 5 Suspect vessels and suspect aircraft

Law enforcement operations to suppress illicit traffic pursuant to this Agreement shall be carried out only against suspect vessels and suspect aircraft, including those aircraft and vessels without nationality, and those assimilated to ships without nationality.

Article 6 Verification of nationality

1. For the purpose of this Agreement, a vessel or aircraft has the nationality of the State whose flag it is entitled to fly or in which the vessel or aircraft is registered, in accordance with domestic laws and regulations.

2. Requests for verification of nationality of vessels claiming registration in, or entitlement to fly the flag of one of the Parties, shall be processed through the competent national authority of the flag State Party.

3. Each request should be conveyed orally and later confirmed by written communication, and shall contain, if possible, the name of the vessel, registration number, nationality, homeport, grounds for suspicion, and any other identifying information.

4. Requests for verification of nationality shall be answered expeditiously and all efforts shall be made to provide such answer as soon as possible, but in any event within four (4) hours.

5. If the claimed flag State Party refutes the claim of nationality made by the suspect vessel, then the Party that requested verification may assimilate the suspect vessel to a ship without nationality in accordance with international law.

Article 7 National measures with regard to suspect vessels and suspect aircraft

1. Each Party undertakes to establish the capability at any time to:
    (a)   respond to requests for verification of nationality;
    (b)   authorise the boarding and search of suspect vessels;
    (c)   provide expeditious disposition instructions for vessels detained on its behalf;
    (d)   authorise the entry into its waters and air space of law enforcement vessels and law enforcement aircraft and aircraft in support of law enforcement operations of the other Parties.

2. Each Party shall notify the Depositary of the authority or authorities defined in Article 1 to whom requests should be directed under paragraph 1 of this Article.

Article 8 Authority of law enforcement officials

1. When law enforcement officials are within the waters or territory, or on board a law enforcement vessel or law enforcement aircraft, of another Party, they shall respect the laws and naval and air customs and traditions of the other Party.

2. In order to carry out the objectives of this Agreement, each Party authorises its designated law enforcement and aviation officials, or its competent national authority if notified to the Depositary, to permit the entry of law enforcement vessels, law enforcement aircraft and aircraft in support of law enforcement operations, under this Agreement into its waters and air space.

Article 9 Designation and authority of embarked law enforcement officials

1. Each Party (the designating Party) shall designate qualified law enforcement officials to act as embarked law enforcement officials on vessels of another Party.

2. Each Party may authorise the designated law enforcement officials of another Party to embark on its law enforcement vessel. That authorisation may be subject to conditions.

3. Subject to the domestic laws and regulations of the designating Party, when duly authorised, these law enforcement officials may:

(a) embark on law enforcement vessels of any of the Parties;

(b) enforce the laws of the designating Party to suppress illicit traffic in the waters of the designating Party, or seaward of its territorial sea in the exercise of the right of hot pursuit or otherwise in accordance with international law;

(c) authorise the entry of the law enforcement vessels on which they are embarked into and navigation within the waters of the designating Party;

(d) authorise the law enforcement vessels on which they are embarked to conduct counter-drug patrols in the waters of the designating Party;

(e) authorise law enforcement officials of the vessel on which the law enforcement officials of the designating Party are embarked to assist in the enforcement of the laws of the designating Party to suppress illicit traffic; and

(f) advise and assist law enforcement officials of other Parties in the conduct of boardings of vessels to enforce the laws of those Parties to suppress illicit traffic.

4. When law enforcement officials are embarked on another Party's law enforcement vessel, and the enforcement action being carried out is pursuant to the authority of the law enforcement officials, any search or seizure of property, any detention of a person, and any use of force pursuant to this Agreement, whether or not involving weapons, shall, without prejudice to the general principles of Article 11, be carried out by these law enforcement officials. However:

(a) crew members of the other Party's vessel may assist in any such action if expressly requested to do so by the law enforcement officials and only to the extent and in the manner requested. Such a request may only be made, agreed to, and acted upon if the action is consistent with the applicable laws and procedures of both Parties; and

(b) such crew members may use force in accordance with Article 22 and their domestic laws and regulations.

5. Each Party shall notify the Depositary of the authority responsible for the designation of embarked law enforcement officials.

6. Parties may conclude agreements or arrangements between them to facilitate law enforcement operations carried out in accordance with this Article.

Article 10 Boarding and search

1. Boarding and searches pursuant to this Agreement shall be carried out only by teams of authorised law enforcement officials from law enforcement vessels.

2. Such boarding and search teams may operate from law enforcement vessels and law enforcement aircraft of any of the Parties, and from law enforcement vessels and law enforcement aircraft of other States as agreed among the Parties.

3. Such boarding and search teams may carry arms.

4. A law enforcement vessel of a Party shall clearly indicate when it is operating under the authority of another Party.

LAW ENFORCEMENT OPERATIONS IN AND OVER TERRITORIAL WATERS

Article 11 General principles

1. Law enforcement operations to suppress illicit traffic in and over the waters of a Party are subject to the authority of that Party.

2. No Party shall conduct law enforcement operations to suppress illicit traffic in the waters or air space of any other Party without the authorisation of that other Party,

granted pursuant to this Agreement or according to its domestic legal system. A request for such operations shall be decided upon expeditiously. The authorisation may be subject to directions and conditions that shall be respected by the Party conducting the operations.

3. Law enforcement operations to suppress illicit traffic in and over the waters of a Party shall be carried out by, or under the direction of, the law enforcement authorities of that Party.

4. Nothing in this Agreement shall be construed as authorising a law enforcement vessel, or law enforcement aircraft of one Party, independently to patrol within the waters or air space of any other Party.

Article 12 Assistance by vessels for suppression of illicit traffic

1. Subject to paragraph 2 of this Article, a law enforcement vessel of a Party may follow a suspect vessel into the waters of another Party and take actions to prevent the escape of the vessel, board the vessel and secure the vessel and persons on board awaiting an expeditious response from the other Party if either:

(a) the Party has received authorisation from the authority or authorities of the other Party defined in Article 1 and notified pursuant to Article 7; or

(b) on notice to the other Party, when no embarked law enforcement official or law enforcement vessel of the other Party is immediately available to investigate. Such notice shall be provided prior to entry into the waters of the other Party, if operationally feasible, or failing this as soon as possible.

2. Parties shall elect either the procedure set forth in paragraph 1a or 1b, and shall so notify the Depositary of their election. Prior to receipt of notification by the Depositary, Parties shall be deemed to have elected the procedure set forth in paragraph 1a.

3. If evidence of illicit traffic is found, the authorising Party shall be promptly informed of the results of the search. The suspect vessel, cargo and persons on board shall be detained and taken to a designated port within the waters of the authorising Party unless otherwise directed by that Party.

4. Subject to paragraph 5, a law enforcement vessel of a Party may follow a suspect aircraft into another Party's waters in order to maintain contact with the suspect aircraft if either:

(a) the Party has received authorisation from the authority or authorities of the other Party defined in Article 1 and notified pursuant to Article 7; or

(b) on notice to the other Party, when no embarked law enforcement official or law enforcement vessel or law enforcement aircraft of the other Party is immediately available to maintain contact. Such notice shall be provided prior to entry into the waters of the other Party, if operationally feasible, or failing this as soon as possible.

5. Parties shall elect either the procedure set forth in paragraph 4a or 4b, and shall so notify the Depositary of their election. Prior to receipt of notification by the Depositary, Parties shall be deemed to have elected the procedure set forth in paragraph 4a.

Article 13 Assistance by aircraft for suppression of illicit traffic

1. A Party may request aircraft support from other Parties for assistance, including monitoring and surveillance, in suppressing illicit traffic.

2. Any assistance under this Article within the air space of the requesting Party shall be conducted in accordance with the laws of the requesting Party and only in the specified areas and to the extent requested and authorised.

3. Prior to the commencement of any assistance, the Party desiring to assist in such activities (the requested Party) may be required to provide reasonable notice, communication

frequencies and other information relative to flight safety to the appropriate civil aviation authorities of the requesting Party.

4. The requested Parties shall, in the interest of safe air navigation, observe the following procedures for notifying the appropriate aviation authorities of such overflight activity by participating aircraft:

(a)   In the event of planned bilateral or multilateral law enforcement operations, the requested Party shall provide reasonable notice and communications frequencies to the appropriate authorities, including authorities responsible for air traffic control, of each Party of planned flights by participating aircraft in the air space of that Party.

(b)   In the event of unplanned law enforcement operations, which may include the pursuit of suspect aircraft into another Party's air space, the law enforcement and appropriate civil aviation authorities of the Parties concerned shall exchange information concerning the appropriate communications frequencies and other information pertinent to the safety of air navigation.

(c)   Any aircraft engaged in law enforcement operations or activities in support of law enforcement operations shall comply with such air navigation and flight safety directions as may be required by each concerned Party's aviation authorities, in the measure in which it is going across the airspace of those Parties.

5. The requested Parties shall maintain contact with the designated law enforcement officials of the requesting Party and keep them informed of the results of such operations so as to enable them to take such action as they may deem appropriate.

6. Subject to paragraph 7 of this Article, the requesting Party shall authorise aircraft of a requested Party, when engaged in law enforcement operations or activities in support of law enforcement operations, to fly over its territory and waters; and, subject to the laws of the authorizing Party and of the requested Party, to relay to suspect aircraft, upon the request of the authorising Party, orders to comply with the instructions and directions from its air traffic control and law enforcement authority, if either:

(a)   authorisation has been granted by the authority or authorities of the Party requesting assistance defined in Article 1, notified pursuant to Article 7; or

(b)   advance authorisation has been granted by the Party requesting assistance.

7. Parties shall elect either the procedure set forth in paragraph 6a or 6b, and shall so notify the Depositary of their election. Prior to receipt of notification by the Depositary, Parties shall be deemed to have elected the procedure set forth in paragraph 6a.

8. Nothing in this Agreement shall affect the legitimate rights of aircraft engaged in scheduled or charter operations for the carriage of passengers, baggage or cargo or general aviation traffic.

9. Nothing in this Agreement shall be construed as authorising aircraft of any Party to enter the air space of any State not party to this Agreement.

10. Nothing in this Agreement shall be construed as authorising an aircraft of one Party independently to patrol within the air space of any other Party.

11. While conducting air activities pursuant to this Agreement, the Parties shall not endanger the lives of persons on board or the safety of civil aviation.

Article 14 Other situations

1. Nothing in this Agreement shall preclude any Party from otherwise expressly authorising law enforcement operations by any other Party to suppress illicit traffic in its territory, waters or air space, or involving vessels or aircraft of its nationality suspected of illicit traffic.

2. Parties are encouraged to apply the relevant provisions of this Agreement whenever evidence of illicit traffic is witnessed by the law enforcement vessels and law enforcement aircraft of the Parties.

Article 15 Extension to internal waters

Upon signing, ratification, acceptance or approval of this Agreement, or at any time thereafter, a Party may notify the Depositary that it has extended the application of this Agreement to some or all of its internal waters directly adjacent to its territorial sea or archipelagic waters, as specified by the Party.

OPERATIONS SEWARD OF THE TERRITORIAL SEA

Article 16 Boarding

1. When law enforcement officials of one Party encounter a suspect vessel claiming the nationality of another Party, located seaward of any State's territorial sea, this Agreement constitutes the authorisation by the claimed flag State Party to board and search the suspect vessel, its cargo and question the persons found on board by such officials in order to determine if the vessel is engaged in illicit traffic, except where a Party has notified the Depositary that it will apply the provisions of paragraph 2 or 3 of this Article.

2. Upon signing, ratification, acceptance or approval of this Agreement, a Party may notify the Depositary that vessels claiming the nationality of that Party located seaward of any State's territorial sea may only be boarded upon express consent of that Party. This notification will not set aside the obligation of that Party to respond expeditiously to requests from other Parties pursuant to this Agreement, according to its capability. The notification can be withdrawn at any time.

3. Upon signing, ratification, acceptance or approval of this Agreement, or at any time thereafter, a Party may notify the Depositary that Parties shall be deemed to be granted authorisation to board a suspect vessel located seaward of the territorial sea of any State that flies its flag or claims its nationality and to search the suspect vessel, its cargo and question the persons found on board in order to determine if the vessel is engaged in illicit traffic, if there is no response or the requested Party can neither confirm nor deny nationality within four (4) hours following receipt of an oral request pursuant to Article 6. The notification can be withdrawn at any time.

4. A flag State Party that has notified the Depositary that it shall adhere to paragraph 2 or 3 of this Article, having received a request to verify the nationality of a suspect vessel, may authorise the requesting Party to take all necessary actions to prevent the escape of the suspect vessel.

5. When evidence of illicit traffic is found as the result of any boarding conducted pursuant to this Article, the law enforcement officials of the boarding Party may detain the vessel, cargo and persons on board pending expeditious disposition instructions from the flag State Party. The boarding Party shall promptly inform the flag State Party of the results of the boarding and search conducted pursuant to this Article, in accordance with paragraph 1 of Article 26 of this Agreement.

6. Notwithstanding the foregoing paragraphs of this Article, law enforcement officials of one Party may board a suspect vessel located seaward of the territorial sea of any State, claiming the nationality of another Party for the purpose of locating and examining the documents of that vessel when:

  (a)   it is not flying the flag of that other Party;
  (b)   it is not displaying any marks of its registration;
  (c)   it is claiming to have no documentation regarding its nationality on board; and

(d)   there is no other information evidencing nationality.

7. In the case of a boarding conducted pursuant to paragraph 6 of this Article, should any documentation or evidence of nationality be found, paragraph 1, 2 or 3 of this Article shall apply as appropriate. Where no evidence of nationality is found, the boarding Party may assimilate the vessel to a ship without nationality in accordance with international law.

8. The boarding and search of a suspect vessel in accordance with this Article is governed by the laws of the boarding Party.

Article 17 Other boardings under international law

Except as expressly provided herein, this Agreement does not apply to or limit boarding of vessels, conducted by any Party in accordance with international law, seaward of any State's territorial sea, whether based, *inter alia*, on the right of visit, the rendering of assistance to persons, vessels, and property in distress or peril, or an authorisation from the flag State to take law enforcement action.

IMPLEMENTATION

Article 18 Identification of point of contact

In designating the authorities and officials as defined in Article 1 that exercise responsibilities under this Agreement, each Party is encouraged to identify a single point of contact with the capability to receive, process and respond to requests and reports at any time.

Article 19 Maritime law enforcement co-operation and co-ordination programmes for the Caribbean Area

1. The Parties shall establish regional and sub-regional maritime law enforcement co-operation and co-ordination programmes among their law enforcement authorities. Each Party shall designate a co-ordinator to organise its participation and to identify the vessels, aircraft and law enforcement officials involved in the programme to the other Parties.

2. The Parties shall endeavour to conduct scheduled bilateral, sub-regional and regional operations to exercise the rights and obligations under this Agreement.

3. The Parties undertake to assign qualified personnel to regional and sub-regional co-ordination centres established for the purpose of co-ordinating the detection, surveillance and monitoring of vessels and aircraft and interception of vessels engaged in illicit traffic by and over the sea.

4. The Parties are encouraged to develop standard operating procedures for law enforcement operations pursuant to this Agreement and consult, as appropriate, with other Parties with a view to harmonising such standard operating procedures for the conduct of joint law enforcement operations.

Article 20 Authority and conduct of law enforcement and other officials

1. Subject to its constitutional principles and the basic concepts of its legal system, each Party shall take such measures as may be necessary under its domestic law to ensure that foreign law enforcement officials, when conducting actions in its water under this Agreement, are deemed to have like powers to those of its domestic law enforcement officials.

2. Consistent with its legal system, each Party shall take appropriate measures to ensure that its law enforcement officials, and law enforcement officials of other Parties

acting on its behalf, are empowered to exercise the authority of law enforcement officials as prescribed in this Agreement.

3. In accordance with the provisions in Article 8 and without prejudice to the provisions in Article 11, each Party shall ensure that its law enforcement officials, when conducting boardings and searches of vessels, and air activities pursuant to this Agreement, act in accordance with their applicable national laws and procedures and with international law and accepted international practices.

4. In taking such action under this Agreement, each Party shall take due account of the need not to endanger the safety of life at sea, the security of the vessel and cargo, and not to prejudice any commercial or legal interest. In particular, they shall take into account:

(a)   the dangers involved in boarding a vessel at sea, and give consideration as to whether this could be more safely done in port; and

(b)   the need to avoid unduly detaining or delaying a vessel.

Article 21 Assistance by vessels

1. Each Party may request another Party to make available one or more of its law enforcement vessels to assist the requesting Party effectively to patrol and conduct surveillance with a view to the detection and prevention of illicit traffic by sea and air in the Caribbean area.

2. When responding favourably to a request pursuant to paragraph 1 of this Article, each requested Party shall provide to the requesting Party via secure communication channels:

(a)   the name and description of its law enforcement vessels;

(b)   the dates at which, and the periods for which, they will be available;

(c)   the names of the Commanding Officers of the vessels; and

(d)   any other relevant information.

Article 22 Use of force

1. Force may only be used if no other feasible means of resolving the situation can be applied.

2. Any force used shall be proportional to the objective for which it is employed.

3. All use of force pursuant to this Agreement shall in all cases be the minimum reasonably necessary under the circumstances.

4. A warning shall be issued prior to any use of force except when force is being used in self-defence.

5. In the event that the use of force is authorised and necessary in the waters of a Party, law enforcement officials shall respect the laws of that Party.

6. In the event that the use of force is authorised and necessary during a boarding and search seaward of the territorial sea of any Party, the law enforcement officials shall comply with their domestic laws and procedures and the directions of the flag State.

7. The discharge of firearms against or on a suspect vessel shall be reported as soon as practicable to the flag State Party.

8. Parties shall not use force against civil aircraft in flight.

9. The use of force in reprisal or as punishment is prohibited.

10. Nothing in this Agreement shall impair the exercise of the inherent right of self-defence by law enforcement or other officials of any Party.

Article 23 Jurisdiction over offenses

1. Each Party shall take such measures as may be necessary to establish its jurisdiction over the offences it has established in accordance with Article 3, paragraph 1, of the 1988 Convention, when:

   (a)   the offence is committed in waters under its sovereignty or where applicable in its contiguous zone;

   (b)   the offence is committed on board a vessel flying its flag or an aircraft which is registered under its laws at the time the offence is committed;

   (c)   the offence is committed on board a vessel without nationality or assimilated to a ship without nationality under international law, which is located seaward of the territorial sea of any State;

   (d)   the offence is committed on board a vessel flying the flag or displaying the marks of registry or bearing any other indication of nationality of another Party, which is located seaward of the territorial sea of any State.

Article 24 Jurisdiction over detained vessels and persons

1. In all cases arising in the waters of a Party, or concerning a Party's flag vessels seaward of any State's territorial sea, that Party has jurisdiction over a detained vessel, cargo and persons on board including seizure, forfeiture, arrest, and prosecution. Subject to its Constitution and its laws, the Party in question may consent to the exercise of jurisdiction by another State in accordance with international law and in conformity with any condition set by it.

2. Each Party shall ensure compliance with its notification obligations under the Vienna Convention on Consular Relations.

Article 25 Dissemination

1. To facilitate implementation of this Agreement, each Party shall ensure that the other Parties are fully informed of its respective applicable laws and procedures, particularly those pertaining to the use of force.

2. When engaged in law enforcement operations under this Agreement, the Parties shall ensure that their law enforcement officials are knowledgeable concerning the pertinent operational procedures of other Parties.

Article 26 Results of enforcement action

1. A Party conducting a boarding and search pursuant to this Agreement shall promptly inform the other Party of the results thereof.

2. Each Party shall, on a periodic basis and consistent with its laws, inform the other Party on the stage which has been reached of all investigations, prosecutions and judicial proceedings resulting from law enforcement operations taken pursuant to this Agreement where evidence of illicit traffic was found on vessels or aircraft of that other Party. In addition, the Parties shall provide each other with information on results of such prosecutions and judicial proceedings, in accordance with their national legislation.

3. Nothing in this Article shall require a Party to disclose details of the investigations, prosecutions and judicial proceedings or the evidence relating thereto; or affect rights or obligations of Parties derived from the 1988 Convention or other international agreements and instruments.

Article 27 Asset seizure and forfeiture

1. Assets seized, confiscated or forfeited in consequence of any law enforcement operation undertaken in the waters of a Party pursuant to this Agreement shall be disposed of in accordance with the laws of that Party.

2. Should the flag State Party have consented to the exercise of jurisdiction by another State pursuant to Article 24, assets seized, confiscated or forfeited in consequence of any law enforcement operation of any Party pursuant to this Agreement shall be disposed of in accordance with the laws of the boarding Party.

3. To the extent permitted by its laws and upon such terms as it deems appropriate, a Party may, in any case, transfer forfeited property or proceeds of their sale to another Party or intergovernmental bodies specialising in the fight against illicit traffic in and abuse of narcotic drugs and psychotropic substances.

Article 28 Claims

Claims against a Party for damage, injury or loss resulting from law enforcement operations pursuant to this Agreement, including claims against its law enforcement officials, shall be resolved in accordance with international law.

FINAL PROVISIONS

Article 29 Preservation of rights and privileges

1. Nothing in this Agreement shall be construed as altering the rights and privileges due to any individual in any legal proceeding.

2. Nothing in this Agreement shall be construed as altering the immunities to which vessels and aircraft are entitled under international law.

3. For the purposes of this Agreement, in no case shall law enforcement vessels or law enforcement aircraft be considered suspect vessels or suspect aircraft.

Article 30 Effect on claims concerning territory or maritime boundaries

Nothing in this Agreement shall prejudice the position of any Party under international law, including the law of the sea; nor affect the claims to territory or maritime boundaries of any Party or any third State; nor constitute a precedent from which rights can be derived.

Article 31 Relationship to other agreements

1. The Parties are encouraged to conclude bilateral or multilateral agreements with one another on the matters dealt with in this Agreement, for the purpose of confirming or supplementing its provisions or strengthening the application of the principles embodied in Article 17 of the 1988 Convention.

2. Nothing in this Agreement shall alter or affect in any way the rights and obligations of a Party which arise from agreements in force between it and one or more other Parties on the same subject.

Article 32 Meetings of the Parties

1. There shall be a meeting of the Parties at the end of the second year following the year in which this Agreement enters into force. After this term, subsequent meetings of the Parties shall be held no sooner than ninety (90) days after a request of fifty percent of the Parties made in conformity with the usual diplomatic practice.

2. Meetings of the Parties shall examine, *inter alia*, compliance with the Agreement, and adopt, if necessary, measures to enhance its effectiveness, and review measures in the field of regional and sub regional co-operation and co-ordination of future actions.

3. Meetings of the Parties convened pursuant to paragraph 2 of this Article shall consider amendments to this Agreement proposed in accordance with Article 33.

4. All decisions taken by the meetings of the Parties shall be by consensus

Article 33 Amendments

1. Any Party may at any time after entry into force of the Agreement for that Party propose an amendment to this Agreement by providing the text of such a proposal to the Depositary. The Depositary shall promptly circulate any such proposal to all Parties and Signatories.

2. An amendment shall be adopted at a meeting of the Parties by consensus of the Parties therein represented.

3. An amendment shall enter into force thirty days after the Depositary has received instruments of acceptance or approval from all of the Parties.

Article 34 Settlement of disputes

If there should arise between two or more Parties a question or dispute relating to the interpretation or application of this Agreement, those Parties shall consult together with a view to the settlement of the dispute by negotiation, inquiry, mediation, conciliation, arbitration, recourse to regional bodies, judicial process or other peaceful means of their choice.

Article 35 Signature

This Agreement shall be open for signature by any State party to the 1988 Convention that is located in the Caribbean area, or any State that is responsible for the foreign relations of a territory located in the Caribbean area, at San José, Costa Rica, from 10 April 2003.

Article 36 Entry into force

1. States may, in accordance with their national procedures, express their consent to be bound by this Agreement by;
   (a) signature without reservation as to ratification, acceptance or approval; or
   (b) signature subject to ratification, acceptance or approval, followed by ratification, acceptance or approval.

2. This Agreement shall enter into force 30 days after five States have expressed their consent to be bound in accordance with paragraph 1 of this Article.

3. For each State consenting to be bound after the date of entry into force of this Agreement, the Agreement shall enter into force for that State 30 days after the deposit of its instrument expressing its consent to be bound.

Article 37 Reservations and exceptions

Subject to its Constitution and laws and in accordance with international law, a Party may make reservations to this Agreement, except when they are incompatible with the object and purpose of the Agreement. No reservations may be made regarding Articles 2, 12, 13 and 16.

Article 38 Declarations and statements

Article 37 does not preclude a State, when signing, ratifying, accepting or approving this Agreement, from making declarations or statements, however phrased or named, with a view, *inter alia*, to the harmonisation of its laws and regulations with the provisions of this Agreement, provided that such declarations or statements do not purport to exclude or to modify the legal effect of the provisions of this Agreement in their application to that State.

Article 39 Territorial application

This Agreement shall only apply to the Caribbean area, as defined in Article 1, paragraph j.

Article 40 Suspension

Parties to this Agreement may temporarily suspend in specified areas under their sovereignty their obligations under this Agreement if such suspension is required for imperative reasons of national security. Such suspension shall take effect only after having been duly published.

Article 41 Withdrawal

1. Any Party may withdraw from this Agreement. Withdrawal will take effect twelve months after receipt of the notification of withdrawal by the Depositary.

2. This Agreement shall continue to apply after withdrawal with respect to any administrative or judicial proceedings arising out of actions taken pursuant to this Agreement in respect of the withdrawing Party.

Article 42 Depositary

1. The original of this Agreement shall be deposited with the Government of the Republic of Costa Rica, which shall serve as the Depositary.

2. The Depositary shall transmit certified copies of the Agreement to all signatories.

3. The Depositary shall inform all signatories and parties to the Agreement of:
   (a) all designations of law enforcement authorities pursuant to Article 1, paragraph c.
   (b) all designations of authorities to whom requests for verification of registration are to be made, and for authorisation to enter national waters and air space and board and search, and for disposition instructions, pursuant to Articles 6 and 7.
   (c) all officials designated as being responsible for the designation of embarked law enforcement officials pursuant to Article 9, paragraph 5.
   (d) all notification of elections regarding authorisation for pursuit or entry into territorial waters and air space to effect boardings and searches pursuant to Article 12.
   (e) all notification of elections regarding authorisation for aircraft support pursuant to Article 13.
   (f) all declarations of territorial applicability under Article 15.
   (g) all notifications of elections not to provide advance authorisation for boarding pursuant to Article 16, paragraphs 2 and 3.
   (h) all proposals to amend the Agreement made pursuant to Article 33.
   (i) all signatures, ratifications, acceptances, and approvals deposited pursuant to Article 36.
   (j) the dates of entry into force of the Agreement pursuant to Article 36.
   (k) all reservations made pursuant to Article 37.
   (l) all declarations made pursuant to Article 38.
   (m) all declarations made pursuant to Article 40.
   (n) all notifications of withdrawal pursuant to Article 41.

4. The Depositary shall register this Agreement with the United Nations pursuant to Article 102 of the Charter of the United Nations.

IN WITNESS WHEREOF, the undersigned, being duly authorised by their respective Governments, have signed this Agreement.

DONE at San José, this tenth day of April 2003, in the English, French and Spanish languages, each text being duly authentic.

Interdiction Principles for the Proliferation Security Initiative
(Paris Principles)

Agreed at Paris, 4 September 2003
http://www.state.gov/t/isn/rls/fs/23764.htm[1]

The Proliferation Security Initiative (PSI) is a response to the growing challenge posed by the proliferation of weapons of mass destruction (WMD), their delivery systems, and related materials worldwide. The PSI builds on efforts by the international community to prevent proliferation of such items, including existing treaties and regimes. It is consistent with and a step in the implementation of the UN Security Council Presidential Statement of January 1992, which states that the proliferation of all WMD constitutes a threat to international peace and security, and underlines the need for member states of the UN to prevent proliferation. The PSI is also consistent with recent statements of the G8 and the European Union, establishing that more coherent and concerted efforts are needed to prevent the proliferation of WMD, their delivery systems, and related materials. PSI participants are deeply concerned about this threat and of the danger that these items could fall into the hands of terrorists, and are committed to working together to stop the flow of these items to and from states and non-state actors of proliferation concern.

The PSI seeks to involve in some capacity all states that have a stake in non-proliferation and the ability and willingness to take steps to stop the flow of such items at sea, in the air, or on land. The PSI also seeks cooperation from any state whose vessels, flags, ports, territorial waters, airspace, or land might be used for proliferation purposes by states and non-state actors of proliferation concern. The increasingly aggressive efforts by proliferators to stand outside or to circumvent existing non-proliferation norms, and to profit from such trade, requires new and stronger actions by the international community. We look forward to working with all concerned states on measures they are able and willing to take in support of the PSI, as outlined in the following set of 'Interdiction Principles.'

Interdiction Principles for the Proliferation Security Initiative

PSI participants are committed to the following interdiction principles to establish a more coordinated and effective basis through which to impede and stop shipments of WMD, delivery systems, and related materials flowing to and from states and non-state actors of proliferation concern, consistent with national legal authorities and relevant international law and frameworks, including the UN Security Council. They call on all states concerned with this threat to international peace and security to join in similarly committing to:

1. Undertake effective measures, either alone or in concert with other states, for interdicting the transfer or transport of WMD, their delivery systems, and related materials to and from states and non-state actors of proliferation concern. 'States or non-state actors of proliferation concern' generally refers to those countries or entities that the PSI participants involved establish should be subject to interdiction activities because they are engaged in proliferation through: (1)

---

[1] At the Fifth Anniversary of the Proliferation Security Initiative PSI participating States met in Washington, DC, on 28 May 2008, and adopted the Washington Declaration which states in the relevant part: 'The 91 PSI participating states have endorsed the September 4, 2003 PSI Statement of Interdiction Principles, also known as the "Paris Principles". Today, the PSI participating states recommit to and reaffirm the value of implementing those Principles.' (http://www.state.gov/r/pa/prs/ps/2008/may/105268.htm).

efforts to develop or acquire chemical, biological, or nuclear weapons and associated delivery systems; or (2) transfers (either selling, receiving, or facilitating) of WMD, their delivery systems, or related materials.

2. Adopt streamlined procedures for rapid exchange of relevant information concerning suspected proliferation activity, protecting the confidential character of classified information provided by other states as part of this initiative, dedicate appropriate resources and efforts to interdiction operations and capabilities, and maximize coordination among participants in interdiction efforts.

3. Review and work to strengthen their relevant national legal authorities where necessary to accomplish these objectives, and work to strengthen when necessary relevant international law and frameworks in appropriate ways to support these commitments.

4. Take specific actions in support of interdiction efforts regarding cargoes of WMD, their delivery systems, or related materials, to the extent their national legal authorities permit and consistent with their obligations under international law and frameworks, to include:

   (a) Not to transport or assist in the transport of any such cargoes to or from states or non-state actors of proliferation concern, and not to allow any persons subject to their jurisdiction to do so.

   (b) At their own initiative, or at the request and good cause shown by another state, to take action to board and search any vessel flying their flag in their internal waters or territorial seas, or areas beyond the territorial seas of any other state, that is reasonably suspected of transporting such cargoes to or from states or non-state actors of proliferation concern, and to seize such cargoes that are identified.

   (c) To seriously consider providing consent under the appropriate circumstances to the boarding and searching of its own flag vessels by other states, and to the seizure of such WMD-related cargoes in such vessels that may be identified by such states.

   (d) To take appropriate actions to (1) stop and/or search in their internal waters, territorial seas, or contiguous zones (when declared) vessels that are reasonably suspected of carrying such cargoes to or from states or non-state actors of proliferation concern and to seize such cargoes that are identified; and (2) to enforce conditions on vessels entering or leaving their ports, internal waters or territorial seas that are reasonably suspected of carrying such cargoes, such as requiring that such vessels be subject to boarding, search, and seizure of such cargoes prior to entry.

   (e) At their own initiative or upon the request and good cause shown by another state, to (a) require aircraft that are reasonably suspected of carrying such cargoes to or from states or non-state actors of proliferation concern and that are transiting their airspace to land for inspection and seize any such cargoes that are identified; and/or (b) deny aircraft reasonably suspected of carrying such cargoes transit rights through their airspace in advance of such flights.

   (f) If their ports, airfields, or other facilities are used as transshipment points for shipment of such cargoes to or from states or non-state actors of proliferation concern, to inspect vessels, aircraft, or other modes of transport reasonably suspected of carrying such cargoes, and to seize such cargoes that are identified.

Agreement between the Government of the United States of America and the Government of the Republic of Liberia Concerning Cooperation to Suppress the Proliferation of Weapons of Mass Destruction, Their Delivery Systems, and Related Materials by Sea

Done at Washington, 11 February 2004; entry into force, 8 December 2004
http://www.state.gov/t/isn/trty/32403.htm

The Government of the United States of America and the Government of the Republic of Liberia (hereinafter, 'the Parties');

Deeply concerned about the proliferation of weapons of mass destruction (WMD), their delivery systems, and related materials, particularly by sea, as well as the risk that these may fall into the hands of terrorists;

Recalling the 31 January 1992 United Nations Security Council Presidential statement that proliferation of all WMD constitutes a threat to international peace and security, and underlines the need for Member States of the UN to prevent proliferation;

Further recalling the International Ship and Port Facility Security Code, adopted by the International Maritime Organization on 12 December 2002;

Mindful of the Convention on the Prohibition of the Development, Production, Stockpiling and Use of Chemical Weapons and on their Destruction, done at Paris 13 January 1993; the Treaty on Nonproliferation of Nuclear Weapons, done at Washington, London and Moscow 1 July 1968; and the Convention on the Prohibition of the Development, Production and Stockpiling of Bacteriological (Biological) and Toxin Weapons and on their Destruction, done at Washington, London and Moscow 10 April 1972;

Acknowledging the widespread consensus that proliferation and terrorism seriously threaten international peace and security;

Convinced that trafficking in these items by States and non-state actors of proliferation concern must be stopped;

Inspired by the efforts of the International Maritime Organization to improve the effectiveness of the Convention for the Suppression of Unlawful Acts against the Safety of Maritime Navigation, done at Rome 10 March 1988;

Reaffirming the importance of customary international law of the sea, and mindful of the provisions in that respect of the 1982 United Nations Convention on the Law of the Sea;

Committed to cooperation to stop the flow by sea of WMD, their delivery systems, and related materials to or from States or non-state actors of proliferation concern;

Have agreed as follows:

Article 1 Definitions

In this Agreement, unless the context otherwise requires:

1. 'Proliferation by sea' means the transportation by ship of weapons of mass destruction, their delivery systems, and related materials to or from States or non-state actors of proliferation concern.

2. 'Weapons of mass destruction' (WMD) means nuclear, chemical, biological and radiological weapons.

3. 'Related materials' means materials, equipment and technology, of whatever nature or type, that are related to and destined for use in the development, production, utilization or delivery of WMD.

4. 'Items of proliferation concern' means WMD, their delivery systems, and related materials.

5. 'States or non-state actors of proliferation concern' means those countries or entities that should be subject to interdiction activities because they are or are believed to be engaged in: (1) efforts to develop or acquire WMD or their delivery systems; or (2) trafficking (either selling, receiving, or facilitating) of WMD, their delivery systems, or related materials.

6. 'Security Force Officials' means:

(a) for the United States, uniformed or otherwise clearly identifiable members of the United States Coast Guard and the United States Navy, who may be accompanied by clearly identifiable law enforcement officials of the Departments of Homeland Security and Justice, and other clearly identifiable officials duly authorized by the Government of the United States of America and notified to the Competent Authority of the Republic of Liberia; and

(b) for Liberia, uniformed or otherwise clearly identifiable members of the armed forces or law enforcement authorities of Liberia, duly authorized by the Government of the Republic of Liberia and notified to the Competent Authority of the United States.

7. 'Security Force vessels' means warships and other vessels of the Parties, or of third States as may be agreed upon by the Parties, on which Security Force Officials of either or both Parties may be embarked, clearly marked and identifiable as being on government service and authorized to that effect, including any vessel and aircraft embarked on or supporting such vessels.

8. 'Suspect vessel' means a vessel used for commercial or private purposes in respect of which there are reasonable grounds to suspect it is engaged in proliferation by sea.

9. 'International waters' means all parts of the sea not included in the territorial sea, internal waters and archipelagic waters of a State, consistent with international law.

10. 'Competent Authority' means for the United States, the Commandant of the United States Coast Guard (including any officer designated by the Commandant to perform such functions), and for Liberia, the Agent of the Commissioner of Maritime Affairs appointed under section 13 of Title 21 (the Maritime Law) of the Laws of the Republic of Liberia.

Article 2 Object and purpose of Agreement

1. The object and purpose of this Agreement is to promote cooperation between the Parties to enable them to prevent the transportation by vessel of items of proliferation concern.

2. The Parties shall carry out their obligations and responsibilities under this Agreement in a manner consistent with the principles of international law pertaining to the sovereign equality and territorial integrity of States.

3. The Parties shall cooperate to the fullest extent possible, subject to the availability of resources and in compliance with their respective laws.

Article 3 Cases of suspect vessels

Operations to suppress proliferation by sea pursuant to this Agreement shall be carried out only against suspect vessels, including suspect vessels without nationality, suspect vessels assimilated to vessels without nationality, and suspect vessels registered under the law of one of the Parties under a bareboat charter notwithstanding an underlying registration in another State not party to this Agreement, but not against a vessel registered under the law of one of the Parties while bareboat chartered in another State not party to this Agreement.

Article 4 Operations in international waters

1. Authority to Board Suspect Vessels. Whenever the Security Force Officials of one Party ('the requesting Party') encounter a suspect vessel claiming nationality in the other Party ('the requested Party') located seaward of any State's territorial sea, the requesting Party may request through the Competent Authority of the requested Party that it:

(a) confirm the claim of nationality of the suspect vessel; and

(b) if such claim is confirmed:

  (i) authorize the boarding and search of the suspect vessel, cargo and the persons found on board by Security Force Officials of the requesting Party; and

  (ii) if evidence of proliferation is found, authorize the Security Force Officials of the requesting Party to detain the vessel, as well as items and persons on board, pending instructions conveyed through the Competent Authority of the requested Party as to the actions the requesting Party is permitted to take concerning such items, persons and vessels.

2. Contents of Requests. Each request should contain the name of the suspect vessel, the basis for the suspicion, the geographic position of the vessel, the IMO number if available, the homeport, the port of origin and destination, and any other identifying information. If a request is conveyed orally, the requesting Party shall confirm the request in writing by facsimile or e-mail as soon as possible. The requested Party shall acknowledge to the Competent Authority of the requesting Party in writing by e-mail or facsimile its receipt of any written or oral request immediately upon receiving it.

3. Responding to Requests.

(a) If the nationality is verified, the requested Party may:

  (i) decide to conduct the boarding and search with its own Security Force Officials;

  (ii) authorize the boarding and search by the Security Force Officials of the requesting Party;

  (iii) decide to conduct the boarding and search together with the requesting Party; or

  (iv) deny permission to board and search.

(b) The requested Party shall answer through its Competent Authority requests made for the verification of nationality within two hours of its acknowledgment of the receipt of such requests.

(c) If the nationality is not verified within the two hours, the requested Party may, through its Competent Authority:

  (i) nevertheless authorize the boarding and search by the Security Force Officials of the requesting Party; or

  (ii) refute the claim of the suspect vessel to its nationality.

(d) If there is no response from the Competent Authority of the requested Party within two hours of its acknowledgment of receipt of the request, the requesting Party will be deemed to have been authorized to board the suspect vessel for the purpose of inspecting the vessel's documents, questioning the persons on board, and searching the vessel to determine if it is engaged in proliferation by sea.

4. Right of Visit. Notwithstanding the foregoing paragraphs of this Article, the Security Force Officials of one Party ('the first Party') are authorized to board suspect vessels claiming nationality in the other Party that are not flying the flag of the other Party, not displaying any marks of its registration or nationality, and claiming to have no documentation on board the vessel, for the purpose of locating and examining the vessel's documentation. If documentation or other physical evidence of nationality is located, the

foregoing paragraphs of this Article apply. If no documentation or other physical evidence of nationality is available, the other Party will not object to the first Party assimilating the vessel to a ship without nationality consistent with international law.

5. Use of Force. The authorization to board, search and detain includes the authority to use force in accordance with Article 9 of this Agreement.

6. Shipboarding Otherwise in Accordance with International Law. This Agreement does not limit the right of either Party to conduct boardings of vessels or other activities consistent with international law whether based, *inter alia*, on the right of visit, the rendering of assistance to persons, vessels, and property in distress or peril, or an authorization from the Flag or Coastal State, or other appropriate bases in international law.

Article 5 Exercise of jurisdiction over detained vessels, as well as items and persons on board

1. Jurisdiction of the Parties. In all cases covered by Article 4 concerning the vessels of a Party located seaward of any State's territorial sea, that Party shall have the primary right to exercise jurisdiction over a detained vessel, cargo or other items and persons on board (including seizure, forfeiture, arrest, and prosecution), provided, however, that the Party with the right to exercise primary jurisdiction may, subject to its Constitution and laws, waive its primary right to exercise jurisdiction and authorize the enforcement of the other Party's law against the vessel, cargo or other items and persons on board.

2. Jurisdiction in the contiguous zone of a Party. In all cases not covered by Article 4 involving the vessel of a Party that arise in the contiguous zone of a Party and in which both Parties have authority to board and to exercise jurisdiction to prosecute –

(a) except as provided in paragraph (b), the Party which conducts the boarding shall have the primary right to exercise jurisdiction;

(b) in cases involving suspect vessels fleeing from the territorial sea of a Party in which that Party has the authority to board and to exercise jurisdiction, that Party shall have the primary right to exercise jurisdiction.

3. Disposition Instructions. Consultations as to the exercise of jurisdiction pursuant to paragraphs 1 and 2 of this Article shall be undertaken without delay between the Competent Authorities.

4. Form of waiver. Where permitted by its Constitution and laws, waiver of jurisdiction may be granted verbally, but as soon as possible it shall be recorded in a written note from the Competent Authority and be processed through the appropriate diplomatic channel, without prejudice to the immediate exercise of jurisdiction over the suspect vessel by the other Party.

Article 6 Exchange of information and notification of results of actions of the Security Forces

1. Exchange of Operational Information. The Competent Authorities of both Parties shall endeavor to exchange operational information on the detection and location of suspect vessels and shall maintain communication with each other as necessary to carry out the purpose of this Agreement.

2. Notification of Results. A Party conducting a boarding and search pursuant to this Agreement shall promptly notify the other Party of the results thereof through their Competent Authorities.

3. Status Reports. The relevant Party, in compliance with its laws, shall timely report to the other Party, through their Competent Authorities, on the status of all investigations, prosecutions and judicial proceedings and other actions and processes, arising out of the application of this Agreement.

Article 7 Conduct of Security Force Officials

1. Compliance with Law and Practices. Each Party shall ensure that its Security Force Officials, when conducting boardings and searches pursuant to this Agreement, act in accordance with its applicable national laws and policies and consistent with international law and accepted international practices.

2. Boarding and Search Teams.

(a) Boardings and searches pursuant to this Agreement shall be carried out by Security Force Officials from Security Force vessels and vessels and aircraft embarked on or otherwise supporting such Security Force vessels, as well as by vessels and aircraft of third States as agreed between the Parties.

(b) The boarding and search teams may operate from Security Force vessels of the Parties and from such vessels of other States, according to arrangements between the Party conducting the operation and the State providing the vessel and notified to the other Party.

(c) The boarding and search teams may carry arms.

Article 8 Safeguards

1. Where a Party takes measures against a vessel in accordance with this Agreement, it shall:

(a) take due account of the need not to endanger the safety of life at sea;

(b) take due account of the security of the vessel and its cargo;

(c) not prejudice the commercial or legal interests of the Flag State;

(d) ensure within available means, that any measure taken with regard to the vessel is environmentally sound under the circumstances;

(e) ensure that persons on board are afforded the protections, rights and guarantees provided by international law and the boarding State's law and regulations;

(f) ensure the master of the vessel is, or has been, afforded the opportunity to contact the vessels' owner, manager or Flag State at the earliest opportunity.

2. Reasonable efforts shall be taken to avoid a vessel being unduly detained or delayed.

Article 9 Use of force

1. All uses of force pursuant to this Agreement shall be in strict accordance with the applicable laws and policies of the Party conducting the boarding and applicable international law.

2. Each Party shall avoid the use of force except when and to the degree necessary to ensure the safety of Security Force Officials and vessels or where Security Force Officials are obstructed in the execution of their duties.

3. Only that force reasonably necessary under the circumstances may be used.

4. Boarding and search teams and Security Force vessels have the inherent right to use all available means to apply that force reasonably necessary to defend themselves or others from physical harm.

5. Whenever any vessel subject to boarding under this Agreement does not stop on being ordered to do so, the Security Force vessel should give an auditory or visual signal to the suspect vessel to stop, using internationally recognized signals. If the suspect vessel does not stop upon being signaled, Security Force vessels may take other appropriate actions to stop the suspect vessel.

Article 10 Exchange and knowledge of laws and policies of other party

1. Exchange of Information. To facilitate implementation of this Agreement, each Party shall take steps necessary to ensure the other Party is appropriately informed of its respective applicable laws and policies, particularly those pertaining to the use of force.

2. Knowledge. Each Party shall take steps necessary to ensure that its Security Force Officials are knowledgeable concerning the applicable laws and policies in accordance with this Agreement.

Article 11 Points of contact

1. Information. Each Party shall inform the other Party, and keep current, the points of contact for communication, decision and instructions under Articles 4 and 5, and notifications under Articles 6 and 10 of this Agreement. Such information shall be updated by and exchanged between the Competent Authorities.

2. Availability. The Parties shall ensure that the points of contact have the capability to receive, process and respond to requests and reports at any time.

Article 12 Disposition of seized property

1. Except as otherwise agreed by the Parties, cargo and other items seized in consequence of operations undertaken onboard vessels subject to the jurisdiction of a Party pursuant to this Agreement, shall be disposed of by that Party in accordance with its laws.

2. The Party exercising jurisdiction may, in any case, transfer forfeited cargo and other items or proceeds of their sale to the other Party. Each transfer generally will reflect the contribution of the other Party to facilitating or effecting the forfeiture of such assets or proceeds.

Article 13 Claims

1. Injury or Loss of Life. Any claim for injury to or loss of life of a Security Force Official of a Party while carrying out operations arising from this Agreement shall normally be resolved in accordance with the laws of that Party.

2. Other Claims. Any other claim submitted for damage, harm, injury, death or loss resulting from an operation carried out by a Party under this Agreement shall be resolved in accordance with the domestic law of that Party, and in a manner consistent with international law.

3. Consultation. If any loss, injury or death is suffered as a result of any action taken by the Security Force Officials of one Party in contravention of this Agreement, or any improper or unreasonable action is taken by a Party pursuant thereto, the Parties shall, without prejudice to any other legal rights which may be available, consult at the request of either Party to resolve the matter and decide any questions relating to compensation or payment.

Article 14 Disputes and consultations

1. Disputes. Disputes arising from the interpretation or implementation of this Agreement shall be settled by mutual agreement of the Parties.

2. Evaluation of Implementation. The Parties agree to consult as necessary to evaluate the implementation of this Agreement and to consider enhancing its effectiveness. The evaluation shall be carried out at least once a year.

3. Resolving Difficulties. In case a difficulty arises concerning the operation of this Agreement, either Party may request, through the Competent Authorities, consultations with the other Party to resolve the matter.

Article 15 Effect on rights, privileges and legal positions

Nothing in this Agreement:

(a) alters the rights and privileges due any person in any administrative or judicial proceeding conducted under the jurisdiction of either Party.

(b) shall prejudice the position of either Party with regard to international law.

Article 16 Cooperation and assistance

1. The Competent Authority of one Party may request, and the Competent Authority of the other Party may authorize, Security Force Officials to provide technical assistance, such as specialized assistance in the conduct of search of suspect vessels, for the boarding and search of suspect vessels located in the territory or waters of the requesting Party.

2. Nothing in this Agreement precludes a Party from authorizing the other Party to suppress proliferation in its territory, waters or airspace, or to take action involving suspect vessels or aircraft claiming its nationality, or from providing other forms of cooperation to suppress proliferation.

Article 17 Entry into force and duration

1. Entry into Force. This Agreement shall enter into force upon an exchange of notes indicating that the necessary internal procedures of each Party have been completed.

2. Provisional Application. Beginning on the date of signature of this Agreement, the Parties shall, to the extent permitted by their respective national laws and regulations, apply it provisionally. Either Party may discontinue provisional application at any time. Each Party shall notify the other Party immediately of any constraints or limitations on provisional application, of any changes to such constraints or limitations, and upon discontinuation of provisional application.

3. Termination. This Agreement may be terminated by either Party upon written notification of such termination to the other Party through the diplomatic channel, termination to be effective one year from the date of such notification.

4. Continuation of Actions Taken. This Agreement shall continue to apply after termination with respect to any administrative or judicial proceedings regarding actions that occurred during the time the Agreement was in force.

Article 18 Rights for third States

1. The Parties agree that the Government of the Republic of Liberia may extend, *mutatis mutandis*, all rights concerning suspect vessels claiming its nationality under the present Agreement to such third States as it may deem appropriate, on the understanding that such third States shall likewise comply with all conditions set forth in the present Agreement for the exercise of such rights, and subject to agreement by that Party and such third States on the designation of points of contact in accordance with Article 11.

2. Such third States shall enjoy rights and be subject to all conditions governing their exercise as set forth in paragraph 1 of this Article effective on the date of a notification by the third State to that Party that it will comply with the conditions for the exercise of those rights.

3. Such rights shall be revocable by that Party or the third State in writing. Such rights shall be revoked, and the conditions governing their exercise shall cease to apply, effective on the date of notification.

4. Such rights shall be subject to modification by mutual concurrence in writing of that Party and the third State. Upon establishment of such mutual written concurrence by that Party and the third State in question, such rights shall be modified effective on the date agreed between that Party and the third State.

IN WITNESS WHEREOF, the undersigned, being duly authorized by their respective Governments, have signed this Agreement.

DONE at Washington, this eleventh day of February 2004, in duplicate, both texts being equally authentic.

Guidelines on the Treatment of Persons Rescued at Sea

IMO Resolution MSC.167(78), adopted on 20 May 2004[1]

1 PURPOSE

1.1   The purpose of these Guidelines are to provide guidance to Governments[2] and to shipmasters with regard to humanitarian obligations and obligations under the relevant international law relating to treatment of persons rescued at sea.

1.2   The obligation of the master to render assistance should complement the corresponding obligation of IMO Member Governments to co-ordinate and co-operate in relieving the master of the responsibility to provide follow up care of survivors and to deliver the persons retrieved at sea to a place of safety. These Guidelines are intended to help Governments and masters better understand their obligations under international law and provide helpful guidance with regard to carrying out these obligations.

2 BACKGROUND

IMO Assembly resolution A.920(22)

2.1   The IMO Assembly, at its twenty-second session, adopted resolution A.920(22) on the review of safety measures and procedures for the treatment of persons rescued at sea. That resolution requested various IMO bodies to review selected IMO Conventions to identify any gaps, inconsistencies, ambiguities, vagueness or other inadequacies associated with the treatment of persons rescued at sea. The objectives were to help ensure that:

.1   survivors of distress incidents are provided assistance regardless of nationality or status or the circumstances in which they are found;

.2   ships, which have retrieved persons in distress at sea, are able to deliver the survivors to a place of safety; and

.3   survivors, regardless of nationality or status, including undocumented migrants, asylum seekers and refugees, and stowaways, are treated, while on board, in the manner prescribed in the relevant IMO instruments and in accordance with relevant international agreements and long-standing humanitarian maritime traditions.

2.2   Pursuant to resolution A.920(22), the Secretary-General brought the issue of persons rescued at sea to the attention of a number of competent United Nations specialized agencies and programmes highlighting the need for a co-ordinated approach among United Nations agencies, and soliciting the input of relevant agencies within the scope of their respective mandates. Such an inter-agency effort focusing on State responsibilities for

---

[1] The Guidelines are set out in the Annex to Resolution MSC.167(78). Part 4 (International Aeronautical Search and Rescue Manual) and Appendix omitted.

[2] Footnote in original: Where the term Government is used in these Guidelines, it should be read to mean Contracting Government to the International Convention for the Safety of Life at Sea (SOLAS), 1974, as amended, or Party to the International Convention on Maritime Search and Rescue, 1979, as amended, respectively.

non-rescue issues, such as immigration and asylum that are beyond the competence of IMO, is an essential complement to IMO efforts.

SOLAS and SAR Convention amendments

2.3   At its seventy-eighth session, the Maritime Safety Committee (MSC) adopted pertinent amendments to chapter V of the International Convention for the Safety of Life at Sea (SOLAS) and to chapters 2, 3 and 4 of the Annex to the International Convention on Maritime Search and Rescue Convention (SAR Convention). These amendments are expected to enter into force on 1 July 2006. At the same session the MSC adopted the current guidelines; these amendments provide for the development of such guidelines. The purpose of these amendments and the current guidelines is to help ensure that persons in distress are assisted, while minimizing the inconvenience to assisting ships and ensuring the continued integrity of SAR services.

2.4   Specifically, paragraph 1-1 of SOLAS regulation V/33 and paragraph 3.1.9 of the Annex to the SAR Convention, as amended, impose upon Governments an obligation to co-ordinate and co-operate to ensure that masters of ships providing assistance by embarking persons in distress at sea are released from their obligations with minimum further deviation from the ship's intended voyage.

2.5   As realized by the MSC in adopting the amendments, the intent of new paragraph 1-1 of SOLAS regulation V/33 and paragraph 3.1.9 of the Annex to the International Convention on Maritime Search and Rescue, 1979, as amended, is to ensure that in every case a place of safety is provided within a reasonable time. The responsibility to provide a place of safety, or to ensure that a place of safety is provided, falls on the Government responsible for the SAR region in which the survivors were recovered.

2.6   Each case, however, can involve different circumstances. These amendments give the responsible Government the flexibility to address each situation on a case-by-case basis, while assuring that the masters of ships providing assistance are relieved of their responsibility within a reasonable time and with as little impact on the ship as possible.

2.7   Some comments on relevant international law are set out at the appendix.

3   PRIORITIES

3.1   When ships assist persons in distress at sea, co-ordination will be needed among all concerned to ensure that all of the following priorities are met in a manner that takes due account of border control, sovereignty and security concerns consistent with international law:

Lifesaving
>All persons in distress at sea should be assisted without delay.

Preservation of the integrity and effectiveness of SAR services
>Prompt assistance provided by ships at sea is an essential element of global SAR services; therefore it must remain a top priority for shipmasters, shipping companies and flag States.

Relieving masters of obligations after assisting persons
>Flag and coastal States should have effective arrangements in place for timely assistance to shipmasters in relieving them of persons recovered by ships at sea.

5 SHIPMASTERS

General guidance

5.1   SAR services throughout the world depend on ships at sea to assist persons in distress. It is impossible to arrange SAR services that depend totally upon dedicated shore-based rescue units to provide timely assistance to all persons in distress at sea. Shipmasters have certain duties that must be carried out in order to provide for safety of life at sea, preserve the integrity of global SAR services of which they are part, and to comply with humanitarian and legal obligations. In this regard, shipmasters should:

.1   understand and heed obligations under international law to assist persons in distress at sea (such assistance should always be carried out without regard to the nationality or status of the persons in distress, or to the circumstances in which they are found);

.2   do everything possible, within the capabilities and limitations of the ship, to treat the survivors humanely and to meet their immediate needs;

.3   carry out SAR duties in accordance with the provisions of Volume III of the IAMSAR Manual;

.4   in a case where the RCC responsible for the area where the survivors are recovered cannot be contacted, attempt to contact another RCC, or if that is impractical, any other Government authority that may be able to assist, while recognizing that responsibility still rests with the RCC of the area in which the survivors are recovered;

.5   keep the RCC informed about conditions, assistance needed, and actions taken or planned for the survivors (see paragraph 6.10 regarding other information the RCC may wish to obtain);

.6   seek to ensure that survivors are not disembarked to a place where their safety would be further jeopardized; and

.7   comply with any relevant requirements of the Government responsible for the SAR region where the survivors were recovered, or of another responding coastal State, and seek additional guidance from those authorities where difficulties arise in complying with such requirements.

5.2   In order to more effectively contribute to safety of life at sea, ships are urged to participate in ship reporting systems established for the purpose of facilitating SAR operations.

6 GOVERNMENTS AND RESCUE CO-ORDINATION CENTRES

Responsibilities and preparedness

6.1   Governments should ensure that their respective rescue co-ordination centres (RCCs) and other national authorities concerned have sufficient guidance and authority to fulfil their duties consistent with their treaty obligations and the current guidelines contained in this resolution.

6.2   Governments should ensure that their RCCs and rescue units are operating in accordance with the standards and procedures in the IAMSAR Manual and that all ships operating under their flag have on board Volume III of the IAMSAR Manual.

6.3   A ship should not be subject to undue delay, financial burden or other related difficulties after assisting persons at sea; therefore coastal States should relieve the ship as soon as practicable.

6.4   Normally, any SAR co-ordination that takes place between an assisting ship and any coastal State(s) should be handled via the responsible RCC. States may delegate to their respective RCCs the authority to handle such co-ordination on a 24-hour basis, or may task other national authorities to promptly assist the RCC with these duties. RCCs should be prepared to act quickly on their own, or have processes in place, as necessary, to involve other authorities, so that timely decisions can be reached with regard to handling survivors.

6.5   Each RCC should have effective plans of operation and arrangements (interagency or international plans and agreements if appropriate) in place for responding to all types of SAR situations. Such plans and arrangements should cover incidents that occur within its associated SAR region, and should also cover incidents outside its own SAR region if necessary until the RCC responsible for the region in which assistance is being rendered (see paragraph 6.7) or another RCC better situated to handle the case accept responsibility. These plans and arrangements should cover how the RCC could co-ordinate:

   .1   a recovery operation;

   .2   disembarkation of survivors from a ship;

   .3   delivery of survivors to a place of safety; and

   .4   its efforts with other entities (such as customs and immigration authorities, or the ship owner or flag State), should non-SAR issues arise while survivors are still aboard the assisting ship with regard to nationalities, status or circumstances of the survivors; and quickly address initial border control or immigration issues to minimize delays that might negatively impact the assisting ship, including temporary provisions for hosting survivors while such issues are being resolved.

6.6   Plans of operation, liaison activities and communications arrangements should provide for proper co-ordination in advance of and during a rescue operation with shipping companies and with national or international authorities that may need to be involved in response or disembarkation efforts.

6.7   When appropriate, the first RCC contacted should immediately begin efforts to transfer the case to the RCC responsible for the region in which the assistance is being rendered. When the RCC responsible for the SAR region in which assistance is needed is informed about the situation, that RCC should immediately accept responsibility for co-ordinating the rescue efforts, since related responsibilities, including arrangements for a place of safety for survivors, fall primarily on the Government responsible for that region. The first RCC, however, is responsible for co-ordinating the case until the responsible RCC or other competent authority assumes responsibility.

6.8   Governments and the responsible RCC should make every effort to minimize the time survivors remain aboard the assisting ship.

6.9   Responsible State authorities should make every effort to expedite arrangements to disembark survivors from the ship; however, the master should understand that in some cases necessary co-ordination may result in unavoidable delays.

6.10   The RCC should seek to obtain the following information from the master of the assisting ship:

   .1   information about the survivors, including name, age, gender, apparent health and medical condition and any special medical needs;

   .2   the master's judgment about the continuing safety of the assisting ship;

   .3   actions completed or intended to be taken by the master;

   .4   assisting ship's current endurance with the additional persons on board;

   .5   assisting ship's next intended port of call;

.6   the master's preferred arrangements for disembarking the survivors;

.7   any help that the assisting ship may need during or after the recovery operation; and

.8   any special factors (e.g., prevailing weather, time sensitive cargo).

6.11   Potential health and safety concerns aboard a ship that has recovered persons in distress include insufficient lifesaving equipment, water, provisions, medical care, and accommodations for the number of persons on board, and the safety of the crew and passengers if persons on board might become aggressive or violent. In some cases it may be advisable for the RCC to arrange for SAR or other personnel to visit the assisting ship to better assess the situation onboard, to help meet needs on board, or to facilitate safe and secure disembarkation of the survivors.

Place of safety

6.12   A place of safety (as referred to in the Annex to the 1979 SAR Convention, paragraph 1.3.2) is a location where rescue operations are considered to terminate. It is also a place where the survivors' safety of life is no longer threatened and where their basic human needs (such as food, shelter and medical needs) can be met. Further, it is a place from which transportation arrangements can be made for the survivors' next or final destination.

6.13   An assisting ship should not be considered a place of safety based solely on the fact that the survivors are no longer in immediate danger once aboard the ship. An assisting ship may not have appropriate facilities and equipment to sustain additional persons on board without endangering its own safety or to properly care for the survivors. Even if the ship is capable of safely accommodating the survivors and may serve as a temporary place of safety, it should be relieved of this responsibility as soon as alternative arrangements can be made.

6.14   A place of safety may be on land, or it may be aboard a rescue unit or other suitable vessel or facility at sea that can serve as a place of safety until the survivors are disembarked to their next destination.

6.15   The Conventions, as amended, indicate that delivery to a place of safety should take into account the particular circumstances of the case. These circumstances may include factors such as the situation on board the assisting ship, on scene conditions, medical needs, and availability of transportation or other rescue units. Each case is unique, and selection of a place of safety may need to account for a variety of important factors.

6.16   Governments should co-operate with each other with regard to providing suitable places of safety for survivors after considering relevant factors and risks.

6.17   The need to avoid disembarkation in territories where the lives and freedoms of those alleging a well-founded fear of persecution would be threatened is a consideration in the case of asylum-seekers and refugees recovered at sea.

6.18   Often the assisting ship or another ship may be able to transport the survivors to a place of safety. However, if performing this function would be a hardship for the ship, RCCs should attempt to arrange use of other reasonable alternatives for this purpose.

Non-SAR considerations

6.19   If survivor status or other non-SAR matters need to be resolved, the appropriate authorities can often handle these matters once the survivors have been delivered to a place of safety. Until then, RCCs are responsible for co-operation with any national or international authorities or others involved in the situation. Examples of non-SAR considerations that may require attention include oil spills, onscene investigations, salvage, survivors who are migrants or asylum seekers, needs of survivors once they have been delivered to a place of safety, or security or law enforcement concerns. National authorities other than the RCC typically have primary responsibility for such efforts.

6.20   Any operations and procedures such as screening and status assessment of rescued persons that go beyond rendering assistance to persons in distress should not be allowed to hinder the provision of such assistance or unduly delay disembarkation of survivors from the assisting ship(s).

6.21   Although issues other than rescue relating to asylum seekers, refugees and migratory status are beyond the remit of IMO, and beyond the scope of the SOLAS and SAR Conventions, Governments should be aware of assistance that international organizations or authorities of other countries might be able to provide in such cases, be able to contact them rapidly, and provide any instructions that their RCCs may need in this regard, including how to alert and involve appropriate national authorities. States should ensure that their response mechanisms are sufficiently broad to account for the full range of State responsibilities.

6.22   Authorities responsible for such matters may request that RCCs obtain from the assisting ship certain information about a ship or other vessel in distress, or certain information about the persons assisted. Relevant national authorities should also be made aware of what they need to do to co-operate with the RCC (especially with regard to contacting ships), and to respond as a matter of urgency to situations involving assisted persons aboard ships.

Adoption of Mandatory Ship Reporting System in the Western European Particularly Sensitive Sea Area

IMO Resolution MSC.190(79), adopted on 6 December 2004

The Maritime Safety Committee,

Recalling article 28(b) of the Convention related to the creation of the International Maritime Organization concerning the functions of the Committee,

Recalling also regulation V/11 of the International Convention for the Safety of Life at Sea (SOLAS), 1974 concerning the adoption by the Organization of ship-reporting systems,

Recalling further resolution A.858(20), which authorizes the Committee to perform the function of adopting ship-reporting systems on behalf of the Organization,

Taking into account the Guidelines and criteria for ship-reporting systems, adopted by resolution MSC.43(64), as amended by resolution MSC.111(73),

Having considered the recommendations of the Sub-Committee on Safety of Navigation at its fiftieth session,

Having also noted that the Marine Environment Protection Committee, at its fifty-second session, endorsed the recommendations of the Sub-Committee on Safety of Navigation at its fiftieth session and designated the Western European Waters as a Particularly Sensitive Sea Area (PSSA) by resolution MEPC.121(52),

1. *Adopts*, in accordance with SOLAS regulation V/11, the ship-reporting system in the Western European Particularly Sensitive Sea Area as described in the Annexes to this resolution;

2. *Decides* that this mandatory ship-reporting system will enter into force at 0000 hours UTC on 1 July 2005;

3. *Requests* the Secretary-General to bring this resolution and its Annexes to the attention of Contracting Governments to the SOLAS Convention and to members of the Organization who are not parties to the Convention.

ANNEX 1

DESCRIPTION OF THE MANDATORY SHIP REPORTING SYSTEM FOR THE WESTERN EUROPEAN PARTICULARLY SENSITIVE SEA AREA[1]

The West European Tanker Reporting System (WETREP) is established in the Western European Particularly Sensitive Sea Area.

1   Categories of ships required to participate in the system
1.1   Ships required to participate in the mandatory ship reporting system WETREP:
Every kind of oil tanker of more than 600 tonnes deadweight, carrying a cargo of:
- heavy crude oil, meaning crude oils with a density at 15°C of higher than 900 kg/m^3;
- heavy fuel oils, meaning fuel oils with a density at 15°C of higher than 900 kg/m^3, or a kinematic viscosity at 50°C of higher than 180 mm^2/s;
- bitumen and tar and their emulsions.

1.2   Pursuant to SOLAS, the mandatory ship reporting system WETREP does not apply to any warship, naval auxiliary or other vessel owned or operated by a contracting government and used, for the time being, only on government non-commercial service.

2   Geographical coverage of the system, and number and edition of the reference chart used for the delineation of the system
2.1   The area covered by the reporting system WETREP is defined within the following co-ordinates and are also shown in the chartlet attached at appendix 3: [...].[2]

2.2   The reference chart is Admiralty Chart No. 4011 (World Geodetic System 1984 Datum (WGS 84)).

3   Format, contents of report, times and geographical positions for submitting report. Authorities to whom the reports must be sent and available services
3.1   Format
3.1.1   WETREP reports shall be sent to the nearest participating coastal or communication station listed in annex 1, appendix 1 and shall be drafted in accordance with the format as shown in appendix 2.

3.1.2   The format of the report described below is in accordance with resolution A.851(20) appendix, paragraph 2.
3.2   Contents of report
3.2.1   The report required from participating ships contains information that is essential to achieve the objectives of the system:
  .1   the ship's name, call sign, IMO number/MMSI number and position are needed for establishing the identity of the ship and its initial position (letters A, B and C);
  .2   the ship's course, speed and destination, are important in order to maintain track of the ship so as to be able to implement search and rescue measures if a report from a ship fails to appear; to be able to instigate measures for the safe navigation of the ship; and to prevent pollution in the areas where weather

---
[1] Appendixes 1-3 omitted.
[2] Co-ordinates omitted.

conditions are severe (letters E, F, G and I). Proprietary information obtained as a requirement of the mandatory ship reporting system WETREP will be protected under this system consistent with the Guidelines and Criteria for Ship Reporting Systems, as amended (resolution A.851(20));

.3   the number of persons on board and other relevant information are important in relation to the allocation of resources in a search and rescue operation (letters P, T and W); and

.4   in accordance with the provisions of the SOLAS and MARPOL conventions, ships will provide information on defects, damage, deficiencies or other limitations (under 'Q') as well as, additional information (under 'X').

3.3   Time and geographical position for submitting report

3.3.1   Ships must report:

.1   on entry into the Reporting Area as defined in paragraph 2; or

.2   immediately on departing from a port, terminal or anchorage within the Reporting Area; or

.3   when they deviate from routeing to their original declared destination port/ terminal/anchorage or position, for orders, given at time of entry into Reporting Area; or

.4   when deviation from planned route is necessary due to weather or equipment malfunction or a change in the navigational status; and

.5   when finally exiting from Reporting Area.

3.3.2   Ships need not report if, while on normal passage routeing during transit of Reporting Area, the boundary of the Reporting Area is crossed on other occasions apart from the initial entry and final exit.

3.4   Shore-based authorities to whom reports are sent

3.4.1   Upon entering the WETREP reporting area, ships will notify the co-ordination centre of the responsible authority of the Coastal State participating in the system. The vessel traffic services, RCC, coastal radio station or others facilities to whom the reports must be sent to are listed in appendix 1.

3.4.2   Should the ship be unable to send the report to the nearest coastal radio station or other facility, the report shall be sent to the next-nearest coastal radio station or other facility as listed in appendix 1.

3.4.3   Reports may be sent by any modern communication form, including Inmarsat-C, telefax and e-mail as appropriate.

4   Information to be given to participating ships and procedures to be followed

4.1   If requested, coastal States can provide ships with information of importance for the safety of navigation in the ship reporting area, from broadcasting devices set up in the coastal States.

4.2   If necessary, individual information can be provided to a ship in relation to the special local conditions.

5   Communications required for the system, frequencies on which reports should be transmitted and information to be reported

5.1   The vessel traffic services, RCC, coastal radio station or others facilities to whom the reports must be sent to are listed in appendix 1.

5.2   The reports required from a ship entering and navigating in the reporting area shall begin with the word WETREP and shall contain a two-letter abbreviation for identification of the report (Sailing Plan, Final Report or Deviation Report). Telegrams so prefixed are dispatched free of charge to ships.

5.3   Dependent on the type of report, the following information shall be included as referred to under paragraph 6 of appendix 2:

A: Ship identification (ship name, call sign, IMO identification number and MMSI Number)

B: Date time group

C: Position

E: True course

F: Speed

G: Name of last port of call

I: Name of next port of call with the ETA

P :   Oil cargo type(s), quantity, grade(s) and density. If those tankers carry other hazardous cargo simultaneously: the type, quantity and IMO class of that cargo, as appropriate

Q: To be used in cases of defects or deficiency affecting normal navigation

T: Address for the communication of cargo information

W: Number of persons on board

X: Various information applicable for those tankers:
- characteristics and estimated quantity of bunker fuel, for tankers carrying more than 5,000 tonnes of bunker fuel
- navigational status, (for example, under way with engines, restricted in ability to manoeuvre, etc.)

5.4   Reports shall be in a format consistent with IMO resolution A.851(20).

5.5   Reports shall be free of charge for reporting ships.

6   Relevant Rules and Regulations in force in the area of the system

6.1   Regulations for the Preventing Collisions at Sea

The International Regulations for Preventing Collisions at Sea, 1972 (COLREGs), as amended, apply throughout the area covered by the system.[3]

6.2   Traffic separation schemes and other routeing measures

6.2.1   The following IMO adopted Traffic Separation Schemes:

West of the Scilly Isles
South of the Scilly Isles
Off Land's End, between Seven Stones and Longships
South of the Scilly Isles
West of the Scilly Isles
Off Ushant
Off Casquets
In the Strait of Dover and adjacent waters
Off Fastnet RockOff Smalls
Off Tuskar Rock
Off Skerries
In the North Channel
Off Finisterre
Off Cape Roca
Off Cape S. Vicente

6.2.2   The following IMO adopted Deep-Water Routes:

Deep-water route leading to the Port of Antifer

---

[3] Footnote in original: Ships carrying dangerous or polluting goods coming from or bound for a port within the reporting area must comply with the European Community Directive on *Vessel Traffic Monitoring* (2002/59/EC).

Deep-water route forming part of the north-eastbound traffic lane of the Strait of Dover and adjacent waters traffic separation scheme

Deep-water route west of the Hebrides

6.2.3   The following IMO adopted Areas to be Avoided:

In the region of the Rochebonne Shelf

In the English Channel and its approaches

In the Dover Strait

Around the F3 station within the separation scheme 'In the Strait of Dover and adjacent waters'

In the region of the Orkney Islands

In the region of the Fair Isle

In the region of the Shetland Islands

Between the Smalls Lighthouse and Grassholme Island

In the region of the Berlengas Islands

6.2.4   The following other IMO adopted Routeing Measures:

Recommended directions of traffic flow in the English Channel

Recommended routes in the Fair Isle Channel

Recommendations on navigation around the United Kingdom coast

6.2.5   The following IMO adopted Mandatory Ship Reporting Systems:

Off 'Les Casquets' and the adjacent coastal area

In the Dover Strait/Pas-de-Calais

Off Ushant

Off Finisterre

6.2.6   The following Coastal Vessel Traffic Services (VTS):

Corsen VTS

Dover, Channel Navigation Information Service (CNIS)

Finisterre VTS

Gris-Nez VTS

7   Shore-based facilities to support the operation of the system

7.1   The vessel traffic services, RCC, coastal radio stations or others facilities to whom the reports must be sent to are listed in appendix 1.

7.2   The vessel traffic services, RCC, coastal radio stations or others facilities that form a part of the service, will at all times be manned.

7.3   All communications facilities

7.3.1   All IMO approved communication methods are accepted and available as detailed in appendix 1.

7.4   Staff training and qualification

7.4.1   Personnel are trained according to national and international recommendations. The training of personnel comprises an overall study of the navigation safety measures, the relevant international (IMO) and national provisions with respect to the safety of navigation.

8   Procedures to be followed if shore-based communications fail

Should the ship be unable to send the report to the nearest coastal radio station or other facility, the report shall be sent to the next-nearest coastal radio station or other facility as listed in appendix 1.

9   Measures to be taken if a ship fails to comply with the requirements of the system

The objectives of the system are to initiate SAR and measures to prevent pollution as fast and effective as possible if an emergency is reported or a report from a ship fails to appear, and it is impossible to establish communication with the ship. All means will be used to obtain the full participation of ships required to submit reports. If reports are not submitted and the offending ship can be positively identified, then information will be passed on to the relevant flag State Authorities for investigation and possible prosecution in accordance with national legislation. The mandatory ship reporting system WETREP is for the exchange of information only and does not provide any additional authority for mandating changes in the vessel's operations. This reporting system will be implemented consistent with UNCLOS, SOLAS and other relevant international instruments so that the reporting system will not provide the basis to impinge on a transiting vessel's passage through the reporting area.

Strengthening Australia's Offshore Maritime Security

Announcement by the Australian Government, Department of Transport and Regional Services, Office of Transport Security, February 2005
www.dotars.gov.au/transport/security/maritime/pdf/Strengthening_offshore.pdf

Introduction

Australia is further strengthening its offshore maritime security through a series of linked initiatives that will be implemented progressively through 2005.

These measures build on previously announced border protection and maritime security initiatives. They focus, in particular, on the protection of Australia's offshore oil and gas facilities, and on ensuring that any terrorist threat to Australia's maritime assets and the Australian coastline can be quickly detected and defeated.

An integrated approach to offshore maritime security

Australia intends to achieve effective security for offshore oil and gas platforms and enhanced security measures within Australia's exclusive economic zone and territorial sea, in accordance with international and domestic law, through an integrated approach that combines:

- warning and maritime domain awareness (achieved through intelligence, cooperative international action, surveillance and the integrated use and analysis of available maritime information);
- deterrence (achieved through cooperative bilateral and multilateral action, increased patrolling and the demonstration of the intent and capability to achieve effective offshore maritime security);
- response (based on informed and effective planning and preparedness, clear command and control and sufficient available capabilities);
- enhanced protective security measures for offshore platforms, related onshore facilities and ports; and
- clear and practised consequence management arrangements.

Australian Maritime Identification System[1]

Based on cooperative international arrangements, including with neighbouring countries, in accordance with international and domestic law, the Australian Government proposes to establish a Maritime Identification System as a framework for seeking,

---

[1] An almost identical Notice, published on 25 January 2005, used the term 'Australian Maritime Identification Zone'. Similarly, in a Press Release of 15 December 2004, Australian Prime Minister John Howard also spoke of 'Maritime Identification Zone' (http://www.pm.gov.au/news/media_releases/media_Release1173.html).

analysing and managing information on vessel identity, crews, cargoes and ship movements to support Australia's maritime security needs, particularly in relation to vessels seeking to enter Australian ports.

The development of this proposal takes into account the limited circumstances in which positional information can be required from non-Australian flagged vessels.

Through the establishment of this identification system, the Australian Government aims to centrally coordinate and integrate the maritime information that is already collected by a number of Australian Government and State agencies. The collection of information on known and forecast vessel movements will assist in the more effective conduct of maritime surveillance within Australia's exclusive economic zone and territorial sea.

This identification system would have graduated application in the following manner:

- Up to 1,000 nautical miles or 48 hours steaming from the Australian coast, Australia will seek advanced arrival information from International Ship and Port Security Code vessels whose next port of call is in Australia. This information, on ship identity, crew, cargo, location, course, speed, and intended port of arrival is already collected for Australian Customs and International Ship and Port Security Code (ISPS Code) purposes. Similar advanced arrival information is collected by other countries for the same domestic and international purposes.

- Up to 500 nautical miles or 24 hours steaming from Australia, information will be sought, on a wholly voluntary basis, on identity, course and speed from vessels proposing to transit Australia's exclusive economic zone or territorial sea.

- Within Australia's exclusive economic zone, the aim will be to identify all vessels, other than day recreational boats. Such information is already sought for purposes such as fisheries protection and is often provided voluntarily for maritime safety purposes.

Joint Offshore Protection Command

A Joint Offshore Protection Command is being established to link the Australian Defence Force responsibility for counter-terrorism prevention and response within Australia's maritime zones with the existing civil maritime surveillance and regulatory roles that are undertaken or coordinated by the Coastwatch Division of the Australian Customs Service.

This new Command will simplify and strengthen planning and command and control arrangements for offshore counter-terrorism response. The Command will also make the best use of all available resources.

The Director-General of Coastwatch, presently Rear Admiral Russ Crane, will also be the Commander of the Joint Offshore Protection Command. The Command will have a joint accountability structure, being responsible.

- to the Chief of the Defence Force for military offshore maritime protection functions, including the conduct of ADF offshore patrol, prevention, and response capabilities and activities in relation to counter-terrorism, the protection of offshore oil and gas platforms and the offshore interdiction of ships within Australia's exclusive economic zone and territorial sea; and

- to the Chief Executive Officer of Customs for the conduct of civil maritime surveillance, the coordination of maritime regulatory and law enforcement functions and support for activities such as border protection and control, immigration, quarantine and fisheries protection.

The protection of offshore oil and gas facilities

A programme of augmented security patrols of Australia's oil and gas fields in the Timor Sea and on the North West Shelf is proposed to increase the security of these offshore facilities and to actively deter those who may be contemplating or planning an attack on these assets.

Augmented security patrolling, using available Defence Force and Customs patrol boats and aircraft, essentially involves the periodic but unpredictable saturation of selected areas with patrol assets for pre-determined periods of time.

Some of the oil and gas facilities in the Timor Sea that will be a focus of these enhanced patrols are in areas where Australia shares jurisdiction with Indonesia or East Timor.

The Minister for Foreign Affairs is writing to his counterparts to seek the cooperation of those countries in introducing these mutually-beneficial enhanced counterterrorism security measures. Matters that Australia will be seeking to address include the enforcement of the existing safety zones around offshore facilities (established in accordance with the 1982 Convention on the Law of the Sea); and arrangements that would permit the boarding of suspect vessels within such sensitive areas.

The Australian Government also will continue to support the further development of multilateral and bilateral arrangements to strengthen offshore maritime security and counter-terrorism measures.

The direct protection of each offshore platform through the provision of appropriate security measures is the final element of the Government's integrated approach to enhanced offshore maritime security. The provision of such measures is an industry responsibility.

To assist industry in the development of protective security measures for offshore facilities, the *Maritime Transport Security Act 2003* is being extended to apply to offshore oil and gas facilities to provide the necessary advice and oversight in the implementation of any additional security measures.

Directive 2005/35/EC of the European Parliament and of the Council of 7 September 2005 on Ship-Source Pollution and on the Introduction of Penalties for Infringements

Official Journal L 255, 30 September 2005, 11, and L 33, 4 February 2006, 87[1]

The European Parliament and the Council of the European Union,

Having regard to the Treaty establishing the European Community, and in particular Article 80(2) thereof,

Having regard to the proposal from the Commission,

Having regard to the opinion of the European Economic and Social Committee,

After consulting the Committee of the Regions,

---

[1] Footnotes omitted. Directive 2005/35/EC was initially supplemented by Council Framework Decision 2005/667/JHA of 12 July 2005 to Strengthen the Criminal-Law Framework for the Enforcement of the Law Against Ship-Source Pollution (Official Journal L 255, 30 September 2005, 164). On 23 October 2007, the European Court of Justice annulled the Framework Decision on the ground that several of its provisions fall within the legislative competence of the Community (Case C-440/05 *Commission* v. *Council* [2007] ECR I-9097, para. 69). On 11 March 2008, the Commission presented a proposal for a Directive of the European Parliament and of the Council amending Directive 2005/35/EC (COM(2008) 134 final) which will in effect incorporate in the Directive the provisions of the annulled Framework Decision. The proposed amendments to Directive 2005/35/EC, which will be renamed 'Directive of the European Parliament and of the Council on Ship-Source Pollution and on the Introduction of Penalties, Including Criminal Penalties, for Pollution Offences', are reproduced in the footnotes. Both Parliament and Council have suggested changes to the Commission's proposal. For the amendments adopted by Parliament on 5 May 2009, see Council of the European Union, Doc. 9315/09, 18 May 2009.

Acting in accordance with the procedure laid down in Article 251 of the Treaty,

Whereas:

(1)   The Community's maritime safety policy is aimed at a high level of safety and environmental protection and is based on the understanding that all parties involved in the transport of goods by sea have a responsibility for ensuring that ships used in Community waters comply with applicable rules and standards.

(2)   The material standards in all Member States for discharges of polluting substances from ships are based upon the Marpol 73/78 Convention; however these rules are being ignored on a daily basis by a very large number of ships sailing in Community waters, without corrective action being taken.

(3)   The implementation of Marpol 73/78 shows discrepancies among Member States and there is thus a need to harmonise its implementation at Community level; in particular the practices of Member States relating to the imposition of penalties for discharges of polluting substances from ships differ significantly.

(4)   Measures of a dissuasive nature form an integral part of the Community's maritime safety policy, as they ensure a link between the responsibility of each of the parties involved in the transport of polluting goods by sea and their exposure to penalties; in order to achieve effective protection of the environment there is therefore a need for effective, dissuasive and proportionate penalties.

(5)   To that end it is essential to approximate, by way of the proper legal instruments, existing legal provisions, in particular on the precise definition of the infringement in question, the cases of exemption and minimum rules for penalties, and on liability and jurisdiction.

(6)   This Directive is supplemented by detailed rules on criminal offences and penalties as well as other provisions set out in Council Framework Decision 2005/667/JHA of 12 July 2005 to strengthen the criminal law framework for the enforcement of the law against ship-source pollution.

(7)   Neither the international regime for the civil liability and compensation of oil pollution nor that relating to pollution by other hazardous or noxious substances provides sufficient dissuasive effects to discourage the parties involved in the transport of hazardous cargoes by sea from engaging in substandard practices; the required dissuasive effects can only be achieved through the introduction of penalties applying to any person who causes or contributes to marine pollution; penalties should be applicable not only to the shipowner or the master of the ship, but also the owner of the cargo, the classification society or any other person involved.

(8)   Ship-source discharges of polluting substances should be regarded as infringements if committed with intent, recklessly or by serious negligence. These infringements are regarded as criminal offences by, and in the circumstances provided for in, Framework Decision 2005/667/JHA supplementing this Directive.

(9)   Penalties for discharges of polluting substances from ships are not related to the civil liability of the parties concerned and are thus not subject to any rules relating to the limitation or channelling of civil liabilities, nor do they limit the efficient compensation of victims of pollution incidents.

(10)   There is a need for further effective cooperation among Member States to ensure that discharges of polluting substances from ships are detected in time and that the offenders are identified. For this reason, the European Maritime Safety Agency set up by Regulation (EC) No 1406/2002 of the European Parliament and of the Council of 27 June 2002 has a key role to play in working with the Member States in developing technical solutions and providing technical assistance relating to the implementation of this Directive and in assisting the Commission in the performance of any task assigned to it for the effective implementation of this Directive.

(11)   In order better to prevent and combat marine pollution, synergies should be created between enforcement authorities such as national coastguard services. In this context, the Commission should undertake a feasibility study on a European coastguard dedicated to pollution prevention and response, making clear the costs and benefits. This study should, if appropriate, be followed by a proposal on a European coastguard.

(12)   Where there is clear, objective evidence of a discharge causing major damage or a threat of major damage, Member States should submit the matter to their competent authorities with a view to instituting proceedings in accordance with Article 220 of the 1982 United Nations Convention on the Law of the Sea.

(13)   The enforcement of Directive 2000/59/EC of the European Parliament and of the Council of 27 November 2000 on port reception facilities for ship-generated waste and cargo residues is, together with this Directive, a key instrument in the set of measures to prevent ship-source pollution.

(14)   The measures necessary for the implementation of this Directive should be adopted in accordance with Council Decision 1999/468/EC of 28 June 1999 laying down the procedures for the exercise of implementing powers conferred on the Commission.

(15)   Since the objectives of this Directive, namely the incorporation of the international ship-source pollution standards into Community law and the establishment of penalties – criminal or administrative – for violation of them in order to ensure a high level of safety and environmental protection in maritime transport, cannot be sufficiently achieved by the Member States and can therefore be better achieved at Community level, the Community may adopt measures, in accordance with the principle of subsidiarity as set out in Article 5 of the Treaty. In accordance with the principle of proportionality, as set out in that Article, this Directive does not go beyond what is necessary in order to achieve those objectives.

(16)   This Directive fully respects the Charter of fundamental rights of the European Union; any person suspected of having committed an infringement must be guaranteed a fair and impartial hearing and the penalties must be proportional,

Have adopted this Directive:

Article 1 Purpose

1. The purpose of this Directive is to incorporate international standards for ship-source pollution into Community law and to ensure that persons responsible for discharges are subject to adequate penalties as referred to in Article 8, in order to improve maritime safety and to enhance protection of the marine environment from pollution by ships.

2. This Directive does not prevent Member States from taking more stringent measures against ship-source pollution in conformity with international law.

Article 2 Definitions

For the purpose of this Directive:

1. 'Marpol 73/78' shall mean the International Convention for the Prevention of Pollution from Ships, 1973 and its 1978 Protocol, in its up-to-date version;

2. 'polluting substances' shall mean substances covered by Annexes I (oil) and II (noxious liquid substances in bulk) to Marpol 73/78;

3. 'discharge' shall mean any release howsoever caused from a ship, as referred to in Article 2 of Marpol 73/78;

4. 'ship' shall mean a seagoing vessel, irrespective of its flag, of any type whatsoever operating in the marine environment and shall include hydrofoil boats, air-cushion vehicles, submersibles and floating craft.

Article 3 Scope

1. This Directive shall apply, in accordance with international law, to discharges of polluting substances in:

    (a)   the internal waters, including ports, of a Member State, in so far as the Marpol regime is applicable;

    (b)   the territorial sea of a Member State;

    (c)   straits used for international navigation subject to the regime of transit passage, as laid down in Part III, section 2, of the 1982 United Nations Convention on the Law of the Sea, to the extent that a Member State exercises jurisdiction over such straits;

    (d)   the exclusive economic zone or equivalent zone of a Member State, established in accordance with international law; and

    (e)   the high seas.

2. This Directive shall apply to discharges of polluting substances from any ship, irrespective of its flag, with the exception of any warship, naval auxiliary or other ship owned or operated by a State and used, for the time being, only on government non-commercial service.

Article 4 Infringements

Member States shall ensure that ship-source discharges of polluting substances into any of the areas referred to in Article 3(1) are regarded as infringements if committed with intent, recklessly or by serious negligence. These infringements are regarded as criminal offences by, and in the circumstances provided for in, Framework Decision 2005/667/JHA supplementing this Directive.[2]

Article 5 Exceptions

1. A discharge of polluting substances into any of the areas referred to in Article 3(1) shall not be regarded as an infringement if it satisfies the conditions set out in Annex I, Regulations 9, 10, 11(a) or 11(c)[3] or in Annex II, Regulations 5, 6(a) or 6(c) of Marpol 73/78.[4]

2. A discharge of polluting substances into the areas referred to in Article 3(1)(c), (d) and (e) shall not be regarded as an infringement for the owner, the master or the crew when acting under the master's responsibility if it satisfies the conditions set out in Annex I, Regulation 11(b) or in Annex II, Regulation 6(b) of Marpol 73/78.[5]

---

*6

[2] According to Article 1 (3) of the Commission's proposal for a Directive amending Directive 2005/35/EC Article 4 is to be replaced by the following:

    Article 4 Criminal offences

    1. Member States shall ensure that ship-source discharges of polluting substances into any of the areas referred to in Article 3 (1) are regarded as criminal offences if committed with intent, recklessly or with serious negligence.

    2. Each Member State shall take the measures necessary to ensure that inciting or aiding and abetting a criminal offence referred to in paragraph 1 is punishable by criminal law.

[3] The regulations in Annex I of MARPOL 73/78 have been revised and renumbered. The equivalent provisions are now regulations 4, 15 and 34.

[4] The regulations in Annex II of MARPOL 73/78 have been revised and renumbered. The equivalent provisions are now regulations 13 and 3.

[5] According to Article 1 (2) of the Commission's proposal for a Directive amending Directive 2005/35/EC, in Articles 5 (1) and (2), the term 'infringement' is to be replaced by 'criminal offence'.

[6] According to Article 1 (4)-(6) of the Commission's proposal for a Directive amending Directive 2005/35/EC the following Articles are to be inserted after Article 5:

    Article 5a Penalties against natural persons

    1. Each Member State shall take the necessary measures to ensure that the criminal offences referred to in Article 4 are punishable by effective, proportionate and dissuasive criminal penalties.   *(Cont.)*

Article 6 Enforcement measures with respect to ships within a port of a Member State

1. If irregularities or information give rise to a suspicion that a ship which is voluntarily within a port or at an off-shore terminal of a Member State has been engaged in or is engaging in a discharge of polluting substances into any of the areas referred to in Article 3(1), that Member State shall ensure that an appropriate inspection, taking into account the relevant guidelines adopted by the International Maritime Organisation (IMO), is undertaken in accordance with its national law.

2. In so far as the inspection referred to in paragraph 1 reveals facts that could indicate an infringement within the meaning of Article 4, the competent authorities of that Member State and of the flag State shall be informed.[7]

Article 7 Enforcement measures by coastal States with respect to ships in transit

1. If the suspected discharge of polluting substances takes place in the areas referred to in Article 3(1)(b), (c), (d) or (e) and the ship which is suspected of the discharge does not call at a port of the Member State holding the information relating to the suspected discharge, the following shall apply:

    (a) If the next port of call of the ship is in another Member State, the Member States concerned shall cooperate closely in the inspection referred to in Article 6(1) and in deciding on the appropriate measures in respect of any such discharge;

    (b) If the next port of call of the ship is a port of a State outside the Community, the Member State shall take the necessary measures to ensure that the next port of call of the ship is informed about the suspected discharge and shall request the State of the next port of call to take the appropriate measures in respect of any such discharge.

2. Where there is clear, objective evidence that a ship navigating in the areas referred to in Article 3(1)(b) or (d) has, in the area referred to in Article 3(1)(d), committed an infringement resulting in a discharge causing major damage or a threat of major damage to the coastline or related interests of the Member State concerned, or to any resources of the

---

2. Each Member State shall take the measures necessary to ensure that the criminal penalties referred to in paragraph 1 apply to any person who is found responsible by a court for a criminal offence within the meaning of Article 4.

Article 5b Liability of legal persons

1. Each Member State shall take the measures necessary to ensure that legal persons can be held liable for the criminal offences referred to in Article 4, committed for their benefit by any natural person acting either individually or as part of an organ of the legal person, who has a leading position within the legal person, based on:

(a) a power of representation of the legal person, or
(b) an authority to take decisions on behalf of the legal person, or
(c) an authority to exercise control within the legal person.

2. Apart from the cases provided for in paragraph 1, each Member State shall take the measures necessary to ensure that a legal person can be held liable where lack of supervision or control by a natural person referred to in paragraph 1 has made possible the commission of the criminal offence referred to in Article 4 for the benefit of the legal person by a natural person under its authority.

3. The liability of a legal person under paragraphs 1 and 2 shall not exclude criminal proceedings against natural persons who are involved as perpetrators, instigators or accessories in the criminal offences referred to in Article 4.

Article 5c Penalties against legal persons

1. Each Member State shall take the measures necessary to ensure that a legal person held liable pursuant to Article 5b (1) and (2) is punishable by effective, proportionate and dissuasive penalties.

2. Each Member State shall take the measures necessary to ensure that the penalties referred to in paragraph 1 apply to any legal person who is found responsible by a court for a criminal offence within the meaning of Article 4.

[7] According to Article 1 (2) of the Commission's proposal for a Directive amending Directive 2005/35/EC the term 'infringement' in Article 6 (2) is to be replaced by 'criminal offence'.

areas referred to in Article 3(1)(b) or (d), that State shall, subject to Part XII, Section 7 of the 1982 United Nations Convention on the Law of the Sea and provided that the evidence so warrants, submit the matter to its competent authorities with a view to instituting proceedings, including detention of the ship, in accordance with its national law.[8]

3. In any event, the authorities of the flag State shall be informed.

Article 8 Penalties[9]

1. Member States shall take the necessary measures to ensure that infringements within the meaning of Article 4 are subject to effective, proportionate and dissuasive penalties, which may include criminal or administrative penalties.

2. Each Member State shall take the measures necessary to ensure that the penalties referred to in paragraph 1 apply to any person who is found responsible for an infringement within the meaning of Article 4.

Article 9 Compliance with international law

Member States shall apply the provisions of this Directive without any discrimination in form or in fact against foreign ships and in accordance with applicable international law, including Section 7 of Part XII of the 1982 United Nations Convention on the Law of the Sea, and they shall promptly notify the flag State of the vessel and any other State concerned of measures taken in accordance with this Directive.

Article 10 Accompanying measures

1. For the purposes of this Directive, Member States and the Commission shall cooperate, where appropriate, in close collaboration with the European Maritime Safety Agency and taking account of the action programme to respond to accidental or deliberate marine pollution set up by Decision No 2850/2000/EC and if appropriate, of the implementation of Directive 2000/59/EC in order to:

(a) develop the necessary information systems required for the effective implementation of this Directive;

(b) establish common practices and guidelines on the basis of those existing at international level, in particular for:

— the monitoring and early identification of ships discharging polluting substances in violation of this Directive, including, where appropriate, on-board monitoring equipment,

— reliable methods of tracing polluting substances in the sea to a particular ship, and

— the effective enforcement of this Directive.

2. In accordance with its tasks as defined in Regulation (EC) No 1406/2002, the European Maritime Safety Agency shall:

(a) work with the Member States in developing technical solutions and providing technical assistance in relation to the implementation of this Directive, in actions such as tracing discharges by satellite monitoring and surveillance;

(b) assist the Commission in the implementation of this Directive, including, if appropriate, by means of visits to the Member States, in accordance with Article 3 of Regulation (EC) No 1406/2002.

---

[8] According to Article 1 (2) of the Commission's proposal for a Directive amending Directive 2005/35/EC the term 'infringement' in Article 7 (2) is to be replaced by 'criminal offence'.

[9] According to Article 1 (7) of the Commission's proposal for a Directive amending Directive 2005/35/EC Article 8 is to be deleted.

Article 11 Feasibility Study

The Commission shall, before the end of 2006, submit to the European Parliament and the Council a feasibility study on a European coastguard dedicated to pollution prevention and response, making clear the costs and benefits.

Article 12 Reporting

Every three years, Member States shall transmit a report to the Commission on the application of this Directive by the competent authorities. On the basis of these reports, the Commission shall submit a Community report to the European Parliament and the Council. In this report, the Commission shall assess, *inter alia*, the desirability of revising or extending the scope of this Directive. It shall also describe the evolution of relevant case-law in the Member States and shall consider the possibility of creating a public database containing such relevant case-law.

Article 13 Committee procedure

1. The Commission shall be assisted by the Committee on Safe Seas and the Prevention of Pollution from Ships (COSS), established by Article 3 of Regulation (EC) No 2099/2002 of the European Parliament and of the Council, of 5 November 2002.

2. Where reference is made to this Article, Articles 5 and 7 of Decision 1999/468/EC shall apply, having regard to the provisions of Article 8 thereof. The period laid down in Article 5(6) of Decision 1999/468/EC shall be set at one month.

Article 14 Provision of information

The Commission shall regularly inform the Committee set up by Article 4 of Decision No 2850/2000/EC of any proposed measures or other relevant activities concerning the response to marine pollution.

Article 15 Amendment procedure

In accordance with Article 5 of Regulation (EC) No 2099/2002 and following the procedure referred to in Article 13 of this Directive, the COSS may exclude amendments to Marpol 73/78 from the scope of this Directive.

Article 16 Implementation

Member States shall bring into force the laws, regulations and administrative provisions necessary to comply with this Directive by 1 April 2007 and forthwith inform the Commission thereof.

When Member States adopt those provisions, they shall contain a reference to this Directive or be accompanied by such a reference on the occasion of their official publication. Member States shall determine how such reference is to be made.

Article 17 Entry into force

This Directive shall enter into force on the day following its publication in the Official Journal of the European Union.

Article 18 Addressees

This Directive is addressed to the Member States.

ANNEX

Summary, for reference purposes, of the Marpol 73/78 discharge regulations relating to discharges of oil and noxious liquid substances, as referred to in Article 2.2

Part I: Oil (Marpol 73/78, Annex I)

For the purposes of Marpol 73/78 Annex I, 'oil' means petroleum in any form including crude oil, fuel oil, sludge, oil refuse and refined products (other than petrochemicals which are subject to the provisions of Marpol 73/78 Annex II) and 'oily mixture' means a mixture with any oil content.

Excerpts of the relevant provisions of Marpol 73/78 Annex I:

Regulation 9: Control of discharge of oil

1. Subject to the provisions of Regulations 10 and 11 of this Annex and paragraph 2 of this Regulation, any discharge into the sea of oil or oily mixtures from ships to which this Annex applies shall be prohibited except when all the following conditions are satisfied:

   (a)   for an oil tanker, except as provided for in subparagraph (b) of this paragraph:

      (i)   the tanker is not within a special area;

      (ii)   the tanker is more than 50 nautical miles from the nearest land;

      (iii)   the tanker is proceeding en route;

      (iv)   the instantaneous rate of discharge of oil content does not exceed 30 litres per nautical mile;

      (v)   the total quantity of oil discharged into the sea does not exceed for existing tankers 1/15000 of the total quantity of the particular cargo of which the residue formed a part, and for new tankers 1/30000 of the total quantity of the particular cargo of which the residue formed a part; and

      (vi)   the tanker has in operation an oil discharge monitoring and control system and a slop tank arrangement as required by Regulation 15 of this Annex.

   (b)   from a ship of 400 tons gross tonnage and above other than an oil tanker and from machinery space bilges excluding cargo pump-room bilges of an oil tanker unless mixed with oil cargo residue:

      (i)   the ship is not within a special area;

      (ii)   the ship is proceeding en route;

      (iii)   the oil content of the effluent without dilution does not exceed 15 parts per million; and

      (iv)   the ship has in operation (monitoring, control and filtering equipment) as required by regulation 16 of this Annex.

2. In the case of a ship of less than 400 tons gross tonnage other than an oil tanker whilst outside the special area, the (flag State) Administration shall ensure that it is equipped as far as practicable and reasonable with installations to ensure the storage of oil residues on board and their discharge to reception facilities or into the sea in compliance with the requirements of paragraph (1)(b) of this Regulation.

3. [...].

4. The provisions of paragraph 1 of this Regulation shall not apply to the discharge of clean or segregated ballast or unprocessed oily mixtures which without dilution have an oil content not exceeding 15 parts per million and which do not originate from cargo pump-room bilges and are not mixed with oil cargo residues.

5. No discharge into the sea shall contain chemicals or other substances in quantities or concentrations which are hazardous to the marine environment or chemicals or other substances introduced for the purpose of circumventing the conditions of discharge specified in this regulation.

6. The oil residues which cannot be discharged into the sea in compliance with paragraphs 1, 2 and 4 of this Regulation shall be retained on board or discharged to reception facilities.

7. [...].

Regulation 10: Methods for the prevention of oil pollution from ships while operating in special areas

1. For the purpose of this Annex, the special areas are the Mediterranean Sea area, the Baltic Sea area, the Black Sea area, the Red Sea area, the 'Gulfs area', the Gulf of Aden area, the Antarctic area and the North-West European waters, (as further defined and specified).

2. Subject to the provisions of regulation 11 of this Annex:

(a)   Any discharge into the sea of oil or oily mixture from any oil tanker and any ship of 400 tons gross tonnage and above other than an oil tanker shall be prohibited while in a special area. [...];

(b)   [...] Any discharge into the sea of oil or oily mixture from a ship of less than 400 tons gross tonnage, other than an oil tanker, shall be prohibited while in a special area, except when the oil content of the effluent without dilution does not exceed 15 parts per million.

3.   (a)   The provisions of paragraph 2 of this Regulation shall not apply to the discharge of clean or segregated ballast.

(b)   The provisions of subparagraph (2)(a) of this regulation shall not apply to the discharge of processed bilge water from machinery spaces, provided that all of the following conditions are satisfied:

(i)   the bilge water does not originate from cargo pump-room bilges;

(ii)   the bilge water is not mixed with oil cargo residues;

(iii) the ship is proceeding en route;

(iv)   the oil content of the effluent without dilution does not exceed 15 parts per million;

(v)   the ship has in operation oil filtering equipment complying with Regulation 16(5) of this Annex; and

(vi)   the filtering system is equipped with a stopping device which will ensure that the discharge is automatically stopped when the oil content of the effluent exceeds 15 parts per million.

4.   (a)   No discharge into the sea shall contain chemicals or other substances in quantities or concentrations which are hazardous to the marine environment or chemicals or other substances introduced for the purpose of circumventing the conditions of discharge specified in this regulation.

(b)   The oil residues which cannot be discharged into the sea in compliance with paragraph 2 or 3 of this Regulation shall be retained on board or discharged to reception facilities.

5. Nothing in this Regulation shall prohibit a ship on a voyage only part of which is in a special area from discharging outside the special area in accordance with Regulation 9 of this Annex.

6. [...].

7. [...].

8. [...].

Regulation 11: Exceptions

Regulations 9 and 10 of this Annex shall not apply to:

(a) the discharge into the sea of oil or oily mixture necessary for the purpose of securing the safety of a ship or saving life at sea; or

(b) the discharge into the sea of oil or oily mixture resulting from damage to a ship or its equipment:

    (i) provided that all reasonable precautions have been taken after the occurrence of the damage or discovery of the discharge for the purpose of preventing or minimising the discharge; and

    (ii) except if the owner or the master acted either with intent to cause damage, or recklessly and with knowledge that damage would probably result; or

(c) the discharge into the sea of substances containing oil, approved by the (flag State) administration, when being used for the purpose of combating specific pollution incidents in order to minimise the damage from pollution. Any such discharge shall be subject to the approval of any Government in whose jurisdiction it is contemplated the discharge will occur.

Part II: Noxious liquid substances (Marpol 73/78 Annex II)

Excerpts of the relevant provisions of Marpol 73/78 Annex II:

Regulation 3: Categorisation and listing of noxious liquid substances

1. For the purpose of the Regulations of this Annex, noxious liquid substances shall be divided into four categories as follows:

(a) Category A: noxious liquid substances which if discharged into the sea from tank cleaning or deballasting operations would present a major hazard to either marine resources or human health or cause serious harm to amenities or other legitimate uses of the sea and therefore justify the application of stringent anti-pollution measures;

(b) Category B: noxious liquid substances which if discharged into the sea from tank cleaning or deballasting operations would present a hazard to either marine resources or human health or cause harm to amenities or other legitimate uses of the sea and therefore justify the application of special anti-pollution measures;

(c) Category C: noxious liquid substances which if discharged into the sea from tank cleaning or deballasting operations would present a minor hazard to either marine resources or human health or cause minor harm to amenities or other legitimate uses of the sea and therefore require special operational conditions;

(d) Category D: noxious liquid substances which if discharged into the sea from tank cleaning or deballasting operations would present a recognisable hazard to either marine resources or human health or cause minimal harm to amenities or other legitimate uses of the sea and therefore require some attention in operational conditions.

2. [...].

3. [...].

4. [...].

(Further guidelines on the categorisation of substances, including a list of categorised substances are given in Regulation 3(2) to (4) and Regulation 4 and the Appendices to Marpol 73/78 Annex II)

Regulation 5: Discharge of noxious liquid substances

Category A, B and C substances outside special areas and Category D substances in all areas

Subject to the provisions of [...] Regulation 6 of this Annex,

1. The discharge into the sea of substances in Category A as defined in Regulation 3(1)(a) of this Annex or of those provisionally assessed as such or ballast water, tank washings, or other residues or mixtures containing such substances shall be prohibited. If tanks containing such substances or mixtures are to be washed, the resulting residues shall be discharged to a reception facility until the concentration of the substance in the effluent to such facility is at or below 0,1 % by weight and until the tank is empty, with the exception of phosphorus, yellow or white, for which the residual concentration shall be 0,01 % by weight. Any water subsequently added to the tank may be discharged into the sea when all the following conditions are satisfied:

(a)   the ship is proceeding en route at a speed of at least 7 knots in the case of self-propelled ships or at least 4 knots in the case of ships which are not self-propelled;

(b)   the discharge is made below the waterline, taking into account the location of the seawater intakes; and

(c)   the discharge is made at a distance of not less than 12 nautical miles from the nearest land in a depth of water of not less than 25 m.

2. The discharge into the sea of substances in Category B as defined in Regulation 3(1)(b) of this Annex or of those provisionally assessed as such, or ballast water, tank washings, or other residues or mixtures containing such substances shall be prohibited except when all the following conditions are satisfied:

(a)   the ship is proceeding en route at a speed of at least 7 knots in the case of self-propelled ships or at least 4 knots in the case of ships which are not self-propelled;

(b)   the procedures and arrangements for discharge are approved by the (flag State) administration. Such procedures and arrangements shall be based upon standards developed by the (IMO) and shall ensure that the concentration and rate of discharge of the effluent is such that the concentration of the substance in the wake astern of the ship does not exceed 1 part per million;

(c)   the maximum quantity of cargo discharged from each tank and its associated piping system does not exceed the maximum quantity approved in accordance with the procedures referred to in subparagraph (b) of this paragraph, which shall in no case exceed the greater of 1 m³ or 1/3000 of the tank capacity in m³;

(d)   the discharge is made below the waterline, taking into account the location of the seawater intakes; and

(e)   the discharge is made at a distance of not less than 12 nautical miles from the nearest land and in a depth of water of not less than 25 m.

3.   The discharge into the sea of substances in Category C as defined in Regulation 3(1)(c) of this Annex or of those provisionally assessed as such, or ballast water, tank washings, or other residues or mixtures containing such substances shall be prohibited except when all the following conditions are satisfied:

(a)   the ship is proceeding en route at a speed of at least 7 knots in the case of self-propelled ships or at least 4 knots in the case of ships which are not self-propelled;

(b)   the procedures and arrangements for discharge are approved by the (flag State) administration. Such procedures and arrangements shall be based upon standards developed by the (IMO) and shall ensure that the concentration and rate of discharge of the effluent is such that the concentration of the substance in the wake astern of the ship does not exceed 10 parts per million;

(c)   the maximum quantity of cargo discharged from each tank and its associated piping system does not exceed the maximum quantity approved in accordance with the procedures referred to in subparagraph (b) of this paragraph, which shall in no case exceed the greater of 3 m^3 or 1/1000 of the tank capacity in m^3;

(d)   the discharge is made below the waterline, taking into account the location of the seawater intakes; and

(e)   the discharge is made at a distance of not less than 12 nautical miles from the nearest land and in a depth of water of not less than 25 m.

4. The discharge into the sea of substances in Category D as defined in Regulation 3(1)(d) of this Annex, or of those provisionally assessed as such, or ballast water, tank washings, or other residues or mixtures containing such substances shall be prohibited except when all the following conditions are satisfied:

(a)   the ship is proceeding en route at a speed of at least 7 knots in the case of self-propelled ships or at least 4 knots in the case of ships which are not self-propelled;

(b)   such mixtures are of a concentration not greater than one part of the substance in ten parts of water; and

(c)   the discharge is made at a distance of not less than 12 nautical miles from the nearest land.

5. Ventilation procedures approved by the (flag State) administration may be used to remove cargo residues from a tank. Such procedures shall be based upon standards developed by the (IMO). Any water subsequently introduced into the tank shall be regarded as clean and shall not be subject to paragraphs 1, 2, 3 or 4 of this Regulation.

6. The discharge into the sea of substances which have not been categorised, provisionally assessed, or evaluated as referred to in Regulation 4(1) of this Annex, or of ballast water, tank washings, or other residues or mixtures containing such substances shall be prohibited.

Category A, B and C substances within special areas (as defined in Marpol 73/78 Annex II, Regulation 1, including the Baltic Sea)

Subject to the provisions of [...] Regulation 6 of this Annex,

7. The discharge into the sea of substances in Category A as defined in Regulation 3(1)(a) of this Annex or of those provisionally assessed as such, or ballast water, tank washings, or other residues or mixtures containing such substances shall be prohibited. If tanks containing such substances or mixtures are to be washed, the resulting residues shall be discharged to a reception facility which the States bordering the special area shall provide in accordance with Regulation 7 of this Annex, until the concentration of the substance in the effluent to such facility is at or below 0,05 % by weight and until the tank is empty, with the exception of phosphorus, yellow or white, for which the residual concentration shall be 0,005 % by weight. Any water subsequently added to the tank may be discharged into the sea when all the following conditions are satisfied:

(a)   the ship is proceeding en route at a speed of at least 7 knots in the case of self-propelled ships or at least 4 knots in the case of ships which are not self-propelled;

(b)   the discharge is made below the waterline, taking into account the location of the seawater intakes; and

(c)   the discharge is made at a distance of not less than 12 nautical miles from the nearest land and in a depth of water of not less than 25 m.

8. The discharge into the sea of substances in Category B as defined in Regulation (3)(1)(b) of this Annex or of those provisionally assessed as such, or ballast water, tank washings, or other residues or mixtures containing such substances shall be prohibited except when all the following conditions are satisfied:

    (a)   the tank has been prewashed in accordance with the procedure approved by the (flag State) Administration and based on standards developed by the (IMO) and the resulting tank washings have been discharged to a reception facility;

    (b)   the ship is proceeding en route at a speed of at least 7 knots in the case of self-propelled ships or at least 4 knots in the case of ships which are not self-propelled;

    (c)   the procedures and arrangements for discharge and washings are approved by the (flag State) Administration. Such procedures and arrangements shall be based upon standards developed by the (IMO) and shall ensure that the concentration and rate of discharge of the effluent is such that the concentration of the substance in the wake astern of the ship does not exceed 1 part per million;

    (d)   the discharge is made below the waterline, taking into account the location of the seawater intakes; and

    (e)   the discharge is made at a distance of not less than 12 nautical miles from the nearest land and in a depth of water of not less than 25 m.

9. The discharge into the sea of substances in Category C as defined in Regulation 3(1)(c) of this Annex or of those provisionally assessed as such, or ballast water, tank washings, or other residues or mixtures containing such substances shall be prohibited except when all the following conditions are satisfied:

    (a)   the ship is proceeding en route at a speed of at least 7 knots in the case of self-propelled ships or at least 4 knots in the case of ships which are not self-propelled;

    (b)   the procedures and arrangements for discharge are approved by the (flag State) adminstration. Such procedures and arrangements shall be based upon standards developed by the (IMO) and shall ensure that the concentration and rate of discharge of the effluent is such that the concentration of the substance in the wake astern of the ship does not exceed 1 part per million;

    (c)   the maximum quantity of cargo discharged from each tank and its associated piping system does not exceed the maximum quantity approved in accordance with the procedures referred to in subparagraph (b) of this paragraph which shall in no case exceed the greater of 1 m^3 or 1/3000 of the tank capacity in m^3;

    (d)   the discharge is made below the waterline, taking into account the location of the seawater intakes; and

    (e)   the discharge is made at a distance of not less than 12 nautical miles from the nearest land and in a depth of water of not less than 25 m.

10. Ventilation procedures approved by the (flag State) administration may be used to remove cargo residues from a tank. Such procedures shall be based upon standards developed by the (IMO). Any water subsequently introduced into the tank shall be regarded as clean and shall not be subject to paragraphs 7, 8 or 9 of this Regulation.

11. The discharge into the sea of substances which have not been categorised, provisionally assessed or evaluated as referred to in Regulation 4(1) of this Annex, or of ballast water, tank washings, or other residues or mixtures containing such substances shall be prohibited.

12. Nothing in this regulation shall prohibit a ship from retaining on board the residues from a Category B or C cargo and discharging such residues into the sea outside a special area in accordance with paragraphs 2 or 3 of this Regulation, respectively.

Regulation 6: Exceptions

Regulation 5 of this Annex shall not apply to:

(a) the discharge into the sea of noxious liquid substances or mixtures containing such substances necessary for the purpose of securing the safety of a ship or saving life at sea; or

(b) the discharge into the sea of noxious liquid substances or mixtures containing such substances resulting from damage to a ship or its equipment:

    (i) provided that all reasonable precautions have been taken after the occurrence of the damage or discovery of the discharge for the purpose of preventing or minimising the discharge; and

    (ii) except if the owner or the master acted either with intent to cause damage, or recklessly and with knowledge that damage would probably result; or

(c) the discharge into the sea of noxious liquid substances or mixtures containing such substances, approved by the (flag State) administration, when being used for the purpose of combating specific pollution incidents in order to minimise the damage from pollution. Any such discharge shall be subject to the approval of any government in whose jurisdiction it is contemplated the discharge will occur.

Convention for the Suppression of Unlawful Acts Against the Safety of Maritime Navigation, 2005

Done at London, 14 October 2005; not yet in force
1678 UNTS 222 [Registration Number 29004]
and IMO Doc. LEG/CONF.15/21, 1 November 2005[1]

Article 1

1. For the purposes of this Convention:

(a) 'ship' means a vessel of any type whatsoever not permanently attached to the sea-bed, including dynamically supported craft, submersibles, or any other floating craft.

(b) 'transport' means to initiate, arrange or exercise effective control, including decision-making authority, over the movement of a person or item.

(c) 'serious injury or damage' means:

    (i) serious bodily injury; or

    (ii) extensive destruction of a place of public use, State or government facility, infrastructure facility, or public transportation system, resulting in major economic loss; or

---

[1] The Convention for the Suppression of Unlawful Acts Against the Safety of Maritime Navigation was originally adopted on 10 March 1988 and entered into force on 1 March 1992. The Convention was revised on 14 October 2005 by the Protocol of 2005 to the Convention for the Suppression of Unlawful Acts Against the Safety of Maritime Navigation. According to Article 15 (2) of the Protocol 'Articles 1 to 16 of the Convention, as revised by this Protocol, together with articles 17 to 24 of this Protocol and the Annex thereto, shall constitute and be called the Convention for the Suppression of Unlawful Acts against the Safety of Maritime Navigation, 2005 (2005 SUA Convention).' The text reproduced is a consolidated version of the Convention as amended by the Protocol.

      (iii) substantial damage to the environment, including air, soil, water, fauna, or flora.

(d) 'BCN weapon' means:

    (i) 'biological weapons', which are:

        (1) microbial or other biological agents, or toxins whatever their origin or method of production, of types and in quantities that have no justification for prophylactic, protective or other peaceful purposes; or

        (2) weapons, equipment or means of delivery designed to use such agents or toxins for hostile purposes or in armed conflict.

    (ii) 'chemical weapons', which are, together or separately:

        (1) toxic chemicals and their precursors, except where intended for:

        (A) industrial, agricultural, research, medical, pharmaceutical or other peaceful purposes; or

        (B) protective purposes, namely those purposes directly related to protection against toxic chemicals and to protection against chemical weapons; or

        (C) military purposes not connected with the use of chemical weapons and not dependent on the use of the toxic properties of chemicals as a method of warfare; or

        (D) law enforcement including domestic riot control purposes,
as long as the types and quantities are consistent with such purposes;

        (2) munitions and devices specifically designed to cause death or other harm through the toxic properties of those toxic chemicals specified in subparagraph (ii)(1), which would be released as a result of the employment of such munitions and devices;

        (3) any equipment specifically designed for use directly in connection with the employment of munitions and devices specified in subparagraph (ii)(2).

    (iii) 'nuclear weapons' and other 'nuclear explosive devices'.

(e) 'toxic chemical' means any chemical which through its chemical action on life processes can cause death, temporary incapacitation or permanent harm to humans or animals. This includes all such chemicals, regardless of their origin or of their method of production, and regardless of whether they are produced in facilities, in munitions or elsewhere.

(f) 'precursor' means any chemical reactant which takes part at any stage in the production by whatever method of a toxic chemical. This includes any key component of a binary or multicomponent chemical system.

(g) 'Organization' means the International Maritime Organization (IMO).

(h) 'Secretary-General' means the Secretary-General of the Organization.

2. For the purposes of this Convention:

(a) the terms 'place of public use', 'State or Government facility', 'infrastructure facility', and 'public transportation system' have the same meaning as given to those terms in the International Convention for the Suppression of Terrorist Bombings, done at New York on 15 December 1997; and

(b) the terms 'source material' and 'special fissionable material' have the same meaning as given to those terms in the Statute of the International Atomic Energy Agency (IAEA), done at New York on 26 October 1956.

Article 2

    1. This Convention does not apply to:

(a) a warship; or

(b) a ship owned or operated by a State when being used as a naval auxiliary or for customs or police purposes; or

(c) a ship which has been withdrawn from navigation or laid up.

    2. Nothing in this Convention affects the immunities of warships and other Government ships operated for non-commercial purposes.

Article 2*bis*

    1. Nothing in this Convention shall affect other rights, obligations and responsibilities of States and individuals under international law, in particular the purposes and principles of the Charter of the United Nations and international human rights, refugee and humanitarian law.

    2. This Convention does not apply to the activities of armed forces during an armed conflict, as those terms are understood under international humanitarian law, which are governed by that law, and the activities undertaken by military forces of a State in the exercise of their official duties, inasmuch as they are governed by other rules of international law.

    3. Nothing in this Convention shall affect the rights, obligations and responsibilities under the Treaty on the Non-Proliferation of Nuclear Weapons, done at Washington, London and Moscow on 1 July 1968, the Convention on the Prohibition of the Development, Production and Stockpiling of Bacteriological (Biological) and Toxin Weapons and on their Destruction, done at Washington, London and Moscow on 10 April 1972, or the Convention on the Prohibition of the Development, Production, Stockpiling and Use of Chemical Weapons and on their Destruction, done at Paris on 13 January 1993, of States Parties to such treaties.

Article 3

    1. Any person commits an offence within the meaning of this Convention if that person unlawfully and intentionally:

(a) seizes or exercises control over a ship by force or threat thereof or any other form of intimidation; or

(b) performs an act of violence against a person on board a ship if that act is likely to endanger the safe navigation of that ship; or

(c) destroys a ship or causes damage to a ship or to its cargo which is likely to endanger the safe navigation of that ship; or

(d) places or causes to be placed on a ship, by any means whatsoever, a device or substance which is likely to destroy that ship, or cause damage to that ship or its cargo which endangers or is likely to endanger the safe navigation of that ship; or

(e) destroys or seriously damages maritime navigational facilities or seriously interferes with their operation, if any such act is likely to endanger the safe navigation of a ship; or

(f) communicates information which that person knows to be false, thereby endangering the safe navigation of a ship.

    2. Any person also commits an offence if that person threatens, with or without a condition, as is provided for under national law, aimed at compelling a physical or juridical person to do or refrain from doing any act, to commit any of the offences set forth in paragraphs 1 (b), (c), and (e), if that threat is likely to endanger the safe navigation of the ship in question.

Article 3*bis*

1. Any person commits an offence within the meaning of this Convention if that person unlawfully and intentionally:

  (a) when the purpose of the act, by its nature or context, is to intimidate a population, or to compel a Government or an international organization to do or to abstain from doing any act:

   (i) uses against or on a ship or discharges from a ship any explosive, radioactive material or BCN weapon in a manner that causes or is likely to cause death or serious injury or damage; or

   (ii) discharges, from a ship, oil, liquefied natural gas, or other hazardous or noxious substance, which is not covered by subparagraph (a)(i), in such quantity or concentration that causes or is likely to cause death or serious injury or damage; or

   (iii) uses a ship in a manner that causes death or serious injury or damage; or

   (iv) threatens, with or without a condition, as is provided for under national law, to commit an offence set forth in subparagraph (a)(i), (ii) or (iii); or

  (b) transports on board a ship:

   (i) any explosive or radioactive material, knowing that it is intended to be used to cause, or in a threat to cause, with or without a condition, as is provided for under national law, death or serious injury or damage for the purpose of intimidating a population, or compelling a Government or an international organization to do or to abstain from doing any act; or

   (ii) any BCN weapon, knowing it to be a BCN weapon as defined in article 1; or

   (iii) any source material, special fissionable material, or equipment or material especially designed or prepared for the processing, use or production of special fissionable material, knowing that it is intended to be used in a nuclear explosive activity or in any other nuclear activity not under safeguards pursuant to an IAEA comprehensive safeguards agreement; or

   (iv) any equipment, materials or software or related technology that significantly contributes to the design, manufacture or delivery of a BCN weapon, with the intention that it will be used for such purpose.

2. It shall not be an offence within the meaning of this Convention to transport an item or material covered by paragraph 1(b)(iii) or, insofar as it relates to a nuclear weapon or other nuclear explosive device, paragraph 1(b)(iv), if such item or material is transported to or from the territory of, or is otherwise transported under the control of, a State Party to the Treaty on the Non-Proliferation of Nuclear Weapons where:

  (a) the resulting transfer or receipt, including internal to a State, of the item or material is not contrary to such State Party's obligations under the Treaty on the Non-Proliferation of Nuclear Weapons and,

  (b) if the item or material is intended for the delivery system of a nuclear weapon or other nuclear explosive device of a State Party to the Treaty on the Non-Proliferation of Nuclear Weapons, the holding of such weapon or device is not contrary to that State Party's obligations under that Treaty.

Article 3*ter*

Any person commits an offence within the meaning of this Convention if that person unlawfully and intentionally transports another person on board a ship knowing that the person has committed an act that constitutes an offence set forth in article 3, 3*bis* or 3*quater* or an offence set forth in any treaty listed in the Annex, and intending to assist that person to evade criminal prosecution.

Article 3*quater*

Any person also commits an offence within the meaning of this Convention if that person:

(a)   unlawfully and intentionally injures or kills any person in connection with the commission of any of the offences set forth in article 3, paragraph 1, article 3*bis*, or article 3*ter*; or

(b)   attempts to commit an offence set forth in article 3, paragraph 1, article 3*bis*, paragraph 1(a)(i), (ii) or (iii), or subparagraph (a) of this article; or

(c)   participates as an accomplice in an offence set forth in article 3, article 3*bis*, article 3*ter*, or subparagraph (a) or (b) of this article; or

(d)   organizes or directs others to commit an offence set forth in article 3, article 3*bis*, article 3*ter*, or subparagraph (a) or (b) of this article; or

(e)   contributes to the commission of one or more offences set forth in article 3, article 3*bis*, article 3*ter* or subparagraph (a) or (b) of this article, by a group of persons acting with a common purpose, intentionally and either:

(i)   with the aim of furthering the criminal activity or criminal purpose of the group, where such activity or purpose involves the commission of an offence set forth in article 3, 3*bis* or 3*ter*; or

(ii)   in the knowledge of the intention of the group to commit an offence set forth in article 3, 3*bis* or 3*ter*.

Article 4

1.   This Convention applies if the ship is navigating or is scheduled to navigate into, through or from waters beyond the outer limit of the territorial sea of a single State, or the lateral limits of its territorial sea with adjacent States.

2.   In cases where the Convention does not apply pursuant to paragraph 1, it nevertheless applies when the offender or the alleged offender is found in the territory of a State Party other than the State referred to in paragraph 1.

Article 5

Each State Party shall make the offences set forth in articles 3, 3*bis*, 3*ter* and 3*quater* punishable by appropriate penalties which take into account the grave nature of those offences.

Article 5*bis*

1.   Each State Party, in accordance with its domestic legal principles, shall take the necessary measures to enable a legal entity located in its territory or organized under its laws to be held liable when a person responsible for management or control of that legal entity has, in that capacity, committed an offence set forth in this Convention. Such liability may be criminal, civil or administrative.

2.   Such liability is incurred without prejudice to the criminal liability of individuals having committed the offences.

3.   Each State Party shall ensure, in particular, that legal entities liable in accordance with paragraph 1 are subject to effective, proportionate and dissuasive criminal, civil or administrative sanctions. Such sanctions may include monetary sanctions.

Article 6

1.   Each State Party shall take such measures as may be necessary to establish its jurisdiction over the offences set forth in articles 3, 3*bis*, 3*ter* and 3*quater* when the offence is committed:

    (a)   against or on board a ship flying the flag of the State at the time the offence is committed; or

    (b)   in the territory of that State, including its territorial sea; or

    (c)   by a national of that State.

    2. A State Party may also establish its jurisdiction over any such offence when:

    (a)   it is committed by a stateless person whose habitual residence is in that State; or

    (b)   during its commission a national of that State is seized, threatened, injured or killed; or

    (c)   it is committed in an attempt to compel that State to do or abstain from doing any act.

    3. Any State Party which has established jurisdiction mentioned in paragraph 2 shall notify the Secretary-General. If such State Party subsequently rescinds that jurisdiction, it shall notify the Secretary-General.

    4. Each State Party shall take such measures as may be necessary to establish its jurisdiction over the offences set forth in articles 3, 3*bis*, 3*ter* and 3*quater* in cases where the alleged offender is present in its territory and it does not extradite the alleged offender to any of the States Parties which have established their jurisdiction in accordance with paragraphs 1 and 2 of this article.

    5. This Convention does not exclude any criminal jurisdiction exercised in accordance with national law.

Article 7

    1. Upon being satisfied that the circumstances so warrant, any State Party in the territory of which the offender or the alleged offender is present shall, in accordance with its law, take him into custody or take other measures to ensure his presence for such time as is necessary to enable any criminal or extradition proceedings to be instituted.

    2. Such State shall immediately make a preliminary inquiry into the facts, in accordance with its own legislation.

    3. Any person regarding whom the measures referred to in paragraph 1 are being taken shall be entitled to:

    (a)   communicate without delay with the nearest appropriate representative of the State of which he is a national or which is otherwise entitled to establish such communication or, if he is a stateless person, the State in the territory of which he has his habitual residence;

    (b)   be visited by a representative of that State.

    4. The rights referred to in paragraph 3 shall be exercised in conformity with the laws and regulations of the State in the territory of which the offender or the alleged offender is present, subject to the proviso that the said laws and regulations must enable full effect to be given to the purposes for which the rights accorded under paragraph 3 are intended.

    5. When a State Party, pursuant to this article, has taken a person into custody, it shall immediately notify the States which have established jurisdiction in accordance with article 6, paragraph 1 and, if it considers it advisable, any other interested States, of the fact that such person is in custody and of the circumstances which warrant his detention. The State which makes the preliminary inquiry contemplated in paragraph 2 of this article shall promptly report its findings to the said States and shall indicate whether it intends to exercise jurisdiction.

Article 8

1. The master of a ship of a State Party (the 'flag State') may deliver to the authorities of any other State Party (the 'receiving State') any person who the master has reasonable grounds to believe has committed an offence set forth in article 3, 3*bis*, 3*ter*, or 3*quater*.

2. The flag State shall ensure that the master of its ship is obliged, whenever practicable, and if possible before entering the territorial sea of the receiving State carrying on board any person whom the master intends to deliver in accordance with paragraph 1, to give notification to the authorities of the receiving State of his intention to deliver such person and the reasons therefor.

3. The receiving State shall accept the delivery, except where it has grounds to consider that the Convention is not applicable to the acts giving rise to the delivery, and shall proceed in accordance with the provisions of article 7. Any refusal to accept a delivery shall be accompanied by a statement of the reasons for refusal.

4. The flag State shall ensure that the master of its ship is obliged to furnish the authorities of the receiving State with the evidence in the master's possession which pertains to the alleged offence.

5. A receiving State which has accepted the delivery of a person in accordance with paragraph 3 may, in turn, request the flag State to accept delivery of that person. The flag State shall consider any such request, and if it accedes to the request it shall proceed in accordance with article 7. If the flag State declines a request, it shall furnish the receiving State with a statement of the reasons therefor.

Article 8*bis*

1. States Parties shall co-operate to the fullest extent possible to prevent and suppress unlawful acts covered by this Convention, in conformity with international law, and shall respond to requests pursuant to this article as expeditiously as possible.

2. Each request pursuant to this article should, if possible, contain the name of the suspect ship, the IMO ship identification number, the port of registry, the ports of origin and destination, and any other relevant information. If a request is conveyed orally, the requesting Party shall confirm the request in writing as soon as possible. The requested Party shall acknowledge its receipt of any written or oral request immediately.

3. States Parties shall take into account the dangers and difficulties involved in boarding a ship at sea and searching its cargo, and give consideration to whether other appropriate measures agreed between the States concerned could be more safely taken in the next port of call or elsewhere.

4. A State Party that has reasonable grounds to suspect that an offence set forth in article 3, 3*bis*, 3*ter* or 3*quater* has been, is being or is about to be committed involving a ship flying its flag, may request the assistance of other States Parties in preventing or suppressing that offence. The States Parties so requested shall use their best endeavours to render such assistance within the means available to them.

5. Whenever law enforcement or other authorized officials of a State Party ('the requesting Party') encounter a ship flying the flag or displaying marks of registry of another State Party ('the first Party') located seaward of any State's territorial sea, and the requesting Party has reasonable grounds to suspect that the ship or a person on board the ship has been, is or is about to be involved in the commission of an offence set forth in article 3, 3*bis*, 3*ter* or 3*quater*, and the requesting Party desires to board,

    (a)   it shall request, in accordance with paragraphs 1 and 2 that the first Party confirm the claim of nationality, and

    (b)   if nationality is confirmed, the requesting Party shall ask the first Party (hereinafter referred to as 'the flag State') for authorization to board and to take appropriate measures with regard to that ship which may include stopping, boarding and searching the ship, its cargo and persons on board, and questioning the persons on board in order to determine if an offence set forth in article 3, 3*bis*, 3*ter* or 3*quater* has been, is being or is about to be committed, and

(c)   the flag State shall either:

(i)   authorize the requesting Party to board and to take appropriate measures set out in subparagraph (b), subject to any conditions it may impose in accordance with paragraph 7; or

(ii)   conduct the boarding and search with its own law enforcement or other officials; or

(iii) conduct the boarding and search together with the requesting Party, subject to any conditions it may impose in accordance with paragraph 7; or

(iv)   decline to authorize a boarding and search.

The requesting Party shall not board the ship or take measures set out in subparagraph (b) without the express authorization of the flag State.

(d)   Upon or after depositing its instrument of ratification, acceptance, approval or accession, a State Party may notify the Secretary-General that, with respect to ships flying its flag or displaying its mark of registry, the requesting Party is granted authorization to board and search the ship, its cargo and persons on board, and to question the persons on board in order to locate and examine documentation of its nationality and determine if an offence set forth in article 3, 3*bis*, 3*ter* or 3*quater* has been, is being or is about to be committed, if there is no response from the first Party within four hours of acknowledgment of receipt of a request to confirm nationality.

(e)   Upon or after depositing its instrument of ratification, acceptance, approval or accession, a State Party may notify the Secretary-General that, with respect to ships flying its flag or displaying its mark of registry, the requesting Party is authorized to board and search a ship, its cargo and persons on board, and to question the persons on board in order to determine if an offence set forth in article 3, 3*bis*, 3*ter* or 3*quater* has been, is being or is about to be committed.

The notifications made pursuant to this paragraph can be withdrawn at any time.

6.   When evidence of conduct described in article 3, 3*bis*, 3*ter* or 3*quater* is found as the result of any boarding conducted pursuant to this article, the flag State may authorize the requesting Party to detain the ship, cargo and persons on board pending receipt of disposition instructions from the flag State. The requesting Party shall promptly inform the flag State of the results of a boarding, search, and detention conducted pursuant to this article. The requesting Party shall also promptly inform the flag State of the discovery of evidence of illegal conduct that is not subject to this Convention.

7.   The flag State, consistent with the other provisions of this Convention, may subject its authorization under paragraph 5 or 6 to conditions, including obtaining additional information from the requesting Party, and conditions relating to responsibility for and the extent of measures to be taken. No additional measures may be taken without the express authorization of the flag State, except when necessary to relieve imminent danger to the lives of persons or where those measures derive from relevant bilateral or multilateral agreements.

8.   For all boardings pursuant to this article, the flag State has the right to exercise jurisdiction over a detained ship, cargo or other items and persons on board, including seizure, forfeiture, arrest and prosecution. However, the flag State may, subject to its constitution and laws, consent to the exercise of jurisdiction by another State having jurisdiction under article 6.

9. When carrying out the authorized actions under this article, the use of force shall be avoided except when necessary to ensure the safety of its officials and persons on board, or where the officials are obstructed in the execution of the authorized actions. Any use of force pursuant to this article shall not exceed the minimum degree of force which is necessary and reasonable in the circumstances.

10. Safeguards:

(a) Where a State Party takes measures against a ship in accordance with this article, it shall:

   (i) take due account of the need not to endanger the safety of life at sea;

   (ii) ensure that all persons on board are treated in a manner which preserves their basic human dignity, and in compliance with the applicable provisions of international law, including international human rights law;

   (iii) ensure that a boarding and search pursuant to this article shall be conducted in accordance with applicable international law;

   (iv) take due account of the safety and security of the ship and its cargo;

   (v) take due account of the need not to prejudice the commercial or legal interests of the flag State;

   (vi) ensure, within available means, that any measure taken with regard to the ship or its cargo is environmentally sound under the circumstances;

   (vii) ensure that persons on board against whom proceedings may be commenced in connection with any of the offences set forth in article 3, 3*bis*, 3*ter* or 3*quater* are afforded the protections of paragraph 2 of article 10, regardless of location;

   (viii) ensure that the master of a ship is advised of its intention to board, and is, or has been, afforded the opportunity to contact the ship's owner and the flag State at the earliest opportunity; and

   (ix) take reasonable efforts to avoid a ship being unduly detained or delayed.

(b) Provided that authorization to board by a flag State shall not *per se* give rise to its liability, States Parties shall be liable for any damage, harm or loss attributable to them arising from measures taken pursuant to this article when:

   (i) the grounds for such measures prove to be unfounded, provided that the ship has not committed any act justifying the measures taken; or

   (ii) such measures are unlawful or exceed those reasonably required in light of available information to implement the provisions of this article.

States Parties shall provide effective recourse in respect of such damage, harm or loss.

(c) Where a State Party takes measures against a ship in accordance with this Convention, it shall take due account of the need not to interfere with or to affect:

   (i) the rights and obligations and the exercise of jurisdiction of coastal States in accordance with the international law of the sea; or

   (ii) the authority of the flag State to exercise jurisdiction and control in administrative, technical and social matters involving the ship.

(d) Any measure taken pursuant to this article shall be carried out by law enforcement or other authorized officials from warships or military aircraft, or from other ships or aircraft clearly marked and identifiable as being on government service and authorized to that effect and, notwithstanding articles 2 and 2*bis*, the provisions of this article shall apply.

(e) For the purposes of this article 'law enforcement or other authorized officials' means uniformed or otherwise clearly identifiable members of law enforcement or other government authorities duly authorized by their Government. For the specific purpose of law enforcement under this Convention, law enforcement or other authorized officials shall provide appropriate government-issued identification documents for examination by the master of the ship upon boarding.

11.   This article does not apply to or limit boarding of ships conducted by any State Party in accordance with international law, seaward of any State's territorial sea, including boardings based upon the right of visit, the rendering of assistance to persons, ships and property in distress or peril, or an authorization from the flag State to take law enforcement or other action.

12.   States Parties are encouraged to develop standard operating procedures for joint operations pursuant to this article and consult, as appropriate, with other States Parties with a view to harmonizing such standard operating procedures for the conduct of operations.

13.   States Parties may conclude agreements or arrangements between them to facilitate law enforcement operations carried out in accordance with this article.

14.   Each State Party shall take appropriate measures to ensure that its law enforcement or other authorized officials, and law enforcement or other authorized officials of other States Parties acting on its behalf, are empowered to act pursuant to this article.

15.   Upon or after depositing its instrument of ratification, acceptance, approval or accession, each State Party shall designate the authority, or, where necessary, authorities to receive and respond to requests for assistance, for confirmation of nationality, and for authorization to take appropriate measures. Such designation, including contact information, shall be notified to the Secretary-General within one month of becoming a Party, who shall inform all other States Parties within one month of the designation. Each State Party is responsible for providing prompt notice through the Secretary-General of any changes in the designation or contact information.

Article 9

Nothing in this Convention shall affect in any way the rules of international law pertaining to the competence of States to exercise investigative or enforcement jurisdiction on board ships not flying their flag.

Article 10

1.   The State Party in the territory of which the offender or the alleged offender is found shall, in cases to which article 6 applies, if it does not extradite him, be obliged, without exception whatsoever and whether or not the offence was committed in its territory, to submit the case without delay to its competent authorities for the purpose of prosecution, through proceedings in accordance with the laws of that State. Those authorities shall take their decision in the same manner as in the case of any other offence of a grave nature under the law of that State.

2.   Any person who is taken into custody, or regarding whom any other measures are taken or proceedings are being carried out pursuant to this Convention, shall be guaranteed fair treatment, including enjoyment of all rights and guarantees in conformity with the law of the State in the territory of which that person is present and applicable provisions of international law, including international human rights law.

Article 11

1.   The offences set forth in articles 3, 3*bis*, 3*ter* and 3*quater* shall be deemed to be included as extraditable offences in any extradition treaty existing between any of the States Parties. States Parties undertake to include such offences as extraditable offences in every extradition treaty to be concluded between them.

2.   If a State Party which makes extradition conditional on the existence of a treaty receives a request for extradition from another State Party with which it has no extradition

treaty, the requested State Party may, at its option, consider this Convention as a legal basis for extradition in respect of the offences set forth in articles 3, 3*bis*, 3*ter* and 3*quater*. Extradition shall be subject to the other conditions provided by the law of the requested State Party.

3. States Parties which do not make extradition conditional on the existence of a treaty shall recognize the offences set forth in articles 3, 3*bis*, 3*ter* and 3*quater* as extraditable offences between themselves, subject to the conditions provided by the law of the requested State Party.

4. If necessary, the offences set forth in articles 3, 3*bis*, 3*ter* and 3*quater* shall be treated, for the purposes of extradition between States Parties, as if they had been committed not only in the place in which they occurred but also in a place within the jurisdiction of the State Party requesting extradition.

5. A State Party which receives more than one request for extradition from States which have established jurisdiction in accordance with article 6 and which decides not to prosecute shall, in selecting the State to which the offender or alleged offender is to be extradited, pay due regard to the interests and responsibilities of the State Party whose flag the ship was flying at the time of the commission of the offence.

6. In considering a request for the extradition of an alleged offender pursuant to this Convention, the requested State shall pay due regard to whether his rights as set forth in article 7, paragraph 3, can be effected in the requesting State.

7. With respect to the offences as defined in this Convention, the provisions of all extradition treaties and arrangements applicable between States Parties are modified as between States Parties to the extent that they are incompatible with this Convention.

Article 11*bis*

None of the offences set forth in article 3, 3*bis*, 3*ter* or 3*quater* shall be regarded for the purposes of extradition or mutual legal assistance as a political offence or as an offence connected with a political offence or as an offence inspired by political motives. Accordingly, a request for extradition or for mutual legal assistance based on such an offence may not be refused on the sole ground that it concerns a political offence or an offence connected with a political offence or an offence inspired by political motives.

Article 11*ter*

Nothing in this Convention shall be interpreted as imposing an obligation to extradite or to afford mutual legal assistance, if the requested State Party has substantial grounds for believing that the request for extradition for offences set forth in article 3, 3*bis*, 3*ter* or 3*quater* or for mutual legal assistance with respect to such offences has been made for the purpose of prosecuting or punishing a person on account of that person's race, religion, nationality, ethnic origin, political opinion or gender, or that compliance with the request would cause prejudice to that person's position for any of these reasons.

Article 12

1. States Parties shall afford one another the greatest measure of assistance in connection with criminal proceedings brought in respect of the offences set forth in articles 3, 3*bis*, 3*ter* and 3*quater*, including assistance in obtaining evidence at their disposal necessary for the proceedings.

2. States Parties shall carry out their obligations under paragraph 1 in conformity with any treaties on mutual assistance that may exist between them. In the absence of such treaties, States Parties shall afford each other assistance in accordance with their national law.

Article 12*bis*

1. A person who is being detained or is serving a sentence in the territory of one State Party whose presence in another State Party is requested for purposes of identification, testimony or otherwise providing assistance in obtaining evidence for the investigation or prosecution of offences set forth in article 3, 3*bis*, 3*ter* or 3*quater* may be transferred if the following conditions are met:

   (a)   the person freely gives informed consent; and

   (b)   the competent authorities of both States agree, subject to such conditions as those States may deem appropriate.

2. For the purposes of this article:

   (a)   the State to which the person is transferred shall have the authority and obligation to keep the person transferred in custody, unless otherwise requested or authorized by the State from which the person was transferred;

   (b)   the State to which the person is transferred shall without delay implement its obligation to return the person to the custody of the State from which the person was transferred as agreed beforehand, or as otherwise agreed, by the competent authorities of both States;

   (c)   the State to which the person is transferred shall not require the State from which the person was transferred to initiate extradition proceedings for the return of the person;

   (d)   the person transferred shall receive credit for service of the sentence being served in the State from which the person was transferred for time spent in the custody of the State to which the person was transferred.

3. Unless the State Party from which a person is to be transferred in accordance with this article so agrees, that person, whatever that person's nationality, shall not be prosecuted or detained or subjected to any other restriction of personal liberty in the territory of the State to which that person is transferred in respect of acts or convictions anterior to that person's departure from the territory of the State from which such person was transferred.

Article 13

1. States Parties shall co-operate in the prevention of the offences set forth in articles 3, 3*bis*, 3*ter* and 3*quater*, particularly by:

   (a)   taking all practicable measures to prevent preparation in their respective territories for the commission of those offences within or outside their territories;

   (b)   exchanging information in accordance with their national law, and co-ordinating administrative and other measures taken as appropriate to prevent the commission of offences set forth in articles 3, 3*bis*, 3*ter* and 3*quater*.

2. When, due to the commission of an offence set forth in article 3, 3*bis*, 3*ter* or 3*quater*, the passage of a ship has been delayed or interrupted, any State Party in whose territory the ship or passengers or crew are present shall be bound to exercise all possible efforts to avoid a ship, its passengers, crew or cargo being unduly detained or delayed.

Article 14

Any State Party having reason to believe that an offence set forth in article 3, 3*bis*, 3*ter* or 3*quater* will be committed shall, in accordance with its national law, furnish as promptly as possible any relevant information in its possession to those States which it believes would be the States having established jurisdiction in accordance with article 6.

Article 15

1. Each State Party shall, in accordance with its national law, provide to the Secretary-General, as promptly as possible, any relevant information in its possession concerning:

(a)   the circumstances of the offence;

(b)   the action taken pursuant to article 13, paragraph 2;

(c)   the measures taken in relation to the offender or the alleged offender and, in particular, the results of any extradition proceedings or other legal proceedings.

2. The State Party where the alleged offender is prosecuted shall, in accordance with its national law, communicate the final outcome of the proceedings to the Secretary-General.

3. The information transmitted in accordance with paragraphs 1 and 2 shall be communicated by the Secretary-General to all States Parties, to Members of the Organization, to other States concerned, and to the appropriate international intergovernmental organizations.

Article 16

1. Any dispute between two or more States Parties concerning the interpretation or application of this Convention which cannot be settled through negotiation within a reasonable time shall, at the request of one of them, be submitted to arbitration. If, within six months from the date of the request for arbitration, the parties are unable to agree on the organization of the arbitration any one of those parties may refer the dispute to the International Court of Justice by request in conformity with the Statute of the Court.

2. Each State may at the time of signature or ratification, acceptance or approval of this Convention or accession thereto, declare that it does not consider itself bound by any or all of the provisions of paragraph 1. The other States Parties shall not be bound by those provisions with respect to any State Party which has made such a reservation.

3. Any State which has made a reservation in accordance with paragraph 2 may, at any time, withdraw that reservation by notification to the Secretary-General.

Article 16*bis* Final clauses of the Convention

The final clauses of this Convention shall be articles 17 to 24 of the Protocol of 2005 to the Convention for the Suppression of Unlawful Acts against the Safety of Maritime Navigation. References in this Convention to States Parties shall be taken to mean references to States Parties to that Protocol.

FINAL CLAUSES

Article 17 Signature, ratification, acceptance, approval and accession

1. This Protocol shall be open for signature at the Headquarters of the Organization from 14 February 2006 to 13 February 2007 and shall thereafter remain open for accession.

2. States may express their consent to be bound by this Protocol by:

(a)   signature without reservation as to ratification, acceptance or approval; or

(b)   signature subject to ratification, acceptance or approval, followed by ratification, acceptance or approval; or

(c)   accession.

3. Ratification, acceptance, approval or accession shall be effected by the deposit of an instrument to that effect with the Secretary-General.

4. Only a State which has signed the Convention without reservation as to ratification, acceptance or approval, or has ratified, accepted, approved or acceded to the Convention may become a Party to this Protocol.

Article 18 Entry into force

1. This Protocol shall enter into force ninety days following the date on which twelve States have either signed it without reservation as to ratification, acceptance or approval, or have deposited an instrument of ratification, acceptance, approval or accession with the Secretary-General.

2. For a State which deposits an instrument of ratification, acceptance, approval or accession in respect of this Protocol after the conditions in paragraph 1 for entry into force thereof have been met, the ratification, acceptance, approval or accession shall take effect ninety days after the date of such deposit.

Article 19 Denunciation

1. This Protocol may be denounced by any State Party at any time after the date on which this Protocol enters into force for that State.

2. Denunciation shall be effected by the deposit of an instrument of denunciation with the Secretary-General.

3. A denunciation shall take effect one year, or such longer period as may be specified in the instrument of denunciation, after the deposit of the instrument with the Secretary-General.

Article 20 Revision and amendment

1. A conference for the purpose of revising or amending this Protocol may be convened by the Organization.

2. The Secretary-General shall convene a conference of States Parties to this Protocol for revising or amending the Protocol, at the request of one third of the States Parties, or ten States Parties, whichever is the higher figure.

3. Any instrument of ratification, acceptance, approval or accession deposited after the date of entry into force of an amendment to this Protocol shall be deemed to apply to the Protocol as amended.

Article 21 Declarations

1. Upon depositing its instrument of ratification, acceptance, approval or accession, a State Party which is not a party to a treaty listed in the Annex may declare that, in the application of this Protocol to the State Party, the treaty shall be deemed not to be included in article 3*ter*. The declaration shall cease to have effect as soon as the treaty enters into force for the State Party, which shall notify the Secretary-General of this fact.

2. When a State Party ceases to be a party to a treaty listed in the Annex, it may make a declaration as provided for in this article, with respect to that treaty.

3. Upon depositing its instrument of ratification, acceptance, approval or accession, a State Party may declare that it will apply the provisions of article 3*ter* in accordance with the principles of its criminal law concerning family exemptions of liability.

Article 22 Amendments to the Annex

1. The Annex may be amended by the addition of relevant treaties that:
   (a)   are open to the participation of all States;
   (b)   have entered into force; and

(c) have been ratified, accepted, approved or acceded to by at least twelve States Parties to this Protocol.

2. After the entry into force of this Protocol, any State Party thereto may propose such an amendment to the Annex. Any proposal for an amendment shall be communicated to the Secretary-General in written form. The Secretary-General shall circulate any proposed amendment that meets the requirements of paragraph 1 to all members of the Organization and seek from States Parties to this Protocol their consent to the adoption of the proposed amendment.

3. The proposed amendment to the Annex shall be deemed adopted after more than twelve of the States Parties to this Protocol consent to it by written notification to the Secretary-General.

4. The adopted amendment to the Annex shall enter into force thirty days after the deposit with the Secretary-General of the twelfth instrument of ratification, acceptance or approval of such amendment for those States Parties to this Protocol that have deposited such an instrument. For each State Party to this Protocol ratifying, accepting or approving the amendment after the deposit of the twelfth instrument with the Secretary-General, the amendment shall enter into force on the thirtieth day after deposit by such State Party of its instrument of ratification, acceptance or approval.

Article 23 Depositary

1. This Protocol and any amendments adopted under articles 20 and 22 shall be deposited with the Secretary-General.

2. The Secretary-General shall:

(a) inform all States which have signed this Protocol or acceded to this Protocol of:
    (i) each new signature or deposit of an instrument of ratification, acceptance, approval or accession together with the date thereof;
    (ii) the date of the entry into force of this Protocol;
    (iii) the deposit of any instrument of denunciation of this Protocol together with the date on which it is received and the date on which the denunciation takes effect;
    (iv) any communication called for by any article of this Protocol;
    (v) any proposal to amend the Annex which has been made in accordance with article 22, paragraph 2;
    (vi) any amendment deemed to have been adopted in accordance with article 22, paragraph 3;
    (vii) any amendment ratified, accepted or approved in accordance with article 22, paragraph 4, together with the date on which that amendment shall enter into force; and

(b) transmit certified true copies of this Protocol to all States which have signed or acceded to this Protocol.

3. As soon as this Protocol enters into force, a certified true copy of the text shall be transmitted by the Secretary-General to the Secretary-General of the United Nations for registration and publication in accordance with Article 102 of the Charter of the United Nations.

Article 24 Languages

This Protocol is established in a single original in the Arabic, Chinese, English, French, Russian and Spanish languages, each text being equally authentic.

DONE AT LONDON this fourteenth day of October two thousand and five.

IN WITNESS WHEREOF the undersigned, being duly authorized by their respective Governments for that purpose, have signed this Protocol.

ANNEX

1   Convention for the Suppression of Unlawful Seizure of Aircraft, done at The Hague on 16 December 1970.

2   Convention for the Suppression of Unlawful Acts against the Safety of Civil Aviation, done at Montreal on 23 September 1971.

3   Convention on the Prevention and Punishment of Crimes against Internationally Protected Persons, including Diplomatic Agents, adopted by the General Assembly of the United Nations on 14 December 1973.

4   International Convention against the Taking of Hostages, adopted by the General Assembly of the United Nations on 17 December 1979.

5   Convention on the Physical Protection of Nuclear Material, done at Vienna on 26 October 1979.

6   Protocol for the Suppression of Unlawful Acts of Violence at Airports Serving International Civil Aviation, supplementary to the Convention for the Suppression of Unlawful Acts against the Safety of Civil Aviation, done at Montreal on 24 February 1988.

7   Protocol for the Suppression of Unlawful Acts against the Safety of Fixed Platforms Located on the Continental Shelf, done at Rome on 10 March 1988.

8   International Convention for the Suppression of Terrorist Bombings, adopted by the General Assembly of the United Nations on 15 December 1997.

9   International Convention for the Suppression of the Financing of Terrorism, adopted by the General Assembly of the United Nations on 9 December 1999.

Protocol for the Suppression of Unlawful Acts against the Safety of Fixed Platforms Located on the Continental Shelf, 2005

Done at London, 14 October 2005; not yet in force
1678 UNTS 304 [Registration Number 29004]
and IMO Doc. LEG/CONF.15/22, 1 November 2005[1]

Article 1

1. The provisions of article 1, paragraphs 1(c), (d), (e), (f), (g), (h) and 2(a), of articles 2*bis*, 5, 5*bis*, and 7 and of Articles 10 to 16, including articles 11*bis*, 11*ter* and 12*bis*, of the Convention for the Suppression of Unlawful Acts against the Safety of Maritime Navigation, as amended by the Protocol of 2005 to the Convention for the Suppression of Unlawful Acts against the Safety of Maritime Navigation shall also apply *mutatis mutandis* to the offences set forth in articles 2, 2*bis* and 2*ter* of this Protocol where

---

[1] The Protocol for the Suppression of Unlawful Acts against the Safety of Fixed Platforms Located on the Continental Shelf was originally adopted on 10 March 1988 and entered into force on 1 March 1992. The 1988 Protocol was revised on 14 October 2005 by the Protocol of 2005 to the Protocol for the Suppression of Unlawful Acts Against the Safety of Fixed Platforms Located on the Continental Shelf. According to Article 6 (2) of the 2005 Protocol 'Articles 1 to 4 of the 1988 Protocol, as revised by this Protocol, together with articles 8 to 13 of this Protocol shall constitute and be called the Protocol for the Suppression of Unlawful Acts against the Safety of Fixed Platforms Located on the Continental Shelf, 2005 (2005 SUA Fixed Platforms Protocol).' The text reproduced is a consolidated version of the 1988 Protocol as amended by the 2005 Protocol.

such offences are committed on board or against fixed platforms located on the continental shelf.

    2. In cases where this Protocol does not apply pursuant to paragraph 1, it nevertheless applies when the offender or the alleged offender is found in the territory of a State Party other than the State in whose internal waters or territorial sea the fixed platform is located.

    3. For the purposes of the Protocol, 'fixed platform' means an artificial island, installation or structure permanently attached to the sea-bed for the purpose of exploration or exploitation of resources or for other economic purposes.

Article 2

    1. Any person commits an offence if that person unlawfully and intentionally:

    (a)   seizes or exercises control over a fixed platform by force or threat thereof or any other from of intimidation; or

    (b)   performs an act of violence against a person on board a fixed platform if that act is likely to endanger its safety; or

    (c)   destroys a fixed platform or causes damage to it which is likely to endanger its safety; or

    (d)   places or causes to be placed on a fixed platform, by any means whatsoever, a device or substance which is likely to destroy that fixed platform or likely to endanger its safety.

    2. Any person also commits an offence if that person threatens, with or without a condition, as is provided for under national law, aimed at compelling a physical or juridical person to do or refrain from doing any act, to commit any of the offences set forth in paragraphs 1(b) and (c), if that threat is likely to endanger the safety of the fixed platform

Article 2*bis*

    Any person commits an offence within the meaning of this Protocol is that person unlawfully and intentionally, when the purpose of the act, by its nature or context, is to intimidate a population, or to compel a Government or an international organization to do or to abstain from doing any act:

    (a)   uses against or on a fixed platform or discharges from a fixed platform any explosive, radioactive material or BCN weapon in a manner that causes or is likely to cause death or serious injury or damage; or

    (b)   discharges, from a fixed platform, oil, liquefied natural gas, or other hazardous or noxious substance, which is not covered by subparagraph (a), in such quantity or concentration that causes or is likely to cause death or serious injury or damage; or

    (c)   threatens, with or without a condition, as is provided for under national law, to commit an offence set forth in subparagraph (a) or (b).

Article 2*ter*

    Any person also commits an offence within the meaning of this Protocol if that person:

    (a)   unlawfully and intentionally injures or kills any person in connection with the commission of any of the offences set forth in article 2, paragraph 1, or article 2*bis*; or

    (b)   attempts to commit an offence set forth in article 2, paragraph 1, article 2*bis*, subparagraph (a) or (b), or subparagraph (a) of this article; or

(c)   participates as an accomplice in an offence set froth in article 2, article 2*bis*, or subparagraph (a) or (b) of this article; or

(d)   organizes or directs others to commit an offence set forth in article 2, article 2*bis* or subparagraph (a) or (b) of this article; or

(e)   contributes to the commission of one or more offences set forth in Article 2, article 2*bis* or subparagraph (a) or (b) of this article, by a group of persons acting with a common purpose, intentionally and either:

    (i)   with the aim of furthering the criminal activity or criminal purpose of the group, where such activity or purpose involves the commission of an offence set forth in article 2 or 2*bis*; or

    (ii)   in the knowledge of the intention of the group to commit an offence set forth in article 2 or 2*bis*.

Article 3

1. Each State Party shall take such measures as may be necessary to establish its jurisdiction over the offences set forth in articles 2, 2*bis* and 2*ter* when the offence is committed:

(a)   against or on board a fixed platform while it is located on the continental shelf of that State; or

(b)   by a national of that State.

2. A State Party may also establish its jurisdiction over any such offence when:

(a)   it is committed by a stateless person whose habitual residence is in that State;

(b)   during its commission a national of that State is seized, threatened, injured or killed; or

(c)   it is committed in an attempt to compel that State to do or abstain from doing any act.

3. Any State Party which has established jurisdiction mentioned in paragraph 2 shall notify the Secretary-General. If such State Party subsequently rescinds that jurisdiction, it shall notify the Secretary-General.

4. Each State Party shall take such measures as may be necessary to establish its jurisdiction over the offences set forth in article 2, 2*bis* and 2*ter* in cases where the alleged offender is present in its territory and it does not extradite the alleged offender to any of the States Parties which have established their jurisdiction in accordance with paragraphs 1 and 2.

5. This Protocol does not exclude any criminal jurisdiction exercised in accordance with national law.

Article 4

Nothing in this Protocol shall affect in any way the rules of international law pertaining to fixed platforms located on the continental shelf.

Article 4*bis*   Final clauses of the Protocol

The final clauses of this Protocol shall be articles 8 to 13 of the Protocol of 2005 to the Protocol for the Suppression of Unlawful Acts against the Safety of Fixed Platforms Located on the Continental Shelf. References in this Protocol to States Parties shall be taken to mean references to States Parties to the 2005 Protocol.

FINAL CLAUSES

Article 8 Signature, ratification, acceptance, approval and accession

1. This Protocol shall be open for signature at the Headquarters of the Organization from 14 February 2006 to 13 February 2007 and shall thereafter remain open for accession.

2. States may express their consent to be bound by this Protocol by:

(a)   signature without reservation as to ratification, acceptance or approval; or

(b)   signature subject to ratification, acceptance or approval followed by ratification, acceptance or approval; or

(c)   accession.

3. Ratification, acceptance, approval or accession shall be effected by the deposit of an instrument to that effect with the Secretary-General.

4. Only a State which has signed the 1988 Protocol without reservation as to ratification, acceptance, or approval, or has ratified, accepted, approved or acceded to the 1988 Protocol may become a Party to this Protocol.

Article 9 Entry into force

1. This Protocol shall enter into force ninety days following the date on which three States have either signed it without reservation as to ratification, acceptance or approval, or have deposited an instrument of ratification, acceptance, approval or accession with the Secretary-General. However, this Protocol shall not enter into force before the Protocol of 2005 to the Convention for the Suppression of Unlawful Acts against the Safety of Maritime Navigation has entered into force.

2. For a State which deposits an instrument of ratification, acceptance, approval or accession in respect of this Protocol after the conditions in paragraph 1 for entry into force thereof have been met, the ratification, acceptance, approval or accession shall take effect ninety days after the date of such deposit.

Article 10 Denunciation

1. This Protocol may be denounced by any State Party at any time after the date on which this Protocol enters into force for that State.

2. Denunciation shall be effected by the deposit of an instrument of denunciation with the Secretary-General.

3. A denunciation shall take effect one year, or such longer period as may be specified in the instrument of denunciation, after the deposit of the instrument with the Secretary-General.

Article 11 Revision and amendment

1. A conference for the purpose of revising or amending this Protocol may be convened by the Organization.

2. The Secretary-General shall convene a conference of States Parties to this Protocol for revising or amending the Protocol, at the request of one third of the States Parties, or five States Parties, whichever is the higher figure.

3. Any instrument of ratification, acceptance, approval or accession deposited after the date of entry into force of an amendment to this Protocol shall be deemed to apply to the Protocol as amended.

Article 12 Depositary

1. This Protocol and any amendments adopted under article 11 shall be deposited with the Secretary-General.

2. The Secretary-General shall:

(a) inform all States which have signed this Protocol or acceded to this Protocol of:

(i)   each new signature or deposit of an instrument of ratification, acceptance or approval or accession together with the date thereof;

(ii) the date of the entry into force of this Protocol;

(iii) the deposit of any instrument of denunciation of this Protocol together with the date on which it is received and the date on which the denunciation takes effect;

(iv) any communication called for by any article of this Protocol; and

(b) transmit certified true copies of this Protocol to all States which have signed or acceded to this Protocol.

3. As soon as this Protocol enters into force, a certified true copy of the text shall be transmitted by the Secretary-General to the Secretary-General of the United Nations for registration and publication in accordance with Article 102 of the Charter of the United Nations.

Article 13 Languages

This Protocol is established in a single original in the Arabic, Chinese, English, French, Russian and Spanish languages, each text being equally authentic.

DONE AT LONDON this fourteenth day of October two thousand and five.

IN WITNESS WHEREOF the undersigned, being duly authorized by their respective Governments for that purpose, have signed this Protocol.

Revised Guidelines for the Identification and Designation of Particularly Sensitive Sea Areas

IMO Resolution A.982(24), adopted on 1 December 2005

1 Introduction

1.1   The Marine Environment Protection Committee (MEPC) of the International Maritime Organization (IMO) began its study of the question of Particularly Sensitive Sea Areas (PSSAs) in response to a resolution of the International Conference on Tanker Safety and Pollution Prevention of 1978. The discussions of this concept from 1986 to 1991 culminated in the adoption of Guidelines for the Designation of Special Areas and the Identification of Particularly Sensitive Sea Areas by Assembly resolution A.720(17) in 1991. In a continuing effort to provide a clearer understanding of the concepts set forth in the Guidelines, the Assembly adopted resolutions A.885(21) and A.927(22). This document is intended to clarify and, where appropriate, strengthen certain aspects and procedures for the identification and designation of PSSAs and the adoption of associated protective measures. It sets forth revised Guidelines for the Identification and Designation of Particularly Sensitive Sea Areas (the Guidelines or PSSA Guidelines).

1.2   A PSSA is an area that needs special protection through action by IMO because of its significance for recognized ecological, socio-economic, or scientific attributes where such attributes may be vulnerable to damage by international shipping activities. At the time of designation of a PSSA, an associated protective measure[1], which meets the requirements of the

---

[1] Footnote in original: The term 'associated protective measure' or 'measure' is used both in the singular and plural throughout these Guidelines. It is important to recognize that an identified vulnerability may be addressed

appropriate legal instrument establishing such measure, must have been approved or adopted by IMO to prevent, reduce, or eliminate the threat or identified vulnerability. Information on each of the PSSAs that has been designated by IMO is available at www.imo.org.

1.3   Many international and regional instruments encourage the protection of areas important for the conservation of biological diversity as well as other areas with high ecological, cultural, historical/archaeological, socio-economic or scientific significance. These instruments further call upon their Parties to protect such vulnerable areas from damage or degradation, including from shipping activities.

1.4   The purpose of these Guidelines is to:

.1   provide guidance to IMO Member Governments in the formulation and submission of applications for designation of PSSAs;

.2   ensure that in the process all interests – those of the coastal State, flag State, and the environmental and shipping communities – are thoroughly considered on the basis of relevant scientific, technical, economic, and environmental information regarding the area at risk of damage from international shipping activities and the associated protective measures to prevent, reduce, or eliminate that risk; and

.3   provide for the assessment of such applications by IMO.

1.5   Identification and designation of any PSSA and the adoption of associated protective measures require consideration of three integral components: the particular attributes of the proposed area, the vulnerability of such an area to damage by international shipping activities, and the availability of associated protective measures within the competence of IMO to prevent, reduce, or eliminate risks from these shipping activities.

2 International Shipping Activities and the Marine Environment

2.1   Shipping activity can constitute an environmental hazard to the marine environment in general and consequently even more so to environmentally and/or ecologically sensitive areas. Environmental hazards associated with shipping include:

.1   operational discharges;

.2   accidental or intentional pollution; and

.3   physical damage to marine habitats or organisms.

2.2   Adverse effects and damage may occur to the marine environment and the living resources of the sea as a result of shipping activities. With the increase in global trade, shipping activities are also increasing, thus including greater potential for adverse effects and damage. In the course of routine operations, accidents, and wilful acts of pollution, ships may release a wide variety of substances either directly into the marine environment or indirectly through the atmosphere. Such releases include oil and oily mixtures, noxious liquid substances, sewage, garbage, noxious solid substances, anti-fouling systems, harmful aquatic organisms and pathogens, and even noise. In addition, ships may cause harm to marine organisms and their habitats through physical impact These impacts may include the smothering of habitats, contamination by anti-fouling systems or other substances through groundings, and ship strikes of marine mammals.

3 Process for the Designation of Particularly Sensitive Sea Areas

3.1   The IMO is the only international body responsible for designating areas as Particularly Sensitive Sea Areas and adopting associated protective measures. An application to IMO for designation of a PSSA and the adoption of associated protective measures, or an amendment thereto, may be submitted only by a Member Government. Where two or more Governments have a common interest in a particular area, they should formulate a co-

by only one or by more than one associated protective measure and that therefore the use of this terminology in the singular or plural should not be taken as any indication to the contrary.

ordinated proposal.[2] The proposal should contain integrated measures and procedures for co-operation between the jurisdictions of the proposing Member Governments.

3.2   Member Governments wishing to have IMO designate a PSSA should submit an application to MEPC based on the criteria outlined in section 4, provide information pertaining to the vulnerability of this area to damage from international shipping activities as called for in section 5, and include the proposed associated protective measures as outlined in section 6 to prevent, reduce or eliminate the identified vulnerability. Applications should be submitted in accordance with the procedures set forth in section 7 and the rules adopted by IMO for submission of documents.

3.3   If, in preparing its submission for a PSSA proposal, a Member Government requires technical assistance, that Government is encouraged to request such assistance from IMO.

4   Ecological, Socio-Economic, or Scientific Criteria for the Identification of a Particularly Sensitive Sea Area

4.1   The following criteria apply to the identification of PSSAs only with respect to the adoption of measures to protect such areas against damage, or the identified threat of damage, from international shipping activities.

4.2   These criteria do not, therefore, apply to the identification of such areas for the purpose of establishing whether they should be protected from dumping activities, since that is implicitly covered by the London Convention 1972 (the Convention on the Prevention of Marine Pollution by Dumping of Wastes and Other Matter, 1972) and the 1996 Protocol to that Convention.

4.3   The criteria relate to PSSAs within and beyond the limits of the territorial sea. They can be used by IMO to designate PSSAs beyond the territorial sea with a view to the adoption of international protective measures regarding pollution and other damage caused by ships. They may also be used by national administrations to identify areas within their territorial seas that may have certain attributes reflected in the criteria and be vulnerable to damage by shipping activities.

4.4   In order to be identified as a PSSA, the area should meet at least one of the criteria listed below and information and supporting documentation should be provided to establish that at least one of the criteria exists throughout the entire proposed area, though the same criterion need not be present throughout the entire area. These criteria can be divided into three categories: ecological criteria; social, cultural, and economic criteria; and scientific and educational criteria.

Ecological criteria

4.4.1   Uniqueness or rarity – An area or ecosystem is unique if it is 'the only one of its kind'. Habitats of rare, threatened, or endangered species that occur only in one area are an example. An area or ecosystem is rare if it only occurs in a few locations or has been seriously depleted across its range. An ecosystem may extend beyond country borders, assuming regional or international significance. Nurseries or certain feeding, breeding, or spawning areas may also be rare or unique.

4.4.2   Critical habitat – A sea area that may be essential for the survival, function, or recovery of fish stocks or rare or endangered marine species, or for the support of large marine ecosystems.

---

[2] Footnote in original: It is clear that the Guidelines recognize that an application for designation of a PSSA may be submitted by one or more Governments. For ease of drafting, however, the use of the word 'Government' will be used throughout the text and it should be recognized that this term applies equally to applications where there is more than one Government involved.

4.4.3   Dependency – An area where ecological processes are highly dependent on biotically structured systems (e.g. coral reefs, kelp forests, mangrove forests, seagrass beds). Such ecosystems often have high diversity, which is dependent on the structuring organisms. Dependency also embraces the migratory routes of fish, reptiles, birds, mammals, and invertebrates.

4.4.4   Representativeness – An area that is an outstanding and illustrative example of specific biodiversity, ecosystems, ecological or physiographic processes, or community or habitat types or other natural characteristics.

4.4.5   Diversity – An area that may have an exceptional variety of species or genetic diversity or includes highly varied ecosystems, habitats, and communities.

4.4.6   Productivity – An area that has a particularly high rate of natural biological production. Such productivity is the net result of biological and physical processes which result in an increase in biomass in areas such as oceanic fronts, upwelling areas and some gyres.

4.4.7   Spawning or breeding grounds – An area that may be a critical spawning or breeding ground or nursery area for marine species which may spend the rest of their life-cycle elsewhere, or is recognized as migratory routes for fish, reptiles, birds, mammals, or invertebrates.

4.4.8   Naturalness – An area that has experienced a relative lack of human-induced disturbance or degradation.

4.4.9   Integrity – An area that is a biologically functional unit, an effective, self-sustaining ecological entity.

4.4.10   Fragility – An area that is highly susceptible to degradation by natural events or by the activities of people. Biotic communities associated with coastal habitats may have a low tolerance to changes in environmental conditions, or they may exist close to the limits of their tolerance (e.g., water temperature, salinity, turbidity or depth). Such communities may suffer natural stresses such as storms or other natural conditions (e.g., circulation patterns) that concentrate harmful substances in water or sediments, low flushing rates, and/or oxygen depletion. Additional stress may be caused by human influences such as pollution and changes in salinity. Thus, an area already subject to stress from natural and/or human factors may be in need of special protection from further stress, including that arising from international shipping activities.

4.4.11   Bio-geographic importance – An area that either contains rare biogeographic qualities or is representative of a biogeographic type or types, or contains unique or unusual biological, chemical, physical, or geological features.

Social, cultural and economic criteria

4.4.12   Social or economic dependency – An area where the environmental quality and the use of living marine resources are of particular social or economic importance, including fishing, recreation, tourism, and the livelihoods of people who depend on access to the area.

4.4.13   Human dependency – An area that is of particular importance for the support of traditional subsistence or food production activities or for the protection of the cultural resources of the local human populations.

4.4.14   Cultural heritage – An area that is of particular importance because of the presence of significant historical and archaeological sites.

Scientific and educational criteria

4.4.15   Research – An area that has high scientific interest.

4.4.16   Baseline for monitoring studies – An area that provides suitable baseline conditions with regard to biota or environmental characteristics, because it has not had substantial perturbations or has been in such a state for a long period of time such that it is considered to be in a natural or near-natural condition.

4.4.17   Education – An area that offers an exceptional opportunity to demonstrate particular natural phenomena.

4.5   In some cases a PSSA may be identified within a Special Area and vice versa. It should be noted that the criteria with respect to the identification of PSSAs and the criteria for the designation of Special Areas are not mutually exclusive.

5   Vulnerability to Impacts from International Shipping

5.1   In addition to meeting at least one of the criteria listed in 4.4, the recognized attributes of the area should be at risk from international shipping activities. This involves consideration of the following factors:

Vessel traffic characteristics

5.1.1   Operational factors – Types of maritime activities (e.g. small fishing boats, small pleasure craft, oil and gas rigs) in the proposed area that by their presence may reduce the safety of navigation.

5.1.2   Vessel types – Types of vessels passing through or adjacent to the area (e.g. high-speed vessels, large tankers, or bulk carriers with small under-keel clearance).

5.1.3   Traffic characteristics – Volume or concentration of traffic, vessel interaction, distance offshore or other dangers to navigation, are such as to involve greater risk of collision or grounding.

5.1.4   Harmful substances carried – Type and quantity of substances on board, whether cargo, fuel or stores, that would be harmful if released into the sea.

Natural factors

5.1.5   Hydrographical – Water depth, bottom and coastline topography, lack of proximate safe anchorages and other factors which call for increased navigational caution.

5.1.6   Meteorological – Prevailing weather, wind strength and direction, atmospheric visibility and other factors which increase the risk of collision and grounding and also the risk of damage to the sea area from discharges.

5.1.7   Oceanographic – Tidal streams, ocean currents, ice, and other factors which increase the risk of collision and grounding and also the risk of damage to the sea area from discharges.

5.2   In proposing an area as a PSSA and in considering the associated protective measures to prevent, reduce, or eliminate the identified vulnerability, other information that might be helpful includes the following:

.1   any evidence that international shipping activities are causing or may cause damage to the attributes of the proposed area, including the significance or risk of the potential damage, the degree of harm that may be expected to cause damage, and whether such damage is reasonably foreseeable, as well as whether damage is of a recurring or cumulative nature;

.2   any history of groundings, collisions, or spills in the area and any consequences of such incidents;

.3   any adverse impacts to the environment outside the proposed PSSA expected to be caused by changes to international shipping activities as a result of PSSA designation;

.4   stresses from other environmental sources; and

.5   any measures already in effect and their actual or anticipated beneficial impact.

6   Associated Protective Measures

6.1   In the context of these Guidelines, associated protective measures for PSSAs are limited to actions that are to be, or have been, approved or adopted by IMO and include the following options:

6.1.1   Designation of an area as a Special Area under MARPOL Annexes I, II or V, or a SO_x emission control area under MARPOL Annex VI, or application of special discharge restrictions to vessels operating in a PSSA. Procedures and criteria for the designation of Special Areas are contained in the Guidelines for the Designation of Special Areas set forth in annex 1 of Assembly resolution A.927(22). Criteria and procedures for the designation of SO_x emission control areas are found in Appendix 3 to MARPOL Annex VI;

6.1.2   Adoption of ships' routeing and reporting systems near or in the area, under the International Convention for the Safety of Life at Sea (SOLAS) and in accordance with the General Provisions on Ships' Routeing and the Guidelines and Criteria for Ship Reporting Systems. For example, a PSSA may be designated as an area to be avoided or it may be protected by other ships' routeing or reporting systems; and

6.1.3   Development and adoption of other measures aimed at protecting specific sea areas against environmental damage from ships, provided that they have an identified legal basis.

6.2   Consideration should also be given to the potential for the area to be listed on the World Heritage List, declared a Biosphere Reserve, or included on a list of areas of international, regional, or national importance, or if the area is already the subject of such international, regional, or national conservation action or agreements.

6.3   In some circumstances, a proposed PSSA may include within its boundaries a buffer zone, in other words, an area contiguous to the site-specific feature (core area) for which specific protection from shipping is sought. However, the need for such a buffer zone should be justified in terms of how it would directly contribute to the adequate protection of the core area.

7 Procedure for the Designation of Particularly Sensitive Sea Areas and the Adoption of Associated Protective Measures

7.1   An application for PSSA designation should contain a proposal for an associated protective measure that the proposing Member Government intends to submit to the appropriate IMO body. If the measure is not already available under an IMO instrument, the proposal should set forth the steps that the proposing Member Government has taken or will take to have the measure approved or adopted by IMO pursuant to an identified legal basis (see paragraph 7.5.2.3).

7.2   Alternatively, if no new associated protective measure is being proposed because IMO measures are already associated with the area to protect it, then the application should identify the threat of damage or damage being caused to the area by international shipping activities and show how the area is already being protected from such identified vulnerability by the associated protective measures. Amendments to existing measures may be introduced to address identified vulnerabilities.

7.3   In the future, additional associated protective measures may also be introduced to address identified vulnerabilities.

7.4   The application should first clearly set forth a summary of the objectives of the proposed PSSA designation, the location of the area, the need for protection, the associated protective measures, and demonstrate how the identified vulnerability will be addressed by existing or proposed associated protective measures. The summary should include the reasons why the associated protective measures are the preferred method for providing protection for the area to be identified as a PSSA.

7.5   Each application should then consist of two parts.

7.5.1   Part I – *Description, significance of the area and vulnerability*

.1   *Description* – a detailed description of the location of the proposed area, along with a nautical chart on which the location of the area and any associated protective measures are clearly marked, should be submitted with the application.

.2   *Significance of the area* – the application should state the significance of the area on the basis of recognized ecological, socio-economic, or scientific attributes and should explicitly refer to the criteria listed above in section 4.

.3   *Vulnerability of the area to damage by international shipping activities* – the application should provide an explanation of the nature and extent of the risks that international shipping activities pose to the environment of the proposed area, noting the factors listed in section 5. The application should describe the particular current or future international shipping activities that are causing or may be expected to cause damage to the proposed area, including the significance of the damage and degree of harm that may result from such activities, either from such activity alone or in combination with other threats.

7.5.2   Part II – *Appropriate associated protective measures and IMO's competence to approve or adopt such measures*

.1   The application should identify the existing and/or proposed associated protective measures and describe how they provide the needed protection from the threats of damage posed by international maritime activities occurring in and around the area. The application should specifically describe how the associated protective measures protect the area from the identified vulnerability.

.2   If the application identifies a new associated protective measure, then the proposing Member Government must append a draft of the proposal which is intended to be submitted to the appropriate Sub-Committee or Committee or, if the measures are not already available in an IMO instrument, information must be provided with regard to its legal basis and/or the steps that the proposing Member Government has taken or will take to establish the legal basis.

.3   The application should identify the legal basis for each measure. The legal bases for such measures are:

(i)   any measure that is already available under an existing IMO instrument; or

(ii)   any measure that does not yet exist but could become available through amendment of an IMO instrument or adoption of a new IMO instrument. The legal basis for any such measure would only be available after the IMO instrument was amended or adopted, as appropriate; or

(iii)   any measure proposed for adoption in the territorial sea,[3] or pursuant to Article 211(6) of the United Nations Convention on the Law of the Sea where existing measures or a generally applicable measure (as set forth in subparagraph (ii) above) would not adequately address the particularized need of the proposed area.

.4   These measures may include ships' routeing measures; reporting requirements discharge restrictions; operational criteria; and prohibited activities, and should be specifically tailored to meet the need of the area to prevent, reduce,

---

[3] Footnote in original: This provision does not derogate from the rights and duties of coastal States in the territorial sea as provided for in the United Nations Convention on the Law of the Sea.

or eliminate the identified vulnerability of the area from international shipping activities.

.5 The application should clearly specify the category or categories of ships to which the proposed associated protective measures would apply, consistent with the provisions of the United Nations Convention on the Law of the Sea, including those related to vessels entitled to sovereign immunity, and other pertinent instruments.

7.6 The application should indicate the possible impact of any proposed measures on the safety and efficiency of navigation, taking into account the area of the ocean in which the proposed measures are to be implemented. The application should set forth such information as:

.1 consistency with the legal instrument under which the associated protective measure is being proposed;

.2 implications for vessel safety; and

.3 impact on vessel operations, such as existing traffic patterns or usage of the proposed area.

7.7 An application for PSSA designation should address all relevant considerations and criteria in these Guidelines, and should include relevant supporting information for each such item.

7.8 The application should contain a summary of steps taken, if any, by the proposing Member Government to date to protect the proposed area.

7.9 The proposing Member Government should also include in the application the details of action to be taken pursuant to domestic law for the failure of a ship to comply with the requirements of the associated protective measures. Any action taken should be consistent with international law as reflected in the United Nations Convention on the Law of the Sea.

7.10 The proposing Member Government should submit a separate proposal to the appropriate Sub-Committee or Committee to obtain the approval of any new associated protective measure. Such a proposal must comply with the requirements of the legal instrument relied upon to establish the measure.

8 Criteria for Assessment of Applications for Designation of Particularly Sensitive Sea Areas and the Adoption of Associated Protective Measures

8.1 IMO should consider each application, or amendment thereto, submitted to it by a proposing Member Government on a case-by-case basis to determine whether the area fulfils at least one of the criteria set forth in section 4, the attributes of the area meeting section 4 criteria are vulnerable to damage by international shipping activities as set forth in section 5, and associated protective measures exist or are proposed to prevent, reduce, or eliminate the identified vulnerability.

8.2 In assessing each proposal, IMO should in particular consider:

.1 the full range of protective measures available and determine whether the proposed or existing associated protective measures are appropriate to prevent, reduce, or eliminate the identified vulnerability of the area from international shipping activities;

.2 whether such measures might result in an increased potential for significant adverse effects by international shipping activities on the environment outside the proposed PSSA; and

.3 the linkage between the recognized attributes, the identified vulnerability, the associated protective measure to prevent, reduce, or eliminate that vulnerability, and the overall size of the area, including whether the size is commensurate with that necessary to address the identified need.

8.3   The procedure for considering a PSSA application by IMO is as follows:

1.   the MEPC should bear primary responsibility within IMO for considering PSSA applications and all applications should first be submitted to the MEPC:

     .1   the Committee should assess the elements of the proposal against the Guidelines and, as appropriate, should establish a technical group, comprising representatives with appropriate environmental, scientific, maritime, and legal expertise;

     .2   the proposing Member Government is encouraged to make a presentation of the proposal, along with nautical charts and other supporting information on the required elements for PSSA designation;

     .3   any technical group formed should prepare a brief report to the Committee summarizing their findings and the outcome of its assessment; and

     .4   the outcome of the assessment of a PSSA application should be duly reflected in the report of the MEPC;

2.   if appropriate following its assessment, the MEPC should designate the area 'in principle' and inform the appropriate Sub-Committee, Committee (which could be the MEPC itself), or the Assembly that is responsible for addressing the particular associated protective measures proposed for the area of the outcome of this assessment;

3.   the appropriate Sub-Committee or Committee which has received a submission by a proposing Member Government for an associated protective measure should review the proposal to determine whether it meets the procedures, criteria, and other requirements of the legal instrument under which the measure is proposed. The Sub-Committee may seek the advice of the MEPC on issues pertinent to the application;

4.   the MEPC should not designate a PSSA until after the associated protective measures are considered and approved by the pertinent Sub-Committee, Committee, or Assembly. If the associated protective measures are not approved by the pertinent IMO body, then the MEPC may reject the PSSA application entirely or request that the proposing Member Government submit new proposals for associated protective measures. A proper record of the proceedings should be included in the report of the MEPC;

5.   for measures that require approval by the Maritime Safety Committee (MSC), the Sub-Committee should forward its recommendation for approval of the associated protective measures to the MSC or, if the Sub-Committee rejects the measures, it should inform the MSC and MEPC and provide a statement of reasons for its decision. The MSC should consider any such recommendations and, if the measures are to be adopted, it should notify the MEPC of its decision;

6.   if the application is rejected, the MEPC shall notify the proposing Member Government, provide a statement of reasons for its decision and, if appropriate, request the Member Government to submit additional information; and

7.   after approval by the appropriate Sub-Committee, Committee, or, where necessary, the Assembly of the associated protective measures, the MEPC may designate the area as a PSSA.

8.4   IMO should provide a forum for the review and re-evaluation of any associated protective measure adopted, as necessary, taking into account pertinent comments, reports, and observations of the associated protective measures. Member Governments which have ships operating in the area of the designated PSSA are encouraged to bring any concerns with the associated protective measures to IMO so that any necessary adjustments may be made. Member Governments that originally submitted the application for designation with the associated protective measures, should also bring any concerns and proposals for additional measures or modifications to any associated protective measure or the PSSA itself to IMO.

8.5 After the designation of a PSSA and its associated protective measures, IMO should ensure that the effective date of implementation is as soon as possible based on the rules of IMO and consistent with international law.

8.6 IMO should, in assessing applications for designation of PSSAs and their associated protective measures, take into account the technical and financial resources available to developing Member Governments and those with economies in transition.

9 Implementation of Designated PSSAs and the Associated Protective Measures

9.1 When a PSSA receives final designation, all associated protective measures should be identified on charts in accordance with the symbols and methods of the International Hydrographic Organization (IHO).

9.2 A proposing Member Government should ensure that any associated protective measure is implemented in accordance with international law as reflected in the United Nations Convention on the Law of the Sea.

9.3 Member Governments should take all appropriate steps to ensure that ships flying their flag comply with the associated protective measures adopted to protect the designated PSSA. Those Member Governments which have received information of an alleged violation of an associated protective measure by a ship flying their flag should provide the Government which has reported the offence with the details of any appropriate action taken.

Revised Pilotage Requirements for Torres Strait

Australian Maritime Safety Authority, Marine Notices 8/2006 and 16/2006

MARINE NOTICE 8/2006

The purpose of this Marine Notice is to advise ship-owners and operators of new requirements for pilotage in the Torres Strait to be introduced by the Australian and Papua-New Guinean governments in 2006.

On 22 July 2005, the IMO's Marine Environment Protection Committee approved the extension of the Great Barrier Reef Particularly Sensitive Sea Area (PSSA) to include the Torres Strait. As one of the associated protective measures for the area, the Committee also adopted Australia's proposal to extend the system of pilotage within the Great Barrier Reef to the Torres Strait. Australia has operated a system of compulsory pilotage within the great Barrier Reef since 1991.

These decisions are reflected in IMO Resolution MEPC.133(53), which recommends that Governments recognize the need for effective protection of the Torres Strait and inform ships flying their flag that they should act in accordance with Australia's system of pilotage for merchant ships 70m in length and over or oil tankers, chemical tankers, and liquefied gas carriers, irrespective of size, when navigating the Torres Strait and the Great North East Channel.

Amendments to the Commonwealth *Navigation Act 1912* (the Act) make it an offence under new section 186I to navigate in a compulsory pilotage area without a pilot. A new compulsory pilotage area for the Torres Strait will be specified in Marine Orders Part 54 and further details of that area are reproduced below. Significant penalties will apply to a master or owner who fails to comply with the compulsory pilotage requirements in the Navigation Act and Marine Orders Part 54.

Under the new requirements, section 186J of the Act will require the pilot to provide a certificate to the master in the approved form specifying details about the completed piloted voyage before disembarking the ship. Such a certificate will provide an owner and master evidence that they engaged a pilotage service and complied with the compulsory pilotage requirements of the Act.

In certain circumstances, a master or owner may apply to AMSA to seek an exemption from the requirement to navigate with a pilot in a compulsory pilotage area – see section 186K of the Act and provision 11 of Marine Orders Part 54. The latter will shortly be made available on the AMSA internet site, www.amsa.gov.au.

The compulsory pilotage requirements under the Act and Marine Orders Part 54 will complement the existing pilotage requirements under the *Great Barrier Reef Marine Park Act 1975* concerning pilotage through the Great Barrier Reef.

The new requirements concerning pilotage will commence on 06 October 2006.

Owners, operators, or Masters of vessels which routinely use Torres Strait routes, but are not currently engaging pilots to do so, are encouraged to make at least two piloted transits before 06 October. This will allow the masters to become familiar with the pilots' operating procedures.

Application

Marine Orders Part 54 specifies the Torres Strait as a Compulsory Pilotage Area in the following terms,

The Torres Strait Pilotage Area is bound on the south by the line of latitude 10° 41′ S, and on the north by Australia's EEZ, and divided into the following two parts:
Torres Strait Pilotage Area A is bound by the longitudes 141° 50′ E and 142° 05′ E.
Torres Strait Pilotage Area B is bound by the longitudes 142° 05′ E and 143° 24′ E.

The application is as follows:

All vessels of 70 metres or more in overall length, and all loaded tankers, chemical tankers and liquefied gas carriers, except defence force vessels, when transiting through Torres Strait Pilotage Area A with a draught of 8 metres or more must have a pilot on board.

All vessels (irrespective of draught) of 70 metres or more in overall length, and all loaded tankers, chemical tankers and liquefied gas carriers, except defence force vessels, when transiting through Torres Strait Pilotage Area B must have a pilot on board [...].

MARINE NOTICE 16/2006

The purpose of this Marine Notice is to provide final guidance information on the new requirements for pilotage in the Torres Strait, as advised by Marine Notice 8 of 2006 issued in May 2006.

Ship-owners, masters and operators are advised that, as a condition of entry into an Australian port, failure to carry a pilot as prescribed may result in a prosecution under Australian law. Relevant authorities such as the vessel's flag state administration and the IMO will also be advised of the failure to embark a pilot.

Australia has extended the current system of pilotage within the Great Barrier Reef into the Torres Strait to ensure a safe passage regime is in place.

Australian pilots will have access to the latest real time maritime safety information, including:
- Hydrographic, meteorological and oceanographic data
- Aids to navigation availability, performance and correction data
- Dynamic traffic information associated with participation in the Vessel Traffic System and Navigational warnings

The carriage of an Australian pilot will have the effect of enhancing transit passage, with the ability to maximise tidal window opportunities for transit and ensuring adequate margins for safety and environmental protection.

The new pilotage arrangements do not apply to sovereign immune vessels, including defence and other government owned vessels.

In accordance with UNCLOS Articles 42.2 and 44, Australian authorities will not suspend, deny, hamper or impair transit passage and will not stop, arrest or board ships that do not take on a pilot while transiting the Strait. However, the owner, master and/or operator of the ship may be prosecuted on the next entry into an Australian port, for both ships on voyages to Australian ports and ships transiting the Torres Strait en route to other destinations.

The Australian domestic legislation also includes a defence from prosecution if a pilot could not be carried because of stress of weather, saving life at sea or other unavoidable cause.

Nairobi International Convention on the Removal of Wrecks

Done at Nairobi, 18 May 2007; not yet in force
IMO Doc. LEG/CONF.16/19, 23 May 2007[1]

The States Parties to the present Convention,

Conscious of the fact that wrecks, if not removed, may pose a hazard to navigation or the marine environment,

Convinced of the need to adopt uniform international rules and procedures to ensure the prompt and effective removal of wrecks and payment of compensation for the costs therein involved,

Noting that many wrecks may be located in States' territory, including the territorial sea,

Recognizing the benefits to be gained through uniformity in legal regimes governing responsibility and liability for removal of hazardous wrecks,

Bearing in mind the importance of the United Nations Convention on the Law of the Sea, done at Montego Bay on 10 December 1982, and of the customary international law of the sea, and the consequent need to implement the present Convention in accordance with such provisions,

Have agreed as follows:

Article 1 Definitions

For the purposes of this Convention:

1. 'Convention area' means the exclusive economic zone of a State Party, established in accordance with international law or, if a State Party has not established such a zone,

---

[1] Footnotes and Annex omitted.

an area beyond and adjacent to the territorial sea of that State determined by that State in accordance with international law and extending not more than 200 nautical miles from the baselines from which the breadth of its territorial sea is measured.

2. 'Ship' means a seagoing vessel of any type whatsoever and includes hydrofoil boats, air-cushion vehicles, submersibles, floating craft and floating platforms, except when such platforms are on location engaged in the exploration, exploitation or production of sea-bed mineral resources.

3. 'Maritime casualty' means a collision of ships, stranding or other incident of navigation, or other occurrence on board a ship or external to it resulting in material damage or imminent threat of material damage to a ship or its cargo.

4. 'Wreck', following upon a maritime casualty, means:

(a)   a sunken or stranded ship; or

(b)   any part of a sunken or stranded ship, including any object that is or has been on board such a ship; or

(c)   any object that is lost at sea from a ship and that is stranded, sunken or adrift at sea; or

(d)   a ship that is about, or may reasonably be expected, to sink or to strand, where effective measures to assist the ship or any property in danger are not already being taken.

5. 'Hazard' means any condition or threat that:

(a)   poses a danger or impediment to navigation; or

(b)   may reasonably be expected to result in major harmful consequences to the marine environment, or damage to the coastline or related interests of one or more States.

6. 'Related interests' means the interests of a coastal State directly affected or threatened by a wreck, such as:

(a)   maritime coastal, port and estuarine activities, including fisheries activities, constituting an essential means of livelihood of the persons concerned;

(b)   tourist attractions and other economic interests of the area concerned;

(c)   the health of the coastal population and the well-being of the area concerned, including conservation of marine living resources and of wildlife; and

(d)   offshore and underwater infrastructure.

7. 'Removal' means any form of prevention, mitigation or elimination of the hazard created by a wreck. 'Remove', 'removed' and 'removing' shall be construed accordingly.

8. 'Registered owner' means the person or persons registered as the owner of the ship or, in the absence of registration, the person or persons owning the ship at the time of the maritime casualty. However, in the case of a ship owned by a State and operated by a company which in that State is registered as the operator of the ship, 'registered owner' shall mean such company.

9. 'Operator of the ship' means the owner of the ship or any other organization or person such as the manager, or the bareboat charterer, who has assumed the responsibility for operation of the ship from the owner of the ship and who, on assuming such responsibility, has agreed to take over all duties and responsibilities established under the International Safety Management Code, as amended.

10. 'Affected State' means the State in whose Convention area the wreck is located.

11. 'State of the ship's registry' means, in relation to a registered ship, the State of registration of the ship and, in relation to an unregistered ship, the State whose flag the ship is entitled to fly.

12. 'Organization' means the International Maritime Organization.

13. 'Secretary-General' means the Secretary-General of the Organization.

Article 2 Objectives and general principles

1. A State Party may take measures in accordance with this Convention in relation to the removal of a wreck which poses a hazard in the Convention area.

2. Measures taken by the Affected State in accordance with paragraph 1 shall be proportionate to the hazard.

3. Such measures shall not go beyond what is reasonably necessary to remove a wreck which poses a hazard and shall cease as soon as the wreck has been removed; they shall not unnecessarily interfere with the rights and interests of other States including the State of the ship's registry, and of any persons, physical or corporate, concerned.

4. The application of this Convention within the Convention area shall not entitle a State Party to claim or exercise sovereignty or sovereign rights over any part of the high seas.

5. States Parties shall endeavour to co-operate when the effects of a maritime casualty resulting in a wreck involve a State other than the Affected State.

Article 3 Scope of application

1. Except as otherwise provided in this Convention, this Convention shall apply to wrecks in the Convention area.

2. A State Party may extend the application of this Convention to wrecks located within its territory, including the territorial sea, subject to article 4, paragraph 4. In that case, it shall notify the Secretary-General accordingly, at the time of expressing its consent to be bound by this Convention or at any time thereafter. When a State Party has made a notification to apply this Convention to wrecks located within its territory, including the territorial sea, this is without prejudice to the rights and obligations of that State to take measures in relation to wrecks located in its territory, including the territorial sea, other than locating, marking and removing in accordance with this Convention. The provisions of articles 10, 11 and 12 of this Convention shall not apply to any measures so taken other than those referred to in articles 7, 8 and 9 of this Convention.

3. When a State Party has made a notification under paragraph 2, the 'Convention area' of the Affected State shall include the territory, including the territorial sea, of that State Party.

4. A notification made under paragraph 2 above shall take effect for that State Party, if made before entry into force of this Convention for that State Party, upon entry into force. If notification is made after entry into force of this Convention for that State Party, it shall take effect six months after its receipt by the Secretary-General.

5. A State Party that has made a notification under paragraph 2 may withdraw it at any time by means of a notification of withdrawal to the Secretary-General. Such notification of withdrawal shall take effect six months after its receipt by the Secretary-General, unless the notification specifies a later date.

Article 4 Exclusions

1. This Convention shall not apply to measures taken under the International Convention relating to Intervention on the High Seas in Cases of Oil Pollution Casualties, 1969, as amended, or the Protocol relating to Intervention on the High Seas in Cases of Pollution by Substances other than Oil, 1973, as amended.

2. This Convention shall not apply to any warship or other ship owned or operated by a State and used, for the time being, only on Government non-commercial service, unless that State decides otherwise.

3. Where a State Party decides to apply this Convention to its warships or other ships as described in paragraph 2, it shall notify the Secretary-General thereof specifying the terms and conditions of such application.

4.   (a)   When a State Party has made a notification under article 3, paragraph 2, the following provisions of this Convention shall not apply in its territory, including the territorial sea:

   (i)   Article 2, paragraph 4

   (ii)   Article 9, paragraphs 1, 5, 7, 8, 9 and 10

   (iii)   Article 15

   (b)   Article 9, paragraph 4, insofar as it applies to the territory, including the territorial sea of a State Party, shall read:

   'Subject to the national law of the Affected State, the registered owner may contract with any salvor or other person to remove the wreck determined to constitute a hazard on behalf of the owner. Before such removal commences, the Affected State may lay down conditions for such removal only to the extent necessary to ensure that the removal proceeds in a manner that is consistent with considerations of safety and protection of the marine environment.'

Article 5   Reporting wrecks

1. A State Party shall require the master and the operator of a ship flying its flag to report to the Affected State without delay when that ship has been involved in a maritime casualty resulting in a wreck. To the extent that the reporting obligation under this article has been fulfilled either by the master or the operator of the ship, the other shall not be obliged to report.

2. Such reports shall provide the name and the principal place of business of the registered owner and all the relevant information necessary for the Affected State to determine whether the wreck poses a hazard in accordance with article 6, including:

   (a)   the precise location of the wreck;

   (b)   the type, size and construction of the wreck;

   (c)   the nature of the damage to, and the condition of, the wreck;

   (d)   the nature and quantity of the cargo, in particular any hazardous and noxious substances; and

   (e)   the amount and types of oil, including bunker oil and lubricating oil, on board.

Article 6   Determination of hazard

When determining whether a wreck poses a hazard, the following criteria should be taken into account by the Affected State:

   (a)   the type, size and construction of the wreck;

   (b)   depth of the water in the area;

   (c)   tidal range and currents in the area;

   (d)   particularly sensitive sea areas identified and, as appropriate, designated in accordance with guidelines adopted by the Organization, or a clearly defined area of the exclusive economic zone where special mandatory measures have been adopted pursuant to article 211, paragraph 6, of the United Nations Convention on the Law of the Sea, 1982;

   (e)   proximity of shipping routes or established traffic lanes;

   (f)   traffic density and frequency;

   (g)   type of traffic;

   (h)   nature and quantity of the wreck's cargo, the amount and types of oil (such as bunker oil and lubricating oil) on board the wreck and, in particular, the

damage likely to result should the cargo or oil be released into the marine environment;
  (i)   vulnerability of port facilities;
  (j)   prevailing meteorological and hydrographical conditions;
  (k) submarine topography of the area;
  (l)   height of the wreck above or below the surface of the water at lowest astronomical tide;
  (m) acoustic and magnetic profiles of the wreck;
  (n) proximity of offshore installations, pipelines, telecommunications cables and similar structures; and
  (o) any other circumstances that might necessitate the removal of the wreck.

Article 7 Locating wrecks

1. Upon becoming aware of a wreck, the Affected State shall use all practicable means, including the good offices of States and organizations, to warn mariners and the States concerned of the nature and location of the wreck as a matter of urgency.

2. If the Affected State has reason to believe that a wreck poses a hazard, it shall ensure that all practicable steps are taken to establish the precise location of the wreck.

Article 8 Marking of wrecks

1. If the Affected State determines that a wreck constitutes a hazard, that State shall ensure that all reasonable steps are taken to mark the wreck.

2. In marking the wreck, all practicable steps shall be taken to ensure that the markings conform to the internationally accepted system of buoyage in use in the area where the wreck is located.

3. The Affected State shall promulgate the particulars of the marking of the wreck by use of all appropriate means, including the appropriate nautical publications.

Article 9 Measures to facilitate the removal of wrecks

1. If the Affected State determines that a wreck constitutes a hazard, that State shall immediately:
  (a) inform the State of the ship's registry and the registered owner; and
  (b) proceed to consult the State of the ship's registry and other States affected by the wreck regarding measures to be taken in relation to the wreck.

2. The registered owner shall remove a wreck determined to constitute a hazard.

3. When a wreck has been determined to constitute a hazard, the registered owner, or other interested party, shall provide the competent authority of the Affected State with evidence of insurance or other financial security as required by article 12.

4. The registered owner may contract with any salvor or other person to remove the wreck determined to constitute a hazard on behalf of the owner. Before such removal commences, the Affected State may lay down conditions for such removal only to the extent necessary to ensure that the removal proceeds in a manner that is consistent with considerations of safety and protection of the marine environment.

5. When the removal referred to in paragraphs 2 and 4 has commenced, the Affected State may intervene in the removal only to the extent necessary to ensure that the removal proceeds effectively in a manner that is consistent with considerations of safety and protection of the marine environment.

6. The Affected State shall:
  (a) set a reasonable deadline within which the registered owner must remove the wreck taking into account the nature of the hazard determined in accordance with article 6;

(b)　inform the registered owner in writing of the deadline it has set and specify that, if the registered owner does not remove the wreck within that deadline, it may remove the wreck at the registered owner's expense; and

(c)　inform the registered owner in writing that it intends to intervene immediately in circumstances where the hazard becomes particularly severe.

7.　If the registered owner does not remove the wreck within the deadline set in accordance with paragraph 6(a), or the registered owner cannot be contacted, the Affected State may remove the wreck by the most practical and expeditious means available, consistent with considerations of safety and protection of the marine environment.

8.　In circumstances where immediate action is required and the Affected State has informed the State of the ship's registry and the registered owner accordingly, it may remove the wreck by the most practical and expeditious means available, consistent with considerations of safety and protection of the marine environment.

9.　States Parties shall take appropriate measures under their national law to ensure that their registered owners comply with paragraphs 2 and 3.

10.　States Parties give their consent to the Affected State to act under paragraphs 4 to 8, where required.

11.　The information referred to in this article shall be provided by the Affected State to the registered owner identified in the reports referred to in article 5, paragraph 2.

Article 10　Liability of the owner

1.　Subject to article 11, the registered owner shall be liable for the costs of locating, marking and removing the wreck under articles 7, 8 and 9, respectively, unless the registered owner proves that the maritime casualty that caused the wreck:

(a)　resulted from an act of war, hostilities, civil war, insurrection, or a natural phenomenon of an exceptional, inevitable and irresistible character;

(b)　was wholly caused by an act or omission done with intent to cause damage by a third party; or

(c)　was wholly caused by the negligence or other wrongful act of any Government or other authority responsible for the maintenance of lights or other navigational aids in the exercise of that function.

2.　Nothing in this Convention shall affect the right of the registered owner to limit liability under any applicable national or international regime, such as the Convention on Limitation of Liability for Maritime Claims, 1976, as amended.

3.　No claim for the costs referred to in paragraph 1 may be made against the registered owner otherwise than in accordance with the provisions of this Convention. This is without prejudice to the rights and obligations of a State Party that has made a notification under article 3, paragraph 2, in relation to wrecks located in its territory, including the territorial sea, other than locating, marking and removing in accordance with this Convention.

4.　Nothing in this article shall prejudice any right of recourse against third parties.

Article 11　Exceptions to liability

1.　The registered owner shall not be liable under this Convention for the costs mentioned in article 10, paragraph 1 if, and to the extent that, liability for such costs would be in conflict with:

(a)　the International Convention on Civil Liability for Oil Pollution Damage, 1969, as amended;

(b)　the International Convention on Liability and Compensation for Damage in Connection with the Carriage of Hazardous and Noxious Substances by Sea, 1996, as amended;

(c) the Convention on Third Party Liability in the Field of Nuclear Energy, 1960, as amended, or the Vienna Convention on Civil Liability for Nuclear Damage, 1963, as amended; or national law governing or prohibiting limitation of liability for nuclear damage; or

(d) the International Convention on Civil Liability for Bunker Oil Pollution Damage, 2001, as amended;

provided that the relevant convention is applicable and in force.

2. To the extent that measures under this Convention are considered to be salvage under applicable national law or an international convention, such law or convention shall apply to questions of the remuneration or compensation payable to salvors to the exclusion of the rules of this Convention.

Article 12 Compulsory insurance or other financial security

1. The registered owner of a ship of 300 gross tonnage and above and flying the flag of a State Party shall be required to maintain insurance or other financial security, such as a guarantee of a bank or similar institution, to cover liability under this Convention in an amount equal to the limits of liability under the applicable national or international limitation regime, but in all cases not exceeding an amount calculated in accordance with article 6(1)(b) of the Convention on Limitation of Liability for Maritime Claims, 1976, as amended.

2. A certificate attesting that insurance or other financial security is in force in accordance with the provisions of this Convention shall be issued to each ship of 300 gross tonnage and above by the appropriate authority of the State of the ship's registry after determining that the requirements of paragraph 1 have been complied with. With respect to a ship registered in a State Party such certificate shall be issued or certified by the appropriate authority of the State of the ship's registry; with respect to a ship not registered in a State Party it may be issued or certified by the appropriate authority of any State Party. This compulsory insurance certificate shall be in the form of the model set out in the annex to this Convention, and shall contain the following particulars:

(a) name of the ship, distinctive number or letters and port of registry;

(b) gross tonnage of the ship;

(c) name and principal place of business of the registered owner;

(d) IMO ship identification number;

(e) type and duration of security;

(f) name and principal place of business of insurer or other person giving security and, where appropriate, place of business where the insurance or security is established;

(g) period of validity of the certificate, which shall not be longer than the period of validity of the insurance or other security.

3. (a) A State Party may authorize either an institution or an organization recognized by it to issue the certificate referred to in paragraph 2. Such institution or organization shall inform that State of the issue of each certificate. In all cases, the State Party shall fully guarantee the completeness and accuracy of the certificate so issued and shall undertake to ensure the necessary arrangements to satisfy this obligation.

(b) A State Party shall notify the Secretary-General of:

(i) the specific responsibilities and conditions of the authority delegated to an institution or organization recognized by it;

(ii) the withdrawal of such authority; and

(iii) the date from which such authority or withdrawal of such authority takes effect.

An authority delegated shall not take effect prior to three months from the date on which notification to that effect was given to the Secretary-General.

(c)   The institution or organization authorized to issue certificates in accordance with this paragraph shall, as a minimum, be authorized to withdraw these certificates if the conditions under which they have been issued are not maintained. In all cases the institution or organization shall report such withdrawal to the State on whose behalf the certificate was issued.

4.   The certificate shall be in the official language or languages of the issuing State. If the language used is not English, French or Spanish, the text shall include a translation into one of these languages and, where the State so decides, the official language (s) of the State may be omitted.

5.   The certificate shall be carried on board the ship and a copy shall be deposited with the authorities who keep the record of the ship's registry or, if the ship is not registered in a State Party, with the authorities issuing or certifying the certificate.

6.   An insurance or other financial security shall not satisfy the requirements of this article if it can cease for reasons other than the expiry of the period of validity of the insurance or security specified in the certificate under paragraph 2 before three months have elapsed from the date on which notice of its termination is given to the authorities referred to in paragraph 5 unless the certificate has been surrendered to these authorities or a new certificate has been issued within the said period. The foregoing provisions shall similarly apply to any modification, which results in the insurance or security no longer satisfying the requirements of this article.

7.   The State of the ship's registry shall, subject to the provisions of this article and having regard to any guidelines adopted by the Organization on the financial responsibility of the registered owners, determine the conditions of issue and validity of the certificate.

8.   Nothing in this Convention shall be construed as preventing a State Party from relying on information obtained from other States or the Organization or other international organizations relating to the financial standing of providers of insurance or financial security for the purposes of this Convention. In such cases, the State Party relying on such information is not relieved of its responsibility as a State issuing the certificate required by paragraph 2.

9.   Certificates issued and certified under the authority of a State Party shall be accepted by other States Parties for the purposes of this Convention and shall be regarded by other States Parties as having the same force as certificates issued or certified by them, even if issued or certified in respect of a ship not registered in a State Party. A State Party may at any time request consultation with the issuing or certifying State should it believe that the insurer or guarantor named in the certificate is not financially capable of meeting the obligations imposed by this Convention.

10.   Any claim for costs arising under this Convention may be brought directly against the insurer or other person providing financial security for the registered owner's liability. In such a case the defendant may invoke the defences (other than the bankruptcy or winding up of the registered owner) that the registered owner would have been entitled to invoke, including limitation of liability under any applicable national or international regime. Furthermore, even if the registered owner is not entitled to limit liability, the defendant may limit liability to an amount equal to the amount of the insurance or other financial security required to be maintained in accordance with paragraph 1. Moreover, the defendant may invoke the defence that the maritime casualty was caused by the wilful misconduct of the registered owner, but the defendant shall not invoke any other defence, which the defendant might have been entitled to invoke in proceedings brought by the

registered owner against the defendant. The defendant shall in any event have the right to require the registered owner to be joined in the proceedings.

11. A State Party shall not permit any ship entitled to fly its flag to which this article applies to operate at any time unless a certificate has been issued under paragraphs 2 or 14.

12. Subject to the provisions of this article, each State Party shall ensure, under its national law, that insurance or other security to the extent required by paragraph 1 is in force in respect of any ship of 300 gross tonnage and above, wherever registered, entering or leaving a port in its territory, or arriving at or leaving an offshore facility in its territorial sea.

13. Notwithstanding the provisions of paragraph 5, a State Party may notify the Secretary-General that, for the purposes of paragraph 12, ships are not required to carry on board or to produce the certificate required by paragraph 3, when entering or leaving a port in its territory or arriving at or leaving from an offshore facility in its territorial sea, provided that the State Party which issues the certificate required by paragraph 2 has notified the Secretary-General that it maintains records in an electronic format, accessible to all States Parties, attesting the existence of the certificate and enabling States Parties to discharge their obligations under paragraph 12.

14. If insurance or other financial security is not maintained in respect of a ship owned by a State Party, the provisions of this article relating thereto shall not be applicable to such ship, but the ship shall carry a certificate issued by the appropriate authority of the State of registry stating that it is owned by that State and that the ship's liability is covered within the limits prescribed in paragraph 1. Such a certificate shall follow as closely as possible the model prescribed by paragraph 2.

Article 13 Time limits

Rights to recover costs under this Convention shall be extinguished unless an action is brought hereunder within three years from the date when the hazard has been determined in accordance with this Convention. However, in no case shall an action be brought after six years from the date of the maritime casualty that resulted in the wreck. Where the maritime casualty consists of a series of occurrences, the six-year period shall run from the date of the first occurrence.

Article 14 Amendment provisions

1. At the request of not less than one third of States Parties, a conference shall be convened by the Organization for the purpose of revising or amending this Convention.

2. Any consent to be bound by this Convention expressed after the date of entry into force of an amendment to this Convention shall be deemed to apply to this Convention, as amended.

Article 15 Settlement of disputes

1. Where a dispute arises between two or more States Parties regarding the interpretation or application of this Convention, they shall seek to resolve their dispute, in the first instance, through negotiation, enquiry, mediation, conciliation, arbitration, judicial settlement, resort to regional agencies or arrangements or other peaceful means of their choice.

2. If no settlement is possible within a reasonable period of time not exceeding twelve months after one State Party has notified another that a dispute exists between them, the provisions relating to the settlement of disputes set out in Part XV of the United Nations Convention on the Law of the Sea, 1982 shall apply *mutatis mutandis*, whether or not the States party to the dispute are also States Parties to the United Nations Convention on the Law of the Sea, 1982.

3. Any procedure chosen by a State Party to this Convention and to the United Nations Convention on the Law of the Sea, 1982 pursuant to Article 287 of the latter shall apply to the settlement of disputes under this Article, unless that State Party, when ratifying, accepting, approving or acceding to this Convention, or at any time thereafter, chooses another procedure pursuant to Article 287 for the purpose of the settlement of disputes arising out of this Convention.

4. A State Party to this Convention which is not a Party to the United Nations Convention on the Law of the Sea, 1982 when ratifying, accepting, approving or acceding to this Convention or at any time thereafter shall be free to choose, by means of a written declaration, one or more of the means set out in Article 287, paragraph 1, of the United Nations Convention on the Law of the Sea, 1982 for the purpose of settlement of disputes under this Article. Article 287 shall apply to such a declaration, as well as to any dispute to which such State is party, which is not covered by a declaration in force. For the purpose of conciliation and arbitration, in accordance with Annexes V and VII of the United Nations Convention on the Law of the Sea, 1982 such State shall be entitled to nominate conciliators and arbitrators to be included in the lists referred to in Annex V, Article 2, and Annex VII, Article 2, for the settleme nt of disputes arising out of this Convention.

5. A declaration made under paragraphs 3 and 4 shall be deposited with the Secretary-General who shall transmit copies thereof to the States Parties.

Article 16 Relationship to other conventions and international agreements

Nothing in this Convention shall prejudice the rights and obligations of any State under the United Nations Convention on the Law of the Sea, 1982, and under the customary international law of the sea.

Article 17 Signature, ratification, acceptance, approval and accession

This Convention shall be open for signature at the Headquarters of the Organization from 19 November 2007 until 18 November 2008 and shall thereafter remain open for accession.

(a) States may express their consent to be bound by this Convention by:
   (i)   signature without reservation as to ratification, acceptance or approval; or
   (ii) signature subject to ratification, acceptance or approval, followed by ratification, acceptance or approval; or
   (iii) accession.

(b) Ratification, acceptance, approval or accession shall be effected by the deposit of an instrument to that effect with the Secretary-General.

Article 18 Entry into force

1. This Convention shall enter into force twelve months following the date on which ten States have either signed it without reservation as to ratification, acceptance or approval or have deposited instruments of ratification, acceptance, approval or accession with the Secretary-General.

2. For any State which ratifies, accepts, approves or accedes to this Convention after the conditions in paragraph 1 for entry into force have been met, this Convention shall enter into force three months following the date of deposit by such State of the appropriate instrument, but not before this Convention has entered into force in accordance with paragraph 1.

Article 19 Denunciation

1. This Convention may be denounced by a State Party at any time after the expiry of one year following the date on which this Convention comes into force for that State.

2. Denunciation shall be effected by the deposit of an instrument to that effect with the Secretary-General.

3. A denunciation shall take effect one year, or such longer period as may be specified in the instrument of denunciation, following its receipt by the Secretary-General.

Article 20 Depositary

1. This Convention shall be deposited with the Secretary General.

2. The Secretary-General shall:

   (a) inform all States which have signed or acceded to this Convention of:

      (i)   each new signature or deposit of an instrument of ratification, acceptance, approval or accession, together with the date thereof;

      (ii) the date of entry into force of this Convention;

      (iii) the deposit of any instrument of denunciation of this Convention together with the date of the deposit and the date on which the denunciation takes effect; and

      (iv) other declarations and notifications received pursuant to this Convention; and

   (b) transmit certified true copies of this Convention to all States that have signed or acceded to this Convention.

3. As soon as this Convention enters into force, a certified true copy of the text shall be transmitted by the Secretary-General to the Secretary-General of the United Nations for registration and publication in accordance with Article 102 of the Charter of the United Nations.

Article 21 Languages

This Convention is established in a single original in the Arabic, Chinese, English, French, Russian and Spanish languages, each text being equally authentic.

Done at Nairobi this eighteenth day of May two thousand and seven.

In witness whereof the undersigned, being duly authorized by their respective Governments for that purpose, have signed this Convention.

Piracy and Armed Robbery against Ships in Waters off the Coast of Somalia

IMO Resolution A.1002(25), adopted on 29 November 2007[1]

The Assembly,

Recalling Article 15(j) of the Convention on the International Maritime Organization concerning the functions of the Assembly in relation to regulations and guidelines concerning maritime safety and the prevention and control of marine pollution from ships,

Recalling also article 1 of the Charter of the United Nations, which includes, among the purposes of the United Nations, the maintenance of international peace and security,

---

[1] Resolution A.1002(25) replaced Resolution A.979(24) on Piracy and Armed Robbery against Ships in the Waters off the Coast of Somalia, adopted on 23 November 2005. Footnotes omitted.

Also recalling article 100 of the United Nations Convention on the Law of the Sea (UNCLOS), which requires all States to co-operate to the fullest possible extent in the repression of piracy on the high seas or in any other place outside the jurisdiction of any State,

Further recalling article 105 of UNCLOS which, *inter alia*, provides that, on the high seas or in any other place outside the jurisdiction of any State, every State may seize a pirate ship or aircraft, or a ship or aircraft taken by piracy and under the control of pirates and arrest the persons and seize the property on board,

Bearing in mind article 110 of UNCLOS which, *inter alia*, enables warships, military aircraft, or other duly authorized ships or aircraft clearly marked and identifiable as being on government service to board any ship, other than a ship entitled to complete immunity in accordance with article 95 and article 96 of UNCLOS, when there are reasonable grounds for suspecting that the ship is, *inter alia*, engaged in piracy,

Reaffirming resolution A.545(13) on 'Measures to prevent acts of piracy and armed robbery against ships', adopted on 17 November 1983; resolution A.683(17) on 'Prevention and suppression of acts of piracy and armed robbery against ships', adopted on 6 November 1991; and resolution A.738(18) on 'Measures to prevent and suppress piracy and armed robbery against ships', adopted on 4 November 1993,

Bearing in mind resolution A.922(22), through which the Assembly adopted the Code of Practice for the Investigation of the Crimes of Piracy and Armed Robbery against Ships ('the Code') and which, *inter alia*, urges Governments to take action, as set out in the Code, to investigate all acts of piracy and armed robbery against ships occurring in areas or on board ships under their jurisdiction; and to report to the Organization pertinent information on all investigations and prosecutions concerning these acts,

Bearing in mind also resolution A.979(24) on 'Piracy and armed robbery against ships in waters off the coast of Somalia', by means of which the Assembly, *inter alia*:

   – recommended a number of measures to protect ships from piracy and armed robbery attacks in waters off the coast of Somalia and by means of which the situation was brought to the attention of the Security Council of the United Nations ('the Security Council');

   – requested the Secretary-General to continue monitoring the situation in relation to threats to ships sailing in waters off the coast of Somalia and to report to the Council, as and when appropriate, on developments and any further actions which might be required; and

   – requested the Council to monitor the situation in relation to threats to ships sailing in waters off the coast of Somalia and to initiate any actions it might deem necessary to ensure the protection of seafarers and ships sailing in waters off the coast of Somalia,

Noting with satisfaction the actions taken by the Council and the Secretary-General pursuant to resolution A.979(24),

Considering that the Maritime Safety Committee has approved MSC/Circ.622/Rev.1 and MSC/Circ.623/Rev.3 containing recommendations to Governments and guidance to shipowners and ship operators, shipmasters and crews on preventing and suppressing acts of piracy and armed robbery against ships and has established a special signal for use by ships under attack or threat of attack,

Noting that the General Assembly of the United Nations, at its sixty-first session, by resolution A/RES/61/222 on 'Oceans and the law of the sea', adopted on 20 December 2006, *inter alia*:

   .1 encourages States to co-operate to address threats to maritime safety and security, including piracy, armed robbery at sea, smuggling and terrorist acts against shipping, offshore installations and other maritime interests, through bilateral and multilateral instruments and mechanisms aimed at monitoring, preventing and responding to such threats;

.2   urges all States, in co-operation with the Organization, to combat piracy and armed robbery at sea by adopting measures, including those relating to assistance with capacity building through training of seafarers, port staff and enforcement personnel in the prevention, reporting and investigation of incidents, bringing the alleged perpetrators to justice, in accordance with international law, and by adopting national legislation, as well as providing enforcement vessels and equipment and guarding against fraudulent ship registration; and

.3   calls upon States to become parties to the Convention for the Suppression of Unlawful Acts against the Safety of Maritime Navigation and the Protocol for the Suppression of Unlawful Acts against the Safety of Fixed Platforms Located on the Continental Shelf; invites States to consider becoming parties to the 2005 Protocols amending those instruments; and also urges States parties to take appropriate measures to ensure the effective implementation of those instruments, through the adoption of legislation, where appropriate,

Noting also, with great concern, the increasing number of incidents of piracy and armed robbery against ships occurring in waters off the coast of Somalia, some of which have reportedly taken place more than 200 nautical miles from the nearest land,

Mindful of the grave danger to life and the serious risks to navigational safety and the environment to which such incidents may give rise,

Being particularly concerned that the Monitoring Group on Somalia, in its report of 27 June 2007 to the Security Council, confirmed, *inter alia,* that piracy and armed robbery against ships in waters off the coast of Somalia, unlike in other parts of the world, is caused by the lack of lawful administration and inability of the authorities to take affirmative action against the perpetrators, which allows the 'pirate command centres' to operate without hindrance at many points along the coast of Somalia,

Being aware of the serious safety and security concerns the shipping industry and the seafaring community continue to have as a result of the attacks against ships sailing in waters off the coast of Somalia referred to above,

Being concerned at the negative impact such attacks continue to have on the prompt and effective delivery of food aid and of other humanitarian assistance to Somalia and the serious threat this poses to the health and well-being of the people of Somalia,

Noting, with appreciation, the 'Sub-regional seminar and workshop on piracy and armed robbery against ships' held by IMO in Sana'a, Yemen, from 9 to 13 April 2005, for Oman, from 14 to 18 January 2006,

Being aware that the Security Council has, through resolution S/Res/1425(2002), adopted on 22 July 2002, stipulated that the arms embargo on Somalia prohibits the direct or indirect supply to Somalia of technical advice, financial and other assistance, and training related to military activities,

Noting that the Security Council, by resolution S/Res/1766 (2007) adopted on 23 July 2007, decided, *inter alia,* to re-establish the Monitoring Group on Somalia and directed it to continue to investigate, in coordination with relevant international agencies, all activities, including in the financial, maritime and other sectors, which generate revenues used to commit violations of the embargo on all delivery of weapons and military equipment to Somalia, which the Security Council had established by resolution S/Res/733 (1992),

Noting also that the Security Council, being concerned at the continuing incidence of acts of piracy and armed robbery against ships in waters off the coast of Somalia:

.1 on 15 March 2006, in response to resolution A.979(24), through a Statement by the President of the Security Council, *inter alia*, encouraged Member States of the United Nations, whose naval vessels and military aircraft operate in international waters and airspace adjacent to the coast of Somalia, to be vigilant to any incident of piracy therein and to take appropriate action to protect merchant shipping, in particular the transportation of humanitarian aid, against any such act, in line with relevant international law and further urged co-operation among all States, particularly regional States, and active prosecution of piracy offences; and

.2 on 20 August 2007, in operative paragraph 18 of resolution S/Res/1772 (2007) encouraged Member States of the United Nations, whose naval vessels and military aircraft operate in international waters and airspace adjacent to the coast of Somalia, to be vigilant to any incident of piracy therein and to take appropriate action to protect merchant shipping, in particular the transportation of humanitarian aid, against any such act, in line with relevant international law,

Noting with appreciation the action taken by the Secretary-General of the United Nations in response to the request of the Council, at its ninety-eighth session, in particular, to bring the Organization's concerns to the President of the Security Council with a request to bring them to the attention of the members of the Security Council,

Recognizing that the particular character of the present situation in Somalia requires an exceptional response to safeguard the interests of the maritime community making use of the sea off the coast of Somalia,

Recognizing also the strategic importance of the navigational routes along the coast of Somalia for regional and global seaborne trade and the need to ensure that they remain safe at all times,

Recognizing further, in view of the continued situation in Somalia giving rise to grave concern, the need for the immediate establishment of appropriate measures to protect ships sailing in waters off the coast of Somalia from piracy and armed robbery attacks,

Appreciating the efforts of those who have responded to calls from, or have rendered assistance to, ships under attack in waters off the coast of Somalia; acknowledging the efforts of a number of international organizations in raising awareness amongst, and providing guidance for, their respective memberships and reporting to the Organization in relation to this issue; and noting with appreciation the work done by the International Maritime Bureau of the International Chamber of Commerce in providing the industry with warnings in relation to incidents occurring in waters off the coast of Somalia and assistance in resolving cases where ships have been hijacked and the seafarers on board have been held hostage,

Respecting fully the sovereignty, sovereign rights, jurisdiction and territorial integrity of Somalia and the relevant provisions of international law, in particular UNCLOS,

Having considered the actions taken, following the adoption of resolution A.979(24), by the Council, at its ninety-eighth regular and twenty-fourth extraordinary sessions, and by the Secretary-General in the light of the prevailing situation in the waters off the coast of Somalia,

1. *Condemns and deplores* all acts of piracy and armed robbery against ships irrespective of where such acts have occurred or may occur;

2. *Appeals* to all parties which may be able to assist to take action, within the provisions of international law, to ensure that:

.1 all acts or attempted acts of piracy and armed robbery against ships are terminated forthwith and any plans for committing such acts are abandoned; and

.2   any hijacked ships, seafarers serving in them and any other persons on board are immediately and unconditionally released and that no harm is caused to them;

.3   *Strongly urges* Governments to increase their efforts to prevent and suppress, within the provisions of international law, acts of piracy and armed robbery against ships irrespective of where such acts occur and, in particular, to co-operate with other Governments and international organizations, in the interests of the rule of law, safety of life at sea and environmental protection, in relation to acts occurring or likely to occur in the waters off the coast of Somalia;

4.   *Also strongly urges* Governments to promptly:

.1   issue, to ships entitled to fly their flag, as necessary, specific advice and guidance on any appropriate additional precautionary measures ships may need to put in place when sailing in waters off the coast of Somalia to protect themselves from attack, which may include, *inter alia*, areas to be avoided;

.2   issue, to ships entitled to fly their flag, as necessary, advice and guidance on any measures or actions they may need to take when they are under attack, or threat of attack, whilst sailing in waters off the coast of Somalia;

.3   encourage ships entitled to fly their flag to ensure that information on attempted attacks or on acts of piracy or armed robbery committed whilst sailing in waters off the coast of Somalia is promptly conveyed to the nearby coastal States and to the nearest most appropriate Rescue Coordination Centre;

.4   provide a point of contact through which ships entitled to fly their flag may request advice or assistance when sailing in waters off the coast of Somalia and to which such ships can report any security concerns about other ships, movements or communications in the area;

.5   bring to the attention of the Secretary-General information on attempted attacks or on acts of piracy or armed robbery committed against ships entitled to fly their flag whilst sailing in waters off the coast of Somalia for him to take appropriate action in the circumstances;

.6   encourage ships entitled to fly their flag to implement expeditiously, for the ship's protection and for the protection of other ships in the vicinity, any measure or advice the nearby coastal States or any other State or competent authority may have provided;

.7   establish, as necessary, plans and procedures to assist owners, managers and operators of ships entitled to fly their flag in the speedy resolution of hijacking cases occurring in the waters off the coast of Somalia;

.8   investigate all acts or attempted acts of piracy and armed robbery against ships entitled to fly their flag occurring in the waters off the coast of Somalia and to report to the Organization any pertinent information;

.9   take all necessary legislative, judicial and law enforcement action so as to be able, subject to national law, to receive and prosecute or extradite any pirates or suspected pirates and armed robbers arrested by warships or military aircraft, or other ships or aircraft clearly marked and identifiable as being on government service; and

.10   with respect to ships entitled to fly their flag employed by the World Food Programme for the delivery of humanitarian aid to Somalia, where such ships are to be escorted by warships or military aircraft, or other ships or aircraft clearly marked and identifiable as being on government service, to conclude, taking into account operative paragraph 6.4, any necessary agreements with the State(s) concerned;

5. *Requests* Governments to instruct national Rescue Coordination Centres or other agencies involved, on receipt of a report of an attack, to promptly initiate the transmission of relevant advice and warnings, through the World-Wide Navigation Warning Service, the International SafetyNet Service or otherwise, to ships sailing in the waters off the coast of Somalia so as to warn shipping in the immediate area of the attack;

6. *Requests also* the Transitional Federal Government of Somalia to:

.1   take any action it deems necessary in the circumstances to prevent and suppress acts of piracy and armed robbery against ships originating from within Somalia and thus depriving them of the possibility of using its coastline as a safe haven from where to launch their operations;

.2   take appropriate action to ensure that all ships seized by pirates and armed robbers and brought into waters within its territory are released promptly and that ships sailing off the coast of Somalia do not henceforth become victims of acts of piracy or armed robbery;

.3   advise the Security Council that, in response to the pressing request of the Council of the International Maritime Organization, it consents to warships or military aircraft, or other ships or aircraft clearly marked and identifiable as being on government service, operating in the Indian Ocean, entering its territorial sea when engaging in operations against pirates or suspected pirates and armed robbers endangering the safety of life at sea, in particular the safety of crews on board ships carrying, under the World Food Programme, humanitarian aid to Somalia or leaving Somali ports after having discharged their cargo, together with any conditions attached to the consent given; and

.4   advise also the Security Council of its readiness to conclude, taking into account operative paragraph 4.10, any necessary agreements so as to enable warships or military aircraft, or other ships or aircraft clearly marked and identifiable as being on government service to escort ships employed by the World Food Programme for the delivery of humanitarian aid to Somalia or leaving Somali ports after having discharged their cargo;

7. *Calls upon* Governments in the region to conclude, in co-operation with the Organization, and implement, as soon as possible, a regional agreement to prevent, deter and suppress piracy and armed robbery against ships;

8. *Also calls upon* all other Governments, in co-operation with the Organization and as requested by those Governments in the region, to assist these efforts;

9. *Requests further* the Secretary-General to:

.1   transmit a copy of the present resolution to the Secretary-General of the United Nations for consideration and any further action he may deem appropriate;

.2   continue monitoring the situation in relation to threats to ships sailing in waters off the coast of Somalia and to report to the Council, as and when appropriate, on developments and any further actions which may be required;

.3   establish and maintain co-operation with the Monitoring Group on Somalia; and

.4   consult with interested Governments and organizations in establishing the process and means by which technical assistance can be provided to Somalia and nearby coastal States to enhance the capacity of these States to give effect to the present resolution as appropriate;

10. *Requests* the Maritime Safety Committee to review and update, as a matter of urgency, MSC/Circ.622/Rev.1, MSC/Circ.623/Rev.3 and resolution A.922(22), taking into account current trends and practices;

11. *Also requests* the Council to continue to monitor the situation in relation to threats to ships sailing in waters off the coast of Somalia and to initiate any actions which it may deem necessary to ensure the protection of seafarers and ships sailing in waters off the coast of Somalia;

12. *Revokes* resolution A.979(24).

Ilulissat Declaration

Adopted at the Arctic Ocean Conference, Ilulissat, Greenland, 28 May 2008
http://www.cop15.dk/

[1]   At the invitation of the Danish Minister for Foreign Affairs and the Premier of Greenland, representatives of the five coastal States bordering on the Arctic Ocean – Canada, Denmark, Norway, the Russian Federation and the United States of America – met at the political level on 28 May 2008 in Ilulissat, Greenland, to hold discussions. They adopted the following declaration:

[2]   The Arctic Ocean stands at the threshold of significant changes. Climate change and the melting of ice have a potential impact on vulnerable ecosystems, the livelihoods of local inhabitants and indigenous communities, and the potential exploitation of natural resources.

[3]   By virtue of their sovereignty, sovereign rights and jurisdiction in large areas of the Arctic Ocean the five coastal states are in a unique position to address these possibilities and challenges. In this regard, we recall that an extensive international legal framework applies to the Arctic Ocean as discussed between our representatives at the meeting in Oslo on 15 and 16 October 2007 at the level of senior officials. Notably, the law of the sea provides for important rights and obligations concerning the delineation of the outer limits of the continental shelf, the protection of the marine environment, including ice-covered areas, freedom of navigation, marine scientific research, and other uses of the sea. We remain committed to this legal framework and to the orderly settlement of any possible overlapping claims.

[4]   This framework provides a solid foundation for responsible management by the five coastal States and other users of this Ocean through national implementation and application of relevant provisions. We therefore see no need to develop a new comprehensive international legal regime to govern the Arctic Ocean. We will keep abreast of the developments in the Arctic Ocean and continue to implement appropriate measures.

[5]   The Arctic Ocean is a unique ecosystem, which the five coastal states have a stewardship role in protecting. Experience has shown how shipping disasters and subsequent pollution of the marine environment may cause irreversible disturbance of the ecological balance and major harm to the livelihoods of local inhabitants and indigenous communities. We will take steps in accordance with international law both nationally and in cooperation among the five states and other interested parties to ensure the protection and preservation of the fragile marine environment of the Arctic Ocean. In this regard we intend to work together including through the International Maritime Organization to strengthen existing measures and develop new measures to improve the safety of maritime navigation and prevent or reduce the risk of ship-based pollution in the Arctic Ocean.

[6]   The increased use of Arctic waters for tourism, shipping, research and resource development also increases the risk of accidents and therefore the need to further

strengthen search and rescue capabilities and capacity around the Arctic Ocean to ensure an appropriate response from states to any accident. Cooperation, including on the sharing of information, is a prerequisite for addressing these challenges. We will work to promote safety of life at sea in the Arctic Ocean, including through bilateral and multilateral arrangements between or among relevant states.

[7]   The five coastal states currently cooperate closely in the Arctic Ocean with each other and with other interested parties. This cooperation includes the collection of scientific data concerning the continental shelf, the protection of the marine environment and other scientific research. We will work to strengthen this cooperation, which is based on mutual trust and transparency, inter alia, through timely exchange of data and analyses.

[8]   The Arctic Council and other international fora, including the Barents Euro-Arctic Council, have already taken important steps on specific issues, for example with regard to safety of navigation, search and rescue, environmental monitoring and disaster response and scientific cooperation, which are relevant also to the Arctic Ocean. The five coastal states of the Arctic Ocean will continue to contribute actively to the work of the Arctic Council and other relevant international fora.

UN Security Council Resolution 1816 (2008)

UN Doc. S/RES/1816 (2008) of 2 June 2008

The Security Council,

Recalling its previous resolutions and the statements of its President concerning the situation in Somalia,[1]

---

[1] Three previous resolutions in particular dealt with question of piracy off the Somali coast:
Resolution 1772 (2007) of 20 August 2007
The Security Council, [...]
Stressing its concern at the upsurge in piracy off the Somali coast described in paragraph 51 of the Secretary-General's report, and *taking note* of the joint communiqué of the International Maritime Organization and the World Food Programme of 10 July 2007, [...]
Determining that the situation in Somalia continues to constitute a threat to international peace and security in the region,
Acting under Chapter VII of the Charter of the United Nations, [...]
18. *Encourages* Member States whose naval vessels and military aircraft operate in international waters and airspace adjacent to the coast of Somalia to be vigilant to any incident of piracy therein and to take appropriate action to protect merchant shipping, in particular the transportation of humanitarian aid, against any such act, in line with relevant international law; [...].
Resolution 1801 (2008) of 20 February 2008
The Security Council, [...]
Stressing concern at the upsurge in piracy off the Somali coast described in paragraph 22 of the Secretary-General's report, and *recalling* the joint communiqué of the International Maritime Organization and the World Food Programme of 10 July 2007, [...]
Determining that the situation in Somalia continues to constitute a threat to international peace and security in the region,
Acting under Chapter VII of the Charter of the United Nations, [...]
12. *Encourages* Member States whose naval vessels and military aircraft operate in international waters and airspace adjacent to the coast of Somalia to be vigilant to any incidents of piracy therein and to take appropriate action to protect merchant shipping, in particular the transportation of humanitarian aid, against any such act, in line with relevant international law, and *welcomes* the contribution made by France to protect the World Food Programme naval convoys and the support now provided by Denmark to this end; [...].
Resolution 1814 (2008) of 15 May 2008
The Security Council, [...]
Determining that the situation in Somalia continues to constitute a threat to international peace and security in the region, [...[

Gravely concerned by the threat that acts of piracy and armed robbery against vessels pose to the prompt, safe and effective delivery of humanitarian aid to Somalia, the safety of commercial maritime routes and to international navigation,

Expressing its concerns at the quarterly reports from the International Maritime Organization (IMO) since 2005, which provide evidence of continuing piracy and armed robbery in particular in the waters off the coast of Somalia,

Affirming that international law, as reflected in the United Nations Convention on the Law of the Sea of 10 December 1982 ('the Convention'), sets out the legal framework applicable to combating piracy and armed robbery, as well as other ocean activities,

Reaffirming the relevant provisions of international law with respect to the repression of piracy, including the Convention, and *recalling* that they provide guiding principles for cooperation to the fullest possible extent in the repression of piracy on the high seas or in any other place outside the jurisdiction of any state, including but not limited to boarding, searching, and seizing vessels engaged in or suspected of engaging in acts of piracy, and to apprehending persons engaged in such acts with a view to such persons being prosecuted,

Reaffirming its respect for the sovereignty, territorial integrity, political independence and unity of Somalia,

Taking into account the crisis situation in Somalia, and the lack of capacity of the Transitional Federal Government (TFG) to interdict pirates or patrol and secure either the international sea lanes off the coast of Somalia or Somalia's territorial waters,

Deploring the recent incidents of attacks upon and hijacking of vessels in the territorial waters and on the high seas off the coast of Somalia including attacks upon and hijackings of vessels operated by the World Food Program and numerous commercial vessels and the serious adverse impact of these attacks on the prompt, safe and effective delivery of food aid and other humanitarian assistance to the people of Somalia, and the grave dangers they pose to vessels, crews, passengers, and cargo,

Noting the letters to the Secretary-General from the Secretary-General of the IMO dated 5 July 2007 and 18 September 2007 regarding the piracy problems off the coast of Somalia and the IMO Assembly resolution A.1002 (25), which strongly urged Governments to increase their efforts to prevent and repress, within the provisions of international law, acts of piracy and armed robbery against vessels irrespective of where such acts occur, and *recalling* the joint communiqué of the IMO and the World Food Programme of 10 July 2007,

Taking note of the Secretary-General's letter of 9 November 2007 to the President of the Security Council reporting that the Transitional Federal Government of Somalia (TFG) needs and would welcome international assistance to address the problem,

Taking further note of the letter from the Permanent Representative of the Somali Republic to the United Nations to the President of the Security Council dated 27 February 2008, conveying the consent of the TFG to the Security Council for urgent assistance in securing the territorial and international waters off the coast of Somalia for the safe conduct of shipping and navigation,

---

Acting under Chapter VII of the Charter of the United Nations, [...]

11. *Reiterates* its support for the contribution made by some States to protect the World Food Programme maritime convoys, *calls upon* States and regional organizations, in close coordination with each other and as notified in advance to the Secretary-General, and at the request of the TFG, to take action to protect shipping involved with the transportation and delivery of humanitarian aid to Somalia and United Nations-authorized activities, *calls upon* AMISOM troop-contributing countries, as appropriate, to provide support to this end, and *requests* the Secretary-General to provide his support to this effect; [...].

Determining that the incidents of piracy and armed robbery against vessels in the territorial waters of Somalia and the high seas off the coast of Somalia exacerbate the situation in Somalia, which continues to constitute a threat to international peace and security in the region,

Acting under Chapter VII of the Charter of the United Nations,

1. *Condemns and deplores* all acts of piracy and armed robbery against vessels in territorial waters and the high seas off the coast of Somalia;

2. *Urges* States whose naval vessels and military aircraft operate on the high seas and airspace off the coast of Somalia to be vigilant to acts of piracy and armed robbery and, in this context, *encourages*, in particular, States interested in the use of commercial maritime routes off the coast of Somalia, to increase and coordinate their efforts to deter acts of piracy and armed robbery at sea in cooperation with the TFG;

3. *Urges* all States to cooperate with each other, with the IMO and, as appropriate, with the relevant regional organizations in connection with, and share information about, acts of piracy and armed robbery in the territorial waters and on the high seas off the coast of Somalia, and to render assistance to vessels threatened by or under attack by pirates or armed robbers, in accordance with relevant international law;

4. *Further urges* States to work in cooperation with interested organizations, including the IMO, to ensure that vessels entitled to fly their flag receive appropriate guidance and training on avoidance, evasion, and defensive techniques and to avoid the area whenever possible;

5. *Calls upon* States and interested organizations, including the IMO, to provide technical assistance to Somalia and nearby coastal States upon their request to enhance the capacity of these States to ensure coastal and maritime security, including combating piracy and armed robbery off the Somali and nearby coastlines;

6. *Affirms* that the measures imposed by paragraph 5 of resolution 733 (1992) and further elaborated upon by paragraphs 1 and 2 of resolution 1425 (2002) do not apply to supplies of technical assistance to Somalia solely for the purposes set out in paragraph 5 above which have been exempted from those measures in accordance with the procedure set out in paragraphs 11 (b) and 12 of resolution 1772 (2007);

7. *Decides* that for a period of six months from the date of this resolution, States cooperating with the TFG in the fight against piracy and armed robbery at sea off the coast of Somalia, for which advance notification has been provided by the TFG to the Secretary-General, may:

   (a) Enter the territorial waters of Somalia for the purpose of repressing acts of piracy and armed robbery at sea, in a manner consistent with such action permitted on the high seas with respect to piracy under relevant international law; and

   (b) Use, within the territorial waters of Somalia, in a manner consistent with action permitted on the high seas with respect to piracy under relevant international law, all necessary means to repress acts of piracy and armed robbery;

8. *Requests* that cooperating states take appropriate steps to ensure that the activities they undertake pursuant to the authorization in paragraph 7 do not have the practical effect of denying or impairing the right of innocent passage to the ships of any third State;

9. *Affirms* that the authorization provided in this resolution applies only with respect to the situation in Somalia and shall not affect the rights or obligations or responsibilities of member states under international law, including any rights or obligations under the Convention, with respect to any other situation, and underscores in particular that it shall not be considered as establishing customary international law, and affirms further that this authorization has been provided only following receipt of the letter from the Permanent Representative of the Somalia Republic to the United Nations

to the President of the Security Council dated 27 February 2008 conveying the consent of the TFG;

10. *Calls upon* States to coordinate their actions with other participating States taken pursuant to paragraphs 5 and 7 above;

11. *Calls upon* all States, and in particular flag, port and coastal States, States of the nationality of victims and perpetrators or piracy and armed robbery, and other States with relevant jurisdiction under international law and national legislation, to cooperate in determining jurisdiction, and in the investigation and prosecution of persons responsible for acts of piracy and armed robbery off the coast of Somalia, consistent with applicable international law including international human rights law, and to render assistance by, among other actions, providing disposition and logistics assistance with respect to persons under their jurisdiction and control, such victims and witnesses and persons detained as a result of operations conducted under this resolution;

12. *Requests* States cooperating with the TFG to inform the Security Council within 3 months of the progress of actions undertaken in the exercise of the authority provided in paragraph 7 above;

13. *Requests* the Secretary-General to report to the Security Council within 5 months of adoption of this resolution on the implementation of this resolution and on the situation with respect to piracy and armed robbery in territorial waters and the high seas off the coast of Somalia;

14. *Requests* the Secretary-General of the IMO to brief the Council on the basis of cases brought to his attention by the agreement of all affected coastal states, and duly taking into account the existing bilateral and regional cooperative arrangements, on the situation with respect to piracy and armed robbery;

15. *Expresses* its intention to review the situation and consider, as appropriate, renewing the authority provided in paragraph 7 above for additional periods upon the request of the TFG;

16. *Decides* to remain seized of the matter.

UN Security Council Resolution 1838 (2008)

UN Doc. S/RES/1838 (2008) of 7 October 2008

The Security Council,

Recalling its resolutions 1814 (2008) and 1816 (2008),

Gravely concerned by the recent proliferation of acts of piracy and armed robbery at sea against vessels off the coast of Somalia, and by the serious threat it poses to the prompt, safe and effective delivery of humanitarian aid to Somalia, to international navigation and the safety of commercial maritime routes, and to fishing activities conducted in conformity with international law,

Noting with concern also that increasingly violent acts of piracy are carried out with heavier weaponry, in a larger area off the coast of Somalia, using long-range assets such as mother ships, and demonstrating more sophisticated organization and methods of attack,

Reaffirming that international law, as reflected in the United Nations Convention on the Law of the Sea of 10 December 1982 ('the Convention'), sets out the legal framework applicable to combating piracy and armed robbery at sea, as well as other ocean activities,

Commending the contribution made by some States since November 2007 to protect the World Food Programme ('WFP') maritime convoys, and, the establishment by the European Union of a coordination unit with the task of supporting the surveillance and protection activities carried out by some member States of the European Union off the coast of Somalia, and the ongoing planning process towards a possible European Union naval operation, as well as other international or national initiatives taken with a view to implementing resolutions 1814 (2008) and 1816 (2008),

Noting recent humanitarian reports that as many as three-and-a-half million Somalis will be dependent on humanitarian food aid by the end of the year, and that maritime contractors for the WFP will not deliver food aid to Somalia without naval warship escorts, *expressing its determination* to ensure long-term security of WFP deliveries to Somalia and *recalling* that it requested the Secretary-General in resolution 1814 (2008) to provide his support for efforts to protect WFP maritime convoys,

Reaffirming its respect for the sovereignty, territorial integrity, political independence and unity of Somalia,

Taking note of the letter dated 1 September 2008 of the President of Somalia to the Secretary-General of the United Nations expressing the appreciation of the Transitional Federal Government ('TFG') to the Security Council for its assistance and expressing the TFG's willingness to consider working with other States, as well as regional organizations, to provide advance notifications additional to those already provided, in accordance with paragraph 7 of resolution 1816 (2008), to combat piracy and armed robbery at sea off the coast of Somalia,

Recalling that in the statement of its President dated 4 September 2008 (S/PRST/2008/33) it welcomed the signing of a peace and reconciliation agreement in Djibouti and commended the Special Representative of the Secretary-General for Somalia, Mr. Ahmedou Ould-Abdallah, for his ongoing efforts, and *emphasizing* the importance of promoting a comprehensive and lasting settlement in Somalia,

Recalling also that in the statement of its President dated 4 September (S/PRST/2008/33) it took note of the parties' request in the Djibouti Agreement that the United Nations, within a period of 120 days, authorize and deploy an international stabilization force and *looking forward* to the Secretary-General's report due 60 days from its passage, in particular a detailed and consolidated description of a feasible multinational force, as well as a detailed concept of operations for a feasible United Nations peacekeeping operation,

Emphasizing that peace and stability, the strengthening of State institutions, economic and social development and respect for human rights and the rule of law are necessary to create the conditions for a full eradication of piracy and armed robbery at sea off the coast of Somalia,

Determining that the incidents of piracy and armed robbery against vessels in the territorial waters of Somalia and the high seas off the coast of Somalia exacerbate the situation in Somalia which continues to constitute a threat against international peace and security in the region,

Acting under Chapter VII of the Charter of the United Nations,

1. *Reiterates that it condemns and deplores* all acts of piracy and armed robbery at sea against vessels off the coast of Somalia;

2. *Calls upon* States interested in the security of maritime activities to take part actively in the fight against piracy on the high seas off the coast of Somalia, in particular by deploying naval vessels and military aircraft, in accordance with international law, as reflected in the Convention;

3. *Calls upon* States whose naval vessels and military aircraft operate on the high seas and airspace off the coast of Somalia to use on the high seas and airspace off the coast of Somalia the necessary means, in conformity with international law, as reflected in the Convention, for the repression of acts of piracy;

4. *Urges* States that have the capacity to do so to cooperate with the TFG in the fight against piracy and armed robbery at sea in conformity with the provisions of resolution 1816 (2008);

5. *Urges* also States and regional organizations, in conformity with the provisions of resolution 1814 (2008), to continue to take action to protect the World Food Programme maritime convoys, which is vital to bring humanitarian assistance to the affected populations in Somalia;

6. *Urges* States, as requested in particular by International Maritime Organization resolution ('IMO') A-1002(25), to issue to ships entitled to fly their flag, as necessary, advice and guidance on appropriate precautionary measures to protect themselves from attack or actions to take if under attack or the threat of attack when sailing in waters off the coast of Somalia;

7. *Calls upon* States and regional organizations to coordinate their actions pursuant to paragraphs 3, 4 and 5 above;

8. *Affirms* that the provisions in this resolution apply only with respect to the situation in Somalia and shall not affect the rights or obligations or responsibilities of member States under international law, including any rights or obligations under the Convention, with respect to any situation, and *underscores* in particular that this resolution shall not be considered as establishing customary international law;

9. *Looks forward* to the report of the Secretary-General requested in paragraph 13 of resolution 1816 (2008) and *expresses* its intention to review the situation with respect to piracy and armed robbery at sea against vessels off the coast of Somalia with a view, in particular, upon the request of the TFG, to renewing the authority provided in paragraph 7 of resolution 1816 (2008) for an additional period;

10. *Decides* to remain seized of the matter.

UN Security Council Resolution 1846 (2008)

UN Doc. S/RES/1846 (2008) of 2 December 2008

The Security Council,

Recalling its previous resolutions concerning the situation in Somalia, especially resolutions 1814 (2008), 1816 (2008) and 1838 (2008),

Continuing to be gravely concerned by the threat that piracy and armed robbery at sea against vessels pose to the prompt, safe and effective delivery of humanitarian aid to Somalia, to international navigation and the safety of commercial maritime routes, and to other vulnerable ships, including fishing activities in conformity with international law,

Reaffirming its respect for the sovereignty, territorial integrity, political independence and unity of Somalia,

Further reaffirming that international law, as reflected in the United Nations Convention on the Law of the Sea of 10 December 1982 ('the Convention'), sets out the legal framework applicable to combating piracy and armed robbery at sea, as well as other ocean activities,

Taking into account the crisis situation in Somalia, and the lack of capacity of the Transitional Federal Government ('TFG') to interdict pirates or patrol and secure either the international sea lanes off the coast of Somalia or Somalia's territorial waters,

Taking note of the requests from the TFG for international assistance to counter piracy off its coasts, including the 1 September 2008 letter from the President of Somalia to the Secretary-General of the United Nations expressing the appreciation of the TFG to the Security Council for its assistance and expressing the TFG's willingness to consider working with other States and regional organizations to combat piracy and armed robbery at sea off the coast of Somalia, the 20 November 2008 letter conveying the request of the TFG that the provisions of resolution 1816 (2008) be renewed, and the 20 November request of the Permanent Representative of Somalia before the Security Council that the renewal be for an additional 12 months,

Further taking note of the letters from the TFG to the Secretary-General providing advance notification with respect to States cooperating with the TFG in the fight against piracy and armed robbery at sea off the coast of Somalia and from other Member States to the Security Council to inform the Council of their actions, as requested in paragraphs 7 and 12 of 1816 (2008), and encouraging those cooperating States, for which advance notification has been provided by the TFG to the Secretary-General, to continue their respective efforts,

Expressing again its determination to ensure the long-term security of World Food Programme (WFP) maritime deliveries to Somalia,

Recalling that in its resolution 1838 (2008) it commended the contribution made by some States since November 2007 to protect (WFP) maritime convoys, and the establishment by the European Union (EU) of a coordination unit with the task of supporting the surveillance and protection activities carried out by some member States of the European Union off the coast of Somalia, as well as other international and national initiatives taken with a view to implementing resolutions 1814 (2008) and 1816 (2008),

Emphasizing that peace and stability within Somalia, the strengthening of State institutions, economic and social development and respect for human rights and the rule of law are necessary to create the conditions for a full eradication of piracy and armed robbery at sea off the coast of Somalia,

Welcoming the signing of a peace and reconciliation Agreement ('the Djibouti Agreement') between the TFG and the Alliance for the Re-Liberation of Somalia on 19 August 2008, as well as their signing of a joint ceasefire agreement on 26 October 2008, *noting* that the Djibouti Agreement calls for the United Nations to authorize and deploy an international stabilization force, and *further noting* the Secretary-General's report on Somalia of 17 November 2008, including his recommendations in this regard,

Commending the key role played by the African Union Mission to Somalia (AMISOM) in facilitating delivery of humanitarian assistance to Somalia through the port of Mogadishu and the contribution that AMISOM has made towards the goal of establishing lasting peace and stability in Somalia, and *recognizing* specifically the important contributions of the Governments of Uganda and Burundi to Somalia,

Welcoming the organization of a ministerial meeting of the Security Council in December 2008 to examine ways to improve international coordination in the fight against piracy and armed robbery off the coast of Somalia and to ensure that the international community has the proper authorities and tools at its disposal to assist it in these efforts,

Determining that the incidents of piracy and armed robbery against vessels in the territorial waters of Somalia and the high seas off the coast of Somalia exacerbate the situation in Somalia which continues to constitute a threat to international peace and security in the region,

Acting under Chapter VII of the Charter of the United Nations,

1. *Reiterates* that it condemns and deplores all acts of piracy and armed robbery against vessels in territorial waters and the high seas off the coast of Somalia;

2. *Expresses* its concern over the finding contained in the 20 November 2008 report of the Monitoring Group on Somalia that escalating ransom payments are fuelling the growth of piracy off the coast of Somalia;

3. *Welcomes* the efforts of the International Maritime Organization ('IMO') to update its guidance and recommendations to the shipping industry and to Governments for preventing and suppressing piracy and armed robbery at sea and to provide this guidance as soon as practicable to all Member States and to the international shipping community operating off the coast of Somalia;

4. *Calls upon* States, in cooperation with the shipping industry, the insurance industry and the IMO, to issue to ships entitled to fly their flag appropriate advice and guidance on avoidance, evasion, and defensive techniques and measures to take if under the threat of attack or attack when sailing in the waters off the coast of Somalia;

5. *Further calls upon* States and interested organizations, including the IMO, to provide technical assistance to Somalia and nearby coastal States upon their request to enhance the capacity of these States to ensure coastal and maritime security, including combating piracy and armed robbery at sea off the Somali and nearby coastlines;

6. *Welcomes* initiatives by Canada, Denmark, France, India, the Netherlands, the Russian Federation, Spain, the United Kingdom, the United States of America, and by regional and international organizations to counter piracy off the coast of Somalia pursuant to resolutions 1814 (2008), 1816 (2008) and 1838 (2008), the decision by the North Atlantic Treaty Organization (NATO) to counter piracy off the Somalia coast, including by escorting vessels of the WFP, and in particular the decision by the EU on 10 November 2008 to launch, for a period of 12 months from December 2008, a naval operation to protect WFP maritime convoys bringing humanitarian assistance to Somalia and other vulnerable ships, and to repress acts of piracy and armed robbery at sea off the coast of Somalia;

7. *Calls upon* States and regional organizations to coordinate, including by sharing information through bilateral channels or the United Nations, their efforts to deter acts of piracy and armed robbery at sea off the coast of Somalia in cooperation with each other, the IMO, the international shipping community, flag States, and the TFG;

8. *Requests* the Secretary-General to present to it a report, no later than three months after the adoption of this resolution, on ways to ensure the long-term security of international navigation off the coast of Somalia, including the long-term security of WFP maritime deliveries to Somalia and a possible coordination and leadership role for the United Nations in this regard to rally Member States and regional organizations to counter piracy and armed robbery at sea off the coast of Somalia;

9. *Calls upon* States and regional organizations that have the capacity to do so, to take part actively in the fight against piracy and armed robbery at sea off the coast of Somalia, in particular, consistent with this resolution and relevant international law, by deploying naval vessels and military aircraft, and through seizure and disposition of boats, vessels, arms and other related equipment used in the commission of piracy and armed robbery off the coast of Somalia, or for which there is reasonable ground for suspecting such use;

10. *Decides* that for a period of 12 months from the date of this resolution States and regional organizations cooperating with the TFG in the fight against piracy and armed robbery at sea off the coast of Somalia, for which advance notification has been provided by the TFG to the Secretary-General, may:

(a) Enter into the territorial waters of Somalia for the purpose of repressing acts of piracy and armed robbery at sea, in a manner consistent with such action permitted on the high seas with respect to piracy under relevant international law; and

(b) Use, within the territorial waters of Somalia, in a manner consistent with such action permitted on the high seas with respect to piracy under relevant international law, all necessary means to repress acts of piracy and armed robbery at sea;

11. *Affirms* that the authorizations provided in this resolution apply only with respect to the situation in Somalia and shall not affect the rights or obligations or responsibilities of Member States under international law, including any rights or obligations under the Convention, with respect to any other situation, and underscores in particular that this resolution shall not be considered as establishing customary international law; and *affirms further* that such authorizations have been provided only following the receipt of the 20 November letter conveying the consent of the TFG;

12. *Affirms* that the measures imposed by paragraph 5 of resolution 733 (1992) and further elaborated upon by paragraphs 1 and 2 of resolution 1425 (2002) do not apply to supplies of technical assistance to Somalia solely for the purposes set out in paragraph 5 above which have been exempted from those measures, in accordance with the procedure set out in paragraphs 11 (b) and 12 of resolution 1772 (2007);

13. *Requests* that cooperating States take appropriate steps to ensure that the activities they undertake pursuant to the authorization in paragraph 10 do not have the practical effect of denying or impairing the right of innocent passage to the ships of any third State;

14. *Calls upon* all States, and in particular flag, port and coastal States, States of the nationality of victims and perpetrators of piracy and armed robbery, and other States with relevant jurisdiction under international law and national legislation, to cooperate in determining jurisdiction, and in the investigation and prosecution of persons responsible for acts of piracy and armed robbery off the coast of Somalia, consistent with applicable international law including international human rights law, and to render assistance by, among other actions, providing disposition and logistics assistance with respect to persons under their jurisdiction and control, such victims and witnesses and persons detained as a result of operations conducted under this resolution;

15. *Notes* that the 1988 Convention for the Suppression of Unlawful Acts Against the Safety of Maritime Navigation ('SUA Convention') provides for parties to create criminal offences, establish jurisdiction, and accept delivery of persons responsible for or suspected of seizing or exercising control over a ship by force or threat thereof or any other form of intimidation; *urges* States parties to the SUA Convention to fully implement their obligations under said convention and cooperate with the Secretary-General and the IMO to build judicial capacity for the successful prosecution of persons suspected of piracy and armed robbery at sea off the coast of Somalia;

16. *Requests* States and regional organizations cooperating with the TFG to inform the Security Council and the Secretary-General within nine months of the progress of actions undertaken in the exercise of the authority provided in paragraph 10 above;

17. *Requests* the Secretary-General to report to the Security Council within 11 months of adoption of this resolution on the implementation of this resolution and on the situation with respect to piracy and armed robbery in territorial waters and the high seas off the coast of Somalia;

18. *Requests* the Secretary-General of the IMO to brief the Council on the basis of cases brought to his attention by the agreement of all affected coastal States, and duly

taking into account the existing bilateral and regional cooperative arrangements, on the situation with respect to piracy and armed robbery;

19. *Expresses* its intention to review the situation and consider, as appropriate, renewing the authority provided in paragraph 10 above for additional periods upon the request of the TFG;

20. *Decides* to remain seized of the matter.

UN Security Council Resolution 1851 (2008)

UN Doc. S/RES/1851 (2008) of 16 December 2008

The Security Council,

Recalling its previous resolutions concerning the situation in Somalia, especially resolutions 1814 (2008), 1816 (2008), 1838 (2008), 1844 (2008), and 1846 (2008),

Continuing to be gravely concerned by the dramatic increase in the incidents of piracy and armed robbery at sea off the coast of Somalia in the last six months, and by the threat that piracy and armed robbery at sea against vessels pose to the prompt, safe and effective delivery of humanitarian aid to Somalia, and *noting* that pirate attacks off the coast of Somalia have become more sophisticated and daring and have expanded in their geographic scope, notably evidenced by the hijacking of the M/V Sirius Star 500 nautical miles off the coast of Kenya and subsequent unsuccessful attempts well east of Tanzania,

Reaffirming its respect for the sovereignty, territorial integrity, political independence and unity of Somalia, including Somalia's rights with respect to offshore natural resources, including fisheries, in accordance with international law,

Further reaffirming that international law, as reflected in the United Nations Convention on the Law of the Sea of 10 December 1982 (UNCLOS), sets out the legal framework applicable to combating piracy and armed robbery at sea, as well as other ocean activities,

Again taking into account the crisis situation in Somalia, and the lack of capacity of the Transitional Federal Government (TFG) to interdict, or upon interdiction to prosecute pirates or to patrol and secure the waters off the coast of Somalia, including the international sea lanes and Somalia's territorial waters,

Noting the several requests from the TFG for international assistance to counter piracy off its coast, including the letter of 9 December 2008 from the President of Somalia requesting the international community to assist the TFG in taking all necessary measures to interdict those who use Somali territory and airspace to plan, facilitate or undertake acts of piracy and armed robbery at sea, and the 1 September 2008 letter from the President of Somalia to the Secretary-General of the UN expressing the appreciation of the TFG to the Security Council for its assistance and expressing the TFG's willingness to consider working with other States and regional organizations to combat piracy and armed robbery off the coast of Somalia,

Welcoming the launching of the EU operation Atalanta to combat piracy off the coast of Somalia and to protect vulnerable ships bound for Somalia, as well as the efforts by the North Atlantic Treaty Organization, and other States acting in a national capacity in cooperation with the TFG to suppress piracy off the coast of Somalia,

Also welcoming the recent initiatives of the Governments of Egypt, Kenya, and the Secretary-General's Special Representative for Somalia, and the United Nations Office on Drugs and Crime (UNODC) to achieve effective measures to remedy the causes, capabilities, and incidents of piracy and armed robbery off the coast of Somalia, and *emphasizing* the need for current and future counter-piracy operations to effectively coordinate their activities,

Noting with concern that the lack of capacity, domestic legislation, and clarity about how to dispose of pirates after their capture, has hindered more robust international action against the pirates off the coast of Somalia and in some cases led to pirates being released without facing justice, and *reiterating* that the 1988 Convention for the Suppression of Unlawful Acts Against the Safety of Maritime Navigation ('SUA Convention') provides for parties to create criminal offences, establish jurisdiction, and accept delivery of persons responsible for or suspected of seizing or exercising control over a ship by force or threat thereof or any other form of intimidation,

Welcoming the report of the Monitoring Group on Somalia of 20 November 2008 (S/2008/769), and *noting* the role piracy may play in financing embargo violations by armed groups,

Determining that the incidents of piracy and armed robbery at sea in the waters off the coast of Somalia exacerbate the situation in Somalia which continues to constitute a threat to international peace and security in the region,

Acting under Chapter VII of the Charter of the United Nations,

1. *Reiterates* that it condemns and deplores all acts of piracy and armed robbery against vessels in waters off the coast of Somalia;

2. *Calls* upon States, regional and international organizations that have the capacity to do so, to take part actively in the fight against piracy and armed robbery at sea off the coast of Somalia, in particular, consistent with this resolution, resolution 1846 (2008), and international law, by deploying naval vessels and military aircraft and through seizure and disposition of boats, vessels, arms and other related equipment used in the commission of piracy and armed robbery at sea off the coast of Somalia, or for which there are reasonable grounds for suspecting such use;

3. *Invites* all States and regional organizations fighting piracy off the coast of Somalia to conclude special agreements or arrangements with countries willing to take custody of pirates in order to embark law enforcement officials ('shipriders') from the latter countries, in particular countries in the region, to facilitate the investigation and prosecution of persons detained as a result of operations conducted under this resolution for acts of piracy and armed robbery at sea off the coast of Somalia, provided that the advance consent of the TFG is obtained for the exercise of third state jurisdiction by shipriders in Somali territorial waters and that such agreements or arrangements do not prejudice the effective implementation of the SUA Convention;

4. *Encourages* all States and regional organizations fighting piracy and armed robbery at sea off the coast of Somalia to establish an international cooperation mechanism to act as a common point of contact between and among states, regional and international organizations on all aspects of combating piracy and armed robbery at sea off Somalia's coast; and *recalls* that future recommendations on ways to ensure the long-term security of international navigation off the coast of Somalia, including the long-term security of WFP maritime deliveries to Somalia and a possible coordination and leadership role for the United Nations in this regard to rally Member States and regional organizations to counter piracy and armed robbery at sea off the coast of Somalia are to be detailed in a report by the Secretary-General no later than three months after the adoption of resolution 1846;

5. *Further encourages* all states and regional organizations fighting piracy and armed robbery at sea off the coast of Somalia to consider creating a centre in the region to coordinate information relevant to piracy and armed robbery at sea off the coast of Somalia, to increase regional capacity with assistance of UNODC to arrange effective

shiprider agreements or arrangements consistent with UNCLOS and to implement the SUA Convention, the United Nations Convention against Transnational Organized Crime and other relevant instruments to which States in the region are party, in order to effectively investigate and prosecute piracy and armed robbery at sea offences;

6. In response to the letter from the TFG of 9 December 2008, *encourages* Member States to continue to cooperate with the TFG in the fight against piracy and armed robbery at sea, *notes* the primary role of the TFG in rooting out piracy and armed robbery at sea, and *decides* that for a period of twelve months from the date of adoption of resolution 1846, States and regional organizations cooperating in the fight against piracy and armed robbery at sea off the coast of Somalia for which advance notification has been provided by the TFG to the Secretary-General may undertake all necessary measures that are appropriate in Somalia, for the purpose of suppressing acts of piracy and armed robbery at sea, pursuant to the request of the TFG, provided, however, that any measures undertaken pursuant to the authority of this paragraph shall be undertaken consistent with applicable international humanitarian and human rights law;

7. *Calls on* Member States to assist the TFG, at its request and with notification to the Secretary-General, to strengthen its operational capacity to bring to justice those who are using Somali territory to plan, facilitate or undertake criminal acts of piracy and armed robbery at sea, and *stresses* that any measures undertaken pursuant to this paragraph shall be consistent with applicable international human rights law;

8. *Welcomes* the communiqué issued by the International Conference on Piracy around Somalia held in Nairobi, Kenya, on 11 December 2008 and *encourages* Member States to work to enhance the capacity of relevant states in the region to combat piracy, including judicial capacity;

9. *Notes* with concern the findings contained in the 20 November 2008 report of the Monitoring Group on Somalia that escalating ransom payments are fuelling the growth of piracy in waters off the coast of Somalia, and that the lack of enforcement of the arms embargo established by resolution 733 (1992) has permitted ready access to the arms and ammunition used by the pirates and driven in part the phenomenal growth in piracy;

10. *Affirms* that the authorization provided in this resolution apply only with respect to the situation in Somalia and shall not affect the rights or obligations or responsibilities of Member States under international law, including any rights or obligations under UNCLOS, with respect to any other situation, and underscores in particular that this resolution shall not be considered as establishing customary international law, and *affirms further* that such authorizations have been provided only following the receipt of the 9 December 2008 letter conveying the consent of the TFG;

11. *Affirms* that the measures imposed by paragraph 5 of resolution 733 (1992) and further elaborated upon by paragraphs 1 and 2 or resolution 1425 (2002) shall not apply to weapons and military equipment destined for the sole use of Member States and regional organizations undertaking measures in accordance with paragraph 6 above;

12. *Urges* States in collaboration with the shipping and insurance industries, and the IMO to continue to develop avoidance, evasion, and defensive best practices and advisories to take when under attack or when sailing in waters off the coast of Somalia, and *further urges* States to make their citizens and vessels available for forensic investigation as appropriate at the first port of call immediately following an act or attempted act of piracy or armed robbery at sea or release from captivity;

13. *Decides* to remain seized of the matter.

Code of Conduct Concerning the Repression of Piracy and Armed Robbery against Ships in the Western Indian Ocean and the Gulf of Aden

Done in Djibouti, 29 January 2009; effective as from 29 January 2009
IMO Doc. C 120/14, 3 April 2009

The Governments of Comoros, Djibouti, Egypt, Eritrea, Ethiopia, France, Jordan, Kenya, Madagascar, Maldives, Mauritius, Mozambique, Oman, Saudi Arabia, Seychelles, Somalia, South Africa, Sudan, the United Arab Emirates, the United Republic of Tanzania and Yemen (hereinafter referred to as 'the Participants'),

Deeply concerned about the crimes of piracy and armed robbery against ships in the Western Indian Ocean and the Gulf of Aden and the grave dangers to the safety and security of persons and ships at sea and to the protection of the marine environment arising from such acts;

Reaffirming that international law, as reflected in UNCLOS, sets out the legal framework applicable to combating piracy and armed robbery at sea;

Noting that the Assembly of the International Maritime Organization (hereinafter referred to as 'IMO'), at its twenty-fifth regular session, adopted, on 27 November 2007, resolution A.1002(25) on Piracy and armed robbery against ships in waters off the coast of Somalia which, among other things, called upon Governments in the region to conclude, in co-operation with IMO, and implement, as soon as possible, a regional agreement to prevent, deter and suppress piracy and armed robbery against ships;

Noting also that the General Assembly of the United Nations, at its sixth-third session, adopted, on 5 December 2008, resolution 63/111 on Ocean and the law of the sea which amongst others:

— recognizes the crucial role of international cooperation at the global, regional, sub-regional and bilateral levels in combating, in accordance with international law, threats to maritime security, including piracy, armed robbery at sea, terrorist acts against shipping, offshore installations and other maritime interests, through bilateral and multilateral instruments and mechanisms aimed at monitoring, preventing and responding to such threats, the enhanced sharing of information among States relevant to the detection, prevention and suppression of such threats, the prosecution of offenders with due regard to national legislation and the need for sustained capacity-building to support such objectives;

— emphasizes the importance of prompt reporting of incidents to enable accurate information on the scope of the problem of piracy and armed robbery against ships and, in the case of armed robbery against ships, by affected vessels to the coastal State, underlines the importance of effective information-sharing with States potentially affected by incidents of piracy and armed robbery against ships, and takes note of the important role of the IMO;

— calls upon States to take appropriate steps under their national law to facilitate the apprehension and prosecution of those who are alleged to have committed acts of piracy;

— urges all States, in cooperation with the IMO, to actively combat piracy and armed robbery at sea by adopting measures, including those relating to assistance with capacity-building through training of seafarers, port staff and enforcement personnel in the prevention, reporting and investigation of incidents, bringing the alleged perpetrators to justice, in accordance with international law, and by adopting national legislation, as well as providing enforcement vessels and equipment and guarding against fraudulent ship registration;

— welcomes the significant decrease in the number of attacks by pirates and armed robbers in the Asian region through increased national, bilateral and trilateral initiatives as well as regional cooperative mechanisms, and calls upon other States to give immediate attention to adopting, concluding and implementing cooperation agreements on combating piracy and armed robbery against ships at the regional level;

— expresses serious concern regarding the problem of increased instances of piracy and armed robbery at sea off the coast of Somalia, expresses alarm in particular at the recent hijacking of vessels, supports the recent efforts to address this problem at the global and regional levels, notes the adoption by the Security Council of the United Nations of resolutions 1816 (2008) of 2 June 2008 and 1838 (2008) of 7 October 2008, and also notes that the authorization in resolution 1816 (2008) and the provisions in resolution 1838 (2008) apply only to the situation in Somalia and do not affect the rights, obligations or responsibilities of Member States of the United Nations under international law, including any rights or obligations under the United Nations Convention on the Law of the Sea (hereinafter referred to as 'UNCLOS'), with respect to any other situation, and underscores in particular that they are not to be considered as establishing customary international law;

— notes the initiatives of the Secretary-General of the IMO, following up on resolution A.1002(25) to engage the international community in efforts to combat acts of piracy and armed robbery against ships sailing the waters off the coast of Somalia; and

— urges States to ensure the full implementation of resolution A.1002(25) on acts of piracy and armed robbery against ships in waters off the coast of Somalia;

Noting further that the Security Council of the United Nations has adopted resolutions 1816 (2008), 1838 (2008), 1846 (2008) and 1851 (2008) in relation to piracy and armed robbery in waters off the coast of Somalia;

Recalling the Assembly of IMO, at its twenty-second regular session, adopted, on 29 November 2001, resolution A.922(22) on the Code of Practice for the Investigation of the Crimes of Piracy and Armed Robbery against Ships which amongst others invited Governments to develop, as appropriate, agreements and procedures to facilitate co-operation in applying efficient and effective measures to prevent acts of piracy and armed robbery against ships;

Taking into account the Special measures to enhance maritime security adopted on 12 December 2002 by the Conference of Contracting Governments to the International Convention for the Safety of Life at Sea, 1974 as amended, including the International Ship and Port Facility Security Code;

Inspired by the Regional Cooperation Agreement on Combating Piracy and Armed Robbery against Ships in Asia adopted in Tokyo, Japan on 11 November 2004;

Recognizing the urgent need to devise and adopt effective and practical measures for the suppression of piracy and armed robbery against ships;

Recalling that the Convention for the Suppression of Unlawful Acts Against the Safety of Maritime Navigation (hereinafter referred to as 'SUA Convention') provides for parties to create criminal offences, establish jurisdiction, and accept delivery or persons responsible for or suspected of seizing or exercising control over a ship by force or threat thereof or any other form of intimidation;

Desiring to promote greater regional co-operation between the Participants, and thereby enhance their effectiveness, in the prevention, interdiction, prosecution, and punishment of those persons engaging in piracy and armed robbery against ships on the basis of mutual respect for the sovereignty, sovereign rights, sovereign equality, jurisdiction, and territorial integrity of States;

Welcoming the initiatives of IMO, the United Nations Office on Drugs and Crime, the United Nations Development Programme, European Commission, League of Arab States, and other relevant international entities to provide training, technical assistance and other forms of capacity building to assist Governments, upon request, to adopt and implement practical measures to apprehend and prosecute those persons engaging in piracy and armed robbery against ships;

Welcoming the creation in New York on 14 January 2009 of the Contact Group on Piracy off the coast of Somalia which will help mobilize and co-ordinate contributions to international efforts in the fight against piracy and armed robbery against ships in the waters off the coast of Somalia, pursuant to United Nations Security Council resolution 1851(2008);

Noting further the need for a comprehensive approach to address the poverty and instability that create conditions conducive to piracy, which includes strategies for effective environmental conservation and fisheries management, and the need to address the possible environmental consequences of piracy;

Have agreed as follows:

Article 1 Definitions

For the purposes of this Code of conduct, unless the context otherwise requires:

1. 'Piracy' consists of any of the following acts:
   a.   any illegal acts of violence or detention, or any act of depredation, committed for private ends by the crew or the passengers of a private ship or a private aircraft, and directed:
      (i)   on the high seas, against another ship or aircraft, or against persons or property on board such ship or aircraft;
      (ii) against a ship, aircraft, persons or property in a place outside the jurisdiction of any State;
   b.   any act of voluntary participation in the operation of a ship or of an aircraft with knowledge of facts making it a pirate ship or aircraft;
   c.   any act of inciting or of intentionally facilitating an act described in subparagraph (a) or (b).

2. 'Armed robbery against ships' consists of any of the following acts:
   a.   unlawful act of violence or detention or any act of depredation, or threat thereof, other than an act of piracy, committed for private ends and directed against a ship or against persons or property on board such a ship, within a State's internal waters, archipelagic waters and territorial sea;
   b.   any act of inciting or of intentionally facilitating an act described in subparagraph (a).

3. 'Secretary-General' means the Secretary-General of the International Maritime Organization

Article 2 Purpose and Scope

1. Consistent with their available resources and related priorities, their respective national laws and regulations, and applicable rules of international law, the Participants intend to co-operate to the fullest possible extent in the repression of piracy and armed robbery against ships with a view towards:

(a) sharing and reporting relevant information;

(b) interdicting ships and/or aircraft suspected of engaging in piracy or armed robbery against ships;

(c) ensuring that persons committing or attempting to commit piracy or armed robbery against ships are apprehended and prosecuted; and

(d) facilitating proper care, treatment, and repatriation for seafarers, fishermen, other shipboard personnel and passengers subject to piracy or armed robbery against ships, particularly those who have been subjected to violence.

2. The Participants intend this Code of conduct to be applicable in relation to piracy and armed robbery in the Western Indian Ocean and the Gulf of Aden.

Article 3 Protection Measures for Ships

The Participants intend to encourage States, ship owners, and ship operators, where appropriate, to take protective measures against piracy and armed robbery against ships, taking into account the relevant international standards and practices, and, in particular, recommendations,[1] adopted by IMO.

Article 4 Measures to Repress Piracy

1. The provisions of this Article are intended to apply only to piracy.

2. For purposes of this Article and of Article 10, 'pirate ship' means a ship intended by the persons in dominant control to be used for the purpose of committing piracy, or if the ship has been used to commit any such act, so long as it remains under the control of those persons.

3. Consistent with Article 2, each Participant to the fullest possible extent intends to co-operate in:

(a) arresting, investigating, and prosecuting persons who have committed piracy or are reasonably suspected of committing piracy;

(b) seizing pirate ships and/or aircraft and the property on board such ships and/or aircraft; and

(c) rescuing ships, persons, and property subject to piracy.

4. Any Participant may seize a pirate ship beyond the outer limit of any State's territorial sea, and arrest the persons and seize the property on board.

5. Any pursuit of a ship, where there are reasonable grounds to suspect that the ship is engaged in piracy, extending in and over the territorial sea of a Participant is subject to the authority of that Participant. No Participant should pursue such a ship in or over the territory or territorial sea of any coastal State without the permission of that State.

6. Consistent with international law, the courts of the Participant which carries out a seizure pursuant to paragraph 4 may decide upon the penalties to be imposed, and may also determine the action to be taken with regard to the ship or property, subject to the rights of third parties acting in good faith.

7. The Participant which carried out the seizure pursuant to paragraph 4 may, subject to its national laws, and in consultation with other interested entities, waive its primary right to exercise jurisdiction and authorize any other Participant to enforce its laws against the ship and/or persons on board.

8. Unless otherwise arranged by the affected Participants, any seizure made in the territorial sea of a Participant pursuant to paragraph 5 should be subject to the jurisdiction of that Participant.

---

[1] Footnotes in original: (1) MSC/Circ.622/Rev.1 on Recommendations to Governments for preventing and suppressing piracy and armed robbery against ships as it may be revised. (2) MSC/Circ.623/Rev.3 on Guidance to shipowners and ship operators, shipmasters and crews on preventing and suppressing acts of piracy and armed robbery against ships as it may be revised.

Article 5 Measures to Repress Armed Robbery against Ships

1. The provisions of this Article are intended to apply only to armed robbery against ships.

2. The Participants intend for operations to suppress armed robbery against ships in the territorial sea and airspace of a Participant to be subject to the authority of that Participant, including in the case of hot pursuit from that Participant's territorial sea or archipelagic waters in accordance with Article 111 of UNCLOS.

3. The Participants intend for their respective focal points and Centres (as designated pursuant to Article 8) to communicate expeditiously alerts, reports, and information related to armed robbery against ships to other Participants and interested parties.

Article 6 Measures in All Cases

1. The Participants intend that any measures taken pursuant to this Code of conduct should be carried out by law enforcement or other authorized officials from warships or military aircraft, or from other ships or aircraft clearly marked and identifiable as being in government service and authorized to that effect.

2. The Participants recognize that multiple States, including the flag State, State of suspected origin of the perpetrators, the State of nationality of persons on board the ship, and the State of ownership of cargo may have legitimate interests in cases arising pursuant to Articles 4 and 5. Therefore, the Participants intend to liaise and co-operate with such States and other stakeholders, and to coordinate such activities with each other to facilitate the rescue, interdiction, investigation, and prosecution.

3. The Participants intend, to the fullest possible extent, to conduct and support the conduct of investigations in cases of piracy and armed robbery against ships taking into account the relevant international standards and practices, and, in particular, recommendations[2] adopted by IMO.

4. The Participants intend to co-operate to the fullest possible extent in medical and decedent affairs arising from operations in furtherance of the repression of piracy and armed robbery against ships.

Article 7 Embarked Officers

1. In furtherance of operations contemplated by this Code of conduct, a Participant may nominate law enforcement or other authorized officials (hereafter referred to as 'the embarked officers') to embark in the patrol ships or aircraft of another Participant (hereafter referred to as 'the host Participant') as may be authorized by the host Participant.

2. The embarked officers may be armed in accordance with their national law and policy and the approval of the host Participant.

3. When embarked, the host Participant should facilitate communications between the embarked officers and their headquarters, and should provide messing and quarters for the embarked officers aboard the patrol ships or aircraft in a manner consistent with host Participant personnel of the same rank.

4. Embarked officers may assist the host Participant and conduct operations from the host Participant ship or aircraft if expressly requested to do so by the host Participant, and only in the manner requested. Such request may only be made, agreed to, and acted upon in a manner that is not prohibited by the laws and policies of both Participants.

---

[2] Footnote in original: (3) Resolution A.922(22) on the Code of Practice for the Investigation of the Crimes of Piracy and Armed Robbery against Ships as it may be revised.

Article 8 Coordination and Information Sharing

1. Each Participant should designate a national focal point to facilitate coordinated, timely, and effective information flow among the Participants consistent with the purpose and scope of this Code of conduct. In order to ensure coordinated, smooth, and effective communications between their designated focal points, the Participants intend to use the piracy information exchange centres Kenya, United Republic of Tanzania and Yemen (hereinafter referred to as 'the Centres'). The Centres in Kenya and the United Republic of Tanzania will be situated in the maritime rescue co-ordination centre in Mombasa and the sub-regional co-ordination centre in Dar es Salaam, respectively. The Centre in Yemen will be situated in the regional maritime information centre to be established in Yemen based on the outcomes of the sub-regional meetings held by IMO in Sana'a in 2005 and Muscat in 2006 and Dar es Salaam. Each Centre and designated focal point should be capable of receiving and responding to alerts and requests for information or assistance at all times.

2. Each Participant intends to:

(a) declare and communicate to the other Participants its designated focal point at the time of signing this Code of conduct or as soon as possible after signing, and thereafter update the information as and when changes occur;

(b) provide and communicate to the other Participants the telephone numbers, telefax numbers, and e-mail addresses of its focal point, and, as appropriate, of its Centre and thereafter update the information as and when changes occur; and

(c) communicate to the Secretary-General the information referred to in subparagraphs (a) and (b) and thereafter update the information as and when changes occur.

3. Each Centre and focal point should be responsible for its communication with the other focal points and the Centres. Any focal point which has received or obtained information about an imminent threat of, or an incident of, piracy or armed robbery against ships should promptly disseminate an alert with all relevant information to the Centres. The Centres should disseminate appropriate alerts within their respective areas of responsibility regarding imminent threats or incidents to ships.

4. Each Participant should ensure the smooth and effective communication between its designated focal point, and other competent national authorities including search and rescue coordination centres, as well as relevant non-governmental organizations.

5. Each Participant should make every effort to require ships entitled to fly its flag and the owners and operators of such ships to promptly notify relevant national authorities, including the designated focal points and Centres, the appropriate search and rescue coordination centres and other relevant contact points[3], of incidents of piracy or armed robbery against ships.

6. Each Participant intends, upon the request of any other Participant, to respect the confidentiality of information transmitted from a Participant.

7. To facilitate implementation of this Code of conduct, the Participants intend to keep each other fully informed concerning their respective applicable laws and guidance, particularly those pertaining to the interdiction, apprehension, investigation, prosecution, and disposition of persons involved in piracy and armed robbery against ships. The Participants may also undertake and seek assistance to undertake publication of handbooks and convening of seminars and conferences in furtherance of this Code of conduct.

---

[3] Footnote in original: (4) For example the Maritime Liaison Office Bahrain (MARLO), the United Kingdom Maritime Trade Office Dubai (UKMTO).

Article 9 Incident Reporting

1. The Participants intend to undertake development of uniform reporting criteria in order to ensure that an accurate assessment of the threat of piracy and armed robbery in the Western Indian Ocean and the Gulf of Aden is developed taking into account the recommendations,[4] adopted by IMO. The Participants intend for the Centres to manage the collection and dissemination of this information in their respective geographic areas of responsibility.

2. Consistent with its laws and policies, a Participant conducting a boarding, investigation, prosecution, or judicial proceeding pursuant to this Code of conduct should promptly notify any affected flag and coastal States and the Secretary-General of the results.

3. The Participants intend for the Centres to:
   (a) collect, collate and analyze the information transmitted by the Participants concerning piracy and armed robbery against ships, including other relevant information relating to individuals and transnational organized criminal groups committing piracy and armed robbery against ships in their respective geographical areas of responsibility; and
   (b) prepare statistics and reports on the basis of the information gathered and analyzed under subparagraph (a), and to disseminate them to the Participants, the shipping community, and the Secretary-General.

Article 10 Assistance among Participants

1. A Participant may request any other Participant, through the Centres or directly, to co-operate in detecting any of the following persons, ships, or aircraft:
   (a) persons who have committed, or are reasonably suspected of committing, piracy;
   (b) persons who have committed, or are reasonably suspected of committing, armed robbery against ships;
   (c) pirate ships, where there are reasonable grounds to suspect that those ships are engaged in piracy; and
   (d) ships or persons who have been subjected to piracy or armed robbery against ships.

2. A Participant may also request any other Participant, through the Centres or directly, to take effective measures in response to reported piracy or armed robbery against ships.

3. Co-operative arrangements such as joint exercises or other forms of co-operation, as appropriate, may be undertaken as determined by the Participants concerned.

4. Capacity building co-operation may include technical assistance such as educational and training programmes to share experiences and best practice.

Article 11 Review of National Legislation

In order to allow for the prosecution, conviction and punishment of those involved in piracy or armed robbery against ships, and to facilitate extradition or handing over when prosecution is not possible, each Participant intends to review its national legislation with a view towards ensuring that there are national laws in place to criminalize piracy and armed robbery against ships, and adequate guidelines for the exercise of jurisdiction, conduct of investigations, and prosecutions of alleged offenders.

---

[4] Footnotes in original: (5) MSC/Circ.622/Rev.1 on Recommendations to Governments for preventing and suppressing piracy and armed robbery against ships as it may be revised. (6) MSC/Circ.623/Rev.3 on Guidance to shipowners and ship operators, shipmasters and crews on preventing and suppressing acts of piracy and armed robbery against ships as it may be revised.

Article 12 Dispute Settlement

The Participants intend to settle by consultation and peaceful means amongst each other any disputes that arise from the implementation of this Code of conduct.

Article 13 Consultations

Within two years of the effective date of this Code of conduct, and having designated the national focal points referred to in Article 8, the Participants intend to consult, with the assistance of IMO, with the aim of arriving at a binding agreement.

Article 14 Claims

Any claim for damages, injury or loss resulting from an operation carried out under this Code of conduct should be examined by the Participant whose authorities conducted the operation. If responsibility is established, the claim should be resolved in accordance with the national law of that Participant, and in a manner consistent with international law, including Article 106 and paragraph 3 of Article 110 of UNCLOS.

Article 15 Miscellaneous Provisions

Nothing in this Code of conduct is intended to:

(a) create or establish a binding agreement, except as noted in Article 13;

(b) affect in any way the rules of international law pertaining to the competence of States to exercise investigative or enforcement jurisdiction on board ships not flying their flag;

(c) affect the immunities of warships and other government ships operated for non-commercial purposes;

(d) apply to or limit boarding of ships conducted by any Participant in accordance with international law, beyond the outer limit of any State's territorial sea, including boardings based upon the right of visit, the rendering of assistance to persons, ships and property in distress or peril, or an authorization from the flag State to take law enforcement or other action;

(e) preclude the Participants from otherwise agreeing on operations or other forms of co-operation to repress piracy and armed robbery against ships;

(f) prevent the Participants from taking additional measures to repress piracy and armed robbery at sea through appropriate actions in their land territory;

(g) supersede any bilateral or multilateral agreement or other co-operative mechanism concluded by the Participants to repress piracy and armed robbery against ships;

(h) alter the rights and privileges due to any individual in any legal proceeding;

(i) create or establish any waiver of any rights that any Participant may have under international law to raise a claim with any other Participant through diplomatic channels;

(j) entitle a Participants to undertake in the territory of another Participant the exercise of jurisdiction and performance of functions which are exclusively reserved for the authorities of that other Participant by its national law;

(k) prejudice in any manner the positions and navigational rights and freedoms of any Participant regarding the international law of the sea;

(l) be deemed a waiver, express or implied, of any of the privileges and immunities of the Participants to this Code of conduct as provided under international or national law; or

(m) preclude or limit any Participant from requesting or granting assistance in accordance with the provisions of any applicable Mutual Legal Assistance Agreement or similar instrument.

Article 16 Signature and Effective Date

The Code of conduct is open for signature by Participants on 29 January 2009 and at the Headquarters of IMO from 1 February 2009.

The Code of conduct will become effective upon the date of signature by two or more Participants and effective for subsequent Participants upon their respective date of deposit of a signature instrument with the Secretary-General.

Article 17 Languages

This Code of Conduct is established in the Arabic, English and French languages, each text being equally authentic.

DONE in Djibouti this twenty-ninth day of January two thousand and nine

IN WITNESS WHEREOF the undersigned, being duly authorized by their respective Governments for that purpose, have signed this Code of conduct.

APPENDIX 1: RATIFICATIONS OF THE UNITED NATIONS CONVENTION ON THE LAW OF THE SEA AND ITS IMPLEMENTATION AGREEMENTS

(as at 1 June 2009)

Country	UNCLOS	IA 1994	IA 1995	Country	UNCLOS	IA 1994	IA 1995
Afghanistan	*[1]			Albania	23.06.2003	23.06.2003	
Algeria	11.06.1996	11.06.1996		Andorra			
Angola	05.12.1990			Antigua and Barbuda	02.02.1989		
Argentina	01.12.1995	01.12.1995	*	Armenia	09.12.2002	09.12.2002	
Australia	05.10.1994	05.10.1994	23.12.1999	Austria	14.07.1995	14.07.1995	19.12.2003
Azerbaijan				Bahamas	29.07.1983	28.07.1995	16.01.1997
Bahrain	30.05.1985			Bangladesh	27.07.2001	27.07.2001	*
Barbados	12.10.1993	28.07.1995	22.09.2000	Belarus	30.08.2006	30.08.2006	
Belgium	13.11.1998	13.11.1998	19.12.2003	Belize	13.08.1983	21.10.1994	14.07.2005
Benin	16.10.1997	16.10.1997		Bhutan	*		
Bolivia	28.04.1995	28.04.1995		Bosnia and Herzegovina	12.01.1994		
Botswana	02.05.1990	31.01.2005		Brazil	22.12.1988	25.10.2007	08.03.2000
Brunei Darussalam	05.11.1996	05.11.1996		Bulgaria	15.05.1996	15.05.1996	13.12.2006
Burkina Faso	25.01.2005	25.01.2005	*	Burundi	*		
Cambodia	*			Cameroon	19.11.1985	28.08.2002	
Canada	07.11.2003	07.11.2003	03.08.1999	Cape Verde	10.08.1987	23.04.2008	
Central African Republic	*			Chad	*		
Chile	25.08.1997	25.08.1997		China	07.06.1996	07.06.1996	*
Colombia	*			Comoros	21.06.1994		
Congo	09.07.2008	09.07.2008		Cook Islands	15.02.1995	15.02.1995	01.04.1999
Costa Rica	21.09.1992	20.09.2001	18.06.2001	Côte d'Ivoire	26.03.1984	28.07.1995	*
Croatia	05.04.1995	05.04.1995		Cuba	15.08.1984	17.10.2002	
Cyprus	12.12.1988	27.07.1995	25.09.2002	Czech Republic	21.06.1996	21.06.1996	19.03.2007
DPR of Korea	*			DR of the Congo	17.02.1989		
Denmark	16.11.2004	16.11.2004	19.12.2003	Djibouti	08.10.1991		
Dominica	24.10.1991			Dominican Republic	*		
Ecuador				Egypt	26.08.1983	*	*
El Salvador	*			Equatorial Guinea	21.07.1997	21.07.1997	
Eritrea				Estonia	26.08.2005	26.08.2005	07.08.2006
Ethiopia	*			European Community	01.04.1998	01.04.1998	19.12.2003
Fiji	10.12.1982	28.07.1995	12.12.1996	Finland	21.06.1996	21.06.1996	19.12.2003
France	11.04.1996	11.04.1996	19.12.2003	Gabon	11.03.1998	11.03.1998	*
Gambia	22.05.1984			Georgia	21.03.1996	21.03.1996	
Germany	14.10.1994	14.10.1994	19.12.2003	Ghana	07.06.1983		
Greece	21.07.1995	21.07.1995	19.12.2003	Grenada	25.04.1991	28.07.1995	
Guatemala	11.02.1997	11.02.1997		Guinea	06.09.1985	28.07.1995	16.09.2005

---

[1] * indicates that the treaty has been signed but not yet ratified.

Country	UNCLOS	IA 1994	IA 1995	Country	UNCLOS	IA 1994	IA 1995
Guinea-Bissau	25.08.1986		*	Guyana	16.11.1993	25.09.2008	
Haiti	31.07.1996	31.07.1996		Honduras	05.10.1993	28.07.2003	
Hungary	05.02.2002	05.02.2002	16.05.2008	Iceland	21.06.1985	28.07.1995	14.02.1997
India	29.06.1995	29.06.1995	19.08.2003	Indonesia	03.02.1986	02.06.2000	*
Iran	*		17.04.1998	Iraq	30.07.1985		
Ireland	21.06.1996	21.06.1996	19.12.2003	Israel			*
Italy	13.01.1995	13.01.1995	19.12.2003	Jamaica	21.03.1983	28.07.1995	*
Japan	20.06.1996	20.06.1996	07.08.2006	Jordan	27.11.1995	27.11.1995	
Kazakhstan				Kenya	02.03.1989	29.07.1994	13.07.2004
Kiribati	24.02.2003	24.02.2003	15.09.2005	Kuwait	02.05.1986	02.08.2002	
Kyrgyzstan				Lao PDR	05.06.1998	05.06.1998	
Latvia	23.12.2004	23.12.2004	05.02.2007	Lebanon	05.01.1995	05.01.1995	
Lesotho	31.05.2007	31.05.2007		Liberia	25.09.2008	25.09.2008	16.09.2005
Libyan Arab Jamahiriya	*			Liechtenstein	*		
Lithuania	12.11.2003	12.11.2003	01.03.2007	Luxembourg	05.10.2000	05.10.2000	19.12.2003
Madagascar	22.08.2001	22.08.2001		Malawi	*		
Malaysia	14.10.1996	14.10.1996		Maldives	07.09.2000	07.09.2000	30.12.1998
Mali	16.07.1985			Malta	20.05.1993	26.06.1996	11.11.2001
Marshall Islands	09.08.1991		19.03.2003	Mauritania	17.07.1996	17.07.1996	*
Mauritius	04.11.1994	04.11.1994	25.03.1997	Mexico	18.03.1983	10.04.2003	
Micronesia	29.04.1991	06.09.1995	23.05.1997	Moldova	06.02.2007	06.02.2007	
Monaco	20.03.1996	20.03.1996	09.06.1999	Mongolia	13.08.1996	13.08.1996	
Montenegro	23.10.2006	23.10.2006		Morocco	31.05.2007	31.05.2007	*
Mozambique	13.03.1997	13.03.1997	10.12.2008	Myanmar	21.05.1996	21.05.1996	
Namibia	18.04.1983	28.07.1995	08.04.1998	Nauru	23.01.1996	23.01.1996	10.01.1997
Nepal	02.11.1998	02.11.1998		Netherlands	28.6.1996²	28.06.1996	19.12.2003
New Zealand	19.07.1996	19.07.1996	18.04.2001	Nicaragua	03.05.2000	03.05.2000	
Niger	*			Nigeria	14.08.1986	28.07.1995	
Niue	11.10.2006	11.10.2006	11.10.2006	Norway	24.06.1996	24.06.1996	30.12.1996
Oman	17.08.1989	26.02.1997	14.05.2008	Pakistan	26.02.1997	26.02.1997	*
Palau	30.09.1996	30.09.1996	26.03.2008	Panama	01.07.1996	01.07.1996	16.12.2008
Papua New Guinea	14.01.1997	14.01.1997	04.06.1999	Paraguay	26.09.1986	10.07.1995	
Peru				Philippines	08.05.1984	23.07.1997	*
Poland	13.11.1998	13.11.1998	14.03.2006	Portugal	03.11.1997	03.11.1997	19.12.2003
Qatar	09.12.2002	09.12.2002		Republic of Korea	29.01.1996	29.01.1996	01.02.2008
Romania	17.12.1996	17.12.1996	16.07.2007	Russian Federation	12.03.1997	12.03.1997	04.08.1997
Rwanda	*			Saint Kitts and Nevis	07.01.1993		
Saint Lucia	27.03.1985		09.08.1996	Saint Vincent and the Grenadines	01.10.1993		
Samoa	14.08.1995	14.08.1995	25.10.1996	San Marino			
Sao Tome and Principe	03.11.1987			Saudi Arabia	24.04.1996	24.04.1996	
Senegal	25.10.1984	25.07.1995	30.01.1997	Serbia	12.03.2001	28.07.1995	
Seychelles	16.09.1991	15.12.1994	20.03.1998	Sierra Leone	12.12.1994	12.12.1994	

² For the Netherlands Antilles, 13 February 2009.

Country	UNCLOS	IA 1994	IA 1995	Country	UNCLOS	IA 1994	IA 1995
Singapore	17.11.1994	17.11.1994		Slovakia	08.05.1996	08.05.1996	06.11.2008
Slovenia	16.06.1995	16.06.1995	15.06.2006	Solomon Islands	23.06.1997	23.06.1997	13.02.1997
Somalia	24.07.1989			South Africa	23.12.1997	23.12.1997	14.08.2003
Spain	15.01.1997	15.01.1997	19.12.2003	Sri Lanka	19.07.1994	28.07.1995	24.10.1996
Sudan	23.01.1985	*		Suriname	09.07.1998	09.07.1998	
Swaziland	*	*		Sweden	25.06.1996	25.06.1996	19.12.2003
Switzerland	01.05.2009	01.05.2009		Syrian Arab Republic			
Tajikistan				Thailand	*		
The FYR of Macedonia	19.08.1994	19.08.1994		Timor-Leste			
Togo	16.04.1985	28.07.1995		Tonga	02.08.1995	02.08.1995	31.07.1996
Trinidad and Tobago	25.04.1986	28.07.1995	13.09.2006	Tunisia	24.04.1985	24.05.2002	
Turkey				Turkmenistan			
Tuvalu	09.12.2002	09.12.2002	02.02.2009	Uganda	09.11.1990	28.07.1995	*
Ukraine	26.07.1999	26.07.1999	27.02.2003	United Arab Emirates	*		
United Kingdom	25.07.1997	25.07.1997	10.12.2001, 19.12.2003	United Rep. of Tanzania	30.09.1985	25.06.1998	
United States of America		*	21.08.1996	Uruguay	10.12.1992	07.08.2007	10.09.1999
Uzbekistan				Vanuatu	10.08.1999	10.08.1999	*
Vatican City				Venezuela			
Viet Nam	25.07.1994	27.04.2006		Yemen	21.07.1987		
Zambia	07.03.1983	28.07.1995		Zimbabwe	24.02.1993	28.07.1995	

APPENDIX 2: DECLARATIONS AND STATEMENTS UNDER ARTICLES 287, 298 AND 310 OF THE UNITED NATIONS CONVENTION ON THE LAW OF THE SEA

(Unless otherwise indicated, the declarations were made upon ratification, formal confirmation, accession or succession)[1]

ALGERIA

[...] The People's Democratic Republic of Algeria does not consider itself bound by the provisions of article 287, paragraph 1 (b), of the United Nations Convention on the Law of the Sea dealing with the submission of disputes to the International Court of Justice.

The People's Democratic Republic of Algeria declares that, in order to submit a dispute to the International Court of Justice, prior agreement between all the parties concerned is necessary in each case.

The Algerian Government declares that, in conformity with the provisions of Part II, section 3, subsections A and C, of the Convention, the passage of warships in the territorial sea of Algeria is subject to an authorization fifteen (15) days in advance, except in cases of force majeure as provided for in the Convention.

ANGOLA

The Government of the People's Republic of Angola reserves the right to interpret any and all articles of the Convention in the context of and with due regard to Angolan Sovereignty and territorial integrity as it applies to land, space and sea. Details of these interpretations will be placed on record at the time of ratification of the Convention. [...].[2]

ARGENTINA

(a) With regard to those provisions of the Convention which deal with innocent passage through the territorial sea, it is the intention of the Government of the Argentine Republic to continue to apply the regime currently in force to the passage of foreign warships through the Argentine territorial sea, since that regime is totally compatible with the provisions of the Convention.

(b) With regard to Part III of the Convention, the Argentine Government declares that in the Treaty of Peace and Friendship signed with the Republic of Chile on 29 November 1984, which entered into force on 2 May 1985 and was registered with the United Nations Secretariat in accordance with Article 102 of the Charter of the United Nations, both States reaffirmed the validity of Article V of the Boundary Treaty of 1881 whereby the Strait of Magellan (Estrecho de Magallanes) is neutralized forever with free navigation assured for the flags of all nations. The aforementioned Treaty of Peace and Friendship also contains specific provisions and a special annex on navigation which includes regulations for vessels flying the flags of third countries in the Beagle Channel and other straits and channels of the Tierra del Fuego archipelago.

(c) The Argentine Republic accepts the provisions on the conservation and management of the living resources of the high seas, but considers that they are insufficient, particularly the provisions relating to straddling fish stocks or highly migratory fish stocks,

---

[1] Statements that are not related to the law of the sea such as non-recognition statements have been omitted. For the full text of all statements see http://www.un.org/Depts/los/convention_agreements/convention_declarations.htm.
[2] Declaration made upon signature on 10 December 1982.

and that they should be supplemented by an effective and binding multilateral regime which, *inter alia*, would facilitate cooperation to prevent and avoid overfishing, and would permit the monitoring of the activities of fishing vessels on the high seas and of the use of fishing methods and gear. The Argentine Government, bearing in mind its priority interest in conserving the resources of its exclusive economic zone and the area of the high seas adjacent thereto, considers that, in accordance with the provisions of the Convention, where the same stock or stocks of associated species occur both within the exclusive economic zone and in the area of the high seas adjacent thereto, the Argentine Republic, as the coastal State, and other States fishing for such stocks in the area adjacent to its exclusive economic zone should agree upon the measures necessary for the conservation of those stocks or stocks of associated species in the high seas.

Independently of this, it is the understanding of the Argentine Government that, in order to comply with the obligation laid down in the Convention concerning the conservation of the living resources in its exclusive economic zone and the area adjacent thereto, it is authorized to adopt, in accordance with international law, all the measures it may deem necessary for the purpose.

(d) The ratification of the Convention by the Argentine Government does not imply acceptance of the Final Act of the Third United Nations Conference on the Law of the Sea. In that regard, the Argentine Republic, as in its written statement of 8 December 1982 (A/CONF.62/WS/35), places on record its reservation to the effect that resolution III, in annex I to the Final Act, in no way affects the 'Question of the Falkland Islands (Malvinas)', which is governed by the following specific resolutions of the General Assembly: 2065 (XX), 3160 (XXVIII), 31/49, 37/9, 38/12, 39/6, 40/21, 41/40, 42/19, 43/25, and Assembly decisions: 44/406, 45/424, 46/406, 47/408 and 48/408, adopted within the framework of the decolonization process.

In this connection, and bearing in mind that the Malvinas and the South Sandwich and South Georgia Islands form an integral part of Argentine territory, the Argentine Government declares that it neither recognizes nor will recognize the title of any other State, community or entity or the exercise by it of any right of maritime jurisdiction which is claimed to be protected under any interpretation of resolution III that violates the rights of Argentina over the Malvinas and the South Sandwich and South Georgia islands and their respective maritime zones. Consequently, it likewise neither recognizes nor will recognize and will consider null and void any activity or measure that may be carried out or adopted without its consent with regard to this question, which the Argentine Government considers to be of major importance.

The Argentine Government will accordingly interpret the occurrence of acts of the kind referred to above as contrary to the aforementioned resolutions adopted by the United Nations, the objective of which is the peaceful settlement of the sovereignty dispute concerning the islands by means of bilateral negotiations and through the good offices of the Secretary-General of the United Nations.

The Argentine Republic reaffirms its legitimate and inalienable sovereignty over the Malvinas and the South Georgia and South Sandwich islands and their respective maritime and island zones, which form an integral part of its national territory. The recovery of those territories and the full exercise of sovereignty, respecting the way of life of the inhabitants of the territories and in accordance with the principles of international law, constitute a permanent objective of the Argentine people that cannot be renounced.

Furthermore, it is the understanding of the Argentine Republic that the Final Act, in referring in paragraph 42 to the Convention together with resolutions I to IV as forming an integral whole, is merely describing the procedure that was followed at the Conference to avoid a series of separate votes on the Convention and the resolutions. The Convention itself clearly establishes in article 318 that only the Annexes form an integral part of the Convention; thus, any other instrument or document, even one adopted by the Conference, does not form an integral part of the United Nations Convention on the Law of the Sea.[3]

(e) The Argentine Republic fully respects the right of free navigation as embodied in the Convention; however, it considers that the transit by sea of vessels carrying highly radioactive substances must be duly regulated.

The Argentine Government accepts the provisions on prevention of pollution of the marine environment contained in Part XII of the Convention, but considers that, in the light of events subsequent to the adoption of that international instrument, the measures to prevent, control and minimize the effects of the pollution of the sea by noxious and potentially dangerous substances and highly active radioactive substances must be supplemented and reinforced.

(f) In accordance with the provisions of article 287, the Argentine Government declares that it accepts, in order of preference, the following means for the settlement of disputes concerning the interpretation or application of the Convention: (a) the International Tribunal for the Law of the Sea; (b) an arbitral tribunal constituted in accordance with Annex VIII for questions relating to fisheries, protection and preservation of the marine environment, marine scientific research and navigation, in accordance with Annex VIII, article 1. The Argentine Government also declares that it does not accept the procedures provided for in Part XV, section 2, with respect to the disputes specified in article 298, paragraph 1 (a), (b) and (c).

AUSTRALIA

The Government of Australia declares, under paragraph 1 of article 287 of the United Nations Convention on the Law of the Sea [...] that it chooses the following means for the settlement of disputes concerning the interpretation or application of the Convention, without specifying that on has precedence over the other:

(a) The International Tribunal for the Law of the Sea established in accordance with Annex VI of the Convention; and

(b) The International Court of Justice.

The Government of Australia further declares, under paragraph 1 (a) of article 298 of the United Nations Convention on the Law of the Sea [...], that it does not accept any of the procedures provided for in section 2 of Part XV (including the procedures referred to in paragraphs (a) and (b) of this declaration) with respect of disputes concerning the interpretation or application of articles 15, 74 and 83 relating to sea boundary delimitations as well as those involving historic bays or titles.

These declarations by the Government of Australia are effective immediately.[4]

AUSTRIA

In the absence of any other peaceful means to which it would give preference, the Government of the Republic of Austria hereby chooses one of the following means for the settlement of disputes concerning the interpretation or application of the two Conventions in accordance with article 287 of the Convention on the Law of the Sea, in the following order:

1. The International Tribunal for the Law of the Sea established in accordance with Annex VI;

---

[3] Paragraph (d), with the exception of subparagraph 4, is largely identical with the Argentine declaration made upon signature on 5 October 1984 which has been omitted.

[4] Declaration under articles 287 and 298 made after ratification, on 22 March 2002.

2. A special arbitral tribunal constituted in accordance with Annex VIII;

3. The International Court of Justice.

Also in the absence of any other peaceful means, the Government of the Republic of Austria hereby recognizes as of today the validity of special arbitration for any dispute concerning the interpretation or application of the Convention on the Law of the Sea relating to fisheries, protection and pre2servation of the marine environment, marine scientific research and navigation, including pollution from vessels and by dumping.

The Permanent Mission of Austria to the United Nations would like to draw the attention of the Secretary-General to the fact that, as a member of the European Union, Austria has transferred competence to the Union in certain matters governed by the Convention. A detailed declaration on the nature and extent of the competence transferred to the European Union will be made in due course in accordance with the provisions of Annex IX of the Convention.

BANGLADESH

1. The Government of the People's Republic of Bangladesh understands that the provisions of the Convention do not authorize other States to carry out in the exclusive economic zone and on the continental shelf military exercise or manoeuvres, in particular, those involving the use of weapons or explosives, without the consent of the coastal State.

2. The Bangladesh Government is not bound by any domestic legislation or by any declaration issued by other States upon signature or ratification of this Convention. Bangladesh reserves the right to state its position concerning all such legislation or declarations at the appropriate time. In particular, Bangladesh ratification of the Convention in no way constitutes recognition of the maritime claims of any other State having signed or ratified the Convention, where such claims are inconsistent with the relevant principles of international law and which are prejudicial to the sovereign rights and jurisdiction of Bangladesh in its maritime areas.

3. The exercise of the right of innocent passage of warships through the territorial sea of other States should also be perceived to be a peaceful one. Effective and speedy means of communication are easily available and make the prior notification of the exercise of the right of innocent passage of warships reasonable and not incompatible with the Convention. Such notification is already required by some States. Bangladesh reserves the right to legislate on this point.

4. Bangladesh is of the view that such a notification requirement is needed in respect of nuclear-powered ships or ships carrying nuclear or other inherently dangerous or noxious substances. Furthermore, no such ships shall be allowed within Bangladesh waters without the necessary authorization.

5. Bangladesh is of the view that the sovereign immunity as envisaged in article 236 does not relieve a State from the obligation, moral or otherwise, in accepting responsibility and liability for compensation and relief in respect of damage caused by pollution of the marine environment by any warship, naval auxiliary, other vessels or aircraft owned or operated by the State and used on government non-commercial service.

6. Ratification of the Convention by Bangladesh does not *ipso facto* imply recognition or acceptance of any territorial claim made by a State party to the Convention, nor automatic recognition of any land or sea border.

7. The Bangladesh Government does not consider itself bound by any of the declarations or statements, however phrased or named, made by other States when signing, accepting, ratifying or acceding to the Convention and that it reserves the right to state its position on any of those declarations or statements at any time.

8. The Bangladesh Government declares, without prejudice to article 303 of the Convention on the Law of the Sea, that any objects of an archaeological and historical nature found within the maritime areas over which it exercises sovereignty or jurisdiction shall not be removed, without its prior notification and consent.

9. The Government of Bangladesh shall, at an appropriate time, make declarations provided for in articles 287 and 298 relating to the settlement of disputes.

10. The Government of Bangladesh intends to undertake a comprehensive review of existing domestic laws and regulations with a view to harmonizing them with the provisions of the Convention.

BELARUS

1. In accordance with article 287 of the Convention, the Republic of Belarus accepts as the basic means for the settlement of disputes concerning the interpretation or application of the Convention an arbitral tribunal constituted in accordance with Annex VII. For the settlement of disputes concerning fisheries, protection and preservation of the marine environment, marine scientific research or navigation, including pollution from vessels and by dumping, the Republic of Belarus will use a special arbitral tribunal constituted in accordance with Annex VIII. The Republic of Belarus recognizes the jurisdiction of the International Tribunal for the Law of the Sea over questions concerning the prompt release of detained vessels or their crews, as envisaged in article 292 of the Convention;

2. In accordance with article 298 of the Convention, the Republic of Belarus does not accept compulsory procedures entailing binding decisions for the consideration of disputes concerning military activities, including by government vessels and aircraft engaged in non-commercial service, or disputes concerning law enforcement activities in regard to the exercise of sovereign rights or jurisdiction, or disputes in respect of which the Security Council of the United Nations is exercising the functions assigned to it by the Charter of the United Nations.[5]

BELGIUM

The Government of the Kingdom of Belgium has decided to sign the United Nations Convention on the Law of the Sea because the Convention has a very large number of positive features and achieves a compromise on them which is acceptable to most States. Nevertheless, with regard to the status of maritime space, it regrets that the concept of equity, adopted for the delimitation of the continental shelf and the exclusive economic zone, was not applied again in the provisions for delimiting the territorial sea. It welcomes, however, the distinctions established by the Convention between the nature of the rights which riparian States exercise over their territorial sea, on the one hand, and over the continental shelf and their exclusive economic zone, on the other.

It is common knowledge that the Belgian Government cannot declare itself also satisfied with certain provisions of the international régime of the sea-bed which, though based on a principle that it would not think of challenging, seems not to have chosen the most suitable way of achieving the desired result as quickly and surely as possible, at the risk of jeopardizing the success of a generous undertaking which Belgium consistently encourages and supports. Indeed, certain provisions of Part XI and of Annexes III and IV

---

[5] Upon signature on 10 December 1982, the Byelorussian Soviet Socialist Republic had declared, inter alia, that 'in accordance with article 298 of the Convention, it does not accept compulsory procedures entailing binding decisions in the consideration of disputes concerned with the delimitation of marine limits, disputes relating to military activity and disputes in relation to which the United Nations Security Council performs functions entrusted to it under the United Nations Charter.'

appear to it to be marred by serious defects and shortcomings which explain why consensus was not reached on this text at the last session of the Third United Nations Conference on the Law of the Sea, in New York, in April 1982. These shortcomings and defects concern in particular the restriction of access to the Area, the limitations on production and certain procedures for the transfer of technology, not to mention the vexatious implications of the cost and financing of the future International Sea-Bed Authority and the first mine site of the Enterprise. The Belgian Government sincerely hopes that these shortcomings and defects will in fact be rectified by the rules, regulations and procedures which the Preparatory Commission should draw up with the twofold intent of facilitating acceptance of the new régime by the whole international community and enabling the common heritage of mankind to be properly exploited for the benefit of all and, preferably, for the benefit of the least favoured countries. The Government of the Kingdom of Belgium is not alone in thinking that the success of this new régime, the effective establishment of the International Sea-Bed Authority and the economic viability of the Enterprise will depend to a large extent on the quality and seriousness of the Preparatory Commission's work: it therefore considers that all decisions of the Commission should be adopted by consensus, that being the only way of protecting the legitimate interests of all.

As the representatives of France and the Netherlands pointed out two years ago, the Belgian Government wishes to make it abundantly clear that, notwithstanding its decision to sign the Convention today, the Kingdom of Belgium is not here and now determined to ratify it. It will take a separate decision on this point at a later date, which will take account of what the Preparatory Commission has accomplished to make the international régime of the sea-bed acceptable to all, focusing mainly on the questions to which attention has been drawn above.

The Belgian Government also wishes to recall that Belgium is a member of the European Economic Community, to which it has transferred powers in certain areas covered by the Convention; detailed declarations on the nature and extent of the powers transferred will be made in due course, in accordance with the provisions of Annex IX of the Convention.

It also wishes to draw attention formally to several points which it considers particularly crucial. For example, it attaches great importance to the conditions to which Articles 21 and 23 of the Convention subject the right of innocent passage through the territorial sea, and it intends to ensure that the criteria prescribed by the relevant international agreements are strictly applied, whether the flag States are parties thereto or not. The limitation of the breadth of the territorial sea, as established by Article 3 of the Convention, confirms and codifies a widely observed customary practice which it is incumbent on every State to respect, as it is the only one admitted by international law: the Government of the Kingdom of Belgium will not therefore recognize, as territorial sea, waters which are, or may be, claimed to be such beyond 12 nautical miles measured from baselines determined by the riparian State in accordance with the Convention. Having underlined the close linkage which it perceives between Article 33, paragraph 1 (a), and Article 27, paragraph 2, of the Convention, the Government of the Kingdom of Belgium intends to reserve the right, in emergencies and especially in cases of blatant violation, to exercise the powers accorded to the riparian State by the latter text, without notifying beforehand a diplomatic agent or consular officer of the flag State, on the understanding that such notification shall be given as soon as it is physically possible. Finally, everyone will understand that the Government of the Kingdom of Belgium chooses to emphasize those provisions of the Convention which entitle it to protect itself, beyond the limit of the territorial sea, against any threat of pollution and, *a fortiori*, against any existing pollution resulting from an accident at sea, as well as those provisions which recognize the validity of rights and obligations deriving from specific conventions and agreements concluded previously or which may be concluded subsequently in furtherance of the general principles set forth in the Convention.

In the absence of any other peaceful means to which it obviously gives priority, the Government of the Kingdom of Belgium deems it expedient to choose alternatively, and in order of preference, as Article 287 of the Convention leaves it free to do, the following means of settling disputes concerning the interpretation or application of the Convention:

1. an arbitral tribunal constituted in accordance with Annex VIII;
2. the International Tribunal for the Law of the Sea established in accordance with Annex VI;
3. the International Court of Justice.

Still in the absence of any other peaceful means, the Government of the Kingdom of Belgium wishes here and now to recognize the validity of the special arbitration procedure for any dispute concerning the interpretation or application of the provisions of the Convention in respect of fisheries, protection and preservation of the marine environment, marine scientific research or navigation, including pollution from vessels and by dumping.

For the time being, the Belgian Government does not wish to make any declaration in accordance with Article 298, confining itself to the one made above in accordance with Article 287. Finally, the Government of the Kingdom of Belgium does not consider itself bound by any of the declarations which other States have made, or may make, upon signing or ratifying the Convention, reserving the right, as necessary, to determine its position with regard to each of them at the appropriate time.[6]

The Kingdom of Belgium notes that, as a State member of the European Community, it has transferred competence to the Community for some matters provided for in the Convention, which are listed in the declaration made by the European Community upon formal confirmation of the Convention by the European Community on 1 April 1998.

In accordance with article 287 of the Convention, the Kingdom of Belgium hereby declares that it chooses, as a means for the settlement of disputes concerning the interpretation or application of the Convention, in view of its preference for pre-established jurisdictions, either the International Tribunal for the Law of the Sea established in accordance with Annex VI (art. 287.1 (a)) or the International Court of Justice (art. 287.1(b)), in the absence of any other means of peaceful settlement of disputes that it might prefer.

BOLIVIA

1. The Convention on the Law of the Sea is a perfectible instrument and, according to its own provisions, is subject to revision. As a party to it, Bolivia will, when the time comes, put forward proposals and revisions which are in keeping with its national interests.

2. Bolivia is confident that the Convention will ensure, in the near future, the joint development of the resources of the sea-bed, with equal opportunities and rights for all nations, especially developing countries.

3. Freedom of access to and from the sea, which the Convention grants to land-locked nations, is a right that Bolivia has been exercising by virtue of bilateral treaties and will continue to exercise by virtue of the norms of positive international law contained in the Convention.

4. Bolivia wishes to place on record that it is a country that has no maritime sovereignty as a result of a war and not as a result of its natural geographic position and

---

[6] Declaration made upon signature on 5 December 1984.

that it will assert all the rights of coastal States under the Convention once it recovers the legal status in question as a consequence of negotiations on the restoration to Bolivia of its own sovereign outlet to the Pacific Ocean.[7]

BRAZIL

I. Signature by Brazil is *ad referendum*, subject to ratification of the Convention in conformity with Brazilian constitutional procedures, which include approval by the National Congress.

II. The Brazilian Government understands that the régime which is applied in practice in maritime areas adjacent to the coast of Brazil is compatible with the provisions of the Convention.

III. The Brazilian Government understands that the provision of article 301, which prohibits 'any threat or use of force against the territorial integrity or political independence of any State, or in any other manner inconsistent with the principles of international law embodied in the Charter of the United Nations', apply, in particular, to the maritime areas under the sovereignty or the jurisdiction of the coastal State.

IV. The Brazilian Government understands that the provisions of the Convention do not authorize other States to carry out in the exclusive economic zone military exercises or manoeuvres, in particular those that imply the use of weapons or explosives, without the consent of the coastal State.

V. The Brazilian Government understands that, in accordance with the provisions of the Convention, the coastal State has, in the exclusive economic zone and on the continental shelf, the exclusive right to construct and to authorize and regulate the construction, operation and use of all types of installations and structures, without exception, whatever their nature or purpose.

VI. Brazil exercises sovereignty rights over the continental shelf, beyond the distance of two hundred nautical miles from the baselines, up to the outer edge of the continental margin, as defined in article 76.

VII. The Brazilian Government reserves the right to make at the appropriate time the declarations provided for in articles 287 and 298, concerning the settlement of disputes.[8]

I. The Brazilian Government understands that the provisions of article 301 prohibiting 'any threat or use of force against the territorial integrity of any State, or in other manner inconsistent with the principles of international law embodied in the Charter of the United Nations' apply in particular to the maritime areas under the sovereignty or jurisdiction of the coastal State.

II. The Brazilian Government understands that the provisions of the Convention do not authorize other States to carry out military exercises or manoeuvres, in particular those involving the use of weapons or explosives, in the exclusive economic zone without the consent of the coastal State.

III. The Brazilian Government understands that in accordance with the provisions of the Convention the coastal State has, in the exclusive economic zone and on the continental shelf, the exclusive right to construct and to authorize and to regulate the construction, operation and use of all kinds of installations and structures, without exception, whatever their nature or purpose.

---

[7] Declaration made upon signature on 27 November 1984.
[8] Declaration made upon signature on 10 December 1982.

CANADA

With regard to article 287 of the Convention on the Law of the Sea, the Government of Canada hereby chooses the following means for the settlement of disputes concerning the interpretation or application of the Convention without specifying that one has precedence over the other:

    (a)   the International Tribunal for the Law of the Sea established in accordance with Annex VI of the Convention; and

    (b)   an arbitral tribunal constituted in accordance with Annex VII of the Convention.

With regard to Article 298, paragraph 1 of the Convention on the Law of the Sea, Canada does not accept any of the procedures provided for in Part XV, section 2, with respect to the following disputes:

    –   Disputes concerning the interpretation or application of articles 15, 74 and 83 relating to sea boundary delimitations, or those involving historic bays or titles;

    –   Disputes concerning military activities, including military activities by government vessels and aircraft engaged in non-commercial service, and disputes concerning law enforcement activities in regard to the exercise of sovereign rights or jurisdiction excluded from the jurisdiction of a court or tribunal under article 297, paragraph 2 or 3;

    –   Disputes in respect of which the Security Council of the United Nations is exercising the functions assigned to it by the Charter of the United Nations, unless the Security Council decides to remove the matter from its agenda or calls upon the parties to settle it by the means provided for in the Convention.

According to Article 309 of the Convention on the Law of the Sea, no reservations or exceptions may be made to the Convention unless expressly permitted by other articles of the Convention. A declaration or statement made pursuant to article 310 of the Convention cannot purport to exclude or to modify the legal effect of the provisions of the Convention in their application to the state, entity or international organization making it. Consequently, the Government of Canada declares that it does not consider itself bound by declarations or statements that have been made or will be made by other states, entities and international organizations pursuant to article 310 of the Convention and that exclude or modify the legal effect of the provisions of the Convention and their application to the State, entity or international organization making it. Lack of response by the Government of Canada to any declaration or statement shall not be interpreted as tacit acceptance of that declaration or statement. The Government of Canada reserves the right at any time to take a position on any declaration or statement in the manner deemed appropriate.

CAPE VERDE

The Government of the Republic of Cape Verde signs the United Nations Convention on the Law of the Sea with the following understandings:

I. This Convention recognizes the right of coastal States to adopt measures to safeguard their security interests, including the right to adopt laws and regulations relating to the innocent passage of foreign warships through their territorial sea or archipelagic waters. This right is in full conformity with articles 19 and 25 of the Convention, as it was clearly stated in the Declaration made by the President of the Third United Nations Conference on the Law of the Sea in the plenary meeting of the Conference on 26 April 1982.

II. The provisions of the Convention relating to the archipelagic waters, territorial sea, exclusive economic zone and continental shelf are compatible with the fundamental objectives and aims that inspire the legislation of the Republic of Cape Verde concerning its sovereignty and jurisdiction over the sea adjacent to and within its coasts and over the seabed and subsoil thereof up to the limit of 200 miles.

III. The legal nature of the exclusive economic zone as defined in the Convention and the scope of the rights recognized therein to the coastal state leave no doubt as to its character of a *sui generis* zone of national jurisdiction different from the territorial sea and which is not a part of the high seas.

IV. The regulations of the uses or activities which are not expressly provided for in the Convention but are related to the sovereign rights and to the jurisdiction of the coastal State in its exclusive economic zone falls within the competence of the said State, provided that such regulation does not hinder the enjoyment of the freedoms of international communication which are recognized to other States.

V. In the exclusive economic zone, the enjoyment of the freedoms of international communication, in conformity with its definition and with other relevant provisions of the Convention, excludes any non-peaceful use without the consent of the coastal State, such as exercises with weapons or other activities which may affect the rights or interests of the said state; and it also excludes the threat or use of force against the territorial integrity, political independence, peace or security of the coastal State.

VI. This Convention does not entitle any State to construct, operate or use installations or structures in the exclusive economic zone of another State, either those provided for in the Convention or those of any other nature, without the consent of the coastal State.

VII. In accordance with all the relevant provisions of the Convention, where the same stock or stocks of associated species occur both within the exclusive economic zone and in an area beyond and adjacent to the zone, the States fishing for such stocks in the adjacent area are duty bound to enter into arrangements with the coastal State upon the measures necessary for the conservation of these stock or stocks of associated species.[9]

I. The Republic of Cape Verde reaffirms in its entirety its declaration dated 10 December 1982, handed over upon signature of the United Nations Convention on the Law of the Sea.

II. The Republic of Cape Verde declares, without prejudice to article 303 of the United Nations Convention on the Law of the Sea, that any objects of an archaeological and historical nature found within the maritime areas over which it exerts sovereignty or jurisdiction shall not be removed without its prior notification and consent.

III. The Republic of Cape Verde declares that, in the absence of or failing any other peaceful means, it chooses, in order of preference and in accordance with article 287 of the United Nations Convention on the Law of the Sea, the following procedures for the settlement of disputes regarding the interpretation or application of the said Convention:

(a) The International Tribunal for the Law of the Sea;

(b) The International Court of Justice.

IV. The Republic of Cape Verde, in accordance with article 298 of the United Nations Convention on the Law of the Sea, declares that it does not accept the procedures provided for in Part XV, section 2, of the said Convention for the settlement of disputes concerning military activities, including military activities by Government-operated vessels and aircraft engaged in non-commercial service, as well as disputes concerning law enforcement activities in regard to the exercise of sovereign rights or jurisdiction

---

[9] Declaration made upon signature on 10 December 1982 and confirmed upon ratification on 19 August 1987.

excluded from the jurisdiction of a court or tribunal under article 297, paragraphs 2 and 3, of the aforementioned Convention.

CHILE

In exercise of the right conferred by article 310 of the Convention, the delegation of Chile wishes first of all to reiterate in its entirety the statement it made at [the April 1982] meeting when the Convention was adopted, which statement is reproduced in document A/CONF.62/SR.164. In particular [it wishes to refer] to the Convention's pivotal legal concept, that of the 200 mile exclusive economic zone to the elaboration of which [Chile] made an important contribution, having been the first to declare such a concept, 35 years ago in 1947, and having subsequently helped to define and earn it international acceptance. The exclusive economic zone has a *sui generis* legal character distinct from that of the territorial sea and the high seas. It is a zone under national jurisdiction, over which the coastal State exercises economic sovereignty and in which third States enjoy freedom of navigation and overflight and the freedoms inherent in international communication. The Convention defines it as a maritime space under the jurisdiction of the coastal State, bound to the latter's territorial sovereignty and actual territory, on terms similar to those governing other maritime spaces, namely the territorial sea and the continental shelf. With regard to straits used for international navigation, the delegation of Chile wishes to reaffirm and reiterate in full the statement made last April, as reproduced in document A/CONF.62/SR.164 referred to above, as well as the content of the supplementary written statement dated 7 April 1982 contained in document A/CONF.62/WS/19.

With regard to the international sea-bed régime, [the Government of Chile wishes] to reiterate the statement made by the Group of 77 at [the April 1982] meeting regarding the legal concept of the common heritage of mankind, the existence of which was solemnly confirmed by consensus by the General Assembly in 1970 and which the present Convention defines as a part of *jus cogens*. Any action taken in contravention of this principle and outside the framework of the sea-bed régime would, as [the April 1982] debate showed, be totally invalid and illegal.[10]

1. The Republic of Chile reiterates in its entirety the statement it made when signing the United Nations Convention on the Law of the Sea, on 10 December 1982 as regards the *sui generis* legal character and the definition of the exclusive economic zone. It also reiterates the statement it made on the same day with regard to 'straits used for international navigation'.

2. The Republic of Chile declares that the Treaty of Peace and Friendship signed with the Argentine Republic on 29 November 1984, which entered into force on 2 May 1985, shall define the boundaries between the respective sovereignties over the sea, seabed and subsoil of the Argentine Republic and the Republic of Chile in the sea of the southern zone in the terms laid down in articles 7 to 9.

3. With regard to part II of the Convention:

   (a) In accordance with article 13 of the Treaty of Peace and Friendship of 1984, the Republic of Chile, in exercise of its sovereign rights, grants to the Argentine Republic the navigation facilities through Chilean internal waters described in that Treaty, which are specified in annex 2, articles 1 to 9.

   In addition, the Republic of Chile declares that by virtue of this Treaty, ships flying the flag of third countries may navigate without obstacles through

---

[10] Statement made upon signature on 10 December 1982 and confirmed upon ratification on 25 August 1997.

the internal waters along the routes specified in annex 2, articles 1 and 8, subject to the relevant Chilean regulations.

In the Treaty of Peace and Friendship of 1984, the two Parties agreed on the system of navigation and pilotage in the Beagle Channel defined in annex 2, articles 11 to 16. The provisions on navigation set forth in that annex replace any previous agreement on the subject that might exist between the Parties.

We reiterate that the navigation systems and facilities referred to in this paragraph were established in the 1984 Treaty of Peace and Friendship for the sole purpose of facilitating maritime communication between specific maritime points and areas, along the specific routes indicated, so that they do not apply to other routes existing in the zone which have not been specifically agreed on.

(b) The Republic of Chile reaffirms the full validity and force of Supreme Decree No. 416 of 1977, of the Ministry of Foreign Affairs, which, in accordance with the principles of article 7 of the Convention - which have been fully recognized by Chile - established the straight baselines which were confirmed in article 11 of the 1984 Treaty of Peace and Friendship.

(c) In cases in which a State places restrictions on the right of innocent passage for foreign warships, the Republic of Chile reserves the right to apply similar restrictive measures.

4. With regard to part III of the Convention, it should be noted that in accordance with article 35 (c), the provisions of this part do not affect the legal regime of the Strait of Magellan, since passage through that strait is 'regulated by long-standing international conventions in force specifically relating to such straits' such as the 1881 Boundary Treaty, a regime which is reaffirmed in the Treaty of Peace and Friendship of 1984.

In article 10 of the latter Treaty, Chile and Argentina agreed on the boundary at the eastern end of the Strait of Magellan and agreed that this boundary in no way alters the provisions of the 1881 Boundary Treaty, whereby, as Chile declared unilaterally in 1873, the Strait of Magellan is neutralized forever with free navigation assured for the flags of all nations under the terms laid down in article V. For its part, the Argentine Republic undertook to maintain, at any time and in whatever circumstances, the right of ships of all flags to navigate expeditiously and without obstacles through its jurisdictional waters to and from the Strait of Magellan.

Furthermore, we reiterate that Chilean maritime traffic to and from the north through the Estrecho de Le Maire shall enjoy the facilities laid down in annex 2, article 10 of the 1984 Treaty of Peace and Friendship.

5. Having regard for its interest in the conservation of the resources in its exclusive economic zone and the adjacent area of the high seas, the Republic of Chile believes that, in accordance with the provisions of the Convention, where the same stock or stocks of associated species occur both within the exclusive economic zone and in the adjacent area of the high seas, the Republic of Chile, as the coastal State, and the States fishing for such stocks in the area adjacent to its exclusive economic zone must agree upon the measures necessary for the conservation in the high seas of these stocks or associated species. In the absence of such agreement, Chile reserves the right to exercise its rights under article 116 and other provisions of the United Nations Convention on the Law of the Sea, and the other rights accorded to it under international law.

6. With reference to part XI of the Convention and its supplementary agreement, it is Chile's understanding that, in respect of the prevention of pollution in exploration and exploitation activities, the Authority must apply the general criterion that underwater mining shall be subject to standards which are at least as stringent as comparable standards on land.

7. With regard to part XV of the Convention, the Republic of Chile declares that:

(a) In accordance with article 287 of the Convention, it accepts, in order of preference, he following means for the settlement of disputes concerning the interpretation or application of the Convention:

    (i) The International Tribunal for the Law of the Sea established in accordance with annex VI;

    (ii) A special arbitral tribunal, established in accordance with annex VIII, for the categories of disputes specified therein relating to fisheries, protection and preservation of the marine environment, and marine scientific research and navigation, including pollution from vessels and by dumping.

(b) In accordance with articles 280 to 282 of the Convention, the choice of means for the settlement of disputes indicated in the preceding paragraph shall in no way affect the obligations deriving from the general, regional or bilateral agreements to which the Republic of Chile is a party concerning the peaceful settlement of disputes or containing provisions for the settlement of disputes.

(c) In accordance with article 298 of the Convention, Chile declares that it does not accept any of the procedures provided for in part XV, section 2 with respect to the disputes referred to in article 298, paragraphs 1 (a), (b) and (c) of the Convention.

CHINA

1. In accordance with the provisions of the United Nations Convention on the Law of the Sea, the People's Republic of China shall enjoy sovereign rights and jurisdiction over an exclusive economic zone of 200 nautical miles and the continental shelf.

2. The People's Republic of China will effect, through consultations, the delimitation of the boundary of the maritime jurisdiction with the States with coasts opposite or adjacent to China respectively on the basis of international law and in accordance with the principle of equitability.

3. The People's Republic of China reaffirms its sovereignty over all its archipelagos and islands as listed in article 2 of the Law of the People's Republic of China on the territorial sea and the contiguous zone, which was promulgated on 25 February 1992.[11]

4. The People's Republic of China reaffirms that the provisions of the United Nations Convention on the Law of the Sea concerning innocent passage through the territorial sea shall not prejudice the right of a coastal State to request, in accordance with its laws and regulations, a foreign State to obtain advance approval from or give prior notification to the coastal State for the passage of its warships through the territorial sea of the coastal State.

---

[11] In this regard, on 7 June 1996, the UN Secretary-General received from the Government of Viet Nam, the following declaration:

1. The People's Republic of China's establishment of the territorial baselines of the Hoang Sa archipelago (Paracel), part of the territory of Viet Nam, constitutes a serious violation of the Vietnamese sovereignty over the archipelago. the Socialist Republic of Viet Nam has on many occasions reaffirmed its indisputable sovereignty over the Hoang Sa as well as the Truong Sa (Spratly) archipelagoes. The above-mentioned act of the People's Republic of China which runs counter to the international law, is absolutely null and void. Furthermore, the People's Republic of China correspondingly violated the provisions of the 1982 United Nations Convention on the Law of the Sea by giving the Hoang Sa archipelago the status of an archipelagic state to illegally annex a vast sea area into the so-called internal water of the archipelago.

2. In drawing the baseline at the segment east of the Leizhou peninsula from point 31 to 32, the People's Republic of China has also failed to comply with the provisions, particularly articles 7 and 38, of the 1982 United Nations Convention on the Law of the Sea. By so drawing, the People's Republic of China has turned a considerable sea area into its internal water which obstructs the rights and freedom of international navigation including those of Viet Nam through the Qiongzhou strait. This is totally unacceptable to the Socialist Republic of Viet Nam.

Declaration under article 298

The Government of the People's Republic of China does not accept any of the procedures provided for in Section 2 of Part XV of the Convention with respect to all the categories of disputes referred to in paragraph 1 (a) (b) and (c) of Article 298 of the Convention.[12]

COSTA RICA

The Government of Costa Rica declares that the provisions of Costa Rican law under which foreign vessels must pay for licences to fish in its exclusive economic zone, shall apply also to fishing for highly migratory species, pursuant to the provisions of articles 62 and 64, paragraph 2, of the Convention.[13]

CROATIA

The Republic of Croatia considers that, in accordance with article 53 of the Vienna Convention on the Law of Treaties of 29 May 1969, there is no peremptory norm of general international law which would forbid a coastal State to request by its laws and regulations foreign warships to notify their intention of innocent passage through its territorial waters, and to limit the number of warships allowed to exercise the right of innocent passage at the same time (articles 17 to 32 of the Convention).[14]

Declaration under article 287

In implementation of article 287 of the [Convention], the Government of Croatia [declares] that, for the settlement of disputes concerning the application or interpretation of the Convention and of the Agreement adopted on 28 July 1994 relating to the Implementation of Part XI, it chooses, in order of preference, the following means:

i)   The International Tribunal for the Law of the Sea established in accordance with annex VI;

ii) The International Court of Justice.[15]

CUBA

With regard to article 287 on the choice of procedure for the settlement of disputes concerning the interpretation or application of the Convention, the Government of the Republic of Cuba declares that it does not accept the jurisdiction of the International Court of Justice and, consequently, will not accept the jurisdiction of the Court with respect to the provisions of articles 297 and 298.

With regard to article 292, the Government of the Republic of Cuba considers that once financial security has been posted, the detaining State should proceed promptly and without delay to release the vessel and its crew and declares that where this procedure is not followed with respect to its vessels or members of their crew it will not agree to submit the matter to the International Court of Justice.

DENMARK

The Kingdom of Denmark makes the following declaration: It is the position of the Government of the Kingdom of Denmark that the exception from the transit passage regime provided for in article 35 (c) of the Convention applies to the specific regime in the

---

[12] Declaration made after ratification, on 25 August 2006.

[13] Declaration made upon signature on 10 December 1982.

[14] Statement made upon succession on 5 April 1995.

[15] Declaration made after succession on 4 November 1999.

Danish straits (the Great Belt, the Little Belt and the Danish part of the Sound), which has developed on the basis of the Copenhagen Treaty of 1857. The present legal regime of the Danish straits will therefore remain unchanged.

The Government of the Kingdom of Denmark declares pursuant to article 287 of the Convention that it chooses the International Court of Justice for the settlement of disputes concerning the interpretation or application of the Convention.

The Government of the Kingdom of Denmark declares pursuant to article 298 of the Convention that it does not accept an arbitral tribunal constituted in accordance with Annex VII for any of the categories of disputes mentioned in article 298.

The Government of the Kingdom of Denmark declares, in accordance with article 310 of the Convention, its objection to any declaration or position excluding or amending the legal scope of the provisions of the Convention. Passivity with respect to such declarations or positions shall be interpreted neither as acceptance nor rejection of such declarations or positions.

The Kingdom of Denmark recalls that, as a member of the European Community, it has transferred competence in respect of certain matters governed by the Convention. In accordance with the provisions of Annex IX of the Convention, a detailed declaration on the nature and ex tent of the competence transferred to the European Community was made by the European Community upon deposit of its instrument of formal confirmation. This transfer of competence does not extend to the Faroe Islands and Greenland.

EGYPT

Declaration concerning the territorial sea
1. The Arab Republic of Egypt establishes the breadth of its territorial sea at 12 nautical miles, pursuant to article 5 of the Ordinance of 18 January 1951 as amended by the Decree of 17 February 1958, in line with the provisions of article 3 of the Convention.

2. The Arab Republic of Egypt will publish, at the earliest opportunity, charts showing the baselines from which the breadth of its territorial sea in the Mediterranean Sea and in the Red Sea is measured, as well as the lines marking the outer limit of the territorial sea, in accordance with usual practice.

Declaration concerning the contiguous zone
The Arab Republic of Egypt has decided that its contiguous zone (as defined in the Ordinance of 18 January 1951 as amended by the Presidential Decree of 17 February 1958) extends to 24 nautical miles from the baselines from which the breadth of the territorial sea is measured, as provided for in article 33 of the Convention.

Declaration concerning the passage of nuclear-powered and similar ships through the territorial sea of Egypt
Pursuant to the provisions of the Convention relating to the right of the coastal State to regulate the passage of ships through its territorial sea and whereas the passage of foreign nuclear-powered ships and ships carrying nuclear or other inherently dangerous and noxious substances poses a number of hazards,

Whereas article 23 of the Convention stipulates that the ships in question shall, when exercising the right of innocent passage through the territorial sea, carry documents and observe special precautionary measures established for such ships by international agreements, the Government of the Arab Republic of Egypt declares that it will require the aforementioned ships to obtain authorization before entering the territorial sea of Egypt, until such international agreements are concluded and Egypt becomes a party to them.

Declaration concerning the passage of warships through the territorial sea of Egypt

[With reference to the provisions of the Convention relating to the right of the coastal State to regulate the passage of ships through its territorial sea] Warships shall be ensured innocent passage through the territorial sea of Egypt, subject to prior notification.

Declaration concerning passage through the Strait of Tiran and the Gulf of Aqaba

The provisions of the 1979 Peace Treaty between Egypt and Israel concerning passage through the Strait of Tiran and the Gulf of Aqaba come within the framework of the general regime of waters forming straits referred to in Part III of the Convention, wherein it is stipulated that the general regime shall not affect the legal status of waters forming straits and shall include certain obligations with regard to security and the maintenance of order in the State bordering the strait.

Declaration concerning the exercise by Egypt of its rights in the exclusive economic zone

The Arab Republic of Egypt will exercise as from this day the rights attributed to it by the provisions of Parts V and VI of the United Nations Convention on the Law of the Sea in the exclusive economic zone situated beyond and adjacent to its territorial sea in the Mediterranean Sea and in the Red Sea.

The Arab Republic of Egypt will also exercise its sovereign rights in this zone for the purpose of exploring and exploiting, conserving and managing the natural resources, whether living or non-living, of the seabed and subsoil and the superjacent waters, and with regard to all other activities for the economic exploration and exploitation of the zone, such as the production of energy from the water, currents and winds.

The Arab Republic of Egypt will exercise its jurisdiction over the exclusive economic zone according to the modalities laid down in the Convention with regard to the establishment and use of artificial islands, installations and structures, marine scientific research, the protection and preservation of the marine environment and the other rights and duties provided for in the Convention.

The Arab Republic of Egypt proclaims that, in exercising its rights and performing its duties under the Convention in the exclusive economic zone, it will have due regard for the rights and duties of other States and will act in a manner compatible with the provisions of the Convention.

The Arab Republic of Egypt undertakes to establish the outer limits of its exclusive economic zone in accordance with the rules, criteria and modalities laid down in the Convention.

[The Arab Republic of] Egypt declares that it will take the necessary action and make the necessary arrangements to regulate all matters relating to its exclusive economic zones.

Declaration concerning the procedure chosen for the settlement of disputes in conformity with the Convention

[With reference to the provisions of article 287 of the Convention] the Arab Republic of Egypt declares that it accepts the arbitral procedure, the modalities of which are defined in Annex VII to the Convention, as the procedure for the settlement of any dispute which might arise between Egypt and any other State relating to the interpretation or application of the Convention.

The Arab Republic of Egypt further declares that it excludes from the scope of application of this procedure those disputes contemplated in article 297 of the Convention.

Statement concerning the Arabic version of the text of the Convention

The Government of the Arab Republic of Egypt is gratified that the Third United Nations Conference on the Law of the Sea adopted the new Convention in six languages, including Arabic, with all the texts being equally authentic, thus establishing absolute equality between all the versions and preventing any one from prevailing over another.

However, when the official Arabic version of the Convention is compared with the other official versions, it becomes clear that, in some cases, the official Arabic text does not exactly correspond to the other versions, in that it fails to reflect precisely the content of certain provisions of the Convention which were found acceptable and adopted by States in establishing a legal régime governing the seas.

For these reasons, the Government of the Arab Republic of Egypt takes the opportunity afforded by the deposit of the instruments of ratification of the United Nations Convention on the Law of the Sea to declare that it will adopt the interpretation which is best corroborated by the various official texts of the Convention.

EQUATORIAL GUINEA

Declaration under article 298

The Government of the Republic of Equatorial Guinea hereby enters a reservation and declares that, under article 298, paragraph 1, of the United Nations Convention of 1982 on the Law of the Sea, it does not recognize as mandatory *ipso facto* with respect to any other State any of the procedures provided for in part XV, section 2, of the Convention as regards the categories of disputes set forth in article 298, paragraph 1 (a).[16]

ESTONIA

1. As a member state of the European Community, the Republic of Estonia has transferred competence in certain matters governed by the Convention to the European Community according to the declaration made by the European Community on April 1, 1998 while acceding to the United Nations Convention on the Law of the Sea.

2. Pursuant to Article 287, paragraph 1 of the Convention the Republic of Estonia chooses the International Tribunal for the Law of the Sea established in accordance with Annex VI and the International Court of Justice as means for the settlement of disputes concerning the interpretation or application of this Convention.

EUROPEAN COMMUNITY

On signing the United Nations Convention on the Law of the Sea, the European Economic Community declares that it considers that the Convention constitutes, within the framework of the Law of the Sea, a major effort in the codification and progressive development of international law in the fields to which its declaration pursuant to Article 2 of Annex IX of the Convention refers. The Community would like to express the hope that this development will become a useful means for promoting co-operation and stable relations between all countries in these fields.

The Community, however, considers that significant provisions of Part XI of the Convention are not conducive to the development of the activities to which that Part refers in view of the fact that several Member States of the Community have already expressed their position that this Part contains considerable deficiencies and flaws which require rectification. The Community recognises the importance of the work which remains to be

---

[16] Declaration made after ratification, on 20 February 2002.

done and hopes that conditions for the implementation of a sea bed mining regime, which are generally acceptable and which are therefore likely to promote activities in the international sea bed area, can be agreed. The Community, within the limits of its competence, will play a full part in contributing to the task of finding satisfactory solutions.

A separate decision on formal confirmation[17] will have to be taken at a later stage. It will be taken in the light of the results of the efforts made to attain a universally acceptable Convention.

Competence of the European Communities with Regard to Matters Governed by the Convention on the Law of the Sea
(Declaration made pursuant to Article 2 of Annex IX to the Convention)

Article 2 of Annex IX to the Convention on the Law of the Sea stipulates that the participation of an international organisation shall be subject to a declaration specifying the matters governed by the Convention in respect of which competence has been transferred to the organisation by its Member States.

The European Communities were established by the Treaties of Paris and of Rome, signed on 18 April 1951 and 25 March 1957, respectively. After being ratified by the Signatory States the Treaties entered into force on 25 July 1952 and 1 January 1958.[18]

In accordance with the provisions referred to above this declaration indicates the competence of the European Economic Community in matters governed by the Convention.

The Community points out that its Member States have transferred competence to it with regard to the conservation and management of sea fishing resources. Hence, in the field of sea fishing it is for the Community to adopt the relevant rules and regulations (which are enforced by the Member States) and to enter into external undertakings with third states or competent international organisations.

Furthermore, with regard to rules and regulations for the protection and preservation of the marine environment, the Member States have transferred to the Community competences as formulated in provisions adopted by the Community and as reflected by its participation in certain international agreements (see Annex).

With regard to the provisions of Part X, the Community has certain powers as its purpose is to bring about an economic union based on a customs union.

With regard to the provisions of Part XI, the Community enjoys competence in matters of commercial policy, including the control of unfair economic practices.

The exercise of the competence that the Member States have transferred to the Community under the Treaties is, by its very nature, subject to continuous development. As a result the Community reserves the right to make new declarations at a later date.

---

[17] Footnote in original: Formal confirmation is the term used in the Convention for ratification by international organisations (see Article 306 and Annex IX, Article 3).

[18] Footnote in original: The Treaty of Paris establishing the European Coal and Steel Community was registered at the Secretariat of the United Nations on 15.3.1957 under No. 3729; the Treaties of Rome establishing the European Economic Community and the European Atomic Energy Community (Euratom) were registered on 21 April and 24 April 1958, respectively under Nos 4300 and 4301. The current members of the Communities are the Kingdom of Belgium, the Kingdom of Denmark, the Federal Republic of Germany, the Hellenic Republic, the French Republic, Ireland, the Italian Republic, the Grand Duchy of Luxembourg, the Kingdom of the Netherlands and the United Kingdom of Great Britain and Northern Ireland. The United Nations Convention on the Law of the Sea shall apply, with regard to matters transferred to the European Economic Community, to the territories in which the Treaty establishing the European Economic Community is applied and under the conditions laid down in that Treaty.

Annex

Community texts applicable in the sector of the protection and preservation of the marine environment and relating directly to subjects covered by the Convention:

Council Decision of 3 December 1981 establishing a Community information system for the control and reduction of pollution caused by hydrocarbons discharged at sea (81/971/EEC) (OJ No L 355, 10.12.1981, p. 52).

Council Directive of 4 May 1976 on pollution caused by certain dangerous substances discharged into the aquatic environment of the Community (76/464/EEC) (OJ No L 129, 18.5.1976, p. 23).

Council Directive of 16 June 1975 on the disposal of waste oils (75/439/EEC)(OJ No L 194, 25.7.1975, p. 23).

Council Directive of 20 February 1978 on waste from the titanium dioxide industry (78/176/EEC) (OJ No L 54, 25.2.1978, p. 19).

Council Directive of 30 October 1979 on the quality required of shellfish waters (79/923/ EEC) (OJ No L 281, 10.11.1979, p. 47).

Council Directive of 22 March 1982 on limit values and quality objectives for mercury discharges by the chlor-alkali electrolysis industry (82/176/EEC) (OJ No L 81, 27.3.1982, p. 29).

Council Directive of 26 September 1983 on limit values and quality objectives for cadmium discharges (83/513/EEC) (OJ No L 291, 24.10.1983, p. 1 et seq.).

Council Directive of 8 March 1984 on limit values and quality objectives for mercury discharges by sectors other than the chlor-alkali electrolysis industry (84/156/EEC) (OJ No L 74, 17.3.1984, p. 49 *et seq.*).

Annex

The Community has also concluded the following Conventions:

Convention for the prevention of marine pollution from land-based sources (Council Decision 75/437/EEC of 3 March 1975 published in OJ No L 194, 25.7.1975, p. 5).

Convention on long-range transboundary air pollution (Council Decision of 11 June 1981 published in OJ No L 171, 27.6.1981, p. 11).

Convention for the protection of the Mediterranean Sea against pollution and the Protocol for the prevention of pollution of the Mediterranean Sea by dumping from ships and aircraft (Council Decision 77/585/EEC of 25 July 1977 published in OJ No L 240, 19.9.1977, p. 1).

Protocol concerning co-operation in combating pollution of the Mediterranean Sea by oil and other harmful substances in cases of emergency (Council Decision 81/420/EEC of 19 May 1981 published in OJ No L 162, 19.6.1981, p. 4).

Protocol of 2 and 3 April 1983 concerning Mediterranean specially protected areas (OJ No L 68/36, 10.3.1984).[19]

Declaration Concerning the Competence of the European Community with Regard to Matters Governed by the United Nations Convention on the Law of the Sea of 10 December 1982 and the Agreement of 28 July 1994 Relating to the Implementation of Part XI of the Convention

[...] By depositing this instrument [of formal confirmation], the Community has the honour of declaring its acceptance, in respect of matters for which competence has been

---

[19] Declaration made upon signature on 7 December 1984.

transferred to it by those of its Member States which are parties to the Convention, of the rights and obligations laid down for States in the Convention and the Agreement. The declaration concerning competence provided for in Article 5(1) of Annex IX to the Convention [follows].

The Community also wishes to declare, in accordance with Article 310 of the Convention, its objection to any declaration or position excluding or amending the legal scope of the provisions of the United Nations Convention on the Law of the Sea, and in particular those relating to fishing activities. The Community does not consider the Convention to recognize the rights or jurisdiction of coastal States regarding the exploitation, conservation and management of fishery resources other than sedentary species outside their exclusive economic zone.

The Community reserves the right to make subsequent declarations in respect of the Convention and the Agreement and in response to future declarations and positions.

(Declaration made pursuant to article 5(1) of Annex IX to the Convention and to Article 4(4) of the Agreement)

Article 5(1) of Annex IX of the United Nations Convention on the Law of the Sea provides that the instrument of formal confirmation of an international organization shall contain a declaration specifying the matters governed by the Convention in respect of which competence has been transferred to the organization by its member States which are Parties to the Convention.[20]

Article 4(4) of the Agreement relating to the implementation of Part XI of the United Nations Convention the Law of the Sea of 10 December 1982[21] provides that formal confirmation by an international organization shall be in accordance with Annex IX of the Convention.

The European Communities were established by the Treaties of Paris (ECSC) and of Rome (EEC and Euratom), signed on 18 April 1951 and 25 March 1957 respectively. After being ratified by the Signatory States, the Treaties entered into force on 25 July 1952 and 1 January 1958. They have been amended by the Treaty on European Union, which was signed in Maastricht on 7 February 1992 and entered into force, after being ratified by the Signatory States, on 1 November 1993, and most recently by the Accession Treaty signed in Corfu on 24 June 1994, which entered into force on 1 January 1995.[22]

The current Members of the Communities are the Kingdom of Belgium, the Kingdom of Denmark, the Federal Republic of Germany, the Hellenic Republic, the Kingdom of Spain, the French Republic, Ireland, the Italian Republic, the Grand Duchy of Luxembourg, the Kingdom of the Netherlands, the Republic of Austria, the Portuguese Republic, the Republic of Finland, the Kingdom of Sweden and the United Kingdom of Great Britain and Northern Ireland.

The United Nations Convention on the Law of the Sea and the Agreement relating to the Implementation of Part XI of the Convention shall apply with regard to the competences

---

[20] Footnote in original: When it signed the Convention, the Community made the requisite declaration, in accordance with Article 2 of Annex IX, in which it specified the matters dealt with by the Convention for which competence had been transferred to it by its Member States.

[21] Footnote in original: Signed by the Community on 29 July 1994 and applied by it provisionally with effect from 16 November 1994.

[22] Footnote in original: The Treaty of Paris establishing the European Coal and Steel Community was registered with the Secretariat of the United Nations on 15 March 1957 under No. 3729; the Treaties of Rome establishing the European Economic Community and the European Atomic Energy Community (Euratom) were registered on 21 April and 24 April 1958 respectively under Nos. 4300 and 4301. The Treaty on European Union was registered on 28 December 1993 under No. 30615; the Accession Treaty of 24 June 1994 was published in *Official Journal of the European Communities* C 241 of 29 August 1994.

transferred to the European Community, to the territories in which the Treaty establishing the European Community is applied and under the conditions laid down in that Treaty, in particular Article 227 thereof.

This declaration is not applicable to the territories of the Member States in which the said Treaty does not apply and is without prejudice to such acts or positions as may be adopted under the Convention and the Agreement by the Member States concerned on behalf of and in the interests of those territories.

In accordance with the provisions referred to above, this declaration indicates the competence that the Member States have transferred to the Community under the Treaties in matters governed by the Convention and the Agreement.

The scope and the exercise of such Community competence are, by their nature, subject to continuous development, and the Community will complete or amend this declaration, if necessary, in accordance with Article 5(4) of Annex IX to the Convention.

*****

The Community has exclusive competence for certain matters and shares competence with its Member States for certain other matters.

1. Matters for which the Community has exclusive competence

– The Community points out that its Member States have transferred competence to it with regard to the conservation and management of sea fishing resources. Hence in this field it is for the Community to adopt the relevant rules and regulations (which are enforced by the Member States) and, within its competence, to enter into external undertakings with third States or competent international organizations. This competence applies to waters under national fisheries jurisdiction and to the high seas. Nevertheless, in respect of measures relating to the exercise of jurisdiction over vessels, flagging and registration of vessels and the enforcement of penal and administrative sanctions, competence rests with the Member States whilst respecting Community law. Community law also provides for administrative sanctions.

– By virtue of its commercial and customs policy, the Community has competence in respect of those provisions of Parts X and XI of the Convention and of the Agreement of 28 July 1994 which are related to international trade.

2. Matters for which the Community shares competence with its Member States

– With regard to fisheries, for a certain number of matters that are not directly related to the conservation and management of sea fishing resources, for example research and technological development and development cooperation, there is shared competence.

– With regard to the provisions on maritime transport, safety of shipping and the prevention of marine pollution contained *inter alia* in Parts II, III, V, VII and XII of the Convention, the Community has exclusive competence only to the extent that such provisions of the Convention or legal instruments adopted in implementation thereof affect common rules established by the Community. When Community rules exist but are not affected, in particular in cases of Community provisions establishing only minimum standards, the Member States have competence, without prejudice to the competence of the Community to act in this field. Otherwise competence rests with the Members States. A list of relevant Community acts appears in the appendix. The extent of Community competence ensuing from these acts must be assessed by reference to the precise provisions of each measure, and in particular, the extent to which these provisions establish common rules.

–   With regard to the provisions of Parts XIII and XIV of the Convention, the Community's competence relates mainly to the promotion of cooperation on research and technological development with non-member countries and international organizations. The activities carried out by the Community here complement the activities of the Member States. Competence in this instance is implemented by the adoption of the programmes listed in the appendix.

3. **Possible impact of other Community policies**

–   Mention should also be made of the Community's policies and activities in the fields of control of unfair economic practices, government procurement and industrial competitiveness as well as in the area of development aid. These policies may also have some relevance to the Convention and the Agreement, in particular with regard to certain provisions of Parts VI and XI of the Convention.

Appendix

COMMUNITY ACTS WHICH REFER TO MATTERS GOVERNED
BY THE CONVENTION AND THE AGREEMENT

In the maritime safety and prevention of marine pollution sectors

Council Decision of 25 February 1992 on radionavigation systems for Europe (92/143/EEC) (OJ No L 59, 4.3.1992, p. 17)

Council Directive of 21 December 1978 concerning pilotage of vessels by deep sea pilots in the North Sea and English Channel (79/115/EEC) (OJ No L 33, 8.2.1979, p. 32)

Council Directive of 13 September 1993 concerning minimum requirements for vessels bound for or leaving Community ports and carrying dangerous or polluting goods (93/75/EEC) (OJ No L 247, 5.10.1993, p. 19)

Council Directive of 23 November 1993 concerning the minimum safety and health requirements for work on board fishing vessels (thirteenth individual Directive within the meaning of Article 16(1) of Directive 89/391/EEC) (93/103/EC) (OJ No L 307, 13.12.1993, p. 1)

Council Directive of 22 November 1994 on common rules and standards for ship inspection and survey organizations and for the relevant activities of maritime administrations (Classification Societies Directive) (94/57/EC) (OJ No L 319, 12.12.1994, p. 20)

Council Directive of 22 November 1994 on the minimum level of training of seafarers (94/58/EC) (OJ No L 319, 12.12.1994, p. 28)

Council Directive of 19 June 1995 concerning the enforcement, in respect of shipping using Community ports and sailing in the waters under the jurisdiction of the Member States, of international standards for ship safety, pollution prevention and shipboard living and working conditions (port State control (95/21/EC) (OJ No L 157, 7.7.1995, p. 1)

Council Directive of 20 December 1996 on marine equipment (96/98/EC) (OJ No L 46, 17.2.1997,p. 25)

Council Regulation of 4 March 1991 on the transfer of ships from one register to another within the Community (91/613/EEC) (OJ No L 68, 15.3.1991, p.1) and Commission Regulation of 28 July 1993 concerning the application of amendments to the International Convention for the Safety of Life at Sea, 1974, and to the International Convention for the Prevention of Pollution from Ships, 1973, for the purpose of Council Regulation (EEC) No 613/91 (2158/93/EEC) (OJ No L 194, 3.8.1993, p. 5)

Council Regulation of 21 November 1994 on the implementation of IMO Resolution
A.747(18) on the application of tonnage measurement of ballast spaces in
segregated ballast oil tankers (2978/94/EEC) (OJ No L 319, 12.12.1994, p. 1)

Council Regulation of 8 December 1995 on the safety management of roll-on/roll-
off passenger ferries (ro-ro ferries) (3051/95/EEC) (OJ No L 320, 30.12.1995,
p. 14)

**In the field of protection and preservation of the marine environment Part XII of the
Convention**

Council Decision of 3 December 1981 establishing a Community information system
for the control and reduction of pollution caused by hydrocarbons discharged at
sea (81/971/EEC) (OJ No L 355, 10.12.1981, p. 52)

Council Decision of 6 March 1986 establishing a Community information system for
the control and reduction of pollution caused by the spillage of hydrocarbons
and other harmful substances at sea (86/85/EEC) (OJ No L 77, 22.3.1986, p.
33)

Council Directive of 16 June 1975 on the disposal of waste oils (75/439/EEC) (OJ
No L 194, 25.7.1975, p. 23)

Council Directive of 15 July 1975 on waste (75/442/EEC) (OJ No L 194, 25.7.1975,
p. 39)

Council Directive of 8 December 1975 concerning the quality of bathing water
(76/160/EEC) (OJ No L 31, 5.2.1976, p. 1)

Council Directive of 4 May 1976 on pollution caused by certain dangerous substances
discharged into the aquatic environment of the Community (76/464/EEC) (OJ
No L 129, 18.5.1976, p. 23)

Council Directive of 20 February 1978 on wastes from the titanium dioxide industry
(78/176/EEC) (OJ No L 54, 25.2. 1978, p. 19)

Council Directive of 30 October 1979 on the quality required of shellfish waters
(79/923/EEC) (OJ No L 281, 10.11.1979, p. 47)

Council Directive of 15 July 1980 on air quality limit values and guide values
for sulphur dioxide and suspended particulars (80/779/EEC) (OJ No L 229,
30.8.1980, p. 30)

Council Directive of 22 March 1982 on limit values and quality objectives for
mercury discharges by the chlor-alkali electrolysis industry (82/176/EEC) (OJ
No L 81, 27.3.1982, p. 29)

Council Directive of 24 June 1982 on the major-accident hazards of certain industrial
activities (82/501/EEC) (OJ No L 230, 5.8.1982, p. 1)

Council Directive of 3 December 1982 on procedures for the surveillance and
monitoring of environments concerned by waste from the titanium dioxide
industry (82/883/EEC) (OJ No L 378, 31.12.1982, p. 1)

Council Directive of 3 December 1982 on a limit value for lead in the air (82/884/
EEC) (OJ No L 378, 31.12.1982, p. 15)

Council Directive of 26 September 1983 on a limit values and quality objectives for
cadmium discharges (83/513/EEC) (OJ No L 291, 24.10.1983, p. 1)

Council Directive of 8 March 1984 on limit values and quality objectives for mercury
discharges by sectors other than the chlor-alkali electrolysis industry (84/156/
EEC) (OJ No L 74, 17.3.1984, p. 49)

Council Directive of 28 June 1984 on the combating of air pollution from industrial
plants (84/360/EEC) (OJ No L 188, 16.7.1984, p. 20)

Council Directive of 9 October 1984 on limit values and quality objectives for
discharges of hexachlorocyclohexane (84/491/EEC) (OJ No L 274, 17.10.1984,
p. 11)

Council Directive of 7 March 1985 on air quality standards for nitrogen dioxide (85/203/EEC) (OJ No L 87, 27.3.1985, p. 1)

Council Directive of 27 June 1985 on the assessment of the effects of certain public and private projects on the environment (85/337/EEC) (OJ No L 175, 5.7.1985, p. 40)

Council Directive of 12 June 1986 on limit values and quality objectives for discharges of certain dangerous substances included in List 1 of the Annex to Directive 76/464/EEC (86/280/EEC) (OJ No L 181, 4.7.1986, p. 16)

Council Directive of 24 November 1988 on the limitation of emissions of certain pollutants into the air from large combustion plants (88/609/EEC) (OJ No L 336, 7.12.1988, p. 1)

Council Directive of 8 June 1989 on the prevention of air pollution from new municipal waste incineration plants (89/369/EEC) (OJ No L 163, 14.6 1989, p. 32)

Council Directive of 21 June 1989 on the reduction of air pollution from existing municipal waste incineration plants (89/429/EEC) (OJ No L 203, 15.7 1989, p. 50)

Council Directive of 21 May 1991 concerning urban waste water treatment (91/271/EEC) (OJ No L 135, 30.5.1991, p. 40)

Council Directive of 12 December 1991 concerning the protection of waters against pollution caused by nitrates from agricultural sources (91/676/EEC) (OJ No L 375, 31.12. 1991, p. 1)

Council Directive of 12 December 1991 on hazardous waste (91/689/EEC) (OJ No L 377, 31.12. 1991, p. 20)

Council Directive of 21 May 1992 on the conservation of natural habitats and of wild fauna and flora (92/43/EEC) (OJ No L 206, 22.7.1992, p. 7)

Council Directive of 15 December 1992 on procedures for harmonizing the programmes for the reduction and eventual elimination of pollution caused by waste from the titanium dioxide industry (92/112/EEC) (OJ No L 409, 31.12.1992, p. 11)

Council Directive of 16 December 1994 on the incineration of hazardous waste (94/67/EEC) (OJ No L 365, 31.12.1994, p. 34)

Council Regulation of 1 February 1993 on the supervision and control of shipments of waste within, into and out of the European Community (259/93/EEC) (OJ No L 30, 6.2.1993, p. 1)

In the marine environment research and scientific and technological cooperation sector

Marine Science and Technology Programme

Environment and Climate Programme

Cooperation with third countries and international organizations: Scientific and technological cooperation with developing countries Programme (INCO-DC)

Conventions to which the Community is a party

Convention for the prevention of marine pollution from land-based sources, Paris, 4 June 1974 (Council Decision 75/437/EEC of 3 March 1975, published in OJ No L 194, 25.7.1975, p. 5)

Protocol amending the Convention for the prevention of marine pollution from land-based sources, Paris, 26 March 1986 (Council Decision 87/57/EEC of 28 December 1986, published in OJ No L 24, 27.1.1987, p. 47)

Protocol for the protection of the Mediterranean Sea against pollution from land-based sources, Athens, 17 May 1980 (Council Decision 83/101/EEC of 28 February 1983, published in OJ No L 67, 12.3.1983, p.1)

Convention for the protection of the Mediterranean Sea against pollution and the Protocol for the prevention of the pollution of the Mediterranean Sea by dumping from ships and aircraft, Barcelona, 16 February 1976, (Council Decision 77/585/EEC of 25 July 1977, published in OJ No L 240, 19.9.1977, p. 1)

Protocol concerning cooperation in combating pollution of the Mediterranean Sea by oil and other harmful substances in cases of emergency, Barcelona, 16 February 1976 (Council Decision 81/420/EEC of 19 May 1981, published in OJ No L 162, 19.6 1981, p. 4)

Convention on long-range transboundary air pollution, Geneva, 13 November 1979, (Council Decision 81/462/EEC of 11 June 1981, published in OJ No L 171, 27.6.1981, p. 11)

Protocol of 23 April 1982 concerning Mediterranean specially protected areas, Geneva, 3 April 1982, (Council Decision 84/132/EEC of 1 March 1984, published in OJ No L 68, 10.3.1984, p. 36)

Agreement for cooperation in dealing with pollution of the North Sea by oil and other harmful substances, Bonn, 13 September 1983, (Council Decision 84/358/EEC of 28 June 1984, published in OJ No L 188, 16.7. 1984, p. 7)

Cooperation agreement for the protection of the coasts and waters of the north-east Atlantic against pollution, Lisbon, 17 October 1990, (Council Decision 93/550/EEC of 20 October 1993, published in OJ No L 267, 28.10.1993, p. 20)

Basel Convention on the control of transboundary movements of hazardous wastes and their disposal, signed in Basel on 22 March 1989, (Council Decision 93/98/EEC of 1 February 1993, published in OJ No L 39, 16.2.1993, p. 1)

FINLAND

As regards those parts of the Convention which deal with innocent passage through the territorial sea, it is the intention of the Government of Finland to continue to apply the present régime to the passage of foreign warships and other government-owned vessels used for non-commercial purposes through the Finnish territorial sea, that régime being fully compatible with the Convention. [...].[23]

1. As declared upon signature, it is the understanding of Finland that the exception from the transit passage regime in straits provided for in article 35 (c) of the Convention is applicable to the strait between Finland (the Aland islands) and Sweden. Since in that strait the passage is regulated in part by a long-standing international convention in force, the present legal regime in that strait will remain unchanged after the entry into force of the Convention.

2. In accordance with article 287 of the Convention, Finland chooses the International Court of Justice and the International Tribunal for the Law of the Sea as means for the settlement of disputes concerning the interpretation or application of the Convention as well as of the Agreement relating to the implementation of its Part XI.

3. Finland recalls that, as a State member of the European Community, it has transferred competence to the Community in respect of certain matters governed by the Convention. A detailed declaration on the nature and extent of the competence transferred to the European Community will be made in due course in accordance with the provisions of Annex IX of the Convention.

---

[23] Declaration made upon signature on 10 December 1982. The second paragraph is identical with the first paragraph of the declaration made upon ratification.

FRANCE

1. The provisions of the Convention relating to the status of the different maritime spaces and to the legal régime of the uses and protection of the marine environment confirm and consolidate the general rules of the law of the sea and thus entitle the French Republic not to recognize as enforceable against it any foreign laws or regulations that are not in conformity with those general rules.

2. The provisions of the Convention relating to the area of the sea-bed and ocean floor beyond the limits of national jurisdiction show considerable deficiencies and flaws with respect to the exploration and exploitation of the said area which will require rectification through the adoption by the Preparatory Commission of draft rules, regulations and procedures to ensure the establishment and effective functioning of the International Sea-Bed Authority.

To this end, all efforts must be made within the Preparatory Commission to reach general agreement on any matter of sub- stance, in accordance with the procedure set out in rule 37 of the rules of procedure of the Third United Nations Conference on the Law of the Sea.

3. With reference to article 140, the signing of the Convention by France shall not be interpreted as implying any change in its position in respect of resolution 1514 (XV).

4. The provisions of article 230, paragraph 2, of the Convention shall not preclude interim or preventive measures against the parties responsible for the operation of foreign vessels, such as immobilization of the vessel. They shall also not preclude the imposition of penalties other than monetary penalties for any willful and serious act which causes pollution.[24]

1. France recalls that, as a State member of the European Community, it has transferred competence to the Community in certain matters covered under the Convention. A detailed statement of the nature and scope of the areas of competence transferred to the European Community will be made in due course in accordance with the provisions of Annex IX of the Convention.

2. France rejects declarations or reservations that are contrary to the provisions of the Convention. France also rejects unilateral measures or measures resulting from an agreement between States which would have effects contrary to the provisions of the Convention.

3. With reference to the provisions of article 298, paragraph 1, France does not accept any of the procedures provided for in Part XV, section 2, with respect to the following disputes:

- Disputes concerning the interpretation or application of articles 15, 74 and 83 relating to sea boundary delimitations, or those involving historic bays or titles;
- Disputes concerning military activities, including military activities by government vessels and aircraft engaged in non-commercial service, and disputes concerning law enforcement activities in regard to the exercise of sovereign rights or jurisdiction excluded from the jurisdiction of a court or tribunal under article 297, paragraph 2 or 3;
- Disputes in respect of which the Security Council of the United Nations is exercising the functions assigned to it by the Charter of the United Nations, unless the Security Council decides to remove the matter from its agenda or calls upon the parties to settle it by the means provided for in the Convention.

---

[24] Declaration made upon signature on 10 December 1982.

GABON

Declaration under article 298, paragraph 1

[The] Government of the Republic of Gabon pursuant to article 298, paragraph 1 of the Convention, does not accept any of the procedures provided for in section 2 of Part XV of the said Convention with respect to the categories of disputes referred to in paragraph 1(a) of article 298.[25]

GERMANY

Statements

I. The Federal Republic of Germany recalls that, as a member of the European Community, it has transferred competence to the Community in respect of certain matters governed by the Convention. A detailed declaration on the nature and extent of the competence transferred to the European Community will be made in due course in accordance with the provisions of Annex IX of the Convention.

II. For the Federal Republic of Germany the link between Part XI of the United Nations Convention on the Law of the Sea of 10 December 1982 and the Agreement of 28 July 1994 relating to the implementation of Part XI of the United Nations Convention on the Law of the Sea as foreseen in article 2(1) of that Agreement is fundamental.

III. In the absence of any other peaceful means, which would be given preference by the Government of the Federal Republic of Germany, that Government considers it useful to choose one of the following means for the settlement of disputes concerning the interpretation or application of the two Conventions, as it is free to do under article 287 of the Convention on the Law of the Sea, in the following order:

  1. The International Tribunal for the Law of the Sea established in accordance with Annex VI;
  2. An arbitral tribunal constituted in accordance with Annex VII;
  3. The International Court of Justice.

Also in the absence of any other peaceful means, the Government of the Federal Republic of Germany hereby recognizes as of today the validity of special arbitration for any dispute concerning the interpretation or application of the Convention on the Law of the Sea relating to fisheries, protection and preservation of the marine environment, marine scientific research and navigation, including pollution from vessels and by dumping.

Declaration

With reference to similar declarations made by the Government of the Federal Republic of Germany during the Third United Nations Conference on the Law of the Sea, the Government of the Federal Republic of Germany, in the light of declarations already made or yet to be made by States upon signature, ratification of or accession to the Convention on the Law of the Sea, declares as follows:

Territorial sea, archipelagic waters, straits

The provisions on the territorial sea represent in general a set of rules reconciling the legitimate desire of coastal States to protect their sovereignty and that of the international community to exercise the right of passage. The right to extend the breadth of the territorial sea up to 12 nautical miles will significantly increase the importance of the right of innocent passage through the territorial sea for all ships including warships, merchant ships and fishing vessels; this is a fundamental right of the community of nations.

---

[25] Declaration made after ratification, on 23 January 2009.

None of the provisions of the Convention, which in so far [as they] reflect existing international law, can be regarded as entitling the coastal State to make the innocent passage of any specific category of foreign ships dependent on prior consent or notification.

A prerequisite for the recognition of the coastal State's right to extend the territorial sea is the regime of transit passage through straits used for international navigation. Article 38 limits the right of transit passage only in cases where a route of similar convenience exists in respect of navigational and hydrographical characteristics, which include the economic aspect of shipping.

According to the provisions of the Convention, archipelagic sea lane passage is not dependent on the designation by the archipelagic States of specific sea lanes or air routes in so far as there are existing routes through the archipelago normally used for international navigation.

Exclusive economic zone

In the exclusive economic zone, which is a new concept of international law, coastal States will be granted precise resource-related rights and jurisdiction. All other States will continue to enjoy the high-seas freedoms of navigation and overflight and of all other internationally lawful uses of the sea. These uses will be exercised in a peaceful manner, and that is, in accordance with the principles embodied in the Charter of the United Nations.

The exercise of these rights can therefore not be construed as affecting the security of the coastal State or affecting its rights and obligations under international law. Accordingly, the notion of a 200-mile zone of general rights of sovereignty and jurisdiction of the coastal State cannot be sustained either in general international law or under the relevant provisions of the Convention.

In articles 56 and 58 a careful and delicate balance has been struck between the interests of the coastal State and the freedoms and rights of all other States. This balance includes the reference contained in article 58, paragraph 2, to articles 88 to 115 which apply to the exclusive economic zone in so far as they are not incompatible with Part V. Nothing in Part V is incompatible with article 89 which invalidates claims of sovereignty.

According to the Convention, the coastal State does not enjoy residual rights in the exclusive economic zone. In particular, the rights and jurisdiction of the coastal State in such zone do not include the rights to obtain notification of military exercises or manoeuvres or to authorize them.

Apart from artificial islands, the coastal State enjoys the right in the exclusive economic zone to authorize, construct, operate and use only those installations and structures which have economic purposes.

The high seas

As a geographically disadvantaged State but a State with important interests in the traditional uses of the seas, the Federal Republic of Germany remains committed to the established principle of the freedom of the high seas. This principle, which has governed all uses of the sea for centuries, has been affirmed and, in various fields, adapted to new requirements in the provisions of the Convention, which will therefore have to be interpreted to the furthest extent possible in accordance with that traditional principle.

Land-locked States

As to the regulation of the freedom of transit enjoyed by land-locked States, transit through the territory of transit States must not interfere with the sovereignty of these States. In accordance with article 125, paragraph 3, the rights and facilities provided for in Part X in no way infringe upon the sovereignty and legitimate interests of transit States. The precise content of the freedom of transit has in each single case to be agreed upon by the transit State and the land-locked State concerned. In the absence of such agreement concerning the terms and modalities for exercising the right of access, the access of persons and goods to transit through the territory of the Federal Republic of Germany is only regulated by national law, in particular with regard to means and ways of transport and the use of traffic infrastructure.[26]

Marine scientific research

Although the traditional freedom of research suffered a considerable erosion by the Convention, this freedom will remain in force for States, international organizations and private entities in some maritime areas, e.g., the seabed beyond the continental shelf and the high seas. However, the exclusive economic zone and the continental shelf, which are of particular interest to marine scientific research, will be subject to a consent regime, a basic element of which is the obligation of the coastal State under article 246, paragraph 3, to grant its consent in normal circumstances. In this regard, promotion and creation of favourable conditions for scientific research, as postulated in the Convention, are general principles governing the application and interpretation of all relevant provisions of the Convention.

The marine scientific research regime on the continental shelf beyond 200 nautical miles denies the coastal State the discretion to withhold consent under article 246, paragraph 5(a), outside areas it has publicly designated in accordance with the prerequisites stipulated in paragraph 6. Relating to the obligation, to disclose information about exploitation or exploratory operations in the process of designation is taken into account in article 246, paragraph 6, which explicitly excluded details from the information to be provided.

GREECE

1. In ratifying the United Nations Convention on the Law of the Sea, Greece secures all rights and assumes all the obligations deriving from the Convention.

Greece shall determine when and how it shall exercise those rights, according to its national strategy. This shall not imply that Greece renounces these rights in any way.

2. Greece wishes to reiterate the interpretative declaration on straits which it deposited at the time of the Convention's adoption and at the time of its signature, the original English-language text of which reads as follows:

'The present declaration concerns the provisions of Part III on "straits used for international navigation" and more especially the application in practice of articles 36, 38, 41 and 42 of the Convention on the Law of the Sea.

In areas where there are numerous spread-out islands that form a great number of alternative straits which serve in fact one and the same route of international navigation, it is the understanding of Greece that the coastal State concerned has the responsibility to designate the route or routes, in the said alternative straits, through which ships and aircraft of third countries could pass under a transit passage regime, in such a way as on the one hand the requirements of international navigation and overflight are satisfied, and on the other hand the minimum security requirements of both the ships and aircraft in transit as well as those of the coastal State are fulfilled.'[27]

3. Pursuant to article 287 of the United Nations Convention on the Law of the Sea, the Government of the Hellenic Republic hereby chooses the International Tribunal for the

---

[26] Upon depositing its instrument of ratification, the Government of the Czech Republic made the following declaration: The Government of the Czech Republic having considered the declaration of the Federal Republic of Germany of 14 October 1994 pertaining to the interpretation of the provisions of Part X of the [said Convention], which deals with the right of access of land-locked States to and from the sea and freedom of transit, states that the [said] declaration of the Federal Republic of Germany cannot be interpreted with regard to the Czech Republic in contradiction with the provisions of Part X of the Convention.

[27] This interpretative declaration on the subject of straits had been made upon signature 10 December 1982.

Law of the Sea established in accordance with Annex VI to the Convention as the means for the settlement of disputes concerning the interpretation or application of the Convention.

4.   Greece, as a State member of the European Community, has given the latter jurisdiction with respect to certain issues relating to the Convention. Following the deposit by the European Union of its instrument of formal confirmation, Greece will make a special declaration specifying in detail the issues dealt with in the Convention for which it has transferred jurisdiction to the European Union.

5.   Greece's ratification of the United Nations Convention on the Law of the Sea does not imply that it recognizes the former Yugoslav Republic of Macedonia and does not, therefore, constitute the establishment of treaty relations with the latter.[28]

---

[28] On 21 December 1995, the UN Secretary-General received from the Government of Turkey the following communication:

1.   The signature and ratification of the Convention by Greece and the subsequent declaration in this regard shall neither prejudice nor affect the existing rights and legitimate interests of Turkey with respect to maritime jurisdiction areas in the Aegean. Turkey fully reserves her rights under international law.

Turkey wishes to state that she will not acquiesce in any claim or attempt designed to upset the long-standing status quo in this respect, that would deprive Turkey of her existing rights and interests. Any unilateral act in this respect that would constitute an abuse of the provisions of the Convention would entail totally unacceptable consequences. Turkey has registered her opposition in this regard actively and persistently from the very outset.

2.   In view of the interpretative statement of Greece concerning the provisions of the Convention on the Law of the Sea on the 'Straits used for International Navigation', Turkey wishes to reiterate her statement of 15 November 1982, contained in document A/CONF.62/WS/34, which remains fully valid at present and reads as follows:

'In connection with the views expressed by the Greek delegation in the written statement contained in document A/CONF.62/WS/26 of May 1982 the Delegation of Turkey wishes to make the following statement:

The scope of the regime of straits used for international navigation and the rights and duties of States bordering straits are clearly defined in the provisions contained in Part III of the Convention on the Law of the Sea. With the limited exceptions provided in articles 35, 36, 38, paragraph 1 and 45, all straits used for international navigation are subject to the regime of transit passage.

In the written statement referred to above Greece is attempting to create a separate category of straits, i.e. spread out islands that form a great number of alternative straits which is not envisaged in the Convention nor in international law. Thereby Greece wishes to retain the power to exclude some of the straits which link the Aegean Sea to the Mediterranean from the regime of transit passage. Such arbitrary action is not permissible under the Convention nor under the rules and principles of international law.

It seems that Greece, failing in the Conference in its efforts to ensure the application of the regime of archipelagic States to the islands of the continental States, is now trying to circumvent the provisions of the Convention by a unilateral and arbitrary statement of understanding.

The reference in the Greek written statement to article 36 is of particular concern as it is an indication of Greece's intention to exercise discretionary powers not only over straits, but also over high seas.

With regard to the air routes, the Greek statement is contrary to the International Civil Aviation Organization (ICAO) rules according to which air routes are established by ICAO regional meetings with the consent of all interested parties and approved by the ICAO Council.

In view of the above considerations, the Delegation of Turkey finds the Greek views expressed in the document A/CONF.62/WS/26 legally unfounded and totally unacceptable.'

3.   Turkey reserves its right to make further declarations as may be required under the circumstances in the future.

Subsequently, on 30 June 1997, the Secretary-General received from the Government of Greece, the following communication:

Turkey has neither signed nor acceded to the [said Convention]. It is, therefore, clear the above-mentioned notification cannot have any legal effect, whatsoever.

With regard to the substance of the Turkish notification, Greece rejects all the allegations therein and would like to make the following observations, in this connection:

The purpose of the Greek statement is to interpret certain provisions of the Convention in full accordance with the spirit and the true meaning of the Convention. It is clear, therefore, that Greece neither wishes nor intends, in any way whatsoever, to create any separate category of straits used for international navigation, nor does she intend to circumvent the provisions of the Convention, in any manner.

(Cont.)

GUATEMALA

The Government of Guatemala declares, that:

(a)   Approval of the Convention by the Congress of the Republic of Guatemala shall under no circumstances affect the rights of Guatemala over the territory of Belize, including the islands, cays and islets, or its historical rights over Bahía de Amatique;

(b)   Accordingly, the territorial sea and maritime zones cannot be delimited until such time as the existing dispute is resolved.[29]

Greece observes, in particular, that the reference of Turkey to art. 36 is misleading, since the part of the high seas referred to in that article constitutes simply an element of the straits in question. Therefore, reference of Greece to this article in no way can be interpreted as an intention to exercise any discretionary powers over the high seas.

Regarding the allegation that Greece violates ICAO rules and regulations, Greece states emphatically that she respects all the rules and regulations established within the ICAO framework. It must be noted, in this respect, that the institution of transit passage is new and, for the time being, it does not influence the ICAO rules and regulations. In view of this, Greece does not see how her statement could interfere with the ICAO international air routes, in any way.

The Turkish allegations amount to a direct and unequivocal threat by a non-party to the Convention, addressed to a party thereto, with the obvious purpose of compelling Greece to abstain from exercising legitimate rights deriving from international law.

Finally, Greece Notes that Turkey makes in her statement repeatedly reference to the provision of the United Nations Law of the Sea, 1982, attempting to draw legal conclusions. Greece interprets these references as an indication that Turkey – a non signatory to the Convention – accepts its provisions as reflecting general customary law.

[29] On 11 September 1997, Belize made the following declaration: Belize cannot accept any declaration or statement made by a State which is not in conformity with articles 309 and 310 of the Convention. Article 309 prohibits reservations or exceptions unless expressly permitted by other articles of the Convention. Under article 310, declarations or statements made by a State cannot exclude or modify the legal effect of the provisions of the Convention in their application to that State. Belize considers that declarations and statements not in conformity with articles 309 and 310 of the Convention include, *inter alia*, those which are not compatible with the dispute resolution mechanism provided in Part XV of the Convention as well as those which purport to subordinate the interpretation or application of the Convention to national laws and regulations, including constitutional provisions. The recent declaration made by the Government of Guatemala on ratification of the Convention is inconsistent with the aforesaid articles 309 and 310 in the following respects:

(a) Any alleged 'rights' over land territory referred to in paragraph (a) of the declaration are outside the scope of the Convention, so that part of the declaration does not fall within the range permitted by article 310.

(b) With regard to the alleged 'historical rights' over Bahia de Amatique, the declaration purports to preclude the application of the Convention, in particular article 310 which defines bays, and Part XV which enjoins that State Parties shall settle any disputes between them concerning the interpretation or application of the Convention in accordance with the procedure prescribed therein.

(c) With regard to paragraph (b) of the Guatemalan declaration that 'the territorial sea and maritime zones cannot be delimited until such time as the existing dispute is resolved', article 74 of the Convention requires States with opposite or adjacent coasts to delimit their respective Exclusive Economic Zones by agreement or, if no agreement can be reached within a reasonable time, by recourse to the dispute settlement mechanism under Part XV of the Convention. As for the delimitation of territorial sea, article 15 of the Convention provides that States with opposite or adjacent coast may not extend their respective territorial seas beyond the median line unless they so agree. To the extent that Guatemala is purporting to make a reservation as to, or to exclude or modify the effect of the aforesaid articles 15 or 74, or Part XV of the Convention, the declaration is inconsistent with articles 309 and 310 of the Convention.

For the reasons given above, the Government of Belize hereby categorically rejects as unfounded and misconceived the Guatemala declaration *in toto*.

GUINEA

The Government of the Republic of Guinea reserves the right to interpret any article of the Convention in the context and taking due account of the sovereignty of Guinea and of its territorial integrity as it applies to the land, space and sea.[30]

GUINEA-BISSAU

The Government of the Republic of Guinea-Bissau declares that, as regards article 287 on the choice of a procedure for the settlement of disputes concerning the interpretation or application of the United Nations Convention on the Law of the Sea, it does not accept the jurisdiction of the International Court of Justice and consequently will not accept that jurisdiction with respect to articles 297 and 298.

HONDURAS

Declaration under article 287

In accordance with article 287, paragraph 1, of the United Nations Convention on the Law of the Sea, the State of Honduras chooses the International Court of Justice as the means for the settlement of disputes of any kind concerning the interpretation or application of the said Convention.

Notwithstanding the foregoing, the State of Honduras reserves the possibility of considering any other means of peaceful settlement, including the International Tribunal for the Law of the Sea, as agreed on a case-by-case basis.[31]

HUNGARY

In accordance with article 287 of the said Convention, the Government of the Republic of Hungary shall choose the following means for the settlement of disputes concerning the interpretation or application of the Convention in the following order:
1. The International Tribunal for the Law of the Sea;
2. The International Court of Justice;
3. A special tribunal constructed in accordance with Annex VIII for all the categories of disputes specified therein.

ICELAND

Under article 298 of the Convention the right is reserved that any interpretation of article 83 shall be submitted to conciliation under Annex V, section 2, of the Convention.

INDIA

(a) The Government of the Republic of India reserves the right to make at the appropriate time the declarations provided for in articles 287 and 298, concerning the settlement of disputes.

(b) The Government of the Republic of India understands that the provisions of the Convention do not authorize other States to carry out in the exclusive economic zone and

---

[30] Declaration made upon signature on 4 October 1984.
[31] Declaration made after ratification, on 18 June 2002.

on the continental shelf military exercises or manoeuvres, in particular those involving the use of weapons or explosives without the consent of the coastal State.[32]

IRAN (ISLAMIC REPUBLIC OF)

In accordance with article 310 of the Convention on the Law of the Sea, the Government of the Islamic Republic of Iran seizes the opportunity at this solemn moment of signing the Convention, to place on the records its 'understanding' in relation to certain provisions of the Convention. The main objective for submitting these declarations is the avoidance of eventual future interpretation of the following articles in a manner incompatible with the original intention and previous positions or in disharmony with national laws and regulations of the Islamic Republic of Iran.

It is [...] the understanding of the Islamic Republic of Iran that:

1) Notwithstanding the intended character of the Convention being one of general application and of law making nature, certain of its provisions are merely product of *quid pro quo* which do not necessarily purport to codify the existing customs or established usage (practice) regarded as having an obligatory character. Therefore, it seems natural and in harmony with article 34 of the 1969 Vienna Convention on the Law of Treaties, that only states parties to the Law of the Sea Convention shall be entitled to benefit from the contractual rights created therein.

The above considerations pertain specifically (but not exclusively) to the following:
–   The right of Transit passage through straits used for international navigation (Part III, Section 2, article 38).
–   The notion of 'Exclusive Economic Zone' (Part V).
–   All matters regarding the International Seabed Area and the Concept of 'Common Heritage of mankind' (Part XI).

2) In the light of customary international law, the provisions of article 21, read in association with article 19 (on the Meaning of Innocent Passage) and article 25 (on the Rights of Protection of the Coastal States), recognize (though implicitly) the rights of the Coastal States to take measures to safeguard their security interests including the adoption of laws and regulations regarding, *inter alia*, the requirements of prior authorization for warships willing to exercise the right of innocent passage through the territorial sea.

3) The right referred to in article 125 regarding access to and from the sea and freedom of transit of Land-locked States is one which is derived from mutual agreement of States concerned based on the principle of reciprocity.

4) The provisions of article 70, regarding 'Right of States with Special Geographical Characteristics' are without prejudice to the *exclusive right* of the Coastal States of enclosed and semi-enclosed maritime regions (such as the Persian Gulf and the Sea of Oman) with large population predominantly dependent upon relatively poor stocks of living resources of the same regions.

5) Islets situated in enclosed and semi-enclosed seas which potentially can sustain human habitation or economic life of their own, but due to climatic conditions, resource restriction or other limitations, have not yet been put to development, fall within the provisions of paragraph 2 of article 121 concerning 'Regime of Islands', and have,

---

[32] On 24 November 1995, Italy made the following statement with respect to the declaration made by India upon ratification, as well as for the similar ones made previously by Brazil, Cape Verde and Uruguay: Italy wishes to reiterate the declaration it made upon signature and confirmed upon ratification according to which 'the rights of the coastal State in such zone do not include the right to obtain notification of military exercises or manoeuvres or to authorize them'. According to the declaration made by Italy upon ratification this declaration applies as a reply to all past and future declarations by other States concerning the matters covered by it.

therefore, full effect in boundary delimitation of various maritime zones of the interested Coastal States.

Furthermore, with regard to 'Compulsory Procedures Entailing Binding Decisions' the Government of the Islamic Republic of Iran, while fully endorsing the Concept of settlement of all international disputes by peaceful means, and recognizing the necessity and desirability of settling, in an atmosphere of mutual understanding and cooperation, issues relating to the interpretation and application of the Convention on the Law of the Sea, at this time will not pronounce on the choice of procedures pursuant to articles 287 and 298 and reserves its positions to be declared in due time.[33]

IRAQ

1. [...].

2. Iraq interprets the provisions applying to all types of straits set forth in Part III of the Convention as applying also to navigation between islands situated near those straits if the shipping lanes leaving or entering those straits and defined by the competent international organization lie near such islands.[34]

IRELAND

Ireland recalls that, as a State member of the European Community, it has transferred competence to the Community in regard to certain matters which are governed by the Convention. A detailed declaration on the nature and extent of the competence transferred to the European Community will be made in due course in accordance with the provisions of Annex IX of the Convention.

ITALY

Upon depositing its instrument of ratification Italy recalls that, as a State member of the European Community, it has transferred competence to the Community with respect to certain matters governed by the Convention. A detailed declaration on the nature and extension of the competence transferred to the European Community will be made in due course in accordance with the provisions of Annex IX of the Convention.

Italy wishes also to reconfirm the following declarations made when it signed the Convention:

'– According to the Convention, the coastal State does not enjoy residual rights in the exclusive economic zone. In particular, the rights and jurisdiction of the coastal State in such zone do not include the right to obtain notification of military exercises or manoeuvres or to authorize them. Moreover, the rights of the coastal States to build and to authorize the construction, operation and the use of installations and structures in the exclusive economic zone and on the continental shelf is limited only to the categories of such installations and structures as listed in article 60 of the Convention.

– None of the provisions of the Convention, which corresponds on this matter to customary international law, can be regarded as entitling the coastal State to make innocent passage of particular categories of foreign ships dependent on prior consent or notification.'

---

[33] Declaration made upon signature on 10 December 1982.
[34] Declaration made upon signature on 10 December 1982.

Italy has the honour to declare, under paragraph 1(a) of article 298 of the Convention, that it does not accept any of the procedures provided for in section 2 of Part XV with respect to disputes concerning the interpretation of articles 15, 74 and 83 relating to sea boundary delimitations as well as those involving historic bays or titles.

In any case, the present declarations should not be interpreted as entailing acceptance or rejection by Italy of declarations concerning matters other than those considered in it, made by other States upon signature or ratification.

Italy reserves its right to make further declarations relating to the Convention and to the Agreement whose instrument of ratification is hereby deposited.

In implementation of article 287 of the United Nations Convention on the Law of the Sea, the Government of Italy has the honour to declare that, for the settlement of disputes concerning the application or interpretation of the Convention and of the Agreement adopted on 28 July 1994 relating to the Implementation of Part XI, it chooses the International Tribunal for the Law of the Sea and the International Court of Justice, without specifying that one has precedence over the other.

In making this declaration under article 287 of the Convention on the Law of the Sea, the Government of Italy is reaffirming its confidence in the existing international judicial organs. In accordance with article 287, paragraph 4, Italy considers that it has chosen 'the same procedure' as any other State Party that has chosen the International Tribunal for the Law of the Sea or the International Court of Justice.[35]

KIRIBATI

In exercise of the right conferred by Article 310 of the Convention, the Republic of Kiribati, upon accession to the United Nations Convention on the Law of the Sea (UNCLOS), declares that in accepting the provisions of Part IV of Article 47 of the said Convention, wishes to highlight its concerns relating to the formula used for drawing archipelagic baselines.

Part IV calculations for archipelagic waters do not allow a baseline to be drawn around all the islands of each of the three Groups of islands that make up the Republic of Kiribati. These Group of islands are spread over an expanse of over three million square kilometres of ocean, and the existing formula as spelt out in Part IV of the Convention, will divide Kiribati's three island groups into three distinct exclusive zone waters and international waters.

The Government of Kiribati wishes to propose that the formula used for drawing archipelagic baselines be revisited in the future to take into consideration the above-mentioned concerns of Kiribati.

Accession by Kiribati to the UN Convention on the Law of the Sea does not in any way prejudice its status as an archipelagic state or its legal rights to declare all or part of its maritime territory as archipelagic waters under the said Convention.

LATVIA

Declaration under article 287

In accordance with paragraph 1 of the Article 287 of the United Nations Convention on the Law of the Sea the Republic of Latvia declares that it chooses the following means for the settlement of dispute concerning the interpretation or application of this Convention:

---

[35] Declaration made after ratification, on 26 February 1997.

1) The International Tribunal for the Law of the Sea established in accordance with Annex VI of the Convention,
2) The International Court of Justice.[36]

LITHUANIA

[...] in accordance with paragraph 1 of Article 287 of the Convention, the Republic of Lithuania chooses the following means for the settlement of dispute concerning the interpretation or application of this Convention:

(a) The International Tribunal for the Law of the Sea established in accordance with Annex VI;
(b) The International Court of Justice.

LUXEMBOURG

The Government of the Grand Duchy of Luxembourg has decided to sign the United Nations Convention on the Law of the Sea because it represents, in the context of the law of the sea, a major contribution to the codification and progressive development of international law.

Nevertheless, in the view of the Government of Luxembourg, certain provisions of Part XI and Annexes III and IV of the Convention are marred by serious shortcomings and defects which, moreover, explain why it was not possible to reach a consensus on the text at the last session of the Third Conference on the Law of the Sea, held in New York in April 1982.

These shortcomings and defects concern, in particular, the mandatory transfer of technology and the cost and financing of the future Sea-Bed Authority and the first mine site of the Enterprise. They will have to be rectified by the rules, regulations and procedures to be drawn up by the Preparatory Commission. The Government of Luxembourg recognizes that the work remaining to be done is of great importance and hopes that it will be possible to reach agreement on the modalities for operating a sea-bed mining régime that will be generally acceptable and therefore conducive to promoting the activities of the international zone of the sea-bed.

As the representatives of France and the Netherlands pointed out two years ago, [the Government of Luxembourg] wishes to make it abundantly clear that, notwithstanding its decision to sign the Convention today, the Grand Duchy of Luxembourg is not here and now determined to ratify it.

It will take a separate decision on this point, at a later date, which will take account of what the Preparatory Commission has accomplished to make the international régime of the sea-bed acceptable to all.

[The Government of Luxembourg] also wishes to recall that Luxembourg is a member of the European Economic Community and, by virtue thereof, has transferred to the Community powers in certain areas covered by the Convention. Detailed declarations on the nature and extent of the powers transferred will be made in due course, in accordance with the provisions of Annex IX of the Convention.

Like other members of the Community, the Grand Duchy of Luxembourg also reserves its position on all declarations made at the final session of the Third United Nations Conference on the Law of the Sea, at Montego Bay, that may contain elements of interpretation concerning the provisions of the United Nations Convention on the Law of the Sea.[37]

---

[36] Declaration made after accession, on 31 August 2005.
[37] Declaration made upon signature on 5 December 1984.

MALAYSIA

1. The Malaysian Government is not bound by any domestic legislation or by any declaration issued by other States upon signature or ratification of this Convention. Malaysia reserves the right to state its position concerning all such legislations or declarations at the appropriate time. In particular, Malaysia's ratification of the Convention in no way constitutes recognition of the maritime claims of any other State having signed or ratified the Convention, where such claims are inconsistent with the relevant principles of international law and the provisions of the Convention on the Law of the Sea and which are prejudicial to the sovereign rights and jurisdiction of Malaysia in its maritime areas.

2. The Malaysian Government understands that the provisions of article 301, prohibiting 'any threat or use of force against the territorial integrity or political independence of any State, or in any other manner inconsistent with the principles of international law embodied in the Charter of the United Nations', apply in particular to the maritime areas under the sovereignty or jurisdiction of the coastal State.

3. The Malaysian Government also understands that the provisions of the Convention do not authorize other States to carry out military exercises or manoeuvres, in particular those involving the use of weapons or explosives in the exclusive economic zone without the consent of the coastal State.

4. In view of the inherent danger entailed in the passage of nuclear-powered vessels or vessels carrying nuclear material or other material of a similar nature and in view of the provision of article 22, paragraph 2, of the Convention on the Law of the Sea concerning the right of the coastal State to confine the passage of such vessels to sea lanes designated by the State within its territorial sea, as well as that of article 23 of the Convention, which requires such vessels to carry documents and observe special precautionary measures as specified by international agreements, the Malaysian Government, with all of the above in mind, requires the aforesaid vessels to obtain prior authorization of passage before entering the territorial sea of Malaysia until such time as the international agreements referred to in article 23 are concluded and Malaysia becomes a party thereto. Under all circumstances, the flag State of such vessels shall assume all responsibility for any loss or damage resulting from the passage of such vessels within the territorial sea of Malaysia.

5. The Malaysian Government also wishes to reiterate the statement relating to article 233 of the Convention in its application to the Straits of Malacca and Singapore which was annexed to a letter dated 28 April 1982 from the representative of Malaysia at the Third United Nations Conference on the Law of the Sea, addressed to the President of the Conference.[38]

6. The ratification of the Convention by the Malaysian Government shall not in any manner affect its rights and obligations under any agreements and treaties on maritime matters entered into which the Malaysian Government is a party.

7. The Malaysian Government interprets article 74 and article 83 to the effect that, in the absence of agreement on the delimitation of the exclusive economic zone or continental shelf or other maritime zones, for an equitable solution to be achieved, the boundary shall be the median line, namely a line every point of which is equidistant from the nearest points of the baselines from which the breadth of the territorial sea of Malaysia and of such other States is measured.

Malaysia is also of the view that, in accordance with the provisions of the Convention, namely article 56 and article 76, if the maritime area is less [than] or to a distance of 200

---

[38] Footnote in original: Official Records of the Third United Nations Conference on the Law of the Sea, vol. XVI, Documents of the Conference, p. 251, document A/CONF.62/L.145, annex.

nautical miles from the baselines, the boundary for the continental shelf and the exclusive economic zone shall be on the same line (identical).

8. The Malaysian Government declares, without prejudice to article 303 of the Convention on the Law of the Sea, that any objects of an archaeological and historical nature found within the maritime areas over which it exerts sovereignty or jurisdiction shall not be removed, without its prior notification and consent.

MALI

On signing the United Nations Convention on the Law of the Sea, the Republic of Mali remains convinced of the interdependence of the interests of all peoples and of the need to base international co-operation on, in particular, mutual respect, equality, solidarity at the international, regional and sub-regional levels, and positive good-neighbourliness between States.

It thus reiterates its statement of 30 April 1982, reaffirming that the United Nations Convention on the Law of the Sea, in the negotiation and adoption of which the Government of Mali participated in good faith, constitutes a perfectible international legal instrument.

Nevertheless, Mali's signature of the said Convention is without prejudice to any other instrument concluded or to be concluded by the Republic of Mali with a view to improving its status as a geographically disadvantaged and land-locked State. It is likewise without prejudice to the elements of any position which the Government of Mali may deem it necessary to take with regard to any question of the Law of the Sea pursuant to article 310.

In any case, the present signature has no effect on the course of Mali's foreign policy or on the rights it derives from its sovereignty under its Constitution or the Charter of the United Nations and any other relevant rule of international law.[39]

MALTA

The ratification of the United Nations Convention on the Law of the Sea is a reflection of Malta's recognition of the many positive elements it contains, including its comprehensiveness and its role in the application of the concept of the common heritage of mankind.

At the same time, it is realized that the effectiveness of the regime established by the Convention depends to a great extent on the attainment of its universal acceptance, not least by major maritime States and those with technology which are most affected by the regime.

The effectiveness of the provisions of Part IX on 'enclosed or semi-enclosed seas', which provide for cooperation of States bordering such seas, like the Mediterranean, depends on the acceptance of the Convention by the States concerned. To this end, the Government of Malta encourages and actively supports all efforts at achieving this universality.

The Government of Malta interprets articles 69 and 70 of the Convention as meaning that access to fishing in the exclusive economic zone of third States by vessels of developed land-locked and geographically disadvantaged States is dependent upon the prior granting of access by the coastal States in question to the nationals of other States which have habitually fished in the said zone.

The baselines as established by Maltese legislation for the delimitation of the territorial sea and related areas, for the archipelago of the islands of Malta and which incorporate the island of Filfla as one of the points from which baselines are drawn, are fully in line with the relevant provisions of the Convention.

[39] Declaration made upon signature on 19 October 1983.

The Government of Malta interprets article 74 and article 83 to the effect that in the absence of agreement on the delimitation of the exclusive economic zone or the continental shelf or other maritime zones, for an equitable solution to be achieved, the boundary shall be the median line, namely a line every point of which is equidistant from the nearest points of the baselines from which the breadth of the territorial waters of Malta and of such other States is measured.[40]

The exercise of the right of innocent passage of warships through the territorial sea of other States should also be perceived to be a peaceful one. Effective and speedy means of communication are easily available and make the prior notification of the exercise of the right of innocent passage of warships reasonable and not incompatible with the Convention. Such notification is already required by some States. Malta reserves the right to legislate on this point.

Malta is also of the view that such a notification requirement is needed in respect of nuclear-powered ships or ships carrying nuclear or other inherently dangerous or noxious substances. Furthermore, no such ships shall be allowed within Maltese internal waters without the necessary authorization.

Malta is of the view that the sovereign immunity contemplated in article 236 does not exonerate a State from such obligation, moral or otherwise, in accepting responsibility and liability for compensation and relief in respect of damage caused by pollution of the marine environment by any warship, naval auxiliary, other vessels or aircraft owned or operated by the State and used on government non-commercial service.

Legislation and regulations concerning the passage of ships through Malta's territorial sea are compatible with the provisions of the Convention. At the same time, the right is reserved to develop further this legislation in conformity with the Convention as may be required.

Malta declares itself in favour of establishing sea lanes and special regimes for foreign fishing vessels transversing its territorial sea.

Note is taken of the statement by the European Community made at the time of signature of the Convention regarding the fact that its member States have transferred competence to it with regard to certain aspects of the Convention. In view of Malta's application to join the European Community, it is understood that this will also become applicable to Malta on membership.

The Government of Malta does not consider itself bound by any of the declarations which other States may have made, or will make upon signing or ratifying the Convention, reserving the right as necessary to determine its position with regard to each of them at the appropriate time. In particular, ratification of the Convention does not imply automatic recognition of maritime or territorial claims by any signatory or ratifying State.

MEXICO

Declarations under articles 287 and 298

In accordance with the terms of article 287 of the United Nations Convention on the Law of the Sea, the Government of Mexico declares that it chooses, in no order of preference, one of the following means for the settlement of disputes concerning the interpretation or application of the Convention:

---

[40] On 22 February 1994, the UN Secretary-General received from the Government of Tunisia the following communication with regard to the declaration concerning articles 74 and 83 of the Convention: The Tunisian Government believes that such an interpretation is not in the least consistent with the spirit and letter of the provisions of these articles, which do not provide for automatic application of the median line with regard to delimitation of the exclusive economic zone or the continental shelf.

1. The International Tribunal for the Law of the Sea established in accordance with annex VI;
2. The International Court of Justice;
3. A special arbitral tribunal constituted in accordance with annex VIII for one or more of the categories of disputes specified therein.

The Government of Mexico declares that, pursuant to article 298 of the Convention, it does not accept the procedures provided for in part XV, section 2, with respect to the following categories of disputes:

1. Disputes relating to sea boundary delimitations, or those involving historic bays or titles, pursuant to paragraph 1 (a) of article 298;
2. Disputes concerning military activities and the other activities referred to in paragraph 1 (b) of article 298.[41]

MOLDOVA

As a country without seashore and geographically disadvantaged bordering a sea poor in living resources. Republic of Moldova affirms the necessity to develop international cooperation for the exploitation of the living resources of the economic zones, on the basis of just and equitable agreements that should ensure the access of the countries from this category to the fishing resources in the economic zones of other regions or sub regions.

MONTENEGRO

1. Proceeding from the right that State Parties have on the basis of article 310 of the United Nations Convention on the Law of the Sea, the [Government of Montenegro] considers that a coastal State may, by its laws and regulations, subject the passage of foreign warships to the requirement of previous notification to the respective coastal State and limit the number of ships simultaneously passing, on the basis of the international customary law and in compliance with the right of innocent passage (articles 17-32 of the Convention).

2. The [Government of Montenegro] also considers that it may, on the basis of article 38, para.1, and article 45, para. 1 (a) of the Convention, determine by its laws and regulations which of the straits used for international navigation in the territorial sea of [Montenegro] will retain the regime of innocent passage, as appropriate.

3. Due to the fact that the provisions of the Convention relating to the contiguous zone (article 33) do not provide rules on the delimitation of the contiguous zone between States with opposite or adjacent coasts, the [Government of Montenegro] considers that the principles of the customary international law, codified in article 24, para. 3, of the Convention on the Territorial Sea and the Contiguous Zone, signed in Geneva on 29 April 1958, will apply to the delimitation of the contiguous zone between the Parties to the United Nations Convention on the Law of the Sea.[42]

MOROCCO

The laws and regulations relating to maritime areas in force in Morocco shall remain applicable without prejudice to the provisions of the United Nations Convention on the Law of the Sea.

---

[41] Declaration made after ratification, on 6 January 2003.
[42] Declaration confirmed upon succession on 23 October 2006.

The Government of the Kingdom of Morocco affirms once again that Sebta, Melilia, the islet of Al-Hoceima, the rock of Badis and the Chafarinas Islands are Moroccan territories.

Morocco has never ceased to demand the recovery of these territories, which are under Spanish occupation, in order to achieve its territorial unity.

On ratifying the Convention, the Government of the Kingdom of Morocco declares that ratification may in no way be interpreted as recognition of that occupation.

The Government of the Kingdom of Morocco does not consider itself bound by any national legal instrument or declaration that has been made or may be made by other States when they sign or ratify the Convention and reserves the right to determine its position on any such instruments or declarations at the appropriate time.

The Government of the Kingdom of Morocco reserves the right to make, at the appropriate time, declarations pursuant to articles 287 and 298 relating to the settlement of disputes.

NETHERLANDS

A. Declaration in Respect of Article 287 of the Convention

The Kingdom of the Netherlands hereby declares that, having regard to article 287 of the Convention, it accepts the jurisdiction of the International Court of Justice in the settlement of disputes concerning the interpretation and application of the Convention with States Parties to the Convention which have likewise accepted the said jurisdiction.

B. Objections

The Kingdom of the Netherlands objects to any declaration or statement excluding or modifying the legal effect of the provisions of the United Nations Convention on the Law of the Sea. This is particularly the case with regard to the following matters:

I. Innocent passage in the territorial sea

The Convention permits innocent passage in the territorial sea for all ships, including foreign warships, nuclear-powered ships and ships carrying nuclear or hazardous waste, without any prior consent or notification, and with due observance of special precautionary measures established for such ships by international agreements.

II. Exclusive economic zone

1. Passage through the exclusive economic zone

Nothing in the Convention restricts the freedom of navigation of nuclear-powered ships or ships carrying nuclear or hazardous waste in the exclusive economic zone, provided such navigation is in accordance with the applicable rules of international law. In particular, the Convention does not authorize the coastal State to make the navigation of such ships in the exclusive economic zone dependent on prior consent or notification.

2. Military exercises in the exclusive economic zone

The Convention does not authorize the coastal State to prohibit military exercises in its exclusive economic zone. The rights of the coastal State in its exclusive economic zone are listed in article 56 of the Convention, and no such authority is given to the coastal State. In the exclusive economic zone all States enjoy the freedoms of navigation and overflight, subject to the relevant provisions of the Convention.

3. Installations in the exclusive economic zone

The coastal State enjoys the right to authorize, operate and use installations and structures in the exclusive economic zone for economic purposes. Jurisdiction over the establishment and use of installations and structures is limited to the rules contained in article 56 paragraph 1, and is subject to the obligations contained in article 56 paragraph 2, article 58 and article 60 of the Convention.

4. Residual rights

The coastal State does not enjoy residual rights in the exclusive economic zone. The rights of the coastal State in its exclusive economic zone are listed in article 56 of the Convention, and cannot be extended unilaterally.

III. Passage through straits

Routes and sea lanes through straits shall be established in accordance with the rules provided for in the Convention. Considerations with respect to domestic security and public order shall not affect navigation in straits used for international navigation. The application of other international instruments to straits is subject to the relevant articles of the Convention.

IV. Archipelagic States

The application of Part IV of the Convention is limited to a State constituted wholly by one or more archipelagos, and may include other islands. Claims to archipelagic status in contravention of article 46 are not acceptable.

The status of archipelagic State, and the rights and obligations deriving from such status, can only be invoked under the conditions of part IV of the Convention.

V. Fisheries

The Convention confers no jurisdiction on the coastal State with respect to the exploitation, conservation and management of living marine resources other than sedentary species beyond the exclusive economic zone.

The Kingdom of the Netherlands considers that the conservation and management of straddling fish stocks and highly migratory species should, in accordance with articles 63 and 64 of the Convention, take place on the basis of international cooperation in appropriate subregional and regional organizations.

VI. Underwater cultural heritage

Jurisdiction over objects of an archaeological and historical nature found at sea is limited to articles 149 and 303 of the Convention.

The Kingdom of the Netherlands does however consider that there may be a need to further develop, in international cooperation, the international law on the protection of the underwater cultural heritage.

VII. Baselines and delimitation

A claim that the drawing of baselines or the delimitation of maritime zones is in accordance with the Convention will only be acceptable if such lines and zones have been established in accordance with the Convention.

VIII. National legislation

As a general rule of international law, as stated in articles 27 and 46 of the Vienna Convention on the Law of Treaties, States may not rely on national legislation as a justification for a failure to implement the Convention.

IX. Territorial claims

Ratification by the Kingdom of the Netherlands does not imply recognition or acceptance of any territorial claim made by a State party to the Convention.

X. Article 301

Article 301 must be interpreted, in accordance with the Charter of the United Nations, as applying to the territory and the territorial sea of a coastal State.

XI. General declaration

The Kingdom of the Netherlands reserves its right to make further declarations relative to the Convention and to the Agreement, in response to future declarations and statements.

C. Declaration in Accordance with Annex IX of the Convention

Upon depositing its instrument of ratification the Kingdom of the Netherlands recalls that, as State member of the European Community, it has transferred competence to the Community with respect to certain matters governed by the Convention. A detailed declaration on the nature and extent of the competence transferred to the European Community will be made in due course in accordance with the provisions in Annex IX of the Convention.

NICARAGUA

In accordance with article 310, Nicaragua declares that such adjustments of its domestic law as may be required in order to harmonize it with the Convention will follow from the process of constitutional change initiated by the revolutionary State of Nicaragua, it being understood that the Convention and the Resolutions adopted on 10 December 1982 and the Annexes to the Convention constitute an inseparable whole.

For the purposes of articles 287 and 298 and of other articles concerning the interpretation and application of the Convention, the Government of Nicaragua shall, if and as the occasion demands, exercise the right conferred by the Convention to make further supplementary or clarificatory declarations.[43]

In accordance with article 310 of the United Nations Convention on the Law of the Sea, the Government of Nicaragua hereby declares:

1. That it does not consider itself bound by any of the declarations or statements, however phrased or named, made by other States when signing, accepting, ratifying or acceding to the Convention and that it reserves the right to state its position on any of those declarations or statements at any time.

2. That ratification of the Convention does not imply recognition or acceptance of any territorial claim made by a State party to the Convention, nor automatic recognition of any land or sea border.

In accordance with article 287, paragraph 1, of the Convention, Nicaragua hereby declares that it accepts only recourse to the International Court of Justice as a means for the settlement of disputes concerning the interpretation or application of the Convention.

Nicaragua hereby declares that it accepts only recourse to the International Court of Justice as a means for the settlement of the categories of disputes set forth in subparagraphs (a), (b) and (c) of paragraph 1 of article 298 of the Convention.

NORWAY

Declaration pursuant to article 310 of the Convention

According to article 309 of the Convention, no reservations or exceptions other than those expressly permitted by its provisions may be made. A declaration pursuant to its article 310 cannot have the effect of an exception or reservation for the State making it. Consequently, the Government of the Kingdom of Norway declares that it does not consider itself bound by declarations pursuant to article 310 of the Convention that are or will be made by other States or international organizations. Passivity with respect to such declarations shall be interpreted neither as acceptance nor as rejection of such declarations. The Government reserves Norway's right at any time to take a position on such declarations in the manner deemed appropriate.

---

[43] Declaration made upon signature on 9 December 1984.

Declaration pursuant to article 287 of the Convention

The Government of the Kingdom of Norway declares pursuant to article 287 of the Convention that it chooses the International Court of Justice for the settlement of disputes concerning the interpretation or application of the Convention.

Declaration pursuant to article 298 of the Convention

The Government of the Kingdom of Norway declares pursuant to article 298 of the Convention that it does not accept an arbitral tribunal constituted in accordance with Annex VII for any of the categories of disputes mentioned in article 298.

OMAN

It is the understanding of the Government of the Sultanate of Oman that the application of the provisions of articles 19, 25, 34, 38 and 45 of the Convention does not preclude a coastal State from taking such appropriate measures as are necessary to protect its interest of peace and security.[44]

Pursuant to the provisions of article 310 of the Convention and further to the earlier declaration by the Sultanate of Oman dated 1 June 1982 concerning the establishment of straight baselines at any point on the coastline of the Sultanate of Oman and the lines enclosing waters within inlets and bays and waters between islands and the coastline, in accordance with article 2 (c) of Royal Decree No. 15/81 and in view of the desire of the Sultanate of Oman to bring its laws into line with the provisions of the Convention, the Sultanate of Oman issues the following declarations:

Declaration No. 1, on the territorial sea

1. The Sultanate of Oman determines that its territorial sea, in accordance with article 2 of Royal Decree No. 15/81 dated 10 February 1981, extends 12 nautical miles in a seaward direction, measured from the nearest point of the baselines.

2. The Sultanate of Oman exercises full sovereignty over its territorial sea, the space above the territorial sea and its bed and subsoil, pursuant to the relevant laws and regulations of the Sultanate and in conformity with the provisions of this Convention concerning the principle of innocent passage.

Declaration No. 2, on the passage of warships through Omani territorial waters

Innocent passage is guaranteed to warships through Omani territorial waters, subject to prior permission. This also applies to submarines, on condition that they navigate on the surface and fly the flag of their home State.

Declaration No. 3, on the passage of nuclear-powered ships and the like through Omani territorial waters

With regard to foreign nuclear-powered ships and ships carrying nuclear or other substances that are inherently dangerous or harmful to health or the environment, the right of innocent passage, subject to prior permission, is guaranteed to the types of vessel, whether or not warships, to which the descriptions apply. This right is also guaranteed to submarines to which the descriptions apply, on condition that they navigate on the surface and fly the flag of their home State.

Declaration No. 4, on the contiguous zone

The contiguous zone extends for a distance of 12 nautical miles measured from the outer limit of the territorial waters, and the Sultanate of Oman exercises the same prerogatives over it as are established by the Convention

---

[44] Declaration made upon signature on 1 July 1983.

Declaration No. 5, on the exclusive economic zone

1. The Sultanate of Oman determines that its exclusive economic zone, in accordance with article 5 of Royal Decree No. 15/81 dated 10 February 1981, extends 200 nautical miles in a seaward direction, measured from the baselines from which the territorial sea is measured.

2. The Sultanate of Oman possesses sovereign rights over its economic zone and also exercises jurisdiction over that zone as provided for in the Convention. It further declares that, in exercising its rights and performing its duties under the Convention in the exclusive economic zone, it will have due regard to the rights and duties of other States and will act in a manner compatible with the provisions of the Convention.

Declaration No. 6, on the continental shelf

The Sultanate of Oman exercises over its continental shelf sovereign rights for the purpose of exploring it and exploiting its natural resources, as permitted by geographical conditions and in accordance with this Convention.

Declaration No. 7, on the procedure chosen for the settlement of disputes under the Convention

Pursuant to article 287 of the Convention, The Sultanate of Oman declares its acceptance of the jurisdiction of the International Tribunal for the Law of the Sea, as set forth in annex VI to the Convention, and the jurisdiction of the International Court of Justice, with a view to the settlement of any dispute that may arise between it and another State concerning the interpretation or application of the Convention.

PAKISTAN

(i) The Government of the Islamic Republic of Pakistan shall, at an appropriate time, make declarations provided for in articles 287 and 298 relating to the settlement of disputes.

(ii) The Law of the Sea Convention, while dealing with transit through the territory of the transit State, fully safeguards the sovereignty of the transit State. Consequently, in accordance with article 125, the rights and facilities of transit to the land-locked State ensure that it shall not in any way infringe upon the sovereignty and the legitimate interest of the transit State. The precise content of the freedom of transit consequently, in each case, has to be agreed upon by the transit State and the land-locked State concerned. In the absence of such an agreement concerning the terms and modalities for exercising the right of transit, through the territory of the Islamic Republic of Pakistan shall be regulated only by national laws of Pakistan.

(iii) It is the understanding of the Government of the Islamic Republic of Pakistan that the provisions of the Convention on the Law of the Sea do not in any way authorize the carrying out in the exclusive economic zone and in the continental shelf of any coastal State military exercises or manoeuvres by other States, in particular where the use of weapons or explosives is involved, without the consent of the coastal State concerned.

PALAU

Declaration under article 298

The Government of the Republic of Palau declares under paragraph 1 (a) of Article 298 of the 1982 United Nations Convention on the Law of the Sea that it does not accept compulsory procedures entailing binding decisions relating to the delimitation and/or interpretation of maritime boundaries.[45]

---

[45] Declaration made after accession, on 27 April 2006.

PANAMA

The Republic of Panama, in depositing its instrument of ratification of the United Nations Convention on the Law of the Sea (adopted by Law No. 38 of 4 June 1996 and promulgated in Official Journal No. 23.056 of 12 June 1996), declares that it has exclusive sovereignty over the 'historic Panamanian bay' of the Golfo de Panamá, a well-marked geographic configuration the coasts of which belong entirely to the Republic of Panama. It is a large indentation or inlet to the south of the Panamanian isthmus, where sea-waters superjacent to the seabed and subsoil cover the area between latitudes 7°28′00″ North and 7°31′00″ North and longitudes 79°59′53″ and 78°11′40″, both west of Greenwich, these being the positions of Punta Mala and Punta Jaqué respectively, west and east of the entrance of the Golfo de Panamá. This large indentation penetrates fairly deep into the Panamanian isthmus. The width of its entrance, from Punta Mala to Punta de Jaqué is some 200 kilometres and it penetrates inland a distance of 165 kilometres (measured from the imaginary line joining Punta Mala and Punta Jaqué to the mouths of the Rio Chico east of Panama City).

Given its present and potential resources, the historic bay of the Golfo de Panamá is a vital necessity for the Republic of Panama, both in terms of security and defence (this has been the case since time immemorial) and in economic terms, as its marine resources have been utilized since ancient times by the inhabitants of the Panamanian isthmus.

It is oblong in shape, with a coastal outline that roughly resembles a calf's head, and its coastal perimeter, which measures some 668 kilometres, is under the maritime control of Panama. According to this delimitation, the historic bay of the Golfo de Panamá has an area of approximately 30,000 square kilometres.

The Republic of Panama declares that, in the exercise of its sovereign and territorial rights and in compliance with its duties, it will act in a manner compatible with the provisions of the Convention and reserves the right to issue further statements on the Convention if necessary.

PHILIPPINES

1. The signing of the Convention by the Government of the Republic of the Philippines shall not in any manner impair or prejudice the sovereign rights of the Republic of the Philippines under and arising from the Constitution of the Philippines.[46]

---

[46] On 3 August 1988, Australia made the following objection: Australia considers that [the] declaration made by the Republic of the Philippines is not consistent with article 309 of the Law of the Sea Convention, which prohibits the making of reservations, nor with article 310 which permits declarations to be made 'provided that such declarations or statements do not purport to exclude or to modify the legal effect of the provisions of this Convention in their application to that State.'

The declaration of the Republic of the Philippines asserts that the Convention shall not affect the sovereign rights of the Philippines arising from its Constitution, its domestic legislation and any treaties to which the Philippines is a party. This indicates, in effect, that the Philippines does not consider that it is obliged to harmonise its law with the provisions of the Convention. By making such an assertion, the Philippines is seeking to modify the legal effect of the Convention's provisions.

This view is supported by the specific reference in the declaration to the status of archipelagic waters. The declaration states that the concept of archipelagic waters in the Convention is similar to the concept of internal waters held under former constitutions of the Philippines and recently reaffirmed in article 1 of the New Constitution of the Philippines in 1987. It is clear, however, that the Convention distinguishes the two concepts and that different obligations and rights are applicable to archipelagic waters from those which apply to internal waters. In particular, the Convention provides for the exercise by foreign ships of the rights of innocent passage and of archipelagic sea lanes passage in archipelagic waters.

Australia cannot, therefore, accept that the statement of the Philippines has any legal effect or will have any effect when the Convention comes into force and considers that the provisions of the Convention should be observed without being made subject to the restrictions asserted in the declaration of the Republic of the Philippines.

Similar objections were made by Belarus, Bulgaria, Ukraine, and the USSR.

2. Such signing shall not in any manner affect the sovereign rights of the Republic of the Philippines as successor of the United States of America, under and arising out of the Treaty of Paris between Spain and the United States of America of 10 December 1898, and the Treaty of Washington between the United States of America and Great Britain of 2 January 1930.

3. Such signing shall not diminish or in any manner affect the rights and obligations of the contracting parties under the Mutual Defence Treaty between the Philippines and the United States of America of 30 August 1951 and its related interpretative instruments; nor those under any other pertinent bilateral or multilateral treaty or agreement to which the Philippines is a party.

4. Such signing shall not in any manner impair or prejudice the sovereignty of the Republic of the Philippines over any territory over which it exercises sovereign authority, such as the Kalayaan Islands, and the waters appurtenant thereto.[47]

5. The Convention shall not be construed as amending in any manner any pertinent laws and Presidential Decrees or Proclamation of the Republic of the Philippines; the Government of the Republic of the Philippines maintains and reserves the right and authority to make any amendments to such laws, decrees or proclamations pursuant to the provisions of the Philippines Constitution.

6. The provisions of the Convention on archipelagic passage through sea lanes do not nullify or impair the sovereignty of the Philippines as an archipelagic State over the sea lanes and do not deprive it of authority to enact legislation to protect its sovereignty, independence and security.

7. The concept of archipelagic waters is similar to the concept of internal waters under the Constitution of the Philippines, and removes straits connecting these waters with the economic zone or high sea from the rights of foreign vessels to transit passage for international navigation.

8. The agreement of the Republic of the Philippines to the submission for peaceful resolution, under any of the procedures provided in the Convention, of disputes under article 298 shall not be considered as a derogation of Philippines sovereignty.[48]

PORTUGAL

1. Portugal reaffirms, for the purpose of delimitation of the territorial sea, the continental shelf and the exclusive economic zone, its rights under domestic law in respect of the mainland and of the archipelagos and the islands incorporated therein;

---

[47] On 12 June 1985, the UN Secretary-General received from the Government of China the following communication: The so-called Kalayaan Islands are part of the Nansha Islands, which have always been Chinese territory. The Chinese Government has stated on many occasions that China has indisputable sovereignty over the Nansha Islands and at the adjacent waters and resources.

On 23 February 1987, the UN Secretary-General received from the Government of Viet Nam the following communication concerning the declarations made by the Philippines and by China: [...] The Republic of the Philippines, upon its signature and ratification of the 1982 UN Convention on the Law of the Sea, has claimed sovereignty over the islands called by the Philippines as the Kalaysan [see paragraph 4 of the declaration]. The People's Republic of China has likewise claimed that the islands, called by the Philippines as the Kalaysan, constitute part of the Nansha Islands which are Chinese territory. The so-called 'Kalaysan Islands' or 'Nansha Islands' mentioned above are in fact the Truong Sa Archipelago which has always been under the sovereignty of the Socialist Republic of Vietnam. The Socialist Republic of Vietnam has so far published two White Books confirming the legality of its sovereignty over the Hoang Sa and Truong Sa Archipelagoes. The Socialist Republic of Vietnam once again reaffirms its indisputable sovereignty over the Truong Sa Archipelago and hence its determination to defend its territorial integrity.

[48] Understanding made upon signature on 10 December 1982 and confirmed upon ratification on 8 May 1984.

2. Portugal declares that, within a 12 nautical mile zone contiguous to its territorial sea, it shall take such control measures as it deems to be necessary, in accordance with the provisions of article 33 of the Convention;

3. Pursuant to the provisions of the United Nations Convention on the Law of the Sea, Portugal enjoys sovereign rights and jurisdiction over an exclusive economic zone of 200 nautical miles from the baselines from which the breadth of the territorial sea is measured;

4. The maritime boundary lines between Portugal and the States whose coasts are opposite or adjacent to its own coasts are those which historically have been established on the basis of international law;

5. Portugal expresses its understanding that the Resolution III of the United Nations Third Conference on the Law of the Sea shall fully apply to the non-self-governing Territory of East Timor, of which it remains the administering Power, under the United Nations Charter and the relevant Resolutions of the General Assembly and of the Security Council. Accordingly, the application of the Convention, in particular a delimitation, if any, of the maritime areas of the territory of East Timor, shall take into consideration the rights of its people under the Charter and the Resolutions and, furthermore, the responsibilities incumbent upon Portugal as administering Power of the Territory of East Timor;

6. Portugal declares, without prejudice to the provisions of Article 303 of the United Nations Convention on the Law of the Sea and to the application of other legal instruments of international law regarding the protection of the underwater archaeological heritage, any objects of a historical or archaeological nature found in the maritime zones under its sovereignty or jurisdiction may be removed only after prior notice to and subject to the consent of the competent Portuguese authorities;

7. Ratification by Portugal of this Convention does not imply the automatic recognition of any maritime or land boundary;

8. Portugal does not consider itself bound by the declarations made by other States and it reserves its position as regards each declaration to be expressed in due time;

9. Bearing in mind the available scientific information and with a view to the protection of the environment and the sustained growth of economic activities based on the sea, Portugal will, preferably through international cooperation and taking into account the precautionary principle, carry out control activities beyond the areas under national jurisdiction;

10. For the purposes of Article 287 of the Convention, Portugal declares that, in the absence of non-judicial means for the settlement of disputes arising out of the application of this Convention, it will choose one of the following means for the settlement of disputes:

    (a)   the International Tribunal for the Law of the Sea, established in pursuance of Annex VI;

    (b)   the International Court of Justice;

    (c)   an arbitral tribunal constituted in accordance with Annex VII;

    (d)   a special arbitral tribunal, constituted in accordance with Annex VIII;

11. In the absence of any other peaceful means for the settlement of disputes, Portugal will, in accordance with Annex VIII to the Convention, choose the recourse to a special arbitral tribunal in so far as the application of the provisions of this Convention, or the interpretation thereof, to the matters relating to fisheries, protection and preservation of living marine resources and marine environment, scientific research, navigation and marine pollution are concerned;

12. Portugal declares that, without prejudice to the provisions contained in Section 1, Part XV of this Convention, it does not accept the compulsory procedures referred to in Section in Section 2 of the said Part, with respect to one or more of the categories specified in Article 298 (a) (b) (c) of this Convention;

13. Portugal notes that, as a Member State of the European Community, it has transferred to the Community competence over a few matters governed by this Convention. A detailed declaration will be submitted in due time, specifying the nature and extent of the matters in respect of which it has transferred competence to the Community, in accordance with the provisions of Annex IX of the Convention.

REPUBLIC OF KOREA

Declaration pursuant to Article 298

1. In accordance with paragraph 1 of Article 298 of the Convention, the Republic of Korea does not accept any of the procedures provided for in section 2 of Part XV of the Convention with respect to all the categories of disputes referred to in paragraph 1(a), (b) and (c) of Article 298 of the Convention.

2. The present declaration shall be effective immediately.

3. Nothing in the present declaration shall affect the right of the Republic of Korea to submit a request to a court or tribunal referred to in Article 287 of the Convention to be permitted to intervene in the proceedings of any dispute between other States Parties, should it consider that it has an interest of a legal nature which may be affected by the decision in that dispute.[49]

ROMANIA

1. As a geographically disadvantaged country bordering a sea poor in living resources, Romania reaffirms the necessity to develop international cooperation for the exploitation of the living resources of the economic zones, on the basis of just and equitable agreements that should ensure the access of the countries from this category to the fishing resources in the economic zones of other regions or subregions.

2. Romania reaffirms the right of coastal States to adopt measures to safeguard their security interests, including the right to adopt national laws and regulations relating to the passage of foreign warships through their territorial sea.

The right to adopt such measures is in full conformity with articles 19 and 25 of the Convention, as it is also specified in the Statement by the President of the United Nations Conference on the Law of the Sea in the plenary meeting of the Conference on 26 April 1982.

3. Romania states that according to the requirements of equity - as it results from articles 74 and 83 of the Convention on the Law of the Sea - the uninhabited islands without economic life can in no way affect the delimitation of the maritime spaces belonging to the mainland coasts of the coastal States.[50]

RUSSIAN FEDERATION

1. The Union of Soviet Socialist Republics declares that, under article 287 of the United Nations Convention on the Law of the Sea, it chooses an arbitral tribunal constituted in accordance with Annex VII as the basic means for the settlement of disputes concerning the interpretation or application of the Convention. It opts for a special arbitral tribunal constituted in accordance with Annex VIII for the consideration of matters relating to fisheries, the protection and preservation of the marine environment, marine scientific

---

[49] Declaration made after ratification, on 18 April 2006.
[50] Declaration made upon signature on 10 December 1982 and confirmed upon ratification on 17 December 1996.

research, and navigation, including pollution from vessels and dumping. It recognizes the competence of the International Tribunal for the Law of the Sea, as provided for in article 292, in matters relating to the prompt release of detained vessels and crews.

2. The Union of Soviet Socialist Republics declares that, in accordance with article 298 of the Convention, it does not accept the compulsory procedures entailing binding decisions for the consideration of disputes relating to sea boundary delimitations, disputes concerning military activities, or disputes in respect of which the Security Council of the United Nations is exercising the functions assigned to it by the Charter of the United Nations.[51]

The Russian Federation declares that, in accordance with article 298 of the United Nations Convention on the Law of the Sea, it does not accept the procedures, provided for in section 2 of Part XV of the Convention, entailing binding decisions with respect to disputes concerning the interpretation or application of articles 15, 74 and 83 of the Convention, relating to sea boundary delimitations, or those involving historic bays or titles; disputes concerning military activities, including military activities by government vessels and aircraft, and disputes concerning law-enforcement activities in regard to the exercise of sovereign rights or jurisdiction; and disputes in respect of which the Security Council of the United Nations is exercising the functions assigned to it by the Charter of the United Nations.

The Russian Federation, bearing in mind articles 309 and 310 of the Convention, declares that it objects to any declarations and statements made in the past or which may be made in future when signing, ratifying or acceding to the Convention, or made for any other reason in connection with the Convention, that are not in keeping with the provisions of article 310 of the Convention. The Russian Federation believes that such declarations and statements, however phrased or named, cannot exclude or modify the legal effect of the provisions of the Convention in their application to the party to the Convention that made such declarations or statements, and for this reason they shall not be taken into account by the Russian Federation in its relations with that party to the Convention.

SAO TOME AND PRINCIPE

I. The signing of the Convention by the Government of the Democratic Republic of Sao Tome and Principe will in no way affect or prejudice the sovereign rights of the Democratic Republic of Sao Tome and Principe embodied in and flowing from the Constitution of Sao Tome and Principe;

II. The Government of the Democratic Republic of Sao Tome and Principe reserves the right to adopt laws and regulations relating to the innocent passage of foreign warships through its territorial sea or its archipelagic waters and to take any other measures aimed at safeguarding its security;

III. The Government of the Democratic Republic of Sao Tome and Principe considers that the provisions of the Convention relating to archipelagic waters, the territorial sea and the exclusive economic zone are compatible with the legislation of the Republic of Sao Tome and Principe as regards its sovereignty and its jurisdiction over the maritime space adjacent to its coasts;

IV. The Government of the Democratic Republic of Sao Tome and Principe considers that, in accordance with the provisions of the Convention, where the same stock area adjacent thereto, the States fishing for such stocks in the adjacent area are under an obligation to agree with the coastal State upon the measures necessary for the conservation of the stock or stocks of associated species;

[51] Declaration made upon signature on 10 December 1982.

V. The Government of the Democratic Republic of Sao Tome and Principe, in accordance with the relevant provisions of the Convention, reserves the right to adopt laws and regulations to ensure the conservation of highly migratory species and to co-operate with the States whose nationals harvest these species in order to promote the optimum utilization thereof.[52]

SAUDI ARABIA

1. The Government of the Kingdom of Saudi Arabia is not bound by any domestic legislation or by any declaration issued by other States upon signature or ratification of this Convention. The Kingdom reserves the right to state its position concerning all such legislation or declarations at the appropriate time. In particular, the Kingdom's ratification of the Convention in no way constitutes recognition of the maritime claims of any other State having signed or ratified the Convention, where such claims are inconsistent with the provisions of the Convention on the Law of the Sea and prejudicial to the sovereign rights and jurisdiction of the Kingdom in its maritime areas.

2. The Government of the Kingdom of Saudi Arabia is not bound by any international treaty or agreement which contains provisions that are inconsistent with the Convention on the Law of the Sea and prejudicial to the sovereign rights and jurisdiction of the Kingdom in its maritime areas.

3. The Government of the Kingdom of Saudi Arabia considers that application of the provisions of Part IX of the Convention concerning the cooperation of States bordering enclosed or semi-enclosed areas is subject to the acceptance of the Convention by all States concerned.

4. The Government of the Kingdom of Saudi Arabia considers that the provisions of the Convention relating to application of the system for transit passage through straits used for international navigation which connect one part of the high seas or an exclusive economic zone with another part of the high seas or an exclusive economic zone also apply to navigation between islands adjacent or contiguous to such straits, particularly where the sea lanes used for entrance to or exit from the strait, as designated by the competent international organization, are situated near such islands.

5. The Government of the Kingdom of Saudi Arabia considers that innocent passage does not apply to its territorial sea where there is a route to the high seas or an exclusive economic zone which is equally suitable as regards navigational and hydrographic features.

6. In view of the inherent danger entailed in the passage of nuclear-powered vessels or vessels carrying nuclear material or other material of a similar nature and in view of the provision of article 22, paragraph 2, of the Convention on the Law of the Sea concerning the right of the coastal State to confine the passage of such vessels to sea lanes designated by the State within its territorial sea, as well as that of article 23 of the Convention, which requires such vessels to carry documents and observe special precautionary measures as specified by international agreements, the Kingdom of Saudi Arabia, with all of the above in mind, requires the aforesaid vessels to obtain prior authorization of passage before entering the territorial sea of the Kingdom until such time as the international agreements referred to in article 23 are concluded and the Kingdom becomes a party thereto. Under all circumstances, the flag State of such vessels shall assume all responsibility for any loss or damage resulting from the innocent passage of such vessels within the territorial sea of the Kingdom of Saudi Arabia.

---

[52] Declaration made upon signature on 13 July 1983.

7. The Kingdom of Saudi Arabia shall issue its internal procedures for the maritime areas subject to its sovereignty and jurisdiction, so as to affirm the sovereign rights and jurisdiction and guarantee the interests of the Kingdom in those areas.

SERBIA

1. Proceeding from the right that States parties have on the basis of article 310 of the United Nations Convention on the Law of the Sea, the Government of [Yugoslavia] considers that a coastal State may, by its laws and regulations, subject the passage of foreign warships to the requirement of previous notification to the respective coastal State and limit the number of ships simultaneously passing, on the basis of the international customary law and in compliance with the right of innocent passage (articles 17 to 32 of the Convention).

2. The Government of [Yugoslavia] also considers that it may, on the basis of article 38, paragraph 1, and article 45, paragraph 1 (a) of the Convention, determine by its laws and regulations which of the straits used for international navigation in the territorial sea of [Yugoslavia] will retain the regime of innocent passage, as appropriate.

3. Owing to the fact that the provisions of the Convention relating to the contiguous zone (article 33) do not provide rules on the delimitation of the contiguous zone between States with opposite or adjacent coasts, the Government of [Yugoslavia] considers that the principles of the customary international law, codified in article 24, paragraph 3, of the Convention on the Territorial Sea and the Contiguous Zone, signed at Geneva on 29 April 1958, will apply to the delimitation of the contiguous zone between the parties to the United Nations Convention on the Law of the Sea.[53]

SLOVENIA

The Republic of Slovenia does not consider itself to be bound by the declaratory statement on the basis of article 310 of the Convention, given by the former Socialist Federal Republic of Yugoslavia.

Proceeding from the right that States Parties have on the basis of article 310 of the United Nations Convention on the Law of the Sea, the Republic of Slovenia considers that its Part V 'Exclusive Economic Zone', including the provisions of article 70, 'Right of Geographically Disadvantaged States', forms part of the general customary international law.[54]

Declaration pursuant to article 287
The Government of the Republic of Slovenia declares pursuant to article 287 of the Convention that it chooses an arbitral tribunal constituted in accordance with Annex VII for the settlement of disputes concerning the interpretation or application of the Convention.

Declaration pursuant to article 298
The Government of the Republic of Slovenia declares pursuant to article 298 of the Convention that it does not accept an arbitral tribunal constituted in accordance with Annex VII for any of the categories of disputes mentioned in article 298.[55]

---

[53] Declaration confirmed upon succession on 12 March 2001.
[54] Declaration made upon succession on 16 June 1995.
[55] Declaration made after succession, on 11 October 2001.

SOUTH AFRICA

[...] The Government of the Republic of South Africa shall, at an appropriate time, make declarations provided for in Articles 287 and 298 of the Convention relating to the settlement of disputes.

SPAIN

1. The Spanish Government, upon signing this Convention, declares that this act cannot be interpreted as recognition of any rights or situations relating to the maritime spaces of Gibraltar which are not included in article 10 of the Treaty of Utrecht of 13 July 1713 between the Spanish and British Crowns. The Spanish Government also considers that Resolution III of the Third United Nations Conference on the Law of the Sea is not applicable in the case of the Colony of Gibraltar, which is undergoing a decolonization process in which only the relevant resolutions adopted by the United Nations General Assembly apply.

2. It is the Spanish Government's interpretation that the régime established in Part III of the Convention is compatible with the right of the coastal State to issue and apply its own air regulations in the air space of the straits used for international navigation so long as this does not impede the transit passage of aircraft.

3. With regard to article 39, paragraph 3, it takes the word 'normally' to mean 'except in cases of *force majeure* or distress'.

4. With regard to Article 42, it considers that the provisions of paragraph 1 (b) do not prevent it from issuing, in accordance with international law, laws and regulations giving effect to generally accepted international regulations.

5. The Spanish Government interprets articles 69 and 70 of the Convention as meaning that access to fishing in the economic zones of third States by the fleets of developed land-locked and geographically disadvantaged States is dependent upon the prior granting of access by the coastal States in question to the nationals of other States who have habitually fished in the economic zone concerned.

6. It interprets the provisions of Article 221 as not depriving the coastal State of a strait used for international navigation of its powers, recognized by international law, to intervene in the case of the casualties referred to in that article.

7. It considers that Article 233 must be interpreted, in any case, in conjunction with the provisions of Article 34.

8. It considers that, without prejudice to the provisions of Article 297 regarding the settlement of disputes, Articles 56, 61 and 62 of the Convention preclude considering as discretionary the powers of the coastal State to determine the allowable catch, its harvesting capacity and the allocation of surpluses to other States.

9. Its interpretation of Annex III, Article 9, is that the provisions thereof shall not obstruct participation, in the joint ventures referred to in paragraph 2, of the States Parties whose industrial potential precludes them from participating directly as contractors in the exploitation and resources of the Area.[56]

1. The Kingdom of Spain recalls that, as a member of the European Union, it has transferred competence over certain matters governed by the Convention to the European Community. A detailed declaration will be made in due course as to the nature and extent of the competence transferred to the European Community, in accordance with the provisions of Annex IX of the Convention.

---

[56] Declaration made upon signature on 4 December 1984.

2. In ratifying the Convention, Spain wishes to make it known that this act cannot be construed as recognition of any rights or status regarding the maritime space of Gibraltar that are not included in article 10 of the Treaty of Utrecht of 13 July 1713 concluded between the Crowns of Spain and Great Britain. Furthermore, Spain does not consider that Resolution III of the Third United Nations Conference on the Law of the Sea is applicable to the colony of Gibraltar, which is subject to a process of decolonization in which only relevant resolutions adopted by the United Nations General Assembly are applicable.

3. Spain understands that:

(a) The provisions laid down in Part III of the Convention are compatible with the right of a coastal State to dictate and apply its own regulations in straits used for international navigation, provided that this does not impede the right of transit passage.

(b) In article 39, paragraph 3 (a), the word 'normally' means 'unless by *force majeure* or by distress'.

(c) The provisions of article 221 shall not deprive a State bordering a strait used for international navigation of its competence under international law regarding intervention in the event of the casualties referred to in that article.

4. Spain interprets that:

(a) Articles 69 and 70 of the Convention mean that access to fisheries in the exclusive economic zone of third States by the fleets of developed landlocked or geographically disadvantaged States shall depend on whether the relevant coastal States have previously granted access to the fleets of States which habitually fish in the relevant exclusive economic zone.

(b) With regard to article 297, and without prejudice to the provisions of that article in respect of settlement of disputes, articles 56, 61 and 62 of the Convention do not allow of an interpretation whereby the rights of the coastal State to determine permissible catches, its capacity for exploitation and the allocation of surpluses to other States may be considered discretionary.

5. The provisions of article 9 of Annex III shall not prevent States Parties whose industrial potential does not enable them to participate directly as contractors in the exploitation of the resources of the zone from participating in the joint ventures referred to in paragraph 2 of that article.

6. In accordance with the provisions of article 287, paragraph 1, Spain chooses the International Court of Justice as the means for the settlement of disputes concerning the interpretation or application of the Convention.

Declarations under articles 287 and 298

Pursuant to article 287, paragraph 1, the Government of Spain declares that it chooses the International Tribunal for the Law of the Sea and the International Court of Justice as means for the settlement of disputes concerning the interpretation or application of the Convention.

The Government of Spain declares, pursuant to the provisions of article 298, para. 1(a) of the Convention, that it does not accept the procedures provided for in part XV, section 2, with respect to the settlement of disputes concerning the interpretation or application of articles 15, 74 and 83 relating to sea boundary delimitations, or those involving historic bays or titles.[57]

---

[57] Declaration made after ratification, on 19 July 2002.

SUDAN

[...] [The Sudan] wishes to reiterate [the statement by the President of the Conference] in plenary meeting during the Third United Nations Conference on the Law of the Sea, on 26 April 1982, concerning article 21, in which deals with the laws and regulations of the coastal State relating to innocent passage: namely, that the withdrawal of the amendment submitted at the time by a number of States did not prejudge the right of coastal States to take all necessary measures, particularly in order to protect their security, in accordance with article 19 on the meaning of the term 'innocent passage' and article 25 on the rights of protection of the coastal State.

The Sudan also wishes to state that, according to its interpretation, the definition of the term 'geographically disadvantaged States' given in article 70, paragraph 2, applies to all the parts of the Convention in which this term appears. [...].[58]

SWEDEN

It is the understanding of the Government of Sweden that the exception from the transit passage régime in straits, provided for in Article 35 (c) of the Convention is applicable to the strait between Sweden and Denmark (Oresund) as well as to the strait between Sweden and Finland (the Aland islands). Since in both those straits the passage is regulated in whole or in part by long-standing international conventions in force, the present legal régime in the two straits will remain unchanged.

As regards those parts of the Convention which deal with innocent passage through the territorial sea, it is the intention of the Government of Sweden to continue to apply the present régime for the passage of foreign warships and other government-owned vessels used for non-commercial purposes through the Swedish territorial sea, that régime being fully compatible with the Convention.

It is also the understanding of the Government of Sweden that the Convention does not affect the rights and duties of a neutral State provided for in the Convention concerning the Rights and Duties of Neutral Powers in case of Naval Warfare (XIII Convention), adopted at The Hague on 18 October 1907.[59]

It is the understanding of the Government of the Kingdom of Sweden that the exception from the transit passage regime in straits, provided for in article 35 (c) of the Convention is applicable to the strait between Sweden and Denmark (Oresund), as well as to the strait between Sweden and Finland (the Aland islands). Since in both those straits the passage is regulated in whole or in part by long-standing international conventions in force, the present legal regime in the two straits will remain unchanged.

The Government of the Kingdom of Sweden hereby chooses, in accordance with article 287 of the Convention, the International Court of Justice for the settlement of disputes concerning the interpretation or application of the Convention and the Agreement Implementing Part XI of the Convention.

The Kingdom of Sweden recalls that, as a member of the European Community, it has transferred competence in respect of certain matters governed by the Convention. A detailed declaration on the nature and extent of the competence transferred to the European Community will be made in due course in accordance with the provisions of Annex IX of the Convention.

[58] Declarations made in plenary meeting at the Final Part of the Eleventh Session of the Third United Nations Conference on the Law of the Sea, held at Montego Bay, Jamaica, from 6 to 10 December 1982, and reiterated upon signature on 10 December 1982.

[59] Declaration made upon signature on 10 December 1982.

TRINIDAD AND TOBAGO

Declaration under article 287
The Republic of Trinidad and Tobago [...] declare[s] that in the absence of or failing any other peaceful means, The Republic of Trinidad and Tobago chooses the following means in order of priority for the settlement of disputes concerning the interpretation or application of the United Nations Convention on the Law of the Sea:

a. The International Tribunal for the Law of the Sea established in accordance with Annex VI;

b. The International Court of Justice.

Declaration under article 298
[The] Minister of Foreign Affairs of the Republic of Trinidad and Tobago, do hereby declare under paragraph 1 (a) of article 298 of the United Nations Convention on the Law of the Sea done at Montego Bay on the tenth day of December one thousand nine hundred and eighty-two, that the Republic of Trinidad and Tobago does not accept any of the procedures provided for in Part XV, section 2 of the Convention with respect to the categories of disputes concerning the interpretation or application of articles 15, 74 and 83 relating to sea boundary delimitations as well as those involving historic bays or titles.[60]

TUNISIA

[...] Declaration 2
The Republic of Tunisia, in accordance with the provisions of article 311, and in particular paragraph 6 thereof, declares its adherence to the basic principle relating to the common heritage of mankind and that it will not be a party to any agreement in derogation thereof. The Republic of Tunisia calls upon all States to avoid any unilateral measure or legislation of this kind that would lead to disregard of the provisions of the Convention or to the exploitation of the resources of the seabed and ocean floor and the subsoil thereof outside of the legal regime of the seas and oceans provided for in this Convention and in the other legal instruments pertaining thereto, in particular resolution I and resolution II.

Declaration 3
The Republic of Tunisia, in accordance with the provisions of article 298 of the United Nations Convention on the Law of the Sea, declares that it does not accept the procedures provided for in part XV, section 2, of the said Convention with respect to the following categories of disputes:

(a) (i) Disputes concerning the interpretation or application of articles 15, 74 and 83 relating to sea boundary delimitations, or those involving historic bays or titles, provided that a State having made such a declaration shall, when such a dispute arises subsequent to the entry into force of this Convention and where no agreement within a reasonable period of time is reached in negotiations between the parties, at the request of any party to the dispute, accept submission of the matter to conciliation under annex V, section 2; and provided further that any dispute that necessarily involves the concurrent consideration of any unsettled dispute concerning sovereignty or other rights over continental or insular land territory shall be excluded from such submission;

(ii) After the conciliation commission has presented its report, which shall state the reasons on which it is based, the parties shall negotiate an

---

[60] Declaration made after ratification, on 13 February 2009.

agreement on the basis of that report; if these negotiations do not result in an agreement, the parties shall, by mutual consent, submit the question to one of the procedures provided for in section 2, unless the parties otherwise agree;

(iii) This subparagraph does not apply to any sea boundary dispute finally settled by an arrangement between the parties, or to any such dispute which is to be settled in accordance with a bilateral or multilateral agreement binding upon those parties;

(b) Disputes concerning military activities, including military activities by government vessels and aircraft engaged in non-commercial service, and disputes concerning law enforcement activities in regard to the exercise of sovereign rights or jurisdiction excluded from the jurisdiction of a court or tribunal under article 297, paragraph 2 or 3;

(c) Disputes in respect of which the Security Council of the United Nations is exercising the functions assigned to it by the Charter of the United Nations, unless the Security Council decides to remove the matter from its agenda or calls upon the parties to settle it by the means provided for in this Convention.

Declaration 4

The Republic of Tunisia, in accordance with the provisions of article 310 of the United Nations Convention on the Law of the Sea, declares that its legislation currently in force does not conflict with the provisions of this Convention. However, laws and regulations will be adopted as soon as possible in order to ensure closer harmony between the provisions of the Convention and the requirements for completing Tunisian legislation in the maritime sphere.

Declaration under article 287

In accordance with the provisions of article 287 of the United Nations Convention on the Law of the Sea, the Government of Tunisia declares that it accepts, in order of preference, the following means for the settlement of disputes relating to the interpretation or implementation of the above-mentioned Convention:

(a) The International Tribunal for the Law of the Sea;

(b) An arbitral tribunal established in accordance with Annex VII.[61]

UKRAINE

1. Ukraine declares that, in accordance with article 287 of the United Nations Convention on the Law of the Sea of 1982, it chooses as the principal means for the settlement of disputes concerning the interpretation or application of this Convention an arbitral tribunal constituted in accordance with Annex VII. For the consideration of disputes concerning the interpretation or application of the Convention in respect of questions relating to fisheries, protection and preservation of the marine environment, marine scientific research and navigation, including pollution from vessels and by dumping, Ukraine chooses a special arbitral tribunal constituted in accordance with Annex VIII.

Ukraine recognizes the competence, as stipulated in article 292 of the Convention, of the International Tribunal for the Law of the Sea in respect of questions relating to the prompt release of detained vessels or their crews.

2. Ukraine declares, in accordance with article 298 of the Convention, that it does not accept, unless otherwise provided by specific international treaties of Ukraine with relevant States, the compulsory procedures entailing binding decisions for the consideration of

---

[61] Declaration made after ratification, on 22 May 2001.

disputes relating to sea boundary delimitations, disputes involving historic bays or titles, and disputes concerning military activities.

3. Ukraine declares, taking into account articles 309 and 310 of the Convention, that it objects to any statements or declarations, irrespective of when such statements or declarations were or may be made, that may result in a failure to interpret the provisions of the Convention in good faith, or are contrary to the ordinary meaning of terms in the context of the Convention or its object and purpose.

4. As a geographically disadvantaged country bordering a sea poor in living resources, Ukraine reaffirms the necessity to develop international cooperation for the exploitation of the living resources of economic zones, on the basis of just and equitable agreements that should ensure the access to fishing resources in the economic zones of other regions and sub-regions.

UNITED KINGDOM OF GREAT BRITAIN AND NORTHERN IRELAND

(a) General

The United Kingdom cannot accept any declaration or statement made or to be made in the future which is not in conformity with articles 309 and 310 of the Convention. Article 309 of the Convention prohibits reservations and exceptions (except those expressly permitted by other articles of the Convention). Under article 310 declarations and statements made by a State cannot exclude or modify the legal effect of the provisions of the Convention in their application to the State concerned.

The United Kingdom considers that declarations and statements not in conformity with articles 309 and 310 include, *inter alia*, the following:

- those which relate to baselines not drawn in conformity with the Convention;
- those which purport to require any form of notification or permission before warships or other ships exercise the right of innocent passage or freedom of navigation or which otherwise purport to limit navigational rights in ways not permitted by the Convention;
- those which are incompatible with the provisions of the Convention relating to straits used for international navigation, including the right of transit passage;
- those which are incompatible with the provisions of the Convention relating to archipelagic states or waters, including archipelagic baselines and archipelagic sea lanes passage;
- those which are not in conformity with the provisions of the Convention relating to the exclusive economic zone or the continental shelf, including those which claim coastal state jurisdiction over all installations and structures in the exclusive economic zone or on the continental shelf, and those which purport to require consent for exercises or manoeuvres (including weapons exercises) in those areas;
- those which purport to subordinate the interpretation or application of the Convention to national laws and regulations, including constitutional provisions.

(b) European Community

The United Kingdom recalls that, as a Member of the European Community, it has transferred competence to the Community in respect of certain matters governed by the Convention. A detailed declaration on the nature and extent of the competence to the European Community will be made in due course in accordance with the provisions of Annex IX of the Convention.

(c)   The Falkland Islands

With regard to paragraph (d) of the Declaration made upon ratification of the Convention by the Government of the Argentine Republic, the Government of the United Kingdom has no doubt about the sovereignty of the United Kingdom over the Falkland Islands and over South Georgia and the South Sandwich Islands. The Government of the United Kingdom, as the administering authority of both Territories, has extended the United Kingdom's accession to the Convention and ratification of the Agreement to the Falkland Islands and to South Georgia and the South Sandwich Islands. The Government of the United Kingdom, therefore, rejects as unfounded paragraph (d) of the Argentine declaration.

(d)   Gibraltar

With regard to point 2 of the declaration made upon ratification of the Convention by the Government of Spain, the Government of the United Kingdom has no doubt about the sovereignty of the United Kingdom over Gibraltar, including its territorial waters. The Government of the United Kingdom, as the administering authority of Gibraltar, has extended the United Kingdom's accession to the Convention and ratification of the Agreement to Gibraltar. The Government of the United Kingdom, therefore, rejects as unfounded point 2 of the Spanish declaration.

(e)   Extent

These instruments of accession and of ratification extend to: The United Kingdom of Great Britain and Northern Ireland; The Bailiwick of Jersey; The Bailiwick of Guernsey; The Isle of Man; Anguilla; Bermuda; British Antarctic Territory; British Indian Ocean Territory; British Virgin Islands; Cayman Islands; Falkland Islands; Gibraltar; Montserrat; Pitcairn, Henderson, Ducie and Oeno Islands; St. Helena and Dependencies; South Georgia and South Sandwich Islands; Turks and Caicos Islands.

Declaration on the choice of procedure under article 287

In accordance with Article 287, paragraph 1, of the United Nations Convention on the Law of the Sea, the United Kingdom of Great Britain and Northern Ireland chooses the International Court of Justice for the settlement of disputes concerning the interpretation or application of the Convention.

The International Tribunal for the Law of the Sea is a new institution, which the United Kingdom hopes will make an important contribution to the peaceful settlement of disputes concerning the law of the sea. In addition to those cases where the Convention itself provides for the compulsory jurisdiction of the Tribunal, the United Kingdom remains ready to consider the submission of disputes to the Tribunal as may be agreed on a case-by-case basis.[62]

Declaration pursuant to article 298, paragraph 1

[...] the United Kingdom of Great Britain and Northern Ireland does not accept any of the procedures provided for in section 2 of Part XV of the Convention with respect to the categories of disputes referred to in paragraph 1(b) and (c) of article 298.[63]

UNITED REPUBLIC OF TANZANIA

In accordance with article 287 of the United Nations Convention on the Law of the Sea, the United Republic of Tanzania declares that it chooses the International Tribunal for the Law of the Sea for the settlement of disputes concerning the interpretation or application of the Convention.

---

[62] Declaration made after accession, on 12 January 1998.
[63] Declaration made after accession, on 7 April 2003.

URUGUAY

(A) The provisions of the Convention concerning the territorial sea and the exclusive economic zone are compatible with the main purposes and principles underlying Uruguayan legislation in respect of Uruguay's sovereignty and jurisdiction over the sea adjacent to its coast and over its bed and subsoil up to a limit of 200 miles.

(B) The legal nature of the exclusive economic zone as defined in the Convention and the scope of the rights which the Convention recognizes to the coastal State leave room for no doubt that it is a '*sui generis*' zone of national jurisdiction different from the territorial sea and that it is not part of the high seas.

(C) Regulation of the uses and activities not provided for expressly in the Convention (residual rights and obligations) relating to the rights of sovereignty and to the jurisdiction of the coastal State in its exclusive economic zone falls within the competence of that State, provided that such regulation does not prevent enjoyment of the freedom of international communication which is recognized to other States.

(D) In the exclusive economic zone, enjoyment of the freedom of international communication in accordance with the way it is defined and in accordance with other relevant provisions of the Convention excludes any non-peaceful use without the consent of the coastal State - for instance, military exercises or other activities which may affect the rights or interests of that State; and it also excludes the threat or use of force against the territorial integrity, political independence, peace or security of the coastal State.

(E) This Convention does not empower any State to build, operate or utilize installations or structures in the exclusive economic zone of another State, neither those referred to in the Convention nor any other kind, without the consent of the coastal State.

(F) In accordance with all the relevant provisions of the Convention, where the same stock or stocks of associated species occur both within the exclusive economic zone and in an area beyond and adjacent to the zone, the States fishing for such stocks in the adjacent area are duty bound to agree with the coastal State upon the measures necessary for the conservation of these stocks or associated species.

(G) When the Convention enters into force, Uruguay will apply, with respect to other States parties, the provisions established by the Convention and by Uruguayan legislation, on the basis of reciprocity.

(H) Pursuant to the provisions of article 287, Uruguay declares that it chooses the International Tribunal for the Law of the Sea for the settlement of such disputes relating to the interpretation or application of the Convention as are not subject to other procedures, without prejudice to its recognition of the jurisdiction of the International Court of Justice and of such agreements with other States as may provide for other means for peaceful settlement.

(I) Pursuant to the provisions of article 298, Uruguay declares that it will not accept the procedures provided for in part XV, section 2, of the Convention, in respect of disputes concerning law enforcement activities in regard to the exercise of sovereign rights or jurisdiction excluded from the jurisdiction of a court or tribunal under article 297, paragraphs 2 and 3.

(J) Uruguay reaffirms that, as stated in article 76, the continental shelf is the natural prolongation of the territory of the coastal State to the outer edge of the continental margin.[64]

---

[64] Declarations made upon signature on 10 December 1982 on and confirmed upon ratification on 10 December 1992.

VIET NAM

The Socialist Republic of Viet Nam, by ratifying the 1982 United Nations Convention on the Law of the Sea, expresses its determination to join the international community in the establishment of an equitable legal order and in the promotion of maritime development and cooperation.

The National Assembly reaffirms the sovereignty of the Socialist Republic of Viet Nam over its internal waters and territorial sea; the sovereign rights and jurisdiction in the contiguous zone, the exclusive economic zone and the continental shelf of Viet Nam, based on the provisions of the Convention and principles of international law; and calls on other countries to respect the above-said rights of Viet Nam.

The National Assembly reiterates Viet Nam's sovereignty over the Hoang Sa and Truong Sa archipelagoes and its position to settle those disputes relating to territorial claims as well as other disputes in the Eastern Sea through peaceful negotiations in the spirit of equality, mutual respect and understanding, and with due respect of international law, particularly the 1982 United Nations Convention on the Law of the Sea, and of the sovereign rights and jurisdiction of the coastal States over their respective continental shelves and exclusive economic zones; the concerned parties should, while exerting active efforts to promote negotiations for a fundamental and long-term solution, maintain stability on the basis of the status quo, refrain from any act that may further complicate the situation and from the use of force or threat of force.

The National Assembly emphasizes that it is necessary to [differentiate] between the settlement of the dispute over the Hoang Sa and Truong Sa archipelagoes and the defence of the continental shelf and maritime zones falling under Viet Nam's sovereignty, rights and jurisdiction, based on the principles and standards specified in the 1982 United Nations Convention on the Law of the Sea.

The National Assembly [authorizes] the National Assembly's Standing Committee and the Government to review all relevant national legislation to consider necessary amendments in conformity with the 1982 United Nations Convention on the Law of the Sea, and to safeguard the interests of Viet Nam.

The National Assembly authorizes the Government to undertake effective measures for the management and defence of the continental shelf and maritime zones of Viet Nam.

YEMEN

1. The People's Democratic Republic of Yemen will give precedence to its national laws in force which require prior permission for the entry or transit of foreign warships or of submarines or ships operated by nuclear power or carrying radioactive materials.

2. With regard to the delimitation of the maritime borders between the People's Democratic Republic of Yemen and any State having coasts opposite or adjacent to it, the median line basically adopted shall be drawn in a way such that every point of it is equidistant from the nearest points on the baselines from which the breadth of the territorial sea of any State is measured. This shall be applicable to the maritime borders of the mainland territory of the People's Democratic Republic of Yemen and also of its islands.[65]

---

[65] The Yemen Arab Republic had signed the Convention on 10 December 1982 with the following declarations:
1. The Yemen Arabic Republic adheres to the rules of general international law concerning rights to national sovereignty over coastal territorial waters, even in the case of the waters of a strait linking two seas.

2.   The Yemen Arab Republic adheres to the concept of general international law concerning free passage as applying exclusively to merchant ships and aircraft; nuclear-powered craft, as well as warships and warplanes in general, must obtain the prior agreement of the Yemen Arab Republic before passing through its territorial waters, in accordance with the established norm of general international law relating to national sovereignty.

3.   The Yemen Arab Republic confirms its national sovereignty over all the islands in the Red Sea and the Indian Ocean which have been its dependencies since the period when the Yemen and the Arab countries were a Turkish administration.

4.   The Yemen Arab Republic declares that its signature of the Convention on the Law of the Sea is subject to the provisions of this declaration and the completion of the constitutional procedures in effect. [...].

In response to this declaration, Ethiopia on 8 November 1984 made the following statement: Paragraph 3 of the declaration relates to claims of sovereignty over unspecified islands in the Red Sea and the Indian Ocean which clearly is outside the purview of the Convention. Although the declaration, not constituting a reservation as it is prohibited by article 309 of the Convention, is made under article 310 of same and as such is not governed by articles 19-23 of the Vienna Convention on the Law of Treaties providing for acceptance of and objections to reservations, nevertheless, the Provisional Military Government of Socialist Ethiopia wishes to place on record that paragraph 3 of the declaration by the Yemen Arab Republic cannot in any way affect Ethiopia's sovereignty over all the islands in the Red Sea forming part of its national territory.

APPENDIX 3: CLAIMS TO MARITIME JURISDICTION

(as at 15 February 2009)[1]

Country	Landlocked State	National legislation provides for straight baselines along all or part of the coast (including straight lines across river mouths and bays)	Claim to archipelagic status	Territorial Sea	Contiguous Zone	Exclusive Economic Zone	Fisheries Zone	Continental Shelf (as reflected in national legislation)	Submission to the CLCS
				Breadth of the zones in nautical miles					
Afghanistan	×								
Albania		×		12					
Algeria		×		12	24		32 or 52	D²	
Andorra	×								
Angola		×		12	24	200			
Antigua and Barbuda			×	12	24	200		CM/200³	
Argentina		×		12	24	200		CM/200	×
Armenia	×								
Australia		×		12 *⁴	24	200		CM/200	×
Austria	×								
Azerbaijan	×								
Bahamas			×	12		200			
Bahrain				12	24				
Bangladesh		×		12	18	200		CM⁵	
Barbados		×		12		200			×
Belarus	×								
Belgium				12	24	CP⁶	CP	D	
Belize		×		12 *		200			
Benin				200					
Bhutan	×								
Bolivia	×								
Bosnia and Herzegovina									
Botswana	×								
Brazil		×		12	24	200		CM/200	×
Brunei Darussalam				12		200			
Bulgaria		×		12	24	200		D	
Burkina Faso	×								
Burundi	×								
Cambodia		×		12	24	200		200	
Cameroon		×		12				CM/200	

[1] Appendix 3 is based on the Table of claims to maritime jurisdiction prepared by the Division for Ocean Affairs and the Law of the Sea, Office of Legal Affairs of the United Nations. For the latest Table see http://www.un.org/Depts/los/LEGISLATIONANDTREATIES/claims.htm.

[2] D indicates that according to national legislation the limits of a given zone are to be established by a delimitation agreement with other States. In the absence of such an agreement the boundary is to be median (equidistant) line.

[3] CM/200 indicates a claim extending to the outer edge of the continental margin, or to 200 nautical miles where the outer edge does not extend up to that distance.

[4] * indicates that a different rule applies to parts of the sea area concerned.

[5] CM indicates a claim extending to the outer edge of the continental margin.

[6] CP indicates that the breadth of the zone is defined by coordinates of points.

Country	Landlocked State	National legislation provides for straight baselines along all or part of the coast (including straight lines across river mouths and bays)	Claim to archipelagic status	Territorial Sea	Contiguous Zone	Exclusive Economic Zone	Fisheries Zone	Continental Shelf (as reflected in national legislation)	Submission to the CLCS
				Breadth of the zones in nautical miles					
Canada		×		12	24	200		CM/200	
Cape Verde			×	12	24	200		200	
Central African Republic	×								
Chad	×								
Chile		×		12	24	200			
China		×		12	24	200		CM/200	
Colombia		×		12		200		unspecified	
Comoros			×	12		200			
Congo				200					
Cook Islands				12		200		CM/200	×
Costa Rica		×		12		200			
Côte d'Ivoire		×		12		200			×
Croatia		×		12		CP[7]		D	
Cuba		×		12	24	200			×
Cyprus		×		12	24	200	EXP[8]		
Czech Republic	×								
DPR of Korea				12	50[9]	200			
DR of the Congo				12		D			
Denmark		×		12 *	24	200/ D[10]	200[11]	200 m[12]/ EXP	×
Djibouti		×		12	24	200			
Dominica		×		12	24	200			
Dominican Republic		×	×	12	24	200		CM/200	
Ecuador		×		200[13]				200	
Egypt		×		12	24	×[14]			
El Salvador				200					
Equatorial Guinea		×		12		200			
Eritrea				12		×[15]			
Estonia		×		12 *		CP		CP	
Ethiopia	×								
Fiji			×	12		200		200 m/EXP	×
Finland		×		12 *	14[16]	D	CP	200 m/EXP	

[7] The Ecological and Fisheries Protection Zone proclaimed only certain elements of the EEZ. The outer limit of the Zone is defined by a list of geographical coodinates.

[8] EXP indicates a claim up to the depth of exploitability.

[9] 50-nautical mile military zone in the Sea of Japan and to EEZ limit in the Yellow Sea.

[10] Applies also to Greenland.

[11] For Greenland and Færoe Islands.

[12] 200m indicates a claim up to a depth of 200 metres.

[13] Only between the continental territorial sea of Ecuador and its insular territorial sea around the Galápagos Islands.

[14] In March 2003, Cyprus and Egypt signed an agreement on the delimitation of their respective exclusive economic zones.

[15] The exclusive economic zone has been delimited in arbitration Eritrea-Yemen, Award in phase II: Maritime delimitation.

[16] Two miles beyond the outer limits of the territorial sea.

Country	Landlocked State	National legislation provides for straight baselines along all or part of the coast (including straight lines across river mouths and bays)	Claim to archipelagic status	Territorial Sea	Contiguous Zone	Exclusive Economic Zone	Fisheries Zone	Continental Shelf (as reflected in national legislation)	Submission to the CLCS
						Breadth of the zones in nautical miles			
France		×		12	24	200 *		200 m/EXP	×
Gabon		×		12	24	200			
Gambia				12	18		200		
Georgia				12		D		D	
Germany		×		12 *		CP		200 m/EXP	
Ghana				12	24	200		200	×
Greece				6[17]				200 m/EXP	
Grenada		×		12		200			
Guatemala				12		200		unspecified	
Guinea				12		200			
Guinea-Bissau		×		12		200			
Guyana		×		12		200		CM/200	
Haiti		×		12	24	200		EXP	
Honduras		×		12	24	200		unspecified	
Hungary	×								
Iceland		×		12		200		CM/200	×
India				12	24	200		CM/200	×
Indonesia			×	12		200			×
Iran		×		12	24	D		D	
Iraq				12				unspecified	
Ireland		×		12	24	200	200	CP	×
Israel				12 *				EXP	
Italy		×		12		D		200 m/EXP	
Jamaica			×	12	24	200		CM/200	
Japan		×		12 *	24	200		CM/200	×
Jordan				3					
Kazakhstan	×								
Kenya		×		12		200			×
Kiribati		×	×	12		200			
Kuwait				12				CP	
Kyrgyzstan	×								
Lao PDR	×								
Latvia		×		12		D		CM/200	
Lebanon				12					
Lesotho	×								
Liberia				200					
Libyan Arab Jamahiriya		×		12			62		
Liechtenstein	×								
Lithuania		×		12	CP	D		D	
Luxembourg	×								
Madagascar		×		12	24	200		200[18]	

[17] Ten-mile limit applies for the purpose of regulating civil aviation.
[18] 200 nautical miles or delimitation agreement or 100 nautical miles from isobath 2,500m.

Country	Landlocked State	National legislation provides for straight baselines along all or part of the coast (including straight lines across river mouths and bays)	Claim to archipelagic status	Territorial Sea	Contiguous Zone	Exclusive Economic Zone	Fisheries Zone	Continental Shelf (as reflected in national legislation)	Submission to the CLCS
				Breadth of the zones in nautical miles					
Malawi	×								
Malaysia				12		200		200 m/EXP	×
Maldives			×	12	24	200			
Mali	×								
Malta		×		12	24		25	200 m/EXP	
Marshall Islands			×	12	24	200			
Mauritania		×		12	24	200		CM/200	
Mauritius		×		12	24	200		CM/200	×
Mexico		×		12	24	200		CM/200	×
Micronesia				12		200			×
Moldova	×								
Monaco				12					
Mongolia	×								
Montenegro									
Morocco		×		12	24	200		200 m/EXP	
Mozambique		×		12	24	200		CM/200	
Myanmar		×		12	24	200		CM/200	×
Namibia				12	24	200		CM/200	×
Nauru		×		12	24	200			
Nepal	×								
Netherlands		×		12	24	CP		200 m/EXP	
New Zealand		×		12	24	200		CM/200	×
Nicaragua				12	24	200		CM	
Niger	×								
Nigeria				12		200		200 m/EXP	×
Niue				12		200			
Norway		×		12	24	200	200[19]	CM/200	×
Oman		×		12	24	200		unspecified	
Pakistan		×		12	24	200		CM/200	×
Palau				3			200		×
Panama				12	24	200		CM/200	
Papua New Guinea			×	12 *			200	200 m/EXP	×
Paraguay	×								
Peru				200				200	
Philippines			×	CP[20]		200		EXP	×
Poland		×		12		D			
Portugal		×		12	24	200		EXP	×
Qatar				12	24	D			
Republic of Korea		×		12	24	200			
Romania		×		12	24	200			
Russian Federation		×		12	24	200		CM/200	×

[19] Jan Mayen and Svalbard.
[20] Rectangle defined by coordinates; claim extends beyond 12 nautical miles.

Country	Landlocked State	National legislation provides for straight baselines along all or part of the coast (including straight lines across river mouths and bays)	Claim to archipelagic status	Territorial Sea	Contiguous Zone	Exclusive Economic Zone	Fisheries Zone	Continental Shelf (as reflected in national legislation)	Submission to the CLCS
				Breadth of the zones in nautical miles					
Rwanda	×								
Saint Kitts and Nevis		×		12	24	200		CM/200	
Saint Lucia				12	24	200		CM/200	
Saint Vincent and the Grenadines			×	12	24	200			
Samoa		×		12	24	200			
San Marino	×								
Sao Tome and Principe			×	12		200			
Saudi Arabia		×		12	18			unspecified	
Senegal		×		12	24	200		CM/200	
Serbia	×								
Seychelles			×	12	24	200		CM/200	×
Sierra Leone				12	24	200		200	
Singapore				12[21]		D			
Slovakia	×								
Slovenia		×		12/D		D		D	
Solomon Islands			×	12		200		200	×
Somalia		×		200					
South Africa		×		12	24	200		CM/200	×
Spain		×		12	24	200[22]	CP[23]		×
Sri Lanka		×		12	24	200		CM/200	×
Sudan		×		12	18			200 m/EXP	
Suriname				12		200			×
Swaziland	×								
Sweden		×		12		D		200 m/EXP	
Switzerland	×								
Syrian Arab Republic		×		12	24	200		CM	
Tajikistan	×								
Thailand		×		12	24	200			
The FYR of Macedonia	×								
Timor-Leste				12	24	200		CM/200	
Togo				30		200			
Tonga		×		12		200			×
Trinidad and Tobago			×	12	24	200		CM/200	×
Tunisia		×		12	24	D	×[24]		
Turkey				6–12[25]		200[26]			
Turkmenistan	×								

[21] In case of overlap with the territorial sea of neighbouring countries, negotiations with a view to arriving at agreed delimitations in accordance with international law will be undertaken. The same applies to the EEZ.
[22] In the Atlantic Ocean.
[23] In the Mediterranean.
[24] Up to 50-m isobath - Off the Gulf of Gabès.
[25] Six nautical miles in the Aegean Sea, 12 nautical miles in the Black Sea.
[26] In the Black Sea.

Country	Landlocked State	National legislation provides for straight baselines along all or part of the coast (including straight lines across river mouths and bays)	Claim to archipelagic status	Territorial Sea	Contiguous Zone	Exclusive Economic Zone	Fisheries Zone	Continental Shelf (as reflected in national legislation)	Submission to the CLCS
				Breadth of the zones in nautical miles					
Tuvalu			×	12	24	200			
Uganda	×								
Ukraine		×		12		200			
United Arab Emirates		×		12	24	200		CM/200	
United Kingdom		×		12 *		200[27]	200 or 12[28]	CP	×
United Republic of Tanzania				12		200			
United States of America				12	24	200		CM/200	
Uruguay		×		12	24	200		CM	×
Uzbekistan	×								
Vanuatu		×	×	12	24	200		CM/200	
Vatican City	×								
Venezuela		×		12	15	200		200 m/EXP	
Viet Nam		×		12	24	200		CM/200	×
Yemen		×		12	24	200		CM/200	×
Zambia	×								
Zimbabwe	×								

[27] Bermuda, Pitcairn, South Georgia and South Sandwich Islands.
[28] 12 nautical miles in Guernsey; 200 nautical miles in United Kingdom, Anguilla, British Indian Ocean Territory, British Virgin Islands, Cayman Islands, Falkland Islands, Monserrat, St. Helena and Dependencies, and Turks and Caicos Islands.

INDEX

Nomenclature used in the index

The numbers in bold print refer to the document numbers which can be found in the top outside corner of each page; the numbers in normal type refer to the regulation, rule, article, paragraph, subparagraph or other numbers within a document. For example, **36** 298(1)(a)(ii) denotes article 298, paragraph 1, subparagraph (a), sub-subparagraph (ii), of the United Nations Convention on the Law of the Sea which is reproduced as document number 36.

References to the preamble of a document are indicated by use of the letter P followed by the paragraph number of the preamble in square brackets. For example, **56** P[5] denotes the fifth preambular paragraph of the Agreement for the Implementation of the Provisions of the United Nations Convention on the Law of the Sea Relating to the Conservation and Management of Straddling Fish Stocks and Highly Migratory Fish Stocks. Similarly, references to the Introduction of a document are indicated by use of 'Intro' following the document number. For example, **58** Intro denotes the Introduction to the Code of Conduct for Responsible Fisheries.

References to articles, paragraphs and sub-paragraphs in the Annex to a document are in the form 'document number + Annex' (including Annex number, if applicable) in bold print, followed by the section, article and paragraph numbers in normal type. For example, **36 Annex VI** 8(2) refers to the United Nations Convention on the Law of the Sea, Annex VI, article 8, paragraph 2. Similarly, references to articles, paragraphs and subparagraphs in a Protocol, Schedule or Regulations attached to a document are in the form 'document number + Prot (including protocol number, if applicable), 'document number + Schedule' or 'document number + Reg' in bold, followed by the article and paragraph numbers in normal type. For example, **20 Reg** 3(b) denotes Rule 3, paragraph (b), of the International Regulations for Preventing Collisions at Sea annexed to the Convention on the International Regulations for Preventing Collisions at Sea.

Citations for sections of the Annex to the Agreement Relating to the Implementation of Part XI of the United Nations Convention on the Law of the Sea are in the form '**37 Annex** S' followed by the number of the relevant section of the Annex and the paragraph and subparagraph, as appropriate. For example, **37 Annex** S6(1)(f)(i) refers to section 6, paragraph 1, subparagraph (f), sub-subparagraph (i) of the Annex to the Agreement.